"A remarkably learned, wise, and substantial study of the history of Christian doctrine. Written by an Anglican who is also an evangelical, this volume interacts with the entire scope of Christian theology in all of its major ecclesial trajectories. This book will stand the test of time—in the best tradition of Newman, Harnack, and Pelikan."

Timothy George, Distinguished Professor of Divinity, Beeson Divinity School, Samford University

"Despite its breadth, one that covers the centuries, *A History of Christian Theology* also plumbs the depths of numerous doctrines throughout the church's last two thousand years. This volume is an excellent resource for students, pastors, and scholars, and for anyone who wants to study the organic development of the church's theology. This will prove to be an invaluable resource for generations to come."

J. V. Fesko, Harriet Barbour Professor of Systematic and Historical Theology, Reformed Theological Seminary, Jackson

"Under Gerald Bray's able pen, the history of Christian thought comes to life. Bray's Trinitarian way of framing the story of Christian doctrine is a creative and helpful contribution to the discipline. His familiarity with the sources from every branch of the Christian tree is refreshing—and enviable! His evenhanded narrative—mixed with periodic personal commentary that is often witty, always insightful, and occasionally provocative—makes this book a delight to read. *A History of Christian Theology* will be essential reading for scholars and students for years to come. Highly recommended."

Nathan A. Finn, Provost and Dean of the University Faculty, North Greenville University

A HISTORY OF CHRISTIAN THEOLOGY

A HISTORY OF CHRISTIAN THEOLOGY

A TRINITARIAN APPROACH

GERALD BRAY

CROSSWAY®

WHEATON, ILLINOIS

A History of Christian Theology: A Trinitarian Approach

Formerly published as *God Has Spoken: A History of Christian Theology*

Published by Crossway
1300 Crescent Street
Wheaton, Illinois 60187

First printing 2014

Reprinted with new title 2024

Printed in Colombia

All emphases in Scripture quotations have been added by the author.

Trade paperback ISBN: 978-1-4335-8919-5
ePub ISBN: 978-1-4335-8922-5
PDF ISBN: 978-1-4335-8920-1

Library of Congress Cataloging-in-Publication Data

Names: Bray, Gerald Lewis, author.
Title: A history of Christian theology : a trinitarian approach / Gerald Bray.
Other titles: God has spoken
Description: Wheaton, Illinois : Crossway, 2024. | Includes bibliographical references and index.
Identifiers: LCCN 2024000862 (print) | LCCN 2024000863 (ebook) | ISBN 9781433589195 (trade paperback) | ISBN 9781433589201 (pdf) | ISBN 9781433589225 (epub)
Subjects: LCSH: Theology, Doctrinal—History.
Classification: LCC BT21.3 .B73 2024 (print) | LCC BT21.3 (ebook) | DDC 230.09—dc23/eng/20240329
LC record available at https://lccn.loc.gov/2024000862
LC ebook record available at https://lccn.loc.gov/2024000863

Crossway is a publishing ministry of Good News Publishers.

NP 34 33 32 31 30 29 28 27 26 25 24
13 12 11 10 9 8 7 6 5 4 3 2 1

Contents

Preface 13

PART ONE

The Israelite Legacy

1 *Christianity and Judaism* 27

The Parting of the Ways

Christianity and the Hebrew Canon of Scripture

Christianity and Jewish Biblical Interpretation

Christianity and the Prehistory of Israel

The Christian Interpretation of Israel's History

2 *A Shared Inheritance* 68

God Is One

The Divine Act of Creation

The Image of God in Man

The Nature of Sin and Evil

Election and Redemption

PART TWO

The Person of the Father

3 *God as Father* 99

Judaism and the Fatherhood of God

Non-Jewish Conceptions of Divine Fatherhood

Jesus and His Father

The Father as the Principle of Divinity

The Unbegotten and Almighty God-in-Himself

The Father and the Creator

4 *The Father and His Children* 133

A New Relationship with God

A New Understanding of Scripture

PART THREE

The Work of the Father

5 *The Reconciliation of the World* 151
The Work of the Father from a Jewish Perspective
The Work of the Father from a Gentile Perspective
The Christian Doctrine of Creation
6 *Providence and Predestination* 175
The Image and Likeness of God
The Call to Holiness
7 *The Work of the Father and the Trinity* 188
The Father and His Creation
The Divine Hierarchy
The Eclipse of the Father

PART FOUR

The Person of the Son

8 *The Challenge of the Incarnation* 211
The Church Confronts the Roman World
Jesus and His Contemporaries
Jesus in Early Christian Teaching
Adoptianism
9 *The Son of God* 232
Arianism
The Way to Nicea
The Aftermath of Nicea
A New Departure in Christology
The Triumph of Athanasius
The Trinitarian Synthesis
10 *The Christian Theological Vocabulary* 293
Hebrew, Greek, and Latin
What Is God?
What Is God Like?
Who Is God?
11 *The Son of Man* 323
The Divine Word in Human Flesh
Nestorianism

The Chalcedonian Definition
The Definition of Humanity
The Will of Christ
The Portrait of Christ
Retrospect and Prospect

PART FIVE

The Work of the Son

12 *The Body of Christ* . . . 405
The Man from Heaven
The Water and the Blood
The Likeness of Sinful Flesh
The Second Adam
13 *The Death of Christ* . . . 434
The Only Sacrifice for Sin
The Cost of Reconciliation
The Centrality of the Lord's Supper
The Memorial of Christ's Sacrifice
The Sacramental System
The Invention of Purgatory
The Justification of Sinners
The Glory of the Cross
Prophet, Priest, and King
14 *The Coming of Christ's Kingdom* . . . 542
The Eternal Reign of Christ
The Crisis of Authority
The Heavenly Kingdom
The New Covenant

PART SIX

The Person of the Holy Spirit

15 *The Forgotten Person of the Trinity?* . . . 607
The Road Less Traveled
The Spirit of God in the Bible
The Paraclete and Personhood
The Holy Spirit in the Ancient Creeds

16 *Spirit of the Father, Spirit of the Son* . . . 637
Double Procession?
Augustine and the Holy Spirit
The Origins of Controversy
Anselm and the Holy Spirit
The Course of the Controversy
The Parting of East and West
The *Filioque* Question Today

PART SEVEN

The Work of the Holy Spirit

17 *The Presence of God* . . . 723
From Glory to Glory
The Indwelling Power of God
18 *The Inspiration of Holy Scripture* . . . 736
The Prophetic Word of God
The Rule of Faith
The Handbook of the Christian Life
19 *The Preservation of the Church* . . . 764
The Mind of Christ
The Wisdom of the Ages
The Source of Truth
20 *The Pathway to Heaven* . . . 803
Angels and Archangels
The Peace That Passes Understanding
The Imitation of Christ
21 *The Mystical Body of Christ* . . . 836
The Gift of Righteousness
The True Church
Life in the Spirit
The Scope of the Covenant
The Extent of Christ's Atonement
The Assurance of Salvation
The Fellowship of the Spirit
The Devoted Life
The Pentecostal Mission

PART EIGHT

One God in Three Persons

22 *The Classical Doctrine of God* 985

The Patristic Synthesis

The God of the Philosophers

The Reformation Breakthrough

The Emergence of Unitarianism

23 *The Eclipse of Theology* 1021

The Cult of Reason

The Reconstruction of Theology

The Crisis of Authority: Roman Catholicism

The Crisis of Authority: Protestantism

The Crisis of Authority: Eastern Orthodoxy

24 *The Trinitarian Revival* 1147

The Protestant World

The Roman Catholic Church

The Eastern Orthodox Tradition

25 *The Challenge of God Today* 1205

A Suffering God?

The Credibility of Theology

Where Are We Now?

Chronological List of Persons 1227

Chronological List of Events 1235

General Index 1238

Scripture Index 1258

God hath spoken—by his prophets,
Spoken his unchanging word,
Each from age to age proclaiming
God the One, the righteous Lord:
Mid the world's despair and turmoil
One firm anchor holdeth fast,
God is king, his throne eternal,
God the first and God the last.

God hath spoken—by Christ Jesus,
Christ, the everlasting Son,
Brightness of the Father's glory,
With the Father ever one;
Spoken by the Word Incarnate,
God of God, ere time began,
Light of Light, to earth descending,
Man, revealing God to man.

God yet speaketh—by his Spirit
Speaketh to the hearts of men,
In the age-long word expounding
God's own message, now as then;
Through the rise and fall of nations
One sure faith yet standing fast,
God abides, his word unchanging,
God the first and God the last.

George Wallace Briggs (1875–1959)

Preface

Until the nineteenth century, there was no such thing as the "history of Christian doctrine." The doctrines themselves were contained in the creeds and confessions of the church, but how they had come into being was seldom examined in any detail. Protestants were aware that there had been developments over time, since otherwise the sixteenth-century Reformation would have been incomprehensible. If no change of any kind was possible, the Reformation should have been rejected as an innovation that was incompatible with eternally revealed truth, which is just what their Roman Catholic adversaries argued. Claiming the authority of the apostle Peter as the appointed successor of Jesus and the first bishop of Rome, the popes and their supporters assumed that what they believed and taught had come directly from the Lord himself.

The Eastern Orthodox churches had never accepted papal jurisdiction over them. On the whole, they agreed with Rome about the *content* of the church's theology, but not about the nature of the *authority* that had defined it. To them, Rome not only claimed a power that Jesus had not given to Peter, but it had corrupted the church's teaching in the process. This was the significance of adding the word *filioque* ("and [from] the Son") to the Nicene Creed's statement that the Holy Spirit proceeds from the Father (John 15:26). Did the pope have the power to authorize such an addition as this without the backing of a universal ("ecumenical") church council? Rome said that he did, but the East replied that he did not. Each side believed that the other had misread the Bible, in particular the words of Jesus in Matthew 16:18–19:

> . . . you are Peter, and on this rock I will build my church, and the gates of hell shall not prevail against it. I will give you the keys of the kingdom of heaven, and whatever you bind on earth shall be bound in heaven, and whatever you loose on earth shall be loosed in heaven.

It was the use made of this statement to undergird papal power that split the church apart. In 1054, papal legates excommunicated the patriarch of Constantinople because he would not submit to their authority, and in the sixteenth century Rome did the same to the Protestants, who also looked back to the eleventh century as the time when things had started to go seriously wrong in the church.

It soon became apparent that the Protestant rejection of papal authority was not like that of the Eastern churches, but no one thought to appeal to history as an explanation for this difference. Change and development over time were dimly understood, but their significance was not properly appreciated. Martin Luther, for example, did not hesitate to tell his students that Paul's epistle to the Galatians was of special relevance to them because Germans and Galatians were both of Celtic stock, and so it was only to be expected that the problems of ancient Galatia would be paralleled in contemporary Germany! It was not until the nineteenth century that historical development was used to explain the divisions that had occurred over time and the emergence of the doctrines that the different churches held, either in common or in opposition to one another. Since none of those doctrines was clearly stated in the New Testament, the suspicion began to grow that the very concept of doctrine had evolved in postbiblical times and had been imposed on the church by a priesthood determined to secure its own power.

To men who believed that the Christian faith ought to be grounded on Scripture alone (*sola Scriptura*), this came to mean that theology (or "dogma," as they usually preferred to call it) was a corruption of the primitive faith. They believed that if dogma could be sidelined or even dismantled, Christians might come together again, not in the churches (because they too were the product of postbiblical deviations) but in their hearts. Believers who demonstrated the spirit of Christ in their lives were more likely to persuade others of the truth of the gospel message than institutions which imposed their own orthodoxies on people who did not understand what they meant.

This was a one-sided view, of course, but the notion that what the church(es) taught was significantly different from what could be found in the Bible took root and gave birth to what we now call the "history of Christian doctrine." Of course, by no means everyone agreed with the thesis that postbiblical developments were corruptions of Christ's original teaching. That interpretation was promoted mainly among liberal Protestants, though over the course of the nineteenth century it became dominant in the Protestant world.

Roman Catholics, by contrast, initially found it hard to reconcile their beliefs with any notion of doctrinal development, but after the proclamation of papal infallibility in 1870 (which clearly was an innovation of sorts), the idea was taken over and used to explain why the papacy could introduce such apparent innovations and make them compulsory parts of Catholic belief. In Roman Catholic eyes, doctrine developed under the guidance of the Holy Spirit, who worked through the pope in order to confront and confound the errors of the age. They agreed with liberal Protestants that some of their teaching had been unknown in the early days of Christianity but argued that it had been made clear to the church in response to changing historical circumstances. The history of Christian doctrine was therefore to be understood not as a corruption of the original message of the New Testament but as a work of the Holy Spirit, adapting and bringing to perfection over time the revelation that had been given once and for all in Jesus Christ.

Conservative Protestants, and eventually even the Eastern Orthodox churches, gradually accepted the concept of the historical development of doctrine along lines broadly similar to the Roman Catholic view, but they interpreted the work of the Holy Spirit very differently. To them, the history of Christian doctrine was a struggle to maintain the truth of the gospel over against predators of different kinds—the popes, of course, but also the ancient heretics and the liberals of modern times.

Today, these nineteenth-century positions have been greatly modified, if not entirely abandoned, by all sides in the debate. No one now believes that Christian doctrine is a corruption of the teaching of Jesus, even if it is still widely claimed that much of it is different from anything he would have recognized. Similarly, very few people would now assert that what their particular church teaches is absolute truth to the exclusion of everything else. The concept of doctrinal orthodoxy still exists and is defended by conservatives from very different backgrounds, but everyone recognizes that it has often been formulated by political and other extraneous factors whose influence must be transcended if we are going to recover the sense of unity that lies beneath the surface of our divisions. Whether this recovery will lead to a reunion of the churches is doubtful, because the force of tradition and the staying power of institutions militate against it, but it can certainly be said that there is now a kind of spiritual ecumenism in the Christian world that brings people together across traditional barriers, both individually and in a plethora of parachurch organizations.

All this means that it is no longer possible to write a history of Christian doctrine whose main purpose is to debunk or defend a particular denominational tradition. We all have our preferences, of course, but anyone who argues that only the Baptists, or only the Roman Catholics (or the Reformed, the Eastern Orthodox, the Lutherans, or whoever) are right while everyone else is wrong is now regarded as a propagandist, not as a historian—and is dismissed accordingly. At the present time it is universally agreed that the historian must rise above his own bias and be as fair as he can be to others, accepting that even disagreeable facts must be analyzed and explained in their context, even if he might privately wish that the past had been different.

To some extent, the course of recent secular history has helped make this more "objective" approach easier and more natural. If we look back over the twentieth century, which one of us does not wish that it had been different from what it was? No one in 1900 wanted world war, routine genocide (a word that did not then exist), or the invention of weapons of mass destruction, and no one wants them now. But we cannot pretend that they never happened, nor can we blame one side for having caused all the trouble. The Western Allies (the United Kingdom, France, and the United States) tried that on Germany after the First World War, and look what they got—the revenge of Adolf Hitler! We do not want to make that mistake again, and this feeling has rubbed off on church historians as much as on others. Responsibility for what happened in the past is shared by all involved, because human beings are inherently sinful, and no one should be more aware of this than Christians, whose business it is to preach sin, righteousness, and judgment to an unbelieving world.

Of course, if we are to write a history of Christian doctrine at all, it must have some unifying principle, and if denominational or ideological allegiance will no longer do, something must be found to take its place. One possible approach is to take individual doctrines and trace their history, which is basically what Gregg Allison has done in his recent book *Historical Theology* (Zondervan, 2011). This is useful for students who are asked to write a paper on the development of something like the doctrine of the atonement, for example, because the information relating to it is gathered in one place. It also corresponds to a general tendency in modern research, which likes to make its material manageable by chopping it into bite-sized chunks and examining each one of them in depth, often to the virtual exclusion of anything else. Thus we can study the Trinity or justification by faith as discrete doctrines that have developed over time and look at how they have come to be what they are today, without getting bogged down in apparently irrelevant things like papal authority or original sin.

The trouble with that approach is that it oversimplifies and therefore distorts the history that it wants to explain. There has never been a time when people have held to individual doctrines as if the rest of theology did not exist. Even those who have stressed one particular thing—the sacraments, for example, or biblical inerrancy—have done so in a context that affects everything they believe. They may be accused of having distorted their theological inheritance by an undue emphasis on one part of it, but they have never believed that one point to the exclusion of the rest. Theology has always come as a complete package, even if the arrangement of its materials has changed over time and may now be quite different from what it once was.

Today we live in a climate where the doctrine of the Trinity has assumed a new prominence in theological discussion. Why this is so can be debated, but however we got to this point, this is where we are now. It therefore seems logical and appropriate to adopt a Trinitarian framework as the basis for explaining historical theology in the current context. Everyone agrees that the doctrine of the Trinity as we know it did not spring fully grown out of the New Testament. Whether we think that its emergence was a deformation of the original divine revelation or the natural outcome of godly reflection on it, no one can doubt that the result has commanded the assent of the vast majority of Christians over the centuries. Disputes there have certainly been, but every branch of the Christian church confesses that "we believe in one God, Father, Son, and Holy Spirit."

Furthermore, we also agree that each of these three persons is active in a distinct way. The Son came into the world as Jesus Christ; the Holy Spirit comes into the hearts of believers, giving them the power to cry "Abba, Father!"—and the Father is the one to whom our prayers are directed. Theologians differ about whether priority should be given to who the persons are or to what they do. The former is the more logical approach, since the authority of what a person does depends on who that person is, although it is possible to argue that the first Christians saw what God was doing in their midst and only later figured out how each of the divine persons was involved. Nevertheless, an understanding of who God is must come before there can be a proper appreciation of what God does, an order that is borne out by the way Christian theology actually developed.

When Jesus proclaimed his relationship with the Father, he introduced a subtle but significant shift in the Jewish picture of God, which now had to allow for a Father-Son relationship that could embrace both a divine incarnation and the ongoing transcendence of the supreme being. Nevertheless, the early Christians gave a priority to the Father that was in direct continuity with the Old Testament, and the revelation of the Son did not entail any departure from its transcendent monotheism. It was the organizing principle on which everything else depended, but the confession of the Son as Lord made it necessary to determine what his relationship to the one God was. Similarly with the Holy Spirit. Was he to be regarded as a person like the Father and the Son, as a personification of the divine being, or simply as another name for the Father? Were Christians expected to relate to God as one, as three, or as some combination of the two, depending on the circumstances?

These questions were inherent in the New Testament revelation, but resolving them was not an immediate priority for the first generation of Christians. Awareness of their importance and the need to get to grips with them grew over time and became urgent when false teachers emerged who tried to lead the church astray by equating the Father with God and denying the divinity of the Son and of the Holy Spirit. Some people today argue that these questions should never have been raised and that had they remained dormant the church would not have been divided in the way that it was, but this is naive and contrary to the teaching of the New Testament, where Christians were told that they must move on from the milk of the word to its meat.[1] That meant coming to terms with problems that did not appear on the surface but that would threaten to destroy the gospel message if they were not resolved. Laying a firm foundation involved going beyond what was immediately visible, and that is what the church found itself obliged to do. One thing led to another, and in the course of church history different aspects of Christian doctrine came to the fore and demanded resolution. Each time this happened, theologians had to take another look at their inheritance and examine it from a different angle. Just as a piece of cut glass reveals different aspects of the light according to how it is held, so the New Testament appears in a new light when looked at in response to the different theological questions that have been put to it.

This is the essence of historical theology, whose task is to explain how and why this happened. Theological developments did not occur arbitrarily but appeared in a logical sequence over time. The resolution of one problem led naturally to the next one, a process that we can observe from the beginning of the church up to the present time. Whether we have now arrived at the "end" of Christian theological development is impossible to say. Our perspective can only be governed by where we are, because each generation has a complete theology of its own. Future ages may well have to recast the tradition in order to explain developments that are as yet hidden from our eyes, but this we cannot tell. It may also be that we have reached the end of the present age and that Christ will come again before that can happen. This we do not know either. All we can do now is look at where we have come from, try to understand where we are, and suggest where we might go from here. What happens next remains hidden in the mind and purposes of God.

If these basic principles are understood, the organization of this book will be easy to grasp. Christian theology began with its Jewish inheritance, which it appropriated *in toto* and claimed was to be understood only in and through Jesus Christ. The nature of that inheritance and its impact on the early church must therefore be considered first. Next there comes the person of God the Father, whom Jesus introduced to his disciples. As good Jews, they knew about

[1] 1 Cor. 3:2; Heb. 5:12–13.

the one God, but they did not address him as their Father, and Jesus became known for this teaching. His signature cry was *Abba* (Aramaic for "father")—it is one of the few words of his that has been preserved in the original language.

Christians who prayed to God as their Father had to stress that he was the God of the Old Testament—the Creator and the Redeemer are one. This was disputed by the so-called "Gnostics" but it was fundamental to the integrity of Christianity. The Father was not a superior deity who intervened in order to rescue the work of an inferior Creator, but was himself the Creator who stepped in to put right what had gone wrong with his creation.

After that was established, the identity of the Son was next on the theological agenda. The incarnation of the Son could not really be understood until it was agreed that created matter was not the work of an inferior deity, because in that case, God could not have become man without ceasing to be divine. The great disputes of the fourth and fifth centuries over the person of Christ arose out of attempts to express this great mystery in a way that would affirm both the divinity and the humanity of the incarnate Son without compromising the integrity of either. That was not an easy task and it produced many serious disagreements, but the end result was the great creedal theology that has commanded the assent of virtually the entire Christian world and has stood the test of time.

Once the person of the Son had been defined to most people's satisfaction, the church had to move in two different directions. On the one hand, it had to link the person of the Son to his work, just as it had previously connected who the Father is to what the Father does. But it also had to move on to define the person of the Holy Spirit, who was neither a second Son nor an attribute of the Father's divinity. Which of these two would be dealt with first was not logically determined in advance, and it is fair to say that the Eastern (Orthodox) churches generally moved on to the person of the Holy Spirit, whose identity and relationship to the other persons would preoccupy them for centuries, whereas the Western church (the ancestor of today's Roman Catholics and Protestants) concentrated more on the work of Christ. Anselm of Canterbury (1033–1109) wrote on both subjects, but his treatise on the Holy Spirit was directed toward the controversy between the West (which he represented) and the East, whereas his discourse on Christ's atonement was intended for a purely Western audience, which gives us a good picture of how theology was developing in the eleventh century. It is also typical of the Western tradition that it is for his work on the atonement that Anselm is now famous, whereas his arguments for the double procession of the Holy Spirit have attracted far less attention.

By 1500 East and West had gone their separate ways because they could not agree about the Holy Spirit's identity. It was clear that what was central for the East was relatively peripheral in the West, where the procession of the Spirit from the Father (or from the Father and the Son) was something rarely discussed outside the polemics connected with East-West relations. What they concentrated on was the work of Christ, especially as this was communicated to the believer through his presence in the sacraments. The sixteenth-century Reformation had nothing to do with the double procession of the Holy Spirit but was preoccupied with the sacrifice of Christ: was it a once-for-all, unrepeated historical event, or did it miraculously reappear every time the priest celebrated Holy Communion? This was a question that few people in the East understood (let alone had an opinion about), but it split the Western church in two.

The disputes between papal loyalists, whom we now call Roman Catholics, and their opponents, whom we lump together as "Protestants" even though this term originally applied only to Martin Luther and his immediate followers, was not really about the work of Christ, however. Rather, it was about the way the effects of his saving work were received in the church, and that was the work of the Holy Spirit. Did the Spirit work primarily through objective means like the papacy, the institutional church, the sacraments, and so on, as the Roman Catholics claimed, or did he work subjectively, in the hearts and minds of individual believers, as the Protestants insisted? To understand the difference, ask yourself the following question: "When did you become a Christian?" A faithful Catholic would answer, "When I was baptized," but no true Protestant would say that. However important baptism may be, Protestants would insist that ceremonial water cannot make someone a believer. Without the inner working of the Holy Spirit, the outward rite we call "baptism" is of no intrinsic value. The same principle applies to everything else. A minister's vocation is "valid" not because of his ordination but because of his calling by God. Anyone can be ordained by the church authorities, but not everyone is called by God, as both Protestants and Catholics recognize. But where most Protestants would accept the ministry of an independent person like John Bunyan or Billy Graham, whether he was properly "ordained" or not, they would be less inclined to sit under the ministry of an immoral preacher. Many Catholics, on the other hand, would be more likely tolerate a bad priest than a do-it-yourself evangelist, because it is the authority of the church that counts for them, and not the personal holiness of its individual representatives.

Finally, in the modern world, the historical antagonisms between different groups of Christians have had to compete with something quite different. This is the suspicion that either there is no God at all, or that all religious beliefs point to the same transcendent deity. From the triumph of Christianity in the fourth century until about 1700, no theologian had been forced to argue the case for New Testament monotheism—the belief that there is one God who reveals himself in three persons—unless he was engaged in dialogue with Jews or Muslims. Such dialogues did take place from time to time, but they were rare and peripheral to the main body of the church. For the most part, Christians persecuted Jews and fought against Muslims with no questions being asked on either side.

All this changed in the eighteenth century, when men brought up in "Christian" Europe and America began to challenge their own religious inheritance in the name of "reason." First to go was the Trinity, which seemed to them to be illogical and even incomprehensible. From there it was a short step to open atheism, because if God was a distant power with no direct connection to everyday life on earth, what was the point of believing in him? Admittedly, many atheists hedged their bets and declared themselves to be "agnostics," if only because they realized that disproving the existence of God was even harder than proving it, but the practical result was the same. God was removed from the mental furniture of educated Westerners, a situation that continues to the present time. Christians (and others) enjoy "religious freedom" in Western countries, but only to the extent that their beliefs do not matter. If a religious conviction interferes with the atheistic mind-set, then it must be silenced, or at least sidelined. You will not get a doctorate today if you claim (as Isaac Newton did) that your research is primarily intended to explore the mind of God at work in the universe!

It is in this Babylonian exile of the modern church that the doctrine of the Trinity has returned to center stage. Christians of different traditions have come together, realizing that if they do not hang together they will be hanged separately. Where this will lead (if anywhere) is impossible to say, and it is not the business of the historian to indulge in prophecy. All we can affirm is that this is the point that we have come to at the present time, and those of us who believe in the providence of God (as this author does) are confident that he is working out his purposes for us and for his church as much today as in the past. This was the confidence of the late Archdeacon George Wallace Briggs, who after living through two world wars and an unprecedented "rise and fall of nations" could still write the forward-looking words of the hymn with which this preface began. The God who has spoken in the past continues to speak in the present, but his message is the same now as it has always been. The forms change over time and new developments occur in the way that the truth is expressed, but its substance remains unaltered. How this has happened and what it means for us today is what the following pages are all about.

The aim of this book is to make the history of Christian theology comprehensible to nonspecialists while at the same time providing a useful resource for those who want to take the subject further. Technical terms are explained in simple language, and background information is provided when it is necessary for understanding the subject and is unlikely to be part of the average person's general knowledge. At the same time, original sources are given in the footnotes, where it is assumed that serious students will be able to consult works not only in Latin and Greek but also in French and German. Works in other languages (Danish, Dutch, Romanian, Russian, Swedish) are also cited when theological developments in those countries are being discussed. However, English translations are also noted when they are available.

In the main body of the text, quotations from other languages have been freshly translated, and biblical references have been taken from a form of the text that the original author of the quote would have been familiar with, not from a modern translation based on a critical edition.

This book began life at Moore Theological College in Sydney, an institution of higher learning that shines as a beacon of light in an Anglican Communion that is currently beset by the storm clouds of schism, heresy, and apostasy. Special thanks are due to the former principal John Woodhouse and his wife, Moya, for the warm hospitality which they have always shown the author, and to the current principal Mark Thompson and his wife, Kathryn, on whose kitchen table the first draft slowly emerged. Different parts of it were subsequently written at Beeson Divinity School in Birmingham, Alabama; at Knox Theological Seminary in Fort Lauderdale, Florida; and at Tyndale House in Cambridge, all of which have been spiritual homes to me over the years. In addition, I must thank my employers, the Latimer Trust, whose constant support and encouragement have made this work possible.

As it happens, the volume reached completion on a return visit to Moore College, where a rapidly assembled team of critics put it through the final test of relevance to its intended audience. Special thanks are due to Joel Atwood, Matt Baker, Katherine Cole, Nick Davies, Matt Dodd, Tom Habib, Hank Lee, Matt Simpson, Mike Turner, Luke Wagenaar and Mike Weeks, who kept the author on his toes and did much to make this book accessible to its intended audience. It is to them and to the many godly men and women who over the years have passed through Moore College as teachers, staff, and students, that this book is humbly dedicated as a small token of my abiding affection for them. To them and to all who read this book, may the Lord God of Israel preserve and protect you in your earthly pilgrimage and bring you safely home to rest in his eternal glory.

Gerald Bray
The Feast of St. Luke the Evangelist
October 18, 2013

A Note on Transliteration

Greek and Cyrillic words that occur in the text have been transliterated into the Latin alphabet so as to make it easier to read them. In the footnotes, the standard international conventions that govern transliteration have been followed where names and publications are concerned, unless there is a generally recognized English equivalent (for example, *Tolstoy*, not *Tol'stoj*). Ancient Greek names have been given in their English or Latin forms (for example, *Aristotle* and *Plato*, not *Aristotelês* or *Platôn*). Unfamiliar Greek names have been Latinized, because a form like Autolycus looks less outlandish to most readers than pseudo-Greek alternatives like *Autolukos*, *Autolykos*, or *Aytolykos*. Modern Greek names are transliterated according to the same principles unless the writers concerned have adopted their own form of transliteration. So, for example, John Zizioulas is widely known under that name, not as Iôannês Zêzioulas, and so the more familiar form is adopted here.

The titles of ancient works have been given in Latin, which is the standard way of tracing them, even when they are written in Greek and there are English equivalents. Thus, Augustine's *City of God* is given in the footnotes as *De civitate Dei*, Basil of Caesarea's book on the Holy Spirit is *De Spiritu Sancto*, and so on. Scholarly monographs that have been translated into English from another language are referenced in both the original and the translated editions, but when no English translation exists only the original title is given.

Otherwise the system of transliteration has been designed to make it as easy as possible both for readers who know the original languages to reproduce the forms in the appropriate script and for others to pronounce the different words and names correctly.

With respect to Greek, most of the transliterations are straightforward. However,

> Ypsilon has been rendered as *y* when it stands alone but as *u* in diphthongs (*au*, *eu*, *ou*).
>
> Long vowels have been indicated with a circumflex (*ê* for Eta and *ô* for Omega).

With respect to Cyrillic, the soft sign after certain consonants has been indicated by an apostrophe (') but the hard sign has been ignored. The Russian letter *ë* (which is always stressed) has been rendered as *yo*, in accordance with the pronunciation—Solovyov, for example, and not Soloviev, as is often found in Western publications. Likewise Fyodor and not Fedor. An occasional exception has been made when a Russian writer has adopted a particular form of his name in the Latin alphabet, but the phonetic equivalent is indicated in parentheses where a reader might otherwise mispronounce it, as for example, Zernov (Zyornov). This is not done, however, for the descendants of Russian exiles who have no real connection with their ancestral homeland. Thus, for example, Bouteneff is not accompanied by Butenyov.

Soft vowels have usually been indicated by a preceding *j* (in the footnotes) or *y* (in the main text) but omitted after a soft sign or a preceding *i*. Thus, for example, *rasp'atie* ("crucifixion") rather than *raspjatije* or *raspyatiye*. Greek and Latin loan words in Russian have been transliterated according to the standard Russian conventions, even when this leads to inconsistency. For example, *typographia* from Greek becomes *tipografia* when it is from Russian, even though it is the same Greek word.

Note also that because the Cyrillic alphabet lacks the Greek *Xi*, a name like Maxim(us) becomes Maksim. Since 1917 Greek Theta has been written as *f* in Russian, which is how it has always been pronounced. Thus the Greek name Theophanes becomes Russian Feofan, Theodore is Fyodor, and so on. This is not a problem with modern writers, whose names are usually preserved intact, but it can cause some confusion when dealing with pre-1917 Western publications, which often Hellenized or Latinized them. It should also be remembered that Russian names can be "Latinized" according to different systems that correspond to different Western languages. Thus, for example, we can find Yeltsin (English), Eltsine (French) or Jelzin (German) instead of the more technically correct El'cyn, Jel'cyn or Yel'cyn, but all six of these forms transliterate the same Russian original! Most Russian émigrés of the early twentieth century preferred the French form of their name, which has now become standard in their family—e.g., Zouboff instead of Zubov, which would be the form more likely to be used today.

PART ONE

The Israelite Legacy

1

Christianity and Judaism

The Parting of the Ways

Why are Christianity and Judaism different religions? Today we are used to this and seldom give it much thought, but for the historian it is a question that demands an answer. Consider the evidence. Jesus was a Jew and so were his disciples. Neither he nor they expressed any desire to break away from Israel. Jesus made it clear that his message was intended primarily for Jews, and his disciples followed him in this.[1] He regarded the Hebrew Bible as authoritative Scripture, quoted it often, and even stated that not one word of it would be overruled by his teaching.[2] His message was that he had come to fulfill the promises made in the law and by the prophets, and there were many Jews in Jesus' time who were actively waiting for that to happen. They expected a charismatic Messiah figure who would come and deliver Israel from its bondage to the Romans, and to some of them at least, Jesus looked like a plausible candidate for the role. They may have been wrong to interpret his mission in political terms, but that was a mistake that could be corrected by a more spiritual interpretation of the promises made to Israel—it was not a new idea that was alien to the hopes and aspirations of the nation.

Furthermore, although the Jewish world of Jesus' day stood apart from its non-Jewish (or "Gentile") surroundings as a distinct religious and national entity, it was not a monolith. Alongside the temple establishment in Jerusalem, which all Jews recognized as their central religious authority, there were many subgroups competing for influence among them. In the New Testament we meet the Pharisees and the Sadducees, who are well known from other sources. There was also the Qumran community, which was not mentioned by anyone in ancient times but which we know a lot about thanks to the discovery of the Dead Sea scrolls in 1947. Among several other groups there were many "Hellenized" Jews, people who had adopted Gentile ways and the Greek

[1] See, for example Matt. 15:26; John 4:22; Acts 2:36.
[2] Matt. 5:17–19.

language but without abandoning their ancestral faith.[3] We might even include the Samaritans, who were Jews of a kind even though they were rejected by the mainstream. Why could Jesus not have launched a messianic sect similar to one of these and remained within the fold of historic Judaism?

In fact, some modern scholars think that this is more or less what Jesus wanted to do. They portray him as a great rabbi whose intentions were traduced by others after his death.[4] What propelled his disciples (or perhaps *their* disciples) to develop a belief in Jesus as the Son of God that was incompatible with the Jewish understanding of monotheism remains something of a mystery to them. They generally conclude that this development occurred under non-Jewish influence, but why that was able to supersede traditional Jewish beliefs is unclear and remains controversial.[5]

There were always many Jews who rejected Jesus and his message, but only when his followers started admitting Gentile believers to their fellowship without obliging them to become Jews first did it become clear that Christianity was not just another form of Judaism. Within a couple of generations, Jewish converts to the new faith tailed off and the church became a largely Gentile body to whom the political heritage and religious culture of Israel were alien. Once that happened, it was inevitable that Jews and Christians would emphasize their differences and downplay what they held in common. In many ways Jews found this easier to do than Christians did. Jews could always dismiss Christianity as an aberration based on a false interpretation of their sacred Scriptures, but Christians could not reject their Jewish inheritance so easily. They insisted that Christ had come to fulfill those Scriptures, and they knew that he had ministered almost exclusively to his fellow Jews. They also realized that his teaching and work could not be understood if the Jewish background to them was not recognized. The few Christians who tried to reject the Hebrew Bible were condemned as heretics, and the church continued to emphasize not only *that* Jesus had fulfilled the promises contained in it but also *how* he had done so.

The stages by which Christians separated from Judaism are obscure, though we may assume that the process was not the same everywhere. What is universally agreed is that by about AD 100 a Christian church had emerged that claimed a Jewish origin and heritage by appropriating the Hebrew Bible as its own, but that no longer thought of itself as Jewish.[6] The Jerusalem temple had

[3] They were numerous enough to form a distinct group in the early Jerusalem church. See Acts 6:1.

[4] See, for example, Geza Vermes, *Jesus the Jew: A Historian's Reading of the Gospels* (Philadelphia: Fortress, 1981); idem, *The Religion of Jesus the Jew* (Minneapolis: Fortress, 1994).

[5] See J. Carleton Paget, *Jews, Christians, and Jewish Christians in Antiquity* (Tübingen: Mohr Siebeck, 2010), 1–39, for a good discussion of the current state of the question.

[6] For a recent study of this process, see Thomas Robinson, *Ignatius of Antioch and the Parting of the Ways: Early Jewish-Christian Relations* (Peabody, MA: Hendrickson, 2009).

been destroyed by the Romans in AD 70, so whatever connections the church continued to have with it after the resurrection of Jesus were automatically severed. The Old Testament food laws and other aspects of traditional Jewish practice that survived the initial conversion of Jews to Christ were gradually ignored or abandoned, and any knowledge of Hebrew was quickly lost. Christians read the Greek translation of the Bible as their sacred text and used it to argue that Jesus was the promised Messiah. Somewhat oddly, although Christians advocated loyalty to the Roman authorities, it was they who were persecuted for their beliefs and not the Jews, despite the Jewish tendency to rebel against Rome. The reason for this was that Judaism was a legally recognized religion, while Christianity was not. Even as early as AD 64, when most of the apostles were still alive, the emperor Nero could distinguish Christians from Jews to the extent of blaming the former, but not the latter, for having started the great fire of Rome in that year. This unfair discrimination inevitably caused bad feelings, and some Christians believed that Jewish agitators were the main cause of their suffering. How true that was is hard to say, but that there was an abiding tension between two otherwise similar communities is certain.

How did this happen? A comparison between Christianity and Samaritanism may help us understand the process more clearly. The Samaritan schism seems to have been political in origin, as much as anything else, and with a scriptural text that contained only six books (Genesis to Joshua), Samaritanism was less developed than full-blown Judaism. Christianity, on the other hand, was everything that Judaism was and more. Not only did it take over the whole of the Hebrew Bible, it added to it quite considerably. The Old Testament that the church preferred to use was a Greek version that contained a number of books (and parts of books) that were missing from the Hebrew text,[7] and what we now call the New Testament was gradually added to it—in Greek, not in Hebrew. The New Testament is less than a third as long as the Old, but its significance for Christians is at least as great as that of the Old Testament, if not greater. The reason for this is that the church regards it not only as equally authoritative (and therefore just as divinely inspired) as the Hebrew Bible but also as a kind of commentary on it, giving principles of interpretation that the church can use to read and interpret its Israelite legacy.

It is the New Testament that tells us what the essential difference between Christianity and Judaism was, and we must look to it for clues to explain how the two became separated. Let us start with the teaching of Jesus. Was he a rabbi with new and challenging ideas, or was he something quite different?

[7] These books constitute what are now known as the Apocrypha. In Protestant Bibles they are usually omitted or printed separately between the Old and New Testaments.

What was his take on the law of Moses, and why was his view rejected by the Jewish leaders of his day?

What is certain is that Jesus was not a rabbi in the usual sense of the term. He was not trained in a rabbinical school in the way that the apostle Paul was, and as far as we know, his only contact with the rabbinic world before he began his public ministry occurred when he went to Jerusalem at the age of twelve and spent several days with the teachers in the temple.[8] However there is no indication that he learned anything from them; on the contrary, it appears that even as a boy he was teaching them as their equal. It is true that during his adult ministry he was frequently addressed as "rabbi," but this was a courtesy title bestowed on him by people who did not know what else to call him.[9] Neither his training (if he had any) nor his message could be described as "rabbinical" in the usual sense of the word.

Admittedly, rabbinical Judaism was still developing in Jesus' day, so there may have been more freedom for Jews to recognize the kind of freelance teacher that Jesus was than would have been the case later on. But even if that is true, what Jesus said was often quite different from standard rabbinical teaching. The main differences between them can be sketched as follows:

1. The rabbis were concerned to interpret the law and apply it to situations that were not envisaged in the original text, or not fully expounded there. Jesus said that he had come to fulfill the law and make it redundant. In this sense, he was not really messianic, as Jews understood it, because he did not see his mission as the establishment of a Jewish state in which the law of Moses would be perfectly observed. On the contrary, he said that his kingdom was not of this world, something that was beyond the comprehension of most Jews of his time.[10] Messianic movements remained active among Jews until AD 135, when the defeat of Bar-Kochba's rebellion finally put an end to them, but Christians did not get involved in them because, in their view, the Messiah had already come!

2. The rabbis understood the law essentially as the performance of particular tasks, whereas Jesus saw it more as the adoption of a certain attitude. While it is too simple to say that the rabbis thought of righteousness as something external whereas Jesus internalized it, there was definitely a difference of emphasis between them along these lines, as can be seen from particular incidents in the life of Jesus. For example, the rabbis believed that it was wrong to heal people on the Sabbath because it was a sacred day of rest, whereas Jesus

[8] Luke 2:41–52.
[9] It is also confined to the Fourth Gospel. See John 1:38, 49; 3:2; 6:25; 20:16.
[10] John 18:36.

thought it was appropriate and sometimes even necessary, because meeting human needs was more important than observing divinely appointed regulations that might get in the way.[11]

3. The rabbis took their cue from Moses the lawgiver, whereas Jesus went back to Abraham as the true source of Israel's faith. According to Jesus, Moses stepped in to bolster that faith because the people were unable to keep it, but his law was a stopgap to prevent further degeneration, and not a pathway to eternal life.[12]

4. The rabbis wanted to *protect* Israel from contamination by the outside world, whereas Jesus wanted to *transform* Israel by raising it to a higher plane. For Jesus, the things of the world could not pollute those who were pure in heart, and so there was no need to fear or avoid them as a matter of principle, even if they had to be used with discretion.[13]

None of these things by themselves, or even all of them taken together, need have caused a breach between the Christian church and the Jewish world. If Jesus had been no more than a reformer within the Jewish culture of his time, it is quite possible that his ideas would have been taken on board after his death. After all, the Jews had persecuted the prophets but then canonized their message, and presumably the same thing could have happened to Jesus.[14] What made him different was the nature of the authority on which his teaching was based. Both the rabbis and Jesus believed that all authority came from God and that it was contained in the law of Moses. But Jesus taught that the written law pointed to him as its author, its content, and its fulfillment, and he claimed authority over it.[15] If Jesus was right, it could only mean that, in his view, the Hebrew Bible taught that he was God in human flesh, come to earth as the prophets had promised that he would.[16] The signs of this are there in the Gospels. Not only did Jesus reinterpret the law, but he forgave sins, which was something only God could do.[17] In his duel with the Devil at the beginning of his ministry, he was tempted in ways that only God could be. A mere man could not have turned stones into bread, but the Creator of all things could do so.[18] Once that is understood, the rest of Jesus' ministry falls into place and his resurrection becomes inevitable—how could death have held the One who made all things and who is eternal life in himself?

[11] Mark 2:27–28; Luke 6:5.
[12] Matt. 19:7–9; compare John 7:19–22 with John 8:39–40.
[13] Matt. 15:16–20.
[14] Matt. 5:12; John 15:20.
[15] John 5:39–40; Mark 2:28.
[16] Isa. 7:14; 9:6–7; Mic. 5:2.
[17] Mark 2:5–12.
[18] Matt. 4:1–11.

Putting Jesus at the center and interpreting the law as something that was meant to be fulfilled in him caused a seismic shift in biblical interpretation as it affected Christians. No longer was it a matter of applying the law to previously unknown (or unforeseen) circumstances, as the rabbis typically did. Now the main subject of discussion became how the law revealed Jesus—who he was, where he came from, and what his relationship was to God, whom he called his Father. It was questions of that kind that brought Christian theology into being and set the church on an intellectual journey quite different from anything that could be found in rabbinical Judaism.

Theology as an academic discipline did not exist in Old Testament times, nor has it developed very much in modern Judaism, where "theological studies" focus more on religious laws and their interpretation than on the being of God. The ancient Israelites knew that their beliefs were different from those of the surrounding peoples, but they never developed a "doctrine of God" to explain this. That term did not exist in ancient Hebrew, but if it had, it would have meant something quite different from what we mean by it today. When we talk about the doctrine of God in the writings of Paul, we focus on what Paul taught about God. But if Paul had used the term, he would have meant not what he (or anyone else) thought about God, but what God had told them about himself. The "doctrine of God" would have been the teaching received from God, not what its recipients thought about him, and in thinking this way Paul would have been typical of his time.

The ancient Israelites knew about other belief "systems," if we can call them that, but they were not interested in dialoguing with those who held them or in trying to persuade them to accept Israel's understanding of God instead. Foreigners could worship the God of Israel if they wanted to, but it was extremely difficult for them to become Israelites, if only because they were not descended from the ancestors to whom God had revealed himself.[19] Jews saw little need to explain their faith to outsiders, and their leaders were more concerned with the practice of worshiping God than with developing a theory of monotheism.[20] Of course they knew that there was only one God, but that knowledge was less important than the fact that he had established a relationship with them, a "covenant" that demanded obedience to a set of laws rather than a confession of certain beliefs.[21] But what for Jews was their

[19] Apart from specific cases like Ruth and Naaman (2 Kings 5:15–17), there are a number of references to "all the nations of the earth" who will be blessed by Israel (Gen. 18:18) and worship the true God (Psalm 67). But on the whole, the message was that salvation belongs to the Jews, as Jesus told the Samaritan woman (John 4:22), and if non-Jews were to benefit from it, it could only be in and through Israel.

[20] See the encounter between Elijah and the prophets of Baal for a good example of this (1 Kings 18:20–40).

[21] See Isa. 35:8, where the prophet says that even fools will not go astray if they do the right thing.

national covenant became for Christians the *Old* Testament, a body of law and tradition that was superseded by a new and fuller revelation of God in Jesus Christ. That revelation was not another law but a new relationship with God that was rooted in a deeper understanding of who he is and of what he has done to save us.

Instead of creating new laws, the Christian church developed theology, which is the understanding of God based on his self-revelation.[22] In itself, the New Testament is not a textbook of theology any more than the Old Testament is, but what it says shows us why the church would have to create such a discipline. Christians had a commission to preach the gospel to the nations, which meant that they had to explain what it was and why it mattered. People who did not understand even the rudiments of Jewish thought would find it very difficult to grasp the Christian message, as Paul discovered when he went to Athens.[23] Furthermore, Jewish beliefs had to be presented to them in a coherent and systematic way, since otherwise they would either have made no sense at all or else would have been absorbed in a piecemeal fashion, which might have been even worse.

A religion or culture that adopted certain Jewish beliefs without understanding the context in which they had emerged might easily end up misunderstanding and even perverting them. A good example of this was the widespread adoption of the Hebrew week in non-Jewish circles. A cycle of time that for Jews was closely connected to creation and the worship of the Creator was borrowed by others and applied to the seven recognized planets—the sun, the moon, Mars, Mercury, Jupiter, Venus, and Saturn. It was then used for astrological purposes that had nothing to do with Judaism. The Christian church was eventually able to rescue the week from this aberration and restore the sense of harmony with the created order that had originally been intended, but the fact that most Western European languages still use the planetary names for the individual days serves as a reminder of how the biblical concept had been misinterpreted by those who did not understand or accept the context in which it first appeared.[24]

---

[22] It should be said that Christians did not use the word "theology" to describe their beliefs for a very long time. They preferred to call it their "doctrine" (*didachê* in Greek; *doctrina* in Latin) or their "teaching" (Greek *didaskalia*; Latin *disciplina*). The Greek word *theologia* first appeared in the writings of Plato (429–347 BC), who used it to mean what we would now call "mythology," and it may have been avoided by Christians for that reason.

[23] Acts 17:16–34.

[24] In English, the names of the Roman gods have been replaced by Germanic equivalents, but the principle is the same (Mars=Tiw; Mercury=Woden; Jupiter=Thor; Venus=Freya). The main exception in Western Europe is Portuguese, which numbers the days as "second," "third," "fourth," and so on. The same is also true in many Eastern European languages, particularly where the influence of the Greek Orthodox church has been strong. It may be noted in passing that Muhammad also adopted the Christian names for the days of the week, with the result that many Islamic societies use them in their Arabic forms without realizing where they originally came from.

Jews believed that God was eternal, almighty, and so on, but they seldom speculated about the implications of these attributes for their understanding of how he interacted with the world. Their approach was essentially practical and subjective. As far as they were concerned, God was who he said he was because what he did demonstrated that his claims were true. Rather than speculate about mysteries that were too great for the human mind to bear, they thought that it was better to do what God commanded and reap the rewards that obedience would bring. This does not mean that the ancient Israelites were free to ignore the nature of God's being. On the contrary, they were forbidden to make idols representing him, because he was invisible and could not be contained within limitations imposed by the human mind.[25] Neither were they encouraged to speculate about how an invisible, infinite Creator could enter into a relationship with his finite creatures. They often talked about God in human terms, but at the same time they insisted that he was not a man, and the possibility that he might become one never crossed their minds.[26] When the Jews of Jesus' day were presented with that idea, most of them rejected it as blasphemy and left it at that.[27]

It was in the Gentile world that questions about the nature of God's being were important. Greek philosophers had long speculated about the nature of ultimate reality, and they wanted to know how the God of the Bible fitted into that picture. Lacking a doctrine of creation or an understanding of how spiritual and material realities interacted, Gentile converts needed clear guidance about these things. In the Gentile imagination, the line between the divine and the human was permeable, so why should the incarnation of the Son as Jesus Christ be regarded as unique? Jesus was not the first or the only man to claim divinity; nor were his claims particularly impressive. He may have risen from the dead, but how could he have died in the first place if he was God? Could he do that and still be the ultimate good and transcendent being? The gospel had to be explained to Gentiles in ways that most Jews had never thought about, and Christian theology was to some extent a result of the struggle to do this.

The church also had to explain how Jesus Christ was related to the Jewish God. This meant that biblical monotheism had to be interpreted in a way that could accommodate the divinity of Christ. The Old Testament talked about the Word of God, the Spirit of God, and the Wisdom of God in ways that sounded personal, but Jews understood those terms as poetic metaphors more than anything else. On the whole, Christians agreed with them about this, but

[25] Ex. 20:4–6.
[26] See Ps. 50:7–15.
[27] Matt. 26:65; John 10:31–33.

they also had to consider such expressions in a wider context in which Jesus Christ was identified with the divine Word and Wisdom, and the Spirit was a distinct person, not just the breath of the one God.

Given their different perspective on such matters, could Christians not simply have abandoned Judaism and created an entirely new religion? The snag with that solution was that Jesus had come to fulfill the promises of the law that had been proclaimed and renewed by the prophets of ancient Israel. So even if parts of the Old Testament were no longer applicable after the coming of Christ, abandoning the Hebrew Bible was not an option for the early church. Whether they liked it or not, Christians shared a common inheritance with Jews, although they interpreted it in different ways. We cannot appreciate what the origins of Christian theology were unless we come to grips with this two-edged phenomenon, which has been the cause of so much misunderstanding between the Old and the New Testament people of God.

The relationship between Christians and Jews is complex and has often been the subject of intense controversy. It has always been possible for a Jew to become a Christian without ceasing to be Jewish, a situation that was all but universal in the time of the apostles, but the other way around is more problematic. There were Jews in the early church who thought that non-Jewish converts to Christianity had to become Jews in order to be Christians, but that was vigorously contested by Paul and the idea was soon rejected.[28] Paul was not against the Jewish law as such; nor did he see anything wrong with Jews who observed it. He did so himself,[29] and when he took Timothy on as his assistant, he had him circumcised so as not to offend Jewish opinion.[30] This was important to Paul because in the first Christian churches there were many people who retained close business and family ties with fellow Jews who remained unconvinced of the claims of Christ. Only as those bonds weakened over two or three generations was there a clear separation between Jews and Christians at the grassroots level.[31] Gradually non-Jewish converts became more numerous and Jewish Christians mixed more readily with them than with other Jews. When that happened, the sense of a

[28] Gal. 2:11–3:29; Rom. 2:17–4:25.

[29] See Acts 21:20–26.

[30] Acts 16:1–3. Timothy was the son of a mixed marriage. His father was a Gentile, so he was not circumcised as a baby, but his mother was Jewish, which in the eyes of other Jews made him Jewish as well. Interestingly enough, Timothy had been brought up as a Christian by his mother and grandmother, who were both believers (2 Tim. 1:5). We do not know whether they had wanted Timothy to be circumcised, but his father (presumably an unbelieving Gentile) probably did not allow it.

[31] It must however be remembered that the Romans distinguished Christians as a separate group at a very early date. The emperor Nero blamed them (and not the Jews) for having caused the great fire of Rome in AD 64, and Pliny the Younger recognized them as a distinct group when he was governor of Bithynia (AD 111–112). Apparently Pliny had no idea that Christians were related to Jews, which gives us a clear indication of how they were perceived less than three generations after the beginnings of the church.

wider Jewish solidarity disappeared and the two communities went their separate ways.

By the mid-second century Christians were writing treatises against the Jews, and it was even possible for Marcion of Pontus (fl. c. 144) to argue that Jewish influence had no place in the Christian church, that the Hebrew Scriptures should be rejected, and that any sign of dependence on them ought to be rooted out of the New Testament.[32] Marcion's was an extreme view, and he never persuaded a significant number of people to adopt his position, but the fact that it could be aired at all shows how far the church had moved away from its Jewish origins in little over a century. At the same time, Judaism was also developing its own postbiblical identity, which in many respects was no closer to the Old Testament than Christianity was. While modern Jews have never rejected their ancient Scriptures, they depend for religious guidance more on the Mishnah and the Talmud, both of which were the products of rabbinical teaching in the centuries after the birth of Christ, than they do on the Bible.[33] In sum, both religions draw on the inheritance of the Hebrew Scriptures and claim them for their own, but each has moved on from them in its own way and each has become a stranger to the other.[34]

Christianity and the Hebrew Canon of Scripture

It is obvious to anyone reading the Gospels that Jesus assumed that the Jewish Scriptures were of divine origin. The redemption Jesus proclaimed was the inheritance of the Jewish people that had been promised to them by the law and the prophets, and he told them that he was fulfilling it before their eyes.[35] His disciples claimed the same thing, using the Hebrew Bible in order to preach the gospel of salvation by grace through faith in Christ. To the apostles, the law of Moses pointed to Christ because it established the standards of holiness that God required of his people. It reminded them that they could never attain those standards on their own, and it outlined a way of escape that would eventually be realized through the once-for-all sacrifice of the Great High Priest, the sinless Son of God who had given his life for theirs. As they and their associates produced the books that would form the New Testament, they were conscious that they were expounding the Hebrew Bible and explaining what they were convinced was its true meaning.

[32] See Sebastian Moll, *The Arch-heretic Marcion* (Tübingen: Mohr Siebeck, 2010).
[33] See Hermann L. Strack and Günter Stemberger, *Introduction to the Talmud and Midrash* (Minneapolis: Fortress, 1992).
[34] See Marcel Simon, *Verus Israel: A Study of the Relations between Christians and Jews in the Roman Empire AD 135–425* (Oxford: Oxford University Press, 1986); originally published in French (Paris: E. de Boccard, 1964).
[35] Luke 4:21.

In principle, the text of the Old Testament used by the first Christians was the same as that used by their Jewish contemporaries. The Christians made no attempt to add to it or to modify it because they believed it was the Word of God that had been fulfilled in Jesus Christ. Because they thought that every part of it pointed to him, they were convinced that if they were to doctor it in some way they would lose or misunderstand the meaning of some aspect of Christ's mission. As Jesus himself had said, "Until heaven and earth pass away, not an iota, not a dot, will pass from the Law."[36] They also knew that it would have been impossible to preach the gospel to Jews if they had modified the biblical text merely to suit their own theological preferences. The church therefore had powerful motives for keeping its Old Testament as close to the Jewish original as it could, although the text was not fixed to the degree that it is now, nor had the limits of the canon been finally determined.

As far as the Old Testament text is concerned, the discovery of the Dead Sea scrolls at Qumran in 1947 has shown that in the time of Jesus even the Hebrew original was not as uniform as it later became. The extent of the variations should not be exaggerated, and generally speaking the Qumran scrolls are close to the now standard Masoretic form of the text, but sometimes the latter preserves inferior readings that can be corrected by appealing to the evidence from Qumran.[37] There are even cases where Hebrew versions discovered at Qumran support the readings of the Greek translation begun at Alexandria in the third century BC and known to us as the Septuagint or "Seventy" (LXX), because it was supposedly produced by seventy (or seventy-two) scholars.[38] The origin of this translation is covered in legend, but it seems likely that a group of Jews in Alexandria, aware that their community was rapidly losing its knowledge of Hebrew, decided to translate the Pentateuch (Genesis–Deuteronomy) into Greek so that their faith would be maintained by the younger generation. This probably occurred around 250 BC, and the rest of the Hebrew Scriptures were gradually translated over the next 200 years or so. By the time Jesus was born, most if not all of the Hebrew Bible was available in Greek, though the standard of translation was extremely variable. Books like Job and Daniel were paraphrased rather than translated literally, and the LXX version of the Psalms

---

[36] Matt. 5:18.

[37] The Masoretic text was prepared by the so-called Masoretes, whose name derives from the Hebrew word *masorah* ("fetter"). By fixing the form of the biblical text, the Masoretes were meant to be putting limits, or fetters, on its interpretation. They were active from the seventh to the eleventh centuries AD.

[38] "Septuagint" derives from the Latin word for "seventy," the approximate number of translators, which explains the abbreviation LXX, the Roman numeral for seventy. On the nature of this translation and its authority in the early church, see Karen H. Jobes and Moisés Silva, *Invitation to the Septuagint* (Grand Rapids, MI: Baker, 2000); and Martin Hengel, *The Septuagint as Christian Scripture: Its Prehistory and the Problem of Its Canon* (Edinburgh: T & T Clark, 2002). See also Abraham Wasserstein and David Wasserstein, *The Legend of the Septuagint: From Classical Antiquity until Today* (Cambridge: Cambridge University Press, 2006).

often bore little relation to the original. Some passages were either omitted or transposed elsewhere, and a number of mistakes were made by the translators.

Doubts about the accuracy of the Greek version were apparently quite widespread and seem to have led an anonymous Jewish writer to compose the so-called *Letter of Aristeas* sometime around 150 BC, with the purpose of shoring up the prestige and authority of the Greek Pentateuch. The Pseudo-Aristeas, as this writer is known, claimed to be one of the seventy-two scholars who had been sent from Jerusalem to Alexandria in order to undertake the translation, which (he assured his readers) enjoyed the approval of the temple establishment. But although this argument might have persuaded Jews outside Palestine who had abandoned the use of Hebrew to accept the LXX, there were always those who had not lost contact with Jerusalem, where there were Greek-speaking synagogues and many people (like the young Saul of Tarsus) who were fluent in both Hebrew and Greek. People in those circles were well aware of the defects of the LXX, and from time to time they produced revisions of the text in order to make it reflect the Hebrew more accurately. These revisions circulated freely, making what we now call the LXX more like a family of translations than a single text.

As this was happening, the legends attributed to Aristeas were taking on a life of their own. By the time of Philo (d. AD 50) it was being claimed that the seventy translators had worked independently but had all come up with exactly the same version—evidence that the LXX was divinely inspired![39] That gave it an entirely new status and made it possible for advocates of the LXX to explain the differences between it and the Hebrew text as the will of God. Philo's endorsement of the LXX undoubtedly strengthened its authority among Diaspora Jews, though it did not displace that of the Hebrew originals, at least not among those who were able to consult them.

By the time the New Testament was written, the LXX was circulating in a number of different forms that were tolerated as long as there was no definitive Hebrew text against which they could be judged. That situation began to change after the destruction of Jerusalem in AD 70. The dispersal of the temple establishment led to a retrenchment that eventually eliminated the various Hebrew versions in favor of the one that later became the Masoretic text. Once that happened, the pressure was on to make the Greek versions conform to the increasingly standardized Hebrew one as much as possible. Despairing of the LXX, some individual Jews undertook the task of translating afresh, preparing one very literal translation (Aquila) and at least two relatively idiomatic

[39] Philo, *De vita Mosis (Moysi)* 2, ll. 33–44.

ones (Symmachus and Theodotion). There is some evidence that the text now attributed to Theodotion was actually much older, but if so, it shows that the need for a more accurate translation than the LXX was felt even before the fall of Jerusalem. Theodotion's version is important mainly because its text of Daniel quickly replaced that of the earlier LXX, a fact which proves that the legend of the LXX's divine inspiration was not universally believed!

Much of the knowledge we have of this translation process comes from Origen (185?–254?), a Christian from Alexandria who tried to provide the church with a viable LXX text by revising it in the light of these subsequent Jewish versions. His corrected form of the LXX became the Old Testament of the Greek church, which it remains to the present day. Jews, however, soon abandoned the LXX almost entirely, preferring to use Aquila's translation or to revert to the original Hebrew, which they eventually did.

As for the books that were included in the biblical canon, we know that the Pentateuch, which the Jews called the Torah or the five books of Moses, was foundational to all forms of Judaism and that Christians agreed with this. Jesus frequently referred to "Moses" (Matt. 8:4; Mark 1:44; 10:3; 12:26; Luke 24:44; John 5:45–46; 7:19) as the presumed author of the Torah, which is often quoted in the New Testament. Next came the section known as the Prophets (Nevi'im). This included Joshua to 2 Kings (but not Ruth) and Isaiah to Malachi (but not Lamentations or Daniel). Here again there was general agreement by the time of Jesus, although the LXX separated the historical from the more obviously prophetic books, putting the former immediately after the Torah and the latter at the end of the canon.

More problematic were the books that are now included in the third section of the Hebrew Bible, where they are known simply as the Writings (*Ketuvim*). These are the Psalms, Job, Proverbs, Ruth, the Song of Songs, Ecclesiastes, Lamentations, Esther, Daniel, Ezra–Nehemiah (a single book) and Chronicles, in that order. It is an interesting fact that while the New Testament often refers to "the Law and the Prophets,"[40] it never mentions the Writings as a distinct collection of books. Does this mean that the Writings were not regarded as Scripture in the first century AD? That is hard to say. The books themselves were certainly in existence and enjoyed canonical status among the Jews, and there is no reason to think that Christians disagreed with that assessment. After all, the Psalms are quoted in the New Testament more than any other book, and their prophetic quality was highly valued. The early Christians could refer to the "Law" in a way that included the entire canon of Scripture (see, e.g.,

[40] Matt. 5:17; 7:12; 22:40; Luke 16:16; Acts 13:15; 24:14; Rom. 3:21.

1 Cor. 14:21), so we cannot assume that the New Testament phrase "the Law and the Prophets" was meant to exclude the Writings.

The only book that produced serious doubts among Jews was Esther, which is not found among the Qumran scrolls and is not quoted in the New Testament either. The main reason for these doubts appears to have been that Esther does not mention the name of God, which made it seem unlikely that it could be inspired Scripture. It is not mentioned in the New Testament, but that cannot be taken as evidence that Christians rejected its canonicity, since several other Old Testament books are not quoted in the New Testament either,[41] and they were certainly regarded as inspired Scripture. Arguments from silence prove nothing, and there is no indication that the early church ever rejected Esther in the way that some Jews were thought to have done.

Much less clear is the status of a number of books or parts of books that are found in the LXX but not in the Hebrew Bible. Some of these were probably translated from Hebrew into Greek, but the original text has been lost and only the Greek now survives. In the case of Esther, the LXX version contains substantial additions to the Hebrew text that mention God frequently, making us suspect that they may have been added for that reason! The additions to Daniel and Jeremiah take the form of appendices (*Bel and the Dragon*, for example, or the *Letter of Baruch*) which can stand alone if need be. Most of the other texts are either historical (like the books of the *Maccabees*) or form part of the wisdom literature that is associated with the name of Solomon.

Taken together, these books have come to be known as the Apocrypha and have been clearly rejected by the Jewish tradition, even though they are all of Jewish origin.[42] None of them is quoted in the New Testament, though there are possible allusions to some of them, and they are included in Christian editions of the LXX. It seems that they were used in the church as morally edifying texts without being regarded as divinely inspired Scripture, though the tendency to canonize them as such grew over time. Debate about the status of the LXX, and therefore of the Apocrypha as well, flared up between Augustine and Jerome in the late fourth century. As a distinguished Hebrew scholar, Jerome plumped for the exclusive inspiration of the Hebrew original while Augustine, as a theologian, argued that because the apostles used the LXX it should be the canonical text adopted by the church. Augustine's view prevailed and the Apocrypha later had some influence on the development of medieval

[41] There are no quotations in the New Testament from Ruth, 2 Kings, 1 and 2 Chronicles, Ezra, Nehemiah, Song of Solomon, Lamentations, or Obadiah.

[42] The word "apocrypha" means "hidden," which the books in question obviously are not! A more accurate term, and the one now generally preferred by scholars, is "deuterocanonical," though it must be admitted that it has not caught on outside specialist circles.

theology, but in the earliest period of Christianity it was an irrelevance. No commentaries were written on it, which means that it was not in regular use in the church's preaching and teaching ministry.[43] In the sixteenth century, the Protestant Reformers revived the position of Jerome, which they regarded as more scientific, so that today Protestant Bibles follow the Hebrew text, though the influence of the LXX can still be seen in the names given to some of the books and in the order in which they are placed in the canon.[44]

Having said this, it must be admitted that the New Testament, which was originally written in Greek, normally uses the LXX when it quotes from the Hebrew Bible, even when the Hebrew text is different. Various explanations for this have been given, which may be summarized as follows:

1. Quoting the LXX was mainly a matter of convenience. Christians were writing in Greek for Greek-speakers who were already familiar with that translation. It was more important for the early Christian evangelists to tap into that tradition than to correct it by referring back to the original Hebrew, because they were claiming that Christ had come to fulfill the Scriptures, a point that could only be credibly made if people recognized those Scriptures when they heard them. Had the evangelists translated directly from the Hebrew, many Greek-speaking Jews might have thought that they were doctoring the text to make it fit their agenda. Since Christians were not trying to bend the text to suit themselves but only to communicate the gospel to their hearers, using the LXX seemed to be the best means to that end. Given that neither the Hebrew nor the LXX then existed in a single form, it was always possible for a New Testament writer to use a version of the Greek that was closer to the Hebrew than the original LXX, and that seems to be what Paul actually did, particularly when he was quoting from Isaiah.

2. The differences between the Hebrew and the LXX did not really matter. The exact meaning of many Hebrew words, especially those that refer to plants and animals not found outside the Middle East, was unknown even to the original translators. What on earth is a pygarg, for example?[45] Would it matter if the lilies of the field turned out to be daffodils or daisies? Not really, and in cases like these the LXX readings may be just as good as any others. It would have been different if Christians had been expected to obey the Jewish food laws, but since they were not bound to them, they could allow the identity of

[43] An exception may be made for Tobit, on which Ambrose (339?–397) wrote a commentary, and also for Ecclesiasticus, which was commented on by Theodoret (d. 466?). But both of these were late and they had no imitators until the time of Bede (673–735).

[44] This influence, such as it is, was mediated through the Latin Vulgate, translated by Jerome from the original Hebrew and Greek.

[45] Deut. 14:5 (KJV); the ESV has "ibex."

many of the "unclean" creatures they mention to remain uncertain, since this did not affect their faith in any practical way.[46] That was the approach taken by the early church and even by Jews, who were forced to admit that they did not always know exactly what they were supposed to avoid eating.

It also happens that the Hebrew can sometimes be read in different ways because the original text had no vowels. A famous example of this occurs in Genesis 47:31, which says that Jacob "bowed himself upon the head of his *mth*." The Hebrew word *mth* can be read either as *mittah* (bed) or as *matteh* (staff). The Masoretic text preferred the former, which makes more sense, but the LXX chose the latter, and its version is the one given in Hebrews 11:21.[47] The only way to reconcile these two readings is to translate the Genesis text as "staff," taking the Hebrews citation of the LXX as evidence for that, but this seems to be forced.[48] Perhaps the writer to the Hebrews knew that "bed" was a better reading, but thought that his audience was used to the LXX and would have spotted an "error" had he used it instead of "staff." What can we do about something like this? Does it matter one way or the other? Whatever solution we prefer, we should be able to admit that it makes little difference in practice, and this was the way that most early Christians looked at discrepancies of this kind.

3. Christians believed that the LXX was a divinely inspired translation and so if it diverged from the Hebrew, it was to be preferred as a more recent (and therefore superior) revelation from God. That was certainly what many Christians in later times maintained, but the New Testament writers were too conversant with the Hebrew text to say this. They were happy to quote the LXX as the Word of God because to them the inspiration of Scripture was "plenary" but not "verbal." This is a modern distinction that requires some adaptation when applied to ancient Israel and the early church, but it is important nonetheless.[49] Both Jews and Christians believed that the Hebrew Bible was fully inspired by God and that, as Jesus famously said, not "one jot or one tittle" of it would be unfulfilled or made redundant.[50] But neither Jews nor Christians attached so much importance to the precise words of the text that only one version of it could be authoritative. Above all, they did not think that translation into another language was impossible or that Scripture could only be read in the original Hebrew.

---

[46] This is the case in Deut. 14:12–18.

[47] The ESV follows the Masoretic text in Genesis, but leaves the word "staff" in Hebrews.

[48] It is, however, what the New International Version does.

[49] In modern times, "plenary" inspiration has sometimes been used to allow translators to paraphrase the original text, as long as its basic meaning is preserved, with the result that it is suspect in the eyes of those who maintain "verbal" inspiration and prefer more literal translations. In the ancient world, however, belief in "verbal inspiration" would have meant excluding the possibility of translation altogether.

[50] Matt. 5:18 (KJV). The "jot" is the letter *yod* (equivalent to our *i*) and a tittle is a small stroke that distinguishes some Hebrew letters from others (e.g., *resh* from *daleth*, *nun* from *waw*, and *beth* from *resh*). It may be compared to the distinctions made in our alphabet between C and G, between O and Q and between P and R.

In later centuries Jews would retreat to their Hebrew text and adopt a strictly "verbal" doctrine of divine inspiration that ruled out translation. This view would also be adopted by Muslims, who believe that their Qur'an can only be truly read in the original (and divinely inspired) Arabic, but Christians have never embraced so narrow an approach to the biblical text. The Eastern churches retained the LXX as a divinely inspired translation and forgot the Hebrew, though they were not averse to translating their Greek version into other languages.[51] For its part, the Western church regarded the Latin translation made by Jerome in the late fourth century (known as the Vulgate) as infallible, and insisted that it should be used to the exclusion of all others, although it never went so far as to say that it was divinely inspired.[52] The Roman Catholic Church canonized it at the Council of Trent in 1546, at a time when humanist scholars and Protestants were challenging both the authority and the accuracy of the Latin.[53]

Protestants wanted to go back to the original languages but also to translate the Bible directly from them into the vernacular tongues of Europe. In doing this they returned to the view of the early church, which was that the text was fully inspired but not in a way that rules out any possibility of translation. The big difference between the sixteenth-century Protestant (and generally modern) approach and that of the ancients is that the original texts are now fully recognized as the standard by which the church's teaching and preaching must be measured. Not everyone learns the languages concerned, but there is now no danger that they will be lost or disregarded as they were for many centuries; nor can any translation take their place in the way that the LXX and the Vulgate once did. Today all serious theology and scholarship must engage with the original texts, and even make new translations of them if the existing ones are unable to convey their meaning with sufficient accuracy.

At the same time, we have to recognize that our standards were not those of the early church, which was often prepared to advance theological arguments on the basis of readings that would be universally rejected today. Whether (and to what extent) the conclusions drawn from such a procedure must also

[51] But note that a Modern Greek version is called an "interpretation" (*hermêneia*) and not a "translation" (*metaphrasis*).

[52] The distinction between "Eastern" and "Western" churches is based on the division of the Roman empire in the late fourth century. For the most part, the West was Latin-speaking, so that "Western" and "Latin" can be used synonymously for theological purposes. The Eastern situation was more complex. Greek was the *lingua franca* in the Eastern part of the empire, but there were important communities where it was not spoken, and translation into the different vernaculars was more common. The Western church was also united around the see of Rome, whereas the East recognized four centers of authority—Constantinople, Alexandria, Antioch, and Jerusalem, each of which constituted a separate "church."

[53] The decree was issued at Session 4 on April 8, 1546. See *Conciliorum oecumenicorum decreta* (Bologna: Istituto per le Scienze Religiose, 1973), 664–665.

be rejected is a matter of debate. In some cases, the points being made can be supported from other texts that have not been so misinterpreted, and so they can be allowed to stand for that reason. Other cases are more problematic, and Christians have differed as to how much weight should be given to the force of tradition as a guide for interpretation. All that can be said here is that the texts concerned have to be considered on their own merits and that blanket judgments either for or against accepting traditional understandings of them must be avoided.

In the course of time Christians and Jews would come to differ about what the text of the Old Testament was, as well as about how particular verses should be interpreted, but this did not worry the New Testament writers or the churches to which they wrote. It was only after the Hebrew text was standardized that this became a significant issue, particularly in dialogue with Jews. The desirability of making the Greek text correspond to the Hebrew was often accepted by educated Christians, but not when it came to Isaiah 7:14, where an important theological principle was involved. The LXX says that "a virgin shall conceive," using the Greek word *parthenos* to translate the Hebrew *almah*, which means "young woman" (Greek, *neanis*).[54] It is probable that the translators thought that sexual intercourse marked the transition from youth to adulthood, making the two words virtually synonymous. Christians naturally relied on *parthenos* as a prophecy of the virgin birth of Christ, and the verse is quoted to this effect in the New Testament.[55] No one objected to this at the time, but the issue came to a head in the mid-second century when Aquila and others corrected this apparent error by using *neanis* instead of *parthenos* in their translations.

The threat that this kind of revision posed to the church is amply demonstrated by Justin Martyr's *Dialogue with Trypho*, which may be dated to about AD 155.[56] Trypho, who is usually identified as the Jewish rabbi Tarphon, challenged the accuracy of the LXX translation, and Justin responded by offering two counterarguments to this. First, he said (quite rightly, it would seem) that there is nothing special about a young woman giving birth. That is so commonplace that it could hardly be regarded as a special sign, as the text indicates it would be. If a young woman who was not a virgin had had a son, how would anyone have guessed that something unique had occurred? Less persuasively, Justin followed Philo and argued that the LXX was a divinely inspired translation, of which this verse was an outstanding example. The Hebrew was am-

[54] The Hebrew word for "virgin" is *bethulah*.

[55] Matt. 1:23.

[56] Justin Martyr, *Dialogus cum Tryphone* 43.3–8; 67.1; 68.9; 71.3; 77.3; 84.1, 3.

biguous and somewhat banal but the Greek was clear and prophetic, as inspired Scripture ought to be. In this instance, which was of supreme importance for the teaching of the church, Justin felt that he needed the Philonic myth to buttress his theological position, and later generations generally accepted his logic. The long-term effect of this was that Christians began to ignore the Hebrew and even to regard it as having been corrupted by anti-Christian Jews. Only the LXX could be relied on for theological construction—a belief that was to remain unchanged in the Eastern churches and is occasionally still advocated by some very conservative Western Christians today.

The LXX was to have an enormous impact on the choice of theological vocabulary used by the New Testament writers and by the early Christians in general. It is to the LXX that we owe the translation of "Torah" as "law" (*nomos*), when it might just as easily have been rendered as "teaching" or "instruction" (*didachê*). Likewise, it was the LXX that translated *berith* as *diathêkê* ("testament" or "covenant") and most importantly, *panim* ("face") as *prosôpon*, the word later used to mean "person" in the theological sense. The LXX thus created a biblical terminology that prepared the way for the coming of Christ by making the Greek language capable of absorbing Christian theological concepts. Without that, preaching the gospel would have been much harder and the church's theological tradition would not have developed as quickly and as (relatively) painlessly as it did. In this way, Hellenistic Jews played an important part in the life of the early church without being aware of it. Later Judaism would move off in a different direction, and the Hellenists would cease to exist as an identifiable group within Israel—but by the time that happened the seeds they had sown had grown and helped to produce the fruit that we now call Christian theology.

Christianity and Jewish Biblical Interpretation

Most Christians today do not realize that the New Testament writers often used rabbinical methods of interpreting the Old Testament, despite the great revival of interest in the Judaism of Jesus' day that has occurred over the past century and revolutionized our understanding of this phenomenon.[57] It had always been known that Paul received the best rabbinical education available in his time, because he said so himself.[58] But for centuries little attention was paid to the possibility that Jewish influences seriously affected his interpretation of

[57] See W. D. Davies, *Paul and Rabbinic Judaism* (London: SPCK, 1948). For a Jewish perspective, see Jacob Neusner, *Christian Faith and the Bible of Judaism: The Judaic Encounter with Scripture* (Grand Rapids, MI: Eerdmans, 1987). For an overall summary of the different views held on the subject, see David L. Baker, *Two Testaments, One Bible*, 2nd ed. (Leicester: Apollos, 1991).

[58] Acts 22:3.

the Bible. Now, however, we know enough about Jewish biblical exegesis in the first century AD to be able to assess its impact on the New Testament, and the results show us how important it was, especially when Christians were arguing with Jews. Methods of interpretation that were used in the rabbinical schools are echoed not only by Paul but throughout the New Testament, and they help us to understand how arguments that seem strange to us were accepted by Jews at that time. For example, in Matthew 2:23 we read,

> And he [Joseph] went and lived in a city called Nazareth, so that what was spoken by the prophets might be fulfilled, that he [Jesus] would be called a Nazarene.

On the surface, this does not appear to make much sense. Joseph was already living in Nazareth before Jesus was born,[59] so he was returning home, though Matthew gives the impression that Joseph was going there for the first time. More importantly, there is nothing in the prophets to say that Jesus would come from Nazareth, a place that is not even mentioned in the Old Testament. Matthew was presumably referring to Judges 13:5, where the angel of the Lord says to the wife of Manoah of Zorah, the future mother of Samson,

> . . . behold, you shall conceive and bear a son. No razor shall come upon his head, for the child shall be a Nazirite to God from the womb, and he shall begin to save Israel from the hand of the Philistines.

The Nazirites were members of a strict Jewish sect, and the word has nothing to do with Nazareth. But "Nazirite" sounds like "Nazarene," and that was enough to permit this kind of word play, which was very common among the rabbis. Furthermore, there are other, more substantial similarities between the two stories. Like Manoah and his wife, Mary was visited by an angel who told her that she would bear a son, who would also save Israel from its enemies. Samson, the son of Manoah, was certainly not the promised Messiah, but as a judge of Israel he was a prototype of the Savior who was to come and he is mentioned in the list of the great heroes of faith in Hebrews 11.[60] The fact that Jesus succeeded where Samson failed was further proof that the two men were connected, because the Old Testament was interpreted as a record of Israel's failure to achieve what only the Messiah could do. Christ therefore fulfilled the promise made concerning Samson just as much as he fulfilled those made to Abraham and Moses. A verse that appears to be mistaken in linking

[59] Luke 2:4.
[60] Heb. 11:32.

"Nazarene" to "Nazirite" turns out to have a profound theological meaning and provides a good example of how the early Christians found Christ in all the Scriptures, as he taught them to do.[61]

Here we meet a kind of interpretation that we would not accept if someone were to make it today but that seemed perfectly valid to those to whom it was addressed.[62] The rabbis were accustomed to the idea that divine truths were hidden beneath the surface of mundane realities and did not care that "Nazirite" and "Nazarene" are etymologically unrelated. To them, both words pointed to a higher reality, the clear outlines of which could be discerned only by those who understood the spirit of prophecy. Their relationship transcended human reason, and only those able to rise up to that higher sphere of knowledge could perceive it. They also believed that, in a world ruled by a sovereign God, nothing happened by accident. Joseph went to Nazareth for a reason, even if he did not understand what it was. With hindsight everything became clear, and the "signs" were discovered and interpreted accordingly.

Jewish biblical interpretation can be analyzed into four different types, though in practice these were often combined and can sometimes be difficult to distinguish. The first, and in the New Testament by far the most common of them was literal exegesis. This took the text as it stood and read it accordingly. Clear examples of this can be found in the story of the temptation of Jesus, who answers the Devil by quoting three verses from Deuteronomy.[63] It can also be found in Paul, who often quotes the Torah in a perfectly straightforward way.[64] Stephen's speech to the Jewish leaders, in which he recapitulates the history of Israel, is another outstanding example.[65] The early church was firmly grounded in actual events, and it never lost sight of the fundamental importance of the literal meaning of the Old Testament.

Nonliteral Jewish interpretation can be classified as *midrash*, *pesher*, or allegory. Only the last of these is familiar to us today, probably because it is of Greek origin and was applied to nonreligious as well as to religious texts. In the first century it was mainly used by Philo, as we might expect, and hardly at all elsewhere, and its virtual absence from the New Testament shows us that the mind-set of Hellenistic Judaism barely touched the apostles and their colleagues. As the apostle to the Gentiles, Paul did make some use of allegory, though it is noticeable that this was of a Pharisaic rather than a

---

[61] See Luke 24:44–47.

[62] On this tension and how it might be dealt with, see Peter Enns, *Inspiration and Incarnation: Evangelicals and the Problem of the Old Testament* (Grand Rapids, MI: Baker Academic, 2005).

[63] Deut. 8:3; 6:16, and 6:13, quoted in Matt. 4:4, 7, and 10 respectively. Deuteronomy is the most frequently quoted book of the Torah in the New Testament, and it was almost always read literally.

[64] See, for example, Rom. 7:7 (Ex. 20:12–17); 1 Cor. 6:16 (Gen. 2:24); and 2 Cor. 13:1 (Deut. 19:15).

[65] Acts 7:1–53. The same can be said for Heb. 11:1–38.

Philonic type.[66] In other words, it was closer to what we would now call typology, using genuine historical events to illustrate spiritual principles rather than ignoring the historicity of the Old Testament stories altogether. The best known example of this is found in Galatians 4:21–31, where Paul compares Jews and Christians to the two sons of Abraham. Ishmael, the son of the slave concubine Hagar, represents Israel because he was the natural son, whereas Isaac stands for the church of Christ because he was the spiritual child and the true heir of the covenant that God had made with his father. Ishmael and Israel both came into being as a result of the natural process of human reproduction, but Isaac and the church existed only because of a promise made by God.

Much more common was *midrash*, a form of interpretation whose goal was to penetrate the spirit of the biblical text in order to uncover meanings that were not immediately obvious. As a method, it was not as fully defined in Jesus' day as it was to be later on, but it was already very popular among the Pharisees and an attempt to regulate it had been made by the great rabbi Hillel in the first century BC. Jesus often used midrashic interpretation when arguing with Jewish leaders, and it seems that it was particularly popular in one-on-one debates.[67] Paul, as a Pharisee himself, made considerable use of it, often in quite a sophisticated way.[68] In particular, the influence of Hillel can be detected in several places, much more often than it can be in the teaching of Jesus, perhaps because Jesus had not been taught by rabbis.[69]

The most popular method of Jewish interpretation used by the early Christians, however, was *pesher*. *Pesher* is an Aramaic word meaning "solution," and its stands in opposition to *raz*, which means "puzzle" or "riddle." This is the kind of interpretation we have already met with in the example of Nazirite-Nazarene given above. It assumes that everything has a veiled meaning, which has to be extracted from the text by methods that may seem strange to us. Jews believed that God had revealed mysteries (*raz*) to the prophets and had given the gift of interpretation (*pesher*) to others.[70] In the Qumran community, the gift of interpretation belonged to the enigmatic Teacher of Righteousness, who was himself a prophetic, semi-eschatological figure. *Pesher* interpretation was not scholarly analysis but had its own charismatic and revelatory quality, which made it particularly suited to the ministry of Jesus. A famous example of it can

[66] 1 Cor. 9:9; 10:1–4; Gal. 4:21–31.

[67] For examples, see Matt. 7:11; 10:25; Mark 2:25–28; 12:26: Luke 12:28.

[68] See Rom. 3:10–18; 9:19–29; 10:18–21; Gal. 3:10–13.

[69] See Rom. 4:1–12; 5:15–21; 13:8–10; Gal. 3:8–17. It is probable that links between Jesus and Hillel (as in Matt. 7:11) were accidental, whereas Paul would have known his teaching and is more likely to have used it deliberately.

[70] Note the similarity here to what Paul says about speaking in tongues and their interpretation, in 1 Cor. 14:13–19.

be found in the story of Jesus' preaching in the synagogue at Nazareth, when he read from Isaiah and then told the startled congregation that the prophet's words had been fulfilled in their hearing![71] Another famous example of the same phenomenon occurs in Peter's speech on the day of Pentecost, in which he compared the events of that day to the prophetic vision of Joel.[72]

Pesher interpretation lent itself naturally to the theme of the fulfillment of prophecy, and so we should not be surprised to find that it is common in the Gospels, in the opening chapters of Acts, and in the epistle to the Hebrews. Nor should we be surprised to discover that it is relatively rare in Paul, who was less immediately concerned with the theme of prophetic fulfillment.[73]

It is the Christocentric dimension of New Testament interpretation that distinguishes it most obviously from its Jewish counterparts. Rabbinic methods were used when they could be useful, but they were means to an end that was essentially foreign to the rabbis. As Richard Longenecker has put it,

> In the preaching of the early Christians, . . . one looks almost in vain for any clear consciousness of employing various methods of interpretation in quoting the Old Testament. For purposes of analysis we may (rightly, I believe) catalogue their methods and trace out their respective patterns. But the first Christian preachers seem to have made no sharp distinction between literalist treatments of the text, Midrash exegesis, Pesher interpretation, and the application of accepted predictive prophecies. All of these were employed, and at times there appears a blending and interweaving of methods. What they were conscious of, however, was interpreting the Scriptures from a Christocentric perspective, in conformity with the exegetical teaching and example of Jesus, and along Christological lines. In their exegesis there is the interplay of Jewish presuppositions and practices, on the one hand, and Christian commitments and perspectives on the other, which produced a distinctive interpretation of the Old Testament.[74]

However strange these methods may seem to us, we have to remember that the people and the circumstances that the apostles were addressing were quite different from anything we are familiar with. In seeking to evaluate their approach, what matters most is that their audiences accepted its validity and were often persuaded by their arguments. Today we think differently, and our message has to be adapted to meet the needs and expectations of our time, but it is still possible to defend a Christological interpretation of the Old Testament,

[71] Luke 4:18–19, quoting Isa. 61:1–2.
[72] Acts 2:17–21, quoting Joel 2:28–32.
[73] Paul does occasionally use it, though. See Rom. 16:25–27; Eph. 3:1–11.
[74] Richard Longenecker, *Biblical Exegesis in the Apostolic Period* (Grand Rapids, MI: Eerdmans, 1975), 103.

even among Jews.[75] God speaks to us where we are, not because he approves of our situation or agrees with our way of thinking, but because unless he does so we shall never hear his voice.[76] As Paul put it,

> To the Jews I became as a Jew, in order to win Jews. To those under the law I became as one under the law (though not being myself under the law) that I might win those under the law. To those outside the law I became as one outside the law (not being outside the law of God but under the law of Christ) that I might win those outside the law. To the weak I became weak, that I might win the weak. I have become all things to all people, that by all means I might save some.[77]

Jewish methods of interpreting the Bible faded out of the church as it turned from preaching to them and went to the Gentiles instead. What they took with them was the Old Testament and their conviction that it prophesied the coming of the Messiah for all nations—to the Jews first, but also to the rest of the world. Preaching to non-Jewish people required a different approach, but the underlying message remained the same and the inheritance of Israel was recycled to make it speak to a different intellectual and religious climate. *Midrash* and *pesher* interpretations disappeared and were replaced by allegory, but the literal meaning of the text remained fundamental and determined how the other methods would be used.

In early Christian exegesis, the appeal to allegory was normally permitted only when the plain sense of the text seemed to require it, either because the text as it stood was immoral or unsatisfactory, or because it was not intended to be taken literally to begin with. Thus we find allegorical interpretations of the parables of Jesus (which were not accounts of historical events) and of those psalms that advocated the murder of little children.[78] The Song of Songs was in a category of its own. Its eroticism seemed strange for a work of spiritual edification, and so it was almost always interpreted in an allegorical way, as an illustration of the relationship either between Christ and the church or between Christ and the individual believer.[79] But these were exceptional cases, and easily explained by the nature of the texts involved. On the whole, the church read the Old Testament as history, and disputed with the Jews the right to claim it as children of Abraham. But the way they interpreted its details was quite

[75] The difference of course is that, for Jews, the messianic prophecies have yet to be fulfilled.
[76] He even spoke to the wise men through astrology! See Matt. 2:2.
[77] 1 Cor. 9:20–22.
[78] See Ps. 137:9, for example.
[79] See Mark W. Elliott, *The Song of Songs and Christology in the Early Church 381–451* (Tübingen, Mohr Siebeck, 2000).

different and of great significance for the emergence of the Christian church as a missionary organization that was not attached to, and did not create, a distinct ethnicity.

Christianity and the Prehistory of Israel

Differences between the way in which Jews and Christians read the Bible can be discerned from its very beginning. In New Testament times, Jews and Christians both interpreted the pre-Abrahamic period (recounted in Genesis 1–11) as essentially "prehistoric." This did not mean that they thought the stories were mythical, but that they thought those accounts had been transmitted orally over many generations before being written down. Nothing in Genesis 1–11 could be regarded as an eyewitness account of the events being described, and many of the names that appear in the narrative were either unknown to later history or else "generic"—the eponymous ancestors of historical nations, for example. People read of their existence and of the place they occupied in the development and differentiation of the human race, but did not relate to them as individuals in the way that they related to Abraham, Isaac, and Jacob, who were the recognized ancestors of their faith community in a way that Enoch and Methuselah were not.

From the prehistoric period the Jews learned that all human beings were descended from Adam and Eve, and are therefore related to one another. Every man and woman, however "primitive" he or she might be in cultural terms, was made in the image and likeness of God and shared in the dominion over creation that was given to Adam. Jewish tradition always accepted that principle, at least in theory, even if it did not make much of it in practice. This was because their reading of the narrative placed the emphasis on the progressive differentiation of the human race, leading eventually to the emergence of the chosen people of Israel. To them, the appearance of other nations was rather like the creation of the other planets. It was nice to know about them, but with the exception of their near neighbors and close relations, they did not impinge on Israel most of the time and made little difference to their everyday lives.

Christians however, could not adopt a detached attitude to the existence of non-Jews (or unbelievers). With its calling to preach the gospel of Christ to the ends of the earth, the church had to come to terms with the common humanity of all people, not just of those whom Israel recognized as Gentiles but also of those who are not mentioned in the Old Testament at all. There was never any suggestion that northern Europeans, for example, were excluded from the promises of God merely because their names did not appear in Genesis. The unity of the human race went back to the beginning and covered everyone. In that sense Jesus Christ was regarded as the "new Adam" who came to die for people of every tribe and nation, and the history of the human race was brought together in him.[80]

The creation account in Genesis teaches that men and women are fundamentally equal, since both were created in the image and likeness of God, but that within this equality there is an order of priority and a certain differentiation. The woman was taken out of the man and intended to be his helper, a belief which in later times was enshrined in the concept of male "headship."[81] This headship was intrinsic to their relationship. The woman was expected to submit to her husband's authority, and in return the man was expected to take care of his wife and sacrifice his interests to hers.[82] The pattern established in the garden of Eden carried over into the life of the church, which was called to model male-female relationships as they were originally meant to be.[83] Here again, Jews and Christians were in fundamental agreement, but Judaism was (and is) patriarchal in a way that Christianity has never been. The most obvious example of this is that while among Jews only men were given the covenant sign of circumcision, the church has always baptized men and women without distinction because we are all one in Christ.[84]

The creation story also tells us that Adam and Eve had a knowledge of God that might be described as a "personal relationship" with him, but that this relationship was both inferior to what God intends for us now and compromised by their disobedience. On the first point, Theophilus of Antioch (late second century) wrote,

> Because he was still a child, Adam was unable to receive knowledge in the right way. . . . The reason God commanded him not to eat [of the tree of] knowledge was not that God was trying to be nasty to him, as some people think. In reality, God wanted to test Adam, to see whether he would obey his commands. At the same time, he wanted man, child that he was, to remain simple and innocent a little while longer.[85]

As for their disobedience, Irenaeus of Lyon (130?–200) had this to say:

[80] 1 Cor. 15:22, 45.
[81] 1 Cor. 11:4–16.
[82] Eph. 5:22–33.
[83] 2 Cor. 5:17; Gal. 6:15; 1 Tim. 2:11–15.
[84] Gal. 3:28.
[85] Theophilus of Antioch, *Ad Autolycum* 2.25.

> Disobedience to God brings death. For that reason, Adam and Eve were subjected to the penalty of death. From that very moment, they were handed over to it. They died the same day that they ate . . .[86]

As a result of their sin, human beings can no longer fulfill the tasks that God assigned to them or enjoy the blessings that they were meant to inherit, even though the original divine command has not been rescinded nor have the promised blessings been annulled. Sin has not reduced humanity to the level of the animals, but it has introduced an anomalous situation that is in conflict with God's original intention for us. For this sad state of affairs, human beings are entirely responsible, because it is we who have rejected God and not the other way around. Jews and Christians both agreed that the main purpose of the biblical revelation was to show how God has overcome this problem and restored the right relationship between himself and at least some of his human creatures. Where they differed was over the means he had chosen to accomplish that—the law of Moses or the gospel of Christ.

The first Christians shared the traditional Jewish belief that sin could be atoned for only by sacrifice. Because sin had cut Adam and Eve off from the God of life and brought death into the world, this sacrifice had to include death, but in prehistoric times that was imperfectly understood. The story of Cain and Abel shows us that Abel realized it but Cain did not. Abel's sacrifice of a slaughtered lamb was acceptable to God, but Cain, whose offering of vegetables was rejected as inadequate, turned around and killed him out of jealousy. The lesson drawn from that was that persecution and martyrdom was symptomatic of what would happen to those who offered true worship to God, and Christians did not hesitate to refer to the blood of righteous Abel, whose witness was powerful in the early church.[87] The apostle Paul boasted of his sufferings for the gospel, and warned Timothy that "all who desire to live a godly life in Christ Jesus will be persecuted."[88] Furthermore, the early Christians were convinced that the attacks against them would begin among their own Jewish people, who had murdered the prophets of old because of their unwelcome faithfulness to God.[89]

The only other prehistoric patriarchs who made much of an impact on the early Christians were Enoch and Noah. There was a certain fascination with Enoch among Jews in New Testament times, and prophecies attributed to him

[86] Irenaeus of Lyon, *Adversus omnes haereses* 5.23.2.
[87] Heb. 11:4.
[88] 2 Tim. 3:11–12. See also 2 Cor. 11:23–33.
[89] Matt. 23:35–37, which mentions the murder of Zechariah the son of Berachiah (Zech. 1:1) as well as that of Abel. Note too that there was another Zechariah, the son of Jehoiada the high priest, who was also murdered in Jerusalem (2 Chron. 24:20–22).

circulated widely. One of them was actually quoted by Jude, though whether he thought it was authentic is impossible to say.[90] The book of *Enoch* never became canonical Scripture, partly because the Jewish authorities did not believe that anything written by Enoch could have survived the flood and partly because they had no interest in anything that claimed to be pre-Mosaic.[91] But Enoch retained his fascination among Christians for another reason: he was the seventh in the descent of Adam and had been taken up to God without passing through death, which was a sign of his exceptional righteousness.[92] As understood by Christians, that righteousness was the fruit of Enoch's faith, and he was held up among them as a prime example of someone who had been justified by faith alone. Moreover, whereas the other patriarchs had enjoyed exceptionally long lives, which the Jews attributed to their good behavior,[93] Enoch went up to heaven remarkably young—a mere lad of 365! For Christians this was a sign that to be cut off in the prime of life, as so many of them were, was not a curse but a blessing, especially if they died as witnesses to their faith—even though that interpretation has nothing to do with the text.[94]

Noah was the other prehistoric figure who made a great impression on later generations. As the only righteous man left in his time, he was spared during the great flood that God sent to wipe out the world that had fallen into sin. Because he was faithful, Noah received God's promise that the world would never again be destroyed on account of its sinfulness.[95] Both Jews and Christians recognized that the world was an evil place, and that it continued to exist only because of this divine promise. Salvation would therefore have to come by redeeming this sinful world, and not at the expense of its destruction. That this promise had implications for the future of Israel was made clear by the prophet Isaiah,[96] but Ezekiel taught that Noah's righteousness had no power to save anyone but himself.[97] The conclusion must be that the covenant of preservation that God had given to Noah was not a form of salvation, but only the necessary preliminary for what would later be made available to those who were righteous.

At first sight, it might seem as though the Jews believed that only Israel was

[90] Jude 14–15, quoting *1 Enoch* 1:9.

[91] Surprising as it seems to us, they may not have realized that Enoch's prophecies were of recent origin, and did not come from him.

[92] Gen. 5:22–24, quoted in Heb. 11:5. Jude (v. 14) mentions that he was the seventh from Adam—a significant number.

[93] See Gen. 47:9 for confirmation of this.

[94] On Enoch, see Clement of Rome, *Epistula I* 9; Irenaeus of Lyon, *Adversus omnes haereses* 5.5.1; Tertullian, *De anima* 50.

[95] Gen. 8:21–22.

[96] Isa. 54:9.

[97] Ezek. 14:14, 20.

destined to receive that salvation, but although that is true, it must be carefully qualified. It was not Israel as a whole that would be saved but only a remnant, as Isaiah had said.[98] This remnant theology, as it is often called, characterized later Judaism, particularly after the exile, and gave the story of Noah its particular poignancy.[99] This was brought home by Jesus, who used the flood as a paradigm of the coming judgment.[100] Remnant theology is also found in Paul's great discourse about the future of the Jewish people, and the theme recurs in Hebrews and the Petrine epistles, with specific reference to Noah.[101] Peter compared the washing away of sin by the flood to the washing away of sin in baptism, using Noah as a prophetic witness of what God intended to do in Christ.[102]

The main difference between Jewish and Christian interpretations of Noah and the flood was seen in the way in which they understood the righteousness that was needed for salvation. For Jews this meant keeping the law, even though that could not have been true of Noah, who lived centuries before the law was given. Christians, however, interpreted it as the righteousness of faith, and in this respect they were undoubtedly closer to the meaning of the text, since it was because of his enduring faithfulness that God had agreed to spare Noah in the first place.[103] What was true of Noah was also true of Enoch and of all those who had lived before the law was given, as Irenaeus stated quite clearly:

> Enoch pleased God without being circumcised. He was God's messenger to the angels even though he was a man, and was taken up into heaven where he has been preserved until now as a witness of the just judgment of God. . . . Moreover, all the other righteous men who lived before Abraham, and those patriarchs who came before Moses, were justified quite apart from the law and its demands.[104]

Both Jews and Christians believed that the human race got off to a new start after the flood, but that rebellion against God continued and grew worse as time went on. In the end, that rebellion led to the emergence of distinct ethnic groups that could not communicate with one another—the curse of the tower of Babel.[105] The loss of a shared language set the seal on mankind's alienation from God, because it was no longer possible for everyone to be of one mind

[98] Isa. 1:9. The ESV translates this as "a few survivors." See also Isa. 10:22–23, quoted by Paul in Rom. 9:27.
[99] See, for example, Jer. 23:3; 31:7; 40:15; Ezek. 6:8; Mic. 5:7–8; Zeph. 2:7; Hag. 1:12–14; Zech. 8:12.
[100] Matt. 24:36–39.
[101] Rom. 11:5; Heb. 11:7; 2 Pet. 2:5.
[102] 1 Pet. 3:18–21.
[103] Gen. 6:9.
[104] Irenaeus of Lyon, *Adversus omnes haereses* 4.16.2.
[105] Gen. 11:1–9.

and one understanding with respect to him. If God spoke to one nation, the others would not understand what he was saying and so would not share in the blessing that his word brought. This clearly suited the Jews, who saw themselves as God's chosen people to the exclusion of everyone else. They had a common language, a common law and government, and a common worship with only one recognized center of authority, all of which set them apart as a distinct nation.[106]

The Christian church did not deny the validity of this Jewish interpretation of the destiny of Israel, but transcended it. Rather than set up a physical nation-state that would exclude outsiders while at the same time harboring unworthy members within its ranks in the way that Israel did, the church established itself as a spiritual society bound together by the indwelling power of the Holy Spirit, who gave it its common language and a unity of heart and mind that was otherwise lacking.[107] Somewhat ironically perhaps, it is in their respective answers to the curse of Babel that we can see the essential similarities and differences between Israel and the church most clearly. Both were pledged to worship the one God with one heart and one mind, but what Israel worked out in material terms that were given a spiritual meaning, the church expressed spiritually in ways that made use of material signs like water, bread, and wine, but that were not bound by them. In the church, external rites like baptism had their place, but they did not define the people of God in the physical way that circumcision had defined ancient Israel.[108]

The Christian Interpretation of Israel's History

The differences between Jewish and Christian interpretations of Israel's prehistory were only magnified when it came to the historical period. The first question that divided them was also the most fundamental—when did Israel's history begin? Jews traced their national origins to Moses and the law that he gave the people in the desert. That law continued to be the foundation of their religious life long after the political framework created by David and Solomon had fallen apart and the nation found itself exiled, dispersed, and subject to foreign control. According to Jewish tradition, Moses was the author of all five books of the Torah (Pentateuch), but only the last four of them described events contemporary with him. Genesis was important for Israel's self-understanding, but it was essentially a prologue that explained why the law of Moses took the shape it did.[109] Christians, on the other hand, looked back behind Moses and

[106] For the importance of this, see 1 Kings 11:25–33 and John 4:20–22.
[107] Acts 2:5–11.
[108] See, for example, 1 Cor. 11:27–30; 1 Pet. 3:21.
[109] A classic example of this can be seen in the fourth commandment, which establishes the Sabbath as a day of rest by comparing it with God's rest after he had created the world. Compare Ex. 20:11 with Gen. 2:2–3.

based their claims to be the people of God on the promises he had made to Abraham. They regarded Abraham, not Moses, as the true founder of Israel because he was the father of all who believe and trust in God.[110] Who was right?

The complexity of this dispute can perhaps be understood by comparing it with a well-known modern example. When did the history of the United States begin? Some people would say that it started with the migrations of the Amerindian tribes from Siberia, but this is prehistory, just as Genesis 1–11 is prehistory. No one denies that it happened, but it is shrouded in mist and uncertainty and its relevance to modern conditions is hard to discern. However sympathetic we may be to the Amerindians, we must accept that history in North America began with the European invasions of the sixteenth and seventeenth centuries. Between 1492 and 1763 Spain, France, and Britain established colonies and fought for supremacy in what they thought was a virtually uninhabited wilderness. This colonial period can be likened to the age from Abraham to Moses. It is historical and in direct continuity with what came later, yet at the same time it is distinct and separate from it. The United States as we know it today began to emerge only after 1763, when the French were expelled from America and the British colonies came together and rebelled against their mother country. The nation that exists now was created in the years from 1776 to 1789 by a series of events that may be compared to the exodus and the giving of the law at Mount Sinai.

So when did American history begin? Americans themselves are divided on how they answer this. Those who think in terms of the nation state look to the revolution and the constitution as the basis of American society just as the ancient Jews looked back to Moses. But those who think more in terms of spiritual and cultural values are liable to go back to the Pilgrim Fathers of 1620 and trace their origins to the idealism of a group of religious believers who set out to establish a new kind of society in an unknown land. This was what Abraham had done, and the Jews never forgot his call from God, even though it was interpreted through the prism of the Mosaic law. The two origin stories coexisted in ancient Israel, rather in the way that the Fourth of July and Thanksgiving coexist in the United States today.

In both Israel and the USA, the two perspectives can usually be harmonized reasonably well at the level of civil society, but they tend to diverge when religious questions are raised. In the American example, secularists appeal to the constitutional separation of church and state to justify their vision of American society, whereas believers look back to the Pilgrims as the founders of a Christian

[110] Rom. 4:1–25.

America. Similarly, in ancient Israel, those who thought of righteousness in terms of keeping the law appealed to Moses, but Christians, who saw faith as the essence of their identity, looked back to Abraham instead. The difference between the two cases is that whereas modern Americans have (so far) been able to live together in spite of their contrasting perceptions, Jews and Christians were forced apart because the Christian understanding of justification by faith was incompatible with the Jewish insistence on the need to do the works of the law, however much faith those who did such works may have had.[111]

For Jews, the legacy of Abraham was both ethnic and religious. It was ethnic because all Jews were physically descended from him, at least in theory.[112] It was religious because God made a covenant with him that he would find a new home in the land of Canaan and become the ancestor of a great nation. To this day, it is that promise which undergirds the claim of the Jewish people to the land of Palestine, as Canaan is now called.[113] That claim has never been uncontested, and only seldom has it been fully realized: under David and Solomon (tenth century BC), at the time of the Maccabees (c. 164–63 BC), and in our own day (since 1967).[114] Nevertheless, it has never ceased to be Israel's national ideal, and over the centuries Jews tried to maintain a presence in the "Promised Land" even when they had no hope of ruling it themselves. "Next year in Jerusalem" is the ancient Jewish Passover toast, but only recently has it once again become a reality for a significant number of Jews.

The religious and ethnic ingredients of Abraham's covenant were combined in the rite of circumcision, which explains why it was so important to Israelite nationhood. God gave it to Abraham as a reward for his faithful obedience, so its ultimate origin was religious, but it soon became a badge of ethnic identity, because Abraham was told to circumcise all his male descendants. Those who escaped it were not to be regarded as part of the nation or as inheritors of the covenant promises.[115]

The early Christians also regarded Abraham as their father, as Paul and James both testified.[116] They appealed to Abraham as the classic example of what a true child of God was—a man who was justified by his faith and not by the works of the law. When Jews (and Jewish Christians) tried to insist that

[111] Gal. 2:15–16.
[112] See John 8:39, 53, 56.
[113] The name Palestine is derived from Philistine, though modern Palestinians have no more connection to the Philistines than they have to the Canaanites. Both of those peoples vanished centuries ago, but the name Palestine survived because it was adopted by the Greeks and the Romans as the country's name.
[114] Israel became an independent state in May 1948, but only since the "six-day war" in June 1967 has it occupied the whole of ancient Palestine.
[115] Gen. 17:10–14.
[116] Rom. 4:16; James 2:21.

circumcision was necessary for Gentile converts to Christianity, Paul countered with a lengthy exposition of how the rite had come into existence. It had been given to Abraham, not as a precondition of his adherence to the covenant God made with him but as a sign of the faith which made that covenant possible in the first place.[117]

The Christian appeal to Abraham was primarily a spiritual one, and the early church saw itself as the heir to the covenant promises that had been handed down through the generations, symbolically represented in the trilogy of "Abraham, Isaac, and Jacob."[118] In this connection it is important to note that Christians did not claim alternative descent from Abraham in the way that Muslims were later to do. According to Islamic tradition, Muhammad and the Arabs are descended from Ishmael, Abraham's son by his concubine Hagar.[119] The early Christians did not say anything like that. They took over the stories of Isaac and Jacob without any difficulty, but they made less of them than they did of Abraham. Jacob was important to Jews because he was the ancestor of the twelve tribes of Israel, to each of whom a portion of the Promised Land had been given, but this was less significant for Christians.[120]

Paul knew that he was a Benjamite, so some memory of the ancient tribes persisted in New Testament times, but this had no bearing on the church. Ten of the tribes had been "lost" as long ago as 722 BC, when the northern kingdom of Israel had been carried away into Assyrian exile, so only Judah and Benjamin were left, though the phrase "twelve tribes" continued to be used to describe the Jews who were dispersed across the ancient world, and the first Christians followed this practice, at least when they were talking to fellow Jews.[121] In the fullness of time, said Paul, all Israel would be saved, and we should not be surprised to find him speaking of the twelve tribes in that context.[122] For Christians, the tribes of Israel had an eschatological significance that did not correspond to the earthly membership of the church, where Jew and Gentile mingled to form a new people of God.

Of the sons of Jacob, the one who made the greatest impression on the early Christians was Joseph, partly because of the way he had been persecuted by his brothers and had been rescued by God, but mostly because he was the

---

117 Gal. 3:1–4:31.

118 Heb. 11:9. See Irenaeus of Lyon, *Adversus omnes haereses* 4.21.1–3.

119 Qur'an, Sura 2:122–128. The Bible tells us that Ishmael became a desert nomad (Gen. 21:20–21; 25:12–18), so some link between him and the Arabs is possible, but it has to be said that the Islamic claim is more fantasy than fact.

120 Levi was an exception. As the priestly tribe, the Levites were not allotted any particular territory to dwell in.

121 See James 1:1. Whether Jesus chose his twelve disciples to represent the Israelite tribes is uncertain, but if he did, it makes his betrayal by Judas, the disciple who bore the name of the tribe of Judah, which had given its name to the Jewish people, even more poignant.

122 See Rom. 11:25–26.

one who led Israel into Egypt, where it had time to grow and multiply before persecution led to the exodus and the establishment of the nation as it came to be known in later times.[123] Joseph also figures (instead of his son Ephraim) in the list of the twelve tribes that we find in the great vision of the saved in the book of Revelation, though no explanation for this is given.[124]

But however important Abraham, Isaac, and Jacob were to Jews at the time of Jesus, there can be no doubt that for most of them Israel had been formed into a nation by Moses, their great liberator and lawgiver. It was Moses who had set up the priesthood and sacrifices that would eventually find their home in the temple at Jerusalem, and it was through him that God had given the law that would bind the nation together in a common set of observances. Even a cursory reading of the Gospels and Acts will demonstrate how significant this was.[125] As it turned out, the followers of Jesus belonged to the last generation of Jews who would have direct experience of the temple and its worship. The temple plays a major role in the Gospels and even in the Acts of the Apostles, where we are told that the apostle Paul went to worship there on his last visit to Jerusalem, regardless of the antagonism which his preaching had provoked among the Jews and the danger of arrest that he faced. On that occasion he was accused of having taken Trophimus, a Gentile from Ephesus, into the temple with him (though he claimed that he had not done so)—a reminder that the temple could not be a focus for Christian worship in the same way that it was for Jews, because non-Jewish members of the church would not have been admitted to it.[126]

That incident highlights the dilemma that the Mosaic law posed for the early church. Jewish Christians were free to observe it as much as they liked, and many of them did so. But at the same time, Paul insisted that Gentile Christians were free *not* to practice Jewish rituals as long as they avoided giving unnecessary offense to Jews.[127] The logic that justified this was that the rituals of the Mosaic law had become redundant traditions that Christians could dispense with because they were superfluous to belief in Christ.

Discontent with the way pious Jews observed the law of Moses is an inescapable feature of the New Testament. We find it in the teaching of Jesus, who was born under the law and lived according to it all his life, but who nevertheless found it wanting for different reasons.[128] In some respects, Jesus thought

[123] See Acts 7:9–16; Heb. 11:21–22.
[124] Rev. 7:8.
[125] Mark 10:3; Luke 20:37; John 5:46; 7:19–23; 9:28–29; Acts 3:22.
[126] Acts 21:26–29.
[127] By eating meat that had been sacrificed to idols, for example; Rom. 14:1–23; 1 Cor. 8:1–13; Acts 15:19–20.
[128] See Matt. 5:17–48.

that the way the rabbis interpreted the law was too lenient. This was the case with its permission of divorce, which Jesus told his disciples Moses had allowed because of the people's hardness of heart, but which was not God's original intention.[129] In other ways, though, it was too strict, particularly in the details of its food laws.[130] Nothing that God made could be called unclean, and yet the law of Moses had set up a barrier between what could and could not be eaten that had become a distinguishing mark of Jews in wider society.[131]

In essence Jesus and his disciples taught that the law of Moses was a rescue operation, designed to preserve a semblance of Abraham's faith in a nation which was not capable of rising to the spiritual heights that had so distinguished him.[132] In that sense it was a straitjacket that tied Israel to the right pathway despite their inveterate tendency to err. When the jacket was too tight for comfort, Jewish leaders had a way of letting it out by reinterpreting its more difficult prescriptions in ways that made it easier to bear. Thus, for example, the command to "honor father and mother," which involved taking care of them in old age, could be avoided by paying a tax to the temple in lieu. This tax, known as *corban*, dispensed the person who paid it from any obligation to his parents, and was a superficially pious means of escaping responsibility for them.[133] Yet from the standpoint of those who devised such interpretations, it was a practical way of applying a law that was otherwise vague and difficult to keep.

Jesus' criticism of this approach shows that he and his Jewish interlocutors disagreed about what the law really meant. For Jesus it verbalized spiritual principles which, if they were taken seriously, were far more demanding than the literal fulfillment of the written prescription. To the Jewish leaders of his day, however, the law was a set of axioms that had to be spelled out in detail if they were to have any force, and they were afraid that if its commands were unmanageable no one would obey them. They probably thought that Jesus was being impossibly idealistic, which in a sense was true. Neither Jesus nor his followers believed that people could keep the law by following its external rules and precepts. Only a change of heart brought about by the Holy Spirit could do that, and if that happened, the detailed prescriptions of the written law would lose much of their meaning. Who would worry about what he ate if he knew that sin and corruption came from his heart and mind, and not from the food he consumed?

The apostle Paul followed Jesus' teaching about the law closely and developed

---

[129] Matt. 19:7–9.
[130] Matt. 15:17–20.
[131] Acts 10:28.
[132] Matt. 19:7–9; Gal. 3:17–26.
[133] Mark 7:9–13.

it even further. Like Jesus, he had also been born under the law and had done his best to keep and defend it before his conversion. But when he realized what Jesus was saying, the scales fell from his eyes and he understood Moses in a completely new way. Like Jesus, he never doubted that the law of Moses was the word of God. In itself, the law was holy, righteous, and perfect, but it could not be kept to the letter.[134] A man who had the Holy Spirit of God dwelling in his heart did not need to be circumcised in the flesh because he possessed something more powerful than that. Circumcision was an outward reminder to Jews of what they were supposed to subscribe to, but the presence of the Spirit was an inward compulsion to do what the law required, whether the resulting actions were the same as what it prescribed or not. As Origen (185?–254?) put it,

> Christianity was introduced into the world through Mosaic worship and the prophetic writings, but once that introduction had been made, there was progress through the interpretation and explanation of those things. . . . Those who grow in the faith of Christ do not treat the law with disrespect. On the contrary, they give it greater honor, showing what depth of wise and mysterious reasoning those writings contain, something that the Jews do not fully understand.[135]

The consensus of the New Testament was that the law of Moses, good as it was in itself, had to be transcended. This had dramatic implications for the priestly system of sacrifices that Moses had set up and invested in his brother Aaron. It was still in operation in Jesus' time, but as he had come to be the Great High Priest who would make the one, perfect, and sufficient sacrifice that would be valid forever, the days of the sacrificial system were numbered. Jews who believed in Jesus had no more need of the temple sacrifices, and when they disappeared after the destruction of Jerusalem in AD 70, Christians had no desire to see them restored. Everything the sacrifices had pictured had been fulfilled in Christ, and so the end of the earthly sacrifices made no difference to them. On the contrary, the end of the sacrifices strengthened their case, because they could claim that God had permitted the destruction of the temple once it was no longer needed. Like the prophets, the early Christians insisted that the temple was merely a symbol, a convenient way of remembering God's presence in Israel, but not essential to his sovereign rule over his people.[136]

Of the post-Mosaic period the early Christians had surprisingly little to say. In the two extended accounts of Israel's history that we find in the New

---

[134] Rom. 7:7–23.
[135] Origen, *Contra Celsum* 2.4.
[136] Acts 7:48–51, quoting Isa. 66:1–2.

Testament, that of Stephen, the first Christian martyr, ends with Solomon, and that of the writer to the Hebrews peters out with David and a vague reference to the prophets.[137] This can hardly be an accident, especially given the fact that Jesus was hailed as the "son of David," the new Solomon who was greater than the old.[138] It was Solomon who had built the original temple, of course, and Jesus saw himself very much in that tradition; his body was to be the temple of the new covenant that God was making with his people, and in him priest, sacrifice, and temple would all be rolled into one.[139]

The identification of Jesus with the Davidic monarchy was important because it was the fulfillment of the prophecy that David would never lack for a successor to reign over Israel. In human terms it could be argued that not only had that prophecy not been fulfilled, it had been denied by the destruction of Jerusalem in 586 BC and the deportation of the Davidic royal family to Babylon.[140] Later kings of Israel were not of the Davidic line, and the Herodians were actually Edomites (Idumaeans), a related but nevertheless non-Israelite nation.[141] By reestablishing the connection to David, the kingship that the New Testament claimed for Jesus fulfilled the ancient prophecy but in an unexpected way. Many of his followers believed that he would be the new David, but they thought of this in a purely worldly sense. Jesus was expected to raise the standard of revolt against Rome, set up a new Israelite kingdom, and rule over it in the way that Solomon had.

Instead, Jesus proclaimed the message that his kingdom was "not of this world."[142] Many of his would-be followers were disappointed, and the state authorities of the time mocked his pretensions. But in doing that, they unwittingly confirmed the promises God had made to his people long before and brought about the union of monarchy and priesthood that had eluded Israel throughout its historic existence. The crucified Christ was proclaimed "King of the Jews." He wore a crown of thorns and his throne was the cross, yet it was in these symbols that the true nature of his kingship was revealed. Jesus was not merely the new Solomon but the eternal king who had triumphed over sin and death, which the old Solomon could never have done. Jesus appropriated the legacy of David but interpreted it in a new and more spiritual way, as he did with the rest of the Old Testament.

---

[137] Acts 7:47; Heb. 11:32.

[138] Matt. 22:42; John 7:42; Luke 11:31.

[139] Matt. 26:61; John 2:19–21; Heb. 7:11–10:17.

[140] The promise made to David, that his descendants would reign forever on the throne of Judah, is a persistent theme of 2 Chronicles (see 2 Chron. 7:18; 21:7; 33:7), a book which also recounts the decline and fall of the Jerusalem monarchy.

[141] They were descended from Esau, Jacob's twin brother.

[142] John 18:36.

For the early Christians, the history of Israel culminated in the building of the temple by Solomon, and the rest was merely commentary. They made virtually nothing of the subsequent history of the kingdoms of Israel and Judah. The traumatic experience of the exile and return is largely passed over in silence. James and 1 Peter were addressed to the twelve tribes or "elect exiles" of the Dispersion, but what this meant is unclear. Most probably it was just a way of referring to those Jews who lived outside of Palestine, since none of the places mentioned was connected to the historical exile, nor were all twelve tribes removed at the same time.[143] As an event of theological significance, the exile plays no obvious part in the New Testament at all.

On the other hand, the first half of the millennium that separated Jesus from the time of Solomon was the age of the prophets, who pointed out how the dreams of David and Solomon had failed to materialize, how time and again the people had turned away from God and been punished for it, and how God had raised up spiritual giants to pass judgment on these failures and to proclaim that there would be a future divine intervention that would put everything right.

All the prophets played a part in this, but two stood out above the rest. The first of them was Elijah, whom the early Christians ranked with Enoch in importance and whose ministry was not yet completed. As Tertullian (160?–220?) put it,

> Enoch was translated and so was Elijah. They did not experience death because it was postponed (and only postponed). They have been reserved for the suffering of death, so that by their blood they may extinguish the Antichrist.[144]

The second important prophet was Isaiah, who, more clearly than any of the others, foretold the coming of Jesus in quite specific terms. He would be the son of a virgin, the incarnation of God, and the suffering servant who would pay the price for the people's sins.[145] Other prophets provided additional details that rounded out this picture, but it was Isaiah who was regarded as the great evangelist of the Old Testament.[146]

It was the coming together of the priesthood and the kingship in the life and death of Jesus that most impressed the early Christians, as we can see

---

[143] James 1:1 mentions the "twelve tribes" and 1 Peter 1:1 the "elect exiles" in Pontus, Galatia, Cappadocia, Asia and Bithynia, all of which are in what is now Turkey, not in Babylonia (Iraq). The historical exile occurred in two phases—the ten northern tribes were exiled in 722 BC and permanently "lost"; Judah and Benjamin went in 586 BC.

[144] Tertullian, *De anima* 50.

[145] Isa. 7:14; 53:1–12.

[146] The New Testament quotes his book more often than any other in the Old Testament except the Psalms. On the Christian reading of Isaiah, see Brevard S. Childs, *The Struggle to Understand Isaiah as Christian Scripture* (Grand Rapids, MI: Eerdmans, 2004).

from the way they picked up and interpreted the story of Melchizedek. The historical Melchizedek was a king of Salem (Jerusalem) to whom Abraham offered a tenth of the spoils he had gained after the so-called "battle of the kings."[147] Exactly who Melchizedek was and why Abraham did this was a mystery. Melchizedek was obviously not an Israelite, but nor could he have been like Enoch, a descendant of Adam who had somehow preserved the worship of the true God. He must have been a descendant of Noah, just as Abraham was, but how he had escaped the sinfulness of the world around him is unknown. The incident recorded in Genesis was sufficiently odd to have impressed itself on the Israelites, who long before the appearance of Jesus had spoken openly of a "priest forever, after the order of Melchizedek," clearly distinguishing him from the existing (and implicitly inferior) priesthood of Aaron.[148]

We do not know if Jesus taught that he was the new Melchizedek, but the writer to the Hebrews certainly thought that he was, and he developed the idea as his main interpretation of the life and work of Christ.[149] Identifying Jesus with Melchizedek not only put him on a higher plane than any of the priests of Israel, but it made him greater than Abraham, because even Abraham had paid him a tithe as a mark of his submission to Melchizedek's priestly ministry. Furthermore, it linked Jesus to that mysterious pre-Abrahamic era in which there were great men who knew God even though they were not recipients of a divine covenant. Jesus was born and lived under the law, and as an Israelite he was the heir to the covenant promises, but there was something about him that went beyond that. In the final analysis, he was not the servant of the covenant promises, even though he fulfilled them, but their lord and master. The covenant, whether in the form given to Abraham, Moses, or David, was a vehicle, a means to an end, a guide to a deeper revelation. That deeper revelation was incarnated in Melchizedek, the priest-king who had neither beginning nor end and who was not bound by any human ties to those who were called to worship him.

The uniqueness of Jesus was that he was a priest forever, like Melchizedek. Of all the prophets and teachers of Israel, he was the only one who came to speak about himself. When talking with the Pharisees, he reproached them for claiming to have a knowledge of the Scriptures but failing to see that they spoke about him.[150] It was an audacious thing to say, but it is the key to understanding his earthly ministry. By focusing on himself, Jesus was changing the way his

[147] Gen. 14:18–20.
[148] Ps. 110:4. The psalm is attributed to David.
[149] Heb. 5:5–10; 6:13–20; 7:1–20.
[150] John 5:39–40.

disciples thought about God. That Jesus was more than just an extraordinary spiritual figure was made clear right at the beginning, in the episode of the healing of the paralytic who had been let down through the roof.[151] The man had obviously been brought to Jesus for healing, but Jesus did not heal him as expected—or at least, not straightaway. Instead, he told the man that his sins had been forgiven. This was a dimension of healing outside the purview of a prophet or faith healer because, as the Jewish leaders who heard him were quick to point out, God alone can forgive sins. It was only in reaction to them that Jesus healed the man physically, as evidence that he had the power to forgive him spiritually. He then went on to make the point that, as the Son of Man, he was in control not only of natural phenomena but also of the law of Moses, which had been given to the people as their infallible spiritual guide.

By these actions, Jesus changed the terms of what we would now call the theological debate. He was the paradigm-shifting factor who made all the difference regarding the way in which the material that was otherwise shared by both Jews and Christians was interpreted by the latter. In Christian terms, the purpose of the law was to lead people to Jesus, and it had to be read in that light. With his coming, some parts of the old law ceased to be relevant, either because he had fulfilled them or because circumstances had made them redundant. The temple sacrifices were no longer necessary, so the rules governing them were effectively overturned. The various regulations governing the civic life of Israel were also outdated, because Israelite society had moved on and no longer needed them. On the other hand, there were some laws, especially those contained in the Ten Commandments, that remained valid for all time. "You shall not kill" was just as much a law for Christians as it was for Jews, with the difference that Jesus had extended it to include evil thoughts and desires of the human heart as well as explicit criminal action.[152]

But whatever effect Jesus' teaching had on particular laws, the overall impact was the same—he was at the center of the way(s) in which they were to be interpreted. This is important because laws are usually given for the well-being of a state or social community. This was true of the law of Moses, which looked forward to the time when Israel would be settled in the Promised Land and governed by a king. It was no accident that Jesus preached the coming of the kingdom, and hardly surprising that his disciples and others believed that what he meant was that he himself would lead a revolt against the Romans. But for Jesus, the coming of the kingdom was the presence of the king among his

[151] Mark 2:1–12.
[152] Matt. 5:21–22.

people. To be under his rule was to be united to him, and it was in that union that the destiny of Israel would be realized.

To sum up, the early Christians read the same Bible as the Jews and fully identified themselves with the history of Israel. The fact that they concentrated on Abraham, Moses, and David did not set them apart from their Jewish counterparts, who did much the same thing. Jews interpreted Abraham through the lens of Moses whereas Christians did the opposite, but that difference of perspective need not have provoked a lasting division between them. Where Christians really differed from Jews was in their estimation of the status of Jesus and the meaning of his life and death. Christians believed that the Hebrew Bible pointed to the coming of Christ, that the law of Moses was intended to preserve Israel until that happened (but only until then), and that the covenant God made with Abraham was fulfilled in him. In practical terms, that meant that many of the legal prescriptions in the Old Testament became redundant after Christ's death and resurrection, but the text itself remained the Word of God and continued to function as the Christian Bible, to which the New Testament was later added. The New Testament writers assumed this inherited tradition and built on it; they did not invent something new. It is to a consideration of what these fundamental and enduring principles were that we must now turn our attention.

2

A Shared Inheritance

God Is One

Of all the theological concepts found in the Hebrew Bible, none is more fundamental than its monotheism, which the Christian church embraced without reservation. There was never the slightest suggestion that Christians believed in another god (or gods), and when the apostles preached the gospel to Jews it was on the understanding that the God of Abraham had revealed himself to them in a new way. If there was any difference in the way that Christians approached him, it was only that they replaced the unpronounced divine name *YHWH* (usually vocalized nowadays as Yahweh) with *kyrios* ("Lord"), a common Jewish habit but one that was not often indicated in writing.[1] This difference can sometimes help modern scholars decide whether a manuscript (of the LXX, for example) is of Jewish or Christian origin, but that is all. Christian monotheism was entirely Jewish in origin and shows no sign of having been influenced by any other religion or philosophy. The early Christians never identified the God of Jesus Christ with a pagan deity, nor did they allow non-Jewish concepts of a "high god" to affect their theology, even if evangelists occasionally appealed to such a god when preaching the gospel to Gentiles who knew nothing of Judaism.[2] Pagan monotheists did exist, but they were very different from Christians because they either worshiped an object like the sun or an idea like the "supreme mind," but never a personal being.[3] It is sometimes claimed that early Christian doctrines were couched in Greek philosophical terms alien to the Jewish mind, but this is debatable, and it is safe to say that, without its Jewish inheritance, Christian monotheism would never have become what it was.

Some scholars argue that Old Testament monotheism began as "henothe-

---

[1] Jews usually wrote an abbreviated form of *YHWH* (*YH*, for example) or sometimes vocalized it by supplying the vowels of *Adonai* ("my Lord"), producing the hybrid form *Yahowah*, which has become Jehovah in English.

[2] See Acts 17:16–34 for an example of this.

[3] Monotheistic sun-worship had a brief flowering in Egypt during the reign of Akhenaten or Amenhotep IV (1353?–1336? BC), but as far as we can tell there was no link between this and Judaism, let alone Christianity. Belief in the supreme mind or supreme being was common among pagan Greek philosophers, but it was not identified as a specific god.

ism," that is to say, as the worship of a single deity that did not exclude the possibility that other gods might also exist. It is impossible to answer this question one way or the other, but it makes little difference in practice. The spiritual leaders of Israel clung to the uniqueness of *YHWH* and did all they could to suppress the worship of other deities. Even if they thought that the pagan gods were real, they believed that they were powerless, which reduced the question of their existence to the level of an academic exercise.[4] Certainly there is no doubt that, by the time of Jesus, Israel was monotheistic in the modern sense, and in that respect it was unique in the ancient world. Empires like the Roman one thought of religious unity not in terms of worshiping a single god but as an open-ended polytheism that could absorb the deities of subject peoples and even assimilate them into existing Roman or Greek cults. Scholars tell us that the pagan pantheon was multilayered, consisting of primitive chthonic deities like Uranus, Olympian gods like Zeus (Jupiter), and exotic imports like Mithras, who was introduced from Persia, and Osiris, who came from Egypt. In that world, Jews stood out as unassimilable, even if some pagans occasionally tried to identify the God of the Bible as Saturn.[5]

In preexilic times many Jews had been tempted into various forms of pagan worship, but this disappeared after the return from Babylon. No doubt there were individuals who assimilated into the surrounding Gentile culture, but polytheism no longer posed a serious threat to Israel's religious identity. On the contrary, there were a number of non-Jewish people who were attracted to biblical monotheism and attended the synagogues, though relatively few of them became Jews. These so-called "God-fearers" formed an important element in the early Christian churches, but they acted on their own initiative. No non-Jewish city or state embraced the God of the Bible as its own, not least because that would have entailed rejecting their ancestral gods. There could be no compromise between biblical monotheism and Gentile polytheism, and it was their intransigence on this point, as much as anything else, that made both Jews and Christians so unpopular in the ancient world. To the pagan mind they were both atheists, because they denied the existence of the pagan pantheon.

By embracing the witness of the Old Testament as divine self-revelation, the early Christians signaled their acceptance of an essentially Jewish theology. This is particularly significant, because even though the church developed a Trinitarian view of God and ran the risk of being accused of tritheism, it clung tenaciously to monotheistic principles and embarked on centuries of theological argument designed to reconcile the Three and the One, an effort that would

[4] See 1 Kings 18:20–40.

[5] A connection made because the Jews worshiped God on Saturn's day (Saturday).

hardly have been necessary if some form of polytheism had been a viable option. Later on there would be theologians who would attempt to preserve the oneness of God by denying or relativizing the divinity of the persons of the Trinity, but no one ever tried to say that there were three gods. If Christians had been forced to choose, they would always have put the One ahead of the Three. The doctrine of the Trinity might be complicated to the point of being incomprehensible, but however it was expressed, it never involved the abandonment of biblical monotheism.

The God of Israel was not only one; he was also entirely spiritual in nature. Pagan gods might have a spiritual dimension to them, but they could be depicted in material terms and even as being contained to some extent in particular objects. Virtually all the non-Israelite peoples of antiquity made idols of their gods and worshiped them, something that was an abomination to Israel from the beginning.[6] No one had ever seen God and no one could ever see him. It might be claimed that Moses was an exception to this because God knew him "face to face,"[7] but it was accepted by Jews and Christians alike that this meant only that Moses had had a spiritual encounter with God. He had "seen" God in the wind, in the cloud, and in the fire that accompanied the people of Israel in the desert and that met him with particular intensity on Mount Sinai, but these sightings could not be depicted or idolized. God could not even be confined to a temple made with human hands, and the holy of holies where he supposedly "dwelt" was empty, apart from the ark of the covenant and the cherubim, symbolizing the fact that he could not be reduced to any kind of material limitation.[8] This was expressed very well by the Latin writer Minucius Felix (late second century), who said,

> God cannot be seen because he is brighter than light. Nor can he be grasped because he is purer than touch. He cannot be measured, because he is greater than all perceptions of him. He is infinite and immense. His greatness is known to him alone. Our hearts are too limited to be able to understand him. . . . Anyone who thinks he knows the greatness of God is in fact diminishing his greatness.[9]

The early Christians had exactly the same understanding of God's spiritual nature as Jews had, and they were just as condemning of idolatry and the theological misconceptions that lay behind it as the Old Testament prophets

---

[6] Ex. 20:4–6.
[7] Deut. 34:10.
[8] See Acts 7:48–50 for a clear statement of this.
[9] Minucius Felix, *Octavius* 18.

had been. At the same time, the incarnation of the Son of God as Jesus Christ introduced a complication that had not troubled the ancient Israelites. As the apostle John put it, "The Word became flesh and dwelt among us, and we have seen his glory, glory as of the only Son from the Father, full of grace and truth."[10] Likewise, the apostle Paul told the Colossian church that in Christ "the whole fullness of deity dwells bodily."[11] As a man, the Son of God could presumably have been painted, and if he were on earth today he would certainly be photographed, but what would that reveal about God? The same John who beheld his divine glory also said, "No one has ever seen God; the only Son, who is at the Father's side, he has made him known."[12] Even after the incarnation, the spiritual character of divinity ensured that it continued to be invisible, and Jesus could only be known for who he really was if God revealed that knowledge to the people concerned.[13]

The key characteristics of this inherited monotheism were that God is personal, that he is eternal, and that he is sovereign over everything that exists because he made it and sustains it in being. Today we take these beliefs for granted and it is hard for us to appreciate how radical this theology was for its time. Let us begin with the assertion that God is a personal being. This seems so obvious to us that we are surprised to discover that the ancient Israelites never referred to him in that way. The Hebrew language had no word for "person," although the God of the Bible was always a "he" and never an "it." He thought, spoke, and acted like a person and not like some blind or abstract force. Most importantly, we know that he was personal because he made human beings in his image and likeness and we describe ourselves as "persons." In the Judeo-Christian worldview, it is this shared characteristic of personhood that determines the nature of divine revelation, which comes to us as communication from one person to another. There is no doubt about this, yet the Bible never uses the word "person" to describe it!

Most ancient peoples, on the other hand, had no trouble in depicting their gods in personal terms. The problem was that, in their case, personhood was a sign of relativity and imperfection. To be personal was to be relational, which meant that they were not absolute, because there were other beings that they related to. A personal deity could not be uniquely self-existent, as we find when we look at the pagan pantheon, where the gods and goddesses formed a celestial community that in many ways was patterned on what we observe in

[10] John 1:14.
[11] Col. 2:9.
[12] John 1:18 (ESV mg).
[13] Matt. 16:17.

this life. The difference between the pagan gods and human beings was often more a matter of degree than of kind, and passing from one world to the other was by no means impossible. Kings and heroes were regularly deified after their deaths, and men could easily find themselves doing battle with gods who had come down to earth. In sharp contrast to this, though, the ancient Greeks also had a concept of a Supreme Being that was above and beyond anything personal. The Supreme Being was a universal and abstract idea that could be imagined but not a person to whom one could relate, and therefore not at all like the God of the Bible.

It was this philosophical incompatibility between the personal and the absolute that the biblical revelation contradicted. The God of Israel had the characteristics of a personal being but he was also absolute and transcendently unique. He was, if you like, the "supreme being" by default. That term was not used of him but it was strongly hinted at, as the identification of the secret name of God (*YHWH*) with the verb "to be" indicates.[14] The early Christians were totally committed to understanding God as an absolute personal being in the biblical sense, even though many of them had been converted out of paganism. As far as they were concerned, the names and attributes of God expressed things that were true about him but that could never capture the fullness of his essence. As Clement of Alexandria (150?–215?) put it,

> If we name God, we do not do so properly. We can call him the One, the Good, the Mind, the Absolute Being, the Father, God, Creator or Lord. But we are not giving him a name when we do this. Rather, we use good names in order that our minds might have points of reference, so that we should not go wrong in other ways. None of these terms expresses God in itself, but taken together they are indicative of the power of the Almighty.[15]

The personal character of the supreme being meant that a relationship with him was possible, and here the Hebrew Bible was unequivocal. Pagan philosophers could believe that man was the measure of all things, and judge what they saw around them in that light, but this option was not open to Jews or Christians. For them, it was God who determined what reality was and how it should be understood, and man who was privileged to be given a share of that understanding. The Jewish and Christian view of the universe was therefore much more stable than anything found in pagan thought.[16] From a biblical perspective, motion and change were not signs of chaos and disorder but acts

[14] Ex. 3:14–15.
[15] Clement of Alexandria, *Stromateis* 5.12.
[16] This is a basic difference between the book of Ecclesiastes and any form of pagan Greek philosophy.

of God that express the control he exercises over his creation. Human beings may not understand everything God does, but we have the capacity to investigate his acts and the assurance that they make sense within the framework of a coherent universe.

Jews and Christians both agreed that God was eternal. Before the heavens were created he was already there, and his years would never cease.[17] The Old Testament expressed his eternity as never-ending time, but the Israelites knew better than to interpret that literally. As they understood it, a thousand years in God's eyes were like a single day, or a matter of hours.[18] Time as we measure it had no significance for God because he was beyond its grasp. Origen expressed this succinctly when he wrote,

> With God, all time is today. There is no evening with him . . . and no morning. There is nothing but time that stretches out, along with his unbeginning and unseen life.[19]

God's independence of time was why he did not change, and why he was always ready and able to help his people. This constancy contrasts favorably with the comings and goings of the pagan gods, who could never be relied on to be available when they were needed.[20] Pagan gods could be born and even die, though that was rare.[21] But the God of Israel knew neither birth nor death—he was simply there. Jews did not speculate about how he could live outside time and yet be closely involved with it; they assumed that he knew everything that would happen in our future without speculating about mysteries like freedom of the will and determinism. For them, such matters were subsumed in the covenant that God had made with Israel, to which he would remain faithful whatever happened.[22]

As the quotation from Origen shows, the early Christians did nothing to alter this picture of God, even though it caused them some difficulty. The problem they faced was the need to explain how the Son of God could exist within the divine eternity. If the Father had begotten him, as the Bible says, was there a time when the Son had not existed? This logical conundrum would take the church many centuries to resolve, but it is important to note that Christians who tried to reconcile eternity with generation did not conclude that God must dwell in time and space. Those who had a problem with the Son's eternity

---

[17] Ps. 102:25–27.
[18] Ps. 90:4.
[19] Origen, *Commentarium in Iohannis Evangelium* 1.32.
[20] 1 Kings 18:26–29.
[21] It was true of the Greek god Pan and the Egyptian god Osiris, but that was about all.
[22] Isa. 43:1–7.

preferred to say that if he had been born or had come into existence at some point in time, he could not have been God in the full sense of the word. The early Christians were determined to protect the Old Testament picture of the one eternal God, even at the cost of relativizing the divinity of the Son if they had to.

The sovereignty of God over everything he has made was another biblical idea that the early church took over from the Old Testament. The Israelites acknowledged the rule of God over the entire universe and were aware that he had the pagan nations under his control, but they concentrated on his special love for them and tended to interpret divine sovereignty in terms of God saving them from their enemies. The early Christians believed the same thing, but their emphasis was different. They saw universal divine sovereignty as the basis for the mission of preaching the gospel to the ends of the earth—winning the world for Christ rather than keeping it at bay in the interests of their own survival.[23] As the encyclical letter of the church of Smyrna concerning the martyrdom of its bishop Polycarp (69?–155) put it,

> All the martyrdoms were blessed and noble, and they took place according to the will of God. For it befits those who profess greater piety than others to ascribe to God the authority over all things.[24]

In a world created and governed by the God of the Bible there was no room for accidents or surprises, no scope for any power that was not subject to his will. Even Satan was under God's control.[25] As Irenaeus wrote,

> Not a single thing that has been made, or that will be made, escapes the knowledge of God. Through his providence, every thing has received its nature, rank, number, and uniqueness. Nothing has come about by accident or for no purpose. Everything has been made with exact appropriateness and by the exercise of transcendent knowledge.[26]

The God of the Old Testament also possessed a strong moral character that Christians readily affirmed. In himself, he was "holy," a term that could be interpreted in different ways, but all of them set him apart from anything that is unworthy of him. For the Jews, this included certain types of food and behavior that were regarded as "unclean," and the law of Moses contained a number of ritual prescriptions designed to procure or maintain a state of "holiness" in the

[23] See Matt. 28:19–20.
[24] *The Martyrdom of Polycarp* 2.
[25] Irenaeus of Lyon, *Adversus omnes haereses* 5.22.2.
[26] Ibid., 2.26.3.

presence of God. Christians usually ignored these precepts, but the underlying idea that a believer must be holy because God is holy remained as fundamental for them as it was for Jews.[27] In practice, this meant that Christians were expected to avoid certain people and things if they were liable to lead the unwary astray, and in this respect there was probably less difference between Jews and Christians in New Testament times than the evidence might suggest. This is because the New Testament concentrates on things like the Jewish food laws, where Christian practices were different, and tends to pass over the many other ways in which Jewish and Christian practices were similar, if not identical. In one case, however, the New Testament is just as clear in its demands as the Old. This was the command given to God's people not to marry outside the faith. The danger of that as a source of religious corruption was well known in Old Testament times, and the early Christians thought exactly the same. Paul gave Christians great freedom in the choice of a marriage partner, but the one thing he insisted on was that they should marry another believer.[28]

Later Christian writers were just as strict about this, if not more so. Tertullian, for example, was uncompromising:

> Believers contracting marriages with Gentiles are guilty of fornication and are to be excommunicated, as the apostle taught. As he said, it is wrong even to eat with such a person.[29]

It is true that Tertullian was a noted rigorist in such matters, but Cyprian of Carthage (200?–258) was just as firm as he was and may even have been quoting Tertullian when making his own statements on the subject.[30]

The early Christians also took over from Judaism a firm belief in the goodness of God.[31] In a world where supernatural forces were often propitiated because people were afraid of their malign influence, Jews and Christians stood out in affirming the opposite. It is true that in the Old Testament there were occasions when obedience to the will of God produced results that would not be considered "good" in purely human terms. This was the case, for example, of the divine command to slay the Amalekites and of the marriage between Hosea and a prostitute.[32] Both these things were violations of the Ten Commandments, and neither of them would have been acceptable in the New Testament church, but that was because the context had changed, not because the

[27] 1 Thess. 4:3.
[28] 1 Cor. 7:35, 39; 2 Cor. 6:14.
[29] Tertullian, *Ad uxorem* 2.3.
[30] Cyprian of Carthage, *De lapsis* 6; *Ad Quirinum* 3.62.
[31] Ex. 34:6; Neh. 9:25, 35; Ps. 31:19; 52:1; Zech. 9:17; Rom. 2:4; 11:22.
[32] 1 Sam. 15:3; Hos. 1:2.

principle behind them was any different. For example, hospitality was considered to be a good thing, but it was not to be offered to false teachers. If they appeared in a congregation and started leading people astray, they were to be thrown out without further ado, even if the demands of hospitality dictated otherwise.[33] Just as Israel could not tolerate the Amalekites in their midst, so the early church could not tolerate heretics, however much they were told to "love their enemies." Obedience to the commands of God determined what was good or not good in his sight, and on this Jews and Christians were agreed. As Clement of Alexandria wrote,

> God is not involuntarily good, the way a fire is involuntarily hot. In him, goodness is voluntary. . . . he does not do good by necessity, but by his own free choice.[34]

Jews and Christians were also expected to treat one another as they wanted others to treat them. The love of God and the love of one's neighbor went hand in hand and were the twin pillars of the law. Ritual practices might be abolished or abandoned, but the fundamentals of the law remained the same for both Jews and Christians, because they reflected the character of God that we are called to imitate.[35] Jesus condemned the Jewish leaders of his time because they often put legal niceties ahead of the moral principles that the law was supposed to uphold, but he did not see this as a new revelation from God. The criticism was made because Jesus expected his hearers to understand what he was saying and agree with him about what the true foundation of Old Testament religion was.[36]

Finally, the God of the Old Testament had a rational nature that is reflected in human beings, and both Jews and Christians felt obliged to respect that. This did not mean that the mind of God was exactly the same as the mind of man; Israel had to be reminded that his ways are "higher" than our ways, and his thoughts are "higher" than our thoughts.[37] Christians followed the same principle and agreed that, although we cannot always understand why God does what he does, we can know that there is an inner logic and purpose in his actions that is not arbitrary or self-contradictory.

The significance of divine rationality was clearly visible in the inner coherence of the created order. Everything is in its proper place and functions to further God's greater glory. Because we have minds that are analogous to his, albeit on a much reduced scale, we can learn the principles or "laws" of nature and

---

[33] 2 John 10–11.
[34] Clement of Alexandria, *Stromateis* 7.7.
[35] Matt. 22:37–40, quoting Deut. 6:5 and Lev. 19:18.
[36] Matt. 23:23–24.
[37] Isa. 55:8–9; Job 38–41.

make the created order work to our benefit.[38] Best of all, we can hear God's Word as it is revealed to us, we can understand it, and we can put it into practice. Our knowledge of God is not confined to secret oracles of mysterious interpretation, even if such things are not entirely excluded. There have always been prophecies whose meaning has been unclear, and there are things about God's plans that he has chosen not to reveal. But leaving those aside, there is plenty that we have been told, and we know enough to be able to live in a way that is pleasing to him. This was true of the Jews, and it was true of the early Christians also. God's people were expected to use the rationality that he had graciously imparted to them in order to develop the creation over which he had placed them. In the words of Clement of Alexandria,

> Many things in life arise from the exercise of human reason, which has received its kindling spark from God. Some examples are health through medicine, soundness of body through gymnastics, and wealth from trade. All these things have their origin and existence because of divine providence, though not without human cooperation as well.[39]

More revelation meant more opportunity, but it also entailed greater responsibility on the part of the recipients. The Jews, who knew God's law, were more guilty of failing to uphold it than were the Gentiles, who did not have comparable knowledge.[40] Similarly, Christians had a greater obligation to do God's will than the ancient Jews had had, because they knew more about it. But these differences were ones of degree, not of kind, and the basic principle was the same. God has a mind and has given us minds so that we can understand what his purposes are, to the extent that he has revealed them to us. In their understanding of what God is like and of what his expectations are, Jews and Christians started from the same principles and ended up in the same place, which was that obedience is the key to faithfulness.[41] On this both religions were agreed, and the Christian church has continued to appeal to the saints of the Old Testament as models for the Christian life, because they put flesh on the skeleton of the principles that make up the monotheistic faith of the Bible.

The Divine Act of Creation

Belief in the divine creation of the material universe is another important legacy to the church from ancient Israel. All ancient peoples had myths of origins,

[38] Job 42:3; Ps. 19:1–14; 139:6.
[39] Clement of Alexandria, *Stromateis* 6.17.
[40] Paul makes this argument in Rom. 2:1–24.
[41] 1 Sam. 15:22. Compare Heb. 5:8.

but none of them bears more than a superficial resemblance to the Old Testament account. For the most part, pagan peoples either thought that the world was the product of a series of conflicts between opposing forces which eventually achieved some kind of balance, or that it had emerged from something else—a great monster perhaps, or the head of one of the gods. None of them believed that the universe was a coherent whole, created by a God whose own being lay outside the system that he had made.

It was fundamental to both Jewish and Christian belief that God is above and beyond the created order, because if he were not, the universe would be an extension of his being and just as divine as he is. The Bible assumes that God already existed and was perfect in himself before he made the world. It also says that creation was an act of divine speech, and therefore cannot be understood as an extension of his own being.[42] God is nothing like his creatures, which means that no created thing can be divinized or worshiped. The prohibition of idolatry was one of the most basic elements of the Old Testament law, and the early Christians agreed wholeheartedly with that.[43] As Tertullian put it,

> From the beginning idolatry has been forbidden, and practice of it has been punished. . . . There is no offense so presumptuous in God's eyes as this kind of sin.[44]

Jews and Christians also believed that everything made by God was fundamentally good.[45] The goodness of creation meant that evil could not be inherent in any part of it. This belief stood in sharp contrast to the widespread pagan idea that the material world was evil. But for Jews and Christians, not even Satan was bad by nature. To quote Tertullian,

> God made Satan good, along with his other works. Before he became the Devil, Satan stood out as the wisest of the creatures. . . . If you turn to the prophecy of Ezekiel, you will quickly realize that he was created good. It was by his own choice that he became corrupt.[46]

The existence of evil was the result of disobedience and rebellion, not something that was part of creation itself. The implications of this were far-reaching. First, it meant that God's people did not have to be afraid of the world around them. God had given the human race dominion over the other

[42] Gen. 1:3.
[43] Ex. 20:4–6; 1 John 5:21.
[44] Tertullian, *Scorpiace* 2.
[45] Gen. 1:31.
[46] Tertullian, *Adversus Marcionem* 2.10. See Origen, *De principiis* 1.5.4, for a similar analysis of Satan. The prophecies of Ezekiel 28:1–19, apparently aimed at the king of Tyre, were generally regarded as referring to Satan.

creatures and told them to exercise the authority which that dominion conferred.[47] The Old Testament does not say whether this dominion extended to the spiritual creatures as well, but Paul told the Romans that nothing in heaven or on earth could separate believers from the love of God, and to the Corinthians he said that they would participate in God's judgment of the angels.[48] In the latter case he assumed that they should have known that already, which suggests that it was a natural extension of the dominion given to Adam and Eve in the garden.

The doctrine of the goodness of creation and the consequent reconfiguration of the nature of evil became a fundamental building block of Christian theology. The incarnation of the Son of God, on which the whole gospel hangs, would have been inconceivable otherwise.[49] The resurrection of the body would have made no sense,[50] and the promise of a new heaven and a new earth would have been absurd if salvation had been interpreted as an escape from them![51] So important were these beliefs that there were more commentaries written on Genesis 1–3 in the early centuries of the church, and by a wider range of theologians, than on any other part of the Bible.[52] Christians may have elaborated on the details to a degree that is not explicitly stated in the Old Testament, but there can be no doubt that fundamentally they agreed with Jews on this all-important question.

Jews and Christians also shared the belief that there is an order in creation. The world was governed by laws that had been established by God from the beginning and that remained subject to his providential control.[53] The cycle of the agricultural year, so important to human survival, was not arbitrary, and would continue unchanged to the end of time.[54] Nothing in the world is superfluous or disposable, even if we do not immediately see what its purpose is, and God takes care of creatures great and small.[55]

Christians also inherited from ancient Israel the belief that human beings are expected to live in harmony with creation and be responsible stewards of what God has given them. This was the purpose of the week, a rhythm of work and rest that God's people were meant to enjoy in their own lives.[56] The church

[47] Gen. 1:26–28.
[48] Rom. 8:38–39; 1 Cor. 6:3.
[49] John 1:14. How could the divine Word have become flesh, if flesh were fundamentally evil?
[50] 1 Cor. 15:35–38.
[51] Rev. 21:1.
[52] See Andrew Louth, ed., *Genesis 1–11*, vol. 1 in *The Ancient Christian Commentary on Scripture*, *Old Testament*, Thomas C. Oden, gen. ed. (Downers Grove, IL: InterVarsity Press, 2001), for a representative selection of examples.
[53] Ps. 19:1–14.
[54] Gen. 8:22.
[55] Matt. 6:26–30; Ps. 104:24–25.
[56] Ex. 20:8–11.

adopted this principle without hesitation but made two important modifications to it. First, Christians rejected the almost superstitious reverence that some Jews had for the Sabbath, insisting that although it was meant to be a day of rest and worship, it could not be so hedged about with legalism that the weightier matters of the law had to be ignored out of deference to it.[57] Second, they changed the day of rest from the seventh to the first day of the week. The Jewish Sabbath was the logical culmination of the creating work of God, who rested on the seventh day, but the first (or eighth) day symbolized the beginning of the new creation that had been established and fulfilled in Christ. According to the anonymous epistle attributed to Barnabas (second century),

> Look how God speaks to the Jews: "Your sabbaths are not acceptable to me . . . but I shall make a new beginning on the eighth day, a beginning of another world."[58] This is why we keep the eighth day with joyfulness, the day on which Jesus rose from the dead.[59]

Unlike the Jewish Sabbath, which was confined to this world, the Christian Sabbath pointed to the eternal rest of the people of God, which was promised to all believers but that could not be fulfilled in this life.[60]

In making these modifications, the Christian church may have downplayed the significance of the material creation to some degree, but if so, this has to be understood in context. The Christian belief that this present world will eventually give way to a new and better one was meant to give believers hope that the limitations of this present age, most notably death, would one day be overcome.[61] Not even the most zealous keeper of the Old Testament law could halt or reverse the process of decay that is inherent in the natural world, though the ancient Israelites knew that somehow God would redeem them from it, even if they were not sure how.[62] It was the purpose of the Christian gospel to explain God's plan in that respect—the mystery that had been hidden from the beginning of time was now revealed in Jesus Christ, who died and rose again, thereby overcoming the limitations of created nature and opening up a whole new vista of eternal life.

New and glorious as the gospel message was, it did not entail a rejection of the material creation. Christians were called to wait in eager anticipation for the coming of Christ, and to greet their own death as the beginning of a

[57] Mark 2:27–28.
[58] A loose allusion to Isa. 1:13.
[59] *Barnabas* 15.
[60] Ps. 95:6–11, quoted and discussed in Heb. 3:7–4:7.
[61] Rev. 21:1–4.
[62] Job 19:25.

new and eternal life in him, but they were not told to commit suicide or do anything that might unduly hasten their earthly end.[63] Their material bodies would decay and die, but while they were still in them it was their duty to treat them properly because they are the temple of the Holy Spirit.[64] Created things were not an end in themselves but vehicles for God to work out his purposes, and for that reason believers were expected to take care of them. As the early Christians saw it, God hates nothing that he has made, there are no "unclean" things or people, and we have no right to harm or destroy what properly belongs to God.[65] Christians knew that they had a hope of eternal life that had not been revealed to Israel, but that hope was the extension and fulfillment of the Old Testament promises and not a complete change of direction. In their approach to this life they stood shoulder to shoulder with Jews, receiving God's blessings with gratitude and rejecting any kind of otherworldly "spirituality" that would have persuaded them that the material universe was evil or unworthy of their attention.

The Image of God in Man

An essential ingredient of the Judeo-Christian worldview was the belief that the human race is unique in creation. Modern scientists discuss how human beings are related to animals, but this was of little interest to the biblical writers. What concerned them was not how we resemble other creatures but how (and why) we differ from them. It was obvious to them that dogs and horses were more like each other than either is like human beings, despite the close relationships which ancient people often had with their domestic animals. They knew that among pagans, this sense of kinship with animals could take on a religious significance, as we see in a number of ancient cultures where human and animal combinations were invented and worshiped. The Egyptian sphinx, the Assyrian lions with human faces, and the centaurs of Greek imagination blurred a distinction that for the biblical writers was axiomatic. There is only one instance in the Scriptures where this absolute separation between humans and animals may be somewhat compromised, and that is in the vision of Ezekiel, which was also seen by John.[66] In this vision there are four living creatures, one like a lion, one like an ox, one like an eagle, and one like a man. In John they are clearly distinct from one other, but they appear to be merged together in Ezekiel. It is hard to know what to make of this because the vision was meant

[63] 1 Thess. 4:13.
[64] 1 Cor. 6:19; 2 Cor. 6:16.
[65] Isa. 11:9; 65:25.
[66] Ezek. 1:5–10; Rev. 4:6–7.

to be surreal, but it is certain that neither Jews nor Christians ever thought of fusing these extraordinary creatures together and worshiping them.[67]

In the context of ancient society it is remarkable how the biblical tradition consistently upheld the dignity of the entire human race. Many ancient peoples regarded slaves and even women as little more than animals and denied them their full humanity. Neither Jews nor Christians could accept this. To their minds, the place of man in the universe was defined by the belief that all human beings have been created in the "image and likeness of God."[68] Although this is not mentioned very often in either Testament, the fact that it occurs in the story of creation shows that it was fundamental to the biblical understanding of human identity. We have to admit that the early Christians did not do justice to the biblical teaching, because they mistook "image" and "likeness" for two different things, when in fact they were the same. To their minds, when Adam and Eve fell, they lost the likeness of God but not his image. The loss of the likeness was taken to be the result of sin, but the preservation of the image was seen as a reminder that, in spite of human error and disobedience, mankind retained a special character in God's eyes that nothing could take away.[69] As Origen said,

> All men are inclined to sin by nature . . . but not all are incapable of complete transformation. In every school of philosophy, and in the Word of God, there are examples of people who were so completely changed that they may be held up as models of the perfect life.[70]

The ancient Christian interpretation of the image of God as something different from his likeness was due to a failure to appreciate the Hebraic use of synonymity and parallelism, not to any intentional difference of doctrine between the church and the Old Testament. It never occurred to Christians that their view differed from that of the Jews, and Jews did not reproach them for having misunderstood biblical teaching on this point. We are therefore justified in saying that this was a belief that Christians took over from Judaism, which they developed further by saying that God became a man in Jesus Christ, in whom the true image and likeness of God became visible.[71] Moreover, human

[67] In later Christian tradition, the creatures came to represent the four Evangelists. The man was the symbol of Matthew, the lion of Mark, the ox of Luke, and the eagle of John. By far the best known of these today is the lion of St. Mark, because it was adopted by the city of Venice, which claims Mark as its patron saint.

[68] See Gen. 1:26–27.

[69] On this subject, see Gerald L. Bray, "The Significance of God's Image in Man," *Tyndale Bulletin* 42 (1991): 195–225.

[70] Origen, *Contra Celsum* 3.66.

[71] See Philip E. Hughes, *The True Image: The Origin and Destiny of Man in Christ* (Leicester: Inter-Varsity Press, 1989).

beings were unique in relation to the spiritual creation just as much as they were in relation to the material one. As the writer to the Hebrews put it, quoting the Old Testament, "To which of the angels has he ever said, 'Sit at my right hand until I make your enemies a footstool for your feet'?"[72] He then went on to develop this theme:

> It was not to angels that God subjected the world to come, of which we are speaking. It has been testified somewhere, "What is man, that you are mindful of him, or the son of man, that you care for him? You made him for a little while lower than the angels; you have crowned him with glory and honor, putting everything in subjection under his feet."[73]

The Jewish and Christian view of man was not that he was the measure of all things, but that he was the governor of the material world that had been placed under him. Lions and elephants might have qualities of size and physical prowess than human beings lack, but they are not greater than we are because of that. Dragons and monsters lurking in the deep are creatures of the imagination only; they have no power over us. In a world where such fantasies could exert a powerful influence, the biblical teaching liberated people from the fears of their own imagination and set them free to serve God as they were meant to.

Another consequence of this belief was that witchcraft had no place in Israel or in the Christian church because it was a denial both of the goodness of creation and of the glory of mankind.[74] If there was a difference between Jews and Christians on this point, it was that ancient Israel was commanded to put witches to death, whereas the apostles cast out the evil spirits that made the black arts possible.[75] Either way, there was no tolerance shown for sorcery, and both Israel and the church did all they could to suppress it. In the words of Origen,

> The names of Abraham, Isaac, and Jacob possess such power when combined with the name of God that Israelites pray to him and exorcize demons with the words: "God of Abraham, God of Isaac, God of Jacob." Moreover, the invocations "God of Israel," "God of the Hebrews," and "God who drowned Pharaoh and the Egyptians in the Red Sea" are frequently used against demons and wicked powers.[76]

[72] Heb. 1:13, quoting Ps. 110:1.
[73] Heb. 2:5–8, quoting Ps. 8:4–6.
[74] Ex. 22:18; Deut. 18:10.
[75] Acts 16:16–18.
[76] Origen, *Contra Celsum* 4.33–34.

The Nature of Sin and Evil

Jews and Christians both agreed that sin, like evil, was not inherent in the created order but was the result of a rebellion against God that had been made possible because God had given both angels and men the free will to disobey him. It was among the angels that disobedience to God first manifested itself. The Bible does not say much about this, but it is clear that the forces of evil were led by Satan, an angelic being who rebelled against God along with a host of his fellow angels.[77] As a result, God cut them off from him but did not destroy them. Satan was allowed to continue his rebellious activity as the "prince of this world" until some future time when God would defeat him, remove his power, and banish evil from his creation.

In particular, Satan was permitted to tempt Adam and Eve, the only other creatures who had a free will similar to that of the angels. By listening to Satan and falling for his deception, they sinned and were likewise banished from God's presence, with the result that the human race is now in bondage to sin. Adam and Eve did not choose to sin against God on their own initiative—they were led astray by a spiritual power greater than themselves and were therefore trapped in a situation from which there was no escape unless God himself were to intervene to rescue them. It was that rescue plan of God to which both Jews and Christians believed they had access. They understood it in different ways, but their analysis of the problem was essentially the same. The fall of mankind was an anomaly that God could not tolerate, because it would mean a surrender to the forces of evil and the consequent loss of his own sovereignty. As Irenaeus put it,

> Man was created by God for life. However, he was injured by the serpent who had corrupted him. Now if man, after losing life, never returned to it but was utterly abandoned to death, God would have been conquered. The wickedness of the serpent would have prevailed over the will of God.[78]

Jews and Christians agreed that sin was a personal act of disobedience against God that broke the relationship he had given to his creatures. Once that happened, the disobedient creatures could not put things right again, and sin was here to stay. It might be possible to mitigate its effects by obeying God's revealed will, but no matter how hard we try, we shall never restore the original relationship. Because sin is a personal act, it can only be committed by personal

[77] The clearest statement of this is in Jude 6, followed by 2 Pet. 2:4. The Old Testament says nothing about it directly, but offers parallels in the fall of earthly kings who tried to make themselves gods. See Ezek. 28:12–19 and Isa. 14:12–20.

[78] Irenaeus of Lyon, *Adversus omnes haereses* 3.23.1.

beings and does not affect their created nature in any fundamental way. When the angels rebelled against God they were cast out of his presence, but they did not cease to be spiritual beings. Similarly, when human beings followed them in their rebellion, they were subjected to death and to all the material consequences of living in what was now a hostile environment, but they did not cease to be human.

It was this worldview that put Judaism and Christianity in a league quite different from anything else that could be found in the ancient world. Everyone knew that evil was a problem, but the explanations of how it originated were not only very different from the one found in the Bible but quite incompatible with its teaching. Some people argued that good and evil were equal forces in opposition to each other. This view is called "dualism." It was held by the Zoroastrians in Persia and spread from there into the Roman world. The Bible implicitly denied this because it claimed that evil is the work of a creature made by the good God, who remains in control of what he has made. Whatever the Evil One does he can do only because God allows him to do it, and when that permission is denied or withdrawn, he will be impotent.[79] There is certainly no possibility that Satan might defeat God in open combat and take over the universe—on the contrary, he and his works will ultimately be destroyed.[80] Perhaps the early Christians were more detailed in their descriptions of this than most Jews were, but if so, this was a difference of degree and not of kind. In essence, they both thought along similar lines and believed that good would triumph over evil in the end. As Clement of Alexandria wrote,

> God does not actively produce suffering, but he does not prevent those beings who cause it from doing so. But in the end, he overrules for good the crimes of his enemies.[81]

This positive Judeo-Christian outlook stood out in a world where many people believed that nonmaterial things were naturally good and material ones were naturally evil. According to them, human beings were souls imprisoned in material bodies, which gave rise to the inner conflict between good and evil that we all experience. On that model, the only way for a human being to become good was to escape from the body, either by a rigorous program of spiritual exercises, by a mystical experience, or by death. The challenge posed to the church by this view was that potential points of contact with it could be found in the New Testament, where we read about the struggle between the "flesh"

---

[79] Job 1:6–12.
[80] Rev. 12:7–12; 20:7–10.
[81] Clement of Alexandria, *Stromateis* 4.12.

and the "spirit."[82] Such language could easily be misunderstood by those who thought in pagan terms, so it is essential to emphasize that the Christian interpretation of these things was shaped by Judaism and not by the Gentile culture that it was trying to evangelize. Like the Jews, Christians believed that the struggle between good and evil was a spiritual one and was meaningful only in that context. Neither Jews nor Christians could say that diseases, natural disasters, or defects in matter (such as bodily disabilities) were the result of someone's personal sin, which is what many at the time assumed.[83]

Other people thought of evil as a decline from the perfect good. According to that view, anything that was not identical with absolute good was evil to the degree that it was distinct from it. This meant that every creature must be at least partly evil because only God was the perfect good. Absolute evil was the complete denial of good, which meant total alienation from God and therefore from being itself. In this way of thinking, evil became "nonbeing"—it did not exist! This view was implicitly rejected by the Bible, which states quite clearly that evil does exist and is manifested in the person of Satan and his demons. To deny that is to succumb to his ultimate temptation, because when those who are subject to him cease to be aware of the fact, evil has triumphed and there is no further conflict between it and the good in the minds of those who have surrendered to the Devil.

Why God chose to let Satan survive and exercise power as the prince of this world is a mystery than neither Jews nor Christians were able to explain. Origen wrote,

> Regarding the Devil, his angels and forces opposed [to God], the church teaches that such beings do indeed exist. But it has not explained what they are or how they exist. Most Christians think that the Devil was an angel who rebelled and persuaded as many other angels as he could to follow him.[84]

Some suggested that because God made creatures with free will, he had to respect their decision when it went against him and allow them to go on existing in their rebellious state. Others claimed that it was always God's intention to allow evil to come into the world, but because he could not be the author of that evil himself, he created Satan, fully aware that Satan would rebel against him. In that scenario, the existence of evil was supposed to highlight the contrasting goodness of God and give free will a real meaning by presenting human beings with a stark choice. If Adam and Eve had rejected Satan and done what God expected of them,

---

[82] Rom. 7:15, 18, 25; 8:1–13; 1 Cor. 5:5; 2 Cor. 10:2–3; Gal. 3:3; 1 Pet. 3:18.
[83] See John 9:1–3. The entire book of Job is a refutation of this idea.
[84] Origen, *De principiis*, preface, 6.

they would have earned his approval and the natural goodness given to them at creation would have become a moral goodness as well. Theories of this kind circulated among both Jews and Christians, but they were speculative, and the origin of evil remained a mystery beyond human comprehension. What is important for our present purposes is that Jews and Christians thought alike on this matter, and the early church found itself having to persuade a pagan world to accept a biblical doctrine that was alien to their way of thinking and essentially "Jewish."

Jews and Christians also agreed that the rebellion of mankind against God was universal. The importance of the creation story of Adam and Eve was that their sin is the common inheritance of the entire human race. Every one of us is heir to their humanity, and so we share in their responsibility for sin. I may not do what they did, and I may even object to it and try to put it right, but I am still affected by it because I have inherited a rebellious spirit from them. Just as I must accept responsibility for the actions of the state of which I am a citizen, whether I have participated in them personally or not, so I must accept responsibility for the sinfulness of the human race to which I belong. What this means is that whatever "free will" I have, I can only exercise within the context of my inherited sinfulness. I am not free to choose to be sinless, nor am I able to escape from my sinful condition by my own efforts.

The idea that people can somehow improve themselves or even live totally blameless lives was alien to both Jewish and Christian thought because both agreed that sin is universal. For this reason, Jews and Christians have often thought that human beings are sinful "by nature," but this term is open to serious misunderstanding. If "nature" refers to the way we were created, then it is not accurate, since what God created was (and still is) naturally good. In that sense, human sinfulness is "unnatural," which is how the early Christians understood it.[85] On the other hand, it was also accepted that every human being is "sinful" whether he or she has committed actual sins or not, because we have inherited the universal human separation from God. In this sense, even a newborn baby must be regarded as "sinful," even though it has not committed any actual sin. As Tertullian said when speaking about the sinlessness of Christ,

> The flesh of Christ committed no sin itself, but it was just like sinful flesh. What I mean is that it had the same nature, but without the corruption that our flesh has inherited from Adam. This is why we declare that Christ had the same flesh as that which has become naturally sinful in [fallen] man.[86]

[85] Sin does not belong to our physical makeup, and for that reason the term "natural" should be avoided when discussing it.

[86] Tertullian, *De carne Christi* 16.

Jews and Christians agreed that sinfulness was a state of being independent of any actual sins we may have committed. There have been many attempts by both religions to establish grades of sin, and it is undoubtedly true that some sinful acts are worse than others, but a man's spiritual state before God is not determined by that. It is the brokenness of our relationship with him that produces sinfulness, and the actual sins we commit are the expression of that basic fault. Good works may be of some use in reversing the effects of actual sins, but they cannot touch the underlying state of sinfulness, which does not depend on any action we take, whether it is good or bad.

For Christians, this Jewish view of sin was of the utmost importance because it was the only way that the incarnation of the Son of God in Jesus Christ could be understood. For many pagans, an incarnation of the supreme good was a logical impossibility, because contact with matter would inevitably corrupt it. Even if he lived a perfect human life, a person claiming to be the incarnation of goodness would still be sinful, because sin was inherent in matter. Jews ruled out a divine incarnation because of the spiritual nature of God, not because matter was evil and sinlessness was an impossible condition for human beings. After all, Adam and Eve had been sinless before they fell, and they were fully human. In this respect as in so many others, the worldview of the early church was that of Judaism and not of the pagan culture that it was called to evangelize.

Election and Redemption

Given that Jews and Christians held the same beliefs about the fundamental goodness of creation and about the fall of mankind into sin, it is not surprising that they also agreed that God planned to put matters right. What they differed about was how this would happen. Judaism and Christianity developed in mutually exclusive ways because of that disagreement, but that took some time to become apparent. In the earliest days of the church, most Christians were Jewish and preached to their fellow Jews that Christ was the fulfillment of the hope of Israel.[87] Fundamental to this was the belief that everything God had done for his people was an act of *grace*, which meant that no one could do anything to earn his salvation. If God has decided to save people from their sinfulness and its consequences, he has done so entirely of his own free will. As Clement of Rome (late first century) wrote,

> We have been called by God's will in Christ Jesus, and are not justified by ourselves. We are not justified by our own wisdom, understanding, godliness,

[87] See Acts 28:20.

or works that we have done with the right intentions. We are justified by that faith by which Almighty God has justified all men from the beginning.[88]

Jews were taught that there was nothing special about them in worldly terms and that they owed their special position as God's chosen people to his love for them.[89] Yet in spite of this, many of them came to believe that their descent from Abraham was a guarantee that God would be gracious to them, regardless of the way they lived. Jesus pointed out that physical descent from Abraham meant nothing if it was not accompanied by Abraham's faith, and Paul repeated that message at some length when he wrote to the church at Rome.[90] Abraham had been given the sign of circumcision to mark his faith in that covenant, but although he had circumcised both Ishmael and Isaac, Ishmael had been rejected and only Isaac had inherited the covenant promise, a point that Paul made when arguing against relying on circumcision for salvation.[91] Likewise, Isaac had twin sons, Esau and Jacob, but although Esau was more highly favored physically and Jacob was not a very likeable character, it was Jacob and not Esau who was chosen to inherit the blessing.[92]

The early Christians accepted that salvation had come to the Jews first, and Paul almost always went to the synagogue to preach the gospel when he arrived in a new city. The problem was that not every Jew who heard the message believed it, and many of those who rejected it did so with considerable violence, as Paul's experiences in different places remind us.[93] When that happened, Paul replied that by rejecting Christ, they were in turn being rejected by God in spite of their ancestral claims.[94] Salvation by grace through faith demanded personal commitment, and no one could claim to be saved by virtue of his or her ancestors, even if Israel did have a special place in God's affection because of them.[95]

What the Jews believed and what Christians agreed with was that God's grace is not hidden or mysterious, even if the causes of it are unknown. His purposes have been worked out historically in the lives of real people whom he has chosen to be his witnesses. The biblical term for this is *election*, and both Jews and Christians based their faith and practice on the assumption that they were the ones whom God had chosen to be his.[96]

---

[88] Clement of Rome, *Epistula I* 32.
[89] Deut. 7:6–8.
[90] Luke 3:8; John 8:33–58; Rom. 4:1–13.
[91] Gal. 4:21–31.
[92] Rom. 9:10–13.
[93] See Acts 14:4–5, 19; 17:5, 13; 18:12.
[94] Acts 13:46. See also Acts 18:6; 1 Thess. 2:16; and the extended discussion in Romans 9–11.
[95] Phil. 3:4–14; Rom. 11:28; Eph. 2:8.
[96] That the Israelites were God's chosen people is a commonplace in the Old Testament, but the doctrine is prominent in the New Testament as well. See, for example, Matt. 24:22–31; Luke 18:7; Rom. 8:33; Col. 3:12; Titus 1:1; 1 Pet. 1:1–2; 2 John 1.

In the Bible and in the early centuries of the church, election was understood primarily in a corporate sense. That is to say, it was a body of people that had been elected rather than isolated individuals, though we must not create an artificial distinction in our minds between the individual and the group. A body is made up of different parts, as Paul reminded the Corinthians, and each part must perform its proper task if the body is to function as it should.[97] It would make no sense to say that the body was elect but not its parts, just as it would be silly to think that each of the parts had been chosen but not the body. Nevertheless, the emphasis among both Jews and Christians was on the community of faith in which individuals found their proper place, and not on individuals who were expected to recognize each other and constitute a body of their own making.

In principle Israel was the elect nation, God's chosen people, and both Jews and Christians were happy to affirm that. In the words of Clement of Alexandria,

> The covenant of salvation, reaching down to us from the foundation of the world, through different generations and times, is one and the same, even if the way it works is different. There is still only one unchangeable gift of salvation, given by one God through one Lord . . .[98]

The difficulty came when it was asked whether the number of the elect was coterminous with the members of the Israelite nation. Allowing for a few exceptions like Naaman the Syrian, that essentially had been the understanding in Old Testament times.[99] To be elect without being part of Israel was perhaps possible but it was anomalous, and unless there was very clear indication to the contrary, it was safe to assume that non-Israelites had not been chosen by God. But what about Israelites who did not live up to their calling? There were plenty of them around, even after the great purges of antiquity. Could a Jew claim to be a child of God if he blasphemed the name of the Lord, ignored the law of Moses, and scandalized the Gentile world by his behavior?[100]

This was a more difficult question, and there was no easy answer to it. The rite of circumcision, administered shortly after birth, guaranteed that a Jewish male would be marked for life. Even if he tried to deny it, evidence that he belonged to the elect nation was still present in his body, and other people would recognize that. A Jew who misbehaved was in a worse position than a Gentile who did the same things in ignorance, because his election worked against him.

[97] 1 Cor. 12:12–30.
[98] Clement of Alexandria, *Stromateis* 6.13.
[99] For Naaman, see 2 Kings 5:1–19.
[100] See Rom. 2:17–29.

A Gentile might be excused for not knowing what he should do, but an Israelite would be punished because, as one of the elect, he ought to have known better.

It is apparent from this that the early Christians did not think that all the elect were necessarily saved. They did not deny that the Jewish people had a special place in God's plan, but when individual Jews disgraced themselves, Christians were quite prepared to say that God had rejected them because of their sins. As they saw it, election was an act of God's grace but it was not an automatic guarantee of salvation, and Jews who thought that it was were deceiving themselves.

The early Christians also had to come to terms with the large numbers of Gentiles who sought admission to the church because of their faith in Christ. After some initial doubts and disagreements about how to proceed with this, the apostles decided that Gentiles could join the church as equal members without submitting to the demands of the law of Moses.[101] Were those Gentiles also to be regarded as elect?

That could be done only by changing the terms of election, eliminating the physical requirements of descent from Abraham and acceptance of the law of Moses, and replacing them with purely spiritual criteria. The Christian church was a body of the elect because God had formed it by the indwelling presence and power of his Holy Spirit.[102] Christians had been set apart from the "world," not by physical differences but by an inward spiritual commitment that would naturally express itself in changed lives and behavior. They constituted a holy nation, a special people, a "royal priesthood" in the service of God, and were meant to demonstrate this by the way they lived.[103]

It soon turned out that even in the church there was a gap between theory and practice. Holy people behaved in unholy ways and had to be corrected. They could not just be cut off from the body, because if that practice were consistently adopted, there would be no church left—all have sinned and come short of the glory of God![104] In a few extreme cases, excommunication (as this cutting off was called) might be the best solution, especially for those who had no intention of changing their behavior, but the majority were not that bad.[105] For the most part, they meant well but did not achieve the high standards required of them. Sometimes they were ignorant, sometimes they were lazy, sometimes they came up against obstacles (like an unbelieving spouse) that made living the Christian life in its fullness either impossible or very difficult.

[101] Acts 15:1–29; Gal. 3:28–29.
[102] Acts 2:38–41.
[103] 1 Pet. 2:9.
[104] Rom. 3:23.
[105] See 1 Tim. 1:20.

The New Testament epistles were written to help such people, and so we know a good deal about the problems they faced. Moreover, those epistles have become part of the sacred Scriptures of the church, because what they say strikes a chord with believers everywhere—we struggle with much the same things that the early Christians did, even though the precise details and circumstances may be quite different.

Inevitably, therefore, the question of the relationship between election and salvation came up once more, albeit in a new guise. In later times this would become a major topic of discussion and disagreement among Christians, but that was not the case in the early church. The approach it took was to treat those who had made a profession of faith in Christ and been baptized as members of the elect community, without assuming either that they were perfect or that they were automatically going to be saved. We see this in those exhortations where the apostles write to saints in order to tell them that they ought to behave in a way that corresponds to their profession.[106] The obvious conclusion must be that they were not doing so, since if they had been, it would have been unnecessary for the apostles to write to them.

The apostles wrote to their congregations assuming that they would be obeyed and that people would want to make their behavior conform to their profession of faith as much as possible, but they were prepared for rejection and disobedience in individual cases. The story of the New Testament church is not one of unalloyed success, and discipline often had to be exercised in order to maintain the purity of its witness. In one extreme case, that of Ananias and Sapphira, the guilty parties were struck dead because they had lied to the Holy Spirit![107]

In essence, the apostles saw the church as the continuation of historic Israel. Both were a mixed company of sheep and goats, of wheat and tares, and only the last judgment would make it clear which was which.[108] Individual believers had the assurance of salvation and did not have to fear that they would be rejected when the judgment came, but they also had to realize that assurance is not the same thing as presumption. The context in which grace and election were to be worked out was that of God's covenant with his people, a belief that Jews and Christians shared. Because there is only one God there can be only one covenant, since anything else would destroy the unity of the divine plan. Neither Jews nor Christians could imagine that God would promise salvation to one group of people in one way (through the law of Moses or through Jesus Christ) and to others in quite dif-

---

[106] Phil. 2:12; 1 Pet. 1:2.
[107] Acts 5:1–11.
[108] See Matt. 13:24–40; 25:32–33.

ferent ways. This stood in sharp contrast to the dominant feeling among pagans, who saw no essential difference between religions and who were quite happy to accept that whatever benefit was conveyed by one could equally well be conveyed by the others. This was not an irresponsible eclecticism but a belief that underneath the apparent differences there lay a common bedrock of truth that was the same for everyone, even if different people expressed it in different ways.

Neither Jews nor Christians could accept that kind of relativism. For them there was only one way to salvation, and that was by obeying the voice of the God who had entered into covenant with Abraham, Isaac, and Jacob. Christians understood the outworking of that covenant in ways that were different from what the rabbis taught, but on the fundamental principle they were agreed. For the early church there was "one Lord, one faith, one baptism."[109] In modern times there has been a tendency to analyze the covenant idea into different parts, the suggestion being that God made a covenant with Adam, and then another one with Abraham, another one with Moses, another one with David, and finally a new and different one with Christians in and through Jesus Christ. This analysis has some merit in distinguishing different aspects of the covenant that were revealed at different times in Israel's history, but it must not be pressed to the point of suggesting that the covenant lacked an overall unity. The Jews of Jesus' day saw no difference between God's word to Abraham, to Moses, and to David; for them, it was all one and the same.

The early church saw the covenant made in Christ as something new, but not to the point that it abandoned the old covenant and started afresh. As the words of Clement of Alexandria quoted above suggest, it understood the distinction as one of *dispensation*, or *administration*—legal terms which signified that the same fundamental principles were now to be applied in a new context. Tertullian described it as follows:

> The two dispensations are distinguished by reformation, amplification, and progress. For example, fruit is separate from the seed, even though it originally comes from the seed. Likewise, the gospel is separate from the law, even though it originally developed out of the law. It is a different thing, but not an alien one. It is distinct from the law, but not foreign to it.[110]

How this worked may perhaps be grasped by using a modern, secular analogy. Some cities still have bylaws that forbid tethering a horse in front of certain buildings. Those laws were passed in the days before the invention of the automobile

[109] Eph. 4:5.
[110] Tertullian, *Adversus Marcionem* 4.11.

and now they are redundant, but they may be interpreted to mean that no one should park a car in those places, on the ground that the car is the modern equivalent of the horse. That is not what the law *says* but it is what it *means*, and it is applied accordingly. In the same way, the life and work of Jesus Christ altered the conditions in which the law of Moses functioned, making many of its provisions obsolete, but the principles were still valid and they were applied according to what the Bible calls the "spirit" of the text and not the "letter."[111]

It is in this way that the "new" covenant made in Christ's blood differed from the old one revealed to Moses and the prophets. Whereas before there had been a prophet who received a word from God and proclaimed it to the nation, now Jesus was the incarnation of that Word and proclaimed himself as the fulfillment of God's promises. Where there had once been priests who offered sacrifices in the temple for the sins of the people, now Jesus was the Great High Priest who offered the perfect sacrifice of himself in the temple that was his body. In the past there had been a king ruling over a territory he called his kingdom, but now Jesus was the king who ruled over his people by uniting them to himself. The ancient covenant roles (called "offices" in traditional theological language) had been united and brought to their logical fulfillment by Jesus. A new dispensation had arrived, but only because the old one had been fulfilled and was no longer needed, not because it had been fundamentally mistaken all along and had therefore been abolished.

It was at this point that Jews and Christians disagreed. They spoke the same covenantal language but interpreted it differently, because Jews did not accept that a new dispensation had arrived. From the Christian point of view, the tragedy was that while Jews watched the old dispensation disappear under their eyes as the Romans destroyed the temple and traditional Israelite society, they were unable to see that this was the logical and inevitable consequence of the fact that those things had served their purpose and were no longer required. By claiming that those promises had been fulfilled in Christ, either already or in the age to come, Christians stepped into the shoes of the ancient Israelites and appropriated what had been promised to them as their own inheritance.

The hope of future fulfillment was another thing that Jews and Christians had in common, though their different interpretations of the covenant meant that they interpreted the details differently. We do not know how many Israelites in the time of Jesus were actively looking for the Messiah, or what they thought he would do if he came. The general impression we get is that somehow the "kingdom would be restored to Israel," and it seems that most

[111] 2 Cor. 3:6.

people imagined that a new David would come along and restore the empire that he and his son Solomon had briefly ruled a thousand years before.[112] There were certainly a few people who appeared and claimed to be such a figure, though the movements they started quickly fizzled out or were suppressed by the Romans. Had one of them succeeded, no doubt everyone would have rallied behind him and any earlier skepticism would have been swept away. No one likes to argue with success, but as failure was the invariable result, few people wanted to be identified with that either. Some even saw the Roman empire as a bulwark against impending disaster. As Tertullian said,

> We must pray for the stability of the empire and for Roman interests in general, because we know that a mighty cataclysm is impending. The end of all things threatens dreadful calamities which are only being held back by the continued existence of the Roman empire. We have no desire to be overtaken by these dire events, and in praying that their coming may be delayed, we are supporting Rome's duration.[113]

Perhaps the best way to look at this is to compare the situation then with what we find in the church now. Officially, Christians are still committed to the belief that Christ will come again to judge the living and the dead, and we repeat that phrase every time we say one of the classical creeds. There are also occasional "prophecies" that the end is coming, and a few hopefuls gather to wait for it, but most people ignore such activities and regard them with a mixture of amusement and disdain. No one knows when Christ will come again, and it has to be said that hardly anyone is seriously preparing for it. Most of us believe (and so far experience has confirmed us in this) that we shall die and go to meet him long before he comes back to earth. Yet the belief itself is still there, and with it the hope that everything will work out for the best in the end. Jews still await the coming of their Messiah, with much the same mixture of hope and indifference that we find among Christians. When Jesus told his disciples that the coming of the Son of Man would be as much of a surprise as Noah's flood, and the apostles told the church that the Lord would come like a thief in the night and catch us unawares, they could have been speaking as much to Jews of their own time as to Christians today.[114]

Having said that, hope for the future is widespread among both Jews and Christians, and is intrinsic to our relationship with God. We may not know exactly what will happen to us or when, but we believe that it will ultimately

---

[112] Acts 1:6.
[113] Tertullian, *Apologeticum* 32.
[114] Matt. 24:36–44; 1 Thess. 5:2; 2 Pet. 3:10.

be good and that God will keep faith with us in the end.[115] Compare that to what most pagan peoples of antiquity believed. For them, the best days were in the distant past, the "golden age" from which the present time of sorrow and corruption had dramatically declined. The future, such as it was, could only be worse, and it would all end in a great conflagration or disaster that would mark the end of the world. This disaster scenario is by no means absent today, of course, and the existence of nuclear weapons makes it a real possibility now in a way that the ancients could not have imagined. But whereas most of them would have accepted their fate as inevitable, most of us cling to the belief that where there is life, there is hope. We do this because the God of the Bible has taught us that he is the first and the last, the One who is and who was and who is to come, the Almighty.[116] Disasters there will be aplenty, but the world belongs to God and in the end he will reclaim it, along with his faithful people in it, for himself.

To sum this up, Judaism and Christianity both have an "eschatology," a doctrine of the future which will also be the divinely appointed culmination of the past and the present. We do not cling to the past as something better than what we have now, and we look to the future with optimism and hope. We do not believe that time is essentially cyclical, so that what goes around will come around again in an endless series of repetitions, none of which will be noticeably better or worse than the last. Jews and Christians believe in "progress," not in the humanistic sense that science will eventually solve all the world's problems, but in the sense that God has a purpose for our lives that will one day be fulfilled, and that gives us the will to live and act in the present. We are building for the future, but we are also building for eternity, and we believe that, in the end, these two will merge into one. Christians understand the details of this differently from Jews but our basic outlook is the same, and it sets us apart from every other religion or philosophy that the world has to offer.

[115] Rom. 8:28.
[116] Rev. 1:8.

PART TWO

The Person of the Father

3

God as Father

Judaism and the Fatherhood of God

It is no exaggeration to say that Christian theology began when Jesus called God his Father and taught his disciples to do the same. That was something previously unknown in Israel, and the Jews who heard Jesus say this reacted against him because of it. There are passages in the Old Testament where the language of fatherhood is used of God, but they are relatively few and their meaning is sometimes unclear. Jesus never appealed to those passages to support his teaching, and those who heard him were astonished and upset because what he said seemed to indicate a degree of familiarity with God that they thought was blasphemous. As the story is recounted in the New Testament, what provoked this reaction was the fact that Jesus was healing people on the Sabbath day. This is significant because Israel kept the Sabbath rest out of respect for the completion of the divine work of creation in six days.[1] In this way, the Israelites sought to order their national life according to the pattern laid down by God when he made the world. By resting on the seventh day they observed a sacred time that reminded them that God's work was complete and all-sufficient for their needs.

But in spite of that deeply ingrained tradition and its spiritual significance, Jesus did things on the Sabbath that apparently contradicted the law of God and its teaching about creation. He justified healing people on the Sabbath day by arguing that God was still at work, not in creating new things but in restoring a world that had been corrupted by human sin. When the Jewish leaders challenged him over his behavior, Jesus replied, "My Father is working until now, and I am working."[2] He claimed to know that God was not at rest in eternity because as his Father's Son, he was still doing God's work. The implications of that claim were not lost on his audience. In John's words,

[1] Ex. 20:8–11.
[2] John 5:17.

> This was why the Jews were seeking all the more to kill him, because not only was he breaking the Sabbath, but he was even calling God his own Father, making himself equal with God.[3]

But why would those Jews draw such an unlikely conclusion? After all, when we call God our Father today we are not making ourselves equal to him but are simply proclaiming our acceptance of his authority over us. Why did the Jews not think that Jesus was saying the same thing then as we are now? Even if the novelty of his claim caused them some discomfort, why did they not see it in the light of the allusions to divine fatherhood that occasionally appear in the Old Testament? One reason was that Jesus' assertion of his sonship was coupled with the claim that he had the power to override the Old Testament law. That alone made it obvious that Jesus was claiming to have a relationship with God unlike anything previously known in Israel. On the few occasions when God had spoken of the Israelites as his children, he did not mean that they shared his divine power or that they could modify his commandments in the way that Jesus did. The only time when the Jewish people are known to have called on God as their Father occurs in Isaiah, where the prophet, speaking as the voice of the nation, says,

> You are our Father,
> though Abraham does not know us,
> and Israel does not acknowledge us;
> you, O Lord, are our Father,
> our Redeemer from old is your name.
> O Lord, why do you make us wander from your ways
> and harden our heart, so that we fear you not?
> Return for the sake of your servants,
> the tribes of your heritage.[4]

The context is one of sin and judgment, in which the prophet's voice calls out to God for the redemption that he has promised his people. It is in that way that God appears as their Father, as he also does a little later on, when Isaiah uses the image of the potter and the clay, which the apostle Paul later borrowed to great effect:[5]

> O Lord, you are our Father;
> we are the clay, and you are our potter;

[3] John 5:18.
[4] Isa. 63:16–17.
[5] Rom. 9:20–21, alluding to Isa. 64:8–9.

we are all the work of your hand.
Be not so terribly angry, O LORD,
and remember not iniquity forever.[6]

To the modern reader, it seems that the Israelites were addressing God as their Creator, but we must be cautious about this. First, the context is not creation but redemption—the people have sinned and they are begging God for mercy and restoration. Second, if Isaiah was thinking of God primarily as Creator, Israel would not have been any different from the other nations. According to the Hebrew Bible, everyone was descended from Adam, who was created in God's image and was the ancestor of all human beings.[7] If that were the meaning here, Isaiah would be praying on behalf of the entire human race, when in fact he is adopting the persona of Israel alone. It is not the universal relationship between humanity and God that he is alluding to but the covenant relationship that God had granted to Israel. When God first spoke to Abraham and to Moses, the human clay (to use Isaiah's image) was already there. The divine potter did not create Israel out of nothing but took what he found and shaped it according to his will. Finally, as Paul pointed out when he alluded to this verse, a potter's relationship to his clay is not reciprocal, so that Israel could not pray to God as its Father in the way that Jesus taught his disciples to do.[8] The poetic image of God's fatherhood is powerful but it is also more distant than what we find in the Gospels, and we must remember that Jesus never referred to this text when teaching his disciples how to pray, though he often quoted Isaiah and could easily have done so if the text had been relevant to his purpose.

Furthermore, when Jews thought about their ancestry they usually did not look back as far as Adam, the generic founder of the human race.[9] They preferred Abraham, Isaac, and Jacob, whom God had made the ancestor of a chosen people. Abraham had other children, but it was through the line of Isaac that Israel came into being. Jacob was his younger son but was preferred over his older brother. It was he who was given the name Israel, and after that, all his sons belonged to the chosen people. In this sense Israel's origin was supernatural, a constant reminder to the Jews that they were special in the eyes of God. Jesus understood this, of course, and he did not hesitate to criticize the Jews for failing to live up to their high calling. As he put it to them,

[6] Isa. 64:8–9.
[7] Gen. 1:26–27.
[8] Matt. 6:9.
[9] Apart from the genealogies in Genesis and 1 Chronicles, Adam never appears in the Old Testament, apart from possible allusions in Deut. 32:8 and Job 31:33, neither of which is certain. Contrast this with the apostle Paul, who discusses the importance of Adam on three separate occasions (Rom. 5:12–14; 1 Cor. 15:22, 45; 1 Tim. 2:13–14).

> I know that you are offspring of Abraham; yet you seek to kill me because my word finds no place in you. I speak of what I have seen with my Father, and you do what you have heard from your father.[10]

In human terms, Jesus was a descendant of Abraham just as much as his hearers were, yet here he was saying that they were not from the same stock at all. Jesus claimed that he was doing what his Father had told him, and that if they were really the children of Abraham as they said they were, they would recognize that what he was doing came from God. When the Jews heard this, they were provoked into declaring that God was their Father, rejecting Jesus' claims and accusing him of being possessed by a demon. In other words, they tried to turn Jesus' argument on its head—they were the children of God and he was of the Devil, not the other way around! At that point Jesus told them that Abraham had known who he was and had looked forward to his future coming. Needless to say, this seemed absurd to the Jews. How could Jesus and Abraham have known each other when Abraham had lived nearly two thousand years earlier? Jesus then replied that he was in existence long before Abraham was born, an assertion that could only mean that he was claiming to be God.[11]

The important thing to notice here is how Jesus subtly moved his Jewish opponents from the material to the spiritual dimension in the discussion about their ancestry. He could hardly have denied that Jews were physically descended from Abraham just as he was, but he was more concerned to tell them that they had nothing in common with him at the spiritual level, whereas Abraham did. Abraham's relationship to God was enshrined in the covenant that God had made with him, and if God was their Father, it was because they were bound to him by that covenant. The Jews maintained the outward signs of belonging to the covenant, most notably circumcision, but in their hearts and minds many of them had long since rejected it. The tragedy was that they mistook the outward signs as evidence that they possessed the spiritual reality that those signs represented, which was simply not true.

It was in the context of this spiritual dimension that Jesus pressed home the point that their true father was neither God nor Abraham, but the Devil. Of course, the Devil had not given them physical birth as Abraham had, nor was he their Creator, as God was. But they had a relationship with him that made him their spiritual master, and their opposition to Jesus showed that they were doing the Devil's will. In denouncing the Jewish leaders, Jesus was not

[10] John 8:37–38.
[11] John 8:39–59.

introducing a new idea about God of which they had never heard (and therefore could not be blamed for not knowing); rather, he was recalling the way in which their relationship to God was presented in the Old Testament. Consider what Moses said to them in Deuteronomy:

> You are the sons of the Lord your God. . . . For you are a people holy to the Lord your God, and the Lord has chosen you to be a people for his treasured possession, out of all the peoples who are on the face of the earth.[12]

Moses described the Israelites as God's sons because they were the heirs to the covenant promises, and were therefore expected to manifest the holiness that matched their status. God was their Father by implication, but the resemblance that made such a relationship possible was their holiness. Holiness was not a thing in itself, but a description of what made both God and Israel different from everything else. God was holy because he was not a creature and was not bound by the power of Satan over a fallen world, and Israel was called to be equally holy by detaching itself from the other nations, which were so bound, and obeying God instead. This theme recurs in Psalm 103, where the fatherhood of God is mentioned as the reason he would rescue Israel from the sins that had so obscured the nation's holiness:

> He does not deal with us according to our sins,
> nor repay us according to our iniquities. . . .
> As a father shows compassion to his children,
> so the Lord shows compassion to those who fear him.[13]

In this verse God is compared to a human father, but whether this proves that the psalmist thought of God as the Father of Israel is hard to say for sure. God is compared to many things in the Bible—a rock, a fortress, fire, and so on—but he is not identified with any of them, so a comparison of this kind must be interpreted with caution.[14] Nevertheless, the image of fatherhood is a powerful and significant one, and speaks movingly of the love that God has for the people he has chosen. The association it seems to have with the people's sin and their plea for God's forgiveness comes out with special force during the exile, as we can see from what God said to Jeremiah:

> Is Ephraim my dear son?
> Is he my darling child?

[12] Deut. 14:1–2. The small-capital style (Lord) indicates the use of the personal name of God, *YHWH* (Yahweh).
[13] Ps. 103:10, 13.
[14] See, for example, 2 Sam. 22:2; Psalm 71:3; Deut. 4:24; Heb. 12:29.

For as often as I speak against him,
    I do remember him still.
Therefore my heart yearns for him;
    I will surely have mercy on him,
        declares the LORD.[15]

The text is striking, but although the fatherhood of God is assumed, it is implied rather than explicitly stated. Furthermore, as with most of the other Old Testament references to God as Father, this verse is also somewhat negative in character. God was perceived to be Israel's Father in the context of the covenant he made with Abraham and later confirmed with Moses, but apart from the initial statement of this in Deuteronomy 14, the fact is mentioned only to point out the contrast between what God had originally intended and the harsh reality that Israel had betrayed his trust and rebelled against him. The Israelites do not seem to have appealed to God's fatherly nature except when they were in need of compassion and forgiveness; it was not part of their daily worship or felt to be fundamental to their experience of him. We can therefore say with some assurance that when Jesus called God his Father and taught his disciples to do the same he was doing something new, and the reaction of the Jewish leaders who heard him confirms us in this perception.

Non-Jewish Conceptions of Divine Fatherhood

If the ancient Jews seldom referred to God as their Father and, when they did, were careful about how they did so, pagans showed no such reticence. Their pantheons often had divine father-figures, and procreation, both of other gods and of superhuman beings, was common in their mythology. The most obvious example of this is the Roman god Jupiter, whose name is a shortened form of *Iovispater* ("Jove-father"), but he was far from alone. To pagan minds, the gods were closely associated with physical forces of all kinds, both good and evil, and the description of creativity as fatherhood was natural to them. They had a sense that human beings were directly dependent on supernatural powers that held the universe together. Who or what they were remained essentially mysterious, though the Greek philosophers used words like *psychê* (soul), *nous* (mind) and *logos* (reason), which over time tended to merge into a single concept—the Supreme Being. The apostle Paul picked up on this tendency when speaking to the philosophers of Athens and even cited one of the Greek poets to that effect.[16] The

[15] Jer. 31:20. The name Ephraim stands for the ten tribes of Israel that were deported in 722 BC (about 130 years before Jeremiah received this message), and the verse is a lament for the tragic fate that had befallen them.
[16] "For we are indeed his offspring" (Acts 17:28). The poet was Aratus (d. 240 BC) and the quotation is from *Phaenomena* 5; see also his contemporary Cleanthes, *Hymn to Zeus* 4, where he expresses the same thought.

gist of Paul's discourse was that he had come to reveal the God who had previously been unknown to the Gentiles, as they themselves occasionally admitted.[17]

It has sometimes been claimed that Jews were reluctant to embrace the concept of divine fatherhood because of its pagan associations, but we must be cautious about this. It is certainly true that the gods of the other nations were often pictured as superhuman beings, and their kings and heroes were frequently deified. The Roman emperor was officially proclaimed a "son of God" after the posthumous deification of his predecessor, although it must be said that many Romans found this practice barbaric and alien to their traditions. The Old Testament frequently portrays God in semi-human terms by speaking of his eyes, his hands, and so on, but it emphatically denies that he is a glorified man. The deification of earthly rulers was incompatible with biblical teaching and alien to Jewish practice, which made it impossible for them to participate in the rituals of allegiance that were expected of Romans, but the biblical anthropomorphisms show us that the writers of the Old Testament did not avoid saying things merely because they might sow confusion among the Jewish people.

If pagan notions of divine fatherhood had been creeping into Judaism and distorting it, we would know about it from prophetic denunciations of the phenomenon, but there were none. If there had been a right way to worship God as Father, the prophets or the psalmists would surely have said so and made it perfectly clear how their view of the matter differed from that of the surrounding peoples. There is plenty of rhetoric in the Hebrew Bible against idolatry and the fertility cults that went with it, and there was every opportunity for such statements to be made, so the silence of the Old Testament probably indicates that there was no problem of this kind. In the Israelite mind, the God of the Bible was the Creator who had made a world outside himself that had no more connection to him than the clay had to the potter who worked on it. The similarity of nature and inevitability of relationship implied by the word "father" had no place in their vision of God and therefore seems to have been ignored by the Old Testament writers as being completely irrelevant to what they were saying.

Much more important for the Jewish and Christian traditions was the influence of Greek philosophy, and in particular that of Plato (429–347 BC) and his followers. Plato often spoke about the highest principle, using different terms to describe it. In the *Republic* he called it the "good," in the *Symposium* it was the "beautiful," and in the *Parmenides* the "one."[18] His most sustained treatment

[17] On this subject, see Robert M. Grant, *Gods and the One God: Christian Theology in the Graeco-Roman World* (London: SPCK, 1986).

[18] Plato, *Respublica* 502d–509c, 517b–521b; *Symposium* 210e–212b; *Parmenides* 137c–166c.

of the theme, however, was in the *Timaeus*, which later became almost required reading among both Jews and Christians, and for most of the Middle Ages it was the only work of Plato known in Western Europe. In this treatise, Plato developed the theme of the creator (*dêmiourgos*) or maker (*poiêtês*), whom he also called the father. This creator was good, and he decided to make an orderly universe (*kosmos*) out of disordered matter, which apparently already existed, using a model based on abstract forms or ideas. The creator wanted his *kosmos* to be as good as it could be, though he recognized that because it was material it could not rise to the same level as himself.[19] From the matter available to him, he made a world and gave it both a mind and a soul, so that it became a second, somewhat inferior god. In addition to this, the creator also made the stars and planets along similar lines.[20]

In all of these new worlds he planted immortal souls and told them that if they should happen to fall into a material body, they must try to live as virtuous a life as possible. After the death of that body they would return to the stars from which they had come. If they failed to be virtuous, however, they would fall back into another body and become women. If they failed a third time, they would fall even further and become animals, and so on. The stars and planets, as secondary or "young" gods, imitated the creator and made material bodies out of the elements of earth, air, fire, and water. They then put immortal souls into those bodies, with unfortunate results. The souls, who were by nature intelligent, lost their understanding when they were incarnated, and could regain it only by severe self-discipline.[21]

Plato's thought was not systematic, and there was much that he left unsaid. For example, we do not know where he thought the forms/ideas came from. Did the creator make them, or were they already there, just as eternal as he was? Nor is it clear whether the creator can be identified with the good, the beautiful, or the one. For Plato, these three may just as easily have been abstractions as agents, and therefore not capable of making anything. Such loose ends were subsequently debated and eventually systematized by Plato's followers, the most influential of whom (for our purposes) was Alcinous (150 BC?). According to his interpretation, the father was the highest god, the ultimate cause of all things, the first mind, the supreme good, and the god who dwelt above the heavens. The forms and ideas that went to make up the world were his thoughts. His most important act was to give birth to the creator, a lesser god, who was nevertheless the mind of heaven and the soul of the world. It was this

[19] Plato, *Timaeus* 28c–34b.
[20] Ibid., 41a–42e.
[21] Ibid., 42e–44e.

lesser god who entered into contact with matter, something that the purity of the highest god prevented him from doing.[22]

Alcinous was followed by other philosophers of his generation, and it was in this form that the ideas of their master reached Jews like Philo of Alexandria (d. AD 50). Philo was strongly attracted to Platonism but always made sure that it was adjusted to the teaching of the Old Testament. His commitment to biblical monotheism ensured that he would never accept the idea that the father and the creator were two different gods, still less that the former was superior to the latter! Others were less cautious, however, and their attempts to harmonize Platonic teachings with the Bible and the revelation of Jesus Christ would cause big problems for the early church.[23] Christians could accept that the terms "Creator" and "Father" were different—the former referred to the origin of the entire universe whereas the latter was restricted to the covenant people of God who were united to him in Christ—but they could never agree that they could be separated into two distinct deities. The two concepts had to be held together within the one God, though as time would show, that would prove to be more difficult than it could ever seem to us.

Jesus and His Father

We know that Jesus called God his Father in a way that his Jewish hearers found strange and that others would not have understood at all. We also know that he was not talking about the distant Creator of the universe but about a being to whom he was so close that his words and actions were effectively the same as the Father's. As he told his disciples, "I and the Father are one."[24] If he had been content to say that God was his Father because he kept the Abrahamic covenant more faithfully than other Israelites did, people might have disagreed with him but he would not have been considered blasphemous. In that case, Jesus could perhaps have been compared to men like Enoch, Moses, and Elijah, who were exceptionally close to God without being divine.[25] But when the New Testament writers looked for analogies to Jesus' claims in the Old Testament, the only one they could find was the promise made concerning King Solomon and his promised messianic successor who would restore Israel and give it a glory even greater than what it had had in Solomon's day.

That promise had been revealed to the prophet Nathan, who had been told to explain to King David why he could not build a temple at Jerusalem that

[22] See John Whittaker and Pierre Louis, *Alcinoos. Enseignement des doctrines de Platon* (Paris: Les Belles Lettres, 1990).
[23] See Riemer Roukema, *Gnosis and Faith in Early Christianity* (London: SCM, 1989).
[24] John 10:30.
[25] See Matt. 16:13–14.

would house the ark of the covenant and be the center of the people's worship. The reason was that David had acquired his kingdom by bloodshed and violence, and although God had honored him in many ways, he wanted the builder of his temple to be a man of peace.[26] As he explained to David,

> When your days are fulfilled to walk with your fathers, I will raise up your offspring after you, one of your own sons, and I will establish his kingdom. He shall build a house for me, and I will establish his throne forever. I will be to him a father, and he shall be to me a son. I will not take my steadfast love from him, as I took it from him who was before you, but I will confirm him in my house and in my kingdom forever, and his throne shall be established forever.[27]

Nathan was referring to Solomon and his descendants, but the chronicler who recorded his words knew that the promise would not be literally fulfilled. Since he was writing after the fall of Jerusalem and the extinction of the Davidic monarchy in 586 BC, he could have understood Nathan's words only in an eschatological sense. That he was not alone in this can be seen from the Psalms:

> I [God] have set my King
> on Zion, my holy hill.
>
> I will tell of the decree:
> The Lord said to me: "You are my Son;
> today I have begotten you.
> Ask of me, and I will make the nations your heritage,
> and the ends of the earth your possession."[28]

Psalm 89 says of the eschatological king that,

> He shall cry to me, "You are my Father,
> my God, and the Rock of my salvation."
> And I will make him the firstborn,
> the highest of the kings of the earth.[29]

In the New Testament, the writer to the Hebrews picked up on this and made it the starting point of his exposition of the Old Testament and

[26] The name "Solomon" means "his peace."
[27] 1 Chron. 17:11–14. See Heb. 1:5.
[28] Ps. 2:6–8. See Heb. 1:5; 5:5.
[29] Ps. 89:26–27. See Rom. 8:29; Col. 1:15, 18; Heb. 1:5.

the way that Jesus has fulfilled it.[30] But the way he did so underscores the fact that the predictions of the eternal reign of the house of David did not suggest that the Messiah would be anything more than a human being. He would be "greater than Solomon," but his superiority would be one of degree, not of kind.[31]

Is there any evidence to suggest that Jesus accepted that concept of his sonship? He often called himself the Son of Man, a term that refers to the heavenly being seen by Daniel,[32] but there is no evidence that anyone else used it of him. In Hebrew, the expression "son of" is commonly used in an adjectival sense, so that a "son of man" is simply a "human being."[33] God regularly addressed the prophet Ezekiel as "son of man," meaning no more than that he was human.[34] When Jesus called himself Son of Man he also meant it in a generic sense, but unlike Ezekiel, who could have been any child of Adam, Jesus was a very specific Man who had come down from heaven to share our humanity in a uniquely representative way.[35] Furthermore, Jesus did not use the title Son of Man as proof of his relationship to God the Father. The title emphasized his humanity in an apocalyptic, heavenly setting, but it was not particularly relational—there was no Man the Father to complement the Son!

Jesus' relationship to his Father is expressed in his title "Son of God," an identity that could be known only by those to whom the Father had revealed it.[36] Here we are dealing with something other than the Son's divine nature, because Jesus could not have been the archetypal God in the same way that he was the archetypal Man. The reason for this is obvious: human beings exist in plurality, and so Jesus could be a man without being the only one. But there is only one God, so it makes no sense to say that Jesus represented him, unless he was that one God himself. But although Jesus identified himself with the Father, he still spoke of the Father as if he were someone else. The matter was further complicated by his claim that it was only in and through the Son that the Father could be known:

[30] The author of the epistle remains unknown, but internal evidence strongly suggests that he was a Hellenistic Jew who moved in the same circles as the apostle Paul, with whom he was later identified. He was probably writing sometime between AD 60 and AD 65, shortly before the Jewish revolt and the destruction of the temple in AD 70. See Peter T. O'Brien, *The Letter to the Hebrews* (Grand Rapids, MI: Eerdmans, 2010) for a full discussion.

[31] Matt. 12:42; Luke 11:31.

[32] Dan. 7:13.

[33] Compare Mark 3:17, where we are told that Jesus surnamed James and John, the sons of Zebedee, "Boanerges," meaning "Sons of Thunder," a colorful description of their character, not a definition of their nature.

[34] The phrase first appears in Ezek. 2:1 and last in Ezek. 47:6—ninety-three times in all!

[35] John 3:13–15.

[36] See Matt. 16:13–17, where the terms "Son of Man" and "Son of God" are brought together and equated with each other.

> No one has ever seen God; the only begotten Son, who is in the bosom of the Father, he has made him known.[37]

In himself, God is invisible, but the Son, who shares the Father's nature in a way that no one else does, became a man and revealed the Father for the first time. The implication is that because the ancient Israelites lived before the coming of the Son, they did not know the Father, and could not have known him for that reason. This inevitably raised questions about the connection between the "Father" of John 1:18 and the God of the Old Testament, who had frequently revealed himself to the patriarchs and was well known to the Israelites, even if they could not see him. Were the first Christians supposed to believe that by making the Father known, Jesus had revealed the God of Israel for the first time? Here was a relationship that had to be clarified in order to make sense of the message of the gospel. If the Father of Jesus Christ were someone different from the God of the Old Testament, how could Jesus have claimed to be fulfilling the Hebrew Scriptures which had been given by that God and bore witness to him? What continuity with Israel would his life and ministry have had? But if the Father were the Old Testament God without qualification, then who or what was the Son? He could not have been God, but how could he claim to be revealing the Father as his Son if he were a different (and necessarily inferior) being?

The evidence of the Gospels makes it clear that Jesus thought of the Father as someone greater than himself.[38] This is seen in the Son's conscious submission to his Father's will, which was the foundation of his earthly life and ministry. As he once told his disciples when they offered him something to eat, "My food is to do the will of him who sent me and to accomplish his work."[39] This submission was voluntary, but it had the same inevitability about it that eating has. It is possible to abstain from food, but only at the price of self-destruction, and we may conclude that if Jesus had *not* done his Father's will his life would have lost its purpose. There was something about the Father that made the Son's submission to him seem natural and even essential to the right ordering of their relationship.

This becomes even clearer when we realize that there is no sign that the Father was expected to submit to the Son's will in return. The Father had sent the Son without having to ask the Son for his agreement, but the Son did not

[37] John 1:18. The Greek text is disputed, with some manuscripts reading "God" instead of "Son" after "only begotten." The ESV translation, which prefers "God" to "Son," omits "begotten," and avoids using the word "bosom," is inadequate here.
[38] John 14:28.
[39] John 4:34.

have comparable authority over the Father. When he wanted the Father to do something, he had to ask him to grant his request(s).[40] Of course the Son knew that he would be heard, but the fact that he had to ask shows that their relationship was not one of "equals," as we would understand that term today. Jesus even taught his disciples that there were things about him, like the date of his future return in glory, that were known only to the Father.[41] This admission of ignorance on his part has always puzzled Christian theologians, who have found it hard to accept that there could be something that the Son does not know. To their minds, God knows everything, so if the Son admits that there is something that he does not know, it must mean that he is not fully God. To counter this unwelcome conclusion, they may say that the Son really did know when he would return but because he had not been authorized to reveal the date to his disciples he professed ignorance when speaking to them. The difficulty with this solution is that it means that the Son told a "little white lie," as parents sometimes do when they do not want their children to know more than is good for them. Such behavior seems unworthy of God.

It is easy to see how Jesus might have treated his disciples that way, but the evidence suggests that when this problem arose elsewhere, Jesus told them that he was unable to speak clearly to them because they could not bear it,[42] not because he did not know what to say; so when he said he was ignorant as to the date of his return, we should take his statement at face value.[43] How the Father can know things that the Son does not know is a mystery bound up with their relationship which no outsider can fully penetrate. The nature of that relationship is expressed in the language of generation, according to which the Father has begotten the Son. This is an analogy taken from human experience and cannot be interpreted literally, but it does indicate that the Father enjoys a certain primacy within the Godhead that the Son recognizes and adheres to, so that in revealing himself as the Son he simultaneously reveals what is distinctive about the Father who sent him.

This relational structure also affects the Holy Spirit, who Jesus said proceeds from the Father.[44] Generation and procession are not the same thing, just as the Son and the Holy Spirit are not identical to one another, but the divinity of both is expressed in terms of a relation of dependence on the Father. However, this is not true of the Father, whose divinity is not explained by reference

[40] John 17:1–26.
[41] Matt. 24:36; Mark 13:32. See also Acts 1:7.
[42] This may explain what Paul meant when he said that "The Spirit searches everything, even the depths of God" (1 Cor. 2:10). The Holy Spirit is the third person of the divine Trinity, and so not an outsider to the relationship between the Father and the Son.
[43] John 16:12.
[44] John 15:26.

to anyone else. Even if it seems obvious that the Father could not be called a Father without having a Son, the Son is revealed as one who depends on the Father in a way that is not true in reverse. To know the Father is to acknowledge his primacy and centrality within the Godhead. The primacy of the Father is one of order, not of being. He is greater than the Son (and the Holy Spirit) because he has the authority to send the other persons of the Trinity to accomplish his will. This is made clear in the opening verses of 1 Peter, where we are told that Christians have been chosen according to the foreknowledge of God the Father, whom Peter goes on to praise in the following terms:

> Blessed be the God and Father of our Lord Jesus Christ! According to his great mercy, he has caused us to be born again to a living hope through the resurrection of Jesus Christ from the dead . . .[45]

The Father as the Principle of Divinity

The Son's work is the accomplishment of what the Father has willed and planned from the beginning. This perspective is common throughout the New Testament, sometimes without specifically naming the Father, as in the famous words of John 3:16: "God so loved the world, that he gave his only Son, that whoever believes in him should not perish but have eternal life." The context makes it clear that John is talking about the Father, but the fact that he can speak in this way reminds us that the Father can be called God in some absolute sense that does not apply to the other persons of the Trinity. The Father enjoys a primacy within the Trinity that the other persons respect, not because they are inferior to him but because the order inside the being of God has determined that their mutual relationships will be worked out in this way. The Father is the one to whom the other persons refer (and defer), making that role an essential part of his distinctiveness. It is his particular function to represent the being or substance of God in himself, as well as in his relations to the other divine persons. When God is spoken of as one, it is the Father who is primarily in view, not because he is God to a degree that the Son and the Holy Spirit are not, but because he represents the divine being in a way that is unencumbered by other considerations. The Son became a man and died for our sins, the Holy Spirit was sent at Pentecost and dwells in our hearts by faith, but the Father remains what God is and has always been in himself—sovereign and transcendent. The other persons make it possible for us to relate to him, but in himself he remains hidden from our eyes and totally different from anything we are or can ever imagine.

[45] 1 Pet. 1:3.

The New Testament does not speak about God in abstract terms of substance, but whatever his being is, it is expressed in and through the Father. This is what Paul told the Corinthians:

> Then comes the end, when he [the Son] delivers the kingdom to God the Father after destroying every rule and every authority and power. For he must reign until he has put all his enemies under his feet. The last enemy to be destroyed is death. . . . When all things are subjected to him, then the Son himself will also be subjected to him who put all things in subjection under him, that God may be all in all.[46]

Later on, he said much the same thing to the Philippians:

> God has highly exalted him [Jesus] and bestowed on him the name that is above every name, so that at the name of Jesus every knee should bow, in heaven and on earth and under the earth, and every tongue confess that Jesus Christ is Lord, to the glory of God the Father.[47]

These and other passages like them show us that in the New Testament, the Father was the ultimate reference point in the Godhead to whom the Son was responsible for accomplishing his mission. When the Son delivers the kingdom to the Father it will be perfect—there will be nothing further for the Father to add, because the Son is able to do everything that the Father can do. But the Son's work will not finally be registered as "accomplished" in the heavenly realms until the Father receives it, because that is his role in the divine order. The language of subjection that Paul used is subtle and must not be misunderstood. The world is subject to the Son because it is inferior to him by nature, but the Son is subject to the Father, not because he is naturally inferior to him, but in order to reveal how the members of the Trinity relate to one another. God will be all in all, not because the Father will claim possession of the Son and his work but because their presence in heaven will be the sign that the Father's plan and purpose have been accomplished. The worship of the Son does not detract from the Father's glory but adds to it, and indeed is necessary for that glory to be fully revealed.

It is the Father's special privilege to glorify the Son in the light of what the Son has done for our salvation. The Father can do this because he retains the eternal glory of God which neither the incarnation of the Son nor the sending of the Holy Spirit has modified or diminished in any way.[48] In the New Testament it was

[46] 1 Cor. 15:24–26, 28.
[47] Phil. 2:9–11.
[48] John 17:5.

not the adequacy of the Son's work that was at stake so much as its authenticity, because it had to be ratified by the Father before it could become effective and be revealed to the world. It was also the Father's prerogative to determine what would happen to those whom the Son had saved. As Jesus put it,

> I am no longer in the world, but they are in the world, and I am coming to you. Holy Father, keep them in your name, which you have given me, that they may be one, even as we are one.[49]

Here we see how the Son appealed to the Father to protect the unity of the church as a reflection of their own unity in the Godhead, giving the Father the same role among believers as he already had in his relationship to the other divine persons.

The structure of personal relations within the Godhead made it natural for the early Christians to think of the Father as the one who identifies himself with those attributes in a way that is not true of the other persons. This does not mean that the Son and the Holy Spirit lack these qualities or possess them to an inferior degree, but that when we think of God as holy, eternal, all-powerful, and so on, we personify these attributes in the Father more readily than in the other divine persons, a habit that can be traced back to the New Testament and that became standard in the early church. This identification of the divine attributes with the person of the Father was to cause considerable difficulties later on, but it can claim biblical support. As James says,

> Every good gift and every perfect gift is from above, coming down from the Father of lights with whom there is no variation or shadow due to change. Of his own will he brought us forth by the word of truth, that we should be a kind of firstfruits of his creatures.[50]

This suggests that the Father is unchanging (and therefore eternal, since change would imply time), that he is perfect light, and that he created us out of nothing. All of these ideas were to be prominent themes in the theology of the early church, and all were held to be especially characteristic of the Father.

The Unbegotten and Almighty God-in-Himself

When it came to distinguishing the Father from the Son, the early Christians did not think in terms of a relationship of equals as we would today. To them, relationships were determined by things inherent in who or what were related.

[49] John 17:11.
[50] James 1:17–18.

In other words, the Father possessed something that complemented what the Son possessed, thereby forming the harmonious and perfect connection that constituted their relationship. The New Testament described the Son as the "only begotten" of the Father, and so on the basis of that, the early Christians concluded that the Father was "unbegotten" (*agennêtos*), the term that became the hallmark of his identity.[51] The Bible does not use that term of God in either Testament, but it is easy to see why it was adopted. God was eternal and the Creator of the universe, so it would have seemed obvious that he could not have been born from any higher being, nor did he give birth to any of his creatures—they were made out of nothing.

The term "unbegotten" expressed what Christians wanted to say about the Father, but it was not invented by them. It had already been used by Plato in the *Timaeus*, as a description of the highest form, which he categorized as "unchanging, unbegotten, and indestructible, admitting no modification and entering no combination, imperceptible to sight or other senses, the object of thought."[52] Those Christians who adopted the word to describe the Father of Jesus Christ knew where it had come from and interpreted it accordingly. This does not mean that they succumbed to Platonism as opposed to biblical faith. On the contrary, they accepted what Plato said because they believed that it agreed with the scriptural picture of God. The terminology may have come from Plato, but the reality it described was compatible with biblical revelation, even though it was not found in Scripture itself.

It seems that the first Christian theologian to use the term "unbegotten" was Justin Martyr (100?–165), who urged his readers to "follow the only unbegotten God through his Son,"[53] and wrote of him,

> To the Father of all, who is unbegotten, there is no name given. For anyone who is called by a name is dependent on the person who gives him that name. These words—Father, God, Creator, Lord, and Master—are not names, but titles derived from his good deeds and functions.[54]

Shortly afterwards, the same theme was developed at greater length by Theophilus of Antioch:

> He [God] is without beginning, because he is unbegotten, and he is unchangeable, because he is immortal. . . . He is Lord because he rules over the universe; Father, because he is before all things; Creator (*dêmiourgos*) and

[51] John 1:14, 18; 3:16, 18; 1 John 4:9 (KJV, NASB).
[52] Plato, *Timaeus* 52a.
[53] Justin Martyr, *Apologia I* 14.
[54] Justin Martyr, *Apologia II* 6.

> Maker (*poiêtês*), because he is creator (*ktistês*) and maker (*poiêtês*) of the universe; the Highest, because of his being above all; and Almighty, because he himself rules and embraces all.[55]

Theophilus listed a number of divine names and attributes like light, word, mind, spirit, wisdom, strength, power, Lord, judge, and so on, including Father in this list, with the observation that, "if I call him Father, I speak of all things as being from him."[56] The same thought was expressed by Tertullian (fl. 186–212) when he wrote, "God is the Supreme Being, existing in eternity, unbegotten, unmade, without beginning, without end."[57]

In all of these early writers, the term "unbegotten" was an adjective used to describe the nature of God, with particular reference to the Father. It may have been introduced into Christian usage in order to distinguish the Father from the Son, who was the "only begotten," but the word's Platonic origins soon made themselves felt and it was applied to the being of God as a whole. In this way, "unbegotten" was a term that served to merge the particular identity of the Father with the universal nature of God, making it inevitable that the two concepts, which were already very close, would become synonymous in Christian thinking. It took longer for "unbegotten" to develop to the point where it almost became a title of the Father, but by the fourth century it was being used as the standard designation of his particularity within the Godhead. Alexander of Alexandria (d. 328), the bishop who led the campaign against Arius that culminated in the summoning of the First Council of Nicea in AD 325, wrote,

> We must maintain the dignity proper to the unbegotten Father by saying that there is no cause of his being. . . . By all means let us ascribe to the Son the honor that is due to him, recognizing that he was begotten of the Father before all ages and worshiping him accordingly as the only one who was always in existence. We must not deny the Son's divinity but recognize in him the exact likeness of the Father's image and character in every respect. Nevertheless, we also believe that it is the Father's unique property to be unbegotten, for the Savior himself said: "The Father is greater than I."[58]

A generation later Gregory of Nyssa (335?–395?) was able to write that "the Father is without beginning and is unbegotten, and he has always been regarded as the Father."[59] His contemporary Epiphanius of Salamis (315?–403)

---

[55] Theophilus of Antioch, *Ad Autolycum* 4.
[56] Ibid., 3.
[57] Tertullian, *Adversus Marcionem* 1.3. His exact words are, "summum esse magnum, in aeternitate constitutum, innatum, infectum, sine initio, sine fine."
[58] Alexander of Alexandria, *Epistula de haeresi Arianorum* 12. The quotation is from John 14:28.
[59] Gregory of Nyssa, *Contra Eunomium* 1.33.

filled this out with reference to the other persons of the Trinity for good measure:

> The Father is unbegotten, uncreated, and incomprehensible. The Son is begotten, but he is also uncreated and incomprehensible. The Holy Spirit is not begotten or created. He is not the Son's twin brother, nor his uncle, nor his grandfather nor his grandson . . .[60]

From there it was but a short step to the so-called Athanasian Creed, composed in southern Gaul sometime in the late fifth or early sixth century, where the Father was declared to be "made of none, neither created nor begotten," a definition that was then passed on to the Western church, where it became standard until the time of the Reformation and beyond.

If "unbegotten" went from being an adjectival description of the divine nature to being virtually a personal title bestowed on the Father, "Almighty" might be said to have migrated in the opposite direction. In origin it was one of the names given to God in the Old Testament, *El-Shaddai*, where it appears no fewer than forty-eight times, thirty-one (or nearly two-thirds) of which occur in the book of Job. Of the remainder, slightly more than half are in the Pentateuch, with Ruth, the Psalms, and the Prophets accounting for the rest. It is the Pentateuchal occurrences that are the most significant theologically, because from them we learn that *El Shaddai* was the name by which God was known to Abraham, Isaac, and Jacob.[61] It was therefore a term of considerable importance because it went to the heart of the covenant that God had made with Israel. It also emphasized the sovereignty and oneness of Yahweh, because while there could be many gods and many lords, there could be only one Almighty whose power was supreme over everything else.[62]

Given its prominence in the Old Testament, it comes as a surprise to discover that the name "Almighty" (Greek, *Pantokratôr*) barely figures in the New Testament at all. Leaving aside the book of Revelation, it occurs only once, when the apostle Paul is quoting directly from the Hebrew Bible.[63] It definitely seems to have a flavor of the Old Testament about it, which may explain its use in John's Apocalypse, where it occurs no fewer than nine times, almost all of them in expressions of praise and triumph for God's victory over the forces of evil and death. What is less clear is whether it was predicated of the Father alone or of the Trinity taken together. In a majority of cases it occurs in the

---

[60] Epiphanius of Salamis, *Ancoratus* 7.
[61] Ex. 6:2–3.
[62] This point was not lost on the early Christians. See, for example, Theophilus of Antioch, *Ad Autolycum* 1.4; and Origen, *De principiis* 3.6.5.
[63] 2 Cor. 6:18. The "quotation" is actually a series of different sources that Paul strung together.

phrase "Lord God Almighty," which is ambiguous, because it may refer to either the Father alone or the Trinity.[64] However, there are two verses where it seems to be applied specifically to the Father, even though he is not named as such. The first of these is Revelation 15:3, which reads,

> And they sing the song of Moses, the servant of God, and the song of the Lamb, saying,
>
> "Great and amazing are your deeds,
> O Lord God the Almighty!"

The mention of Moses suggests that this is the covenant God of the Old Testament who is being praised, and the addition of the Lamb indicates that it is the Father alone who is being addressed. The same differentiation between God and the Lamb appears in the other occurrence, where John says that the temple in the heavenly city is replaced by "the Lord God the Almighty and the Lamb,"[65] which reinforces the impression that the title "Almighty" applies primarily to the Father.

The all but universal creedal formula "I believe in God the Father, the Almighty," which was standard from the second century onward and may go back to New Testament times, shows us that this was the common understanding of the early church.[66] The transition from "Almighty" as a divine name to "almighty" as a descriptive adjective of God's being seems to have been an accident of translation, at least at the beginning. Greek had adjectives like *pantodynamos* ("all-powerful") and *apeirodynamos* ("boundlessly powerful") which could be used to describe the almighty will of God, while reserving *Pantokratôr* for the divine name.[67] But Latin was not so rich, and was forced to use the adjective *omnipotens* for the name of God as well as for the divine attribute associated with it. As a result, the two things fused into a single concept, which they have remained ever since, at least in the Western theological tradition. Furthermore, the creedal tradition has ensured that "Almighty" continues to be attached to the name of the Father in the first instance, though this does not necessarily mean that it cannot apply to the other two persons of the Trinity as well.

In the third century, Hippolytus of Rome interpreted John's use of the title *Pantokratôr* in Revelation as referring to Christ, and the controversies sur-

[64] See Rev. 4:8; 11:17; 15:3; 16:7; 19:6; 21:22. In 2 Cor. 6:18 the word "God" is omitted and in Rev. 16:14 and 19:15, "Lord" is left out. Rev. 1:8 omits both.

[65] Rev. 21:22.

[66] See Novatian, *De Trinitate* 1–2.

[67] See Hippolytus of Rome, *Contra Berona et Helica* 1.

rounding his divinity that erupted in the fourth century resulted in making this attribution standard among the orthodox.[68] By the time the Athanasian Creed was written (AD 500?), the Trinitarian dimension of the name had become part of the church's confession: "The Father is almighty, the Son almighty, and the Holy Spirit almighty, and yet there are not three Almighties but one Almighty." Even so, it was hard to escape the tradition of ascribing the title to the Father, and it was that attribution that was to have the deepest impact on later theological development.

Reinforcing this tendency was a parallel movement that attempted to define the uniqueness of the Father by claiming that he was God in a way that the Son and the Holy Spirit were not. When commenting on the complex description of the Word of God in the opening verses of John's Gospel, Origen tried to explain the difference between the Father and the Son by saying that the Father is *autotheos*, or "God-in-himself," while the Son is merely *theos* or "God" in some more generic sense of the term. To support this interpretation Origen relied on two arguments. First, he said that John made a clear distinction between "God" with the definite article (*ho theos*), which he used to refer to the God of the Old Testament, and "God" without the article (*theos*), which he used of the Word (*logos*) or Son. Second, Origen quoted the words of Jesus, which he believed supported his interpretation:

> God is *autotheos*, as the Savior says in his prayer to the Father: "that they know you, the only true God."[69] Everything in addition to the *autotheos* is made God by participation in his divinity and is not to be called *ho theos* but rather *theos*. . . . The Word of God, . . . by being with God is always God, not possessing that of himself, but by his being with the Father; and not continuing to be God . . . except by remaining always in uninterrupted contemplation of the depths of the Father.[70]

Of course, to be *autotheos* was to be God not only in relation to the Son but also in relation to the divine attributes, of which the Father was not just the unique expression but also the unique possessor. From there it was a short step toward identifying the Father with the One God, a move which inevitably led to a certain downgrading of the status of the Son. Origen resolved the problem of the Son's divinity by saying that it was a natural reproduction of the Father's in the same way that children possess the same human nature as

[68] Hippolytus of Rome, *Contra Noetum* 6. For the fourth century, see Cyril of Jerusalem, *Cathecheses* 4.5; 8.3; and Rufinus of Aquileia, *Commentarium in Symbolum Apostolorum* 5.
[69] John 17:3.
[70] Origen, *Commentarium in Iohannis Evangelium* 2.2.

their parents. He had greater difficulty with the Holy Spirit, whom he regarded as a creature of the Father through the Son and as being divine only because of his total dependence on them. It is easy to see why Origen was forced into such a position. If the Father alone is *autotheos* and the Holy Spirit is not a second Son, it is hard to see what other possibility there could be.

There is no doubt that Origen got himself into difficulty with his *autotheos* doctrine. On the one hand, he was quite clear that there had never been a time when the Word or Wisdom of God had not existed:

> Whoever assigns a beginning to the Word or Wisdom of God must be careful not to become guilty of impiety toward the unbegotten Father. For whoever does this denies that there has always been a Father, who had always generated the Word and had possessed Wisdom from eternity.[71]

He also affirmed that the Father as *autotheos* has bestowed all his own nature and power on the Son:

> The God and Father of all things is not the only being who is great in our judgment. He has imparted himself and his greatness to his only begotten and firstborn of every creature, in order that he, being the image of the invisible God, might preserve the image of the Father in his greatness.[72]

But in his commentary on the opening verses of John's Gospel, Origen distinguished the Son from the Father in a way that made him subtly inferior:

> The light that shines in the darkness [the Son] is not necessarily the same as the light in which there is no darkness at all [the Father]. . . .[73] God is the Father of truth, which makes him greater than the truth [the Son].[74] He is the Father of wisdom, which makes him greater and more excellent than wisdom [the Son].[75] Likewise, as the Father of the true light, he is greater than the true light itself.[76]

In Origen's mind, these things held together because the *autotheos* (Father) had bestowed his nature on his Word and his Wisdom, which he had from all eternity. It apparently never occurred to him that others might take his words and use them to mean that the Son and the Holy Spirit were inferior to the

[71] Origen, *De principiis* 1.2.3.
[72] Origen, *Contra Celsum* 6.69.
[73] Origen is alluding here to James 1:17, where God is described as "the Father of lights with whom there is no variation or shadow due to change."
[74] An allusion to John 14:6.
[75] Possibly an allusion to Prov. 8:22. See also 1 Cor. 1:29.
[76] Origen, *Commentarium in Iohannis Evangelium* 2.18.

Father, who alone was truly God. Yet that is what happened in the generation after Origen's death, and it led to the great theological crisis in the early-fourth-century church.

The Father and the Creator

If the early church was ready to acknowledge the Father as the unbegotten, Almighty, and *autotheos*, it might seem obvious that it would also have accepted him as the unchallenged Creator of the universe, but things were not that simple. As we have already seen, Jewish Christians had no problem recognizing the God of the Old Testament as the Creator, but were less sure whether he could be called Father. By contrast, Gentile Christians, especially those familiar with Plato's *Timaeus*, could easily have pictured the Father as the supreme being, but it would have been more difficult for them to accept that he was directly involved in the creation of the world because of the Platonic doctrine that matter was evil. Resolving this question was therefore one of the more delicate problems facing the early Christians, and it provoked far more debate than any other issue.

The New Testament was quite clear that the Son had taken part in the divine act of creation. At the beginning of his Gospel, John said that "all things were made through him, and without him was not any thing made that was made."[77] Paul said the same thing to the Colossians:

> He [Christ] is . . . the firstborn of all creation. For by him all things were created, in heaven and on earth, visible and invisible, whether thrones or dominions or rulers or authorities—all things were created through him and for him.[78]

Today we tend to read this as a rhetorical flourish on Paul's part, but it was not understood like that at the time. For many of his early readers, things invisible were more real than the visible world around them, and the thrones, dominions, rulers, and authorities referred to specific powers that not only existed but held sway over the earth. To claim that Christ had created them and that they served him was to restructure the mental image that people had of the world in which they lived, and it is hardly surprising that it led to a great deal of discussion and speculation about the nature of reality.

According to our earliest Christian sources, the first attempt to elaborate a cosmology that could rival the standard biblical account arose in Samaria.

[77] John 1:3.
[78] Col. 1:15–16.

The Samaritans were an aberrant Jewish sect of uncertain origin, but the general impression we get from the Scriptures is that they had deviated from the norms that were taught and practiced at Jerusalem. The beginnings of this may be traceable as far back as the time of King Jeroboam I (900 BC?), who set up altars at Bethel and Dan in order to prevent his people from going to the Jerusalem temple to worship.[79] Later on, people from Samaria opposed the reestablishment of the Jewish community after the exile and had to be fought off, with the help of the Persian authorities who ruled the country.[80] In New Testament times Jews and Samaritans were no longer on speaking terms, and Jesus caused a sensation when he reached out to them.[81] This action apparently produced a number of converts, and just before his ascension Jesus specifically told his disciples to preach the gospel in Samaria.[82] But something seems to have gone wrong with the Samaritan mission. In Acts 8 we are told that the Samaritans had been baptized in the name of Jesus only, an omission of the Holy Spirit that the apostles in Jerusalem took so seriously that they went there themselves in order to put matters right.[83]

It was at that point that Simon the magician, a Samaritan who had been baptized along with so many others, approached the apostles and asked if they would sell him the power to confer the Holy Spirit. The apostles were horrified and urged Simon to repent of his wickedness, which he apparently did.[84] No more is heard of him in the New Testament, but a century later he was credited with having invented a creation myth that had become the origin of the so-called Gnostics. "Gnostic" is the name now used to describe people who believed that the pathway to salvation lay through esoteric knowledge that was given only to a few enlightened ones, who were truly spiritual (*pneumatikoi*). The rest remained unspiritual, or "soulish" (*psychikoi*), and of course they were the great majority, even within the church. The distinction between *pneumatikoi* and *psychikoi* was recognized by the apostle Paul, but it is unclear whether he thought that professing Christians could be *psychikoi* or whether this word applied only to unbelievers.[85] For the Gnostics, of course, anyone who rejected their teachings was by definition *psychikos*, whether he or she believed in Christ or not. They adopted the Pauline distinction but applied it to suit their own purposes, which were far removed from what Paul had in mind. But as we shall see, this contrast was fundamental

[79] 1 Kings 12:25–33.
[80] Neh. 4:1–14.
[81] John 4:1–42.
[82] Acts 1:8.
[83] Acts 8:14–17.
[84] Acts 8:18–24.
[85] 1 Cor. 2:14–15.

to the Gnostic outlook and was to be foundational to its way of interpreting the world.

How accurate the traditional account of Gnostic origins is has been much debated, and the role of Simon in particular has usually been discounted by modern scholars. But the first mention of Simon as a Gnostic occurs in Justin Martyr, who was also from Samaria (though he was not a Samaritan, but a Greek) and who may well have had access to information that has since been lost. Justin tells us that Simon was widely worshiped in Samaria and that he was later succeeded by Menander, one of his disciples, who, Justin says, was inspired by devils and deceived many people in Antioch.[86] The story was picked up by Irenaeus, whose refutation of the Gnostics was based on the assumption that they were of Samaritan origin. Such early testimony is an argument in favor of the tradition and should not be set aside lightly.

What these Samaritan Gnostics supposedly taught went as follows.[87] In the beginning, the Father, who is the highest God, thought about creating angels. This Thought (*ennoia*) emerged from him and fell down to lower regions where, in disobedience to the Father, she gave birth to angelic powers. Those powers then created the world we know, but they could not accept that they owed their origin to anyone higher than they were. For that reason they captured the Thought and imprisoned her in a human body. Throughout the course of history she reappeared in different incarnations, like Helen of Troy for example, but in every one she was humiliated. When Simon the magician found her, she was living as a prostitute in Tyre. He regarded her as the "lost sheep" that Jesus had talked about.[88]

All this time, the angelic powers that governed the world were completely ignorant of God the Father, but eventually he decided to intervene and rescue the Thought from her captivity. The angelic powers were governing the world badly, and human beings were suffering under their rule, so the Father decided to rescue them along with the Thought. In this way, human beings were given a knowledge of the Father that even the angels had not possessed. In order to come into the world without being detected, the Father had disguised himself first as an angel and then, when he arrived on earth, as a man, even though in fact he was neither. This man was said to have suffered on a cross in Judea, but in reality he had not done so.

Simon's followers looked up to him as the highest manifestation of God, but they recognized that there were others as well. They seem to have believed

[86] Justin Martyr, *Apologia I* 26.
[87] Irenaeus of Lyon, *Adversus omnes haereses* 1.23.1–4.
[88] See Luke 15:6.

that God had appeared to the Samaritans as the Father, to the Jews as the Son, and to the other nations as the Holy Spirit! God did not care what people called him, so to him all three names were the same. But they did not think that God had inspired the Old Testament. Its message had come from the angelic powers that had created the world, which is why it had led people into spiritual slavery by its arbitrary laws and customs. Those people were trying to save themselves by keeping the laws, but Simon would set them free by his grace, the only way that anyone could be saved. Later on, Menander apparently taught that he was the Redeemer, who would save those who were baptized in his name, a clear caricature of the teaching of Jesus.[89]

For our present purposes, what is important about this myth is that it portrays the Father as a higher being than the creators, who did not even know of the Father's existence and refused to accept that there could be anything higher than themselves. But the creators were finite and therefore incapable of producing perfect beings, which is why their attempts to govern the world ended up as a kind of tyranny. Salvation was a work undertaken by the Father in order to deliver us humans from the unjust rule of our creators. As the myth developed it incorporated a number of Christian themes, like the Trinity and the doctrine of salvation by grace and not by works, but the form in which these doctrines appeared was so far removed from the New Testament as to be virtually unrecognizable.

Nevertheless, it was this myth, and the variant forms of it that developed in the course of the second century, that posed one of the greatest threats to the early church. A disciple of Menander by the name of Saturninus (or Satornilus), developed his master's teaching still further by making it clear that the God of Israel was one of the created angels, whom he called "rulers" (*archontes*). As part of his plan of salvation, the Father was going to destroy these rulers, which meant that he would destroy the Jewish God as well. Oddly enough, Saturninus apparently believed that the Old Testament was inspired both by the God of Israel and by Satan, who was his archenemy![90] An intriguing "Christianized" version of this was attributed by Irenaeus to Basilides of Alexandria, who was active in the first half of the second century:

> The unoriginated and ineffable Father, seeing the catastrophic fate [of men], sent his firstborn Nous (he is the one who is called Christ) to deliver those who believe in him from the power of the ones who made the world. He appeared to the nations on earth as a man and performed miracles. He did not

[89] Irenaeus of Lyon, *Adversus omnes haereses* 1.23.5.
[90] Ibid., 1.24.1–2.

> suffer, but a certain Simon of Cyrene was forced to carry his cross.[91] Simon was transformed by Jesus so as to appear to be Jesus himself, and was crucified through ignorance and error. Jesus meanwhile took the form of Simon and stood by, laughing at them. Since he was an incorporeal power and the Nous of the unbegotten Father, he could be transformed into anything he wanted. In this way he ascended to the one who had sent him, laughing at them, because he could not be bound and was invisible to them all.[92]

Somewhat different from this was the teaching of the Ophites, or Naassenes, which has been recorded for us by both Irenaeus and Origen.[93] According to the Ophites, there is a supreme divine trinity consisting of Bythus (the first Man), the son whom he has begotten (the second Man), and the Holy Spirit (the First Woman), who was borne over the lower elements of the waters, the darkness, the abyss, and chaos.[94] However, at some point the Holy Spirit had intercourse with each of the two Men and, being unable to contain the result, she gave birth to two aeons. The first of these was Christ, who immediately took refuge with his mother and now forms an aeon in the heavenly realm, or *plêrôma*, which is completely cut off from the chaos below. The second aeon was Sophia (Wisdom), who fell downward into the lower elements, where she was imprisoned. But as she fell, she determined to hang onto as much of the divine light as she could, and eventually that light gave her the power to escape from her captivity. She rose up above the elements and created the "visible heaven" as a kind of substitute for the one she had lost. Unable to return to the realm of the two Men, she gave birth to a son without their permission. This was Ialdabaoth, who was defective because he was born from a woman alone.[95]

Ialdabaoth inherited his mother's spiritual power, but as he grew stronger he turned against her and chose to give birth to six sons, whom he called "rulers" (*archontes*). Taken together, the sons and their father constituted a holy hebdomad, variously known as the seven heavens and the seven angels (or powers). They were also connected to the seven planets and the seven days of the week, and would eventually each be assigned a messenger whose duty it

[91] See Luke 23:26.
[92] Irenaeus of Lyon, *Adversus omnes haereses* 1.24.4.
[93] Ibid., 1.30; Origen, *Contra Celsum*, 6.22–32. The Ophites took their name from the serpent (Greek, *ophis*; Hebrew, *naas*). For a recent presentation of their views, see Thomas Holsinger-Friesen, *Irenaeus and Genesis: A Study of Competition in Early Christian Hermeneutics* (Winona Lake, IN: Eisenbrauns, 2009), 56–75.
[94] This is meant to be an interpretation of Gen. 1:2.
[95] This story is contained in the *Apocryphum Iohannis*, or *Secret Book of John* 28. For the complete text, see James M. Robinson, ed., *The Nag Hammadi Library in English* (Leiden: Brill, 1996). See also Alastair H. B. Logan, *Gnostic truth and Christian heresy* (Edinburgh: T & T Clark, 1996) for a thorough analysis of it. The name Ialdabaoth probably means "child of chaos" but may also be "Yahweh of hosts" in Hebrew.

would be to proclaim his own *archôn* as a suitable object of worship.[96] This hebdomad was originally intended to rule over heaven and earth, but at some point the sons rebelled against their father. To counter this, Ialdabaoth reached down into the material world and begot a son, whom he shaped like a serpent and called the Nous (Mind). In his anger at his sons' rebellion, Ialdabaoth cried out: "I am Father and God, and above me there is no other," an allusion to Isaiah 45:5, which confirms that Ialdabaoth was meant to be understood as the God of the Old Testament.

As the Ophites understood it, the creation story in Genesis was incomplete because Moses, whom they portrayed as the prophet of Ialdabaoth, had no knowledge of the supreme trinity. That is why he mistakenly made Ialdabaoth the creator (*dêmiourgos*) of heaven and earth and the supreme God. But when Ialdabaoth set himself up in that position, he was sternly rebuked by his mother, Sophia, who revealed to him the existence of the higher realm in which the trinity was located. Repenting of her own fall, which she realized was the ultimate cause of Ialdabaoth's behavior, she dedicated herself to the task of bringing the celestial hierarchy, including the holy hebdomad, back into line with the supreme trinity.

Meanwhile, fed up with his mother, Ialdabaoth summoned his sons and urged them to create man in their own image.[97] Seeing her opportunity, Sophia instructed the sons to give man an awkward and sluggish material body, and when it was ready, Ialdabaoth breathed his own spirit into it.[98] This gave the newly formed man a spark of the divine, which he used to worship Bythus, whom Sophia revealed to him. The man was therefore able to bypass Ialdabaoth and the other *archontes* by going straight to the supreme Father of all, even though as a creature he was greatly inferior to what Ialdabaoth had intended to bring into being. Outsmarted by his mother, Ialdabaoth decided to take his revenge by creating woman out of the body of the man. His aim was to deprive the man of his spiritual power by pouring it into the woman instead. When his sons saw this woman they fell in love with her and used her to produce a race of angels, who may perhaps be identified with the "sons of God" who mysteriously appear in Genesis 6:2.

Ialdabaoth hoped that the angels would worship him, since he had created their mother, but Sophia could not allow that to happen. She intervened and made sure that the woman was deprived of her divine light by persuading her

[96] Note that in the Roman calendar, the days of the week were assigned to the sun, the moon, Mars, Mercury, Jupiter, Venus, and Saturn, who was identified with Ialdabaoth.
[97] This is how the Ophites interpreted the use of the plural in Gen. 1:26.
[98] Compare Gen. 2:7.

to rebel against the commands of Ialdabaoth. The woman then persuaded the man from whom she was created to do the same, with the result that both were cut off from the divine. The agent of this rebellion was the Nous, whom Sophia had incited to act against his father Ialdabaoth. The end result was that, while the original supreme trinity remained undisturbed in their heavenly abode, Ialdabaoth, who had tried to set himself up as the highest God and had made the world in order to demonstrate his power, was left with chaos and destruction, thanks to the machinations of Sophia. Once this background was understood, the subsequent history of Israel as recounted in the Bible fell into place within the Gnostic scheme. Ialdabaoth did his best to force human beings to worship him, but he failed, and ended up destroying them instead, though Noah and his family escaped the flood with the help of Sophia. Later on, Ialdabaoth chose Abraham in the hope that he would worship him, and he gave his law to Moses, but he could offer them nothing beyond his own ignorant and defective self. In the end, of course, Sophia's unfallen brother aeon, Christ, came to the rescue, overthrew Ialdabaoth and led his creatures back to the heavenly trinity, which is what Sophia had wanted all along.

To sum all this up, according to this Gnostic myth, Christ the Redeemer was the offspring of the heavenly trinity (but not one of them), and he was the uncle of the God of the Old Testament (Ialdabaoth), who had wrongly claimed to be the supreme God and had employed Moses to propagate that false message. As the creator (*dêmiourgos*) of heaven and earth, Ialdabaoth had made human beings in his own image, but his plans for them had been thwarted by his son, the serpent Nous, acting at the behest of his mother Sophia. They were quite a family!

It is easy for us to be put off by this bizarre story, but if we dismiss it too readily we shall miss the important theological points that it was making. These can be summed up as follows:

1. The true God dwells so far above us that we cannot approach him or understand him.
2. The first falling away from the true God occurred in the spiritual realm.
3. The creator god (*dêmiourgos*) emerged out of a rebellion against the true God.
4. The creator god has tried to pretend that he is the true God.
5. The creation has gone astray because it was imperfect to begin with.
6. The redeemer god has to destroy the creator god and all his works.
7. The Father remains above and beyond both the creator and the redeemer.
8. The redeemer is closer to the Father than the creator is, but he is still not part of the divine trinity.

From the Christian standpoint, this Gnostic myth went wrong because it separated the true God from both creation *and* redemption. The material world was imperfect and therefore incapable of connecting with the realm in which the true God dwelt. The Christian message was the exact opposite of this: the creation is good; sin is rebellion against God rather than something inherent in matter; the Creator and the Redeemer are one. Above all, Christians taught that the Creator/Redeemer had become a man in Jesus Christ, something that the Gnostic myth was designed to deny. Later Gnostics would tone down the more eccentric aspects of this account, to be sure, but the fundamental inability to reconcile God and the created order would remain characteristic of Gnosticism as long as it existed.

Sometime around AD 150 there appeared a man called Valentinus, who was apparently an active member of the Roman church and did not leave it until he failed in his ambition of becoming a bishop.[99] Valentinus was much more closely connected to the church than the Ophites were, and therefore more sensitive to points in their mythology that Christians might find offensive. Nevertheless, it seems that in general terms he subscribed to their teachings, modifying them only when the Ophite positions seemed too extreme.[100]

The Valentinians seem to have been aware of the inadequacy of the Ophite trinity, because they replaced it with something much closer to standard Christian teaching. In their theology, as transmitted by a certain Ptolemy (one of Valentinus's followers),[101] the archetypal Father, Bythus, impregnated his fellow aeon, Sige, who gave birth to a son, whom they called the Nous. At the same time, Sige also brought forth Aletheia (Truth), though it is not clear how. Nous in turn gave birth to Logos and Zoe (Life), and from them came Anthropos (Man) and Ecclesia (Church). This went on until there was a total of thirty aeons, organized in a hierarchy of eight, ten, and twelve, all of which constituted the divine Fullness (*plêrôma*). The lowest of these aeons was Sophia (Wisdom), who made the mistake of trying to inquire into the depths of Bythus, which she was not authorized to do. She might have been destroyed by this, but for the intervention of Horus (Boundary), who separated out her desire, ignorance, and grief. These he formed into Achamoth, whom he cast out of the Fullness, allowing the purified Sophia to retain her position in heaven.[102]

To keep the Fullness in order, Nous then gave birth to Christ and the Holy Spirit, the former to calm the restlessness of the aeons and give them peace, and

---

[99] Tertullian, *Adversus Valentinianos* 4.1. We know about Valentinus only from his opponents, so information of this kind about him must be treated with caution.

[100] See Holsinger-Friesen, *Irenaeus and Genesis*, 75–98, for an exposition of the Valentinian approach.

[101] Not to be confused with Ptolemy the astronomer.

[102] Achamoth is the Hebrew *hokhma*, or "wisdom," i.e., just another name for Sophia.

the latter to make them grateful for what they already had. In this process, all the aeons contributed to form Christ, so that all the fullness of God could be said to dwell in him, as the Father wanted it to.[103] Meanwhile, Achamoth was forced to live in conditions of darkness and formlessness until Christ took pity on her and gave her a shape to ease her existence. From then on, Achamoth's only desire was to be reunited with Sophia, a struggle out of which the creator (*dêmiourgos*) and the world were both made. Her tears and grief produced the elements out of which all matter was made, and they were of two types. The first was evil and beyond redemption. The second was the *psychikon*, a base substance which nevertheless had the capacity to be converted into something higher, and it was out of this substance that she made the creator. As she was gradually released from her passions in this way, her joy was such that she voluntarily produced a third substance, the *pneumatikon*, which is the spiritual element that she scatters through the world by manipulating an ignorant creator.

As in the Ophite scheme, the creator produced seven heavens, but was not himself one of this hebdomad. Instead, he hovered above it as Hebdomas itself. The Ophite notion that this lower hebdomad was a caricature of the higher one inside the Fullness was replaced by a scheme in which Achamoth took the place of Bythus, the creator that of Nous, and the angels brought forth by the creator the other aeons in the Fullness. However, once Achamoth made the creator she hid herself from him, while nevertheless urging him to create the world as both "soul" (*pyschikon*) and "matter" (*hylikon*). The creator did not realize where this impulse was coming from, however, and genuinely believed that he was the ultimate source of everything he made. That is why he said, "I am the Lord, . . . besides me there is no God."[104] The Valentinians modified the Ophite story to make the creator merely ignorant of what he was doing, and not vindictive or rebellious against his mother, but he was still defective because of his ignorance and did not understand spiritual things because he was *psychikos* and not *pneumatikos*. Ironically, even the Devil, whom the Valentinians called the Cosmocrator, understood more than his creator did, because he at least was a spiritual being!

The upshot of all this was a hierarchy of being in which the highest region, the one immediately below the Fullness, was occupied by Achamoth; the lowest region belonged to the Cosmocrator; and the middle zone was the domain of the creator. The highest realm was beyond human understanding, but the creator dwelt in "heaven" and the Cosmocrator in the "world," of which he was the prince. Interestingly, when the creator made the human race, Achamoth

---

[103] See Col. 1:19.

[104] Isa. 45:5.

secretly intervened to add a spiritual element (*pneumatikon*) to the soul and matter that the creator was able to give by himself. Worshipers of the creator would naturally be lifted up from matter to contemplate the things of the soul, which is what we find in the Old Testament. As Ptolemy put it,

> If the law [of Moses] was not given by the perfect God himself, as we have already said, and certainly not by the Devil either . . . the lawgiver must be a third party who exists alongside the other two. This is the creator and maker of the whole world and everything in it. Because he is essentially different from the other two and stands between them, we might rightly term him the Mediator.[105]

Only the enlightened would be able to unlock their inner spiritual potential, and they of course were the followers of Valentinus. This breakthrough was accomplished by Christ, who entered the world and took on all three levels of reality in order to give those trapped in the flesh or soul the chance to rise higher. In this Valentinian form, Gnosticism posed a real threat to the early church. It is hard to believe it now, but in their different ways, Irenaeus, Tertullian, Origen, and Hippolytus were all preoccupied with the need to refute Gnosticism. Broadly contemporary with each other, they came from the four corners of the Roman world, proof that this was no local or passing concern. Even in the fourth century, when the main battles against Gnosticism were over, Epiphanius of Salamis (315?–403) recorded it in great detail, to the point of preserving Gnostic works that would otherwise be unknown to us.

The opponents of Gnosticism all recognized that the root of the problem lay in the opposition the Gnostics made between God the Father and the creator, whom they regarded as an inferior being. It was therefore necessary to emphasize that this was not the case. As they read the Bible, the God of the Old Testament, the Father of Jesus Christ, and the Creator of the universe were all one and the same.[106] This unity of identity undergirded a corresponding unity of purpose in creation and redemption, and in the end it proved to be far more satisfying to believers. No one put the case for this unity more forcefully or more consistently than Irenaeus:

> I ought to begin with the most important point, which is that God the Creator made heaven and earth and everything in them. . . . and demonstrate that there is nothing above him or behind him, as well as that he made everything

[105] Ptolemy, quoted in Epiphanius of Salamis, *Panarion* 33.7.3–4.

[106] For a comprehensive study of this theme in the early church, see Paul M. Blowers, *Drama of the Divine Economy: Creator and Creation in Early Christian Theology and Piety* (Oxford: Oxford University Press, 2012).

> of his own free will, uninfluenced by anyone else. He is the only God, the only Lord, the only Creator, the only Father, the only one who contains all things and who commanded everything else to come into existence. How can there be any other fullness, principle, power, or god above him, since it is necessary for God, who is the fullness of all these things, to contain them in his immensity without being himself contained by anyone?[107]

As for the aeons, *archontes*, and so on, Irenaeus had this to say:

> God has always had in himself the Word and Wisdom, the Son and the Spirit, by whom and in whom, freely and spontaneously, he made everything that exists. This is the Creator who has granted the world to the human race and whose greatness is unknown to any of those who have been made by him.[108]

Irenaeus went farther, and explained how there were different facets to the being of God, the most fundamental and personal of which bound him to us as our Father:

> In respect of his love, the Creator is our Father; but in respect of his power, he is our Lord, and in respect of his wisdom, he is our maker and designer. By transgressing his commandment, we become his enemies.[109]

In other words, not only is sin a matter of disobedience, but it affects our relationship to God as our Father. We cannot do anything to diminish his power, nor can we detract from his wisdom, but we can hurt his love for us, and when that happens our relationship to him changes for the worse. After Irenaeus, the identification of the Father with the Creator of all things seemed so natural that it would be many centuries before it would be challenged. Novatian had no hesitation in writing,

> God the Father, the founder and Creator of all things, who alone knows no beginning, invisible, infinite, immortal, eternal, is one God. To his greatness, majesty, and power I would say that not only can nothing be preferred, but nothing can be compared.[110]

Clement of Alexandria picked up the *Timaeus* of Plato and quoted it without embarrassment, an important reminder that in some ways the master was

[107] Irenaeus of Lyon, *Adversus omnes haereses* 2.1.1–2.
[108] Ibid., 4.20.4.
[109] Ibid., 5.17.1.
[110] Novatian, *De Trinitate* 31.

closer to the truth than some of his disciples.[111] Clement's disciple Origen said much the same thing:

> No one is able to speak with certainty about God the Father, but it is possible for some knowledge of him to be gained from the visible creation and the natural feelings of the human mind. Such knowledge can then be confirmed by the Holy Scriptures.[112]

So deeply ingrained did this identification become that even as late as the early fourth century, when its inadequacy would be exposed by the Arian controversy, Arnobius of Sicca (d. 330?) could write,

> By the unanimous judgment of all, and by the common admission of the human race, the Almighty God is regarded as unbegotten. . . . Rather, he himself is the source of all things, the Father of ages and of seasons.[113]

What Arnobius regarded as the unanimous opinion of everyone who thought about the subject was that God was the Father and Creator of all things. He certainly knew that the Father was unbegotten, in contrast to the Son. If pressed, he would probably have agreed that his unbegottenness within the Trinity was different from his unbegottenness in relation to the world, but he was not forced to make such a distinction. It was only when Arius (d. 336) started to claim that because the Son was begotten of the Father, he had to be a creature because only the Father was unbegotten, that any difficulty with this scheme was perceived. It then had to be resolved in order to protect the divinity of the Son, but by then the belief that the Father was also the Creator had become so deeply ingrained that it would never again be disputed, let alone dislodged from the Christian theological consensus.

[111] Clement of Alexandria, *Stromateis* 5.12, quoting Plato, *Timaeus* 28c.
[112] Origen, *De principiis* 1.3.1.
[113] Arnobius of Sicca, *Adversus gentes* 34.

4

The Father and His Children

A New Relationship with God

Most of the Jews rejected Jesus' teaching, but those who accepted it soon realized that it challenged their traditional understanding of monotheism in subtle ways. At one level, God remained what he had always been—the Creator, the Redeemer, and the protector of Israel. His steadfast love for them, so characteristic of the covenant, did not change when its promises were fulfilled. But in another sense, there was much that was different. Israel worshiped a God who was invisible and far above anything he had created, but the Son had come into the world as the man Jesus Christ.[1] Without denying the transcendent character of the divine, he had revealed God to the human race in an entirely new way. Furthermore, his message was that those who believed in him would have a relationship with the Father similar to his.[2]

Jesus therefore taught his disciples to think of God as their Father and to pray to him as such, but in doing so he was inviting them to share in something that was true of him in a unique sense. To put it simply, what Jesus was by nature, his disciples were to become by adoption, as the apostle Paul put it.[3] The shared nature of this relationship comes across clearly in what Jesus said to Mary Magdalene after his resurrection:

> Do not cling to me, for I have not yet ascended to the Father; but go to my brothers and say to them, "I am ascending to my Father and your Father, to my God and your God."[4]

Here Jesus was about to ascend to heaven, something that was unique to him, but he was also associating his disciples with him in his wider relationship to the Father. Jesus told his disciples that the Father had sent the Son into the

[1] John 1:18.
[2] See Heb. 11:39–40 for confirmation of this last point.
[3] See Rom. 8:15; Gal. 4:5; Eph. 1:5.
[4] John 20:17.

world as an expression of his love.[5] What did he mean by that? The Father did not love the world only because it was his creation, but also because it contained the inheritance he had promised to his Son. If God had sent his Son to us because of his love for the created order, then everything in creation would have been redeemed. But that is expressly denied in the New Testament, which states that at the end of time, the world we know will be wound up and there will be a new heaven and a new earth.[6] At a purely physical level, Christians were promised new spiritual bodies that would be quite different from the ones they already had.[7] God's love for them was not expressed by prolonging or transforming their earthly life but by giving them an eternal relationship with him that transcended material things.

This new relationship was fundamental to the Christian understanding of God. Those who are united to the Son know his Father too, and can rely on him for all their needs.[8] That assurance gave the early Christians a new way of looking at their lives. People who did not know God as their Father were lost in a hostile universe against which they had to protect themselves as best they could. Christians, on the other hand, were free to live in the world without fear, because they knew that their heavenly Father was taking care of them.[9]

It was this sense of a new standing before God that made Christians different from Jews. As adopted children of their heavenly Father, Christians had access to him in a way that had not been possible until then.[10] They were no longer dependent on the intermittent and fundamentally inadequate intercession of priests or other mediators, but had a relationship with God that had been lifted out of this world and anchored in heaven. Union with Christ introduced them to an understanding of the Father's will and the importance of obeying it. The work of the Holy Spirit made it possible for believers to share the Father's character, which the Bible describes as "holiness."[11] God's holiness had been well known and understood in Old Testament times, but for the most part, it was thought of as something that distanced him from his people. For example, the secret place in the temple where only the high priest could enter, and then only once a year, in order to make the sacrifice of atonement was called the "holy of holies."[12] The ground surrounding the burning bush in the desert where Moses met with God was "holy," which meant that he had to

[5] John 3:16–17.
[6] Rev. 21:1–4.
[7] 1 Cor. 15:42–50.
[8] Matt. 6:25–34.
[9] For an exposition of this, see Melito of Sardis, *Apology* 1. The text dates from the mid-second century.
[10] Rom. 8:15–17; Eph. 2:4–6.
[11] 1 Thess. 4:3 (ESV mg.).
[12] Ex. 26:34; 2 Chron. 4:22 (NASB).

take his shoes off because he could not stand there without humbling himself.[13] Isaiah had a vision of God in the temple, "high and lifted up," in which the angels addressed their Lord as "holy, holy, holy," thereby emphasizing just how far above and beyond the human world he was.[14]

When the people of Israel were called to be holy, it meant that they were expected to cut themselves off from the surrounding nations, so as not to be contaminated by them.[15] The Christian concept of holiness was somewhat different from this. It did not involve physical or ritual separation from the world, but a change of heart and mind. As the apostle Paul put it, "to the pure, all things are pure."[16] A Christian could live in the world and associate with unbelievers without being contaminated by them because he had the Holy Spirit of God dwelling in his heart by faith. Rather than put up external barriers to that world that did nothing to lessen the inner sinfulness of those who erected them, Christians were called to experience a spiritual transformation that would enable them to live in God's presence and be made holy by a relationship with him as their Father.

This is expressed throughout the New Testament, but nowhere more clearly and consistently than in the Sermon on the Mount (Matthew 5–7). The Sermon is a compendium of Jesus' teaching in which the difference between the old and the new experience of God is made very clear. As he put it to his disciples,

> You have heard that it was said, "You shall love your neighbor and hate your enemy."[17] But I say to you, Love your enemies and pray for those who persecute you, so that you may be sons of your Father who is in heaven. For he makes his sun rise on the evil and on the good, and sends rain on the just and on the unjust. For if you love those who love you, what reward do you have? Do not even the tax collectors do the same? And if you greet only your brothers, what more are you doing than others? Do not even the Gentiles do the same? You therefore must be perfect, as your heavenly Father is perfect.[18]

As Jesus taught his disciples, the Christian's relationship to his heavenly Father is one that gives him God's perspective on human affairs. The natural tendency for people to congregate with others like themselves and fend off the rest of the world must be overcome by believers, because God treats all his creatures alike and in principle everyone is welcome in the kingdom of heaven.

[13] Ex. 3:5.
[14] Isa. 6:1, 3.
[15] Lev. 20:7; 1 Pet. 1:15–16.
[16] Titus 1:15.
[17] A popular misreading of Lev. 19:17–18.
[18] Matt. 5:43–48.

This does not mean that there is no such thing as right and wrong, but Jesus said that God loves and cares for those who have turned against him, and his children must do likewise. Christians will act in ways quite different from what the world expects and may suffer because of that, but it is the only way to be conformed to the Father's character, which is what Jesus expected of his followers.

At the heart of the Sermon on the Mount and central to the Christian's devotional life is the Lord's Prayer, which Jesus taught his disciples.[19] The prayer was widely used in the early church and is remarkable for the way in which it expresses what the Christian's relationship with God as Father is like. First, it emphasizes his transcendence. The Father is in heaven and is to be revered as holy. Knowing him personally does not mean that he can be approached with undue familiarity. To be able to enter his presence remains a privilege that can only be granted to those who respect his essential otherness. Next comes the recognition that it is the Father's will that is done in his kingdom, which is fully present in heaven and is in the process of being established on earth. This means that the work of the Son and the Holy Spirit is furthering the spread of the Father's kingdom and that Christians can take part in this by praying directly to the Father.

The Father also appears as the one who provides for our daily needs, a theme that recurs later on in the Sermon.[20] Just as Christians are called to look to the Father as their Creator, so they are expected to turn to him for their preservation in this life and for their salvation in the next. The Father may have given everything he possesses to the Son, but that does not mean that he has relinquished his responsibilities for his creatures, and believers are taught to approach him in the first instance. Even when the blessings they receive come through one of the other divine persons, Christians are expected to recognize that it is the plan and purpose of the Father that is being worked out in their lives. This becomes clear in the concluding lines, where the prayer moves from the material to the spiritual realm. It is the Father who forgives and who protects his people from the attraction and the power of evil. Once again, this does not exclude the work of the Son and the Holy Spirit, but focuses our attention on the guiding and directing mind of the Father to whom they, like we, must answer.

It is this awareness of the Father and the privilege of having access to him that made the church quite different from Israel. To know God as Father not only

[19] Matt. 6:9–13. A shorter form of it is found in Luke 11:2–4. It seems likely that the Lukan version is the one Jesus actually taught and that the Matthaean one has been developed for liturgical use. The Matthaean text is repeated in the *Didache*, an anonymous Christian work roughly contemporary with the New Testament, and it has always been the one in common use.

[20] Matt. 6:25–34.

implied that he would look after his children—that was also a prominent Old Testament theme—but that they would be expected to know his mind and reflect his will insofar as they could. Church membership would not be determined by physical descent from Abraham (or anyone else) but by personal commitment and the indwelling presence of the Holy Spirit. The boundary between God's people and the rest of the world would be redrawn, allowing non-Jews into the fold if they believed in Christ and keeping unbelieving Jews out. Christians would recognize each other as brothers and sisters because of their common relationship to the Father, a relationship that would negate merely human ties.[21] The implications of this mental and spiritual restructuring would touch every aspect of life, a fact that would be of great importance for the reading of Scripture. The Jewish law remained in force as the Word of God, but the way it was read inevitably changed as the implications of this new relationship with him gradually sank in.

A New Understanding of Scripture

One thing that united Jews, Christians, and most Gnostics was their acceptance of an authoritative Scripture as the basis of their faith. There may have been some uncertainty about the canonical status of a book like Esther, but in principle what we now call the Old Testament was accepted as the Word of God by all three groups. The problem was that each of them read it in a different way. In a sense, the Jewish approach was the most straightforward. For Jews, the Law of Moses was the bedrock of the Bible, with the Prophets, Psalms, and other Writings added on to it. Their main concern was to know how the law should be applied to daily life, and for this they relied on the interpretations handed down by the elders who preserved Jewish traditions and identity after the destruction of the temple in AD 70. They understood that the written text was often no longer applicable because circumstances had changed, and that new conditions had arisen which the ancient law had not addressed. But many of them also thought that the ancient laws contained hidden meanings that had to be discovered by allegorical interpretation, or else divined in other curious ways that often strike modern readers as extremely odd.[22]

The rabbis saw their task as working out how the Mosaic law could be adapted to fit current needs by looking at its underlying principles and

[21] Luke 14:25–26.

[22] For a good introduction to the subject, see James L. Kugel, "Early Jewish Biblical Interpretation," in John J. Collins and Daniel C. Harlow, eds., *The Eerdmans Dictionary of Early Judaism* (Grand Rapids, MI: Eerdmans, 2010), 121–141. See also Marcel Simon, *Verus Israel: A Study of the Relations between Christians and Jews in the Roman Empire AD 135–425* (Oxford: Oxford University Press, 1986); and Nicholas R. M. De Lange, *Origen and the Jews: Studies in Jewish-Christian Relations in Third-century Palestine* (Cambridge: Cambridge University Press, 1976).

extrapolating from them. A good example of this technique can be found in 1 Corinthians 9:9, where Paul quoted the Old Testament text that says, "You shall not muzzle an ox when it is treading out the grain."[23] Without denying the literal meaning, Paul extended it to say that Christians had to provide for the material needs of those who ministered to them. The principle was clear—the laborer deserves his wages, as Jesus himself had said.[24]

As this example demonstrates, Christians had no problem with this kind of interpretation and readily adopted it. But the church required something more than this from its reading of Scripture. One of the fundamental claims of the gospel was that the Hebrew Bible prophesied the coming of Christ. Sometimes that was obvious, but often it was not and Christians had to look beneath the surface of the text to discover what its Christological implications were. How could that be done with consistency and integrity? That it was possible, they had no doubt. As Luke the Evangelist recorded,

> Then he [Jesus] said to them, "These are my words that I spoke to you while I was still with you, that everything written about me in the Law of Moses and the Prophets and the Psalms must be fulfilled." Then he opened their minds to understand the Scriptures, and said to them, "Thus it is written, that the Christ should suffer and on the third day rise from the dead, and that repentance and forgiveness of sins should be proclaimed in his name to all nations, beginning from Jerusalem."[25]

For the early Christians, the study of the Hebrew Bible was above all a Christological search, looking for the message of the gospel in the words that God had spoken to Moses and the prophets. The conviction that it was there to be found by those who were prepared to look for it gave them the freedom to employ a wide range of hermeneutical methods, many of which we would hesitate to use today. But the church was not guided by the historical context or the supposed "original intention" of the human authors of the texts, neither of which was self-evident. Christians read the Bible as Jesus had taught them to, and as long as they found him in it, they felt that they had discerned its true meaning.[26] This was the essence of their disagreement with Judaism:

---

[23] Deut. 25:4.

[24] Luke 10:7. Paul alludes to that as well in 1 Cor. 9:14. The example is also cited by Origen, *De principiis* 4.12, in support of a spiritual, as opposed to a purely literal reading of Scripture.

[25] Luke 24:44–47.

[26] An essential guide to early Christian exegesis is Charles Kannengiesser, *Handbook of Patristic Exegesis*, 2 vols. (Leiden: Brill, 2004). It covers the ground both by book of the Bible and by writer. Also very useful is Thomas C. Oden, gen. ed., *The Ancient Christian Commentary on Scripture*, 29 vols. (Downers Grove, IL: InterVarsity Press, 1998–2010).

> We [Jews and Christians] seek to have clear evidence about the person proclaimed in ancient times, and to find out what kind of person was prophesied, what he was to do and (if possible) when he would come. . . . Neither Jews nor Christians are wrong to believe that the prophets were divinely inspired, but the Jews mistakenly believe that the promised Christ is still awaited.[27]

The Gnostics also made use of the Scriptures, but their aims were different from those of either Jews or Christians. They believed that Moses was the prophet of Ialdabaoth and that he had truncated the story of creation, either wittingly or in ignorance—it did not matter which. That led them to reconstruct what they believed was the truth by rearranging the text and supplying the details that Moses had left out. They vastly expanded verses like Genesis 1:2, which they claimed was full of hidden meanings, but virtually ignored the details of the six days of creation, which were of little interest to them. It is easy to dismiss Gnostic biblical interpretation because of its obvious mistakes and exaggerations, but we have to recognize that in many ways it was the Gnostics who faced up to the problems that interpreting the Hebrew Bible posed for non-Jews. In essence, the Mosaic law struck most Gentiles as being too provincial, too particular in its demands, and too far removed from the elevated discourse of universal spiritual truth which they expected to find in a genuinely divine revelation. The Gnostics' conclusions were mistaken but, while the church dismissed them, it was also forced to develop a viable alternative that would reveal the text's true meaning.

The basic problem that the church had to face was this: If Gentile believers did not have to submit to the demands of a law that was obviously imperfect and inadequate, how could they be expected to accept that the same law was the Word of God? As Ptolemy the Valentinian put it,

> It is obvious that the Law was not given by the perfect God who is the Father . . . because it is imperfect and needs to be completed by someone else [Christ], and it contains commandments that cannot be in accordance with the nature and thought of a perfect God.[28]

One solution to this problem was to abandon the Hebrew Bible altogether, on the Gnostic (or semi-Gnostic) assumption that it was the work of an inferior deity and could have no authority for those who followed Jesus Christ. That was the approach taken by Marcion (mid-second century AD), who originated from Pontus on the Black Sea but made his career in Rome. Marcion rejected

[27] Origen, *Contra Celsum* 3.4.

[28] Epiphanius of Salamis, *Panarion* 33.3.4.

the Old Testament completely, but what is of special interest to Christians is that he also tried to expunge its influence from the books that now constitute the New Testament. Marcion was teaching at a time when those books were still in the process of being canonized and so his witness to them, perverse though it is, is valuable evidence for what the church of his day regarded as authoritative Scripture. The books that Marcion expurgated were essentially those of the canon as we know it today, which is proof that they were circulating and being accorded apostolic authority in the early second century. After removing everything Jewish, he was left with the Gospel of Luke and the Pauline epistles, but even they had to be censored to some degree. By doing this, Marcion proved that the books that would eventually make up the New Testament could not be understood without the Hebrew Bible, nor could Christianity reject its Jewish heritage without losing the substance of the gospel. What Marcion ended up with was not a canon but only selected extracts that suited his own purposes, and so his project for establishing the church on the basis of a new scriptural authority quickly collapsed.

Ptolemy's understanding of the Old Testament was considerably more moderate than Marcion's and doubtless more representative of mainstream opinion, but he also had great difficulty in accepting the authority of the canonical text:

> You need to know that the Law contained in the five books of Moses was not composed by a single author. What I mean is that it did not all come from God alone, but also contains some commandments of human origin. The words of our Savior teach us that the Law is divided into three parts. The first part must be attributed to God himself and to his legislative activity, the second to Moses, who added certain commandments to it, not because he was inspired by God but because he was driven by personal considerations, and the third to the elders of the people, who from the very beginning seem to have introduced certain precepts into the main body of the Law on their own authority.[29]

As evidence to support this statement, Ptolemy cited what Jesus had said about divorce.[30] Moses had permitted this, in spite of the fact that at creation God had decreed that "a man shall leave his father and his mother and hold fast to his wife, and they shall become one flesh."[31] Following the teaching of Jesus, Ptolemy interpreted this to mean that while God had originally established

[29] Ibid., 33.4.2.
[30] Matt. 19:3–9.
[31] Gen. 2:24, cited in Matt. 19:5. The permission to divorce is in Deut. 24:1–4.

lifelong matrimony, Moses had introduced divorce because of the hardness of people's hearts. The Jewish scribes and Pharisees accepted this and tried to determine the precise circumstances in which a divorce decree might be issued, but Jesus undercut the whole discussion by taking them back to the original creation principle. The mission of Christ was to restore the commandments of God as they were meant to be from the beginning, a move that would abolish the perceived laxity of Moses and the devious interpretations of the Jewish elders.

Ptolemy was a Gnostic, but he was by no means alone in his views. Tertullian did not hesitate to interpret Jesus' saying that "unless your righteousness exceeds that of the scribes and Pharisees, you will never enter the kingdom of heaven"[32] in exactly the same way:

> Since there are some who say that they have nothing to do with the law (which Christ has not dissolved but fulfilled)[33] but nevertheless sometimes insist on keeping the parts of it that suit them, we also assert that the law has passed away in the sense that its burdens, which (according to the apostles) not even the patriarchs were able to bear,[34] have completely ceased, but the parts that relate to righteousness have not only been retained, they have been amplified, so that our righteousness may exceed the righteousness of the scribes and the Pharisees.[35]

Like the Gnostics, Tertullian saw Jesus' command as a recipe for greater strictness, which in his case meant insisting that Christian monogamy was so absolute that even after the death of a spouse the surviving partner was forbidden from marrying again. That view never became official church policy, but it is probably wrong to think that Tertullian held it only because he had been attracted to the ultra-strict Montanist sect.[36] No doubt his rigorist approach reflected his temperament, but it is likely that there were many in the church who shared his outlook. The eruption of Donatism, another rigorist North African sect that appeared just after the legalization of Christianity in 313, suggests that there was a reserve of popular sympathy for hard-line interpretations of the Bible, especially at times when it must have seemed as if laxity and indiscipline were on the rise.

In their different ways, both Ptolemy and Tertullian appealed to the teaching

---

[32] Matt. 5:20.
[33] Matt. 5:17.
[34] Acts 15:10.
[35] Tertullian, *De monogamia* 7.
[36] On the Montanists, see Christine Trevett, *Montanism: Gender, Authority, and the New Prophecy* (Cambridge: Cambridge University Press, 1996).

of Jesus as the final arbiter in disputes about the meaning of the Mosaic law, but as the examples given above illustrate, their selective approach could create more problems than it resolved. What the church needed was a hermeneutic, an overall principle of interpretation that could make sense of the Old Testament and avoid the pick-and-choose approach that characterized the Gnostic schools and that so irritated Tertullian, without falling into an even stricter legalism than the one Jesus had overturned.

The first Christian who had a clear view of the Scriptures as a coherent body of divinely inspired books that together constituted the teaching authority of the church was Irenaeus. He knew that the books themselves had been in existence and widely used long before his time, but there was no authorized collection based on a defined theological principle. It was this lack that he set out to supply:

> It is wrong to say that the apostles preached before they received perfect knowledge. . . . After the Lord rose from the dead, they were filled with power from on high—with the Holy Spirit. Because they were completely filled, they had perfect knowledge and went off to the ends of the earth, preaching the good news of the blessing we had received from God. . . . Matthew also issued a written Gospel among the Hebrews, in their own language, while Peter and Paul were preaching at Rome and laying the foundations of the church. After their departure, Mark, the disciple and interpreter of Peter, handed down in writing what Peter had preached. Luke, the companion of Paul, recorded in a book the gospel preached by him. Afterwards John, the disciple of the Lord who had leaned on his breast, also published a Gospel during his time of residence at Ephesus.[37]

To the suggestion that the apostolic writings were not the whole story, and that there might be more information about the teaching of Jesus to be had, Irenaeus retorted:

> If the apostles had possessed hidden knowledge that they were in the habit of sharing privately with those who were "perfect," then surely they would have committed this knowledge to those whom they were putting in charge of the churches. After all, the apostles wanted their successors to be perfect and blameless in all things.[38]

How much of what Irenaeus wrote was true to historical fact is hard to determine, but even if some of his details are wrong, the basic thrust of his argu-

[37] Irenaeus of Lyon, *Adversus omnes haereses* 3.1.1.
[38] Ibid., 3.3.1.

ment is probably sound. The New Testament was written by a core of apostles and their associates who worked closely together, agreed with each other, and held nothing back from the church on the ground that it was secret information, too difficult for ordinary believers to absorb. As they saw it, the whole labor was guided by the Holy Spirit and so the texts they produced carried the stamp of divine approval. Irenaeus did not speculate about whether the New Testament canon was "closed," but the logic of his argument suggests that he believed that no more potentially canonical books would be forthcoming. The appearance of the Montanist sect in Asia Minor around AD 170 brought that question to a head. Montanus and his followers claimed to be prophets with messages from God, but they were rejected on the ground that revelation of that kind had come to an end. Even Tertullian, who was sympathetic to the Montanists and quoted some of their prophecies, never put them on the same plane as the apostolic writings, which he regarded as divinely inspired in a uniquely authoritative way.[39]

What marked Irenaeus and Tertullian out from earlier exegetes, including Christian ones, was the way they treated the Hebrew Bible. For them, it was no longer the only canonical Scripture, which the apostolic deposit merely helped to illuminate, but the Old Testament in our sense of the term. It had been supplemented and to a considerable degree superseded by a New Testament, which was now the authorized interpreter of the Hebrew texts.

One important effect of this development was that biblical history was understood in a new way. Most of the early church writers accepted its basic truthfulness, but historicity in the modern sense was much less important to them than it is to us today. The main reason for this is that they had little interest in the secular history of Israel. Unlike Jews, Christians were not looking for a physical restoration of the kingdom of David, nor did they much care about the literal application of the food laws and so on. To them, these were curiosities that had ceased to have any practical meaning after the coming of Christ. David and his descendants were the prophetic forebears who had kept alive the promise of the coming Messiah until he appeared. Once that happened, memory of the Davidic line faded out and the historic links with ancient Israel were severed. The food laws spoke of God's holiness, a concept that Christians internalized and maintained with as much zeal as any Jew had ever done, but in a way that made many of the provisions in the law of Moses seem alien and inapplicable in their literal sense. The boast of Christians was that theirs was the true spiritual holiness, a commitment of

[39] Tertullian, *De anima* 21; *De oratione* 22.

heart and mind and not the outward observance of essentially meaningless rituals.

To apply this understanding of the Old Testament, the early Christians developed a hermeneutical structure based on the principle of the "economy" or "dispensation." This stated that the covenant that God had made with Abraham was worked out in two different modes. Within Israel it followed the precepts of the Mosaic law, which had been given to the people because they were unable to maintain the faith of Abraham in its original purity.[40] In Christ there was a new dispensation, available to the entire world and erected on the basis of internal, spiritual faith. Everything that was external or physical in the Old Testament was thus reinterpreted, a process that was already going on in the New Testament itself, as we can see from the example of the temple, which was taken to mean both the body of Christ and the body of every believer who was filled with the Holy Spirit.[41] Tertullian summed up the church's approach when he wrote,

> The commandments were given carnally to the people of Israel long ago. It follows that there would one day come a time when the precepts of the old law and its ceremonies would cease. There would then come the promise of a new law, the recognition of spiritual sacrifices, and the promise of a new covenant dispensation.[42]

One unforeseen consequence of this dispensational approach was that if God is a Trinity, his revelation might be thought to come in three parts instead of only two. It was fairly easy to link the Old Testament to the self-disclosure of God the Father and the New Testament to the incarnation of God the Son, but what about the Holy Spirit? The Montanists claimed that their prophecies were a latter-day outpouring of God's Spirit, and that they constituted a third testament of sorts, bringing the history of divine revelation to its logical conclusion. It is therefore of more than passing interest to note that this claim was rejected by the rest of the church, which concluded that scriptural revelation had come to an end, even if not all the books that would eventually make up the canon had been formally agreed upon.

Following the two-dispensation model, Irenaeus opened the door to typology as the best means of bringing out the significance of God's Word for the church. Typology took the historical details of the Old Testament seriously but saw them as teaching the Israelites what Christ would do when he came. Irenaeus interpreted that as "recapitulation," a word he took from Ephesians

40 Gal. 3:16–18.

41 Mark 14:58; 1 Cor. 3:16–17; 6:19; 2 Cor. 6:16; Eph. 2:21.

42 Tertullian, *Adversus Iudaeos* 6.

1:10, where Paul described God's purpose having been set forth in Christ "as a plan for the fullness of time, to unite all things in him." This was understood to mean that Christ came to earth as the new Adam and undid all the wrong that the sin of the first Adam had caused.[43] To put it another way, the Creator God of the Old Testament was doing something new. As the Father of Jesus Christ, he was bringing into being the church, a host of brothers and sisters whom he had adopted in and through his Son.

This new hermeneutic, as we might call it, came to maturity in the work of Origen, and from there it passed into the heritage of the medieval church. Origen moved on from Irenaean typology into full-blown allegory. The formal distinction between typology and allegory is a modern one and would not have been as apparent to Origen's contemporaries as it is to us, but there is an important difference between them nonetheless. Typology took history seriously and regarded the Old Testament as a preparation for the coming of Christ. Allegory paid less attention to the historical development of divine revelation, preferring to see each stage of it as a window onto another world. Its basic premise was that although Abraham and Moses lived in material circumstances that were quite different from ours, their spiritual experience of God was the same because God does not change. It was the task of the biblical interpreter to penetrate beyond the time-bound letter of the text to the eternal message that it contains. Origen believed that someone who showed too much interest in the literal sense of the Scriptures might fail to discern their spiritual meaning and end up in the bondage of Judaism from which Christ came to set us free.[44] To quote his precise words,

> The simpler members of the church believe that there is no God greater than the Creator, and they are right about that. But they imagine things about him that would not be said about the most savage and unjust human beings. In all the cases I have mentioned, the basic cause of the false opinions, ungodly statements, and false assertions made about God seems to be nothing other than a failure to understand the spiritual meaning of Scripture. Such errors come from reading the Bible too literally.[45]

[43] 1 Cor. 15:45.

[44] Origen, *De principiis* 4.8–21. See Henri Crouzel, *Origen* (Edinburgh: T & T Clark, 1989), 61–84, for a comprehensive and nuanced examination of Origen's hermeneutical principles. Originally published as *Origène* (Paris: Lethielleux, 1985); also Peter W. Martens, *Origen and Scripture: The contours of the exegetical life* (Oxford: Oxford University Press, 2012). Other studies of Origen's exegesis are R. P. C. Hanson, *Allegory and Event: A Study of the Sources and Significance of Origen's Interpretation of Scripture*, 2nd ed. (Louisville: Westminster John Knox, 2002); Joseph W. Trigg, *Origen: The Bible and Philosophy in the Third-century Church* (Atlanta: John Knox, 1983); Henri de Lubac, *History and Spirit: The Understanding of Scripture according to Origen* (San Francisco: Ignatius, 2007). Originally published as *Histoire et Esprit: L'intelligence de l'Ecriture d'après Origène* (Paris: Aubier, 1950); Manlio Simonetti, *Origene esegeta e la sua tradizione* (Brescia: Morcelliana, 2004); Elizabeth A. Dively Lauro, *The Soul and Spirit of Scripture within Origen's Exegesis* (Atlanta: Society of Biblical Literature, 2005).

[45] Origen, *De principiis* 4.8–9.

Origen believed that the revelation had been given by God to the whole man—body, soul, and spirit. For that reason, he claimed that the text had three levels of meaning, corresponding to each one of these. The literal sense spoke to the body, the intellectual (or moral) sense spoke to the soul, and the spiritual sense informed the human spirit. In his words,

> The way we ought to deal with the Scriptures and extract their meaning is the following, which has been derived from the Scriptures themselves. Solomon in his Proverbs gives us the following rule: "Portray them in a threefold manner, in counsel and knowledge, to answer words of truth to them who propose them to you."[46] The individual ought to portray the ideas of Holy Scripture in a threefold manner on his own soul, so that the simple man may be edified by the "flesh" of Scripture (as we call the literal sense), while the one who has ascended higher may be edified by its "soul." The perfect man . . . will be edified by the spiritual law, which is a shadow of the good things to come. For as a man consists of body, soul, and spirit, so in the same way does Scripture, which God has given us for our salvation.[47]

Leaving aside Origen's misinterpretation of Proverbs, which was due to an inaccurate Greek translation, it is clear from the above that he saw the Bible as a three-layered word from God designed to communicate with us at every level of our being. We start with what is outward and material, which is why the letter of the text addresses our human flesh. From there we move on to the higher senses represented by the soul (intellect) and spirit, and discover that, in many cases, the Bible can sensibly be interpreted at only one or both of those levels. This is how it is meant to be, because the knowledge of God also progresses from an appreciation of the phenomena of everyday life through a more intellectual understanding to a spiritual awareness which alone can begin to grasp the mysteries of Almighty God. To quote Origen again,

> It is enough for us to conform our minds to the rule of faith, and not to think of the words of the Holy Spirit as some ornate concoction of fallible human rhetoric. Rather, we must believe that "all the glory of the king is within,"[48] which is to say that the treasure of divine meaning is hidden inside the frail vessel of the common letter. And if anyone is curious about the meaning of particular points, let him listen to the apostle Paul, who . . . exclaimed in despair and amazement, "O, the depth of the riches of the knowledge and

[46] Prov. 22:20–21 (LXX). The ESV reads, "Have I not written for you thirty sayings of counsel and knowledge, to make you know what is right and true, that you may give a true answer to those who sent you?"
[47] Origen, *De principiis* 4.11.
[48] Ps. 45:13, misquoted. The ESV says, "All glorious is the princess in her chamber."

wisdom of God."[49] Paul did not say that God's judgments were hard to discover, but that they were past finding out.[50]

The aim of reading the Scriptures was to come to a deeper knowledge of God, one that was "past finding out" according to the canons of human reason. This was something quite different from anything found in Judaism or in pagan Greek thought. The Jews read the Bible in order to hear the law of God and apply it to their lives. The Greeks speculated about ultimate reality and wrote down what they imagined it to be like. But Christians read their Scriptures as God's Word to them, a personal communication meant to be heard and experienced. The Bible might be a rule book for daily living, and it might also contain much useful information about the being and behavior of God, but these things were incidental to its main purpose. Those who were enlightened by the Holy Spirit and who could therefore read it as it was meant to be read would find in it the presence of God himself. This was the Father speaking to his children and drawing them closer to him. Once Jesus had made the Father known, there was no other way the Bible could be read properly. The text of the Bible was the voice of the Father himself, pointing us to the way of salvation prepared for us in Christ and leading us through the three stages of our humanity to that deeper knowledge that only a personal relationship with him could provide.

There can be no doubt that the career of Origen marked a decisive turning point in the history of Christian theology. Before his time there were apologists who discussed particular aspects of the subject, often (though not always) in response to the challenges posed by heretics and opponents, both Jewish and Christian. With Origen, however, we come to the work of a theologian whose main concern was to develop the internal logic of God's self-revelation and show how its different parts come together in a coherent whole. For 150 years after Origen's death he was universally admired and copied; the great debates of the fourth century were in many respects disputes about the way his theological legacy should be interpreted. Yet by AD 400 he was coming under attack, and in the end he would be denounced as a heretic and his writings would be destroyed.

The first broadside against Origen came from Jerome (340?–420), the translator of the Latin Bible, who was appalled by Origen's exegesis and did his best to stamp it out wherever he could. Like most of his contemporaries, Jerome had started out as an admirer of Origen and encouraged his friend Rufinus to translate his works into Latin. Rufinus did a good job and remained devoted

[49] Rom. 11:33.
[50] Origen, *De principiis* 4.26.

to his subject, but that only caused Jerome to fall out with him. Fortunately for us, Rufinus's translations have largely survived, giving us a knowledge of Origen that would otherwise be much poorer than it is. More seriously for his reputation, Origen also came under suspicion in the Eastern church, not so much because of his biblical interpretation as because of the Platonizing tendencies of his theology. In particular, he was attacked for believing that the human soul was preexistent and "fell" into the body at the moment of conception. Incautious statements by some of his admirers did not help matters, and eventually Origen was condemned, though not until 553.[51]

By the time that happened, Origen's legacy to the church was so deeply rooted that it could not be eradicated. Whatever the arguments were over details, the basic principles of his theology and especially of his spiritual interpretation of the Bible had become part of the mainstream Christian tradition. His failings were those of any pioneer who tries to open up paths where no one has gone before, and his greatness was such that even his condemnation could not suppress his reputation entirely. Even those who repudiated him believed that the Scriptures were the pathway to a knowledge and experience of God, and God was primarily the Father, whom we come to know in and through the Son and the Holy Spirit. Origen's allegorizing vision would be modified and expanded over time, but it would not be seriously challenged until the Protestant Reformation—or abandoned until modern times by those who rejected the teaching of the Reformers. Indeed, in some conservative, monastic circles it continues to flourish to this day. Origen may belong firmly in the past, but his achievement has cast a long shadow, and the church today would not have become what it is without it.

[51] See Elizabeth A. Clark, *The Origenist Controversy* (Princeton, NJ: Princeton University Press, 1992). On Origen's alleged Platonism, see Mark J. Edwards, *Origen against Plato* (Aldershot: Ashgate, 2002).

PART THREE

The Work of the Father

5

The Reconciliation of the World

The Work of the Father from a Jewish Perspective

As we saw in the last section, those with a Jewish background or a good understanding of the Hebrew Bible could easily identify the Father of Jesus Christ with the God of the Old Testament. When Jesus taught his disciples to pray to their Father in heaven, they could hardly have imagined they were praying to anyone else, and once they had become accustomed to the novel form of address there would have been no further problem. To their minds, whatever the Father did was done by God, and God could do anything. It was God who had sent the Son into the world, and God who had raised him from the dead. In cases like these, God and the Father had to be identical, and the principle was readily extended from there. They would likewise have had no difficulty in identifying the Father as the Creator of the world because they believed that the universe was made by the one God. In this way everything that pertained to divine activity was automatically attributed to the Father, who was the Preserver, Judge, and Redeemer of mankind. The tradition of monotheism was so deeply entrenched in Jewish minds that they could not envisage any other possibility. Pharisees and Sadducees might disagree about something like the resurrection of the body,[1] but the sovereignty of God was not in dispute. Neither side doubted that the Creator was also the Redeemer, whatever his work of redemption might look like in practice. As Job put it,

> I know that my Redeemer lives, and at the last he will stand upon the earth.
> And after my skin has been thus destroyed, yet in my flesh I shall see God.[2]

The details of the end times might be argued over (as they are among Christians today), but not the basic principle that God was in control of whatever

[1] Acts 23:8.
[2] See Job 19:25–26.

might happen. For Jewish Christians, difficulties arose only when it came to defining how the Son was different from the Father. If the Son did the work of God but was not the Father, the Father had to be distinguished in some way from the Son. The two might cooperate, as the New Testament says they did in the creation of the world, but since there were things that only the Son did (like become a man), it was logical to suppose that there must be other things that were unique to the Father. This was confirmed by the Gospels, where we find that the Son not only revealed the existence of the Father as a distinct person but also pointed to his work, much of which had to do with the sending of the Son into the world.

The incarnation of the Son was not an accident, nor is there any indication that the Son wanted to become a man independently of his Father's will. The New Testament makes it clear that his coming into the world was the result of a foreordained plan conceived and executed by the Father, and not something that he decided to do on his own.[3] From what it says, we may conclude that the Father's motives in sending the Son were two: First, he loved the world and wanted us to live in eternal fellowship with him.[4] Second, because we have sinned and cannot return to God on our own, direct intervention on God's part was necessary in order to bring that fellowship into being.[5] The Father's love for us was manifested by the Son, whose incarnation at the Father's behest is an indication of the Father's guiding role within the Godhead.

The Father revealed himself to us in his Son's incarnation in a way that is complete in one sense but partial in another. It is complete because the fullness of the Godhead dwelt bodily in the Son.[6] There is no other God and no hidden dimension to God that has not been revealed in the Son, so that to see him is to see the Father also.[7] But although the *quality* of the Father's self-revelation in the Son cannot be improved upon, the *quantity* of information which the Father chose to reveal through him was limited. We know this because when the mother of James and John asked Jesus to give her sons the places of greatest honor in his kingdom, Jesus replied that it was the Father's responsibility, and not his, to decide to whom those places should be given.[8] Likewise, we know that the Son was not commissioned to tell his disciples when the kingdom would be restored to Israel, even though he held out that promise to them and they knew that he would be their king. When he ascended into heaven, he told

---

[3] 1 Pet. 1:20.
[4] John 3:16.
[5] Rom. 3:23–26.
[6] Col. 2:9.
[7] John 14:9.
[8] Matt. 20:20–23.

them specifically that the Father had fixed the date of his return by his own authority, which tells us that in certain respects the Father can and does act independently of the Son.[9]

In the fourth century and later, theologians debated whether the Son was genuinely ignorant of these aspects of the Father's will, because men like the famous "arch-heretic" Arius (256?–336) believed that if he was, it would be proof that he was not truly God. The opponents of Arius therefore argued that Jesus must have known what the Father's intentions were but deliberately withheld the information from his disciples, which to modern minds suggests that he was lying to them. John Chrysostom (d. 407) did not hesitate to compare Jesus to a parent who conceals things from his children:

> Just as when we see a child crying and stubbornly wishing to take something from us that he does not really need, we hide the thing in question, show him our empty hands and say, "See, we do not have it," so Christ also behaved toward the apostles. And when the child, even after we have shown him our empty hands, continues to cry, knowing he has been deceived, we leave him with the excuse, "Someone is calling me," and in our desire to divert him from his first choice, we give him something else, which we tell him is wonderful, and then we hasten away. This is what Christ also did. The disciples asked for something and he told them he did not have it. The first time [in Mark 13] he frightened them, but the second time [in Acts 1] . . . he gave them the plausible excuse that the Father had set the date by his own authority.[10]

Thus, by the fourth century, the person of the Father had been so completely merged in people's minds with the being of God that for the Son not to share in the Father's knowledge could only mean that he was not fully divine. The complexity of the Father-Son relationship to which the New Testament bears witness had been ironed out by a particular interpretation of the Father and his work, and it was no longer possible for theologians to do justice to his distinctiveness as a person without diminishing the Son and falling into heresy.

The third great act of the Father was that he commissioned the Son to teach and do particular things that would allow those who believed in the Son to gain access to the Father's presence.[11] This picture is especially clear in the Fourth Gospel, where Jesus referred his words and deeds back to the Father's will, which he had come to accomplish.[12] No one could approach the Father

[9] Mark 13:32; Acts 1:7.

[10] John Chrysostom, *Homiliae in Acta Apostolorum* 2.

[11] Eph. 2:6, 18.

[12] John 4:34; 6:38–40.

in any other way, which meant that the Father had established this pattern as a fundamental part of the plan that he had sent the Son to execute.

The fourth great act of the Father was that he vindicated his Son in the face of the opposition that his teaching encountered. When the Jewish authorities condemned him and he was put to death, the Father raised him from the dead in order to prove that the Son was accomplishing his will for the salvation of his chosen people.[13] It is easy to overlook the importance of the fact that the atoning sacrifice which the Son offered to the Father was both acceptable to, and accepted by, him. It was the Father's acceptance that gave the Son's sacrifice its validity—not the degree of pain that the Son suffered, or even his willingness to go to the cross. The church has usually concentrated so much on what Christ did that it has tended to overlook the relational context in which he did it and downplay the importance of the Father's role, but the apostle Paul understood it very well. When he was describing the consequences of Jesus' obedience, even to the point of death, he wrote,

> Therefore God has highly exalted him and bestowed on him the name that is above every name, so that at the name of Jesus every knee should bow, in heaven and on earth and under the earth, and every tongue confess that Jesus Christ is Lord, to the glory of God the Father.[14]

As these verses indicate, the fifth great act of the Father was his delegation of power and authority over the creation to the Son. The New Testament tells us that when the Son went up to heaven he "led captivity captive," a Hebraic expression which means that he accomplished his task victoriously.[15] He then sat down at the right hand of the Father, another Hebraic expression meaning that he took up his authority to rule.[16] The Son's authority was not his own, but was given to him by the Father for the Father's own glory, and at the end of time the Son will return it to him, his mission accomplished.[17] In later times the Arians would claim that the Son's submission to the Father's authority meant that he was inferior to the Father and thus not fully or truly God, but that question did not arise in the first two centuries. To the apostles and their immediate followers, it was clear that the Son's power and authority were a gift from the Father and not something that he could claim by right, even though as a person of the Godhead he was the Father's equal.

The sixth and last of the great acts of the Father was the sending of the

[13] Col. 2:12–14.
[14] Phil. 2:9–11.
[15] Eph. 4:8 (KJV), quoting Ps. 68:18.
[16] Col. 3:1; Heb. 1:3; 1 Pet. 3:22. The right hand was the hand of power.
[17] 1 Cor. 15:28.

Holy Spirit in order to seal the adoption of believers in Christ.[18] The sending was a joint work of the Father and the Son, as Jesus made clear, but he did not hesitate to give pride of place to the Father as the ultimate authority behind it.[19] Later on the apostle Paul told the Galatians that God had sent the Holy Spirit into their hearts in order to enable them to cry "Abba, Father"—in other words, to establish in Christians the same relationship of filial dependence on the Father that the Son enjoys by nature.[20] Our participation in the life of heaven depends on the Holy Spirit and would not be possible without our union with Christ, but behind it lie the plan and purpose of the Father, who initiated the great work of reconciliation and to whom the other persons of the Trinity defer when performing the tasks needed to bring it about.

In all these ways, the Father appears in the New Testament as an agent in his own right. He often works through the Son and the Holy Spirit, but he also takes an active role that cannot be ascribed to anyone else. Because of their strict monotheism, Jewish Christians could only acknowledge the particular work of the Father by seeing it in the context of his relationship to the other divine persons. Without them, the Father was unknowable, and any work ascribed to him could only be understood as referring to God in general. There is some evidence that Jews who had been influenced by the surrounding Greek culture were prepared to call God their Father in a metaphorical sense, meaning that he was the Creator of all mankind.[21] But this was a concession to Hellenism, not something that sprang naturally from their reading of the Old Testament, and it could not have been applied to Jesus because it would have meant that he was less than fully God. There is no sign of this Hellenistic influence in the New Testament, where creation is clearly the work of the Son just as much as it is of the Father.[22] Hellenism would make its impact on the theology of the early church, but it would do so in quite a different way, as we shall see.

The Work of the Father from a Gentile Perspective

The interaction between the early Christians and the Gentile world began when Peter stood up in Jerusalem on the day of Pentecost and preached the gospel to pilgrims from the far corners of the Roman empire, but its success was influenced by forces that had been at work for at least three centuries before that. Most of

[18] Rom. 8:15.
[19] John 15:26.
[20] Gal. 4:6.
[21] See Justin Martyr, *Dialogus cum Tryphone* 2, 6, 60, 127, where God the Creator is called Father without any apparent objection on the part of Trypho (probably the rabbi Tarphon, known to us from other sources). It must be remembered that we have to take Justin's word for it; what Trypho/Tarphon thought about it is otherwise unknown.
[22] John 1:3; Col. 1:15.

those who heard Peter would probably have been Jews belonging to families that had migrated out of Palestine and settled elsewhere in the Mediterranean basin. Many of them no longer spoke Hebrew or Aramaic, though almost all of them must have been fluent in Greek, the trade language of the time.[23] These expatriate or "diaspora" Jews were often highly integrated into the prevailing Greco-Roman culture, as can be seen from the writings of Philo of Alexandria (d. AD 50). A contemporary of both Jesus and Paul, Philo wrote extensive commentaries on the Old Testament, seeking to demonstrate the fundamental compatibility of Greek philosophy with Hebrew revelation. Since Moses had lived several centuries before Homer, not to mention Socrates or Plato, Philo and others argued that the Greeks had read the Pentateuch and adapted it to serve the needs of their own culture. In this way, Philo could explain why there was so much similarity between the teachings of the Old Testament and the pagan philosophers, and could also account for the many differences of detail between them.[24]

Philo's impact on the writers of the New Testament is disputed, and nowadays most scholars tend to discount it, but there can be no doubt that he influenced a number of second- and third-century Christian writers, particularly those who came from Alexandria.[25] He has always been a marginal figure in the history of Judaism, which developed along fundamentally different lines, but his synthesis of Hebrew and Greek thought was attractive to many early Christians, who used him as a model for their own preaching and teaching. Thus it happened that although Philo never knew Jesus, he became a kind of honorary father of the church as it looked for a way to explain the meaning of the Old Testament to non-Jewish converts.

By AD 200, the belief that the Greeks had stolen their best ideas from Moses and the prophets was commonplace throughout the Christian world. Clement of Alexandria was especially insistent about this:

> Before the coming of the Lord the Greek philosophers received fragments of the truth from the Hebrew prophets. They claimed them as their own teachings, without really understanding them.[26]

In the Latin-speaking West, his contemporary Tertullian remarked,

> In their curiosity, the philosophers apparently investigated the sacred Scriptures because of their great antiquity, and misunderstood them. This proves

[23] Acts 2:11.
[24] See Philo, *De aeternitate mundi*, in *The Works of Philo*, trans. C. D. Yonge (Peabody, MA: Hendrickson, 1993), 707–724. For a Christian assertion of this, see Justin Martyr, *Apologia I* 59–60.
[25] See Eric Osborn, *Clement of Alexandria* (Cambridge: Cambridge University Press, 2005).
[26] Clement of Alexandria, *Stromateis* 1.17. Similar statements occur frequently in his writings.

that either they despised them completely or else that they only partially understood them.[27]

In addition to the diaspora Jews, there were a number of Gentiles on the fringes of the synagogues who had been attracted to Judaism. They were known as the "God-fearers" (*sebomenoi* or *theosebeis* in Greek),[28] and although they were less likely to go on pilgrimage to Jerusalem, they understood Jesus' teaching and often became enthusiastic converts to Christianity. To a significant degree, the early church was the fruit of a mission by diaspora Jews like Paul and Barnabas to the God-fearers, who formed the core of its Gentile membership in New Testament times. Paul occasionally preached to people who had no understanding of Judaism, but when he did so there was little to show for his efforts.[29] It was only in post-apostolic times that Gentiles who were entirely outside the Jewish orbit became Christians in large numbers, and when that happened, a different set of theological questions had to be addressed.

The basic problem was that Gentile converts who had little or no previous exposure to Judaism had to be converted not only to Christ but to the biblical worldview within which his mission and message made sense. It seems that the need for this deeper conversion had already been realized by the so-called "false apostles" who trailed Paul and his companions across Asia Minor. They wanted the God-fearers who had accepted Jesus to submit to the Jewish law, which meant that they had to be circumcised.[30] We are so familiar with Paul's fierce reaction to them that we forget that the false apostles had a reasonable case, even if the way they went about making it was superficial and mistaken. Although the outward symbols of Judaism could perhaps be dispensed with, as Paul insisted, the fundamental beliefs on which they rested could not. For example, there was nothing wrong with eating meat that had been sacrificed to idols, but those who did so had to understand that the idols in question did not exist and that eating meat sacrificed to them did not constitute a form of pagan worship.[31]

Similarly, although there was no need to impose strict Sabbath observance on everyone, the Sabbath nevertheless bore witness to the Old Testament doctrine of creation, and disregarding it was clearly wrong if it meant denying that doctrine.[32]

---

[27] Tertullian, *Ad nationes* 2.2.

[28] Acts 13:16.

[29] Acts 17:22–34. See also Acts 14:8–18.

[30] Gal. 2:1–5:15. In the course of his argument, Paul revealed that many Jews ignored the food laws and other inconvenient aspects of the Mosaic law when they were among Gentiles (see Gal. 2:12). Circumcision, however, was not optional.

[31] 1 Cor. 8:1–13.

[32] Rom. 14:5–9.

Gentiles had to accept that there was only one God, that he had made the world, that his creation was good, and that sin was rebellion against his will. None of these things were obvious to non-Jews, and even the Greek philosophers, who had risen above the common understanding of their time, had not got this right. A fair assessment of the situation was given by Justin Martyr (d. AD 156):

> The Sibyl and Hystaspes said that all corruptible things would be dissolved by God. The Stoic philosophers teach that even God will be dissolved into fire, after which the cycle of world history will start again. But we understand that God, the Creator of all things, is above and beyond what is to be changed. It may be that on some points our teaching is the same as that of the philosophers and poets whom you honor, but in other ways it is fuller and more divine. We are the only ones who offer proof of our assertions, so why are we unjustly hated more than anyone else? When we say that everything has been produced and arranged in a universe by God, it sounds as though we are Platonists, and when we say that everything will be burned up, we sound like Stoics. When we say that the souls of the wicked, retaining their sense perceptions after death, are punished, while those of the good are delivered from punishment and live a blessed life, we sound like the poets and philosophers. When we maintain that people should not worship things they have made, we are merely repeating the words of the comic poet Menander, and writers like him, who have said that the workman is greater than his work.[33]

As this passage indicates, Justin was by no means hostile to the ancient Greek philosophical tradition, but he insisted that even at its best, it fell far short of the divine revelation in Christ. Consider his remarks about Socrates, the great martyr to the cause of Greek thought:

> Our doctrines are greater than any human teaching, because Christ appeared on our behalf as a complete rational being—body, mind, and soul. When lawgivers and philosophers spoke well, it was because they were elaborating some part of the Word (*logos*) that they had discovered and meditated on. But since they did not know the Word (*logos*) in its entirely, which is Christ, they often contradicted themselves. When those who lived before Christ tried to analyze and demonstrate things by reason, they were accused of being impious troublemakers. Socrates, who pursued these matters more than anyone else, was accused of exactly the same crimes as we are. They said he was introducing new gods and did not believe in the ones recognized by the state. He rejected Homer and the other poets and taught people to turn away from

[33] Justin Martyr, *Apologia I* 20.

> the evil spirits and those who did what the poets spoke of. Instead, he exhorted them to get to know the unknown God, using their rational faculty to do so. He said that it was not easy to find the Father and Creator of all, nor, having found him, was it safe to declare his existence to everyone. But Christ did both these things by his own power. No one had enough faith in Socrates to die for his teaching, but philosophers and scholars have believed in Christ, as have craftsmen and uneducated people. Even Socrates had some knowledge of him, because he was and is the Word (*logos*) who is in everyone.[34]

Justin's appreciation of Greek culture was much the same as that of the apostle Paul, and may be regarded as typical of the early church.[35] When the Greeks got things right, it was because they were using their rational faculties correctly, but the capacities of the human mind were severely limited and the logic of the philosophers was not popular with the masses. Greco-Roman society was a mishmash of good and bad that lacked any logical coherence. On the one hand, people worshiped things they had made themselves and persecuted anyone who protested against such obvious folly. On the other hand, intellectuals came up with theories about the universe that lacked any objective basis; it was one man's imagination against another's, yet each of them claimed to possess the truth and denounced those who did not agree with them. Given such chaos, the Gentile world needed an orderly and credible foundation on which the message of the incarnate Word could be built.

The root of the problem was that the ancient Greeks believed that there was a radical disjunction between the rational and the material world. In the rational world things stayed the same because truth cannot change. In the material world, however, everything ebbed and flowed because matter lacked the stability that was inherent in eternal truth. From there it was but a short step to saying that whatever was rational was good and whatever was material was bad. As they saw it, the human dilemma is that we are rational souls trapped in material bodies—good beings ensnared by evil and locked in a prison from which only death can provide a complete escape. Not everyone in the Greek world thought exactly alike about these things, but the impact of this dualistic approach was inescapable. For example, the Epicureans believed that matter was good and to be enjoyed, but because of that, they were condemned as "hedonists" and their philosophy was often rejected by others as inferior and morally suspect. The Stoics were out-and-out materialists who believed that the soul was a highly refined form of matter, but they escaped the charge of

[34] Justin Martyr, *Apologia II* 10. See John 1:9.
[35] Acts 17:28.

hedonism because they looked for the triumph of the more refined over the cruder forms of matter and were very ascetic in the way they lived.

What was missing from the Greek paradigm was any notion of the spiritual dimension of reality as this was understood by Jews and Christians. Modern observers tend to assume that when the ancients talked about the rational soul they meant what Christians would later call the spirit, but this is not correct. In the biblical worldview, soul and spirit were alike in that neither of them was material, but in every other way they were quite different. In the New Testament, Paul described unspiritual people as *psychikoi* ("soulish") and contrasted them with those who were spiritual (*pneumatikoi*).[36] Elsewhere, we find that the Word of God was sharper than a two-edged sword, and penetrated so deeply that it could separate soul from spirit.[37] In other words, it could cut away what was unspiritual and reveal the truth in all its purity and grandeur. The New Testament writers knew what they were doing when they made this distinction between the soul and the spirit, because it corresponded to traditional Jewish thought. In the Hebrew Bible, man was both *basar* (flesh) and *nephesh* (soul). *Basar* and *nephesh* could both be used of living people without implying any moral overtones.[38] "Spirit" (*ruach*) was a word generally reserved for God or the elements in man or angels that resembled God. It was therefore possible to be or to have an evil spirit, but not an evil *nephesh*, because moral awareness belonged to what was spiritual. On the other hand, a *nephesh* could sin by turning away from God, and if it did, it would die.[39] What happened after that was unclear. The Hebrews had a notion of Sheol as a place of the departed, but what it was like remained extremely vague. All they knew for sure was that God ruled it as he ruled everything else, and they trusted him to look after them wherever they were in time or eternity.[40]

To the Greek mind, man was a composite of flesh (*sarx*) and soul (*psychê*), which were opposites to one another, because the former was matter while the latter was not.[41] No one really knew how these two incompatible elements had come together, but many theories were proposed. Perhaps the most common of them said that the soul was a fragment or a spark of something much bigger and all-embracing, from which it had broken away and to which it longed to return. Unlike the *nephesh*, the *psychê* was immortal, and after death it went to a place called Hades, which was ruled over by the god Pluto. What Hades

[36] 1 Cor. 2:14.
[37] Heb. 4:12.
[38] See Isa. 40:5.
[39] Ezek. 18:4, 20.
[40] Ps. 139:8. See also Ps. 23:4–6.
[41] An exception must be made for the Stoics, but even they thought that the soul was highly refined matter.

was like was impossible to say, but there was a belief that great men and heroes of the past were living in the so-called Elysian Fields, a paradise in which they were enjoying the reward due to them for their triumphs on earth.[42] This reward did not have a moral character as we would understand it; indeed, one of the oddities of the Greek gods is that they were often highly immoral in human terms.

The gods were usually portrayed as superhuman beings, and it was common to erect statues of them, which were then worshiped. The philosophers derided this practice, which they realized could not be correct, but they did not know what to put in its place. They tended to believe that the universal "soul" from which all individual human souls derived was also a rational mind (*nous* or *logos*), but this was because they possessed rational minds themselves and projected them onto ultimate reality. There was no question of being able to communicate with a rational divine mind, and the voice of the supernatural in human affairs was usually associated with some kind of mental abnormality, as the New Testament testifies.[43] The Greeks fantasized about the divine world and saw its influence in the forces of nature, but it remained a closed book to them. The most they hoped for was deliverance from the burdens of the flesh and a return to the world of the rational soul in which their individual existence would disappear, as the sparks of their particular lives were reabsorbed into the universal divine fire. Tertullian expressed the confusion inherent in this with his usual terseness:

> According to the school of Epicurus, there is nothing after death. Likewise [the Stoic] Seneca says that after death all things come to an end, even death itself. But Pythagoras, Empedocles, and the Platonists say the exact opposite, and claim that the soul is immortal. They even argue, much as we do, that the soul returns to bodies, though not to the same ones, and not always to the bodies of human beings.[44]

People who thought like that had no trouble with the biblical language about the spirit being at war with the flesh, because they interpreted this to mean that nonmaterial good will eventually triumph over material evil.[45] To them, the gospel message was that at the end of time, evil would be destroyed and matter would disappear. The Bible might speak of it as being transformed into something spiritual,[46] but for most people with a Greek background, such

[42] The Champs Elysées, one of the most famous (and chic) boulevards of Paris, was named for them.
[43] See Acts 16:16–18.
[44] Tertullian, *De resurrectione carnis* 1.
[45] See, for example, John 3:6; Rom. 8:1–13; 1 Cor. 5:5; Gal. 3:13; 5:16.
[46] 1 Cor. 15:50–58.

a transformation amounted to destruction. Flesh and blood could not inherit the kingdom of God because they were material things and were therefore slated to vanish along with everything else that was like them.

But if matter was evil, where did it come from? Pagans influenced by dualism had to say that evil had been made by a power that was capable of producing it (and therefore somewhat similar to God) but incapable of attaining the moral and spiritual heights that characterized the Father of Jesus Christ. Plato, whom many Christians honored as the greatest and most spiritual of the pagans, had called this creator-god the *Demiurge* (from the Greek word *dêmiourgos*, meaning "artisan" or "craftsman"), but he was greatly inferior to the God whom Jesus called his Father. For a start, the *Demiurge* was not a true Creator, but only a Designer, working on matter that was already there.[47] To the Platonist mind, matter was just as eternal as the *Demiurge*, and if there was a God who redeemed the soul from matter he must be a completely different being. The Christian God and the *Demiurge* may have been like each other in terms of the supernatural power they possessed, but when it came to moral and spiritual values they were opposites. How the two powers related to each other and where they originally came from was impossible to say. The Bible teaches that the world was made by God and that the powers of evil are spiritual beings who revolted against him and whom he will eventually punish and destroy. But this solution to the problem of good and evil was not available to the ancient Greeks because they had no concept of an all-powerful Creator. Origen expressed it very clearly:

> It might be maintained that if everything was made through the *logos* and evil is a part of all things, then sin and everything wicked was also made by the *logos*. But we have to say that this is false. . . . The Devil is not God's handiwork with respect to his sinfulness, but as a creature, God made him because he is the only Creator there is. A murderer is not made such by God, but as a man, he too is a divine creature.[48]

Greeks who professed faith in Christ without having embraced the Jewish worldview were confronted by a dilemma. On the one hand, they had to believe that Jesus had been sent into the world by his Father, who to all intents and purposes appeared to be the one Almighty God. They also had to believe that the universe was a coherent system created by a single and all-powerful Deity. In human terms, fatherhood and (pro)creation went together, so it seemed per-

[47] Plato, *Timaeus* 32d–33a.
[48] Origen, *Commentarium in Iohannis Evangelium* 2.7.

fectly logical to conclude that the Father was the Creator, and vice versa. Thus it was that a connection that was never explicitly made in the New Testament became standard in the Greco-Roman world. To this day, the classical creeds begin, "I believe in God the Father, the Almighty, Maker of heaven and earth (and of all things visible and invisible)."[49] And despite more than seventeen centuries of theological development, that remains all that most Christians ever confess about the Father as a person in his own right![50]

The importance of this doctrine for the mission of the early church to the Gentile world can scarcely be overstated. The first generation of post-apostolic writers said little about it, because they were still working within a framework shaped by Judaism. But when Justin Martyr made the first serious attempt to reach out to pagan intellectuals, this is what he wrote:

> It is for your sake that we say these things. Under cross-examination, we can always deny that we are Christians, but we do not want to live a lie. We are driven by desire for an eternal and pure life, and want to dwell with God, the Father and Creator of all things, and so we are ready to confess our faith. We are convinced that those who have shown God by their works that they have followed him and desired to live with him in sinless tranquility, can obtain these things.[51]

Justin went on to add that it was Christ who taught this and made it possible for others to enter the presence of God, but he never doubted that the destiny of the Christian was to be reconciled to the Father and Creator of all things.

A generation later, Irenaeus of Lyon refuted the idea that the world had been created by angels or a *Demiurge* who was less than the most high God on the ground that even if the Father had made use of intermediaries as instruments to help him create, he alone was ultimately responsible for what came into being. As Irenaeus put it,

> He [the Father] himself, in a way that we cannot describe or imagine, predestined all things and formed them as he pleased, ordering them in harmony and giving each its own place at the beginning of their creation. Thus on spiritual things he bestowed a spiritual and invisible nature, on celestial things a celestial nature . . . on everything, in short, a nature suited to the kind of life assigned to them.[52]

[49] The opening line of the Apostles' Creed, with the addition inserted in the Nicene Creed in parentheses.
[50] It cannot really be said, for example, that the Reformation confessions or the decrees of the Roman Catholic "ecumenical" councils have got much beyond this.
[51] Justin Martyr, *Apology* I 8.
[52] Irenaeus of Lyon, *Adversus omnes haereses* 2.2.4.

Later writers would take up this theme and develop it further, but after Irenaeus the basic principles were clear. The Father is the Creator who has given the world the order it now possesses. There are no freak occurrences, no flukes that have somehow evaded his control, no aspects of life over which he is not sovereign. Spiritual forces do not fight one another for mastery nor is the material world alien to the plan and purpose of God. The Father-Creator holds it all together. Disorder, such as it is, is not the inevitable result of some primordial chaos but the fruit of disobedience to his will which he has permitted but which never escapes his control. Those who know and worship him do not have to be afraid of what might happen to them in this life, because as the apostle Paul put it, "all things work together for good, for those who are called according to his purpose."[53]

The Christian Doctrine of Creation

In order to make the Bible's teaching comprehensible to non-Jewish people, Christians had to begin with the most fundamental proposition of all—that the created order is essentially good. This is stated with great clarity in Genesis 1, where the phrase is ritually repeated at the end of each day: "God saw everything that he had made, and behold, it was very good."[54] Very few people realize it, but the six days of creation in the opening chapters of Genesis, known in Greek as the *hexaêmeron*, was the part of the Bible most frequently commented on in the early church. Even the great Augustine of Hippo (354–430), who was not a biblical commentator in the usual sense of the term, wrote on it no less than four times![55] Virtually every other ancient Christian writer took a stab at it as well, because they understood how important it was in evangelizing their pagan environment. As Theophilus of Antioch put it,

> No one can give a worthy explanation and description of every aspect of the six days' work; even if he had ten thousand tongues and mouths or lives ten thousand years, he would still not be able to say anything worthy of these things, because of the exceeding greatness and riches of the wisdom of God that can be found in the six days' work narrated in Genesis 1.[56]

The goodness of creation had several aspects to it, each of which was equally important for the preaching of the Christian message. The first and

---

[53] Rom. 8:28.

[54] Gen. 1:31, cf. vv. 10, 12, 18, 25.

[55] Augustine of Hippo, *Confessiones* 11–13; *De civitate Dei* 11.4–34; *De Genesi ad litteram*; *De Genesi adversus Manichaeos*. There is even a fragment of a fifth commentary, known to us as *De Genesi ad litteram liber imperfectus*.

[56] Theophilus of Antioch, *Ad Autolycum* 2.12.

most basic point that Christians had to make was that whatever evil might be, it was not to be located in material objects. When Genesis 1 says that the universe is good, it is not speaking in moral or spiritual terms, but in physical ones. As we would express it today, what God made was "fit for purpose" and operated according to principles that we can understand and use to our own benefit. In moral terms, matter lacks a mind and will of its own and so is neither good nor evil in itself, though it can be used for good or evil purposes. In the latter case it is being abused, but the blame for this belongs to the abuser and not to the material object itself.

It was the essential goodness of matter that made it possible for the Son of God to become a man. He could not have done that if matter had been evil, because God cannot be joined to something that is unworthy of him. If matter had been evil it would have been necessary to get rid of the body altogether for there to have been any change for the better, but that would have made a nonsense of biblical teaching. For not only had the Son of God become a man in Jesus Christ, he had died and risen again in order to make it possible for us to be resurrected from the dead. The resurrection was not a purely spiritual affair but included the material body—in a transformed state to be sure, but a material body nonetheless. In sum, the belief that matter was evil was the antithesis of Christianity and had to be rejected if there was to be any hope that the gospel message would remain intact in the Gentile world.

The second point that Christians had to make was that creation has an order that is not intrinsic to its being but has been given to it by God, who makes sure that it does not cease to function in the way it is supposed to. It may be too much to attribute the rise of modern scientific thought exclusively to the influence of Christianity, but it is hard to deny that the two are connected. Belief in an orderly universe preceded the discovery and application of that order, and for that belief the teaching of the Bible was largely responsible. Many early Christian writers examined the world around them in great detail, and by claiming that everything they observed went back to the providence of a good Creator they were able to make sense of the universe to a degree that had not been achieved before. It is true that they did not develop experimental science as we know it today, a failure that left a good many natural phenomena unexplained, but the basic principles were clear, as Hippolytus (c. 250) reminds us:

> First, God made the different elements out of which everything else would then come into being—fire, spirit, water, and earth. He formed some objects from a single element, but others he made compounds of two, three, and four of them. Those formed from a single element were immortal, since they can

> never be dissolved into their component parts. Those that are compounds, however, can be dissolved, which is why they are termed mortal.[57]

Belief in divine providence also allowed the early Christians to avoid saying that the world is a closed system in which the unexpected is impossible. The fact that God was in active control of his creation and could do with it whatever he chose allowed for the possibility of miracles without destroying the assurance that the universe could be relied upon to behave in predetermined ways. Christian teaching about the plan and purpose of the Creator provided a basis for determining what was "normal" and what was not, an important advance that allowed people to have confidence in the created order and to be set free from superstition and the fear of chaos. At the same time, the Creator was by definition sovereign over his creation, and so his creatures were not locked into a system from which there was no escape.

Third, the doctrine of creation teaches that the world, including its spiritual elements, is not part of God but has been made "outside" him, or as theologians normally put it, *ex nihilo* (out of nothing). The Bible says that God spoke and the world was created, the only link between him and what he has made being his will to make it.[58] Obviously, if God is the Creator, what exists must somehow reflect his nature, but what that connection is cannot be determined solely by examining the creation. It is rather like the famous analogy of the watch and the watchmaker that was used by William Paley (1743–1805) to prove that the world was created by an intelligent being. A watch must have been made by someone capable of producing it, but looking at it will not tell us much about what the watchmaker is like. This comparison is instructive because it helps us to understand why we can say that the Creator is unknowable and transcendent in himself, even though his existence and some of his characteristics can be known in and through what he has made.

The early Christians developed what we would now call "natural theology" along these lines, taking their cue from those biblical passages that speak of the sovereignty of God in and over nature. But they never fell into the trap of suggesting that a created object could be worshiped as divine, even by extension. In the Christian vision the material universe was "desacralized," as we would say today. This means that the idea that it contained hidden mysteries that were susceptible to the pull of magic or the occult was dismissed and human beings were set free from the notion that their lives

[57] Hippolytus of Rome, *Adversus haereses* 10.32 (28).

[58] See Gen. 1:1; Rom. 4:17; 1 Cor. 1:28; Heb. 11:3.

were bound up with the movement of the stars. Tertullian was especially forthright about this:

> After the [coming of the] Gospel, you will nowhere find other sophists, Chaldeans, enchanters, diviners, or magicians—except as clearly punished. You know nothing, astrologer, if you do not know that you should be a Christian. If you did know it, you should have known this also—that you should have nothing more to do with that profession of yours.[59]

Early Christian writers loved to poke fun at pagans for believing in things like astrology, and they never tired of producing examples to prove just how foolish such beliefs were. To their minds, even Plato was blind and failed to understand what the world was really like, in spite of his apparently genuine desire to discover the truth.[60]

The Christian doctrine of creation also teaches that God takes care of the world that he has made. Nothing that happens in it escapes his knowledge or control. For the early Christians, the sovereignty of God in the universe was comparable to the rule of law in human society. Those who have lived in places where law and order have broken down know how frightening and insecure those places can be. They know that the restoration of normal administration is not the imposition of tyranny but freedom from the curse of lawlessness. This is how the first Christians saw their universe. Far from being subject to the whims of unknown and uncontrollable forces, the world was held together by the will of a good and just God who has given to each of his creatures a secure place within his overall order. To reject that order was to court destruction, as Adam and Eve discovered to their cost. Death came into the world because of their sin and not because some blind fate had decreed it, which made it possible to hope that if that sin could be overcome, a new and eternal life might come into being. This was the promise of the gospel, made to those who believed in Christ.

The biggest problem the early Christians had to tackle was the question of the origin of evil. If the world was created good, and if it is governed by a perfect, just, and good God, where did evil come from and why is its presence tolerated? Christians could not accept the idea that evil was the result of a mingling of superior spirit with inferior matter, especially as the Bible taught that there were evil spirits who had rebelled against God and had somehow enticed human beings into their rebellion. Unfortunately, the details of how

[59] Tertullian, *De idololatria* 9. A Chaldean was a magus, like the wise men who visited the infant Jesus.
[60] On the spiritual and intellectual limitations of Plato, see Justin Martyr, *Oratio ad Graecos* 22–23.

and why this happened were not clearly revealed in Scripture, forcing Christians to speculate to an unusually high degree. As Origen put it,

> The church teaches that the Devil, his angels, and the forces opposed [to God] do indeed exist. But it has never explained with sufficient clarity what they are or how they exist. Most Christians think that the Devil was an angel who became an apostate and persuaded as many other angels as he could to fall away with him.[61]

It was common for Christians to suppose that the pagan gods were demons in disguise, but they still saw them as spirits who had originally been created just as good as anything else that God had made. Evil was something they had freely chosen, and God had respected their choice. In Tertullian's words,

> Where did the Devil's malice of lying and deceit originate? Certainly not with God! God made the angel good, and before he became the Devil, he stood out as the wisest of all the creatures. . . . If you turn to the prophecy of Ezekiel, you will quickly realize that this angel was good by creation and that it was by his own choice that he became corrupt.[62]

The identification of the Creator with pure being made it easier to tie the concepts of creation and redemption together. In a world where the danger of separating them was ever-present, the significance of this linkage should not be underestimated. The early Christians portrayed the redemptive work of the Creator as a fulfillment of his original purposes for the human race. As they saw it, Adam and Eve had been created sinless but they were not "perfect" beings. They had no knowledge of good and evil, and without an understanding of the good it is hard to see how they could have had genuine fellowship with God. After all, if God's being and his goodness are inseparably connected, Adam and Eve's inability to appreciate the nature of that good must have been due to some defect in their being. This defect, it was decided, was their mortality. Whether Adam and Eve would have died if they had not sinned was unclear, but the fact that their sin brought death into the world—which Satan's sin against God had not done because Satan is immortal by nature—shows that there was a weakness in the original creation that the forces of evil could (and did) exploit. Justin Martyr was very clear about this:

> God ordained that if man kept his commandments, he would share in immortal life. But if he disobeyed them, his fate would be the exact opposite. Being

[61] Origen, *De principiis*, preface, 6.
[62] Tertullian, *Adversus Marcionem* 2.10. The biblical reference is to Ezek. 28:11–19.

> made the way he was, man soon took the path of transgression and became subject to corruption. This is how corruption became inherent in nature. That is why it was necessary for him who wanted to save us to be someone who would destroy the root cause of corruption. . . . if he had simply waved death away, death would not have approached us on account of his will. But we would have become corruptible again, because we would have carried about in ourselves [the seed of] that natural corruption.[63]

One of the most basic consequences of the adoption of the biblical worldview is that the dimensions of space and time were placed under the immediate control of a God who was not bound by either. How an infinite and eternal divine being can relate to a time-and-space-bound universe is an ancient problem that for Christians is closely tied to the connection between God as Creator and as Redeemer. A divine Creator who made the world and then let it run under its own steam would be less problematic, because he would not be involved in the internal workings of what he had made and could happily dwell outside time and space, quite unconnected with us.

But a Creator who is also the Redeemer must be involved in his creation, since otherwise redemption would have no meaning. How is this possible? At the macro-level, God must be present at every moment in time and everywhere in space. He cannot be located in a particular place, because to locate him would be to define him and limit him to the dimensions of our world. If that were to happen, he would not be able to save us because there would be a part of our universe that he did not inhabit and which would therefore lie outside his control. If that part could not be redeemed, the work of the Redeemer could not be universal or guaranteed, and the corruption that caused the fall would be able to survive and spread again. In a Christian worldview, there can be no escape from the presence and power of God, as Clement of Rome (c. 95) reminded his readers:

> Where can any of us escape from God's mighty hand? Scripture says, "Where shall I go [from your Spirit] or where shall I flee from your presence? If I ascend to heaven, you are there. . . . if I make my bed in Sheol, you are there . . ." Where then can we go? Where can we flee from him who embraces the universe?[64]

When it came to time, the early Christians rejected the cyclical view that dominated most ancient cultures and replaced it with a linear understanding

[63] Justin Martyr, in a lost work cited by Leontius of Byzantium, *Adversus Eutychianos* 2. See Tertullian, *Adversus Marcionem* 2.8, for a similar statement.
[64] Clement of Rome, *Epistula prima* 28. The passage quoted is Ps. 139:7–8.

derived from the Bible. Cyclical time was based on the rotation of the sun, the moon, and the seasons. Even if these were imperfectly understood, they set a pattern for daily life that repeated itself on a daily or annual basis. Most pagan religious rites were connected to this cycle in some way, either by a deification of the sun and moon or by the development of fertility cults and harvest festivals that marked the pattern of life. In their understanding, dying and rising again were commonplace and even predictable. The sun that set in the evening would return the following morning; nature that died in the autumn would spring back to life after a period of hibernation, or "wintering."

In contrast to this, the biblical view of time was primarily linear. The seasons were not denied, of course, but they were relativized and placed in a wider context. God created the world in the distant past with a purpose that was being progressively realized over time, but he himself dwelt above and beyond it. As Origen put it,

> With God, all time is today. There is no evening in him, nor is there morning. There is nothing but time that stretches out, along with his unbeginning and unseen life.[65]

The coming of Christ was the culmination of the divine purpose, and in a sense it marked the end of time. Now we are living in the last days, in expectation of the imminent end of all things. There were pagan beliefs that might be compared to this in some respects but there was nothing exactly the same. The Stoics believed that the world would come to a catastrophic end when matter would be dissolved in fire, but it would then be reborn and continue in another cycle similar to the one we are now living in. Christians rejected this. The end would be catastrophic only for those who rejected Christ; those who had received him as their Savior would rejoice at being finally vindicated and established in the heavenly presence of God. The contrast is fully described by Hippolytus:

> By means of this knowledge [of salvation] you will escape the approaching threat of the fire of judgment and the sunless scenery of gloomy Tartarus, where there never shines a beam from the irradiating voice of the Word. You will also escape the boiling flood of Gehenna's eternal lake of fire. . . . these things you will avoid by being instructed in a knowledge of the true God. You will possess an immortal body, beyond the possibility of corruption, just like the soul. And you will receive the kingdom of heaven.[66]

[65] Origen, *Commentarium in Iohannis Evangelium* 1.32.
[66] Hippolytus of Rome, *Philosophumena* 10.30.

This vision of time changed the way Christians looked at their earthly life and therefore it also changed the way they treated the world around them. They were called to live each day as if it were their last, and when they were persecuted by the state and ran the risk of having to pay for their beliefs with their lives, this sense of urgency was very real. They learned the hard way not to store up treasure on earth but to prepare themselves for the coming of Christ, either to judge the world or to take them home to glory. This sense of otherworldliness might seem at first sight to be an encouragement to despise the created order, but often it turned out to be the very opposite. Pagans had little incentive to do anything, because life would just go on as it had always done and there was nothing they could do to influence the course of events. But Christians knew that history had a purpose in which they were involved, and that their work would count for something at the judgment seat of God. They therefore dedicated every aspect of their lives to him and cherished each moment as an opportunity for service and witness that would not come again. The end of time was not a disaster to be feared but a goal to be aimed at and welcomed because it would be the final fulfillment of God's purposes for his people.

Another aspect of the changed worldview of Christians was the way in which they reordered the hierarchy of being and relationships. Pagans had always been aware of such a hierarchy but they could only speculate about how it had come into existence and what its purpose was, if indeed it had one. Generally speaking, they tended to think that past ages were superior to the present and that all change and development has been for the worse. Human beings might be higher than animals and inert things like plants or rocks, but they were lower than the gods, who were subject in their turn to the fates that controlled all existence. Theirs was a deterministic universe in which everything had its place. Any attempt to escape from that, especially if it were an attempt to rise higher on the scale of being, would be severely punished by those who were in a position to do so, because the hierarchy of being could not be overturned.

Christians did not think like that. They agreed with pagans that there were beings that were both higher and lower than the human race, but not that mankind was subject to spiritual forces that were in turn subject to some absolute and impersonal power. The biblical doctrine of God made it necessary to believe that ultimate power was personal, and that human beings had a special relationship with that power because we have been created in his image and likeness. Clement of Alexandria expressed this as follows:

> Human beings are dear to God because they are his workmanship. The other works of creation, God made by his word of command alone. But he framed

> the human race by his own hand and breathed into them what was peculiar to himself. What God made after his own likeness was either held by him to be desirable in itself or else desirable for some other purpose. . . . It seems logical that God made man because he found him desirable in himself, and not for some ulterior motive. What is desirable is loveable, and so man is loved by God.[67]

But just as important, that power had entered the human race as a man, making it possible for us to die and rise with him to the level of the divine. This did not mean that human beings would one day be deified in the pagan sense, but that we have been given a relationship with ultimate reality that enables us to live not just in harmony but also in fellowship with him. As Irenaeus put it,

> The Creator has granted the world to the human race but his greatness is unknown to any of those whom he has made. . . . Yet as regards his love, God is always known through him by whose means he ordained all things. This is his Word, our Lord Jesus Christ.[68]

Christians were called not merely to be seated in the heavenly places with Christ but to reign with him there and to take part in the judgment of the world.[69] Such a belief utterly transformed the Christian understanding of the place of believers in the created order. Having access to the Father meant being able to share in the Father's plan for his creatures and to live in the world as its rulers, not as victims of forces beyond our control. The liberating power of that message could be properly understood only by those who had been blinded by belief in such forces and reduced to living in fear of them. To know that the world is the work of a loving heavenly Father who has made it for his children to enjoy brought an entirely new perspective to bear on it. Far from being spiritual beings who have been imprisoned in a material body from which we must try to escape, we are creatures whose spiritual and material dimensions make us the link between the two aspects of God's creation and therefore superior to both of them. We may be a little lower than the angels in the hierarchy of being but we are called to judge them, because our relationship with God gives us a higher status than they can ever have. The fourth-century Latin writer Lactantius summed this up perfectly:

> God designed the world for the sake of mankind, but he made mankind for its own sake. People were called to be priests of the divine temple, observers

[67] Clement of Alexandria, *Paedagogus* 1.3.
[68] Irenaeus of Lyon, *Adversus omnes haereses* 4.20.4.
[69] 2 Tim. 2:12; Rev. 20:6; 1 Cor. 6:3.

> of God's works and of heavenly things. They are the only earthly beings who can understand God, being intelligent and rational. . . . everything was put under their control, so that they might be under the control of God, their Maker and Creator.[70]

Finally, in reconciling the world to himself, the Father has given the world meaning by appointing it for judgment. At first sight, this may seem strange to us, because to our minds judgment sounds negative and destructive. We imagine that when God judges the living and the dead the world as we know it will be destroyed. There is an element of truth in that, but it is not the whole story. To be slated for judgment is to be given a sense that our lives have meaning. Judgment is possible only when there are criteria by which it can take place. If it is true that we have all fallen short of the glory of God and deserve condemnation, this demonstrates that what we do and have done matters to God. There are standards that we are supposed to respect and live up to, even if we cannot. Our lives have meaning and purpose that can be understood only by considering the mind of the Judge. As Cyprian of Carthage explained,

> How great will that Day [of judgment] be when it comes! The Lord will begin to count up his people and to recognize what each one of them deserves. . . . he will send the guilty to Gehenna, . . . but he will pay us the reward of our faith and devotion. How great will be the glory, and how great will be the joy, to be admitted to see God![71]

That Judge is our heavenly Father. It is his responsibility to pronounce sentence on us and determine what punishment we must suffer for our sin against him. That punishment is death, because to sin against God is to sin against the source of our life and cut ourselves off from it. The Judge cannot waive the sentence, because to do so would be to accept that there is nothing he can do to put right the wrong that has been done. We sometimes do this in human life because we recognize that there are some wrongs that can never be put right and that forgetting about them is the only practical way we can move forward. But God has the power to put things right and does not have to content himself with a second-best solution to an otherwise insoluble problem.

Our Judge has not only decreed the sentence of death but has also carried it out by sending his Son into the world to take our place on the cross and pay the price for our sins. The punishment we deserve has fallen on him and has therefore been paid in full—there is no outstanding debt that we shall have to

[70] Lactantius, *De ira Dei* 14.
[71] Cyprian of Carthage, *Epistula* 55.10.

make up at some future point. It is in judgment that the work of the Father is seen at its deepest level. By judging the world the Creator gives it its value and sets a price on it. By sending his Son to pay that price the Father redeems the world and restores it to what it ought to be. Only the Creator has the authority to judge in a definitive manner, and only he has the capacity to redeem what he has judged. Creation and redemption meet in the last judgment, and it is here more than anywhere else that we see how the two are reconciled in the overarching work of the Father. As Irenaeus put it,

> In the first Adam, we offended God himself. . . . But in the second Adam we are reconciled to God, being made obedient even unto death. For we were debtors to no one else but to him whose commandment we had transgressed at the beginning. . . . By transgressing God's commandment, we became his enemies. Therefore, in the last times, the Lord has restored us to his friendship through his incarnation. He has become the Mediator between God and man, propitiating the Father against whom we have sinned. He has cancelled our disobedience by his obedience and conferred upon us the gift of communion with, and subjection to, our Maker.[72]

[72] Irenaeus of Lyon, *Adversus omnes haereses* 5.17.1.

6

Providence and Predestination

The Image and Likeness of God

That God had made the universe for a purpose was one of the most important early Christian doctrines. In sharp contrast to that, the pagan vision of the cosmos was eclectic and relatively disordered. In a general way, pagans believed that things were getting worse all the time, but they could not know for sure how this would affect them or what would happen to them beyond the grave. Even if matter re-formed and souls transmigrated to other bodies, it was impossible to say how this would occur or what we might be like in our next life. The past was a lost paradise and the future was an unknown void, isolating the present in a kind of illusion that was more transient than permanent.

To a pagan world which thought like that, the Christian gospel came as a message of stability and reassurance. The biblical universe was not a random jumble of accidental occurrences but a planned system controlled by the loving power of God our Father. He made it for our benefit and placed us in it to rule over it and enjoy its blessings. Far from being the end product of a series of progressive declines from an original ideal, the human race was the crowning glory of creation. Very few Christians interpreted the Genesis story literally, because they recognized that it was not intended to be a straightforward account of what happened when the world was made. They were not bothered by this, because to them the orderly structure of creation was the most important thing, and it was this that captured their imagination. As Origen put it,

> Who can believe that the first three days, with their evenings and mornings, existed before the creation of the sun, moon, and stars? Who would think that there was a first day with no sky? . . . No one doubts that these things are symbolic of certain mysteries. What is presented as history is not to be taken literally.[1]

[1] Origen, *De principiis* 4.1.16.

What mattered was that each of the six days of creation represented a higher, more detailed development than what had gone before. Instead of decline there was incremental improvement, as God decorated his universe with both the necessities and the pleasures of life. The world as we know it was not a minimalist collection of the basic essentials needed for survival, which is what it would be if the evolutionary theory were to be taken to its logical conclusion. We can understand why some creatures might develop particular organs or limbs in order to achieve certain tasks, but there are many things in the world that seem to have no pragmatic purpose at all. Why do we have roses, for example? Are hedgehogs really necessary? To ask this kind of question is to reduce the created order to something less than what it is, and the early Christians did not think in such utilitarian terms. To them, everything in the world was God-given, everything had its reason for existing, and everything was designed to benefit the human race, who appeared last of all and was placed over the rest of the created order as the crowning achievement of God's work.

Because the early Christians attributed this order to their loving heavenly Father, there was a relationship to him built into it from the beginning. This was expressed in the Old Testament assertion that man was created in the image and likeness of God.[2] Scholars recognize that these terms can be found in pagan cultures from Mesopotamia to Greece, and there is some possibility that the biblical phrase echoes ancient Egyptian or Babylonian thought, but the general consensus today is that there is nothing quite like the Hebrew combination anywhere else in the ancient world.[3] Furthermore, although the expression is found more than once in Genesis, it was not expounded in the rest of the Old Testament or in postbiblical Judaism to any significant extent.[4] Real theological development of the idea came only with Christianity, and then it seems that it was the Gnostics who were the first to make the most of it, forcing the rest of the church to state its own position more clearly.

The Gnostic view was remarkably uniform, given the variety of systems that went by that name. In essence, it regarded the image as the form in which man had been created and the likeness as the substance with which that form had been endued. The image and likeness were equivalent to the human soul, which was modeled after the Demiurge. The difference between the two terms was that the image represented a copy of a (superior) original, whereas the likeness was a reproduction of something essentially on the same level of being

---

[2] Gen. 1:26–27.

[3] For a survey of the evidence, see Jacques Fantino, *L'homme image de Dieu chez saint Irénée de Lyon* (Paris: Cerf, 1986), 4–44.

[4] Gen. 5:1–3; 9:6. See Fantino, *L'homme image*, 8–16.

as itself. What this meant was that, as the image of God, Adam was created by the Demiurge to resemble the Father-God who dwelt above and beyond the creation. But as the divine likeness, Adam was made like the Demiurge, not like the Father, who was above and beyond anything to be found in this world. The challenge for the Gnostics was to make the likeness conform to the image by rising from the "psychic" to the spiritual level, of which they had some notion—because they were created in its image—but no direct experience.[5]

The Christian view was very different from this. Before Gnostic ideas became widespread, most Christians made little or no distinction between "image" and "likeness," believing them to be virtually synonymous (as indeed they are). But as Gnostic thought grew more familiar, the church was obliged to counter it by proposing an alternative explanation for the terms the Bible uses. One early attempt to do this was made by Tatian (c. 150), who claimed that it is not the human soul that is of divine origin but the human spirit, making a distinction between soul and spirit that was incompatible with Gnosticism. Tatian then went on to say that the image represented the potential given to the human spirit to become like God, whereas the likeness was the realization of that potential, an order that reversed the Gnostic one.[6] Adam had sinned and turned away from God's plan for him, with the result that he lost the likeness of God and brought death into the human race instead of eternal life. As Melito of Sardis (c. 160) put it,

> For man was being divided by death;
> for a strange disaster and captivity were enclosing him,
> and he was dragged off a prisoner under the shadows of death,
> and desolate lay the Father's image.[7]

Melito tells us, almost in passing, that Adam was created in the image of the Father, another clearly anti-Gnostic statement that was to become axiomatic for future theological reflection. By the late second century the church was moving toward this view, but it was left to Irenaeus to give it a coherent theological foundation.

Irenaeus tackled the Gnostic challenge head-on and in the process produced a full-blown Christian answer to its claims. Where the Gnostics had interpreted the image and likeness of God in purely anthropological terms, Irenaeus added a soteriological and a Christological dimension. What this means is that the

[5] "Psychic" here translates the Greek *psychikos* and refers to the soul, as opposed to *pneumatikos*, which refers to the spirit.
[6] Tatian, *Oratio ad Graecos* 12.
[7] Melito of Sardis, *De Pascha* 56.

Gnostics saw the image and likeness as a description of what human beings are like as creatures, but did not take the matter any further than that. Some Christians, like Tatian, moved in the direction of seeing the image and likeness as holding out the promise of future development, but this had been cut short by the fall and it was not clear whether it would have any further role to play. Irenaeus picked up these threads and wove them into a complete theology by connecting the creation of Adam to the reality of the second Adam, who was the eternal Son of God, made in the image of the Father in heaven.

This approach put a whole new interpretation on the Genesis story. Now, Adam and Eve were seen as having been created in the image and likeness of the Son, who was in turn the image and likeness of the Father. By falling into sin, they lost the likeness but the image was indelible. When he came into the world as Jesus Christ, the Son brought the likeness back to the Adamic image and held it out as the promise of salvation to those who believed in him. As Irenaeus put it,

> The Son of God did not begin to exist [at his incarnation] because he was with the Father from the beginning, but when he became incarnate and was made man, he started the long line of human beings all over again and provided us, once and for all, with salvation. So what we lost in Adam, the image and likeness of God, we may now recover in Christ Jesus.[8]

Irenaeus gives the impression here that Adam lost both the image and the likeness, but elsewhere in the course of his argument he makes it clear that it was the likeness that disappeared, making the remaining image of less value and of no importance as far as salvation is concerned. The Christian was someone in whom the likeness of God was being restored to what the Father had originally intended, but this restoration could happen only in and through the one who had never lost the likeness in the first place. This doctrine formed the centerpiece of Irenaeus's grand scheme of *recapitulation* (Greek, *anakephalaiôsis*), which he based on what Paul said in Ephesians 1:3–10.[9]

Oddly enough, Irenaeus never mentioned the Pauline concept of the new creation, although much of what he had to say was closely connected to it. This may have been because he thought that salvation was the restoration of the world that already exists, not the production of something new, but as that is doubtless what Paul meant, this does not seem like the right explanation.

---

[8] Irenaeus of Lyon, *Adversus omnes haereses* 3.18.1.

[9] Ibid., 3.22.1. For a detailed study of this whole question, see Thomas Holsinger-Friesen, *Irenaeus and Genesis: A Study of Competition in Early Christian Hermeneutics* (Winona Lake, IN: Eisenbrauns, 2009). Also valuable is Eric Osborn, *Irenaeus of Lyons* (Cambridge: Cambridge University Press, 2001).

Irenaeus had to be careful not to fall into the Gnostic trap, where a phrase like "new creation" might be taken to mean rebirth in the world of the Father as opposed to ongoing life in the realm of the Demiurge, and it may well have been this danger that forced him to choose his words carefully. Here we come up against a problem that would often recur in Christian theology and is still something we have to grapple with today. In wanting to be faithful to the teaching of Scripture, Irenaeus found that he had to avoid certain biblical expressions because they were liable to be misunderstood. He was not in dialogue with the apostles, after all, but with a church that had been influenced by alien ideas that cloaked themselves in biblical terminology. To get around that, Irenaeus was forced to express the gospel in a way that would not be mistaken for something else, and this is a prime example of how he went about it.

Another aspect of recapitulation which may not be immediately apparent to modern eyes is that it is the way in which Irenaeus affirmed the biblical doctrine of predestination, another word that he avoided because of probable misunderstanding. In the ancient world it was widely believed that human beings are subject to fate (*moira*), which even the gods are powerless to overcome. In witnessing to the Gentile world, Christian writers were insistent that no one is subject to fate and that every human being has the free will to choose what is good if he so desires. They were primarily concerned to point out that the suffering and punishment that befell the wicked were justly deserved and that God could not be accused of having programmed people in advance, leaving them no option but to take what was coming to them. Justin Martyr expressed this feeling very well:

> Lest some suppose from what we have said that we claim that whatever occurs happens by a fatal necessity because it is foretold as known beforehand, let us explain what we mean. We have learned from the prophets, and we hold it to be true, that punishments, chastisements, and good rewards are rendered according to the merit of each man's actions. If this is not true, and if everything happens by fate, then there is nothing at all in our power. For if it is predetermined that this man will be good and the other man will be evil, neither is the first one meritorious nor the second culpable. Again, unless the human race has the power to avoid evil and choose good freely, no one is accountable for his actions.[10]

Justin recognized the reality of divine foreknowledge, but whatever that was, it did not relieve anyone of responsibility for his or her own actions:

[10] Justin Martyr, *Apologia I* 43.

> Men or angels who were foreknown to be unrighteous are not made wicked by God's fault. Rather, each one is what he will appear to be through his own fault.[11]

Irenaeus followed the same line of argument, but he was aware that God had a purpose in his creation, and that Adam's fall into sin was not his intention for the human race that he had made. As he put it,

> God has always preserved freedom and the power of self-government in man. Yet at the same time, he issued his own exhortations, in order that those who do not obey him would be righteously judged because they have not obeyed him. And those who have obeyed and believed on him should be honored with immortality.[12]

It was the Marcionites and other Gnostic heretics who objected to this by pointing to those passages of Scripture that speak of God hardening the hearts of those who are disobedient—Pharaoh in the first instance, because he would not let the people of Israel go, then the Jews who did not believe in Christ, and finally the world in general, which is blinded by its unbelief.[13] Irenaeus could not ignore this challenge, and he came out strongly in favor of the idea that God knew what he was doing, even though he was not responsible for the sinful actions of those who disobeyed him:

> Even at the present time, God knows the number of those who will not believe because he foreknows everything. He has given them over to unbelief and turned his back on them, leaving them in the darkness which they have chosen for themselves. So why be surprised that he did the same with Pharaoh and with all those who were with him?[14]

Irenaeus undoubtedly believed in predestination because he asserted that God was in control of the universe he had created, but in a context where the concept was closely associated with paganism and Gnosticism, he had to tread carefully in the way that he expressed it. This he did by saying that Adam was created in the image and likeness of Christ with the intention that he should do on earth what Christ did in heaven—rule over the world that had been given to him. Adam's failure to fulfill his commission could not be allowed to thwart God's eternal plan, and so Christ came to earth as the second Adam in order to get the human race back on track.

---

[11] Justin Martyr, *Dialogus cum Tryphone* 140.
[12] Irenaeus of Lyon, *Adversus omnes haereses* 4.15.2.
[13] See, for example, Ex. 7:13; Rom. 11:7; 2 Cor. 4:4.
[14] Irenaeus of Lyon, *Adversus omnes haereses* 4.29.2.

Did Irenaeus believe that everyone would be saved? No. At first sight it might seem logical that if every human being has perished because of the sin of the first Adam, so every human being ought to be saved by the obedience of the second. It would even have been possible for him to quote the apostle Paul in his defense if he had chosen to say that.[15] Instead, he was very clear about the fate reserved for the wicked:

> God has prepared darkness suitable for those who oppose the light, and he has afflicted those who refuse to obey him with an appropriate punishment. . . . He has prepared eternal fire for the Devil, who is the chief of the apostates, and for those who revolted with him.[16]

Reconciling God's foreknowledge with human freedom is ultimately impossible within the limited sphere of human perception, so it would be most unfair to blame Irenaeus for having failed to do so. What matters is that he allowed for both God's controlling power and man's responsibility for the choices he makes, and that he sought to reconcile them by using the concept of the image and likeness of God. In Irenaeus's view, it was because Adam possessed that image that he was free to make the choice he did. Interestingly, that awareness shifts the mystery of the fall from the mind of God to the mind of man. The question is not so much why God created a human being, knowing that he was going to disobey him, as why the man so created chose to exercise his freedom in a way that effectively killed it. What God did was consistent with his nature, but what Adam did was not. It is not the divine plan that is incomprehensible but the human response to it, and it was this that Irenaeus wanted the Gnostics to see.

Once that principle was established, the pattern of salvation became clear. God could not ignore what man had done to himself, nor could he accept that his purpose for his creation could be thwarted by human sin. For Irenaeus, recapitulation was the obvious answer, because only the eternal image and likeness of the Father could put right the disobedience of Adam, the temporal image of the eternal. As long as the image and likeness of God in man were interpreted in this way, the solution to human sin proposed by Irenaeus would dominate Christian theological thought.[17] It was only when Augustine of Hippo (354–430) proposed that the image of God in man was the image of the Trinity and not of the Father through the Son that a new approach to the

[15] He could have interpreted 1 Cor. 15:22 ("As in Adam all die, so also in Christ shall all be made alive") in this way, but significantly, he did not do so.

[16] Irenaeus of Lyon, *Adversus omnes haereses* 4.40.1.

[17] See, for example, Tertullian, *Adversus Marcionem* 2.5, who says essentially the same thing.

mystery of predestination became necessary. By then, of course, the threat of Gnosticism had receded and Augustine was not obliged to combat Marcion in the way that Irenaeus and his contemporaries had to do.

The Call to Holiness

An essential ingredient of the process of recapitulation was the need for human beings to be conformed to the divine likeness. This was not an automatic result of professing faith in Christ but involved a process of transformation similar to what later generations would call "sanctification." In the nature of things, some people would be more successful than others in this endeavor. Irenaeus was well aware of that and believed that the bliss of heaven would be calibrated to take account of it. In a curious interpretation of the words of Jesus, he explained what would happen as follows:

> As the elders say, those who are deemed worthy of an abode in heaven will go there, others will enjoy the delights of paradise, and others will possess the splendors of the city [the New Jerusalem]. For everywhere the Savior will be seen, depending on the worthiness of those who see him. There is this distinction between the habitation of those who produce a hundredfold, and those who produce sixtyfold, and those who produce thirtyfold.[18] The first will be taken up to heaven, the second will dwell in paradise, the last will inhabit the city. It was for this reason that the Lord declared, "In my Father's house are many mansions . . ."[19]

How would a believer become worthy of his reward? The answer was that because God is holy, he wants us to be holy too.[20] Holiness was understood as a form of ritual purification, similar to what was found both in Judaism and in many pagan cults. In Rome it was especially linked to chastity, a connection that grew stronger as time went on. We now know that this was a misinterpretation of what the New Testament meant by holiness, but in purely historical terms there is no getting away from the fact that the early church thought in that way. It was the Father's will for us that we should be holy; it was the purpose of his plan that he would provide the means by which that goal might be reached; and it was the duty of the believer to put that plan into practice.

We can see how this worked by looking at the writings of Tertullian, the earliest Latin-speaking Christian writer and the one whose works have survived more prolifically that those of any other writer before the fourth

[18] See Matt. 13:23, the outcome of the parable of the sower.
[19] Irenaeus of Lyon, *Adversus omnes haereses* 5.36.1–2. The biblical quote is from John 14:2.
[20] See 1 Thess. 4:3.

century.[21] Tertullian is especially valuable as a witness to early Christian beliefs because he wrote on a vast array of subjects, ranging from highly complex philosophical questions to very practical matters about how Christians should behave in civil society. He believed that Christians should imitate the holiness of God himself, and his practical treatises tell us how he thought this should be done. The basic principle was that the righteousness of the Christian ought to exceed that of the scribes and Pharisees, as Jesus had taught his disciples.[22] But what did that mean? As far as Tertullian was concerned, Christians were supposed to be even stricter in their observance of the law than the Pharisees were and not allow any concessions to the weakness of the flesh. As he put it in his exhortation to the martyrs who were awaiting their fate,

> We know from what the Lord said that "the spirit is willing but the flesh is weak."[23] Let us not use this as an excuse [to justify our weakness]. . . . He put the spirit first in order to show that the flesh ought to be subject to it as the weaker to the stronger, so that it might be strengthened by it. The flesh may be afraid of the sword, the cross, the beasts, the fire, and the torture, but the spirit reminds both itself and the flesh that these things, hard as they are, have been calmly accepted and even sought after, not only by men but also by women.[24]

The call to holiness was given to male and female alike, so it is not surprising that the demand for it came across most insistently in the realm of sexual ethics. Tertullian found himself in the curious position of approving matrimony as a social institution but rejecting sexual intercourse. Roman religion was an ancestor cult, but one in which the guardians of Rome were the vestal virgins, whose celibacy was held to be especially holy. An ancestor cult can thrive only if there are children to preserve it, so Tertullian's desire to break with that led him to disapprove of having children. There was also the snag that if Christ were to return when a woman was pregnant, she would be pregnant in eternity, and who would want that? As he said to his wife,

> Why did the Lord say, "Alas for women who are pregnant and for those who are nursing infants in those days"?[25] It must have been because he was saying that when we are set free from the cares of the flesh having the burden of

[21] Tertullian lived in Carthage, in the Roman province of Africa.
[22] Matt. 5:20, quoted in Tertullian, *De monogamia* 7.
[23] Matt. 26:41.
[24] Tertullian, *Ad martyras* 4.
[25] Matt. 24:19.

> children will be an inconvenience. . . . At the sound of the trumpet widows will spring forth unencumbered . . . with no burdensome fruit of marriage heaving in their wombs.[26]

From Tertullian's point of view, living in the end times made it unnecessary to have children because there would be no future, and to think otherwise was a sign of lack of faith. To the obvious objection that Jesus had permitted marriage and procreation, Tertullian replied that this was because he was living in a time of transition from the old to the new dispensation of God's law, and that temporary provisions had to be made to account for the weakness of the flesh that could not make the change overnight. But after 160 years, the coming of the Holy Spirit, and the imminent end of the world, it was time to annul those transitional provisions and apply the full force of the new law—from now on, no sexual intercourse and no children![27]

In saying this, of course, Tertullian was rejecting one of the most basic commandments of God in the creation account. Was it right to be fruitful and multiply and replenish the earth? Why had God told Adam and Eve to do that if by doing so all they were doing was bringing more sinners into being? To this Tertullian had a ready answer: the law of God was unchanged, but there were different dispensations under which different conditions might apply. Jesus had indicated as much when he told his disciples that Moses had permitted divorce. Divorce was wrong, but the hardness of the people's hearts was such that it could not be completely abolished. In those circumstances it was better to regulate what was in principle undesirable, in order to limit the degree of damage it caused. However, when the perfect came, as it did in Christ, the imperfect was done away with and so Jesus quite logically withdrew the Mosaic permission to divorce. All Tertullian was saying is that the same principle applies across the board!

It is often assumed that Tertullian adopted his strict position because of his attraction to Montanism, a millenarian sect from Asia Minor. It does not take much effort to show, however, that this was not the case. Tertullian was attracted to the Montanists, not because he agreed with them but because they agreed with him! He did not change his views because of their influence; indeed, his views were much more mainstream than many people today would like to believe. As for being a rigorist, the generations who followed him were often stricter than he was.[28]

---

[26] Tertullian, *Ad uxorem* 1.5.

[27] Tertullian, *De monogamia* 14.

[28] After all, he never discounted matrimony for the spiritually minded, a directive that they gladly followed.

To be holy was to be celibate, regardless of what God had permitted people to do before the coming of Christ. The Christian life was meant to be a foretaste of heaven, and in heaven there is no giving or taking in marriage, let alone procreation. My identity has been established by the Father who calls me his child, not because he has made me by sexual intercourse but because he has brought me into new life by the indwelling presence of his Holy Spirit in my life. When we think of the third person of the Trinity today, our emphasis usually falls on the word "Spirit," but for Tertullian it lay in the word "holy," because that is the attribute of God that he shares with us as adopted children of the heavenly Father.

It was the work of the Father to raise us to a spiritual level where we would see that it is our duty to have spiritual children, men and women who profess faith in Christ. Evangelism, not sexual intercourse, was the way the church was meant to grow and spread. But evangelism was to be of a very special and particular kind. The Greek word for "witness" is *martys* or *martyr*, and its modern meaning shows very clearly what professing faith in Christ entailed. It was the blood of the martyrs that was the seed of the church, said Tertullian in one of his most famous remarks.[29] His was not a world of youth ministries and family services with church weddings every Saturday in the summer season. The members of Tertullian's church were made of sterner stuff than that. They were spiritual warriors on their way to heaven, and baptism was their oath of allegiance to the army of Christ. This was taken quite literally—the Latin word for "oath" is *sacramentum*, a term that for a long time was applied primarily to baptism as the sacrament of adherence to the Lord of hosts.

The significance of martyrdom in the early church is best understood as the outworking of the doctrine of predestination. The Son of God had come into the world to die, and his followers were not greater than he was. "Take up [your] cross and follow me" was the message of Jesus,[30] and for the early Christians that was the destiny that awaited them. Paul said that those who suffered with Jesus would also reign with him.[31] The heavenly courts were populated by those who had shed their blood in honor of the Lamb who was slain from before the foundation of the world.[32] As far as Tertullian was concerned, this is what it meant to worship the Lord in spirit and in truth—these were the kind of people the Father wanted to worship him. Today we would say, "Put your money where your mouth is," but the early Christians expressed the same thought as, "Lay down your life for what you believe in." Then as now, if you are sincere, that is what you will do.

[29] Tertullian, *Apologeticum* 50.13.
[30] Matt. 16:24.
[31] 2 Tim. 2:12.
[32] Rev. 13:8.

How could a Christian know who was chosen for salvation and who was not? The ultimate test was martyrdom. Tertullian expressed this very clearly when he wrote,

> God had foreseen the weaknesses inherent in the human condition . . . that faith, even after baptism, would be endangered, that most of those who had obtained salvation would be lost again . . . and have to be sought for over mountains and through forests, and be carried back on his shoulders. He therefore provided a second source of comfort, a last chance of help, which is martyrdom and the baptism of blood that sets a man free from danger.[33]

Those who were prepared to lose their lives for the sake of Christ demonstrated beyond doubt that they had been called to share in the marriage supper of the Lamb. They were in heaven, pleading with the Father around the throne for us, begging that he might shorten the time for the sake of his chosen ones. Those who had avoided martyrdom, on the other hand, were suspect. Failure to suffer when suffering was what was expected was a bad sign. People like that were possibly two-faced and unreliable—certainly they were not guaranteed a place in heaven. Yet it was often they who ended up as the leaders of the church, if only because the others were dead or behind bars.

When Christianity was finally legalized, in the fourth century, this problem came out into the open and produced a split in North Africa, where the followers of a certain Donatus claimed that those who had avoided martyrdom were not true Christians. Elsewhere Donatism was avoided, but the thought behind it did not go away easily. It is no accident that when persecution ceased the question of predestination suddenly surfaced, because it was no longer clear who would go to heaven once martyrdom had ceased to be an option.

Martyrdom was a reality for many early Christians, but in the nature of things it was usually only a future hope. Persecutions were sporadic and seldom comprehensive, though none could be sure that it would not happen to them at some point. What they did know was that their daily prayer and spiritual exercises were a preparation for the day when they might be called into the arena to do battle with the lions. In the words of Ignatius of Antioch,

> Allow me to become food for the wild beasts, through whom I will be able to reach God. I am God's wheat, so let me be ground by the teeth of the wild beasts, in order that I may become the pure bread of Christ.[34]

---

[33] Tertullian, *Scorpiace* 6.

[34] Ignatius of Antioch, *Epistula ad Romanos* 4. Ignatius wrote this when he was on his way to Rome to be martyred, sometime around AD 108.

Communicating with their heavenly Father was a vital part of this process, a providential blessing that God had given to his people as they trained for battle. In theory, providence could be traced back to Noah, to whom God had pledged that he would never again flood the earth because of mankind's sinfulness.[35] In practice, it was God's promise that he would protect his people and keep them until they could fulfill the tasks appointed to them in his eternal plan. The world would continue to exist until the fullness of the Gentiles had been gathered in, a process that Christians like Tertullian believed was on the verge of completion. Was it not true that the name of Christ had been proclaimed to the whole of the known world?[36] Were there not believers in such far-off places as Britain and Ethiopia? The preaching of the gospel had been made possible by the Father's providential stay of execution, but the end was drawing near. Today was the day of salvation, and if those who heard his voice did not respond to him they would soon learn to regret it.

Modern scholars have often claimed that the early church settled down over time and abandoned the hope of the imminent return (*parousia*) of Christ, but if that was true of later ages, when Christianity became part of the established order of things, it was not true of this early period. Every new soul won, every new land evangelized was one step closer to the consummation of all things, to the outworking of the providence that made the ingathering of the elect possible.

[35] Gen. 9:11–15.

[36] Tertullian, *Apologeticum* 37.4.

7

The Work of the Father and the Trinity

The Father and His Creation

When Jesus spoke about his Father, it was often in the context of what the Father was doing, either in and through the Son or independently of him. Given that he taught that the only way that anyone could know the Father was by the Son's revelation of him, it is hardly surprising that he would also explain how the Father was using him to fulfill his purposes. Jesus emphasized that he and the Father were one, so that whoever has seen him has seen the Father also.[1] He had to say this, because if the Son were inferior to the Father, he would have been unable to reveal him, at least not fully. If the Father was God in a unique sense, the Son would be someone less than God and therefore unable to reveal the Father as he really is, since no inferior being could portray the absolute One in the fullness of his being. The Son therefore had to be equal to the Father in order to be able to reveal him, but did this equality of being mean that the Son must also do whatever the Father does—and vice versa?

This is a difficult question to answer, because if the Father can do things that the Son cannot do, the question of whether the Son is truly God is bound to arise. Anyone who attempts to demonstrate the Son's divinity will almost certainly insist that the Son can do everything the Father does in order to avoid the conclusion that he is intrinsically inferior to the Father and therefore not really God. But if what the two persons do is identical, how can they be distinguished from each other? If we experience the same divine power at work in exactly the same way, what difference does it make if we attribute it to the Son, to the Father, or to both? To turn the argument for the Son's divinity around, will we end up saying that the incarnation, crucifixion, and resurrection of the Son are the work of the Father too, on the ground that the work of one is the

[1] John 10:30; 14:9.

work of the other? And if we get to that degree of union, is there any reason to distinguish the Father from the Son at all? Are they not just different names for the same God? Surely we have to find something that is particular to each of the persons if we want to avoid confusing them with each other!

The leaders of the early church were well aware of this problem and tried to solve it in different ways. Common to their way of thinking was what we now call "monarchianism." The word derives from "monarch" but in the sense of "single source" rather than the sense of "single ruler" with which we are more familiar today.[2] Some form of monarchianism was all but universal among Christians before AD 200 because of the close association they made between the Father and the absolute being of the One God. Whatever God did they automatically ascribed to the Father, and the question of how (or to what extent) the Son and the Holy Spirit were involved in the Father's activities was a secondary issue, if not a complete afterthought. The divine act of creation, for example, was generally understood to mean that the Father made the world, using the Son and the Holy Spirit as his agents. In this way, the supremacy of the Father was affirmed but the divinity of the other persons of the Trinity was also safeguarded because they belonged to the Creator and were not creatures like everything else. This monarchian tendency was pervasive, but it took different forms, some of which were more aberrant than others.

At one extreme was what we now call "modalism." This was the belief that, although God manifested himself under different names, behind the scenes he was the same being who was playing different parts in a cosmic drama. In the role of Creator, God appeared as the Father of his creatures. In the role of Redeemer, he came into the world as Jesus Christ, who was known as the Son. Finally, in the role of Sanctifier, he now comes into the hearts of believers as the Holy Spirit. The names emphasize the different aspects, or modes, of his divine activity in the world. From that perspective, it seemed perfectly logical to insist that the Father had suffered and died on the cross, because the Father was just another name for the Son. It might even be said that this represented a first attempt at systematizing theology by linking the different activities of God as the work of a single being. Creation and redemption, which to the Gnostics appeared to be incompatible, in fact belonged together because they were just different aspects of the work of the One God.

Today we call this view "patripassianism," which is the belief that the

---

[2] The dual meaning occurs in Greek because the Greek word *archê* can mean either "beginning" or "rule." Compare the English word "archetype," in which both Greek definitions are present. An archetype is both the original form and the one that sets the standard, or rule, for all subsequent copies.

Father suffered and died on the cross. Most of what we know about it comes from Tertullian, who condemned it unreservedly. In his words,

> The Devil has counterfeited the truth in different ways. Sometimes he has claimed to be defending it when in fact he has been destroying it instead. He claims that there is only one Lord, the Almighty Creator of the world, but only in order to make a heresy out of his oneness. He says that the Father himself came down to a virgin, that he himself was born of her, that he suffered—in a word, that he was Jesus Christ.[3]

Tertullian believed that the Devil's agent was a certain Praxeas, who had gone from Asia Minor to Rome sometime in the late second century in order to denounce the Montanists and introduce his patripassian ideas at the same time.[4] As Tertullian somewhat colorfully put it, when he got to Rome, Praxeas drove out the Paraclete (Holy Spirit) and crucified the Father![5]

Why did Tertullian denounce what must have seemed to many to be an eminently sensible interpretation of what Paul had said to the Corinthians: "In Christ God was reconciling the world to himself"?[6] One answer is that in the New Testament accounts of the crucifixion, the Father and Son appear at their most distinct. As Jesus said to the Father, "Not my will, but your will be done."[7] This would have made no sense if the Son had been talking to himself! Tertullian seems to have been more bothered by Praxeas's refusal to accept the authenticity of the Montanist prophecies. These claimed to come from the Paraclete, but in Praxeas's monotheism the Paraclete could only be either the One God or a diabolical imposter, and there is little doubt which of the two Praxeas thought he was. From Praxeas's point of view, recognizing the Montanists might have entailed rejecting the gospel on the ground that God had moved on from what he had done as the Son and was now doing a new work in the form (mode) of the Holy Spirit.

The rest of the church rejected the Montanist claims but was just as horrified by patripassianism as Tertullian was. This was because almost all the early Christians clung to the belief that the Father remained transcendent throughout the earthly life of the Son, whose saving work was done at the Father's

[3] Tertullian, *Adversus Praxean* 1.

[4] Praxeas is otherwise unknown, and his name may be a pseudonym, meaning "busybody" in Greek. Perhaps he is to be identified with Noetus, a man who held similar opinions and who was refuted a generation later by Hippolytus. The Montanists followed Montanus (c. AD 170?), who claimed to have revelations from the Paraclete (Holy Spirit) telling him that the New Jerusalem would descend at a village called Pepuza in Phrygia. The prophecies obviously failed to materialize, but the Montanists practiced a rigorous spiritual discipline that impressed many, including Tertullian.

[5] Tertullian, *Adversus Praxean* 1.

[6] 2 Cor. 5:19.

[7] See Matt. 26:39.

behest but was not something that the Father was directly involved in. As the one who represented the divine being in the Trinity, the Father had to remain what God was—invisible, immutable, and impassible. Had he abandoned that role, not only would he have ceased to be himself but the entire Godhead would have been dissolved, making nonsense of any notion of salvation. After all, there could hardly have been a redemption if the Redeemer had been forced to commit suicide in order to achieve it!

Patripassianism was easy to refute and was never a widely held doctrine. It was an extreme form of a more sophisticated kind of modalism, known today as "economic Trinitarianism." The name comes from the Greek word *oikonomia*, which means "order" or "arrangement" and was usually translated as "dispensation," the term most often preferred today. Economic Trinitarianism was a series of attempts to explain the work of God in the world according to the different dispensations of his revelation. The Old Testament was the age of God the Father/Creator, the Gospels were the story of God the Son/Redeemer, and the post-Pentecostal period belongs to God the Holy Spirit/Sanctifier. The Trinity was confined to the world of time and space as the explanation of how God revealed himself in different ways according to the dispensation of his power that was then in operation. But beneath the surface there was only the one God, and so neither the Son nor the Holy Spirit had any real or objective existence of their own. This was probably what Praxeas taught, in which case Tertullian's portrayal of it is a simplified caricature that suited his rhetorical purpose very well. If that is correct, then patripassianism never existed at all but was invented by Tertullian to show where economic Trinitarianism would lead if it were taken to its logical conclusion.

Tertullian's treatise against Praxeas has survived and has become an important source for Christian doctrine, not because of the circumstances that led to its composition, which were soon forgotten, but because it forced a leading Christian theologian to grapple with the underlying problems that the church was facing in trying to express its faith. In the course of doing this, Tertullian exposed the weakness of the theology he had inherited and proposed a new construction of it, one that has remained foundational for Christian belief ever since.

What Tertullian inherited was the standard assumption that the Father was God in the absolute sense, and that the Son and the Holy Spirit derived their existence from him. They were not created out of nothing in the way that the world was, but were produced from inside the being of God, where they had always resided. The Son was the eternal Word (*logos*), of whom John had written:

> In the beginning was the Word, and the Word was with God, and the Word was God. He was in the beginning with God. All things were made through him, and without him was not any thing made that was made.[8]

To explain how this had occurred, second-century Christian apologists had recourse to a concept that was already familiar to them from the teaching of the Stoics. This said that the *logos* existed in two forms. Inside the supreme being it was the "indwelling *logos*" or *logos endiathetos*. In this form it determined what the supreme being was like—a totally rational mind that governed all things. Stoics did not believe that this *logos* had created the world out of nothing, but that was of secondary importance to them. Their main concern was to insist that the *logos* was the organizer who had established what we would call the scientific laws governing matter and who kept them in being as a *cosmos*, or universal order. In order to do this, the indwelling *logos endiathetos* had had to express itself as the *logos prophorikos*.[9] When applied to the teaching of the New Testament, this doctrine was adapted to the figure of the Son, who had dwelt inside the Father from all eternity but who was brought forth at the beginning of creation in order to execute the great work that had been planned by the Father. The Holy Spirit had also been present inside the Father and first appeared in a distinct form at the creation, but beyond acknowledging this, little or nothing was said about it in the second century.[10]

A doctrine of this kind enabled the early Christians to attribute the work of creation to Christ, who as the Father's *logos prophorikos* had fashioned the universe according to the rational principles that the Father continued to uphold by his power. From this perspective the Son was merely an agent acting on behalf of the Creator, who was (and remained) the Father alone. As an explanation for the origin and order of the universe this *logos* doctrine might have been sufficient, but the Christian faith went well beyond that. The message of the gospel was not just one of creation and preservation but also one of redemption and eventual transformation. After explaining the Son's role in creation, John had gone on to say that the Word became flesh, with the express purpose of dying in that flesh in order to pay for the sins of the whole world.[11] This was well beyond the scope of the Platonic *logos prophorikos* which, like the supreme being from which it sprang, was immortal and impassible. If Christ were this *logos*, and if he had also suffered on the cross, then patripassianism

---

[8] John 1:1–3.

[9] Intimations of this can be found in Justin Martyr (d. 165). See Erwin R. Goodenough, *The Theology of Justin Martyr* (Jena: Frommannsche Buchhandlung, 1923), 151. The distinction first appears in Theophilus of Antioch, *Ad Autolycum* 2.1, and again in Irenaeus of Lyon, *Adversus omnes haereses* 2.12.5.

[10] See Gen. 1:2 for evidence that the Spirit of God was present at creation.

[11] John 1:14; 1 John 2:2.

was inevitable because the *logos* was inherent in God and his death would automatically entail the death of the Father to whom he belonged.

The great struggle against the Gnostics made it clear that for orthodox Christians there could be no disjunction between a transcendent dimension of eternal tranquility and the world of time and space. Different though they were, they were united in the mind and work of the God who was their Father as well as their Creator. At the same time, God the Father was a transcendent being who was quite different from the world he had made. Even his human creatures, who were made in his image and likeness, could not approach him directly but could experience him only in and through the work of the mediators whom he had used to make the world in the first place. These mediators were revealed to Christians as the Son, who became a man in Jesus Christ, and the Holy Spirit, who was sent after the Son's return to heaven to dwell in the hearts of believers. Christians recognized that the Son and the Holy Spirit were both divine, so that through them they had an access to the Father that would otherwise have been denied them, but precisely how the three related to each other remained undefined.

Every attempt to explain how the Son and the Holy Spirit belonged to the being of God started from the axiom that God, considered as the one supreme being in himself, was the Father. The Son and the Holy Spirit were part of him, but it was here that the difficulties began. In the earliest phase of Christian theology, they were identified as the Word and Wisdom of God, inherent in the Father's being and brought forth by him in order to create the world. This way of thinking made it possible to distinguish them from creatures without compromising the unity of God. If asked whether the Son and the Holy Spirit were just as eternal as the Father, the answer could be either yes or no, depending on how the matter was perceived. If the Father was thought of as always possessing his Word and his Wisdom, then the answer was yes—there was never a time when God was without these aspects of his being. But if asked whether the Son and the Holy Spirit could be identified as such from the beginning, the answer might well be no, because they were concealed in the inner being of God and not openly manifested as they would be later on.

However the question was approached, the Son and the Holy Spirit came into focus only in relation to the creation, even if they had existed in some form beforehand. In later times it became customary to regard the Word as the Son and the Holy Spirit as the Wisdom of God, but this was not a distinction found in the New Testament[12] and was not characteristic of second-century

[12] 1 Cor. 1:24.

writers. The following statement by Justin Martyr may be taken as typical of the period:

> The Scriptures say that before the creation God gave birth to a beginning, a rational power proceeding from himself, who is called either the Holy Spirit, or the Glory of the Lord, or the Son, or Wisdom, or an angel. . . . He can be called by all those names because he ministers to the Father's will and was begotten of the Father by an act of his will.[13]

The use of the imagery of generation suggests that it is the Son that Justin has in view here, and the general context supports that view, but the freedom with which he uses the different names interchangeably must not be underestimated. In the very next paragraph he goes on to talk about "the Word of Wisdom, who is himself the God who is begotten of the Father of all things, the Word, the Wisdom, the Power and the Glory of the Begetter" and claims that it is he who has revealed himself to mankind in the Scriptures. The biblical text which Justin cited to back up his assertion was Proverbs 8:22, "The Lord made me the beginning of his ways for his works," a phrase put in the mouth of the divine Wisdom, but which he and the later tradition understood to be a reference to the first appearance of the Son.

Language of this kind may suggest that the Son was somehow inferior to the Father, but that is not at all what Justin was trying to say. In his mind, the appearance of the Son was to be compared to the lighting of one fire from another. As he said,

> When one fire is kindled from another, the fire from which it is kindled is not diminished but remains the same, while the fire that is kindled from it exists independently, without diminishing the original fire.[14]

Statements of this kind can easily be multiplied from other second-century authors. Tatian said almost exactly the same thing, though he made a sharper distinction than Justin did between the Word as latent in the mind of the Father and his creative activity, which he described as the Father's "primordial work," using the same term as Paul employed in Colossians 1:15 to describe the Son as the "firstborn" of all creation.[15] Similar views were expressed a little later by Theophilus of Antioch and Athenagoras of Athens.[16] Theophilus stands out

[13] Justin Martyr, *Dialogus cum Tryphone* 61.
[14] Ibid., 61.
[15] Tatian, *Oratio ad Graecos* 5.1.
[16] Theophilus of Antioch, *Ad Autolycum* 2.10; Athenagoras of Athens, *Supplicatio* 10. Athenagoras also quoted Prov. 8:22 in support of his argument.

from the others because it was he who identified the Son with the Word and the Holy Spirit with Wisdom, basing his distinction on the Septuagint translation of Psalm 33:6.[17]

How the Holy Spirit was supposed to fit into this vision of the Creator God is not altogether clear. That the second-century writers mentioned above believed in a Trinity of divine identities is plainly stated in a number of passages. Justin Martyr said that Christians worshiped "the Father of righteousness, the Son who came forth from him and taught us these things, and the prophetic Spirit."[18] Athenagoras picked up the same theme and claimed that Christians knew what kind of fellowship the Father has with the Son and also what the Spirit is, concluding that "all three are both distinct and united."[19] What they do not tell us is precisely how they saw the Spirit acting in a way that was distinct from the Son. Sometimes Justin attributed the inspiration of the Old Testament prophets to the Holy Spirit, but on other occasions he claimed that they received their message from the Word, so it would appear that the Son and the Spirit performed many of the same functions, although only the former became incarnate in Jesus Christ.[20]

As we might expect, the Trinitarian theology of Irenaeus was more sophisticated than that of his immediate predecessors, but continuities with them are not hard to find in his work. Like Justin, Theophilus, and Athenagoras before him, Irenaeus gave full play to the work of the Son and the Holy Spirit in the divine act of creation, going so far as to call them the "two hands" of the Father and insisting that only these hands were capable of making man in the image and likeness of God:

> It was not angels who made us, for they had no power to make an image of God, nor was it anyone but the Word of the Lord. . . . For God had no need of such beings to accomplish what he had determined to do, since he had his own hands to do it. The Word and Wisdom, the Son and the Spirit, by whom and in whom he freely and spontaneously made all things, were always present in him.[21]

Irenaeus also had a clearer idea of the distinctiveness of the Holy Spirit, claiming that just as God was rational and had his Word (*logos*), so he was also

[17] This is not apparent in the Hebrew, nor in English translation, where the ESV reads, "By the word of the LORD the heavens were made, and by the breath of his mouth all their host."
[18] Justin Martyr, *Apology I* 6.
[19] Athenagoras of Athens, *Supplicatio* 12.
[20] See, for example, Justin Martyr, *Dialogus cum Tryphone* 4 (where the Spirit inspired the prophets) and compare it with *Apologia I* 33, where this function is attributed to the *logos*.
[21] Irenaeus of Lyon, *Adversus omnes haereses* 4.20.1.

spiritual and had his Spirit to demonstrate that.[22] The Word revealed God by becoming a man, but the role of the Spirit could not be overlooked, because without him it was impossible to recognize the Word. As he put it,

> The knowledge of the Father is the Son, and the knowledge of the Son of God can only be obtained through the Spirit. It is according to the Father's good pleasure that the Son ministers and dispenses the Spirit to whomever the Father wills.[23]

Irenaeus had no doubt that the Son was fully God and implied that the Spirit was too, though he did not explicitly say so.[24] It was Tertullian who took matters to the next stage and developed a doctrine of the Trinity that was no longer dependent on the axiom that only the Father was truly God. More clearly than any of his predecessors, he realized that the Son could not be seen as an extension of the Father's divinity, so that whatever he did was essentially the work of the Father. The illogicality of patripassianism made it clear to him that the Son had to be capable of doing things (like dying for the sins of the world) that the Father could not do. At the same time, the Son's divine status had to be affirmed, since otherwise he would be no more than a creature, which the opening verses of John's Gospel explicitly denied. Tertullian also realized, perhaps because of his involvement with the Montanists, that the specific work of the Holy Spirit had to be acknowledged and affirmed.

A Trinitarian doctrine that made the Son and the Spirit equally dependent on the Father was always liable to confuse them with one another, or worse still, make the Spirit appear to be unnecessary. Montanism, with its emphasis on the Paraclete who had come to make holiness a reality in the church as it awaited the imminent return of Christ, provided a rationale for the distinctive work of the Holy Spirit that was lacking in most second-century Christian writing, and Tertullian made the most of it. His pro-Montanist stance was repudiated by the rest of the church, but so successful was the Trinitarian doctrine that emerged from his pen that both it and his pro-Montanist statements survived the censor's knife. This was unique in the history of the early church and tells us more than anything else just how important Tertullian's contribution was.[25]

Tertullian approached the doctrine of the Trinity by saying that the oneness

[22] Irenaeus of Lyon, *Demonstratio* 5.

[23] Ibid., 7.

[24] Ibid. See *Adversus omnes haereses* 5.12.2, where Irenaeus said that God's Spirit was constantly welling up from his being.

[25] Compare what happened to Origen's works after he was condemned for heresy three centuries after his death. Most of them were destroyed, and today we have only a small selection of his total output, whereas Tertullian's works have survived more or less intact.

and the threeness in God belonged to different categories of thought. In other words, the three coexisted with the one and did not derive from it, as the traditional picture had claimed. As a being, or substance, God is one, and totally unlike any of his creatures. But in our experience of him, he is three—Father, Son, and Holy Spirit.[26] Since there was no fixed terminology to express this distinction, Tertullian used various comparisons to make his point. In tabular form they were as follows:

Oneness	**Threeness**
status	*gradus*
substantia	*forma*
potestas (power)	*species*

Tertullian treated these terms as contrasting pairs. The first and third appear to have been his own invention, but the opposition between form and substance was a commonplace of ancient thought, going back at least as far as Aristotle (384–322 BC). It is therefore interesting to note that although Tertullian settled on *substantia* as an adequate way of expressing the real existence of the divine unity, he did not contrast it with *forma* in his explanation of the Trinity. Instead, he chose the word *persona*, which had never been used in any philosophical system and which he derived from the theater, by way of the Roman law courts. As Tertullian understood the term, a *persona* was much more than a mere *forma*—he was an identifiable agent who could act in relation to other similar agents.[27] From the evidence of the Bible, this was obviously true of the Father, Son, and Holy Spirit within the Godhead, just as it was true of all human beings, who were created in the image and likeness of God.[28] *Persona* could therefore be used not only as a way of linking the three members of the Trinity to each other, but also as a way of tying us humans to them.

Most importantly, Tertullian believed that the three divine *personae* were just as objectively real as the one divine *substantia*. Indeed, at first he did not hesitate to call both the Son and the Holy Spirit "substances" in their own right, and it was only as his thought developed and he saw more clearly the need to distinguish the oneness of God from the three persons that he began to reserve the term *substantia* for the former and to use the phrase *substantiva*

[26] Tertullian, *Adversus Praxean* 2. See also his *Apologeticum* 21.
[27] Tertullian, *Apologeticum* 7.
[28] In Roman law, anyone who could either bring an action or be sued in court was a *persona*, which excluded women, children, slaves, and noncitizens. In contrast to that, Tertullian's definition extended the term to include all human beings.

res ("substantive thing") when referring to one of the latter.[29] The importance of this is that the Father was a *persona* like the Son and the Holy Spirit, and not just the personification of the divine *substantia*. Thus the traditional belief that the divine persons were to be derived from the substance of God, which is basically what the different kinds of monarchianism taught about the origin of the Son and the Holy Spirit, was excluded.

One important consequence of this development was that once a clear distinction between the one divine substance and the three equally divine persons was established, the work of the Father could no longer be regarded as the work of the One God without qualification. Instead, it had to be interpreted as the work of one person of the Trinity in relation to the others. Whether and how far the Father's work extended to the human race and the rest of the created order was more problematic, because the Father was not known outside the Godhead except in and through the Son and the Holy Spirit. Following New Testament practice, the Father might continue to be called "God" without further qualification, but this was because of his role within the Trinity with respect to the other two persons, and not because he was identified with the divine substance in a way that the Son and the Holy Spirit were not. It would take many centuries for the church to sort out the confusion that this distinction caused in minds that had grown accustomed to regarding "God" and the Father as synonymous, but the basic lines on which Trinitarian theology would proceed were now established. Tertullian's formula of three persons in one substance would stand the test of time, not just because of its brilliance but also because it expressed the essential teaching of the Bible and gave Christians a viable framework in which to develop their theological thought.

The eventual success of Tertullian's formula was possible because it translated Hebrew (biblical) thought into categories that the Gentile world could recognize and accept. From the beginning, the church had been faced with the competing claims of two very different worldviews, one which it had inherited from the Old Testament and the other which it had to address as part of its evangelistic mission. Its long-term aim was to persuade the Gentile world to accept the Hebraic way of looking at the universe, but that could not be accomplished until that world had been converted to Christ. In order to achieve that, the church had to speak to Gentiles in a way they could understand, giving new meanings to familiar words and reshaping the way those words were used so as to make them conform to the teaching and thought world of the Jewish Scriptures.

[29] Tertullian, *Apologeticum* 26.

In the process, biblical concepts (like the eternity of God) that had been assumed rather than expressly stated, and Gentile vocabulary (like "substance") that had never been precisely defined, fused into the new discipline of systematic Christian theology. Words that had long been in common use became technical terms to describe a God whose being and acts could be known, sometimes with great precision, not by the analysis of an inert object but by participation in a living relationship with him. From beginning to end, it was the objective reality of the biblical God that determined how the vocabulary used to describe him would be developed and understood. The suitability of any particular term would be decided not by the way it was used in everyday life (or in ancient Greek philosophy) but by the degree to which it could be applied to the character of the living God who revealed himself in Scripture. Christians might debate whether the words *persona* and *substantia* were the best ones to use for this purpose, but they agreed about the realities they were trying to describe. If they had doubts about the words it was because they felt them to be inadequate to express their experience of God, which in some respects went beyond anything that human language could communicate. In the end they compromised, accepting that no words could ever be wholly adequate but agreeing to use those that were available to them, since otherwise they would be unable to say anything about the God whom they worshiped and adored. As Augustine (354–430) would later put it,

> I am attempting to say things that cannot really be said as they are thought by a man, or at least not as they are thought by me. When we think about God the Trinity we know that our thoughts are quite inadequate to their object and incapable of grasping him as he is. . . . I ask my readers to forgive me whenever they notice that I am trying and failing to say something which they understand better, or which they are prevented from understanding because I am expressing myself so badly, just as I will forgive them when they are too slow to understand what I am saying.[30]

The Divine Hierarchy

Tertullian's achievement was magnificent, but it was in advance of his time. For reasons that we can only guess at, his lead was not generally followed by his contemporaries or by the generations that immediately succeeded them. Perhaps this was because he wrote in Latin, which was little known in the Greek world and seldom translated. It may also be that his sympathy for Montanism made him suspect, though there was little sign of that in the

[30] Augustine of Hippo, *De Trinitate* 5.1.

writings of Cyprian or Augustine, both of whom borrowed extensively from him. Or it may be due to the fact that he was a North African provincial, though Carthage was hardly a backwater of Roman culture during his lifetime. Whatever the reasons, the rest of the Christian world developed its theology along lines that were more "conservative," in the sense that they stood in clearer succession to what Irenaeus and others like him had said. This tendency is very clear in the work of Hippolytus of Rome (d. 235?), who repeated the teaching about the indwelling Word (*logos endiathetos*) familiar since the time of Justin Martyr.[31] He also stated that God (i.e., the Father) brought forth his Word and used him to create the universe, which he subsequently decorated with the aid of his Wisdom.[32] When God decided to save mankind, he made the Word visible as his Son, a relational term which Hippolytus thought was appropriate to use only after the incarnation.[33] When speaking of the relationship between God and his Word, Hippolytus explained this view as follows:

> When I speak of "another" I do not mean two Gods, but rather light from light, water from its source, a ray from the sun. For there is only one power (*dynamis*), which flows out from the All (*to pan*). The All is the Father, and the power issuing from it is the Word. . . . Everything that exists [comes into being] through him, but he comes from the Father alone.[34]

Perhaps the most interesting thing that Hippolytus said is that there are two "persons" (*prosôpa*) in God, which together with the Holy Spirit made up the Trinity.[35] What Hippolytus understood by "person" is not altogether clear, but the names "Father" and "Son," unlike Spirit, certainly indicate what we would call personal beings. It is possible that he picked up the term "person" from Tertullian, but if so it was most likely at second hand, since Tertullian would never have countenanced leaving the Spirit out of the equation! In any case, Hippolytus was the first Greek-speaking theologian to use the word in something approaching its later (and now orthodox) sense, even if his particular usage raises more questions than it answers.

Hippolytus is also known for his refutation of modalism. He wrote a tract against Noetus, a man who held views very similar to those of Praxeas (and who may even have *been* Praxeas) from which the statements made above are taken, and also against Sabellius, another little-known heretic who was to give

---

[31] Hippolytus of Rome, *Philosophumena* 10.33.1.
[32] Hippolytus of Rome, *Contra Noetum* 10–11.
[33] Ibid., 15.
[34] Hippolytus of Rome, *Contra Noetum* 11.
[35] Ibid., 7.

his name to modalism in later centuries.[36] What Sabellius believed is hard to say, but it appears that he took up the views of Noetus and refined them in order to meet objections that others had raised to his rather simplistic presentation. It is possible that he thought of the Father as the ultimate essence of God, who projected himself as the Son when he wanted to redeem the world and then as the Spirit when he wanted to dwell in the hearts of men.[37] If so, then he was closer to the Greek theologians of the second century than either Noetus or Praxeas was, but as our sources are all secondhand, late, and confused, it is impossible to say any more than that. Later opponents of Sabellianism would accuse those who held that doctrine of teaching that the "persons" of the Trinity were no more than masks (the original meaning of the word *prosôpon*), but there is no indication that Sabellius ever said that, and given that the word was used quite freely by his antagonist Hippolytus, it seems unlikely that he did so. Sabellianism is thus best regarded as a construct made up by later controversialists and not as a real third-century theological position.

Whether Hippolytus knew Tertullian's work is uncertain, but the same cannot be said for Novatian (c. 250), another member of the Roman church who wrote slightly later, and in Latin. Novatian definitely knew Tertullian's work, as well as that of Hippolytus, but the way in which he appropriated it shows how hard it was for him and his contemporaries to break with established tradition. Novatian was happy to call both the Father and the Son "persons," and he saw quite clearly that these terms could not be restricted to the time and space framework of creation. If the Father was the Father in eternity, as he obviously was, then he must always have had a Son.[38] But the Son is not of the same being or substance as the Father. Whatever divinity he possessed was given to him by the Father and reverted to the Father when his work was accomplished. As for the Holy Spirit, Novatian said simply that every spirit is a creature, leaving us to assume that he put the third person of the Godhead in that category too.[39] Novatian's claim to be Trinitarian was very thin, but the fact that he was accepted as such in his own time (and is sometimes still so regarded now) shows how little Tertullian's theology had sunk in, a generation after his death.

Both Hippolytus and Novatian lived and worked in Rome, though neither was a member in good standing of the local church there. Nevertheless, there is every indication that they faithfully represented the kind of theology that

[36] Hippolytus of Rome, *Philosophumena* 9, 11–12.
[37] Epiphanius of Salamis, *Adversus haereses* 62.1.
[38] Novatian, *De Trinitate* 31.
[39] Ibid., 7.

dominated the church in the imperial capital. Rome was exceptionally slow to adopt new ideas and practices, a tendency that could still be observed hundreds of years later. There is certainly no sign that Rome set the tone for the rest of the Christian world or exercised any authority over it at this time, so we should not make too much of the fact that Tertullian's ideas seem to have had little impact there.

It might be possible to explain Tertullian's lack of influence by referring to his uncertain ecclesiastical status, but that excuse hardly applies to men like Clement of Alexandria and Origen, who by this time had already developed an alternative approach to Trinitarian theology that was initially no more influential at Rome than Tertullian's was. Clement inherited the tradition of Justin and Irenaeus but developed it in a way that clearly reveals the influence of contemporary Platonism. For Clement, the Father was the supreme being that can be known only through the Word, who was both his image and his mind. Like the Platonic *nous*, this Word was multifaceted, containing within himself both the Father's ideas and the Father's power to give life to the created universe.[40] The Holy Spirit was the light emanating from the Word, that gives understanding to those who believe. He was also the power of the Word at work in the world, drawing men and women to God.[41] What we see here is the emergence of a hierarchy that starts with the supreme being, who is above and beyond human perception, and then moves down, first to the supreme mind and then to the experience that we can have of that mind at work in our lives. The important point to notice here is that Clement saw no contradiction between this schema and the teaching of the New Testament. As far as he was concerned, all truth is one, and if Platonism and the Bible can be reconciled, then so much the better. Later generations would go much further than Clement did, but he can fairly claim to have been the founder of what was to become the great tradition of Christian philosophical theology.

However, it was in the work of Origen that the Eastern theological tradition reached a level of sophistication that could compare with that of Tertullian. To explain the Trinity, Origen started with his belief that the Father alone was God-in-himself (*autotheos*). But because his power must always have been fully exercised, this God had brought forth other beings that were equally eternal with himself.[42] The *autotheos* does not relate to these beings directly, but only through a mediator, who is his Son. Being outside time and space, the Father gave birth to the Son in a timeless dimension of reality, so it cannot be said

[40] Clement of Alexandria, *Stromateis* 4.156.1–2; 5.1.3; 7.2.2.
[41] Ibid., 6.138.1–2; 7.9.4; 7.79.4.
[42] Origen, *De principiis* 1.2.10; 1.4.3; 2.9.1.

that there was ever a time when he did not exist.[43] This Son was a second God (*deuteros theos*), who was like his Father in every respect except that his divinity is derived from someone other than himself. That meant that the Son was eternally subject to his Father as a second-in-command, employed to do things in and with the created order that the transcendent Father either could not or would not do himself.

Origen's understanding of the Father-Son relationship was remarkably similar to what we find in contemporary Platonism, but unlike Clement, he realized that the Trinity could not be reduced to the level of philosophical speculation. What made the difference was the Holy Spirit, who was,

> the most honorable of all the beings brought into existence through the Word, the chief in rank of all the beings originated by the Father through Christ.[44]

There is a clear order of precedence here that is hierarchical in structure, but despite that, Origen insisted that Father, Son, and Holy Spirit were three "identities" (*hypostases*) in the eternal being of the one God. As with *substantia* in Tertullian, the word *hypostasis* as used by Origen was at first ambiguous, in that it could refer to the one divine being as well as to the three identities, but as his thought matured it came to be used more of the three than of the one, which was characterized as an *ousia* ("being") instead. Here it is important to note that whereas, for Tertullian, *substantia* gravitated toward the divine unity, for Origen the equivalent Greek word *hypostasis* evolved more in the direction of designating the three. Thus over time what had originally been one concept came to be used to designate either the one or the three in God, depending on which tradition one was following and what language one was using. The underlying reality was the same in both systems, but the terminology developed differently and was to cause confusion and even scandal later on, when customary usage on both sides had hardened and the cultural areas served by Latin and Greek went their separate ways and gradually lost touch with one another.

Origen firmly believed that Father and Son were one in the unity of the Godhead, but he understood this unity to be a matter of shared mind and will rather than something forced on them by unavoidable necessity.[45] This sense of individual freedom and voluntary participation in a common divinity was important to him because it underscored the freedom believers have in Christ, but it does make it hard for us to follow his logic in describing who and what the Son is in relation to the Father. On the one hand, the Son was begotten, not

[43] Origen, *Contra Celsum* 5.39.
[44] Origen, *Commentarium in Iohannis Evangelium* 2.10.75.
[45] Origen, *Contra Celsum* 8.12.

created, and shared the Father's nature.[46] On the other hand, there is no sign that Origen thought of the Son as being "consubstantial" (*homoousios*) with the Father, and the impression we get from his writings is that he regarded them as substantially different.[47] As for the Holy Spirit, Origen saw him as deriving from the Father through the Son, who was the immediate source of his power and attributes.[48]

In what was to become the classic text of Greek Trinitarian theology, Origen defined the Father as the "fountainhead of deity" and added,

> The Son and the Spirit are also divine in their own degrees. By derivation they possess all the characteristics of deity. They do not belong to the world of the creatures but co-operate with the Father and communicate [to those creatures] the divine life that flows from him.[49]

In other respects, however, Origen's theology would later be superseded. His notion that there was a world of spiritual beings coeternal with the Father came from Platonism and not from any Christian source, and it would later be abandoned as heretical. Likewise, his insistence that prayer could be directed only to the Father, because he alone was truly God whereas the Son was just the agent who did the Father's bidding, was subsequently abandoned as implying that the Son and the Holy Spirit were inferior divinities.[50] Particularly troubling to later generations was his statement that the Father's action extends to the entire universe, whereas the Son's is limited to rational creatures and the Spirit's to those who are being sanctified.[51] Such a narrowing down of the Son's and the Spirit's activities might appear to correspond to what we observe in the life of the church, but it is a clear denial of the work that all three undertook in creation and cannot be accepted as a truly orthodox expression of Trinitarian theology.

How far Origen's theology influenced the wider church and how far it merely reflected what was already being said is hard to determine. There were a number of theologians of the following generation who appear to have had the same ideas but who expressed them somewhat differently. For example, Theognostus, who ran the catechetical school at Alexandria (fl. c. 250–280),

[46] Origen, *Commentarium in Iohannis Evangelium* 2.2.16; 2.10.76; 19.2.6.
[47] A surviving fragment of his commentary on Hebrews suggests that he did accept the *homoousios* doctrine, but as this has come down to us only in a Latin translation that was made by Rufinus, a man concerned to "clean up" Origen's more dubious theological remarks, we cannot accept it as genuine without hesitation. See J.-P. Migne, ed., *Patrologiae cursus completus: Series graeca*, 162 vols. [hereafter PG] (Paris: 1857–1886), 14, col. 1308.
[48] Origen, *De principiis* 2.10.76.
[49] Ibid., 2.3.20.
[50] Origen, *Contra Celsum* 7.57.
[51] Origen, *De principiis* 1.3.8.

said that the Son's "being" (*ousia*) was derived from the Father's, which suggests that he was using the word as the equivalent of Origen's *hypostasis*, and the same thing can be found in the language used by his successor Pierius (fl. c. 280–300).[52] Writing a little later, Gregory Thaumaturgus of Pontus (d. 270?) is even reputed to have said that the Son was a "creature" (*ktisma, poiêma*), using language that recalled Origen but that would be denounced as heretical a generation later.[53]

One man who definitely did take up where Origen left off was Dionysius of Alexandria, who wrote sometime around AD 260 to a group of churches in Libya that had apparently fallen into a form of Sabellianism. Determined to stamp that out, Dionysius was very forceful in his denunciation and occasionally left himself wide open to the charge that he had exaggerated the counterposition to the point of heresy. One of the churches he attempted to discipline complained to Rome about his behavior, accusing him of making so great a separation between the Father and the Son that the latter was regarded as a creature.[54] Our knowledge of this incident comes mainly from Athanasius (296–373), who tried to exonerate him at a time when such views were clearly regarded as heretical, and it was embarrassing for Athanasius to have to acknowledge him as one of his predecessors as bishop of Alexandria. Athanasius also tells us that Dionysius's position caused shock waves at Rome, where another Dionysius replied to him, accusing him of virtual tritheism because of his insistence that Father, Son, and Holy Spirit were three equal *hypostases* in the one being of God.[55] Dionysius of Rome evidently did not realize how the word *hypostasis* had developed in a direction very different from what he and others in the West had learned from Tertullian's use of *substantia*. It seems that Dionysius of Alexandria was eventually able to explain himself and escape condemnation, but that such misunderstandings could occur did not bode well for the future.

This incident, obscure as it now is, shows us that the churches in the Western half of the Roman empire were beginning to drift away from those in the Eastern half, because their theological assumptions were different. The Westerners had always started from the fundamental unity of God and tried to make room in that for the existence of three realities that they had come to call "persons," mainly because there did not seem to be any better word to describe them. In the East however, the dominance of the concept of a divine hierarchy made it easier

[52] This at least is what the ninth-century Byzantine patriarch and scholar Photius said about them. See his *Bibliotheca* 106, 119.
[53] He is cited to this effect by Basil of Caesarea, *Epistula* 210.5.
[54] Athanasius, *De sententia Dionysii* 5, 9–10.
[55] Athanasius, *De decretis Nicaenae synodi* 26.

to conceive of the distinctiveness of the three identities (*hypostases*) in God. But that concept came at the cost of developing a model in which the second and third rungs of that hierarchy could easily slip down into the realm of the creatures, made by the Father in order to bring the rest of the world into being. To that extent, the doctrine of the Trinity continued to be bound up with the work of the Father, however hard Christian theologians tried to ensure that the Son and the Holy Spirit stayed on the right side of the abyss that separated the Creator from his creation.

The Eclipse of the Father

If the history of Christian theology had ended in the third century, there would be no doubt that the person and work of the Father would be regarded as its most fundamental feature. The God of the Old Testament had been successfully identified with him, and Gnostic challenges to the unity of creation and redemption had largely been overcome. Both the Son and the Holy Spirit were understood to have come from him in some way, even if the details were not as clear as they would later become. The Fatherhood of God was celebrated by Christians because it combined the universal nature of his creation with the special relationship that he had established with his chosen people in Christ. It was a theme that would continue to resonate in Christian theology as long as paganism was a serious threat, and the great creeds of the early church open with a clear acknowledgment of the Father's person and work: "I believe in God, the Father Almighty, Maker of heaven and earth," as the Apostles' Creed puts it and as Christians have confessed ever since.

Yet from the standpoint of the modern world, and indeed for many centuries now, the picture looks very different. Books on the work of Christ and the work of the Holy Spirit are easy to find, but who has written anything on the work of the Father, considered as one of the Trinity and not just as a personification of the divine? It is hard not to conclude that once the Gnostic danger was over, the doctrine of the Father ceased to be a major theological concern. What was said of him in the creeds was concise but it remained unproductive, especially when compared with the other persons of the Godhead. For centuries debates about the person and work of the Son raged furiously and split the church, as did arguments about the person and work of the Holy Spirit. But of the Father, little or nothing has been said, and he has seldom (if ever) been the focus of theological discussion. Why is this?

This relative lack of interest in the person and work of the Father is certainly not due to a dearth of biblical material. As we have seen, the New Testament is full of statements, many of them attributed directly to Jesus, about who the Father is and what he has done. That he is a person who can act independently of the other members of the Trinity seems obvious if we read the Gospels, yet little has been done to expound this, and at least one theologian has seen fit to draw attention to the curious absence of the Father from modern theological discourse.[56]

The explanation for this has to be sought in the course which the development of Christian theology followed in the late third and early fourth centuries. The question that came to the fore at that time concerned the identity of the Son. Could the Son be divine but at the same time inferior to the Father? That he was subordinate to the Father was universally agreed, but was this because he voluntarily submitted to the Father's will or because he was a lesser deity and had no choice but to do what the Father wanted him to? Once it was decided that the relationship between the Father and the Son was determined by mutual agreement and not by some essential inferiority in the latter, it became problematic to admit that there were things the Father could do that the Son could not do. Those who denied that the Son was equal to the Father were quick to pounce on anything of that kind and use it as evidence that the Father was God in a way that the Son was not, a conclusion that the orthodox leadership of the church sought at all costs to avoid.

Thus it was that anything that suggested independent action on the Father's part was glossed over or reinterpreted in a way that avoided making the Son inferior to him. Sometimes, as we have seen, this led theologians to say that the Son concealed the Father's will from his disciples by feigning ignorance, an awkward solution that called the Son's honesty (and the nature of our relationship with him) into question. It must have seemed odd that the one who called himself "the way, and the truth, and the life"[57] should lie in order to protect the Father's secrets, but given the nature of the theological dilemma that controversy over the Son's divinity posed, even that was preferable to risking the danger that an open acceptance of the Father's uniqueness might have posed.

The end result was that the person and work of the Father was effectively eclipsed. He was still the Almighty, but so too were the Son and the Holy Spirit. He remained the Maker of heaven and earth, but the Son was also the Creator, as too (though less obviously) was the Holy Spirit. There was nothing the Father did or could do that the Son did not share, and given the doubts that were raised about the Son's divinity, it seemed only natural to put the emphasis on him rather than on the Father. There, by and large, it has remained ever since.

[56] Thomas A. Smail, *The Forgotten Father* (London: Hodder & Stoughton, 1980).
[57] John 14:6.

The time when argument raged fast and furious over the Father now seems almost impossibly remote and unfamiliar, so much so that it is now hard to imagine how Jesus could have excited so much opposition when he called God his Father. Whether this descent into relative oblivion has been a good thing or not is hard to say, and it is not the historian's task to pass judgments of that kind. All we can do is record the fact of what has happened and move on to examine how Christian theology actually developed over the course of time.

PART FOUR

The Person of the Son

8

The Challenge of the Incarnation

The Church Confronts the Roman World

With the advantage of hindsight, we can see that around AD 250 a marked change took place in the social status of the Christian church. Before AD 200 it had been a relatively small and cohesive group in which it was possible for someone like Irenaeus of Smyrna in Asia Minor to become the bishop of Lyon in southern Gaul (now France). Christian literature, such as it was, consisted mostly of occasional pieces written to address particular problems that had arisen within the church. Pagan Romans were aware that Christians existed, but they did not know much about them. The emperor Nero (54–68) had launched the first great persecution against them in AD 64, apparently because he needed someone to blame for having started the great fire of Rome. In AD 111 Pliny the Younger, who was the governor of Bithynia for that year, wrote to the emperor Trajan (98–117), asking him to confirm whether he had handled accusations brought against local Christians in the right way. Pliny gave a brief description of Christian worship but he seems to have been ignorant of the church's beliefs, beyond its devotion to Christ (of whom Pliny knew almost nothing) and its rejection of idolatry. The modern reader gets the impression that Pliny was puzzled as to why such a peculiar sect should be regarded as dangerous, but he never questioned the imperial policy that had outlawed it.[1]

On the Christian side, the Roman empire was a fact of life but its officials were avoided as much as possible. Luke the Evangelist mentioned that Jesus was born in Bethlehem because the emperor Augustus (27 BC—AD 14) had ordered a census to be carried out that forced Joseph and Mary to return

[1] Pliny the Younger, *Epistulae* 10.96–97. Pliny's letter quickly became well known, and Tertullian discusses both the letter and Trajan's reply, pointing out that it was illogical of the emperor to insist that Christians should not be hunted down like criminals but at the same time to approve punishing them as criminals if they were denounced and confessed. See *Apologeticum* 2.6–9.

to their ancestral city in order to be counted.[2] Later on, Pontius Pilate, the Roman governor of Judea, put Jesus to death, though only at the behest of the Jewish establishment whom he needed to appease.[3] It is ironic that, because of that, the unbelieving Pilate, who wanted nothing to do with Jesus, became the only human being (other than the Virgin Mary) to be commemorated in the great creeds of the early church! The apostle Paul also had occasional brushes with the Roman law, but these were circumstantial, and Paul used his Roman citizenship as a device for escaping from the clutches of his Jewish adversaries, who in his eyes were far more dangerous.[4] On the whole, Paul had a favorable attitude toward the state authorities and urged his congregations to respect them as God's agents for administering justice.[5] If the tradition that he was put to death in Rome is correct, it would have been because he was accidentally caught up in Nero's persecution, not because the empire and the church had come into open confrontation with each other.

Even when the empire turned against the Christians, there was still a residual appreciation for it among the latter. Irenaeus, for instance, said that "because of the Romans the world is at peace. We walk on the highways without fear and sail wherever we want to."[6] Tertullian wrote,

> If we look at the empire, it is surely obvious enough that it is daily becoming better cultivated and more populous than it used to be. Everywhere in the world is now accessible, well known and open to trade, . . . everywhere there are houses, inhabitants, stable government and civilized life.[7]

It was not until the middle of the second century that Christians began to address the problem of persecution and question its rationale. Unlike the Jews, who had fomented a series of rebellions against the empire and suffered the consequences, Christians never opposed the state directly. Instead, they attacked the spiritual foundations on which it rested in a series of writings known as "apologies" or explanations of the Christian faith. The first of them was composed by Justin Martyr about AD 150, and it was followed by a number of others. The gist of these apologies was that Greco-Roman polytheism made no sense, that there was one supreme God and Father of mankind, and that he had revealed himself in his Son, Jesus Christ. The Son had become a man in order

---

[2] Luke 2:1.
[3] Matt. 27:15–23.
[4] Acts 16:37–38; 22:25–29; 25:10–12.
[5] Rom. 13:1–7.
[6] Irenaeus of Lyon, *Adversus omnes haereses* 4.30.3.
[7] Tertullian, *De anima* 30.

to pay the price of human sin, to overcome the power of death, and to make it possible for anyone who believed in him to have eternal life. Transcendent monotheism was the essential foundation of this belief, because anything else would have called its universal application into question, but the person and work of Jesus were equally central to it. It was not enough to believe that there was only one God and to keep his law in the way that the Jews tried to do, even if that were possible. Mankind's separation from God was the result of sin, and that sin had to be paid for by the death of the only sacrifice capable of wiping it out—the voluntary death of the Son of God on the cross.

As the apologists saw it, Jews and Romans had come together in an effort to stamp out God's revelation of himself in Christ, but his resurrection from the dead showed that they were powerless to do so. Instead of moldering in a borrowed tomb, the Son of God ascended into heaven, took up his seat at the right hand of the Father, and ruled the world whether the imperial authorities liked it or not. Pagan Rome had been defeated by a higher power, and its people had to choose which one they would serve. Either they could submit to Christ and his rule, in which case the empire would be transformed into a new kind of society, or they could resist to the bitter end and perish as Nineveh and Babylon had perished before them. What the apologists hoped was that the emperors could be persuaded to see the error of their ways and repent before it was too late. They wanted to live in an empire that recognized the true God and allowed them freedom of worship. It never seems to have occurred to them that if that were to happen, Christianity would displace paganism as the state religion and the church would be forced to play a political role that it did not desire and for which it was not designed.

Whether anyone in authority at Rome read these apologetic works is impossible to say. They were usually addressed to the emperor, but there is no sign that they affected official policy, so even if they were read at the imperial court, they made no impact. Only among some Greek philosophers was there any reaction, and this was generally hostile. Sometime around AD 160–180 a man called Celsus wrote a diatribe against Christianity, in which he endeavored to prove that the new faith was nonsensical. Celsus started with the Christian claims and refuted them one at a time by arguing that they lacked inner coherence and made no sense. Unfortunately, everything we know about Celsus comes from Origen, whose great book *Against Celsus* was a full-scale rebuttal of his position. The scale of Origen's reply shows us how seriously he took the challenge, and it shows that he was successful, because his work survives whereas that of Celsus has been lost.

Origen was writing at least a generation after Celsus, so we are not dealing here with a living controversy between two contemporary thinkers. But Celsus, or the views he represented, must have had some influence, since otherwise Origen would hardly have felt the need to answer him at such length, nor is it likely that his refutation would have been preserved. *Against Celsus* is best seen, not as a personal confrontation between a Christian theologian and an individual Greek philosopher, but as a frontal assault by the church on the basic assumptions of pagan culture. As with the earlier apologists, the heart of Origen's argument was to be found in the person and work of Jesus Christ. He did not ignore the philosophical questions of monotheism, but it was on history and prophecy that he rested his case. Christianity stood or fell with Christ, the man whose life and work ensured that belief in him was not just a satisfying intellectual theory but a life-changing experience. As Origen put it,

> God forbid that anyone who has received the love of God in Christ Jesus should be unsettled by the words of someone like Celsus. When Paul gave a list of all the things which separate men from the love of Christ and from the love of God in Christ Jesus, . . . he did not include arguments [of those opposed to Christianity] among them. What he said was, "Who shall separate us from the love of Christ?"[8]

While this struggle was brewing in the Greek-speaking world, a parallel (though in some ways quite different) development was taking place in the Western, or Latin-speaking half of the empire. Tertullian, whose corpus of writings has survived almost intact, represents it better than any other individual. He composed defenses of the faith along the lines already laid down by Justin Martyr and others, but he also wrote philosophical treatises like his great book on the soul (*De anima*), in which he engaged the leading pagan thinkers of his time. Tertullian was fully aware of the social and political dimensions of Christian faith and wrote about them to an extent that was unparalleled for centuries afterwards. Everything from loyalty to the emperor, the legitimacy of military service, the nature of public entertainment (an important socializing force in the ancient world) and matrimonial practice came within his purview. Like Origen, he understood that becoming a Christian was not just an intellectual decision or a spiritual experience but a total transformation of heart, mind, and life. That this would lead to conflict with existing customs was only to be expected, but for Tertullian that was part of a wider battle for the triumph of the gospel.

As Tertullian and his Christian contemporaries saw it, the Roman world

[8] Origen, *Contra Celsum*, preface, 3.

was corrupt and decaying, having long since abandoned the high ideals of the ancient founders and heroes of Rome. The empire lacked the strength to renew itself from within because its spiritual foundation was incoherent and essentially false. The pagan pantheon could expand to allow for belief in anything and everything, but as Tertullian realized, the result was that it ended up believing in nothing. It could only unite to persecute the Christians who were challenging its principles and demonstrating by their lives and behavior that their way was superior. The imperial establishment could take fright and react against this but it had nothing to put in its place. In Tertullian's words,

> There was an old decree that made it unlawful for a god to be created by an emperor without the senate's agreement. . . . This is another point that supports our contention. With you pagans, divinity is something decided by human desire, so if a god is unpopular with men he will not be a god for long. But it is men who ought to be pleasing to God! Tiberius, in whose reign the name "Christian" made its appearance in the world, informed the senate of the events that had been reported to him from Palestine, events that had revealed the truth of the divinity of Christ, and he had a favorable opinion of it. But the senate, without bothering to check the reports, voted against [making Christ a god].[9]

Tertullian knew that political infighting was hardly the way to decide the truth or falsehood of a claim to divinity, but Rome had nothing better to offer. It is not that alternatives were not suggested. In the philosophical sphere, Plotinus (200?–270) revamped Platonism and turned it into a quasi-religion that he thought could compete with Christianity. Neoplatonism had considerable success among the intellectual elite and was to prove influential in the development of Christian theology in later centuries, but it never acquired a wider social appeal, and in the end its followers were isolated and defeated.

Meanwhile, the spiritual crisis of the empire was getting steadily worse. The emperor Aurelian (270–275), perhaps the most competent Roman ruler of the third century, tried to introduce a form of imperial monotheism in the form of a cult of the sun god, but this suffered from obvious weaknesses and looked pathetic when put next to Christianity. The sun could be called a life-giving force, but it remained an impersonal object with no power to move the human spirit. It had no sacred texts to back it up, its priests were few, and the temples that existed or were built in its honor were public monuments more than centers of worship. Furthermore, the sun cult had no monopoly, if only

[9] Tertullian, *Apologeticum* 5.1–2.

for the obvious reason that rain is also necessary for survival, and sun and rain are mutually incompatible! Too much sun was not good for anyone. Aurelian's cult was nonsense and got nowhere, its only legacy being the compromise introduced by the emperor Constantine in AD 321, when he declared that the day of the sun, which also happened to be the day of Christ's resurrection from the dead, would be declared a weekly holiday.

Aurelian did not last long, but one of his successors, Diocletian (285–305) made a serious effort to restructure the Roman empire before it was too late. Diocletian did not have a religious alternative to propose, but he saw Christianity as a major menace to the established order and embarked on what was to be the longest and most devastating persecution of the church in ancient times. From the Roman point of view it is easy to see why he felt compelled to do this. The church was highly organized with a network of congregations stretching across the empire and a leadership which (by and large) coordinated its activities across vast distances. Heresies came and went but they failed to break the church's cohesion, while schisms were localized and contained. Every year the church grew stronger, and by AD 300 it had put down roots that made it virtually ineradicable. In the West, the Greek language gave way to Latin, while in Egypt and Syria Greek had to share the public space with Coptic and Syriac (a form of Aramaic). This linguistic diversification was a sure sign that the faith was penetrating beyond the urban elite to the local populations, whose remoteness from the centers of power made them relatively less vulnerable to persecution. In the countryside it was often easy to hide until the storm blew over, and that is what many people did. What is interesting is that our evidence for this comes not from reports by the state authorities who were frustrated in their attempts to eradicate this esoteric sect, but from Christian leaders who did not know how to handle the runaways when they sought to be readmitted to the church after the danger of persecution had passed.

At the official level, Christians were unfazed by martyrdom and even welcomed it as an opportunity to demonstrate that their faith was worth dying for. Apostate Christians gained nothing. They were not honored by the Roman empire as loyalists to its cause, and they were obviously rejected by the church, whose martyrs became its uncontested heroes. For the state to create more of them was counterproductive, though (as is often the case) it took the authorities a long time to realize the folly of their ways. This, however, was not because Christians did not point it out to them. One of the standard arguments they used against persecution was its complete wrongheadedness. Christians were loyal subjects of the empire who wanted nothing more than to live in peace with it. The pagan habit of blaming natural disasters and other calamities on them was absurd. If the Romans understood themselves, as their philosophers kept urging them to, they would become Christians, because (as Tertullian put it) the soul is naturally Christian, having an innate knowledge of God that paganism had only corrupted and obscured.[10]

In the final analysis, the Roman empire was a state that was persecuting its best citizens, a sure sign of its fundamental weakness. It could only be a matter of time before rival candidates for the imperial throne would seek Christian support, and if they were successful, they would be obliged to reward the church accordingly. The way for this was prepared by the desert queen Zenobia of Palmyra, who rebelled against Rome in AD 260 and conquered most of Syria. When she occupied Antioch, she appointed the Christian bishop there, Paul of Samosata, governor of the city in her name, the first recorded instance of a Christian leader occupying a secular office. Zenobia must have felt that Paul would be loyal to her because the church would have no desire to return to the persecuting empire, but here she was only half-correct. Paul himself remained faithful to her, but the church declared him a heretic and deposed him in 268. Paul was censured because his understanding of the divinity of Christ was inadequate, but it is possible that some of the animosity toward him sprang from opposition to his involvement with Zenobia. Four years later, when Aurelian recaptured the city, Paul disappeared from view, but the Antiochene church was initially well treated, which may have been a tacit acknowledgment of its underlying loyalty to Rome.[11]

Later on, the titanic struggle of Constantine to secure the empire for himself, which began in 306 and was not finally over until 324, brought him into an alliance with the church. Claiming to have seen a burning cross in the sky the night before the battle that would decide the fate of Rome, Constantine had the Christian emblem painted on his soldiers' shields as a talisman for the fight. When they won, he prepared an edict legalizing Christianity and an informal alliance with the church was soon in place. It cannot have escaped Constantine's notice that, after the seizure of Rome, it was the eastern half of the empire that he had to conquer, and that Christians formed a substantial percentage of the population there. By making concessions to them which could not be implemented in a given province until he took it over, Constantine created a climate of expectation that could no longer be reversed or denied. It is pointless to speculate how far his own involvement with Christianity was genuine rather than merely political; what matters from the historian's point of view is that it was irreversible. By the time the war for the empire was over,

[10] Ibid., 17.6.

[11] The evidence, such as it is, comes from Eusebius of Caesarea, *Historia ecclesiastica* 7.30.19–21.

the church had come out of the shadows and was on the point of becoming a pan-imperial institution. Christianity was not yet the official state religion—it would not be given that status until 380—but it could no longer be ignored or suppressed. For better or for worse, it had become (and would remain) central to the fortunes of the Roman empire and the embryonic European nations that would emerge from its ruins.

What Constantine did not realize was that by associating himself with the Christian church he was also committing himself to involvement in its internal affairs. He probably knew little about them at first, but if so, his ignorance would soon be dispelled. In North Africa, the official recognition of Christianity produced a schism that was to last for centuries. It came to be associated with a man called Donatus, who was one of its leaders.[12] To the Donatists, the true church would always be persecuted because it was fundamentally at odds with the world. If persecution ceased, this could only be because the church had lost its cutting edge and forces hostile to the gospel had taken it over. For people who still had a vivid memory of martyrdom and who were appalled at the way in which those who had denied their faith were being readmitted to the church once the danger had past, the appeal of Donatism was obvious. The foolish decision of some church leaders to attack them by using imperial troops to crush their rebellion only provided grist to their mill, and once new martyrs had been created, healing and reconciliation became impossible. Donatism was not a heresy, but it forced Christians to ask questions that had never surfaced before.[13] What was the church? Who could belong to it, or more to the point, who ought to be excluded from it?

The church was the body of Christ, so any answer to such questions would inevitably bring him into the picture. Was his body pure and sinless as he himself was, or was it marked with all the sins and failings of mankind, for which he had suffered and died? How could sinful human beings be united to Christ, and what happened to them when they were? Were Christians sinners who were saved in spite of themselves, or were they people who had been enlightened by the truth and were now expected to live according to its light? Finding answers to these questions would not be easy, but that is what the church now had to do.

The emergence of the church into the public arena made Christians realize that there is more to Christianity than simple monotheism. The incarnation of the Son of God as Jesus of Nazareth is the church's central doctrine. Everything

[12] The story is told by many ancient sources, the most important of which is Optatus of Milevis, *De schismate Donatistarum*. For a modern interpretation of Donatism, see William H. C. Frend, *The Donatist Church*, 2nd printing (Oxford: Oxford University Press, 1971).

[13] A "heresy" is a movement that denies some aspect of Christian doctrine. The Donatists did not do that, but they cut themselves off from the church in what is known as a "schism."

else derives from it, makes sense only because of it, and has to be believed along with it. Christ's supernatural conception in the womb of a virgin undergirds his divinity and would be superfluous otherwise. Once it is accepted that Jesus was God in human flesh, his teaching, miracles, and resurrection from the dead all flow naturally and without difficulty. If he is God, his teaching is automatically divine both in content and in authority. Miracles would come naturally to him, because God is not bound by the constraints of the created order. If the incarnation was permanent, the resurrection of the body would be inevitable because God cannot die. Only his crucifixion would be hard to explain, because God is not subject to pain or suffering inflicted by outside forces that have no power over him. It is therefore not surprising that theologians soon found themselves arguing over how an impassible God could suffer and die for sins that were alien to his nature. It was a question that could not be avoided, because in his death and resurrection lay the promise of our salvation and eternal life with him in heaven.

In a sense, this problem had already surfaced in debate with the Gnostics. One of the problems the Gnostics faced was how to account for the historical figure of Jesus Christ. If his Father dwelt in a realm far above that of the created order, how was it that Jesus had access to him in a way that no one else did? Was he a creature made by the Demiurge or was he something different, an emissary from the world of the Father who was not contaminated by the limitations of matter, time, and space, and therefore immune to suffering? For a truly consistent Gnostic, the only possible answer was that he was a revelation of the Father who had entered the world made by the Demiurge but who was not part of it. Jesus Christ was not a human being at all, but a heavenly figure who appeared in human form, rather like a higher kind of angel. The miracles that he did were demonstrations of this because they showed how he could overrule the Demiurge by transcending the laws of the created universe. Needless to say, every action of this supernatural figure would have the character of the miraculous, and the Gnostic Gospels give full rein to this tendency. In one of them the child Jesus made clay birds and then turned them into real ones, and anyone who got in his way suffered the consequences.[14] Other accounts are less flamboyant than this, but the impression that Jesus was a man not of this earth is unmistakable.

Today we call this tendency "docetism" from the Greek verb *dokei* ("it seems") because the essence of it is that Jesus was a divine apparition and not a real man. How widespread or influential docetism was is hard to say. In modern

[14] See *The infancy Gospel of Thomas*. An English translation is available in James K. Elliott, ed., *The Apocryphal New Testament* (Oxford: Clarendon, 1993), 68–83.

times there have been scholars who have asserted that later orthodoxy reflected docetic elements because of the difficulty that some of its defenders had in trying to explain the humanity of Jesus, which always seemed to be compromised to some extent by his divinity. There may be some truth in this charge, but it hardly amounts to full-scale docetism. Reconciling the divine and the human in the incarnate Christ was never easy, but the theologians who fashioned what is now orthodox Christology were at least trying to do so—they did not think that Jesus' human nature was fictitious or incomplete. Docetism in the true sense stood and fell with Gnosticism, and the defeat of the latter led naturally to the disappearance of the former.

The reasons for the failure of Gnostic docetism are not hard to find. If Jesus had been so divine that he was incapable of becoming a man in any true sense of the word, the Gospels would make no sense. An apparition would not need to be born, grow up, or live in obscurity for thirty years before beginning a somewhat pointless earthly ministry. An apparition's divinity would have been detected much more easily than that of Jesus, whose identity as the Son of God was known only to those to whom it had been revealed. An apparition could not have suffered and died, making nonsense of the passion narratives that form the main part of the Gospels and depriving the resurrection of any significance. From beginning to end, docetism did not do justice to the evidence, and so it is not surprising that it never got off the ground. But if docetism was not a viable option, what was there to put in its place? Answering that question was not easy, and it would take the church the best part of half a millennium to come up with a reasonably satisfactory solution.

Jesus and His Contemporaries

No one who knew Jesus in the flesh ever doubted that he was a man. As the Gospels indicate, there were plenty of people who knew him well, and he had a number of relatives who could confirm his Israelite ancestry. He is frequently portrayed eating, drinking, and sleeping like any other mortal being, and presumably he could catch cold, stub his toe, or cut his finger just as we can, though the New Testament does not go into such details. We know that he grew up in Nazareth without anyone suspecting that he was different from them, because when he went back there to preach and told them who he really was, they refused to believe it.[15] That Jesus was a man who had come from God was also widely accepted, and not only by his disciples.[16] His credentials as a religious teacher

[15] Luke 4:16–30.
[16] John 3:2.

were suspect to some because of his Galilean origins and lack of formal rabbinical education, but there were no hard and fast rules about who could be a teacher of the law, and the common people accepted him in that capacity. Even the temple establishment in Jerusalem had to recognize that a man who did miracles was no ordinary mortal, though as his fame spread there were some who tried to ascribe his healing powers to the Devil.[17] But this unpleasant reaction only underlines the fact that Jesus could do things that normal people could not do, and some explanation for this extraordinary ability had to be found.

The belief that Jesus was a prophet seemed plausible enough to many, and the reappearance of prophecy in the person of John the Baptist shortly before Jesus began his earthly ministry made it relatively easy to put him in that category. But Jesus had a transforming effect on people that no prophet ever had. John the Baptist had followers, but after his death they either scattered or turned to Jesus instead—there was never a Johannine movement dedicated to preserving his memory, and John himself pointed his followers to Jesus as the one whose coming he had been sent to proclaim.[18] Looking further back, none of the Israelite prophets had left that kind of legacy either. Elijah had been succeeded by Elisha, but there was no Elijah cult. Much later on, schools had formed around prominent rabbis like Gamaliel and Hillel, but they cannot be called religious movements, and after their master's death they faded away. The sectarian groupings that existed in or on the fringes of Judaism had obscure origins, but we never hear of the Pharisees, Sadducees, Essenes, or Samaritans tracing themselves back to a charismatic founder in the way that the different schools of Greek philosophy did. Only Moses enjoyed that kind of reputation, but that was because he was the great lawgiver of Israel, not because he prophesied or tried to attract a personal following. No one ever called himself a Mosaean (or a Mosaic!).

In this respect, Jesus was unique. Not only did he have followers during his lifetime, but they multiplied greatly after his death—the very opposite of what normally happened to people like him. Like him? That of course is the rub—was there anyone like him? The Christian church insisted that there was not. For all his humanity and connections with other people, there was something about Jesus that was irreducibly different, and it was that difference that counted the most. The evidence we have shows that, right from the beginning, Jesus was put on a pedestal next to God the Father, whether he was openly called "God" or not.[19] No one else ever came close to this, and no Jewish

[17] Matt. 12:22–32.

[18] John 3:28–30.

[19] For a recent study of the evidence, see Larry W. Hurtado, *Lord Jesus Christ: Devotion to Jesus in Earliest Christianity* (Grand Rapids, MI: Eerdmans, 2005).

person would have shown Jesus such honor without having the best of reasons for doing so. Even if it took a while to get the formula circulating, there is no doubt that the early Christians were worshiping Jesus as their Lord and Savior well within the lifetime of those who had known him in the flesh.

The most remarkable thing is that Jesus achieved all this out of some very unpromising human material. To quote Clement of Rome,

> Our Lord Jesus Christ did not come in the pomp of pride or arrogance, although he could have done so. Instead, he came in lowliness, as the Holy Spirit had declared, . . . He has no form nor glory. . . . His form was without distinction and deficient when compared to that of ordinary men.[20]

Jesus was an uneducated Galilean who grew up far from the centers of power and influence in the Jewish world. His active ministry was very short—not more than three years at the most. His followers ran away when he got into trouble, and he himself rebuffed many of those who wanted to follow him. He left no son or other recognized successor who could carry on his mission and ministry. There were some who believed that he might be the promised Messiah, the descendant of David who would resurrect the ancient kingdom of Israel and rule over it on a new and even more glorious basis than before, but Jesus did nothing to encourage that belief and may even have tried to suppress it.[21] If someone were going to invent a god in human flesh, Jesus was not the sort of person they would have come up with. His only real claim to fame was his descent from David, but although much is made of that in the Gospels, he was far from being the only man with that pedigree. No doubt just about everyone in Bethlehem had Davidic ancestry, and that was certainly true of Jesus' relatives. It made him special but not unique, and if he had tried to establish a kingdom on that basis alone he would probably have had to face any number of rivals, whose claim would have been just as authentic as his.

Jesus' Jewish critics recognized that he called God his Father but thought that he was blaspheming against God by doing so.[22] Their reaction tells us that on this point Jesus' teaching was clear and unambiguous. Elsewhere we are told that he taught people in parables because they could neither understand nor share in the divine wisdom that he was transmitting to his disciples.[23] The perception of some and the incomprehension of others seem to have gone together, even among Jesus' followers. Peter recognized that Jesus was the Christ,

---

[20] Clement of Rome, *Epistula I* 16.
[21] Acts 1:6–7.
[22] John 5:18.
[23] Matt. 13:10–11.

the Son of the living God, but Jesus quickly informed him that this recognition was not the result of his own deduction based on the available evidence. On the contrary, Peter was able to say what he did only because the Father himself had revealed it to him.[24] That this did not amount to an unshakable personal conviction of Jesus' divinity became clear later on when Peter denied Jesus as he was led away to trial and crucifixion.[25]

The fact is that even those who were closest to Jesus had difficulty in trying to understand him, despite their high expectations of what he would do to restore the kingdom to Israel and fulfill Old Testament prophecy. This shows that the transition from belief in Jesus as a great man who had a special relationship to God to acceptance of him as the divine Son who has an intrinsic and indelible relationship to the Father within the Godhead was not natural or inevitable. As Jesus indicated to Peter, it could only have been the product of divine revelation which was given to particular people on special occasions.

One of those occasions was the baptism of Jesus, when a voice was heard from heaven saying, "This is my beloved Son, with whom I am well pleased."[26] The Father is not mentioned by name but the context makes it clear that the voice must have been his. What did this mean to those who heard it? John the Baptist knew who Jesus was, and some of his disciples were tempted to follow this new and greater prophet.[27] But there is little sign that their awareness of who Jesus was went any further than that. Later on, we hear of Jesus praying to his Father, but as these prayers were private, they were presumably unknown to the disciples at the time and were communicated to them only later. It was on the cross that Jesus' relationship to the Father would be most clearly and publicly revealed, but even then there are only two "words" that refer to it explicitly, and both of these are in Luke's Gospel. In the first of them Jesus asks the Father to forgive those who have condemned him to death, and in the second he commends himself to the Father just as he is about to expire.[28]

The early church's confession of Jesus as the Son of God did not spring from the way his disciples (or others) perceived him. Had he not taught it himself, and then confirmed the truth of his teaching by his resurrection and ascension into heaven, it is hard to see what could have motivated his followers to claim divinity for him. To their minds, God was an invisible, transcendent being, and no man, however charismatic or inspired he might be, could be divine. We can therefore say with some confidence that the church's teaching that

[24] Matt. 16:16–17.
[25] Matt. 26:69–75.
[26] Matt. 3:17.
[27] John 1:35–37.
[28] Luke 23:34, 46.

Jesus Christ was the Son of God in human flesh was not a deduction made by his disciples from the evidence, but part and parcel of the gospel message that the Son had come to proclaim.

Jesus in Early Christian Teaching

In the early days of the church, confessional statements about Jesus were simple and unsophisticated, but they were always there. From the very beginning, no one could join the Christian community without professing Jesus as Lord and Savior.[29] If there was some reticence in the early church about describing Jesus as "God" without further qualification, this was probably because of the ingrained habits of Jewish monotheism, combined with the need to defend that monotheism in a world where a plurality of gods was the norm. But the question of who the Son was and how his being was connected to that of the Father would not go away. If the Father and the Son were "one," as Jesus claimed,[30] and if it was generally agreed that the Father was God, it would not be long before the question of the Son's divinity would come to the fore. As the Father's role as both Creator and Redeemer was affirmed in opposition to the Gnostic challenge, the need to clarify the Son's place in the divine plan of salvation became acute. Since no one could see the Father or approach him except through the Son,[31] who the Son was and how far he could reveal the Father to mankind became matters of central importance for understanding the gospel.

If Jesus had been worshiped as God from earliest times, why had the need for doctrinal definition of his identity and status not been so pressing before the early fourth century? The main reason seems to have been that, as long as there was doubt about the goodness of the created order, there was little scope for developing a doctrine of the Son's incarnation. Until it could be assumed that all Christians believed that matter was essentially good, it was impossible to explain how God could become a man. Anyone who thought that matter was evil would be forced to reject the notion of a divine incarnation, because that would have meant that the supremely good being had been corrupted by entering sinful human flesh. In that case, the divine being would have become no more than another fallen angel, which was obviously not true of Jesus and would have been impossible for God the Father. There was a philosophical dilemma here that could not be resolved until it was generally accepted that the created order is good in itself. Even then, many people had considerable difficulty in believing that it was possible to be a human being without being sinful,

[29] Acts 2:38.
[30] John 10:30.
[31] John 14:6.

because sinfulness is part of the legacy of Adam. Since to be truly human was to be a descendant of Adam, all human beings must be sinners by definition, even if sinfulness is a corruption of our nature and not an intrinsic part of it. The Son of God might conceivably assume the outward trappings of humanity and appear as a man in the way that angels did, but this would not have been enough to make him human. Nor was it immediately clear that the claim that he was born of a virgin who had been impregnated by the Holy Spirit would make him genuinely human either. Could it be that he was some mixture of God and man, or perhaps an intermediate being who had some characteristics of each without being completely either?

Here there seemed to be a logical contradiction that the early Christians found impossible to resolve within the limits of their inherited worldview. The options, as it seemed to them, were as follows:

A. Jesus Christ was a normal human being who had been taken up into God and deified. This obviously happened at his ascension, but it might be pushed back to his resurrection, to his baptism, or even to his conception in his mother's womb. Whatever moment was chosen, the fundamental reality was that he started out as a man and at some point he was raised to the level of the divine. Did this mean that Jesus was the first Christian? Were his followers expected to imitate his example and be transformed into something supernatural just as he had been, or was there something different about him that gave him a power and authority that no one else can aspire to, however much God comes into our lives and draws us closer to him?

B. Jesus Christ was God in human form but not human in the way that we are, because he did not (and could not) sin. He could talk like a man, live like a man, and even die like a man, but all this was superficial and did not touch the core of his being. His appearance as a human being was a kind of accommodation to the limits of our understanding, which was necessary if the infinite Creator was ever going to communicate with the finite creation. If we follow this line of thought, however, we must ask whether the finite is capable of communicating the infinite without limiting and distorting it. If Jesus of Nazareth was a finite manifestation of the infinite being of God, could he have been anything more than a partial revelation of the divine? And is it possible for anyone to be only partially God?

C. Jesus Christ was a combination of divine and human elements that met in him but did not mix. Sometimes we see his God-side at work (as in his miracles) and sometimes we see his man-side (as in his suffering and death on the cross), but these two realities were distinct from each other. On the cross, it was the man that died because the God who was present in Jesus Christ could not share that experience. This would explain why the man Jesus cried out, "My God, my God, why have you forsaken me?"[32] The God-side and the man-side in Jesus had parted company, and only the man actually died. This solution preserved the integrity of both sinless, infinite divinity, and sinful, finite humanity but left people wondering whether God was involved in Christ's suffering at all. If he was not, how was Jesus' death any different from that of the thieves who were crucified with him? It is not the nature or degree of his sacrifice that has saved us but the fact that he was God in human flesh, and if the divine element is removed his crucifixion loses its special character and meaning.

These were the basic options available to the Christian church, and each of them found supporters at different times and places. Very probably the majority of believers inclined to one or other of them, perhaps without fully realizing it, just as they often do today. The attraction of these solutions was not confined to the early church, and one or other of them is always rearing its head somewhere in the Christian world because it offers a neat and comprehensible answer to a complex theological problem. The truly remarkable thing is that the church has never bought into any of them. Despite the difficulties of constructing a doctrine of Christ that does justice to the biblical evidence, and regardless of the fact that the result is harder to understand than any of the alternatives sketched above, the church knew no peace until the theological conundrum had been satisfactorily resolved. That took a long time, and there are still some loose ends that have not been fully tied up, but it is fair to say that the majority consensus reached in the fourth and fifth centuries has survived all the challenges it has had to face and remains the bedrock of Christian orthodoxy to this day. If a body like the World Council of Churches has to decide whether a particular church is Christian or not, it is to the answers that emerged from the struggle over the identity of Christ that it will appeal. Those answers are contained in what we now call the Nicene Creed, a document that remains foundational for our understanding of who Jesus is and what his followers are expected to believe about him.[33] That more might be said about him, no one would deny, but that something less can be accepted as a profession of Christian faith is universally rejected. The Nicene Creed acquired and still retains the prestige it has because it represents the decisions arrived at by the church as it moved toward a definition of who Jesus was and what he had come to do. The controversies that lay behind the creed dealt with essential matters that had to be resolved if the integrity of

[32] Matt. 27:46; Mark 15:34.

[33] This creed is associated with the First Council of Nicea in 325, but it probably comes from the First Council of Constantinople, held in 381 and intended to clarify specific aspects of the doctrine proclaimed at Nicea.

the gospel message was to be preserved, and it is in that light that they must be studied and assessed.

Adoptianism[34]

The first attempt to explain who Jesus was started with the premise that he was born as a normal human being, with a father and mother who were both descended from Adam. This had the advantage of being simple and comprehensible, and was especially appealing to Jews who could not abandon their strict monotheism. Since no one had doubted Jesus' humanity during his lifetime and the people who knew him best were among the most reluctant to accept his claims to special status, it was not hard to argue that we ought to begin with what was commonly agreed. There had been other men in Israel's history, like Enoch and Elijah, who had been "taken up into God," so the idea that Jesus might have followed in their footsteps was not unprecedented. There were also echoes of such things in pagan society, where the deification of emperors and heroes after their death was common practice. Best of all, this solution allowed Christians to identify with the sufferings of Jesus on the cross. He was not a remote deity, incapable of sharing human life, but a man like other men, whose obedience and suffering had earned him the place of honor that was now his.[35] What had happened to him would also be possible for us if only we could follow his example in our own lives and spiritual experience.[36]

This was the view associated with Paul of Samosata, for which he was condemned in 268. As we have already seen, Paul's career was closely entwined with secular politics, and as we only know about him from the testimony of his enemies, it is hard to know what he really believed. This is unfortunate because it clouds the issue—were the charges made against him accurate, or were they motivated by other considerations? Did Paul really believe what later generations thought he taught? We may assume that his enemies presented the evidence about him in an unfavorable light, and the most extensive account of him that we have makes it clear that he was disliked as much for his behavior and the way he conducted public worship as for anything else.[37] Even so, two observations need to be made about this. First, although the positions attributed to Paul may not have been held by him in the same form, they have their own integrity and can be examined without reference to him or his circumstances. What Paul was supposed to have taught is wrong, whether he said it or not.

[34] This is the correct spelling of a word that is often written as "adoptionism" because of the influence of the word "adoption."

[35] See Heb. 5:7–10.

[36] See Heb. 12:1–2.

[37] See Eusebius of Caesarea, *Historia ecclesiastica* 7.30.6–16.

Second, if Paul had been right and his accusers wrong, the truth would probably have emerged at a later stage and his name would have been vindicated. The example of Athanasius (296?–373), who was several times condemned and exiled, only to be canonized in the end as the great orthodox teacher of the church, serves to remind us of this. Paul himself might have suffered, but his disciples would surely have won the day and his reputation would have been restored.

That this did not happen suggests that the accusations leveled against Paul, if not entirely accurate as a statement of his teaching, were close enough to the truth to make such a posthumous vindication impossible. We know that at the First Council of Nicea in 325, the suggestion that the word "consubstantial" (Greek *homoousios*) should be used to describe the Son in his relation to the Father was contested by some because the word had been used by Paul of Samosata, though with a different meaning.[38] This shows that, a generation after his death, Paul's name was still anathema, so the weight of probability suggests that the charges against him contained more truth than the hostile and inadequate nature of the sources might lead us to think.

The view attributed to Paul of Samosata is known as "adoptianism" because he allegedly taught that Jesus of Nazareth was a man whom God had adopted as his Son, but adoptianism came in many forms, and it is not at all clear which of them (if any) Paul espoused. One of the more popular varieties of adoptianism was common among some second-century Jewish Christians, notably the sect known as the Ebionites. They placed great emphasis on the baptism of Jesus, one of the few incidents in his earthly life that is recorded in all four Gospels, as the moment when he was adopted by God. Why had Jesus been baptized? John the Baptist had a ministry of calling people to repentance, and baptism was a symbol of this. But Jesus had no need to repent, so that could not have been the reason for his baptism. That was certainly the view that John himself took, and initially he refused to baptize Jesus because he was unworthy to do so. But Jesus insisted that John should baptize him in order "to fulfill all righteousness."[39] What righteousness was that? The law of Moses did not say anything about baptism; it was a practice that had grown up in the Intertestamental period and had never been formalized. We

[38] Athanasius, *De synodis Arimini et Seleuciae* 45. According to Athanasius, what Paul was trying to guard against was the belief that if Christ was not a man who had been adopted by God, he would necessarily have been an emanation from the Father's essence (*ousia*). In that case the Trinity would consist of three essences, those of the Son and Holy Spirit being derivative from the Father's. By using the term *homoousios* of the Son, Paul was rejecting that idea and saying that the Father shared his own essence with him. It was because they denied this, that those who condemned Paul rejected the use of the term *homoousios*. The next generation retained their aversion to the term without realizing that the meaning the Nicene fathers gave it was quite different from what they were objecting to.
[39] Matt. 3:15.

can understand why Jesus had to be circumcised to fulfill all righteousness, but baptized?

The Jewish Christian interpretation of this seems to have been that the baptism of Jesus was necessary because his descent into the water was symbolic of his descent into hell, where he did battle with the demons and delivered mankind from their power by rising again. Baptism by water was also associated with baptism by fire, the punishment from which Jesus sets us free.[40] Moreover, baptism was to become the indispensable rite of entry into the Christian church, and to the adoptianist mind the baptism of Jesus shows us why it was so important. Christians must be baptized because we too are adopted into the Father's family and given the Spirit of adoption. In other words, Jesus was the first and greatest Christian, the author and pioneer of our salvation who set us the example of what we must do to be saved.

Is this what Paul of Samosata believed? The surviving fragments tell us that he thought that Jesus was a man who had been taken over by the Word (*logos*) and Wisdom (*sophia*) of God, which would make him a kind of modalist, if not actually a Sabellian.[41] The main difference between Sabellian modalism and Paul's doctrine seems to have been that whereas Sabellius downplayed the humanity of Jesus, Paul emphasized it to the point of exaggeration. He did not think that the Son was a temporal manifestation of God but that he was a man whom God had entered and possessed. That made him more of an adoptianist, and that is how he has been consistently viewed in the history of the church, even if it is unlikely that he held the views attributed to a group of second-century Jewish Christians.[42] The evidence of Athanasius suggests that Paul believed that Jesus was conceived by the Holy Spirit, which he took to mean that Jesus was morally superior to other human beings and therefore capable of achieving sinlessness in a way that others were not.[43] If Athanasius was correct, then Paul was an adoptianist of a very special kind, and any association he may have had with the Ebionites was insignificant.

The appeal of the adoptianist message, whatever form it takes, is that it gives us a model to follow and a goal that is achievable. The underlying argument is that, if Jesus could do it, so can we. Far from trying to repel us, this message is intended to draw us closer to him because we can identify with his life and death by trying to imitate it. Jesus is presented as a friend and brother who holds out hope for us. God has set his seal of approval on what Jesus did

[40] See Justin Martyr, *Dialogus cum Tryphone* 88.2–4.
[41] Paul's affinity with Sabellius, if genuine, was almost certainly accidental.
[42] See Aloys Grillmeier, *Christ in Christian Tradition, Volume 1: From the Apostolic Age to Chalcedon (451)*, 2nd ed. (London: Mowbray, 1975), 65–68, for an extended discussion of the issues involved.
[43] Athanasius, *De synodis* 45.

by exalting him and giving him a name that is above every other name, seating him at his own right hand and entrusting the kingdom of heaven to him. In the light of that, Christians are called to work out their own salvation with fear and trembling, a command which can easily be made to fit the adoptianist agenda.[44] Jesus was duly rewarded for his faithfulness, and does the New Testament not hold out the promise that if we suffer with him, we shall also reign with him in his glory?[45]

Adoptianism in its different forms was attractive to many because it promised them a reward comparable to that obtained by Jesus. It also reassured people that their efforts to lead a good life were not in vain and that if they had to suffer for it they would receive a commensurate blessing in the life to come. It was a more or less pure form of salvation by works, which is always a comforting doctrine to those who are ambitious and want to get ahead. The fact that Jesus had already obtained his reward was a further incentive to persevere. The philosophers told their followers to lead good lives in the hope of some future benefit, but they did not know what that would be, nor could they claim that their forebears had actually received it. Who could say what had happened to Plato after he died? Jesus, however, was alive and well and reigning in heaven, something we can be confident of because the Spirit of adoption given to us by God the Father is also his Spirit—the Spirit of the Son, crying "Abba! Father!"[46]

Adoptianism made sense, it was reassuring, and it was challenging at the same time, because it was up to the individual believer as to whether he would follow Jesus to the end and obtain the promised reward. The appeal of adoptianism was broad, and we should not be surprised to discover that many ordinary Christians must have found it very attractive. They still do today. Adoptianism in the ancient sense is long gone, but the underlying appeal is still there, as we can see from the periodic attempts to encourage us to "imitate Christ." In one sense that is a perfectly valid thing to do, and it was even recommended by the apostle Paul (not the man from Samosata!), who told people that he did the same thing.[47] But of course, Paul's context was totally different. The New Testament concept of imitation is focused on the principle of obedience to the will of God, something that is common to Christians and to the incarnate Son. The difference is that the commands given to us are not the same as the ones that were given to Jesus, because his life and mission were not the same as ours.

[44] Phil. 2:9–13.
[45] 2 Tim. 2:12.
[46] Rom. 8:15.
[47] 1 Cor. 11:1.

The Son of God was sent into the world in order to die for our salvation, something that we are not called to do and would be incapable of achieving if we were. In practical terms, our obedience works out differently because we are different. We are sinners saved by grace through faith, which Jesus was not. However you look at it, Jesus was not the first Christian—indeed, he was not a Christian at all and could not have become one even if he had wanted to. Christians are sinners who have been saved, whereas Jesus was sinless and did not need salvation. He acquired it for us but not for himself. He has power and authority over us, not because he was the first one to achieve salvation by his own efforts and has graciously shared his secret formula with us, but because he was God in human flesh with a preexisting entitlement to do what he did.

The fatal weakness of adoptianism is that it does not do justice either to the evidence of the New Testament concerning Jesus or to the more general pattern of salvation that the New Testament reveals. Jesus achieved what he did because he was the right person and had an ability to do it that no one else has or can ever have. It was not because he was stronger, or cleverer, or even more "spiritual" than others that he managed to save us, but because he was the Son of God who had come down from heaven. It was that aspect of the matter that escaped people like Paul of Samosata, and fatally undermined his doctrine of salvation in and through Christ. It was simply not possible to believe in what Jesus did without first believing in who Jesus was, and it was on that stumbling block that Paul of Samosata's construction of the life and work of the Savior ultimately came to grief.

Logical and appealing though adoptianism was to some, to others it appeared to be an inadequate analysis of Jesus as he is presented to us in the Gospels. For all his undoubted humanity, there were things about Jesus that set him apart from the rest of the human race. His conception and birth from a virgin, for example, was unique. Why was such an improbable thing considered to be necessary? It did not fit with adoptianism and was the first reason why that idea had to be abandoned. Then there were the miracles, and especially Jesus' resurrection from the dead, which went beyond anything known elsewhere, even if elements of them had occurred before. But most of all, there was Jesus' own teaching about himself. He was the Son of Man who had come down from heaven, not a boy from Nazareth who had been taken up into God. The weight of the Gospel evidence pointed away from an adoptianist solution, to something that was more like its exact opposite. However Jesus of Nazareth was to be explained, he was a divine being who had come down to earth. But how divine was he? This was the question that the next stage of Christological analysis had to answer.

9

The Son of God

Arianism[1]

Much more subtle and persuasive than adoptianism was the view that the Son who made himself known in Jesus Christ was a divine being who could become a man because, although he was closer to God than anyone else, he was not God himself. He was "divine" in the moral sense of being perfectly good and holy, but he did not possess the characteristics of God that would have prevented him from entering the created world—infinity, eternity, immutability, and so on. Because of this, he did not have to resort to some kind of docetic apparition in order to reveal himself within the created order. At the same time, he was superior to anything in the material world and the highest of the spiritual creatures in heaven. The difference between him and the rest of us was great, but it was essentially one of degree, not of kind. His being was not incompatible with the material universe because he was himself a creature and able to adapt to the finite conditions of this world in a way that would have been impossible if he had been God in the absolute sense of the term.

This was the view espoused by Arius and his followers. As with Paul of Samosata, it is not easy to say what Arius believed, because he is known to us mainly from the reports of his enemies. There is also the added difficulty that Arius had a number of followers and admirers who modified his views in different ways, so that what passed as "Arianism" later on does not necessarily reflect what Arius himself taught.[2] Having said that, there is no doubt that Arius stirred up controversy from the beginning and that, if misunderstanding had been the only problem, there would have been plenty of opportunities to

[1] Arianism is a much-studied and highly controversial subject. The most thorough study of it is by R. P. C. Hanson, *The Search for the Christian Doctrine of God* (Edinburgh: T & T Clark, 1988). Also important are Rowan Williams, *Arius: Heresy and Tradition* (London: Darton, Longman & Todd, 1987); and Aloys Grillmeier, *Christ in Christian Tradition, Volume 1: From the Apostolic Age to Chalcedon (451)*, 2nd ed. (London: Mowbray, 1975), 219–248. Frequently cited in other works, but generally repudiated as a reliable guide to the thought of Arius, is Robert C. Gregg and Dennis E. Groh, *Early Arianism: A View of Salvation* (London: SCM, 1981).

[2] See Hanson, *Search for the Christian Doctrine of God*; and Michel D. Barnes and Daniel H. Williams, *Arianism after Arius: Essays on the Development of the Fourth Century Trinitarian Conflicts* (Edinburgh: T & T Clark, 1993).

put it right. It is hard to believe that the Roman world would have been shaken to its foundations and troubled to varying degrees for the better part of three centuries by nothing more serious than a failure to grasp what Arius was really saying. Misrepresented and wrongly accused though he may have been, there was enough in what he said to cause genuine anxiety, and the condemnation of his teaching at the First Council of Nicea in 325 was never reversed, despite the emergence of a large pro-Arian party and numerous attempts to revise the Nicene decision in a direction more favorable to him.

In assessing the impact of Arius and Arianism, therefore, several questions have to be asked. These may be tabulated as follows:

1. Who was the historical Arius, and what did he believe? Can his teaching now be recovered with any degree of certainty, and what difference would it make if it could be?

2. Why did Arianism survive the condemnation of Arius? How was it possible for him to fade out of the picture while a movement claiming allegiance to his Christology became a major force in the late Roman world?

3. Was the eventual triumph of the opponents of Arius and of Arianism theologically inevitable, or was it the accidental result of secular forces that, for a variety of reasons, happened to be ranged against it? In other words, was anti-Arian orthodoxy a recovery of the true biblical teaching (as it claimed to be) or was it an intellectual tyranny imposed on the church by unscrupulous ecclesiastical politicians?

4. Are there any grounds for rehabilitating Arius and his followers today, or must we accept their condemnation in ancient times as definitive for the subsequent history of the church?

In answer to the first of these questions, many scholars have approached the historical Arius by way of Paul of Samosata, whose distant disciple he may have been. One popular supposition is that Paul's ideas were passed on to Arius by Lucian of Antioch, a somewhat obscure figure who is sometimes thought to have been both a follower of Paul and a teacher of the young Arius.[3] The main problem with this reconstruction is that although there are superficial similarities between what Paul supposedly believed and what Arius taught, they do not encourage us to think that Arius was indebted to Paul. For example, although both men taught that Jesus was less than fully God, Arius regarded him as a divine creature who became a man, whereas Paul of Samosata apparently

[3] For a summary of the discussion and the reasons why this intellectual succession is unlikely, see Rowan Williams, *Arius*, 162.

thought that he had never been anything more than a human being. If what we know of Paul's teaching is accurate, it would have struck Arius as Sabellian and almost certainly would have been rejected by him for that reason.

Paul of Samosata had an absolute concept of both divine and human natures which made them mutually incompatible. That is why God could adopt the man Jesus as his Son but not become a man himself. Arius agreed that the natures of God and man were incompatible, but thought that the biblical evidence demanded a different solution to the question of the Son's identity. To his mind, there really was a heavenly being called the Son of God who became incarnate; the difficulty was to define what the relationship was between that Son and the Father. In a confession of faith that Arius sent c. AD 320 to Alexander, the bishop of Alexandria who had excommunicated him two years earlier, Arius said the following:

> [The Father] gave birth to the only begotten Son before all ages, through whom he made the worlds and everything, producing him not in appearance but in truth, giving him existence by his own will, [making him] unchangeable and unalterable, a perfect creature of God but not like one of the [other] creatures, a product but not like one of the [other] products. . . . He was created by the will of God before times and ages, and having received life and being from the Father, and various kinds of glory (since he gave him existence) alongside himself. For when the Father made him heir of all things he did not deprive himself of what he intrinsically possesses in himself, for he is the source of everything. Thus there are three existing identities (*hypostases*) and God [the Father] is the cause of them all, for he is the supreme One who has no beginning. The Son, who was begotten outside time by the Father, created and established before all worlds, did not exist before he was begotten. Rather he was begotten outside time before anything else and has alone been given existence by the Father. He is not eternal or co-eternal to the Father, nor is he without beginning as the Father is, nor does he possess a being parallel to the Father's. . . . God is prior to everything because he is the supreme One and origin of all things; therefore he is also prior to the Son.[4]

As this quotation shows, Arius did not deny the Trinity but interpreted it in the hierarchical way that had become traditional after the time of Origen. The Father alone was "God" in the absolute sense, and both the Son and the Holy Spirit derived their existence from him.[5] That was the generally held view,

[4] Athanasius, *De synodis* 16; Epiphanius of Salamis, *Panarion* 69.7.

[5] Arius does not mention the Spirit by name, but his affirmation of three divine "identities" (*hypostases*) points in that direction.

but it was unclear whether this derivation took place in time or not. The belief of men like Irenaeus that the Father had brought forth the Son and the Holy Spirit as the two hands with which he would create the world is ambiguous on this point. As they understood it, the Son and the Holy Spirit must have come into existence before the creation and so were not "creatures" in the proper sense of the word. But if there was a divine act that produced them, it is hard to see how there could not have been some kind of time before the world was made. Most people, though, including Irenaeus and Origen, believed that God was above and beyond time, so explaining how the generation of the Son could have occurred remained impossible for them. It was a divine mystery and had to be respected as such.[6]

Arius followed this traditional teaching, which he claimed was shared by any number of people, including Bishop Alexander who had condemned him! He agreed with them that the generation of the Son took place outside time and creation, but he argued that it had nevertheless occurred, making it necessary to say that God (the Father) was there before the Son came into being. The language of Scripture says that the Son is the only begotten of the Father, and since generation is a process, there must have been a time before the Father became Father. As God, he was always there, but he was not called the Father, just as he was not called the Lord until he had made something to be Lord of. This is a technicality to do with the appropriate use of certain names, not a statement about the objective existence of the being to whom those names were given. It did, however, imply that the Trinity is a created phenomenon and not an eternal reality. Arius refused to say that the Son emerged out of the Father's inner being, because to him this would have meant that God was composite and could be divided up into several parts. He was particularly insistent on making a clear distinction between the eternal *logos* of the Father, which was his inherent rational capacity, and the created *logos* that became the incarnate Son or Word and Wisdom of God. The two *logoi* were quite distinct from one another, making it wrong to suggest that the Son was consubstantial (*homoousios*) with the Father.

Arius based his thinking on biblical texts like Proverbs 8:22, which in the Greek Septuagint version says, "He created me as a beginning for his works." According to Arius, this verse (and the rest of the chapter that follows it) is a revelation of the heavenly creation of the Son of God. In Arius's defense, it should be said that this interpretation of Proverbs 8 was universal among Christians at the time. Those who opposed him did not dispute his Christological

[6] Irenaeus of Lyon, *Adversus omnes haereses* 2.2.5.

reading of the text but argued that it had to be read in conjunction with the rest of Scripture and not in isolation.[7] The allusion to "creation" was a poetic metaphor not to be taken literally, and the same had to be said for words like "only begotten" and "firstborn," both of which were applied to the Son in the New Testament.[8]

Arius's theology was attractive to many because it affirmed that the universe was neither eternal (and therefore beyond redemption) nor a chance creation (and therefore outside the control of God). It was planned by God from the beginning, and the creation of Wisdom before that plan was put into operation was an essential precondition for its fulfillment. It also explained how the rest of creation had been made through Christ, as both John and Paul stated in the New Testament.[9] Lastly, in the eyes of many, Arius made sense of a number of things said by Jesus, such as that the Father was greater than he was, that the Father knew things that he did not know, and so on. As Arius understood it, had the Son been God in the strict sense of the term, it would be hard to see how such statements about him could be true, but if he was a divine creature, then it made perfect sense to say that his Creator was a being who was superior to him. Or so Arius thought.

What ultimately undid Arius was the contradiction inherent in the way he understood the relationship between time and eternity, between finitude and infinity. His opponents never ceased repeating that Arius believed there was a time when the Son did not exist, even while claiming that the Son's generation was outside time. For Arius, the concept of eternal generation was a contradiction in terms, but he could not explain how generation outside time was not eternal. Was there a divine time outside its created counterpart? Nor could Arius explain how it was possible for the Son to be a divine creature. Either a being is divine or it is a creature—it cannot be both, because to be divine is to be eternal and therefore uncreated. This is where Arius came unstuck. He might insist that the Son was the highest of the creatures, quite unlike any of the others, but that was still a far cry from being the uncreated God. The chasm that separates the Creator from his creatures is unbridgeable, something that Arius himself acknowledged when he drew a clear distinction between the *logos* of the Father and the created *logos* that is the Son. If the created *logos* was unlike the divine mind of the Father, how could it be called the Word and Wisdom of God? In the end, Arius's attempt to create a divine being in time

[7] Proverbs 8 is about wisdom, and because Jesus was the wisdom of God, it seemed clear to the ancients that this chapter must be about him.
[8] John 1:14 (KJV); Col. 1:15.
[9] John 1:3; Col. 1:16.

was not logically coherent, which is why his Christology failed to capture the mind of the church.

It must be said, however, that Arianism did not go down without a fight. Unlike earlier heresies, which disappeared with the men who invented them, Arianism attracted a large following and was not finally suppressed until the late sixth century, nearly three hundred years later and long after definitive answers to his questions had been given. Why was this? One reason was that it was not immediately apparent that Arius was saying anything new or heretical. His claim that Bishop Alexander and many others preached the same thing as he did is almost certainly true, the main difference being that Arius had taken his assertions to a logical extreme and had drawn conclusions that others had not. Consequently, when they heard his teaching, they were divided in their response. Some saw nothing wrong with it because it seemed to be no more than a clarification of what the church had always taught, but others (and these would have included Alexander) sensed that something was amiss and reacted against it.

Sometime in or shortly after 318, Arius was put on trial in Alexandria and was condemned by the local synod there. He fled to Nicomedia, where Eusebius summoned a synod and exonerated him, but shortly afterwards Arius was condemned again in Caesarea Maritima. Arius was protected by his friends and lived a further eighteen years, but despite their support, his personal influence in the church was never great. He was not a bishop, and so lacked the prestige and the support base that episcopal office conferred. He was not much of a writer either, and relatively few people knew what he taught. Had there been no more to it that that, Arianism might never have got off the ground and our knowledge of it would be no greater than our knowledge of adoptianism or most of the other early heresies. However, it soon became apparent that the controversy would not go away because, at bottom, it was not about the opinions of one man but about different ways of interpreting the church's common theological inheritance, each of which claimed to be legitimate because no authoritative decision concerning the issues involved had ever been made.

Those who thought the way Arius did came to be called "Arian," and their views were attributed to Arius whether he actually held them or not. In the absence of any substantial body of material that can be attributed to Arius himself, distinguishing what came from him from what later got attached to his name is almost impossible. Nevertheless, it is fairly clear that the teachings of the Arians were not so far removed from that of Arius that they could be regarded as alien to his way of thinking, even if he had expressed himself somewhat differently. Arianism was up and running well before Arius died, so if it had been substantially different from what he taught he would have had ample opportunity to say so and to dissociate himself from it, which he never did. In that case, what we call Arianism would probably not have disappeared but would have been attributed to someone else—because its inner logic had a life and an appeal of its own. Classical Arianism was catalogued and defined by Richard Hanson (1916–1988), following the lead of Rudolf Lorenz, as a series of beliefs that can be expressed in propositional form as follows:[10]

1. *God was not always Father. He was originally just God and not Father.* This doctrine was definitely held by Arius himself.
2. *The* logos *or Son is a creature, whom God made out of nothing.* This was also the view of Arius himself, though he was careful not to press the point that God made him "out of nothing," because of the offense that would have caused to a wide range of church opinion.
3. *There are two* logoi *and two* sophiai, *as well as several other powers in God.* Arius definitely believed in two *logoi* and two *sophiai*, but it is not clear what he thought about the existence of other powers in God.
4. *The Son is variable by nature but remains the same by the grace of God.* This was definitely not held by Arius and was an interpretation of his teaching that may have been due to misunderstanding by his enemies.
5. *The* logos *is alien to the divine being and not true God because he has come into existence.* Arius believed that the *logos* was a created being, distinct from the Father but not "alien" to him, because the Son was dependent on the Father and in constant relation to him.
6. *The Son's knowledge of God is imperfect.* This was the teaching of Arius and of his followers in the West, though it was abandoned by some of his supporters in the East.
7. *The Son's knowledge of himself is limited.* Again, this was held by Arius and his Western followers but denied by some later Arians in the East.
8. *The Son was created for our benefit, as an instrument for creating us.* Arius and the Arians both believed this.
9. *A Trinity of dissimilar* hypostases *exists.* It is not clear whether Arius thought this or not. This accusation was frequently leveled at later Arians who tried hard to deny it, so perhaps not.
10. *Arius attributed eternal wisdom and reason to God, but not to the creation, so the Son can only be called Word or Wisdom in a secondary or loose sense.* This was the teaching of Arius himself, though it seems to have been stressed more by later Arians than it was by him.

[10] See Hanson, *Search for the Christian Doctrine of God*, 19–27; Rudolf Lorenz, *Arius Iudaizans? Untersuchungen zur dogmengeschichtlichen Einordunung des Arius* (Göttingen: Vandenhoeck und Ruprecht, 1979).

11. *The Holy Spirit is subordinate to the Son just as the Son is subordinate to the Father.* Arius probably thought this, though there is no evidence for it in the fragments that survive. Later Arians agreed with it, though they also believed that the Holy Spirit proceeds from the Father.
12. *God the Son had to be a creature in order to be able to suffer and die.* It is not clear whether Arius taught this, but his earliest supporters certainly did. They believed that the Son's divinity was minimized to the point where it could experience suffering (though without ceasing to be divine) and that, in the incarnation, the Son had acquired a material body but without a human soul. They remained convinced that somehow God had to suffer for men in order for them to be saved, but because they could not reconcile suffering with the being of the Father they insisted that the Son's divinity had to be diluted in order to make his incarnate life and death possible.

From this list it is possible to see that while the Arians occasionally said things that went beyond what can be attributed to Arius, they did not go against his teaching, except on the question of the Son's knowledge, which some of his Eastern followers thought was greater than what Arius had allowed for. They also rejected Arius's belief that the Son had been made by the Father "out of nothing," but there are signs that Arius himself retreated from that position, perhaps at the urging of his friend Eusebius of Nicomedia, and it subsequently faded into the background.[11] Developments like this should not be seen as a repudiation of Arius but as a refinement of his teaching, of the kind that often happens in the second generation of an intellectual movement. On the other hand, there is no sign that there was a cult of Arius after his death. His works, such as they were, were neither edited nor copied, and many people whom we would now label as Arians denied that they had any connection with him. To the extent that he was known at all, he was respected by later generations but not much more. Richard Hanson's judgment is fair:

> Arius was respected by later Arians, and some of his scanty literary works [were] sometimes quoted. But he was not usually thought of as a great man by his followers. They would all have said that they were simply carrying on the teaching of the Bible and the tradition of the Fathers.[12]

Arius claimed that his views were shared by many others who had studied with him under Lucian of Antioch, which may well be true. Certainly he was supported from the beginning—and, despite his condemnation, for the rest of

[11] See Hanson, *Search for the Christian Doctrine of God*, 24.
[12] Ibid., 128.

his life—by one of them, Eusebius of Nicomedia (d. 341). Eusebius (not to be confused with his contemporary and namesake, the famous church historian Eusebius of Caesarea) was closely associated with Licinius, the emperor in the East whom Constantine had to defeat in order to unite the Roman empire under his scepter. This was an unfortunate connection, not only because Licinius lost the contest with Constantine but also because, after having been initially tolerant of Christians, he resumed the persecution of the church in a last-ditch attempt to rally support for his cause. Eusebius of Nicomedia survived these reverses but he was clearly out of favor in the Constantinian empire, and his support for Arius brought the latter into even greater disrepute. Nevertheless, Eusebius was a brilliant organizer and did a great deal to establish the church in the hinterland of Nicomedia and Antioch, creating a base of loyal supporters there who kept the flame of Arianism alive into the next generation, when it became politically influential once more.

More theologically significant was the contribution of Asterius the Sophist (d. 341?), another contemporary of Arius who had studied under Lucian of Antioch. Asterius had compromised his credentials during the great persecution of Diocletian by sacrificing to a pagan god, and for that reason he was never ordained to the Christian ministry, despite his recantation and return to the church. Nevertheless, Asterius had a good mind and he was widely regarded as a leading theologian whose support for Arius raised the profile of the latter's Christology. Asterius also seems to have ironed out some of Arianism's difficulties, making it more coherent and attractive to those who found some of Arius's statements too crude. His major contribution was that he redefined what Arius meant when he said that the Son was a creature. In its original form, this doctrine had stated that God the Father had made the Son out of nothing, just as he had made the rest of the universe, but Asterius realized that that was too simplistic and rejected it. Instead, he said that God the Father had always possessed a generative capacity inside his own being, and that he exercised that in bringing forth his Son just as he was preparing to create the universe:

> When God decided to make created nature, he saw that it could not endure a direct experience of his uncovered hand. So before doing that he made and created a single being all by himself, and called that being his Son and *logos*, which made it possible for the rest to be created though this intermediary.[13]

[13] Athanasius, *Orationes contra Arianos* 2.24 (Athanasius was describing the views of Asterius). Asterius evidently thought of God as a "consuming fire" (see Heb. 12:29), too hot to handle without protection. The word translated here as "intermediary" is *mesitês*, which also means "mediator" and recalls 1 Tim. 2:5.

By conceding that the Father had produced the Son from inside himself, Asterius made a significant move in the direction of Arius's opponents, though he continued to insist that what the Father had produced was inferior to his own being. Asterius did not realize it, but this concession opened the way for his opponents to argue that he was inconsistent, because something that the Father produced from within himself must by definition share his nature and therefore be equal to him. That, however, was for another day. It was Asterius who, more than anyone else, developed the notion of a suffering God, which he and later Arians regarded as fundamental. As he put it,

> When you hear that the One who created Adam was crucified, that he was strung up, that he was nailed in the flesh, do not say [that he was] a mere man (*psilos anthrôpos*) but [that he was] God in the flesh, making the suffering and death of the flesh his own.[14]

Asterius also clung to the Arian doctrine that the Son was produced from the Father's will, not from his substance, but once again his language came surprisingly close to that of his opponents and made it possible for them to use his words in defense of their own position:

> The Father who begot the only begotten *logos* and firstborn of all creation from himself is a different [being]. He who is alone begot the unique one, he who is perfect begot the one who is perfect, the King begot the King, the Lord the Lord and God God, the exact image (*aparallaktos eikôn*) of his being (*ousia*), will, glory, and power.[15]

In the light of what would happen later, Asterius's language may strike us as somewhat surprising. Why would someone who said that the Son was the exact image of the Father's being find it impossible to agree that he was consubstantial (*homoousios*) with the Father, as Asterius's opponents insisted was the case? Is there a real distinction between these two positions, or is this the kind of hair-splitting that has so often given theology a bad name? Like all Arians, Asterius rejected the notion of consubstantiality because he thought it was a form of modalism. To him it implied that the Son was either a manifestation of the Father in a different guise or a part of the Father that had become detached from him. In order to avoid that, he emphasized that the Father's *hypostasis* was quite different from that of the Son, a solution which would later be recognized as orthodox, though only when a clear distinction had been

[14] Asterius the Sophist, *Commentarium in Psalmos* 22.3. Asterius was commenting on Psalm 22, which he took to refer prophetically to the suffering and death of Christ on the cross.
[15] Eusebius of Caesarea, *Contra Marcellum* 1.4.

made between *hypostasis* and *ousia* (being, substance). Until that happened, maintaining a distinction of *hypostases* implied denying the consubstantiality of the Father and the Son, and the result of that denial was Arianism.

The subtlety of the arguments on both sides, and the uncertainty that surrounded the whole question as long as the terminology being used was not sufficiently defined, is exemplified in the life and work of Eusebius of Caesarea (264?–339). An almost exact contemporary of Arius, Eusebius sympathized with him but managed to avoid being labeled an Arian and retained the confidence of all sides in the debate throughout his lifetime. This is all the more remarkable considering his prominence. He became bishop of Caesarea Maritima in Palestine sometime around 313, attended the First Council of Nicea in 325, played an important part in a number of subsequent church councils in the East, and was a close supporter and confidant of the emperor Constantine.

In theological terms, Eusebius is best understood as the heir to Origen, who had lived and taught in Caesarea and whose influence had subsequently spread to the entire Greek-speaking church. But Eusebius was far from being a slavish follower of his intellectual master. Where Origen had believed in the eternal generation of the Son, Eusebius made a clear distinction between the Father, whose being had no origin or beginning, and the Son, whom he describes as a "second substance" (*deutera ousia*) whom the Father, as the first cause of all things, had brought into being.[16] In support of this position he quoted a wide range of Old Testament texts, naturally giving a prominent place to Proverbs 8:22–36.[17]

On the tricky question of the origin of the Son from the Father, Eusebius refused to be drawn into the discussion, quoting in his defense the words of Isaiah 53:8 as they were rendered in the Greek Septuagint text: "Who can declare his generation?"[18] But there can be no escaping his fundamental conviction that the Father was unoriginated while the Son was originated, and as he put it, "Anyone would allow that a father exists before a son."[19] In many ways it seems that Eusebius lived in a kind of twilight zone that could still be tolerated as long as the two opposing positions in the Arian debate had not decisively hardened. He wanted to maintain a clear distinction between the *hypostases* of the Father and the Son but not at the cost of saying that the Father created the Son out of nothing. Like Arius, he believed that the *logos* had become incarnate in a human body, but he did not specifically reject the idea that the Savior's

[16] Eusebius of Caesarea, *Praeparatio evangelica VII* 12.1.2.
[17] Other verses quoted were Gen. 1:26; 19:2; Job 28:20; Ps. 2:7–8; 33:6, 9; 110:3; and Prov. 8:12, 15. He also made use of the apocryphal *Wisdom of Solomon* 7:22–26.
[18] Eusebius of Caesarea, *Ecclesiastica theologia* 1.12.70–72; 3.6.103.
[19] Eusebius of Caesarea, *Demonstratio evangelica* 1.20.

body possessed a rational soul. The Bible spoke about Jesus being troubled in his soul, and Eusebius accepted its teaching, but he asserted that Jesus' soul was troubled for our sake, and not for his own.[20] Like many people of his time, Eusebius could find nothing for the rational soul of Jesus to do that would make it theologically significant, and he tried to write as if it did not matter. As for the Holy Spirit, he had little to say other than that the Spirit is neither God (the Father) nor the Son, to whom he is entirely subordinate.[21]

A generation later, Eusebius would have been condemned for heresy, but his brilliance and versatility, combined with the fact that the issues at stake still had not been clearly defined, allowed him to escape that fate. His pro-Arian inclinations are clear, not least in his assertion that as the mediator between God and man, the Son could not be either of them, so as to avoid bias![22] He also consistently maintained that the Son worshiped the Father, a statement that most people at the time would have regarded as clearly Arian.[23] On the other hand, he never denounced the decisions taken at the First Council of Nicea or said anything either for or against consubstantiality once it had been approved by that council. It was a politic stance for someone whose sympathies were on the losing side. Fortunately for him, he died at the very moment that the real battle over the implications of Arius's condemnation was beginning in earnest. He escaped just in time to save his reputation for posterity.

Many attempts have been made to find the origins of Arianism in theological and philosophical currents that were popular in the third century. There can be no doubt that Arius and his colleagues were influenced to some degree by Origen, since almost every Christian thinker at that time was, and he must have picked up ideas from people in Alexandria as well as from Lucian of Antioch. Nor is it surprising to find echoes of Platonism and Aristotelianism in his theology, if only because philosophers and theologians were interested in the same things and could easily pick up ideas from one another. It is easy for us to forget that the ancient world was an oral culture dominated by discussion and debate, not by the written word. Our disadvantage is that the latter is all that we have and we are forced to try to piece together a logical system from fragments that to our minds have little or no connection with each other. Numerous attempts to make Arius dependent on a particular school of thought have proved unsatisfactory, and Richard Hanson was probably right to conclude that the only constant factor in Arius's teaching was his devotion to the Bible and his desire

[20] See Hanson, *Search for the Christian Doctrine of God*, 64, for the details.
[21] Eusebius of Caesarea, *Ecclesiastica theologia* 3.6.3.
[22] Eusebius of Caesarea, *Contra Marcellum* 1.1.8.
[23] Eusebius of Caesarea, *Historia ecclesiastica* 10.4.68; *Commentarium in Psalmos* 70(69):23.

to understand its teaching correctly.[24] Like others before and after him, he used the material available to him for that purpose and felt free to alter it whenever the evidence of Scripture seemed to demand it. Later Arians were more self-disciplined in their thinking, but their basic approach was almost certainly closer to that of Arius than to anyone else.

The fundamental problem that Arius set out to resolve was how God could enter his creation, and then suffer and die within it, without ceasing to be divine. As he saw it, the only way to do this was to reduce or dilute divinity so as to make communication with a finite world possible, but not to remove it altogether (as Paul of Samosata apparently did) because then there would be no authentic revelation of God at all. However, the divinity of the Father could not be compromised, so the Son whom he begot in order to act as an intermediary between himself and the world was necessarily inferior to him, even if he shared something of the Father's divine nature. This was made clear by a certain Julian (late fourth century?), whom we call "the Arian" because we know nothing else about him. He wrote,

> When God [the Father] gives birth he does not beget according to his inner feelings (*pathos*), nor does he divide his own being (*ousia*). When he creates, he does not need matter or movement or any kind of instrument, natural or artificial. He generates and creates by his will and power, . . . and by his authority he creates and controls whatever he produces.[25]

According to Julian, the Father created the Son by his will power alone, and left the rest of creation to him. The Son made the Holy Spirit first and then the rest of the universe, an arrangement that preserved the immutability of God the Father, the divine status of the Son, and the inner coherence of the rest of creation. It also made it unnecessary to try to distinguish the purely human acts of Jesus from the ones that require divine intervention, because as a created divinity he always acted in an intermediate way that was partly human and partly divine.

This inner unity of the incarnate Christ's being meant that his weaknesses and limitations applied equally to his divinity and to his humanity, something that was taken as further evidence of the Son's natural inferiority to the Father. A favorite text used to support this was Mark 10:18, where Jesus asks the rich young ruler, "Why do you call me good? No one is good except God alone." The subtlety of Jesus' remark completely escaped the Arians and seemed to

[24] See Hanson, *Search for the Christian Doctrine of God*, 60–98.
[25] Julian the Arian, *Commentarium in Iob* 270.19–271.3.

them to offer irrefutable biblical evidence that Jesus recognized his own inferiority to the Father. That this assertion stung their opponents is clear from the many attempts that were made to interpret the verse "correctly."[26] Hilary of Poitiers (315?–368?) was especially diligent in collecting Arian proof-texts from Scripture and refuting them as best he could, mainly by saying that it was illogical for the Arians to attribute everything Jesus said and did in his human nature to the supposed defects of his divinity.[27] An important corollary of this approach is that the Arians used the biblical evidence that Jesus worshiped God as proof of the Son's inferiority to the Father. John 20:17 was frequently quoted to that effect, and again, the attempts that were made to refute it reveal how important it was to the Arian case.[28] Their interpretation of Scripture may have been naive and simplistic, but it was never far from their thoughts, and that must be regarded as one of their great strengths in the context of a church that was determined to live by the teaching of the Bible.

The inferiority of the Son to the Father was a belief that came into its own when the subject of divine suffering was raised. The belief that God suffered was a fundamental tenet of Arianism just as it was of classical Christian orthodoxy—the difference lying in the way that each side understood the suffering of God. The Arian explanation of it was that the inferior divinity of the *logos* had assumed a soulless body. Jesus Christ was not a "mere man" (*psilos anthrôpos*) but a divine being in human flesh. What the rational soul is and does in us, that divine being was and did in him. As Eudoxius, who was bishop of Antioch, Germanicia, and Constantinople in quick succession, put it,

> [The Son] became flesh, not man, for he did not take a human soul, but he became flesh, in order that he might be called "God for us." . . . There were not two natures because he was not a complete man, but he was God in the flesh instead of a soul. The whole was a single composite nature. He was passible by his [incarnate] dispensation, because if only soul and body suffered, he could not have saved the world. How then could this passible and mortal being be consubstantial with God, who is beyond such things as suffering and death?[29]

Lastly, Arianism stood out in the way that it emphasized the holy life that the incarnate *logos* led. By dwelling in a human body and overcoming

[26] See, for example, Epiphanius of Salamis, *Ancoratus* 18.1, 2, 26; *Panarion* 69.19.1–6; Hilary of Poitiers, *De Trinitate* 7.6.
[27] Hilary of Poitiers, *De Trinitate* 9.15.
[28] See Gregory of Nyssa, *Contra Eunomium* 12.1.
[29] Eudoxius of Constantinople, in a Vatican manuscript edited and published by Franz Diekamp, *Doctrina patrum de incarnatione Verbi* (Münster in Westfalen: Aschendorff, 1907), 64–65.

its weaknesses, the *logos* set an example to his followers, who could have the courage to believe that they might do the same. As the anonymous Arian author of an incomplete commentary on Matthew put it,

> Just as it was not characteristic of human nature to have no hunger for forty days, so it was not characteristic of God ever to feel hunger at all. Therefore, Jesus fasted for forty days for two reasons: first, to give us an example of fasting against temptations, and second, to limit our fasts to forty days. He hungered, however, so that it would not be obvious that he was God by his fasting far beyond human limits. That would have made it impossible for the Devil to tempt him and likewise impossible for him to gain victory over the Devil. . . . When the Devil saw that he was truly hungry, he approached him [with his temptations], but discovered that the one who was outwardly hungry was never so inwardly. So the Devil tempted the one who was hungry but was defeated by the one who was not.[30]

At the heart of Arianism was the belief that, in the incarnation of the *logos*, the Son of God suffered and died for us. To that extent, the Arians understood the cross of Christ better than their opponents did, for all the latter's profession of impeccable orthodoxy. The trouble was that they could achieve that understanding only by allowing for the existence of two Gods, an impassible and unapproachable Father, and a Son who could become a man because he was an inferior kind of God. That combination was perilously close to Gnosticism, and it was inherent in the kind of theology that predominated in the third century. The opponents of Arius concentrated on asserting that the divinity of Christ had to be equal in all respects to that of the Father, because if it were not, the Son would not be truly divine and the Arian insistence that "God suffered" would have no meaning. Their task was to show that Arianism was incoherent and could not survive a serious examination of its own inconsistencies. That it took them two generations to achieve their aim shows how subtle Arianism was and what a powerful impact it had on the church of its day.

The Way to Nicea

The emperor Constantine had probably never heard of Arius when he legalized Christianity in 313, but he was soon forced to come to terms with him in order to save the hard-won peace of his empire. His rival Licinius had already put a stop to theological controversy in the parts of the Eastern empire that he controlled, and Constantine had no desire to rekindle it when he took over. It was not practically

[30] *Opus imperfectum in Matthaeum* 5.2.

possible to gather the whole church together until 324, when he completed his conquest of the East, but once that had been accomplished, solving the Arian problem was the first item on his agenda. At first, he thought that the whole dispute was trivial and sent his faithful aide and adviser, Hosius of Corduba (now Córdoba, in Spain), to Alexandria with the brief to sort it out and restore the peace of the local church. If Hosius originally shared Constantine's belief about Arius, his mind was changed when he met Bishop Alexander. Alexander persuaded Hosius that the matters raised by the controversy over Arius were far from trivial and that they could not be resolved by goodwill alone.

Very little of what Alexander wrote has survived, and the two long letters of his that we have are of uncertain value. One of them was addressed to all the bishops and contains an extended denunciation of Arius, but apart from producing some biblical texts that appear to contradict Arian doctrine, Alexander had almost nothing to say in reply to him.[31] More satisfactory in this respect is his letter to Alexander of Constantinople, which was written after the controversy had been raging for several years and represents a better-thought-out position than would have been likely before 325. The key to his thinking can be found in the following extract:

> You can tell that the theory of [the Son's] creation out of nothing is most ungodly because the Father is always present with the Son. Indeed, this is why he is called "Father." The Father is perfect in the eternal presence of the Son with him. He needs nothing to supplement his goodness, and begot the only begotten Son not in time, nor after an interval, nor out of nothing.[32]

Like the pro-Arian Asterius, Alexander also believed that the Son is the "exact image (*aparallaktos eikôn*) of the Father," a phrase he used to stress the Son's equality with the Father in every respect except that of generation, which applies to him but not to the Father.[33]

Alexander was deeply indebted to Origen, whom he followed closely in his assertions of the eternal generation of the Son. This is perhaps most evident in his willingness to use the word *hypostasis* in a sense approximating that of "person" and his avoidance of the word *ousia*. For him, Father and Son were distinct *hypostases* who shared the same divinity, but although this sounds

[31] Alexander of Alexandria, *Epistula ad omnes episcopos catholicos*. The biblical texts he quotes include Ps. 45:2; 110:3; Mal. 3:6; John 1:1; 3:18; Col. 1:15; and Heb. 1:3.

[32] Alexander of Alexandria, *Epistula ad Alexandrum Constantinopoleos* 7. It has been suggested that this Alexander was bishop of Thessalonica, not Constantinople (which did not exist as such until 330), but it is now clear that there was an Alexander who migrated from Heraclea, the mother church of Byzantium, when Constantine refounded it, and was bishop there until his death in 337. He seems to have been the addressee of this letter, which was probably intended for the emperor's eyes as much as for his.

[33] Alexander of Alexandria, *Epistula ad Alexandrum Constantinopoleos* 12.

very much like later orthodoxy (and can be readily assimilated to it), Alexander did not use these words as technical terms because they had not yet been developed as such. There were several occasions when he could have used the word *homoousios* ("consubstantial") to describe the divinity that was common to the two *hypostases*, but he never did so. He also spoke of Father and Son as two different "natures" (*physeis*), which would have been anathema to later orthodoxy, although in his mind the word seems to have meant no more than "distinct identities." Alexander's verbal handicaps reveal, more clearly than anything else, the disarray of Arius's opponents and the difficulty they had in getting their message across because they lacked a clearly defined vocabulary.

Both Alexander and Hosius realized that the church had a number of internal difficulties which had to be sorted out and that finding a common theological terminology was not the most pressing of them. More important by far was that there was no agreed date for the celebration of Easter. That had been true for at least two hundred years, with the main argument being whether it should be celebrated in line with the Jewish Passover or on the first day of the week, whether that coincided with Passover or not.[34] By 324 all sides were agreed that it should be celebrated on a Sunday, but the methods of calculating which Sunday it should be differed across the empire. This was not a theological issue, but it had practical implications for everyday church life, and a body that was still fighting for public acceptance of its beliefs could not afford to differ about when its most important festival should be observed. As a result, the need to fix the date of Easter was felt by many to be a more pressing reason for summoning a universal council of the whole church than resolving the Arian question was, though inevitably that would also figure on the agenda.[35]

On his way home from Alexandria, Hosius took the land route, which meant that he passed through Antioch toward the end of 324. In a very short space of time, he was able to gather fifty-nine bishops together, all but three of whom put their names to a statement of faith very similar to what we might have expected from Alexander, though of course he was not present. The original statement must have been in Greek, but copies of it survive only in Syriac and they were unknown until one of them was published in 1905.[36] The inter-

[34] Those who supported the Jewish Passover were called the "Quartodecimans" or "fourteenthers" because they wanted to celebrate Easter on Nisan 14, according to the Jewish calendar.

[35] It may be noted in passing that the solution for calculating the date of Easter that was adopted at Nicea remained in universal use only until 457, when the Roman church unilaterally decided to adopt a slightly different method. As a result, West and East once again celebrate Easter on different days, though they usually coincide every five or six years. Arianism was eventually defeated, but the Easter controversy, which Nicea was supposed to settle once and for all, is still with us.

[36] See Hanson, *Search for the Christian Doctrine of God*, 146–151, for the details. Of course, the fact that it was unknown to modern scholars does not mean that contemporaries were unaware of it.

esting thing about this statement is that it represents the teaching of Alexander of Alexandria *before* the First Council of Nicea, which shows that his views enjoyed wide currency in the church even before they were officially imposed. Most remarkably of all, the statement does not use the word "consubstantial," which is important evidence that this term, which would be so controversial in years to come, was not yet regarded as definitive. The most important points that the statement makes are,

1. The Son did not come into existence from nothing but was begotten in the way that was most appropriate for him, which is beyond our understanding.
2. The Son is the image of the Father's *hypostasis*.

These two points were to form the basis of the anti-Arian opposition that gathered some months later in Nicea. They were not much to go on, but the overwhelming support they received at Antioch (of all places) shows that the Arians were up against widespread resistance in the church as a whole. At some point during Hosius's travels, the emperor Constantine ordered a council of bishops to meet at Ancyra[37] to sort out their differences. For reasons of convenience the venue was shifted to Nicea, though probably not before Hosius returned to Nicomedia, where the emperor was then residing. It is possible that Hosius was the mastermind behind the whole idea of summoning a council, and the emperor certainly appointed him to organize it and preside over its sessions as his deputy. The synod gathered from May to July 325 and has gone down as one of the greatest events in the history of the church. The widespread use of the so-called Nicene Creed, which is popularly supposed to derive from this council and represent its decisions, has become the basis of classical Christian orthodoxy and ensured the council's enduring fame, though in fact it was not connected to the council at all. As with so many things, the reputation of the First Council of Nicea belies the reality, which was less impressive than later tradition made it out to be. It did not represent the whole church, because the Latin-speaking West was hardly present, despite the fact that Hosius came from Spain.

In addition, many of the Eastern bishops were less than thrilled that the emperor was its sponsor; after all, it was only a year since persecution had ceased in the East, and who could tell what the future might bring? The notion that a secular ruler could interfere, however benignly, in church affairs did not sit well with a large segment of church opinion. It was small comfort to them that Constantine did not care about the issues and only wanted peace,

[37] Now Ankara, the capital of modern Turkey.

because his theological indifference might easily have led him to take the wrong side for purely political reasons. Constantine was not baptized and was not seeking church membership at the time, but he attended the council and, in collaboration with Hosius, he directed its affairs from behind the scenes. At his insistence, both pro- and anti-Arian bishops were present, though we do not know how many there were on either side.[38] Even Arius and Asterius were supposed to have been there, though they could not have participated in the debates because neither of them was in episcopal orders.[39]

The proceedings of the First Council of Nicea are known to us only from their results. We know that Arius was condemned and went into exile, that the orthodoxy of Eusebius of Caesarea was vindicated despite strong suspicions of his pro-Arian leanings, that Eusebius of Nicomedia was hissed and booed when he presented his own statement of faith, and that at the end a creed was drawn up in which it was declared that the Son was "consubstantial" with the Father. We also know that this creed was phrased in such a way as to make it possible for the more moderate pro-Arians to sign it, which they did. We are told of two bishops who refused and who were exiled as a result, but there must have been many more who swallowed their scruples and conformed to the majority view, whether they really agreed with it or not.

The First Council of Nicea was a historical turning point not so much because of what it said or did but because of what it was—the first church council to be held under the aegis of the state, whose decisions would have the force of law and be applied by imperial authority. For this reason it was called an "ecumenical" council, *oikoumenê* being the Greek word normally used to describe the Roman empire.[40] The council did what was expected of it and condemned Arius's teaching by decreeing that the Son is "consubstantial" (*homoousios*) with the Father, a word that was meant to exclude the possibility that he was a creature born in time. To remove any doubt as to what it was getting at, the council appended the following clarification to its creed:

> Those who say that "there was a time when he [the Son] did not exist" and "before being begotten he did not exist," or who allege that the Son of God

[38] The total number of bishops present was calculated anywhere from 250 to over 300. The classical number that was eventually adopted was 318, because this was the number of Abraham's men who went out to rescue Lot (Gen. 14:14). When referring to Nicea and its statement of faith, ancient sources usually called it "the council/faith of the 318 Fathers."

[39] For Arius, see Rufinus, *Historia ecclesiastica* 1.7.73. For Asterius (and his fellow Arian, Leontius of Antioch), see Epiphanius of Salamis, *Panarion* 69.4.

[40] It is used in this sense in Luke 2:1, for example. The word itself means "inhabited" or "civilized" and was intended to distinguish the empire from the barbarian (uncivilized) nations that lay beyond its borders.

is of another *hypostasis* or *ousia*, or is alterable or changeable, these the universal (*katholikê*) and apostolic church condemns.[41]

The testimony of Eusebius of Caesarea is of particular interest because he signed the creed, even though its tone and content were uncongenial to him. He realized that he had to justify his action to his own supporters, which is how we know that he was able to swallow the term *homoousios* on the understanding that it meant that the Son was from the Father but was not to be regarded as a part of him. He was also heartened to note that it underscored the fact that the Son was quite unlike any of the other creatures, which Arius also believed. When it came to the anathemas contained in the paragraph just quoted, Eusebius could only say that he accepted them because they condemned terms that were not found in the Bible (though that was true of *homoousios* as well, of course!) and that everyone agreed that the Son had existed in heaven before his incarnation on earth as Jesus Christ. What saved the day for him was that the creed did not explicitly affirm the eternal generation of the Son, a statement which he and other pro-Arians wished at all costs to avoid.

This concession to the feelings of the pro-Arians, if concession it was, did not alter the substance of what the creed was proclaiming. Arius had clearly denied the consubstantiality of the Son with the Father and Nicea affirmed it, making Arius a heretic and excluding from the fellowship of the church those who followed Arius consistently. Eusebius and others like him who wanted a kind of compromise were pushed into a position where they had to accept the phraseology of Arius's opponents and try to interpret it in a way that would not exclude the Arian approach completely.

Of particular interest in this creed is the way in which it condemned those who said that the Son was a different *hypostasis* to the Father, a statement that must have seemed modalistic to many and was to cause great confusion and embarrassment to the anti-Arian party later on. Some claimed that *hypostasis* and *ousia* were synonymous, a solution that was often adopted by Latin translators who rendered the two words as *substantia* and *essentia* respectively. It is hard to know whether the drafters of the anathema thought that, but it is even harder to believe that they consciously opted for modalism (Sabellianism) or had any intention of denying that there were three *hypostases* in God and not just one. Whatever the truth of the matter may be, all sides in the debate agreed

[41] For a discussion of this creed and its possible origin, see J. N. D. Kelly, *Early Christian Creeds*, 3rd ed. (London: Longman, 1972), 205–230. See also the update provided by Hanson, *Search for the Christian Doctrine of God*, 163–172. The original text of the creed was edited by Giuseppe L. Dossetti, *Il simbolo di Nicea e di Constantinopoli* (Rome: Herder, 1967), 77–78, from a letter written by Eusebius of Caesarea to his church, explaining why he signed it. That letter can be found among the works of Eusebius in PG 20, 1535–1544.

that the wording was extremely clumsy and unhelpful, something that became more and more obvious as the debate progressed. What this shows more than anything else is that until the terminology of theological discourse was defined with sufficient clarity, dissensions rooted in misunderstanding would be inevitable.

The Aftermath of Nicea

The anti-Arian Alexandrians and their allies felt vindicated by the council's decisions and regarded them as nonnegotiable in any future discussion of the subject, but the pro-Arians refused to admit defeat. The Son might have to be acknowledged as being consubstantial with the Father, but what did that mean? In the immediate aftermath of the council the emphasis was on the reconciliation of as many moderate Arians as possible, and in that climate, the implications of *homoousios* were played down and the word disappeared from view for the next twenty years. By the time it reemerged, the theological landscape had changed almost beyond recognition. Some of the defenders of Nicea had moved in the direction of modalism, which they regarded as implicit in the council's anathemas, and in reaction to that, sympathy for what might be seen as a pro-Arian position increased.

The anti-Arian tendency to veer in the direction of modalism can be observed in the writings of Eustathius of Antioch (fl. 320–337). He had been elected bishop shortly before the Council of Nicea, had attended it as his church's representative, and went back to apply its decisions until he was deposed from office, which was probably sometime in 330 or 331. His tenure of the bishopric was controversial and divisive, but although it did not last long, it was to have a significant impact. On the one hand, he acquired a devoted following that would insist on his orthodoxy for a generation or more after his departure, but on the other hand, he drove a number of his opponents out of the city, dispersing them (and their ideas) around the eastern Mediterranean, where they would take root and be influential in developing a counter movement of ideas.

One important manifestation of Eustathius's anti-Arianism was his affirmation of the existence of a human soul in Christ that suffered in all the ways that Arius had predicated of the divine *logos*, since to Eustathius the *divinity* of the *logos* made it impossible for him to suffer. This clear affirmation of the complete humanity of the incarnate Son of God was to become one of the cardinal points of so-called "Antiochene" Christology, which would gradually emerge as the great rival to its Alexandrian counterpart. In the next generation it would become painfully apparent that on this point, at least, Arius was fairly typical of Alexandria, and that his opponents there were closer to him than they were to men like Eustathius. But along with his assertion of Christ's complete humanity, Eustathius also insisted that "there is one *hypostasis* of the Godhead," a phrase that was to become the watchword of his followers.[42]

By making a radical distinction between the divinity and the humanity of Christ, Eustathius was able to say that the Son of God was "begotten" as the New Testament states (John 1:14), but not "created" as the Arians insisted, thereby making a clear distinction between two terms that had previously been regarded as virtually synonymous. What he could not do was distinguish clearly between the Father and the Son *within* the Godhead, because his insistence on the one *hypostasis* in God made it impossible for him to do so. To his mind, the Son was therefore begotten *as a man* but (apparently) not as God. The circumstances surrounding Eustathius's deposition remain obscure, but it seems most likely that he was condemned for Sabellianism, a charge that is certainly understandable in the light of what he had to say about the one *hypostasis*, even if it was not what he intended. Once again we find that a man who wanted to say the right thing did not know what words to use or how to piece the different aspects of his Christology together into a coherent whole.

Similar to Eustathius was Marcellus (280?–370?), who became bishop of Ancyra sometime around 310, was at Nicea in 325, where he was strongly anti-Arian, and was deposed around 336. He was important enough for Eusebius of Caesarea to write a treatise denouncing his theology, and from it we are left to surmise that it was because of a book he had written against Asterius that he was forced to vacate his see. Whatever the truth was, Marcellus found support in the West and was vindicated by a council held at Rome in 341 and (more importantly) by one that met at Serdica two years later.[43] Whether he was able to go back to Ancyra after the council is disputed, but he is supposed to have lived to the age of ninety, and he remained a controversial figure his entire life.

Marcellus believed that there is only one *hypostasis* and one *ousia* in God, and he denied that the Son had existed as such before his incarnation. As far as Marcellus was concerned, it was the *logos* that had dwelt eternally in God and that had come forth from him in order to become a man. He did not use the term "begotten" to refer to the relationship between God and his *logos*, regarding the latter as eternally present in the former. With a theology like this, it is

[42] Michel Spanneut, *Recherches sur les écrits d'Eustache d'Antioche* (Lille: Facultés Catholiques, 1948), fr. 38, known to us now only in a Syriac translation.

[43] Serdica is now Sofia, the capital of Bulgaria. At that time it was part of the Western church, although it fell under the secular jurisdiction of the Eastern emperor. It was not transferred to the East until 733.

not surprising that he was accused of Sabellianism in the East. As time went on, he modified his *logos* doctrine in the hope of avoiding this charge, but his basic orientation remained the same and his anti-Arianism, though welcome in certain respects, was also something of an embarrassment to men like Athanasius, on whose shoulders the main burden of defending the Nicene definition fell.

Athanasius has gone down in the history of the church as the lone defender of orthodox Christian doctrine against numerous and powerful opponents. In the West especially, his reputation for this was very high even during his lifetime, and after his death his name became a byword for sound doctrine. It became a tradition that still has echoes today.[44] As an Alexandrian by birth, it is quite possible that the young Athanasius heard Arius preach and may even have met him, despite the gap in their respective ages. Athanasius went to Nicea in 325 as the bishop's secretary, and three years later he succeeded him as head of the Alexandrian church. The position came with its own very clear job description: Athanasius had to defend the Nicene *homoousios* and the honor of his own church against any sign of Arianism, a task that determined the rest of his career and ensured that his name would forever be attached to the Nicene cause as its chief champion.

To achieve his objective, Athanasius was forced to play politics in both church and state, and he did not always come off well. He was exiled no fewer than five times by emperors who wanted to silence him, and he could be inconsistent in forming alliances within the church. Having started off with a Christology not far removed from that of Eustathius and Marcellus, he gradually shifted to a position they could never have accepted but which he regarded as vital if the Nicene doctrine was to triumph in the East. This was his abandonment of the one *hypostasis* idea in favor of Origen's three *hypostases* in the Godhead, a move that led him to deny the judgment in favor of Marcellus at the Council of Serdica, and even to omit the embarrassing words "*hypostasis* or" from his version of the Creed of Nicea. We can therefore say that while Athanasius made history, he also rewrote it, and (on the whole) he got away with it.

In his early years as bishop, Athanasius was preoccupied with the Meletians, a schismatic group not unlike the Donatists. He seems to have used violent methods to suppress them and was condemned for this at a council held in Tyre in 335. Deposed from his see, Athanasius took his case to Constantinople where, after initially making a good impression on the emperor, he soon found himself in even deeper trouble. Constantine, now near death,

[44] See, for example, Khaled Anatolios, *Athanasius* (London: Routledge, 2004); Thomas G. Weinandy, *Athanasius: A Theological Introduction* (Farnham: Ashgate, 2004); and Peter J. Leithart, *Athanasius* (Grand Rapids, MI: Baker, 2011).

exiled Athanasius to Trier, and as soon as he was out of the way, the supporters of Arius saw their opportunity. They petitioned the emperor to support the reinstatement of Arius as a presbyter in good standing, and that would have gone ahead had Arius not died before the process could be completed. His death was soon followed by that of Constantine, and Athanasius's first exile came to an abrupt end. He took his time getting back home, though, visiting a number of key churches on the way and giving whatever support he could to the anti-Arians within them.

In Alexandria, the Meletians were waiting for him, and they immediately denounced him to the new emperor, Constantius II (337–361), in the hope that he would send Athanasius back into exile. Similar attacks were emanating from Eusebius of Nicomedia and his circle, allowing Athanasius to summon a council at Alexandria and accuse his enemies of trying to overturn not just him but the decisions of the Council of Nicea. Athanasius then sent this judgment to Rome for its approval, but on the way there the delegation from Alexandria bumped into another one from Antioch, which was also heading to Rome to petition the church there for support *against* Athanasius! The two delegations conferred, and the result was a request to summon another council to sort everything out. Meanwhile, Eusebius of Nicomedia was translated to Constantinople and tried to make good the earlier deposition of Athanasius by appointing a new bishop of Alexandria who would be favorable to him. At just this moment, the desert monk Anthony (250–356), who was widely revered for his ascetic lifestyle, appeared in Alexandria to support Athanasius. This had the effect of weakening the appeal of the Meletians, leaving Athanasius free to pursue what would soon become an anti-Arian crusade.

A council was eventually held at Rome in 341, and it exonerated both Athanasius and (as we have already seen) Marcellus of Ancyra. Bishop Julius of Rome, claiming appellate jurisdiction in the case, annulled the Council of Tyre that had deposed Athanasius, reversed its condemnations, and even contrived to declare Marcellus fully orthodox in his theology, despite his latent Sabellianism. When these verdicts were confirmed at Serdica in 343, the alliance between Rome and Alexandria was sealed, but in many Eastern minds it was associated with the modalism of Marcellus. Arianism could now be promoted as an antidote to Sabellianism, the heresy with which Athanasius and Rome both seemed to be tarred.

While Rome was busily trying to establish a preeminent position in church affairs by backing Athanasius, the opponents of the Nicene doctrine were not idle. They convened a rival council at Antioch, which also met in 341. Whereas the Roman synod had passed legal judgments, the Antiochene council preferred to compose creedal statements and challenge the rest of the church to accept them as orthodox or else be rejected as heretics. The first of these statements rejected the suggestion that the bishops would follow a man like Arius, on the ground that he was only a presbyter. It is important to note that Arius was disowned because of his *status*, not because of his *doctrine*, of which little was said. The council's first creed also stated that Christ remains King and God forever, which was a subtle attack on Marcellus of Ancyra, who at that point was still claiming that when his work was accomplished, the Son went back into the Father and surrendered his independent existence.

In a second creed, the fathers of the Council of Antioch made explicit their rejection of Sabellianism (modalism). The creed was not specifically anti-Marcellan, but it was clearly moving away from his position, not least by its reaffirmation that there were three *hypostases* in the Godhead and not merely one. It also rejected Arianism, but in a less obvious way. Arius would not have liked its description of the Son as "the exact image of the Godhead and the substance and will and power and glory of the Father,"[45] a phrase which was characteristic not only of Alexander of Alexandria but also of Asterius, who may have attended the council in person. The creed did not say that the Son was a creature, although it calls him the "firstborn of all creation" in line with Colossians 1:15. More significantly, it avoided using the word *homoousios*, which in 341 could only mean that it was deliberately distancing itself from Nicea. Hanson's conclusion that it was intended as a substitute for the controversial creed produced in 325 is hard to avoid.

Two further creeds, one composed at the council and clearly intended as yet another attack on Sabellianism, and one composed by a smaller group after the council had finished, complete the picture. This last document is significant because it never used the word *ousia* or any of its compounds, but replaced it with *hypostasis*. The result was that it confessed only one *hypostasis* in God and allowed room for those who believed that the Son was a creature "begotten" from God in time, though it was careful not to stress this point or make it compulsory. Yet despite its obvious deficiencies, it was this fourth creed that survived and became the basis for the next round of discussions about the divinity of Christ and the relationship of the Son to the Father in God.

This was the state of affairs prevailing when the Council of Serdica met in 343. Fresh from their deliberations at Antioch and armed with the last of its four creeds, the Eastern delegation wanted to sort out the theological issues raised by Arianism once and for all. The Western bishops, on the other hand, having just come from their own council at Rome, were more interested in

[45] For the text, see Hanson, *Search for the Christian Doctrine of God*, 286–287.

restoring the deposed Eastern bishops to their sees and asserting what they believed was the jurisdictional authority of the Roman bishop in the East. Minds failed to meet, with the result that the Easterners accused the Westerners of Sabellianism and the Westerners anathematized the Easterners as Arians. In such an atmosphere little could be achieved, but in the longer term it had the effect of making each side more sensitive to the likely reaction of the other. As a result, the Easterners went out of their way to reassure their Western colleagues that when they confessed that there were three *hypostases* in the Godhead they did not mean that there were three different Gods. For their part, the Westerners insisted that by *hypostasis* they meant the same thing as *ousia*, leaving the door open for a reconciliation on that basis.

Despite this, it was soon apparent to all that a damaging rift had opened up in the church, and within a year attempts to heal it had begun. Unfortunately, things started out badly when two Western bishops turned up in Antioch in 344. For reasons known only to himself, Stephen of Antioch decided he would ensnare Euphrates of Cologne, one of the Westerners, in scandal by planting a prostitute in his bedroom and then accusing him of fornication! The plot was discovered, Stephen was deposed (and unfrocked), and the Westerners retired in disgust. Most fatefully of all, when the emperors (Constans in the West and his brother Constantius II in the East) heard of this, they realized that they could not leave church affairs in the hands of the bishops, and from this time onward they took a more active part in the developing theological debates.

Remarkably, the Antiochene Council of 344 was able to produce another creed, which was sent to Milan, where a Western council met the following year and considered it. It was much the same as the document that had been sent to Serdica, but with further explanations of the points that were liable to provoke adverse reaction in the West. In particular, it avoided affirming Origen's belief in the eternal generation of the Son, and said nothing about the existence of three *hypostases* in God. As the West would do, it did not use the term *ousia*, leaving the impression that the oneness of God would have to be described as his *hypostasis*. They even used the word *prosôpon* ("person") to refer to three "objects" in God, something which seems to have been unprecedented in an Eastern confessional document. Unfortunately, the Council of Milan was in no mood to appreciate these remarkable gestures in the Western direction. Instead, it insisted that the Eastern church should condemn Arius outright, and readmit Athanasius to his see of Alexandria, an idea that was unpopular in the East for other reasons.[46] The

[46] Athanasius was seen as a troublemaker and prone to use violence to get his way. Doctrinal issues were secondary, though Athanasius's anti-Arianism and his close association with Marcellus of Ancyra were additional reasons why he was not particularly welcome in the East.

Easterners gave way on these matters in order to keep the peace, but it was clear that real reconciliation was still some way off. And the emperor Constantius II was losing patience with a process that seemed to be getting nowhere.

A New Departure in Christology

When Constantine I died in 337, the empire was divided among his three sons, Constantine II, Constans, and Constantius II. Before long, conflict between the first two of these had eliminated Constantine II, and Constans ruled in the West until he was murdered by his general Magnentius in 350. That led to an invasion by Constantius II. After a few years of campaigning, Magnentius was decisively defeated in 353, leaving Constantius II as the sole ruler of the empire until his death in 361. There is no doubt that Constantius desired the peace of the church and the unity of his empire, and he realized that the Arian controversy would have to be settled if those aims were to be achieved. As he saw it, the only way to reach his goal was to work out which theological position was likely to command the most widespread assent and then to impose it on a council of bishops. He took his time deciding what solution to the Christological question he would adopt, and those who did not like his policy accused him of inconsistency, but in the end he settled on one particular view and hoped that others would eventually come around to agreeing with it.

The first sign of impending change appeared at a council held at Sirmium[47] in 351, which adopted a creed almost identical to the Fourth Creed of Antioch (341) and added twenty-six extra anathemas, most of them directed against Sabellianism and the teaching of Marcellus of Ancyra. However, there was an unwillingness at Sirmium to use the word *ousia* and its compounds, which points to an anti-Nicene influence, even if it could not be called pro-Arian at this stage. Constantius II was now in the West and did what he could to get the churches there to sign the Creed of Sirmium. At first it seemed as though he might succeed, but Western minds were acutely tuned to anything that might smack of Arianism, and they soon found the creed unsatisfactory. The most famous nonsignatory was Hilary of Poitiers, who was exiled to Cappadocia as a result of his objections, but he was only one of many who suffered a similar fate.

Constantius II quickly discovered that he was up against some formidable opponents, but he did not give in to them. One of the most prominent of these was Hosius of Córdoba, now nearly a hundred years old, who had presided at Nicea in 325 and may be assumed to have been a leading supporter of its deci-

[47] Now Sremska Mitrovica in Serbia.

sions. Hosius was dragged from Spain to Sirmium, where, at a third council held in 357, he was told to denounce Athanasius and sign a clearly anti-Nicene Creed that had just been produced at a second council there. Hosius would not renounce Athanasius but he did sign the creed under pressure, though once back in Córdoba he recanted, and before he died he was able to warn all and sundry against succumbing to the danger of Arianism. The other opponent whom Constantius had to crack was Liberius, bishop of Rome (352–366). In theory this should have been easier, because in his earlier days Liberius had shown some pro-Arian leanings, and his emissaries at different councils had proved to be compliant with the emperor's wishes. But as it turned out, Liberius was more obstinate than Constantius had expected, and he was exiled to Berea in Thrace, where his resistance was finally broken and he too signed the Sirmian Creed of 357.[48]

The Second Council of Sirmium was small, and anyone who openly opposed the policies of Constantius II stayed away or was prevented from coming. Athanasius was in hiding in Upper Egypt, having been exiled from Alexandria for a third time, and Hilary, one of our main sources for our knowledge of the council, was languishing in Cappadocia. The creed it composed was almost certainly the work of a second string of pro-Arian bishops, and it was denounced from the start as blasphemous by all who supported Nicea. It was not explicitly Arian, because it said nothing about the Son having been created, either in time or out of nothing, but the Arian tinge was clearly visible in the way it attributed a unique status to the Father and insisted on the eternal subordination of the Son to him. It also stated that the Son suffered in his human body, something that the Father, as God, could never have done. God suffered on the cross, according to this creed, but only because God the Son was somehow an inferior kind of deity, the classic sign of Arianism.

The Second Creed of Sirmium explicitly rejected the use of the word *ousia* to describe the being of God, and forbade the use both of the Nicene *homoousios* ("of the same being") and of the compromise *homoiousios* ("of a similar being"), which had come into use alongside it and was first mentioned in this document. Unsophisticated and extreme as the Second Creed of Sirmium was, it turned out to be of lasting significance because it forced all sides in the Arian debate to define their position in relation to it. The creed was presented to a council held at Antioch in 358, at which point many in the East woke up to realize that they were not able to sign so clearly Arian a statement of faith. After the Third Council of Sirmium, the battle lines were more clearly drawn,

[48] Berea in Thrace is not to be confused with Berea in Macedonia, which the apostle Paul visited (Acts 17:10–15). It lay near the modern city of Edirne (Turkey), known in ancient times as Adrianople.

and those who had preferred to sit on the fence were forced to show their hand. One of these was Basil of Ancyra, the man who had been selected to replace Marcellus when he was deposed in 336.[49] In 358 Basil called a synod where he presented a new creed, composed by himself on the basis of the Second Antiochene Creed of 341.[50] As recorded by Epiphanius of Salamis, Basil explained his theological views like this:

> We are not baptized into a "creator and a created" but into a Father and a Son. . . . The Son is like the Father. We must not allow the idea of passibility to enter into this relationship, . . . nor of bodily existence, but with these safeguards we can apply the words "creature" and "creator" to the Son and the Father. When every elimination and allowance has been made, what we have left is the single concept of likeness.[51]

What Basil was saying was that human beings are consubstantial with each other, since we are all members of the same species, so the same logic could be applied to the divine Father and Son. They could be *like* one another without being identical. As a man, I share my humanity with all other men and women, and in that sense I am *homoousios* with them. But I am also a distinct individual and not identical with anyone else. For me to say that I am of the same being with them means only that my being is *like* theirs—it is similar and compatible with theirs—not that we are exactly the same people. As the Greeks would say, this makes me *homoousios* with them in the sense of being *homoiousios* ("of a like or similar being"). They are similar in being but not absolutely identical, and if *homoousios* could have been interpreted in that way there would have been no problem in accepting at least the moderate Arians back into the church. It was, after all, only an iota of difference that was at stake.

The snag was that it was an iota that made all the difference. This interpretation of *homoousios*, while perfectly possible in the case of humanity, does not work for divinity because there is only one God. It is therefore impossible to be *homoiousios* with God, except perhaps in a very superficial or metaphorical way. We might say that human beings are like God because we are made in his image, or that angels are like God because they are spiritual beings. But such similarities to God serve to highlight how *unlike* him we are in actual fact. A created spirit is like God only to those who are not spirits themselves and who

[49] Basil seems to have held onto the see despite periodic attempts by Marcellus to reclaim it.
[50] Or possibly the fourth. See Hanson, *Search for the Christian Doctrine of God*, 351–352, for an assessment of the evidence.
[51] Epiphanius of Salamis, *Panarion* 73.4.2.

therefore tend to lump all forms of spirituality together under one heading. An image need bear no more than a formal resemblance to its prototype, in the way that a portrait does to the person it portrays. In reality, we are not *homoiousioi* with God, and certainly not *homoousioi*. The Son, however, was in a different category. It was possible to say that he was *homoiousios* with the Father, but because God is one and divinity cannot be manifested in a multiplicity of different individuals, if the Son is *homoiousios* with the Father he must also be *homoousios* with him, and therefore identical with the Father at the level of his being. For Basil of Ancyra, however, such identity of being is possible only for material substances that can be cut into pieces. Spiritual beings cannot be cut up in that way, and so they are all fundamentally independent of one another. That is why they cannot be *homoousioi*, however similar to one another they may appear to be.

Basil's doctrine soon found itself under attack from more consistently pro-Arian quarters. One of these is associated with the name of Acacius of Caesarea (d. 365?), Eusebius's successor to the bishopric there and a faithful representative of his teaching, and also with Eudoxius, who died as archbishop of Constantinople in 360. Lack of evidence and distorted reporting of their views by their opponents make it impossible to be certain of their teaching in every detail, but the broad outlines are clear and consonant with traditional Arianism. They are:

1. The *homoiousios* idea is right about *homoios* but wrong about *ousia*. The Son is like the Father in terms of his power, nature, and authority over (the rest of) creation. This point must be stressed, but since God is not a "substance," words employing *ousia* should be avoided when describing him.

2. The Bible must be the guide to all doctrinal formulation. Words not found in it (like *homoousios*) should not be used to express doctrine. This assertion was intended to embarrass the Nicene party, but of course it could be applied one way or another to everyone engaged in the debate, as the pro-Nicenes did not hesitate to point out.

3. The Father is God in a way that no other being is or can be. He alone is "ingenerate" (*agennêtos*), and since not being born is a fundamental characteristic of divinity, he alone is truly God.

4. The Son was not created out of nothing, but neither was he begotten in the human sense of the term. He came into existence by the express will of the Father, which is what makes the term "begotten" meaningful in the case of God.

5. The Son was a divine being capable of suffering. He did not assume a human soul in his incarnation, because his divine nature took its place and suffered instead.

6. The Son worships the Father as his God; they are in no sense equals.

7. The term *homoousios* suggests Sabellianism and must be rejected. The pro-Nicene retort that this forces their opponents to deny the likeness of the Son to the Father is mistaken. That likeness is real, but it does not inhere in the substance or being of God.

This Homoean teaching, as it is called, did not win favor with everyone who objected to the Nicene *homoousios*. Some thought that it was too much of a compromise and wanted a more logically coherent alternative, which its opponents labeled "Anhomoean" but which its supporters would have preferred to call "Heterousian." The leaders of this group were Aetius (d. 367), a man of humble origins who came to theology somewhat late in life, and his more sophisticated disciple Eunomius of Cyzicus (330?–390?), some of whose writings survive and give us the clearest picture of what they believed and how their Arianism differed from that of the more popular Homoeans.[52] In general terms, where Acacius and his colleagues sought to be biblical and disliked using abstract terms like *ousia* when speaking about God, Aetius and his followers were philosophical in their outlook and made little use of the Bible. The specific points on which the neo-Arians or Heterousians differed from the Homoeans were:

1. God is comprehensible. Anyone can understand him, because he is completely rational. There is no need of special revelation; proper philosophical training is enough.

2. The Son is immutable by nature and not merely by grace (as the Homoeans thought). He cannot become any more (or less) divine than he already is. This means that there could be no self-emptying (*kenôsis*) on the Son's part when he became a man,[53] because whatever "emptying" there was had occurred already—when he was created.

3. The Son is like the Father to the extent that they share the same will, but they have different *ousiai*. This is why Aetius and Eunomius spoke of the Son as *heterousios* ("of a different substance") to the Father, and not as *anhomoios* ("unlike") with respect to him. Far from shying away from unbiblical terms like *ousia*, the neo-Arians were perfectly happy to use them for the sake of logical clarity.

[52] On this group, see Thomas A. Kopecek, *A History of Neo-Arianism*, 2 vols. (Cambridge, MA: Philadelphia Patristic Foundation, 1979).

[53] See Phil. 2:7.

Basil of Ancyra's attempted solution to the Christological problem was neither profound nor consistent, but it appealed to the emperor Constantius II, who promptly ordered that the more extreme Arians who were in control at Antioch should be removed from their posts. He also summoned a further council, to meet at Sirmium in 358, which was intended to ratify Basil's views and bring peace to the church. It was around this time that Liberius of Rome was recalled from exile, having signed a document in which he condemned Athanasius. Did Liberius also sign Basil's creed, or something very much like it? Hilary of Poitiers said that he did and condemned him for it, but Athanasius was more positive about him, which is surprising considering that Liberius had been persuaded to anathematize him personally.[54] What is certain is that the more extreme Arians in Antioch, led by the now deposed Eunomius, tried to claim that Liberius had rejected the *homoousios* doctrine at Sirmium in favor of their own ("anhomoean" or "unlike") doctrine, which said that the Father and the Son were completely different at the level of being (*ousia*). Whatever the truth of the matter, Liberius had certainly given some kind of approval to a formula that the pro-Nicene party in the church regarded as heretical.

The immediate result of this was that the emperor's policy seemed to have triumphed. The extreme Arians in Antioch were isolated just as much as Athanasius was, but the rest, and the Western church under the leadership of Liberius, seemed prepared to reach an agreement. The moderate Arians would have preferred to say that the Son is "like" the Father without mentioning the word *ousia*, but it was generally felt that the compromise formula *homoiousios* was not so different from their position that they would refuse to accept it. This agreement was not left to chance but was composed by Basil, probably at Constantinople, and sent to two synods of the church, one for the East at Seleucia in Cilicia (near Tarsus), and the other at Ariminum (Rimini) in Italy, for the Western bishops. The whole theological program was carefully set out in a letter attributed to George of Laodicea (300?–361) but almost certainly written at Basil's direction.[55]

George's letter is remarkable because it wastes no time in asserting that the Son is an *ousia*, quite distinct from the Father and not to be restricted to the divine *logos* or assimilated to created things that do not exist on their own. In George's thinking, *ousia* and *hypostasis* are synonymous, the only difference being that modern theologians (his contemporaries) preferred *hypostasis* where the ancients had said *ousia* to describe the identity of the Son. He was

[54] Hilary of Poitiers, *Collectio Ariana* B.7.7; Athanasius, *Apologia secunda* 89.3.

[55] It can be found in Epiphanius of Salamis, *Panarion* 73.12.1–73.22.4. We do not know whether the letter was written before or after the councils held in 359, but it scarcely matters for our purposes.

especially opposed to the extreme neo-Arianism then being propagated by the Antiochene theologians mentioned above. In his own words,

> When we hold that the Son is like the Father in every respect, we oppose those who teach that he is only like him in will and power, but that in being (*to einai*) he is unlike (*anhomoios*) the Father. They say that he is not begotten from God but that he is only a creature, different from other creatures [only] because of his higher status, in that everything else was made by him and he alone was made directly by God.[56]

George clearly saw the neo-Arian Anhomoeans as his main enemies, though occasionally he took a swipe at "Sabellians," who may have been pro-Nicene Homoousians. Quite remarkably, George went on to establish a link between Eastern and Western thought, which he obviously hoped would persuade the Westerners to change their suspicious attitude toward what they imagined was the "tritheism" of the East. As he said,

> No one should be disturbed by the word *hypostases*, because the Easterners use the plural to express the subsisting and existing properties of the persons. Each person, including the Holy Spirit, can be described as "subsisting" so that when speaking of three *hypostases* they do not mean three ultimate principles or three gods.[57]

This was actually the first time in the Arian controversy that anyone had made a clear distinction between the three persons and the one substance of God and related the Eastern to the Western terminology. It was also one of the few occasions when the Holy Spirit was mentioned alongside the Father and the Son. George went on later to elaborate how he saw the third person, who "exists from the Father through the Son."[58]

In distinguishing the Son from the Father, George insisted that the Son acts only as the Father's servant, and does not take decisions without consultation, in the way that the Father can.[59] Most of the rest of the letter is taken up with an extended argument against the neo-Arian tendency to distinguish the Father from the Son by using the terms "unbegotten" for the former and "begotten" for the latter, because this distinction implied that the Son belonged to the rest of the created order. The names "Father" and "Son" imply a built-in relationship that must be eternal, which is not true of the pair "unbegotten/begotten."

[56] Epiphanius of Salamis, *Panarion* 73.13.3.4.
[57] Ibid., 73.16.2.
[58] Ibid., 73.16.4.
[59] Ibid., 73.18.3–8.

George and Basil retained the subordinationism inherent in all Eastern theology from the time of Origen, but in other respects they were remarkably close to the pro-Nicene position. Certainly they were less bothered by it than they were by extreme Arianism, and within a few years pro-Nicene theologians would be making use of their insights as they sought to refine their own theological position.

The imperial desire to impose this way of thinking on the church failed dismally. The Council of Seleucia gave Basil's creed a cool reception, with many present preferring the more pro-Arian formula put forward by Acacius of Caesarea. He wanted to drop all the competing terms (*homoousios, homoiousios*, and *anhomoios*) and say only *homoios* ("like") instead. Acacius did not get very far with this suggestion, which was extremely simplistic and unsatisfactory, but that simplicity had its own appeal. All sides petitioned the emperor, hoping that he would incline to their views and ban the rest, but as it happened, Acacius reached Constantinople first and managed to persuade the emperor to side with him. The Council of Ariminum meanwhile wanted nothing to do with Basil's innovations and preferred to stick with the Creed of Nicea, which it thought was perfectly adequate. Its bishops also appealed to Constantius, who promptly put as much pressure on them as he could. In the end, the majority gave in and signed the emperor's creed, as did the delegates from Seleucia.

By the end of 359 it looked as though Constantius's policy had succeeded and the whole empire had submitted to the Homoean theology as propounded by Acacius, even if it was stretched by some people to include what they really believed. This was a broad church in which relatively few individuals encompassed the breadth but many found shelter in one corner of it or another. Things might have continued indefinitely in this vein, but within weeks of the apparently final decision, a revolt broke out, led by Constantius's cousin Julian. At first the emperor ignored it, but eventually he had to take it seriously and decided to suppress it. He fell ill on campaign and died, bequeathing the empire to Julian, who would renounce Christianity and try to restore the ancient pagan gods. Constantius's policies were in ruins, not least in Alexandria, where his replacement for Athanasius was lynched by the mob and the rightful bishop was summoned back to his see.

The Triumph of Athanasius

By 361, Athanasius was an accomplished theologian whose writings had become well known for their defense of Nicene orthodoxy against the resurgence of Arianism. His first and perhaps greatest book is now subdivided into two and known as the *Contra gentes* and *De incarnatione*, but originally they were a single work.[60] There is considerable disagreement about the date of its composition, but it seems most likely to have been sometime around 335, followed shortly afterwards by his lectures against the Arians (*Orationes contra Arianos*), whose beliefs had to be exposed and refuted even if it appeared that the danger they posed for the church had receded. In this early period, Athanasius was prepared to use terminology, like that of the "precise image [*eikôn aparallaktos*] of the Father," that he would later reject because of the unfortunate way it was being used by his adversaries. By trial and error, he was helping to shape a technical vocabulary that would be adequate for the needs of Nicene orthodoxy and that would form the basis for the theological synthesis that emerged after his death.

Basic to Athanasius's approach was his belief that God created the world without an intermediary. God did not generate his *logos* as the Son in order to create the universe; rather, the Son was with the Father in eternity. As he put it,

> [Christ is] the good offspring of the Good and by origin the true Son. He is the power, wisdom and *logos* of the Father, not by participation nor because these attributes are attached to him externally. . . . He is wisdom in himself, *logos* in himself, the power of the Father in himself, light in himself, truth in himself, righteousness in himself, virtue in himself, the character, reflection, and image [of the Father]. He is the wholly perfect offspring of the Father, the only Son, the Father's precise image [*eikôn aparallaktos*].[61]

In his diatribes against the Arians, Athanasius spent a good deal of time expounding the key biblical texts they used to defend their position, and especially Proverbs 8:22–36, which he claimed applied only to the incarnate Christ and not to the eternal Son.[62] Modern readers cannot accept Athanasius's exegesis of this text any more than that of his Arian opponents, because their common assumption that it is Christological in intention is mistaken. But we must not let this deter us from recognizing that Athanasius understood that the word "mediator," when applied to Christ, does not mean some intermediary between the Father and the created order, but refers to the substitutionary sacrifice by which the Son reconciled us to God. Obvious as this seems to us, it was a new idea in the theological climate of the fourth century. At one stroke Athanasius removed the need, felt by the Gnostics as well as by the Arians, to look for a being that could mediate between God and the world without

[60] Athanasius, *Contra gentes* and *De incarnatione*, ed. Robert W. Thomson (Oxford: Oxford University Press, 1971).
[61] Athanasius, *Contra gentes* 46.52–61.
[62] Athanasius, *Orationes contra Arianos* 2.73–74.

belonging wholly to either. It also made it possible to locate the Trinity inside the eternal being of God rather than see it as a series of emanations from the Father designed to reach out to his creatures in time and space.

The strength of Athanasius's theology lay in its basic principles. First, he insisted on the unity, indivisibility, and eternity of God. That made it impossible for him to accept that the *logos* had emerged from the divine being, whether in time or out of it. Next, he believed that Jesus of Nazareth was the *logos* incarnate, whose purpose in coming to earth was to redeem the human race from the sin of Adam. In Christ, God had revealed himself to the world as he truly is and not as some intermediary might interpret his being to us. The one weakness, which the Arians were quick to perceive and which Athanasius never fully overcame, was that he found it hard to explain how the incarnate *logos* could suffer and still be divine. The Arians had explained his suffering by diluting the quality of his divinity, but that solution was anathema to Athanasius. What he needed, but did not have ready to hand, was a way of preserving the Son's divine impassibility without limiting or discounting the reality of his human suffering.

In describing how the Son is related to the Father, Athanasius was fond of using biblical imagery. To him, as to the apostles, Christ was the image, reflection, and stamp of the Father.[63] But he never interpreted these expressions to mean that the Son was inferior to the Father in the way that a copy is inferior to the original. He was particularly concerned to avoid the Arian belief that the Father had created the Son in order for the Son to take his place in circumstances (like suffering) where it would have been impossible for the Father to act. As far as Athanasius was concerned, what the Son did, the Father did also.[64] What sealed their unity and made the Son's divinity fundamental to understanding it was his conviction that the Son revealed the Father. If the Son were inferior to the Father in some way, he would not have been able to do that, because whatever notion of the Father he might convey would inevitably be partial and distorted. Furthermore, if the Son were not fully God, it would be impossible for us to be integrated into the divine life and become "gods" as Jesus promised us that we would.[65]

Athanasius did not mean that believers would rise to the same level of being as the Son's, because the Son is God by nature (*physis*) whereas we are "divine" only by what we would now call grace.[66] He also pointed out that, while it is

[63] See 2 Cor. 4:4; Col. 1:15; Heb. 1:3.

[64] Athanasius, *Orationes contra Arianos* 2.24.

[65] Ibid., 3.6. See John 10:34–35.

[66] Athanasius does not use the word "grace" (*charis*) but expresses the same idea by saying "position" (*thesis*) instead.

possible to imagine God as Creator or Maker without specifying what he has created or made, it is not possible to say the same of the term "Father." For God to be a Father implies that he must have a Son, and so eternal fatherhood logically brings eternal sonship with it.[67]

Athanasius's main target was Arianism, but he was also aware of the opposite danger of Sabellianism and did what he could to avoid it. In his words,

> [Father and Son] are one, not like a one who is named twice over, so that sometimes he is the Father and sometimes the Son. . . . They are one in the uniqueness of their inherent nature and in the identity of the one Godhead. Everything that can be said of the Father can also be said of the Son, except that he is not the Father.[68]

Here we can see how Athanasius had the substance of the matter but lacked the terminology to describe it satisfactorily. He could have spoken of two *hypostases* or even of two *prosôpa* ("persons") but he did not, probably because the first would have sounded to his Western readers like tritheism and the second would have come across in the East as Sabellianism. The terminology needed to solve the problem was available, but an intellectual climate in which it could be received without ambiguity or misunderstanding had still to be created.

The biggest hurdle that Athanasius had to surmount was the Arian assertion that the Father was unbegotten (*agennêtos*) and uncreated (*agenetos*), whereas the Son was begotten (*gennêtos*). If "unbegotten" and "uncreated" are practically synonymous, did it follow that the same must be true of "begotten" and "created"?[69] Athanasius insisted that this way of thinking reflected Greek philosophy and was unbiblical.[70] The eternity of the Father implied the eternity of the Son, and any references to the Son's birth or "creation" must therefore refer to his incarnation, not to his relationship with the Father within the Godhead. Here Athanasius was on unsure ground, and the weakness of his exegetical principles did not help. What he lacked was a knowledge of Hebrew that would have enabled him to see that the language which he regarded as temporal was in fact relational and juridical—to be

[67] Some people today might wonder why the Father could not have had a daughter instead of a son. The answer is that a daughter would not have been identical to him but a contrast, which the absence of sexuality in God makes impossible.

[68] Athanasius, *Orationes contra Arianos* 3.4.

[69] The Greek words are very similar and so are easily associated with one another, but it is not true to say (as some commentators do) that they were confused because they were pronounced alike. The difference lay not in the single versus the double *n*, which makes no difference in Greek, but in the middle vowel, which is long in "unbegotten" and short in "uncreated"—and was pronounced differently enough for the distinction to be heard.

[70] Athanasius, *Orationes contra Arianos* 1.34; *De decretis* 5–6.

the "firstborn" was to be the heir, whether the statement was literally true or not.

On the other hand, the Arian argument that birth is a process and that fathers must precede their children in time was rightly dismissed by Athanasius as pressing the analogy too far. What is true in the created order has no meaning in the sphere of the divine; what matters there is the relationship, not the origin, of which there can be none. The Son did not come into being as an act of the Father's will, but was present in God all along. Of course, his existence did not go *against* the Father's will but was in harmony with it. As he put it,

> The Son does not exist without the Father willing his existence. The existence of the Son is obviously according to the Father's will, just as God is [willing to be] good without having willed it deliberately. The Son does not originate from the Father's will but his existence does not go against it either. The fact that the Father and Son love each other and that the Son honors the Father demonstrates this.[71]

Nothing illustrates the development of Athanasius's theology in the wake of controversy better than the use he made of the term *homoousios*. Odd though it may seem, this word appeared only once in his early writings, in what amounted to a quotation from Nicea, and he did not expound it.[72] After that, he was silent on the subject for twenty years, which seems surprising in the circumstances but is a reminder that *homoousios* was less significant in the immediate aftermath of Nicea than it would later become. To many people it sounded Sabellian and suggested that the Son was "a chip off the old block," as it were—a part of God that had been cut loose rather than a distinct being in his own right. As we have already seen, there were some who wanted to avoid *ousia* terminology altogether and find another way of expressing the unity of Father and Son, who were "like in all respects" or "identical in nature" because the Son was the "exact image" of the Father.[73] It seems that it was only when creedal formulas began to emerge that were intended to replace the Nicene one, and the emperor offered his support to them in the interest of maintaining church unity, that Athanasius felt compelled to defend the decision of 325 and came to see that *homoousios*, properly understood, offered the surest bulwark against the renewed threat of Arianism. Thus it was that in his *De decretis*, written around 357, when Constantius II was just beginning to impose his own preferred solution to the Arian problem, Athanasius retreated

[71] Athanasius, *Orationes contra Arianos* 3.66.
[72] Ibid., 1.21 (repeated in 1.23).
[73] Ibid., 3.22, 26.

to the Nicene formulation, which quickly became the defining symbol of his Christology.

Athanasius explained that, at Nicea, *homoousios* had been introduced because the Arians were able to interpret phrases such as "like the Father" and "exact image of the Father" in a way that accorded with their theology.[74] To the objection that *homoousios* was normally used of material substances and not of spiritual realities, Athanasius pointed out that everyone spoke of the sun and its rays, which are distinct but inseparable. The same could be said for light and its reflection, which are consubstantial but conceptually distinct.[75] Finally, he traced the word back through a series of earlier writers, culminating with Origen, all of whom had used it in spite of the fact that it cannot be found in the Bible.[76] It was therefore not a Nicene innovation, but an ancient term hallowed by usage that long predated the Arian controversy.

With the emergence of the Homoeousian doctrine of Basil of Ancyra,[77] Athanasius returned to the defense of *homoousios* in his work on the councils (*De synodis*), but this time he went into even greater detail. He began with a demolition of the teaching of Acacius of Caesarea and defended the use of the nonbiblical *homoousios* by reminding objectors that they also used any number of nonbiblical expressions (like *agenetos* and "exact image"). At one point Athanasius even condemned the Arians for saying that the Son was from a different *hypostasis* than that of the Father, thereby inadvertently revealing that he still believed that *hypostasis* and *ousia* were synonymous.[78] In tackling the Homoeousians, he based his analysis of their doctrine on the letter of George of Laodicea, which he treated with remarkable gentleness. He did not regard the Homoeousians as heretics but as would-be orthodox believers who lacked an adequate understanding of the oneness of God. What he apparently did not realize was that the Homoeousians were gradually moving toward a much needed conceptual distinction between the one and the three in the divine being that had previously eluded almost everyone and had led to the widespread feeling that the Nicene use of *homoousios* was Sabellian.[79]

After rehearsing the pro-Nicene arguments that the Son cannot merely participate in the Father's divinity but must be fully united with him if he is to reveal God to us and transform us by his indwelling power, Athanasius summed up his approach as follows:

[74] Athanasius, *De decretis* 20.1–3.
[75] Ibid., 23.1–2.
[76] Ibid., 26–27.
[77] "Homoeousian" is the Latin spelling of "Homoiousian."
[78] Athanasius, *De synodis* 40.3.
[79] Ibid., 41.2–5.

> We do not speak of two gods, we do not think of the unity of the Son with the Father in terms of the similarity of their teaching, but in terms of being (*ousia*) and reality. So we speak . . . of one God who exists as one form of divinity, like the relationship of light to its ray.[80]

Keen though he was to defend the *homoousios*, Athanasius realized that it was not adequate merely to explain the Son's relationship to the Father, because although it accounted for their identity of being it did not explain how they were distinguished from one another. Just as human beings share a common nature without being identical with each other in every respect, so believers will be made like Christ in heaven without being exactly the same as he is. Similarity and distinctiveness coexist at every level, even within the Godhead.[81] Here we reach the limits, and see the limitations, of Athanasius's theology. He knew that there were distinctions within the one *ousia* of God but had no word to explain them, because as yet neither *hypostasis* nor *prosôpon* was sufficiently well defined to describe them. That breakthrough would not come until the next phase of theological development, which Athanasius did not live to see.

In theological terms, the Homoean and Homoeousian controversies were of little significance, but in other ways they came to matter more than the Nicene condemnation of Arius. This was because it was in the form of Homoeanism that Arianism entered political life in the late fourth and fifth centuries. The imperial family of Constantius II (apart from the eccentric Julian the Apostate) remained faithful to the Homoean doctrine, which did not lose state support until the Constantinian dynasty was extinguished in 378. That put an end to Arianism as a serious force among the Romans, but by a curious turn of events, the doctrine acquired a new lease of life that extended its influence for another two centuries.

That happened because in the fourth century there was a growing number of Christians among the Gothic tribesmen who lived north of the Black Sea. They had been converted by slaves they had seized from the Romans, but they needed further instruction in their new faith. One of their number, a young man called Wulfila (310?–383), or Ulfilas (in Greek and Latin), went to Constantinople for instruction toward the end of Constantius's reign, when Homoean Arianism was in the ascendant there. He picked it up and translated most of the Bible into his native language as a way of furthering the conversion of the Goths and other Germanic tribes like them. Before long, many of

[80] Ibid., 52.1.
[81] Ibid., 55.1–3.

them had become Christians, but in the eyes of the Romans they were heretical Arians.[82]

In 376 they invaded the Roman empire, defeated the emperor Valens at Adrianople two years later, and remained on imperial territory. They gradually migrated westward and established semi-independent kingdoms in Spain (409), North Africa (430), and Italy (476), which thus came under Arian rule. These Germanic tribesmen were a tiny minority who clung to Arianism as a way of maintaining their distinctiveness, and therefore also their power, over the vast majority of the populations they ruled. Those populations identified themselves as Romans, in communion with the bishop of Rome, who was the Western representative of the universal or Catholic church. To be Roman was to be Catholic and vice versa, and it was only a matter of time before their demographic weight made itself felt.

With the help of these Catholic Romans, Italy and North Africa were reconquered by the Eastern empire in the early sixth century and Arianism was extinguished. In Spain, however, the Visigoths (Western Goths) held out longer. They were not converted to Catholicism until 589, and only after that did Arianism, which had long ceased to be a serious theological position, finally die out. Nevertheless, the memory of it survived, ensuring that future generations would come to regard Arius as the arch-heretic who had fatally threatened the integrity of the church and its witness to Christ. Just as important, they would also come to regard Athanasius (whom they saw as the Arians' chief theological opponent) as the savior of the church and the final authority on matters of theological orthodoxy. When a monk in late fifth-century Gaul (now France) set out to compose a statement of faith that would communicate Nicene orthodoxy to a wider public, it came to be dubbed the "Athanasian" Creed, even though it had nothing to do with Athanasius and contained statements that he would have found alien and would almost certainly have rejected.[83] Just as the Arianism of the Visigoths bore little relation to the teaching of Arius, so the orthodoxy of the Athanasian Creed had moved beyond what Athanasius would have recognized, though not nearly as far as Arianism had moved from its own roots. By then Nicene orthodoxy in its original form had been transformed by a second wave of theological reflection that in many ways made the controversies of the fourth century seem increasingly obsolete.

[82] Gothic is related to English, as the name Wulfila ("little wolf") makes clear.

[83] For the details of this creed, see J. N. D. Kelly, *The Athanasian Creed* (London: A. & C. Black, 1964). For a more recent appraisal, see Gerald L. Bray, "Whosoever Will Be Saved: The Athanasian Creed and the Modern Church," in *Evangelicals and Nicene Faith: Reclaiming the Apostolic Witness*, ed. Timothy F. George (Grand Rapids, MI: Baker, 2011).

The Trinitarian Synthesis

From the vantage point of hindsight it is clear that what was missing in the Christological debates of the mid-fourth century was an adequate means of distinguishing the oneness of God from the divine Trinity confessed by the church. We are now so used to speaking of three persons in the one substance (or being) of God that it is hard to understand why the greatest minds of the post-Nicene era were unable to reach agreement on this. But finding a formula that would be acceptable to all was difficult because battle lines had hardened and people were suspicious of anything that sounded like a concession to their opponents. The different sides were often closer on matters of substance than they realized, but it was hard to find theological terms to describe their beliefs that were both meaningful and relatively free of preconceived bias. To get a clear view of the issues, it is helpful to remind ourselves of what the parameters of the debate were. The points of agreement and disagreement can be set out as follows:

1. God is one, the Father and the Almighty. This belief was enshrined in the opening lines of the Creed of Nicea and was accepted by all parties in the subsequent debates. It represented a victory over the Gnostics of an earlier era, some of whose followers still existed in the fourth century, which made what to us seems like a banal confession a matter of some importance. Whatever was said about the Son or the Holy Spirit could not be allowed to compromise this basic belief about God the Father.

2. The Son is subordinate to the Father, as his name indicates and as the witness of Jesus in the New Testament also affirms. On this everyone was agreed, but what did it imply for the being and identity of the Son? At one end of the spectrum were those who said that the Son is a creature, higher than the others and the means by which the Father made the rest of the universe, but nevertheless still a creature. This was generally believed to be the essence of Arianism, though many who were tarred with that brush by the pro-Nicene party held a more nuanced view of the matter. As time went on, there was an increasing tendency among the so-called Arians to emphasize the Son's divinity, which led many of them to assert that he was produced by the Father's will at some point outside the human understanding of time.

At the other end of the spectrum were the modalistic Sabellians, who believed that the Son was no more than a manifestation of the one God in a different form. In reality, neither the Father nor the Son were distinct beings in their own right but only names assumed by the one God when he revealed himself to mankind. As with Arianism, very few people seem to have held the

Sabellian view in its pure form, but those who emphasized the divinity of the Son without making it clear as to how he differed from the Father laid themselves open to this charge.

3. The Holy Spirit stands in a special relationship to both the Father and the Son, but its exact nature remains a mystery. Even Athanasius was content with this:

> It is enough to know that the Spirit is not a creature and is not mentioned among the created things. Nothing alien to it is associated with the Trinity, which is indivisible and coherent in itself. This teaching is enough for believers; beyond that, the cherubim cover [the mystery] with their wings.[84]

Insofar as the subject was developed at all, it was generally agreed that the Holy Spirit stood in much the same relationship to the Son as the Son did to the Father. In other words, what a man thought about the divinity of Christ would determine what he thought about the divinity of the Holy Spirit, a fact that made the question one of extreme urgency once it was decided that the Son was *homoousios* with the Father. If the parallelism between Father/Son and Son/Holy Spirit was correct, did it mean that the Holy Spirit was *homoousios* with the Son, and would that imply that he must therefore be *homoousios* with the Father too? This was the logical comparison that would lead from Christology to the Trinity and determine the course of theological development in the late fourth century. The germ of it can already be detected in the second creed produced by the Council of Antioch in 341:

> The Father is really Father, the Son is really Son, and the Holy Spirit is really Holy Spirit. These names have not been given lightly or carelessly but signify exactly the particular *hypostasis* and order and glory of each one who is named, so that they are three in *hypostasis* but one in agreement (*symphônia*).[85]

A later generation would find this inadequate because it located the unity of the three in their mutual agreement rather than in their common essence (*ousia*), but the general drift is clear. The three *hypostases* are distinct but they belong together—the challenge to theologians was to work out precisely how.

It is easy to portray the debates over Arianism and Sabellianism in simple terms of opposition, but as often happens in such cases, most people were somewhere in between the two extremes. To complicate matters still further,

[84] Athanasius, *Epistulae ad Serapionem* 1.11.
[85] Athanasius, *De synodis* 23.

quite a number of theologians modified their positions in the course of debate, making it difficult to place them in one camp or the other. Not a few were prepared to sign any document that was put in front of them, either for the sake of peace or simply in order to escape the peril of exile. Others are known to us only through their opponents, who naturally tended to exaggerate what they disagreed with, whether it was "Arianism" or "Sabellianism." There were even one or two people like Cyril of Jerusalem (313?–386), the great catechist of the fourth-century church, who managed to avoid the controversy altogether by saying as little as possible about it and taking care not to use words that would be picked up by the protagonists on either side and used against them.[86] The church could not go on like this forever, of course, and we must sympathize with the attempts of the emperor Constantius II (337–361) to knock the bishops' heads together, even if we cannot accept the validity of the solution he wanted them to accept. Even so, it was the emperor, more than anyone else, who kept the church focused on the need for unity, and it was in the fallout from his botched interventions in church affairs that the first signs of a consensus started to emerge.

We can detect this emerging consensus for the first time in the letter of Gregory of Laodicea, who realized that the oneness of God and the Trinity were different concepts that had to be analyzed separately. Trying to turn the one into the three did not work, because it diminished the absolute uniqueness of the Father without making either the Son or the Holy Spirit fully divine. Gregory saw the problem but he could not resolve it because he lacked the conceptual terminology needed to do so. To call God a "being" (*ousia*) was fine if it referred only to the Father, but the term could not be stretched to cover the Son as well because it blurred his distinctiveness from the Father. To say that the Son was "consubstantial" (*homoousios*) with the Father was therefore either a form of Sabellianism (failing to recognize the Son's distinctiveness adequately) or of tritheism, imagining that Father, Son, and Holy Spirit were like separate people, made out of the same basic substance but otherwise quite different from one another. The difficulties which the word *ousia* caused were such that it is hardly surprising to find that some theologians wanted to dispense with it and its compounds altogether, which was easier to do in that they were not biblical terms.

There was always the alternative of *hypostasis*, which was used (and preferred) by many, but the problem was that no one could distinguish this word from *ousia* with sufficient clarity. Origen had said that there were three

[86] On these people, see Hanson, *Search for the Christian Doctrine of God*, 387–413.

hypostases in God, but very few people were prepared to follow him and many thought that his solution was basically a form of tritheism that ought to be avoided. Other terms, like *prosôpon* ("person") and *physis* ("nature") were occasionally employed to describe the plurality and the singularity (respectively) of God, but they never caught on in popular discourse. *Prosôpon* suffered from its connections to the theater, where it meant "mask," and so those who applied it to the Godhead ran the risk of being called Sabellians. *Physis* was too vague; it described what a thing is *like* rather than what it *is*. It may be true that this distinction is blurred in the case of God because his perfection means that what he is (divine being) is also what he is like (good, just, etc.), but the two concepts cannot be confused. We pray to a God whom we recognize as the supremely good divine being, but we do not pray to "Goodness," which is something that we attribute to that being but that does not define it completely.

Such was the inadequacy of the terminology available to the theologians of the Eastern (Greek) church, from which they tried but failed to escape. In the Latin West it was a very different story. There, Tertullian had laid down that God was "three persons in one substance," a formula that survived the heat of every subsequent theological battle and is now generally accepted by all Christians as the best one available. The neatness of the formula was such that almost no one in the Latin world had any desire to tamper with it, though they gradually recognized that it had to be interpreted in the light of later controversy. Tertullian had known nothing of Arianism or Sabellianism, and so had not been careful to guard against them. For example, he could speak of the Son as a "portion" (*portio*) of the Godhead without having to specify what he meant by the term, a luxury that later generations could not afford.[87] There was also some reluctance to refer to him as an authority because of his schismatic tendencies. In a generation faced with Donatism in North Africa, Tertullian's strained relationship with the church could not be mentioned without showing disapproval.[88] But these were minor quibbles that did not affect the main argument. The definition of God as "three persons in one substance" quickly established itself as a commonplace of theological discussion in the Latin-speaking world, as can be seen from the writings of Hilary of Poitiers.[89]

The major exception to this tendency was Marius Victorinus (275–363), a philosopher who converted to Christianity in adulthood and made it his life's work to define the terms needed for a proper discussion of the being of God.[90]

---

[87] Tertullian, *Adversus Praxean* 9. Hilary of Poitiers picked him up on this; see his *De Trinitate* 2.8.22.

[88] See, for example, Hilary of Poitiers, *Commentarium in Matthaeum* 5.1.

[89] For a detailed examination of Hilary's theology, see Carl L. Beckwith, *Hilary of Poitiers on the Trinity* (Oxford: Oxford University Press, 2008).

[90] On Marius Victorinus, see "Marius Victorinus," *Les Etudes Philosophiques*, Avril 2012, no. 2, 147–256.

Marius had little time for Tertullian and explicitly distanced himself from his theology:

> It is wrong to say "two persons [in] one substance." Instead, there are two, Father and Son, out of one substance. The Father gives of his substance to the Son because he has begotten him, which makes them both *homoousioi*.[91]

It is not hard to see why Marius would have found Tertullian distasteful. Tertullian was anti-philosophical, and anti-Platonic in particular, whereas Marius was a trained philosopher who wanted to reconcile Platonism with Christianity as far as he could. Tertullian was also straightforward to the point of bluntness, whereas Marius was so refined that he was often almost incomprehensible. Marius knew that *persona* was not a word used in philosophical discourse; it meant nothing to a Platonist and must have struck him as a crude and unprofessional way of speaking about God. But Tertullian's preferred term was clear. Everyone knew (or thought they knew) what a person was, which was more than could be said of Marius's preferred alternatives, like *subsistentia* and *existentia*. Marius loved to express his principles as abstractions, but the average Christian could not relate to an abstraction in the way that he could relate to something concrete like a person. As a result, Marius was greatly admired by a few intellectuals but generally ignored by everyone else, though his thought was not without its influence on the subsequent development of Trinitarian doctrine.

Marius's great contribution was that he understood more clearly than anyone had before him that the Trinity is a revelation of the internal life of God, not an external projection of divine power onto the created universe. Understanding the Son and the Holy Spirit is therefore not a matter of figuring out what kind of creatures they are and how they made the world between them, but rather of learning how they relate to each other, and to the Father, within the Godhead. He also realized that the common ingredient that unites all three is "spirit":

> God is spirit and Jesus is spirit and the Holy Spirit is spirit. The three are from one substance and so they are all *homoousioi*. The Holy Spirit is from Christ as Christ is from God, and so the One is Three.[92]

Here Marius managed to be both biblical and comprehensible. What he perhaps did not realize was that by defining the common element in the Trinity

[91] Marius Victorinus, *Adversus Arium* 1.11.
[92] Ibid., 1.14.

as "spirit" he was opening the door to a fresh consideration of the Holy Spirit as an essential partner in the Godhead. It would be fair to say that in most of the Arian debates the Holy Spirit was effectively discounted. If he was mentioned at all, it was as a creature dependent on the Son just as the Son was a creature dependent on the Father, and it was not at all clear to the Arians that he was in any sense divine.

Marius would have none of that. In a striking image which is again surprisingly biblical, he identifies the Three as different kinds of voice. The Father is the divine silence who nevertheless speaks, the Son is his voice, and the Holy Spirit is the voice of that voice.[93] He even says that the Holy Spirit is Jesus Christ in a different form, begotten by the Father in and through the only begotten Son, who speaks in the heart of believers and teaches them the truth about God.[94] Far from trying to suppress the *homoousios* or find an alternative word for it, Marius extended it to cover the Holy Spirit as well, making it a Trinitarian (and not just a Christological) expression. Here there was great promise for the future, but Marius could not move forward to realize it because of his unwillingness to use the word "person" to describe the Three and his inability to find an acceptable alternative. His philosophical bent toward rationalism landed him in a virtual Sabellianism that others were quick to perceive and that he could not shake off. Moreover, to the extent that he was to influence later developments in the West (and his impact on Augustine is particularly noticeable), that Sabellian tinge would be transmitted with it.

While Marius was grappling with Trinitarian problems in the West, a similar development was occurring in the Greek-speaking world, where the issues had been much more fraught. As it turned out, it would not be the ideas of Athanasius so much as those of Basil of Ancyra that would give birth to the next generation of theologians, who would resolve the difficulties that had stymied their predecessors and prevented the full acceptance of Nicene doctrine in the Eastern church. The credit for this achievement belongs mainly to the so-called "Cappadocian fathers," of whom by far the most important were Basil of Caesarea (329?–379), his younger brother Gregory of Nyssa (330?–395?), and his close friend Gregory of Nazianzus (330?–390). Together they represented a new breed of Christian intellectual, much more closely connected with the philosophical schools of Athens (where they had studied) and correspondingly more indebted to the Neoplatonic school of Plotinus, Porphyry (234?–303?), and Iamblichus (242?–327), whose students were still teaching when they were students.

[93] Ibid., 1.13; 3.16.
[94] Ibid., 4.33.

Neoplatonism had made little impact on Christian thinking before this time, but the Cappadocians made use of it to break the logjam that had trapped the church in an apparently irresolvable problem of terminology. This fact has led many modern scholars to accuse them, and with them the subsequent orthodox tradition, of being more Hellenistic than biblical, but the charge is unfair. Basil and his colleagues took from Neoplatonism what they found useful and adapted it to the requirements of Christian teaching; they did not buy into it as such. As an example that illustrates their independence of mind, we may recall the fact that Plotinus spoke of "three principal *hypostases*" underlying the whole of reality.[95] The Cappadocians were glad to take up the concept of "three *hypostases*," which in any case went back to Origen, but discarded the "principal," as Basil made clear:

> There are not "three principal *hypostases*," nor is the Son's activity imperfect. There is only one principle (*archê*) of all things, which creates [them] through the Son and brings [them] to perfection in the Spirit.[96]

Philosophy (of whatever kind) was to be the handmaid of theology but not its mistress. This became very clear in Basil's refutation of the neo-Arians, whom he encountered above all in the teaching of Eunomius, who maintained that *agennêsia* ("unbegottenness") was the *ousia* of God and that it was therefore impossible for him to generate anything. That essentially rationalist concept was given short shrift by Basil, who pointed out that if it were true, God could not be a Father. He was ingenerate (unbegotten) in the sense that he owed his existence to no one else, but that aspect (*epinoia*) of his identity did not prevent him from begetting a Son or bringing forth the Holy Spirit, as the Scriptures say he did.[97] As for the neo-Arian notion that any right-thinking person can come to an adequate knowledge of God, Basil retorted that only the Son and the Holy Spirit know the Father's *ousia*. We cannot know anything about him unless we are enlightened by the Spirit and made aware of the Son, who then reveals the Father to us.[98]

Basil is particularly interesting for the way in which he treated Proverbs 8:22 ("He created me as a beginning for his works" in the Septuagint version). This was the classic proof-text of the Arians, and the inability of their opponents to see that it is not about the Son at all made it especially hard to refute the Arian assertion that the Bible says that the Son was created. But although he

[95] Plotinus, *Enneads* 5.1.

[96] Basil of Caesarea, *De Spiritu Sancto* 16.38.136. On Basil's thought more generally, see Philip Rousseau, *Basil of Caesarea* (Berkeley: University of California Press, 1994).

[97] Basil of Caesarea, *Adversus Eunomium* 1.5,8,11.

[98] Basil of Caesarea, *Epistula* 38.3.

had to work with that handicap, Basil managed to tackle this verse in a highly sophisticated manner. He pointed out that this phrase occurs only once in Scripture, that Proverbs is full of riddles and obscure sayings, and that some interpreters believe that the Hebrew verb is better translated "possessed" and not "created."[99] For someone with no knowledge of Hebrew and no background in biblical exegesis, that was not a bad attempt to explain it!

When it came to the positive construction of Christian doctrine, as opposed to the demolition of the errors of his opponents, Basil had to confront the usual problems of confused terminology and do what he could to sort them out. Sometimes he used *hypostasis* to mean *ousia*, not least in his interpretation of the word in Hebrews 1:3.[100] But more often he made a distinction between the two words and moved in the direction of saying that there are three *hypostases* in the one *ousia* of God. Interestingly, he could also use the word *prosôpon* instead of *hypostasis* and contrast it with the underlying unity of the divine being:

> The Son is in the Father and the Father is in the Son, the first being like the second and the second like the first. It is in this that their unity consists. According to the individuality of the persons (*prosôpa*) they are distinct, but according to the community of their nature, they are both one.[101]

Basil was aware of the theatrical use of *prosôpon* to mean "mask" and of the danger of Sabellianism that lurked behind this, which may be one reason why he did not make more use of the term than he did. But he would also have known that *prosôpon* had no philosophical pedigree, and like Marius Victorinus, he may have hesitated to use it for that reason too. That possibility is strengthened by the fact that he frequently used *hyparxis* ("existence") and *tropos hyparxeôs* ("mode of existence") as substitutes for *hypostasis*, a usage that was to prove very popular among his disciples.

The root of the distinction between being (*ousia*) and existence (*hyparxis*) lay in the difference between eternity and time. Being is eternal; existence is temporal. That made it possible to think of the persons of the Trinity as temporal manifestations of the underlying divine being, with the difference that for Basil these manifestations were also eternal. He thought of them not in terms of time and space but in terms of the universal and the particular—Father, Son, and Holy Spirit were specific forms of the general being of God

[99] Basil of Caesarea, *Adversus Eunomium* 2.20. The ESV follows this suggestion and adopts the translation "possessed."
[100] Ibid., 1.20.
[101] Basil of Caesarea, *De Spiritu Sancto* 18.45.

that constituted them all. This solution would be questioned by subsequent generations of theologians because of what was perceived as its latent Sabellianism, but it represented a huge advance on everything that had gone before. No longer would it be possible to think of the Trinity as a hierarchy of beings, one of which was superior to the others, nor would it be possible to conceive of them coming into existence one after the other. All three would henceforth be regarded as equally eternal within the one being of God. Basil's formulation would require some further tweaking before it could be accepted as fully orthodox, but his intention was clear, and once his perspective took root there would be no going back to the intellectual world that had permitted the emergence of Arianism.

As far as *homoousios* was concerned, Basil accepted it as the teaching of Nicea and applied it to the Holy Spirit, much as Marius Victorinus was doing in the Latin West at the same time. He was prepared to accept *homoiousios* or at least the phrase that the Son was "like the Father according to his *ousia*" as long as it was clear that this "likeness" was unalterable. As he saw it, the danger was that *homoiousios* did not exclude change in the way that *homoousios* did, and so the latter term was preferable for that reason.[102] But although he came down on the side of Nicea in the end, Basil was much more flexible about this than Athanasius was, though he followed Athanasius in one important particular. *Homoousios*, thought by the Arians to be a sign of modalism, was in fact anti-Sabellian, because it preserved the identity of the *hypostases* or *prosôpa*. The reason for that was that it would be nonsense to say that something is consubstantial with itself, so for the Son to be *homoousios* with the Father must mean that although he is different from the Father he is also the same, but the same in another way![103]

Basil's hesitations about the appropriateness of *homoousios* and his willingness to accept *homoiousios* or its equivalents in its place gradually gave way to a more wholehearted commitment to the Athanasian position, which he defended in the last years of his life. What changed his mind seems to have been a correspondence with Apollinarius of Laodicea (310?–390?), a disciple of Athanasius who would later be condemned for heresy but who was regarded as orthodox until about 360. Apollinarius convinced Basil that only *homoousios* could capture the essence of the relationship between the Father and the Son within the one being of God, and from that point on Basil's theology was more closely aligned with that of Alexandria and the pro-Nicene party than it had previously been.[104] This incident would be obscured by those anxious to

[102] Basil of Caesarea, *Epistula* 9.3.
[103] Ibid., 52.3.
[104] See G. L. Prestige, *St. Basil the Great and Apollinaris of Laodicea*, ed. Henry Chadwick (London: SPCK, 1956).

preserve Basil's reputation from association with a notorious heretic, but such thoughts were not in his mind at the time they corresponded, and there seems to be no reason to doubt that this is what actually happened.

Basil's contribution to the evolving theological debate would not be complete until he had tackled and done his best to resolve the lingering doubts about the place of the Holy Spirit in the Trinity, and in particular the question of his relationship to the Son. Athanasius had led the way toward recognizing the Spirit as *homoousios* with both the Father and the Son, and as Basil became more convinced of the need to use that term, he felt no hesitation in extending it to the Holy Spirit as well. Epiphanius of Salamis had already blazed a trail by stating on several occasions that the Holy Spirit proceeds from the Father[105] and "receives" from the Son. Not infrequently he ran the two together by saying that the Spirit proceeds from both, an elision that was to have fateful consequences many centuries later.[106] But the immediate cause of Basil's intervention on the subject was not the growing perception among the pro-Nicenes that something needed to be said about it. Rather, it was a particular theory put forward by Macedonius, bishop of Constantinople from about 340 to 346 and again from 352 until his deposition in 360, along with Basil of Ancyra and other Homoeousians.

Whether Macedonius was the originator of the doctrine that goes by his name is uncertain, but however it originated, it has always been associated with him.[107] Its essence was that it used the *homoousios* teaching of Nicea to break the chain that had traditionally led from the Father through the Son to the Holy Spirit. The Macedonians,[108] or *Pneumatomachoi* ("Attackers of the Spirit") as they were pejoratively called, confessed the Nicene doctrine as far as the Son was concerned but denied that it had any bearing on the Spirit, who in their minds was not *homoousios* with the Father and the Son. This was a crude compromise between the pro-Nicene and the pro-Arian points of view, accepting the former with respect to the Son but the latter with respect to the Spirit. Macedonianism seems to have emerged in the wake of the Second Council of Sirmium and was essentially what Athanasius was combating in his letters to Serapion, written in the early 360s. At about the same time, Macedonian sympathizers took this doctrine to the West, where it was widely circulated and given at least tacit approval by local bishops who did not understand what the fuss was all about. To them, it was clear that the Macedonians were Homoou-

[105] This is John 15:26.

[106] Epiphanius of Salamis, *Ancoratus* 11.3; 73.1–2; *Panarion* 62.4.12; 69.18.4. For the doctrine of the double procession of the Holy Spirit, see Part Six, "The Person of the Holy Spirit."

[107] On this question, see Hanson, *Search for the Christian Doctrine of God*, 760–762.

[108] This term must not be confused with the same word that is used to describe the inhabitants of Macedonia!

sians, at least to some extent, and they suffered along with other pro-Nicenes as long as Homoean Arianism was the favored imperial policy. After 378 they reemerged, along with the other Homoousians, and continued to exist for at least another generation, though after 381 their influence was much less than it had been beforehand.

Macedonianism is best understood as a kind of Arianism applied to the Holy Spirit rather than to the Son. The Macedonians denied that the Spirit was God, although they accepted that he was divine and were prepared to call him "Lord." They believed that it was right to worship God *in* the Spirit but not to worship the Spirit as God. They acknowledged that Jesus had said that God is spirit,[109] but insisted that he had used the word generically as a description of the divine being, and was not talking about a person of the Godhead. To them, the Spirit was an intermediary between God and the creation, with all the ambiguity that such a position implied. For example, they could not agree whether the Spirit was a creature or not.[110] Like the Arians, they amassed a wealth of scriptural texts that seemed to support their position.[111] Some of these strike the modern reader as amusing, like their use of 1 Corinthians 2:10 ("The Spirit searches everything, even the depths of God") to say that the Spirit had to go looking for the truth because he did not know it automatically (as God did)! Other texts appear to have been doctored to suit their purposes, such as Philippians 3:3, which they read as "those who worship God in the Spirit" instead of "those who worship by the Spirit of God" in order to eliminate the unacceptable phrase "Spirit of God," which would imply his divinity.[112]

Macedonianism was the heresy that Basil confronted in his classic work on the Holy Spirit (*De Spiritu Sancto*), which must have been written around 372 or 373, when the controversy was in full swing. Interestingly enough, Basil never came out and said explicitly that the Holy Spirit is God, but by inductive reasoning from the Bible he demonstrated that that is the only conclusion that can be drawn from the evidence. As he put it,

> [The Holy Spirit] proceeds from the Father, not by generation like the Son, but as the breath of his mouth. . . . The Spirit is a living substance (*ousia*), the Lord of sanctification. His affinity [to the Father] is shown in this way, but his mode of existence (*tropos hypaxeôs*) is concealed in silence.[113]

[109] John 4:24.
[110] Pseudo-Didymus the Blind of Alexandria, *De Trinitate* 2.2; anonymous, *Dialogi Macedoniani* 1:8, 20; 2:2.4.
[111] Among them were Amos 4:12–13; Luke 10:22; John 6:46; and 1 Tim. 5:21.
[112] Epiphanius of Salamis, *Ancoratus* 15.1; Pseudo-Didymus, *De Trinitate* 2.11. It should be said that the variant readings involve only minor alterations of the Greek text and have some manuscript support, though it is often impossible to say whether this is because of Macedonian doctoring or not.
[113] Basil of Caesarea, *De Spiritu Sancto* 18.46.

Basil's legacy was inherited by Gregory of Nazianzus.[114] At the time of Basil's death, imperial policy was shifting once more in favor of the pro-Nicene party under the influence of Theodosius I (378–395), who was to be the last ruler of a united Roman empire. In 380 Theodosius declared Christianity to be the official state religion, and preparations began for another council that would confirm this and establish what the imperial church's doctrine would be.[115] Gregory was the man chosen to become the bishop of Constantinople, where the council would be held, though he was so appalled by this honor and frustrated by the attempts of his enemies to unseat him that he resigned before the council was over and retreated to Cappadocia, never to return to the capital again.[116] Gregory was not made of the stuff required for effective leadership, but his *Theological Orations* remain some of the most profound works on the subject ever to have been composed.[117] Generally speaking, he was the mouthpiece of Basil, as can be seen from the following:

> You are surrounded by one light of God and three—three as regards the *hypostases*, if you want to call them that, or *prosôpa* (for we shall not quibble about terminology as long as the meaning is the same), but one in his *ousia*, or divinity, which is, so to speak, divided indivisibly and united in division. The Godhead is one in three and the three are one.[118]

In this passage, Gregory accepted the use of *prosôpon* to describe the threeness of God, but elsewhere he regarded this habit as a Latinism that had been forced on the Western church because the Latin language was unable to distinguish *hypostasis* from *ousia*! Gregory's ignorance of Latin was matched only by his ignorance (or more likely, his deliberate suppression) of the fact that most Greek-speakers had been equally confused until Basil had put them straight!

Gregory was just as clear about the incarnation of Christ as he was in his understanding of the Trinity. It is to him that we owe the famous phrase, "What has not been assumed has not been healed," a succinct explanation of why the Son had to become fully human, and not just assume an outward casing of flesh, as the Arians had insisted.[119] It would be left to later generations to

[114] On Gregory, see John McGuckin, *Saint Gregory of Nazianzus: An Intellectual Biography* (Crestwood, NY: St. Vladimir's Seminary Press, 2001); and Christopher A. Beeley, *Gregory of Nazianzus on the Trinity and the Knowledge of God* (Oxford: Oxford University Press, 2008).

[115] Constantine I had legalized Christianity in 313, but that was not the same thing as making it the official religion, to the exclusion of all others. It was Theodosius who made that move, and it was in his time that the remnants of paganism (such as the Olympic games) were suppressed.

[116] Gregory of Nazianzus, *De vita sua* ll. 1680–1687.

[117] Gregory produced a large number of orations, of which the five so-called "theological" ones are numbered 27–31.

[118] Gregory of Nazianzus, *Orationes* 39.11.

[119] Gregory of Nazianzus, *Epistula* 101.

work out the full implications of that statement, but the main outline of an acceptable Christology was now clear. Whatever else might be said about the incarnate Son, he was God who suffered and died, not in his divinity but in the humanity that he had assumed in order to fulfill the Father's saving purpose.

When dealing with the Holy Spirit, Gregory took over Basil's teaching and drew the logical conclusions from it. Basil had never explicitly said that the Spirit was *homoousios* with the Father and the Son, but he had said that he was "of equal honor" (*isotimos*) to them, and Gregory concluded that that was effectively the same thing.[120] Basil had understood that it was impossible to find precise biblical texts that would confirm the deity of the Holy Spirit, but what he had regarded as a problem Gregory resolved by saying that it is necessary to collect all the evidence that the Scriptures provide and draw the logical conclusion from it.[121]

Another of Basil's heirs was his brother Gregory of Nyssa, who was much more of a systematic theologian than either Basil or Gregory of Nazianzus, and who must therefore be considered as the most important of the Cappadocians as far as spreading their teaching and ensuring their long-term influence is concerned.[122] In this respect, his debt to the Platonic tradition is obvious, but so too are the ways in which he diverged from it. Like Plotinus, Gregory of Nyssa taught that men are called by God to an ever-deepening participation in the divine being, as far as human nature will permit this, but where the Platonists spoke of ideas (*noêta*) and the supreme being (*to ontôs on*), Gregory substituted angels and God the Father. In other words, his ultimate principles were not abstract but personal, and so for him, absorption into the divine is not the end of existence but the beginning of a new kind of life in God. The "static" nature of Platonic perfection gave way in his thinking to a "dynamic" or living relationship that is entirely consonant with the teaching of the Bible, though quite alien to Plotinus and his disciples.

Gregory taught that there are two ways of knowing God, one external and the other internal. The external way proceeds by philosophical contemplation of his attributes, which can be compared and contrasted to human nature. The internal way is that of mystical experience, in which the old self must die and enter the divine "darkness."[123] There it would walk by faith and come to a perfect knowledge of God's incomprehensible being. In this way, Gregory

[120] Basil of Caesarea, *De Spiritu Sancto* 6, 8; Gregory of Nazianzus, *Oratio* 31.14.
[121] Gregory of Nazianzus, *Oratio* 31.24–25. On Basil's hesitations, see his *Adversus Eunomium* 3.7.
[122] On Gregory of Nyssa, see Martin Laird, *Gregory of Nyssa and the Grasp of Faith: Union, Knowledge, and Divine Presence* (Oxford: Oxford University Press, 2004).
[123] For a detailed explanation of this, see Jean Daniélou, *Platonisme et théologie mystique. La doctrine spirituelle de S. Grégoire de Nysse*, 2nd ed. (Paris: Aubier, 1953).

attempted to resolve the problem of how the *ousia* of God could be known when it surpasses human knowledge. It also makes it possible for him to explain the inadequacies of human language when it comes to discussing the reality of the divine, though he insisted that certain distinctions must be preserved, especially the one between *hypostasis* and *ousia*. As he put it,

> The individuality of the *hypostases* makes the distinction of the persons (*prosôpa*) clear . . . and the one Name [of God] present in our statement of faith, indicates the singleness of the *ousia* of the persons.[124]

He went on to say that there is no difference of nature (*physis*) between the persons, but only a distinction that makes it possible to recognize each of them for who he is. Here at last we have reached what we now recognize as Trinitarian orthodoxy. When it came to dealing with the apparent inferiority of the Son to the Father, Gregory usually followed the traditional pro-Nicene path of attributing such statements to the human nature of Christ and not to his divinity. But he also laid considerable stress on the notion of order (*taxis*) in the Trinity, which dispensed with the concept of inferiority and replaced it with a sense of cooperative organization. In his words,

> The order is given to us in the gospel, according to which our creed starts with the Father, passes through the Son in the middle, and ends with the Holy Spirit.[125]

The words and images Gregory used were modified here and there as time went on, but in essence his doctrine has survived to become the bedrock of the church's confession to this day. The immediate reason for this is that they were taken up and codified by a council that met in Constantinople in mid-381 to determine what the doctrine of the newly established state church should be. The council was only about half the size of the one held at Nicea in 325, and it seems that most of the bishops who attended it were dependent on the see of Antioch. As far as we can tell, there was no representation from Alexandria until near the end of the proceedings, and none from Rome or the West either. The acts of the council have not survived, nor are there any firsthand reports from those who were there. More significantly, it is not clear that the council ever composed a creed, though modern scholars have now retreated from the skepticism of their forebears and are inclined to accept that it did.[126] Even so, there seems to have been no explicit mention of it for

[124] Gregory of Nyssa, *Refutatio confessionis Eunomii* 12.
[125] Gregory of Nyssa, *Contra Eunomium* 1.42.
[126] For the details, see Kelly, *Early Christian Creeds*, 296–367.

the next seventy years, when it was produced (and endorsed) at the Council of Chalcedon in 451. Only after that did it acquire the universal authority that it now enjoys.

Popular opinion has conflated the creed of 381 with that of Nicea in 325, but this is incorrect. To some extent (and to the nonspecialist eye) all creeds look alike, but a detailed examination of their contents reveals that the creed of 381 has other antecedents, though we do not now know what they were. However, it fits very well with the theology of Basil and his fellow Cappadocians, particularly in the section devoted to the Holy Spirit, which is greatly expanded as compared to the earlier creed of 325. It summarizes the doctrine of Basil's *De Spiritu Sancto* very accurately, even in the detail that it refuses to say that the Spirit is *homoousios* with the other persons of the Trinity. Such an omission would hardly have been possible at Chalcedon, by which time the consubstantiality of all three persons was taken for granted, and this must have made the creed seem somewhat archaic in 451. That, of course, is an argument in favor of its authenticity as a product of the council of 381, even if we cannot trace its origin any more precisely than that.

The canonization of Cappadocian Trinitarianism at the First Council of Constantinople set the seal on that doctrine in the Eastern church, which has never departed from it. In the West, things were more complicated. There, the creed of 381 was little known until after Chalcedon, and there is no sign that theologians of the stature of Ambrose of Milan (339?–397) and Augustine of Hippo (354–430) had even heard of it. Particularly telling is the fact that a council held at Aquileia in northern Italy later in 381, which was designed to secure Western acceptance of what had been done at Constantinople, made no mention of it, nor did a further council that was held in Rome the following year. There were a number of Eastern representatives at the Roman council who were able to clarify what had been done at Constantinople and secure agreement to its decisions, but there was no mention of any creed. On the other hand, the council did condemn the writings of Apollinarius of Laodicea, a follower of Athanasius who had strayed too far and denied the presence of a human soul in the incarnate Christ. It is hard to see why it would have done this except by way of ratifying what Constantinople had already done in 381, which makes its silence on the creed seem even more surprising.

What Ambrose, who was present at Aquileia, ignored would hardly have made much impression on his devoted disciple Augustine, who went on to write a magnificent study of the Trinity that has remained foundational for Western reflection on the subject. Augustine began writing it in 399 but broke off after a few years and did not finish it until 419. Its importance for the history of doctrine is twofold. First, it was a remarkable synthesis of existing thought in both East and West, though Augustine admitted that his knowledge of the Greek tradition was imperfect.[127] It appeared at the right time, when that thought had finally crystallized and could be "packaged," as we would say today, for wider consumption. Second, it became the undisputed basis for all subsequent Trinitarian theology in the West, and remains so to this day. Modern theologians can follow Augustine, develop his thought further, or even reject him, but they cannot ignore him. His *De Trinitate* lacks the kind of authority that only canonization by a church council can give, but it is indispensable because it represents how the Creed of Constantinople was later received and understood in the West, even if it was originally quite unconnected to it.[128]

Augustine's *De Trinitate* is a work in fifteen "books" (we would call them "chapters" today) which are neatly divided into two halves. Books 1–7 deal with theology proper and reveal the extent to which Augustine based his Trinitarian reflections on the developing Christology of his time.[129] It is clear from the way he approached the subject that it was the need to defend the divinity of the incarnate Son that motivated further reflection on the Trinity, and in this respect the *De Trinitate* faithfully reflects the intellectual milieu in which it was born. Books 9–15 are very different. They concentrate on various analogies of the Trinity that can be found in creation, and especially in the constitution of the human mind. Augustine recognized that he was indulging in speculation here and regarded these books as secondary to his main purpose, but it is thanks to them that he is now sometimes hailed as the founder of the discipline of psychology.[130] Book 8 is a transition from one to the other, explaining how the created order manifests the being and nature of God and can therefore be studied in order to gain a deeper understanding of him.

[127] Augustine of Hippo, *De Trinitate* 3.1: "From the few Greek works that have been translated for us, I do not doubt that everything we might want to know can be found there, but most of us are not well enough acquainted with that language to be able to read Greek books on the subject with any real understanding of them." We do not know what translations Augustine was referring to, but perhaps he had seen Jerome's translation of the work of an otherwise unknown Alexandrian monk called Didymus, *De Spiritu Sancto*. Otherwise, he probably relied on Hilary of Poitiers and Marius Victorinus, both of whom transmitted elements of Greek thought for the Latin world, though they did not translate specific Greek works.

[128] For a translation of the *De Trinitate*, see Augustine of Hippo, *On the Trinity*, trans. Edmund Hill (Brooklyn, NY: New City, 1991). For a comprehensive study of the work, see Lewis Ayres, *Augustine and the Trinity* (Cambridge: Cambridge University Press, 2010).

[129] The first book is essentially an analysis and interpretation of the biblical texts used to support orthodox Christology.

[130] Hence the extraordinary translation by Stephen McKenna, edited by Gareth B. Matthews: Augustine of Hippo, *On the Trinity Books 8–15* (Cambridge and New York: Cambridge University Press, 2002). The translator and editor omit books 1–7, which they think are of little interest to the modern reader, and concentrate instead on Augustine's speculative analogies. He would have been horrified!

Augustine's originality lies not so much in what he said but in the way that he said it. He was concerned to systematize doctrines that had previously been developed to meet particular needs. Thus, for example, in book 1 of *De Trinitate* he stated that, as a general rule, when the Scriptures speak of the Son as being inferior to the Father, they are referring to the Son in his human, not in his divine nature. That was the standard argument of Athanasius and his colleagues against the Arians. Augustine then went on to state that, occasionally, the New Testament gives the impression that the Son is inferior to the Father, not because he is a lesser divinity but because within the established order of the Godhead, the Son does what the Father wills. Finally, he said that there are times when the Son is spoken of in one of his two natures but what he does is more appropriate to the other. Thus it is possible to say that the Son of God suffered and died on the cross (but only in his human nature) and that the Son of man will come to judge the living and the dead (as God). This transposition can get quite complicated, as appears from the following, which is basically an interpretation of Philippians 2:6–11:

> In the form of God the Son is equal to the Father, and so is the Holy Spirit, since neither of them is a creature, as we have already demonstrated. But in the form of a servant, the Son is less than the Father, as he himself said: "The Father is greater than I."[131] The [incarnate] Son is also less than himself, because it is said that "he emptied himself"[132] and he is less than the Holy Spirit, because he said himself, "Whoever speaks a word against the Son of Man will be forgiven, but whoever speaks against the Holy Spirit will not be forgiven."[133]

Books 2 and 3 of the *De Trinitate* are taken up with a lengthy investigation of the Old Testament passages in which God or an angel representing him appeared to the patriarchs and prophets of old. Augustine claimed, in line with almost all the ancients, that these theophanies were pre-incarnation manifestations of the Son. In book 4 he tied them together by stating that they were all part of the preparation for the final act of divine self-revelation in the incarnation of the Son. His life, death, and resurrection made sense of everything that had gone before and laid the foundation for our understanding and experience of God now. On earth, we can see only in part because our faculties are limited, but what we see is a manifestation of the eternal truth that passes human comprehension. To quote Augustine,

[131] John 14:28.
[132] Phil. 2:7.
[133] Matt. 12:32. Augustine of Hippo, *De Trinitate* 1.22.

> Everything that has taken place in time . . . has been designed to elicit the faith by which we must be purified in order to contemplate the truth and has either testified to the Son's mission or been that mission itself.[134]

In book 5 he went on to break the logjam over words like "begotten" that had caused so much heartache in the East because of the implication that there was some kind of change in God (and therefore diminution to his natural perfection). A begotten deity could not be equal to an unbegotten one, or so it was thought, but Augustine pointed out that this terminology referred to the mutual relationship of the Father and the Son, not to the way the Son had come into being. There then follows an extended discussion of the meaning of theological terminology, which takes us to the end of book 7. True to the climate of his time, Augustine recognized how confusing words like *hypostasis* and *ousia* could be:

> The Greeks make a distinction between *hypostasis* and *ousia* that I do not fully understand. Most of them say "one *ousia* and three *hypostases*" which in Latin means "one being and three substances." But for us, being and substance are much the same thing, so we cannot say that. Instead, many Latin authorities have said "three persons" in order to express in words what they had already experienced without words. . . . Human speech is burdened by a great lack of suitable vocabulary. We say "three persons," not because we mean that exactly, but because otherwise we would be reduced to silence.[135]

Finally, after going through the various attributes of divinity that are present in all three persons equally, Augustine concluded,

> Father and Son are one wisdom because they are one being. . . . It does not follow that because the Father is not the Son nor the Son the Father, or because one is "unbegotten" while the other is "begotten" that they are not one being, because these names only declare their relationships. Together they are one wisdom, one being because being and wisdom are the same, but they are not both Word or Son, because that is not a question of being or wisdom, but a matter of relationship.[136]

In book 8, as he transitioned from an examination of God as he is in himself to a consideration of how he has manifested himself to and in the world, Augustine started to consider what would become one of the most important

---

[134] Ibid., 4.25.
[135] Ibid., 5.10.
[136] Ibid., 7.3.

themes of the whole work: love. The Bible commands us to love God with all our heart, mind, soul, and strength, but we cannot love what we do not know. But love is not merely the means to an end. God is love in himself, and so the more we love him, the more we participate in his being. To quote Augustine,

> Embrace love which is God and embrace God with love. This is the love that unites all the good angels and all the servants of God in a bond of holiness. It conjoins us to them and subjoins us to itself. The more we are cured of the tumor of pride, the more we are full of love, and if a man is full of love, what is he full of, if not God?[137]

And then, at last, we come to the culmination of the whole discourse:

> What is this love which the divine Scriptures praise and proclaim so much, but love of the good? Love means having someone who loves, something that is loved, and love itself. Love is a trinity: the lover, the loved, and love. What is love but a kind of life that couples or tries to couple two things, the lover and his beloved? This is true even of the most external and fleshly kinds of love. . . . What does the spirit love in a friend but his spirit? Here again there are three, the lover, the beloved, and love.[138]

The remaining books of the *De Trinitate* work out this theme in creation and, above all, in the mind of man. It was fundamental to Augustine's understanding of humanity that each of us is created in the image and likeness of the Trinity and therefore we possess in ourselves a Trinitarian structure that corresponds to God: our memory, our intellect, and our will. The presence of sin in our lives has distorted the way these things function, but the redemption we have obtained in Christ puts them back in order again. Even so, the image always remains what it is—a picture, and not the reality itself. In the end we must die and go to be with Christ, and then we shall know by direct experience what it means to be enwrapped in the eternal love of God.

With this, we have reached the final development of Trinitarian thought in the West during the centuries when the main theological quest was for an adequate way to understand who the person of the Son was in relation to the Father. Augustine not only explained that with a clarity that others could not match, but he opened the door for further theological development by demonstrating how closely interconnected the heavenly Trinity and the earthly reality of our human creation, fall, and redemption are. As the Western church

137 Ibid., 8.12.
138 Ibid., 8.14.

absorbed this teaching, it began to concentrate more closely on its implications for the work of Christ in obtaining our salvation, and a new chapter in theological reflection was opened up. The Eastern church, however, went in a different direction, being less concerned with the implications of this doctrine for our experience of salvation, and concentrating more on clarifying the difference between the two natures of Christ, the way in which they worked together, and the implications of that for the work of the Holy Spirit in the life of the believer.

10

The Christian Theological Vocabulary

Hebrew, Greek, and Latin

When Pontius Pilate wrote his controversial inscription on the cross of Jesus, he made sure that the message was conveyed in Hebrew (Aramaic), Greek, and Latin, a reminder that the Roman empire was a multilingual state.[1] In Acts 2:7–11 we are told that Peter and the other disciples were heard speaking in many languages on the day of Pentecost, but we are not told what those languages were. Luke mentions some of the places where the pilgrims in Jerusalem had come from, and from that we can at least make a guess. The Parthians and Medes would have spoken Persian and possibly Kurdish, while the Elamites, Mesopotamians, and Judeans would presumably have used Aramaic most of the time. Cappadocia, Pontus, Asia, Phrygia, and Pamphylia would all have been superficially Greek-speaking, with a number of (mostly unrecorded) local languages as well, though it is doubtful whether the sort of people who went on pilgrimage to Jerusalem would have come from those ethnic groups. Egypt was Greek-speaking in Alexandria and some other cities but Coptic-speaking in the countryside, and the same was probably true of Cyrenaica, which was attached to Egypt at that time. The Cretans spoke a Greek dialect and the Arabs presumably spoke some form of Arabic, though the definition of "Arab" is uncertain, and the ones mentioned here may have been Aramaic-speakers from Roman "Arabia."[2] The visitors from Rome that are mentioned could have been Latin-speakers, but it is more likely that they used Greek most of the time, as the members of the Roman church to whom Paul wrote presumably did.

No one would have thought it miraculous to hear Peter speaking Aramaic, or even Greek, which he also knew, though where and when he and the other

[1] See John 19:19–22.

[2] The Romans used "Arabia" to refer to much of what is now Jordan and the Negev of Israel.

disciples picked it up is unknown.[3] Even Jesus may have learned some Greek and used it in conversation with people like Jairus and Pontius Pilate, but the texts are silent on this point. Pilate probably did not speak Aramaic, and even if he did, he would have been unlikely to use it in a formal trial. However, there is no mention of an interpreter being provided for Jesus, so the matter must remain undecided. What is certain is that the three languages pinned to the cross were all of great significance in the development of the early church, though the roles they played were different and their legacy has come down to us in quite distinct ways.

To begin with Hebrew, the language that we know by this name was on the verge of extinction as a living tongue in Jesus' day. It was still used for liturgical purposes, but most Palestinian Jews spoke Aramaic, a closely related Semitic language that outsiders readily dubbed "Hebrew" because that is what it sounded like to Greek or Latin speakers. Aramaic was the trade language used from Palestine to Mesopotamia, having been spread initially by the Assyrians and then taken over by the Babylonians and the Persians. In 701 BC the average inhabitant of Jerusalem did not understand Aramaic, something we know because the Jewish negotiators with the Assyrian army that was then besieging Jerusalem asked the Assyrians to speak Aramaic instead of Hebrew, so that the people inside the city would not know what they were saying.[4]

The Babylonian exile (sixth century BC) changed all that, because the people who were forced to decamp to Mesopotamia had no choice but to learn Aramaic, and when their children returned to Judea a generation later they brought it back with them. By the time of Jesus it had become the commonly spoken language, and it was almost certainly his own mother tongue. He ministered in it and even quoted Psalm 22 in it when he was hanging on the cross.[5] The apostles presumably spoke Aramaic to one another, but they wrote (if at all) in Greek, and Luke thought it was worth a special mention when Paul addressed the Jewish leaders in their own tongue.[6] In the course of his trial before King Agrippa, Paul also mentioned that Jesus spoke to him from heaven in "Hebrew," which probably should be read as Aramaic.[7]

Biblical Hebrew was not regarded by contemporary Jews as a sacred language, and they had already translated their Bible into Greek as well as produced Aramaic glosses on the text (the so-called Targums). It is therefore

[3] For research on this subject, see J. N. Sevenster, *Do You Know Greek? How Much Greek Could the First Jewish Christians Have Known?* (Leiden: Brill, 1968).

[4] 2 Kings 18:26.

[5] Mark 15:34. Matt. 27:46 gives a slightly more Hebraic version, with *Eli* instead if *Eloi*, but that was commonly done in Aramaic texts and proves nothing.

[6] Acts 21:40.

[7] Acts 26:14.

hardly surprising that it held no appeal to the early Christians and entered the church only in a few words that were regularly used in worship—*amen*, *alleluia* (hallelujah), and *hosanna*. We might add *pesach* to this list, which was Hellenized as *pascha* and passed from there into Latin and other languages.[8]

Hebrew had the added disadvantage that it did not possess a large stock of abstract nouns that could be used for theological reflection. There were some, like *hokhma* (wisdom), which was picked up by Gnostics in the form *achama* or its plural *achamot*, but most of them would have had to be invented (as Modern Hebrew has done). Since hardly anyone spoke the language, this was a waste of effort and so it was not attempted. Aramaic, however, thrived in its traditional heartland, and after Christianity became the majority religion, theological works began to appear in it. Some of them were translations of Greek originals, but there was also a respectable tradition of native writing that continued to be creative for several centuries.[9] The form of the language used for this was a northern dialect that we now call Syriac, and modern scholars have recovered a significant number of theological texts whose Greek originals were destroyed (or allowed to decay and disappear) because their authors were condemned as heretics.

A similar development occurred in Egypt, where Christian texts in the native Coptic language, both translations from Greek and original compositions, gradually made their appearance.[10] Later there was also a sizeable production of Christian literature in Armenian which is of similar range to what we have in Coptic.[11] Neither Coptic nor Armenian is a Semitic language, and both were heavily dependent on Greek for their theological vocabulary, as indeed was Syriac, which is quite uninformative about the words actually used by Jesus and his disciples, even though they spoke the same language.

This reflects the fact that the dominant tongue throughout the eastern half of the Roman empire was Greek, a situation that had come about because of the conquests of Alexander the Great (d. 323 BC) and would last until the language was replaced by Arabic in AD 706.[12] The New Testament was written

---

[8] But not English, which uses "Passover" for the Jewish feast and "Easter" (the name of a pagan goddess!) for the Christian one.

[9] Aramaic is little known outside its area of origin, but see the significant studies by Robert Murray, *Symbols of Church and Kingdom: A Study in Early Syriac Tradition* (Cambridge: Cambridge University Press, 1975). For a summary of what is available, see *Patrology: The Eastern Fathers from the Council of Chalcedon to John of Damascus*, ed. Angelo Di Berardino (Cambridge: James Clarke, 2006), 407–490.

[10] See Di Berardino, *Patrology*, 491–570. For a recent study of it, see Stephen J. Davis, *Coptic Christology in Practice: Incarnation and Divine Participation in Late Antique and Medieval Egypt* (Oxford: Oxford University Press, 2008). See also Aloys Grillmeier and Theresia Hainthaler, *Christ in Christian Tradition, Volume 2: From the Council of Chalcedon (451) to Gregory the Great (590–604), Part 4: The Church of Alexandria With Nubia and Ethiopia* (London: Mowbray, 1996).

[11] See Di Berardino, *Patrology*, 571–604.

[12] The Arabs had conquered Syria and Egypt in the decade after 632, but for the first two generations of their rule they continued to use Greek for official purposes.

in Greek as a matter of course, and theologians who wanted to be read by a wide audience wrote in it. It was probably Paul's mother tongue, as is implied in Acts 21:37–39, when a Roman official expressed surprise that he knew it. Greek was the dominant if not the only language used by the church in the first two centuries of its existence, and it has left its imprint on the vocabulary we use to describe its officers, buildings, and elements of worship.

It is particularly interesting to note that Latin, which came to maturity as a written language shortly before the coming of Christ and which could have created translations of Greek words, just as Greek had translated Hebrew, was often prepared to adopt them directly, presumably because the Romans sensed that they had a special meaning that was better preserved in that way. Thus, although they could have said *Unctus* for *Christos* or *nuntius* for *angelos*, they did not. Sometimes they even adopted Greek words that had a different meaning in the original language, but were applied to specific (though not necessarily church) purposes in Latin. A good example of this is the Greek word *basilikê*, which means "royal" but was taken over by the Romans as *basilica*. Originally, a basilica could be any large building built in a certain style (round with a dome), but as time went on it was increasingly restricted to the meaning of "large church" which it retains to this day.[13] The Germanic and Slavic tribes of northern Europe adopted another Greek word, *kyriakê*, which means "dominical" or "belonging to the Lord," and used it to mean "church," something that is completely unknown in Greek.

The Slavonic religious vocabulary is particularly interesting, because it was developed from scratch in the ninth and tenth centuries by Greek missionaries who made no reference to Latin. They did their best to make up suitable words, but they could not always devise native equivalents and were forced to take over the original Greek more or less unchanged, as table 10.1 demonstrates.

The dominance of Greek terminology in these areas of church life is obvious, even if it is not total, and it can only be explained by the fact that the words had come to have a specifically religious connotation that could not be conveyed by ordinary translations. This was even true to some extent within the Greek language itself. The word *angelos*, for example, originally meant "messenger," but whereas it is still possible to use *(par)angelia* for "message," Modern Greek has to say *angeliophoros* ("message-bearer") for "messenger" because *angelos* now means exactly what it means in English—"angel," and nothing else. Likewise, an *ekklêsia* was originally an assembly or parliament, but Modern Greek has to use *boulê* for that, because *ekklêsia*

[13] In Romanian, *biserică* is the normal word for "church."

now means only "church." What were once "ordinary" words have acquired a religious tinge that has usually remained, often to the exclusion of the original meaning.

Table 10.1

Greek	Latin	English	Slavonic
Institutions and government:			
ekklêsia	*ecclesia*	*(Eccles)*[A]	—
(kyriakê)	—	*kirk/church*	*tserkov*
(basilikê)	*basilica*	—	—
katholikê	*catholica*	*catholic*	*soborna(ya)*
monastêrion	*monasterium*	*minster*[B]	*monastir*
synodos	*synodus/ concilium*	*synod/council*	*sobor*
oikoumenikos	*oecumenicus*	*ecumenical*	*vselenniy*
dioikêsis/ eparchia	*dioecesis*	*diocese*	*eparkhia*
Theology:			
theologia	*theologia*	*theology*	*bogoslovie*
orthodoxia	*orthodoxia*	*orthodoxy*	*pravoslavie*
hairesis	*haeresis*	*heresy*	*eres*
Christos	*Christus*	*Christ*	*Khristos*
angelos	*angelus*	*angel*	*angel*
diabolos	*diabolus*	*devil*	*diavol*
Ministers and officials:			
apostolos	*apostolus*	*apostle*	*apostol*
prophêtês	*propheta*	*prophet*	*prorok*
episkopos	*episcopus*	*bishop*	*episkop*
presbyteros	*presbyter*	*priest*[C]	*sv'ashchennik*
papas/pappas[D]	*papa*	*pope/–*[E]	*papa/pop*
diakonos	*diaconus*	*deacon*	*diakon*
abbas[F]	*abbas*	*abbot*	*avva*
patriarchês	*patriarcha*	*patriarch*	*patriarkh*
monachos	*monachus*	*monk*	*monakh*

Greek	Latin	English	Slavonic
Worship:			
liturgia	*cultus/liturgia*	*service/liturgy*	*sluzhba/liturgia*
psalmos	*psalmus*	*psalm*	*psalom*
hymnos	*hymnus*	*hymn*	*pesen'*
symbolon	*symbolum*	*creed*[G]	*simvol*
evangelion	*evangelium*	*gospel/evangel*[H]	*evangel*
epistolê	*epistula*	*epistle*	*poslanie*
kanôn	*canon/regula*	*canon/rule*	*kanon*
eikôn	*imago*	*icon/image*	*ikon/obraz*

Notes: [A]Found only in family and place names, e.g., Eccleston. [B]Also "monastery" in Modern English, of course. [C]The derivation of this word is controversial. It is probably a conflation of *presbyter* and *praepositus*, which has also given us the word "provost." [D]Note the different stress: *pápas* and *pappás*. [E]English normally restricts this word to refer to the bishop of Rome, though some writers also use it of an Eastern Orthodox priest. [F]Taken from Aramaic *abba*. [G]The English word derives from the Latin *credo*, which is the first word of the creed, officially known as the "symbol of faith." [H]A translation of the Greek "good news" as "good spell."

Greek words were adopted for naming church officers and activities, both liturgical and administrative, but they did not normally penetrate much further than that. When we look at the life of Jesus as outlined in the creeds, for example, we find the vocabulary shown in table 10.2.

Table 10.2

Greek	Latin	Slavonic[A]
syllêpsis	*conceptio*	*zachatie*
ensarkôsis	*incarnatio*	*voploshchenie*
theophaneia	*epiphania*	*bogoiavlenie*
peritomê	*circumcisio*	*obrezanie*
baptisma	*baptisma*	*kreshchenie*
peirasmos	*tentatio*	*iskushenie*
metamorphôsis	*transfiguratio*	*preobrazhenie*
staurôsis	*crucifixio*	*rasp'atie*
anastasis	*resurrectio*	*voskresenie*
analêpsis	*ascensio*	*voznesenie*
parousia/erchomos	*adventus*	*prishestvie*

Note: [A]Russified for easier recognition and pronunciation.

Both the Latin and the Slavonic lists are completely different from the Greek one, apart from the Latin borrowing of *baptisma* and *epiphania*, though notice that Greek normally uses a slightly different word for the epiphany.[14] The really surprising thing, though, is that whereas the Slavonic is a translation made from the Greek (so that *bogoiavlenie*, for example, renders *theophaneia* and not *epiphaneia*), English uses the Latin words without translating them, so that a genuine translation is now all but impossible. No one would say "enfleshment" for "incarnation" or "upstanding" for "resurrection," and if they did, the effect would be disconcerting, to say the least.[15]

The reason for this is that Latin became the universal language of the Western church for all purposes—liturgical, administrative, and educational—for a thousand years and was so familiar that the sixteenth-century Reformers saw no need to replace its terminology with made-up English words that no one would have understood. Like it or not, we in the Western tradition remain Latin Christians, even if Latin itself is no longer spoken or even widely known in our culture.

In ancient times, translation from Greek into Latin was a major preoccupation of the Western church. The need to do this well became especially acute after the legalization of Christianity in the fourth century, when controversy made it desirable to standardize theological terminology as much as possible. This was not an easy task. When scholars translated Greek works into Slavonic, they could usually make up words as they went along, because Slavonic had no literary tradition of its own, but Latin did. For example, the Greek word *symphônia* means "agreement" and is made up of two Greek roots—*syn* ("with") and *phônê* ("voice"). In Slavonic, the prefix for "with" is *s-* and the word for voice is *glas* (related to Greek *glôssa*, meaning "tongue"), so it was possible to create *soglashenie*, which also means "agreement." In Latin, however, the prefix for "with" is *con-* and the word for "voice" is *vox*, the combination of which gives us *convocatio*. The problem was that this word already existed in Latin, and it had two closely related meanings—primarily it was a summons to assemble and by extension it also came to mean the assembly so summoned. But it could not mean "agreement." The process by which *soglashenie* was invented did not work, and Latin had to find another word to express *symphônia*. This was usually either *consensus*, which we have adopted into English without change, or the closely related *consensio*, which we have not. "Voice" was replaced by "sense" or "feeling," which is similar

[14] We also recognize *metamorphôsis* but do not use it to mean "the transfiguration of Jesus."

[15] The one (partial) exception is that *adventus* is usually rendered as "coming" in phrases like the "second coming" of Jesus.

but not exactly the same and therefore open to other interpretations that may not reflect *symphônia* at all.[16]

A word like *soglashenie* is what we call a "calque," because it was constructed in direct imitation of the original in another language, but *consensus* is an "equivalent," a word that is taken to mean the same thing as the original but is not exactly parallel to it or specifically created from it. Latin theology has both calques from Greek and equivalents, each of which has created its own difficulties. As an example of a calque, we may pick *essentia*, which is based on the verb "to be" just like *ousia*. But the Romans thought that *essentia* was an artificial creation and seldom used it, preferring *substantia*, which was a calque of *hypostasis* but usually taken to be the equivalent of *ousia*. As long as no one worried about harmonization, this was not a major problem. But when a standard vocabulary had to be devised, and when heretics (or potential heretics) pounced on such ambiguities and insisted that *substantia* must be used of the three persons of the Godhead as well as of the one divine being, how could confusion be avoided? Was it necessary to have two different words, when even the Greeks often failed to see any real difference between *hypostasis* and *ousia*? These were the questions that dominated fourth- and fifth-century theological debate, and to understand what happened, we have to make some effort to grasp what the problems were and how they were resolved.

What Is God?

In evangelizing the pagan world around them, the first problem that the early Christians had to address was how to explain who the biblical God was without causing misunderstanding. To us it seems obvious that he is a person of some kind and that we should start with that. God relates to his people in what can only be described as a personal way, and what little the Bible says about his being is couched in personal terms. "I am" is the way the Scriptures talk about that, and the rest follows from there. Abstractions are generally avoided, and in their place we find God's words and deeds. We can extrapolate from them to say that he is all-powerful, all-knowing, and so on, but if we do, we are creating a conceptual synthesis that is not explicitly stated as such in the Bible itself.

The pagan world did not have a problem with the idea of a God who speaks. Most of their gods did that, but since they were either projections of human beings onto the spiritual world or personifications of natural phenomena, that was only to be expected. The God of biblical revelation is the exact opposite of this. He is uniquely one, and whatever resemblance there may be

[16] Of course, we have also borrowed *symphônia*, but in a specialized musical sense!

between him and us is due to the fact that we are created in his image, not the other way around. But although the Bible says that we are like God enough for us to be able to communicate with him (and vice versa), it also says that there is a huge gulf between the Creator and his creatures that our minds cannot bridge. As God said to the prophet Isaiah,

> As the heavens are higher than the earth,
> so are my ways higher than your ways
> and my thoughts than your thoughts.[17]

Even more explicit was the command God gave to Moses and that was engraved on the heart of every Jew:

> You shall not make for yourself a carved image, or any likeness of anything that is in heaven above, or that is in the earth beneath, or that is in the water under the earth. You shall not bow down to them or serve them.[18]

God is not a material object, and no physical substance can be turned into a representation of him. This was a doctrine that appealed to many Greeks, who sensed that there was something wrong with idolatry and longed to get beyond it to make contact with ultimate reality. But how? What was ultimate reality, and in what way could human beings connect with it? The Jews had no very clear answer to this, but Christians did. As John proclaimed it, "No one has ever seen God; the only Son, who is at the Father's side, he has made him known."[19] The same message was conveyed by the anonymous author of Hebrews:

> . . . in these last days, he [God] has spoken to us by his Son. . . . He is the radiance of the glory of God and the exact imprint of his nature [*hypostasis*], and he upholds the universe by the word of his power.[20]

The God who cannot be contained or portrayed by created things became a man in Jesus Christ, a claim that was scandalous to the Jews, who rejected any such possibility, and foolishness to the Greeks, for whom the abstract cause of all things could not become a particular individual.[21] This was the message that Christians had to proclaim, but they could only do so if they had a convincing picture of who God was and why it was possible for him to act in the way that he did.

---

[17] Isa. 55:9.
[18] Ex. 20:4–5.
[19] John 1:18. Some manuscripts (and the ESV) have "God" instead of "Son."
[20] Heb. 1:2–3.
[21] 1 Cor. 1:23.

Communicating their understanding of God both to Jews and to the pagan world was the main difficulty that the early Christians faced. By their acceptance of the Old Testament as divinely inspired, they were fundamentally committed to Jewish monotheism, but in a way that allowed for the Father, the Son, and the Holy Spirit to be distinct from each other without being substantially different. In approaching the pagan world, they knew that different schools of ancient Greek thought often used the same vocabulary as the New Testament, but that they seldom troubled to define their terms very carefully. Philosophers spoke of the supreme mind (*nous*), the world-soul (*psychê*), and reason (*logos*) as the pillars of universal order, regarding them as expressions of ultimate being (*to on*), but precisely what these things were or how they interacted was vague. Often they were just different names for the same thing, *to hypokeimenon* ("underlying reality") that they assumed must exist but that remained notional and abstract in their minds. To them, the supreme being was a concept, not a person, and it was ludicrous to suggest that one might meet it or have a personal relationship with it, as Christians claimed that they had in Jesus Christ.

Ancient Greek philosophy was cerebral and developed among men of leisure who were often regarded with somewhat amused contempt by their more pragmatically inclined contemporaries.[22] Seldom, if ever, did these people try to put their theories into practice, and the few who did usually came to grief. Stoicism, for example, had a reputation for encouraging men to resist worldly pain and pleasure by mentally distancing themselves from such things, but its call to heroism was elitist by definition. We know about Stoics like Seneca and Marcus Aurelius because they were prominent for other reasons, and it is their isolated individualism that stands out as much as anything else. Tertullian believed that Seneca was virtually a Christian because of his asceticism, but it would be hard to find anyone more remote from the lives and concerns of ordinary people than Seneca was.[23] To put it bluntly, Christians went out into the world to spread the gospel whereas the Stoics, with their superficially similar values, did all they could to isolate themselves from that world. If it is by their fruits that we know them, then, Christians were about as different from most ancient Greek philosophers as it was possible to be.

Nevertheless, Christians had to preach their message in and to a world dominated by such people, so we must not be surprised to find that they used similar words to express what they wanted to say. When they came across the universalist principles of ancient Greek thought, it was inevitable that they

[22] There is a touch of this in Luke's account of Paul in Athens. See Acts 17:21.
[23] Tertullian, *De anima* 20.1.

would link them to the God of the Bible, because he was the ultimate source of all things and the universal principle *par excellence*. But it would be a mistake to think that they set about doing this systematically. The apostle John wrote that the *logos* was God, and he must have been aware that the word was current in different branches of Greek philosophy, but there is no evidence that he was influenced by that, and most scholars today interpret his words in a Hebraic, not in a Hellenistic sense. John never mentioned the *nous*, but he could hardly have separated it from God if it was supposed to be the supreme reality, and would probably have found it hard to say whether it was any different from the *logos*. As far as the definition of the supreme being is concerned, John said that God is *ho ôn* (masculine),[24] a phrase that both parallels the philosophical *to on* (neuter) and stands in contrast to it. Both Greek words are the present participle of the verb *einai* ("to be"), and in that sense they can be said to mean the same thing. In Latin, for example, both have to be translated as *ens*, and modern European languages cannot distinguish between them either, unless, like German, they have both masculine and neuter articles.[25]

The difference between the Christian use of the masculine and the philosophical use of the neuter was important and, on the Christian side at least, deliberate. *Ho ôn* (masculine) was meant to be personal, while *to on* (neuter) was abstract. This is not a trivial matter, because Christians insist that the supreme being is personal and that we, his creatures, relate to him because we share that characteristic. Christian theology uses a number of words that were common in ancient Greek philosophy, but "person" is not one of them, because the ancient Greeks did not conceive of ultimate reality in that way. For Christians, however, "person" is the most important concept of all, because that is how we meet with God. The connection between Greek philosophy and Christian theology was born of historical circumstances, but it was more superficial than is often supposed. Once we go beneath the surface we discover that the resemblances between them are far less significant than the differences.

The most fundamental difference between them was that Christians used words to describe the real existence of the God who had revealed himself in the Bible, which severely limited the scope for speculation and removed much of the abstraction from concepts such as *hypostasis* and *ousia*. These were no longer merely ideas in the mind but descriptions of the God who created the world and who had his own identity, quite apart from the way that others conceived of him. Pagan notions of *hypostasis* and *ousia* may have been abstract, but they were compatible with the structure of the known world and

[24] Rev. 1:8.

[25] *Der Seiende* as opposed to *das Seiende*.

were ultimately derived from it. Whatever the underlying reality was, the things that we perceive were developed out of it—they did not appear from nothing.

This was where the church parted company with pagan philosophy, because the Bible taught that God was quite different from his creation and that he had made what we see out of nothing. But if that was the case, how could words that were used to describe things that we know be transposed to fit a reality that is beyond our imagining? Christian theologians recognized that all human language used to describe God was necessarily analogical, but the objective existence of the God they wanted to describe meant that some analogies were more appropriate than others, even if they sometimes had to be shorn of unwelcome connotations. To put it a different way, whereas pagans had been content to employ many different terms to describe an ultimate reality of which they had no objective knowledge, Christians felt the need to develop a single set of words to describe a God who could not be imagined, but of whom they had direct knowledge, thanks to his self-revelation in the Bible and in Jesus Christ.

Their task was made simpler as Christians came to agree that *hypostasis* and/or *ousia* were the best words to use when trying to describe God. Other terms (such as *hypokeimenon*, "the underlying thing") might occasionally be found, but they never made it into serious theological discourse. But could *hypostasis* and *ousia* be used interchangeably? Was it better to stick with one of them and ignore the other? Or should both be used, but in different ways? Today we know that it was the last of these options which eventually triumphed, but that was by no means clear at the start. In New Testament times, very few people had any idea that *hypostasis* could be used to mean something quite different from *ousia*, and if they showed a preference for one of these terms, it was for other reasons. Only in the fourth century did some people begin to think that an important distinction between the two words could (and should) be made, and even then, it was not until the Council of Chalcedon in 451 that a final decision about their technical meaning gained general acceptance.

Today we might think that *ousia* ("being") would have been the term preferred for describing God, but for many people in the early church, *hypostasis* appeared to be the better option.[26] The main reason for this seems to have been that it occurs in the Bible, especially in Hebrews 1:3, where the Son is described as the image (*charaktêr*) of the Father's *hypostasis*.[27] This verse proved beyond

[26] This was true of writers like Alexander of Alexandria, the chief theological mind behind the First Council of Nicea, and of Cyril of Jerusalem, both of whom seem to have done their best to avoid using *ousia* altogether. See Christopher Stead, *Divine Substance* (Oxford: Oxford University Press, 1977), 160–161.

[27] It occurs four other times as well, in 2 Cor. 9:4; 11:17, and in Heb. 3:14; 11:1, but with a different meaning. The best-known of these verses is the last, which the ESV translates as, "Faith is the *assurance* of things hoped for." It is the assurance because it is the underlying reason for our hope, hence the use of *hypostasis*.

a doubt that the Father was a *hypostasis*, but could the same thing be said of the Son? Was the image of the Father a second *hypostasis* or just a particular manifestation of the single *hypostasis* that was God? The question was complicated by the fact that *hypostasis* can have two quite different meanings. It can mean "underlying reality," in which case it would refer most naturally to what the Father and Son have in common, but it can also mean "individual identity," and in that sense the Son was distinct to the point of being a *hypostasis* in his own right.[28] In God the Father the two meanings coalesced, because he was both an individual identity and ultimate reality. The difficulty was whether the same thing could be said of the Son without creating two gods (or three, if the Holy Spirit is included). There were many people who could agree that the Son was a *hypostasis* in the second sense but not in the first, and for that reason they insisted that he could not be fully divine. In sum, the word *hypostasis* had its uses but it also caused confusion because the range of its possible meanings was too great for it to be unambiguous in a theological context.

That left *ousia*, a word that is not found in the Bible and which also had a wide variety of possible meanings.[29] It overlapped with *hypostasis* in certain contexts, but its semantic range was somewhat different. Derived as it was from the verb "to be," *ousia* focused more on the essence of a thing and less on how that thing was perceived or related to others. In a sense, we might say that *hypostasis* referred to something external, the way a thing manifested itself or was perceived by others, to a degree that *ousia* did not. *Ousia* remained the hidden substance of what a thing really was, whether that could be perceived externally or not.

Theologians who made use of *ousia* had to face the charge that the word was "unbiblical," but this is unfair. The verb *einai* ("to be") is used in both the Old and the New Testament as the name of God, and Jesus even applied it to himself.[30] In the Old Testament there is no question that I AM was the name given to the one God, though usually in the third person form *YHWH* ("he is").[31] There is also no question that Jesus was identifying himself with *YHWH* when he used it. The Bible never says that *YHWH* is the supreme being, because it does not speak in such abstract terms, but the implication is certainly there. The fact that the Bible calls him the sovereign Lord and the Creator of heaven and earth does not leave much room for the existence of

---

[28] For a detailed examination of the evidence, see G. L. Prestige, *God in Patristic Thought*, 2nd ed. (London: SPCK, 1952), 162–178.

[29] For the details, see Stead, *Divine Substance*, 131–156.

[30] Ex. 3:14; Rev. 1:8; John 8:58.

[31] Written Hebrew had no vowels, but normally we supply them and say "Yahweh." "Jehovah" is a corrupt form of the same name, created by using the vowels of *Adonai* ("my Lord"). It appears in Greek as *Iechovas* and in Latin as *Iehova*, from which the English form is derived.

anything greater than he is. Those who know *YHWH* and serve him have the highest knowledge that it is possible to have, and so "supreme being" is not an inappropriate description of who and what he is.

To what extent is this supreme being synonymous with God the Father? That the Father is the supreme being seems to be beyond question, but can we reverse the order and say that the supreme being is the Father, and only the Father? This is where the difficulty arises, because the New Testament teaches that the Son is also the supreme being but that he is not the Father. The Son's identity with the Father as the supreme being is vitally important, because if they are not the same at that level, the Son cannot be truly or fully God. As the Nicene theologians and their followers saw it, the difference between the Father and the Son must be maintained, but not at the expense of compromising the divine nature of the Son.

One major problem that Christians had with the term *ousia* was that in ancient Greek thought it was a finite concept. An *ousia* could be defined by referring to its attributes—its shape, color, weight, and so on. But the God of the Bible is not finite and cannot be defined in the same way. To attempt to do so is a distortion of reality that amounts to a falsification and a form of intellectual idolatry. As a being, God is fundamentally different from anything else because he is the Creator and we are his creatures. We can look at other creatures and contrast them with God by saying that he is not like any of them, but we lack the conceptual tools necessary for defining what he is. Even to say that God is a being runs the risk of limiting him to a definable concept, a fact that led many Christian theologians to insist that God is beyond being, or *to mê on* ("nonbeing"), because he cannot be reduced to any such mental category. Out of that conclusion the Christian mystical tradition was to emerge.

It is important to realize that the encounter between Greek philosophical thought and Christian theology did not lead to a Hellenization of Christianity. Rather, it led to the development of a mysticism whose prime concern was to avoid such intellectual idolatry by ensuring that the worship of God did not get reduced to philosophical categories that corrupted it by their inadequacy. At the time of the First Council of Nicea, mystical theology was still in its infancy, if it existed at all. It might be possible to trace its origins to the life and thought of Anthony, a desert hermit in Egypt, who was a great favorite of Athanasius and was supposed to have lived to the age of 105, but this is not certain, and it is probably better to say that Anthony practiced the sorts of spiritual discipline (fasting, prayer, and so on) that would later undergird mystical theology, rather than that he developed it as such.

The indications are that Christian mysticism emerged only after the Council of Chalcedon, in the writings of the Pseudo-Dionysius (sixth century) and his contemporaries.[32] Yet the fact that the Pseudo-Dionysius was identified as Dionysius the Areopagite is telling. Not only was that Dionysius a New Testament figure (see Acts 17:34) and disciple of the apostle Paul, he was also an ex-philosopher, or at least someone who had moved in those circles before his conversion. The Pseudo-Dionysius was most probably a sixth-century monk who composed what were to become the classic texts of mystical theology, but like his biblical namesake, he may well have been an ex-philosopher and perhaps even one of those who were expelled from Athens in 529. The attribution of the name of the Areopagite to him was false but it was not arbitrary. It indicates that the historic role of mystical theology was to confront and overcome pagan philosophical theology on its own grounds by showing that whatever heights it may have attained, it did not go high enough. To know the true God, it was necessary to transcend the limitations of the human mind and encounter the One who first addressed Moses as I AM and sent him to the people with that message.[33]

Long before that happened, however, the Arian controversy had brought *ousia* into prominence at the First Council of Nicea, where it was used on no fewer than three separate occasions with reference to the relationship between the Father and the Son:

1. The council declared that the Son is "out of" the Father's *ousia* (*ek tês ousias tou Patros*), a phrase which could have many meanings but that was probably intended to guard against any suggestion that he was a creature.[34] Unfortunately, it was possible to interpret this phrase to mean that the Son was a portion of the Father, or something less than the fullness of the Father's being, and some later Arians tried to interpret it in that way as a means of reconciling themselves to the Nicene statement.

2. The council declared that the Son was consubstantial (*homoousios*) with the Father. This word was to become the badge of later orthodoxy, but it too was open to different interpretations, depending on whether *ousia* was understood in a generic or in a specific sense. In a generic sense it would have the same force as "human being" has—one thing manifested in many examples. But in a specific sense, it would imply absolute identity with the one God, which to those who equated him with the Father, sounded like a kind of Sabellianism

[32] On the Pseudo-Dionysius, see René Roques, *L'univers dionysien: Structure hiérarchique du monde selon le Pseudo-Denys* (Paris: Cerf, 1983). See also, Andrew Louth, *Denys the Areopagite* (London: Geoffrey Chapman, 1989); and *Pseudo-Dionysius: The Complete Works*, trans. Colm Luibheid (Mahwah, NJ: Paulist, 1987). The last contains a preface by René Roques and introductions by Jaroslav Pelikan, Jean Leclercq, and Karlfried Froehlich.

[33] Ex. 3:14–15.

[34] See Stead, *Divine Substance*, 226–232.

(modalism). Indeed, it seems that the word was originally used by Gnostics, who interpreted it to mean something like "belonging to the same dimension of reality," and it may have been picked up by Sabellius or even Paul of Samosata, though for what purpose remains unknown. Its use by the council was a novelty of sorts, and the word had little importance for at least a generation. When it reemerged in the 360s it was mainly because it was thought to be inadequate and alternatives to it were being actively canvassed. In the course of the ensuing debate, it was refined in a way that made it both more acceptable and more appropriate to use it as a description of the Son.[35]

3. The council condemned anyone who suggested that the Son was "of a different *hypostasis* or *ousia* from the Father." This statement indicates that *hypostasis* and *ousia* were still being regarded as synonyms for the divine being, a fact that caused embarrassment later on, when it became common to use *hypostasis* of the three in God and *ousia* of the one. By 381 it was no longer possible to accept the Nicene anathema in the form in which it had originally been expressed, because more people were coming to realize that the Son was indeed a different *hypostasis* from the Father, but that they also shared the same *ousia*.

In many ways it was the need to reinterpret the decrees of the council of 325, as these conflicting possibilities became obvious in the next generation, that led to the refinement of the conciliar terminology in ways that we are familiar with today. Inevitably, *ek tês ousias* came to be read as *homoousios*, and any suggestion that *hypostasis* was an equivalent term was airbrushed out of the picture. But it was still not clear what *homoousios* was supposed to convey, and different parties emerged in the church in an attempt to explain it. They were,

1. The Homoeousians, who believed that the Son's *ousia* was like that of the Father, but not identical with it.

2. The Homoeans, who believed that the Son was like the Father in the way he thought and acted, but that he was of a different *ousia*. This group included those who thought that *ousia* was the wrong word to use of God, because it conveyed the image of a physical substance, which God was not. The later Arians were mostly all Homoeans.

3. The Nicene Homoousians, who rejected the Homoean view because it relegated the Son to a lesser order of being, and who wooed the Homoeousians by saying that the distinction between the Son's unity with the Father and his

[35] See R. P. C. Hanson, *The Search for the Christian Doctrine of God* (Edinburgh: T & T Clark, 1988), 190–202 for the details.

distinctiveness, which they were rightly trying to maintain, would be better expressed by using two different words, so as to avoid the confusion caused by trying to make either *ousia* or *hypostasis* do for both. Once that was agreed, it was only a matter of time before *ousia* came to designate the divine oneness and *hypostasis* was recycled and applied exclusively to the divine threeness.

Before leaving *ousia*, we have to look briefly at how the word was translated into Latin. By the time of the great Christological debates of the fourth century, the Latin-speaking Western church was becoming more influential and its perceptions had to be taken into account in the formulation of the church's doctrine. From a purely etymological point of view, the Greek word *ousia* should have been translated by using some form of *esse*, the Latin for "to be." *Ousia* was created out of the feminine form of the present participle, but this was more difficult in Latin, which has only *ens* for all three genders. A form *entia** was theoretically possible, but it is not attested anywhere and probably never existed.[36] Instead, a curious form *essentia*, made by combining the infinitive and the nominal ending, made its appearance. The Romans disliked this artificial concoction, and it was to be many centuries before it became commonplace in Latin. Instead of that, they preferred to say *substantia*, which corresponded to Greek words like *hypostasis* and *hypokeimenon*, which the philosophers used more or less as equivalents to *ousia*. The absence of a fixed technical terminology made this easier to do, of course, because as long as the general idea got across, no one bothered too much about trying to achieve precision.

Thus it happened that when the Christian church was looking for a Latin word to correspond with *homoousios*, the most natural translation was *consubstantialis*, which remains the favorite term to this day—or its close equivalent, *consubstantivus*.[37] It is possible for us to say "coessential," but this is seldom done, perhaps because the artificiality of the word is still subconsciously felt even after all these centuries. The Latin translation is now well established and universally accepted, but it contains problems of its own, not least because the semantic range of *substantia* is different from that of the Greek *ousia*. For a start, a "substance" is more likely to be a material thing than an *ousia* is. If we look at older translations of the Bible, we shall find the word being used to mean "possessions," as in the phrase, "He wasted his substance."[38] For this, Greek uses a different word, in this case *hyparchonta*, which comes from the verb "exist," but even in the sixteenth century it would

[36] Compare *sapiens* ("wise") and *sapientia* ("wisdom").
[37] Both words can be found in Tertullian, though with different meanings. See *Adversus Hermogenem* 44.3 for the former and *Adversus Valentinianos* 12.5; 37.2, for the latter. The fact that both treatises are anti-Gnostic is telling.
[38] Luke 15:13 (KJV).

not have been possible for Western Europeans to say that the Prodigal Son had wasted his "existence"!

In modern times a different problem has emerged as scientists and others have come to doubt whether there are such things as "substances" at all. In a world of atomic energy, what we have traditionally thought of as substances are produced and dissolved by natural forces in such a way that we cannot say that they are permanent. This has caused some people to rethink their doctrine of God, on the ground that to call him a "divine substance" is to use terminology that is no longer meaningful and does not correspond to observable reality. Having mistakenly assumed that "substance" was originally a philosophical term borrowed by Christian theology, they now want to dispose of it because it is incompatible with modern philosophical ideas and replace it with something like "energy." But energy is just a refined form of matter and does not solve the problem created by a supposedly outdated concept of "substance." Here the value of historical perspective is that we can see how a word came to acquire a meaning that does not depend on any material thing, and refute the charges laid against its use by modern theologians. Whether "substance" can be rescued from current trends is hard to say, but if a substitute for it must now be found, let us at least remember that in its original application to Christian theology it did not suffer from the defects that its modern critics have attributed to it.

It was in the struggle over Arianism that problems arose because of misunderstandings and inadequate definitions of words, and these problems had to be addressed if the controversy was ever to be resolved. Modern theologians who claim that the church gave in to the pressures of the surrounding Hellenistic culture and transformed its charismatic, biblically based gospel message into a kind of pseudo-philosophy which it called "theology" have misread their history.

It is true that Christian thinkers and Greek philosophers moved in the same intellectual circles and shared a number of common presuppositions. It could hardly have been otherwise, since communication between them would have been impossible if they had had no common reference points. The church would not have been able to evangelize the Greek world if it spoke a different language, as we can see from the encounter the apostle Paul had with the intellectuals of Athens.[39]

Having said that, it is not true to say that Christians capitulated to the mind-set of the surrounding philosophical culture. On the contrary, the philos-

[39] Acts 17:18–21.

ophers whom they are accused of imitating were the last people in the ancient world to accept the gospel message. So reluctant were they, in fact, that in 529 the emperor Justinian closed the remaining philosophical schools and exiled their members to Persia. If Christianity had been little more than another philosophy, it is hard to see why resistance to it would have been that strong. It is true that intellectuals do have a way of clinging stubbornly to their beliefs, but if the differences that separated pagan philosophers from Christian theologians were only trivial matters of terminology that did not affect the underlying substance, the threat of exile would surely have been enough to make them swallow their differences. The truth was that these differences were not trivial, and exile was the preferred option for those who in conscience could not accept a belief system that was alien to their basic principles.

What Is God Like?

The Homoeans' dissatisfaction with *ousia* led them to propose that it would be better to describe the Father and the Son in terms of their nature (*physis*) rather than of their being. If the Son thought like the Father, spoke like the Father, and acted like the Father, there was clearly some similarity between them, even if this did not depend on sharing a common essence. Today we would say that there was a functional equivalence between them which might be emphasized while leaving the more fundamental ontological questions unanswered, and perhaps unanswerable. For example, in the fourth century almost everyone agreed that both the Father and the Son were holy and good. They might have been able to agree that they were also both eternal, as long as allowance was made to include those who thought that the Son was eternally present in the mind of the Father before being begotten as a distinct *hypostasis*. As for the Son's power and authority, the New Testament said that these had been given to him by the Father and that he would give them back to the Father at the end of time, so there was no real problem there.[40]

Naturally, these shared divine characteristics would be manifested by the Son in a way that was consonant with his particular identity, as we can see when we look at his immortality. The Father was immortal in the sense that he was not subject to death, but the Son could suffer and die. However, the Son was also "immortal" because although he could die, death could not hold him. In this way he was like the Father and unlike him at the same time, but it seemed to make little difference in practice, because in the end, death was defeated and the Son now enjoys the same immortality that the Father has.

[40] See Matt. 28:19; 1 Cor. 15:28.

This solution to the problem of how the Father and the Son could share a common divinity without being identical seemed logical and held considerable appeal, not least to the imperial authorities, who thought they could unite the church around a formula that would cater to a wide range of opinions. It was Athanasius, more than anyone else, who first saw through this way of thinking and denounced it as incompatible with the teaching of the Bible. His argument was based on two fundamental principles:

1. God is absolute, so everything said about him must be absolute too. If he is good, he is the supreme and absolute good, and all other "goodness" is relative to that. If the Son's goodness is absolute, then he is God; if he is not God, then his goodness can only be relative, even if it is deep and impressive to the outside observer.

2. God is "simple," which means that what is said of him applies to the whole of him, and not just to a part of his being. If we say that he is good, holy, and eternal, we must not think of these things as though they were colors in a rainbow that could be distinguished like so many stripes. If God is good, holy, and eternal, then all of him must be each of these things at the same time. You cannot subtract one or more of them and still have God, because these descriptions of him, or "attributes," as we call them, apply to the whole of his being. Therefore, if the Son is really like God, then he must share all the divine attributes in full and equal measure. If he does not, then he is not like God, even if he does a passable imitation of him most of the time. In other words, the Son cannot be like God without actually being God, because in God, being and attributes merge into one.

In nature, there is an unbridgeable gulf between the Creator and his creatures, which can be expressed as the difference between the absolute and the relative, or between the infinite and the finite. Because we have been made in God's image and likeness, we can have some understanding of what the divine attributes are but we cannot define them by projecting our notions of goodness, holiness, eternity (and so on) onto him. For a start, we tend to think of these qualities in terms of their opposites—goodness is defined over against evil, and holiness against corruption. To our finite minds, eternity seems like time that never comes to an end. But God's goodness and holiness are not defined by their opposites, because those opposites do not exist in him. Nor can his eternity be thought of as unending time, because God is beyond time.

This is why the so-called "attributes" of God are mainly expressed as negatives—he is invisible, immortal, impassible, and so on. Occasionally we can use positive terms to describe him, like "holy" and "eternal," but this is because those attributes are communicated to us and we have some understanding of what they are, as opposed to what they are not. But even in these cases, true definition remains beyond our grasp. We know that eternity implies timelessness, but we cannot imagine what that is like. We also know that God's holiness is absolute and essentially mysterious, whereas ours is relative and is most easily defined by what we do *not* do. In the end it amounts to much the same thing—what we say about God sets him apart from us and can only be described in terms that indicate that their substance is beyond our understanding.

In some ways, the Christian approach was similar to that of the pagan philosophers, who also had a list of negative attributes that they ascribed to the supreme being. One of their favorites was *to apeiron* ("the infinite"), which summed up their approach admirably. They concentrated mainly on objective, natural characteristics like infinity, immutability, impassibility, and immortality, to the exclusion of moral and spiritual qualities like goodness and holiness, which to them seemed inapplicable in the realm of the *apeiron*. Christians could not follow this way of thinking because the biblical God revealed that he was holy and good. He was not an incomprehensible being that was indifferent to the fate of mankind but a living and active God who wanted his people to imitate his holiness and goodness. In this respect, Christians were a world away from any form of paganism, as those who came into contact with them quickly realized. Christians agreed with pagan philosophers that God was physically different from his creation, but although he was incompatible with it at that level, he was intimately connected with it in spiritual and moral terms, making it necessary to express his infinite attributes in a finite mode, however contradictory and impossible that might appear to be.

The Christian defense of God's "physical" attributes as incomprehensible to us was conducted not against the philosophers but against the idolatry of pagan religion. This was a battle at grassroots level, but as it seldom had to be argued intellectually, it is difficult to find treatises written on the subject. As far as we know, the first person to systematize the divine attributes was John of Damascus (675?–749?), a late witness but one who eschewed originality and claimed that what he said was the teaching of the ancient fathers, which in this case it undoubtedly was. We can therefore use his schematization in order to understand what fourth-century theologians believed, even if they did not organize their thoughts to the degree that John did. Like any good teacher, John arranged his list of eighteen divine attributes in an order that helps us to understand what the early Christians said about God and why.[41] He began with

[41] John of Damascus, *De fide orthodoxa* 1.8.

God's relationship to time, and then went on to its logical corollary, which was his relationship to space. After that, he explained what God is and what he is like. All but two of his descriptive adjectives are negatives, and the ones that are not begin with the same letter (alpha), a device intended to aid the process of memorization. The adjectives relating to time are the following:

Greek	**Latin**	**English**
anarchos	–	*(without beginning)*
aktistos	*increatus*	*uncreated*
agennêtos	*ingenitus*	*unbegotten*
anolethros	*(imperdibilis)*	*imperishable*
athanatos	*immortalis*	*immortal*
aiônios	*aeternus*	*eternal*

The first three adjectives refer to the beginning of time, the next three to its end, but negation is the common thread that unites them. As we would expect, the Latin words are closer to the English ones than the Greek words are, but note that Latin does not possess generally recognized equivalents for every Greek term. This was one of the reasons why the Greeks often thought that Latin was incapable of expressing the full range of theological categories, but more important, it also helps to explain why John's schematization never caught on in the West. The spatial attributes were categorized as follows:

Greek	**Latin**	**English**
apeiros	*infinitus*	*infinite*
aperigraptos	*(incircumscriptus)*	*uncircumscribed*
aperioristos	*illimitatus*	*unbounded*
apeirodynamos	–[A]	*(of unlimited power)*

Note: [A]No one ever seems to have invented *infinipotens*, and there is certainly no word like "infinipotent" in English or in other Western European languages.

Here again the relative poverty of the Latin vocabulary strikes us, and as a consequence English and other Latin-dependent Western languages are unable to match the subtlety and range of the Greek. As before, the emphasis is on negation—God is not limited or bound by anything, and the words that are used emphasize that fact. The adjectives describing his being are:

Greek	Latin	English
haplês[A]	*simplex*	*simple*
asynthetos	*incompositus*	*uncompounded*
asômatos	*incorporeus*	*incorporeal*
arrheustos	*(influxibilis)*	*(without flux)*

Note: [A]Note that the Greek word begins with an alpha. The "h" was represented by a "rough breathing" mark, like an inverted comma, that was no longer pronounced in John's day.

Once more, the Latin is a translation, in some cases made up for the occasion—*influxibilis* does not appear until the Middle Ages—and English is deficient. Finally, the qualities of the divine being are expressed as:

Greek	Latin	English
apathês	*impassibilis*	*impassible*
atreptos	*immutabilis*	*immutable*
analloiôtos	*(inalterabilis)*	*inalterable*
aoratos	*invisibilis*	*invisible*

Here we come to the attributes that have caused the greatest controversy in modern times, but this is mainly because the original meaning and context have not been understood. John of Damascus was talking about the objective being (*ousia*) of God, not about the way he relates to us in moral and spiritual terms, and this is how his impassibility must be understood. God could not be made to suffer because of some inherent weakness in his constitution that an external force might discover and manipulate, nor could he be influenced by human sacrifices on his behalf, as Elijah had long ago demonstrated to the prophets of Baal.[42]

Western theology has never been entirely comfortable with the divine attributes, as the relative inability of both Latin and modern languages to express them adequately indicates, but on the whole they have been accepted in principle as valid descriptions of God's being. Had the Son not become a man in Jesus Christ, the question of the divine nature might well have faded into the background. That it did not do so was largely due to the next round of controversy, which emerged in the wake of the acceptance of the *homoousios* by the First Council of Constantinople in 381. Once the identity of the Son

[42] 1 Kings 18:20–29.

with the Father was assured, the church could move on to determine how the divine nature could be fully present and manifested in a finite man, and what that might mean for the integrity of his human nature. It was in that context that Christian teaching about the nature of God came into its own.

When we turn to the moral and spiritual attributes of God, we find that John of Damascus treated them differently from the "physical" ones. In fact, he did not list them as attributes at all, but said only that God is the "source of goodness and righteousness," placing the emphasis on the fact that these attributes can be communicated to other beings, and leaving it up to us to assume that God must be good and righteous in himself. It is at this level that believers were expected to participate in the divine nature, a fundamental demand on discipleship that can be traced back to the New Testament.[43] For that reason, the moral and spiritual attributes of God were seldom discussed as such and were never turned into abstractions. From Paul's advice to the Thessalonians to the creed of 381, the message was the same—God expected his people to be holy as he is holy, and those who wanted to know what holiness was had only to read the Bible and put its teachings into practice.[44]

Who Is God?

Moving on from the definition of *ousia* and *physis*, we come naturally to the problem the early Christians had in finding a term to designate the element of threeness in God. In Hebrews 1:3 the Son is described as the *charaktêr* of the Father's *hypostasis*, whatever that is supposed to mean in this context. Translators do their best to find modern equivalents for these words but this is very difficult to do, not least because the words have remained in use and changed their meanings in subtle ways. *Charaktêr* can be fairly easily understood as "stamp" or "imprint," referring to the image created by a rubber stamp or something like that. It is an exact reproduction of the original and derives its authority from that fact (especially if it is used to seal a document), but at the same time it is also derivative. The stamp has the shape and design of the original without being the original itself. In the modern world we are used to the idea that a copy can have the force of an original, and we often accept photocopies of birth certificates and the like as authentic, but this was not so in ancient times. It was a principle of Roman law that a copy did *not* have the force of the original, which had to be made available whenever possible. The *charaktêr* was something of an exception to this rule because its nature permit-

[43] 2 Pet. 1:3–4. See also Matt. 19:16–22.
[44] 1 Thess. 4:3–8.

ted exact reproduction, but it might still be suspect if the original was unknown or unavailable for inspection. In any case, it was a reflection of something else and not an agent in its own right, which made it ambiguous and hard to use as a theological description of the Son.

Charaktêr never got off the ground as a theological term, and as we have already indicated, *hypostasis* had so many possible meanings that it could not be pinned down precisely enough. In Hebrews 1:3 it may be synonymous with *ousia*, in which case the verse would mean that the Son was the exact replica of his Father's being, but even if such a translation is possible, it does not mean that it is the best one. After all, how could a being that was by definition unique be replicated? The biblical text suggests that the Father has a *hypostasis* that the Son can duplicate but does not share. If that is the case, it is only a short step to saying that the Son has his own *hypostasis*, derived from that of the Father but still distinct from it. To put it a different way, the *hypostasis* of the Father gave him his identity, and the fact that the Son also had an identity implied that he also had a *hypostasis* of his own.

This notion of identity is what made it possible for someone like Origen to use *hypostasis* to refer to the threeness in God. Yet as we have seen, his phrase "three *hypostases* in one *ousia*" only became the preferred Greek way of expressing the doctrine of the Trinity around the time of the First Council of Constantinople in 381, when it was becoming clear that a different word was needed to differentiate what was three from the term used to describe what was one. Because *ousia* and *hypostasis* were originally synonymous, there were some people who wanted to say that God was a single *hypostasis* or that he was three *ousiai*, but they were quietly corrected by those who saw that such formulas were only causing confusion and therefore ought to be avoided.

Once it was agreed that *hypostasis* should be used for the three and *ousia* for the one, the two terms had to be distinguished in a way that was real and not just notional. For example, if we were to describe the Trinity as "three substances in one essence" it would be only a matter of time before someone would ask whether this makes sense, since "substance" and "essence" are the same thing. How could there be three *hypostases* but only one *ousia* in God? Another problem was that *hypostasis*, understood to mean "identity," is a word that reflects human perception more than the divine reality. The three *hypostases* are what we see in God, the way in which we describe how he has manifested himself to us. But this does not necessarily imply that each *hypostasis* is a distinct agent, or that they must have a relationship to one another that is similar to our relationship with them. Indeed, there is always the possibility that they are not present in the eternal being of God at all, but are merely manifestations of him in time and space. *Hypostasis* is a useful word insofar as it can be distinguished from *ousia*, but it also has limitations that were not slow to manifest themselves in the fourth-century debates.

In ancient Greek there was a strong tendency, as there still is in many languages, to distinguish between something that *is* in a permanent way and something that only *exists* for the time being. Spanish and Portuguese do this, for example, and foreigners are often caught out by it. Are we to say that we are something permanently (*somos*) or only temporarily (*estamos*)? It may be obvious that I am permanently a man and only temporarily ill, but what verb should I use to describe being married or single? Are these temporary states or permanent realities? Here much depends on the horizon of the speaker, who may interpret "permanent" as "long-lasting" even if it is not strictly "eternal." This is basically what has happened in English and many other languages, where this subtlety is no longer preserved and the verbs "to be" and "to exist" are often synonymous.

In the case of God, however, we must be very careful not to disregard the distinction between what is eternal and what is only temporal. For an ancient Greek to say that God "is" was not the same thing as to say that he "exists," because God "is" in eternity but can only "exist" in time and space. What if this were the difference between *ousia* (eternal) and *hypostasis* (temporal)? In that case, as an *ousia*, God would be eternally one, but in time and space he would be revealed to us as one *hypostasis* or another. This is the essence of modalism, and the fact that it was perceived as a constant danger (even if it was not a doctrine explicitly held by many people) reminds us how significant a distinction this was. Most early Christians realized that God could not be three *hypostases* in a modalistic way, if only because the Son and the Father communicated with each other, but how was this misunderstanding to be avoided?

The answer was provided by introducing another category of thought, drawn in the first instance from Roman law, but ultimately from the Greek theater. Ancient Greek theater was masked drama, which enabled many parts to be played by only a few actors. Spectators would learn from the shape of the mask (*prosôpon*) what sort of character was being portrayed—a long nose might indicate greed, floppy ears might be the sign of a gossip, and so on. Even today, this usage is preserved in Shakespearean plays, which are always prefaced by a list of the so-called *dramatis personae*, who are the characters in the play. In ancient times these *personae* were codified by Theophrastus, who lived in the fourth century BC. His book, called the *Characters*, told people how to read the masks and explained what they represented.[45]

[45] Note that for Theophrastus, *charaktêr* and *prosôpon* were synonymous, which may have some bearing on the interpretation of Heb. 1:3.

From there it was only a short step to transferring the word *prosôpon* from the mask to the face that lay behind it, and to use the habit of reading the mask to read people's faces as a way of discerning their character. This transfer of meaning must have been well underway in Theophrastus's time, because when the Old Testament was translated in the third century BC, *prosôpon* appears in its extended meaning of "face." It is even used in ways that go completely against the notion of mask. Jacob and Moses, for example, are both described as having seen God "face to face," a Hebrew expression that was rendered in Greek as *prosôpon pros prosôpon*.[46] The apostle Paul picked up the phrase and used it to make a sharp contrast to the sort of hiddenness that a mask entails: "Now we see through a glass, darkly; but then *face to face*."[47] In Latin, *prosôpon* became *persona*, and we can even translate Paul in this sense—we shall see God *person to person*. A new theological term was emerging that had no equivalent in any ancient Greek philosophy.

The effects of this would soon be felt in Christian theology, though in a way that might not have been apparent to the writers of the New Testament. When Tertullian wanted to express Christian theology he used *substantia* to represent *hypostasis* in the sense of *ousia*, but then had to find something else to describe the divine threeness. Being familiar with Roman law, he borrowed the word *persona*, which had come to be used in the law courts to mean someone who was capable of acting or being acted against—in other words, a plaintiff or a defendant. Tertullian did not think of God in that way, but he saw the advantage in using a word that implied the ability to act and to take responsibility for action. He therefore said that God was three *personae* in one *substantia*, and his choice of terminology has remained standard in Western (Latin) theology ever since.

At the time, few Greeks bothered reading Latin and not many knew of the legal use of the word *persona*, though some of them did in fact use *prosôpon* in much the same sense. Take Hippolytus, for example:

> If [Noetus] should say: "Jesus himself said, 'I and the Father are one'," let him pay attention and realize that he did not say, "I and the Father *am* one" but "*are*" one. The "are" is not used of one; Jesus was indicating that there are two persons (*prosôpa*) but [only] one power (*dynamis*).[48]

The word could have become just as standard in Greek as it was to become in Latin, but it did not. Perhaps there was a lingering fear of Sabellianism,

[46] Gen. 32:30; Ex. 33:11.
[47] 1 Cor. 13:12 (KJV).
[48] Hippolytus of Rome, *Contra Noetum* 7.

given the underlying meaning of "mask," but more likely it was because most Greek theological discussion was fundamentally philosophical in nature, and *prosôpon* was not a philosophical term. Only in the fourth century did Basil of Caesarea start to use *prosôpon* in the sense of *hypostasis*, but it would be some time yet before the two terms would be regarded as interchangeable.[49] The advantage of *prosôpon* over *hypostasis* was that it emphasized the subject's ability to act. Strictly speaking, a chair or a table could be a *hypostasis* because it was an identifiable form that belonged to a wider species of thing. But neither a chair nor a table could do anything or be responsible for anything, which was an obvious defect when it came to representing God.

Prosôpon added that element of agency, and for that reason it was more suitable than *hypostasis* as a description of God, but in the fifth century it would suffer from the fact that the Nestorians used it to describe the conjunction of divinity and humanity in the womb of Mary. The effect of this was that instead of being the cause of an action, the Nestorian *prosôpon* was the result of one. That reminds us of how flexible the vocabulary still was, but it also shows why more precise definition was needed. In the end, the Council of Chalcedon (451) defined *prosôpon* and *hypostasis* as equivalent terms for the threeness of God, probably hoping that they would merge into a single concept that would avoid the pitfalls just mentioned.

It was little noticed at the time, but the Chalcedonian Definition of the person of Christ brought about a fundamental revolution in the way Christians conceived of theology. Before that time, words like "God" and "man" referred primarily to their respective *ousiai*. When we read in the creeds that Christ was "fully God and fully man," we really ought to say "fully divine and fully human," because although we think of God and man primarily in personal terms, those who composed the creeds did not. To them, God and man were primarily substances that are known to us as Father, Son, and Holy Spirit in the first case and as Adam and Eve in the second. What we call the personal was present, but it was secondary and not conceptualized as such.

Chalcedon made this traditional way of thinking untenable because it made the person/*hypostasis* an agent. Instead of being a manifestation of divinity, the Son was now to be seen as a divine agent who possessed divinity, which he could dispose of as he chose. As long as the *hypostasis* of the Son was thought of as a manifestation of the divine *ousia*, the nature of that *ousia* would control what he could and could not do. An infinite and eternal divine *ousia* could not become finite and temporal without ceasing to be itself, and that inevitably

[49] Basil of Caesarea, *Epistula* 38. Some scholars attribute this letter to Gregory of Nyssa, but this does not matter for our purposes, since we are talking about the same time period.

called the genuineness of the Son of God's incarnation into question. The only way such a thing could be imagined would be by absorbing humanity into his divinity, because the other way around would diminish the divinity and make the resulting combination something less than God.

But if the Son of God is a divine person who possesses a divine nature without being bound by it, what was previously unthinkable suddenly becomes possible. The divine person can take on a human nature in addition to his divine one and operate in and through it without the other one being affected. This is what happened in the incarnation, and it is why the Chalcedonian Definition, despite considerable opposition both then and since, was able to hold its own and win the day among the majority of the churches. Chalcedon represented the culmination of a theological movement that had been going on for more than 250 years. It had begun in the struggle to affirm the person and work of the Father against the Gnostics, had continued in the struggle against Arius, and had reached mature expression in the debates over Nestorianism. But it was not until the council itself that the final building blocks were put in place and what had gone before suddenly had to be read in a new light.

This was particularly painful in the case of those who were living and writing in the immediate buildup to Chalcedon, who had to come to terms with the issues that were finally resolved there but who never got that far themselves. In the east, Cyril of Alexandria's Christology was compatible with that of Chalcedon but his followers rejected the council's decisions because it failed to uphold Cyril's "one nature after the incarnation" formula that had become the hallmark of resistance to Nestorianism in the East. As a result, the Alexandrians condemned Chalcedon as Nestorian, which it was not, and went their separate way. Another theologian who must be put in this category is Augustine of Hippo (354–430), whose theology is so often interpreted in the light of Chalcedon and assumed to be congruent with it that it is difficult to remember that he died twenty-one years before the council was held. Whether he would have accepted its decisions is impossible to say, but there are grounds for thinking that he would have revised his reflections on the Trinity if he had lived into the post-Chalcedonian era.

Why do we think this? Augustine's great work on the Trinity remains a classic of Western theology, the ultimate source of everything that has been written on the subject since.[50] It is still read with profit today, and no one has ever thought to call it unorthodox. By the standards of his time it was not, of course, and Augustine cannot be expected to have foreseen what was to happen

[50] See Lewis Ayres, *Augustine and the Trinity* (Cambridge: Cambridge University Press, 2010); Khaled Anatolios, *Retrieving Nicaea* (Grand Rapids, MI: Baker, 2011), especially 241–280.

after his death. Nevertheless there are certain features of what he had to say about the Trinity that he would not have said after Chalcedon, or at least not in the same way.

The first of them is his objection to the use of the word "person" as a term for describing what was common to the distinctiveness of the Father, Son, and Holy Spirit. He thought that it did not do justice to the identity of the three, and since the term had still not been properly defined, he may have had a case. But would he have said that after Chalcedon? It is impossible to be sure, but the chances are that he would not. Probably he would have accepted the council's logic and regarded "person" as sufficiently well defined that it could now serve as the proper term for the threeness in God. More important, would his understanding of God's love have survived the close scrutiny it would have received had his theology been known and debated in the East? It may be reasonable to think of the lover and the beloved as "persons," but can this be applied to the love that flows between them? The personal identity of the Holy Spirit has always been the most difficult aspect of Augustinian Trinitarianism. Had Augustine known the Chalcedonian Definition and had time to assimilate its implications for his theology, he might have seen the inadequacy of constructing a picture in which the Father and the Son are "persons" in a way that the Holy Spirit is not. A more communitarian picture of the Trinity might have emerged and been less susceptible to the danger of reducing the Spirit, and therefore the presence of God in our lives, to a force or power that is less than fully personal.

Having said that, there can be no doubt that the struggle to define the person of the Son within the Godhead obliged the church to develop a viable Trinitarian doctrine that could allow for an incarnation of one of the divine persons without in any way diminishing the being of God. It is no accident that the classical doctrine of the Trinity emerged at this time, nor that it has remained virtually unchanged in its essentials to the present day.

11

The Son of Man

The Divine Word in Human Flesh

For most of the fourth century, the main theological struggle in the church was centered on the need to define the relationship of the Son to the Father. The Son's incarnation as Jesus of Nazareth was not forgotten, but it was interpreted in the light of what was perceived to be the more fundamental question. Those who had known Jesus during his earthly ministry never doubted that he was a man, whatever his relationship to God the Father might be, and that feeling persisted well into the third century. Adoptianism, which modern observers are inclined to view as a scaling down of Christ's divine glory, could have been regarded by some contemporaries as the exact opposite. Far from being a mere man, Jesus had been taken up into God to a degree previously unknown. Enoch and Elijah had gone up to heaven (and many people were convinced that Moses had done so too), but despite their exalted status, they were never acknowledged by God as his sons in the way that Jesus was. He was in a different category from them, and it remained only to determine what the true nature of his divinity was.

From that perspective, Arius represented a further advance toward acknowledging the divinity of Christ. For him, Jesus was not a man who was taken up into God but a divine creature who came down to earth and assumed a human body in which he suffered and died on the cross. It is important to understand that, like virtually all other Christians of their time, the Arians regarded divinity and humanity as radically incompatible. In order to achieve some kind of union between them in Christ, Arius insisted that each nature had to give way to the other. As the Son of the Father, Jesus was divine without being fully God, but as the son of Mary he was a man without being fully human. In particular, he lacked the nonmaterial elements of humanity (soul, mind, and spirit) which were supplied by his divine being. This was an essential Arian belief because it was the only way the Arians could account for divine suffering on the cross. Had Jesus been an ordinary man, with a human soul, mind, and spirit, his humanity would have borne his suffering but not God. But if that had happened, there would have been nothing extraordinary about the death of Christ and it would have had no saving significance for us, because God would not have been involved in it.

The Nicene opponents of Arius pushed things further by insisting that the Son was fully God, and therefore incapable of suffering and dying in his divine nature. That left them with the problem of having to define who it was that died for our sins and what it was that made his death effective for obtaining our salvation. The logic of Arianism suggested that if God, being immortal, cannot suffer or die, the death of Jesus had no divine dimension and therefore could not save us, even if it might offer an example of self-sacrifice that we should be prepared to imitate. Such a reductionist view of Christ's death held no attraction for the Nicenes, but they lacked the conceptual apparatus they needed for explaining their position properly, a deficiency that became more apparent as the struggle against Arianism moved toward its conclusion.

Arianism was an Alexandrian heresy, and it is to Alexandria that we must look for the first sign of how the suffering and death of Christ would be explained. We are drawn inexorably to Athanasius, who was not only the leader of the struggle against Arianism but also the chief exponent of Alexandrian Christology. We have already seen how important his *De incarnatione* was for defending the full divinity of the Son as the divine *logos*, but while Athanasius was strong on that point, he had relatively little to say about the humanity of the incarnate Son. He recognized that the *logos* had become a man in order to put right the sin of Adam, by which the human race had been led into corruption, but the way he expressed it was vague, and ultimately it proved to be unsatisfactory. To quote his exact words,

> Lest what had been created should perish and the work of the Father among men should be in vain, he took to himself a body, and one that was not any different from ours. He did not want simply to be in a body, nor did he wish merely to appear, because if that had been his aim he could have achieved it by some other and better means. Instead, he took our body, and not just that—he took it from a pure and unspotted virgin, . . . undefiled by intercourse with males.[1]

From this it is clear that Athanasius rejected docetism and thought that Jesus had a body like ours. Yet it was a body without sin, which he evidently believed was passed on by sexual intercourse and was therefore inherent in the

[1] Athanasius, *De incarnatione* 8.

body itself. If we reflect that sin does not inhere in flesh and bones but in the nonmaterial aspects of our being—it is spiritual disobedience, a corruption of the will and a distortion of the mind—we must conclude that Athanasius believed that Jesus possessed all these things. That conclusion is supported by what he went on to say about the image of God in Adam:

> Since God is good, he bestowed on mankind something of his own image, our Lord Jesus Christ. He made men according to his own image and likeness, so that by understanding . . . the image, that is to say, the Word of the Father, they might come to some understanding of the Father through him, and by recognizing their Maker they might live a happy and blessed life.[2]

Here Athanasius explained that human beings are made in the image of Christ, who is in turn the image of the Father—which makes his incarnation the logical solution to the human dilemma. This reinforces the view that Athanasius believed that human beings possess a created spiritual dimension, since otherwise they could not have been made in the divine image. The only snag with that interpretation is that Marcellus of Ancyra, whom Athanasius came to oppose after the Council of Serdica in 343 but who seems to have been a source of inspiration to him at this earlier stage, apparently believed that not just the soul but also the material human body was made in the image of God.[3] We must therefore be cautious about claiming too much for Athanasius on the basis of what he wrote in the *De incarnatione*, especially since there is no further clarification of his views in his later writings.

Today, the general consensus is that Athanasius may have admitted the existence of a human mind, soul, and spirit in the incarnate Christ, but if he did so, he could find nothing for them to do, and so we must conclude that, to his mind, they were of little practical significance. As Aloys Grillmeier (1910–1998) concluded, "In every passage where he gives a positive interpretation of the person of Jesus Christ, his being and his redeeming work, Athanasius has refrained from including the human soul of the Lord in a really visible way."[4] When commenting on John 10:18 ("I have power to lay my soul down, and I have power to take it up again"), Athanasius had this to say:

> To be troubled was natural for the flesh, but to have power to lay down his life and take it back again when he wanted to was not a human property, but

[2] Ibid., 11.

[3] For the evidence of this, see Aloys Grillmeier, *Christ in Christian Tradition, Volume 1: From the Apostolic Age to Chalcedon (451)*, 2nd ed. (London: Mowbray, 1975), 283–284.

[4] Ibid., 1:310. See Athanasius, *De incarnatione* 17 for evidence that Athanasius believed that the *logos* effectively took the place of a human soul in Christ.

> belonged to the power of the *logos*. A man does not die by his own power but by the necessity of nature and against his will, but the Lord, being himself immortal, had power as God to become separate from the body and to take it back again whenever he wanted to.[5]

The existence of the nonmaterial parts of the human being is not denied but neither is it mentioned, and activities natural to them are performed by the *logos*. Athanasius would doubtless have been horrified to think that his understanding of Christ's humanity was similar to that of the Arians, but it is hard to come to any other conclusion on the basis of the evidence. The text that is most favorable to the view that Athanasius believed that the incarnate Christ had a human soul and mind is found in a tract he wrote to the church of Antioch in 362, in which his main purpose was to explain the decision taken by his own church against the teaching attributed to Eustathius of Antioch, whom they suspected of holding to a form of adoptianism. In this text, Athanasius wrote,

> They [the members of the Alexandrian synod] confessed also that the Savior did not have a body without a soul (*apsychon*), without feeling or without a mind. It was not possible, when the Lord had become a man for us, that his body should have lacked reason, nor was the salvation effected in the *logos* a salvation of body only, but of the soul also.[6]

This was as close as Athanasius ever came to recognizing the presence of a human soul in Christ, and the passage has often been cited by those who want to prove that his views conformed to those of later Chalcedonian orthodoxy. It is certainly possible to read his statement in that sense, but whether that is what he consciously intended (or believed) is another matter. The phrase "salvation effected in the *logos*" is a reminder of what remained uppermost in Athanasius's mind. If there was a human soul in Jesus, it was a conduit for the work of the *logos* in and through him, and not an agent in its own right.

Even in ancient times, doubts about Athanasius's doctrine arose from the way in which it was interpreted by Apollinarius, who was one of Athanasius's pupils and who fully endorsed the statement quoted above. But where Athanasius probably (and the great majority of contemporary theologians in the Greek-speaking world certainly) interpreted *apsychon* literally as meaning "without a soul," Apollinarius apparently read it as "without life," which was an alternative (if less likely) possibility. It is at this point that we miss any detailed explanation from Athanasius that would make this interpretation impos-

[5] Athanasius, *Contra Arianos* 3.57.
[6] Athanasius, *Tomus ad Antiochenos* 7.

sible, and that opens him up to the charge that he was essentially Apollinarian in his thinking, even though he denied it. As Athanasius saw it, the trouble with Apollinarius was not that he thought of the *logos* as the principle that effectively controlled the spiritual side of the incarnate Christ, making his human soul redundant, but that he denied the perfection of Christ's humanity. That Athanasius could not accept, and he and Apollinarius went their separate ways.

Apollinarianism and Arianism were very similar in their understanding of the incarnation, so much so that it seems that there must have been some connection between them. Aloys Grillmeier thought that Arianism was an outgrowth of some form of Apollinarianism, which he claimed had existed at Alexandria long before it was attributed to Apollinarius, who lived a generation after Arius.[7] Grillmeier thought that it was easier for the high doctrine of the divine *logos* as held by Apollinarius to degenerate into the semi-divine form proclaimed by Arius than the other way around, but that must be regarded as uncertain. It is also possible to see Apollinarianism as a corrective to Arianism, one that kept its main principles but reinterpreted them in a way that Athanasius and the pro-Nicenes would find more congenial. Since there is no hard evidence of the existence of "Apollinarianism" before Apollinarius, that is the safer option and the one followed here.

Apollinarius taught that the incarnation was the union of the divine spirit of the Son with human flesh, taken from the womb of the Virgin Mary. The Son did not enter an already existing man, as the adoptianists claimed, nor did he unite with flesh on the basis that he too was a creature, as the Arians believed. Instead, the divine *logos* became a man by taking on human flesh. Jesus did not have a human mind, soul, or will, because the *logos* did not need them—he had their divine equivalents already. His humanity consisted only of flesh and bones, which the *logos* had lacked before it became incarnate. Just as ordinary human beings are a compound of body and soul, so Jesus Christ was a compound of flesh and *logos* that formed a single, united whole. Apollinarius called this union his nature (*physis*), because if one part were to be removed there would be no man Jesus Christ left.

Of course it will be obvious that the *logos* and the flesh were not equal partners in this union. The former always dominated the latter and must be regarded as the initiator of the incarnation in the first place. The *logos* could (and did) exist apart from that incarnation, but the human flesh had no independent identity. As Apollinarius put it, "The divine *nous* is ensouled in the flesh of Christ, thereby making it sinless."[8] For Apollinarius, to imagine the existence

[7] Grillmeier, *Christ in Christian Tradition*, 1:329–330.
[8] Ibid., 1:333.

of a principle of humanity in Christ other than the *logos*, that is to say, a human soul, would be to reduce the union of God and man to something accidental and potentially dissoluble, which would be no real union at all. There can be only one mind in the incarnate Christ, and by definition that must be the mind of the *logos*, not of a human being called Jesus of Nazareth.

Most importantly for the future, it followed from this that the elements of Christ's humanity did not constitute a "nature" (*physis*) in their own right, because they could not exist independently. As Apollinarius understood it, only something viable can be called a *physis*, which is why the incarnate Christ had only one "nature"—that of the *logos*, with bits of humanity added on. In fact, Apollinarius used the word *physis* in much the same way as others spoke of a *hypostasis* or even of an *ousia*, as a distinct, definable object, and he was quite prepared to use those words, and even *prosôpon* too, as synonyms.[9] In fact, it is probable that it was he who first applied the term *hypostasis* to the incarnate Christ, though the paucity of our evidence makes it impossible to confirm this. Whether he was also the first person to determine that the incarnate Christ had only "one nature" (*mia physis*) is impossible to say, but the formula was to become paradigmatic of the Alexandrian approach to Christology, and its association with Apollinarianism was to make it suspect to those who did not share it.

The attraction of Apollinarianism lay in the fact that not only did it offer a clear understanding of the principle of unity in Christ but it also ensured that the motivating force in his being was divine, and therefore both immortal and unstoppable. The ability of the incarnate *logos* to suffer and die was ensured by what is called the "transfer of properties" (*communicatio idiomatum*), according to which the divine Son can experience human pain in the elements of his humanity which, because they do not form a separate *physis*, can be predicated of the *logos*. It is only a short step from there to the later position that the incarnate Christ is a single "person," but while Apollinarius would undoubtedly have accepted that, his interpretation of it was different from what was later agreed on. The reason for this was that, for Apollinarius, "person" (*prosôpon* or *hypostasis*) was just another word for "nature" (*physis*), and it was that which controlled the thinking and behavior of Jesus. Apollinarius had words that might be translated as "person" but not the underlying concept, which he assimilated to "nature" in a way that not only denied the full humanity of Christ but also made it impossible to imagine it.

Apollinarius was condemned for heresy at the First Council of Constanti-

[9] Apollinarius of Laodicea, *De fide et incarnatione* 6.

nople in 381, but it would be hard to deny that his views were typical of Alexandrian theology. His mistake, and his misfortune, was that he drew the logical conclusions from them and exposed the Alexandrian approach's fundamental weaknesses. The root of the trouble was that the Alexandrians thought of the incarnation of Christ as a union of *logos* and "flesh," a word that they interpreted to mean something less than full humanity. The biblical source of their thinking is easy to detect: "the Word became flesh and dwelt among us, and we have seen his glory,"[10] though (surprisingly) this verse was seldom quoted directly and cannot be found even in Athanasius's *De incarnatione*. What they did not fully grasp was that the Hebrew word *basar*, normally translated as *sarx* in Greek, has a wider meaning than we would normally ascribe to its English equivalent "flesh." In a verse reminiscent of John 1:14, the prophet Isaiah said, "the glory of the Lord shall be revealed, and all flesh shall see it together."[11] The meaning here is clearly "people," not "skin and bone," but the Alexandrians either did not see this or preferred to ignore it. We can understand their desire to avoid any idea that the union of God and man in Christ was merely superficial, but if the price paid for this was a denial of the full humanity of Jesus, then it was too high. The church quickly realized this and reacted against it by condemning Apollinarius. Whether the Alexandrian tradition as a whole stood under the same judgment was what the next two generations would be asked to decide.

Nestorianism

The realization that the Alexandrian approach to Christology had fundamental weaknesses dawned only slowly in the years after 325. The debates between Arians, semi-Arians, and supporters of Nicea were all governed by the basic belief that there was only one God (the Father), and that he could not experience suffering or death. The Son of God suffered and died on the cross, but for that to be possible either he had to be less than fully God (as the Arians taught) or else only his humanity suffered and died (as everyone else believed). But if the incarnate Son was a single entity (person, being, or whatever one might call it), then the center of his consciousness had to be the divine *logos*, and he could not have had any separate existence as a man.

As the full divinity of Christ was more clearly affirmed, the inadequacy of this view of Christ's humanity became increasingly apparent. The Arians had allowed that the divine *logos*, being a creature, could play the part of a human

[10] John 1:14.
[11] Isa. 40:5.

soul in Christ. Indeed, for them, that was essential, because if Jesus had had a human soul that could suffer and die, they would not have been able to affirm the presence of the divine in the suffering in Christ, which is what the incarnation was all about. The pro-Nicenes successfully resisted this challenge, but what were they going to put in its place? They could hardly follow Apollinarius, who taught that the nonmaterial side of Jesus' being was fully divine. It therefore could not suffer or die, which robbed Christ's sacrifice of any saving significance, since God was not involved in it. With this theory, it was also virtually impossible to understand how Jesus could have been tempted or could have borne our sins, because he did not identify with the rest of humanity at the level where these things occurred—in the rational soul. But as Gregory of Nazianzus famously put it, "What has not been assumed has not been healed,"[12] which means that if the Son did not have a human soul, then human souls were not saved by his sacrificial death and resurrection. In other words, an incomplete humanity in Christ entailed an incomplete salvation for us, and an incomplete salvation was no salvation at all.

A sign that the Alexandrian way of thinking would be contested can be detected in the writings of Marcellus of Ancyra. Marcellus's very high view of the divinity of the *logos* led him to reject the view that it was the image of God, a term that he applied only to the flesh of the incarnate Christ, who made the *logos* visible. Marcellus ascribed everything that appeared to be weak or vulnerable about Jesus to his human flesh, a procedure that inevitably propelled him in the direction of recognizing the existence of a complete human nature in him. This came out very clearly in his assertion that there were two wills in the incarnate Christ, one divine and the other human. His comment on Matthew 26:41 is worth recording:

> When Jesus says, "Father, if possible, let this cup pass from me, yet not my will, but your will be done" and "The spirit is willing but the flesh is weak," he shows that he has two wills—the human will, which is that of the flesh, and the divine will. Because of the weakness of the flesh, the human will begs to be spared suffering, but the divine will is prepared for it.[13]

This statement seems unremarkable to us now, but it was a novelty at the time. Marcellus may have been the first person to articulate the belief that the incarnate Christ had two wills and not just one, as everyone in Alexandria who expressed himself on the subject seems to have thought. In this respect at least,

[12] Gregory of Nazianzus, *Epistula* 101.
[13] Marcellus of Ancyra, *De incarnatione et contra Arianos* 21.

Marcellus was the precursor of later orthodoxy, but it would be wrong to think that his assertion that there were two wills in Christ was exactly the same as the doctrine that was held by later generations.

The reason for this is that Marcellus thought of the *logos* in Christ as the active power (*energeia drastikê*) animating the flesh from the outside, as opposed to the principle (*dynamis*) that gave the flesh its life on the inside. In other words, according to Marcellus, the *logos* accepted suffering and death, not for himself but for the flesh in which he was incarnate. In saying "not my will but your will be done," he was subordinating the will of the flesh that he had assumed to the divine will that he brought with him into that flesh. As God, he could tell the flesh what to do, but he did not have to suffer the consequences. The actions of the flesh were governed by the *logos*, an external force, and did not come from within. There was no agony in the garden of Gethsemane, only the submission of a weak human will to a strong divine one. This was something less than a true picture of Christ's passion, as became apparent in the way in which Marcellus's disciple Photinus picked up his idea and "simplified" it.[14] According to Photinus, Jesus was a man with special divine power (*energeia drastikê*, again), and not the incarnate Son of God at all. This takes us back to adoptianism by another route, and because of this Marcellus's doctrine would be suspect for generations to come. It seemed that the more a theologian emphasized Christ's humanity, the less divine Christ became, and vice versa.[15] Only a new way of thinking about the question could break this particular logjam, but it would take many years for that to emerge.

After Marcellus, the next person who examined this subject in detail was Eustathius of Antioch. Like Marcellus, Eustathius regarded the *logos* as the subject of the incarnation, but unlike him, he found room for spiritual suffering in the human soul of Christ. In that respect, Eustathius came closer than Marcellus to what would eventually be canonized as Christological orthodoxy, but he was still some distance away from it. A Latin fragment of his writings tells us that he referred to the incarnate Christ as *homo deifer*, the "God-bearing man."[16] The adoptianist ring is unmistakable, and reminds us yet again of the

[14] For what little is known about Photinus, see Gustave Bardy, *Paul de Samosate* (Paris: E. Champion, 1923), 407–414.
[15] The problem can be seen most clearly in the epistles attributed to Ignatius of Antioch (d. 118) but most probably dating to the mid-fourth century and now associated with the theology of Eusebius of Emesa (300?–359?). The Pseudo-Ignatian Epistles denounce the views of Marcellus and Photinus, making it clear that they are adoptianist. See, for example, Pseudo-Ignatius, *Epistula ad Philadelphiam* 6.3. The matter is discussed at some length by Grillmeier, *Christ in Christian Tradition*, 1:303–308.
[16] The Greek for this would be *anthrôpos theophoros*. It stands in sharp contrast to the description of Christ as *theos sarkophoros* ("flesh-bearing God") used by Ignatius, the early second-century bishop of Antioch. See Aloys Grillmeier, *Christ in Christian Tradition*, 1:301, for the details.

fundamental problem that all these men had to face when trying to get the balance between the humanity and the divinity of Christ.

Eustathius was not an adoptianist but his language left him open to misunderstanding, and the direction in which that misunderstanding went would in time become associated with the church at Antioch (as opposed to Alexandria). Eustathius himself, however, after having supported the decisions taken at Nicea in 325, was deposed by a pro-Arian faction at Antioch and driven into exile. This had the effect of making him a martyr to the Nicene cause, at least in the eyes of his supporters in Antioch, and when the Christological problem came to the fore a generation later, it was to his legacy that those supporters would appeal.

One of the leaders of this group was a man called Paulinus, who attended the Synod of Alexandria in 362 and gained the support of Athanasius because of his firmly anti-Arian stance. After 362 it became acceptable to say that, in Christ, the *logos* became man, and not merely that he entered into a man, a compromise formula that tried to exclude both adoptianism and Apollinarianism.[17] Yet the fact that Apollinarius was able to interpret the decrees of Alexandria in a way that was compatible with his Christology showed that the struggle against his position was far from over. On the contrary, Apollinarianism soon made its appearance in Antioch and gained a following there, thanks to the energetic preaching of a man called Vitalis. Vitalis was eventually confronted by Epiphanius of Salamis, who turned up in Antioch in 374 and defeated him in open debate. Undeterred, Vitalis then took his case to Rome, where he thought that he could win over Bishop Damasus (366–384), and through him the entire Western church, to his position.

Damasus knew little of what had been going on in the East but he was suspicious of what Vitalis had to say, particularly when he heard his interpretation of the Alexandrian Synod of 362. Instead of supporting Vitalis, Damasus wrote to Paulinus with an outline of his own Christological position. In that letter he upheld the view that Christ was the unique Son of God, the divine Word (*logos*), and Wisdom, who in the incarnation became a complete man, with a body, soul, and mind (*sensus*), though without sin. Damasus made no attempt to expound the subtler points of this image of the incarnate Christ, but the framework was clear and would prove to be enduring. No one at the time could have known it, but in the end it would be Western intervention that would cut through the impasse created by the opposing schools of Christological reflection in the East and produce the

[17] Athanasius, *Contra Arianos* 3.30.

formula that would be accepted as orthodox by the Council of Chalcedon in 451.

More immediately, Damasus's letter prompted the convening of a synod at Antioch in 379, where Meletius (a friend of the recently deceased Basil of Caesarea) and Diodore of Tarsus led the charge against Apollinarius. Meletius was basically pro-Nicene in his theology but he refused to use the term *homoousios* because it was not in the Bible. Athanasius had recognized that this reluctance did not affect the substance of Meletius's teaching, and he had urged a reconciliation with the Paulinians at Antioch, on the ground that they believed the same thing but expressed it in slightly different ways. Diodore, a colleague of Meletius and therefore not particularly close to Paulinus and his circle, was a relative outsider who had come to the debate as a friend and disciple of Eusebius of Emesa (300?–359?), a man whose theology was basically Alexandrian but who made some attempt to modify his inheritance by suggesting that the suffering of the flesh could be regarded as the suffering of the soul by a transfer of properties (*communicatio idiomatum*). That way, the essential impassibility of the soul (and of the divine *logos* in Christ) would be protected but room could also be found for acknowledging a genuine participation by the *logos* in the suffering and death of the incarnate Son.

Diodore first came to prominence through his opposition to the emperor Julian the Apostate (361–363), who lived in Antioch for several months and wreaked considerable havoc among the Christians in the city while he was there. Diodore stood up to him by defending the divinity of Christ, a doctrine that Julian regarded as blasphemous because it introduced suffering into the *logos*. Julian was particularly incensed by the Christian use of the term *Theotokos* ("God-bearer") as a description of the Virgin Mary, because he believed that it confused the divine and the human. Diodore was sensitive to this charge and apparently downplayed the use of *Theotokos* in order to avoid such misunderstanding, but this tactical maneuver must not be misinterpreted. On the essential issue, Diodore distanced himself from any hint of adoptianism by speaking of the duality in the incarnate Christ as that between *logos* and "flesh," in the traditional Alexandrian manner.

Here we can detect the influence of Eusebius of Emesa on Diodore's thought. Just as Eusebius recoiled from the extreme of Apollinarianism, so did Diodore. As the controversy developed, Diodore came to see more clearly that the incarnate Christ must have had a human soul and therefore must have been a complete man. However, he reached this position not by rejecting the use of the term "flesh" but by extending it—as the Bible did—to include the life of the soul. By the time of the First Council of Constantinople in 381, which

Diodore and Meletius both attended, that position was firmly in place and was adopted by the council as the most orthodox formula available.[18]

Of particular importance for the future was Diodore's rejection of the belief that there is only one *hypostasis* in the incarnate Christ. This opinion was not endorsed by the council held at Constantinople in 381, and would later be explicitly rejected by the Council of Chalcedon. But from Diodore's perspective the "one *hypostasis*" doctrine had to be disowned because in his mind it implied that there was a natural unity between the *logos* and the flesh of Christ that dehumanized the latter and resulted in Apollinarianism. For Diodore, the humanity of Christ had to have its own integrity in order for him to be able to take our place on the cross and become our Savior. Anything that fell short of that would compromise (and therefore destroy) our salvation. In the course of time the debate would move on and Diodore's position would be shown to be inadequate, but he was making an important point, and it is fair to say that the substance of his position, if not its precise language, was retained and reaffirmed at Chalcedon.

Another theologian who felt the need to develop Alexandrian Christology further was Didymus the Blind (313?–398). His views are of particular importance because he came from Alexandria and worked within that context. Fragments of his lost *Commentary on the Psalms* that were discovered in the Egyptian desert in 1941 make it clear that he realized what was missing from Athanasius's thought and supplied it. His exact words were, "As the [human] soul that Jesus assumed is something other than the Trinity, it is by nature created to endure the onset of suffering (*propatheia*)."[19] In other words, because the rational soul of the man Jesus was not divine, it did not share the divine attributes that would have prevented it from suffering. Jesus was therefore able to enter into the anguish of humanity and could be tempted just as we are, although he was without sin.[20]

The weakness of Didymus's interpretation lay in his understanding of the origin of Christ's soul, which he derived from Platonism by way of Origen. He believed that all human souls were part of the divine world-soul, from which they had fallen away and become sinful. The only exception to this was the human soul of Christ, which managed to cling to the *logos* from which it sprang and thus avoided the fall. When the *logos* became flesh, he brought this exceptional human soul with him, giving the incarnate Christ a complete

[18] Meletius died during the council, but that did not affect the adoption of his views. See Grillmeier, *Christ in Christian Tradition*, 1:358–360.

[19] See Adolphe Gesché, "La christologie du *Commentaire sur les Psaumes* découvert à Toura," (Gembloux: Editions J. Duculot, 1962), 135.

[20] This, of course, is a New Testament teaching. See Heb. 4:15.

(but sinless) humanity as well as a complete divinity. Didymus was even able to speak of two *prosôpa* in Jesus, a concept that he also referred to as two *morphai* ("forms") and two *charaktêres* ("shapes").[21] These synonyms make it clear that for Didymus, *prosôpon* did not mean "person" in the later sense of an agent, but merely an "appearance," not all that far removed from the word's original meaning of "mask." Nevertheless, the fact that he could speak in terms that made the divinity and humanity of Christ parallel to each other shows that he was moving away from earlier Alexandrian ideas, in which Christ's humanity was always incomplete and subordinate to his divinity.

Given that Didymus was head of the catechetical school at Alexandria, it is not surprising that his ideas were influential to the point that they had become standard in Egypt by the time he died. It is particularly interesting to note that Theophilus of Alexandria (385–412) was a firm exponent of the true manhood of Jesus and held a view of its importance identical to that of Gregory of Nazianzus, namely, that what has not been assumed has not been healed.[22] Theophilus was the uncle of the famous Cyril who would lead the defense of his church's teaching a generation later, which is a reminder to us that Alexandria and Antioch were not as far apart in their theology as many modern scholars like to think.

Outside Alexandria, a similar view was promoted by Epiphanius of Salamis, who tried (unsuccessfully) to get Basil of Caesarea interested in the question. Basil certainly believed that Christ bore all the sufferings of humanity in his flesh, but he was more reticent when it came to saying anything about Christ's soul because he wanted to safeguard its sinlessness. Like Athanasius, he simply did not appreciate the importance of saying that the human soul of Jesus bore our sins on the cross without becoming sinful himself, because his assumption of that burden was an act of supreme obedience to the will of his Father and not the logical consequence of his own finite humanity.

Gregory of Nazianzus, as we have already had occasion to notice, had a more satisfactory understanding of why the incarnate Christ had to be fully human as well as fully divine, but he lacked the conceptual vocabulary required for expressing this within the overall unity of Christ. Was Jesus a flesh-bearing God or a God-bearing man? Gregory canvassed both possibilities and declared his preference for the latter. This makes him sound very Antiochene to later generations, but he himself did not see things so clearly. His real contribution to the ongoing development of Christology was in the way he linked it to the doctrine of the Trinity. He did this by using the Greek adjective *allos* ("other")

[21] Didymus got these terms from Phil. 2:7 and Heb. 1:3 respectively.
[22] Theophilus of Alexandria, *Epistula paschalis* 17.

in both the masculine (personal) and the impersonal neuter form *allo* to explain how both the Trinity and the incarnate Christ were constituted, with the following results:

	Personal	**Impersonal**
The incarnate Christ:	one; no *allos*	two; a divine *allo* and a human *allo*
The Trinity:	three *alloi*	one; no *allo*

In this way Gregory expressed what would later be canonized as orthodox doctrine but without using the terminology of "person" and "nature," which we can read back into it but which was not fully developed at that time. The fact that we can do this without distorting Gregory's meaning shows that he understood the heart of the matter in an orthodox way. After him, defining the doctrine was relatively simple, although it was not as straightforward as it now seems to us. It was not that the vocabulary needed to do this was lacking but that it had not been sufficiently clearly defined and canonized, to the exclusion of other options. The problem was that this lack of clarity could conceal hidden differences of doctrine that had to be sorted out before genuine agreement could be reached. That agreement was never total and still proves elusive today, but it is fair to say that the different positions are not nearly as irreconcilable as they would be if they involved heresies like Arianism, Apollinarianism, or adoptianism.

That, however, is looking ahead. At the time, Gregory of Nazianzus's insights were taken up and developed further by Basil's younger brother, Gregory of Nyssa, who made it clear that in the context of Trinitarian theology, *hypostasis* and *prosôpon* were essentially synonymous and referred to the threeness in God, not to his essential unity. That paved the way for using the terms to refer to the oneness of the incarnate Christ, who was identical to the second member of the Godhead, and Gregory of Nyssa was clearly moving in that direction. What held him back was that he continued to think of the *hypostases*/*prosôpa* as individual manifestations of the underlying essence, rather than as personal agents interacting with one another (in the case of the Trinity) and capable of possessing two otherwise incompatible natures (in the case of the incarnate Christ). As Gregory expressed it,

> The firstfruits of human nature that were taken up into God are mingled in the divine being like drops of vinegar in the sea, and their particular properties are effectively lost. For if the Son were to be known inside the Godhead in

> a different kind of nature that could be recognized by its own characteristics, making one part of him appear weak, limited, corruptible, or temporal, and the other powerful, omnipotent, incorruptible, and eternal, the result would be that there would be two Sons [and not just one.][23]

In the end, Gregory believed that Christ's humanity could only be taken up into God by ceasing to be itself, a contradiction that could not be the last word on the subject. Somehow the human nature of Christ had to remain what it was, even as it was assumed by the Son of God and taken up to glory. If that were not so, our salvation would be compromised, because we too shall be taken up to glory, though without losing the limitations that make us human beings and not God. How then could we be united with Christ if his human nature were not like ours? This was the abiding problem of all fourth-century Christology, and until it was tackled and resolved the doctrine of Christ would remain a point of tension in the life of the church.

The modified Alexandrian approach that we find in the two Gregorys was typical of their time and can be found without significant variation in the thought of men like Hilary of Poitiers and John Chrysostom, both of whom moved in similar theological circles. A real alternative did not emerge until Theodore of Mopsuestia (d. 428) developed one in the years after the First Council of Constantinople.[24] Theodore was a leading light of the theological school of Antioch, and it was because of his influence there that his approach was considered "Antiochene" in later times. Long after his death, Theodore was condemned for heresy and many of his works disappeared, with the result that it is now difficult to get a balanced picture of his achievement. What is clear, though, is that his approach to the person and natures of Christ was based on a broad theological outlook that was rooted in his understanding of the Bible.

For Theodore, divine revelation had two different aspects—the present and the future. By the "present" he meant the whole sphere of time and creation, in which types and symbols spoke of spiritual truth. The Old Testament laid the groundwork for the institution of the church, and the church is the pattern of the life that believers will live in heaven. By the "future," Theodore meant the redeeming work of Christ, which makes the life of heaven a reality in our lives. It begins at baptism, the rite in which the Christian participates in the death and resurrection of the Savior, and is sealed by adoption as a child of God, in which state the believer shares in the Son's relationship with the Father in the Godhead.

---

[23] Gregory of Nyssa, *Ad Theophilum adversus Apollinarium* 126–127.

[24] See F. A. Sullivan, *The Christology of Theodore of Mopsuestia* (Rome: Gregorian University Press, 1956).

This relationship and its benefits are revealed to us in the life of Jesus Christ, who showed his disciples how to live as children of God. For this to mean anything to them, the incarnate Son had to be fully human, since otherwise his example would not have been transferable to them. One of Theodore's prime concerns was to preserve the transcendence of God, whose nature remains above and beyond anything we can know or participate in directly. Human beings cannot become divine, and so the human nature of Jesus could not have been divine either. Instead, Theodore saw the relationship between divinity and humanity in Christ as one of "conjunction" (*synapheia*), a kind of union that allowed each nature to remain what it was but to share in the life of the other. Thus, the presence of the *logos* alongside the human nature of Christ made it possible for the latter to live a life of perfect obedience. Jesus of Nazareth was not sinless because his human nature was transformed into something divine but because, as a man, he was perfectly obedient to the will of his Father. This was the link between him and his followers—the disciples of Jesus were not called to become divine, but they were expected to obey, and the example of Jesus was set out in Scripture in order to demonstrate that this obedience was achievable by any right-thinking human being.

Theodore's approach was quite different from that of the Alexandrians but it did not emerge as a result of conflict with them. The evidence suggests that they moved in different circles and so naturally went their separate ways. Theodore was closer to Didymus the Blind than to anyone else at Alexandria, but there is no evidence that he was directly dependent on him. He opposed both the Arians and the Apollinarians, but that was only to be expected and did not amount to a condemnation of Alexandrian Christology as such. Yet the premise on which his Christology was built conflicts with the Alexandrian belief that the divine *logos* operated on the human flesh of Christ in order to produce the God-man. Alexandrian Christology could allow for a human soul in Jesus if necessary, but it was entirely subordinated to the *logos*.

In Theodore's construction, however, not only did Jesus have a human soul, but that soul was at the heart of the conjunction between divinity and humanity in the incarnate Son. As he put it,

> [The divine Son] co-operated with the one whom he assumed, but where does this imply that his divinity had replaced the human mind (*nous*) in the one whom he had assumed? It was not his custom to replace the *nous* in anyone to whom he extended his co-operation. Even if in this case [i.e., of Jesus] the extent of the co-operation was exceptional, it still does not mean that the divinity took the place of the *nous*. If that had happened, how would he

> [Jesus] have been afraid of suffering? What need would he have had of prayer, especially of the vehement kind that, as the apostle Paul says, he brought before God with a loud voice and many tears?[25]

Where the Alexandrians saw the triumph of Christ as the natural outcome of the work of the *logos* overruling his human flesh, Theodore saw it in the steadfastness of the flesh itself, fortified by divine grace but not replaced by the divine nature.

The portrait of Christ as a man who wrestled with the need to submit his mind and will to that of the Father shifted the focus of Christological speculation dramatically. No longer was it a question of trying to decide how human he was but the exact opposite. What place was there for the presence of the *logos* in Jesus if all he could do was get in the way of the man who was struggling with God? The logic of Theodore's argument seemed to demand that there should be as much distance between Christ's divinity and his humanity as possible, but the further one moved in that direction, the more the unity of the incarnate Son was compromised. What held them together if they had nothing in common?

Theodore saw no difficulty with this and believed that "becoming a man" and "assuming a man" were the same thing—there was no preexistent human being into whom the Son came, as the adoptianists claimed. His words are worth quoting:

> [The fathers of Nicea] said that the Son became a man. It was not through a straightforward divine decision that he emptied himself [cf. Phil. 2:7], nor was it through the grace of powerful help [to a man], which he has so often offered in the past and still offers now. Instead, he took on our very nature. He clothed himself with it and dwelt in it so as to make it perfect through suffering; he united himself to it.[26]

This sounds very much as if Theodore was moving in a thought-world that, if it was not Alexandrian, could at least be reconciled with that view. But while he scored highly on his ability to detect two natures in the one incarnate Christ, he was less sure of himself when it came to describing how these natures were united to each other. The notion of "conjunction" was his preferred way of describing this, but how this conjunction came into being and was maintained through the life, death, and resurrection of Jesus is not so clear. In a fragment

[25] See Henry B. Swete, *Theodori episcopi Mopsuesteni in epistolas B. Pauli commentarii*, 2 vols. (Cambridge: Cambridge University Press, 1880–1882), 2:315. The biblical reference is to Heb. 5:7.
[26] Theodore of Mopsuestia, *Homiliae catecheticae* 7.1.

preserved by the sixth-century theologian Leontius of Byzantium, Theodore apparently wrote,

> When we distinguish the natures, we say that the nature of God the *logos* is complete and that its *prosôpon* is also complete (for it is wrong to speak of a *hypostasis* without its *prosôpon*). We also say that the human nature is complete, as is his *prosôpon*. But when we look at the conjunction, then we say that there is only one *prosôpon*.[27]

If we were able to interpret *prosôpon* here in the later sense of "person," there would be little problem in harmonizing what Theodore said with the definition of the Council of Chalcedon in 451. The difficulty is that we cannot do this, because for Theodore, a *prosôpon* was not a "person" but an "appearance," the visible manifestation of something else that lies behind it. It is true that Theodore started with the *prosôpon* of the *logos*, which was then extended to cover the man Jesus, but the *prosôpon* of their conjunction was not the cause of the incarnation, but its result. Theodore's language can be adapted to fit later orthodoxy but it did not start out that way, as the distinction he made between the terms *hypostasis* and *prosôpon* make clear. For Theodore, *hypostasis* was attached primarily to "nature," which meant that there were two of them in the incarnate Christ and made it hard to see what objective existence his one *prosôpon* could have. The conjunction of the two natures/*hypostases* might look permanent, but it was always dissoluble, and for that reason the unity of Christ was never finally secure.

It is at this point that the third option available to the fathers of the early church came into its own, in the teaching of Nestorius. As with both Paul of Samosata and Arius, Nestorius (381?–451?) is a figure whom we know mainly through his enemies, though in his case a Nestorian church has survived and preserved his teaching in something like its original form. Nestorianism developed over time and to some extent may have distanced itself from Nestorius, but it is accessible to us in a way that adoptianism and Arianism are not.[28] In particular, the discovery in 1897 of the long-lost *Book of Heraclides*, which was quickly recognized as one of Nestorius's works, led to a reassessment of his teaching in the hope of being able to pronounce him orthodox, despite the fact that he had been condemned both at the First Council of Ephesus in 431 and again at the Council of Chalcedon in 451.[29] It is known that Nestorius wrote to

[27] Leontius of Byzantium, fragment 6, cited in Swete, *Theodori episcopi Mopsuesteni*, 2:299.

[28] Late in life, Nestorius wrote a letter to the people of Constantinople in which he disowned the teachings of some of his followers, though it is hard to know how much weight to give to this. See François Nau, *Le livre d'Héraclide de Damas* (Paris: Letouzey et Ané, 1910; repr., Farnborough: Gregg International, 1969), 374.

[29] Luigi I. Scipioni, *Ricerche sulla Cristologia del 'Libro di Eraclide' di Nestorio. La formulazione teologica e il suo contesto filosofico* (Fribourg: Presses Universitaires, 1956).

the latter council protesting his orthodoxy and asking that he be rehabilitated by the church, but this did not happen. Once again, it seems that however misunderstood Nestorius was and however unfair the campaign against him, in the end his views were unable to do justice to the mystery of the incarnation and had to be rejected.[30]

The conflict began in 428, when Nestorius was elected bishop of Constantinople, a city that had traditionally been under Antiochene influence. It was a sensitive appointment, not least because heretics and dissidents of various kinds were drawn to the city as a relatively safe haven. In smaller towns they were easily exposed, but in the capital they could often melt into the crowds and escape notice. This was a problem that Nestorius was determined to confront. On arrival in his new see he launched a kind of inquisition that was designed to root out unacceptable elements, and particularly Arians and Apollinarians, whose views had been condemned by the council held in the city in 381. Unfortunately, Nestorius's zeal seems to have been matched by an inability to appreciate the subtleties of Alexandrian theology, which all sounded Apollinarian to him.

This might not have mattered very much except that he also got embroiled in a Christological controversy in Constantinople which he had to address. On the surface the quarrel appears to have been about the Virgin Mary, but here the modern reader has to be careful not to misunderstand what was going on. Today Mary has been elevated to such a status in the Roman Catholic Church (and to a somewhat lesser degree in the Eastern Orthodox churches as well) that it is hard to distinguish the claims made on her behalf by later generations from what was going on in the fifth century. The dispute at that time was not about her, but about her Son. Was the fetus in her womb God, or not?

This question brought the somewhat rarefied theological controversies down to a level that everyone could understand. Mary had obviously given birth to a human baby, but he was no ordinary child. He had been conceived by the Holy Spirit, not by Joseph, as the New Testament insists at some length.[31] Luke even tells us that when the pregnant Mary went to visit her equally pregnant cousin Elizabeth, the fetus in Elizabeth's womb (the future John the Baptist), leaped in her womb, and that Elizabeth was moved to address Mary as the mother of her Lord.[32] Every Christian knew the story, and any doctrine that tried to downplay it would certainly be rejected by the church. It was therefore to be expected that Christians would confess

[30] For a complete assessment of the arguments and discussion, see Grillmeier, *Christ in Christian Tradition*, 1:559–568.
[31] Matt. 1:18–25; Luke 1:26–38.
[32] Luke 1:41–43.

that the Son of God dwelt in Mary's womb, making her the "God-bearer" (*Theotokos*).

No one seems to have questioned this, but the emergence of Arianism (and later of Apollinarianism) brought the term into some disrepute. The reason was that both groups wanted to stress the *Theotokos* idea as a way of reinforcing their belief that the *logos* entered Mary's womb and took the place of a rational soul in the incarnate Christ. It may be true that for Apollinarius the *logos* was fully God, while for Arius he was a divine creature, but either way, the *Theotokos* doctrine was seen as a means of denying the full humanity of Christ, to which neither Arius nor Apollinarius subscribed. Because of this, the term *Theotokos* had become suspect as being at least potentially Arian or Apollinarian, and there was a group in Constantinople that wanted to remove it from the worshiping life of the church for that reason.

Unfortunately, their suggestion that *Theotokos* should be replaced by *anthrôpotokos* ("man-bearer") was hardly an improvement and probably made the misunderstanding even worse. At one level, there was nothing surprising about saying that Mary was a "man-bearer," since that is true of every woman who has a child. But in the case of Jesus, to insist on a word like that could only mean that his miraculous, divine origin was being denied. Whatever was special about Jesus would not have come from his conception in Mary's womb but from some subsequent act of God in his life—adoptianism once again! But that went against the teaching of the Gospels, and it went against the sense among ordinary Christians that, in Jesus, God was with us—Immanuel, as Isaiah had called him.[33] Nevertheless, the use of *anthrôpotokos* made the point that Jesus was a real man and not just a divine being clothed in human flesh.

At the heart of this controversy, though it was apparently not recognized at the time, was the question of how the word "flesh" should be interpreted. There is reason to believe that Athanasius equated the flesh with the body as a whole but, as we have seen, the implications of this were not properly explored in his theology, leaving open the possibility that it could be interpreted in an Apollinarian sense—as indeed happened. Stating clearly that Mary was *anthrôpotokos* would make that interpretation heretical, which is presumably what its supporters had in mind. When faced with having to adjudicate on the rights and wrongs of this quarrel, Nestorius found himself in an uncomfortable dilemma. He did not want to repudiate the *Theotokos*, which he regarded as true enough in itself, but he also appreciated the merits of *anthrôpotokos* and did not want to deny the insight that it contributed to understanding the incarnation.

[33] Isa. 7:14, quoted in Matt. 1:23.

Like many bishops before him and since, Nestorius decided that the best way forward was to compromise. In his Paschal Letter issued at Easter [April 7] 429, he acknowledged the merits of the arguments on both sides in the dispute and proposed that the best solution would be to discard both terms and replace them with *Christotokos* ("Christ-bearer"), because the child in her womb was not simply God or man but a conjunction (*synapheia*) of the two, which was the most important thing. This of course was the teaching of Theodore of Mopsuestia, who had only recently died, and Nestorius obviously thought that it was the right answer to the problem. Unfortunately, Nestorius did not stop there. He also accused Cyril, who had been bishop of Alexandria since 412, of Apollinarianism and attacked the traditional understanding of the "transfer of properties" (*communicatio idiomatum*), which he thought was responsible for such unfortunate phrases as "Mother of God" and "the suffering God" that appeared to compromise the supreme otherness of the divine nature.[34]

Nestorius was wrong in his assessment of Cyril, but it must be admitted that there were some grounds for his mistake. Cyril said that what had been two natures before (or apart from) the incarnation became one nature after it. "One nature [*mia physis*] of the incarnate Son of God" was his formula, and his followers were never to deviate from it. As they saw it, trying to distinguish human from divine activity in Jesus was pointless because everything Jesus did was both. His humanity was complete and everywhere present in him, but so was his divinity, so his actions were the work of both natures, which had been united by the power of the *logos* in the incarnation and had become indissolubly one.

Cyril's *mia physis* formula was probably derived from Apollinarius, who certainly used it to explain his own conception of what the incarnation was. Only those who realized that Cyril moved on from Apollinarius without divesting himself of this particular Apollinarian formula understood this, but such awareness was rare outside Alexandria. Cyril was forced to develop the *mia physis* formula further by the trenchant criticism of it made by a certain Succensus, who is otherwise unknown. Succensus pointed out that Apollinarius had been able to speak of one nature in the incarnate Christ because, to him, Christ's humanity did not constitute a complete nature. However, once it is granted that the suffering of Christ was not a matter of the flesh only but also

[34] For recent and sympathetic assessments of Cyril, see John McGuckin, *Saint Cyril of Alexandria and the Christological Controversy* (Crestwood, NY: St. Vladimir's Seminary Press, 2004); Thomas G. Weinandy and Daniel A. Keating, eds., *The Theology of St. Cyril of Alexandria* (London: T & T Clark, 2003); and Susan Wessel, *Cyril of Alexandria and the Nestorian Controversy: The Making of a Saint and of a Heretic* (Oxford: Oxford University Press, 2004). Readers of Greek might also consult D. A. Lialiou, *Hermêneia tôn* Hypomnêstikôn *tou Hagiou Kyrillou Alexandreias* (Thessalonica: Pournaras, 2000).

of the rational soul, then Christ possessed a complete human nature as well as his divinity, and the *mia physis* concept of Apollinarius needed to be revised accordingly. That Cyril understood this is clear from the following summary he gives of Succensus's position:

> Whoever says that the Lord suffered only in the flesh makes the suffering irrational and involuntary. But if anyone says that he suffered in a rational soul and voluntarily, there is no objection to saying that he suffered in his human nature. If that is so, how can we not accept that the two natures coexist without separation after the union?[35]

Cyril's assent to this tells us that he understood that the human soul of Christ was the necessary seat of his suffering in a way that Apollinarius denied and that Athanasius failed to affirm with sufficient clarity. Unlike Apollinarius, Cyril believed that the natural life-force of Christ's human body came from his human soul, not from the *logos*, but he also wanted to affirm that it was the presence of the *logos* in that body that made it "life-giving." The death of Christ on the cross was not just a physical event but a spiritual one as well. Christians are not saved by the physical blood of Jesus but by the spiritual outpouring of divine power in and through that blood. To separate the physical from the spiritual was to remove the latter from human experience and so to take away our salvation. The relationship between God and man in Christ could not be accidental but must be substantial and irreversible, which meant that any idea of a mere "conjunction" had to be ruled out.

This was why Cyril clung to the *mia physis* formula even when its original meaning was no longer applicable and was likely to cause confusion to those who were unfamiliar with his intellectual background. Like all the Alexandrians of his type, Cyril could not see that his solution to the Christological problem left the integrity of Jesus' humanity in doubt. If Jesus were the Son of God with added capabilities derived from the human nature he had assumed in his incarnation, did that make him a real human being? If the "control center" of his life was not human in the way that ours is, could he be a man like one of us? That Nestorius saw the problem in these terms is clear from a letter that he later wrote to Theodoret of Cyrus:

> Cyril says: ". . . even if the distinction of the natures is not misunderstood, from which (*ex hôn*) an inexpressible union is achieved." This *ex hôn* makes it sound as if Cyril is speaking of the natures of the Lord as parts which

[35] Cyril of Alexandria, *Epistula 46 ad Succensum*, 2.5.

> combine to make up the whole. He should not have said "from which" (*ex hôn*) but "of which" (*hôn*), because this inexpressible unity is not made up *from* the natures but consists *of* them.[36]

For Cyril, a "nature" is the essence of a thing, which must be shaped into a *hypostasis* in order for it to be identifiable. The two concepts are distinct in the way that "substance" and "form" are distinct, but they also belong inseparably together, so that one can sometimes be used to signify the other. In God, the divine nature is hypostatized in the *logos*, whom we recognize as the Son of the Father. This hypostatized nature is what we would call a "person," and it is this "person" that became incarnate in Jesus Christ. His humanity has different properties (and would therefore be considered a different "nature" by people unfamiliar with Cyril's use of the term *physis*) but the *logos* is the common subject who binds humanity and divinity together. Cyril's Christology can thus be summed up as follows:

1. The *hypostases* or *physeis* of humanity and divinity that make up the incarnate Christ cannot be divided after their union in him.
2. The properties of the incarnate Christ cannot be divided according to *hypostasis* or *physis*. Everything Christ is and does is the essence and action of a single being, the one *hypostasis* of God the *logos* incarnate.[37]
3. The *logos* is united to the flesh by *hypostasis*. There is therefore only one *hypostasis* in Christ and not two, united by "conjunction."

The creed of 381, to which both Cyril and Nestorius subscribed, makes it clear that the Son of God is the single divine subject of both his eternal relationship with the Father and the Holy Spirit in the Trinity, and his descent into the womb of Mary in the incarnation. It was on this basis that Cyril developed his Christology, including his understanding of the "transfer of properties" that Nestorius criticized as inappropriate. Nestorius may have been right to sound a note of caution here, but the way he did so was unhelpful, to say the least. So afraid was he of erring on the side of the divine over the human that he virtually abolished the use of the term *logos*, which implied a divine subject of the incarnation, and substituted "Christ" instead. To the uninitiated that might seem like a harmless modification, or even an improvement, since Christ is clearly a person in the way that the *logos* may not be, but here we have to

[36] For the text, see Friedrich Loofs, *Nestoriana. Die Fragmente des Nestorius gesammelt, untersucht und herausgegeben* (Halle: Niemeyer, 1905), 197–198.

[37] The English is somewhat ambiguous, but in Greek the word "incarnate" must refer either to the *physis* (in which case it is *sesarkômenê*) or to the *logos*, in which case it is *sesarkômenou*. In Cyril, both forms are found, though a distinction between them appeared at a later stage.

remember how Theodore of Mopsuestia had developed his understanding of the word.

For Theodore, and therefore also for Nestorius, "Christ" was the designation applied to the *result* of the conjunction of the two natures, not to its *cause*—to the end, as it were, and not to the beginning. Nestorius was uncomfortable with the idea that the *logos* was the subject of the incarnation if by that was meant that he added a human nature to his already existing divinity, because to his mind such a picture denied the full humanity of Christ. Unfortunately the only alternative he could suggest was that Christ was the sum total of the two natures joined together, without specifying who or what joined them. Was each nature an independent agent that somehow agreed to unite? That made little sense and could only have been viable as a form of adoptianism.

That weakness was seized on by Nestorius's Alexandrian opponents, who used it as one of their main arguments against his position. Nestorius, however, did not intend to deny the unity of Christ's person but wished to affirm the integrity of each of his two natures, which coexisted without the so-called "transfer of properties." As he put it in a sermon he preached at the height of the controversy in 430, "I did not say that the Son was one [person] and God the *logos* another; I said that God the *logos* was by nature one thing and the temple [i.e., his body] by nature another, one Son by conjunction."[38] He makes his position even clearer in another fragment that has survived, though it cannot be precisely dated:

> Even before the incarnation, God the *logos* was Son and God alongside the Father, but in the last days he took the form of a servant.[39] However, since he was already a Son both in name and by nature, he cannot be called a second Son after taking this form, since then we would be acknowledging [the existence of] two Sons.[40]

What Nestorius really believed was that the Son of God was the *logos* in his divine nature who manifested himself as "Christ" in the incarnation. The difficulty seems to have been that he could not make the *logos* the subject of the incarnate Christ's *human* nature because he was already the subject of his divinity. At the same time, though, he strongly rejected the idea that "Christ" was the subject of the human nature who entered into conjunction with the *logos*, and claimed that that was why he rejected the adequacy of the term *anthrôpotokos*.[41] In assessing Nestorius, the following points can be made:

[38] Loofs, *Nestoriana*, 308.
[39] Phil. 2:7.
[40] Loofs, *Nestoriana*, 275.
[41] Ibid., 182, 248–249, 259, 299, 354.

1. He believed that the distinction between divinity and humanity was absolute in terms of their respective natures and remained so after the incarnation. Any confusion on this point would lead either to obscuring the divinity (Arius) or to reducing the extent of the humanity (Apollinarius).

2. He rejected the "transfer of properties" from one nature to the other because, in effect, such a transfer would cancel out the independent identity and coherence of each nature.

3. He understood that the unity of the incarnate Christ was to be found in his *prosôpon* and not in either of his natures, although it was by a conjunction of the natures that this unity emerged.

4. Each of Christ's natures had its own integrity, which Nestorius designated by the term *hypostasis*. He could therefore say that the conjunction of the natures was also a conjunction of *hypostases*, a formula that the Alexandrians could never have accepted because to them it made the human nature of Christ a different being from the eternal Son of God.

Nestorius escaped from the snares of Arianism and Apollinarianism by insisting on the integrity of each of the two natures of the incarnate Christ, and he understood that the unity of these natures had to be expressed by using a different term, in his case *prosôpon*. The weakness of his position was that the meaning he attached to *prosôpon* was not strong enough to bear the weight that he put on it because it was only the external manifestation of some underlying reality and not the agent that shaped and determined that reality. In other words, the *logos* was not the *prosôpon* of the incarnate Christ, but he contributed to its makeup.

Nestorius wanted to do the right thing, but he was unable to come up with an adequate answer to the questions that he had raised by insisting that the incarnate Christ must be a unity of two distinct natures and not some kind of fusion between them. He was condemned, not because of his intentions (which were good) but because his solution to the problem was inadequate. Was this just? Here opinions are bound to differ. Had he *not* been condemned, his followers would have assumed that his Christology was correct as it stood and could be adopted without prejudice to his or their orthodoxy. Unfortunately, it was not possible to separate the man from his ideas, and so Nestorius paid a price for the latter, which his intentions did not merit. For this reason he remains a controversial figure who is still capable of rallying support from those whose primary concern is with "justice" for those who have been wrongly accused. But even those who are sympathetic to him personally have to accept that he did not solve the Christological problem, which soon moved on to another level and effectively made his proposals redundant.[42]

When Cyril of Alexandria learned of Nestorius's views, he realized immediately that his compromise *Christotokos* formula would never do. The principle of unity in Christ was the cause of the incarnation, not its result, and that principle was divine. The natures of divinity and humanity did not come together to form a new entity called Christ, because the Son of God existed with his Father in eternity before becoming incarnate, and in his incarnation he took on human flesh in addition to his divine nature. Nestorius had already communicated his ideas to Rome and elsewhere in an attempt to persuade the Christian world to accept his solution to the Christological question, and Cyril followed suit. This was natural, because Rome was the only theological center of comparable importance to Alexandria and Constantinople. By 430, both sides in the dispute were appealing to the Roman church to support them in their quest for a solution.

It must be said that much of this activity was politically motivated. At the First Council of Nicea an order of precedence had been established for the bishops of the three major centers of the Roman empire. Rome (as the imperial capital) came first, followed by Alexandria as the chief city of the east, and then Antioch, the headquarters of the government of Syria. But less than five years later, on May 11, 330, the emperor Constantine moved the capital from Rome to the ancient Greek city of Byzantium, which he renamed Constantinople after himself. The bishop of Heraclea, which was the nearest important town to Byzantium, transferred his seat to the new city and expected to be accorded the same degree of precedence that would be given to this "New Rome" in secular society. That upset the bishop of Old Rome, who saw this move as the first step in downgrading the status of his own church. It also discomfited Alexandria, which was now demoted to third place in the imperial hierarchy and was no longer recognized as the main city of the East.

It is therefore not altogether surprising that Rome and Alexandria should make common cause against the upstart Constantinople. There was also the fact that Greek had by now ceased to be widely understood at Rome, so the letters of Nestorius had to be translated into Latin, a difficult task when the need to find adequate terms for theological matters is taken into account. Cyril, it seems, took care to translate his messages to Rome before they were sent, which made it easier on the receiving end and ensured that any translation errors could be detected and removed at the source. Of course, it also made

[42] See, for example, Luigi I. Scipioni, *Nestorio e il concilio di Efeso. Storia, dogma, critica* (Milan: Vita e Pensiero, 1974).

it possible for Cyril to doctor his quotations from Nestorius to suit his own interpretation of them. In his submission to Rome, he presented Nestorius as a pure adoptianist, which is wrong but understandable if his statements are taken out of context and read in a certain way.

The Romans, who found the whole question somewhat perplexing, took their time in replying and were careful to consult people whom they thought could decipher what the opposing parties in the East were saying. Leo, who was then the archdeacon of Rome but who would later become the city's bishop (440–461) and play a leading role in the controversy, made a special appeal to John Cassian (360?–435?), an Easterner who had become abbot of the monastery of St. Victor in Marseille and who was supposed to be an expert on Greek theological thought.[43] Unfortunately, Cassian was anything but an impartial observer. He regarded Nestorius as an outright heretic and condemned him in language that sometimes went to the extreme of virtually denying the distinctiveness of the two natures of the incarnate Christ. In the end, he fell back on a traditional Western approach which agreed with the Alexandrian belief that the initiative in the incarnation belonged to the divine *logos*, and reassured both Leo and his bishop, Celestine I (422–432), that Cyril was the man to back. Thus it was that in a synod held in Rome in 430 to discuss the matter, Nestorius was condemned for supposedly denying that the Son of God was a single person. If by "person" Celestine meant *prosôpon* he was clearly wrong, but if he meant *hypostasis* he had a point. Unfortunately, at this time it was still not clear whether the Latin *persona* meant either *prosôpon* or *hypostasis* in the sense that these words were used by Cyril and Nestorius, so the meaning of the Roman opinion was open to interpretation. As subsequent events were to make clear, Cyril was up to the challenge in a way that Nestorius and his followers were not.

To resolve the dispute, the emperor Theodosius II (408–450), who himself supported Nestorius, summoned a council to meet at Ephesus in 431. That council was dominated by Cyril, who attended in person, and the representatives of Rome who supported him, with the result that Nestorius was deposed and forced to leave Constantinople. Two letters from Cyril to Nestorius (the second and the third) were read out, and the former of these (the second) was acclaimed by the council as entirely consonant with the decisions taken at Nicea in 325. The third letter was also read, but no decision about it was taken, perhaps because it contained twelve anathemas against the teaching of Nestorius that the council did not feel able to endorse quite as wholeheartedly. A reply by Nestorius to the second

[43] Cassian's monastery is not to be confused with the one of the same name that appeared in Paris in the twelfth century.

letter was also read out, but it was rejected as heretical. The Council of Ephesus did not finally resolve the Christological disputes, but certain things became apparent as a result of it. The deposition of Nestorius, in spite of the emperor's support for him, was a real triumph for Cyril and proof that the church would not be dominated by the state. The condemnation of 431 was never to be reversed, in spite of the ongoing backing for Nestorius in Antioch and his own attempts to have his name cleared. Instead, a new solution eventually emerged that neither the Nestorians nor the Alexandrians would accept, though the rest of the church would come to regard it as having achieved the right balance between the two opposing and mutually incompatible positions that had fought it out at Ephesus.

The Chalcedonian Definition

The alliance between Alexandria and Rome that ensured the defeat of Nestorius at Ephesus in 431 was not the final word on the subject of Christology. There were still many issues that had to be resolved, particularly on the Alexandrian side. As we have already seen, Cyril's second letter to Nestorius was read and approved, but his third letter, though it was read, was greeted with greater reserve. The main reason for this was that in it Cyril delivered not only the response of Celestine of Rome to Nestorius's proposals, but also twelve additional anathemas which he had composed and expected Nestorius to sign. Needless to say, these anathemas were framed in such a way as to maximize the Alexandrian understanding of Christology and were intended to be an act of surrender on Nestorius's part. They read as follows:

1. If anyone does not confess that Emmanuel is true God, and thus does not accept that the holy Virgin is *Theotokos* (because she brought forth, after the flesh, the divine *logos* made flesh), let him be anathema.
2. If anyone does not confess that the *logos* of God the Father has been hypostatically united to flesh, and is one Christ with his own flesh, both God and man alike, let him be anathema.
3. If anyone divides the divine and human *hypostases* after their union, reducing their connection to one of dignity, authority, or rule, and not a unity of natures, let him be anathema.
4. If anyone attributes what is said of Christ in the Gospels and Epistles to two *hypostases*, one of them a man distinct from the *logos* and another the *logos* alone, let him be anathema.
5. If anyone says that Christ was a "God-bearing man" and denies that he is God in truth, one Son by nature who, as the *logos*, became flesh and shared in our flesh and blood, let him be anathema.

6. If anyone says that the *logos* of the Father is the Master of Christ, rather than both God and man, the *logos* having become flesh according to the Scriptures, let him be anathema.
7. If anyone says that Jesus was a man moved by God the *logos* and invested with the glory of the only begotten, who was someone else, let him be anathema.
8. If anyone says that the man assumed [by the *logos*] ought to be worshiped and glorified as God along with God the *logos*, as if the one was present in the other (as "along with" inevitably suggests), and does not worship the one Emmanuel and offer him the glory of the one *logos* made flesh, let him be anathema.
9. If anyone says that the Lord Jesus Christ was glorified by the [Holy] Spirit, as if the power he exercised belonged to the Spirit and not to him, let him be anathema.
10. If anyone says that it was not the divine *logos* who became our high priest and apostle when he became flesh and man, but someone else, a man born of a woman, and if anyone then says that he offered the sacrifice for himself as well as for us (for he who knew no sin had no need to sacrifice on his own behalf), let him be anathema.[44]
11. If anyone does not confess that the Lord's flesh is life-giving and the flesh of the *logos* of God the Father, but says that it is the flesh of someone else that is only associated with the *logos* and not life-giving in itself, let him be anathema.
12. If anyone does not confess that the *logos* of God suffered, was crucified, tasted death, and became the "firstborn from the dead" in the flesh, let him be anathema.[45]

That Cyril was anti-adoptianist is obvious. Nestorius agreed with him wholeheartedly on that, but the fact that adoptianism is clearly the target of several of the anathemas shows that Cyril was not convinced of this. Most of the twelve condemnations are aimed at the notion of "conjunction," which was central to Nestorius's thinking but alien to the Alexandrians because it struck them as adoptianist, however much Nestorius and his followers might deny it. In fact, Nestorius agreed with Cyril more than Cyril thought, but the two men lacked a common language of discourse in which that fundamental agreement could be expressed with integrity by both of them. In this sense, the anathemas were lopsided, and those who were uncomfortable with that were forced to try to moderate them as best they could.

[44] In support of this statement, Cyril quotes Eph. 5:2 and Col. 1:18.

[45] Cyril of Alexandria, *Epistula* 17 (abbreviated).

One of those men was Theodoret of Cyrus (d. 466?), who rejected the terminology of Cyril but wanted to meet him at least halfway.[46] From a position where he regarded *physis* (nature) and *hypostasis* as virtually synonymous, making it impossible for him to accept that there could have been a union of "natures" in Christ, Theodoret gradually moved toward the view that *hypostasis* was more or less the same as *prosôpon*, a shift that brought him closer to Cyril. He never got to the point of identifying the *prosôpon* of Christ with the divine *logos* completely, but his willingness to equate *prosôpon* with *hypostasis* made it possible for those who sympathized with Nestorius to embrace a compromise formula and restore the unity of the church.

Reconciliation along these lines was much quicker in coming than anyone could have foreseen in the immediate aftermath of the Council of Ephesus. It was brought about by Bishop John of Antioch, who sent Paul of Emesa as his emissary to Alexandria, bearing a creedal statement which said that the Son was "*homoousios* with the Father according to his divinity and *homoousios* with us in his humanity." On that basis the Antiochenes were prepared to confess that Mary was *Theotokos* and to agree that although some of Christ's sayings were more obviously "divine" or "human" than others, the person who uttered them was one and the same.

Cyril responded positively to this overture and recognized that it formed the basis for a genuine agreement. He particularly liked the "perfect God and perfect man" approach but took the liberty of adjusting it in a small but significant way. His formula was, 'the same, perfect in divinity and perfect in humanity."[47] Cyril's concern was not with the perfection of the natures but with the unity of the subject in the incarnate Christ. He did not want to diminish the Son's humanity by seeing it as something that was merely added onto the divine *logos*, but he did want to make sure that the formula "perfect God and perfect man" would not be construed in a way that would allow for the revival of the notion of "conjunction." That was understood and accepted in Antioch, and by 433 peace had been restored.

Another significant player in the negotiations was Nestorius himself. What happened to him after his deposition is unclear, but by 436 (at the latest) he was in exile. He survived until at least 449 and probably a few years longer, because his most important extant work, the *Book of Heraclides*, engages

[46] See Paul B. Clayton, Jr., *The Christology of Theodoret of Cyrus: Antiochene Christology from the Council of Ephesus (431) to the Council of Chalcedon (451)* (Oxford: Oxford University Press, 2007).

[47] Cyril of Alexandria, *Epistula ad Ioannem Antiochenum de pace*. The letter is also known by the opening word of the Latin version, *Laetentur.*

with arguments that were first put forward at that time.[48] Nestorius sought to align himself with orthodox Christology as this was understood in Rome and Constantinople, if not in Alexandria, but he continued to make a distinction between the *logos* (divine) and Christ (divine-human) that the rest of the Christian world found inadequate, if not actually heretical. He was even prepared to accept Cyril of Alexandria's insistence that the union of natures in Christ occurred "according to *hypostasis*" (*kath'hypostasin*), but only if *hypostasis* was interpreted to mean *prosôpon*. In the end, what happened was the reverse—*prosôpon* was defined as equivalent to *hypostasis*. The difference is that Nestorius wanted the "agent" element in Christ's personhood to be reduced to a mere appearance (of the conjunction of two natures), whereas his opponents wanted *prosôpon* to mean "person" as we understand the term—an agent capable of doing things and taking responsibility for them. "Two natures in one person" (Nestorius) was therefore not the same as "one person in two natures."

It is important to bear in mind that Nestorius did not believe that the "personal" union of the two natures in Christ was a mere fiction. On the contrary, he taught that the *prosôpon* of the *logos* became the *prosôpon* of the human nature of Christ and that it could operate either in one or in both natures as it wished. In many ways Nestorius was just as orthodox as any of his contemporaries (and opponents) were, but his failure, inability, or unwillingness to see the *logos* as the agent of the incarnation and the one true *prosôpon* dogged him to the bitter end. With the advantage of hindsight we can see that he did not deserve the condemnation that he received, but neither was his Christological model adequate for the future. His pleas for recognition went unheeded, but his closeness to the position that was worked out at the Council of Chalcedon was such that many of his followers were able to subscribe to that council without difficulty, and so remain in communion with the mainline church.

The approach that was to prevail, at least in Constantinople and the West, began to emerge as the Nestorian crisis was reaching its climax. Its first representative was Proclus, who was bishop of the capital from 434 to 446. He had already made a name for himself because of a sermon he had preached in the presence of Nestorius in which he acknowledged that Mary was *Theotokos* and described her as "the workshop of the union of the natures" who gave birth to one who was neither pure God nor a mere man, but the divine *logos* incarnate.[49] In looking for a word to describe the *logos*, Proclus moved increasingly toward

[48] It is possible that the *Book of Heraclides* was edited after Nestorius's death, with additional material reflecting this later stage, but that is uncertain. See Grillmeier, *Christ in Christian Tradition*, 1:501–502.
[49] For the details, see ibid., 1:520–523.

hypostasis, thereby detaching it from its earlier connection to *ousia* and *physis*, which had caused so much confusion, and making it more closely approximate to *prosôpon*. This naturally pleased the supporters of Nestorius, even though for Proclus the *prosôpon* of Christ was not the result of the incarnation but its cause. As he put it in his response to an enquiry from some Armenians who wanted to know where Theodore of Mopsuestia fitted into all this: "Knowing only one Son . . . I recognize only one *hypostasis* of God the *logos* made flesh."[50] What Proclus did was to take Cyril of Alexandria's formula of the "one *hypostasis* of God the *logos* made flesh" and change the predicate "made flesh" so that it referred not to the *hypostasis* but to the *logos*.[51] Proclus also distanced himself from Theodore of Mopsuestia on the matter of the "conjunction" of the two natures, making it clear that his modification of Cyril was not a surrender to Nestorianism. He arrived at this solution in 435, and three years later he sent it to Antioch for approval, which it received.[52]

The stage was now set for the final act in the drama, which would be played out in Constantinople itself. As long as Cyril and Proclus were alive there was no trouble, but Cyril died in 444 and Proclus followed him to the grave two years later. Cyril was succeeded by Dioscorus, who was considerably less subtle and irenic than his predecessor, and Proclus by Flavian, who was a less gifted theologian. It is tempting to suggest that second-rate men were now in charge, which made it less likely that future disagreements would be resolved as quickly or as amicably as had happened after 431.

Trouble soon came in the person of Eutyches, an Alexandrian archimandrite[53] who went to Constantinople and there delivered a series of lectures on Christology in which he advanced the *mia physis* doctrine of Cyril, but without the qualifications to which Cyril had agreed after the Council of Ephesus. This naturally raised eyebrows in the capital, and when the local synod of bishops next met, one of its number, Eusebius of Dorylaeum, accused Eutyches of heresy. There followed a trial, in the course of which Cyril's second letter to Nestorius and the formula of reunion adopted in 433 were both read out and declared to be the foundation of the orthodox position. Eutyches was duly censured, and the proceedings were closed by Flavian, who announced that

[50] Proclus, *Tomus ad Armenios*. The text can be found in PG 65, col. 864d.

[51] Cyril had apparently used both forms indifferently, but for Proclus it was important to stress that it was the *logos* who became flesh and not the divine *hypostasis*. In other words, the incarnate Christ was a single *hypostasis* (divine) with two natures, one divine and the other human.

[52] The Antiochene leadership accepted Proclus's *Tomus* but disliked the fact that he was trying to use his position as bishop of Constantinople to impose it on them. In this case, however, theology triumphed over politics.

[53] Literally "leader of the flock," an ecclesiastical title that has no exact equivalent in the Western churches. An archimandrite is lower in the hierarchy than a bishop but higher than the ordinary clergy, and may be compared to an archdeacon in the West.

"we recognize that Christ is from two natures after the incarnation, in one *hypostasis* and one *prosôpon* confessing one Christ, one Son, one Lord."[54] This was, or at least was intended to be, the Christology of Proclus, halfway between Cyril and Nestorius and combining the best elements of each in a higher synthesis. It was this formula that Flavian would use to try to bring the two sides together and end the controversy caused by Eutyches's reversion to an earlier state of affairs.

Matters might have ended there but for a certain ambiguity in Flavian's formula "from two natures" and the determination of Eutyches, backed by his bishop Dioscorus, to make their interpretation of it prevail. What Flavian wanted to say was that the incarnate Son of God had two natures that were inextricably conjoined in one *hypostasis* and one *prosôpon*. But by using the phrase "from two natures" instead of "in two natures" he left the door open for different interpretations of how they were combined in the incarnate Christ. Eutyches was prepared to accept this formula, but only on condition that it was understood to mean that after the incarnation the two natures of God and man became one. At the other extreme, there were many in Constantinople who confessed the two natures in one *prosôpon*, as Nestorius did, but who balked at saying there was only one *hypostasis* in the incarnate Christ. This was because, to them, a *hypostasis* could only be the concrete manifestation of an underlying nature, and if there was only one *hypostasis* in Christ, it must be the divine one, in which case his humanity would have no integrity of its own.

In the midst of this uncertainty, a second council was held at Ephesus in 449, at which Dioscorus rammed through the "one *hypostasis*" formula couched in the language of Cyril's anathemas, thereby ruling out any form of compromise with Nestorius and his supporters. In preparation for this council, Eutyches had appealed to the major centers of the Christian world, and especially to Rome, which he hoped to win over. The emperor Theodosius II was also persuaded to back him, even to the point of allowing Dioscorus to preside over the council and excluding Theodoret of Cyrus, Eutyches's most dangerous opponent, from it. Flavian and his supporters were discredited by Dioscorus's manipulative tactics, and when the Roman delegation turned up, it was also declared suspect because it had accepted Flavian's hospitality on the way to Ephesus. In this atmosphere, the result was a foregone conclusion. Eutyches was completely vindicated by the council, and his many enemies, including Flavian and Theodoret, were formally deposed. At one point Dioscorus even threatened military intervention if he did not get his own way. So bad did it

[54] Quoted in Grillmeier, *Christ in Christian Tradition*, 1:524.

get that when Leo of Rome heard about it, he wrote to the Empress Pulcheria telling her that the council was not a court of justice (*iudicium*) but a den of thieves (*latrocinium*), and the name "Robber Synod" has stuck to it ever since.[55]

Flavian had also been actively seeking support, of course, and after some initial hesitation due to ignorance of the true situation, Leo of Rome rallied behind him. Not only did Leo offer Flavian political support, he also sent back a long treatise outlining what he believed to be the true doctrine of Christ. Leo's *Tomus ad Flavianum*, usually known simply as the *Tome*, struck the right note at the right time. Drawing on resources of Western theology that were largely unknown in the East, Leo was able to tighten up some of Flavian's loose and inadequate language, while at the same time recasting the framework of the debate.

It was at this point that Western theology first made a serious impact on discussion in the East and played a decisive role in shaping the church's doctrine. Leo's theological inheritance went back to Tertullian, who dominated the Latin scene as much as Origen influenced Greek writers for centuries after his time. The main difference was that whereas the ambiguities of Origen's thought led to divergent developments and generations of wrangling, because terms like *hypostasis* had many (and sometimes contradictory) meanings, the Latin world was much more united behind Tertullian's Trinitarian formula of three persons in one substance. That has stood the test of time and remained current to the present day, even if its precise meaning has evolved in the centuries since.

The impact of the debates in the East was felt at Rome and elsewhere, but the Westerners were for the most part outsiders and spectators, even at the great councils of Nicea in 325 and Constantinople in 381. Hilary of Poitiers got involved with the arguments over Homoean Arianism in the late 350s, and his subsequent exile in Cappadocia allowed him to make firsthand acquaintance with the Eastern theological world, but the East impacted him much more than he influenced it. Another Westerner, Hilary's older contemporary Marius Victorinus, spent a good deal of time developing and clarifying the Latin theological vocabulary in order to make it conform more closely to the subtleties of the Greek, but of course this was not noticed in the East and had only a limited appeal in the West, where "three subsistences (*hypostases*) in the one essence (*ousia*)" was unlikely to supersede "three persons in the one substance" and in fact never did so.

What united the West was a determination to combat anything that

[55] Leo of Rome, *Epistula 95 ad Pulcheriam Augustam*, dated July 20, 451.

smacked of Arianism. The sorts of compromise that we find in the East after the First Council of Nicea never took hold in the Latin world, despite many attempts to propagate them there. As for Apollinarianism, it was (if anything) even more alien to Western thinking than Arianism was. Hilary of Poitiers was very clear about this. As he said,

> The Son of Man is no one other than the Son of God, nor is the one who was in the form of God any different from the one who was born in the form of a servant as a perfect man.[56]

This quotation shows us that Hilary's starting point was Philippians 2:5–11, where the apostle Paul described the incarnation in terms of a "self-emptying" (*kenôsis*) of the one who was in the form of God. Hilary did not understand this as an abandonment of divinity on the part of the Son. Rather, when he came to earth, the Son concealed or "laid aside" aspects of his divine nature so as not to appear to be superhuman, but he always retained the capacity to act like God and did so in his miracles, for example.

The permanence of the divine nature in the incarnate Son becomes even clearer when we consider what Hilary had to say about the humanity of Christ. He never doubted its completeness, but found it hard to accept that Jesus experienced suffering in the same way that we do. For Hilary, the presence of the divine in the human was a protection for the latter, making it immune to pain and gradually transforming it into the likeness of God that was fully realized in Jesus' ascension and heavenly glory. As he said,

> How can we compare the flesh conceived by the Holy Spirit to an ordinary human body? That flesh is bread from heaven, that humanity is from God. He had a body to suffer and indeed he suffered, but he did not have a nature that could feel pain. His body possessed a unique nature of its own. It was transfigured into heavenly glory on the mountain, it put diseases to flight by its touch, it restored eyesight by its spittle . . .[57]

What we see here is a curious attempt to have it both ways—suffering, yes, but without pain! Hilary never suggested that the earthly events of the life of Jesus were fictitious, but although the Son of God passed through death he did not feel it in the way that we do. Everything he said or did reveals the mixing of the divine with the human, though without losing the distinction between them:

---

[56] Hilary of Poitiers, *De Trinitate* 10.19.
[57] Ibid., 10.23.

> Taking on himself the weakness of our flesh, and remaining both divine and human, he performs, prays, professes, looks for all those things that are ours in such a way that what is naturally his is mingled with them. At one moment he speaks as a man because he was born as a man, and suffered and died as a man. At another moment, he speaks completely as God the Word . . .[58]

The two natures are preserved in their individual integrity, but at the same time, it is clear that the humanity is gradually being taken up into God. That perception would later be modified, but Hilary provides us with an excellent example of how the Western tradition could evolve without altering its basic principles. However inadequate his understanding of Christ's humanity may have been, he clung firmly to the belief that, in the incarnation, two natures were united by the divine subject of the *logos* without compromising their own integrity. His "historical" approach, starting with the preexistence of the Son in heaven, proceeding from there to the "self-emptying" of the incarnation, and then continuing with the progressive glorification of the divinely assumed humanity, chimed in well with the Gospel narratives and made it impossible to think of the person of Christ as the result, rather than as the cause, of the union of God and man. The details still had to be tweaked, but the structure was solid, with the result that Hilary remains a revered doctor of the Western church and has not been rejected in the way that Nestorius would later be.

One of the most acute Western observers of the Eastern scene in the late fourth century was Jerome (340?–420), who wrote that he was deeply attracted to both Apollinarius and Didymus the Blind, both of whom he had met, but whose views he saw as being mutually contradictory.[59] He himself sought a middle way between their extremes, which he explained as follows:

> [Jesus] was crucified as man and glorified as God. . . . We do not believe that God is one [subject] and man another, or that there are two persons in the Son of God, as the new heresy falsely does. Instead, [we hold that] the Son of God and the Son of Man are one and the same, and whatever he says applies both to his divine glory and to our salvation.[60]

Jerome was almost on the point of saying that Christ is one divine person in two natures, but was held back from this because "person" had not yet been defined with sufficient clarity to make such a statement unambiguous. On the other hand, he showed none of the hesitation of Hilary in giving full rein to

[58] Hilary of Poitiers, *Tractatus in Psalmos* 54.
[59] Jerome, *Epistula* 84.3.
[60] Ibid., 120.9.

the human passions of Christ. As far as Jerome was concerned, if the Son of God had a human body he must have had human feelings, and if he had human feelings, then he was capable of suffering in the same way that we are. The difference between Jesus and us was not this, but rather that in suffering for us he did not sin, which is a different thing altogether.[61] It is (at least theoretically) possible to be human without sinning, as Adam and Eve were at the beginning, but not to lack bodily feeling.

In the event, it was Augustine who would make the final breakthrough to what we now recognize as orthodox Christology. Like Hilary, Jerome, and Marius Victorinus before him, he had no difficulty in confessing the two natures of Christ, which he saw as mutually complementary in a way that may sound vaguely Nestorian:

> The whole of humanity, including a rational soul and body, was taken by the Word (*logos*), so that the one Christ, the one God, the Son of God, was not just the Word, but the Word and man. He is the Son of God the Father because he is the Word, and the Son of Man because he is a man. . . . At the same time as being a man, he is also the Son of God thanks to the Word by whom the man was taken. Likewise, at the same time as being the Word, he is the Son of Man, thanks to the man who had been taken up by the Word.[62]

What was missing in Augustine's definition was an adequate term for describing the unity of subject in Christ. The knowledge that this gap would later be filled by the word "person" naturally makes us ask what Augustine understood by that term. In his discussion of the difference between person and nature in the Trinity, he defined "person" as "something singular and individual" as opposed to "nature," which was something held in common.[63] It was the singularity of the Son of God that became a man in Jesus Christ, and Augustine eventually recognized this in what would become the basis of the standard Latin Christological formula: *Persona una ex duabus substantiis constans; una in utraque natura persona*, which may be translated, "One person made up of two substances; one person in each nature."[64]

Yet even Augustine never quite reached the balance that he was looking for and found so hard to express. For him, the union of body and soul in a human being was more problematic than the union of the *logos* and the human soul in Christ, because, like a good Platonist, he believed that the *logos* and the human

[61] Jerome, *Tractatus sive homiliae in Psalmos* 108.
[62] Augustine of Hippo, *Sermones* 214.6.
[63] Augustine of Hippo, *De Trinitate* 7.6.11.
[64] Augustine of Hippo, *Tractatus in Iohannis Evangelium* 99.1.

soul were made of the same spiritual substance and so could mix and mingle without any inner contradiction. He resolved the problem of the body, which was made of a different substance, by saying that the human soul was the mediator between the *logos* and the flesh, the conduit by which the divine passed into the human. This suggestion gave a tremendous boost to the development of human psychology, a discipline of which Augustine is sometimes regarded as the founder, but it was still not enough to provide an adequate description of how the two natures of the incarnate Christ were united.

This was the tradition that Leo of Rome inherited and on which he drew in framing an answer to Flavian which he hoped might reverse the baneful effects of the "Robber Synod" of Ephesus. Leo was careful to cultivate other contacts in Constantinople because he knew that Flavian was not a free agent. His greatest success was with Pulcheria, the emperor's sister, who accepted his arguments and wanted to see his solution put into effect. The main obstacle, however, was the emperor himself. Theodosius II was a firm supporter of Dioscorus and upheld the decisions of the "Robber Synod" in spite of the pressure exerted on him by Leo. He deposed Flavian and replaced him with Anatolius, an Alexandrian whom we may assume would do the bidding of Dioscorus. Refusing to give up, Leo dispatched a high-powered delegation to Constantinople which he hoped might persuade the emperor to change his mind. As things turned out, that was unnecessary, because before Leo's emissaries arrived in the capital, Theodosius II had fallen from his horse and been killed. He was succeeded by Pulcheria and the man she soon chose as her husband, the Latin-speaking Marcian (450–457).

Overnight, the political situation changed and the supporters of Eutyches found themselves suddenly out of favor. Flavian was not restored to his see, because Anatolius, who had been a creature of Dioscorus, adjusted to the new dispensation and demonstrated a willingness to compromise, though of course he still remained an Alexandrian at heart. Whether he asked Pulcheria and Marcian to summon another church council is uncertain, but that is what happened. It met at Chalcedon in October 451.[65] The Council of Chalcedon sought to resolve the apparently interminable Christological debates by adopting an approach that was essentially Alexandrian in conception but that was clothed in the language and terminology of Antioch. It achieved this by adapting the doctrine of the Roman church as expounded by Leo, who approached the question from an independent angle.

[65] Chalcedon is the modern Kadıköy, just across the Bosphorus from Constantinople and within sight of the imperial palace. On the council, see R. V. Sellers, *The Council of Chalcedon: A Historical and Doctrinal Survey* (London: SPCK, 1961).

Leo's exposition of the problem was deceptively and disarmingly simple. He started from the creedal statement that, "We believe in God the Father Almighty and in Jesus Christ his only begotten Son, our Lord, who was born of the Holy Spirit and the Virgin Mary."[66] The two natures derive from this dual origin and coexist in tension with one another in the incarnate Christ. The principle of their union does not lie in some kind of conjunction, nor is it to be ascribed to an assumption of the flesh by God. Instead, it is located in the person of the Son. The idea that there were two natures before the incarnation but only one afterwards must be rejected, because the natures are just as real and internally coherent in the incarnate Christ as they were (or in the case of the humanity would have been) independently of him.

Leo insisted that, in Christ, each nature does what is proper to itself, but in communion with the other, a communion assured by the person who united them.[67] It was here that the gap between his thought and that of the Alexandrians was at its widest. By maintaining that the one divine person acts in each of his natures according to the properties inherent in that nature, Leo effectively undercut the Alexandrian idea that the *logos* was a single subject whose acts engage both natures simultaneously. In contrast to this, Leo could state that, on the cross, the divine person of the Son of God suffered and died in his human flesh but without this affecting the impassibility of his divine nature, whereas the Alexandrians could not envisage such a distinction. For them, the death of Christ was the death of the God-man, insofar as such a thing was conceivable. Here, Leo had clarified a distinction that the Alexandrians were unable to make and that would contribute to the further alienation of Alexandria after the council was over.

Leo can fairly be accused of misrepresenting both Nestorius and Eutyches in his criticism of their positions, but this was due more to ignorance and misunderstanding than to any unwillingness to come to terms with them. Later on, theologians in the East who supported Leo's basic position would feel obliged to clarify it in order to avoid such misunderstandings, and in that process his doctrine would be refined further. But on the main point, Leo's insistence that the person of Christ was the deciding factor that kept the two natures in their proper place was too attractive an idea for the majority of the bishops at the council to ignore it. In essence, it was Leo's Christology that won the day, and his *Tome* became (and to a large extent has remained) the definitive interpretation of what Chalcedon intended to say.

[66] Leo's version of what was later to be known as the Apostles' Creed did not yet have the more precise form of words "who was conceived by the Holy Spirit and born of the Virgin Mary."
[67] Leo of Rome, *Tomus ad Flavianum* 94.

What the council decided can be summed up as follows. First, it said that Jesus Christ is the eternal Son of God who already possessed a divine nature by virtue of that fact. In the incarnation, that divine Son acquired a second, human nature in the womb of Mary, who bore him as God (and so could legitimately be called the *Theotokos*) but who was not the source of his divinity. In themselves, the two natures were incompatible and remained separate. As the Chalcedonian Definition famously expressed it, they were united:

asynchytôs	without confusion
atreptôs	without change
adihairetôs	without separation
achôristôs	without division

The first two of these adverbs may be interpreted as "anti-Eutychian" because they denied that the two natures had merged into one. The last two may be regarded as "anti-Nestorian" because they denied that the two natures could be split apart once they had been united in the incarnation. As for the disputed phrase "from two natures," the council initially hesitated but finally agreed to replace it with "in two natures," rejecting the idea that divinity and humanity had somehow merged into one.

The Chalcedonian Definition appeared to be evenhanded in its rejection of both Eutyches and Nestorius, but on the key issue of the unity of Christ, it came down on the side of the Alexandrians. This is because the council accepted that the principle of unity was to be found in the eternal Son of God who was the agent of the incarnation, which is what the Alexandrians had said all along. The Nestorian view, which was that the unity of Christ was the result of the conjunction of the two independent natures, was weak on this point and so it was rejected. Unfortunately, this rejection was not apparent to the Alexandrians, because the definition used the Nestorian term *prosôpon* (and not *logos*) to describe the principle of unity in Christ. The difference between it and the Nestorian position was that it defined *prosôpon* not as the conjunction (*synapheia*) of two natures but as "person" in the Roman way. This made the word equivalent to *hypostasis*, which for generations had been used in the East to distinguish the Father, Son, and Holy Spirit from each other. In this way the fathers of Chalcedon hoped to unite the Christian world behind a single confession of faith.

The long-term theological significance of the Chalcedonian Definition was that it shifted the terms of discussion from a nature-based understanding of the incarnate Christ to one that started with the intentions of the divine person.[68] All talk of a conjunction of natures or of a transfer of properties from one nature to the other was transformed by a new paradigm, one in which the divine person of the *logos*, the Son of God, took on a second (human) nature in the womb of the Virgin Mary, becoming its defining identity (*hypostasis*) and acting in and through it in exactly the same way as he already acted in and through his divinity. The person of the Son did not suppress or modify the human soul in any way but embraced it, together with its pain and suffering, and as a man died on the cross for our salvation. In other words, the divine person of the Son of God suffered and died in his human nature, a formula that the fathers of Chalcedon believed was the best way to express the reality of the gospel story and that still commands the assent of most of the church. In the words of Aloys Grillmeier,

> The dogma of Chalcedon must always be taken against the background of scripture and the whole patristic tradition. It is not to no purpose that the Definition itself points to the prophets and the sayings of Christ himself . . . and finally to the creed of the Fathers, i.e. to Nicaea, indeed beyond Nicaea to the two succeeding councils and to the letters of Cyril, received with such solemnity, and the Tome of Leo. Few councils have been so rooted in tradition as the Council of Chalcedon. The dogma of Chalcedon is ancient tradition in a formula corresponding to the needs of the hour. So we cannot say that the Chalcedonian Definition marks a great turning point in the christological belief of the early church.[69]

The Chalcedonian Definition of the incarnation was generally well received in the European provinces of the Roman empire. The prestige of Leo of Rome was such that it was virtually unquestioned in the West, particularly as it was also backed by the imperial authorities in Constantinople. This combination was especially important in the late fifth century because the Roman empire in the West was collapsing. In 476 the last Western emperor was deposed and the imperial regalia were sent to Constantinople in formal recognition that there would henceforth be only one emperor for the entire Roman world. In practice, the Eastern emperor would have to reconquer the lost provinces, a goal which was to be partially achieved in the reign of Justinian I (527–565). The Germanic tribes that replaced the Roman governors in the West were either Homoean Arians (Italy, Spain, and North Africa) or pagans (Gaul and Britain), a circumstance that served to unite the interests of both the church and the

[68] See Stephen W. Need, *Human Language and Knowledge in the Light of Chalcedon* (New York: Peter Lang, 1996).
[69] Grillmeier, *Christ in Christian Tradition*, 1:550.

empire. The church wanted the support of the emperor against heretics and enemies of the gospel, while the empire needed the church if it was ever to win back the lands it had lost.

Loyalty to the Chalcedonian Definition quickly came to be associated with these twin aims, and its authority was never seriously challenged in the West. To this day, Chalcedon remains foundational for the Christology of the Western churches, both Roman Catholic and Protestant, and its conclusions have generally been regarded as the successful culmination of centuries of debate.[70] Its decisions were acknowledged and disseminated toward the end of the fifth century by an unknown monk in southern Gaul, who composed a creedal statement now known as the "Athanasian Creed," or (more correctly) by its Latin title, *Quicunque vult*.[71] It was a compendium of Nicene Trinitarianism and Chalcedonian Christology that came to be regarded as one of the three great creeds of the Western church and was the chief vehicle by which the doctrinal decisions of the ancient councils were communicated to ordinary worshipers for the next millennium and beyond. Only in the eighteenth century, when its association with Athanasius was exposed as fictitious and its insistence on strict orthodoxy of belief was questioned by theologians affected by the Enlightenment, did the *Quicunque vult* fade from view, but by then its work was done. For both Catholics and Protestants, the Chalcedonian Definition had become an inseparable part of historic Christian teaching and the entire history of the early church was read in light of it.

In the East it was a different story. The church of Constantinople accepted the council without great difficulty, as did the church of Jerusalem, but only a minority in Alexandria and Antioch could be persuaded to agree to it. The Nestorians, who were based in Antioch and northern Syria, were forced out of the Roman empire in 484 and went to Persia, where they were welcomed and given semiofficial status. From there they spread across central Asia and were very influential for many centuries, but they were eventually persecuted out of existence by the local Turkic tribes after they converted to Islam. Today there are only a handful of them left in their historic homeland of Iraq, where they have suffered persecution in recent times, and the head of the church has emigrated to the United States. In general terms it can be said that over the centuries the theologians of this church have done little more than defend their interpretation of Nestorius. This has helped to preserve some of his writings

[70] On the reception of Chalcedon, see Aloys Grillmeier, *Christ in Christian Tradition, Volume 2, Part 1: From Chalcedon to Justinian I* (London: Mowbray, 1987).

[71] See J. N. D. Kelly, *The Athanasian Creed* (London: A. & C. Black, 1964); Gerald L. Bray, "*Whosoever Will Be Saved*: the Athanasian Creed and the Modern Church," in T. George, ed., *Evangelicals and Nicene Faith: Reclaiming the Apostolic Witness* (Grand Rapids, MI: Baker, 2011), 45–57.

(like the *Book of Heraclides*), which would otherwise have been lost, but neither in ancient times nor since has there been much dialogue with the rest of the Christian world, and as a result, Nestorian theology has remained isolated and undeveloped.[72]

The Alexandrian tradition has fared much better.[73] Dioscorus repudiated Eutyches as an extremist, but he refused to endorse Chalcedon because it did not uphold the "one nature after the incarnation" formula, which he attributed to Cyril of Alexandria and regarded as sacrosanct for that reason. Within a hundred years or so the defenders of this kind of monophysitism (or "miaphysitism," as it is sometimes called nowadays) had spread their interpretation of Christianity to Ethiopia and South India, and they also moved into Syria after the departure of the Nestorians. Eventually they even won over the Kingdom of Armenia, though the Armenian church was careful to safeguard its independence by adopting a modified form of monophysitism. In later centuries the monophysites were frequently persecuted, and they have now been reduced to a minority in Egypt and Syria, but they are still the national church of Ethiopia and Armenia, and a force to be reckoned with in the Middle East and South India. In recent years the fact that the Chalcedonian Definition of faith is similar to their views in substance, though it employs different language, has drawn them closer to the mainstream of the Christian world, where they are no longer regarded as heretics in the way they once were and (like the Nestorians) have been admitted to such bodies as the World Council of Churches.[74]

The legacy of Chalcedon is therefore a mixed one. A source of unity in the West, it has divided the East with consequences that are still with us. From the standpoint of the history of theology, post-Chalcedonian Christological developments are important mainly because they helped to clarify the terminology adopted by the council, and in so doing they have deepened our understanding of what is implied by a confession of two natures in the incarnate Christ.

The Definition of Humanity

The connection between Christology and the doctrine of the Trinity is obvious, but the struggles of the fourth and fifth centuries were also important because

[72] The Nestorian church is now so small that it cannot produce theologians capable of defending its historic position.

[73] See William H. C. Frend, *The Rise of the Monophysite Movement* (Cambridge: Cambridge University Press, 1972), for a general history. Also Stephen J. Davis, *Coptic Christology in Practice: Incarnation and Divine Participation in Late Antique and Medieval Egypt* (Oxford: Oxford University Press, 2008). The theological issues are fully covered in Aloys Grillmeier and Theresia Hainthaler, *Christ in Christian Tradition, Volume 2: From the Council of Chalcedon (451) to Gregory the Great (590–604), Part 4: The Church of Alexandria With Nubia and Ethiopia* (London: Mowbray, 1996).

[74] For a discussion of the issues in a modern context, see Paulos Gregorios, William H. Lazareth, Nikos A. Nissiotis, eds., *Does Chalcedon Divide or Unite? Towards Convergence in Orthodox Christology* (Geneva: World Council of Churches, 1981).

of the way in which they shaped what we mean by humanity. In general terms, of course, everyone knew what human beings were, even though many ancient peoples believed that they were superior to other nations, whom they tended to refer to as "barbarians" or "Gentiles." These labels were not necessarily pejorative but they were not complimentary either, and they made it clear that those who were so designated were excluded from the chosen group. But however low a man's opinion might be of someone who was not like himself, there was never any question that he might confuse other people with animals, let alone with inanimate things. This occurred only at the other end of the scale. There were occasional sightings of angels in human form, and among pagans heroes might be deified after their deaths, but these were exceptional cases and no one really expected to come across them in the normal course of life.

But although human beings were easily recognized, there was little attempt to define what it means to be human. In the Old Testament, different parts of the body are associated with nonmaterial things like the mind or the emotions, something that we still do to some extent. For example, when we say that someone has spoken from the heart we do not mean that his vocal chords have moved to a different part of his body but that he has spoken with feeling and sincerity.

This metaphorical approach does not matter very much as long as there is no need to be too analytical in our thinking. No one would suggest that a heart transplant should be avoided because it would alter a person's emotions, even if the possibility of potentially unpleasant side-effects always has to be considered. The ancients knew nothing about such things, of course, and if they dealt with personality disorders at all, it was in some other way, such as ascribing them to demon possession. But even then they discriminated between conditions that could be cured by recognized means and ones that could not, and they were more sophisticated in their assessments than we often realize.

It was the incarnation of the Son of God that made it necessary for Christians to define what constituted a normal human being. Could Jesus have been a man possessed, either by God or by the Devil? There were those who thought like that; were they right?[75] If God could become a man, what would his humanity have to include in order to make that definition stick? Everyone in the early church agreed that Jesus was different from other people in some ways, but were those differences great enough to make him more than merely human? To look at the question from another angle, how much like Jesus is it possible for us to be? What is it that forces us not only to admit that we cannot save

[75] See Matt. 12:24; Mark 3:22; Luke 11:15.

ourselves but also to confess that Jesus was able to save us instead? Today we have become so used to hearing that the Son of God became a man that we forget how puzzling this was to the early Christians, who had never had to think about such a thing before.

Take the sinlessness of Christ, for example. This is an important theme of the New Testament epistles and became foundational for the Christian doctrine of salvation, but discussion of it played little part in the earthly life and ministry of Jesus. In the Gospels we find that sinlessness, to the extent that the concept was known at all, was an attribute that was claimed not by Jesus but by the Pharisees. It was their proud boast that they had kept the law, which in their eyes meant that they had not sinned. Even the apostle Paul, a Pharisee of the Pharisees, could speak in such terms after he became a Christian. Writing to the Galatians, he described himself and his fellow Jews in terms that set them apart from what he called "Gentile sinners." He may have meant this ironically, because the context tells us that he did not believe that Gentiles were sinners in a way that Jews were not, but if so, the irony made its point in a way that was possible only because that is how most Jews of the time actually thought.[76]

As far as the Pharisees were concerned, Jesus was a great "sinner" because he broke the law in ways that they found scandalous. Before Christians could talk about the sinlessness of Jesus, therefore, the nature of sin had to be redefined. That required a complete rethink about what the relationship between God and man was meant to be, how and why it had gone wrong, and what needed to happen for it to be put right. It also raised the question of whether the restoration of human relationships with God was (or could be) a universal phenomenon, or whether it was confined to a chosen few. The Jews were convinced that God cared about them in a way that he did not care about anyone else, and that salvation was confined to them. Perhaps the temple sacrifices could have made atonement for the sins of Gentiles as well as Jews, but they did not do so, because they were not intended for that purpose—their power was defined by the context in which they were made. Christians believed that Jesus had died for the sins of non-Jews as well as for those of Jews, but there is no sign that they thought that everyone would be saved. Why not? Can human beings reject the grace of God if they choose to do so? If they can, what does that say about the sovereignty of God? If they cannot, why are we told to preach the gospel to everyone when much of the seed we are sowing will fall on unsuitable ground and bear no fruit? What makes human beings tick the way they do, and can we do anything to change that? These are the questions that arise when we

---

[76] See Gal. 2:15.

consider how God can become a real man, dwell on earth as one of us, die for us on the cross, and raise us (or some of us) to eternal life with him.

The ancient Israelites knew that human beings were created in the image and likeness of God and that it was that fact which distinguishes us from other creatures, including the angels. They used words like "soul" (*nephesh*) and "flesh" (*basar*) to refer to humans on the principle that the part can be used to refer to the whole. God did not have either of these things, but he did possess a spirit (*ruach*), as do we. The spirit was therefore the link between God and man, as the apostle Paul reminds us when he says, "The Spirit of himself bears witness with our spirit that we are children of God."[77] At the same time, our human spirit is finite in a way that the divine Spirit is not, and so it is wrong to think of it as a spark of the divine within us, in the way that many Greeks thought of the human soul.

In the New Testament we find that the words "flesh" (*sarx*), "soul" (*psychê*), and "spirit" (*pneuma*) are all used with reference to human beings, not merely in a physical sense but with a moral and spiritual dimension as well. For the apostle Paul, an unregenerate man was a man of flesh or of soul, the two words being virtually interchangeable, whereas those who knew God were men of spirit.[78] Paul did not mean that spiritual people had no flesh or soul, but that what these elements represented—rebellion against God and the spiritual blindness that resulted from that—was not the controlling factor in their lives.

From our perspective, the most important thing is that in the New Testament "flesh" has a metaphysical meaning which has little to do with the physical reality. A spiritual person still has a body of flesh, but he uses that body and governs his flesh in ways that follow spiritual principles. Conversely, a carnal or "soulish" person still has a spirit, but that spirit is governed by desires that come from elsewhere. These desires may not be bad in their proper context, but if they are allowed to determine how a person lives they usurp what belongs to the spirit and become negative influences that take him away from God.

The New Testament writers did not ask whether the incarnate Son of God had flesh, soul, and spirit in the same way that other human beings had. They took that for granted. What made Jesus different from us was that, in him, these elements were ordered in the right way and had the right priorities. His human spirit submitted to the divine will that he had come to earth to accomplish, even if there were times when it had to struggle to achieve that submission. There was no question of either adding to his human nature or detracting from it, and it remained intact and fully compatible with ours.

[77] Rom. 8:16.
[78] See 1 Cor. 2:14.

It was only when the gospel reached out to the pagan world that this biblical understanding of human nature was challenged and had to be rethought in order not to be misunderstood. The problem was that in the Gentile mind, soul and spirit were almost the same thing and the body, being material, was essentially alien to them. As they saw it, the human soul was a spark of the divine spirit that was trapped in matter, which was the body or the flesh. This entrapment was the root cause of sin, and the only way out of it was for the soul to get as far away from the body as possible. In this life, sinlessness was inconceivable because the soul was wrapped up with matter, from which there was no escape. The resurrection of the body/flesh was an absurdity to the Gentiles, because to them it was like saying that something evil will be saved and live forever in the presence of a God whose nature is incompatible with it.

Christians tackled this problem by insisting that created matter was essentially good. The human body could therefore dwell with God in eternity without any moral contradiction. But Christians could not deny the reality of sin and evil, and they believed that human beings were subjected to evil in this life. They did not agree with their Gentile contemporaries that sin and evil resided in matter, nor did they accept the Pharisaical idea that sin was essentially breaking the law. So where was sin to be found, if it was so powerful and all-pervasive?

Their answer was that sin was a spiritual rebellion against God, initiated by Satan in the angelic realm and extended by his successful temptation of Adam and Eve to encompass the entire human race. One might almost say that whereas pagans believed that human beings were divine spirits/souls trapped in evil material bodies, Christians believed the opposite—that rebellious human spirits were living in naturally good bodies that had been perverted by their spiritual rebellion. Jesus did not have a rebellious human spirit, so his body remained unaffected by it and he was sinless. He could suffer all the aches and pains that mortal flesh was heir to, including physical death, but as none of these things was sinful in itself (or even necessarily the result of sin), that did not compromise his fundamental status in relation to the Father.

Once that basic pattern is understood, a divine incarnation is less problematic, but getting people to change their paradigm of good and evil was exceedingly difficult. One of the reasons for that was that most pagans thought that the human mind and will were functions of the soul/spirit. Did the incarnate Son have these things? Did he need them? If he had them, what did he do with them? A sinless Jesus must have thought and willed whatever God thought and willed, but as he was also the incarnate Son of God, it would seem logical to say that his mind and will were part of his divine nature. The trouble was that, if that was the case, then either he had no human equivalents (the teaching of Apollinarius) or the human equivalents were passive and did little or nothing on their own (the apparent teaching of Athanasius). The second of these positions was the more cautious one, and it enjoyed widespread currency in Alexandria, much to the chagrin of those Antiochene theologians who thought that it fatally compromised the full humanity of Jesus.

Even in ancient times, though, it was quickly perceived that if Jesus had a human mind and a human will they must be noticeable, which meant that they had to do something. Hence we find in the Gospels statements to the effect that there were things that the Son did not know, and that he had to submit his human will to that of the Father because they were different. As a man, Jesus did not have a death wish, which is why he prayed in the garden of Gethsemane for the cup to be taken away from him. But at the same time, he knew that he had come to do the will of the Father who had sent him, not his own will, and so he submitted to what he knew was the right thing. That did not come easily or automatically to him in his human nature—he sweated blood in the struggle—but he succeeded because his relationship with the Father was unbroken and he was therefore capable of supreme obedience to the Father's will.[79]

None of this would have made much practical difference had the relationship between the Son and the Father stayed within the realm of the Godhead. The Son's obedience to the Father's will, important as it was, would have remained a matter between the two of them had the incarnation of the Son not had a specific purpose involving the human race. The Son did not come into the world merely to manifest himself to us or to give us an example of a godly life that we might follow if we so chose. Rather, he had come to take our place, to become sin and a curse for us, to die on the cross in order to pay the price of our sin and open up the gates of heaven to us.[80] The Jews had long made atonement with the blood of the spotless lamb, but animal offerings could not take away human sin. Animals do not sin, because they are not responsible for their actions, and so their deaths, however piously intended and performed, do not get to the heart of the matter.[81] A truly effective atonement can be made only by one who has the ability to be our substitute. For that reason, the Son of God must be just as human as we are, since otherwise there would be aspects of our humanity that his sacrifice would not touch because those aspects were not present in him.

Gregory of Nazianzus stated this pithily in his famous statement that "what

[79] Matt. 26:39, 42; Luke 22:41–44.
[80] 2 Cor. 5:21; Gal. 3:13–14; Heb. 9:15.
[81] Heb. 10:4.

has not been assumed has not been healed."[82] Jesus had to have a human mind and will, not merely because we have them but because they are the means by which we sin. If Jesus did not have these things, then our human minds and wills would not have been touched by his sacrifice and we would be no further ahead after it than we were before. Furthermore, Jesus' human mind and will had to be genuinely capable of sinning, not because they were forced to sin nor because they actually did sin, but because unless they had that capacity, Jesus could not have taken our sins upon himself and become sin for us. As the ancients understood it, the rational soul was the seat of sin, but how would Jesus have borne our sins if he had no soul to contain them? Believers need to know that they have been healed and forgiven because Jesus has reached down to us, has taken our place, and has done something for us that we could never have done for ourselves. This is why his human mind and will could never be added extras or superfluous to his being; on the contrary, they were vital to his whole mission and achievement.

The decisions of the Council of Chalcedon did not resolve all the questions surrounding the humanity of Jesus but they did cast them in a new light. For more than two hundred years after 451 those questions would continue to be debated, and only gradually would the remaining problems be clarified and resolved. Indeed, there are many who would say that this process has not been completed even yet. Modern science has uncovered psychological depths to human nature of which the ancients were barely aware and which they had no means of expressing conceptually, so the claim is made that their solution to the Christological problem is not necessarily adequate or even relevant to many modern concerns. In some quarters, voices have been raised to argue that the Chalcedonian Definition may have to be abandoned or at least recast in order to take these modern issues into account. At the very least, there are many who claim that it needs to be revisited to examine how far it is capable of answering modern questions about the nature of the Son's incarnation.

Defenders of the Chalcedonian position point out that its critics know little about the controversies that arose after the council was over and that had to be resolved in its wake. They maintain that if these things were better known today, many (and perhaps most) of the concerns voiced by modern critics would either vanish or be so greatly modified as to make the original objections seem misguided. There is certainly room for further reflection on the Chalcedonian Definition in the light of modern knowledge about the way human beings function, but it can also be argued that the guidelines worked

[82] Gregory of Nazianzus, *Epistula* 101.

out after Chalcedon for defining the human nature of Christ can be extended to cover human nature in general and do not have to be seriously altered in the light of modern concerns, which can be accommodated within the traditional framework.

The difference between the monophysites of the Alexandrian tradition and the Chalcedonians was to some extent terminological (one nature after the incarnation versus a union of two), but behind this disagreement there lay a conceptual difference about what a human being was. The Chalcedonians accepted that the divine *hypostasis* of the Son constituted the humanity of Christ as an objective reality, but they insisted that his humanity had its own integrity and that it was not simply attached to, still less absorbed by, the Son's divine nature. To illustrate what this means from the New Testament, the saliva of Jesus was able to create healing mud to put on the blind man's eyes, not because it was part of the divine-human nature of the incarnate Son, but because the Son willed it to be so.[83] In other words, there was no point in collecting Jesus' saliva in order to heal people because it would not work on its own—it required the direct and personal intervention of the Son for that to happen.

As we have already noted, pre-Chalcedonian theologians called this the "transfer of properties" (*communicatio idiomatum*). According to this theory, it was possible for the Son to transfer some of his divine attributes to his human nature, allowing the latter to do things (like walk on water) of which it would not normally be capable. It is an attractive theory because it offers a way of accounting for many of the extraordinary phenomena recorded in the Gospels about Jesus. But in the end it does not work, for several reasons:

1. There is no sign that the transfer of properties was permanent or comprehensive. Could the Son have shifted only a select number of his divine properties to his human nature, without engaging the rest of his divinity as well? Could his human body have acquired the ability to walk on water without also becoming infinite and invisible? How would God's basic simplicity as a being be affected if his properties could be broken down and split up in this way?

2. Jesus told Peter that he could also walk on water if he had the faith to believe, and Peter actually tried to do so.[84] Would Jesus have said that if he knew that his own ability to walk on water depended on a transfer of properties that would have been impossible for Peter?

3. Why would Jesus transfer properties on relatively trivial and unimportant occasions like the time when he walked on water but not when it might have

[83] See John 9:6–7.

[84] Matt. 14:25–31.

made a significant difference, such as on the day of his crucifixion? As was said at the time, "If you are the Son of God, come down from the cross."[85] Was this a real possibility for Jesus?

4. Could the properties be transferred the other way, that is, from the human nature to the divine, and if so, what would that do to the Son's divine nature and his relationship to the other persons of the Godhead, given that the divine nature was shared between them? This question was not asked in ancient times but it has appeared in recent years in the modern discussion about divine suffering, where a property belonging to his human nature is believed to have been shared by his divine nature as well. But if the Son of God suffered and died in his divine nature, would this not mean that the Father and the Holy Spirit must also have suffered and died in some way, and if so, how does that affect the nature of God? Can we say that although he may have been impassible at one time, when the Son became a man, he transferred his human properties to his divinity? Did God acquire a human characteristic that he previously lacked and so can no longer be regarded as impassible?

For the monophysites, of course, the transfer of properties had become automatic, if not necessarily comprehensive, in and through the incarnation, but it could only go in one direction—the human attributes of Jesus were taken up into his divine nature and transformed by it, but not the other way around. For the Chalcedonians, on the other hand, the transfer of properties, if that is the right term for it, was occasional and voluntary. The human nature of Jesus could be used by the divine person of the Son as, when, and how he chose, and could become the vehicle of divine power at work, but this possibility had not become an integral part of Jesus' human nature. That nature remained the same as ours, which is why it made sense for Jesus to tell Peter that he too could walk on water. All Peter needed for that was what the human Jesus had, which was faith in the power of God to perform a miracle.

Unfortunately the debates between the monophysites and the Chalcedonians were skewed, as earlier debates between Arians and supporters of the First Council of Nicea had been, by political intervention on the part of the emperor in Constantinople. The provinces of Egypt and Syria were in revolt against the imposition of the two-natures Christology of Chalcedon, and the emperor had to keep his remaining empire intact. As a result, the imperial government favored compromise, which was overtly rejected in the West (where the emperor could do nothing to enforce his policy) and covertly in the East,

[85] Matt. 27:40.

where opposition to it went underground and was even persecuted. Of course, that only intensified the opposition and made reconciliation not just difficult (as it had always been) but also reprehensible in the eyes of many.

Dioscorus of Alexandria never accepted the Chalcedonian Definition, and when he died in 454, his church elected an even more intransigent successor. This was Timothy II Aelurus (d. 477), who seized control of Alexandria by instigating the murder of a rival, pro-Chalcedonian bishop, and who ruled there until 460, when he was exiled to the Crimea. This made him a martyr figure to many of his followers, who never came to terms with his imperially designated successor, Timothy III Salophakiolos (460–475). As long as the empire was in the hands of the pro-Chalcedonian emperor Leo I (457–474) there was nothing anyone could do about this, but when Leo died, the succession was disputed, and for a time his brother-in-law Basiliscus was able to claim the throne. This was the signal for a fresh assault on the decisions taken at Chalcedon, and Basiliscus allowed Timothy II to return from exile. He was treated to a hero's welcome in Alexandria, though he had to face down the Eutychians there as he had already done in Constantinople. In spite of the ups and downs of imperial politics, monophysite Christology was now firmly entrenched in Egypt as the "authentic" Alexandrian tradition and was poised to spread its influence far and wide.

Basiliscus was soon overthrown, but not before he could issue an encyclical in which he anathematized both Chalcedon and the *Tome* of Leo, and insisted that the church should stick to the decisions of the three earlier councils of 325, 381, and 431. He avoided mentioning either the one or the two natures of Christ, but the general pro-Alexandrian gist was obvious. One of the encyclical's chief opponents was Acacius, bishop of Constantinople (472–489), who was instrumental in deposing Basiliscus in favor of Zeno (476–491), Leo I's son-in-law and the father of the legitimate heir, Leo II, who had already reigned for a short time in 474. Initially it seemed that Zeno's restoration would lead to a pro-Chalcedonian policy, but the opposition in Alexandria was too strong and the imperial government soon realized that it would have to compromise. The trick was to dismantle Chalcedon without openly condemning either it or Leo's *Tome*, because that would only alienate Rome and the West (as the encyclical of Basiliscus had briefly done.)

The architect of the new policy was to be Acacius, who quickly got to work on a formula that was designed to produce church unity across the board. It was published by Zeno in 482 and is known to us as the *Henôtikon*, from the Greek word for "union" (*henôsis*). The positive theology of the *Henôtikon* was virtually identical to that of Basiliscus's encyclical, but with some nuances designed to make it less abrasive and partisan. Chalcedonians reading it could see their own confession reflected in the reaffirmation of the double *homoousios*—the incarnate Christ was acknowledged as being consubstantial with the Father in his divinity and with us in his humanity—but as this formula went back to the reunion of 433 and had been endorsed by Cyril, it was not a concession on the part of the Alexandrians. More problematic was the omission of anything that might suggest that in Christ there was one *hypostasis* or person but in two natures, though the phrase "one nature" was also left out, perhaps as a concession to the Nestorians. On the other hand, the twelve anti-Nestorian anathemas of Cyril, which had been greeted with such reserve at Ephesus in 431, were warmly endorsed and the following phrase was inserted in defense of this supposedly traditional faith: "Everyone who has thought or thinks anything else, either now or at any time, either at Chalcedon or in any synod whatever, we anathematize."[86]

This did not amount to a condemnation of Chalcedon, but the fact that anything said at it could be called into question was unsettling to those who regarded it as untouchable. The *Henôtikon* also included the phrase "One of the Trinity, God the *logos*, became incarnate" which sounded innocuous enough, but which could be interpreted in a way that would produce a form of Apollinarianism, and it was not long before that happened. In devising the *Henôtikon*, Acacius and Zeno were less interested in theology than in the unity of the church. For Acacius, the advantage was that Alexandria would have to recognize the primacy of Constantinople, and for Zeno, that it would hold the empire together. What neither of them realized is that theological confusion does not create unity, as the commentator Facundus of Hermiane put it.[87] Then as now, attempts to reunite the church on any basis other than theological truth were bound to fail, and in this case the latter state was worse than the first.

The main effect of the *Henôtikon* was to produce schisms all over the Christian world, although this was not immediately apparent in the East. There the churches of Alexandria, Jerusalem, and Antioch were all reconciled under the leadership of Constantinople, or so it seemed. The bishops were once more on speaking terms, but their flocks had other ideas. In all the Eastern churches strong opposition to the *Henôtikon* was stirred up by the monks, who had the ear of the people. They wanted to return to the encyclical of Basiliscus and regarded the *Henôtikon* as a sellout to the pro-Chalcedonians. The leaders of the churches found themselves at odds with their own flocks, a situation that could not last. At first they preferred to interpret the Henôtikon

[86] Text quoted in Grillmeier, *Christ in Christian Tradition, Volume 2, Part 1*, 253.
[87] Facundus of Hermiane, *Pro definitione trium capitum* 12.4.

in as anti-Chalcedonian a way as they could, but in the end they had to abandon it altogether.

In the West, there were some people who were prepared to accept the *Henôtikon*, not least because it did not condemn Chalcedon or Leo, but they were few. For the most part, Acacius was denounced as a heretic and from 484 the churches of Rome and Constantinople were in schism. But whereas Rome was united behind its bishop, Constantinople was not. There the monks known as the "sleepless ones" (*akoimêtai*) agitated in favor of Chalcedon to such an extent that they accused even Rome of going soft on the matter. Chalcedon also gained support from the monks of Jerusalem, led by the long-lived archimandrite Sabas (439–533). There, the monks were able to win over the bishop (Elias), who not only resisted all pressure to accept the *Henôtikon* but also refused to join in the growing campaign to have the Council of Chalcedon annulled.

That campaign was led by Severus of Antioch (456?–538), probably the greatest monophysite theologian of all time, and bishop of the city from 512 to 518.[88] Severus managed to win over Zeno's successor as emperor, Anastasius I (491–518), and in 513 he held a great synod in Antioch that ratified his anti-Chalcedonian policies. With the emperor's help he managed to depose Elias of Jerusalem and extend his influence across the Middle East. That influence would not go unchallenged, but it laid the basis for the establishment of a long-term monophysite church in Syria as well as in Egypt.

Imperial policy changed yet again when Anastasius died and was succeeded by a Latin-speaking general called Justin I (518–527). The real power, however, was exercised by his nephew Justinian, who succeeded him in 527 and reigned until 565. Justin and Justinian quickly adopted a pro-Chalcedonian stance, not least because of the pressure they faced from the *akoimêtai* on the streets of Constantinople. Reconciliation with Rome quickly followed, and Justin recognized its bishop as his legate and the supreme head of the Western church.[89] As with the introduction of the *Henôtikon*, the reconciliation with Rome was more political than theological. The Western church did not understand the subtleties of Alexandrian Christology and condemned it as Eutychian, which it clearly was not. Acacius and his successors in Constantinople could have put the Romans right on this but they did not do so, probably because theology was not their main concern. Imperial policy was focused on the reconquest of

[88] See Pauline Allen and C. T. R. Hayward, *Severus of Antioch* (London: Routledge, 2004); Roberta C. Chesnut, *Three Monophysite Christologies: Severus of Antioch, Philoxenus of Mabbug, and Jacob of Sarug* (Oxford: Oxford University Press, 1976).

[89] This later became one of the justifications for papal power.

the lost Western provinces, and for that, the cooperation of the Western church was essential. This explains the high price that the emperors were prepared to pay in order to get that cooperation.

In order to cement the reconciliation, Hormisdas, the bishop of Rome (514–523) circulated a tract around the Eastern churches in which he claimed that only his see had been preserved from heresy since New Testament times, a "fact" that in his eyes contributed to its theological authority in the Christian world as a whole. On that basis he demanded total adherence to the Chalcedonian Definition and a repudiation of the *Henôtikon*. The latter meant a disavowal not only of the document but also of all those who had agreed to it, which included a number of Chalcedonian bishops in the East who had accepted it as a compromise because they put the unity of the church first. It was a bitter pill for the Eastern churches to swallow, and many bishops refused to cooperate. They were then deposed and sent into exile, where they set up an underground network to keep the faith, as they understood it, alive. By pushing his case too far, Hormisdas succeeded only in dividing the Eastern churches, though for the time being Rome gained an unprecedented ascendancy over Constantinople. The high point came in 536, when Hormisdas's successor Agapetus I (535–536) was able to force the emperor to depose the bishop of Constantinople, a non-Chalcedonian, and have him replaced by someone more acceptable to Rome. Severus was condemned at the same time and died out of communion with the pro-Chalcedonian churches. The prospects for the future unity of the Eastern churches looked bleak.[90]

Severus was a systematic theologian of a kind that had not been seen in the non-Chalcedonian world since Cyril of Alexandria. His basic starting point was the "one nature" formula that he attributed to Cyril but which in fact had crept into Cyril's thought from Apollinarian sources and had never really shed that association. Because of this, Severus could not use the word "nature" to refer to Christ's humanity but only to the eternal, divine *logos*. When that *logos* became flesh, it took on the essence (*ousia*) of humanity, a statement that was clearly anti-Apollinarian (since Apollinarius had denied the existence of a human soul in Christ) but that introduced a strange distinction between "essence" (*ousia*) and "nature" (*physis*) that made no sense to a Chalcedonian, for whom they were practically synonymous. Severus's concern, of course, was to maintain the unity of the incarnate Christ at all costs, and he could not imagine the *logos* operating in his humanity in a way that was distinct from his divinity. If the divine person of the Son of God suffered and died on the

[90] For a good overview of the history and politics, see Volker L. Menze, *Justinian and the Making of the Syrian Orthodox Church* (Oxford: Oxford University Press, 2008).

cross in his human nature (as Chalcedon affirmed), his divinity must also be involved. If it was not, then Christ was divided and the man who died on the cross was not the Son of God.

The nature of Severus's dilemma can be appreciated when we consider that he faced the danger that his interpretation of Christ's incarnation would be interpreted in an Apollinarian direction. This actually happened in the case of Julian of Halicarnassus, who met Severus in Constantinople in 510, was attracted to his Christology, and thought he was interpreting it correctly when he claimed that the human body of Jesus was incorruptible. Severus was horrified by this and denied any such conclusion, but although Julian represented an extreme position, it is hard to deny his logic. If the divine *hypostasis* of the Son gives the human nature of Jesus its identity, an identity that it possesses only because it has been shaped by the *logos*, it is easy to see why it ought to be safe from any kind of harm or corruption. Julian's view came to be known as "aphthartodocetism" and was quickly condemned on all sides, but the fact that it could be proposed at all was a warning to others of the dangers that were inherent in Severus's teaching.[91] It was a sense of those dangers that motivated others to oppose his position, and gradually a school of pro-Chalcedonians grew up to answer him, though it was never influential enough to win over monophysite opinion.

The most important of these defenders of Chalcedon was John of Caesarea, often known as John the Grammarian, who concentrated his attack on Severus's use of theological terms. The main argument revolved around the precise meaning of *physis*, and John tackled this in a roundabout way. First, he analyzed the distinction, already made by Basil of Caesarea with respect to the Trinity, between *hypostasis* and *ousia*. By doing that, he established that *hypostasis* related to the particularity of an object whereas *ousia* referred to its underlying essence, which is why Basil could say that there were three *hypostases* in the one *ousia* of God. John then applied this terminology to the incarnate Christ with a clarity of vision that had never before been achieved. He declared himself willing to accept that prior to the incarnation it would have been possible to speak of "two natures" out of which the one Christ was formed, but only on the understanding that Jesus' human nature had no independent existence until it was conceived in the womb of Mary.

Severus understood "nature" to mean "what exists from birth," which is why he spoke of only one nature in the incarnate Christ, but John challenged him on this. He thought that it would be better to speak of the "two essences,"

[91] The Greek word for "incorruptible" is *aphthartos*, and "docetism" means "appearance." So "aphthartodocetism" is the appearance of incorruptibility.

divinity and humanity, which had at least theoretical existence prior to the incarnation and which were brought together by the divine *hypostasis* of the Son. John even went so far as to claim that Severus was able to speak of Christ being formed "from two natures" only because by "nature" he meant *ousia* and not *physis*.[92] Of course, for John the two *ousiai* were abstractions that were concretized only in the one *hypostasis*. This was not a problem in the Godhead, since it was perfectly understandable that the divine *ousia* should be defined by an equally divine *hypostasis*, but what about the human *ousia*? Severus claimed that it did not have a *hypostasis* of its own and could not have one, because then there would be two *hypostases* and the incarnate Christ would not be a unity. Severus also argued that there could be no *physis* that did not have a *prosôpon*, since the *prosôpon* was the only way that it could be recognized and identified.[93] John agreed with that argument up to a point, but countered Severus by saying that the human nature of Christ was concretized in the divine *hypostasis* of the Son. As he put it,

> We do not define the human *ousia* in Christ as real in the sense of being a *hypostasis* that exists by itself and is a *prosôpon*, but only in the sense that it exists. It is the *hypostasis* that reveals what the *ousia* is . . .[94]

John explained this by using the concept of *enhypostasia*, which meant that an *ousia* could find its identity in a *hypostasis* that was given to it, even if (as in the case of Jesus) that *hypostasis* did not derive from the *ousia* itself.[95] In other words, a divine *hypostasis* could give concrete reality to a human *ousia*, which then would have, like any other *ousia*, its own *physis* or "nature." To use Severus's terminology, John meant that the *prosôpon* of the human *physis* of Christ was the *hypostasis* of the divine *logos*. That he did not state this with complete clarity was due to his concern that if he had done so, he might have run the risk of attributing a separate *hypostasis* to the human nature of Christ, which was the very thing that both sides were trying to avoid.

There was also the danger of suggesting that the divine *hypostasis* might somehow modify the human nature and thereby dehumanize it, which is what John thought that Severus and his fellow monophysites were doing. The truth was that when the *hypostasis* of the Son gave concrete identity to the human nature of Jesus, the characteristics of that nature were fully preserved. Jesus

---

[92] John the Grammarian of Caesarea, *Apologeticum* 1.19.
[93] Ibid., 4.2.
[94] Ibid., 4.6.
[95] John did not actually use the form *enhypostasia*, but preferred the adjective *enhypostaton* and the adverb *enhypostatôs*, words that can be traced back at least as far as Epiphanius of Salamis (*Panarion* 72.11) and Jerome (*Epistula* 15.3).

was a typical Jewish male of first-century Palestine with no physical features that set him apart from others like him, but those features were not the work of the divine *hypostasis*. If Jesus looked like his contemporaries it was because the flesh he took from Mary determined that, and what was true of his physical appearance was also true of his mental capacities, and so on.

John did not help his argument by the way in which he was prepared to use terms like "conjunction" (*synapheia*) to describe the union of the two natures in the incarnate Christ, nor was it helpful that he employed expressions like "the twofold Christ" (*diplasios Christos* or in Latin *Christus duplex*) and "the God-bearing man" (*anthrôpos theophoros* or in Latin *homo deifer*), which tended to weaken the unity of Christ as a single divine subject, even if the expressions themselves had a respectable pedigree and John did not intend them to be interpreted in that way. By pointing out such things, Severus was able to fend off John's challenge to his theology, though the fundamental issue of *enhypostasia* remained important and could not be so easily dismissed.

This was the situation that confronted Leontius of Byzantium, a somewhat obscure sixth-century defender of Chalcedon whose importance has usually been underestimated. One of the main reasons for this is that it is hard to identify who Leontius was and what he wrote. There are at least twenty known contemporaries of his who had the same name, and the writings of one of them, Leontius of Jerusalem, were hopelessly confused with his in the manuscript tradition.[96] We know that Leontius of Byzantium was present at a synod in Constantinople in 536, where the theology of Severus and Julian was condemned, but whether he played any significant part in that is unclear. From his writings, it seems that he was more interested in expounding his Christology than in criticizing others for getting it wrong, but the general uncertainty that surrounds him makes any conclusion about him difficult to substantiate.

It appears that Leontius thought of the *hypostasis* of Jesus Christ as a concrete being who was neither simply divine nor simply human. Those adjectives applied to his natures and not to his person, whom Leontius variously described as Christ, Savior, and Lord. Did Leontius do this because he thought that the *hypostasis* of Christ was neither human nor divine but something else, a third element of some kind (*tertium quid*)? He has certainly been accused of that in modern times, but the evidence does not support such a drastic and abnormal conclusion.[97] Like John the Grammarian before him, Leontius was

---

[96] So far, the best attempt to sort this out has been made by B. E. Daley, *Leontius of Byzantium: A Critical Edition of His Works, with Prolegomena* (unpublished dissertation, Oxford University, 1978).

[97] See Aloys Grillmeier, *Christ in Christian Tradition, Volume 2, From the Council of Chalcedon (451) to Gregory the Great (590–604), Part 2: The Church of Constantinople in the Sixth Century* (London: Mowbray, 1995), 186–191, for a summary of the evidence and discussion.

preoccupied with trying to define the terms used in Christology in a way that would avoid confusion and possibly even lead to agreement among the different factions in the church. Again like John, he distinguished *physis* from *hypostasis* by saying that the former was a general word applied to a substance (*ousia*) whereas the latter was a specific manifestation of a substance. To talk about the nature of a thing is to talk about its general characteristics, whereas a *hypostasis* is a particular example of the thing being analyzed. Leontius helped to clarify the problems that confronted the defenders of Chalcedon, but he did not solve them as many scholars have thought.[98] For that, more thought and reflection would be required.

That definitive solution is now generally attributed to Leontius of Jerusalem, a slightly younger contemporary of Leontius of Byzantium who may have been writing in Constantinople in the decade or so following the condemnation of Severus in 536. Friedrich Loofs made the mistake of confusing him with Leontius of Byzantium, a confusion that has still not been totally dispelled. But an examination of the two works now attributed to Leontius of Jerusalem, one against the monophysites and the other against the Nestorians, makes it clear that he was a deeper and more accomplished theologian than his namesake of Byzantium.

Leontius of Jerusalem was apparently the first person who made a conscious distinction between the concept of "union in or according to nature" and "union in or according to *hypostasis*," arguing that only the latter was applicable to the incarnate Christ. At the same time, he also stated that the *hypostasis* of Jesus was the divine *logos*, an obvious conclusion perhaps, but one that had not been made before.[99] The problem from which even Leontius could not free himself was that, following Basil of Caesarea, a *hypostasis* was considered to be a particular identity assumed by an *ousia*. That was how Basil understood the *hypostases* of the Trinity, and it inhibited generations of theologians from drawing the conclusion that, in Christ, the *hypostasis* of the Son was the agent of a synthesis between divinity and humanity that preserved each nature intact. Leontius was even able to say that the incarnation was a peculiarity of the divine Son's *hypostasis*, a confusion between time and eternity that did nothing to clarify the situation. Leontius was not perfect, but his Christology represented a considerable advance on what had gone before, as the following extract demonstrates:

[98] The problem goes back to Friedrich Loofs, *Leontius von Byzanz und die gleichnamigen Schriftsteller der griechischen Kirche* (Leipzig: J. C. Hinrichs, 1887). Loofs confused Leontius with several contemporaries of the same name and came up with a picture of his Christology that can no longer be regarded as valid. See Grillmeier, *Christ in Christian Tradition, Volume 2, Part 2*, 200–212, for the arguments.

[99] Leontius of Jerusalem, *Contra Nestorianos* 7.4.

> One *hypostasis* is common to both natures. It existed before the *ousia* of the human being, when it belonged to the *logos* in the common *ousia* of divinity. It created the nature of the *kyriakos anthrôpos* for itself, embraced it and joined it to its own nature. At the same time it began to be the *hypostasis* of the fleshly nature [of Christ], and moved from being a simple *hypostasis* to one that was common [to both natures] and therefore multifaceted.[100]

What Leontius was describing was what the apostle Paul had written to the Colossians: "in him [Christ] the whole fullness of deity dwells bodily," which might be called the signature verse of Leontius's entire Christology.[101] His closeness to Pauline theology can be seen throughout Leontius's writings, but especially in his perception that the sinlessness of Christ was the most obvious way to perceive his divinity. The writer to the Hebrews (whom Leontius regarded as Paul) had said that Christ had become like us in all things, except for sin.[102] This was possible only because his human nature was hypostatized in the divine *logos*, from which it acquired the grace to remain sinless. Leontius even spoke about the influence on the human will of the incarnate Christ that came from the divine will dwelling in him. That was how Christ achieved a balance between sinless divinity and grace-filled humanity that was not immune to human failings but was enabled by that same grace to triumph over them.[103] The details would need further refining, but in essence Leontius had understood and expressed the New Testament portrait of Christ to which the Council of Chalcedon had borne eloquent though not yet fully developed witness.

Unfortunately, by then it was too late to achieve a reconciliation with the Eastern churches on the basis of a common acceptance of Chalcedon. Severus and his allies had already established an alternative ecclesiastical organization, and Rome was unwilling to compromise. Justinian tried to keep the peace by supporting Chalcedonian bishops himself but allowing his wife, the empress Theodora, to act on behalf of the non-Chalcedonians. The door was thus left ajar, and some of the latter continued to hope for an eventual change of imperial policy that would favor them. But any such change would have had to include a renunciation of Chalcedon, and since that was out of the question, the schism looked as if it would be permanent (which it turned out to be).

That, however, could not have been foreseen at the time, and the emperor was unwilling to give up attempts to reunite the warring parties. In 553 he summoned another council in Constantinople, which took the bold step of

[100] Ibid., 2.14.
[101] Col. 2:9.
[102] Heb. 2:17–18; 4:15.
[103] Leontius of Jerusalem, *Contra Nestorianos* 1.19.

condemning three theologians who were thought to be pro-Nestorian in their teaching. These were Theodore of Mopsuestia, Ibas of Edessa, and Theodoret of Cyrus. It is true that not everything they wrote was condemned, only those writings that dealt with the Christological question directly, but the implications were clear. The condemnation of the "Three Chapters," as these works came to be known, left a bad taste in many mouths because their authors were long dead and had always been regarded as orthodox. In a separate decree, the council also condemned Origen, whose multifaceted works had long been a source of divergent theological opinions and who had been under suspicion in some quarters for centuries, in spite of his pervasive influence in the East. Like the other three, Origen was a voice from the distant past, and there were some who were uneasy at the blanket condemnation of his theology so long after his death.[104] Nevertheless the ban was put into effect, and is one of the main reasons why relatively few of Origen's works have survived in the original Greek. On the other hand, the council finally endorsed Cyril of Alexandria's third letter to Nestorius including the twelve anathemas, a clear indication of their willingness to make peace with the monophysites as far as they could.

The Second Council of Constantinople, in 553, recognized by the Chalcedonian churches as the fifth ecumenical one, was the closest that those churches would ever come to accommodating the non-Chalcedonians of the East, but by the time it took place the latter had become irreconcilable. The years of persecution after 518 had done their work, and a new church had come into being. How far the theological disputes that lay behind the split touched ordinary church members is hard to say. Outside the eastern provinces of the Roman empire, there was no reaction at all, because there Chalcedon was unchallenged. In the East, there is evidence that a number of people went back and forth from one church to the other, believing that the quarrels were disputes over terminology rather than matters of substance, but the differences had an effect on popular worship, and it was in that way that ordinary people came to feel them most deeply.

A good example of this is the acclamation known as the "Thrice-holy" or *Trishagion*. This originated sometime in the early fifth century and made its first major appearance at the Council of Chalcedon. In its original form it went, "Holy God, holy and strong, holy and immortal, have mercy on us."[105] In that form it was innocuous, but it was not clear whether it applied to the Trinity in general or to Christ in particular. In Constantinople the former interpretation

[104] See Elizabeth A. Clark, *The Origenist Controversy: The Cultural Construction of an Early Christian Debate* (Princeton, NJ: Princeton University Press, 1992).

[105] In Greek, *Hagios ho Theos, hagios ischyros, hagios athanatos, eleēson hēmas.*

held sway, whereas in Antioch it was the latter. In 471 the Antiochenes introduced an expanded version of it into the official liturgy of their church, adding, "who was crucified for us" before the final clause. An attempt to clarify this by making a further addition of the words "Christ the king" immediately before it was rejected, an unfortunate move that aggravated the ambiguity and was to lead to trouble.

After 510 there was considerable pressure put on the church at Constantinople to adopt the Antiochene version of the *Trishagion*, which was declared to be fully orthodox, despite the fact that to some it sounded as if it was confessing that the entire Trinity suffered and died on the cross. After long and somewhat confused debates, even Rome finally agreed that the expanded version could be used in an orthodox sense, but although that decision was never formally repudiated it was discreetly put aside, and by 536 the Chalcedonians were no longer using the longer version. Thus it came about that in their worship the two sides were distinguished by a formula that came to stand for a non-Chalcedonian Christology and that was well known to every worshiper. The schism was complete.

Justinian's attempt to reunite the church was a failure, but unfortunately it was not the end of his theological activity. Having failed with the monophysites, he turned to the Nestorians, hoping to restore links with them in spite of the condemnation of the Three Chapters in 553. Not surprisingly, that also failed, whereupon he went to the other extreme and sought to reconcile the supporters of Julian of Halicarnassus, a move which, if it had succeeded, would have split the monophysites and perhaps destroyed their influence in the East. What actually happened is unclear and has been the subject of considerable scholarly dispute.[106] The tradition is that, toward the end of his life, Justinian issued an edict approving of the aphthartodocetist idea that Christ's human body was incorruptible and impassible. This has been contested in modern times, and it appears that whatever the emperor did, he never intended to depart from the teaching of Chalcedon on which his whole ecclesiastical policy had been based since 518. Regardless of what the truth of the matter is, all attempts at reconciliation with the Julianists died with Justinian in 565 and nothing more was heard of them after that.

The Will of Christ

The death of Justinian I in 565 turned out to be a watershed. His successor Justin II (565–578) was unable to hold onto all the conquests made in the previ-

[106] For the details, see Grillmeier, *Christ in Christian Tradition, Volume 2, Part 2*, 463–475.

ous reign, and after the Lombard invasion of Italy in 568 the political situation in the West became critical once more. Rome remained under imperial control but it was not secure, and its church's policies were less oriented toward Constantinople than they had been before. In Spain, the Visigothic Arians were finally defeated in 589 and Rome then embarked on an evangelistic campaign to restore Christianity to what had once been Roman Britain. The Franks, who had accepted Roman Christianity in 496, gradually established themselves as the mainstay of orthodoxy in the West, and they never fell under the sway of Constantinople.

In the East, the empire was able to hold its own against the Persians, but the problem of what to do about the monophysites and the Nestorians remained acute. Justinian's policies had locked the imperial administration into a pro-Chalcedonian position which it could not repudiate, but its opponents demanded nothing less. Justin II tried to heal divisions by issuing what has become known as a second *Henôtikon*, but it was no more successful than the first one had been. The stalemate continued until 602, when the emperor Maurice (584–602) was overthrown in a revolt that broke out in Constantinople. The Persian king Chosroes (Khusraw) II (590–628) took that as a signal to invade the empire, and before long most of Syria, Palestine, and eventually even Egypt, had fallen to him. Chosroes II had no reason to favor the Chalcedonians, and under his rule both monophysites and Nestorians were tolerated, though the Persian predilection for the latter made the former, who were much stronger in Syria and Egypt, unhappy.

The situation was not reversed until the emperor Heraclius (610–641) was able to defeat the Persians and reconquer the lost provinces in 628. His victory would prove to be short-lived, however, because unknown to him or to the Persians, a new enemy was appearing on the horizon. In the deserts of Arabia, which had been a backwater since time immemorial, the prophet Muhammad was uniting the tribes under the banner of his new religion of Islam. By the time he died in 632, Arabia was poised for dramatic expansion into the exhausted empires of the north, and within a few years all the territories that Heraclius had worked so hard to recover were lost again, this time for good. The Muslims promised religious toleration to the Christians, whatever their internal divisions might be, and the non-Chalcedonians in particular had no incentive to fight for Constantinople. For its part, the empire was now theologically homogeneous to a degree that it had not been before, and eventually it learned to live with this Muslim-imposed solution to the problems of the church.

But this is to look ahead. In 628 none of that could be foreseen and Heraclius was once again faced with the need to find an accommodation between

Chalcedonians and non-Chalcedonians. This had now been made even more difficult by the way in which the latter had used Persian occupation as an excuse for taking advantage of the former. It so happened that the bishop of Constantinople, a man called Sergius (610–638), was a Syrian of monophysite origin, who had a special insight into the Christological problems that divided the two churches and a personal incentive for wanting to overcome them. He decided that the way to go about this was to agree that the center of activity (*energeia*) in the incarnate Christ, which the monophysites naturally thought belonged to his one nature, could be regarded as one as long as it was transferred from the nature of Christ to his person (*hypostasis*). In other words, the person of Christ had a single will that he manifested in both natures. If that formula could be agreed upon, Sergius believed, the insistence of the monophysites on the unity of the incarnate Christ would be catered to and they might be able to reconcile themselves to a "two-nature" formula that did not divide that unity.

Sergius's solution, known as "monenergism," appealed to Heraclius, who put it forward as a compromise that might reconcile the non-Chalcedonians. Sergius pointed out that no one had ever spoken of two wills in Christ, not even Nestorius, who assumed that his divine and human natures worked together in such a way as to give him a common will. This had to be the case, Sergius argued, because if Christ had had two wills they would eventually have come into conflict with each other, but there is no indication of that in the Gospels. Jesus' prayer in the garden of Gethsemane was explained as an expression of his desire to teach us to put God's will before ours, and not as a sign that his human will wanted something different from his divine one.[107]

Sergius had his greatest success in Armenia, which in 633 formally adopted monenergism as its doctrine, an act that distinguished the Armenians from other non-Chalcedonians and remains a hallmark of their church to this day. Unfortunately, the Syrians were less amenable. They had suffered from persecution at the hands of the Chalcedonians in a way that the Armenians had not, and their bitterness toward Chalcedon was impossible to overcome. To make matters worse, in Palestine there was a strong pro-Chalcedonian party that had no desire to reconcile with the monophysites and that began to put pressure on Sergius to retract his compromise solution. He had more success in Egypt, at least initially, but Heraclius's appointment of his aide Cyrus as both bishop of Alexandria and governor of the province made the monenergist doctrine appear as an imperial imposition and stirred up resentment, especially as Cyrus implemented it in a heavy-handed fashion. By the time the Arabs invaded in

[107] Matt. 26:39; Luke 22:42.

634, both Syria and Egypt were on the brink of revolt, and even Palestine was unhappy with the imperial compromise.

Just as the eastern provinces were falling to the Arabs, Heraclius issued his so-called *Ekthesis* ("Explanation"), in which he declared that the incarnate Christ had only one will. This form of monenergism has therefore come to be called "monothelitism," and it sparked the next round of controversy in a church that could ill afford it at the time. Constantinople accepted the emperor's teaching, but it was rejected in the East and West alike. In Egypt the reaction against it was so bitter that it has been credited with driving a number of non-Chalcedonians into the arms of the Muslim invaders.[108] Pro-Chalcedonians were equally incensed. Sophronius, the bishop of Jerusalem who had protested to Sergius against the latter's monenergistic policies, had died by the time the *Ekthesis* was published (and Jerusalem had fallen to the Arabs), but his crusade against the monophysites and their influence was taken up by his disciple, Maximus the Confessor (580–662).[109]

Maximus received considerable support for his position from the West, and in 645 he triumphed in a debate held in Constantinople with its former bishop Pyrrhus, who defended the *Ekthesis*. Three years later the emperor Constans II (641–668), in a vain attempt to restore peace to the church, issued a document known as the *Typos* in which he forbade all discussion of the subject. That merely provoked Martin I, bishop of Rome (649–655) to convene a council at which Maximus's Christology was affirmed. Both Martin and Maximus suffered for their defiance of imperial authority, the former by exile to the Crimea and the latter by bodily mutilation as well as exile. After Maximus's death the controversy continued until 680–681, when a Third Council of Constantinople, now recognized as the sixth ecumenical one, vindicated his position and condemned monothelitism as heresy.

In fact, monothelitism was doomed from the start. First, there was the

---

[108] Frend, *Rise of the Monophysite Movement*, 352.

[109] The literature on Maximus is enormous, perhaps because of his reputation as a bridge-builder between East and West. Modern study of his work goes back to Hans U. von Balthasar, *Die kosmische Liturgie* (Freiburg-im-Breisgau: Herder, 1941), subsequently published as *La liturgie cosmique* (Paris: Aubier, 1947) and in English translation as *Cosmic Liturgy: The Universe according to Maximus the Confessor* (San Francisco: Ignatius, 2003). Since then, there have been important studies by Jean-Miguel Garrigues, *Maxime le Confesseur. La charité, avenir divin de l'homme* (Paris: Beauchesne, 1976); Nikos Matsoukas, *Kosmos, anthrôpos, koinônia kata ton Maximo Homologêtê* (Athens: Grigoris, 1980); Pierre Piret, *Le Christ et la Trinité selon Maxime le Confesseur* (Paris: Beauchesne, 1983); Lars Thunberg, *Man and the Cosmos: The Vision of St. Maximus the Confessor* (Crestwood, NY: St. Vladimir's Seminary Press, 1986); Joseph P. Farrell, *Free Choice in St. Maximus the Confessor* (South Canaan, PA: St. Tikhon's Seminary Press, 1989); Aidan Nichols, *Byzantine Gospel: Maximus the Confessor in Modern Scholarship* (Edinburgh: T & T Clark, 1993); Andrew Louth, *Maximus the Confessor* (London: Routledge, 1996); Jean-Claude Larchet, *Maxime le Confesseur, médiateur entre l'Orient et l'Occident* (Paris: Cerf, 1998); Demetrios Bathrellos, *The Byzantine Christ: Person, Nature, and Will in the Christology of St. Maximus the Confessor* (Oxford: Oxford University Press, 2004); Torstein T. Tollefsen, *The Christocentric Cosmology of St. Maximus the Confessor* (Oxford: Oxford University Press, 2008).

latent theological question. If the will is part of a being's person (*hypostasis*) and not his nature, there would be three wills in God and not just one. That would open up the possibility of disagreement within the Trinity, which is scarcely conceivable. But if God's will is part of his nature and the incarnate Christ has only one will, that will would have to be divine and therefore common to all three persons of the Godhead. Many of those who upheld monothelitism agreed that Christ's will had to be divine, but others thought it was some combination of the divine and the human, known technically as "theandric." Either way, it was not (and could not be) truly human.

But if Christ's will was not fully human, his solidarity with the rest of the human race was called into question. A divine will cannot be tempted, because it cannot go against its own divinity. Were the temptations of Jesus therefore false and meaningless? If sin is an act of the will, and the will of Jesus was divine, how could he have sinned or become sin for us on the cross? As Maximus saw clearly, it was not the will of the Son that was pitted against the will of the Father in the garden of Gethsemane, but the human will that had to struggle to submit to the divine. This was both natural and necessary. As a man, Jesus did not want to die, any more than any mentally balanced human being would. If he had had a death wish, his crucifixion would not have been a conscious atonement for sin but the result of a psychotic condition. It therefore made more sense to say that Jesus had two wills, not one, and that view finally triumphed at the Third Council of Constantinople.

Hidden in that decision and not made explicit at the time, but nevertheless of very great importance for the future development of theology, was the assertion that the will, as part of our nature, does not determine the status of our person or the quality of our personal relationships with others. For example, I may be unwilling to honor my father and mother, but that does not change my relationship with them, which is fixed by other criteria. As a sinner, I am unwilling to obey the commandments of God, but that does not alter the fact that I have been made in his image and likeness and am responsible to him for my thoughts and actions. Ultimately, this means that salvation cannot be an act of the will alone. It is the fruit of a personal relationship (union with Christ) that is established by God and not by the desire of any human being. It also means, although this was not fully perceived in ancient times, that if I lose the function of my will (perhaps through mental disability or hypnosis), I do not lose my relationship with God. A brainwashed person can deny Christ, but this does not count, because he has been deprived of his natural freedom to make decisions. In other words, although our will is a means by which our relationship with God can and ought to be expressed, if it is handicapped for some reason, that relationship still exists and we do not lose our salvation merely because we cannot confess it as a normal person would.

The monothelite controversy was an important milestone in the development of the concept of the person that had emerged at Chalcedon. The defeat of monothelitism can be regarded as the final victory of the church over Apollinarianism and the reductionist view of humanity that it professed. We must never forget that Jesus provided the early Christians with a picture not just of what God is like but also of what it means to be a human being. If his humanity did not include a will, then neither would ours. What we call our "will" would be no more than an expression of our rebellion against God and would have no existence of its own. A perfect human being would be totally subjected to the will of God, the only will that would have real existence.

In the course of the monothelite controversy, pro-Chalcedonian theologians did what they could to work out how the human nature of Christ could be complete without having its own identity (*hypostasis*). The Nestorians had resolved the issue by saying that the human nature of Jesus did have its own *hypostasis*—in other words, there would have been a man, Jesus of Nazareth, whether he was also the Son of God or not. The monophysites, on the other hand, had absorbed the human nature into the divine and so the question did not have to be asked at all. But the Chalcedonian determination to maintain the existence of two distinct natures in the one incarnate person of the Son of God made it necessary to find a way in which this could be done without diminishing the integrity of his human nature.

Maximus tackled the problem and answered it by saying that the incarnate Christ could not be a composite nature formed from two incompatible elements, divinity and humanity, because if he were, he would be neither God nor man, but something in between. Instead of this, Maximus argued that the Son must remain God if he is to have the power to save us, but that he must also become one of us if we are to be truly saved. This can happen only if each nature remains what it is. Given that the divine nature has a will that is shared with the other persons of the Trinity, that will must be present in the divine nature of Christ but it cannot absorb the human will because to do so would be to compromise the sovereign "otherness" of God.

Maximus seems to have been the first theologian who clearly distinguished between person and nature in Christ by saying that his "nature" describes *what* he is whereas his person defines *who* he is.[110] The first is purely objective whereas the second is relational. When we ask who Jesus is, the answer is that

[110] Maximus the Confessor, *Opuscula* 23.

he is the Son of the Father, and therefore divine. But when we ask what he is, we have to say that he is fully God and fully man, because both natures are present in him. It was in this framework that Maximus developed his understanding of the word *hypostasis*, hoping to show that the monophysite and Nestorian perspectives, taken on their own, upset the balance between God and man that was the hallmark of the Chalcedonian position.

Seen from the standpoint of the subject, or agent, of the incarnation, the *hypostasis* of Christ was the one divine *logos* who became a man, which is what the monophysites were concerned to insist on. As a man, he was a union of two natures, not a mixture that would either have created a third nature or suppressed the fullness of his humanity. This was the burden of Nestorius. As Maximus saw it, Chalcedon took both of these concerns and combined them in a higher synthesis, though it too needed to be expressed more carefully than had been the case in the century and a half following the council.

Many Chalcedonians had tried to explain the union of the two natures in Christ by comparing it to the union of body and soul in man. The so-called Athanasian Creed sums it up as follows: "For as the reasonable soul and flesh is one man, so God and man is one Christ." But as Maximus pointed out, the analogy is not perfect. In human beings, the body and soul did not have an independent existence before conception in the womb, whereas in the case of God and man in Christ, the divine *logos* existed from all eternity. In human beings, the coalescence of body and soul creates the individual person, whereas in the incarnation, the person of the Son was already there. In the womb of Mary, that divine person took on a human nature, body and soul, giving it his own *hypostasis*.

As he developed this notion further, Maximus came to realize, to a degree that no one before him seems to have understood, that the controlling factor in the incarnation was the person or *hypostasis* of the *logos*, not his natures. What had occurred in Mary's womb was that the *logos* had acquired a second nature in which he functioned with the same freedom that he had in his divinity. At last, the ancient belief that a person or *hypostasis* was the reflection or expression of an underlying substance was turned on its head, and the two natures became the means by which the person of the Son revealed himself in the world.

This revolution in his way of thinking was necessary for Maximus to be able to resolve the question of the will of the incarnate Christ. Once again, he proceeded by way of linguistic analysis. Abandoning the philosophical tradition, he turned to the New Testament, where "will" is consistently expressed as *thelêma*.[111] Maximus defined this as the faculty of willing or as the ability to will, and distinguished it from the object of willing or the thing willed, which he called *thelêton* or *thelêthen*. The difference can be seen when we apply the terms to the action of both God and man. If we are talking about "will" in the sense of the object of our willing, both God and man can will the same thing—the salvation of the world, for example. But if we are talking about the faculty of willing inherent in our respective natures, then God's will is eternally anchored in his being whereas man's will is created along with the rest of him. As God, Jesus possessed the eternal divine *thelêma*, but as man he also acquired a created human will. Maximus defined "will" in this sense as follows:

> The natural will is a power that desires what is in accordance with its nature. Every being, and especially rational ones, naturally desires what is in accordance with its nature, having been given that power by God as part of its own constitution.[112]

Both of these could focus on the same object and will the same thing, but in their origin they were quite different. In the garden of Gethsemane, Jesus' submission to his Father proceeded from the divine will, not from the human one, which by nature would never want to die, but there was no conflict between them, because in the submission of the human to the divine we discover that both willed the same thing—the suffering, death, and resurrection of the Son of God made man. Once the meaning of our terms is clarified, said Maximus, the two wills in Christ fall into place and the problem of their joint activity (*energeia*) goes away.

The importance of this for our salvation was very clear to Maximus. As he said in his refutation of the monothelites,

> If Adam ate [the fruit of the tree of the knowledge of good and evil] willingly, then the will is the first thing in us that became subject to suffering. Therefore . . . if the *logos* did not assume it along with the [rest of human] nature when he became incarnate, I have not been set free from sin. And if I have not been set free from sin, I have not been saved, since whatever is not assumed has not been saved.[113]

When dealing with the way Christ's human will functioned in practice, Maximus found it difficult to accept that Christ should have been subject to

[111] This term, along with its active form *thelêsis* (found in the Septuagint, cf. Ezek. 18:23; Prov. 8:35), was preferred by Maximus because it was biblical. Pagan Greeks had normally used *boulêsis* for "will," not *thelêma* or *thelêsis*, neither of which occurs in philosophical writing.

[112] Maximus the Confessor, *Opuscula* 16.

[113] Maximus the Confessor, *Disputatio* 325B. The last phrase picks up Gregory of Nazianzus, *Epistula* 101.

the same limitations that afflict sinful human beings. We exercise our wills in selfish and ignorant ways, but that could hardly have been the case for someone who was sinless.[114] Maximus was reluctant to make a clear distinction between the natural limitations of the flesh and those which had entered in as the result of sin, but although he has been criticized for this, he was very clear that the human will of Christ was moved not by the divine will but by the divine person of the *logos*. In other words, Christ's human will was free to make moral choices and was not predetermined by a power greater than itself.[115]

The Christology of Maximus was developed entirely within a Chalcedonian context and made no impression on either the monophysites or the Nestorians, who by then had gone their separate ways. It tightened up the formulas of Leo in his *Tome*, which had been adopted at Chalcedon, and gave new weight to them. Maximus was rewarded by the unflinching support of the West, and his perspectives were finally canonized at the Third Council of Constantinople. Since then they have been the lens through which Chalcedon has been read, though the failure to realize this in modern times has led to criticism of the council that would be unjustified if Maximus's teaching were more widely appreciated than it is.

The Third Council of Constantinople (680–681) was the last time that the Eastern and Western Chalcedonian churches acted in complete harmony with each other. A decade later, another council was called to meet in Constantinople in order to complete the work of the fifth and sixth ecumenical councils by setting out a series of disciplinary canons designed to regulate the everyday life of the church. Because it was an appendix to the fifth and sixth councils, it is sometimes known as the "Quinisext" (Greek, *Penthektê*) council, but as it met in the imperial palace of Trullum, it is usually referred to as the Council *in Trullo*. It was there that the Eastern church decreed that only leavened bread should be used in celebrating the Lord's Supper, on the ground that unleavened bread represented a Judaizing practice, even though Jesus himself undoubtedly used it. It was also there that it was decreed that, in the future, bishops must be celibate. Married men could continue to be ordained as priests, but if a priest's wife died, he could not marry again. These rules, and others like them, created a distinctive framework for the life of the Eastern Orthodox Church which continues to characterize it to this day.

The canons of the Council *in Trullo* were rejected in the West, however, which preferred to set out its own rules. Few people noticed it at the time, but over the centuries this was to produce a different kind of church. The result

[114] On this, see the discussion by Bathrellos, *Byzantine Christ*, especially 148–172.
[115] Maximus the Confessor, *Opuscula* 1, 3, 15; *Ambigua* 1345D.

was that, centuries later, when East and West came face-to-face in the Crusades (after 1096), they met not so much as sister churches but as aliens to one another. More immediately, contacts between Rome and Constantinople were frayed by events beyond the control of either of them. The Arabs who had conquered Syria and Egypt two generations before were on the move once more, and in 698 they extinguished Roman rule in North Africa. By 711 they were invading Spain, led by their intrepid commander Tariq.[116] In a few years they destroyed the Visigothic kingdom there and advanced into Gaul, until the Franks finally repulsed them at Poitiers (732). In the East, they invaded Asia Minor and laid siege to Constantinople in 717, though without success. The survival of the Christian world seemed to be in doubt, and it was at this moment of existential crisis that the next and, as it proved, final act in the drama of Christological definition made its appearance.

The Portrait of Christ

The troubles that befell the worldwide church in the seventh century were to leave lasting scars that are hidden or perhaps misunderstood today because the whole period is obscure in our minds. In 626 Constantinople was besieged by a tribe of pagan barbarians known as the Avars, who have since disappeared from the historical record. The danger they posed may have been exaggerated but it was deeply felt at the time, and in popular opinion the city was delivered only by miraculous divine intervention. In a highly charged emotional atmosphere, the population gave credit for the victory to an image of Christ that (it was said) had not been made by human hands, that had been carried around the walls during the siege. It also prompted Romanus Melodus to compose a hymn in honor of the Virgin Mary, who was regarded as the patron saint of the capital. The *Akathistos* ("not seated") hymn, as it is known, commemorated the all-night vigil held before the decisive battle in which Mary's aid was sought. It subsequently entered the Eastern church's liturgy, where it remains to this day.

These events occurred shortly before the rise of Islam, which was very much opposed to the idea that God could be represented in human terms and which denied both the Trinity and the incarnation of the Son. Between 632 and 642, Muslim Arabs invaded and occupied Syria, Palestine, and Egypt, where they imposed their language and religion so thoroughly that they have never been uprooted. As the impact of these Islamic conquests sank in, it was only natural

[116] They landed at a place they called "the rock of Tariq" or *Jabal-al-Tariq*, which has been corrupted by use into the more familiar "Gibraltar."

that the surviving parts of the Christian empire, which we may now more appropriately call "Byzantine" rather than "Roman," were psychologically and spiritually unsettled.[117] The Council *in Trullo* reflected this to some extent by seeking to regulate and limit the power being ascribed to sacred images as protectors. Canon 73 forbade the decoration of floors with the sign of the cross, canon 82 insisted that Christ should be depicted in human form and not as a lamb, and canon 100 made a distinction between good and bad images, the latter being pictures that stirred up shameful desires and pleasures instead of promoting devotion to God.

Trouble was brewing, and eventually it led to a confrontation between popular and learned theological perceptions about the value of images. Then as now, intellectuals were more moved by the spoken and written word than they were by pictures, but the nonintellectual populace thought differently. For them, images depicted what they believed, and they clung to them with a devotion that to more educated people smacked of paganism. Controversy erupted in the reign of the emperor Leo III (717–741), who had delivered the city from its Arab besiegers and set about rebuilding the fortunes of the empire. Leo came from Isauria, a mountainous region in Asia Minor not far from the Christian-Muslim frontier. Its inhabitants had an austere way of life and may have been influenced by Islamic opposition to images in worship. Whatever the case, it was in Leo's reign that open opposition to images was first expressed. It used to be thought that Leo ordered their destruction in a decree issued in 726, but lack of evidence has cast doubt on this claim.[118] It now seems more likely that real opposition to icons broke out only in the reign of his son, Constantine V (741–775). What is certain is that opposition to icons came to be associated with the Isaurian dynasty and remained a live issue in Byzantine politics as long as the descendants of Leo III remained in power.

The ostensible reason for this iconoclasm, as the controversy is now (somewhat misleadingly) known, is that God cannot be pictured, and so no image of Christ could capture his true identity. The invisibility of the divine is an ancient biblical principle that no one wanted to deny, but the issue was more complicated than that. In Jesus Christ, the Son of God had become a man, and as such he was obviously visible. It must have been possible to paint his picture, though

[117] "Byzantine" from Byzantium, the name of the capital before it was changed to Constantinople. It should be remembered, though, that the rulers there always called themselves Romans and never Byzantines. Even today, Greek Orthodox Christians living in Turkey are known as "Rum," not as "Yunan," which is Turkish for "Greek" (cf. "Ionian").

[118] See Leslie Brubaker, *Inventing Byzantine Iconoclasm* (London: Bristol Classical, 2012), which contains an excellent bibliography of the subject. For original texts, see Daniel J. Sahas, *Icon and Logos: Sources in Eighth-century Iconoclasm* (Toronto: University of Toronto Press, 1986); and for a more general history, now somewhat dated, Edward J. Martin, *A History of the Iconoclastic Controversy* (London: SPCK, 1930).

we have no evidence that anyone did so during his lifetime. Pictures of people undoubtedly affect the way we perceive them, and nowadays many people keep photographs of those who are close to them. Often they display such pictures prominently and they may even kiss them from time to time as a sign of their devotion to the person being pictured. Of course, they would be the first ones to agree that the pictures are no substitute for the reality they represent, but that does not stop them from using the pictures as a visible reminder of what is important to them.

If we are happy to do this with friends and relatives, why should we hesitate when it comes to Jesus? Should he not be even more precious to us than they are? Put like this, the use of icons becomes more comprehensible, and it was not long before the Byzantines perceived the underlying Christological questions that they raised. There were always people who objected to iconoclasm, and some of them went to great lengths to defend the veneration of icons. Outside the empire, John of Damascus (675?–749?), writing from his monastic cell in Jerusalem, put up a spirited defense of icons, despite the fact that he lived under Muslim rule and must have been more sensitive than most to the theological issues involved.

The basic question was whether it is possible to paint a picture of the incarnate Son of God. At one level, the answer to this had to be yes, because Jesus was a man who could be seen by others, whether they believed in him or not. On the other hand, we have no idea what he looked like, and the New Testament gives us no guidance in the matter. We can assume that he must have had the physical features of a Middle Eastern Jew of the first century, because he did not stand out from his contemporaries in any noticeable way. He probably had a beard, because beards were common in the circles in which he moved and because his nomadic lifestyle would have made shaving difficult. Beyond that, we cannot go. If we were meant to make pictures of him, it might be asked, would we not have been given some directions to go on? There is certainly no suggestion that anyone in the New Testament church produced icons, although the catacombs in Rome preserve Christian art from the second century onward.[119]

It seems most likely that the practice of painting pictures of Christ and the saints became common in the fourth century, as large numbers of illiterate people joined the church and had to be instructed in Christian doctrine. These icons were never just artistic creations; they were theological statements that used specific symbolic representations to convey Christ's true humanity and

[119]Interestingly, in the earliest Christian art Jesus is usually portrayed as beardless!

his sinlessness. Around his head were the Greek letters for *ho ôn* ("he who is"), the biblical name of God attributed to Christ in Revelation 1:8. Photographic accuracy was never the aim of the iconographers, and attempts at such realism would almost certainly have been regarded as trivial, if not blasphemous, because the humanity of the Son of God had been glorified by his ascension into heaven.

Having said that, the physical visibility of the incarnate Christ was the theological starting point for iconography and remains so. The issue at stake was the relationship between his human nature and his divine person. His divine nature is invisible and cannot be painted, but his human nature obviously can be. But can we paint a human nature without portraying the person? When we look at portraits today we recognize the person being depicted and focus on him or her, not on the human nature of the accompanying body, which we take for granted. In theological terms, painting the person of Christ in his human nature is an expression of *enhypostasia*. Indeed, we may go further than that and say that *enhypostasia* makes painting pictures of Jesus almost necessary in order to convey the reality of the union between the divine person and the human nature. Pictures tell us, more than words can ever do, what meeting Jesus must have been like for those who saw him in the flesh. They can help us to understand, better than anything else, what awaits us in the kingdom of heaven, when we shall see him in his glorified state. Like everything on earth, icons are no more than a pale reflection of heavenly realities, but they are nevertheless aids to help us imagine what those realities must be like, and those who promoted icons believed that they must be treasured for that reason. They are gateways to the heavenly glory, even though in themselves they fall as far short of that as we do.

When faced with this kind of argument, the Western church has always found itself in something of a dilemma. On the purely theological issue it is difficult to deny the case put forward for icons, because to do so calls into question the reality of Christ's incarnation. *Enhypostasia* is as much a Western doctrine as an Eastern one, and no one in the Christian world objects to making pictures of Christ. The problem does not lie in the pictures but in the use to which they are put. We may treasure photographs of family members but we do not normally talk or pray to them as if they were a means of reaching the people they portray. Even if there are some people who go to such extremes, no one would claim that it is the right way for us to make contact with our loved ones.

Western Christians tend to think this way about icons. The pictures themselves are unobjectionable, and many are very beautiful. They may well focus our minds on Christ and make us reflect more deeply on him. But to argue that they are a means of getting closer to God, that we should venerate them and make them a focus of our worship is another thing altogether. That smacks of idolatry, however much the charge may be denied by the Eastern Orthodox churches. Here we come up against an instance where fundamental doctrinal agreement has produced different reactions to the way that doctrine should be worked out in practice. The main reason for this is that the Eastern churches have been strongly influenced by a mystical theology that is present in the West but remains basically alien to its devotional spirit. The iconoclast controversy is another sign of that fork in the road between East and West that was going to produce very different theological traditions and lead to centuries of hostility and mutual recrimination. Ironically, these have been all the more intense thanks to the large area of theological agreement that undergirds them but was unable to hold them together.

Iconoclasm was the official doctrine of the Byzantine empire until 787, when it was condemned at the Second Council of Nicea. Even then it did not disappear but made a comeback in 815 and was not finally defeated until 843. That defeat was celebrated as the so-called "triumph of Orthodoxy" and is still commemorated in the Eastern Orthodox churches on the first Sunday in Lent. The West, on the other hand, was largely indifferent to this and never took icons on board as part of its devotional life. Roman Catholics decorate their churches with pictures and statues, but although they occasionally pray in front of them, they do not emphasize this in the way that the Eastern Orthodox do. Protestants on the whole reject the practice entirely, though they are quite happy to paint pictures of Jesus, Mary, and the disciples for educational purposes.[120]

What we are faced with here is a good example of what can happen when minds do not meet. Something that is essentially agreed upon at the theological level has worked out very differently in practice, and the distinctiveness of the Eastern and Western traditions is clear for all to see. The Second Council of Nicea was recognized as the seventh (and for the Eastern churches, final) ecumenical council, and its endorsement of icons marked the final stage in the development of ancient Christology. Its reception in the West was more formal than real, however, not least because Byzantine power in Italy had virtually disappeared by then. The imperial capital of Ravenna had fallen to the Lombards in 751, and Rome was in real danger of coming under pagan rule once more.

[120] One of the most detailed critiques of icons can be found in the Anglican homily "Against Peril of Idolatry," printed as the second sermon in the *Second Book of Homilies* issued in 1563. The Anglican author, who was probably Bishop John Jewel of Salisbury, was attacking the superstitious use of images that was common in his time, but he was quite familiar with the Byzantine debate, which he described at length.

To avert that, its bishop, whom we may now refer to as the pope, appealed to the Franks, who were the only remaining Christian power in the West. The Franks duly responded, defeated the Lombards, and handed the former imperial territory in central Italy over to the pope. This was the beginning of the Papal States, which remained independent until they were finally absorbed into the resurgent Kingdom of Italy in 1870. By 787 the popes were looking to the Franks to protect them rather than to the Byzantines, and when Charles the Great, usually known to us by his Old French name "Charlemagne" (772–814), visited Rome in 800, the pope crowned him as emperor of the "restored" Western Roman empire. This restored empire went through a number of changes over time, but as the Holy Roman Empire of the German Nation (as it came to be called in the Middle Ages) it managed to survive until 1806. But by 800 the ancient world of the New Testament and the early church had finally passed into history, and a new era of church life had begun.

Retrospect and Prospect

By the time the iconoclastic controversy came to an end, the Christian world had been preoccupied with the doctrine of the person and natures of Christ for half a millennium—as long as the entire history of the Americas since the time of Christopher Columbus. Creeds had been composed and councils had been held, the decisions of which have remained foundational to the present day. The schism caused by the Council of Chalcedon still remains but it has become fossilized and is no longer divisive in the way that it once was. Both sides now admit that it was a quarrel over words more than substance and that it was exacerbated by personalities and politics on both sides. Formal reunion may still be some way off, but the atmosphere has changed and it is now possible to study the history of ancient Christology with more objectivity than it was in the past.

For most churches, including all those in the Western tradition of Christianity (Roman Catholic and Protestant), the Chalcedonian formula, interpreted through the lens of Leontius of Jerusalem, Maximus the Confessor, and their associates, remains the benchmark of Christological orthodoxy. It is sometimes challenged by individual theologians wanting to make a point, but it has never been overturned. It took the church a long time to reach this conclusion, but it has proved stable and enduring, a genuine achievement in spite of the many failings of those who fought for it and the difficult circumstances in which so much of the doctrine had to be elaborated. Given that history, it is hardly surprising that when the result was finally accepted by the majority of the

Christian world, the desire to call a halt to further theological exploration, with its attendant controversy, was very strong. Among the Eastern Orthodox, the seven councils came to be fixed in the mind of the church, and to this day they constitute the bedrock of its theology and disciplinary practice. The West was less dogmatic about this, but as its theologians were scarcely worthy of the name for several more centuries, that hardly mattered. After 800 there was a definite pause in theological creativity as the churches absorbed the lessons of the past and appropriated their inheritance.

The classical centuries of Christian theological formation were preoccupied with the question of Christology, as we can see from both the Apostles' and the so-called Nicene Creed. Although they are Trinitarian in shape, their longest section deals with the person and life of Jesus Christ, the Son of God. The main events of Jesus' earthly life are detailed in the creeds because they were seen to have theological significance, reminding us that it was not just who Jesus was but what he did that makes him our Lord and Savior. At the same time, we must remember that what we now call "soteriology," that is to say, the doctrine of the Savior and salvation, did not exist as such in the ancient world. Soteriological questions were discussed within the framework of Christology. For example, the adequacy of Christ's atoning sacrifice was not measured by the degree to which it complied with the provisions of the law of Moses. Instead, it was gauged by the extent to which he was a real man and able to be our substitute on the cross. His fitness to be our sacrifice was more important than the act of sacrifice itself, the efficacy of which could be taken as read once his qualifications were verified. This does not mean that Christ's atoning death was unimportant, but that it was interpreted in categories relating to his being and identity as the God-man, rather than in terms of covenant fulfillment.

It was not obvious to anyone at the time, but the resolution of the Christological problems thrown up by Arianism and Nestorianism raised further questions that would have to be answered in due course. One of these was the identity of the Holy Spirit. If the Father was fully God and the Son was equally divine, what could be said about the divinity of the third person of the Trinity? Where did he fit in? The other question was connected to the incarnate life and work of Christ. Why was his sacrifice necessary, and what did it achieve? Where is Jesus now, and what is he doing on our behalf, if anything? These questions were implicit in the development of Christology but they were not developed in ancient times. It was enough to confess that Jesus died, rose again, ascended into heaven, reigns in glory at the Father's right hand, and will come again in judgment. The pattern of Jesus' life, death, and resurrection was clear, but the saving significance of each aspect of it was not fully explored.

Which way would the church's theological development go? Would it concentrate on what we now call the work of Christ (soteriology), or would it move on to the person of the Holy Spirit (pneumatology)? Either direction was possible and in fact both were taken, but with the significant condition that the Western church leaned toward the work of Christ and the Eastern church to the person of the Holy Spirit. We must not press this too far, but after the Third Council of Constantinople in 681, differences appeared that would eventually lead to the separation of the Eastern and Western traditions. It was a very gradual process and was not fully recognized until the late eleventh century, when the crusading movement brought them together in what was supposed to be a common enterprise but turned out to be more of a catalyst for further division. By the time theologians got to work on the issues involved, it had become clear that the two halves of Christendom had gone their separate ways and were no longer in communion with one another, even if it is hard to say exactly when the split became definitive.

Historians who examine these developments cannot pass judgment on them but must record the facts and try to explain the processes by which the separation evolved. Theologians are more likely to want to evaluate the different pathways in terms of "right" and "wrong," and since a high proportion of those who study these matters are theologians or theologically trained historians, their approach cannot be ignored. What is there to be said in favor of (or against) the options actually chosen, even if they were only subconsciously followed by those who were immediately involved?

In favor of moving from the person of the Son to the person of the Holy Spirit, it can be argued that this is the most logical Trinitarian progression. The doctrine of the Holy Spirit was undeveloped before the fourth century, but this was noticed at the time, and attempts were made to put it right. It must have seemed natural to the Cappadocian fathers that "pneumatology" would rise to take its place alongside Christology as a complementary doctrine that would be structured along similar lines. Just as the person of the Son was being defined in order to make his work comprehensible, so the person of the Holy Spirit would have to be expounded for the same reason. The Nicene Creed, with its "expanded" section on the Holy Spirit, shows what they had in mind. The validity of this approach has never been questioned, but it is remarkable how the doctrine of the Holy Spirit was developed by looking at his work and projecting back from there to consider the identity of his person. Basil of Caesarea was the first major theologian to devote a complete work to the Spirit, and that is how he proceeded. It is called the inductive method—starting from the evidence provided by the Spirit's work and building up a case for his divinity, rather than starting with the Trinity and deciding from there what might be said about the person of the Spirit.

This pattern has been continued in Western theology to the present day. There are relatively few books written about the person of the Holy Spirit, and in systematic theologies the question of his identity within the Godhead is usually passed over fairly quickly. What really interests Western theologians is the Holy Spirit's work, which takes up the bulk of their reflection about him. The Eastern churches have followed the Cappadocian approach and paid more attention to the Holy Spirit's personal identity, arguing that once that is defined his work falls naturally into place. In fact, Eastern theologians have never reflected very deeply on the work of either the Son or the Holy Spirit, except when they have been prodded into doing so by the influence of the West.

Western theology moved more naturally from the person and natures of Christ to a detailed consideration of his work. The person of the Holy Spirit was not ignored, but the question of his identity was usually discussed only when the different approach of the Eastern tradition was perceived and it was thought that an answer to it had to be found. Today we can attempt to achieve a balance between these two approaches, but we cannot deny our history. Modern theologians in the West who look to the East for inspiration soon find themselves wondering whether they have to ignore or even reject their own tradition. For some, this is welcome because it seems to offer a way out of the differences created by the Protestant Reformation. Why not resolve the conflicts over justification by faith and predestination by appealing to a kind of theology that does not understand what they are? It is an approach that many find attractive, but it is hardly realistic. The issues that shaped and divided Western Christendom over a millennium did not emerge in a void, nor can they be wished away. The Eastern tradition reminds us that other developments were possible, but in the West those developments either did not occur or played only a secondary role. We may regret this, but we must deal with the inheritance we have received and seek to understand its importance for our perception of Christian truth today and not to try to wish it away.

For its part, the Eastern tradition must also take on board the issues developed and debated in the West for the past one thousand years. Its theologians cannot write them off as heretical deviations caused by schism and the excesses of papal power, as some of them have tried to do. To follow the fathers of the church is to follow the Bible that inspired them, and the Bible makes it clear that the covenant history of Israel is foundational to our faith. The Eastern tradition has largely ignored this and has suffered as a result, though there are signs that this may now be changing.

Whether we should move on from Christology to soteriology or to pneumatology was at one time a matter of preference but has now become a question of tradition. Those of us who write from a Western perspective have little choice—our history takes us to soteriology first and then to pneumatology, though the two things have always been closely connected. Someone writing from an Eastern perspective would probably move on to pneumatology and pass over soteriology altogether because it does not fit easily into this pattern. This book is written from a Western standpoint and so it puts soteriology first, though readers may rest assured that the road less traveled has not been forgotten and will be given due attention in the section (Part Six) that follows the next one.

PART FIVE

The Work of the Son

12

The Body of Christ

The Man from Heaven

At what point in the history of salvation can we begin to speak about the work of the Son as distinct from that of the Father? That the Son was eternally present with the Father is clearly affirmed in the New Testament,[1] but before he became a man in Jesus Christ it is hard to find anything that can be regarded as primarily or exclusively his work. The early Christians combed the Hebrew Bible for references to the eternal Son and were prone to regard every theophany (appearance of God) or reference to the divine Word (or Wisdom) as pertaining to him. The problem with this was that although the Word and Wisdom of God are personified aspects or extensions of the divine being, the Jews never thought of them as persons in their own right. The early Christians, however, identified them with Jesus Christ, because that is how they thought the New Testament presented them. "The Word became flesh and dwelt among us"[2] was one of the best-known texts in the Gospels, and was frequently quoted in that sense. The apostle Paul called Christ the power and wisdom of God,[3] in another verse that was cited at regular intervals. Since both the Word and the Wisdom of God referred to the Son, the two terms were easily conflated with each other, allowing early Christian writers like Origen to cite Proverbs 8:22, where Wisdom says, "The Lord created me at the beginning for his works," as proof that the Son was Co-creator of the world, along with the Father.[4]

It was virtually axiomatic to the early Christians that any Old Testament encounter with God was a vision of the Son. Irenaeus was quite explicit about this:

> The Son of God is embedded everywhere in Moses' writings. At one point he spoke with Abraham as they were about to sit down to eat. On another

[1] John 1:1–3; Col. 1:15–16.
[2] John 1:14.
[3] 1 Cor. 1:24.
[4] Origen, *De principiis* 1.2.1–2. See also Irenaeus of Lyon, *Adversus omnes haereses* 4.20.1, and Clement of Alexandria, *Stromateis* 5.16, for other early examples of this. The text quoted was the Greek Septuagint (LXX) version.

> occasion, he was with Noah, giving him the blueprint [for the ark]. Another time, he asked where Adam was. Yet another time, he called down judgment on the people of Sodom. Sometimes he even became visible, directing Jacob on his journey and speaking with Moses from the [burning] bush.[5]

Of all the Old Testament passages that could be read in this way, by far the most important was the vision of the Son of Man in Daniel 7:

> I saw in the night visions,
> and behold, with the clouds of heaven
> there came one like a son of man,
> and he came to the Ancient of Days
> and was presented before him.
> And to him was given dominion
> and glory and a kingdom,
> that all peoples, nations, and languages
> should serve him;
> his dominion is an everlasting dominion,
> which shall not pass away,
> and his kingdom one
> that shall not be destroyed.[6]

Few if any Old Testament texts are quoted or alluded to in the New Testament as often as this one, which is mentioned five times in the four Gospels and five times in the book of Revelation.[7] To these occurrences may be added such incidents as Jesus' reply to Caiaphas, when he told him that "you will see the Son of Man seated at the right hand of Power and coming on the clouds of heaven."[8] According to Daniel, the Son of Man has been given a universal and eternal kingdom, a gift that is frequently mentioned in the New Testament, not least by the apostle Paul, who told the Philippians that "at the name of Jesus every knee should bow, in heaven and on earth and under the earth, and every tongue confess that Jesus Christ is Lord,"[9] and told the Corinthians that "God has put all things in subjection under his feet."[10] Seen from the perspective of human history, Jesus' glorification followed naturally on his death, resurrection, and ascension, but Jesus himself put it in its wider context in his so-called "high priestly" prayer in John 17:

---

[5] Irenaeus of Lyon, *Adversus omnes haereses* 4.10.1.
[6] Dan. 7:13–14. This text was quoted, for example, by Tertullian, *Adversus Marcionem* 4.10.
[7] Matt. 24:30; 28:18; Mark 13:26; Luke 1:33; John 12:34; Rev. 1:7, 13; 11:15; 14:14; 19:6.
[8] Matt. 26:63–64.
[9] Phil. 2:10–11.
[10] 1 Cor. 15:27.

> I glorified you [the Father] on earth, having accomplished the work that you gave me to do. And now, Father, glorify me in your own presence *with the glory that I had with you before the world existed.*[11]

In the early third century, Hippolytus of Rome picked up this wider dimension and tied it all together:

> Who was in heaven but the Word unincarnate, who was sent in order to demonstrate that he was present on earth as well as in heaven. He was the Word, the Spirit and the power [of God], who took on the name that was common and current among men. From the beginning, he was called the Son of Man because of what he would become, even though he was not yet incarnate, as Daniel testified.[12]

The eternal presence of the Son in heaven with the Father was important to the early Christians because it was the basis for their arguments against the Arians and others who denied his divinity, but their emphasis was Christological rather than soteriological. The Son's divine status was the essential prerequisite for his incarnation, but it was only after he became a man that his work became clearly distinct from that of the Father and acquired a particular significance of its own. Irenaeus expressed this as follows:

> It was the Word of God who became the Son of Man. He received the power to forgive sins from the Father. He was man and he was God. This was so that he could suffer for us as man and have compassion on us as God.[13]

What the Son did in heaven before he came to earth he did in concert with the Father, and it was in the context of the one God that his work had to be understood. This was most obvious in the case of creation, where Father and Son worked together and were practically indistinguishable from each other. The New Testament insists that the Son was the Creator and heir of all things, a confession that clearly differentiated him from any creature and guaranteed his divine status.[14] But important as that was, the creation was never regarded as a work of the Son as such. Tertullian described the Word as "the Lord's right hand, indeed his two hands, by which he operated and made the universe," and Tertullian's way of thinking may be regarded as typical of the time.[15]

---

[11] John 17:4–5.

[12] Hippolytus of Rome, *Contra Noetum* 4.

[13] Irenaeus of Lyon, *Adversus omnes haereses* 5.17.3.

[14] John 1:1–4; Col. 1:15–17.

[15] Tertullian, *Adversus Hermogenem* 45. In the ancient creeds, the article dealing with the Father calls him the Creator and the Almighty, but this confession is not extended to the Son or to the Holy Spirit, even though Chris-

For the early church, the work of the Son, as distinct from that of the Father, began with his incarnation and was expounded in that context. As God the Creator, Father and Son were one, but as God the Redeemer, their roles were differentiated. The Father sent the Son into the world but did not enter it himself. The Son, on the other hand, left his heavenly glory and became a man.[16] At the heart of the distinction between Father and Son was the Son's experience of suffering and death, which was alien to the divine nature but essential for the saving work that the Son had been sent to accomplish. Tertullian explained both the connection and the difference between the work of the two persons by using a familiar analogy:

> How could the Son have suffered, but not the Father? The Father is separate from the Son, without being separated from him as God. A river that flows from a fountain has the same nature as it has and is not separated from it. But if the river becomes polluted with dirt and mud, the harm done to it does not stretch back to the fountain. Of course, it is the fountain's water that suffers, but only after it has flowed downstream. The source itself is left untouched.[17]

The distinctiveness of the Son's work in his incarnate state is clear from the creeds, which devote a lengthy second article to the life, death, resurrection, and return of Jesus Christ, singling out particular high points that had saving significance for believers. Even more important, it is expounded in the New Testament itself:

> . . . he [the Son] is before all things and in him all things hold together. And he is the head of the body, the church. He is the beginning, the firstborn from the dead, that in everything he might be preeminent. For in him all the fullness of God was pleased to dwell, and through him to reconcile to himself all things, whether on earth or in heaven, making peace by the blood of his cross.[18]

In these few words, the apostle Paul delineates for us how the work of the Son would be understood by Christians through the ages. Its component parts can be analyzed as follows:

1. Along with the Father, the Son is the Creator and Preserver of the universe, but as the Redeemer, he is the head of the church, which is his body. The old creation is being transformed and renewed in the church.

---

tians believed that creation was the work of all three persons acting together and was not the exclusive preserve of the Father.

[16] Phil. 2:6–7; John 17:5.

[17] Tertullian, *Adversus Praxean* 29.

[18] Col. 1:17–20.

2. The Son is the initiator of his work and remains sovereign over it. He is not subject to any higher power, nor does he abandon his new creation to its own devices.

3. The Son's death on the cross has reconciled the world to himself. Because of his sacrifice, the universe is now at peace with God, whether his creatures accept that or not. The implication of this is that there is no other way of salvation—those who want to benefit from the reconciliation of God and man can do so only by being united in (and submitted to) Jesus Christ.

4. His death heralded the start of a new life in his resurrected state. The members of his body, the church, have died and risen again with him. They share in his new life as adopted children of God," as the apostle Paul described it.[19]

These were the parameters within which the doctrine of the work of the Son was developed by the early Christians. As the quotation from the apostle Paul implies, the incarnate body of Christ was their point of departure. As they saw it, the Son of God had become a man for a reason. His human nature was an integral part of his mission and an obvious point of contact with us. What happened in and to that body was a demonstration of what he had come to do on earth. The sufferings of his earthly life had a purpose in God's plan of salvation, and the ascension of his body into heaven took the work that he accomplished in time and space and raised it to eternity. The big difference between the Danielic vision of the Son of Man and the Christian confession of the risen, ascended, and glorified Son of God is that Daniel gave no indication that the Son's body played any significant part in his work. The church, however, proclaimed that it was in the suffering and death of that body that Christ's work had been fulfilled and taken up into heaven, where the Lamb slain from before the foundation of the world continues to plead for us before the Father's throne.[20]

To be incorporated into Christ—made part of his body—was not only to benefit from the work that he has done on our behalf but also to be allowed to share in it in some mysterious way:

> Then Jesus told his disciples, "If anyone would come after me, let him deny himself and take up his cross and follow me. For whoever would save his life will lose it, but whoever loses his life for my sake will find it. For what will it profit a man if he gains the whole world and forfeits his soul? Or what shall a man give in return for his soul? For the Son of Man is going to come with

[19] See Gal. 4:1–7; Titus 3:7.
[20] See Rev. 13:8.

> his angels in the glory of his Father, and then he will repay each person according to what he has done.[21]

Later on, Paul wrote to his disciple Timothy in the same vein: "If we have died with him, we will also live with him; if we endure, we will also reign with him."[22] The work of the Son was not something to be observed from a distance but something in which Christians were called to participate, not as equals but as people whose lives had been transformed by his. The external rules of the Jewish law had been done away with by the work of the incarnate Son, who had fulfilled the promises given to the Jews and made their sacrificial and other ritual works redundant. As Paul told the Galatians,

> I have been crucified with Christ. It is no longer I who live, but Christ who lives in me. And the life I now live in the flesh I live by faith in the Son of God, who loved me and gave himself for me. I do not nullify the grace of God, for if righteousness were through the law, then Christ died for no purpose.[23]

The incarnation found its ultimate meaning in the sacrifice and death of Jesus on the cross. Christ, into whose body Christians have been grafted, is the one by whose sufferings we have been healed and through whom we have been born again to a new life.

The Water and the Blood

Being put to death for one's beliefs was extremely rare in the Greco-Roman world, which liked to pride itself on its rationalism. The notorious case of Socrates, who was forced to commit suicide by the Athenians in 399 BC, was held up as an example of supreme virtue in the face of popular stupidity, and the image stuck. In Roman times there were a few intellectuals who suffered a similar fate for political reasons—Cicero in 43 BC and Seneca in AD 65—but as in the case of Socrates, their virtue was quickly recognized. Seneca's death at the command of the emperor Nero even became a factor in blackening the latter's reputation.

The case of Jesus was different. Political considerations played a part in his trial and crucifixion, but they were not decisive. Jesus went to his death because of his claims and his teaching, which offended the Jews far more than anyone else.[24] What is more, Jesus had followers in a way that Socrates and Cicero did

[21] Matt. 16:24–27.
[22] 2 Tim. 2:11–12.
[23] Gal. 2:20–21.
[24] Matt. 27:15–26.

not. As early as AD 64, Nero was able to launch a persecution of Christians based on nothing more than their adherence to the sect. For the next 250 years the Roman authorities regarded Christians as worthy of death without ever managing to explain why—an absurd injustice that Christians were able to turn to their profit in a series of appeals (known as "apologies") to the reason and conscience of the ancient world. Their arguments were irrefutable, but still the persecutions continued. Why?

It was not long before Christians began to claim that they were being persecuted because they represented a spiritual power that was inimical to the world. Furthermore—and this is the important point—death was the supreme manifestation of this. Christianity was all about dying and being born again, in union with Christ's sufferings and resurrection. When they met to worship together, Christians broke bread and drank wine in remembrance of Christ's death, a ceremony so solemn in its implications that anyone who abused it would bring down divine judgment on himself.[25] To be allowed to share in Christ's sufferings was a badge of honor, which every Christian was privileged to share. In the words of Paul,

> Do you not know that all of us who have been baptized into Christ Jesus were baptized into his death? We were buried therefore with him by baptism into death, in order that, just as Christ was raised from the dead by the glory of the Father, we too might walk in newness of life.[26]

Baptism was a kind of death, and the new life was one of suffering on Christ's behalf. It was the experience of particular individuals, to be sure, but their afflictions belonged to the whole church. As Paul told the Corinthians,

> If we are afflicted, it is for your comfort and salvation; and if we are comforted, it is for your comfort, which you experience when you patiently endure the same sufferings that we suffer.[27]

A more explicit link between the sufferings of the believer and those of Christ can be found in what Paul writes to the Colossians:

> Now I rejoice in my sufferings for your sake, and in my flesh I am filling up what is lacking in Christ's afflictions for the sake of his body, that is, the church.[28]

[25] 1 Cor. 11:24–29.
[26] Rom. 6:3–4.
[27] 2 Cor. 1:6.
[28] Col. 1:24.

What is particularly interesting about this statement is Paul's reference to "what is lacking in Christ's afflictions." Does this mean that Christ's suffering and death were not enough for the salvation of his body, the church? Was it necessary for believers to add to Christ's work by contributing their own tribulations to it? Paul nowhere hints at such a conclusion, and much of what he says would seem to rule it out, but to Christians who were trying to make sense of their own travails, the idea that they were somehow contributing to their own salvation had an obvious appeal.

It is also interesting to note that while the New Testament recognizes martyrdom for the name of Christ and even glorifies it in the case of Stephen, the first Christian martyr, it does not make a habit of this.[29] There is a hint at the end of John's Gospel about how Peter would be put to death, but we are told no more than that.[30] Of Paul, nothing is said at all—we last see him dwelling peacefully in his own hired house in Rome, apparently waiting for his case to come to trial.[31] What happened later we are not told, though ancient traditions say that Paul, like Peter, was martyred for his faith, in Rome, and there is no reason to doubt them. Martyrdom was in the air, and dying for Christ was seen as a privilege, but it was never elevated to the status reserved for the crucifixion of Jesus in the Gospels. His death was paradigmatic for his followers but it remained qualitatively different from theirs. Some people apparently thought that any martyr could forgive sins on the strength of his own sacrifice, but Tertullian denounced this error, saying,

> Let a martyr purge his own sins. . . . Who can redeem another's death by his own, apart from the Son of God?[32]

Christians shared in Christ's suffering not by imitating it but by being united to his death by baptism and by feasting on his body and blood in the Lord's Supper.

That message was clear enough to most people, but it raised questions when the nature and effects of baptism were analyzed. Granted that baptism was a dying with Christ and a washing away of sin, the application to the individual believer of an act that had been anticipated by his sacrifice on the cross, what would happen if the believer in question were to sin again *after* being baptized? What did the writer to the Hebrews have in mind when he wrote,

[29] Acts 7:54–60.
[30] John 21:18–19.
[31] Acts 28:30.
[32] Tertullian, *De pudicitia* 22.

> It is impossible, in the case of those who have once been enlightened, who have tasted the heavenly gift, and have shared in the Holy Spirit, . . . and then have fallen away, to restore them again to repentance, since they are crucifying once again the Son of God to their own harm and holding him up to contempt.[33]

What did Jesus mean when he told his disciples that he had another baptism, one that was clearly associated with his suffering and death but of which his disciples had no experience?[34] Tertullian explained it like this:

> We have a second font . . . one of blood. . . . He sent out these two baptisms from the wound in his pierced side, so that those who believed in his blood could be bathed with the water, and those who had been bathed in the water could drink his blood. This second baptism is equivalent to the first, if that one has not been received, and restores it if it has been lost.[35]

Questions like these puzzled the early Christians, who naturally wanted to know how all this affected them. In particular, the problem of what to do about sins committed after baptism ("post-baptismal sins") became a pressing issue. Tertullian was especially exercised by this:

> God had foreseen . . . that even after baptism, faith would be endangered. He saw that most people would fall away again after obtaining salvation . . . and therefore provided another means of comfort and a second chance for salvation—the fight of martyrdom and the baptism of blood.[36]

By the time Tertullian sat down to write about baptism, sometime around AD 200, it was generally agreed that it was the essential initiation rite into the life of the church, the body of Christ. Union with him meant the washing away of sin, which is what baptism did.[37] Most people were baptized on profession of faith, because the majority of church members were converts from the pagan (or occasionally Jewish) world, but the rite was not primarily understood as the confirmation of an already existing faith, as it is among most Baptists (or so-called "credo-baptists") today. No one in the early church doubted the objective efficacy of baptism, as long as it was properly administered in the name of the Trinity. People who had been baptized only in the name of Jesus had to receive

[33] Heb. 6:4–6.
[34] Matt. 20:22–23; Mark 10:38–39; Luke 12:50.
[35] Tertullian, *De baptismo* 16.
[36] Tertullian, *Scorpiace* 6.
[37] For a thorough study of this subject, see Everett Ferguson, *Baptism in the Early Church: History, Theology, and Liturgy in the First Five Centuries* (Grand Rapids, MI: Eerdmans, 2009).

the laying on of hands in order to receive the Holy Spirit, whereas those who had received John's baptism for repentance were presumably baptized again (at least sometimes) because the purpose for which John had baptized was different from Christian baptism.[38]

It is important to understand that when the legitimacy of infant baptism was rejected by Tertullian, it was not because the children who received it lacked the faith needed to make the rite valid. Tertullian was worried because he believed that a small child who received baptism was genuinely cleansed from sin, and feared that he would almost certainly sin again without realizing it, thereby losing his salvation. Like a kind of spiritual vaccination, baptism took effect whether the recipient was aware of it or not, and it was for that reason that Tertullian thought it should be avoided. Once baptized, a person was cleansed from sin and had to continue in that state, which was no easy thing to do. Tertullian suggested that baptism should therefore be delayed as long as possible, so that adolescents could get sin out of their system, so to speak, and be baptized only when they were ready to settle down:

> The delay of baptism is preferable, particularly in the case of little children. Let children come when they are growing up, and when they are learning where they should come. Let them become Christians when they are old enough to know Christ. Why should innocent children rush into asking for forgiveness of their sins? We do not give them responsibility in this world, but we are quite happy to let them have spiritual responsibility. . . . Those who understand how important salvation is will be more afraid of receiving it than delaying it.[39]

Tertullian is often accused of rigorism, but his baptismal policy was remarkably liberal and compassionate, given the assumptions he made about the significance of the rite. He did not want anyone to lose his salvation because of some youthful indiscretion, which is why he advised putting it off as long as possible. But in a society where up to half the babies born died in infancy and life expectancy for those who survived was not high, such a policy was extremely risky. Unwilling to leave things to chance, the church organized catechetical classes in which new converts were instructed in preparation for baptism, which they received as soon as the authorities thought they were ready to handle the responsibilities that it entailed.

Leading a sinless life was possible only if the concept of "sin" was defined in an external and legalistic way, as the Pharisees had done. This was essen-

[38] For the former, see Acts 8:14–17; for the latter, see Acts 19:1–7.
[39] Tertullian, *De baptismo* 18.

tially Tertullian's approach. Of course he insisted that the righteousness of the Christian must exceed that of the scribes and Pharisees, but according to him, the way to achieve this was by being even stricter and more legalistic than they had been.[40] That was not what Jesus had meant by those words, but that did not worry Tertullian. For him, baptism was the gateway to sinless perfection, and if that were not attained, the believer would lose his salvation. It was here that martyrdom came to the rescue. A Christian who sinned after baptism could redeem himself, not by trusting in the shed blood of Christ for salvation (because he had already rejected that) but by shedding his own blood as a martyr. Those who lost their lives because of their faith went to heaven, because the blood of martyrdom was a baptism that cleansed them from all sin. In Tertullian's words,

> We have a second cleansing, which is one and the same, and is that of blood, of which the Lord said, "I have to be baptized with a baptism," although he had already been baptized. For he had come by water and blood, just as John wrote, in order to be made wet by water and glorified by blood, which is why he would make us called by water and chosen by blood. He poured out these two baptisms from the wound of his pierced side, so that those who would believe in his blood would be washed in water, and those who would be washed in water would also bear his blood. This is the baptism that makes a washing that has been rejected available again, and that restores what has been lost.[41]

Tertullian's view was the one that dominated the North African church, but it was by no means peculiar to that province. Writing less than a generation later, Origen put it like this:

> Inasmuch as the martyr receives forgiveness of his sins, he is baptized. For if baptism promises forgiveness of sins, . . . and if one who endures the baptism of martyrdom receives that forgiveness, martyrdom may quite rightly be called a baptism.[42]

Seen in this light, martyrdom was not only beneficial, it was virtually necessary for most church members, who otherwise had no hope of entering heaven because they had sinned after baptism. In this scenario, persecution became a blessing in disguise. It was a second chance at redemption, and one that true

[40] Tertullian, *De monogamia* 7.
[41] Ibid., 16. Tertullian says much the same thing in several other places besides this one. Cf., e.g., *Scorpiace* 6; *De pudicitia* 22; *De resurrectione carnis* 43; *De anima* 58.
[42] Origen, *Commentarium in Matthaei Evangelium* 16.6.

believers would embrace with alacrity. Moreover, there was every indication that it would continue to be available until the return of Christ at the end of time. The fact that the world was at enmity with the people of God guaranteed that persecution would never cease, as Paul had assured Timothy.[43]

Those who did not suffer came under the suspicion that they had escaped it by compromising with the world. In the great persecution that occurred in the reign of Diocletian (285–305), many prominent Christians saved themselves by handing over the Scriptures to the authorities, who then burned them publicly. These "handers-over" (or *traditores* in Latin) were regarded as apostates, and attitudes toward them can be gauged from the fact that our word "traitor" is derived from *traditor*. After the persecution ceased, many of these people sought readmission to the church, which was normally granted if they confessed and demonstrated their contrition by some act of repentance. But there were many who were appalled at such leniency and who believed that the legalization of Christianity had come about because the church had compromised with the enemy. True believers had to reject it and embark on a course that would provoke the state into resuming its customary opposition to the church, which could feel spiritually secure only as long as it was being persecuted by the rulers of this world.

This was the mentality that assured the success of Donatism in North Africa. It was not the only part of the Roman empire to experience a reaction against the legalization of the church, but elsewhere the outcome was different. In Egypt, a certain Meletius, the bishop of a place called Lycopolis, led a group that broke away from the church at Alexandria. However, his schism was fueled by personal animosities between him and the successive bishops of Alexandria, and it seems that the question of showing clemency to repentant *traditores* was just an excuse to continue quarreling.[44] In its initial phase, the reaction against the legalization of Christianity at Carthage was remarkably similar to what happened at Alexandria—a relatively lenient bishop (Caecilian) was opposed by a rigorist (Majorinus) who split the local church. Bishops elsewhere supported Caecilian, but since they also welcomed the state's change of policy toward Christians and were even prepared to ask for the emperor's help in regaining control of the Carthaginian church, that support was highly suspect. Majorinus soon died and was succeeded by Donatus, the man who gave his name to the movement and guaranteed that it would not die out

[43] 2 Tim. 3:12.

[44] The bishops of Alexandria who were involved with the Meletians were Peter (d. 311), Alexander (312–328), and Athanasius (328–373). Meletius had taken over the administration of the Alexandrian church after Peter, whose attitude toward the backsliders was lenient, was imprisoned. When Peter was martyred, Meletius quickly positioned himself against his legitimate successor (Alexander) and the feud developed from there.

when those who had initially been involved passed from the scene.[45] Curiously enough, given the subsequent history of Donatism, Donatus took his case to the emperor Constantine, who referred it to a synod of bishops summoned to meet at Arles in 314. That synod sided with Caecilian, and from then on, the anti-Donatists had the might of the Roman empire on their side.

The result was tragic. On the one hand, secular forces were readily employed by the church against the Donatists, who became rebels against imperial authority as well as schismatics. Even a century later, attempts at reconciliation were bedeviled by this, with each side harking back to the original events and blaming the other for having started the whole thing.

Why did people go on sinning after baptism if they had been cleansed from it? To this the Donatists had a simple answer. The baptism of the mainline church was ineffective because it was administered by unworthy people. They claimed that a man who was himself a sinner could not administer a rite that would take away someone else's sin, and so "baptism" performed by such a person was ineffective. This was why anyone who had been baptized in the mainline church had to be baptized again upon joining the Donatists, and why a person so baptized would then be expected to lead a sinless life. Put like this, there were a number of inconsistencies in the Donatist position that Augustine had no trouble picking up. First, Donatus and the first generation of his followers had all been baptized in the mainline church and did not rebaptize each other when they broke with it, on the ground that they had not been properly baptized to begin with. Furthermore, they had all been ordained, and some had even been consecrated as bishops, by men who had shown leniency to backsliders and who were therefore "sinners." How could they reject a form of church order that they themselves depended on for their authority? For its part, the mainline church did not regard Donatist baptisms as invalid, because it respected Donatist ordinations and recognized all baptisms performed in the name of the Trinity, regardless of who had performed them.

As for the worthiness of the minister, the mainline church thought that this was both unknown and irrelevant. To use a secular analogy, a doctor who is ill is not thereby prevented from giving patients a vaccine to protect them against the same illness, so why should a sinful clergyman be unable to baptize others? As Augustine explained the matter,

> How is someone to be cleansed through baptism when the conscience of the man who is to baptize him is polluted without his knowledge? . . . Will such

[45] See William H. C. Frend, *The Donatist Church: A Movement of Protest in Roman North Africa* (Oxford: Oxford University Press, 1952; repr., 1972).

> a man receive faith or guilt? . . . According to the Donatists' judgment, the salvation of the spirit is uncertain as long as they turn the hope of those who are to be baptized away from the Lord their God and persuade them that it should be placed in man instead. This is in direct opposition to the Holy Scriptures, which say, "It is better to trust in the Lord than to put confidence in man"[46] and, "Cursed be the man who trusts in man."[47] The practical result of this is that salvation becomes not merely uncertain, but null and void.[48]

The validity of baptism did not depend on the spiritual state of the minister, the orthodoxy of the church, or even the faith of the recipient. It depended on the promise of Christ, who had given baptism to his followers and enjoined them to practice it as a means of spreading the gospel.[49] To reject it, or to replace it with something else, was to reject Christ. Given that in baptism we are united to Christ in his death and resurrection, to deny its power was to deny the sufficiency of Christ's atoning work. If post-baptismal sin could cancel the effects of baptism, then there were sins for which Christ had not died and which his sacrifice was unable to remit. In other words, the grace of God the Father revealed in his Son was not enough, and something more was required for salvation.

The Donatists tried to get around this by saying that the original baptism was invalid, but as we have already seen, that was a weak argument. The trouble was that they had nothing else to offer. They could deny that they rebaptized people by claiming that whatever baptism had preceded theirs was no more effective than John's baptism had been. To the charge that there is only one baptism, the Donatists replied that it was administered in three stages, each of which was greater than the previous one. First, there was John's baptism for repentance, then Christ's baptism with the Holy Spirit, and finally the Paraclete's baptism with fire.[50] Augustine answered this by pointing out that John's baptism was qualitatively different and looked forward to a greater baptism that was to come, the baptism of Christ which was in the Holy Spirit and fire simultaneously. As he put it,

> If the water of John refers to the one baptism, it was not right that those who had been baptized by John should have been rebaptized on the orders of the apostle Paul.[51] They already had the water part of baptism, so all that

[46] Psalm 118:8.
[47] Jer. 17:5.
[48] Augustine of Hippo, *Contra epistulam Parmeniani* 1.2–3.
[49] Ibid., 1.5–7. See Matt. 28:19–20.
[50] Ibid., 2.32.75.
[51] Acts 19:1–7.

> remained was the Holy Spirit and fire, because these were lacking in John's baptism, and then theirs would be complete. . . . But because they were ordered to be baptized on the apostle's authority, it is sufficiently clear that the water of John's baptism had nothing to do with the baptism of Christ, but belonged to a different dispensation, adapted to the needs of the times.[52]

It is not hard to see how Augustine was able to refute the Donatist claims, but he still had to address the underlying question about the nature of the church. In the New Testament the church is called the "body of Christ" because it is an extension of his incarnate human nature. In time, the church is "militant here on earth," the community of those who are engaged in spiritual warfare against the world, the flesh, and the Devil as part of their pilgrim journey toward the City of God. But there is also the church triumphant in heaven, consisting of the saints of both the Old and the New Testaments,[53] who are now rejoicing in the presence of their Lord at the victory he has won over the powers that the church militant is still battling against.

What the Donatists believed was that the church militant ought to be victorious here on earth. They agreed that we are called to fight against our spiritual enemies, but those enemies are (or ought to be) external to us. To fight successfully against them we have to be purged of any trace of their influence in our lives, which means that we must become perfect. To the Donatists, real Christians had ceased sinning altogether, and the true church consisted only of such people. To support this contention, they appealed to the human nature of Christ, which was sinless. If the church is his body, then surely it must be sinless too, because otherwise it would not fit into his overall nature. This is a subtle argument and was persuasive to many, but it ignores the difference between the visible and the invisible church. The Donatists quoted Cyprian of Carthage (200?–258) to the effect that "only those who are of one heart and mind dwell in the church of Christ,"[54] but Augustine was able to show that Cyprian was talking to men who were preaching Christ without love. They were

> . . . envious and malevolent, contentious and without love, but even so they used to baptize. Nor did the detestable waywardness which they demonstrated violate or diminish the sacrament of Christ that they handled in the slightest degree.[55]

[52] Augustine of Hippo, *Contra epistulam Parmeniani* 2.32.75.
[53] Heb. 11:39–12:1.
[54] Cyprian of Carthage, *Epistula* 69.5.
[55] Augustine of Hippo, *De baptismo* 7.49.97.

Men like Optatus of Milevis (c. 360–390) and Augustine, both of whom wrote extensively against the Donatists, give us the impression that they were exasperated by their opponents' obstinacy in refusing to rejoin the mainline church. Augustine, in particular, did not hesitate to argue that they should be forced back into it for their own good.[56] To him, Donatism seemed pointless and irrational, a sign that he did not understand its appeal to those whose theology was anchored in the pre-Constantinian era. In a letter written about AD 417, Augustine had this to say about their thirst for martyrdom:

> Every day they kill themselves by jumping off steep precipices, or by drowning or burning themselves. The Devil has taught them these three types of death, so that when they want to die and cannot find anyone they can force to turn their swords on them, they throw themselves onto rocks, or into fires or floods. Who was it but the Devil . . . who quoted the Law to suggest to our Savior that he should jump down from the pinnacle of the temple?[57] If they really had Christ in their hearts, they would surely protect themselves from such temptations.[58]

Donatism never expanded outside Roman Africa, which was one of its chief weaknesses. But although it could not appeal to the witness of the universal church in the way that its opponents did, it was not an ephemeral phenomenon either. Personal animosities played their part in creating the schism, but they are not enough to explain its enduring appeal. North African Christianity had developed a theology of martyrdom that touched not only on the nature of the church but also (and more fundamentally) on the significance of the saving work of Christ. By linking those two things together, Donatism acquired a significance that it would not otherwise have had. The Donatists set up a rival church organization with its own bishops, teachers, and preachers that survived until after the Muslim conquest of North Africa in 698.

As Augustine saw it, however, Donatism was quite literally a dead end. Those who pursued it to its logical conclusion ended up killing themselves, whereas those who did not were hypocrites in separating themselves from the mainline church merely because its members were doing the same thing as they were! The theology of martyrdom had reached the point where it was either self-destructive or inapplicable, but that did not end the controversy, because underlying it was the doctrine of the church, which had not yet been properly worked out. To a faith whose chief symbol is the cross of Christ, martyrdom

[56] Augustine of Hippo, *Epistula* 173.10.
[57] Matt. 4:5–7; Luke 4:9–12.
[58] Augustine of Hippo, *Epistula* 185.12.

was to have an enduring appeal. Long after the doctrine of baptism had lost any obvious connection with it, echoes of the "baptism of blood" could reappear, sometimes in surprising places. Consider, for example, the well-known words of Augustus Toplady's hymn "Rock of Ages":

Let the water and the blood
From thy riven side which flowed
Be of sin the double cure
Cleanse me from its guilt and power

The double cure? The Donatists would have recognized this combination—the water of baptism and the shedding of blood, which together bear witness to our union with Christ and the forgiveness of sin that he brings. The difference is that for Toplady and the mainline Christian tradition, it was only the blood of Christ that cured the effects of sin, and not that of martyrs.

The Likeness of Sinful Flesh

What Augustine did not explicitly say, but what would become apparent after the Council of Chalcedon, was that the church as the body of Christ lived in the dimension of his human nature and not of his divinity, where sinlessness would obviously be taken for granted. Why was Christ's human nature sinless? Was perfection inherent in it, or was it dependent on some other cause? The insistence of most of the church fathers that Jesus was a human being just as we are strongly suggested that Jesus was not sinless by nature, because if he had been, he would not have been like us. Jesus could have sinned, and the apostle Paul even said that the Father had sent him "in the likeness of sinful flesh and for sin,"[59] but he did not. His human nature was preserved from that, not because it possessed any inherently supernatural quality, but by the grace of God. Even if it is true that as the Son of God incarnate, Jesus was better placed to receive that grace than we are, he still needed it in order to remain in the sinless state in which he had come into the world. Jesus did not save us by setting an example of how to behave if we want to be sinless in the way that he was, but by embracing our sinfulness, by *becoming* sin for us even though he was in no sense a sinner himself, and paying the price for that sinfulness that we would otherwise have had to pay.[60]

The body of Christ is a pierced body, a body that has borne the weight of sin and that is no stranger to its effects. Our salvation does not reside in it

[59] Rom. 8:3.
[60] 2 Cor. 5:21.

but in the one to whom it belongs. Of course, we must be part of the body, because the Son of God did not bear our sins in any other form, but it is the means to an end and not the end in itself. This is where Donatism had gone wrong. It had failed to discern the body of Christ, which can be known only in the breaking of the bread that stands for the broken body of the sacrificial Lamb.[61] Instead of recognizing Christ's body broken for them, the Donatists had broken it afresh by claiming that Christ's body did not know the consequences of sin. They had forgotten that Jesus had come to bring sinners to repentance and not to preach to the righteous, who thought they had no need of a Savior. They did not understand that the way to be united to Christ was not to become sinless as he was sinless, which was impossible, but to be grafted into him by means of his wounds and the blood that flowed from those wounds for our redemption. For the branch to be grafted into the tree, the tree must first be cut and its inner life revealed, since otherwise that inner life cannot flow into us.

To look for perfection in the body of Christ, as the Donatists did, was to ignore its wounds, and to ignore them was to ignore our salvation. Their way of thinking makes sense only if we realize that it is the divine person of the Son in his human nature that is being held up as the model for us to follow. Although it never denied any creedal doctrine, Donatism was perceived to be a kind of Christological heresy and it was attacked on that basis. The ensuing controversy brought out the fact that embedded in the doctrine of the two natures of Christ was a particular understanding of what he had achieved for us and for our salvation. The atoning work of the Son was possible because as the Son of his Father he was sinless, but as a man he could become "sin" for us, so that by dying in his human nature he could cancel our debt to God and bring us to heaven. Christians are baptized into Christ's body, not in order to be made perfect but in order to find forgiveness of sins in his atoning blood, to which union with his body gives us access.

Baptism is therefore the beginning of a life lived in the grace of forgiveness, not the end of sin and the beginning of perfection, as the Donatists claimed.[62] The Donatists had put so much emphasis on the outward form of belonging that they had lost its inner substance. Water by itself could never wash away sins; that could only be the work of the reconciling love of God poured out into our hearts by the power of his indwelling Spirit. By separating themselves from other believers, the Donatists had shown that they lacked that love, and so their baptism was an empty sham, however technically "correct" it may have

[61] See 1 Cor. 11:29.
[62] Augustine of Hippo, *De baptismo* 4.18–20 (26–28).

appeared.[63] Augustine had broken through the logjam that had been created by an inadequate understanding of what baptism was, but only because he had addressed the Christological nature of the church. The church was a hospital for sinners and not a club for the perfect; a place of healing and redemption, not of false expectation and hypocrisy—a body, in sum, that ordinary people can join and in which they can find comfort for their souls without being expected to be better than they actually are.

But if the church did not expect its members to be perfect, how sinful were they allowed to be? Could anyone belong to it, or were there some standards that were expected, even if they fell short of the ideal? Augustine soon found himself having to consider those questions, not so much in relation to the Donatists, who were more preoccupied with the church's ministers than with its lay members, as in connection with a different teaching altogether, which was unrelated to Donatism but was just as closely connected to the work of Christ in the life of the believer as Donatism was.

As far as Augustine was concerned, the Donatist controversy was essentially resolved at the Council of Carthage in 411. That was not the end of the schism, of course, but after 411 serious theological debate about it faded into the background. In its place came another challenge to the church's teaching about baptism, which was brought to North Africa by refugees fleeing the sack of Rome by Alaric the Goth in 410, and which first surfaced at the council in the following year. Some of these refugees had absorbed the teaching of a British monk named Pelagius, who had been preaching in Rome and insisting that human beings had the free will to accept or reject the grace of God at work in their lives.[64]

At first Augustine was reluctant to engage in controversy with Pelagius, and tried to suggest that he was merely reporting the assertions of others and not claiming to believe them himself.[65] Augustine was aware of Pelagius's reputation as a holy man and found it hard to believe that he could have been led astray so badly. Pelagius's commentary on the Pauline epistles was so highly regarded that after his condemnation it was recycled under the name of Jerome (340?–420), and later on under that of Cassiodorus (485?–585?), and so it survives to the present day.[66] What is more, in some respects Pelagius's New Testament text was superior to that possessed by Augustine, which often

[63] Ibid., 1.11 (16).

[64] By "British" we mean that he was probably a Romanized Briton, an ancestor of the modern Welsh, Cornish, and Breton peoples. He was certainly not English, because the Anglo-Saxons had not yet invaded Roman Britain.

[65] Augustine of Hippo, *De peccatorum meritis et remissione* 3.1, 5–6.

[66] *Expositiones XIII epistularum Pauli*, ed. Alexander Souter (Cambridge: Cambridge University Press, 1926). An English translation of the commentary on Romans has been published in Theodore De Bruyn, *Pelagius's Commentary on St. Paul's Epistle to the Romans* (Oxford: Oxford University Press, 1993).

makes modern readers more inclined to trust his judgment in places where the two differ.

This was particularly significant in their different interpretations of Romans 5:12, a verse on which Augustine placed considerable weight. As Pelagius read it, the text said, "Therefore, just as through one man sin came into the world, and through sin death, so death passed to all men, in that all sinned."[67] This is a fair representation of the original Greek, but Augustine read something different: "Through one man sin came into the world and through sin death, and thus it was passed on to all men, in whom all have sinned."[68] This misreading, in which it was sin and not death that was passed on to the human race, was not Augustine's fault. It was the translation that had come down to him, and he read it sincerely, but its inaccuracy inevitably makes his interpretation suspect. As a result, Augustine's teaching on this subject has come in for a lot of criticism, and a good many modern commentators have rejected it on the grounds that it is not what Paul was saying.[69] That, however, does not mean that we should prefer the theological interpretation of Pelagius, who commented on it to the effect that sin had come into the world and spread "by example or by pattern":

> Just as through Adam sin came at a time when it did not yet exist, so in the same way through Christ righteousness was recovered at a time when it survived in almost no one. And just as through the former's sin death came in, so also through the latter's righteousness life was regained. . . . As long as people sin in the same way that Adam did, they will die.[70]

In his magisterial commentary on Romans, Charles Cranfield rejected this view because, ". . . it reduces the scope of the analogy between Christ and Adam to such an extent as virtually to empty it of real significance, and fails to do justice to the thought of vv. 18 and 19 and to that solidarity of men with Adam which is clearly expressed in 1 Cor. 15:22."[71] It is quite clear that for Augustine, sin and death were intimately connected—the one led directly to the other. Modern readers will probably disagree with Augustine's belief that the physical death of the human body is the direct result of sin, but although

[67] De Bruyn, *Pelagius's Commentary*, 92.
[68] Augustine of Hippo, *De peccatorum meritis et remissione* 1.10. See the translation of this work by Roland Teske, *Saint Augustine: Selected Writings on Grace and Pelagianism* (New York: New City, 2011), 73–214.
[69] For a full and fair discussion of the exegetical issues, see C. E. B. Cranfield, *A Critical and Exegetical Commentary on the Epistle to the Romans*, 2 vols. (Edinburgh: T & T Clark, 1975, 1979), 1:269–281. Cranfield concludes that although Augustine's reading of the verse must be rejected, his understanding of the theological issues was sound and is supported by the wider context.
[70] See De Bruyn, *Pelagius's Commentary*, 92.
[71] Cranfield, *Romans*, 1:277.

it is true that Augustine did think that, he was also aware that Adam was created as a mortal being and that the death caused by sin was spiritual, not physical.[72] Human beings are spiritually dead without Christ, even though they are physically alive, a contrast that was fundamental to Augustine's thought. When trying to decide whether Augustine was right or wrong in his debate with Pelagius, we must bear in mind that it is possible to abandon some aspects of his argument without denying the validity of its essential thrust.

As Augustine recounted it, his first encounter with Pelagianism was circumstantial:

> A short time ago, when we were in Carthage, I heard in passing from some people who were casually chatting, that infants are not baptized in order to receive the forgiveness of sins, but in order to be sanctified in Christ. I was disturbed by this new idea, but since it was not the right moment for me to say something against it and since they were not the kind of people whose potential influence worried me, I paid no attention. But look at what has happened. That idea is now being zealously defended and even preserved in writing. A crisis has blown up and our brethren are asking us about it, which is why we are being forced to write against it.[73]

Augustine was surprised by what he heard because he thought that everyone agreed that little children were in need of salvation. The question had surfaced more than 150 years previously, in a dispute about whether children should be baptized on the eighth day after their birth (which is when Jewish boys were circumcised) or as soon as they were born. In arguing for the latter position, Cyprian had written,

> Even the most serious transgressors and those who had sinned a lot against God receive the forgiveness of sins when they believe, and we hold no one back from baptism and grace. How much more then, should we refuse to hold back a newly born infant who has committed no sin, apart from having contracted the disease of death by being born in the flesh as a child of Adam? An infant receives forgiveness of sins more easily [than an adult] because it receives forgiveness, not for its own sins but for those of someone else [i.e., Adam].[74]

Augustine did not know it, but he could have quoted both Irenaeus and Origen to the same effect.[75] It is important to bear in mind that infant mortality

---

[72] Augustine of Hippo, *De peccatorum meritis et remissione* 1.4–8.
[73] Ibid., 3.12.
[74] Cyprian of Carthage, *Epistula* 64.5. Quoted by Augustine of Hippo, *De peccatorum meritis et remissione* 3.10.
[75] Irenaeus of Lyon, *Adversus omnes haereses* 2.22.4; Origen, *Homiliae in Leviticum* 8.5.

rates in the ancient world, and in many places until very recently, were extremely high. What to us is an unfortunate (but thankfully rare) occurrence, to them was a daily experience for which a sensitive pastoral response had to be found. In that situation, we can easily understand why Pelagius's teaching would have come as a great relief to many. An infant who had committed no actual sin would not be held guilty before God and would be saved without the need for baptism. We can sum up Pelagius's beliefs as follows:

1. Every human being is born in the innocent state in which Adam and Eve were created.
2. Human beings sin because they do what Adam did, and so they die as he died.
3. There are a few righteous adults who have not sinned, though they are exceptional.
4. Everyone who has sinned needs Christ as his Savior, and must therefore be baptized.
5. Children who die but have not committed an actual sin belong to Christ.
6. Infants who have not sinned do not need to be baptized (though they may be).

In answer to this, Augustine made the following counterassertions:

1. No human being is born in the innocent state in which Adam and Eve were created.
2. Human beings sin because they are born sinful, and die for the same reason.
3. There is no such thing as a sinless person—child or adult—except for Jesus Christ.
4. Everyone has sinned and needs Christ as his Savior, and must therefore be baptized.
5. Children who die without committing actual sin may or may not belong to Christ.
6. Infants who have not sinned still need to be baptized, because they are born sinful.

In the case of adults, the Pelagians accepted that almost all of them were sinners and so needed Christ as their Savior. But Pelagius made an exception of certain people who are described in the Bible as having been "righteous," and he used them as evidence that it was possible to live a sinless life. Here Augustine found himself in something of a dilemma. He did not deny that sinlessness was possible; Jesus of Nazareth was an obvious case in point. But

Augustine went further than this. Noting that God told his people to lead holy lives, he said,

> I cannot doubt that God has not commanded human beings to do anything impossible and that nothing is impossible for God in terms of assisting and helping us to accomplish what he commands. Hence, human beings can, if they so desire, be without sin, if they are helped by God.[76]

But having admitted that, Augustine immediately went on to add that there is not, and never has been, any example of such a person. The men and women praised in the Bible for their righteousness were not sinless, as the case of Job illustrates. Job never did anything wrong, but after his temptations were over, God still rebuked him for his ignorance, and he would not have done that if Job had been perfect.[77] For good measure, Augustine went on to quote Paul, who said that an unbelieving spouse and children were sanctified by the presence of a Christian in the family.[78] For Augustine, this was a clear example of how it was possible to be "holy" and "righteous" without even being a believer. Did this mean that such people were saved in spite of themselves? Not at all. As Augustine observed,

> Whatever their sanctification may be, we must hold it as beyond any doubt that it cannot make them Christians or forgive their sins, unless they become believers by the teaching and sacraments of Christ and the church. No matter how holy and righteous their spouses are, nonbelievers are not cleansed from the sinfulness which forces those who have been excluded from the kingdom of God to enter into condemnation. And no matter how holy and righteous the parents are who begot them, infants are set free from original sin only if they have been baptized in Christ. We must speak all the more earnestly for them because they cannot speak for themselves.[79]

In the end, no one can escape the consequences of Adam's sin because we all inherit the separation from God and the guilt which that entails. This is true even of children who are born to Christian parents. One of the arguments used by the Pelagians was that because parents cannot pass on to their children what they do not have themselves, if they have been cleansed from sin, they will not give birth to sinful offspring.[80] Augustine refuted this conclusion in two ways. First, he said that human beings can only pass on to their children what

[76] Augustine of Hippo, *De peccatorum meritis et remissione* 2.7.
[77] Ibid., 2.14–18.
[78] 1 Cor. 7:14.
[79] Augustine of Hippo, *De peccatorum meritis et remissione* 3.21.
[80] Ibid., 3.15.

they have inherited from Adam and Eve. They may have been regenerated in Christ, but they did not inherit that and therefore cannot pass it on to the next generation. He illustrated this with some graphic examples from everyday life:

> If it bothers people [to think] that a sin which is washed away in baptism is nevertheless present in those to whom baptized parents give birth, how do they explain why the foreskin that is removed by circumcision is present in those who are born of circumcised parents? And how is the chaff which is so carefully removed by human labor still to be found in grain that grows from what that has already been threshed?[81]

But even the Pelagians had to admit that not all children of Christian parents are believers, something that would be impossible if two Christian souls naturally gave birth to a third like themselves. Augustine therefore concluded,

> No one is cleansed from sin by being born, but all are cleansed by being reborn. This is why a human being who has been born from human beings who have been cleansed because they have been born again, must themselves be born again in order to be cleansed. Parents could pass on to their offspring what they did not have, not only as grain passes on chaff and a circumcised man passes on a foreskin, but also as believers pass on unbelief. . . . This defect no longer belongs to those who have been born again by the Spirit, but it still belongs to the mortal seed from which they were generated in the flesh.[82]

The second way in which Augustine refuted the Pelagian claims was even more significant. It was one thing to argue that baptism was given to remedy the defects inherent in human nature but quite another to tie it directly to the saving work of Christ. At every point in his argumentation, Augustine kept returning to the fundamental fact that the Son of God had come into the world, not to save the righteous, but to bring sinners to repentance.[83] No one can enter the kingdom of heaven unless he is born again.[84] Jesus Christ is the way, the truth, and the life—no one can come to the Father except through him.[85] These verses and others like them run like a leitmotiv through everything Augustine wrote on the subject of sin and salvation. To quote but one striking example,

> To heal the sinfulness contracted by birth and increased by our will and to raise up this flesh, the physician came in the likeness of sinful flesh. It is not

[81] Ibid., 3.16.
[82] Ibid., 3.17.
[83] Mark 2:17; Luke 5:32.
[84] John 3:7.
[85] John 14:6.

those who are healthy who need him, but those who are sick, and he did not come to call the righteous, but sinners.[86]

Christ came to bring life to all those who were members of his body. His purpose was to save them, set them free, redeem them, and enlighten them so that they could enter the kingdom of heaven. His intention was to act as our mediator, so that after he had ended the hostility between us and God, we would be reconciled to him and rescued from eternal death. All this presumes that those who are saved need these things. But as Augustine clearly saw,

> Those who do not need life, salvation, liberation, redemption, and enlightenment cannot belong to the dispensation of Christ's grace. . . . Since that includes the baptism by which they are buried with Christ in order to be joined to him as his members (that is, as believers in him), they certainly do not need baptism, since they have no need of the forgiveness and reconciliation that comes through the mediator.[87]

To dispense with baptism was to reject the salvation offered to mankind in Christ. That salvation was the forgiveness of sins and reconciliation to God. The baptism of infants, which Pelagians agreed was desirable even if they did not think it was strictly necessary, made sense only if there was an inherited original sin, because infants have not sinned in their own right. From there, Augustine went on to argue that the baptism of infants was not merely desirable, but essential for their salvation. Quoting the words of Jesus when he said that the sheep hear his voice and that he gives them eternal life, Augustine added,

> Since infants start to belong to his sheep only by baptism, they will certainly perish if they do not receive it, for they will not have the eternal life that Christ gives to his sheep.[88]

Augustine's argument can be summed up as follows:

1. Only those who belong to Christ can be saved.
2. Baptism is the means by which we are incorporated into Christ.
3. Only those who have been baptized can be saved.
4. Infants must therefore be baptized if they are to be saved.

[86] Augustine of Hippo, *De peccatorum meritis et remissione* 3.21. See Matt. 9:12.
[87] Augustine of Hippo, *De peccatorum meritis et remissione* 1.39.
[88] Ibid., See John 10:27–28.

The Second Adam

Pelagianism made the mistake of leaving redemption open-ended and subject to our own will and effort. According to Pelagius's way of thinking, if I want to be saved I can be, and if I do not, I can turn away from God as and when I please. This is what Pelagius meant by free will, and according to him, this is what makes us truly human. Animals do what comes naturally to them and cannot go against that, but human beings are free to shape their own destiny and are even entrusted by God with that responsibility. It all sounds very attractive, but how true is it?

There is a great deal about us as individuals that we have not chosen. None of us has been asked to decide in what century we would be born, who we would have as parents, or what our sex, color, and nationality would be. All this and more has been given to us without our consent, and we have to make the most of our inheritance, whether we like it or not. In the world of time and space we have no freedom to alter these basic facts, and whatever "free will" we may possess is obliged to function within these parameters. Most important, we have not chosen to be sinners. Our sinfulness is part of our existence, not because sin is naturally inherent in all created beings (on account of our finitude) but because our first parents disobeyed God. Their legacy remains with us, and although its consequences can be mitigated and eventually reversed in Christ, we still have to live with them. As Augustine put it,

> You say that no one should have perished because of someone else's sin. It is true that Adam's sin was the sin of another person, but he is our ancestor, and for this reason his sins are ours, by the law of insemination and reproduction. Who can deliver us from this damnation, except the one who came to seek and to save that which was lost?[89] Therefore we find mercy in those whom he sets free but recognize the most secret judgment of God on those whom he does not set free, and we know that this judgment is very just.[90]

In essence, redemption is no more a human choice than creation is. Had God not decided to send his Son into the world, nothing any human being could have done would have altered the fact that we are condemned in his sight. Salvation is a gift of God bestowed on those whom he has chosen to receive it, whether they have asked for it or not. In the New Testament there is only one conversion story that is told at length, that of Saul of Tarsus, and it would be hard to think of anyone who was less interested in becoming a Christian than he was.[91]

---

[89] See Matt. 18:11; Luke 19:10.
[90] Augustine of Hippo, *Contra Iulianum* 1.48.
[91] Acts 9:1–19; 22:3–16.

Jesus met Saul on the road to Damascus in spite of his wishes or expectations, and imposed his will on him. Saul, or Paul as he was later known, really had no choice in the matter, and neither does anyone else. Those who meet with God know whom they have met, and they are powerless to turn away from him. The hallmark of the true convert is not that he has exercised his free will and accepted Christ but that his will is set free for the first time. He realizes that he has been in bondage to Satan, an evil force of whom he was previously unaware, and that he has now been delivered from that bondage. To know Christ is to walk in newness of life, and birth is not something that we can choose for ourselves.[92]

What has this got to do with the person and natures of Jesus Christ? Everything. Jesus is the Creator, the Son of God who came down to earth in order to be our Redeemer. In his incarnation he revealed himself to us as the Creator by his ability to rule the created order and make it bend to his will in ways that are not possible for other human beings. He had been the Creator since before the foundation of the world, and continues in that capacity now. Similarly, although he revealed himself as our Redeemer when he came into the world, his work of redemption did not begin with that. If it had, redemption would be confined to time and space and have no eternal validity. Instead, the Son has been our Redeemer just as long as he has been our Creator—from the beginning and in eternity. As Augustine wrote,

> The Lord says, "You have not chosen me but I have chosen you."[93] At the same time it is clear that they did choose him when they believed, but this was only because he had first chosen them for belief. . . . His mercy stepped in beforehand according to his grace, and not because he owed them a debt for having chosen him. He chose them out of the world while he was in the flesh, but they had already been chosen by him from before the foundation of the world. This is the changeless truth of predestination and grace.[94]

We do not know how that would have worked out if Adam and Eve had not fallen into sin, but the biblical picture of them in Eden is that they were not fully formed as human beings—they lacked the knowledge of good and evil and they did not possess immortality. Whether and how they would have acquired these things if they had not been deceived by Satan is unknown and unknowable, but the Bible tells us that there was room for future improvement even in the garden of Eden.

We do not know what God would have done had there been no fall, but we

[92] Rom. 6:4. Augustine says this in *De correptione et gratia* 13 (42).
[93] John 15:16.
[94] Augustine of Hippo, *De praedestinatione haereticorum* 17.34.

can say that the plan of redemption is just as firm and fixed in his mind as the plan of creation is. He knows who will be saved, when they will be saved, and in what circumstances they will turn to him. For God not to know this would be an admission that he is not truly sovereign, and for him to have delegated the responsibility for our salvation to us would be an abdication of his authority. We do not get to heaven because we want to go there but because God wants us to live with him in eternity—a rather different thing!

Here we are dealing with the mystery of predestination—to eternal bliss but also to eternal damnation (also known as "reprobation"). The two go together. If God has predestined only some to be saved, he must have done something else with the rest of humanity, or his control over the universe would be forfeited. Those who have not been chosen for salvation are condemned to eternal death, not because they have chosen it but because their will is not free to choose anything else. It is Christ who sets us free, and if he does not do that, then we have no other choice but to go to the damnation that awaits all those who turn away from God. Augustine made this point as follows:

> Why did God create people whom he knew would be condemned to hell and not saved by his grace? The blessed apostle explains this as succinctly and as authoritatively as he can when he says . . . that it would indeed be unjust if God had made vessels of wrath for perdition,[95] if they had not belonged to the universal race of the condemned that descends from Adam. What is made a vessel of wrath by birth receives its deserved punishment, but what is made a vessel of mercy by rebirth receives undeserved grace.[96]

This was the teaching that Augustine opposed to the free-will doctrine of Pelagius, which he understood to be a travesty of the truth. To portray God as a well-organized Creator, so skilled that everything in heaven and on earth coheres in a magnificent harmony, and then to add that in his capacity as Redeemer he has left our options open and does not know what we are going to decide, let alone control it, would be a denial of his sovereignty. The deliberate plan and foreknowledge of God was too important for that and could not be left to chance. As Augustine put it,

> If any of the elect perishes, God is mistaken, but of course none of them perishes, because God is not mistaken. If any of them perishes, God is overcome by human sin, but none of them perishes, because God is overcome by nothing.[97]

---

[95] Rom. 9:22.

[96] Augustine of Hippo, *Epistula* 190.3.9.

[97] Augustine of Hippo, *De correptione et gratia* 7 (14).

The Son who went to his death on the cross did so because his Father had already chosen those whom he intended to save.[98] The Son of God knew whom he was coming for, and he will not lay down his responsibilities until his task is fully accomplished.[99] The duty of the church is to bear witness to that, to share in it, and to rejoice that we can already enjoy its firstfruits. This is what union with Christ in his body means, and why predestination is so central to our understanding of what Christianity is. The divine Son of God is in possession of his human body, which includes those who have been, are being, and will be grafted into it in the course of his redemptive mission.

[98] This was the teaching of the apostle Peter. Compare what he says in Acts 2:23 with 1 Pet. 1:2.
[99] See 1 Cor. 15:28.

13

The Death of Christ

The Only Sacrifice for Sin

That Jesus died on the cross and rose again from the dead was universally believed among Christians. The centrality of the cross as the chief symbol of the Christian faith and the frequency of the Eucharistic memorial of his death brought this home to every new generation of believers and continues to do so. But why did the Son of God have to die? What did his death achieve that could not have been done some other way? Surely the most important thing for us is that we should repent of our sins and be forgiven. Was Christ's death really necessary for that to happen? Could not John's baptism, which was an act of repentance for the forgiveness of sins, have been enough? Today there are many people who regard blood sacrifice as something primitive and unworthy of a serious religion. They know that this language is used in the New Testament but prefer to ignore or to spiritualize it. The true sacrifice, they claim, is that of a broken and a contrite heart—something that was understood even in the Old Testament.[1] To their minds, the outward sacrifices might have been visual aids of some use to primitive peoples but they ought to be rejected by anyone who has a more spiritual concept of religion.

In premodern times people were much less squeamish about blood sacrifice than we are now. The slaughter of animals was a daily occurrence in the lives of most people, and grisly public executions were far from unknown. It would be too much to say that those who lived back then had a blood lust, but they were certainly more accustomed to seeing violent death all around them than we are. Even so, there was a general sense that such deaths should occur only in certain contexts. Punishment for crimes was one obvious one, but Jesus was innocent and his crucifixion was a gross injustice. Death in battle was another acceptable way to go, and in Jesus' case the eternal warfare between good and evil could be brought into play to explain what happened to him. But this had its difficulties, because evil was not supposed to get the upper hand. The Devil

[1] Psalm 51:17.

could not have killed the Son of God unless the Father had permitted him to do so, and why would the Father have done that when he had stopped Satan from killing Job?[2] Somehow the death of Christ had to have a purpose in the will of God that was not dependent on any sin or unworthiness in Jesus and was not the work of Satan either.

The answer given in the New Testament was that the Son of God had died in order to reconcile the world to the Father. The principle of reconciliation went back to the Old Testament, but there it was not linked to the incarnation of the Son as it was in the New. God's people had sinned against him, and in order to put matters right, they had to make sacrifices that would demonstrate the sincerity of their repentance and remove the barrier that their sins had erected between them and their Creator. God was the source of life, and to turn away from him was to court death. "The wages of sin is death"[3] was the principle, and so for sin to be taken away it was necessary to die. Strictly speaking, it was those who had committed the sins who ought to have died to pay for them, but that would have been self-destructive. If I died to pay the price for my sins, reconciliation between me and God would be impossible because I would cease to exist. This was already made clear to Abraham, the ancestor of the Jewish people, who was told to sacrifice Isaac, his son and heir, but was then shown a ram, which could be put to death as a substitute for him.[4] The principle of death by proxy was thus established at the very beginning of Israel's life, and it was this principle that was to be enshrined in the Mosaic law of sacrifices.

Jesus had been born under the Mosaic law, and it was in that context that he lived out his earthly life and went to his sacrificial death. He was the Lamb of God who took away the sins of the world by becoming the sin offering for us and dying on our behalf. Because he was the Son of God, his death was not only totally innocent but also immensely powerful. He could (and did) pay the price for every sin ever committed, thereby making the Mosaic pattern of sacrifices redundant. What the blood of animals could not do, the blood of Christ achieved in a way that went beyond the immediate circumstances of time and space and had eternal validity. This was the true and ultimate reconciliation that would never be replaced by anything better or become obsolete.

To what extent did the early church appreciate this New Testament doctrine of the atoning work of Christ? What they said about it was certainly not stated in those terms, a fact that has led some modern scholars to question whether it was part of their teaching at all. That they regarded Christ as the

[2] Job 1:12; 2:6.
[3] Rom. 6:23.
[4] Gen. 22:12–14.

Paschal Lamb who was slain from before the foundation of the world[5] is beyond doubt. The New Testament is perfectly clear about this, early Christian art made it a prominent theme, the cross became the central symbol of Christianity (even though its origins were anything but Christian or Jewish), and the worship of the church kept the memorial of Christ's sacrifice in clear view of the people.[6] Those who became Christians were baptized into his death, and the first day of the week, on which the resurrection occurred, was set aside to commemorate that event.[7] No one could have been around Christians or in a church for long without having these things firmly planted on their minds and in their memory, and what we now call the atoning work of Christ was a fundamental part of their belief and religious experience. But how far was its meaning developed?

We have already seen that in the early church there was a strong concentration on the Christological foundations that made Jesus fit to be the perfect sacrifice. There was also a deep sense that by the death of a sinless man, human sinfulness and alienation from God had been dealt with once and for all. The problem of evil was more than merely human, however. It had a supernatural dimension, in the form of Satan and his angels, that made it impossible for any man to save himself from the powers that rule the world, even if human beings are capable of doing good within a limited sphere. It is one of the apparent paradoxes of Christianity that good deeds on our part get us nowhere in the sight of God. This seems strange and unfair, especially since God himself is good, the world he made is good, and his desire and command for us is that we should also be and do good. Why does God apparently take no notice of our attempts to do what he wants? The trouble is that even if we want to obey him, we are blocked by the power of evil from which there is no escape. The only way out is for God to intervene and rescue us from Satan's power, which is what he did when he sent his Son to die on the cross. What exactly this meant was not immediately clear, however, and various interpretations of it were proposed. The main ones were as follows:

1. Jesus died for the Father, in obedience to his command. The mission of the Son was determined in heaven and then worked out on earth according to this prearranged plan. The Father approved of what his Son accomplished and rewarded him accordingly. This reward for his obedience is the basis of our salvation in eternity.[8] Justin Martyr expressed it well:

---

[5] Rev. 13:8.
[6] 1 Cor. 11:17–34.
[7] Rom. 6:3–4. On Sunday, see Rev. 1:10.
[8] Consider the so-called "high priestly" prayer of Jesus in John 17:1–26.

The entire human race is under a curse. . . . The Father of all wanted his Christ to take upon himself the curse of the whole human family, knowing that after his crucifixion and death, he would raise him up. . . . His Father wanted him to suffer this so that by his stripes the human race might be healed.[9]

2. He was dying for you and me. We need salvation, and he came to provide it by taking our sins on himself and blotting them out by the sacrifice of his blood. We do not have to fear the wrath of the Father when he comes to judge us, because our sins have been paid for by the Son, who is our Mediator and pleads for us to be forgiven. This payment of our debt to God is the basis of our salvation at the last judgment. In the words of Irenaeus,

In the first Adam we offended God, because Adam did not obey the divine commandment. But in the second Adam we have been reconciled to God and made obedient even to death. For we were debtors to no one except to him whose commandment we had transgressed. Therefore, in the last times the Lord has restored us into fellowship through his incarnation. He has become the Mediator between God and man, propitiating the Father against whom we had sinned, by his death. He has cancelled our disobedience by his obedience.[10]

3. He was dying to break the rule of Satan. From the beginning, it was this spiritual warfare that guided Christ's earthly ministry, as we can see from the temptations that came to him and the numerous occasions on which he cast out demons. The defeat of Satan marks the end of the rule of evil over us and sets us free to live for God in the world as he originally intended. This is the basis of our salvation now. As Irenaeus put it,

In these last days the Son was made a man among men, and he re-formed the human race. He destroyed and conquered man's enemy, and by doing that he gave his handiwork victory over the adversary.[11]

It is probably fair to say that the first two of these possibilities have always been widely believed by Christians. The second option is more immediate to us and therefore easier to grasp, which is probably why it is the explanation that we normally encounter. The first one is closely connected to it, because we need to know that the Son's sacrifice carries clout with our Judge in heaven, which

[9] Justin Martyr, *Dialogus cum Tryphone* 95.
[10] Irenaeus of Lyon, *Adversus omnes haereses* 5.16.3–5.17.1.
[11] Ibid., 4.24.1.

is likely only if the Son was doing what the Father wanted him to do in the first place. After all, if the Son had done something that the Father did not envisage or even objected to, we would hardly be assured that he had accomplished our salvation. Instead, we might well fear that if he were to be punished for his temerity we would go down with him.

It is the third option that seems strangest to us today and is the one least likely to be mentioned in the modern church, even though the creeds say of Jesus that "he descended into hell," a phrase that often perplexes modern believers. In the ancient world, however, and still today in many places, the reality of demonic power was never questioned. People who were firmly in the grip of Satan might not be able to express their plight very accurately, but they knew that something was seriously wrong in the spiritual realm and they were looking for an escape from it. One way or another, that is what most ancient religion was about—how to propitiate the malign forces that control our lives so that they will leave us alone and possibly even be driven away. In the New Testament, the word "propitiation" is used not of Satan but of God, something that has occasionally caused great perplexity and led to serious disagreement with the Christian teaching on the subject.[12] It is easy to understand why an evil power would want to be propitiated, but can this be said of a good and loving God?

The answer of course is yes, but we have to appreciate what Christian propitiation is. It is not an attempt to ward off an evil power, but the very opposite. Jesus' death is called a propitiation because it was designed to bring us nearer to God by removing the barriers that separate us from him. These barriers have been caused by our rebellion and the sinfulness that has resulted from that. If we want to get our relationship with God back on track, we have to take responsibility for the wrongs that have offended him, and that includes putting them right. That was accomplished by Jesus' sacrifice, which is why it was a propitiation for our sins. What is perhaps less widely understood is that the reason we cannot offer such a propitiation ourselves is not because of our human weakness, which the incarnate Son also shared. Nor is it because of our fallen human state, which he voluntarily took on himself. The real reason why we cannot do it is because the sin of Adam, the effects of which we have inherited, was not an independent act of his will. Adam and Eve did not decide to disobey God by themselves, but were tempted by Satan and ensnared by him in a way that Jesus never was. The Gospels record that at the beginning of Jesus' ministry, Satan did his best to make him fall into his hands, but Jesus resisted that temptation and went on to do his Father's will.[13]

[12] Rom. 3:25; 1 John 2:2; 4:10.
[13] Matt. 4:1–11; Mark 1:12–13; Luke 4:1–13. See also Heb. 2:18; 4:15.

Putting things right with God therefore meant destroying Satan's power over us as well as paying the price for our wrongdoing. Jesus' propitiation for our sins would hardly have been the definitive solution to the problem of evil if the cause of that evil had not been dealt with as well. A dentist can cap our teeth, but if he does not treat the underlying decay we shall not be cured and the problem will return. A doctrine of the once-for-all sacrifice of Christ cannot contemplate such a possibility and was designed to eliminate it. So even if the Gospel accounts of the crucifixion say almost nothing about Satan, defeating him was one of Jesus' most important priorities. Yet this aspect of his sacrifice had been so long overlooked in modern times that it came as a great surprise when Gustaf Aulén (1879–1977) brought it back to the theological world's attention in his justly famous book, *Christus Victor*.[14] Aulén rejected the then current idea that the early Christians were unconcerned about sin or that they failed to give it its proper weight in their teaching.[15] As he put it, they believed that Christ came down from heaven "in order to destroy sin, overcome death, and give life to man."[16] Irenaeus, for example, was in no doubt about the nature of sin and its consequences:

> [Men are] by nature sons of God because they were created by him, but because of their deeds they are not his sons. For as among men, disobedient sons who have been disowned by their parents are still sons according to nature, but in law they have become alienated because they are no longer the heirs of their natural parents, so with God, those who do not obey him are disowned by him and cease to be his sons.[17]

Because of man's sin, there is an alienation between him and God that can be taken away only by an act of reconciliation, which is the root meaning of "atonement." That act is performed by God himself, "who had pity on men and took away his enmity against them, by flinging it back on the serpent who was its author and whose intention had been to create a permanent enmity between man and God."[18]

Aulén demonstrated that the early church fathers thought of sin and death

[14] Gustaf Aulén, *Christus Victor* (London: SPCK, 1931). It was translated by A. Gabriel Hebert from the original Swedish, *Den kristna försohningstanka* (Stockholm: Svenska kyrkans diakonistyrelses bokförlag, 1930).

[15] Aulén was trying to show that the medieval doctrine of the atonement, usually associated with the name of Anselm of Canterbury, was a departure from ancient tradition, and that Martin Luther had recovered the emphasis of primitive Christianity. Unfortunately, according to Aulén, Luther's followers slipped back into a medieval way of thinking (which they attributed to Luther himself) and failed to appreciate just how radical the great Reformer was. Today, it is fair to say that these aspects of Aulén's thesis have been largely overturned, but his contribution in drawing attention to the existence of a recognizable doctrine of the atonement in ancient times remains indisputable. See Jaroslav Pelikan's introduction to the second edition of *Christus Victor* (New York: Macmillan, 1969).

[16] Aulén, *Christus Victor*, 19. The quotation is from Irenaeus of Lyon, *Adversus omnes haereses* 3.18.7.

[17] Irenaeus of Lyon, *Adversus omnes haereses* 4.41.2–3.

[18] Ibid., 5.40.3. See also 5.14.3.

as essentially the same thing, and believed that when Jesus died on the cross he was destroying not only sin and death but their ultimate cause, which was Satan. In their view, it was this cosmic battle against satanic influences that was the deepest purpose of Christ's mission and ministry, and it was in that context that his victory over sin and death had to be understood. The logic behind this was set out by Irenaeus as follows:

> Man was created by God in order to have life. Now, if after having lost this life and been harmed by the serpent, man were not to be brought back to life but were to be wholly abandoned to death, God would have been defeated and the wickedness of the serpent would have overturned his will. But since God is both invincible and merciful, he showed his mercy in correcting man. . . . Through the Second Man he bound the strong one, spoiled his goods, and annihilated death, giving life to man who had become subject to death.[19] For Adam had become the Devil's possession and the Devil had him in his power. . . . He who had taken man captive was himself taken captive by God, and captive man was set free from the bondage of condemnation.[20]

Aulén was able to marshal an impressive array of evidence to show how the early Christians interpreted the death of Jesus in this light. Of particular interest to them was the concept of "ransom" (*lytron*), a word used in the New Testament to describe how Jesus paid the price for our sins.[21] But *lytron* was an analogy rather than an exact term, and all analogies have their limitations, as the church was soon to discover. Normally, a ransom is something you give to an enemy or criminal who has captured someone whom you want back. You pay off the captor and reclaim the person who has been snatched from you. Is that what Jesus did? If Jesus paid a ransom for us, to whom was it paid? The natural answer was that it must have been given to the Devil, which is what some of the church fathers thought. Origen, for example, said this:

> To whom did Jesus give his soul as a ransom for many? Surely not to God! So could it have been to the Evil One instead? For he had us in his power until the ransom was given to him, [and that ransom was] the soul of Jesus, since he had been deceived and led to think that he could master that soul. He did not see that to hold him [Jesus] involved a trial of strength which was beyond his ability to handle.[22]

---

[19] See Matt. 12:29.
[20] Irenaeus of Lyon, *Adversus omnes haereses* 3.23.1. See also Eph. 4:8; Rom. 8:1.
[21] Matt. 20:28; 1 Tim. 2:6. The latter text has *antilytron* instead of the simpler *lytron*. Note also that the Greek word for "redemption" is *apolytrôsis*, literally a "ransoming." See Luke 21:28; Rom. 3:24; Eph. 4:30; Heb. 9:15; etc.
[22] Origen, *Commentarium in Matthaei Evangelium* 16.8.

But why would God give his Son's life to the Devil in order to get us back on his side? Did he not have the power to crush Satan under his feet? If so, why would he treat him with such respect? The answer the fathers gave to this was subtle. Neither Origen nor anyone else regarded the Devil's control of mankind as legitimate, but many of them were prepared to accept that, because of Adam's sin, Satan had acquired certain rights over the human race and that God respected them. It was therefore inappropriate for him to step in and seize what Satan had obtained by consent. As Gregory of Nyssa put it,

> We sold ourselves [to the Devil] of our own free will, and when God in his goodness wanted to give us our freedom back again, there was a kind of necessity for him not to do this by force, but to accomplish our deliverance in a lawful way. He did it by offering the owner [i.e., the Devil] all he asked as the redemption price of his property.[23]

It should be said that this view did not go unchallenged. No less a person than Gregory of Nazianzus, a close friend and colleague of Gregory of Nyssa, rejected it completely. As far as he was concerned, the Devil was a robber who had no rights, and so he had no entitlement to a ransom. In his own words,

> We were detained in bondage by the Evil One, sold under sin, and receiving [earthly] pleasure in exchange for our wickedness. Now, since a ransom belongs only to him who holds in bondage, I ask to whom was this ransom offered, and for what reason? If it was to the Evil One, what an outrage! How would the robber receive a ransom, not only *from* God, but which *is* God himself. . . . But if it was offered to the Father, how was that possible? He was not the one oppressing us . . .[24]

Gregory's was a minority view, but it shows what the difficulties were in trying to defend the ransom theory. Those who insisted on doing so did not make things any easier for themselves when they developed the idea that the ransom was offered to the Devil, not because he was entitled to it, but because God was intending to deceive him into destroying himself. To this way of thinking, God's offer of a ransom was a snare, rather like the proverbial piece of cheese put in the mousetrap in order to entice the mouse.[25] The Devil was similarly baited by Jesus on the cross, and he jumped at the opportunity to annihilate the Son of God. As Gregory of Nyssa put it,

[23] Gregory of Nyssa, *Oratio catechetica magna* 22.
[24] Gregory of Nazianzus, *Orationes* 45.22.
[25] One of Augustine's favorite analogies. See Augustine of Hippo, *Sermones* 130.2; 263.1; 265/D.5.

> Since the hostile power was not going to enter into relations with a God who was present and unveiled, or endure his appearance in his heavenly glory, God . . . concealed himself under the veil of our nature, so that, just as happens with greedy fish, the hook of the Godhead might be swallowed along with the bait of human flesh. In that way, Life passed over into death and the Light shone in the darkness, so that what is opposed to Life and Light might be destroyed. For darkness cannot survive when the Light shines, nor can death remain in being where Life is active.[26]

Another common argument was that the Devil overreached himself in trying to overcome the power of Christ. This view was expressed quite clearly by John Chrysostom (d. 407), who said that Satan had struck Adam because Adam was guilty of sin, but then he also struck Christ, who was not. What he did to Adam was justified, but what he did to Christ was not. In cutting him down, Satan had overstepped his rights and so he was deprived of his power.[27] Chrysostom's argument is best seen as a moderating variant of the deception theory, though without the moral ambiguity which that entails. According to him, the Devil should have known what he was doing and should have refrained from doing it, but he did not, and as a result he was overthrown by his own pride and greed.

As thus expounded, the ransom theory and its derivatives were at least memorable, but it has to be said that they are of dubious moral value and lack any clear scriptural support. As Gregory of Nazianzus saw, the "ransom" was not paid to Satan but was the Son's gift to the Father, a voluntary sacrifice on the basis of which the Father removed the condemnation against us. Furthermore, Jesus descended into hell, not because he had tricked the Devil into letting him in, but because he had to do what mattered so much to the early Christians—he had to defeat Satan, the source of sin and death, so as to ensure that never again would he have the power to harm God's people.

The Cost of Reconciliation

Once the church fathers had worked out their understanding of Christ's sacrificial death, there was little further development of the subject for several centuries. In the Eastern church the teaching of Gregory of Nazianzus has remained the standard doctrine of the atonement to the present day. In the West, the ransom idea prevailed in the thought of Augustine and especially of Gregory the Great (590–604), whose vivid descriptions of it became popular

[26] Gregory of Nyssa, *Oratio catechetica magna* 24.
[27] John Chrysostom, *Homiliae in Iohannis Evangelium* 12.31.

sermon fare in the Middle Ages.[28] Not until the eleventh century did the question of why God became man once again become one of urgency, for reasons which we do not fully understand. One of them was certainly the emergence of a concept of chivalric justice, which said that an innocent (and unarmed) man should not be put to death for no reason, which Jesus had been. Another may have been the challenge from Islam, which said that Christ did not die on the cross because he was too good and too divine for that.[29]

Whatever the reasons, people in the late eleventh century wanted to know why it was that the Son of God had come into the world to die. Was the blood that Jesus shed on the cross really sufficient to cover the sins of the whole world for all time? What if someone were to sin in a way that had not been foreseen—would that person be able to benefit from Christ's death? On what grounds? All these questions and others like them had to be confronted and answered, and it was in the course of doing this that the doctrine of the work of Christ gradually became the distinct branch of theology that we know as "soteriology."

The theologian who, more than any other, shaped the medieval church's doctrine of the reconciliation of God and man was Anselm, archbishop of Canterbury from 1093 until his death in 1109.[30] His thoughts on the atoning work of Christ are outlined most clearly in his famous treatise called *Cur Deus homo*, or in English, *Why God Became Man*.[31] It consists of two books of roughly equal length, each of which is subdivided into a number of short chapters. In his preface, Anselm tells us that the first book is aimed at answering the objections of unbelievers who regard the Christian faith as irrational. In the second book, he presupposes that his interlocutors know nothing about Christ and argues on the basis of pure logic that human beings were destined for immortality, which only a God-man could bring about.

Anselm wrote his great work in response to a number of requests from people who believed that he had the ability to make difficult things seem simple. He decided to present his doctrine by using the literary device of adopting one of these enquirers, a man called Boso, as his dialogue partner. The argument

[28] See especially Gregory I of Rome, *Moralia in Iob* 33. He picks up the image of the bait and the fishhook and attaches it to Job 41:1, identifying Leviathan with the Devil. There has been relatively little study of Gregory's thought in recent times, but see Kevin L. Hester, *Eschatology and Pain in Saint Gregory the Great* (Milton Keynes: Paternoster, 2007).

[29] Sura 4.156. It should be noted that the Qur'anic verse is unclear and its meaning is disputed among Muslims themselves.

[30] It should be noted that Anselm was not English. He was born in Aosta, now in northwestern Italy, and spent most of his life at the Norman abbey of Bec. For much of his tenure as archbishop of Canterbury he was in exile, traveling as far as the south of Italy. It was there that he finished writing *Cur Deus homo*. On Anselm's life and work, see Richard W. Southern, *Saint Anselm: A Portrait in a Landscape* (Cambridge: Cambridge University Press, 1990).

[31] Whether the title is a statement (as assumed here) or a question ("Why did God become man?") is debated, but for our purposes it makes little difference. The best modern translation is in Brian Davies and Gillian Evans, eds., *Anselm of Canterbury: The Major Works* (Oxford: Oxford University Press, 1998), 260–356.

is developed as a series of questions raised by Boso and answered by Anselm, though the line of thought is Anselm's throughout.

Boso starts by saying that it is right to believe first and seek understanding later, but Anselm says that he is reluctant to inquire into the deeper things of God. To this, Boso replies that Anselm should touch only on matters that impinge on the subject at hand. Anselm retorts that he is afraid that he will not do his subject justice, but Boso will not listen to this excuse and insists that he carry on. Anselm accedes to Boso's request, but asks that Boso will make sure that he does not say anything that cannot be supported by Holy Scripture and the fathers of the church. Boso then presents the unbelievers' argument that the incarnation of the Son is an act unworthy of God, because it reduces the infinite to the dimensions of the finite. Anselm counters this by saying that, on the contrary, the incarnation magnifies God because it shows us what he is capable of doing. God's decision to procure our redemption in this way is therefore a mark of his greatness. Anselm sees a perfect symmetry in God's saving work that ultimately derives from Irenaeus and his theory of "recapitulation," which he expresses as follows:

> It was appropriate that, just as death entered the human race through a man's disobedience, so life should be restored through a man's obedience; and that just as the sin that caused our condemnation originated from a woman, so the originator of our justification and salvation was born of a woman. Also that the Devil, who defeated the man whom he tricked into eating from a tree, should likewise be defeated himself by a man, through a tree-induced suffering that he [the Devil] inflicted.[32]

To this, Boso replies that unbelievers think the incarnation is a myth because it has not been demonstrated to be logically necessary. Anselm replies that God could not allow his highest creature to perish without fulfilling his plan, and that plan could not have been put into effect without direct divine intervention. Boso then replies that it would have been better for an angel or another man to have done that, but Anselm says that if that had happened, the human race would now be beholden to that angel or man as its redeemer, and not be in fellowship with God.[33]

Boso goes on to critique the traditional idea that the Son was a ransom for our sins. How could it be that God was unable to free mankind from bondage without paying a ransom to Satan? The Devil is not more powerful than God,

[32] Anselm of Canterbury, *Cur Deus homo* 1.3.
[33] Ibid., 1.5.

so why should God defer to him? Surely it was not necessary for his Son to become a man, suffer, and die for us, when God could have set us free merely by disposing of the Devil. Satan has no natural jurisdiction over mankind, and if God found us in his power, then he had every right to tear us away from it because the Devil is not our natural master. Even if man deserves to be punished for his rebellion, it is not Satan's right to punish him, but God's. If the Devil does it instead, it is only because God has allowed him to do it. The fact that man deserves God's punishment does not justify the actions of the Devil, who merely seizes the opportunity that has been given to him to do evil. Satan has no right to ensnare man in sin, and can do so only because God has permitted it as our punishment for disobeying him.[34]

Anselm replies to this by appealing to God's will, which is always just even if we do not understand it. Boso agrees, but says that people will not accept this answer if it is irrational. When Anselm asks what is irrational about the incarnation, Boso repeats the charge that it is both beneath God's dignity to enter his own creation and far too laborious a way of saving us. Anselm's answer is that people who say such things have not understood the Christian faith. God cannot be diminished in any way, which is why he could not suffer and die for our sins in his divine nature. The Son became a man in order to acquire a nature capable of suffering and death; this is not a humiliation of God but an exaltation of human nature. As he put it,

> When we say that God is suffering some humiliation or weakness, we do not understand this in terms of the exalted state of his non-suffering [divine] nature, but in terms of the weakness of the humanity that he was taking on himself. So there is no rational objection to our faith . . . in the incarnation there is no humiliation of God; rather, we believe that human nature was exalted.[35]

Boso accepts this but then asks whether it was right for a sinless man to take human sinfulness on himself and die for it. What is just about letting an innocent man die for the guilty? Was God forced to condemn an innocent man in order to save us? What does this tell us about his omnipotence and sense of justice? To this, Anselm replies that God did not force his Son to die for sinful human beings. On the contrary, the Son took this task upon himself, of his own free will.

Boso's answer is that, despite this, it seems that the Son was in fact coerced because "he became obedient, even to death."[36] Obedience implies a command,

[34] Ibid., 1.6–7. By putting these objections in the mouth of Boso and claiming that they come from unbelievers, Anselm disposes of the ransom theory without actually saying so.
[35] Anselm of Canterbury, *Cur Deus homo* 1.8.
[36] Phil. 2:8.

does it not? Anselm's answer was that it is necessary to distinguish between the inevitable consequences of obedience on the one hand, and the suffering the Son underwent even though his obedience did not demand it, on the other. It was an essential part of the incarnate Son's obedience to his Father that he should live a true and godly life on earth, which is what he did. The Jews killed him, because they could not tolerate the presence of a sinless man in their midst. That also explains why Christ suffered death even though he did not deserve it.

To this Boso replies by asking why the Son's obedience to the Father did not demand suffering and death, even though that is what happened. Anselm answers by asking Boso whether a sinless man deserves to die. Human beings were not created sinful, and had they not disobeyed their Creator there would be no reason for putting them to death. Christ's obedience did not lead to an abandonment of his life, which was not required of him, but to rejection by those who could not tolerate an obedient man among them:

> God did not force Christ to die when there was no sin in him. He suffered death of his own accord, not out of an obedience that consisted in abandoning his life, but out of an obedience that consisted in upholding righteousness so bravely and consistently that he incurred death because of it.[37]

Anselm then went on to argue that the Father effectively ordered Christ to die by telling him to do the things that led to his death. This is why the Bible says that he learned obedience by his sufferings.[38] When Jesus told his disciples that he had come not to do his own will but the will of his Father, what he meant was that his desire to do the right thing did not spring from his humanity but from his divinity. When the New Testament says that God did not spare his Son but handed him over, it means that the Father did not release the Son from his duty of obedience.[39] That is why it was impossible for him not to suffer and die, once he had voluntarily agreed to do so.

Next, Anselm says that the Father allowed the Son to die, not because he would rather see him dead than alive, but because the restoration of the human race could be brought about only by the death of a man who was capable of achieving that. The Father's desire does not exclude the possibility that someone else could have suffered and died, but the Son volunteered to do so in order to accomplish the Father's will. It is only in that sense that the Bible tells us that the Father willed the death of the Son. It is in the context of the Son's obedient

---

[37] Anselm of Canterbury, *Cur Deus homo* 1.9.
[38] Heb. 5:8.
[39] Rom. 8:32.

willingness that the Father handed him over to death. God compelled him to sacrifice his life only because the Son was determined to do the Father's will and that is what his will required. The Son could have avoided death if he had wished to, but in that case mankind would not have been saved. What Jesus did, he did of his own free will, as he told his disciples.[40]

Boso retorts that it does not seem fitting for God to have allowed his Son to suffer in this way, even if the Son wanted to. Anselm replies that, on the contrary, it is entirely appropriate for the Father to acquiesce in the Son's desire to suffer and die, because what the Son wanted to do was a necessary and praiseworthy thing in itself, without which we would not have been saved. Boso, however, is still not satisfied. He wants to know how such a solution can be regarded as rational. It seems unfitting for God to have acted like that, and it is not self-evident that Christ's death is an effective means of saving mankind. Anselm concurs with Boso's objection, at least to the extent of admitting that we should not accept any explanation for Christ's death that contradicts the nature and being of God. He concludes this part of the discussion by saying that we all agree that man was created to enjoy a blessedness that cannot be attained in this life, because of our sinfulness. The forgiveness of sins is therefore necessary if we are to enjoy eternal life. To this, Boso wholeheartedly agrees.

At this point, Anselm shifts the discussion to a consideration of the logic of forgiveness.[41] Boso ceases to be the doubting questioner and becomes the patient listener, eager to hear how Anselm will develop this theme. Anselm starts by defining sin as the refusal to give to God what is owed to him. Put simply, this means that we are duty-bound to be obedient to his will, and the same is true of the angels. To disobey God is to take away from him something that is rightfully his. As long as the angel or man who does this does not compensate God for it, that angel or man remains in a state of debt toward him. Moreover, it is not enough simply to give back what is owed. The one who is at fault ought to return the debt with interest, considering that he has not only taken what does not belong to him but has insulted the honor of God as well. Only when he has compensated God for the dishonor caused to him can the sinner be discharged from his debt:

> When someone repays what he has illegally stolen, his obligation to give is not to be equated with what might be asked of him if he had not stolen anything. Everyone who sins has an obligation to repay to God the honor that

[40] See John 10:17–18.

[41] Anselm of Canterbury, *Cur Deus homo* 1.11.

> he has seized from him—this is the satisfaction that every sinner is obliged to give to God.[42]

Having established that point, Anselm goes on to ask whether God can forgive a sin out of mercy alone, without demanding compensation for it.[43] Boso thinks this is possible, so Anselm has to explain that if no compensation is offered for the sin, the only way to put it right is to punish it. If God forgives sin without punishing it, it has not been put right, and it is not fitting for God to tolerate such disorder in his kingdom. It would also mean that there would be no real difference between sinners and non-sinners, because the sinners would all be forgiven with nothing to justify it and so it would appear that nothing had ever gone wrong.

In human affairs, says Anselm, wrongdoing is always paid for by some kind of compensation established by law. If there is no compensation, there is no law, and sinners get away with their evil deeds. Given that the righteous are those who submit to the law of God and keep it, this would mean that sinners are freer than the sinless are, which does not seem right or possible. If that were true, sinners would resemble God in his infinite freedom more than the sinless do.

Boso's reply is that if this is so, why does God tell us to forgive others when he is not prepared to do so himself? Anselm's answer is that this is not contradictory, because God is telling us not to take vengeance, because that is his prerogative. For us to take retribution upon ourselves would be presumptuous, and therefore just as sinful as whatever it was that we were purporting to punish. Anselm goes on to argue that the creature cannot deprive the Creator of something and not pay him for it. God cannot tolerate such an insult to his honor, because if he did, the universe would fall into chaos.[44] The punishment of a sinner upholds God's honor because it shows that sinners belong to him whether they want to or not.[45]

Anselm then gives a long discourse on the fallen angels, saying that the salvation of human beings is designed to make up the numbers of the bands of angels who fell.[46] From there, he goes on to say that mankind cannot be saved without compensation for sin, and argues that the compensation ought to be proportionate to the offense.[47] Boso's problem with this, says Anselm, is that

[42] Ibid.
[43] Ibid., 1.12.
[44] Ibid., 1.13.
[45] Ibid., 1.14–15.
[46] Ibid., 1.16–18. This is a curious argument and led Anselm down the tortuous pathway of trying to decide whether the number of the saved was equal to the number of the fallen angels or greater. In the end, he concluded that there would be at least as many saved human beings as there are fallen angels, and perhaps more, if we accept the possibility that God had not finished his creation when he made the angels in the first place.
[47] Ibid., 1.19–20.

he had not yet considered how heavy the weight of sin is.[48] The insult inflicted on God's honor by human sin is too great for any human action to be able to compensate. What man stole from God cannot be repaid, which creates an impossible dilemma for sinners.[49] Man cannot be happy until the debt is cleared, but he cannot be excused simply because he is unable to pay it back. Logically, he is eternally condemned and there is no escape, because a sinner cannot make either himself or another sinner righteous.[50] This is why the Son of God had to come into the world to save us. Only in that way could the problem of sin be resolved and mankind be set free from the consequences of our disobedience to the will of God.[51]

In the second part of the book, Anselm and Boso take up the same themes again, but this time from a different angle. Anselm begins by saying that it is clear that rational beings were made righteous so that they would be happy. It follows from that, that if we had not sinned we would not die. Furthermore, if there is to be a restoration of fallen man, he must come back in the same body that he would have had if he had remained sinless, since otherwise it would not be a restoration. On that basis, argues Anselm, God will complete the work he has begun and bring his rational creatures to their logical perfection, but he cannot do this as long as there is no recompense paid for the sins that those creatures have committed.

This restoration will necessarily take place, because it was God's purpose from the beginning, but God cannot be forced into it. God cannot be obliged to do anything, because if he could be, our salvation would not be an act of free grace. As Anselm put it,

> Although it is not fitting for God to fail to bring to completion the good work that he has begun, we ought to attribute it all the more to his grace when he does so, since he has begun it for our sake and not for his own. . . . When God created man he knew perfectly well what man was going to do, and yet by his own goodness in creating him, he put himself under obligation to bring what he had started to completion. God does nothing under compulsion, because he is neither forced to do anything nor prevented from doing it.[52]

What God does he does of his own volition, and that makes our salvation a gracious act that is worthy of his nature. But the only recompense great enough to satisfy God's honor is one made by someone who can make sufficient

[48] Ibid., 1.21.
[49] Ibid., 1.22.
[50] Ibid., 1.23.
[51] Ibid., 1.24–25.
[52] Ibid., 2.5.

payment, and no creature is able to do that. Thus we have a situation in which only God himself can pay the price that is demanded from a rational creature. It is for that reason, says Anselm, that it is fitting and necessary for God to become a man.

Furthermore, he says that the God-man must be perfect in both natures, since otherwise he would not correspond to either of them. He must also be a single individual, because if he is not, the recompense required from Adam would not be made. According to Anselm's logic, God cannot pay himself back as God, nor can any man make sufficient payment, so God must pay back what is owed by becoming a man and paying the debt in his human nature.

It is also right that God should take this human nature from the existing race of Adam and not create humanity afresh, because it is the existing race that he intends to save. Anselm then embarks on a long discussion of how God could create a human being and says that there are four possibilities. Either he can create a man from the natural intercourse of man and woman, as he usually does. Or he can create a man from nothing, as he did with Adam. Thirdly, he can create a human being from a man alone, which is how Eve came into being. Lastly, he can create a man from a woman alone, something which he had not done until the coming of Christ. This last option is preferable, argues Anselm, partly because in sending his Son into the world God is doing something he has never done before, and partly because it gives women hope that they will be saved in spite of the sin of the first woman. As Anselm puts it,

> It is extremely appropriate that, just as the sin of mankind and the cause of our damnation originated from a woman, the cure for sin and the cause of salvation should likewise be born of a woman. Women might lose any hope of having a part in the destiny of the blessed ones, considering that such great evil came from a woman, so in order to prevent this, it is right that a correspondingly great good should proceed from a woman too.[53]

Anselm then explains why it was right for the second person of the Trinity to become a man and not one of the others, and repeats his earlier arguments about the voluntary nature of the Son's suffering and death. He also explains that it is right to praise God for his goodness, even if it comes naturally to him, because righteousness is praiseworthy in itself. Likewise, the angels are to be praised for their goodness, because although they could have sinned, they did not do so.[54]

[53] Ibid., 2.8.
[54] Ibid., 2.10.

He goes on to argue that the incarnate Son of God did not have to die because he had a mortal human nature, but chose to do so. He could have lived forever as a man, but he did not come into the world for that purpose. The fact that he shared our limitations during his earthly life does not mean that he was unhappy, nor did he suffer from ignorance in the way that other mortals do. The Son of God took on mortality for a reason, and he always knew exactly what he was doing and why.[55]

Anselm goes on to explain that the death of Christ outweighs the magnitude of all conceivable sin because it is the perfect offering of the perfect person. It even pays the price of the sin incurred by those who put him to death![56] Anselm then outlines how God made a sinless man out of sinful matter, a miracle that he regarded as greater than that of the original creation. Against Augustine, he goes so far as to claim that there has always been at least one human being who was not completely cut off from God, and that Adam and Eve had a part to play in their own reconciliation to him, though he admits that there is nothing in Scripture to that effect. However, it should be noted that Anselm puts these words in the mouth of Boso, who has drawn what he sees as the logical inference from Anselm's argument thus far. That it was also Anselm's view, however, is confirmed by his reply:

> It seems incredible that God excluded Adam and Eve from his plan, considering that he created them and intended to create through them all the human beings whom he would eventually take up to heaven.[57]

Anselm also argues that the Devil cannot be saved, because that would require the death of a God-angel instead of a God-man, and angels cannot die.[58] He points out that all human beings are descended from one man who sinned, and therefore it is logical to think that one man can save us as well. But angels are not descended from a common ancestor, and so each of the demons is responsible for his own sin. Anselm concludes his extended discussion by saying that his exposition of the logic of the incarnation of the Son of God and the consequent salvation of the human race demonstrates the truth of the Old and New Testaments, in which the details of this divine work are set out for our learning.[59]

Anselm's doctrine of the atonement, which we now call the "satisfaction theory" because it claims that on the cross Jesus satisfied the demands of the

55 Ibid., 2.11.
56 Ibid., 2.15.
57 Ibid., 2.16.
58 Ibid., 2.21.
59 Ibid., 2.22.

Father's justice, thereby turning his wrath away from us, became the dominant one in the medieval church, but it was not the only view that was proposed. A different perspective was developed by Peter Abelard (1079?–1142), a Parisian theologian chiefly remembered today for his illicit love for Heloise, the maiden who became a nun as penance for her affair with him. This is somewhat unfortunate because it obscures Abelard's place in the history of Christian thought.[60]

That Abelard was not part of the theological mainstream was obvious in his own time, but how far he diverged from it is unclear. Modern studies of the period usually portray him as an opponent of Anselm's, but in fact Abelard never mentioned Anselm and we do not know whether he had read *Cur Deus homo* or not. He never interacted with it, even though his approach to the atoning work of Christ was very different from Anselm's. More than anything else, Abelard's doctrine resembles the teaching of Gregory of Nazianzus, though Abelard could not have read Gregory and almost certainly came to his opinions independently. This is what Abelard had to say:

> How dreadful and unjust it is that [God] should have demanded innocent blood as a ransom, or that he would take pleasure in the death of an innocent man. Even worse is the idea that the death of his Son was so pleasing to God that the whole world was reconciled to him because of it. . . . It seems to me that we are justified by the blood of Christ and reconciled to God because by the unique grace that he showed us, the grace by which the Son assumed our nature and taught us by his words and example, up to and including his death, he has bound us closer to him in love. Therefore, anyone who receives such grace will not hesitate to respond to it in love and will be prepared to suffer for his sake.[61]

From this, it seems that what Abelard taught was a kind of adoptianism, though it was certainly not as crude as what Paul of Samosata had proposed. At least that is how Bernard of Clairvaux (1090–1153) interpreted Abelard, and it was Bernard's view that prevailed in their own time.[62] Bernard called Abelard a Pelagian, an accusation that stands up when we consider remarks like the following:

---

[60] See John Marenbon, *The Philosophy of Peter Abelard* (Cambridge: Cambridge University Press, 1997); Constant Mews, *Abelard and Heloise* (Oxford: Oxford University Press, 2005). Studies of his theology are harder to find, but see Jean Jolivet, *La théologie d'Abélard* (Paris: Cerf, 1997); and Thomas Williams, "Sin, Grace and Redemption," in Jeffrey E. Brower and Kevin Guilfoy, eds., *The Cambridge Companion to Abelard* (Cambridge: Cambridge University Press, 2004), 256–276.

[61] Peter Abelard, *Commentarium in Epistulam ad Romanos* 3.26.

[62] Bernard of Clairvaux, *Epistula* 190. Bernard wrote that for Abelard, Christ's saving work was not in "the power of the cross or the price of Christ's blood, but in the improvement of our own way of life."

> . . . unless we say that man can love God and cling to him on the basis of his own natural free choice, we cannot avoid the conclusion that grace predetermines our merits.[63]

Ironically, most of what Abelard had to say about the atonement can be found in his commentary on Romans, which drew on similar works which he thought were published by Jerome and Cassiodorus but which were actually the commentary of Pelagius recycled under their names.[64] Thus Abelard could be a Pelagian and yet sincerely believe that he was a staunch representative of the mainstream orthodox tradition!

Today Abelard attracts more sympathy than he did in his own lifetime, and it is by no means uncommon to hear people echoing sentiments similar to his about the "injustice" of Christ's blood sacrifice and condemning the notion of the Father's pleasure at such a thing as sadistic. But then as now, people who think like that suffer from the same drawback as Anselm's dialogue partner Boso: they have not considered how serious sin is. Those who are saved by Christ are saved by the power of his blood, which the Father has deemed sufficient to pay the price of our reconciliation to him. In every generation there will be those who resist this teaching, but it is of the essence of the gospel and will never fail to surface wherever the message of Christ is truly proclaimed. Anselm's was not to be the last word on the subject, but time has shown that it is he and not Abelard who belongs to the faithful line of witnesses to the atoning work of the Savior.

The Centrality of the Lord's Supper[65]

As the body of Christ on earth, the church had to model his work, not only in the behavior of its members but in the structures of its worship and administration. By the fourth century there could be no doubt that the celebration of

---

[63] Peter Abelard, *Sententiae Hermanni* 155.

[64] *Abaelard: Expositio in Epistulam ad Romanos—Römerbriefkommentar*, ed. Rolf Peppermüller, 3 vols. (Freiburg-im-Breisgau: Herder, 2000).

[65] The literature on this subject is vast, and virtually every point of view is fully expounded somewhere or other. Those new to the subject might start with Yngve Brilioth, *Eucharistic Faith and Practice: Evangelical and Catholic* (London: SPCK, 1930). Originally published as *Nattvarden i evangeliskt gudstjänstliv* (Stockholm: Svenska kyrkans diakonistyrelses bokförlag, 1926). A popular introduction that sometimes borders on caricature is Gary Macy, *The Banquet's Wisdom: A Short History of the Theologies of the Lord's Supper*, 2nd ed. (Akron, OH: OSL, 2005). A classic study of the development of the Supper is that by Gregory Dix, *The Shape of the Liturgy* (London: Dacre, 1945), though many of his conclusions have been contested and some rejected by more recent studies. For a more up-to-date version, see Paul F. Bradshaw and Maxwell E. Johnson, *The Eucharistic Liturgies: Their Evolution and Interpretation* (London: SPCK, 2012). For the Eastern church, see A. Schmemann, *The Eucharist: Sacrament of the Kingdom* (Crestwood, NY: St. Vladimir's Seminary Press, 1988), originally published in Russian as *Evkharistija—tainstvo tsarstva* (Paris: YMCA Press, 1984). Extracts from the church fathers on the subject can be found in Daniel J. Sheerin, *The Eucharist* (Wilmington, DE: Michael Glazier, 1986). See also, David N. Power, *The Eucharistic Mystery: Revitalizing the Tradition* (New York: Crossroad, 1994); and Joseph Martos, *Doors to the Sacred: A Historical Introduction to Sacraments in the Catholic Church*, 2nd ed. (Tarrytown, NY: Triumph, 1991), 203–267.

the Lord's Supper, often called the Eucharist, was the single most important act of Christian worship. But how far back did that go, and what did it mean to those who attended it? Here we enter a minefield of controversy, the content of which can be roughly divided into "traditional" and "modern." In the traditional version, the Lord's Supper was instituted by Christ himself on the night of his betrayal as a perpetual memorial of his coming passion, death, and resurrection. The arguments that arose from this can be classified as follows:

1. What exactly is a "memorial"? Is it a re-presentation of the original act, and if so, to what extent does it reproduce what Jesus himself did?
2. Who has the right to preside over this memorial, and how often should it be celebrated? Is there a set form of words (or other procedure) that is required for the memorial to be genuine?
3. What sort of bread and wine should be used in the celebration, and what happens to them in the course of it, if anything?

Most of the familiar arguments that divide Catholics and Protestants fall under one of these headings, and the debates between them continue to this day. The more modern type of discussion focuses on something else: the relationship between the Lord's Supper as we know it and the Last Supper of Jesus. In that discussion, the following questions come to the fore:

1. Was the Last Supper a Passover meal, and is the Lord's Supper the Christian equivalent of it?
2. Did Jesus institute a regular commemoration of his death, or was that a later development, possibly to be attributed to Paul?
3. When the early Christians met to "break bread," were they specifically remembering Christ's death? How important was that to the common meal that they shared?

It is obvious that the second set of questions is more fundamental than the first, because the traditional approach assumed that the answers to them were yes, yes, and yes! It was only in the nineteenth century that liberal skepticism got to work and questioned the New Testament basis of the church's practice, a fact that now makes it difficult to write the history of the celebration's origins. If the skeptics are right, or even just partly right, at what point did the traditional consensus about the meaning of the Eucharist emerge? Did everyone go along with it at the time, or was there resistance to these innovations that was effectively crushed and subsequently concealed?

It will come as no surprise to discover that every conceivable viewpoint (and the odd inconceivable one!) has been expounded by one scholar or another. Their claims cannot all be right, but some are more plausible than others, and it is probably true that different conceptions of the Lord's Supper coexisted for a long time before a general consensus emerged. At the risk of oversimplifying what is a very complex picture, the following things can be said about this development with reasonable certainty:

1. The Lord's Supper was not a direct continuation of the Last Supper, though there was a perceived connection between the two that was clarified as time went on.[66]

2. In the first generation or two of the church, Christians met to eat together in ways that did not always (or necessarily) include a memorial of Christ's death. As congregations grew larger this became less practicable, and a more formalized celebration of the Lord's Supper gradually emerged. This did not happen everywhere at the same time, but the legalization of Christianity gave it added impetus and it soon became the norm.

3. The focus of the celebration of the Lord's Supper was on the unity and fellowship of the members of Christ's body. This included the sense that all who partook of it believed that their sins had been forgiven, though no one analyzed precisely how that had happened. Only much later did people begin to ask questions like, Was it by the death of Christ on the cross, a sacrifice that was remembered but not repeated in the celebration? Was it because those who participated in the Eucharist were expressing their faith in the saving work of Christ that was being reenacted before their eyes? Or was it because the consecrated elements had some power to change those who received them, a power that took effect if the recipients were believers?

4. Just as important as the memorial of Christ's death was the element of thanksgiving—for the first creation, from which the bread and wine were drawn, and for the new creation which they symbolize. Irenaeus expressed this as follows:

> We offer to God what belongs to God, rightly proclaiming the communion and unity of the flesh and the spirit. Just as the bread produced from the earth is no longer ordinary bread once it receives the invocation (*epiklêsis*) of God, and is no longer common bread but the Eucharist, consisting of two

[66] See I. Howard Marshall, *Last Supper and Lord's Supper* (Exeter: Paternoster, 1980).

> realities—the earthly and the heavenly; so also our bodies, when they receive the Eucharist, are no longer corruptible, but have the hope of resurrection.[67]

The difficulties we face in writing the history of the later development of the Eucharistic celebration are two. First, there is precious little evidence to go on. Various reconstructions of what happened are possible but none can be definitive, and we have little way of knowing how widespread the opinions and practices we know about actually were. Second, what evidence there is can be interpreted in different ways. Conservatives naturally tend to read it in the light of what came later, as if there was an unbroken thread of continuity that makes it possible to read later customs back into an earlier and poorly documented era. Others reject this and prefer to find interpretations that involve breaks with earlier practice, though they differ as to what those breaks were and how they were caused.[68]

What is certain is that the apostle Paul believed that Jesus had instituted a commemorative meal that consisted of breaking bread and drinking a cup.[69] As practiced at Corinth, it seems that this memorial was part of a larger meal that was not being properly supervised, because some ate too much while others went hungry. Paul evidently thought that people should come with the intention of commemorating Christ's death, and that they should discern his body and blood in the bread and cup of which they partook. In his view, failure to do this was a serious sin that would come back to haunt those who were guilty of it. But in the light of later practice, it should be said that Paul emphasized the need for self-discipline on the part of the participants—he did not say that the leaders of the church should exclude those whom they deemed unworthy. Nor was there any mention of a ceremony at which the elements were specially consecrated. Nothing was said about the use of wine—it is the "cup," which may have been filled with water.[70] On the other hand, considerable emphasis was put on the bread, which was especially symbolic of the unity of the body of Christ.

Paul did, however, believe that it was not only possible but necessary to "discern the Lord's body" in the Eucharistic elements, but what that meant is hard to say. A century after his time we find Justin Martyr explaining it as follows:

> We do not receive these things as common bread or drink, but just as our Savior Jesus Christ, being incarnate by the Word of God, took both flesh and blood for our salvation, so we have been taught that the food for which

[67] Irenaeus of Lyon, *Adversus omnes haereses* 4.18.5.
[68] For the details, see Bradshaw and Johnson, *Eucharistic Liturgies*, 1–59.
[69] 1 Cor. 11:17–34.
[70] See Andrew B. McGowan, *Ascetic Eucharists* (Oxford: Clarendon, 1999), 151–155.

> thanks had been given in a word of prayer that comes from him, is both the flesh and blood of that incarnate Christ, from which our blood and flesh are fed by transformation [*metabolê*].[71]

Justin's language is quite striking, but it is not clear what he really meant by it. In particular, it seems unlikely that he thought that the bread and wine, which were "transformed" by a prayer of thanksgiving, ceased to be what they naturally were. Writing nearly a century after Justin, Origen explained this realistic language like this:

> God the Word was not saying that the visible bread which he was holding in his hands was his body, but rather the Word, in whose mystery the bread was to be broken. He was not saying that the visible drink was his blood, but the Word, in whose mystery the drink was to be poured out. For what else could the body and blood of God the Word be, except the Word that nourishes and the Word that "makes glad the heart"?[72]

It is only after Origen's time that we encounter clear guidelines as to how the Lord's Supper was celebrated and what it meant. Cyprian of Carthage had occasion to write about this in AD 253 when he wrote to Caecilius of Biltha. In that letter we find a clear indication that, for Cyprian, the Eucharist was a kind of sacrifice. In his words,

> If Jesus Christ, our Lord and God, is himself the high priest (*sacerdos*) of God the Father and first offered himself as a sacrifice to the Father, and commanded this to be done in remembrance of him, then the priest (*sacerdos*) who imitates what Christ did and offers a true and full sacrifice in the church to God the Father, truly functions in the place of Christ if he proceeds to make the offering in the way that he sees that Christ himself offered it.[73]

As far as we know, Cyprian was the first person to think of the bishop, as distinct from the body of the church, as the one who made the sacrificial offering of the Eucharist. Quite how his assertion should be interpreted is a matter of ongoing debate, but whatever Cyprian meant, his words suggested an association between Christ's sacrifice and the Eucharistic offering that would intensify in the following century. They also signaled an all-important move away from the congregation to the bishop and in due course to the presbyters, who would act on the bishop's behalf.

---

[71] Justin Martyr, *Apologia I* 66.2.

[72] Origen, *Commentarium in Matthaei Evangelium* 85. The quote is from Psalm 104:15.

[73] Cyprian of Carthage, *Epistula* 63.14. By *sacerdos* Cyprian meant the bishop, not a presbyter, as would be the case in later times.

The concept of sacrifice has caused enormous controversy, and the evidence of the early church has frequently been used to support positions that were unknown or alien to its way of thinking. Basically there are three ways in which it has been interpreted:

1. The sacrifice is the self-offering of God's people, who are told to present their bodies as a "living sacrifice," which is their spiritual worship.[74]
2. The sacrifice is the offering of praise and thanksgiving.[75]
3. The sacrifice is the offering of bread and wine as the body and blood of Christ.

It was the second of these that was taken up most often by the early Christians and can fairly be regarded as their "standard" view of the subject. The first option was not ignored but it was too general to be restricted to the Eucharist, whereas the second is more obviously tied to an act of worship. The sacrifice and death of Jesus was clearly an important reason for Christians to offer praise and thanksgiving to God, and it seems to have been because of that natural association that emphasis gradually shifted to the elements of bread and wine that were offered. They would become the focus of attention in later centuries, but it is important to remember that this was a later development and not the general understanding of the early church.

What happened next is not entirely clear. Until recently it was believed that the anonymous *Apostolic Tradition* was written by Hippolytus of Rome around the time of Cyprian's letter, and because of this it exercised considerable influence on liturgical revisions made in the second half of the twentieth century. However, it is now argued that it is later (at least in its final form) and probably unconnected to Hippolytus.[76] If that is the case, then our knowledge of pre-Constantinian liturgical rites is considerably diminished and we are unable to say for sure what form was followed in public worship before Christianity was legalized.

What is certain is that the official recognition of the church in 313 led to a transformation in the way that it conducted its affairs. Worship was no longer a secret affair but a public ceremony, attended by hundreds of people who had little idea of what was going on. The effect of this was succinctly described by David Knowles (1896–1974) in these terms:

[74] Rom. 12:1.
[75] Heb. 13:15. Justin Martyr, *Dialogus cum Tryphone* 117.2; Irenaeus of Lyon, *Adversus omnes haereses* 4.17.5; Tertullian, *De oratione* 28.
[76] See Bradshaw and Johnson, *Eucharistic Liturgies*, 40.

> The standards of life and the level of austerity were lowered and the Christian church became what it has in large measure remained ever since, a large body in which a few are exceptionally devout, while many are sincere believers without any pretension to fervor, and a sizeable number, perhaps even a majority, are either on their way to losing the faith, or retain it in spite of a life which neither obeys in all respects the commands of Christ nor shares in the devotional and sacramental life of the church with regularity.[77]

The picture that David Knowles presented is graphically illustrated by some of the homilies of John Chrysostom, who was severely critical of the irreverent behavior of many in his congregations.[78] To remedy this and to instruct the ignorant in the meaning of the Eucharist, Chrysostom and others composed elaborate liturgies that explained in great detail the reasons for commemorating the death of Christ.[79] They also made provision for those who were not communicants and issued warnings to those who were, that they should approach the holy table of the Lord in the right spirit of reverence and fear. His intention was that those who were unfit to come to Communion would amend their lives and then participate as worthy members of the body of Christ, but it seems that, more often than not, his words had the opposite effect. People who knew they were unworthy stayed away or refrained from communicating, thereby increasing the growing sense that the liturgy was a spectacle performed by experts rather than a communion in which every member of the body of Christ was expected to join.

This sense of mystery was also developed by Theodore of Mopsuestia (d. 428), who shared Chrysostom's concerns about irreverence to such a degree that he urged the newly baptized to take the consecrated bread in their hands and venerate it, even to the point of kissing it and addressing prayers to it as if it were Christ himself.[80] Theodore saw the entire Communion rite as a reenactment of the passion, death, and resurrection of Christ in which the invocation of the Holy Spirit was identified with the resurrection and the bread and wine, which had thitherto been symbols of the dead body of Jesus, became symbols of his risen body.[81] This identification was very popular and widespread, but it is hard for us to appreciate it today, because our way of thinking has changed.

For us, a symbol is a convenient way of indicating something else. The

---

77 David Knowles, *Christian Monasticism* (New York: McGraw-Hill, 1969), 12.

78 John Chrysostom, *Homiliae in Matthaei Evangelium* 19.7–9; 73/74.3; *Homiliae in Iohannis Evangelium* 3.1; *Homiliae in Actus Apostolorum* 24.4; *De sacerdotio* 5.8. See Bradshaw and Johnson, *Eucharistic liturgies*, 63–67.

79 The most famous of these are the ones attributed to him and to Basil of Caesarea, both of which are still regularly used in the Eastern churches.

80 Theodore of Mopsuestia, *Homiliae catecheticae* 5.28.

81 Ibid., 5.11–12.

national flag, for example, stands for the authority of the state and is to be respected as such, but no one would suggest that the two are the same thing. For this reason, there are now those who will say that symbolic language is inadequate to convey the reality—those who consume the bread and wine of the Eucharist are not participating in a symbolic action that is generically unrelated to what it is pointing to but are actually receiving the body and blood of Christ, however that is to be defined. In the ancient world, this problem did not exist. The ancients had no difficulty in thinking that visible signs pointed to a higher reality that went beyond what they were but that was not unconnected to them. Bread and wine were not arbitrary symbols in the way that a flag is, and so it would not do to substitute something else for them, but neither were they to be confused with the spiritual reality they represented. Just as the incarnate Christ had two natures in indissoluble union, so the elements of the Eucharist were earthly things that were inseparably joined to the body and blood of Christ which they symbolized.

From the standpoint of later Western theology, the most advanced position held by the church fathers was that of Ambrose (339?–397), whose works contain several striking references to the change that he believed came over the elements of bread and wine in the Eucharist. Ambrose asserted that if Elijah was able to call down fire from heaven, Christ was surely able to change substances, especially as he was their Creator.[82] Elsewhere he wrote,

> Before the sacred words, it is ordinary bread on the altar, but after consecration it becomes Christ's flesh. . . . What was bread before the consecration is now Christ's body, because Christ's word changes the thing he created. Thus the body of Christ is made from bread, and the wine, mixed with water in the chalice, becomes the blood at the consecration of the heavenly word.[83]

As with so many other things, it was Augustine of Hippo who tied everything together in a synthesis that subsequently became the basis of medieval thought. He avoided the flowery language of Ambrose and was much more cautious about how he expressed what happened to the elements when they were consecrated, but that there was something special about them he did not doubt. Augustine brought to the fore what the apostle Paul had taught about presenting our bodies as a living sacrifice in imitation of Christ, our Great High Priest. As he put it in *The City of God*,

---

[82] Ambrose of Milan, *De mysteriis* 9.52.
[83] Ambrose, *De sacramentis* 4.4.14–17, 19.

> The whole redeemed city itself, which is the congregation and fellowship of the saints, is offered as a universal sacrifice to God by the high priest, who offered himself in suffering for us "in the form of a servant,"[84] so that we might be the body of so great a head. . . . The sacrifice of Christians is that "many are one body in Christ,"[85] which the church celebrates in the sacrament of the altar, where it is revealed to her that she herself is offered in the things that she offers.[86]

Here we have moved from the Christological context that governed earlier thinking to a soteriological emphasis that was not new in itself but that would gradually be distinguished from its Christological foundation and developed along rather different lines. More clearly than ever before, we see in this analysis the work of the church in re-presenting the sacrifice of Christ, not as something new or different from what he had accomplished once for all on the cross of Calvary, but as part of his body, which is eternally sacrificed and presented by our Mediator to the Father as the plea for our forgiveness.

This connection points us naturally to something else—the deliberate reappropriation of the Old Testament by the Christian church.[87] Initially, the Old Testament had been regarded as a book of prophecy that had been fulfilled in Christ and was therefore rendered more or less unnecessary. That idea was soon seen to be inadequate, but Christians found themselves resorting to allegory in order to make sense of the text and give it a reasonable application to their own time. The body of the incarnate Christ was the temple of the Holy Spirit, as our bodies are also, and so it is not surprising that the church building came to be seen as the temple too.[88] Some churches were even designed according to the plan of the temple built by Solomon.[89] Perhaps most famously of all, the great church of Constantinople was called the church of the holy wisdom (*hagia sophia*) in conscious recollection of Solomon, the wisest king of Israel. The identification of the church building with the temple subtly turned what had originally been an allegory into typology. The priests of the old dispensation were shadows and types, not just of Christ but of the priests of the new dispensation who served him day and night in the new temple that was the church. There they offered a bloodless sacrifice on the altar and gave it to the

[84] Phil. 2:7.
[85] 1 Cor. 10:17.
[86] Augustine of Hippo, *De civitate Dei* 10.6.
[87] See, for example, Ambrose, *De sacramentis* 4.1, where he develops this theme. For an analysis of this phenomenon and a list of instances where it occurs, see Sheerin, *Eucharist*, 173–186. He quotes Origen on the Pentateuch, Augustine on the Psalms, and both Origen and Theodoret of Cyrus on the Song of Songs.
[88] 1 Cor. 6:19; Rev. 21:22. That the church as a fellowship was the temple of God is of course a New Testament concept also. See Eph. 2:19–22.
[89] The church of St. Polyeuctus in Constantinople, built around AD 520, is a good example of this.

people as part of their participation in the atoning work of Christ. Unlike the old dispensation, where it was necessary to go to Jerusalem to receive this blessing (and then at a particular time of the year), the Christian church made it available to anyone wherever a priest was present. It was even possible to feast on the body and blood of Christ on a daily basis in big churches and other places where priests reenacted the sacrifice of Christ as often as they could.

It has to be said that this reappropriation of the Old Testament was partial and in some ways incongruous. For example, the New Testament priests were compared to the Jewish Levites and entitled to a tenth of the produce of the land for their support, but unlike the Jewish Levites they were discouraged from marrying, in case the goods of the church were alienated by their children and used for secular purposes, such as providing dowries for the priest's daughters. Fasting was central to the monastic and priestly vocation, but there were no food laws in the New Testament comparable to those of the Torah. There were Christian kings and emperors who could be compared to the Old Testament kings of Israel, with a similar admixture of good and bad, but they had no status in the church comparable to that accorded to David, Solomon, and their successors, and there was no suggestion that the king had any control over the priests of the church—if anything, it was the other way around. The church could excommunicate secular rulers if they did something it did not like, and since virtually all the king's subjects were members of the church as well, the resulting civil disobedience could have grave effects.[90] The attempt to remake the body of Christ along Old Testament lines was full of internal contradictions that would eventually discredit the model, but while it lasted it was a powerful influence in shaping what a Christian civilization and culture ought to look like.

The same pattern of reappropriating the Old Testament can be seen in what happened to the form of church worship and the status of those called to celebrate it. Some things had been there all along, like the singing of psalms which gradually became, along with the biblical canticles, the main musical fare of the church. But whereas the Jews had musical instruments, the church generally sang *a capella*. The resulting Gregorian chant became a haunting reminder of the sacredness of the church's vocation, and even today there are some Christians who reject the use of musical instruments in Christian worship.[91]

[90] A famous example of this occurred in England, when Pope Innocent III placed the entire country under an interdict from 1208 to 1213 because King John would not accept Stephen Langton as archbishop of Canterbury. In effect, the clergy went on strike, and the king's loss of prestige was such that two years after the interdict was lifted, his barons were able to force him to grant them a number of concessions in the now-famous *Magna Carta*. Ironically, one of its few provisions still in force today guarantees "the liberties of the English church."

[91] Gregorian chant is named after Pope Gregory II (715–731), not—as is sometimes thought—Gregory the Great. Today, the conservative Churches of Christ and the Free Church of Scotland continue to resist the use of instrumental music, even though it is not prohibited in the Bible.

More important than that, however, was the way in which the priests came to understand what they were doing. The heart of their ministry was the celebration of the Lord's Supper, the memorial of Christ's saving passion and death that we are called to repeat until he comes again.[92] The obvious model for this was the Jewish Passover meal, which remained a powerful influence in deciding what the date of Easter should be. But unlike the Passover meal, which came around only once a year, the Lord's Supper could be celebrated anytime. The evidence we have suggests that from the fourth century onward it was celebrated more and more frequently, although paradoxically it seems that a smaller percentage of the congregation actually took part in it. In Western Europe the language used in the celebration remained Latin, even in places where it was clearly foreign. This did not matter as much as it would have mattered in earlier times, because the decline in the observance of Communion encouraged even regular worshipers to think that what actually went on was really none of their business. The extreme to which that could be taken can be seen in the term by which it became popularly known. This was the "Mass," a word derived from the closing lines of the liturgy, which were, *Ite, ecclesia missa est* ("Go, the church is dismissed"). People who did not understand Latin at least knew that when these words were said the service was over, and so they called it the *missa*, not realizing that the word just means "dismissed" and has no theological significance. That the term eventually acquired significance was due to developments that transformed the way in which people related to it. The result is that now the word "Mass" implies a very specific theological position that is quite different from what was originally understood as the Lord's Supper.

The Memorial of Christ's Sacrifice

The *missa* was the time when people believed that they came closest to God, because it was then that they received the body and blood of Christ. As the medieval Western church understood it, this was the logical outworking of Christ's incarnation. The Son of God had suffered and died in a material body. To say that his atonement was merely a spiritual exercise removed the sacrificial blood, and "without the shedding of blood there is no forgiveness of sins."[93] It was therefore not enough to say that worshipers participated in Christ's sacrifice only "after a heavenly and spiritual manner" as the Protestant Reformers were later to express it.[94] That dimension was certainly present, but the incarnation

[92] 1 Cor. 11:26.

[93] See Heb. 9:22.

[94] See Article 28 of the Thirty-nine Articles of the Church of England.

taught that God works spiritually in and through material things, and especially in the physical body of Jesus of Nazareth. From that it followed that the memorial of his sacrifice must include both the spiritual and the material dimension for it to be a true representation of what Jesus did on the cross.

Most important, the church did not make the memorial of Christ's sacrifice for purely commemorative reasons. No one denied that Jesus of Nazareth had suffered and died on the cross in the time of Pontius Pilate (as the creeds affirmed), but his death was not just a distant historical event. It was also something of immediate significance to believers because it was the payment for their sins. To participate in it was to receive forgiveness, and the more sinful that believers knew themselves to be, the more they recognized their need of the grace that participation in the sacrament brought. Once that fundamental principle was established, it was not long before an elaborate hierarchy of sins and their corresponding merits was put into place. Believers were expected to confess their sins to a priest and receive instructions from him as to what to do in order to show that they were truly sorry. This was the system known as "penance," which was a formalized kind of repentance.[95] When the penance was done, the sinner would return to the priest and be absolved, after which he could receive Holy Communion, the gift of God's grace that would help him to grow in Christ.

The elements were treated as a kind of spiritual medicine, with a power independent of the dispenser, so that even if the priest were living an immoral life or were heretical in his doctrine, the bread and wine would do their appointed work as long as they had been properly consecrated.[96] This idea was not new to the Middle Ages. As long ago as the early second century, Ignatius of Antioch had written that the bread of the Eucharist was "the drug of immortality," though he understood that in a spiritual rather than material way.[97] By the twelfth century, however, a more materialistic view of the elements had taken hold, and for many people they really were medicines like any other.

The medieval Western church believed that when the risen Christ ascended into heaven, he took his sacrifice with him as payment for the sins of the whole world. That payment may be conceived as a lump sum of merit (or credit, as we would say today) deposited with the Father as our inheritance. All that is required now is for us to claim what has been reserved for us. We can do that

[95] Latin does not distinguish between "penance" (the outward act) and "repentance" (the inward disposition) but uses *paenitentia* for both. It is sometimes best to translate this as "penitence," especially when the text is ambiguous and either meaning is possible.

[96] It should be noted that the Protestant Reformers held the same position. See Article 26 of the Thirty-nine Articles.

[97] Ignatius of Antioch, *Epistula ad Ephesios* 20: "Continue to gather together . . . breaking one bread, which is the drug of immortality, the antidote we take so that we shall not die but live forever in Jesus Christ."

by availing ourselves of the ministry of the church, the appointed agent by which this inheritance is distributed to the heirs of salvation. The possibility that someone might receive this benefit outside the church was effectively excluded, because as Cyprian of Carthage had said, "Outside the church there is no salvation."[98]

Given all this, it is hardly surprising that there was an increasing focus on the nature of the elements themselves. Were they just bread and wine, or did something happen to them when they were consecrated by the priest? Obviously, if they were to have the effect that was claimed for them, they must have acquired some special properties, and from there it was but a short step to concluding that the bread and wine used in Holy Communion became the body and blood of Christ in an objective sense. In other words, once the material elements were consecrated by the priest they ceased to be what they had been before and became something different. In the early church there were those who believed that after the consecration the elements became something *more* than what they had been, but no one denied that they were still bread and wine. But medieval theologians came to think that the bread and wine ceased to exist and were changed into the body and blood of Christ.

Here the Eastern churches failed to follow the Western development but clung to the earlier view that what the priest did was to *add* a spiritual dimension to the material bread and wine. The parallel they appealed to was the conception of Jesus in the womb of the Virgin Mary, when the Holy Spirit added a divine dimension to the physical flesh that Mary contributed to him. Something like this became the standard doctrine of the Eastern churches, which taught that the Holy Spirit comes down into the bread and wine during the celebration of the liturgy. Most scholars agree that this was supposed to happen in the so-called *epiklêsis* (epiclesis, or invocation), which is a central part of Eastern Orthodox liturgies to the present day, though whether the transformation of the bread and wine can be pinned down to a particular action is debatable.[99] In Western liturgies, by contrast, the epiclesis is either not present or is minimized to the point of being unrecognizable. Why should that be so?

One of the reasons may be that the epiclesis appeared to Western minds to be covertly Nestorian or even adoptianist. Did the Holy Spirit do no more than add a supernatural dimension to the body of Jesus in Mary's womb? Would she have had a baby boy without that intervention? To some, the epiclesis idea

[98] Cyprian of Carthage, *Epistula* 72.

[99] See Bradshaw and Johnston, *Eucharistic Liturgies*, 137–192. For the question of the centrality of the epiclesis, see Michael Zheltov, "The Moment of Eucharistic Consecration in Byzantine Thought," in Maxwell F. Johnston, ed., *Issues in Eucharistic Praying in East and West* (Collegeville, MN: Liturgical Press, 2010), 263–306.

suggested that the bread and wine did not change during the celebration, even if they received some extra power from on high. If the Eucharistic elements were really the body and blood of Christ, something must have happened to change them, and what that was had to be explained.

The first person to address the issue in any depth was Paschasius Radbertus (785?–865?), who outlined his views in a book called *The Body and Blood of the Lord*, which he published around 832. According to him, Christians who consumed the Eucharistic elements ate the same body that had been born of Mary, had suffered and died on the cross, and had risen from the tomb. It was hidden from sight by the outward forms of bread and wine, but it nevertheless joined our human nature to the human nature of Christ. As far as Paschasius was concerned, this was necessary if Christ's body and blood were to have any saving effect. Paschasius was not unaware of the difficulties his theory caused, but he skated over them by appealing to God's omnipotence. He claimed that God could make Christ's body present all over the place and in enormous quantity simply because he was God and could do anything. Sometime around 844 Paschasius forwarded a copy of his book to King Charles II (known as "the Bald") of France (840–877), who was provoked by it to write to Ratramnus (d. 870?), one of Paschasius's fellow monks, and ask him whether Paschasius was right or not.

In reply, Ratramnus sent the king another book with the same title, in which he upheld the traditional view that communicants received the body and blood of Christ only in a spiritual sense, which was not the same as the flesh that had been born of Mary. Paschasius and Ratramnus seem to have got along quite well, living as they did in the same monastery, which suggests that the question was one on which it was still possible to hold a variety of different views. As time went on, however, it was Paschasius who got the better of the argument, and it would not be until the eleventh century that his position would again be challenged, this time by Berengar of Tours (999?–1088). Berengar picked up Ratramnus's work, which he believed had been written by John Scotus (or Scottus) Eriugena (815?–877?), the greatest philosopher of his time and one of the few people in Western Europe who was conversant with Greek theology, and drew his own conclusions from it.[100]

Berengar drew a sharp distinction between the spiritual and the physical natures of consecrated bread and wine, insisting that they retained their material composition throughout the Eucharist and could only be discerned as signs of Christ's presence by the faith of the recipient. For this he encountered furious opposition, was excommunicated by the pope, and was even jailed by the

[100] See Deirdre Carabine, *John Scottus Eriugena* (Oxford: Oxford University Press, 2000).

king of France. He was eventually released, but the church continued to pursue him. In 1059 he was forced to swear the following oath:

> The bread and wine placed on the altar are not only a sacrament after they have been consecrated, but the true body and blood of our Lord Jesus Christ. They are taken and broken by the hands of the priests and crushed by the teeth of the faithful, not only sacramentally but in truth.[101]

Of course, Berengar did not believe what he had to swear to, and before long he went back to his earlier opinion, for which he was obliged to recant a second time in 1079.[102] Much the same thing happened again as it had in 1059, but there was one significant modification. In his second oath, Berengar had to swear that the bread and wine were *substantially* changed into the body and blood of Christ "not only by the sign and power of the sacrament, but in his proper nature and true *substance*."[103] The crucial addition of the word "substance" reveals the new influence of Aristotelian physics, which was to play a determining role in the development and eventual resolution of the controversy.

The historical Aristotle (384–322 BC) was a disciple of Plato and the teacher of Alexander the Great, so he was obviously not a Christian or a Jew. His philosophical principles were developed over many centuries and eventually passed into the Islamic world, where they were elaborated still further. By the middle years of the eleventh century these "Aristotelian" ideas were starting to filter back into Western Europe, where they had been unknown or forgotten, and they caused an intellectual revolution.[104] People who had had only the Bible as the source of their knowledge now came to see that the human mind was capable of attaining high levels of scientific awareness apart from divine revelation. Aristotle was accepted as an infallible authority for the natural sciences, but the church continued to insist that only the Bible, as interpreted by it, could give meaning and coherence to knowledge as a whole. What God has done can be known only by revelation, and that revelation was an act of his free favor, or grace. Universal knowledge was held to consist of both nature, which the human mind could discover and analyze on its own, and grace, which could be known only by divine revelation. In a rightly ordered universe, grace builds on

[101] The text is in Gratian, *Decretum* 3.2.42. It is also found in Henry Denzinger and Peter Hünermann, eds., *Enchiridion symbolorum, definitiorum et declarationum de rebus fidei et morum*, 37th ed. (Freiburg-im-Breisgau: Herder, 2012), no. 690. This bilingual Latin-English work is hereafter abbreviated simply as "Denzinger, *Enchiridion*."

[102] See Charles M. Radding and Francis Newton, *Theology, Rhetoric, and Politics in the Eucharistic Controversy, 1078–1079: Alberic of Monte Cassino against Berengar of Tours* (New York: Columbia University Press, 2003).

[103] The text is most conveniently found in Denzinger, *Enchiridion*, no. 700.

[104] The main lines of transmission went through Spain and Sicily, where an Arab Muslim elite ruled over a largely Christian population that was slowly reasserting itself and would eventually reclaim these countries for Christendom.

the foundation of nature and perfects it, a belief that secured an essential place for the church and its theology, not only within a society that was embracing scientific thought but on top of it.

Aristotle had maintained that everything that exists in the world is a substance of some kind, but that particular substances could and did appear in different shapes and sizes. These differences he called "accidents" because they were not essential to the substance but only accidental to it. Bread, for example, is a substance, but it can be white, brown, or black. It can be thick or thin, leavened or unleavened. A loaf can be big or small, heavy or light, fresh or stale. All these things are accidents because they can change without affecting the underlying substance, which is still bread. Medieval theologians took this idea and turned it on its head. What happened in the *missa*, they maintained, was that the substance of bread and wine changed into the body and blood of Christ, but the accidents remained the same. In other words, the consecrated elements looked like bread and wine, felt like bread and wine, and tasted like bread and wine, but in reality they were the body and blood of Christ. This was what came to be called "transubstantiation," an idea that was to have a long history and cause intense controversy in later times.[105]

The full development of the doctrine of transubstantiation did not take place immediately, nor was it universally accepted for a long time. Initially, the church did not know what to do with the new philosophy, but before long its theologians were borrowing Aristotelian terminology, though we do not know who first described the Eucharist in terms of substance and invented the term "transubstantiation." A number of textbooks claim that it was Hildebert of Tours (1055?–1133) but without citing any text in support. Another possible candidate is Hugh of St. Victor (1096?–1141), who is now thought to have written the *Tractatus theologicus* traditionally ascribed to Hildebert, but although it is certain that Hugh held the doctrine, it must also be said that in his great treatise *On the Sacraments* he avoided using the word itself. As he expressed it,

> The true substance of bread and the true substance of wine are changed into the true body and blood of Christ, the appearance of bread and wine alone remaining, [one] substance passing over into [another] substance.[106]

A more likely source is Robert Pullen (d. 1146), who may have been teaching at Paris just before Hugh died and who was credited with having invented the

[105] See James F. McCue, "The Doctrine of Transubstantiation from Berengar through the Council of Trent," in *Harvard Theological Review* 61 (1968): 385–430; Joseph Goering, "The Invention of Transubstantiation," in *Traditio* 46 (1991), 147–170.

[106] Hugh of St. Victor, *De sacramentis*, 2.8.10. See Paul Rorem, *Hugh of Saint Victor* (Oxford: Oxford University Press, 2009), 102.

term by an anonymous medieval source.[107] That would mean that it originated sometime around 1140, which seems plausible. The apparent reluctance to use the term "transubstantiation" may have been because the idea had not gained universal acceptance and there was some hesitation in trying to define it. We see this in Peter Lombard's famous *Sentences*, a compilation of ancient authorities with a commentary on them, that was to become the standard theological textbook of the later Middle Ages.[108] Peter summed up the state of the discussion in his time (about 1150) like this:

> If it is asked what the nature of that change is, whether it is formal, substantial, or something else, I am unable to define it. I know it is not formal, because the species of the things remain as they were before, as do their taste and weight. To some, it appears to be substantial. They say that a substance is changed into a substance, so that one becomes the other one in essence. . . . But the following objection is made to this position by others: If the substance of bread or wine is converted into the body and blood of Christ, then every day some substance is made the body or blood of Christ which it was not before. Today, something is the body of Christ, which it was not yesterday, and each day the body of Christ is increased and formed of some matter of which it was not made at conception.[109]

Peter rejected the crude idea that the Eucharistic elements became the body and blood of Christ in the same way that his flesh and blood had been formed in the womb of Mary, but he was forced to admit that his sources said different things, and he tried to find a formula that would do justice to all of them at the same time.[110] That seems to be why he spoke of a "conversion" of the bread and wine into Christ's body and blood, without specifying what this meant in terms of a change of substance. In the next generation, we can detect a gradual movement toward a more definite affirmation of transubstantiation as opposed to other possible ways of expounding the mystery, but a certain hesitation is still visible. Baldwin of Forde (1125?–1190), who became archbishop of Canterbury in 1185, wrote that "although there is a considerable variety of expression in

[107] Cambridge, Peterhouse MS 255, fol. 239r, printed in Goering, "Invention," 168–170.

[108] Peter Lombard, *Sententiae in IV libris distinctae*, ed. Ignatius C. Brady, 2 vols. (Grottaferrata: Editiones Collegii Sancti Bonaventurae ad Claras Aquas, 1971–1981); trans. Guilio Silano, 4 vols., *The Sentences* (Toronto: Pontifical Institute of Mediaeval Studies, 2007–2010). For an analysis and introduction, see Philipp W. Rosemann, *Peter Lombard* (Oxford: Oxford University Press, 2004); and Marcia Colish, *Peter Lombard*, 2 vols. (Leiden: Brill, 1994). See also *Medieval Commentaries on the* Sentences *of Peter Lombard: Current Research*, vol. 1, ed. Gillian R. Evans (Leiden: Brill, 2002); vol. 2, ed. Philipp W. Rosemann (Leiden: Brill, 2009). Peter Lombard (1090?–1160) was an Italian who taught in Paris and became that city's bishop shortly before his death. His *Sentences* was intended to be a theological textbook for students and future priests and remained the standard text in its field until the sixteenth century.

[109] Peter Lombard, *Sententiae* 4.11.1.

[110] In particular, he juxtaposed Ambrose and Augustine, pointing out how they differed from each other.

this confession of faith, there is only one devout belief and an undivided unity of confession."[111] To this he added,

> Therefore we hold, believe, and confess simply and with confidence, firmly and constantly, that the substance of bread is changed into the substance of the flesh of Christ—though the appearance of bread remains—and that this takes place in a way that is miraculous and beyond description or comprehension . . .[112]

Transubstantiation became official church teaching at the Fourth Lateran Council in 1215, the first canon of which declared,

> There is only one universal church of the faithful, outside which absolutely no one is saved and in which Christ himself is both priest and sacrifice. In the sacrament of the altar, his body and blood are truly contained in the species of bread and wine, the bread being transubstantiated into the body and the wine into the blood by divine power, so that, in order to perfect the mystery of unity, we receive from him what he received from us. Moreover, no one can confect this sacrament except a priest who has been legitimately ordained according to the keys of the church, which Jesus Christ himself gave to his apostles and their successors.[113]

This is the doctrine which (with some modifications and clarifications in the sixteenth century) has been the official teaching of the Roman Catholic Church ever since. Even though the Aristotelian theory on which it is based is no longer scientifically tenable, the power of theological tradition has been such that the Roman church has been able to ignore that inconvenient fact and go on teaching its people to regard the consecrated elements as Christ's body and blood. The church may now need to find another theory to explain how this is supposed to come about, something which it has so far failed to do, but that is a theologian's dilemma. As far as the ordinary Catholic is concerned, the real presence of Christ in the *missa* is not to be doubted, because it is tied to the doctrine of the incarnation of the Son of God. Even if Aristotle's contribution to our understanding of it may have to be revised in the light of modern knowledge, the teaching of the church, as a revelation of God's grace, remains what it has always been.

After 1215, transubstantiation was a doctrine in search of a theology to un-

[111] Baldwin of Forde, *Liber de sacramento altaris*, in J.-P. Migne, ed., *Patrologiae cursus completus: Series latina*, 217 vols. [hereafter PL] (Paris: 1844–1864), 204, col. 662.

[112] Baldwin of Forde, *Liber de sacramento altaris*, in PL 204, col. 679–680.

[113] *Conciliorum oecumenicorum decreta* (Bologna: Istituto per le Scienze Religiose, 1973), 230; Denzinger, *Enchiridion*, no. 802.

dergird it. This was the achievement of Thomas Aquinas (1226–1274), who is generally regarded nowadays as the greatest of the medieval theologians in the West. He was certainly the most systematic and voluminous in his output, and his philosophical theology (known as Thomism) continues to attract adherents today, despite its untenability in the light of modern scientific knowledge. Following what had by then become the established tradition, Aquinas argued that, in the Eucharist, the bread and wine changed their substances into the body and blood of Christ, while their accidents remained what they had been before. This meant that Christ's body and blood could not be perceived by the senses—the communicant would be tasting what to him would be bread and wine. The substance of a thing is an abstraction that only the mind can perceive by spiritual discernment:

> Substance as such cannot be seen by the bodily eye, nor is it the object of any sense, nor can it be imagined. It is only open to the intellect, the object of which is the essence of things, as Aristotle says. Hence, the body of Christ . . . can be reached neither by sense nor by imagination; it is open only to the intellect, which may be called a spiritual eye.[114]

How the substance of one thing could appear in the accidents of something else could only be explained as a miracle, which gave added status to the work of the priest who consecrated the elements—he was now a miracle-worker! Aquinas also differed from his predecessors in that when he set out his teaching on transubstantiation, he insisted that alternative views, which had earlier been more or less accepted, even if grudgingly, were heretical.[115] In his words,

> The position that after the consecration the substance of bread remains alongside the true body is inappropriate, impossible, and heretical. It is inappropriate because it stands in the way of the veneration that is owed to this sacrament. . . . It is impossible because it cannot now be something that it was not before, unless it is changed or something else is changed into it. It is heretical because it contradicts the truth of Scripture.[116]

But Thomas's apparently simple explanation, which he developed at great length, had difficulties that even his contemporaries could see. One of them was

[114] Thomas Aquinas, *Summa theologiae* IIIa.76.7. The reference is to Aristotle, *De anima* 3.6.7.

[115] See James F. McCue, "Doctrine of Transubstantiation," 390–400, for a number of examples of the more tolerant position.

[116] Thomas Aquinas, *Commentarium in IV libros Sententiarum* 4.11.1.1. Aquinas's appeal to Scripture is highly dubious. He claims that when Jesus said, "This is my body," using the neuter pronoun *hoc* for "this," he was referring to the bread, whereas if he had meant that he himself was the body, he would have used the masculine pronoun *hic* instead. See Matt. 26:26. Aquinas knew no Greek and (needless to say) his understanding of such linguistic subtleties was rudimentary at best.

Bonaventure (1221–1274), whose differences from Aquinas were exacerbated by the fact that the two men belonged to different religious orders—Thomas was a Dominican, dedicated to preaching and teaching, whereas Bonaventure was a Franciscan, with an emphasis on works of practical piety.[117]

Bonaventure countered Aquinas by taking the well-known case of a mouse that had eaten a piece of consecrated bread. Had such a mouse consumed the body of Christ? This had been a standard subject of discussion in the twelfth century, and many different conclusions had been reached, which subtly revealed what the respective disputants really thought about transubstantiation.[118] According to the principles of Thomas, the mouse would have eaten the body of Christ, because the change of substance was objective and irreversible. Bonaventure rejected this, however, because,

> The body of Christ in no way descends into the stomach of a mouse, because Christ is only present sacramentally insofar as the bread is designed for human use. But if a mouse gnaws it, the sign ceases to exist and therefore so does the body of Christ—the substance of the bread returns.[119]

Other Franciscans were quick to follow Bonaventure's lead. Petrus Iohannes Olivi (1248?–1298?) argued that the Eucharistic body of Christ must have a definite quantity, since otherwise it would be pure spirit and that was heretical. But how much of it could there possibly be? Apparently even the Dominican Robert Holcot (1290?–1349) objected, saying that if God could make one thing appear in the guise of another, he could do the same with everything that exists, making it impossible for us to be certain about the reality of anything![120] Others shared his skepticism, and it was not until the eleventh session of the Council of Trent (October 11, 1551), after the Protestant Reformation and in conscious reaction to it, that the doctrine was finally defined and imposed on what was left of the Roman Catholic Church.[121]

Once the bread and wine had been transubstantiated, they were no longer

---

[117] The two orders were still in their infancy in the thirteenth century. St. Dominic (1170–1221) was a Spaniard who had been active in the Crusades against the Albigensian heretics in the south of France, and St. Francis (1181–1226) was the scion of a wealthy family in Assisi (Italy) who gave up everything for the mendicant life of a beggar. See Clifford H. Lawrence, *The Friars: The Impact of the Early Mendicant Movement on Western Society* (London: Longman, 1994). On Bonaventure, see Christopher M. Cullen, *Bonaventure* (Oxford: Oxford University Press, 2006).

[118] See Artur M. Landgraf, *Dogmengeschichte der Frühscholastik*, III/2, *Die Lehre von den Sakramenten* (Regensburg: Pustet, 1955), 207–222; and Gary Macy, "Of Mice and Manna: *Quid mus sumit* as a Pastoral Question," *Recherches de théologie ancienne et médiévale* 58 (1991): 157–166. Peter Lombard dismissed the question as being unanswerable (*Sententiae* 4.13.1.8).

[119] Bonaventure, *Commentarium in IV libros Sententiarum* 4.13.

[120] Robert Holcot, *In IV libros Sententiarum quaestiones* 4.3.

[121] See Marilyn McC. Adams, *Some Later Medieval Theories of the Eucharist: Thomas Aquinas, Giles of Rome, Duns Scotus, and William Ockham* (Oxford: Oxford University Press, 2010). For the decree of Trent, see *Conciliorum oecumenicorum decreta*, 693–697.

material substances but spiritual ones—they had become the body and blood of Christ and would operate as such independently of the priest or even of the liturgy. It was possible to put consecrated bread and wine aside and use them later, because once they were transubstantiated they would not lose their sacred character. As a result, devotional practices unknown in the early church grew up around the "host" (the consecrated bread), and eventually the body of Christ became the object of a special feast (Corpus Christi), which still exists in the Roman Catholic Church today.[122]

Long before that, however, belief in transubstantiation had been ebbing away even among those who were prepared to defend it. This trend is particularly noticeable in the writings of John Duns Scotus (1266–1308), who admitted that it was more plausible, and more in tune with the teaching of Scripture, to believe that the body and blood of Christ were present alongside the elements of bread and wine, which retained their natural characteristics, than to believe that they were substantially altered. He nevertheless asserted his belief in transubstantiation, not because it made better sense, but because it was the teaching of the church.[123] In effect, this constituted an appeal to authority over reason and logic, an odd position which strongly suggests that he did not believe it but dared not deny it openly. Much the same view was expressed by William of Ockham (1288?–1348?), who discussed transubstantiation at length and pointed out why it was so hard to accept. As for the idea that the bread and wine remained alongside the body and blood, he said,

> If this were true, many of the problems which arise concerning this sacrament would be solved. For there is a problem as to how something can be nourished by this sacrament, and how the species can decay and something be generated from them. All these problems would be solved naturally if one accepted this explanation. . . . But this explanation must not be held, since the church (which in such matters is presumed not to err) has decided the opposite, which is why I hold the other position [i.e., transubstantiation].[124]

In other words, Ockham did not believe what the church taught, because it made no sense, but he was not prepared to say so explicitly. His reserve on this point was shattered in the next generation by John Wyclif (or Wycliffe; 1328–1384), who insisted that the substance of bread and wine remained after consecration and was condemned for that more than thirty years after his

[122] It was inaugurated in 1264 and is celebrated on the Thursday after Trinity Sunday (i.e., eleven days after Pentecost). See Miri Rubin, Corpus Christi*: The Eucharist in Late Medieval Culture* (Cambridge: Cambridge University Press, 1991).
[123] John Duns Scotus, *In IV libros Sententiarum* 4.11.3.9.
[124] William of Ockham, *In IV libros Sententiarum* 4.11.1.15.

death, at the eighth session of the Council of Constance (May 4, 1415).[125] The fathers of the council appealed to the Lateran decision of 1215, even though that decree did not really support their position, which they based more on Aquinas than on anything that had gone before. By then, the harmony that Aquinas and his contemporaries thought they had established between divine revelation and natural science was breaking down, and the intellectual foundation on which the doctrine of transubstantiation rested had eroded away. Only the weight of church authority could save it, and we should not be surprised to discover that it would not be long before the legitimacy of that authority would also be questioned.

In the meantime, the efficacy of transubstantiation was underscored by the practice of excommunication, which (as the name implies) was the withdrawal of access to the sacrament.[126] Anyone who has lost a card in an ATM or been denied credit for some reason will know what this felt like. Like a modern bank, the medieval church reserved the right to restrict the availability of grace (credit), and it did so as punishment for bad behavior. But if access to the sacraments was needed for eternal life, the church could claim the power of life and death over its members, who wanted to die in a "state of grace," i.e., with their spiritual account in the black. Failure to do this could have the most dire consequences and was to be avoided at all costs.

It is obvious that with such a precious gift in its possession, the church had to make sure that it was properly protected and administered. Above all else, that meant ensuring that only properly qualified people could be allowed to celebrate the rite. It is curious, but true, that in all his instructions about how to administer the Lord's Supper, the apostle Paul never once said who ought to preside at it. We assume that it must have been one of the elders of the local church, but that is not stated anywhere in the New Testament. We know that by the time of Ignatius of Antioch it was the bishop who normally presided, and that this privilege was eventually extended to the presbyters as well.[127] But once

[125] See John Wyclif, *De Eucharistia* 2–5, 9. Also his *Trialogus* 4.2–6, 27, 36. For the condemnation, see *Conciliorum oecumenicorum decreta*, 411; Denzinger, *Enchiridion*, no. 1151.

[126] The practice of excommunication went back at least to canon 5 of the First Council of Nicea (325). See *Conciliorum oecumenicorum decreta*, 8. But the way in which it was applied became a major concern only later. After a brief mention in canon 2 of the First Lateran Council (1123), much more was said about it in canons 9–10 of the Second Lateran council (1139), canons 6 and 9 of the Third Lateran Council (1179), canons 47–49 of the Fourth Lateran Council (1215), canons 19–22 of the First Council of Lyon (1245), and canons 20 and 29–31 of the Second Council of Lyon (1274). John Wyclif's objections to the way in which the power was abused were one of the reasons for his condemnation at the Council of Constance (Article 11). For the texts, see *Conciliorum oecumenicorum decreta*, 190, 197, 214–216, 255–257, 291–293, 325, 330–331, 412.

[127] What we do not know is whether this was a development away from the original practice or a return to it. It is hardly a coincidence that the official restriction of celebration to the priest (*sacerdos*) dates only from canon 1 of the Fourth Lateran Council (1215), the same council that defined the doctrine of transubstantiation. See *Conciliorum oecumenicorum decreta*, 230.

a doctrine of transubstantiation was in place, the office of presbyter became something more than that of an elder or supervisor. From now on he would be a priest in the Old Testament sense of the word, empowered to confect and offer the sacrifice of the Mass. He would no longer be an ordinary Christian like everyone else, but someone with special power to change bread and wine into the body and blood of Christ. Since only a bishop could ordain presbyters, this gave them control over the local church's leadership. In the nature of things, that control was not always very effective, but it was there in principle and the bishops did what they could to make it work in practice.

The attempt to regulate who could celebrate the Lord's Supper went hand in hand with a corresponding attempt to control who could receive the consecrated elements. Obviously, only the baptized had a right to sit at the Lord's table, but not all the baptized were equally welcome. Although there could be no objection in theory to giving Communion to infants—a practice that existed (and still exists) in the Eastern churches—the New Testament spoke of the need to discern the Lord's body, which seemed to imply that some understanding of what was going on was required.[128] As a result, infants were baptized but not admitted to Communion until they confirmed their baptism by taking on themselves the promises that had been made for them by their parents and sponsors (godparents).[129] But not all adults were admitted to Communion, because it was necessary to approach the Table in the right spirit of penitence. Therefore, intending communicants were expected to make their confession to the priest beforehand and not to receive the elements until they had been absolved of their sins.[130]

Finally, it was not clear whether a communicant had to receive both the bread and the wine, or whether it was enough to have only one of them. This was debated for much of the fourteenth and early fifteenth centuries because the cup was then being withdrawn from the laypeople. Whether this was a measure of public hygiene in the face of widespread disease and the bubonic plague, or whether it was a theological development connected to the elevation of the priesthood above the laity is not clear, but the effect was the same. Objectors pointed out that this was unbiblical (which it clearly was) and untraditional

---

[128] See 1 Cor. 11:29.

[129] It is telling that the first official mention of confirmation occurs in 1415 in the articles condemning John Wyclif, who had apparently complained that the rite had been reserved to the bishops because they wanted financial gain and worldly prestige (Article 28). See *Conciliorum oecumenicorum decreta*, 412, and also Articles 7–8 on page 422. It was not really defined properly until the seventh session of the Council of Trent (March 3, 1547), in conscious opposition to Protestant objections. See *Conciliorum oecumenicorum decreta*, 686.

[130] The practice was ancient, but it was not until canon 21 of the Fourth Lateran Council (1215) that any serious attempt was made to regulate it. See *Conciliorum oecumenicorum decreta*, 245. Once again, the link with the promulgation of transubstantiation at the same council can hardly be accidental.

(which it also was), but the church justified it by claiming the power to modify ancient teaching when necessary. It also claimed that because the blood is present in the body, receiving the bread was sufficient—the blood was contained in it! The priests, however, continued to drink the cup, and it was argued that they did so on behalf of the people, because, like Christ, they were mediators between them and God.[131]

Interestingly, considering what was supposed to have happened to the bread and wine, much less emphasis was placed on them. There was no stipulation that the bread had to be of a certain kind, though the Roman church continued to use unleavened wafers in accordance with its ancient tradition. Nor was it clear whether the wine had to be fermented or not. It was not even specified that it had to be red (so as to look like blood), though most of the time it probably was. Perhaps it was felt that these details did not matter—after all, once the bread and wine had become Christ's body and blood, what difference did it make what they had been before?

This was the point to which the doctrine of the Mass had developed at the time of the Reformation, and with some minor modifications it has remained largely unchanged in the Roman Catholic Church today. In recent years Catholic priests have sometimes restored the cup to the laypeople, or practiced what is known as intinction—dipping the bread in the wine. But apart from that there has been little or no change, and the Mass continues to be the central act of worship because it is there, more than anywhere else, that the work of Christ is brought home to the people of God who have come to partake of it.

The Sacramental System

The Eucharist was the center and high point of the church's worship, but it was by no means the only thing that characterized the body of Christ in this world. Around the *missa* there grew up a number of subsidiary devotions, some of which were directly dependent on it (like the adoration of the reserved body and blood, set aside after the initial celebration for use in emergencies) and others that led up to it (like litanies of penitence that were supposed to prepare the worshiper to receive the consecrated elements). The church knew that although the Eucharist was the chief means by which God's grace was given to the world, it was not the only one, and before long there were theologians trying to determine how many such ways there were and regulating them accordingly.

The classic formulation of this was made by Peter Lombard, who came up

[131] The controversy came to a head at the Council of Constance, where Jan Hus (1371?–1415), a Czech reformer who insisted that everyone must communicate in both kinds (*sub utraque specie*), was condemned and burned at the stake as a heretic. See *Conciliorum oecumenicorum decreta*, 418–419 for the details of the condemnation.

with the notion that there were seven special rites in which God gave his grace to his people. Peter called these rites the "sacraments," and thus a whole new sub-branch of theology was brought into being.

The term "sacrament" was itself an ancient one. It can be traced back to Tertullian, who used it exclusively of baptism.[132] The Latin word *sacramentum* meant "oath," and the original image was that of the oath of allegiance that a soldier took to the emperor upon entering his service.[133] Tertullian was undoubtedly aware of that, but his use of the word was probably dictated by the fact that Latin-speaking Christians were already employing it as a translation of the Greek *mystêrion*, which occurs about twenty times in the New Testament, often in connection with "faith."[134] Its precise meaning is hard to pin down, but it certainly did not refer to a rite like baptism. More probably it meant the content of the Christian gospel, which could only be known by a divine revelation that was not given until the coming of Christ—hence the note of secrecy or mystery. Tertullian displayed an awareness of this when he argued against those who denied the necessity of baptism on the ground that all that was needed was the faith of Abraham, which was also a "sacrament."[135] His answer to them was that just as Abraham's faith had been augmented by the incarnation, passion, and resurrection of the Lord, so it had also been augmented by the sign of baptism. That sign had been given in order to show that what had previously been a purely intellectual belief (what Tertullian called "naked faith") had now been clothed in flesh and blood, which had to be cleansed because one day they too would be resurrected.

The connection between inward faith and its outward expression became the dominant theme in the later development of the word *sacramentum*. Whereas the Greek term *mystêrion* retained its essentially spiritual character and was only gradually (and tentatively) attached to particular acts, the Latin *sacramentum* soon came to be used of the Eucharist, as well as of baptism. This development was made easier because Latin had also adopted the word *mysterium*. The first person to write about sacraments as a specific category was Ambrose of Milan, who composed two works on the subject, one of them called *De mysteriis* and the other *De sacramentis*! Each of these is a series of sermons that he preached on the meaning of baptism and the Eucharist, and they are rich in allegorical symbolism drawn from Scripture.

Ambrose did not define the word *sacramentum* in the narrow sense that

[132] Tertullian, *De baptismo*, 1.1. For a detailed study of his use of the term, see René Braun, Deus Christianorum*: Recherches sur le vocabulaire doctrinal de Tertullien*, 2nd ed. (Paris: Etudes Augustiniennes, 1977), 435–443.
[133] That the word continued to be used in this sense is attested by *serment*, the modern French word for "oath."
[134] See, for example, Col. 1:27; 1 Tim. 3:9.
[135] Tertullian, *De baptismo* 13.

it was to acquire in later times. Another of his works is called *De incarnationis Dominicae sacramento* (*On the Sacrament of the Lord's Incarnation*), where the underlying sense of "mystery" is clearly dominant, and the same was probably true of his *De sacramento regenerationis* (*On the sacrament of regeneration*), which unfortunately has been lost. Ambrose also wrote a book about penitence, but he did not call it a sacrament in the way that later tradition would do. We must therefore conclude that although he sometimes used "sacrament" to refer specifically to the rites of baptism and the Eucharist, he was still able to employ the word in its more general sense of *mysterium* and had no conception of what we would now call "sacramental theology."

Ambrose's usage and authority remained unchallenged for hundreds of years. The subject of the sacraments was not really tackled again until Hugh of St. Victor took it up in the early twelfth century.[136] It is to him that we owe what was to become the classical definition of a sacrament as the "outward and visible sign of an inward and spiritual grace." As Hugh put it,

> A sacrament is a corporeal or material element set before the outward senses, representing by likeness, signifying by institution, and containing by sanctification some invisible and spiritual grace.[137]

In Hugh's opinion, a sacrament must bear some resemblance to what it is supposed to signify, it must be authorized by divine institution, and it must be sanctified, or set apart for sacred use, by words of consecration—as Augustine had said before him.[138]

Hugh's great work is a compendium of his whole theology, starting with the creation of the world and proceeding through the fall of man to the giving of both the natural and the divine law. The second book begins with the incarnation of Christ and goes on to examine the nature of the church and spiritual authority within it. Finally, Hugh comes to the sacraments themselves. Baptism naturally claims pride of place, with Confirmation tacked on to it as an appendix.[139] Hugh then moves on to the Eucharist before devoting the last half of the book to a series of practices that have a sacramental character even if they are not sacraments in the true sense of the word. This part of the work shows us the state of confusion that existed in Hugh's time, when it was not certain what ought to be counted as sacraments beyond Baptism and the Eucharist. Many of the things he mentioned are best regarded as appendages to the Eucharist

[136] See Rorem, *Hugh of Saint Victor*, 69–115.
[137] Hugh of St. Victor, *De sacramentis* 1.9.2.
[138] Augustine of Hippo, *Tractatus in Iohannis Evangelium* 80.3.
[139] Hugh of Saint Victor, *De sacramentis* 2.7.

or explanations of abuses such as simony, but among the rites he mentions it is possible to distinguish Matrimony, Penance, and perhaps Extreme Unction.[140] Hugh's exposition is inevitably somewhat open-ended, but in it we can discern the outlines of what was soon to become the classical sacramental system of the Middle Ages.

It fell to Peter Lombard to take matters further, balancing Hugh's biblically based, traditional approach, which we would now call "salvation history," with the more analytical method employed by men like Peter Abelard. Peter Lombard's *Sentences* were intended to be a compendium of traditional theology, compiled from the fathers of the church with an accompanying commentary. They were theoretically based on Augustine's *De doctrina Christiana*, dealing first with things that are to be enjoyed, next with things that are to be used, third with things that are to be both enjoyed and used, and finally with the signs that point to them. They appeared in four books, the first of which was devoted to God the Trinity (meant to be enjoyed), the second to creation (meant to be used), and the third to the incarnation of the Son, the point at which God and creation intersect (meant to be both enjoyed and used). The fourth book is devoted to the sacraments (the signs), with a coda at the end dealing with the last things and other miscellanea.

Although the Lombard's general scheme was Augustinian, he went far beyond his ancient master in the way that he treated his subjects, especially in the fourth book. For Peter, access to the grace of God revealed in Christ was the most important thing, and it was in developing that theme that his work was to make its most original contribution and have lasting impact. As he saw it, there were five sacraments that were personal and universal, in the sense that they were meant to be used by every Christian. These were Baptism, Confirmation, Holy Communion, Penance, and Extreme Unction. Alongside them there were two more that were not meant for everyone and which in the Lombard's time were coming to be seen as mutually exclusive. These were Ordination and Matrimony, which made up the total of seven.

As far as anyone knows, Peter invented this number—seven was often used for holy things, and it represented the perfection of God's gifts, just as the seven-day week represented the perfection of his creation. To get to seven, a certain amount of inventiveness was required, but Peter rose to the challenge. Baptism and Holy Communion were obvious contenders, but the others were something of a mixed bag, being practices that were found in the church and could be regarded as giving grace to those who received them, even though

[140] See *De sacramentis* 2.11, 14, and 15, respectively.

they were not called sacraments in the New Testament and matrimony was not exclusive to Christianity. Following the analogy of the seven-day week, Peter believed that although there were seven sacraments, a Christian would normally receive only six of them, because however powerful the grace of God might be, life on earth could never reflect the fullness of life in heaven, just as the six days of human labor could not encompass the Sabbath rest of God that is reserved for us beyond the grave. Following this pattern, we find the following:

Common to all believers	Reserved for some believers
Baptism	Holy Orders
Confirmation	Holy Matrimony
Penance	
Eucharist (Holy Communion)	
Extreme Unction	

After a brief introduction in which he defined what a sacrament was and explained the nature of Old Testament signs like circumcision, Peter treated the Christian sacraments in the order given above, but the amount of space he devoted to each of them varied enormously, as the following table shows:

Sacrament	Distinctions[A]		Pages[B]
[Old Testament signs]	1	(1)	8
Baptism	2–6	(5)	30
Confirmation	7	(1)	2
Holy Communion	8–13	(6)	29
Penance	14–22	(9)	66
Extreme Unction	23	(1)	3
Holy Orders	24–25	(2)	18
Holy Matrimony	26–42	(17)	77
[Last Things, etc.]	43–50	(8)	43

Notes: [A]The text is subdivided into "distinctions," as was common at the time. This was not done by the Lombard himself but by Alexander of Hales (1185?–1245), who was the first to use the *Sentences* as a textbook. After that, the work became the standard introduction to theology for several centuries, and no one could become a professor of the subject without writing a commentary on it. Even Martin Luther did so. See P. Vignaux, *Luther, commentateur des Sentences* (Paris: Vrin, 1935), who brings out Luther's links to the teaching of men like Robert Holcot and William of Ockham, who also wrote commentaries on the *Sentences* in their time; and P. Kärkkäinen, "Martin Luther," in Gillian R. Evans and Philipp Rosemann, eds., *Mediaeval Commentaries on the Sentences of Peter Lombard: Current Research*, 2 vols. (Leiden: Brill, 2002–2010), 2:471–494. [B]In the recent English translation by Giulio Silano (Toronto, 2010).

Baptism and Holy Communion, the two traditional sacraments, each got about the same amount of attention, which is what we would expect. Holy Orders were also fairly extensively treated. Confirmation and Extreme Unction, on the other hand, received hardly any coverage, which probably reflects their somewhat ambiguous status as "sacraments" and the fact that there was relatively little interest in either of them. The real surprise is the amount of space devoted to Penance and to Holy Matrimony, particularly at a time when celibacy was being imposed on the clergy. Penance was a relatively recent sacrament and had not been extensively treated before, which may explain why there is so much about it here. Matrimony stood out from the rest because it was the only sacrament based on the natural law of creation rather than on any special divine revelation, and so it had plenty of non-Christian counterparts. It was what made it "holy" that was of particular concern to theologians as well as being of great practical importance, since by Peter's time, the church had acquired a virtual monopoly on marriage in Western Europe.

In defining what a sacrament was, the Lombard did no more than pick up what Hugh of St. Victor had said, though he managed to put it more succinctly and therefore more memorably—"a sacrament is a visible form of an invisible grace."[141] His take on Old Testament observances is especially noteworthy. As he put it,

> Those things which were instituted only for the sake of signifying are merely signs, and not sacraments; such were the carnal sacrifices and the ceremonial observances of the old law, which could never justify those who offered them.[142]

For Peter, a sacrament was more than just a sign of God's grace; it was also a means by which that grace was conferred on the recipient, with the intention of healing him from sin. Every sacrament consisted of two elements—a word from God to explain and to bless it, and a thing from nature that was used to express it. It was possible to have only the word, particularly in the case of Penance, where God's forgiveness could be received without any corresponding external act, and it would still be valid. It was also possible to have the thing without the word, especially in baptism, where a person could be immersed in water without hearing or receiving the word of salvation accompanying it. In that case, the sacrament would not be valid unless and until the word meant to accompany it was understood and appropriated. In other words, the outward

[141] Peter Lombard, *Sententiae* 4.1.2. There is an allusion here to Augustine of Hippo, *Quaestiones in Heptateuchum* 3.84.
[142] Peter Lombard, *Sententiae* 4.1.4.3.

sign could only express the inward and spiritual grace; if that grace was lacking, the sign had no power of itself to produce it.[143]

It is interesting to note that Peter also regarded the Old Testament practice of circumcision as being sacramental in character.[144] The reason for this was that circumcision was originally given as an outward sign of Abraham's inner faith, which both Paul and Augustine regarded as sufficient for his justification before God.[145] It was eventually replaced by baptism, because as Peter explained,

> The sacrament of baptism is more common [i.e., it is available to women as well as men] and more perfect, being augmented by a fuller grace. For in circumcision sins were only remitted, but neither the grace that assists in good works, nor the possession or increase of the virtues, was granted by it. This happens in baptism, where not only are sins abolished but helping grace is also conferred and the virtues are increased.[146]

Baptism needed no special justification, since it was clearly enjoined in the New Testament. Peter classified John's baptism among the signs of the Old Testament, because like them, it proclaimed the forgiveness that was coming but did not confer it. He explained why some who had received John's baptism were rebaptized as Christians, while others were not, by arguing that the former had put their faith in the efficacy of John's baptism whereas the latter had seen it as a sign of the grace to come and therefore needed only the laying on of hands in order to receive the Holy Spirit.[147] The rest of what Peter had to say about baptism was drawn from a number of early church sources, which is what we would expect. Perhaps the most interesting section is the one devoted to catechesis before baptism, which Peter associated with exorcism and said was standard practice, even though neither could have been at all common in his time.[148]

By the twelfth century, Confirmation had become a rite in which those who had been baptized in infancy made a personal profession of faith, after which they were admitted to Holy Communion. Then as now, the justification for it was debated, but the nature of the discussion then was different from what we normally hear today. In Peter's day the main question was why Confirma-

[143] Ibid., 4.4.2.1–3. This is essentially the position taken today by those who practice infant baptism.
[144] Ibid., *Sententiae* 4.1.7.1.
[145] Rom. 4:1–3; Augustine of Hippo, *De nuptiis et concupiscentia* 2.11.24.
[146] Peter Lombard, *Sententiae* 4.1.9.5.
[147] Ibid., 4.2.6.2–3. The New Testament references are to Acts 19:2–6 for rebaptism and to Acts 1:22 and 2:4 for the filling with the Holy Spirit on top of John's baptism. See also Acts 8:15–17.
[148] Peter Lombard, *Sententiae* 4.6.7.1–4.

tion could be administered only by the bishop, not by the priest who baptized, since in early times the sealing of the candidate with the holy chrism was the concluding act of the baptismal rite and not a distinct ceremony. As baptism became too common for the bishop to administer in every case, it had been delegated to others (usually, though not necessarily, to the presbyters), but the bishops had retained the right to seal the newly baptized with the chrism as a sign that all believers were united under them.[149]

This right was jealously guarded in the Western church, leading people to wonder whether there was something special about it because it was reserved for the highest dignitaries to perform. Peter managed to produce a quotation from Rabanus Maurus (776?–856) to the effect that while Baptism took away sin, Confirmation strengthened the candidate with the Holy Spirit, making it "higher" in that sense and justifying the practice of reserving its administration to the bishops.[150] Beyond that he did not go, but although the practice has frequently been questioned, it continues more or less unaltered in episcopally ordered churches to the present day.[151] Then as now, it reinforced the role of the church hierarchy, and for many that was all the justification they needed.

Holy Communion was for the Lombard the centerpiece of the sacramental system, the rite which made sense of all the others and that bound the church together in a way that nothing else could. As he put it,

> Baptism puts out the fire of [our] vices, but the Eucharist restores [us] spiritually. That is why it is so well called the Eucharist, meaning "good grace," because in this sacrament not only is there an increase of virtue and grace, but he who is the source and origin of all grace is received entire.[152]

After explaining the Old Testament precedents for the Lord's Supper and Christ's institution of it the night before his death, Peter went on to insist on the objective reality of the sacramental change (or "conversion," as he called it) of the bread and wine into the body and blood of Christ. The most interesting thing about his exposition was the distinction he made between the change in the elements, which he regarded as certain, and the spiritual reception of Christ's body, which was reserved to those who partook of the sacrament in the right way. It was therefore possible for a bad minister to celebrate a valid Eucharist, and for those who took part in it unworthily to receive the body and blood of Christ, but only in a "sacramental sense." The meaning of this phrase

[149] This was not the case in the Eastern churches, where chrismation (the nearest equivalent to confirmation) has always been administered immediately after baptism and by the officiating priest, not by the bishop.

[150] Peter Lombard, *Sententiae* 4.7.3.1. See Rabanus Maurus, *De institutione clericorum*, 1.30.

[151] See Martos, *Doors to the Sacred*, 179–202.

[152] Peter Lombard, *Sententiae* 4.8.1.1.

is that although such a person received exactly the same thing as one who was in the right state of mind, he did not experience communion with Christ, but rather ate and drank to his own condemnation, as the apostle Paul said.[153] Peter was determined to retain the essence of transubstantiation without losing the spiritual nature of the sacrament, but his analysis shows how difficult that was to achieve. On the other hand, the open-endedness of his approach was such that it provided a platform for all subsequent discussion of the subject. Even those who rejected transubstantiation in later times could find something in the *Sentences* on which to base their views, and that is perhaps the true measure of Peter's greatness as a teacher and theologian.

The sense that Peter Lombard was writing in an age of transition from one kind of theology to another, and that he was not always sure which way to go, is confirmed when we look at the way he dealt with the sacrament of Penance. The extraordinary amount of attention that he paid to it is a clear sign that he did not know quite what to say. It is hard to believe that he devoted more space to Penance than to Baptism, Confirmation, and Holy Communion *combined*, but that is the case, even if there were only nine distinctions dedicated to it instead of twelve for the others. The first thing Peter had to do was to establish the place Penance occupied within the general sacramental scheme, which he did by quoting Jerome:

> Penance is necessary for those who are far away [from God], to enable them to draw near to him. As Jerome says, "it is the second plank after the shipwreck," because if someone has stained the robe of innocence he received in baptism by sinning again, he can clean it by recourse to penance. . . . Those who have fallen after baptism can be restored by penance, but not by baptism, because it is all right to do penance frequently, whereas rebaptism is forbidden. Baptism is a sacrament only, but penance is both a sacrament and a virtue of the mind. There is an outer penance which is a sacrament, and an inner penance which is a virtue of the mind, but both bring about justification and salvation.[154]

To understand this, we have to appreciate that the Lombard was working with three different levels of grace.[155] These can best be understood by schematizing them as follows:

1. Justification: this is the essence of the thing signified by both inner and outer penance.

[153] Ibid., 4.9.3.1–3.
[154] Ibid., 4.14.1.1–2. The quotation is from Jerome, *Epistula* 130.9.
[155] Ibid., 4.22.2.5.

2. Inner penance: this is the disposition of the heart that the outer penance signifies.
3. Outer penance: this is the act that testifies to both the inner disposition and justification.

In this scheme of things, outer penance is required because it is testimony to the reality of the inner change of heart, which in turn is the fruit of our justification before God. This makes sense in human terms, because how can we know whether a person is sorry for what he has done wrong unless he demonstrates his regret by some act of contrition or reparation? Saying "sorry" is meaningless without a change of behavior, and if that is what outer penance is supposed to encourage, then so be it.

But what if a person is inwardly sorry for what he has done wrong but has not demonstrated this outwardly, either because no one has told him how to go about it or because the nature of the sin makes outward penance inappropriate. For example, if I have bad thoughts toward another person, I may repent of those and be genuinely sorry, but it would not be very helpful to reveal the fact to others who may be quite unaware that I have had them, so I keep quiet and reserve my sorrow for God alone. Am I forgiven if I do that?

To this, Peter had to answer in the affirmative, because the ultimate issue at stake is the sinner's relationship to God, but although he recognized that, it was only very reluctantly that he did so. In his words,

> Just as inner penance is enjoined on us, so too are both the confession of the mouth and outer satisfaction, if the opportunity for them exists. Someone who does not have any desire to confess is not truly penitent. Just as the forgiveness of sins is a gift from God, so the [outer] penance and confession by which sin is erased must also be from God. . . . The penitent must therefore confess if he has the time to do so, but forgiveness is granted to him before his oral confession if the desire is present in his heart.[156]

It is clear that Peter preferred oral confession if at all possible, using as his pretext for this the authority of the apostle James, who said, "Confess your sins to one another."[157] Moreover, the Lombard took it for granted that in normal circumstances, this confession should be made to a priest. As he put it, "It is necessary to make confession to God first, and then to a priest. It is not possible to get to heaven otherwise, if the opportunity [for making such a

[156] Ibid., 4.17.1.13.
[157] James 5:16.

confession] exists."[158] But he reluctantly conceded that there was a second-best option: "If a priest is not available, confession should be made to a neighbor or to a friend."[159]

Yet for all Peter's deference to the institutional church, he was aware that forgiveness is a gift of God, not of man. It was certainly true that Jesus had given Peter the keys of the kingdom of heaven, so that whatever he bound on earth would be bound in heaven, and whatever he loosed (i.e., forgave) on earth would be loosed in heaven.[160] But Peter explained this power as follows:

> We can rightly say and teach that God alone forgives or does not forgive sins, even though he has granted the church the power of binding and loosing. He binds and looses in one way, and the church in another. He forgives sin in a way that cleanses the soul from its inner stain and frees it from the punishment of eternal death. But he has not granted this power to priests. On the contrary, he has given them the power of binding and loosing, which means the power of telling people whether they have been bound or loosed.[161]

In another striking passage, Peter also demonstrated that he understood that the truly penitent heart was one that had been touched by the love of God. Such a person has been set free from the wrath that comes upon unrepentant sinners and can live the penitent life in the right spirit.[162] It is at that point that the role of the priest becomes central to the act of penance, because it is the priest's duty to guide the repentant sinner in deciding how best to manifest the fruits of divine love in the way he lives. Unfortunately, Peter was forced to admit that here the church often failed its members because few priests were sufficiently discerning to be able to be good guides in this respect. His words will be echoed by anyone who has trained men for ministry:

> Many lack the discernment and are devoid of the knowledge that ought to distinguish a priest, yet they presume to enter the ranks of the priesthood, even though they are unworthy of it . . . and cannot discern who is to be bound and who loosed.[163]

Here Peter touched a raw nerve. The theory of penance was a good one, but the practice was hindered, not only by a certain unwillingness (or inability) on the part of church members to confess their sins, but by the lack of pastoral

---

158 Peter Lombard, *Sententiae* 4.17.3.1, 8.
159 Ibid., 4.17.4.2.
160 Matt. 16:19.
161 Peter Lombard, *Sententiae* 4.18.5.5–6.1.
162 Ibid., 4.18.4.6.
163 Ibid., 4.19.1.3.

skills required in those whose duty it was to administer the sacrament. It is hard not to conclude that Peter wanted something that the church could not deliver, and that part of the problem was a misunderstanding of what penance was supposed to be. What was in theory an act of overflowing love too often turned into a ritual that followed on confessing sin to a priest who had little or no idea of how to respond. Penance was intended to ensure that such confessions were sincere and to prepare the penitent for Communion, but although such preparation is clearly beneficial, it is hard to see how the spiritual discernment required to make it work effectively could ever be objectified and regulated in the way that Peter envisaged.

Extreme Unction was originally the anointing of the sick mentioned in James 5:14–15, which over time came to be seen more as a preparation for death, probably because in premodern times many people who fell sick did not recover from their illnesses. Peter believed that the healing of the body was a secondary issue—whether the recipient lived or died, the sacrament brought healing to his soul, and that was what counted.[164] Peter did not say much more about it, except that if the sick person recovered, the sacrament could always be repeated the next time he fell ill. But although the rite was of little consequence to him, it would soon take on much greater importance. As the sacramental system developed, Extreme Unction would come to be seen as a kind of last confession, in the hope that the dying Christian would be in the right state of mind and spirit to face his Maker and Judge. However, it would not be until the fourteenth session of the Council of Trent (November 25, 1551) that the sacrament would be defined in those terms and made part of the Roman Catholic Church's official doctrine.[165]

Alongside these five sacraments, which every Christian was meant to receive at some point in their lives, there were Ordination and Matrimony. By the time Peter was writing, only celibates could be ordained to the ministry of the church, and those who were already married could not enter Holy Orders. This was contrary to the biblical teaching, and also to the ancient practice of the church, but it was imposed as a discipline for other reasons. A married priest had a family to provide for, which would have meant using the resources of the church for private purposes, and many people thought that was an abuse. It also meant that the priest would be tied to his parish in ways that might compromise his ability to minister impartially to everyone in it. A celibate priest did not have this problem and could be more independent. These and other such reasons lay behind the push for universal, compulsory celibacy for the clergy,

164 Ibid., 4.23.3.2.

165 *Conciliorum oecumenicorum decreta*, 710–711.

but it was a long time coming. Even when it was finally imposed, clerical marriage was hard to eradicate, and in Ireland it survived as a canonical irregularity until the sixteenth-century Reformation.

In Peter Lombard's time, a hierarchy of orders had evolved within the church, but the rationale for this remained somewhat elusive. Peter claimed that there were seven orders, corresponding to the sevenfold grace of the Holy Spirit, that Christ himself had given to his church. Where he got this idea from is unclear. There were different ministries mentioned in the New Testament under the general heading of "spiritual gifts,"[166] but Peter's list bore little or no relation to them. Instead, they were cobbled together from a variety of sources and arranged in ascending order as follows:

> Door-keepers: they guard the church doors and prevent unsuitable people from entering.[167]
>
> Lectors: they read the Scriptures and direct public worship.[168]
>
> Exorcists: they rebuke the ungodly and drive away evil spirits.[169]
>
> Acolytes: they light the candles and prepare the church for worship.[170]
>
> Subdeacons: they collect the offerings of the people and prepare the bread and wine for Communion.[171]
>
> Deacons: they correspond to the Levites of the Old Testament and assist the priests.[172]
>
> Priests: they consecrate the Eucharist and normally administer the other sacraments.[173]

Of these orders, only two were properly "holy," because they alone were of apostolic origin—the deacons and the priests (presbyters).[174] Peter did not say anything about compulsory celibacy, possibly because it was too recent or perhaps because he did not agree with it, but it applied only to priests (and bishops). One interesting point is that Peter saw the office of bishop (and therefore also that of pope) as sacramentally part of the priestly order. Bishops were priests with special responsibilities, and as for the pope,

166 Compare Rom. 12:6–8; 1 Cor. 12:8–10, 28; Eph. 4:11.
167 Peter Lombard, *Sententiae* 4.24.5.1.
168 Ibid., 4.24.6.1.
169 Ibid., 4.24.7.1–2.
170 Ibid., 4.24.8.1–2.
171 Ibid., 4.24.9.2.
172 Ibid., 4.24.10.2.
173 Ibid., 4.24.11.3.
174 Ibid., 4.24.12.1.

> The pope is the prince of priests. . . . He is called the highest priest because he is the one who makes priests and deacons; he dispenses all ecclesiastical orders.[175]

In other words, the pope was different from other bishops and priests in function but not in kind, since he also derived his sacramental authority from the priesthood into which he had been ordained. The word "priest" is derived from a combination of *presbyter* and *praepositus* ("provost"), the former meaning "elder" in Greek and the latter "overseer" in Latin.[176] There had been presbyters in the New Testament period, though we are not sure how they were appointed or what exactly they did, though before long they appeared as a group of men in each church who assisted the bishop in his duties. As the church expanded, these duties came to be associated with running local congregations, and the parish priest as we know him came into being. Originally the term had nothing to do with church worship, but gradually it was accepted that the priest would conduct worship and celebrate Holy Communion in the absence of the bishop. Practice varied as to how much delegation there would be from the bishop to the priest. In the Eastern churches, priests administered both baptism and chrismation, which followed immediately on from baptism as its confirmation, but in the Western church, confirmation was never delegated to the presbyteral order.

As time went on, the Lord's Supper was increasingly assimilated to the Old Testament sacrifices and the word "priest" was used for the cultic officials of ancient Israel as well as for the ministers of the Christian church. From there it spread to include pagan "priests," and the words used in Latin (*sacerdos*) and Greek (*hiereus*) for those who offered the sacrifices came to be applied to Christian presbyters as well. English did not have a word for these pagan or Jewish cultic officials, so the word "priest" was extended to cover them, even though the origin of the word was quite different. So strong has that cultic association now become that modern Protestants usually try to avoid using the word "priest" to describe their own ministers, even though, historically speaking, they have every reason to do so.[177]

Having said all that about the church and its officers, Peter then turned to

---

[175] Ibid., 4.24.16.1.

[176] Note that the Greek form of *presbyter* is *presbyteros*. The Latin word for "elder" would be *senior* and the body of elders was the *senatus*, but although the latter form has retained something of its original meaning, the word *senior* has evolved into "lord" or "mister," as in *señor*, *signiore*, *senhor*, *seigneur*, etc. It has never been used to describe an officer of the church.

[177] Another example of how a word can change its meaning and become unusable is "silly," which once meant "blessed" (as does the German equivalent *selig*). King James I (1603–1625) described himself as "God's silly vassal," but he would not do so if he were alive today!

the institution of Matrimony. Unlike the other sacraments, Matrimony was not of Christian origin but went back to the beginning of the creation, when Adam and Eve were told to "be fruitful and multiply."[178] After the fall, matrimony became the approved way of reining in sexual desires, which were held to be uniformly evil unless they were protected by a good marriage.[179] Peter had to face the difficulty that the apostle Paul spoke of marriage as a second-best for those who could not remain celibate,[180] but he not only did so—he succeeded in demonstrating that, properly understood, it was indeed a sacrament and that Paul had said as much elsewhere![181] In his words,

> Marriage is a sacrament, the sacred sign of a sacred thing, which is the union of Christ and the church, as the Apostle says, . . . the bride is joined to the bridegroom spiritually and bodily, both by love and by a likeness of nature. The symbol of both these unions is in marriage, because the harmony of the spouses signifies the spiritual union of Christ and the church that comes about through love, and their sexual union signifies that which comes about through likeness of nature.[182]

At first sight, such a definition of marriage was very appealing, but it came up against the obvious difficulty that it could not apply to what for Peter was the most important marriage of all time—the union of Mary the mother of Jesus with Joseph, which in Peter's view did not involve sexual intercourse. He was forced to admit that their relationship was defective in that respect, but insisted that as a union of heart and mind it surpassed all others and therefore deserved to be called a proper marriage.[183] Most of the rest of the distinctions concerning Matrimony deal with practical issues more closely connected to canon law than to theology proper, a reminder that theory could never be separated from pastoral practice. It is nevertheless worth remembering that, in a church increasingly dominated by a celibate clergy, Matrimony was the one sacrament reserved to the laity, and its importance was underlined by the picture it gave of how Christ bound himself to the church.

Another way the sacraments could be analyzed was by dividing them into those that could be administered only once, those that were normally administered only once but could in exceptional circumstances be repeated, and those

[178] Gen. 1:28.
[179] Peter Lombard, *Sententiae* 4.26.2.3.
[180] 1 Cor. 7:1–2, 6.
[181] Eph. 5:31. Note that Peter interprets the word *mystêrion* in the text not as "mystery" but as "sacrament."
[182] Peter Lombard, *Sententiae* 4.26.6.1.
[183] Ibid., 4.30.2.2–5.

that were meant to be repeated on a regular basis. Following that line of division, what we come up with is,

Once only	**Once usually**	**Repeated**
Baptism	Holy Matrimony	Penance
Confirmation	Extreme Unction	Eucharist
Holy Orders		

Baptism was the grace of the new birth in Christ and could be given only once since it is not possible to be born again a second time. Confirmation, as the corollary of Baptism, was likewise to be administered only once. Holy Orders were regarded as "indelible"—once a priest, always a priest! This caused problems when it was necessary to depose someone from the ministry, but the logic of sacramental grace was inexorable. If a man could not function as a priest, that was for disciplinary reasons. He still possessed the grace of priesthood and could at least theoretically be reinstated in his ministry, because as the Scripture says, "The gifts and the calling of God are irrevocable"![184]

Holy Matrimony was normally to be given only once, but if one of the parties died the other was free to remarry, and in that case the sacrament could be received a second time. There was no allowance for divorce, and to this day those churches that regard Matrimony as having a sacramental character do not remarry divorced people during the lifetime of their former spouse. Extreme Unction, which was originally meant to be the anointing of the sick for recovery but had become a preparation for death instead was also normally administered only once, though if the sick person were to recover there was no reason why he could not receive it again when the need arose.

Penance and the Eucharist were meant to be repeated on a regular basis, and the two became closely interconnected. A person who wanted to receive Holy Communion was supposed to be in a "state of grace," which implied that he had repented of his sins and made his peace with God and his neighbors. In practice this meant confessing to a priest beforehand and being told to perform certain acts that would demonstrate the sincerity of his repentance. Over time this led to a whole "sin industry," with theologians compiling lists of mortal and "venial" (forgivable) sins, each of which came with an appropriate penance attached. The whole thing became a vast calculation, with sins and penances being ticked off against one another just like crimes and punishments.

[184] See Rom. 11:29. The context, of course, is completely different.

Of course it was very likely that a person would die without having confessed every sin or done penance for it, which naturally left him in debt at the end of his life. How could that debt be paid off? Here the church came up with the ingenious invention of purgatory, a place of punishment and cleansing after death where Christians could work off their outstanding debts and gain entry to heaven. It was a brilliant idea because it meant that the church could take punishment for sin seriously without excluding sinners from heaven. Justice would be done, but the guilty would still get their pardon in the end and everyone would be satisfied. Those whom the church had reason to believe had either not gone to purgatory or who had completed their time there and been admitted into heaven were canonized as "saints," to whom others could pray for help and who were capable of performing miracles. In the early days there were few criteria for sainthood, though martyrdom was always a guarantee of it. Reading the history of the first few centuries of the church, it sometimes seems that almost everyone was a saint, even if we know hardly anything about them. Later on, though, the criteria for sainthood became much stricter, and today the Roman Catholic Church sets the bar very high—to become a "saint" you must perform not one but two miracles after your death, and these must be properly authenticated. Modern "sainthood" in this sense is clearly not for everyone!

The sinner who had performed his penance satisfactorily would then return to the priest to seek absolution from him before proceeding to receive Holy Communion. The Eucharist was far and away the most important of the sacraments, so much so that the word "sacrament" is often used to refer to it without further qualification. The reasons for this are several:

1. It is the only sacrament that involves the whole church at the same time. The others are intended for individuals, often in special circumstances. Matrimony is a partial exception in that it involves two people, but it is the exception that proves the general rule, because it does not embrace just *any* two people—terms and conditions apply!

2. It is the heart of regular public worship. Even if only a few of the worshipers communicate, the service is designed to reflect the centrality of the Eucharist, and those who abstain are in effect withdrawing from full participation in the fellowship of the church.

3. It is the only sacrament in which the communicant receives the body and blood of Jesus Christ, which are the tokens and pledges of our salvation. There are many different applications of divine grace but none can ever be as central as this one, because it is on the Son's atoning sacrifice that our forgiveness depends.

It was the last of these reasons that formed the basis for the variety of devotional practices and doctrinal definitions that grew up around the sacrament in the later Middle Ages. The consecrated elements could be (and were) set aside ("reserved"), carried in procession and exposed to public view so that they could be worshiped as if they were Christ himself. Devotional practices of this kind became very popular and their importance should not be underestimated, because it was in this way that the rather abstract doctrine of transubstantiation came to be embedded in popular piety.

The sacramental system developed by Peter Lombard was never officially adopted by the church, but because his *Sentences* became the standard theological textbook that everyone used, its authority was taken for granted. The Eastern churches knew nothing of it, of course, which is why its first official appearance was in the treaty ("bull") of reunion between Rome and the Armenian church, which was promulgated at the eighth session of the Council of Florence (November 22, 1439).[185] That reunion was a failure, and the Eastern churches have never defined the sacraments as closely as their Western counterparts have done, perhaps because they have never been at the center of theological controversy in the East. Peter could not have known it, but his system would be used to construct an entire theology of grace that would capture the mind of the Western church, reshape its pastoral practice, and lead to the lasting schisms of the sixteenth-century Reformation.

The Invention of Purgatory

The sacramental system was developed on the principle that the seven sacraments were the means by which the work of Christ was applied to the life of the believer, who was expected to grow in grace and be progressively transformed into a true child of God. Some of them, especially the Eucharist, had a "corporate dimension," in that they related to the church as a body of believers as much as, if not more than, to particular members, but the system was primarily geared to the needs of individuals. The sacraments were a progression through life, from Baptism at the beginning to Extreme Unction at the end, with the option of Holy Orders or Matrimony at some point in the middle. Eucharistic devotion could not escape this pattern, and students of the subject all agree that it was increasingly privatized as time went on. The idea that a priest could say Mass by himself or on behalf of only one other person would

[185] *Conciliorum oecumenicorum decreta*, 541. It had, however, appeared in the confession of faith which the Byzantine emperor Michael VIII (1258–1282) sent to the Second Council of Lyon in 1274, though the order was different from that of Peter Lombard, with Penance coming before the Eucharist and Extreme Unction relegated to the end of the list. See Denzinger, *Enchiridion*, no. 860.

have been unthinkable in the early church. But in the later Middle Ages private masses became increasingly common, and some priests even made their living by saying them with specific "intentions" for healing, for the departed, or for anything that those willing to pay for them wanted.[186] As one recent study of the phenomenon put it,

> The "fruits" of the Mass—the benefits that it brought—were commonly understood in a quantitative sense, so that two Masses were believed to bring twice as many benefits as one Mass, and this led to a dramatic increase in the number of celebrations. Paying a stipend to a priest to celebrate one or more Masses on one's behalf became one of the accepted ways in which a sinner might seek to expiate his or her fault, and doing the same on behalf of a deceased person in order to purge their sins and secure their salvation also became widespread. The very wealthy would leave money in their wills so that the same might be done for them after their demise. Offering the sacrifice for particular purposes—the "votive" Mass—was what the Eucharist came to be thought of as being all about.[187]

Doing the same on behalf of a dead person in order to purge their sins? It was one thing for the living to ask for Masses to be said on their own behalf, but how could they reach out to the dead and pray for them? The belief that this was somehow possible, and that the dead still needed the prayers of the living, was the catalyst for the next important theological development, which would transform the sacramental system into a way of salvation in its own right.

What happened to people after they died had always been a major concern of the church—not surprisingly, given that eternal salvation was the gift promised to believers. The Old Testament was vague on the subject, and in the time of Jesus Jews were divided over whether there was to be a resurrection of the dead at the end of time or not.[188] Christians had no doubt about that, of course, and Paul told the Philippian church that he would go to be with Christ when he died, which presumably meant that he expected to share in Christ's resurrected life in heaven.[189] But he also said that when Christ comes again, "the dead in Christ will rise first,"[190] which suggests that they were waiting somewhere until that happened, an opinion that was reinforced by a statement in Hebrews about the salvation of the Old Testament saints.[191] To complicate

[186] See Macy, *Banquet's Wisdom*, 144–151.
[187] Bradshaw and Johnston, *Eucharistic Liturgies*, 219. See also Macy, *Banquet's Wisdom*, 114–120; Power, *Eucharistic Mystery*, 226–230, 248–249.
[188] Matt. 22:23–32.
[189] Phil. 1:23.
[190] 1 Thess. 4:16.
[191] Heb. 11:39–40.

matters still further, many people believed that there were some especially holy individuals who had gone to be with the Lord in heaven, either because they had been taken up directly (without passing through death) or because they were considered worthy to stand in God's presence.[192]

The Christian gospel promised a heavenly reward to all believers, irrespective of any merit on their part, but this message proved to be extremely difficult to accept. There was a general feeling that only the good went to heaven and that the church was meant to give people the goodness they needed in order to get there. A few dedicated individuals might succeed in becoming perfect, and it was generally accepted that those who were martyred for their faith had passed through the baptism of suffering mentioned by Jesus and cleansed their remaining sinfulness in the process.[193] These were the saints, who were fit to go to heaven when they died, and that is where they now are. Proof of such sainthood was not always easy to come by, but if it could be demonstrated that prayers to one of them, or to the bones (or other relics) they had left behind on earth, had produced a miracle or two, the likelihood that they had made the grade was greatly increased. The church would set its seal of approval on them by "canonizing" them and allow people to pray to them for assistance. Over time, it came to be thought that some of these saints had particular interests—Christopher was the patron saint of travelers, for example, and Jude of lost causes. People would therefore direct their requests to the appropriate saint, or to the one who was acknowledged as the patron of their village or country. In some cases, pagan gods were simply "baptized" and recycled, as happened with "Saint Denis," the patron saint of France, in whose basilica near Paris the French kings were buried. This Denis never existed—he was the pagan god Dionysus, whose shrine had been turned into a church. He himself was quietly Christianized and integrated into the medieval scheme of salvation without anyone inquiring too deeply into his qualifications for the role![194]

Unfortunately, the majority of people are not as successful in this life as the small band of "saints"—real or imaginary—were. Most of us are far from perfect when we die, and there are undoubtedly sins in our lives that we have not

---

[192] Enoch (Gen. 5:24) and Elijah (2 Kings 2:11) were both taken up directly into heaven. Moses (Matt. 17:3) and Abraham (Luke 16:22) were thought to be there, though they had died a normal human death. On the other hand, Samuel seems to have been somewhere where he was exposed to the danger of being called back to earth by a witch (1 Sam. 28:11–14).

[193] See Mark 10:38–40.

[194] This did not stop Gregory of Tours (538?–594) from inventing (or recycling the legend of) a Denis who was supposed to have been a martyred third-century bishop of Paris. This Denis was said to have demonstrated his sanctity by carrying his severed head ten miles, to the spot where his cathedral now stands (*History of the Franks*, 1.30). Nor did it prevent later generations from identifying him with Dionysius the Areopagite (Acts 17:34), the supposed author of a number of important works of mystical theology. See the article "Denys" in D. H. Farmer, *The Oxford Dictionary of Saints*, 4th ed. (Oxford: Oxford University Press, 1997), 135.

confessed, either because we have not wanted to or because we are unaware of them. What happens to us when we die, if we are not good enough to be let into heaven? At first the church was tempted to say that we shall all go to hell. It had a pessimistic view of human nature and did not find this particularly shocking, but it was soon felt that such a conclusion was too extreme. Many people did their best and were not particularly evil, and it seemed unfair to exclude them from heaven merely because of a few sins they could have repented of in this life but for some reason had failed to. Did not the Bible hold out at least some hope for the eventual salvation of such people? Eventually theologians came up with the idea that there was a place of the dead where they could prepare themselves for eventual entry into heaven. This place was called purgatory, a medieval invention that brought a new sense of order and purpose to previously vague notions of what life after death held in store.

Finding biblical sources for the existence of purgatory was not easy. There was an obscure passage in the apocryphal *2 Maccabees*, where Judas Maccabaeus was portrayed as encouraging prayers for dead soldiers in the hope that their sins might be forgiven, but there is no indication of where they had gone after death.[195] Even so, the passage became (and to some extent still remains) a proof text for the existence of a place of the dead that corresponds to purgatory. Surprising as it may seem to us, the New Testament appeared to many to offer more satisfactory evidence for its existence. Jesus had told his disciples that the blasphemy against the Holy Spirit would not be forgiven "either in this age or in the age to come," an expression which to medieval minds indicated that there was a chance of forgiveness in the age to come (i.e., after death).[196] There was also the story of the rich man and Lazarus, according to which the rich man was agonizing in hell, from where he could see Lazarus enjoying the delights of heaven. The rich man wanted to repent and cross over to join Lazarus in his bliss but was told that he could not.[197] This sounds fairly discouraging, but there were some who thought that the mere fact that there was a dialogue between the rich man and Lazarus allowed for the possibility of some progression from one place to the other.

Most important, though, was the passage in 1 Corinthians where the apostle Paul talks about believers building their spiritual lives on the foundation laid by Christ. He says that if the resulting building turns out to be unsuitable it will be destroyed by fire, but the believer himself will be saved.[198] Here,

[195] *2 Maccabees* 12:41–46.
[196] Matt. 12:32.
[197] Luke 16:19–26.
[198] 1 Cor. 3:11–15.

more than anywhere else in the New Testament, there was some indication that sin could be burned away after death, but the thought was not developed in the early post-apostolic period. All that we find in the early church is a vague awareness of a place where departed souls went, and the suggestion that they were commemorated by those who were still living.[199] For example, the martyr Perpetua had a vision of her seven-year-old brother Dinocrates, who was apparently healed of a wasting disease after his death, but although that vision was frequently appealed to in later literature as justification for the existence of an intermediate state of moral and spiritual cleansing, it is difficult to know whether that was the original intention of the story.[200]

Apart from that, we find nothing but vague allusions to the idea of a cleansing by fire at some future time, most probably at the final judgment, with which it was almost invariably linked.[201] An exception may be made of Augustine, who more than any of the church fathers expounded 1 Corinthians 3:11–15 in a way that would sound familiar to later generations:

> As for the interval between the death of this present body and the coming of the day of judgment and reward at the general resurrection, it may be claimed that it is then that the spirits of the departed suffer this kind of fire. . . . I am not concerned to refute this suggestion, because it may well be true. It is even possible that the death of the body is part of this tribulation.[202]

Augustine's opinion was to be of great importance in later times because he was the first person to call this fire "purgatorial," though what he meant by that is unclear. It is perhaps worth remembering that when he spoke in this way, it was often in the context of dead relatives for whom particular individuals would feel a special concern, and his approach to them was largely pastoral. That Augustine believed that there were two kinds of fire, one that tormented and one that cleansed, seems to be clear enough, but it is virtually certain that he thought of the purifying fire as part of the last judgment and not as a process leading up to that. Even so, Augustine clearly believed that there was room for praying for the departed, especially if their previous manner of life on earth justified it:

---

[199] See, for example, Tertullian, *De corona* 3.2–3.

[200] *Passio sanctarum Perpetuae et Felicitatis* 2.3–4.

[201] See, for example, Origen, *Homiliae in Lucae Evangelium* 24; *Commentarium in Genesim* 6; Lactantius, *Institutiones* 7.21. On this whole subject, see Jacques Le Goff, *The Birth of Purgatory* (Chicago: University of Chicago Press, 1984), 52–95. The book was originally published as *La naissance du purgatoire* (Paris: Gallimard, 1981), and despite some criticisms of its thesis, it remains a classic exposition of the origins of purgatory.

[202] Augustine of Hippo, *De civitate Dei* 21.26.

> Between death and the final resurrection, men's souls are kept in secret storehouses, where they are either at rest or suffering, according to their deserts. . . . They obtain relief by the dutiful service of friends who are still alive, when the Mediator's sacrifice is offered on their behalf or alms are given to the church. But these acts are only of use to those who during their lives had shown themselves deserving of them. Some people live in a way that is not good enough to be able to dispense with such assistance after their deaths, but not bad enough to make it pointless either. . . . The advantage these acts obtain [for the dead] is complete forgiveness of their sin, or at least a mitigation of their punishment.[203]

Much the same view was held by Caesarius of Arles (502–542), who is often mistakenly assumed to have believed in an intermediate state of fiery purgation, and by Gregory the Great (590–604).[204] Caesarius claimed that there were serious sins that would not be wiped away and minor ones that would be, a distinction that was adopted by Gregory and others, which would later give rise to the classical categories of "mortal" (unforgivable) and "venial" (forgivable) sins.[205]

Without a clear lead from either Scripture or tradition, early medieval theologians drifted along in uncertainty, occasionally borrowing ideas from pre-Christian cults of the dead in the newly converted Celtic or Germanic countries of northern Europe but mainly just repeating what they could glean from Augustine and other great men of the past.[206] It was not until the twelfth century, the age of men like Gratian, Hugh of St. Victor, Peter Lombard, and Bernard of Clairvaux, that the nettle of the intermediate state was finally grasped and some attempt was made to bring order out of the conceptual chaos that had prevailed until then. Gratian quoted Augustine as his authority and added a letter sent by Pope Gregory II to St. Boniface sometime around 732, in which he explained that the souls of the dead are delivered from punishment in four different ways: by the sacrifices of the priests, by the prayers of the saints, by the alms of close friends, and by the fasting of relatives.[207]

Like his sources, Gratian says nothing about purgatory as a place, but greater clarity on this subject can be found in the writings of his contemporary, Hugh of St. Victor. Hugh explained it as follows:

---

[203] Augustine of Hippo, *Enchiridion* 109–110. The text acquired great authority in the Middle Ages because it was included in Gratian's *Decretum* (C. 13, q. 2, c. 23).

[204] See Le Goff, *Birth of Purgatory*, 85–95.

[205] Caesarius of Arles, *Sermones* 179; Gregory I the Great, *Dialogi* 4.41. It was Gregory who really laid the groundwork for this distinction in his *Book of Pastoral Rule* or *Pastoral Care*, which became the classic book of spiritual direction in the Middle Ages. See especially Gregory the Great, *De cura pastorali*, 3.33.

[206] See Le Goff, *Birth of Purgatory*, 96–127.

[207] Gratian, *Decretum* C. 13, q. 2, c. 22.

> There is a punishment after death that is called purgatorial. Those who depart this life with certain sins may be righteous and destined for eternal life, but they are tortured there for a while in order to be cleansed. The place where this happens is not definitely fixed, although many instances in which afflicted souls have appeared [as ghosts] suggest that the pain is endured in this world, and probably where the sin was committed. . . . It is hard to know whether such pains are inflicted anywhere else.[208]

Bernard of Clairvaux concurred in this, but he characteristically added a more personal and pastoral note:

> We sympathize with the dead and pray for them, wishing them the joy of hope. We have to feel sorry for their suffering in purgatorial places but must also rejoice at the approach of the moment when "God will wipe away every tear from their eyes, and death shall be no more, neither shall there be mourning, nor crying, nor pain anymore, for the former things have passed away."[209]

Like his contemporaries, Peter Lombard knew nothing of purgatory as a particular place, though he accepted that there was room for penance after this life and made provision for it in the *Sentences*.[210] The importance of this was not so much in what the Lombard said, which was very little, but in the way that later commentators used those passages as a basis on which to build their own, far more elaborate, theories. We must therefore conclude that although the *Sentences* provided the occasion and the justification for their efforts, they did not resolve or even seriously address the question of the existence of purgatory.

According to Jacques Le Goff (1924–2014), the great French historian of the subject, purgatory as a place was first identified by Peter Comestor or Manducator (d. 1178?), writing sometime in or shortly after 1170.[211] The transition from *ignis purgatorius* ("purgatorial fire") or *locus purgatorius* ("purgatorial place") to *purgatorium* ("purgatory") was so easy and natural that it is hard to tell whether it was made deliberately or not. In the oblique cases, the masculine *purgatorius* and the neuter *purgatorium* fall together, and as Le Goff has demonstrated, there is evidence that later copyists simply omitted the accusative forms *ignem* and *locum* that seemed to them unnecessary when accompanied by the qualifying adjective-cum-noun *purgatorium*, thereby giving the false impression that purgatory had been identified as a particular place

208 Hugh of St. Victor, *De sacramentis* 2.16.4.

209 Bernard of Clairvaux *Sermo 16 de diversis*. The biblical quote is Rev. 21:4.

210 Peter Lombard, *Sententiae* 4.21 and 4.45.

211 Le Goff, *Birth of Purgatory*, 155–158, 362–366. Peter became known as "Manducator" ("the Eater") because he devoured books!

some years earlier.[212] Be that as it may, there is no doubt that after 1200, at the very latest, purgatory was established in people's minds as a definite location, though whether it was nearer to heaven or to hell remained uncertain. Those who emphasized the fact that it was a preparation for entry to heaven naturally inclined to the former view, while those who thought in terms of fiery punishment preferred the latter. The great poet Dante Alighieri (1265?–1321), who immortalized purgatory in his great poem, the *Divina commedia*, seems to have placed it somewhere in the middle between the two extremes, though it is noticeable that his guide through both hell and purgatory was the ancient Roman poet Vergil (70–19 BC), who had no access to heaven (paradise) and could not accompany Dante there because he was a pagan.[213]

By the time of the Fourth Lateran Council in 1215, purgatory was an established part of the church's spiritual universe, as can be seen from the important guidebook for priests who were called to hear the confessions of penitent sinners, which was written around that time by Thomas of Chobham (1160?–1236?). Thomas explained that "mass is celebrated for the living and for the dead, but for the dead doubly, because the sacraments of the altar are petitions for the living, thanksgivings for the saints [in heaven], and propitiations for those in purgatory, and result in remission of their punishment."[214] As far as Thomas was concerned, there was nothing anyone could do for those in hell, so the Mass as a propitiation for the dead could apply only to souls in purgatory, which therefore had to exist!

Around the same time, William of Auvergne (1180?–1249) was also making a case for the necessity of purgatory, based on the need for penance.[215] To him it was obvious that most people died with unconfessed sins and that those sins had to be dealt with before the soul of the departed could enter heaven. It was equally obvious to William that some sins were more serious than others—murder, for example, had to be punished, but gluttony or frivolity could be expiated by penance. This was the penitential practice of the church in this world, and there seemed to William to be no reason why it should not be carried on in the next life. He did not believe that this could be used as an excuse for deferring penance in this life; on the contrary, the more sins were expiated now, the fewer there would be to deal with after death, and the soul's time in purgatory would be correspondingly shortened. As an extension of justice on earth, purgatory appealed to William as the supreme example of God's fair-

[212] Ibid., 364–365.
[213] On the importance of Dante for the doctrine of purgatory, see Le Goff, *Birth of Purgatory*, 334–355.
[214] Thomas of Chobham, *Summa confessorum*, ed. Frederick Broomfield (Louvain: Editions Nauwelaerts, 1968), 125–126.
[215] See Le Goff, *Birth of Purgatory*, 241–245 for the details.

ness, but also as an assurance that this life was closely bound up with the next. Interestingly, William seems to have located purgatory on earth, rather than somewhere near to heaven or hell, which merely increased the feeling that it was essentially an extension of the church's ministry to the living.

Moving things on a step further was Alexander of Hales (1185?–1245), the first man to write a commentary on Peter Lombard's *Sentences* and the first teacher to use that book as his main theological text. In his gloss on *Sentences* 4.21 he expounded the Lombard's theory of penance with reference to purgatory, making the following points:

1. Purgatory is a fire that burns up venial sins.
2. Purgatory wipes out penalties for mortal sins that have not been sufficiently paid for.
3. Purgatory is more severe than any earthy punishment.
4. Purgatory is not an unjust or disproportionate punishment.
5. Purgatory is a place of faith and hope, but without the heavenly vision of God.
6. Hardly anyone is good enough to escape the need to pass through purgatory.

Once he had established all that, Alexander went on to examine the relationship between purgatory and the church. Up to this time it was generally assumed that the church could forgive sins in this life, but that its jurisdiction ended at death. But if purgatorial penance was the continuation of what had already started on earth, it seemed logical to assume that the church's jurisdiction would extend beyond the grave. As he put it,

> Just as specific pain brings satisfaction for a particular sin, so the common pain of the universal church, which cries out on behalf of the sins of dead believers . . . is an aid to satisfaction. It does not create satisfaction in itself, but contributes to it along with the pain suffered by the penitent. This is what intercession is all about. Intercession is the merit of the church which is able to lessen the pain of one of its members.[216]

Here we catch a first glimpse of the system of "indulgences," by which the church would claim to remit the sins of the dead and lessen their suffering in purgatory. In the late eleventh century, Ivo of Chartres (1040?–1115) had worked out a theory of dispensation, or non-application of the rules of ecclesiastical law

[216] Alexander of Hales, *Glossa in Magistri Petri Lombardi Sententias* 4.21.

in certain circumstances.[217] According to him, a fundamental distinction had to be made between different kinds of legal principles, as follows:

Praecepta (precepts):	absolute, binding rules.
Consilia (counsels):	suggestions as to how to apply the rules.
Indulgentiae (indulgences):	permitted exceptions to the rules.

Justice demanded obedience to the rules, though of course those rules had to be applied in the right way. The *praecepta* and the *consilia* were therefore interdependent. But human life is seldom as straightforward as the rules would like it to be, and here there was room for a certain tolerance of weakness and failure. It was not easy to determine how much leeway should be granted, and this could be decided only on a case-by-case basis, which is what canon lawyers were employed to do. Indulgences could be granted, but not without good reason, because the rules had to be kept if justice was to be done. The solution was found in penance, which offered payment and restitution for the offenses that had been committed. In the early days, a full indulgence was granted only to those who went on crusade, as a reward for their sacrifice, but in time this would be extended and indulgences would be made readily available to almost anyone who was prepared to pay for them. In special circumstances, they might even be granted *without* such payment, though for obvious reasons such generosity was rare.

To control all of this, it was necessary to establish a form of penance that would be fair to all and universally applicable. The Fourth Lateran Council issued a canon obliging every Christian, both male and female, to confess his or her sins to a priest at least once a year, and to receive an appropriate penance from him.[218] This canon made it necessary to define what sins could be forgiven and what could not—the distinction between "venial" and "mortal" sins mentioned earlier. In this respect, Thomas of Chobham was the right man at the right time, and his little manual became one of the most popular sources for clerical guidance on the subject. The potential for intellectual madness. however, was enormous, as Jacques Le Goff has pointed out:

> Purgatory was dragged down into a whirlpool of delirious scholastic ratiocination, which raised the most otiose questions, refined the most sophisticated

[217] Ivo of Chartres, *Prologus in Decretum*, printed in PL 161, coll. 47–60.

[218] Canon 21. *Conciliorum oecumenicorum decreta*, 245. The extension of the requirement to women is interesting, not only because it is a clear example of gender equality at work in the Middle Ages, but also because it was to lead to frequent accusations of impropriety in later times, when priests were accused of taking advantage of the confessional to seduce vulnerable women.

> distinctions, and took delight in the most elaborate solutions. Can a venial sin become mortal? Does an accumulation of several venial sins equal a mortal sin? What is the fate of a person who dies with both a mortal sin and a venial sin on his head (assuming that it is possible for this to occur, which some authorities doubted)? And so on.[219]

Questions like these kept legions of theologians and canon lawyers occupied and created an immense legal establishment in which the finer points of any and every particular case could be adjudicated. One of the (perhaps unforeseen) results of this kind of analysis was that people came to be seen more and more as individuals with particular problems that were not exactly like anyone else's. Purgatory was therefore not like heaven and hell, where everyone was treated more or less alike. On the contrary, it was a place where every inmate received special treatment, specifically designed for his or her particular requirements. Odd though it may seem, this had a certain appeal, because people like to be treated as individuals with special needs, and there was great assurance in knowing that those needs would be met on a case-by-case basis.

By about 1250 the fundamental outlines of purgatory were clear and it remained only to clear up some of the details. There was ongoing discussion about where purgatory was located, what purgatorial fire consisted of (i.e., was it purely spiritual or partly material as well?), and whether a soul was set free to go to heaven as soon as its penance was complete or had to wait until the last judgment for final acquittal. Bonaventure dealt with each of these, concluding (for example) that purgatory had become a distinct place only after the incarnation of Christ. Before that time, souls had gone to a place called "limbo" or "the bosom of Abraham," where there was no opportunity for active penance but only a place of waiting for judgment.[220] He also thought that purgatorial fire was both spiritual and material—the spiritual fire was redemptive whereas the material one was merely punitive![221] He was also vehemently opposed to any suggestion that a cleansed soul might have to delay its heavenly bliss until the last judgment: once its time in purgatory was done, it was free to go and so away it went![222]

Very similar views were expressed by Bonaventure's contemporary Albert the Great (1206?–1280), a German who joined the Dominican order and lectured in Paris (1242–1248), where he was a major influence on the young Thomas Aquinas. Thomas, despite his immense theological output, had relatively

[219] Le Goff, *Birth of Purgatory*, 217.
[220] Bonaventure, *Commentarium in IV libros Sententiarum* 4.20.
[221] Bonaventure, *Breviloquium* 7.2.
[222] Bonaventure, *Commentarium in IV libros Sententiarum* 4.21.3.

little to say about purgatory and seems to have been uninterested in the subject.[223] He died before getting to it in the course of his *Summa theologiae*, and most of what we know about his opinions was put together by his students and attached to the *Summa* as a supplement. Essentially, he repeated what earlier doctors (and especially his own teacher Albert the Great) had said, adapting it to the needs of the controversies on the subject in which he was periodically engaged.

The relative indifference of Thomas Aquinas to the question of the existence of purgatory reminds us that not only was it far from being universally popular, but it was actually rejected by a large number of people, including virtually everyone who had reason to quarrel with the authority of the papacy. This was something new in the history of theology. Earlier disputes had been much more "objective" in the sense that no one of any stature had opposed a doctrine merely because it was held by Rome or by some other episcopal see. But purgatory was so closely linked to the power claimed by the papacy that it was very difficult, if not impossible, to keep the two things apart. If the pope lacked the power to forgive sins on earth, he could hardly have done so after a sinner's death, and in that case the question of the church's involvement with purgatory would not have arisen. If, on the other hand, the pope did have the power to forgive sins, rejecting his authority would be a dangerous move in this life because of the effect it might have after death. Either way, purgatory and the papacy were bound up together, and to reject the one was to reject the other.

We should therefore not be surprised to discover that, by and large, heretical sects that objected to the papacy also denied that there was a purgatory.[224] Unfortunately, however, it is hard to know what to make of the evidence for this, because almost all of it comes from hostile sources who may have been poorly informed.[225] More important was the declared opposition of the Eastern churches, which is not as well documented as we might like but of which there can be no doubt. Tensions between East and West had been growing for centuries, but at no time had anything been said about the afterlife or the condition of those who died in a state of sin. The conclusion must be that no difference between the two traditions on this point was perceived by those engaged in dialogue.

It was only after the Western doctrine of purgatory had been proposed and

[223] See Le Goff, *Birth of Purgatory*, 266–278.
[224] Ibid., 278–280.
[225] See Walter P. Wakefield and Austin P. Evans, *Heresies of the High Middle Ages* (New York: Columbia University Press, 1969), especially 346–351; 371–373, where we find evidence for early Waldensian beliefs to this effect. See also Gabriel Audisio, *The Waldensian Dissent: Persecution and Survival c. 1170—c. 1570* (Cambridge: Cambridge University Press, 1999); and for a different group, Robert Lerner, *The Heresy of the Free Spirit in the Later Middle Ages* (Notre Dame, IN: University of Notre Dame Press, 1972).

generally accepted at Rome, that the question became one of serious debate. The political situation was deeply unfavorable to the Eastern side, which did not make discussion any easier, but the Western occupation of large parts of the Byzantine empire after the crusaders captured Constantinople in 1204 forced the two churches to examine their differences in the hope of resolving them. Toward the end of 1231, a debate was held at Casole, near Otranto, between George Bardanes, Greek metropolitan of Corfu, and a Franciscan friar sent by the pope, whose name was Bartholomew. The account of it was written by Bardanes, so we need not question the authenticity of his accusation against the Franciscans for approving "the false doctrine that there exists a purgatorial fire to which souls are sent if they die after confession but before completing penance for their sins, where they are purified and delivered from punishment prior to the last judgment."[226]

The papacy was not prepared to give in on this question, however, and on March 6, 1254, Pope Innocent IV (1243–1254) sent an extensive letter to the bishop of Tusculum, his legate to the Greek church, in which he wrote,

> Since the truth of the Gospel asserts that if anyone blasphemes against the Holy Spirit, he will not be forgiven either in this world or in the next (which teaches us that some sins are punished in this life and others in the next one),[227] and since the Apostle also declares that the work of every man will be tried by fire[228] . . . and since the Greeks themselves apparently believe and profess that the souls of those who die without having completed the penance they had already received, or else who die without mortal sin but guilty of venial ones and other minor faults, are cleansed after death and can be helped in this by the intercessions of the church; we, considering that the Greeks tell us that they cannot find any definite designation for this place of purgation in the works of their doctors, and that according to the tradition and authority of the holy fathers this place is called "purgatory," it is our wish that in future they will also accept this term.[229]

A similar statement was appended to the synodal constitution *Cum sacrosancta*, which was promulgated by Pope Gregory X (1271–1276) on November 1, 1274, following the Second Council of Lyon, and sent to the emperor

---

[226] Pellegrino Roncaglia, *George Bardanès métropolite de Corfou et Barthélemy de l'ordre franciscain. Les discussions sur le purgatoire (15 octobre - 17 novembre 1231)* (Rome: Scuola tipografica italo-orientale S. Nilo, 1953), 57–107.
[227] Matt. 12:32.
[228] 1 Cor. 3:11–15.
[229] Denzinger, *Enchiridion*, no. 838.

Michael VIII (1258–1282) in Constantinople for his approval.[230] Michael VIII had already sent a confession of faith to the pope, which had been read at the fourth session of the council on July 6, 1274. In it, he had admitted that,

> True penitents, who die in a state of love but who have not yet completed their penance . . . have their souls purified after death by purifying and purgatory punishments, as Friar John has explained. The intercessions of living believers are useful in alleviating these punishments, in particular, the sacrifice of the mass, prayers, alms, and other works of devotion which believers are in the habit of doing for each other, according to the customs of the church.[231]

Michael VIII, desperate for support and fearful of the possibility that secular Western powers, and especially the Normans in Sicily, might try to overthrow him, was prepared to sign almost anything to keep the pope happy, and he was even prepared to suppress dissent within his own church. In May 1276 his soldiers expelled some recalcitrant monks from Mount Athos, the heart of Greek monasticism, who were subsequently interrogated by Thomas de Lentini (the Dominican who had admitted Thomas Aquinas into the order) and placed under house arrest on Cyprus. During the interrogation, Thomas asked Nicephorus, one of the Greeks, what he thought about purgatory and received a very frank answer: "Not only do we not accept it, we condemn it, as do the fathers meeting in council. In our Lord's words: 'You are wrong because you know neither the Scriptures nor the power of God.'"[232] Nicephorus did not name any particular council at which the doctrine had been condemned, doubtless because there had never been one, nor was his use of Scripture particularly astute, but there can be no doubt about his doctrine, which was (and still is) more representative of the Eastern church's position than anything Michael VIII might have said to the contrary.

The Western church still refused to admit defeat, and when reunion with the Greeks was proposed again in 1439, purgatory was on the list of things that the latter would be asked to accept, using the precise words of Michael VIII's confession.[233] Once again the union failed and the Eastern churches rejected what they considered to be a false doctrine. Purgatory remained prominent in the Western church, however, and was severely attacked by the Protestant

---

[230] Michael VIII had recaptured Constantinople for the Byzantines in 1261 but was always afraid that a new crusade might be launched to dislodge him.

[231] Denzinger, *Enchiridion*, no. 856. Friar John Parastron was a Franciscan who had instructed the emperor in the teachings of the Roman church.

[232] The Greek text, accompanied by a French translation, is in Vitalien Laurent and Jean Darrouzès, *Dossier grec de l'union de Lyon (1273–1277)* (Paris: Institut Français d'Etudes Byzantines, 1976), 496–499. The verse quoted is Matt. 22:29.

[233] *Conciliorum oecumenicorum decreta*, 527.

Reformers. In answer to them, Rome reasserted its traditional belief, conceding only that obscure and difficult points concerning the doctrine should be avoided in popular preaching, and that anything conducive to scandal (like the sale of indulgences) should be forbidden.[234]

Purgatory caught on in the medieval church because it gave people hope for eternity even if they were not perfect in this life.[235] It provided a means by which they could continue to pray for their loved ones after they had died and help them on their way to heaven. It was also possible for them to perform extra acts of penance in this life, or works of supererogation as they were called, and thereby reduce the time that they would have to spend in purgatory themselves.

In time, this structure of penance and the works of supererogation that accompanied it became a burden both for the church and for the penitents. Telling people to stand barefoot in the snow, holding a lighted candle, for hours on end, for example, soon came to be seen as a pointless exercise. It did nothing for the church, and the people so burdened were merely humiliated, which could be almost intolerable if they were prominent members of their local community. For these and other similar reasons, a way out was eagerly sought and over time was hard to resist, despite the anguished protests of reformers who thought that public penance was good for the soul and ought to be continued.

We can perhaps understand the commutation of penance by comparing it with what happens today to people who break the law in minor ways. In theory, lawbreakers should be put in prison, but prisons are often full and seem to do little good for their inmates. To lock someone up merely for speeding, for instance, seems excessive. So the state has devised another means of punishing this sort of infraction. Instead of doing time behind bars, the guilty are fined. The state gets additional revenue, the victim does not have to suffer major inconvenience or unwanted publicity, and everyone is more or less happy with the result. It was this way of thinking that drove the church to commute penance to a fine. Those who paid up were given a certificate of "indulgence" which effectively wrote off their need to do penance. Once it became clear that people could buy indulgences, both for their loved ones and for themselves, why would they want to go to the trouble of doing works of supererogation when they could pay for a certificate instead? And so, gradually the sale of indulgences became an established practice of the church. The ecclesiastical coffers were

---

[234] Ibid., 774. The instructions are contained in a decree of the twenty-fifth session of the Council of Trent (December 3–4, 1563).

[235] This aspect of it still appeals to some people, including those who ought to know better. See, for example, Jerry L. Walls, *Purgatory: The Logic of Total Transformation* (Oxford: Oxford University Press, 2012), written by someone who claims to be an evangelical Protestant!

filled with donations, and the individuals who bought them had the satisfaction of knowing that their time in purgatory had been reduced.

It was a win-win situation for the church and for the penitent sinner, but it meant that the grace of God was up for sale, and to many people that seemed wrong. The church could not charge for administering the sacraments—no one was supposed to pay for baptism or for receiving Holy Communion—so how could it charge for letting people off penance, which was officially regarded as another sacrament? Ordinary people seldom noticed this inconsistency, but theologians became increasingly aware of it, and there were periodic calls for reform of what had become a highly corrupt system. Eventually one of those calls would be heard, and the man who made it, a German monk turned university professor named Martin Luther, found himself leading a movement for reform that neither he nor the church authorities could have imagined possible before it happened. But Luther's Reformation would not have occurred in the way it did without the understanding of God's grace at work in the body of Christ that had grown up in the preceding centuries, and so the Protestant churches are just as much the children of the Western Middle Ages as the Roman Catholic Church is.[236] It is to that understanding that we must now turn.

The Justification of Sinners

At the heart of the church's teaching about the Mass, penance, and purgatory was the question of God's righteousness and how sinful human beings could obtain it.[237] That God was righteous in himself was beyond doubt, but how did this affect his relationship with human beings? Christians have always recognized that fallen human beings are unworthy to stand in the presence of God, and nothing we can do will change that. But God, of his great mercy and love, has reached out to us in spite of our unworthiness and made it possible for us to return to fellowship with him. Those who respond to his appeal are made "righteous," but how does this happen and what does it involve?

The Israelites told stories about righteous men like Abel, Enoch, Noah, and Job, who worshiped the one God and lived in a way that he approved of, though the details of what that meant were tantalizingly vague. In any case,

[236] It is instructive to remember that both Luther and John Calvin were deeply influenced by, and felt very close to, Bernard of Clairvaux. See Franz Posset, *Pater Bernhardus: Martin Luther and Bernard of Clairvaux* (Kalamazoo, MI: Cistercian, 1999); A. N. S. Lane, *John Calvin: Student of the Church Fathers* (Edinburgh: T & T Clark, 1999), 87–150.

[237] The standard treatment of this subject is Alister McGrath, *Iustitia Dei: A History of the Christian Doctrine of Justification*, 3rd ed. (Cambridge: Cambridge University Press, 2005). It covers the ground remarkably well, but must be used with caution, since not all the claims it makes are supported by the evidence alleged for them. For a good overview of the main issues at stake, see Alan J. Spence, *Justification: A Guide for the Perplexed* (London: T & T Clark, 2012).

these men lived long ago and far away, and they were highly unusual. For practical purposes, righteousness of their kind had ceased to exist, and imitating their examples was never a realistic possibility. As far as Israel was concerned, the righteousness that God required was defined by the law of Moses, which the nation had to keep in order to please God. That was a tall order, and by the time of Jesus the law was being interpreted in a way that made it possible to claim that it was being honored, even though it was not. Jesus and his disciples criticized the hypocrisy of those who did this, and pointed out that they were fooling themselves if they thought they were righteous in God's eyes because of it.[238]

Later on, the apostle Paul explained that the law was not only impossible to keep, but that it was a major cause of *un*righteousness, because knowing what it required made people aware of what great sinners they really were.[239] The law was holy and righteous in itself, but it had no power to transform people into its image. Instead, it produced the opposite effect by showing those who were subject to it that they were sinners not "fit for purpose," as we would say today. Trying to force sinful people into attempting what they were incapable of achieving created an impossible dilemma. Either it led people to despair, as Paul claimed, or it led them to reinterpret the law and lose sight of what true righteousness was, as the Jewish leaders of the time had done.

The good news of the gospel was that Jesus had put an end to the law's power by fulfilling its provisions and paying the debt that we owe to God for our sins. His death was the price demanded for our reconciliation to God, but once it was paid, that reconciliation took effect and created an entirely new situation.[240] Those who have been reconciled to God by the sacrifice of Christ's blood have been justified—that is to say, they have been made righteous in God's eyes and have been given a new life. As Paul put it in his letter to the Romans,

> . . . the judgment following one trespass brought condemnation, but the free gift following many trespasses brought justification. For if, because of one man's trespass, death reigned through that one man, much more will those who receive the abundance of grace and the free gift of righteousness reign in life through the one man Jesus Christ.[241]

Exactly what Paul meant by the words "righteousness" and "justification" has become a subject of intense debate in recent years, but this is a modern

---

[238] The theme is constant in the Synoptic Gospels, and especially in Matthew. See Matt. 6:2, 5, 16; 15:7; 16:3; 22:18; 23:13–29.

[239] Rom. 7:8–10.

[240] Rom. 5:6–11.

[241] Rom. 5:16–17.

argument that has been caused by factors that were unknown in New Testament times.[242] Paul was not trying to combat a legacy of anti-Semitism in the church, and he would probably have been puzzled by the way in which people today tend to see "faith" and "works" as irreconcilable opposites. For him, belief in Christ meant being born again into a new life in which the ritual practices of the law (which is what he understood by "works") were redundant. Jews who found it psychologically difficult to abandon them were permitted to go on keeping the law, and non-Jews were told to respect them for that, but this tolerance was possible only because no one's salvation depended on it.[243]

As the church became less Jewish, the issues that had bothered Paul faded into the background. Gentile converts who had never tried to keep the law of Moses (or even heard of it) were not likely to be troubled by the kinds of problems that had plagued the first generation of Christians. For many of them, the idea that morality was connected to religious belief must have come as a novelty, since that was certainly not the case in Greco-Roman paganism, whose gods and goddesses were famous for their immoral behavior. The great defenders of morality in the ancient world were the philosophers, who were often opposed to religion for that reason. Christians therefore had to make a case for believing that God demands high moral standards and that people who lead sinful lives on earth will not go on doing so in heaven. The gospel message of salvation by grace through faith remained the same, but the audience changed and so a new approach to it was required.

Fundamental to this was the Christian insistence that human beings are free to choose between good and evil. Many ancient people did not believe that. They thought that they were only doing what came naturally to them and that they could not change their behavior. This, said the Christians, was false. No human being is bound by his nature to lead a sinful life. We were not created that way, and if we sin now it is because we have become *un*natural, or denatured, by the power of evil at work in us. Christ came to defeat that evil and restore us to the freedom that we had at the beginning. In other words, sinners are not naturally sinful but are held in bondage by the alien power of Satan, the prince of evil who has got us in his grip. This catastrophe came about because the first human beings chose to do his bidding, and now we are all trapped in sinfulness because of the bondage to it that we have inherited from them. Adam and Eve were to blame for their actions, and we have inherited that blame, even if we have done nothing to deserve it ourselves.

---

[242] For a good survey of the modern debates, see Stephen Westerholm, *Perspectives Old and New on Paul: The "Lutheran" Paul and His Critics* (Grand Rapids, MI: Eerdmans, 2004).

[243] Acts 15:1–21; Rom. 14:1–23; 1 Cor. 8:1–13.

It was at this point that difficulties arose. Can one person justly inherit the debts of another? Am I responsible for Adam's sin when I did nothing to incur it and (thanks to what I now know) would have done otherwise if I had been in his place? How can it be right to condemn an entire race of people for the wrongdoing of a single individual? Does not the Bible say that responsibility for the guilt of others will not be passed on from one generation to the next? As Ezekiel told the Jewish exiles in Babylon,

> . . . you say, "Why should not the son suffer for the iniquity of the father? When the son has done what is just and right, and has been careful to observe all my statutes, he shall surely live. The soul who sins shall die. The son shall not suffer for the iniquity of the father, nor the father suffer for the iniquity of the son. The righteousness of the righteous shall be upon himself, and the wickedness of the wicked shall be upon himself."[244]

The promise given to Ezekiel was that, in the future, individuals would be held responsible for their own sins, but not for the sins of their fathers (or of their children either). This idea of personal, as opposed to collective, responsibility for wrongful actions was an important juridical principle that had to be maintained by anyone concerned with law and order. The alternative was what we would now call the "vendetta," gang warfare in which a person can legitimately be killed merely for belonging to a certain family, tribe, or nation. Even in the modern world, this kind of rough and ready "justice" is far from unknown, so we can only imagine what life must have been like when such thinking was the accepted norm in most places. There was also a sense in which it could be said that freedom of choice was an essential prerequisite to the spread of the gospel. How could people have responded to its message if they had not been free to do so? A theologian might say that those who accepted Christ when they heard him preached were moved by the Spirit of God, but that Spirit was put into their hearts and gave them the power to cry "Abba! Father!" in what seemed to the watching world to be a voluntary act on their part.[245] Certainly we never hear of anyone in the early church who claimed that he was forced to join it against his will!

Another complicating factor was that, in the pagan Greek world, sin had been understood not as disobedience to God (who was unknown), but as failure to make the right choices in life. There were stories of flawed heroes like Achilles and flawed people like Alcibiades whose lives drove this lesson home.

[244] Ezek. 18:19–20.
[245] Gal. 4:6.

The message was that if they had been wiser and more prudent, they might have escaped their fate, though it must be admitted that this was improbable. The reason for this was that human beings are flawed by nature. Sooner or later our limitations (finitude) and our mortality will catch up with us, and when they do, there is nothing we can do about it. People who thought like that naturally believed that Christ's triumph over death and the limitations of human finitude was the essence of his saving work. The New Testament expressed this as "paying the price of sin," but that was in the context of Jewish sacrificial laws which were foreign to many Gentile believers. They did not deny it, of course, but their lack of familiarity with the Old Testament meant that it did not strike them with the same force as it struck Paul and his fellow Jews.

The realization that this Gentile interpretation of sin and salvation was superficial and inadequate was slow to take root. In the Eastern church it never did, and Orthodox theologians still speak of human sinfulness in terms of finitude rather than of inherited guilt, a concept that they generally reject.[246] In the Western church, however, a different course was followed, largely because of Augustine's quarrel with the teaching of Pelagius. Augustine saw clearly that any human response to God in faith is a divine gift, because although we have a will that is free to do many things, it cannot escape the overriding power of sin in our lives. Augustine made a distinction between "free will" as *liberum arbitrium*, which is the ability to choose between different possibilities that are set before us, and *libertas* ("freedom"), which belongs to God alone.[247] Thus, for example, I can decide whether I am going to cross the street or not when the light turns green, but the choice I make will not (and cannot) overcome my fundamental separation from God. Even if the reason why I decide to cross the street is that someone on the other side has fallen down and needs my help to get back up again, it still does not improve my standing with God, because my alienation from him goes deeper than my desire to do good. Criminals are capable of doing good things, but those things do not change their basic criminality and cannot be used to excuse it.

Augustine tackled another common misunderstanding when he declared that God's righteousness was not an attribute of his nature but a description of the way he acts toward us. Obviously the two things are connected, but the difference between them is that while we can accept God's merciful actions to-

[246] See John Meyendorff, *Byzantine Theology* (New York: Fordham University Press, 1974), 143–146; Timothy Ware, *The Orthodox Church* (London: Penguin, 1993), 222–225; Peter Bouteneff, "Christ and Salvation," in Mary B. Cunningham and Elizabeth Theokritoff, eds., *The Cambridge Companion to Orthodox Christian Theology* (Cambridge: Cambridge University Press, 2008), 93–106.

[247] The concept of *liberum arbitrium* can also be found in Tertullian, *De anima* 21. On Augustine's doctrine, see McGrath, *Iustitia Dei*, 38–54.

ward us and even seek to imitate them in our dealings with others, we can never become what he is in his own nature. This distinction opened up the possibility of being "righteous" (i.e., pleasing to God) in the way we live without being perfect. In other words, our finitude is not sinful in itself and does not prevent us from being the kind of people God wants us to be. Compare this with what Maximus the Confessor said in answer to a question put to him by a man called Thalassius. In Maximus's words, "the first human beings fell by coming into being," a statement that put the blame for our condition on our natural finitude and denied that there was any original state of bliss in the garden of Eden![248]

To describe the reception of God's righteousness by sinful human beings, Augustine chose the word *iustificare* and its derivatives, and this usage passed into the Western tradition. He himself believed that the word meant "to make righteous," since it was composed of the two Latin words *iustum* ("righteous") and *facere* ("make"), but it was not clear what that entailed. To the extent that it was a translation of the Greek verb *dikaioun* it meant "pass judgment on"—usually taken in a negative sense but in this case understood positively, as "acquit" rather than "condemn"—but Augustine also used *iustificare* to convey the idea of "transforming someone into a righteous person," which *dikaioun* does not (and cannot) mean. This is important, because it was this additional implication that was to cause trouble and misunderstanding later on.

Augustine believed that a man was made righteous by a process of inner transformation that governed not only his actions but also the motivation that lay behind them.[249] In practice this made motivation more important than action, because even if a particular action failed to achieve its purpose, it would still count as righteous in the sight of God if it had been done with the right motive. Righteousness was also a divine attribute in which Christians participated directly, and not merely a word used to express their relationship with a righteous God. It could be obtained only by God's free gift ("grace") but obtained it was, and the person who was made righteous by Christ became a better human being than he had been before. This was possible because, for Augustine, "grace" was not an abstract gift of righteousness but the presence of the Holy Spirit in a person's life. The Spirit is the love of God that makes it possible for those who receive that gift to love God with all their heart and to love their neighbors as themselves, which is what God demands of us.[250]

Faith is the fruit of love, and so, for Augustine, "justification by faith" really

[248] Maximus the Confessor, *Quaestiones ad Thalassium* 61.
[249] Augustine of Hippo, *De spiritu et littera* 26.45.
[250] Augustine of Hippo, *De Trinitate* 15.17.31.

meant "justification by love," which expressed itself in and through faith.[251] Working in a person's life by the power of God, faith gradually overcomes the desires of the flesh (*concupiscentia*) in the way that a medicine overcomes disease. To be effective, the grace of faith in love had to be periodically refreshed and strengthened so as to be able to pursue and eventually complete its work. How this would happen Augustine did not specify, but we may assume that it was an integral part of a believer's relationship with God. This included partaking of the sacraments but it was not limited to them, and Augustine's concept of grace was so broad that it could encompass whatever was conducive to pious devotion. Unbelievers could feel the effects of God's grace but without benefiting spiritually from it, because faith was needed for that. At the same time, believers did not have to worry about missing out on God's promises, because his promises had been made to those whom he had chosen for salvation before the foundation of the world. Sin may have interrupted this process for a time, but it could not thwart the eternal purposes of God, who would justify his people and save them, whatever Satan might get up to.

There matters rested until the late eighth century, when there was a renewed interest in the process by which a believer was justified. No one seriously doubted that this began at baptism, when a child (and by that time virtually all baptisms were of young children) was grafted into the family of God. What was of greater interest to the medieval mind was the way in which that child then grew spiritually. If we look at the matter objectively, this emphasis on the Christian life was both natural and inevitable. There was no need for a baptized infant to be converted in the way that Paul and Augustine had been, because baptism had removed the guilt of their inherited sinfulness (i.e., original sin). Christian nurture, though, was all-important, because without it the child would never live up to the promise of his baptism and inherit the kingdom of God. Alcuin of York (735?–804), the leading theologian at the court of Charlemagne and an important influence on the thought of that period, had no doubt that a sinner was justified by penitence and sincere regret (*compunctio*), though it is not clear what he thought the latter entailed in terms of actual penance.[252] But any doubts on that score were laid to rest by Haimo of Auxerre (d. 855?), who wrote,

> We are redeemed and justified by the passion of Christ, which justifies mankind in baptism through faith, and subsequently by penance. The two are so closely linked that it is impossible to be justified by one without the other.[253]

[251] See Gal. 5:6.

[252] Alcuin of York, *Liber de divinis officiis*, 55.

[253] Haimo of Auxerre, *Expositio in epistulas Sancti Pauli*, in PL 117, col. 391c. The text being commented on is Rom. 3:24: "justified by his grace as a gift."

Much the same thing was said more than two centuries later by Bruno of Cologne (1030?–1101), who made a point of adding that penance was the divinely appointed means of cleansing the soul from sins committed after baptism.[254] The explanation of this process that was given by a French monk called Hervé de Bourg-Dieu (1080?–1150) may be regarded as typical:

> Through the law there comes a recognition of sin, through faith there comes the infusion of grace in opposition to sin, through grace comes the cleansing of the soul from sin's guilt, through the cleansing of the soul comes freedom of the will (*libertas arbitrii*), through the freedom of the will (*liberum arbitrium*) comes the love of righteousness, and through the love of righteousness comes the implementation of the law.[255]

Note the way the process unfolds: the law points out the need for faith, and faith leads to grace, which sets the ball rolling. Purification, freedom, love, and righteousness then follow in quick succession, leading in the end to the fulfilling of the law, which takes us back to where we started from, but now in a way that actually works. Peter Comestor condensed this into a neat triadic scheme describing the stages of justification that, with minor variations, was repeated by most medieval writers. It went as follows:

1. The infusion of grace, given to beginners.
2. The co-operation of free will (*liberum arbitrium*), given to those making progress.
3. The consummation [i.e., remission of sins], given to those who have arrived.[256]

This was subsequently modified into a fourfold pattern, with the second element being divided into two. The classic statement of it was worked out by William of Auxerre (1160?–1231), who expressed it like this:[257]

1. The infusion of grace
2. The movement of the free will (*liberum arbitrium*)
3. Contrition
4. Remission of sins

The inclusion of contrition made it easy to tie this fourfold scheme into the

---

[254] Bruno of Cologne, *Expositio in omnes epistulas Pauli*, in PL 153, col. 55b–c. The text being commented on is Rom. 5:20: "The law came in to increase the trespass."

[255] Hervé de Bourg-Dieu, *Expositio in epistulas Pauli*. The text is in PL 181, col. 642d, relating to Rom. 3:31. Note that Hervé did not distinguish *libertas* from *liberum arbitrium*.

[256] Peter Comestor, *Sermo* 17.

[257] William of Auxerre, *Summa aurea* 3.2.1 (fol. 121v).

developing sacrament of penance, thus encouraging the integration of justification with the sacramental system that was to take place in the thirteenth century. But those who moved in that direction insisted that penance by itself had no power to justify anyone. Justification was from beginning to end a work of divine grace in which penance was only the necessary condition for that grace to be given.[258] This was the pattern adopted by Alexander of Hales,[259] Albert the Great,[260] Bonaventure,[261] and Thomas Aquinas,[262] as we can see from their respective commentaries on the *Sentences* of Peter Lombard. Thomas modified the scheme somewhat by making a clearer distinction between the second and third stages:[263]

1. The infusion of grace
2. The movement of the free will directed toward God through faith (i.e., love)
3. The movement of the free will directed against sin (i.e., contrition)
4. The remission of sin

To understand what effect this had, we must appreciate that for Thomas and his contemporaries, who had been trained in Aristotelian physics and reflected that in their approach, progress from the first to the last item on the list was a process set in motion by the initial infusion of grace, which led inexorably to the forgiveness of sins. Turning toward God in love and against sin in sorrow were integral parts of this process, which could be distinguished in theoretical terms within a chain of cause and effect, but which normally occurred more or less simultaneously.

For Thomas, justification before God was identified with stage two. The infusion of grace involved a real change in the recipient, who was set free from the constraints of his sinful nature and given the ability to subordinate his mind and will to God. When he did so, he was justified in God's eyes because he had demonstrated his desire to do what was right. The infused grace that made this possible was not an extension of God's nature but a created equivalent of it that God implanted in the soul of the believer, giving him an inbuilt disposition (*habitus*) toward righteousness. This made it possible for him to avoid mortal sin, but as he was not yet perfect, he would still fall into venial sin and stand in need of penance. It was at this point that the penitential system described above

[258] Alan of Lille, *Contra haereticos* 1.51.
[259] Alexander of Hales, *In libros Sententiarum* 4.17.7.
[260] Albertus Magnus, *In libros Sententiarum* 4.17a.10.
[261] Bonaventure, *Commentarium in IV libros Sententiarum* 2.16.1.3.
[262] Thomas Aquinas, *In libros Sententiarum* 4.17.1.4; also *Summa theologiae* I.II, 113.6.
[263] Thomas Aquinas, *Summa theologiae* I.II, 113.8.

kicked in. Even justified believers stood in need of further purification because they continued to struggle against the effects of their "lower nature"—what the Bible calls the war of the spirit against the flesh. Very few people would succeed in winning that battle in this life, but the chance to continue the struggle in purgatory ensured that they would triumph in the end.

It was generally agreed that God responded to the movement of a man's free will toward him because he regarded such a movement as meritorious—it was a good thing for the man to do it, and it deserved an appropriate response from God. The question then arose as to how meritorious it actually was. Could a human being do anything that would really please God? In the strict sense, the answer to this had to be no, because human beings are both finite and sinful and therefore incapable of pleasing God in a perfect way. But like little children who want to do something good but cannot because they lack the strength and the knowledge required for success, sinful people who try their best and have the right intentions ought to be applauded for making the attempt, not rejected as failures because they have not managed to achieve something they are incapable of. This, said the theologians of the time, was what happened when souls infused with created grace turned to God. They were justified, not because they had managed to become righteous by their own efforts, but because it was the right response on God's part to those who were doing the best they could. What God honored in them was merit *de congruo* ("appropriate")—they wanted the right thing and so God gave it to them, even though they had not really earned it.

Had sinful souls been able to make the grade on their own, God would have acknowledged their merit as being *de condigno* ("deserved"), but in absolute terms that was impossible. What changed the nature of the equation was God's free decision to bind himself by promises that, if sinners acted in a certain way, he would consider himself obliged to respond to them accordingly. It was impossible for a sinner to earn merit without infused grace, but once that grace was acquired, the sinner could achieve what was necessary within the parameters laid down by God in his covenant with mankind.[264] Since God had done this, acquiring merit *de condigno* became a real possibility, because it was understood as a reward that was proportionate to the penitent's efforts (and therefore "deserved"). In this sense, the divine reward for human achievement was justified and so expected as the logical outworking of God's righteousness.[265] Much of this discussion focused on the status of the Virgin Mary—did God choose her to be the human mother of his Son because she

[264] See William of Auvergne, *Opera omnia* 1.310 aF, where he defines this principle.
[265] Thomas Aquinas, *Summa theologiae* I.II, 114.1.

deserved the honor (merit *de condigno*), or was it something she was given because she showed the right attitude (merit *de congruo*)?[266] The Bible would seem to suggest the latter,[267] but as time went on the reverence shown to Mary was such that more and more people were inclined toward the former view, which effectively meant that Mary was regarded as sinless. Thus it came about that men like Thomas Aquinas, who did not believe that, were outpaced by those who did, though belief in Mary's immaculate (sinless) conception was not made official Roman Catholic dogma until 1854!

Thomas represented the Dominican school of thought, but his contemporary Bonaventure painted a different picture, which became typical of the Franciscans. According to Bonaventure, Christ has purged believers' souls of their inherited guilt, illuminated their minds by the example of his sacrifice, and is now bringing them to perfection by giving them the grace they need to imitate him.[268] Where the Dominican scheme was focused on the forgiveness of sins and conceived in intellectual terms, the Franciscan one, as developed by Bonaventure, concentrated on union with God in Christ and was more psychological in its emphasis. Because of this, the Franciscans held that justification occurred when divine grace was infused into the soul, which merited it *de congruo*, and everything else followed on from that. The Franciscans later abandoned their psychological focus and identified justification with God's act of accepting the sinner *before* the infusion of grace into his soul, but the general pattern remained the same.

A major point of difference between the Dominicans and the Franciscans was that the former believed that the human soul was naturally capable of receiving divine grace whereas the latter insisted that God had to give it that capacity, since otherwise it would not be able to do so. Thomas Aquinas initially defended the Dominican view, as we can see from his commentary on Peter Lombard,[269] but as his thinking matured he changed his mind and moved closer to the Franciscan position on this matter. In his great *Summa theologiae* he wrote, "When it is said that a man does what he has the power to do, this means that what is in man's power is governed by the fact that he is moved by God."[270] Dominicans and Franciscans continued to approach the question of justification from different angles and so they appeared to be quite different from each other, but their conclusions were similar and, from the standpoint of a modern observer, they appear to have been more alike than they knew.

[266] See McGrath, *Iustitia Dei*, 140–141.
[267] See Luke 1:38.
[268] Bonaventure, *Itinerarium mentis in Deum* 4.3.
[269] Thomas Aquinas, *In libros Sententiarum* 2.28.1.4.
[270] Thomas Aquinas, *Summa theologiae* I.II, 109.6.2.

Criticism of this scheme of things began with John Duns Scotus in the generation after Aquinas and Bonaventure. Scotus pointed out that if contrition were necessary before a sinner could receive the sacrament of penance, the nature of the sacrament would be compromised. Instead of being effective in and of itself (*ex opere operato*), it would only work if the person receiving it was in the right spiritual mood (*ex opere operantis*). In that case, it would hardly be necessary, since the intending penitent would have already reached the point to which the sacrament was meant to bring him.[271] Scotus tried to resolve this problem by saying that contrition, by which he meant repentance based on love for God and his commandments, was not a necessary precondition for receiving the sacrament. All that was needed was repentance based on fear of punishment. If such repentance was deep and sincere it might merit the grace of justification *de congruo*, but if not, it might still be enough to allow the sinner to do penance, in and by which he would be justified, since God had covenanted with his people to that effect. Scotus called this kind of repentance "attrition" instead of "contrition," and one of its principal objectives was to put tender consciences at rest. To his mind, a sinner who started out at the lowest level of attrition would gradually be strengthened by sacramental grace to the point where he would be genuinely contrite, and so the final result would be the same as it was in the schemes that insisted on the necessity of contrition.

Scotus's logic was such that he allowed for the possibility that a sinner could be justified without having to do penance at all, but this possibility was more theoretical than real. In actual fact, no one could know for sure whether he had done enough to merit anything, and so in practice the sacrament became more necessary than ever, because it gave penitents the *assurance* that they were in a state of grace.[272] The importance of this should not be missed. Without assurance, justification would be purely theoretical and unlikely to mean much, since the anxious soul would still be wondering whether he had received it or not. In Scotus's scheme, penance resolved that problem, and the suggestion that assurance could be had without much in the way of genuine repentance beforehand made it all the more attractive.[273]

Scotus also made an important distinction between the moral value of an act and the merit that it might obtain in the sight of God. Moral value was determined by the nature of the act itself—almsgiving, for example, or showing hospitality to strangers. Whether there was any merit in such activities, though,

---

[271] John Duns Scotus, *Opus Oxoniense* 4.1.6.10–11.
[272] Ibid., 4.14.4.14.
[273] As it was to Gabriel Biel, who nevertheless rejected it because there was no evidence for it in Scripture. See Gabriel Biel, *Sermones dominicales de tempore* (Cologne: J. Crith, 1619), 1, 38B; *Collectorium circa quattuor Sententiarum libros*, ed. Wilfrid Werbeck, Udo Hofmann, Hanns Rückert, 6 vols. (Tübingen: Mohr, 1973–1992), 4:14.2.1, note 2E.

depended entirely on the will of God. If God chose to call a moral act meritorious and recognize it as such, then well and good. If he did not, it would make no difference one way or the other. Unbelievers were capable of good deeds but they did not earn any merit from them, because their minds were not set on trying to please God. Conversely, believers might do many meritorious things (such as penance!) which had no moral value. Fasting, for example, was not going to make the world a better place, although it might be what God required of the penitent as proof of his sincerity.[274]

Scotus's views were taken over by William of Ockham, the man who, more than anyone else, moved the discussion to a deeper level of philosophical analysis. He has often been criticized for the way in which he separated the moral value of an act from its meritorious value, as if the former had no significance at all, but this is a misunderstanding of his teaching. In fact, Ockham believed that it was God's acceptance of moral acts that gave them meritorious value, and that in the case of believers, this acceptance was a matter of course.[275] Some of Ockham's followers went further than he did and denied that there could be such a thing as merit *de condigno*. In their view, any merit must by definition be *de congruo*, and even that depended entirely on grace.[276] The general drift of their thinking was away from merit altogether, making everything depend entirely on God's grace, which was essentially the position taken by John Wyclif[277] and Jan Hus (1371?–1415).[278]

The full effect of Ockham's ideas can be seen in the work of Gabriel Biel (1420?–1495), which in many ways represents the culmination of medieval theological developments.[279] Unlike Ockham, Biel was not an uncritical admirer of Duns Scotus and firmly rejected any notion of attrition as a prelude to penance. For Biel, only contrition would do, and he believed, along (as he thought) with Peter Lombard, that in the sacrament of penance all the priest could do was declare that the sinner had already been justified on that basis.[280] Biel did not rule out the possibility of pre-sacramental justification, but even if that happened in a few cases, justification could not be understood apart from the sacrament because the latter was always implied. The reason for this was that contrition, with or without the sacrament, only offered remission of

[274] Biel, *Collectorium* 3.19.1.7.

[275] See Gordon Leff, *William of Ockham: The Metamorphosis of Scholastic Discourse* (Manchester: Manchester University Press, 1975).

[276] See, for example, Manuel Santos-Noya, *Die Sünden- und Gnadenlehre des Gregor von Rimini* (Frankfurt-am-Main: Peter Lang, 1990).

[277] John Wyclif, *De scientia Dei*, fo. 61v.

[278] Jan Hus, *In libros Sententiarum* 2.27.5.

[279] See Heiko Oberman, *The Harvest of Medieval Theology: Gabriel Biel and Late Medieval Nominalism*, 3rd ed. (Durham, NC: Labyrinth, 1983). The process of justification is discussed on 146–184.

[280] Biel, *Collectorium* 4.14.2.1, note 2D.

the *guilt* for sin. The removal of guilt meant that the *punishment* for it was downgraded from the eternal to the temporal realm, but as that was the sphere of penance, the sacraments still had an important part to play.

Biel believed that human beings can love God in their own natural strength, without the infusion of divine grace, but he also recognized that it was God's intention that they should accomplish his will in such a state of grace, which was beyond their natural abilities.[281] He was also concerned with the need for believers to demonstrate moral integrity. Sacramental merit was not meant to be a substitute for that, and Biel often warned his hearers not to think that they could remove their sins by good works, if they were not inwardly repentant (i.e., contrite).[282] As he saw the matter, his proposal was a way of avoiding the easygoing pattern of attrition, which many people besides himself thought was a lazy way out of sincere repentance, without demanding the kind of superhuman self-sacrifice that only a spiritual athlete could achieve.

As far as the disposition (*habitus*) needed for sacramental justification was concerned, Biel was insistent that a believer should love God for his own sake, and not for what he could get out of him.[283] The external penance performed in the sacrament had to be matched by internal repentance, without which it would have no effect. In his full-length study of Biel, Heiko Oberman (1930–2001) drew attention to a sermon Biel preached on Luke 17:14 ("Go and show yourselves to the priests") in which he illustrated what he meant by this.[284] The story is that of the ten lepers whom Jesus cleansed, which Biel took to be a prefiguration of the sacrament of penance. As he understood it, the story proved that penance is necessary because it was only *after they left Jesus* that the lepers were cleansed. In other words, they had to obey the divine command in order to see results, and not merely trust in Jesus' promise to them. At the same time, it was not the priests who healed the lepers, because they were cleansed *before they reached the temple*. All the priests could do was testify to the work of Christ, not perform it themselves. When they reached the priests, the lepers were justified, not because of what happened to them in the temple but because of what Jesus had already done for them.

Biel did not deny the power of divine grace in a person's life, but he did not think that it was essential for everyone to experience it all the time. As he saw it, human beings could often act rightly, according to the light of reason given to them, whether they were aided in this by divine grace or not. It was ignorance,

[281] Ibid., 4.14.2.2.
[282] Ibid., 4.4.1.2., concl. 5O.
[283] Biel, *Sermones* 1, 102E.
[284] Oberman, *Harvest of Medieval Theology*, 159.

not the lack of grace, that prevented people from doing the right thing.[285] The church's primary duty therefore was not to infuse grace into sinners but to enlighten them with the correct understanding, so that they could act properly of their own accord. Apparently Biel thought that, if people knew what was right, they would do it automatically![286]

None of this suggested to Biel that the inner disposition (*habitus*) of created grace was superfluous or unnecessary. On the contrary, it was essential, not because of any metaphysical necessity, but because that was the way that God had ordained his plan of salvation. This was the covenant (*pactum*) that set out his requirements of us and his response to our attempts to meet those requirements. By itself, created grace could never determine God's actions, for the simple reason that it was a created thing and not part of his nature.[287] But within the covenant order of things, God has accepted sinners and given them the grace they need to perform acts of meritorious value, and it is for that reason that they are justified. In Heiko Oberman's words,

> The gratuitous character of God's remuneration is therefore not based on the *activity* of the habit of grace nor on the *presence* of the habit of grace, but on God's eternal decree according to which he has decided to accept every act which is performed in a state of grace as a *meritum de condigno*.[288]

As far as merit *de congruo* was concerned, Biel thought of it as the supreme achievement of a man unaided by the infusion of grace. God may accept this and bestow his grace on the penitent sinner, but he is not obliged to, and if he does so it is an act of generosity on his part, not of justice.[289] God's acceptance of the repentant sinner follows on from his covenant promise and is made necessary because of that, and the same must be said of infused grace, because no outside power can force God to do anything.[290] Indeed, it is precisely because God is free (*liber*) and does not operate under any form of external constraint, that he can show his generosity (*liberalitas*) by ignoring any sense of due proportion between an act and its reward, and revealing his superabundant mercy instead.[291]

The strange result of Biel's doctrine is that he managed to believe both in justification by faith alone and in justification by works alone—at the same

[285] Biel, *Sermones* 1, 101D.
[286] Oberman, *Harvest of Medieval Theology*, 165.
[287] Biel, *Collectorium* 1.17.3.3, dub. 2G.
[288] Oberman, *Harvest of Medieval Theology*, 170.
[289] Biel, *Collectorium* 2.27.1.1., note 3.
[290] Ibid., 2.27.1.3., dub. 4O.
[291] Ibid., 2.27.1.2., concl. 4K.

time! The logic of this was that man is saved by grace alone, because without that, there would never have been a covenant or anything connected with it. But at the same time, and for all practical purposes, man is also saved by his works, because without works capable of attracting the infused grace of God, his grace would never be given. The result is that the sinner is unwittingly placed under an extraordinary burden to produce good works deserving of grace. God's righteousness is a principle that brings only judgment and punishment in its wake, and by doing good works, the sinner must hope that the divine wrath can be deflected from falling on him. No one can know for sure whether this will happen or not; as Biel put it, "Man does not know whether he is worthy of [God's] hatred or love."[292] Without that assurance, the sinner can only face the prospect of hearing about God's covenant and the justification it promises with fear and trepidation, because he has no way of knowing whether he will ever be worthy enough to receive it.

The system outlined by William of Ockham and his followers satisfied the demands of many and was seldom seriously questioned in its fundamentals. As the young Martin Luther (1483–1546) put it shortly before he had his great spiritual crisis,

> The doctors are right to say that when people do their best, God inevitably gives them grace. This cannot mean that this preparation for grace is [based on merit] *de condigno*, because they are incompatible, but it can be regarded as *de congruo* because of God's promise and the covenant (*pactum*) of mercy.[293]

To the modern reader, much of the discussion about justification seems arcane and far removed from anything directly related to the work of Christ,[294] but this is a misperception. To us, "good works" include many different things, but although that was theoretically true in the Middle Ages also, people in those days focused on one thing in particular—the sacrifice of the Mass, which was the supreme manifestation of the death of Christ. Those who wanted to get close to God went to Mass and had masses said on their behalf, and so the work of the Son for mankind's salvation remained central to the medieval conception of what constituted "good works."

Very revealing in this respect is the fact that Nicholas Cabasilas (1322?–1391?), a Greek Orthodox spiritual writer with a good knowledge of contemporary Western theology, expressed what he had to say about justification

[292] Biel, *Sermones* 1, 70F.
[293] Martin Luther, *Dictata super Psalterium* 114:1 (Vulgate 113:1).
[294] See McGrath, *Iustitia Dei*, 200.

in the context of the Eucharistic liturgy.[295] Cabasilas was in many respects a typical representative of the Eastern tradition in that he started with the principle that the righteous God had made human beings in his own image. It was their duty to make good their creation by striving to bring it to perfection, but instead they chose to enslave themselves to sin. God respected their freedom of choice and refused to drag them back from their error, which would have been both unloving and unjust. Instead, he chose to educate mankind by purifying human nature in the womb of the Virgin Mary, where the divine Word became flesh. In Jesus Christ the divine Son cooperated with human nature to remove mankind's rebellion against God through a life of obedience which culminated in the death, resurrection, heavenly adoption, and deification of that nature. The work of Christ therefore accomplished two distinct things: it put right the consequences of the fall, and restored human beings to their original destiny.

According to Cabasilas, it is on the basis of an analogous cooperation between flesh and spirit that believers appropriate to themselves the justification won by Christ on their behalf. The supreme manifestation of this is in their participation in the Eucharist, where they experience a communion of flesh and blood with Christ. What starts with the material elements then rises to encompass the mind and the will, both of which are progressively transformed into the image of Christ.[296] This progression can be outlined as follows:

1. Communion in the flesh and blood of Christ (the sacraments)
2. Communion with the mind of Christ (faith)
3. Communion with the will of Christ (good works)

When it is completed, the believer is reunited with Christ, which was the goal of Adam's creation in the first place. Justification thus brings us back to where we started, fulfilling God's original purpose for mankind. Cabasilas was not interested in merits, penance, or purgatory, none of which had any place in the Eastern tradition. Instead, he saw union with Christ as a mystical experience that was achieved in and through the Eucharistic liturgy. It was an emphasis that would have resonated with Bonaventure, but that had been obscured in the Ockhamist tradition. Whether it could be recovered, and if so, in what way, was the challenge that faced the generation of Martin Luther and the early Protestant Reformers.[297]

[295] See Panayiotis Nellas, *Hê peri dikaiôseôs didaskalia Nikolaou tou Kavasila. Symbolê eis tên Orthodoxon sôteriologian*, 2nd ed. (Athens: Indiktos, 1998).
[296] Cf. 1 Cor. 2:16.
[297] See Nellas, *Peri dikaiôseôs*, 203–207.

The Glory of the Cross

Martin Luther (1483–1546) was in some ways an unlikely candidate for the role of church reformer.[298] At the age of nineteen he had a close escape from death when he was thrown from his horse in a thunderstorm, and against his father's wishes, he decided to enter a monastery. There he distinguished himself by his zeal as he struggled with his ever-deepening sense of his own sin and unworthiness. He also gave himself to study, and within a few years was a master of both the Bible and the fathers of the church. The monastic way of life had changed little over the centuries, but the nature of theological study was undergoing a revolution. Thanks to the work of the Renaissance humanists, and especially of Desiderius Erasmus of Rotterdam (1466–1536), whose reputation for scholarship was at its height in the early sixteenth century, it was no longer enough to read the Bible in Latin. A knowledge of the original Hebrew and Greek was now an indispensable requirement for the true interpreter of the Scriptures, and that inevitably brought into focus the inadequacies of those medieval commentators who had relied solely on the Latin translation available to them. Luther learned to take nothing for granted, and when he was appointed professor of biblical studies at the new university of Wittenberg in 1512, he did not hesitate to criticize traditional interpretations of the biblical texts he lectured on when he felt that they were mistaken.

In the process, he had to wrestle with the texts himself in order to bring out their true meaning, and it was as he was doing this that the great theological questions of his day came into focus. The more Luther studied Paul's letters, especially Romans and Galatians, on which he lectured over a period of several years, the more the contrast between what the apostle was saying and what Luther observed in the church around him weighed on his mind. We do not know exactly when or how it happened, but by 1517 at the latest, Luther's understanding of salvation had undergone a radical shift away from the traditional teaching of his time toward what he saw as the real message of the Bible. Sooner or later, his discovery was bound to cause controversy, but such things

[298] Biographies of Luther abound. The standard one-volume introduction in English remains Roland H. Bainton, *Here I Stand, a Life of Martin Luther* (Nashville: Abingdon, 1950). See also Heiko A. Oberman, *Luther: Man between God and the Devil* (New Haven, CT: Yale University Press, 1989). Different parts of Luther's life are covered by Heinrich Boehmer, *Road to Reformation* (Philadelphia: Fortress, 1946), and Heinrich Bornkamm, *Luther in Mid-career, 1521–1530* (Philadelphia: Fortress, 1983). See also the trilogy by Martin Brecht, *Martin Luther: 1. His Road to Reformation, 1483–1521* (Philadelphia: Fortress, 1985), *2. Shaping and Defining the Reformation, 1521–1532* (Philadelphia: Fortress, 1990), *3. The Preservation of the Church, 1532–1546* (Minneapolis: Fortress, 1993). Luther's works are now available on disk, edited by Kurt Aland, *Martin Luther: Gesammelte Werke CD-ROM*, Digitale Bibliothek 63 (Berlin: DirectMedia, 2002). A fairly comprehensive, though not complete, English translation is available, edited by Jaroslav Pelikan and Helmut T. Lehmann, *Luther's Works*, 55 vols. (St. Louis: Concordia, vols. 1–30; and Philadelphia: Fortress, vols. 31–55, 1955–1986). A very useful compendium of Luther's nonbiblical writings is Timothy F. Lull, ed., *Martin Luther's Basic Theological Writings*, 2nd ed. (Minneapolis: Fortress, 2005).

had happened before and, had other factors not intervened, the fallout would probably have been contained within the academic world.

What altered the situation was something that on the surface seemed to be quite unrelated to Luther's biblical studies. In 1514, Albrecht of Hohenzollern (1490–1545), who had just been made archbishop of Magdeburg at the age of twenty-three (in defiance of the canonical rule that no one under thirty should be made a bishop), managed to get himself appointed archbishop of Mainz as well. This made him one of the most powerful men in Germany, because the archbishop of Mainz was one of the seven electors who chose the emperor.[299] Albrecht was a fairly liberal and tolerant man, but it seems that he was more superstitious than truly religious. His acquisition of Mainz had cost him a lot of money, and to help him pay off his debts, the pope allowed him to raise funds by selling indulgences in the archdiocese of Magdeburg, which included Wittenberg. Needless to say, the blatantly political nature of Albrecht's activities was resented, not least by some of the other electors. One of them was Frederick III of Saxony (1486–1525), the founder of the university of Wittenberg and Luther's patron, who was so incensed that he banned Albrecht from campaigning in his territory, even though it fell under Albrecht's spiritual jurisdiction.

Matters might have rested there, except that Luther was stirred by the theological implications that lay behind the sale of indulgences and resolved to attack the unwelcome campaign on those grounds. He could not have known what the impact of his actions would be when he composed his Ninety-five Theses against the practice, but it was not long before he found himself in the midst of a storm that would force him to define his own theological position. The reason for this amazing reaction was ultimately the invention of printing. Johann Gutenberg (1398–1468) had begun printing Bibles with moveable type as early as 1456, but as with all new technologies, printing took some time to get off the ground.[300] It was still regarded as a new technology in Luther's day, and its potential for the rapid and cheap dissemination of information was only beginning to be appreciated. What happened in this case was that someone noticed the theses on the church door at Wittenberg, copied them down, and printed them. Within weeks they were all over Germany, unleashing a reservoir of pent-up resentment against the church and its insatiable appetite for revenue. Luther's protest was widely supported, not least by Frederick III and other rulers who felt that papal taxation, however indirect, was a threat

[299] The Holy Roman Emperor was officially elected, though in practice a member of the Habsburg family was almost always chosen. In the early sixteenth century the electors were the archbishops of Cologne, Mainz, and Trier and the secular rulers of Brandenburg (Albrecht's father), Saxony, Bohemia, and the Rhenish Palatinate.

[300] This is still true today. Television was invented in the 1920s but did not become popular until thirty years later. Similarly, the internet first appeared in 1969 but did not become common until the 1990s.

to them. How much they understood Luther's theological concerns is hard to say, but it soon became clear that the problem would not be resolved merely by stopping the sale of indulgences. Luther's challenge reached to the foundation of the papal authority that had permitted it, and what might otherwise have been swept aside as just one more financial scandal became instead a life-and-death struggle for the soul of Western Christendom.

Luther's theology is difficult to analyze, partly because it is very rich in content, partly because he developed his ideas over time (and usually in response to particular pressures), and partly because his followers have always had a strong tendency to read their own ideas back into their master and interpret him accordingly. Viewed in the context of his own time, Luther can best be understood as a man who was preoccupied with the saving work of Christ. In this respect, he was the direct heir of Anselm of Canterbury and can be ranked with him as one of the greatest expositors of the doctrine of the atonement. Luther was a debater more than a systematician, a fact that shaped his theology and has frequently confused interpreters who have tried to turn his debating points into principles, with the result that not infrequently they have ended up with a one-sided and unbalanced portrait of the great Reformer.

To make his point as forcefully as possible, Luther was in the habit of creating theoretical opposites: law versus gospel, a theology of glory versus a theology of the cross, "active" versus "passive" righteousness, and so on. This approach can be helpful as long as we focus on Luther's main concerns and the reasons why he was dissatisfied with the dominant theology of his time, but it is misleading if we think that he preached the gospel to the exclusion of the law, and so on. In fact, Luther combined these apparent opposites in a dynamic way that transformed the theological landscape and eventually brought a new kind of church into being. In his preaching, the law found its purpose and fulfillment in the gospel which gave it its true meaning. He was very clear about this:

> I want to keep Moses [i.e., the law] and not sweep him under the carpet, because I find three things in him. . . . [First of all], I keep the commandments that Moses has given, not because he gave them, but because they have been implanted in me by nature and are written on everyone's heart. In the second place, I find something in Moses that I do not get from nature—the promises and pledges of God about Christ. . . . In the third place, we read Moses for the beautiful examples of faith, love, and the cross that are shown in the patriarchs—Adam, Abel, Noah, Abraham, Isaac, Jacob, Moses, and the rest. . . . The Old Testament is properly understood when we retain from the prophets the beautiful texts about Christ, when we take note of and grasp

> the fine examples [of godly living it contains], and when we use its laws to our advantage . . .[301]

As this passage shows, Luther's primary concern was to find Christ and his saving work in the Scriptures and apply them to the lives of his hearers. The Jews had turned the law's precepts into a code of works that blinded them to the grace of God, so that when Christ came to fulfill its promises they rejected him, preferring their own attempts to achieve righteousness over the power of God to give them what they could never achieve on their own. Luther was very hard on the Jews for that reason, but although that has understandably caused controversy in modern times, what he said must be interpreted in its own context.[302] For example, he was just as condemning of Christian theologians who sought their salvation in Aristotle as he was of the Jews. Even before he posted his Ninety-five Theses against indulgences, he had already denounced the reigning orthodoxy of his time:

> There is no moral virtue . . . without sin. We do not become righteous by doing righteous deeds, but having been made righteous first, we then do righteous deeds. Virtually the entire *Ethics* of Aristotle is the worst enemy of grace. It is wrong to say that no one can become a theologian without Aristotle. On the contrary, no one can become a theologian unless he does so apart from him.[303]

Luther's attacks on the Jews had no effect on them; they were not listening. But it was a different matter when it came to his fellow Christian theologians. When he lashed out against indulgences, his audience knew what to expect. Luther began with the teaching of Jesus, which the church had misinterpreted:

> When our Lord and Master Jesus Christ said, "Repent,"[304] he wanted the entire life of believers to be one of repentance. This word cannot be understood as referring to the sacrament of penance . . . yet it does not mean just inner repentance, which is worthless unless it produces some outward mortification of the flesh.[305]

Here again we see how wrong it is to interpret Luther in terms of opposites. It is certainly true that he rejected the standard identification of repentance

---

[301] Martin Luther, *How Christians Should Regard Moses*, the reworked text of a sermon preached on Exodus in 1525. The full English translation is in Pelikan and Lehmann, *Luther's Works*, 35:161–174.

[302] See Martin Luther, *On the Jews and Their Lies*, in Pelikan and Lehmann, *Luther's Works*, 47:121–305.

[303] Martin Luther, *Disputation against Scholastic Theology*, 38, 40–41, 43–44. The complete text is in Pelikan and Lehmann, *Luther's Works*, 31:9–16.

[304] Matt. 4:17.

[305] Martin Luther, The Ninety-five Theses, 1–3. The full text is in Pelikan and Lehmann, *Luther's Works*, 31:25–33.

with acts of penance imposed by priests in the confessional, but this does not mean that he was indifferent to the practical effects that repentance should have on a person's life. The difference was that where sacramental penance envisaged a progressive change resulting from it, Luther believed that the spiritual change had to come first and that the works that validated it would then flow naturally on from that.

As for the claim that the pope was able to forgive sins, which was the belief that underpinned indulgences, Luther said,

> The pope neither desires nor is able to remit any penalties except those imposed by his own authority, or by that of the canons. He cannot forgive any guilt, but can only declare and show that it has already been forgiven by God.[306]

In other words, what happens to us after death lies outside the pope's jurisdiction, and nothing he says or does in this world will make any difference to it. Luther had not yet rejected the idea of purgatory, or even the possibility that the pope might grant indulgences to the deserving, but the gist of his remarks was clear: "Christians are to be taught that papal indulgences are useful only if they do not put their trust in them, but very harmful if they lose their fear of God because of them."[307] So indulgences were fine if they were ignored, but harmful if they were taken at face value and treated as an assurance that a person's sins have been forgiven! As for going to purgatory after death in order to work off the remaining debt of sin, Luther declared,

> Any truly repentant Christian has a right to full remission of penalty and guilt, even without indulgences. Any true Christian, living or dead, participates in all the blessings of Christ and the church, and this is granted to him by God, even without indulgences.[308]

Without saying a word about purgatory directly, Luther undercut it by making it unnecessary—who would go there if the debt of his sins was already fully paid? Whether he realized it or not, Luther was arguing himself out of the traditional theology, and once the process had begun it moved very quickly. As early as 1520 he was writing,

> Two years ago I wrote on indulgences, but in such a way that I now deeply regret having published that little book. At that time I still clung with great

[306] Luther, Ninety-five Theses, 5–6.
[307] Ibid., 49.
[308] Ibid., 36–37.

superstition to the tyranny of Rome, so I held that indulgences should not be completely rejected, given that so many people approved of them.[309]

A great deal had happened in a short time, and Luther had now reached the point of no return. In *The Babylonian Captivity of the Church*, he launched a broadside attack on the papacy and the sacramental system which lay at the heart of its power.[310] He rejected four of the traditional seven sacraments outright, keeping only baptism, penance, and the Eucharist, all of which he claimed had been corrupted by Rome.[311] What God intended as food for his people had become poison instead, because the grace of eternal life was being withheld from them and the church was suffering as a result. It is not surprising to discover that Luther allied himself with the Czech Utraquists, whose insistence on Communion in both kinds was both biblical and traditional. More unexpected perhaps was his attack on transubstantiation, which he regarded as an Aristotelian attempt to explain the mystery of Christ's presence in the Eucharist and therefore wrong. A problem arose, however, when Luther tried to find a substitute for what had become the official doctrine of the Catholic church. His rather unsatisfactory conclusion was that ordinary people

> . . . do not understand or dispute whether accidents are present without substance, but believe with a simple faith that Christ's body and blood are truly contained there, and leave to those who have nothing else to do, the argument about what contains them.[312]

Luther never really advanced beyond that view, which was to cause him difficulty when he had to confront the Swiss reformers, led by Huldrych Zwingli (1484–1531). The Swiss held that spirit and matter were two different modes of being that did not overlap. To them it was impossible for Christ's ascended body and blood to be present in earthly bread and wine—the whole idea that spiritual realities could be contained in material objects made no sense. Luther agreed with that up to a point, but argued that the Swiss were being too rationalistic. Christ had told his followers that he would be present with them in the breaking of the bread, and so he was. Rationalistic attempts to explain this were futile, but so were rationalistic denials of it. In Luther's mind, the medieval scholastics and the Swiss had made the same mistake, even though

[309] Martin Luther, *The Babylonian Captivity of the Church*, I. See Lull, *Martin Luther*, 210–211. Luther did not say what he had written on the subject, but it was probably his *Explanation of the Ninety-five Theses*, which appeared in 1518. The text is in Pelikan and Lehmann, *Luther's Works* 31:83–252.

[310] The book's title was highly ironic, because the "Babylonian captivity of the papacy" was the term normally reserved for its Avignon period (1305–1377), when the rot supposedly first set in.

[311] He soon went further and dropped penance. See Pelikan and Lehmann, *Luther's Works* 36:124.

[312] Luther, *Babylonian Captivity of the Church*, I, in Pelikan and Lehmann, *Luther's Works*, 36:32.

they had come to opposite conclusions as a result. But in spite of that, Luther undoubtedly felt closer to Zwingli than he did to the Catholics, as can be seen from the agreed statement they produced after they met at Marburg in 1529 and failed to agree:

> Although we have not at this time agreed whether the true body and blood of Christ are bodily in the bread and wine, each side is able to display Christian love to the other (as far as conscience allows). Both sides are praying diligently to Almighty God that he would confirm us in the right understanding through his Spirit.[313]

Later generations would emphasize the differences between Luther and Zwingli in what became a spirit of mutual antagonism far removed from that of the Marburg Articles, which were then reinterpreted in that light. The truth was that Luther and Zwingli were coming at the question from different starting points, which made agreement difficult to achieve. Luther was not as concerned with what happened to the elements of bread and wine in the Lord's Supper as some of his later followers made him out to be, but he was determined to avoid saying anything that might compromise the recipient's access to the grace of God in Christ that the sacrament promised. It was because he thought that Zwingli's approach was removing that access that he objected to it, not because he had any lingering attachment to transubstantiation.

Could Luther and Zwingli eventually have come to a common mind? It is not impossible to think so, although Zwingli's violent death less than two years after the colloquy of Marburg prevented that from happening. But there were those like Martin Bucer (1491–1551) who never gave up hope of finding a *via media* that would do justice to both positions, and his views greatly influenced John Calvin (1509–1564).[314] Is it too fanciful to think that had Luther and Zwingli lived to read it, Calvin's exposition of the Supper would have united them? Consider the following:

> The flesh and blood of Christ feed our souls just as bread and wine maintain our bodies. The sign would mean nothing if our souls did not find nourishment in Christ. That could not happen unless Christ truly formed one with us and refreshed us by the eating of his flesh and the drinking of his blood. Although it seems incredible that the flesh of Christ, which is so far away

[313] Martin Luther, *The Marburg Articles*, 15. The text is in Pelikan and Lehmann, *Luther's Works*, 38:89.
[314] See David F. Wright, ed., *Martin Bucer: Reforming Church and Community* (Cambridge: Cambridge University Press, 1994); Brian Lugioyo, *Martin Bucer's Doctrine of Justification: Reformation Theology and Early Modern Irenicism* (Oxford: Oxford University Press, 2010). Also Martin Greschat, *Martin Bucer: Ein Reformator und seine Zeit* (Munich: C. H. Beck, 1990); French trans., *Martin Bucer (1491–1551). Un réformateur en son temps* (Paris: Presses Universitaires de France, 2002).

from us in spatial terms, should be food to us, let us remember how the secret power of the Holy Spirit surpasses all our conceptions, and how foolish it is to want to measure its immensity by our feeble capacity.[315]

In the event, only the Church of England really took Bucer's *via media* to heart, largely because it was concerned to preserve as much outward unity as it could.[316] The Germans and the Swiss could shut themselves up in their city-states and anathematize each other, but the English could not afford such luxury. They had to stick together, and so they tried very hard to accommodate both the Lutheran and the Swiss approaches in their liturgies and doctrine, creating an "Anglican" ethos that is neither one nor the other, but that can reach out to both in acceptance and understanding of what each of them was trying to affirm.

As the sacramental controversy revealed, the heart of Luther's theology was access to the saving work of Christ on the cross. In one sense, of course, no one had ever denied the centrality of Christ's death and resurrection, which had always been at the heart of Christian worship and devotion. Luther had no quarrel with Anselm's doctrine of the atonement, and much of what he said can be understood as a restatement of it in the face of scholastic and philosophical accretions that had blurred its force in the four centuries that separated the two men. In Luther's time, the biggest single obstacle to the acceptance of Anselm's teaching was the widespread and growing belief in the freedom of the will. In theory, of course, that had long ago been condemned as Pelagianism, but the Renaissance had breathed new life into it and the Roman sacramental system could easily be adapted to accommodate it.

Matters soon came to a head in a conflict between Luther and Erasmus over this very thing. Erasmus had originally been a supporter of Luther and agreed with him when it came to the problem of corruption in the church. If anything, Erasmus was even more critical of Rome and the papacy than Luther was, and initially he saw his younger contemporary as an ally.[317] That soon changed, however, as Erasmus realized that Luther believed—in line with Augustine—that the human will was enslaved by sin and incapable of doing anything to save itself. Erasmus rejected this severe doctrine, preferring the more Pelagian view that human beings were capable of doing good and were free to choose

[315] John Calvin, *Institutio Christianae religionis* 4.17.10. The standard English translation is now *Calvin: Institutes of the Christian Religion*, ed. John T. McNeill and Ford Lewis Battles (Philadelphia: Westminster, 1960).

[316] Bucer actually went to England and died there in 1551. The extent of his direct influence on the English Reformation is a matter of debate and was probably not great, but the idea of a *via media* appealed to the English, even if the precise details of it were not worked out by Bucer.

[317] See his *In Praise of Folly*, which is a biting satire of the church of his day. It was first published as *Moriae encomium* (Strasbourg: Matthias Schuwerij, 1511).

or reject the salvation offered to them in Christ. In 1524 he wrote a short book on the subject which was aimed directly at Luther.[318] Luther replied almost immediately in what became one of his best works and a classic statement of the opposing view.[319] Erasmus did not give up and wrote three more books on the subject, trying as hard as he could to pour oil on troubled waters, but to no avail.[320] Luther would not hear of any compromise because, in truth, no compromise was possible. To allow for the freedom of the will was to detract from the glory of the work of Christ, the exaltation of which was always his chief passion.

The main lines of Luther's doctrine were already apparent in the theses he composed for a disputation held at Heidelberg in May 1518. This had little to do with indulgences but concentrated heavily on good works and the bondage of the will to sin. It also introduced another great theme of Luther's, the opposition between what he called a "theology of glory" and a "theology of the cross." Listen to what he said:

> The man who does not know Christ does not know God hidden in suffering. Therefore he prefers works to suffering, glory to the cross, strength to weakness, wisdom to folly, and good to evil generally. These are the people whom the apostle calls "enemies of the cross of Christ,"[321] for they hate the cross and suffering, and love works and their glory. They call the good of the cross evil and the evil of [their own] deeds good. God can be found only in suffering and the cross.... Therefore, friends of the cross say that the cross is good and works are evil, for through the cross works are destroyed and the old Adam, who is particularly edified by works, is crucified. It is impossible for a man not to be puffed up by his good works unless he has first been deflated and destroyed by suffering and evil until he knows that he is worthless and that his works are not his but God's.[322]

Once again it is easy to play on the rhetorical oppositions and misunderstand what Luther was trying to say. Worldly glory is the antithesis of the cross of Christ, to be sure, but Luther knew that Paul gloried in the cross, and that

---

[318] Desiderius Erasmus, *De libero arbitrio* (Antwerp: Michael Hillenius Hoochstratanus, 1524). English translation by Ernest F. Winter, *Erasmus and Luther: Discourse on Free Will* (London: Continuum, 2007).

[319] Martin Luther, *De servo arbitrio* (Wittenberg: Johannes Lufft, 1525). English translation in Pelikan and Lehmann, *Luther's Works*, 33:1–295; also J. I. Packer and Olaf R. Johnston, *The Bondage of the Will* (Cambridge: James Clarke, 1957).

[320] Desiderius Erasmus, *Hyperaspistes: Diatribae adversus servum arbitrium Martini Lutheri*, 2 vols. (Basel: Johann Froben, 1526–1527); *De sarcienda ecclesiae concordia deque sedandis opiniomum dissidiis* (Antwerp: Crapheus, 1533).

[321] Phil. 3:18.

[322] Martin Luther, *Proofs of the Thesis Debated in the Chapter at Heidelberg, May 1518*, 21. See Pelikan and Lehmann, *Luther's Works*, 31:39–58 for the full text.

was the point he was trying to make.[323] The wisdom of God is folly to those who are perishing, but to those who are being saved it is the power of God.[324] Not only was this profoundly biblical, it was also very personal. If the atonement theory of Anselm had a defect, it was that it was too objective. According to Anselm, Christ had paid the price for the sins of the whole world, and his successors believed that it was the duty and privilege of the church to offer his payment to those who came seeking the grace made available to them in the sacraments. But for Luther, Christ died for sinners rather than for sins, and it is as sinners in need of grace that the Son of God unites us to himself. The sacraments bear witness to that union and nourish it, but they cannot create it or be manipulated in order to strengthen it. Frequent Communion is of no use to the man whose heart is not right with God, but to the one who is justified by faith, it is the bread of eternal life.[325]

In effect, what Luther did was to adjust the Anselmian theory of atonement by turning it into what we now call "penal substitution." What this means is that Christ took our place on the cross and paid the penalty for our sins that we would otherwise have had to pay for ourselves. Neither of these ideas was new, and both can be found throughout the history of the church. What made them so powerful in Luther's teaching was the combination of them that came at the right time to address a situation that led to misunderstandings (and misapplications) that were effectively concealing the gospel.

As with the original Anselmian theory, penal substitution has always had its detractors, but it became (and has remained) the benchmark of Protestant spirituality because it says something about the sacrifice of Christ that we have to affirm if we are to understand it properly. The substitutionary element is essential, because without that the cross of Christ would be meaningless—indeed, it would be scandalous. Jesus did not have to die for any sins of his own, and the New Testament repeatedly insists on his innocence. If he had not been taking someone else's place, there would be no valid explanation for his death. The penal element is also essential, because if he had died for our sins but not paid the penalty for them, we might still have to die in order to make sure that they were properly punished. Jesus would then be an example to us, perhaps even a reassurance that our death would be followed by resurrection just as his was, but he would not be our Savior and would have no special claim on us as Lord.

People who have rejected penal substitution have done so for different rea-

323 See Gal. 6:14.
324 1 Cor. 1:18.
325 See Luther, *Babylonian Captivity of the Church*, I, in Pelikan and Lehmann, *Luther's Works*, 36:11–57.

sons, but they all boil down to what Anselm said to his dialogue partner Boso: they have not understood how serious the weight of sin really is. God cannot just wipe away our misdeeds as if they do not matter, not because he lacks the power to do so but because they are too important to be ignored. What we do matters to God because we matter to God. The scope of our relationship with him cannot be reduced to moral precepts or good advice, important though such things are in their place. Our sins are not measured by an objective standard of gravity but by the fact that they manifest disobedience to the will of God and are therefore a rejection of our relationship with him. In submitting to the Father's will and restoring that relationship by his sacrificial payment for our sins, Jesus was doing something that was both necessary in itself and impossible for anyone else to do. Penal substitution is the term for this that we normally use today, but although earlier ages expressed it differently, the heart of the matter has remained unchanged since the day that Jesus made that sacrifice on our behalf.

Prophet, Priest, and King

One of the most important aspects of the Reformation was its desire to make sense of the Bible as a whole. The rediscovery of the sacred text and the renewed insistence that it alone should be the basis of Christian theology naturally led scholars to ask how it held together and what its basic principles were. In this endeavor, the work of Christ was central, because the Old Testament had foretold his coming and the New Testament explained how its promises had been fulfilled. One of the main categories in which this could be understood was that of God's covenant with his people. In ancient Israel there were three "offices" (as they were called) that marked the relationship between God and his people, and each of them was distinguished by anointing. Christ ("the anointed one") held them all and fulfilled their functions in such a way as to make them redundant. It was well known that in Jesus' day only one of the traditional offices, the priesthood, was still functioning, but there were indications of a revival of prophecy in the career of John the Baptist, and Jesus himself was widely expected to restore the kingdom of his ancestor David. There was no suggestion in the Gospels that he might usurp a priestly role, but he did indicate that his body was the temple, and the letter to the Hebrews explains that he was indeed the high priest of a new covenant.[326]

In the early church, the greatest amount of attention was paid to the combination of priest and king, which was unknown in ancient Israel but was typified,

[326] Heb. 4:14–16.

even in the Old Testament, by the mysterious figure of Melchizedek. The historical Melchizedek had been the king of Salem (Jerusalem) in the time of Abraham, but his status as a priest of God Most High was already recognized as unique long before the coming of Jesus.[327] The suggestion that the Davidic king would be "a priest forever after the order of Melchizedek" is found in Psalm 110:4, and the whole Melchizedek theme became a major component of the argument made by the author of Hebrews, that Jesus was the one who had fulfilled the ancient covenant promises made to Abraham and Moses.[328]

All of this was well known to the early Christians, who frequently commented on Melchizedek, pointing out that Jesus had offered the very same thing to God as Melchizedek had done—bread and wine, which in his case were his own body and blood.[329] As Augustine of Hippo put it,

> The king fought for us, the priest offered himself for us. In fighting for us, it seemed as though he himself was overcome, but in fact he was a conqueror. He was crucified, and on that cross he slew the Devil, which is what makes him our king. But how is he our priest? Because he offered himself for us.[330]

Mention of all three offices together was less common, but some instances can be found. Eusebius of Caesarea, for example, wrote,

> Of all who in former times were consecrated with holy oil, whether as priests, kings, or prophets, no one received such power of divine virtue as our Savior and Lord Jesus demonstrates. . . . the only high priest of all men, the only king of all creation, and the Father's supreme prophet of prophets.[331]

A century or so later, Peter Chrysologus wrote,

> He was called Christ by anointing and Jesus by name, because he poured himself forth on those anointed with the fullness of the Spirit of divinity which in earlier times had been gathered together by kings, prophets, and priests, into one person, this king of kings, priest of priests, prophet of prophets . . .[332]

In the Middle Ages, the same theme reappeared in the writings of Thomas Aquinas, which may have been the immediate source from which the Reformers picked it up:

---

[327] The story is told in Gen. 14:17–20.
[328] Heb. 7:1–22.
[329] Cyprian of Carthage, *Epistula* 63.4.
[330] Augustine of Hippo, *Tractatus in I Epistulam Iohannis* 3.2.
[331] Eusebius of Caesarea, *Historia ecclesiastica* 1.3.
[332] Petrus Chrysologus, *Sermo* 59.

Christ, as the head of all, has the perfection of all graces. With others, one is a lawgiver, another is a priest, and another is king, but in Christ all three come together because he is the fount of all grace.[333]

Thomas came closer than any of the church fathers to making this theme a part of his systematic theology, but he never developed it any further than this. Martin Luther made frequent references to Christ as priest and king, of which the following is a typical example:

> Christ our high priest has ascended into heaven and sits on the right hand of God the Father, where he makes unending intercession for us. . . . In his death, he is a sacrifice offered up for sins; in his resurrection he is a conqueror; in his ascension he is a king, in making mediation and intercession, he is a high priest.[334]

Luther went further than this, however, because he extended Christ's priestly kingship to the experience of the believer who is united with him:

> Just as Christ obtained these two prerogatives by his birthright, so he imparts them to and shares them with everyone who believes in him. . . . Hence we are all kings and priests in Christ.[335]

Similar statements can be found in the writings of Philipp Melanchthon (1497–1560) and Heinrich Bullinger (1504–1575), among others.[336] There is no sign among the early Lutherans of the threefold office, however, apart from a reference to it by Andreas Osiander (1498–1552), which he made in a deposition to the imperial diet at Augsburg in 1530, when the famous Protestant Confession was presented to the emperor. Osiander wrote,

> "Christ" means "anointed," so one sees that all three offices apply to him—the prophetic office, for he only is our teacher and master;[337] the kingly authority, for he rules forever in the house of Jacob;[338] and the priestly office, for he is a priest forever after the order of Melchizedek.[339] That is now his office, so that he may be our wisdom, righteousness, sanctification, and redemption, as Paul testifies.[340]

---

[333] Thomas Aquinas, *Summa theologiae* III.1.22.1. See John F. Jansen, *Calvin's Doctrine of the Work of Christ* (London: James Clarke, 1956), 31, for the suggestion that Thomas influenced Calvin on this.

[334] Martin Luther, *Table Talk*, 190. The text is not in Pelikan and Lehmann, *Luther's Works*, but an English translation can be found in Martin Luther, *Table Talk*, ed. W. Hazlitt (London: D. Bogue, 1848), 82.

[335] Martin Luther, *On Christian liberty*, in Pelikan and Lehmann, *Luther's Works*, 31:354.

[336] See Jansen, *Calvin's Doctrine*, 34–36, for the relevant evidence.

[337] Matt. 23:8.

[338] Luke 1:32.

[339] Psalm 110:4.

[340] 1 Cor. 1:30. The text is in Wilhelm Gussmann, *Quellen und Forschungen zur Geschichte der Augsburger Glaubensbekenntnisses*, I/1 (Berlin: Teubner, 1911), 302.

John Calvin inherited this tradition and developed it further. Initially he took what Luther said about the twofold office of Christ as priest and king, and repeated it almost word for word in the first edition of his *Institutes*, which appeared in 1536.[341] But in the 1539 edition, he expanded this to include the prophetic office as well: "The prophets have their own anointing, as do the kings and priests, not in an outward ceremony, but spiritually."[342] He did not develop it any further at that time, but in his catechism of 1543 he explained the messianic title as follows:

> By this title is clearly declared his office. He was anointed by the heavenly Father to be ordained as king, priest or sacrifice, and prophet.[343]

After that, the final edition of the *Institutes* (1559) contains an entire chapter on the threefold office(s) of the Messiah, and it would be this that governed the approach taken by subsequent generations of Reformed theologians.[344] As Calvin expressed it,

> The name Christ refers to those three offices, for we know that under the law, prophets as well as priests and kings were anointed with holy oil. This is why the name Messiah was given to the promised Mediator. But although I admit that he was so called with respect to the kingly office, still the prophetic and sacerdotal unctions have their proper place, and must not be overlooked.[345]

Calvin had relatively little to say about the prophetic office, but he recognized its importance. Its scriptural grounding he located in the words of Isaiah that Jesus quoted with reference to himself when he stood up to preach in the synagogue at Nazareth:

> The Spirit of the Lord God is upon me,
> because the Lord has anointed me
> to bring good news to the poor;
> he has sent me to bind up the brokenhearted,
> to proclaim liberty to the captives,

[341] *Calvini opera*, I, 68. The text is the first of fifty-nine volumes devoted to Calvin's works, published in the *Corpus Reformatorum*, ed. G. Baum, E. Cunitz, and E. Reuss (Braunschweig: C. A. Schwetschke und Sohn, 1863–1900), XXIX–LXXXVII.
[342] *Calvini opera*, I, 513.
[343] Ibid., VI, 19 (*Corpus Reformatorum*, XXXIV).
[344] Jansen, *Calvin's Doctrine*, 51–120, did his best to claim that Calvin really adhered to the twofold priest-king formula and that on this point he was misunderstood by his followers. There can be no doubt that Calvin did often use the twofold formula, but that should not be interpreted as excluding the threefold one (including prophecy). The clear evidence of the *Institutes* cannot be set aside so lightly, and subsequent Reformed theologians derived their picture of the offices from that text more than from anything else.
[345] Calvin, *Institutio* 2.15.2.

and the opening of the prison to those who are bound;
to proclaim the year of the LORD's favor.[346]

Both the anointing and the prophetic ministry are clearly indicated in this passage, which Jesus used at the very beginning of his earthly ministry and which set the tone for what was to follow. Calvin believed that the anointing was not just for him but for his whole body (i.e., the church), so that the preaching of the gospel would always be accompanied by the effectual working of the Holy Spirit—though Calvin did not develop that idea. What he did insist on was that Jesus was the prophet who brought prophecy to an end because his teaching was perfect and could not be surpassed. As he put it,

> The purpose of the prophetical dignity in Christ is to teach us that the doctrine that he delivered includes a wisdom that is perfect in all its parts.[347]

Calvin treated Christ's priestly office with comparable brevity, but its fundamental importance is obvious and its implications were fully developed in his treatment of the atonement. His focus was clearly on Christ's role as Mediator. In his own words,

> There is no access to God for us or for our prayers until the priest, purging away our defilements, sanctifies us and obtains for us that favor of which we are deprived because of the impurity of our lives and hearts. If the benefit and efficacy of Christ's priesthood is to reach us, it must start with his death. From there, it follows that the one with whose help we obtain favor must be a perpetual intercessor. This is the basis of confidence not only in prayer but in the tranquillity of godly minds which can rely on the paternal indulgence of God and feel assured that whatever has been consecrated by the Mediator is pleasing to him.[348]

But it was the kingly office, which Calvin treated after the prophetic but before the priestly one, to which he devoted the greatest attention, in line with his recognition that it was the one for which Christ's anointing was primarily intended. The first point that Calvin made was that the kingly office of Christ was spiritual in nature, which meant that it was eternal and not subject to the decay that had afflicted the historical Israelite monarchy to which he laid claim as the "son of David." For Calvin, this reality had two equally important aspects. The first related primarily to the church, which had the assurance that

346 Isa. 61:1–2, quoted in Luke 4:18–19.
347 Calvin, *Institutio* 2.15.2.
348 Ibid., 2.15.6.

whatever disasters might befall it in this world, it would triumph in the end. The second, which he emphasized more than the first, was that it gave every believer the hope of a blessed immortality. As he put it,

> Let each of us, when he hears that the kingdom of Christ is spiritual, be roused by that thought to entertain the hope of a better life, and to expect that as it is now protected by the hand of Christ, so it will be fully realized in a future life.[349]

Calvin was under no illusion that this life would be a paradise for believers. He knew that they would live in a state of constant spiritual warfare, and that the conditions of peace and happiness promised by the gospel properly belonged to the life of heaven. But at the same time, he also insisted that the blessing of Christ's kingdom was a reality in this life:

> Christ enriches his people with all things necessary to the eternal salvation of their souls, and fortifies them with courage to stand unassailable against all the attacks of spiritual foes. He reigns for us more than for himself, both inside and outside us, so that being replenished (insofar as God knows it to be expedient) with the gifts of the Spirit (of which we are naturally destitute) we may feel from their firstfruits that we are truly united to God for perfect blessedness.[350]

To Calvin's mind, the glory of the kingdom of Christ was supremely revealed in the way in which he strengthens his followers to face the battles they have to fight in this world and to overcome the temptations of the flesh and the wiles of the Devil. He summed it up like this:

> Since Christ arms and equips us by his power, adorns us with splendor and magnificence, enriches us with wealth, we find here the most abundant cause of glorying and are also inspired with boldness, so that we can contend fearlessly with the Devil, sin, and death. Clothed with his righteousness, we can bravely surmount all the insults of the world, and as he replenishes us liberally with his gifts, so we can in turn bring forth fruit to his glory.[351]

Quoting the words of the apostle Paul, Calvin went on to explain how the Father had given Christ the kingdom, which he would one day hand back to him in glory. By becoming the Mediator between God and man, the Son left the presence of the Father, where he properly belonged, and drew near to us,

---

[349] Ibid., 2.15.3.
[350] Ibid., 2.15.4.
[351] Ibid., 2.15.4.

so that we in turn might be drawn nearer to God. But we should not forget that his mediation comes with divine authority, which he exercises toward everyone, whether they submit to him or not. Those who understand this have all the more reason to obey him:

> For as he unites the offices of king and pastor toward believers who voluntarily submit to him, so (on the other hand) we are told that he wields an iron scepter to break and bruise the rebellious like a potter's vessel.[352] We are also told that he will judge the Gentiles, that he will cover the earth with dead bodies and lay low every opposing height.[353] Some examples of this can already be seen, but full proof will be given at the last judgment, which may properly be regarded as the final act of his reign.[354]

In Calvin's teaching, the offices of prophet, priest, and king belonged to the divine self-revelation in time and space and would cease to function when all things were finally wound up at the end of the age. But while prophecy would be fulfilled and the priestly sacrifices made redundant by the perfection of heaven, the kingly rule would continue in another form, because it was nothing less than the manifestation on earth of the eternal sovereignty of God.

[352] Psalm 2:9.
[353] Psalm 110:6.
[354] Calvin, *Institutio* 2.15.5.

14

The Coming of Christ's Kingdom

The Eternal Reign of Christ

An important aspect of the work of Christ, but one that has been somewhat neglected in recent times, is that of his eternal reign in glory. This is surprising, given that it is plainly stated in the Nicene Creed:

> He ascended into heaven and sits at the right hand of God. From there he will come to judge the living and the dead, and his kingdom will have no end.

These doctrines continue to figure in theological textbooks, but a number of factors have contributed to their relative decline in practical importance. One of these has been the emphasis on the "finished" nature of Christ's atoning work on the cross. Anxious to avoid Roman Catholic teachings that suggest that the once-for-all sacrifice of the incarnate Son can somehow be continued, re-presented, or extended in and by the church, Protestant theologians have stressed the fact that his atoning work has been accomplished and cannot be repeated. When they speak of the Christian life, their emphasis tends to shift to the work of the Holy Spirit, whose coming at Pentecost is widely regarded as the "birthday" of the church. Another factor is that there has been a negative reaction against some sectarian movements and liberal theologians (mainly of the late nineteenth and early twentieth centuries), who have tried to build the kingdom of God on earth. The sectarians have done this in order to hasten Christ's return or in eager expectation of its imminent (and sometimes predictable) arrival; the liberals have done it in order to make the issue of Christ's "return" irrelevant.

But in spite of these aberrations, it is clear that the eternal reign of Christ is an essential part of his work.[1] We cannot go back to Calvary, but we can

[1] 1 Cor. 15:28. The book of Revelation is almost entirely devoted to this theme.

receive its benefits now because Christ has taken his sacrifice up to the Father, at whose right hand he pleads for us, and from where he dispenses forgiveness and restoration to his faithful servants here below. Because of that, his death remains a valid atonement for us today. The challenge we face is figuring out how to describe it properly and put it into practice in our experience. It was over this, more than anything else, that the Western church divided in the sixteenth century, and differences of opinion about it continue to keep the various denominations apart.

In the centuries before the church turned its attention to the work of Christ, its teaching about his eternal reign was necessarily somewhat vague. The creedal statements remind us that it was always there, but when we look more deeply into it what we find is not particularly encouraging. For the most part, the early Christians seem to have concentrated on what they believed was Christ's imminent return and the subsequent end of the world. New Testament scholars call this the *parousia*, and many of them believe that the earliest Christian communities expected it to arrive at any minute. According to one widely received modern opinion, the *parousia* hope gradually faded and was replaced by a more institutionalized understanding of the church, which we now call "catholicism." Precisely when this happened is a matter of debate. Many think that the process was already underway in the New Testament period and interpret parts of it, notably Luke–Acts and the Pastoral Epistles, as harbingers of what was to come. Others point to the suppression of the Montanist heresy in the late second century as the time when this transition finally occurred, and still others place it as late as the legalization of Christianity in 313. These differences of opinion affect the way we read the New Testament and the church fathers, but they are differences about the speed of the transformation of the early Christian communities into the catholic church, not about the fact of the transformation itself. However long it took—and the pace of development no doubt varied considerably in different places—the end result was the same.

There can be no doubt that an institutional church emerged in the second century, if not before, and that by the time Christianity became a legal religion it was well entrenched. But whether this means that the *parousia* hope had faded is a different matter. Readers of the New Testament had always known that the gospel must be preached to the ends of the earth before Christ comes again, and they registered each new triumph of the gospel as a development toward that end.[2] Already around the year 200, Tertullian was boasting that there were Christians throughout the Roman empire and beyond—the prophecy was

[2] Matt. 28:19–20; Acts 1:8. See also Rom. 15:18–24.

being realized in his own time.[3] To many people in later centuries, the legalization of Christianity was merely a further development along the same lines, the outworking of the claim that "every knee should bow . . . and every tongue confess that Jesus Christ is Lord."[4]

In his great book *The City of God*, Augustine more or less single-handedly rewrote human history and reconfigured the self-understanding of the Romans. Gone were the pagan heroes of antiquity whose virtue and self-sacrifice molded the traditional conception of Roman citizenship. In their place came the saints and martyrs of the church, the model citizens of the kingdom of heaven to which we belong.

Augustine did not repudiate the secular state but he put it in context. Jesus had told the Jews of his day that they were to render unto Caesar the things that were Caesar's, but unto God the things that were God's.[5] Augustine's point was that Caesars come and go, but God is eternally one and the same. Caesar was also a lesser authority than God, so what belonged to him did not matter nearly as much as what belonged to the Lord. As Jesus told his disciples, "Do not fear those who kill the body but cannot kill the soul. Rather fear him who can destroy both soul and body in hell."[6] Modern readers may be tempted to see this relativization of Caesar as a church-state conflict in which the state came off worse, but this would be a misperception. In the teaching of Jesus and the early Christians, church and state each had their proper sphere, but the church's sphere was of eternal significance while that of the state was not. Insofar as Christians had to live in this world, obedience to the state was required of them, but they did not really belong on earth, and their main preoccupation must always be to prepare themselves for the kingdom of heaven.[7]

Augustine traced this difference between the world and the kingdom of God back as far as the conflict between Cain and Abel. In his words,

> Scripture tells us that Cain founded a city, whereas Abel, being a pilgrim, did not. For the city of the saints is up above, even though it produces citizens here below, and in them the city [of God] is on pilgrimage until the time of its kingdom comes. Then it will assemble all those citizens as they rise again in their bodies and they will be given the promised kingdom, where they will reign with their prince, the king of ages, world without end.[8]

[3] Tertullian, *Apologeticum* 37.4.
[4] Phil. 2:10–11.
[5] Matt. 22:21.
[6] Matt. 10:28.
[7] On obedience to the state, see Rom. 13:1–7. Compare this with Heb. 11:10, 16, for example.
[8] Augustine of Hippo, *De civitate Dei* 15.1.

The practical effects of this belief must not be underestimated. Wealthy people who had previously cultivated great estates and taken great pride in their ancestry and descendants turned their properties into monasteries and retired from the world. Officials like Ambrose (339?–397), the prefect (mayor) of Milan, resigned their offices to become priests and bishops in the church. No doubt some of these vocations were opportunistic, like that of Synesius of Cyrene (373?–414?), who is often held up as the model of the worldly ecclesiastic.[9] But many others were genuine, and the church tried to ensure that only those who were rightly motivated would get high office by placing restrictions like poverty and chastity on them that were meant to deter the ungodly.

Basil of Caesarea was supposed to have been the first person to draw up a rule for these monastic communities, and his rule is still the basis for them in the Eastern churches today. Augustine also founded a community in Hippo and devised a rule for it, though his monastery seems to have disappeared after his death and was not used again for nearly a thousand years. In Italy, Basil's rule was taken up and modified by Benedict of Nursia (480?–543) in his great establishment at Monte Cassino, which still exists today. Western monasticism would later develop a variety of different forms, but for the first five hundred years it was Benedictine.

The monks became the shock troops of orthodoxy in the battles against Arianism and later heresies, and the spearhead of evangelization beyond the Roman frontier. They invented no new doctrine, but did what they could to make the reign of Christ a reality in everyday experience. The churches of the British Isles and northern Europe came into existence because of their labors, and monastic fervor characterized those churches for centuries afterwards. To this day, place names ending in -minster or -münster recall abbeys from which the monks set out to establish the local church, and the names of their founders tell the same story. Patrick (Ireland), Columba (Scotland), David (Wales), Augustine (England), Boniface (Germany), Willibrord (Netherlands)—all were monks, dedicated to the same task and prepared to risk their lives for the sake of the gospel.[10]

It was in this spiritual climate that monasticism came to be recognized as the model of a Christian society to which all serious believers should aspire.[11] Monasticism was a counterculture that aimed to express the life of the heavenly kingdom on earth and point the way toward the Christian's eternal

[9] See Bengt A. Roos, *Synesius of Cyrene: A Study in His Personality* (Lund: Lund University Press, 1991).

[10] See Ian Wood, *The Missionary Life: Saints and the Evangelisation of Europe 400–1050* (London: Longman, 2001).

[11] See Clifford H. Lawrence, *Medieval Monasticism: Forms of Religious Life in Western Europe in the Middle Ages* (London: Longman, 1984).

destiny. It soon became the dominant force in church life, so much so that its principles were extended, first to bishops and then more gradually (and only in the West), to the lower clergy. It took many centuries before clerical celibacy became obligatory in the Western church, but the direction was clear and the church never retreated from it. In the East, the tradition that bishops had to be celibate meant that they could not normally be drawn from the lower clergy, most of whom were married, and so they were almost always monks who had been ordained as priests. This created a special class of so-called "hieromonks" from which bishops were—and still are—drawn, a practice that contributed in its own way to the overall monasticization of the church.[12]

In the Western church, Pope Gregory I "the Great" (590–604) tried to impose monastic discipline on the entire clergy, but although he failed, his goals remained in the forefront of people's minds. His will eventually triumphed at the Second Lateran Council in 1139, more than five hundred years after his death, as part of a more widespread reform, which took monasticism as the norm and tried to make the rest of the clergy conform to it. The effects of this can be seen especially in England, where there was a steady movement toward converting "secular" cathedrals (as the non-monastic ones were called) into monastic ones. This eventually led to the elevation of one monastery (Ely) into a bishopric, with the abbey as its cathedral.[13]

The *parousia* hope therefore changed its outward appearance over time but it did not die, and in some vital respects it became more influential than ever. The successful imposition of universal clerical celibacy was its greatest triumph, because those who publicly represented Christ to the world were meant to live like the saints and angels in heaven, demonstrating by their sacrifice and dedication what the future hope of Christians would be like. As the clerical estate became more clearly defined by its celibacy it also became more powerful, and whatever voice laypeople had once had in church affairs was effectively silenced. At one time, bishops had been elected by popular acclamation in a public assembly, but by the eleventh century that was being phased out everywhere, even at Rome, which was more conservative in such matters than most

[12] Readers of Dostoevsky, for example, will be familiar with the hieromonks who figure in his books, but they probably do not understand their significance in the Eastern church.

[13] That happened in 1109, the year that Anselm died. By then about half of the English cathedrals had become monastic, including such famous ones as Canterbury, Durham, Winchester, and Norwich. But others escaped the process—for example, York, London, Lincoln, Exeter, and Salisbury all remained "secular." In two cases there was an attempt to amalgamate a secular cathedral with a monastery but the process was never completed. The effects, however, were long-lasting. Lichfield (a secular cathedral) and Coventry (a monastery) stayed united until 1836, and Bath (a monastery) and Wells (a secular cathedral) remain linked to this day. After the Reformation, King Henry VIII created six new bishoprics, all of which were based in former monasteries (Bristol, Chester, Gloucester, Oxford, Peterborough, and Westminster). Westminster Abbey lost its bishop after only ten years, but it remains a sort of national cathedral and is outside the normal diocesan structure of the Church of England. The monastic footprint has not been eradicated!

other places. In 1059 the newly formed college of "cardinals" was charged with the election of future popes, and of course all the cardinals were men in holy orders.[14] The popes then embarked on a campaign to seize control of the right to appoint bishops and other clergy, a right that had been claimed by kings and noblemen all over Europe. It was a long struggle but the church was eventually successful, at least on the whole, and its character changed as a result.

Ironically, the separation of the clergy from the people (by means of a realized eschatology that tried to reproduce something of heaven on earth) had the effect of secularizing the church in a way that would have horrified its original proponents. The logic of this process is plain enough. If Christians can live the life of heaven in this world, then there is some obligation on them to do so, since they are heading for heaven in any case. If priests can live like monks, the church can surely become a monastery and the whole of our human life can be regulated accordingly. In other words, the *parousia* hope is not just for a few spiritual athletes who can outperform the rest, but for everyone. Once that idea took hold, it was a short step to thinking that the church itself was the kingdom of God on earth, and that its head, the bishop of Rome, was its divinely appointed governor or, as he himself put it, the "vicar of Christ."[15]

The progressive identification of the church with the kingdom of God on earth did not take explicit doctrinal form, but it gave a new dimension to the ancient creedal affirmation of belief in the "one, holy, catholic and apostolic church," which was now identified with the institution that was centered on Rome and its bishop. To be out of line (and/or out of communion) with them was to leave the church and so lose one's salvation. Papal and conciliar decrees of the church, however trivial or bizarre they might seem to be, became equivalent to the word of God. Questions that could not be answered from the Bible were resolved by the church, which then became the privileged interpreter of how (or whether) Scripture was to be applied in particular cases. In this way, the practical authority of the church and its leaders became more important than the Bible itself, and those outside the system were discouraged from reading it on their own. It would be too much to say that the Bible was unknown to ordinary people, but its contents were filtered through the prism of church authority and there was almost no one around who could challenge that effectively.

One important effect of the identification of church and kingdom is that things that had previously been regarded as secular matters, outside the church's competence, were no longer left to Caesar's jurisdiction. The church

[14] The Latin word *cardo* means "hinge," and the cardinals were regarded as the "hinges" of the door of St. Peter that led into the kingdom of heaven.

[15] A title first regularly used by Pope Innocent III (1198–1216) and now standard.

regarded its appropriation of secular authority as the Christianization of society, the application of the gospel to the needs of everyday life, and it must be admitted that in some ways the effects were beneficial. Matrimony is a case in point. In ancient times it had been a purely secular thing—there were no church weddings in the New Testament. Christians were advised not to marry outside the faith, but beyond that nothing much was said about it.

The medieval church changed all that. Even as the clergy became celibate, matrimony became "holy" and marriage outside the church was progressively downgraded. This had two immediate and long-lasting consequences. The first was that the parties to the marriage had to give their consent to it. In theory at least, no one could be married against his (or more importantly, her) will. This was an attack on the ancient social custom of arranged marriages and a blow in favor of individual freedom, even if the practical constraints operating in society were not so easily overcome. The second was that, once it was voluntarily contracted, a marriage could not be dissolved by anything short of death. Legal separation was possible, as was annulment if it could be shown that the original marriage had been unlawful, but divorce (understood as the breaking of a legitimate marriage) was ruled out. This had the long-term effect of raising the status of marriage and of stabilizing families by giving women a security that they had not previously had. Of course there were abuses, and the system was far from perfect, but that is true of any arrangement devised by human beings. What matters most is not the failures but the intentions—and the relatively high level of overall success registered in the longer term.

The church also claimed an important role in education and the upbringing of children. It provided schools and eventually universities where learning could be fostered beyond the walls of the monastery. The fact that colleges in places like Paris, Oxford, and Cambridge followed a monastic pattern of life, even though the students were not monks, is yet another indication of how the monastic ideal spilled over into wider society. Social welfare, such as it was, was also the province of the church. It is not an accident that the words "hospital" and "hotel" were originally the same—guesthouses where those in need of them could be cared for. Even tourism took the form of pilgrimage, and at times it was very popular. People from all over Europe made their way to the great shrine of Santiago de Compostela in northwestern Spain, and after the crusaders captured Jerusalem quite a number went there too. Even in the late-fourteenth century, pilgrimages to sacred sites had lost none of their popularity, as Geoffrey Chaucer's *Canterbury Tales* reminds us.

The church also entered the political sphere, again often to salutary effect. The so-called "truce of God" was introduced in order to cut down on the warfare that so often disrupted feudal societies, and the Crusades were launched as a religious initiative. Western Europeans had nothing to gain by invading the Holy Land, and in worldly terms the Crusades were a spectacular failure. But in popular legend they live on as heroic efforts to spread the gospel by a new kind of spiritual warrior—the knight in shining armor. The natural aggression of the military class was turned into a noble quest for the holy grail. Physical lust was transformed into courtly love, the courtesan being replaced by the damsel in distress. As these ideals trickled down into the lower classes, a new kind of person emerged: the gentleman. There was no such individual in the New Testament or in the early church, but by the end of the Middle Ages gentlemen were becoming the norm in European society, and the words "sir" and "madam," previously reserved for the upper class, became the most common forms of address for everyone. In a word, the church created what we now call the middle class by expecting peasants to act like gentlemen of noble birth—as profound a social revolution as any that has ever occurred.

In these and in myriad other ways, the church touched every aspect of society. Trade and commerce were regulated according to Christian notions of propriety, which effectively forbade people to lend money at interest (usury). Unfortunately, this well-intentioned move went against the natural laws of economics and had the effect of giving a disproportionate share of banking and financial services to Jews, who were not subject to the laws of the church. It is the tragedy of European history that so much of the later animosity toward the Jewish minority can be traced to this, as the figure of Shylock in Shakespeare's *Merchant of Venice* reminds us.[16] A society in which the church controlled everything would never have found it easy to relate to an extraneous minority, but the peculiar virulence of the hatred toward Jews owes at least as much to this accident of medieval history as it does to the conflicts between Christians and Jews recorded in the New Testament. The accusation of "Christ-killers" leveled against Jews in later times was the result, not the cause, of the resentment felt against them for entirely different reasons.

The grip that the church had on medieval society was not successfully challenged for a long time, and there were relatively few attempts to do so. The logic that had produced it was compelling and all-embracing, so that if it failed to take root, most people concluded that the fault lay with the forces that

[16] Shylock's case is especially disturbing, because neither Shakespeare nor any of his audience had any personal experience of Jews and therefore had no way of judging how fair the caricature of them was. The Jews had been expelled from England in 1290 as an act of piety and were not readmitted until 1656—a generation after Shakespeare's death. This behavior was repeated in Spain (1492) and Portugal (1494), who expelled their Jews as an act of thanksgiving for the reconquest of the Iberian peninsula from the Arabs and for the subsequent discovery of America in the same year.

resisted it and not with whatever it was that the church was trying to impose. Thus we find that in Ireland, the custom of accepting married priests and even hereditary abbots of monasteries continued until the sixteenth-century Reformation, but although it was grudgingly tolerated by Rome, it was still regarded as an abuse and was stamped out when the opportunity to do so arose.[17] But that happened only *after* the Reformation, when the Irish church was brought into real conformity with Rome for the first time, just when the churches in neighboring England and Scotland were breaking free of papal control and adopting what had up to then been peculiarly Irish ways!

Given the monastic imprint on medieval church life, it will come as no surprise to discover that movements for reform were mostly monastic in origin. In 909 Duke William I of Aquitaine decided to found a monastery at Cluny (in Burgundy), which was given complete internal autonomy and placed under the protection of the bishop of Rome.[18] That made little difference at the time, but over the next century and a half a combination of gifted abbots and ever closer links with Rome produced a situation in which Cluny acquired an exceptional degree of influence over the Western church. By 1100 it had established branch monasteries all over Europe and secured the election of reform-minded popes, who raised the status of their see (and incidentally their own power) to previously undreamed-of heights. When Pope Gregory VII (1073–1085) fell out with Henry IV of Germany (1056–1105)[19] over the appointment of bishops, it was Abbot Hugh of Cluny who mediated the settlement. The king, who at one point had managed to have the pope deposed from his office, was forced to submit to him at Canossa, a place whose name has become proverbial for abject surrender. In 1095 Pope Urban II (1088–1099) was strong enough to be able to launch the Crusades, in which the fighting men of Western Europe submitted to him and not to their own kings as commander-in-chief.

With power came wealth, and with wealth came the corruption of the monastic ideal. Men who had sworn to live in poverty found themselves living in luxury instead, and this anomaly soon provoked the wrath of those who believed that Christ preferred the simple life. One of the best-known advocates of this was Bernard of Clairvaux, who singlehandedly set out to recreate the original purity of monasticism. Forsaking the existing establishments, Bernard set up his own network of monasteries, giving them a new rule of life that was based on his own abbey at Cîteaux. The Cistercians, as Bernard's monks were

[17] On this subject, see John Ranelagh, *A Short History of Ireland*, 3rd ed. (Cambridge: Cambridge University Press, 2012), 50. Ranelagh writes from a Catholic and nationalist background, so cannot be accused of Protestant bias in his criticisms.

[18] For a popular account, see Edwin Mullins, *Cluny: In Search of God's Lost Empire* (Oxford: Signal, 2006).

[19] He was 'King of the Romans" until 1084, when he was crowned Holy Roman Emperor.

called, soon created their own monastic empire, but they were not alone. Other reforming movements rediscovered the rule of Augustine of Hippo and set up monasteries along those lines, and others followed suit—the Premonstratensians (so called from their mother house at Prémontré), the Carthusians (based at La Grande Chartreuse), and the Gilbertines, an English order named after its founder Gilbert of Sempringham (1083–1190), who lived to be 107. The Gilbertine order was unusual in that their establishments were open to both men and women.

This twelfth-century revival was soon followed by something even more radical—the establishment of the mendicant ("begging") orders, known to us as the "friars" from the Latin word for "brothers" (*fratres*). We have already met the founders of two of the most distinguished orders of friars—Francis of Assisi and Dominic of Caleruega (in Spain). In the thirteenth century the Franciscans (or Minorites) and the Dominicans (or Preachers) were followed by many others—the Servites, the Crutched friars, the Trinitarians (or Mathurins as they were known in France), the Carmelites, and the Austin (Augustinian) friars.[20] To them must be added the military orders formed during the Crusades, notably the Hospitallers or Knights of St. John and the Knights Templar. The first of these still exists as a paramedical order of laymen, but the second succumbed to a tragic fate. Jealous of its wealth, King Philip IV of France (1285–1314) concocted a charge of heresy against them, claiming that they engaged in occult practices imported from the Middle East, and succeeded in having the order suppressed in an orgy of violence and injustice.[21] Its chief monument today is the Temple Church in London, along with the inns of court known as the Inner and the Middle Temple, where many leading English barristers have their offices.

All this activity was a sign of a vibrant spiritual life that developed great internal variety and was capable of renewing itself as soon as the corrupting influence of power and status started to kick in. The Franciscans went through a process of internal reformation in the late fifteenth and early sixteenth century that in some places spilled over into early Protestantism. Elsewhere however, these Observant Franciscans acted as a brake on the Lutheran Reformation, because they had already dealt with many of the problems that the Protestants were complaining about.[22] Nevertheless, the links between monasticism and

[20] See Clifford H. Lawrence, *The Friars: The Impact of the Early Mendicant Movement on Western Society* (London: Longman, 1994).

[21] See Malcolm Barber, *The Trial of the Templars* (Cambridge: Cambridge University Press, 1978); Michael Haag, *The Templars: History and Myth* (London: Profile, 2008). On the order of St. John, see Jonathan Riley-Smith, *Hospitallers: The History of the Order of St. John* (London: Hambledon, 1999).

[22] See John H. Moorman, *A History of the Franciscan Order* (Oxford: Oxford University Press, 1968).

the mendicant orders on the one hand, and Protestantism on the other, were real and their importance has frequently been underestimated. Looking at the monastic world around the year 1500, what we see looks surprisingly like a collection of Protestant denominations, each with its own particular emphasis but all basically sharing the same spiritual goals and rivaling each other in the struggle to attract new members. We should not forget that Martin Luther became an Augustinian monk, a spiritual formation that was to remain with him for the rest of his life, and whose ideals he sought to purify and adapt for the use of the wider church. There is a sense in which Protestantism can be regarded as monasticism for the masses, and later renewal movements within it (like pietism, evangelicalism and even Pentecostalism) can sometimes look astonishingly like the religious orders that sprang up in the twelfth and thirteenth centuries.

What monasticism and the friars did was institutionalize the age-old difference between the committed believers and the more lukewarm or indifferent church members—the ones who read their Bibles every day and evangelized versus those who attended services once a month or only on the major festivals. In the early church they had been known as the *pneumatikoi* ("spirituals") and the *psychikoi* respectively, but as this distinction came to be expressed in terms of rules and orders, new terms for them were devised. In the Middle Ages, a "spiritual person" was someone who lived inside the institutional church, either as a parish priest or as a monk or nun. The law recognized that "spiritual persons" were not subject to ordinary civil jurisdiction. They had a right to be tried within the spiritual estate, by ecclesiastical courts established for that purpose. Even when a spiritual person committed a secular crime, he (or more rarely she) was entitled to special treatment in the civil courts, known in English law as "benefit of clergy."[23]

Spiritual persons were distinguished by their dress, by their celibate way of life, and by their social status. Not surprisingly, perhaps, they came to be seen collectively as the "church," which the rest of the population regarded as a breed apart. The Protestant Reformers would later do what they could to break down those barriers and change popular perceptions, but they persist in the popular mind to the present day. An ordained minister is still thought of as being different from everyone else, whether this is officially sanctioned or not. Without making any formal change to its doctrine, the clergy of the medieval church transformed the way they and their institution were perceived by those

[23] This had a long and tortuous history, and was not finally abolished until 1827. On this and other such privileges, see Richard H. Helmholz, *The Canon Law and Ecclesiastical Jurisdiction from 597 to the 1640s* (Oxford: Oxford University Press, 2004), 505–520.

whom they were meant to serve, and this is probably their deepest legacy to the generations that have followed.

The Crisis of Authority

It was the encounter with Islam that challenged the medieval church more than anything else. This came partly from the Crusades but even more from the Christian reconquest of Spain. Spain had been overrun by the Muslim Arabs in the decade after 711 but it had never been completely subdued. In the northern mountains there were small Christian enclaves that survived and gradually expanded as Arab power weakened and internecine strife tore Muslim Spain apart. Even in the occupied areas, the majority of the population remained Christian and Latin-speaking. By the early thirteenth century most of the peninsula had been liberated, but there was a large Muslim (and Jewish) population under Christian rule, and educated Christians were being deeply influenced by Arab thought. Much the same was also true in Sicily, where Arab, Greek, and Latin worlds met and mingled, especially in the time of the emperor Frederick II (1194–1250), who encouraged this and was anathematized by the church as a result.

Out of this cross-fertilization came a new appreciation among Christians for mathematics and the natural sciences, most of which were of ancient Greek origin but had been appropriated by the Muslim world and developed further. As Aristotle, Galen, and Ptolemy were translated into Latin, usually from Arabic rather than from the original Greek, and the works of Avicenna, Averroes, and the Jewish Maimonides also became known, Western Europe went through an intellectual crisis. Here was a secular learning whose importance could not be denied but that was clearly not the work of Christ, the fount of all true wisdom and knowledge. What should Christians do about this?

The church initially tried to suppress the new learning but with only partial and temporary success. A more positive approach toward it was taken by a number of Christian thinkers who worked toward a synthesis of revealed faith and rational science. This eventually matured into what we now call scholastic theology, whose greatest representative was Thomas Aquinas. What he and his colleagues said was that Christ works in two different ways. The first of these is in and through creation, where the activity of the divine *logos* has produced natural laws that can be observed and catalogued by rational human thought. The second is through revelation, which can come only from the Holy Spirit, and that gives us access to a knowledge that is superior to anything human beings can discover on their own. The first way is the way of nature, given to all the children of Adam; the second is the way of grace, given only to those who have been born again in Christ. The two ways meet and connect in the church, where the gift of God's grace gets to work on created nature and brings it to perfection. To scholastic theologians, the Greek and Arab philosophers were right as far as they went but they did not go far enough, because they could not get past the limitations imposed on them by their humanity. As a result, they had discovered particular truths but were unable to integrate them into a universal truth, which left their philosophy inadequate and to some degree incoherent. It took the supernatural revelation of God in Christ to tie these loose ends together and make sense of the whole.

Scholastic theologians thought that by distinguishing reason from revelation and by subordinating the former to the latter, they could meet the challenge of pagan and Islamic science without surrendering the supremacy of the Christian gospel. What they did not realize was that by accepting the validity of secular learning within its own sphere, they were acknowledging a source of authority that was common to all human beings and therefore not the special preserve of the church. Demarcating where the boundary between the secular and the sacred lay became a problem that inevitably undermined the claims of the church to exercise social hegemony. How could an institution derived from revealed truth interfere in the workings of nature, especially if what it asserted on the basis of revelation could be shown to be incompatible with what human minds had discovered by their own efforts? To put it a different way, could the pope make legitimate pronouncements about things that were outside his sphere of competence?

The challenge to the church's authority first appeared in the political arena, where secular rulers who had previously been put in their place by a succession of powerful popes began to assert themselves. They disputed the church's right to interfere in matters properly reserved to secular government by trying to restrict the pope's right to tax their subjects and by refusing to go on crusade at his bidding. Frederick II even formed alliances with Muslim rulers, which in the church's eyes was the ultimate apostasy.[24] Real trouble erupted when the French king claimed the right to tax the temporal possessions of the church and its clergy, on the ground that control over secular affairs was part of his remit. The church countered with the theory that it constituted a divine society of spiritual persons who were exempt from secular jurisdiction. In 1296 Pope Boniface VIII issued a decree known as *Clericis laicos* in which he tried to forbid any

[24] As Holy Roman emperor and king of Sicily, Frederick II (1194–1250) was the most powerful man in Europe at the time. He even went on crusade to the Holy Land and retook Jerusalem in 1229, largely by clever diplomacy, though it was lost again in 1244.

taxation of the clergy without his consent, but the attempt backfired and set in motion a series of events that would compromise the papacy's independence and weaken its authority irreparably.[25] In the course of diplomatic tug-of-war between the king and the papacy, Boniface summoned the French bishops to a synod in Rome where on November 18, 1302, he issued his famous bull *Unam sanctam*, in which he went as far as to claim that his authority

> . . . although it is given to a man and exercised by a man, is not a human but a divine power, given to Peter by the mouth of God and confirmed to him and to his successors in the same Christ who confessed that Peter was the rock, and who told him: "Whatever you bind on earth, etc."[26] Therefore, whoever resists this divinely-ordained power "resists what God has appointed,"[27] unless like Mani, he imagines that there are two principles [of authority], an opinion we judge to be false and heretical, because as Moses testifies, it was not in [two] principles but in one principle that God created the heavens and the earth.[28] We therefore declare, state and define that it is absolutely necessary for the salvation of any human creature that he should be subject to the Roman pope.[29]

What Boniface said was not particularly new—*Unam sanctam* was a collage of statements made at different times by a wide range of theologians and scholars going back as far as Cyprian of Carthage. Even the statement that it was necessary for anyone who wanted to be saved to be subject to the pope had a precedent of sorts in a claim made a generation earlier by Thomas Aquinas.[30] But however deep its roots in earlier tradition may have been, it was Boniface's decree that defined the church's official position on papal authority, a position that was reaffirmed on the conclusion of another dispute with France less than a year before the outbreak of the Protestant Reformation.[31]

Alas for Boniface VIII, it was one thing to assert papal claims to authority and quite another to implement them. The French king responded by trying to have Boniface arrested and tried for heresy, but although he failed in that attempt, it was not long before he would seize control of the papacy in a different way. Boniface died suddenly in 1303 and his successor, Benedict XI

---

[25] See Walter Ullmann, *A Short History of the Papacy in the Middle Ages* (London: Methuen, 1972), 273–278.
[26] Matt. 16:19.
[27] Rom. 13:2.
[28] Gen. 1:1. The bull plays on the double meaning of the Latin *principium*—"principle" and "beginning."
[29] Text in Denzinger, *Enchiridion*, no. 874–875.
[30] Thomas Aquinas, *Contra errores Graecorum*, 32. Aquinas, however, said that it was necessary to be subject to the Roman *church*, not specifically to the pope.
[31] At the eleventh session of the Fifth Lateran Council (December 19, 1516), when papal control over the appointment of French bishops was successfully reasserted. Text in *Conciliorum oecumenicorum decreta* (Bologna: Istituto per le Scienze Religiose, 1973), 640–645; see especially 643–644.

(1303–1304), lived for only a few months. In 1305 the cardinals were persuaded to elect the pro-French Clement V (1305–1314), who established his residence at Avignon in the south of France and was little more than a puppet of the French king, though he managed to avoid issuing a posthumous condemnation of Boniface VIII, which the king had wanted him to do. The move to Avignon turned out to be an enduring one, and seven popes would spend their reigns there before they finally returned to Rome in 1377. But that return, though dictated by the pope's position as bishop of Rome, was bitterly resented by the cardinals, who did all they could to reverse the decision. The result was a schism that lasted in one form or another until 1429, when there were two (and at one point even three) rival popes who disputed the papal office and forced the powers of Europe to take sides, destroying the unity of Christendom and making a mockery of *Unam sanctam*, though it continued to be asserted as the church's official teaching and remained so after the schism was finally healed.

The departure of the papacy to Avignon raised serious theological questions about the nature of the institution. One of its most important analysts and critics was Marsilius of Padua (1275?–1342?),[32] whose great work *Defensor pacis* (*Defender of the Peace*) became the classic statement of opposition to the papal claims. Marsilius became the prophet of a new world order in which secular rulers would find a legitimate place and the hegemony of the popes would be effectively broken. He began with a number of citations from the church fathers, the Old and (especially) the New Testaments, to the effect that peace ought to be the normal and most desired condition of mankind. He quoted various texts from the Gospels and the epistles of Paul and James to point out what Christians should do to support the Holy Roman Emperor in bringing peace to God's people, which he defined as, "that good condition of a city or realm, in which each of its parts is enabled perfectly to perform the operations appropriate to it according to reason and the way it has been established."[33]

Marsilius believed that as civilization developed, government and a system of justice were instituted in order to provide the regulation needed to ensure the right balance among competing social forces. A military order was created in order to protect the nascent society from enemies that would destroy

---

[32] On Marsilius, see his *Defensor pacis*, translated under that title by Alan Gewirth (Toronto: University of Toronto Press, 1980), and as *The defender of the peace*, translated and annotated by Annabel Brett (Cambridge: Cambridge University Press, 2005). See also Marsiglio of Padua, Defensor minor *and* De translatione imperii, ed. Cary J. Nederman (Cambridge: Cambridge University Press, 1993); George Garnett, *Marsilius of Padua and "the Truth of History"* (Oxford: Oxford University Press, 2006); Hwa-Yong Lee, *Political Representation in the Later Middle Ages: Marsilius in Context* (New York: Peter Lang, 2008); Cary J. Nederman, *Community and Consent: The Secular Political Theory of Marsiglio of Padua's* Defensor pacis (Lanham, MD: Rowman & Littlefield, 1995); Gerson M. Riaño, ed., *The World of Marsilius of Padua* (Turnhout: Brepols, 2006).

[33] Marsilius of Padua, *Defensor* 1.2.3.

it, and financiers came into being in order to budget resources so that they would be properly husbanded and not squandered. The priesthood was more controversial. It was a good thing to worship God, but whether a special class of people was needed for this was not clear. Yet Marsilius recognized that all societies had created a religious establishment, whether its leaders believed in the official religion or not, "in order thereby to induce in men a reverence and fear of God and a desire to avoid the vices and cultivate the virtues."[34] In this respect, the Christian world was superior to others because its priests had a true understanding of God and would not lead people into error.

In chapter 6 Marsilius went back to Adam, who was created in the image of God and without sin. Had he remained in that state, civil government would not have been necessary, nor would there have been any religion as we know it. But as a result of the fall, God took pity on his creatures and sent them guides to give them rites and ceremonies by which they might appease his wrath and find their way back to him. Finally he sent his Son Jesus Christ to preach the gospel, which, if it was observed, would earn for its followers the grace of eternal happiness. Christians are promised blessedness in the next life and strength through the sacraments and the teachings that go with them to live a meritorious life here on earth. It is for that purpose that a Christian priesthood has been instituted, so that we may learn how to obtain eternal salvation. After a lengthy discourse about the character required of secular rulers and how they should be chosen, Marsilius came to the subject that had driven him to write in the first place. This was the need to explain how the civil order originally established by God had recently broken down in a peculiar and particularly intractable way.

He started with the teaching of Christ, who had given his disciples the power to teach the gospel, to celebrate the sacraments, and to forgive sins in his name. But he went on to say, in addition to this, that another kind of priestly power had developed over time. This had originally been granted to the ministers of the church by human authority in order to avoid scandal. It permitted the setting up of one priest over others, whose duty it was to ensure that worship was conducted in the right way and that the funds needed to keep the priestly order viable were obtained legitimately.

Among the disciples to whom Jesus gave his original commission, Peter stood out above the rest. On the basis of that preeminence, Peter's successors in Rome claimed superiority, not just over all other bishops and priests, but over secular rulers as well. They insisted that the emperor Constantine had granted them the right to exercise jurisdiction over all the kings and lords of this earth.[35]

[34] Ibid., 1.5.11.
[35] See Rev. 19:16.

In this way, the bishops of Rome had progressively usurped the powers of secular rulers, who had their own legitimate function in the state. The result was disorder and the loss of the peace that ought to prevail among Christians. Marsilius argued that this was the cause of the current distress, and the pope's usurped authority had to be repelled if peace were to be restored to the world.

Marsilius argued that the papacy had established its rule without the consent of the people and that a simple reading of the New Testament would quickly show how unjustified it was. If the popes were interested in following Christ, they would refuse all temporal authority and jurisdiction, just as Christ did:

> Christ came into the world not to dominate men, nor to judge them [in secular courts], nor to wield temporal rule, but to be subject as regards his status in this life, and moreover that he wanted to (and did) exclude himself, his apostles and disciples, and their successors the bishops and priests, from all such coercive authority or worldly rule, both by his example and by his words of counsel or command.[36]

Marsilius granted that priests had the right to exercise spiritual authority within their appointed sphere, and that they should decide who ought to be excommunicated for heresy. But whether heretics and unbelievers, such as Jews, should be allowed to dwell in a Christian state was for the secular ruler to decide, and it was not his business to enforce the church's laws. Marsilius even claimed that saints should not be canonized without secular consent, and that priests should be allowed to marry as they had done in the early church, unless a good reason for not permitting clerical marriage could be adduced.[37]

Marsilius then went on to explain why Christ instituted poverty as the rule for his servants on earth. They were to be detached from worldly interests and concerns so as to be free to preach the gospel to everyone. A priesthood that had seized power in the world had lost its spiritual authority, not enhanced it, by so doing.[38] Marsilius further insisted that no priest was inherently superior or inferior to any other. The apostles had all been equal to each other, and so were the bishops of later times.[39] Ordination to the priesthood conferred an authority that could be exercised anywhere, subject to mutual agreement and convenience, and priests should be chosen by the people assembled together for that purpose. In particular, secular rulers should have the right to refuse to

[36] Marsilius of Padua, *Defensor* 2.4.3.
[37] Ibid., 2.8.9.
[38] Ibid., 2.11.1–2.14.24.
[39] Ibid., 2.15.1–2.16.19.

accept ecclesiastical promotions and to submit their decisions to the judgment of the people.

Next, Marsilius explained how the papacy had come to make its particular claims, and went on to advocate the supremacy of Holy Scripture over every other law. The interpretation of disputed parts of Scripture ought to be determined by general councils of the church and not by any individual, and the power to convene such councils belonged to the secular ruler. Furthermore, no bishop could excommunicate a priest or exercise any temporal jurisdiction, except insofar as it might have been delegated to him by the state.[40]

Despite his strictures against the papacy, Marsilius was not blind to the advantages of having a central church organization that recognized one bishop as superior to the rest. This primacy could not claim any scriptural authority, nor was there any objective reason why it should belong to the Roman bishop, but custom and tradition had focused on Rome, and changing that would probably be impossible.[41] The primacy should be one of honor and dignity, not one of superior authority that would allow the pope to become a tyrant. Finally, Marsilius explained why the claims that Scripture gave coercive jurisdiction to bishops, and that the papacy had inherited the rights and privileges of the ancient Roman emperors were misinterpretations of the biblical texts.[42] In conclusion, and in direct opposition to *Unam sanctam*, Marsilius stated that,

> . . . in order to gain eternal beatitude, it is necessary to believe only in the truth of divine or canonical Scripture, what follows from it with any kind of necessity, and the interpretation of it that has been made by a common council of the faithful, if this is put to an individual in due fashion.[43]

Marsilius wrapped up his arguments by telling his readers that constant vigilance was the price of freedom and so they must keep a watchful eye on those who exercise power in their name. He ended by declaring his loyalty to the Catholic church and submitted his opinions to the judgment of a general council, which he hoped would be convened in due course. No such council was called in his lifetime, but three generations after his death, the Council of Constance (1414–1417) went a long way toward establishing a conciliar form of government for the Western church along Marsilian lines, and its failure was one of the events that paved the way for the Protestant Reformation.

It is particularly interesting to note how Marsilius appealed to the witness

---

40 Ibid., 2.18.1–2.21.15.

41 Ibid., 2.22.1–2.29.12. It must be remembered that the papacy was in exile at Avignon and not in Rome, making this statement a covert attack on the institution and not an indication of support for it.

42 Ibid., 2.30.1–8.

43 Ibid., 3.2.1.

of Scripture in making his arguments against the claims of the papacy. He not only knew that things had been very different in the early church from what they were in his own time, but believed that it was both possible and necessary for the Christian world to return to the earlier situation if its problems were to have any chance of being resolved. That point of view was taken up in the next generation by John Wyclif (1328–1384), who used Ockhamist thinking to dissect the claims of the Roman church.[44] Wyclif maintained that Scripture was the only true revelation from God. Canon law and its traditions were human inventions and could not be treated as if they were on the same level. It therefore followed that whatever was not to be found in the Bible was not to be imposed on the church as Christian doctrine.[45]

Wyclif's insistence on the unique authority of Scripture can be traced back to the fathers of the church without any difficulty, and in that sense his teaching was neither new nor revolutionary. But the generation that saw the rise of scholastic theology also witnessed a new development in the way that the Bible was read and studied. Until well after the year 1000 it had been customary for the Scriptures to be interpreted in an allegorical, even mystical way. There was little sense of their historicity and almost no awareness that many things in them had been written for people who had lived in very different circumstances. Confronted by texts that they found either incomprehensible or inapplicable, interpreters easily resorted to allegorical meanings. Allegorical interpretation was preserved, transmitted, and developed in the monasteries, where it continued to flourish well into the fourteenth century and later, but after about 1100 it no longer had a monopoly. Literal exegesis and textual criticism were revived in the search for greater accuracy, with the result that interpretations that had become traditional were shown to be mistaken.

One of the leaders of this movement was Andrew of St. Victor (1110?–1175), an Englishman who belonged to the Parisian monastery that was at the forefront of the twelfth-century revival of learning. Andrew specialized in interpreting the Old Testament, which he read with an astonishing independence of mind. The only earlier commentator that he had access to was Jerome, with whom he was not afraid to disagree when he felt that the great father of the church had been mistaken. A good example of that can be found in his interpretation of Jeremiah 1:5: "Before I formed you in the womb I knew you, and before you were born I consecrated you; I appointed you a prophet to

[44] The literature on Wyclif is immense. Among recent studies, see Stephen E. Lahey, *John Wyclif* (Oxford: Oxford University Press, 2009); Gillian R. Evans, *John Wyclif: Myth and Reality* (Oxford: Lion, 2005); Michael Wilks, *Wyclif: Political Ideas and Practice* (Oxford: Oxbow, 2000).

[45] John Wyclif, *On the Truth of Holy Scripture*, trans., introduction and notes by Ian C. Levy (Kalamazoo, MI: Medieval Institute, 2001).

the nations." Jerome interpreted the first part of the verse as a reference to the foreknowledge of God, but read the second as parallel to the case of John the Baptist, who was supposedly sanctified in his mother's womb so that he could prophesy through her when the pregnant Virgin Mary came to visit her before John was born.[46] Jerome also linked the verse to the apostle Paul, who told the Galatians that God had set him apart before he was born and called him to be a preacher of the gospel.[47]

Andrew dismissed Jerome's reference to Paul as irrelevant. Paul may have been "set apart" in the womb but he was still self-evidently a sinner who had persecuted the church and who had to be converted to Christ like anyone else. John the Baptist offered a closer parallel to Jeremiah, but in Andrew's time it was commonly believed that both men had been cleansed of original sin in the womb, an interpretation that Andrew rejected because there was no evidence to support it. Instead of that, Andrew proposed a literal reading:

> While the prophet was still a child, God instituted him as a prophet, to prophesy to barbarian nations and to be given to the people. Therefore God provided him with faith and assurance. . . . When Jeremiah excused himself for his lack of eloquence, he did so solely on the ground that he was a child.[48]

This preference for the literal meaning over any others became increasingly common and was reinforced by the contact that many of these scholars had with Jewish rabbis, whom they sought out for their knowledge of Hebrew and for explanations of obscure details in the Old Testament.[49] Wyclif was heir to this tradition and must be understood in light of it. Even though he was not a biblical scholar in the mold of Andrew of St. Victor, Wyclif had a clear understanding of the importance of Scripture:

> Scripture is the foundation of every Catholic opinion, and within it resides the very salvation of the faithful. Moreover, it is the exemplar and mirror designed to examine and extinguish every sort of error or heretical evil. Surely even a small error in this principle could bring about the death of the church.[50]

Wyclif accepted that his view was not universally shared and dealt with some of the major objections to it. The first of these was the contention that

---

[46] Luke 1:41–45.
[47] Gal. 1:15–16.
[48] Andrew of St. Victor, *Commentarium in Prophetas*, Cambridge MS Pembroke 45, fo. 76c–77b. See B. Smalley, *The Study of the Bible in the Middle Ages*, 3rd ed. (Oxford: Blackwell, 1983), 112–195 and 385–387 for the text quoted above.
[49] See Smalley, *Study of the Bible*, 329–355. Also, Gilbert Dahan, *Les intellectuels chrétiens et les Juifs au moyen âge* (Paris: Cerf, 1999).
[50] Wyclif, *On the Truth of Holy Scripture*, 1.1–2.

the Bible uses obscure metaphorical language, which Augustine warned his readers not to imitate. Wyclif agreed with this, but went on to say that the Bible's forms of speech are appropriate to their subject matter and should be interpreted accordingly. He even said that the writings of the Greek philosophers ought to be corrected by Scripture and not the other way around.[51] As he explained it, the Bible uses earthly things to describe heavenly realities. For example, Christ is compared to a lion, not because he is an animal but because many of the attributes of lions are similar to ones found in him. He added that although the Bible often uses figurative language drawn from nature, this should not be taken to mean that it makes statements about natural science.[52] Wyclif also stated that particular passages of Scripture ought to be read in the light of the whole, so as to avoid taking things out of context, and he gave examples of how misunderstanding them could lead to heresy.[53]

Wyclif went on to defend the authority of the Scriptures over against those who would attack them and claim that they lead people into error. According to Wyclif, the interpreter must first learn to understand the inner logic of Scripture and read it in that light. God speaks in many different ways but his self-revelation is never contradictory; those who think that it is have misunderstood it and failed to interpret it properly. Wyclif expounded the authority of the Old Testament as the law of God given to his people and fulfilled by Jesus. He was quite clear that God was the ultimate author of the text, even though he had used human scribes to write it down. As Wyclif put it,

> It is pointless to quarrel over who was the scribe, or the composer of the manuscript, or the reed-pen of the Lord whom God infused with such knowledge. For it is sufficient to believe that God spoke the given knowledge through some of his saints in particular and through individuals generally.[54]

Thanks to Jerome's preference for the Hebrew text, Wyclif was well aware of the problem posed by the so-called "apocryphal" books of the Old Testament. He dealt with them by saying that everyone should agree on the canonicity of the Hebrew Bible and accept that Jerome's translation is an exact rendering of its meaning. That there were corruptions in the manuscripts available to him Wyclif did not deny, but he attributed them to the laziness and incompetence of the church's copyists and not to any inconsistencies in the texts themselves.[55]

Next, Wyclif dealt with the objection that there are many things in Scrip-

[51] Ibid., 1.2.
[52] Ibid., 1.5.
[53] Ibid., 1.7–8.
[54] Ibid., 1.10.
[55] Ibid., 1.11.

ture that are paralleled in secular writings. He did not deny this, but said that the presence of such material in the Bible lent a sacred authority to the mundane affairs of the world. He also knew that there were many Gospels besides the four that we now recognize, but he trusted the decision of the early church as to which of them we should receive as canonical. He admitted that many of the apocryphal books might be divinely inspired because they have life-giving properties, but he saw no need to make them canonical since there was enough uncontested material to go on. He then turned to an examination of false readings, the source of which he located in human pride:

> It appears that our own theologians walk into the lecture hall one day dressed as sheep with the purpose of commending the law of Scripture, and all of a sudden acquire the teeth of foxes, adding to this the tail of a viper. They say that Holy Scripture is for the most part impossible and even blasphemous when read according to the literal, verbal, and fleshly sense.[56]

Wyclif did not feel bound to the literal sense to the exclusion of all other meanings, but he did not agree with the allegorizers that it was unprofitable, because to his mind, God would not have inspired a text that would lead people astray. Wyclif went on to defend the primacy of truth in interpretation. The fathers of the early church rightly refused to accept theological terms that had no scriptural support unless and until it could be shown that their meaning was clear from the text. Wyclif used this patristic custom to complain that his contemporaries invented all kinds of technical vocabulary that had no biblical basis and that could not be shown to agree with the meaning of the text. Because of that, adherence to the truth meant that they must be rejected.[57]

For Wyclif, Scripture was a pastoral tool that must be used with great care and discernment for the discipline and upbuilding of the people of God. To those who accused him of trying to subvert the church by appealing over its head to Scripture, Wyclif replied,

> In publicly proclaiming the love and veneration I have for my Mother, the Roman Church, I am seeking to protect her privileges and her insignia, and taking care to see that they are thus secured.[58]

In other words, the church had nothing to fear from the proclamation of the truth. Scripture was greater than any human authority because it came straight from God:

---

[56] Ibid., 1.12.
[57] Ibid., 1.13.
[58] Ibid., 1.14.

> Since the entirety of Holy Scripture is the word of the Lord, no testimony could possibly be better, more certain, or more efficacious. For if God, who cannot lie, has spoken something in his own Scripture, which is itself a mirror of his will, then it is true.[59]

Wyclif went on to apply this to every part of the Bible, which he said was equally and fully authoritative in everything it says. But although it is all equally true, some truths are more fundamental than others, and we must recognize this in our teaching and application of the text. He also criticized those who said that the writings of the church fathers or the letters of the pope can be accorded an authority equal to that of the Bible. In Wyclif's view, Christians must make sure that what they say is in accordance with the sacred text before they claim authority for it.

As he warmed to his theme, Wyclif became both more pastoral and more political. He appealed to the law of Christ, the teaching of the gospel, as the basis for the Christian church and told his readers that they should love it in the same way as they loved the one who had given it. The law of Moses was mixed with human traditions and became a burden to the people that Jesus had to lift. Later on, Muhammad weakened the Christian world by introducing a system of law that is contrary to the gospel, and the same thing had been done since then by the leaders of the church. If people did not recognize this and take steps to cleanse the church of these accretions, it would collapse under their weight just as ancient Israel had done, and lose the message that Christ came to bring.[60]

In a statement that would be of great importance for the future, Wyclif explained that the church's first duty must be to foster the preaching of God's Word, because if it was not preached it would not be heard, and if it was not heard it would not be obeyed. Every Christian had a duty to do this and to seek to win others for Christ, but the responsibility fell most heavily on the priesthood because it was appointed for that purpose. Even the sacraments could not be understood without the preaching of the Word, which they confirm and illustrate, and the abuses in the church were often due to the neglect of this essential task.[61]

In Wyclif's eyes, not the least of the Bible's functions was that it laid down rules for pastors, telling them how they ought to live and setting out what to teach and how. It was the duty of the good pastor to preach the whole counsel

[59] Ibid., 1.15.
[60] Ibid., 1.20.
[61] Ibid., 1.21.

of God, including the threat of eternal damnation for those who refuse to hear what he has to say. Some people objected to this because they did not see why every priest should have to become a theologian, but to this Wyclif replied,

> Every Christian must be a theologian, as I have demonstrated elsewhere. For it is essential that every Christian learn the faith of the church, either through infused knowledge, or along with this, knowledge acquired from human teachers. Otherwise, he would not be a person of faith, and faith is the highest theology of all.[62]

Of course, if every Christian were a theologian, then laymen could pass judgment on the clergy, who are not above the law in temporal matters. They could even seize church property if necessary, not least because Christ commanded his followers to be poor and to forsake the riches of this world. On the other hand, they also had a duty to protect the church, as Scripture also indicated.[63]

Wyclif divided the Mosaic law into ceremonial and moral elements, of which the first had been abolished in Christ but the second remained as valid as ever. Christ was the fulfillment of the law, and whatever it says must be interpreted in the light of that.[64]

Finally, Wyclif had a simple definition of heresy—whatever went against the teaching of Holy Scripture was false, and if it was being taught by the church, it was heretical.[65] Although he did not explicitly say so, the subversive character of this assertion is clear. Wyclif was accused of heresy, not because what he said was unscriptural, but because it went against the teachings of the institutional church. In response to that, Wyclif claimed that because those teachings could not be found in Scripture, it was they and those who propagated them who were heretical, not he.

The second aspect of the church's teaching that Wyclif attacked concerned the sacraments. In his view, transubstantiation of bread and wine into the body and blood of Christ was impossible because it violated the laws of creation.[66] The idea that a substance could change while leaving its accidents untouched made no sense to him because, if this were true, it would be impossible to know anything at all. How could someone who was unaware that a piece of bread had been consecrated possibly know that it had become the body of Christ if its accidents remained unchanged? As he put it, if transubstantiation were true,

---

62 Ibid., 1.24.
63 Ibid., 1.26–27.
64 Ibid., 1.31.
65 Ibid., 1.32.
66 For a full discussion, see Lahey, *John Wyclif*, 102–134.

> . . . everyone would be perplexed and unable to discern what material things are—and all of this error derives from the story of the sacrament of the altar. . . . There are thousands of such problems vexing the church, all of them stemming from or based on the most impossible fantasy and cause of heresy that has been introduced by the sacrament of the Eucharist.[67]

The only conclusion to be drawn was that transubstantiation was a false doctrine and that the scriptural authority claimed for it was bogus. Instead of adding to nature, the grace of God used nature just as the Son of God used a human body in order to die for the sins of the world. To think otherwise was to fall into the error of monophysitism, though neither Wyclif nor his opponents called it that. Nevertheless, he made a clear distinction between the material and the spiritual world that liberated the former to be itself and restricted the latter to the sphere of revelation.

For a variety of reasons, Wyclif's attacks on the church of his day were more telling than those that had gone before. He had the support of powerful figures in the English government, who protected him against the ecclesiastical hierarchy when he was being roundly denounced both at home and in Rome. He made a direct appeal to the common people and was heard by them at a time when the ravages of the black death and rising taxation had caused great discontent among the peasantry. He advocated translating the Bible into English, and although he probably did not take part in the work himself, his name became attached to two different translations and he acquired a considerable following among the rising middle classes.[68] Above all, his Latin writings circulated widely and attracted the attention of Jan Hus (1371?–1415) in Bohemia, who was inspired by them to launch a reform program of his own.[69] Like Wyclif, Hus challenged what he saw as the corruptions and aberrations of church teaching and pleaded for a return to the simplicity of an earlier age. He was not particularly interested in Eucharistic questions, but in the climate of the time he found it impossible to escape them.

For reasons that are not entirely clear, the church had withdrawn the cup from the laity and gave them only the bread, which was an obvious violation

---

[67] John Wyclif, *De Eucharistia* 8, ll. 242–243.

[68] His followers were called Lollards, from an old word meaning "murmur," and they survived until the sixteenth century, when they were absorbed by the Protestant Reformation. The extent of their appeal can be gauged by the fact that more than two hundred Lollard Bibles survive in manuscript, an extraordinarily high number. See Richard Rex, *The Lollards* (Basingstoke: Palgrave, 2002).

[69] There is an extensive literature on Hus in Czech and German, though much of it concentrates on social and political questions rather than on theology. For the latter, see Thomas Krzenck, *Johannes Hus: Theologe, Kirchenreformer, Martyrer* (Gleichen: Muster-Schmidt Verlag, 2011); Thomas A. Fudge, *Jan Hus: Religious Reform and Social Revolution in Bohemia* (London: I. B. Tauris, 2010). For an interesting view from the Eastern church and the Hussite attempts to establish communion with Constantinople, see Antônês Protopapas, *To kinêma tôn Chousitôn kai hê Kônstantinoupolê. Koines rizes* (Nicosia: Kentro Meletôn Ieras Monês Kykkou, 1999).

of both scriptural teaching and patristic tradition. Thomas Aquinas discussed this at some length, pointing out that Pope Gelasius I (492–496) had decreed that Communion must be given in both kinds (*sub utraque specie*) because one without the other made the sacrament imperfect, and therefore heretical. He added that because the Eucharist was offered as a memorial of Christ's death, and that his shed blood expressed this more clearly than his broken body, it would be easier to omit the bread than withdraw the cup![70] But Aquinas then went on to argue the opposite case by claiming that a distinction had to be drawn between the consecration of the sacrament and its reception. The priest who consecrated it was obliged to receive it in both kinds, as Gelasius had decreed, but lay recipients were not, the reason being that many of them were likely to spill the cup and some were too young (or too old!) to drink it properly. As long as the priest took the cup, the Gelasian decree would be honored, because he could do it on behalf of the people. In any case, said Aquinas, Christ was fully present in both kinds, so those who received only one were not missing anything!

This rather convoluted argument failed to persuade many people in Bohemia, where there was a Eucharistic revival going on in the late fourteenth century. Preachers were encouraging frequent Communion and apparently succeeding in their attempts to persuade people to participate in the sacrament, which they were increasingly offering to them in both kinds, believing that it was the practice of the early church and that there were no valid reasons for not doing so. Hus tended to agree with them, but it was only when he was summoned to the Council of Constance (Konstanz) in 1415 to defend himself that his views on the subject crystallized. Hus was promised a safe conduct to the council by the emperor, but when he got there the safe conduct was overruled by the church and he was burned at the stake for heresy.[71] This scandal made it clear that Rome would brook no opposition and would treat the civil authorities with contempt if they dared to flout its wishes. The council condemned both him and John Wyclif, and even ordered that Wyclif's remains should be exhumed and scattered, which they duly were.[72]

In the short interval between his condemnation and his execution, Hus wrote a letter to two Czech lords who had supported him (Václav of Dubá and Jan of Chlum), in which he said,

[70] Thomas Aquinas, *Summa theologiae* III.80.12. Gelasius's decree was included in Gratian's *Decretum* as *De cons.*, 2.12.

[71] See Walter Brandmüller, *Das Konzil von Konstanz, 1414–1418*, 2 vols. (Paderborn: Ferdinand Schöningh, 1991–1997).

[72] *Conciliorum oecumenicorum decreta*, 411–431. The decree of exhumation is on 415.

> What great madness it is to condemn as error the Gospel of Christ and the Epistle of Paul, which he said he received not from men, but from Christ. . . . They call it an error that faithful lay people should be allowed to drink of the cup of the Lord, and if a priest should give it to them to drink, that he should then be regarded as being in error and condemned as a heretic if he does not stop. O, Saint Paul! You say to all believers, "as often as you eat this bread and drink the cup, you proclaim the Lord's death until he comes,"[73] that is, until the day of judgment.[74]

The Utraquist controversy, so called from the Latin word *utraque* ("each" or "both"), strikes modern readers as arcane and unnecessary, but when the church was seen as the body of Christ and kingdom of heaven on earth, everything said about that body took on a special importance. The Eucharist was not only the central act of Christian worship, it was also the main way in which the church communicated its message and extended its power among the people.

The reality was that the reaction of the church to the challenge posed by Wyclif, Hus, and their followers was more political than theological, however much it tried to prove the opposite. The primary objective of the Council of Constance was to end the great schism and restore the papacy to its former prestige so that Europe would once more be united and at peace. By electing Martin V (1417–1431) as pope and deposing the other pretenders, it made considerable progress in that direction, and when Martin V died he had only one successor, Eugenius IV (1431–1447), who was universally recognized and who was able to complete Martin V's program of reform. The Council of Constance also decreed that further councils would be summoned every five years as a way of checking papal power, but Martin V did his best to subvert this. He summoned a council to meet at Pavia in 1423, but did not attend it and soon had it transferred to Siena, where it was dissolved after only six months. Martin V then promised to hold another council at Basel in 1431, though he did his best to abort it. Unfortunately for him, he died shortly before the council was due to meet and so it went ahead under Eugenius IV, who (like his predecessor) did not attend and who also dissolved it within a few months.

This time, however, the council refused to disperse and demanded that its authority should be recognized. The emperor, who had been humiliated in the Hus affair, sided with it, and the pope was obliged to give in. The council then

---

[73] 1 Cor. 11:26.

[74] Frantisek Palacký, *Documenta Magistri Iohannis Hus* (Osnabrück: Biblio-Verlag, 1869), letter no. 80. See also the article by Hieromonk Patapios, "*Sub utraque specie*. The Arguments of Jan Hus and Jakoubek of Stříbro in Defense of Giving Communion to the Laity under Both Kinds," *Journal of Theological Studies*, n.s. 53 (2002): 503–522.

proceeded to adopt a radical program of reform, which the pope had little choice but to accept. He was rescued, if that is the word, by a renewed plan for reunion with the Eastern churches. The Second Council of Lyon had attempted that in 1274 but failed, and Eugenius IV was determined to try again. This time, the Easterners were desperate for Western aid against the Turks, who had nearly captured Constantinople and were overrunning the Balkans. They were prepared to travel to the West to conduct the negotiations, but wanted to meet in Italy for geographical reasons. Eugenius IV used this as an excuse to transfer the council to Ferrara and then to Florence, but a rump remained in Basel and suspended Eugenius IV (January 24, 1438) before finally deposing him (June 25, 1439). By then, however, the Easterners were ready to sign the agreements for reunion, and they would recognize only Eugenius IV, a decision that greatly enhanced his authority. The most lasting effect of the Council of Basel was to encourage the French king to proclaim what is known as the Pragmatic Sanction of Bourges (July 7, 1438), a decree that established the financial independence of the French Church from Rome. That remained in force until 1516, when (on the eve of the Protestant Reformation) the French bishops were brought back under the control of the papacy, with the acquiescence of the newly crowned King François I (1515–1547).

The fifteenth-century popes fought tenaciously to restore their authority over the church and were remarkably successful, despite some important setbacks. The reunion with the Eastern churches was never accepted by the latter, and after the fall of Constantinople to the Turks in 1453 it was a dead letter.[75] But the Council of Florence was to have an unintended but more long-lasting impact on the Western church. One of the Greek delegates at it was George Gemistos Plethon (1360?–1452), probably the most learned man of his day and a devotee of Plato.[76] Plethon was not interested in theology, but when he was in Florence he gave a series of lectures comparing Plato and Aristotle, which he later wrote up as a book. Legend, based on two funeral orations in his honor, has it that the entire nobility of Florence turned out to hear him and that he sparked off what soon became a mania for all things Greek. But even if the truth is more modest, there can be no doubt that Plethon's activities pointed to something new. For the first time in Western history, there was an active interest in going back to the sources of civilization and culture. The underlying belief, which was anything but new, was that the earlier the source, the more authentic it would be. People had always known that the Latin Bible was a translation, but now there was a real desire to get back to the original texts and a growing

[75] See Joseph Gill, *The Council of Florence* (Cambridge: Cambridge University Press, 1959).
[76] See Christopher M. Woodhouse, *Gemistos Plethon: The Last of the Hellenes* (Oxford: Clarendon, 1986).

belief that they would turn out to be both different from and superior to what the church was accustomed to using. That conviction led to the acceptance of a new kind of authority, based not on the tradition of the church but on the original divine revelation, mediated to the contemporary public by scholars who had access to it and who could interpret it correctly.

Equally important, Lorenzo Valla (1407–1457), who was one of the new generation of so-called "humanists" who were the forerunners of what became known as the Renaissance, managed to prove that the *Donation of Constantine* by which the first Christian emperor had supposedly granted secular jurisdiction to the papacy, was a ninth-century forgery.[77] In other words, the legal basis on which the popes rested their claims to be able to tax the people of Western Europe for the support of the church were groundless. With France opting out and Bohemia in turmoil over Utraquism, the political triumph of the papacy was therefore more fragile than it looked. Its future would depend on its moral and spiritual prestige, but it was precisely here that trouble was on the horizon.

Martin V and Eugenius IV were disciplinarians who did what they could to check the power of the cardinals and restore civil order to Rome. But as time went on and the Renaissance gained in strength, the semi-independent city-states of Italy started competing with one another to see which of them could outshine the others in wealth and culture. Florence, Venice, and Genoa could rely on trade and finance, but Rome could raise money only in and through the church. As it did so, corruption ran riot, and before long not just indulgences but church offices and even the papacy itself were on offer to the highest bidder. Those who gained promotion in this way had no sense of a spiritual calling, and when Alexander VI (1492–1503) allowed his son, Cesare Borgia, to take over the government of Rome, the pope's credibility was lost completely. Rome survived the Borgias, but things did not improve much. Pope Julius II (1503–1513) felt obliged to call another council, which met in the Lateran Palace at Rome from 1512 until 1517, but its reform efforts were halfhearted and ineffectual.[78] Six months after it closed, Martin Luther posted Ninety-five Theses for debate among his colleagues at the university of Wittenberg, and the church would never be the same again.

The Heavenly Kingdom

The Protestant Reformation began as a protest against abuses in the church and was fortified by an appeal to new sources of learning and authority, of

[77] Lorenzo Valla, *La donation de Constantin*, trans. J.-B. Girard (Paris: Les Belles Lettres, 1993). The original work appeared in 1442.

[78] The decrees of the Fifth Lateran Council are in *Conciliorum oecumenicorum decreta*, 595–655.

which the recovery of the authentic text of Scripture was by far the most important. But the passions that the Reformation aroused and the opposition that it encountered can be properly understood only when we realize that the Reformers struck at the root of the system on which the church they knew was built. As the body of Christ on earth, the church did the work of Christ and mediated it to the people through his vicar, the pope. The theory was that the church derived its authority from Christ, who had given it to Peter, from whom it had descended through his successors to the current bishop of Rome. Those in communion with the papacy had the assurance that they were connected to God because Peter was the rock on which Christ built his church, and the gates of hell could not prevail against it.[79] However dubious this claim might be in biblical or historical terms, it provided a theological rationale for the governance of a Christian society and strong psychological reinforcement to those who feared that their sins would cut them off from the grace of God. Challenging such a system was bound to be difficult and would easily provoke hostility on the part of those who felt that their lifeline to heaven was being severed. It was not enough for the Reformers to point out the church's weaknesses, which were widely acknowledged; it had to be replaced by something better and more credible, at least to those who were willing to risk breaking with the established order of things.

The key to understanding how the Reformers tackled the question of the church and its authority can be found in Martin Luther's Ninety-five Theses, which are generally regarded as the spark that lit the fire of the Reformation. Consider the following:

> Thesis 5. The pope neither desires nor is able to remit any penalties except those imposed by his own authority or that of the canons.
>
> Thesis 6. The pope cannot remit any guilt, except by declaring and showing that it has been remitted by God, or (to be sure) by remitting guilt in cases reserved to his judgment.[80]

Luther couched his language in terms that showed deference to the pope himself and blamed the pope's surrogates for the excesses of which he was complaining, but he must have known that the latter would not have been able to operate freely without the pope's connivance or (as in this case) his explicit direction and approval. Authority that proceeded from the top down could not have functioned in any other way. Opposition to it therefore had to follow the

[79] Matt. 16:18.

[80] Pelikan and Lehmann, *Luther's Works*, 31:26.

approach that Luther took, which was to define what the limits of the pope's authority actually were. Just as God had given Adam dominion over the lower creatures but had reserved control of the higher ones for himself, so the pope could exercise his jurisdiction only over those who were placed under him—the living members of the church militant here on earth. Those who died left his jurisdiction, and he had no power over them.

Luther was soon embroiled in theological controversy over the Ninety-five Theses, but as late as 1520 he could still address the pope in irenic and even deferential terms, reassuring him "that I have never thought ill of you personally, that I am the kind of person who would wish you all good things eternally, and that I have no quarrel with any man concerning his morals . . ."[81] That, however, was merely the preface to a devastating attack on the Roman church:

> As you well know, there has been flowing from Rome these many years—like a flood covering the world—nothing but a devastation of men's bodies and souls and possessions, the worst examples of the worst of all things. All this is clearer than day to all, and the Roman church, once the holiest of all, has become the most licentious den of thieves,[82] the most shameless of all brothels, the kingdom of sin, death, and hell. It is so bad that even Antichrist himself, if he should come, could think of nothing to add to its wickedness.[83]

How a pope could emerge out of such a situation and be fully aware of it, yet remain personally innocent and blameless, Luther did not explain, and there was no need to. Leo X (1513–1521) was as guilty as anyone and indeed more so, since he was in charge of the whole operation. Luther did not quite say that the Pope was the Antichrist, but the appearance of the latter in his argument would not have gone unnoticed by a generation that knew that sectarians had long been identifying the two. After telling the pope why he had given up on the Roman curia and consigned it to hell, Luther added that he "turned to the quiet and peaceful study of the Holy Scriptures" so that he might be of some practical use to those around him.[84] This change of course was hardly an accident. As he said in the treatise *On Christian Liberty*, which he attached to his open letter to the pope,

> Christ was not sent into the world for any ministry other than that of the Word [of God]. Moreover, the entire spiritual estate—all the apostles, bish-

[81] Martin Luther, *Open Letter to Pope Leo X*, dated September 6, 1520, in Pelikan and Lehmann, *Luther's Works*, 31:335.
[82] See Matt. 21:13.
[83] Luther, *Open Letter*, in Pelikan and Lehmann, *Luther's Works*, 31:336.
[84] Ibid., 31:338.

> ops, and priests—has been called and instituted *only* for the ministry of the Word. You may ask: "What then is the Word of God, and how shall it be used, since there are so many words of God?" I answer: The apostle [Paul] explains this in Romans 1. The Word is the Gospel of God concerning his Son. . . . To preach Christ is to feed the soul, make it righteous, set it free, and save it, provided that it believes the teaching.[85]

In other words, the institutional church existed for the ministry of the Word and not the other way around. Just as it was not within the pope's remit to determine what happened to souls after death, so it was beyond his competence to sit in judgment on the Scriptures. On the contrary, they sat in judgment on him and his colleagues, and (as Luther hardly needed to add at this point) the standards set by the Word of God found them sadly wanting.

In succeeding years, as controversy deepened and became more bitter, Luther would develop his ideas further. The prospect of a general council of the church that would attempt to resolve disputed questions and reunite Western Christendom gave him the opportunity to collect his thoughts in what we know as the Smalcald (Schmalkald) Articles of 1537, which he intended to serve as his position paper at that council.[86] By then, Luther had abandoned any pretense of deference toward the papacy, which he now condemned in no uncertain terms:

> Everything the pope has undertaken and done on the basis of false, offensive, blasphemous, arrogant power has been and still is a purely diabolical affair and business, which corrupts the entire holy Christian church. . . . As it has often been said, it [the papacy] is a human fiction. It is not commanded. There is no need for it. And it is useless. The holy Christian church can survive quite well without such a head. It would have been much better if such a head had not been raised up by the Devil. The papacy is not necessary in the church because it exercises no Christian office, and the church must continue and exist without the pope.[87]

A little later on Luther went on to call the pope the Antichrist, because he would "not let Christians be saved without his authority."[88] Of course, Luther was under no illusion that such a bold position would get him anywhere at the forthcoming council. He said so himself:

---

[85] Martin Luther, *On Christian Liberty*, in Pelikan and Lehmann, *Luther's Works*, 31:346.
[86] Martin Luther, *The Schmalkald Articles*, trans. William R. Russell (Minneapolis: Fortress, 1995). In the event the council was deferred until 1545, and the Smalcald Articles were never used for their intended purpose, though they give us a clear idea of what Luther was thinking at the time they were written.
[87] Luther, *Schmalkald Articles*, 2.4.3, 5–6.
[88] Ibid., 2.4.10.

> They [i.e., the papists] neither can nor will allow us the smallest portion of these articles. Of that we may be certain. We can only depend on the hope that Christ our Lord has attacked his enemies and will carry the day, both by his Spirit and at his return. Amen. At the council we will not stand before the emperor or the secular authority, as at Augsburg. . . . We will stand before the pope and the Devil himself, who does not intend to listen, but only to damn, murder, and drive us to idolatry.[89]

Luther knew what was coming to him, and that the envisaged council would be a failure because the pope could not possibly have accepted Luther's assessment of him. Today, in our more ecumenical age, we tend to regret statements like the above, which seem to us to be almost as exaggerated as they must have appeared to the pope's supporters back then, but this natural reluctance to embrace the venom of another age should not blind us to the importance of the underlying issue, which was the nature of the church and the exercise of authority within it. On this subject, Luther said,

> We do not agree with them [the papists] that they are the church, and they are not. We do not want to hear what they command or forbid in the name of the church, because, God be praised, a seven-year-old child knows what the church is: holy believers and little "sheep who hear the voice of their shepherd."[90] This is why children pray in this way: "I believe in one holy Christian church."[91] This holiness does not exist in surplices, shaved heads, long albs, and the other ceremonies they have devised over and above the Holy Scriptures. Its holiness exists in the Word of God and true faith.[92]

Through all the polemic of the intervening years, the foundation of the Word of God and true faith remained the same as it had been two decades before. Luther never developed his understanding of the church beyond this, and as a result many important questions remained unresolved during his lifetime. It was all very well to say that the church consisted of those who had faith in the Word of God, but an institutional structure existed, and some rationale for it had to be found. How did Christ rule his church if not through appointed vicars like the pope? And just as importantly, how could ordinary believers gain access to Christ if it was not clear who had the authority to provide it?

Another problem that the Protestants could not avoid was the question of church-state relations. In sixteenth-century Europe it was impossible for the

[89] Ibid., 2.4.15–16.
[90] John 10:3.
[91] The formula is taken from the Apostles' Creed, with the word "catholic" altered to "Christian."
[92] Luther, *Schmalkald Articles*, 3.12.1–3.

church to exist independently of the state because it was generally assumed that the former was the spiritual expression of the latter. All secular rulers were church members, and they represented the voice of the laity, such as it was. The Reformation broke down the traditional church hierarchy and gave the laity a greater voice in church affairs, but in practice this meant allowing secular rulers a much bigger say than they would otherwise have had in how the church should be organized and governed. Luther depended for support on local rulers in Germany who could protect him against the Holy Roman emperor, who remained Catholic, and although he was a big enough man to be able to resist their pressure, his followers were in a less favorable position.

The need to do something about church-state relations became acutely apparent in 1534, when the Church of England broke with Rome under pressure from King Henry VIII. The English church was unique in that its two ecclesiastical provinces (Canterbury and York) had working synods, known as "convocations," which voted to cut ties with the papacy. That vote was later ratified by the English parliament, which passed an act making the king head of the church.[93] This was a novelty. Never before had a secular ruler been granted such a title, and it raised serious questions about the nature of church government. The king could not simply replace the pope, because the latter had a spiritual jurisdiction that no non-ordained person could usurp. The king might appoint the bishops, but he could not consecrate them, nor could he ordain clergymen lower down the scale. Whether (or to what extent) he could interfere with the church's doctrine or worship was also more than a little doubtful.

What happened in England was soon replicated across northern Germany and in Scandinavia, as one state after another accepted Protestantism. For the most part, responsibility for social welfare passed to the secular authorities, who also assumed control of church appointments, at least at the higher level. Theologians retained greater control over doctrine and worship, but even there, their decisions had to be ratified by the secular authorities before they could be implemented. Luther was not entirely happy with this situation, but political pressures from the states that remained loyal to Rome and their increasingly active attempts to reverse the Reformation, coupled with radical popular movements that sought to overthrow the state altogether, forced him to compromise. After his death war broke out in Germany, the Protestant league of princes was defeated, and a new settlement was imposed by the Catholic emperor. This was the so-called *Interim* of 1548, which made some concessions to

[93] See Gerald L. Bray, ed., *Documents of the English Reformation*, 2nd ed. (Cambridge: James Clarke, 2004), 109–114.

Protestant feeling (such as allowing the marriage of priests) but basically tried to re-Catholicize the church as much as possible.

The *Interim* was opposed by most of the Protestants and received only very lukewarmly by the Catholics, with the result that its implementation was compromised from the start. After further dissension and conflict, peace was finally made at Augsburg in 1555 on the principle that the religion of any given territory would be determined by the decision of its secular ruler (*cuius regio eius religio*). This worked for a while, but it could not be a long-term solution to the problem of church government. For one thing, no one at the time thought of what would happen if the ruler changed his allegiance. That had already occurred in England, where Queen Mary I (1553–1558) had done her best to reverse the Reformation and lead the country back to Rome. Somewhat surprisingly, perhaps, parliament had acquiesced in this, but made her promise that no attempt would be made to recover the land and other goods that had been confiscated from the church after 1534. As things turned out, Mary's religious policy was a failure and (if anything) Protestantism was more firmly entrenched as a result of her persecutions than it had been before, but her example remained to warn the church of what could happen if the ruler did not support it. As late as 1688 the Catholic king James II (VII of Scotland) was driven from his throne because of a fear that he would return the country to Rome, even though he had promised not to do so, and to this day the monarch must be a member of the national church in order to avoid any possible recurrence of that scenario.

The course of events in other European countries differed in the details but the broad picture was much the same. Protestantism was often successful in parts of France that were remote from Paris or semi-independent—it even became the official religion of the tiny kingdom of Navarre in the southwest. But when Henri de Navarre became the king of France by dynastic accident (in 1589), he could not take over the government until he converted to Catholicism. He did that in 1593, but granted a measure of toleration to the Protestants in the famous Edict of Nantes (1598). However, this went against the broader tendency of the French kings toward centralization of their power, and in 1685 the Edict was revoked. The Protestants then had to choose between conversion, death, and emigration, and a surprisingly high number left the country rather than abjure their faith.[94]

In the Holy Roman Empire the peace of Augsburg lasted for a generation but eventually started to fray, and in 1618 war broke out again. It lasted for

[94] The best account is Patrick Cabanel, *L'histoire des Protestants en France, XVIe—XXIe siècle* (Paris: Fayard, 2012).

thirty years and devastated most of central Europe, but the peace of Westphalia, which ended it in 1648, brought a stability that was to last for the next two centuries. Protestant and Catholic territories would no longer change religion at the whim of their rulers, and two parts of the empire that did not fit in with the general pattern were detached from it. The first of these was the Swiss Confederation, which went its own way as a league of Protestant and Catholic city-states, and the other was the United Provinces of the Netherlands, commonly known as the Dutch Republic, which was a Protestant federation with substantial minorities who were granted a degree of freedom unknown elsewhere at that time.[95]

Switzerland and the Netherlands were special cases, partly because they were both leagues of small cities and territories that had a republican form of government but mostly because the form of Protestantism that they preferred was not Lutheran but "Calvinist," or as it is more correctly called, "Reformed." John Calvin did not like the way in which German Protestants had so easily surrendered the autonomy of the church to the state and realized that the only way to prevent that was to devise a system of church government that could maintain itself independently. Working in the city-state of Geneva, he could develop a pattern modeled on its government. Geneva was ruled by a council of elected members who were drawn from the leading families, who imposed strict criteria for citizenship and voting rights.[96] Calvin replicated this in the church by establishing high standards for full membership and then allowing the members to elect their representatives. The resulting synod would then ordain ministers to the different offices of preaching, teaching, and social service.

This synodical structure was ideally suited to small territories and became popular not only in Switzerland, but also in many parts of Germany and in the Netherlands.[97] In France it enabled the Protestants to survive as a coherent minority in a hostile state, and the same was true in Hungary, Poland, and elsewhere. The only kingdom that adopted it was Scotland, but that was possible because the country was small and its monarchy was exceptionally weak. Many Lutherans, including Philipp Melanchthon, were attracted by this model and some of them became Reformed, especially in the south and west of Germany, along the Rhine corridor that linked Switzerland to the Netherlands.[98]

[95] The classic study of this is Jonathan Israel, *The Dutch Republic: Its Rise, Greatness, and Fall, 1477–1806* (Oxford: Oxford University Press, 1995).

[96] Calvin himself was not admitted to citizenship until 1559, only five years before his death!

[97] For the history, see Philip Benedict, *Christ's Churches Purely Reformed: A Social History of Calvinism* (New Haven, CT: Yale University Press, 2002).

[98] For the relationship of Melanchthon to Reformed (Calvinist) thought, see Karin Maag, ed., *Melanchthon in Europe: His Work and Influence beyond Wittenberg* (Grand Rapids, MI: Baker, 1999); John Schofield, *Philip Melanchthon and the English Reformation* (Aldershot: Ashgate, 2006); Timothy J. Wengert and M. Patrick Graham,

However, not all Lutherans were won over, and those who opposed Reformed theology regrouped as "authentic," or as they said, "Gnesio-Lutherans," eventually adopting a *Formula of Concord* (1577) that remains the basis of classical Lutheranism to this day.[99] Unfortunately the Gnesio-Lutherans and the Reformed fought each other almost as much as (and sometimes more than) they fought the Roman Catholics, and bad blood between them persisted for centuries. The Reformed were not recognized in the peace of Augsburg in 1555, but that omission was put right in 1648 and the two Protestant confessions lived in uneasy coexistence after that.[100]

Excluded from all this and marginalized in post-Reformation Europe were the radicals, who are usually grouped together as "Anabaptists" because of their belief that membership in the church was granted only to those who could make a personal profession of faith and be baptized as adults. Since the first generation had all been baptized as infants, they believed that they had to be rebaptized, hence the term "Anabaptist."[101] The radicals were never a single group united around one leader, but as time went on many of them recognized the authority of Menno Simons (1496–1561), a former monk who established communities along quasi-monastic lines. Often called Mennonites, most of them left their European homelands and went to places like Russia, where they were allowed to live in peace. Later they emigrated in considerable numbers to Pennsylvania and elsewhere in the Americas, where conservative Mennonite subgroups, such as the Amish and Hutterites, still flourish. Other Mennonites have become more mainstream, but they still retain a strong sense of local community and even of ethnic identity, which is ironic given that they reject any idea of an inherited Christianity.

How far the different kinds of Protestantism could be said to have established themselves for theological reasons is controversial. They all justified their positions by appealing to the Bible of course, but despite their claims to the contrary, it must be conceded that in most cases they adopted a particular ecclesiology for political reasons and then sought a spiritual justification for what they had already done. The only major exception to this occurred in

---

eds., *Philip Melanchthon (1497–1560) and the Commentary* (Sheffield: Sheffield Academic, 1997). For contemporary criticism of Melanchthon, which was widespread, see B. Kobler, *Die Entstehung des negativen Melanchthones* (Tübingen: Mohr Siebeck, 2013).

[99] *The Book of Concord: The Confessions of the Evangelical Lutheran Church*, ed. Robert Kolb and Timothy J. Wengert (Minneapolis: Fortress, 2000). For the background, see Friedrich Bente, *Historical Introductions to the Book of Concord* (St. Louis, MO: Concordia, 1965).

[100] In 1817 the king of Prussia forcibly united them in his dominions, provoking a backlash among conservative Lutherans that led many of them to emigrate to South Australia, where their influence is still felt, and to the United States, where they constituted themselves as the Missouri Synod. See Christopher Clark, *Iron Kingdom: The Rise and Downfall of Prussia, 1600–1947* (London: Penguin, 2006), 412–424.

[101] "Ana" is the Greek prefix that corresponds to the Latin "re," as in *anastasis* ("resurrection").

England, where a unique chain of events produced a church that did not fit any of the patterns established elsewhere. After Mary I's death in 1558, the throne passed to her half-sister Elizabeth I (1558–1603). In the eyes of the Catholic church, Elizabeth was illegitimate because her mother (Anne Boleyn) had not been canonically married to her father (Henry VIII), a fact which made it impossible for her to continue Mary's religious policy, even if she had wanted to. Elizabeth preferred to go back to the kind of church left by her father and her half brother (Edward VI) but she also wanted to keep as many traditional Catholics and convinced Protestants on board as she could.

The result was a balancing act that could be called Reformed theology in Catholic dress, and for the most part it was successful. The pope did not excommunicate her until 1570, though when he did, the door to Rome was finally closed and Englishmen of Catholic sympathies had to choose their allegiance. Most of them opted to remain within the established church, with only a small minority choosing resistance and exile. The Protestants, many of whom had been radicalized under Mary I, not least by their contacts with continental Reformed people who had welcomed them as exiles, believed that there was no longer any need to compromise with Catholicism and began a campaign for further reform of the church. The great manifesto on which this campaign was based was Thomas Wilcox's *Admonition to the Parliament* of 1572, in which he outlined what was needed to put things right in the spheres of doctrine, worship, and church discipline.[102] Wilcox admitted that the church had adopted the right doctrine, but complained that its ministers were not properly equipped to preach it and that its official liturgy contained traditional Catholic elements that were not fully aligned with it. His proposed solution was a better-trained ministry, a revised form of public worship, and the appointment of elders (whom he called "seniors") in every parish who could aid the minister in the implementation of church discipline.

Wilcox and his supporters were quickly dubbed "Puritans" and the name stuck. Elizabeth I made it clear that she would not tolerate any alteration of the settlement she had agreed to at the beginning of her reign, and so although Reformed theology progressed unhindered, the corresponding modifications to church practice and discipline were laid aside. The queen did not worry about this but her theologians did, because they realized that they had to justify this policy by demonstrating (if they could) that what the Puritans were complaining about were secondary matters or "things indifferent" (*adiaphora*) that could rightly be ignored for the sake of unity in the gospel. This was the

[102] The text is in Iain H. Murray, ed., *The Reformation of the Church: A Collection of Reformed and Puritan Documents on Church Issues* (Edinburgh: Banner of Truth, 1965), 85–98.

position adopted by Richard Hooker (1556?–1600), whose *Laws of Ecclesiastical Polity* was conceived as an answer to the *Admonition*, and whose position later came to be regarded as typical of "Anglicanism."[103]

The accession of James VI of Scotland to the English throne (as James I) in 1603 encouraged the Puritans to think that he would introduce the Reformed discipline of his native land into England, but they were to be disappointed. James wanted to unite the two churches, but on the basis of a modified form of the traditional episcopal system, which he evidently thought would be more amenable to the wider project of the reunion of Christendom, to which he was also committed.[104] Theologically, his professed Calvinism kept the Puritans more or less quiet in the hope of better days to come, but as time went on that hope began to fade, particularly as supporters of the state church were active in defending it by extending the principle of *adiaphora* to include even the office of bishop.[105]

Matters came to a head under Charles I (1625–1649), who not only forbade any public debate about theology, but shut down the parliament and ruled on his own for eleven years. During that time he tried to take the church back to what he saw as the purity of the Elizabethan settlement, but which to the Puritans was little short of a return to Rome. Their chance came in 1640 when the king, facing a revolt in Scotland and the likelihood of one in Ireland, had to recall parliament and ask for a subsidy to wage war. Parliament, which was full of Puritan sympathizers, rejected theses demands and effectively took over the government, forcing the king to flee and initiating a civil war that raged through the 1640s. It was in these circumstances that the Puritan parliament summoned an assembly of divines (i.e., theologians) to meet at Westminster in order to hammer out the theological basis for the reconstruction of the churches of England, Scotland, and Ireland, which they intended to unite on that basis. As a result, it was the Westminster Assembly, rather than any other Protestant body, that found itself having to work out an ecclesiology that could claim to be grounded in Scripture and that could stand a reasonable chance of being applicable in practice.

[103] The best text is now *The Folger Library Edition of the Works of Richard Hooker*, ed. W. Speed Hill, 7 vols. (vols. 1–5, Cambridge, MA: Harvard University Press, 1977–1990; vol. 6, Binghamton, NY: Medieval and Renaissance Texts and Studies, 1993; vol. 7, Tempe, AZ: Medieval and Renaissance Texts and Studies, 1998). Secondary studies are numerous. See Nigel Atkinson, *Richard Hooker and the Authority of Scripture, Tradition, and Reason* (Carlisle: Paternoster, 1997); Philip B. Secor, *Richard Hooker: Prophet of Anglicanism* (London: Burns & Oates, 1999); Nigel Voak, *Richard Hooker and Reformed Theology: A Study of Reason, Will, and Grace* (Oxford: Oxford University Press, 2003). On Hooker's subsequent reputation, see Michael Brydon, *The Evolving Reputation of Richard Hooker: An Examination of Responses, 1600–1714* (Oxford: Oxford University Press, 2006).

[104] See William B. Patterson, *King James VI and I and the Reunion of Christendom* (Cambridge: Cambridge University Press, 1997).

[105] See William Ames, *Concerning a National Church*, in Murray, ed., *Reformation of the Church*, 99–102. Ames was a Puritan replying to these apologists and rejecting their (to him) extravagant and unbiblical claims.

In assessing the Westminster Confession's doctrine of the church it is natural to turn to chapter 25, which is specifically dedicated to the subject, and there we find a balanced compendium of Reformed teaching. First, the Confession states that the catholic church is invisible, because it is the company of the elect of every age and place, but it also has a visible aspect that cannot be overlooked. Following the lines laid down by Luther, Calvin, and the other magisterial (or mainline) reformers, the Confession states,

> The visible church, which is also catholic or universal under the gospel . . . is the kingdom of the Lord Jesus Christ, the house and family of God, out of which there is no ordinary possibility of salvation. Unto this catholic, visible church Christ hath given the ministry, oracles, and ordinances of God, for the gathering and perfecting of the saints in this life, to the end of the world; and doth by his own presence and Spirit, according to his promise, make them effectual . . .[106]

The Confession then goes on, as we might expect, to say that the visibility of the church has fluctuated over time and that particular churches that belong to it are relatively, but never absolutely, pure. Some have even degenerated to the point where they are "no churches of Christ but synagogues of Satan,"[107] a covert reference to Rome, no doubt, but possibly also to the episcopally ordered Church of England, which was their more immediate target.[108] The chapter concludes with a ringing affirmation that "there is no other head of the church but the Lord Jesus Christ" and adds for good measure that the pope is Antichrist, because he has set himself up as a false substitute for the real one.[109]

On the surface this all seems clear enough, but further reflection will show that there are hidden assumptions here that must be taken into account. Article 19 of the Thirty-nine Articles of the Church of England, of which this chapter was meant to be a revision, stated that the visible church "is a congregation of faithful men in which the pure Word of God is preached and the sacraments duly ministered," repeating a formula that was characteristic of Luther and that recurs with great regularity in Puritan writings, but this classic phrase was *omitted* from the Confession![110] Given its almost sacrosanct status, the fact that it was not repeated can only mean that the framers of the Westminster

---

106 Westminster Confession, 25.2–3; see Bray, *Documents of the English Reformation*, 507, for the complete text.
107 Rev. 2:9; 3:9.
108 Westminster Confession, 25.5; Bray, *Documents of the English Reformation*, 507. Extreme as this may sound, it is really only a development and restatement of Article 19 of the Thirty-nine Articles of the Church of England, which actually specifies the erroneous churches it has in mind—Jerusalem, Alexandria, and (of course) Rome.
109 Westminster Confession, 25.6; Bray, *Documents of the English Reformation*, 507.
110 See the *Admonition* of Thomas Wilcox and the response of William Ames, cited above, for examples of the use of this phrase.

Confession were not happy with it as a definition of the true church. Why was that? They would obviously have been in favor of preaching the Word in purity and administering the sacraments in the right way, and these matters are covered elsewhere in the Confession itself. But they are not used to define the church, either in its pure (invisible) or in its visible form. That is expressed quite differently:

> The catholic or universal church which is invisible, consists of the whole number of the elect that have been, are, or shall be gathered into one, under Christ the head thereof; and is the spouse, the body, the fullness of him that filleth all in all.[111]

In other words, the church is not defined in terms of what it does but of what it is—the body of Christ composed of the elect of every age, past, present, and future. To understand that, we have to retrace our steps and go back to an earlier chapter in the Confession, which deals explicitly with the mediatorial role of Christ. There we read,

> It pleased God in his eternal purpose to choose and ordain the Lord Jesus, his only begotten Son, to be the mediator between God and man, the Prophet, Priest, and King, the head and Savior of his church, the heir of all things and judge of the world, unto whom he did from all eternity give a people to be his seed, and to be by him in time redeemed, called, justified, sanctified, and glorified.[112]

This eternal dimension is reinforced later on in the same chapter, which states,

> Although the work of redemption was not actually wrought by Christ till after his incarnation, yet the virtue, efficacy, and benefits thereof were communicated unto the elect, in all ages successively from the beginning of the world, in and by those promises, types, and sacrifices wherein he was revealed, and signified to be the seed of the woman which should bruise the serpent's head, and the lamb slain from the beginning of the world, being yesterday and today the same, and for ever.[113]

What this means is that the earthly work of Christ must be seen as the temporal manifestation of a heavenly principle that is eternally valid. The elect have been saved by his sacrifice, whether they lived before it was made, at the time, or since. None of them have been disadvantaged simply because they had

[111] Westminster Confession, 25.1; Bray, *Documents of the English Reformation*, 506.
[112] Westminster Confession, 8.1; Bray, *Documents of the English Reformation*, 494.
[113] Westminster Confession, 8.6; Bray, *Documents of the English Reformation*, 494–495.

no knowledge of the historical crucifixion and resurrection; the Old Testament saints are enjoying eternal life in heaven just as much as those who lived subsequently are, and so are those who are as yet unborn on earth. The incarnation of the Son was necessary in order to make it possible for believers not only to be redeemed but also to be united to him by virtue of a shared human nature. The elect have been ransomed both by a decree from on high and by specific divine actions in this world—our sins became Christ's wounds and our condemnation became his death, so that by his resurrection from the dead we might also be delivered from destruction and welcomed into the eternal life of heaven.[114]

It is clear that what is at issue here is the relationship between earth and heaven, which in terms of the work of Christ takes us straight to the doctrine of the ascension. That event is clearly recorded in the New Testament—it is the last thing that happens in the Gospels and the first in the Acts of the Apostles, providing the conceptual bridge between the earthly ministry and the heavenly reign of Christ.[115] For centuries the ascension was scarcely examined as an event in its own right, but to the extent that it was, it was seen primarily as the taking up of Christ's earthly sacrifice into heaven, where he now pleads for us as our Mediator before the Father's throne. Our participation in that was assured by the re-presentation of his body and blood in the Eucharist, the central act of Christian worship and the ultimate guarantee that the body of Christ is still present among us in the church. This did not mean that there was no awareness in the early church of the existence of believers before the incarnation of the Son who benefited from his sacrifice, even though it had not yet been made.[116] Augustine wrote,

> All who were righteous from the beginning of time have Christ as their head. They believed that he would come, just as we believe that he has already come, and they were made whole by faith in him just as we are.[117]

But like others of his time and later, Augustine believed that when Christ ascended into heaven he left the church behind to take his place on earth, a belief that then justified regarding its sacraments as manifestations of his real presence among us now.[118] Martin Luther shared that belief, which is why he

---

[114] Westminster Confession, 8.4; See Bray, *Documents of the English Reformation*, 494.

[115] Luke 24:51; Acts 1:9.

[116] This theme has been studied by Johannes Beumer, "Die altchristliche Idee einer präexistierenden Kirche und ihre theologische Anwendung," in *Wissenschaft und Weisheit* IX (1942), 13–22; Gérard Philips, "La grâce des justes de l'Ancien testament," in *Ephemerides Theologicae Lovanienses* XXIII (1947), 521–556; Yves Congar, "Ecclesia ab Abel," in *Abhandlungen über Kirche und Theologie. Festschrift für Karl Adam* (Düsseldorf: Patmos Verlag, 1952), 79–108.

[117] Augustine of Hippo, *Enarratio in Psalmos* XXXVI, 3.4. On Augustine, see William H. Marrevee, *The Ascension of Christ in the Works of St. Augustine* (Ottawa: University of Ottawa Press, 1967).

[118] See, for example, Augustine of Hippo, *Enarratio in Psalmos* XVIII, 2.6; *Sermo* CCLXV, 12.

was so insistent on what he called the "ubiquity" of Christ's ascended body. Luther did not accept the medieval doctrine of transubstantiation, but he did believe that Christ's sacrifice was spiritually present in the Eucharist because Christ himself was spiritually present, and where he was, his body was also. It apparently did not occur to Luther that such a belief undermined the integrity of Christ's human nature, which the Council of Chalcedon had declared was not confused with his divinity. John Calvin and others therefore rejected this notion of "ubiquity," which they regarded as impossible, but in any case they did not need it, because their conception of what happened in the ascension and subsequently was different. As Calvin explained it,

> Being raised to heaven, Christ withdrew his bodily presence from our sight, not that he might cease to be with his followers who are still pilgrims on the earth, but that he might rule both heaven and earth more immediately by his power; or rather, the promise which he made to be with us even to the end of the world, he fulfilled by this ascension, by which, as his body has been raised above all heavens, so his power and efficacy have been propagated and diffused beyond all the bounds of heaven and earth.[119]

In taking his body up to heaven, the Son of God abandoned the limitations of the created order without losing the integrity of his human body and without coming back to earth in the form of transubstantiated bread and wine. The purpose of his ascension was not to return periodically in this way but to raise us up to heaven, where, as Paul said, we are "seated . . . with him in the heavenly places."[120] He has opened the gate that Adam had shut by his disobedience, so that,

> . . . transferring his virtue to us, he may quicken us to spiritual life, sanctify us by his Spirit, and adorn his church with various graces, by his protection preserving it safe from all harm, and by the strength of his hand curbing the enemies that rage against his cross and our salvation; in sum, possessing all power in heaven and on earth until he has utterly routed his foes and ours, and completed the structure of his church.[121]

This is a vision of Christ's sovereignty and active rule that goes far beyond any sacrament, touching the whole of creation and assuring the believer that nothing in heaven or earth can separate him from the love of God.[122]

[119] Calvin, *Institutio* 2.16.14. For a modern study of this, see Douglas Farrow, *Ascension and* ecclesia*: On the Significance of the Doctrine of the Ascension for Ecclesiology and Christian Cosmology* (Edinburgh: T & T Clark, 1999).
[120] Eph. 2:6.
[121] Calvin, *Institutio* 2.16.16.
[122] Rom. 8:38–39.

The New Covenant

Calvin's cosmic vision of the ascended Christ entailed a new understanding of the church as the company of the elect of every age, and that was reflected in the Westminster Confession. But it also paved the way for a new interpretation of Scripture, which we now call "covenant theology." It may come as a surprise to discover that covenant theology was unknown before the sixteenth century, for although the building blocks were certainly there and frequently referred to, the overarching structure was not yet in place.[123] Covenant theology was fully expounded in the Westminster Confession, of course, and what the confession says is now regarded as the best and most complete short statement of it. But where did it come from? Luther knew nothing of it, though he was familiar with the covenant concept and made frequent use of it, especially in his interpretation of Genesis and the law of Moses. According to him, there were two covenants, one made in the flesh and another made in the spirit. In his words,

> The first is the covenant of circumcision, to which Israel also is admitted, yes, the slaves too, whether born in the house of Abraham or purchased. It is for this reason that circumcision was retained also by Ishmael's descendants, who populated almost the entire east and the three parts of Arabia. . . . They all rejoiced in the name of their father Abraham. The second covenant is here established with Isaac. Ishmael is clearly excluded from it. Hence this text proves that besides the covenant of circumcision there is another, which pertains to Isaac alone and not, like the covenant of circumcision, to Ishmael also. What then shall we say was the nature of this covenant? It is obviously the promise concerning Christ, which Abraham understood well.[124]

Luther's supposition that there were two different types of covenant was typical of the distinction he made between law and grace, but for that very reason, it cannot be regarded as the source of later covenant theology. The origins of that more likely go back to Huldrych Zwingli (1484–1531) in Zurich, who used the covenant argument in his controversy with the Anabaptists.[125] It seems that Zwingli had already adopted a covenant perspective before his brush with

---

[123] For a survey of the evidence from a viewpoint sympathetic to the view that covenant theology was a logical development of Calvin's approach, see Peter Lillback, *The Binding of God: Calvin's Role in the Development of Covenant Theology* (Grand Rapids, MI: Baker, 2001).

[124] Martin Luther, *Commentary on Genesis*, 17, in Pelikan and Lehmann, *Luther's Works*, 3:162. Luther clearly believed, as did most people in his time, that the (Muslim) Arabs were the descendants of Ishmael.

[125] This was the thesis of Emanuel Graf von Korff, *Die Anfänge der Föderaltheologie und ihre erste Ausgestaltung in Zürich und Holland* (Bonn: Emil Eisele, 1908), which was later developed and confirmed by Gottlob Schrenk, *Gottesreich und Bund im älteren Protestantismus, vornehmlich bei Johannes Cocceius* (Gütersloh: C. Bertelsmann, 1923). See also Ulrich Gäbler, *Huldrych Zwingli: His Life and Work* (Edinburgh: T & T Clark, 1986), 125–131. Originally published as *Huldrych Zwingli: Leben und Werk* (Munich: C. M. Beck, 1983); and W. Peter Stephens, *Zwingli: An Introduction to His Thought* (Oxford: Oxford University Press, 1992), 85–93.

Anabaptism, but only then did it become a significant element in his theology.[126] Zwingli defended the practice of infant baptism on the ground that there was a covenant of grace between God and man that began with Adam and has continued to the present time, having been renewed in Noah, Abraham, and Jesus. In both the Old and the New Testament there is only one people of God, who are joined together by a common faith in Christ.[127]

Zwingli was not unaware of the differences between the Testaments, but he regarded them as minor when set against the fundamental principle that God and his people were united in the covenant.[128] To his mind, children of New Testament believers were as much a part of the covenant of grace as the children of Old Testament ones were, and baptism was the equivalent of circumcision, given to the recipients long before they were capable of making a personal profession of faith.[129] At the same time, Zwingli also believed that the covenant was a two-way street. It was a gift of grace that did not depend on any human response, but those who received it were expected to live according to its tenets or risk losing their salvation.[130]

Zwingli's early death meant that he never developed his ideas any further than that, but his successor at Zurich, Heinrich Bullinger, picked up where he left off and took matters further.[131] Bullinger argued that in making a covenant with man, God was following human convention in order to make his intentions clear. In developing his understanding of salvation history, Bullinger stayed very close to what Zwingli had said about the one covenant that had been renewed at different times in Israel's history, and he stressed that at each stage the people were reminded of their need to remain faithful to it. Far from distinguishing between two covenants (one physical and the other spiritual) as Luther did, Bullinger provides the first evidence in Protestant theology of the idea that the one covenant stretched back beyond Abraham to Adam:

> The covenant that God made with Abraham was not the first—that was the one he made with Adam. In the covenants that followed, he said: "I will erect"

[126] See Jack W. Cottrell, *Covenant and Baptism in the Theology of Huldreich Zwingli* (unpublished ThD dissertation, Princeton Theological Seminary, 1971), 81, 173, 243, 339.

[127] Huldrych Zwingli, *In catabaptistarum strophas elenchus*, in *Huldreich Zwinglis Sämtliche Werke*, *Corpus Reformatorum* (Zurich: Verlag Berichthaus, 1961), XCIII/1:156–157; 164–166.

[128] Zwingli, *In catabaptistarum strophas*, 169–170. See Lillback, *Binding of God*, 81–109.

[129] Huldrych Zwingli, *Antwort über Balthasar Hubmaiers Taufbuchlein*, in *Zwinglis Werke*, *Corpus Reformatorum* (Leipzig: M. Heinsius Nachfolger, 1927), XCI:617, 629.

[130] Zwingli, *Antwort*, 630.

[131] See J. Wayne Baker, *Heinrich Bullinger and the Covenant: The Other Reformed Tradition* (Athens, OH: Ohio University Press, 1980), 15–18. See also Charles S. McCoy and J. Wayne Baker, *Fountainhead of Federalism: Heinrich Bullinger and the Covenantal Tradition* (Louisville: Westminster/John Knox, 1991); Bruce Gordon and Emidio Campi, *Architect of Reformation: An Introduction to Heinrich Bullinger, 1504–1575* (Grand Rapids, MI: Baker, 2004); Emidio Campi and Peter Opitz, *Heinrich Bullinger: Life, Thought, Influence* (Zurich: Theologischer Verlag, 2007).

> or "I will confirm," or "I will establish my covenant with you," which is to say, "I will always keep firmly the beginning of the covenant [with Adam]." It is often renewed with definite reasons, as with Noah after the flood, with Abraham, and later on with Moses. But it is one and the same covenant that is confirmed and established in each of these cases.[132]

Like Zwingli, but perhaps even more forcefully, Bullinger also insisted that faithfulness and obedience were not unaided human works but were made possible only by the gift and grace of God.[133] He pointed out that the Lord's Supper can be regarded as a covenant in itself, as Jesus had said.[134] It replaced the Passover meal and the Jewish sacrifices, just as baptism replaced circumcision.[135] In his words,

> The Scripture witnesseth that the sacraments of the Old Testament and ours are of the same force, inasmuch that Paul calleth them circumcised which are baptized, and them baptized which are circumcised. And he also teacheth that our fathers did eat that spiritual meat which we eat and drank of that spiritual drink, i.e., the rock.[136]

Of course, following this logic, he saw no good reason to withhold baptism from infants any more than his mentor Zwingli had done.[137] John Calvin said much the same thing, and he may have depended to some extent on Bullinger. In particular, Calvin insisted that those who received the covenant were expected to keep it:

> Why should God keep his promise, when we have broken his covenant? . . . He has become our God upon this condition, that we also should be his people. . . . We must show by our deeds that we are his people, in that we obey him.[138]

Like Zwingli and Bullinger, Calvin understood the covenant to be one of grace, given by God irrespective of human merit and dependent for its fulfillment on the gift of faith and obedience. Like them, Calvin believed that the

---

[132] Heinrich Bullinger, *De testamento seu foedere Dei unico et aeterno*, 13 (Zurich: Christoph Froschauer, 1534). An English translation can be found in McCoy and Baker, *Fountainhead*, 101–138.

[133] Heinrich Bullinger, *The Decades*, trans. Thomas Harding, 5 vols. (Cambridge: Cambridge University Press, 1849–1852), 2:3.6.174.

[134] This was his interpretation of Jesus' words in Luke 22:20: "This cup . . . is the new covenant in my blood." See Bullinger, *Decades* 2:5.9.403.

[135] Bullinger, *Decades*, 2:3.8.249, 269.

[136] Ibid., 2:5.7.298.

[137] Ibid., 2:5.7.322; 5.8.372–390.

[138] *Sermons of Master John Calvin upon the Fifthe Book of Moses called Deuteronomie*, trans. Arthur Golding (London: Henry Middleton for John Harison, 1583), 915b. The sermon was preached on Deut. 26:16–19.

covenant signs in the New Testament were superior to those in the Old, but that this did not alter the fact that, fundamentally, they were identical both in their origin and in their effects. As he put it,

> The covenant made with all the patriarchs is so much like ours in substance and reality that the two are actually one and the same. Yet they differ in the mode of dispensation.[139]

At the same time, Calvin also stressed that there were great differences between the Testaments, differences that were rooted in the contrast between the law and the gospel. He tried to reconcile them by developing a distinction between the "broad" and the "narrow" meaning of each of these key terms.

In the narrow sense, the law was nothing but the proclamation of condemnation and death that "belongs peculiarly to the ministration of Moses." But in the broader sense, it is the teaching of Moses as a whole, which contains not just the commandments that bring death but the promises of eternal life that would one day be fulfilled in Christ.[140] Likewise, the gospel could be taken in its broad sense, which "includes those testimonies of his mercy and Fatherly favor which God gave to the patriarchs of old," but it could also be more narrowly interpreted as the proclamation of grace in the life and death of the incarnate Christ.[141] In the narrow sense, the law and the gospel are opposites, but in the broader sense they are essentially the same.[142] This could be seen with great clarity in Jeremiah 31:31–33, where God told the prophet that he would make a new covenant with his people that would not be like the old one (in the narrow sense) but that would renew its broader purposes in a deeper and more purely spiritual way.[143]

Calvin also followed the sacramental teaching of Zwingli and Bullinger, at least with respect to the fulfillment of the covenant promises. Like them, he regarded the change of dispensation as a minor matter and concluded that, "there is no difference in the inner mystery by which the whole force and character of the sacraments are to be weighed."[144]

Where Calvin went beyond Zwingli and Bullinger was in the way he connected the covenant with election. Here again he made a distinction between the broad, general principle and the narrow, particular application. Broadly speaking, God had chosen Abraham and his descendants through Isaac and

[139] Calvin, *Institutio* 2.10.2.
[140] John Calvin, *Commentary on II Corinthians*, 3:7.
[141] Calvin, *Institutio* 2.9.2.
[142] Ibid., 2.9.4; 2.11.10.
[143] John Calvin, *Commentary on Jeremiah*, 31:31–32.
[144] Calvin, *Institutio* 4.16.4.

had given them the outward signs of the covenant promises. But not all the Israelites had remained faithful to them, because within that broad election there was a narrower one, confined to those who were given the spirit of new birth, which enabled them to live up to their covenant responsibilities and inherit the promises that had been made to the wider body.[145] In other words, Calvin believed that it was possible to belong to the covenant people of God without being one of the elect, a distinction that would be fundamental to the way in which he distinguished between the visible and the invisible church as the body of Christ on earth.

Zwingli, Bullinger, and Calvin all represented what we might call the earliest phase of covenant theology. They used the term covenant quite regularly, understood it to have two dimensions, one of them historical and the other eternal, and applied it to the sacraments, especially in defense of infant baptism. Beyond that they did not go, at least not in any systematic way, and so it would be anachronistic to say that they were covenant theologians in the sense that this came to be understood in the next generation. Yet even in Calvin and Bullinger's lifetime, things were moving toward a more systematic approach which would make them look increasingly conservative and even old-fashioned in the wider Reformed context.

We can trace the beginnings of this development to the work of Wolfgang Musculus (1497–1563), who made "covenant" (*foedus*) a separate subject in his systematic theology, distinguished it from "testament" (*testamentum*), and subdivided it into two distinct types—general (*foedus generale*) and special (*foedus speciale*).[146] But unlike Calvin, whose broader covenant extended only to the nation of Israel, Musculus conceived of the *foedus generale* as pertaining to the whole world, reflecting the promise he made to Noah after the flood that he would never again destroy the earth.[147] In the nature of things, though, this covenant was only for a time and would be wound up when the created order ceased to exist. The special covenant, on the other hand, which Calvin would have called the broader one, was made with Abraham and his descendants, though it could be stretched to include Gentile believers as well. This covenant was everlasting, but it also placed an obligation on those who received it to do their part in keeping it. Musculus never suggested that faith was a human work or that anyone other than those whom God had chosen would be saved,

[145] This is spelled out at great length in ibid., 3.27.5–7.

[146] Wolfgang Musculus, *Commonplaces of Christian religion*, trans. John Man (London: H. Bynneman, 1578), 284–295. See also Jordan J. Ballor, *Covenant, Causality, and Law: A Study in the Theology of Wolfgang Musculus* (Göttingen: Vandenhoeck und Ruprecht, 2012).

[147] Musculus, *Commonplaces*, 285.

but even so, believers were expected to live as if God were constantly watching over them to see that they were behaving properly.[148]

Like his Reformed contemporaries, Musculus agreed that there was only one eternal covenant, made in Jesus Christ and contained in the universal church of those who had been chosen from the beginning of time. But having said that, he went on to subdivide the history of salvation into three distinct periods according to the way in which each period was related to the law. First there was the age from Adam to Moses, *before* the law. At that time there was no covenant in the later sense of the word, but God spoke directly to particular individuals and gave them signs, like circumcision, that would later be formalized and applied under the law. That this dispensation could be understood as a covenant is perhaps demonstrated by the prophet Hosea, who wrote of Israel and Judah, "Like Adam they transgressed the covenant," but the reference is somewhat vague and the verse was seldom appealed to in defense of this idea.[149]

The second period extended from Moses to the coming of Christ, when the law governed the administration of the covenant promises. There was very little about the law that could be described as "new"—it was really just a codification of what had already been given beforehand, especially to Abraham. The main purpose of the law was to protect the Israelites from falling under the influences of the surrounding peoples as they developed into a recognizable nation, with their own king and secular government, and to prepare them for the coming of Christ. That coming ushered in the third and final period of history, the time *after* the law, when the restrictions that it had imposed would be broken down and the promises of God would be extended to all nations. But just as the law of Moses ratified what had gone before, so the new covenant in Christ confirmed what had been given at Mount Sinai. Musculus followed the other Reformed theologians mentioned above in their view of the sacraments, and especially of the validity of infant baptism, but unlike Calvin (at least) he made no effective distinction between the visible members of the covenant people and the remnant that was truly elect.

On the other hand, Musculus did distinguish between "covenant" and "testament," which to his mind were two quite different things. As he understood it, a covenant was broken up by the death of one of the parties to it, whereas a testament only came into force when the testator died. This enabled Musculus to regard the work of Christ as a testament by which he bequeathed everything the Father had given him to his heirs (believers) and appointed the apostles

[148] Ibid., 288.

[149] Hosea 6:7. It is not mentioned in the Westminster Confession, for example, despite the large number of scriptural "proof-texts" that the Confession provides.

as his executors. In that sense, it was a dispensation of the covenant, which remained the same as it had always been, because God cannot die.

Another theologian of this period who developed the doctrine of the covenant in fresh ways, while at the same time reaffirming most of what he had inherited from those who had gone before him, was Zacharias Ursinus (1534–1583). On the main points already mentioned, Ursinus was at one with Bullinger and Calvin and, like them, he made no distinction between "covenant" and "testament" in the way that Musculus did. Ursinus went further than his mentors, though, at least in the early stages of his career, by composing a theological catechism in which the theme of covenant played the central role.[150] That would change in his later work, but it shows us where he was coming from.

Ursinus also claimed that the covenant was not just a promise, but the real reconciliation between God and man that had been achieved through the promises.[151] The centrality of Christ to the covenant was demonstrated by the fact that this reconciliation was his work as Mediator "inasmuch as every mediator is the mediator of some covenant and the reconciler of two opposing parties."[152] By satisfying the wrath of God against our sin, Christ had paved the way toward a reconciliation, which is exactly what a mediator was supposed to do, in Ursinus's opinion.

Ursinus also pioneered another distinction between two types of covenant, this time between a covenant of nature and a covenant of grace, language that reflects the influence of medieval scholasticism on his thought. Previous exponents of the covenant had regarded it as entirely of grace, even when (as with Musculus) the "general" covenant extended to the whole world. But now Ursinus argued that there was a covenant of nature, engraved on the heart of every human being by virtue of his creation as a rational being made in the image of God. The difference between his understanding and that of Calvin and Musculus can perhaps best be appreciated by the following diagram:

Calvin	**Musculus**	**Ursinus**
Broad covenant (Israel)	General covenant (fallen world)	Covenant of nature (creation)
Narrow covenant (elect)	Special covenant (elect)	Covenant of grace (elect)

150 Zacharias Ursinus, *Catechesis, summa theologiae per quaestiones et responsiones exposita in Domini Zachariae Ursini . . . opera theologica*, ed. Quirinus Reuter (Heidelberg: Johannes Lancelott, 1612).

151 Ursinus, *Catechesis*, 11, 21.

152 *The Commentary of Dr. Zacharias Ursinus on the Heidelberg Catechism*, trans. G. W. Williard (Grand Rapids, MI: Eerdmans, 1954), 96. On the Heidelberg Catechism, see Lyle D. Bierma, *The Theology of the Heidelberg Catechism: A Reformation Synthesis* (Louisville: Westminster John Knox, 2013).

According to Ursinus, the innate covenant of nature gave man the ability to distinguish right from wrong, and was contained in the Ten Commandments, though it was not defined by them.[153] As he explained it,

> The law contains the natural covenant which was established by God with men at creation, which means that he is known to men by nature. It requires from us perfect obedience toward God, and to those who keep it, it promises eternal life, but to those who do not, it threatens eternal punishments.[154]

Entry into the covenant of grace was possible only for those who fulfilled the covenant of nature, but human sin had made that impossible. That is why God sent his Son, who was the only one able to do what was required. By being united to him, the believer could gain access to the covenant of grace and complete the righteousness that God requires of his servants. Ursinus emphasized that participation in the covenant promises was more than the fulfillment of a legal requirement—it was personal union with Christ. In this Ursinus was following Calvin, but Calvin had never expressed the need for union with Christ in a covenantal framework. Likewise, Ursinus insisted that it was the Holy Spirit who came to seal in the believer's heart the benefits of forgiveness, righteousness, and eternal life that the covenant promised.[155] Here again, Calvin would have agreed with him, but he did not express these ideas as part of the fulfillment of God's covenant with man. Calvin seems to have reserved the term "covenant" for the relationship that God established with Israel and then with the church, but he did not reject the notion that Adam had been given a natural law that he was expected to uphold. This is what Ursinus later called the "natural covenant," meaning by this term exactly what Calvin had understood by the "natural moral law."

We may therefore conclude that Ursinus ended up in the same place as Calvin, but that he did so within a covenant context to a degree that was foreign to Calvin's usage, even if it was in line with Calvin's thought.[156] In that respect he can be regarded as the first Reformed theologian to have had a genuine "covenant theology," in the sense that the covenant was a fundamental principle that touched every aspect of his understanding of God and salvation.

---

[153] Ursinus, *Catechesis*, 10, 22.

[154] Ibid., 14.

[155] Ibid., 10.

[156] The importance of this distinction, and the error in interpreting the origin of covenant theology that has resulted from ignoring it is well treated by Lyle D. Bierma, "Law and Grace in Ursinus's Doctrine of the Natural Covenant: A Reappraisal," in Carl R. Trueman and R. Scott Clark, eds., *Protestant Scholasticism: Essays in Reassessment* (Carlisle: Paternoster, 1999), 96–110. This article contains a discussion of the twentieth-century debate about this subject and gives an extensive bibliography for the benefit of those who wish to follow it further.

The next stage in the development of covenant theology was represented by Caspar Olevianus (1536–1587).[157] As a young man, Olevianus traveled across central Europe to meet and study with both Bullinger and Calvin, to whom he was especially close, as well as Calvin's assistant and successor, Theodore Beza (1519–1605) and his colleague Guillaume Farel (1489–1565). He studied at the Sorbonne (Paris) and later taught for a time at Heidelberg, ending his days as the first professor of dogmatics at the Herborn Academy, where he had a strong influence on the next generation of Reformed theologians. With a career and contacts like these, Olevianus can truly be called a major link across countries and generations, making it possible to construct a plausible genealogy of covenant theology that connects its origins in the previous generation to its final maturity in the next one.

Olevianus taught that the covenant of grace was established after the fall of Adam and that it took the form of a promise that was sealed by an oath.[158] The significance of this should not be underestimated. Perjury—lying under oath—is a serious crime, and God could not possibly be guilty of such a thing. His promises were therefore certain to be fulfilled, as they eventually were in the sending of his Son. Given that it was the Son's death that ratified the covenant, it was appropriate to call it a testament, and Olevianus saw (more clearly than Musculus) that the sacrifice of Christ was inherent in God's promise from the beginning. At the same time, Olevianus also accepted that there was a place for human response to God because the covenant is more than just a promise of future reconciliation—it is a lived experience of that reconciliation at work in the present. In his words,

> The reconciliation of man with God, or this matter of salvation . . . is called a covenant and the form it takes is set out for us by God, for there is no form or procedure more suitable for creating a mutual agreement among equals and for establishing faith.[159]

Note here that in Olevianus's opinion, God makes his elect in some sense "equal" to him and therefore worthy to be his associates ("confederates"), but this also means that it depends for its fulfillment on the submission and

[157] See Lyle D. Bierma, *German Calvinism in the Confessional Age: The Covenant Theology of Caspar Olevianus* (Grand Rapids, MI: Baker, 1996), reissued as *The Covenant Theology of Caspar Olevianus* (Grand Rapids, MI: Reformation Heritage, 2005); R. Scott Clark, *Caspar Olevian and the Substance of the Covenant: The Double Benefit of Christ* (Grand Rapids, MI: Reformation Heritage, 2005).

[158] For what follows, see Bierma, *German Calvinism*, 63–105.

[159] Caspar Olevianus, *Expositio Symboli Apostolici sive articulorum fidei, in qua summa gratuiti foederis aeterni inter Deum et fideles breviter et perspicue tractatur* (Frankfurt: Andreae Wechel, 1576), 9. The book was translated into English in Olevianus's lifetime by John Field and published as *An Exposition of the Symbole of the Apostles, or Rather of the Articles of Faith: In Which the Chief Points of the Everlasting and Free Covenant between God and the Faithful Is Briefly and Plainly Handled* (London: H. Middleton, 1581).

obedience of those who have been called and chosen to share in it. Furthermore, it is impossible for fallen man to meet the conditions required for this fulfillment, so that the elect's ability to do so can be only because God has made that possible by his free gift.[160] God's covenant with man is quite different from any covenant made between human beings, because in the latter case each party contributes something toward it, whereas in God's covenant, everything must come from him:

> It is God who freely gives. Man can only accept this [gift], for even the ability to accept or believe is the free gift of God.[161]

Even so, Olevianus saw that good works have an important part to play in manifesting the reality of the covenant. Christians are alive in Christ, and therefore they must live as he does in order to show that this life is a reality. They must also do good works out of a sense of gratitude for the blessings they have received, as well as for a witness to others, so that they too may be won for Christ.[162]

Olevianus went on to identify the experience of reconciliation through the covenant with the kingdom of Christ. In his words,

> The universal administration of the kingdom of Christ is that new covenant which God promised through the prophet Jeremiah. . . . This covenant, Christ the priest and king of the church has, by his own merit, ratified for eternity between God and us, and by his effective working he applies it in us on a daily basis.[163]

Objective forgiveness before the judgment seat of the Father and the subjective experience of a new life lived in the power of the Holy Spirit belonged together as the double fruit of the covenant relationship sealed in Christ.[164] Fundamental to all this is the mystical union between the believer and Christ, but it is that which makes everything else possible. Christ is the Mediator through whom we receive the reconciliation promised by the covenant, and it is only to the extent that we are joined to him that we can experience that blessing.[165] It is at this point that the work of Christ merged almost imperceptibly with the

[160] Caspar Olevianus, *De substantia foederis gratuiti inter Deum et electos, itemque de mediis, quibus ea ipsa substantia nobis communicatur* (Geneva: Eustathius Vignon, 1585).
[161] *In Epistolam Divi Pauli Apostoli ad Galatas notae, ex concionibus Gasparis Oleviani excerptae, et a Theodoro Beza editae* (Geneva: Eustathius Vignon, 1578), 69 (on Galatians 3:18).
[162] These thoughts are scattered through Olevianus's works; see Bierma, *German Calvinism*, 70, for the details.
[163] Olevianus, *Expositio*, 4.
[164] Olevianus, *De substantia*, 123.
[165] Ibid., 208–209.

work of the Holy Spirit, because it was he who brought about the union that made the reconciling work of Christ effective.[166]

In developing this theme further, Olevianus tied the atoning work of Christ on the cross, which was the fulfillment of the covenant promise, to his eternal relationship with the Father in heaven. The sacrifice could not have had the effect it did if the priest who made it had not been in the relationship of the Son to the Father, because any lesser being would not have enjoyed the Father's confidence or possessed his authority to act on our behalf. As Olevianus expressed it,

> The foundation and ground of the royal priesthood of Christ and thus of the eternal covenant between God and man is expressed in this article about the person of Christ, to whose person, substance and essence these two natures belong . . . , which are so joined together that they are a real and genuine Christ.[167]

From there Olevianus went on to claim that the salvation of the elect was grounded on an eternal decree, which was "in the counsel of God the beginning and cornerstone of our blessedness."[168] Olevianus did not mean by this that the existence of the Son as a distinct person of the Godhead depended on the eternal decree, but rather that God's determination to save the elect was logically prior to the Father's decision to send the Son in order to make that salvation effectual.[169]

That the outworking of the covenant depended on a prior (and eternal) agreement between the Father and the Son was one of the most fundamental aspects of Olevianus's covenant theology. Long before his incarnation, the Son offered himself to the Father as the guarantor (*sponsor*) of the covenant, promising him that he would justify the elect by his atoning sacrifice and reconcile them to the Father by renewing them in the image of God in which they had been created.[170] This commitment had a twofold aspect to it, in that the fall of Adam was both an offense against God and a corruption of human nature. Whether this guarantee can really be called a covenant in its own right, though, and whether it can be said to have extended to the human race before the latter

[166] Ibid., 226–227.

[167] Caspar Olevianus, *Vester Grundt, das ist, die Artikel des alten, waren, ungezweifelten, christlichen Glaubens, den Christen, die in diesen gefährlichen, trübseligen Zeiten einen gewissen Trost aus Gottes Wort suchen, zu gutem erkeret und zugeschreiben* (Heidelberg: Michael Schirat, 1567), ed. Johann M. Reu (Gütersloh: C. Bertelsmann, 1924), 1355–1356.

[168] Olevianus, *Vester Grundt*, 1355.

[169] This is important because later on there would be a tendency to subject everything, including the existence of the Trinity, to a divine decree that was more fundamental than anything else in God.

[170] Olevianus, *De substantia*, 23–157 passim. See Bierma, *German Calvinism*, 107–112.

was even created, is much less clear. Occasionally, Olevianus used language that might be taken to suggest one or both of those things, but this seems to have been accidental rather than deliberate, and the emphasis is always on a mutual agreement between the Father and the Son which was the inevitable fruit of their common will. In this, it would seem that Olevianus merely restated the classical doctrine of the Trinity, according to which the divine will belongs to the one nature, not to the three persons of the Godhead, and that it is unnecessary to read a covenant context into it.

Olevianus's understanding of the relationship between the substance of the covenant and its administration suggests that they must coincide, in the sense that those for whom Christ died are those to whom the benefits of his sacrifice are applied, and this is indeed what we find in his earlier works.[171] But as time went on, Olevianus modified his understanding of the administration of the covenant in order to accommodate the distinction between the visible church, to which the benefits were outwardly applied, and the company of the elect, in whom alone they were effective. The need to make such a distinction was obvious from the Old Testament, where circumcision was given to all the Israelites but took effect only in those who believed.[172] Similarly, the visible church today includes people who receive the outward signs of the covenant without sharing in its substance, a disconnect that makes them profaners of the covenant and enemies of God.[173]

Contrary to what many modern commentators have tried to argue, the existence of such people was not an argument for free will over against predestination, on the supposition that it was possible to be chosen but to reject the divine call. On the contrary, Olevianus saw it as the ultimate reaffirmation of a double predestination, according to which many were called but few were chosen, because it was God's desire to manifest both his mercy (through election) and his justice (through reprobation).[174]

The intersection between the substance of the covenant and its administration is found primarily in the ministry of the Word and the sacraments, in which the promise of reconciliation is transformed into the reality. Olevianus was quite clear that this effect did not depend on any virtue inherent in the covenant signs:

> From the Scriptures we say that all the sanctification of the signs, that is, their separation from profane things for sacred use, which is above all that they

[171] Olevianus, *Vester Grundt*, 1334; *De substantia*, 71.
[172] Caspar Olevianus, *Der Gnadenbund Gottes* (Herborn: Christoff Raben, 1590), 468.
[173] Olevianus, *De substantia*, 197, 220–221.
[174] Ibid., 20–21. See Bierma, *German Calvinism*, 24–26, 83–84.

> should be visible witnesses of the grace promised by God in Christ crucified, depends on the ordination of God for that use, and is not some quality implanted in the signs themselves.[175]

Nor was God obliged to confine the dispensation of his grace to the covenant signs:

> God has not so bound himself to the sacraments that he cannot establish his covenant or call people effectually apart from them, as can be seen from the thief on the cross. . . . But he has bound us, so that no one can hold them in contempt without holding the covenant in contempt also.[176]

Olevianus was clear that the preaching of the Word was the means by which the elect were brought to faith by the inner working of the Holy Spirit; in normal circumstances, there was no other way of entering the covenant.[177] But the Word was always accompanied by the reality, and it was to emphasize this that the sacraments were given. Baptism is the means by which believers are incorporated into the covenant, and the Lord's Supper is the way in which that incorporation is strengthened and confirmed. In addition, the sacraments represent both the gift of God's grace and the submission of the recipients of that grace, thereby reinforcing the mutuality of the relationship between the Lord and his elect.[178] But at the same time, the sacraments are a reminder that unworthy reception of them is a cause of even greater condemnation.[179] The link between the sacramental signs and the covenant was so close in Olevianus's mind that he not infrequently used the signs to refer to the covenant itself, though he remained conscious of the ontological difference between them:

> There are two parts to the covenant, the promise (*promissio*) and the response (*repromissio*). The sign is even called the covenant, because it is a witness and visible sign. Therefore, since in the audible Word or covenant, [God] makes his promise only under a condition, so he does not do otherwise in the visible Word, that is to say, in the sign.[180]

Olevianus could speak in this way because he saw the sacraments as visible signs, not only of God's promises but also of the oath that he attached to them,

[175] Olevianus, *De substantia*, 412–413.
[176] Ibid., 422. The thief on the cross was told that he would go to Paradise without being baptized (Luke 23:43).
[177] Ibid., 249.
[178] This subject is developed at length in ibid., 407–414.
[179] Olevianus, *Der Gnadenbund Gottes*, 348.
[180] C. Olevianus, *In Epistolam Divi Pauli Apostoli ad Romanos notae, ex Gasparis Oleviani concionibus excerptae et a Theodoro Beza editae* (Geneva: Eustathius Vignon, 1578), 109 (commenting on Rom. 2:17).

making them the certain affirmation that he would keep his covenant.[181] As always, however, they took effect only when they were received by the elect in the same Spirit in which they were given.[182] In this, Olevianus was unwittingly echoing the words of Thomas Cranmer in the service of Holy Communion in the *Book of Common Prayer*:

> Ye that do truly and earnestly repent you of your sins, and are in love and charity with your neighbors, and intend to lead a new life, following the commandments of God, and walking from henceforth in his holy ways; draw near with faith, and take this holy sacrament to your comfort . . .[183]

It has to be stressed that Olevianus did not think that an unbeliever could receive the body and blood of Christ in the sacrament, however the presence of that body and blood might be understood. He was naturally hostile to the Roman Catholic doctrine of transubstantiation, but he did not accept the Lutheran idea that it was possible for an unworthy person to consume Christ in any objective sense.[184] In that respect, he retained what in English theology is called a "receptionist" view of the Eucharist, in line with mainstream Reformed (including Anglican) tradition.

With respect to infant baptism, Olevianus followed the line already taken by Calvin and others, but it must be admitted that his particular way of understanding the distinction between the substance and the administration of the covenant created difficulties that he apparently never resolved. On the one hand, baptism was a sure sign of a child's ingrafting into Christ and gave its parents the assurance that, if he should die in infancy, he would go to heaven. But if the same child were to reach maturity and reject the promises made on his behalf as an infant, he would be cast out of the covenant community and lose his salvation.[185] Ultimately, the salvation of such a person would have to depend on election (as it does with everyone else), but it would be impossible to know whether he was elect or not until there was some evidence of it one way or another. This difficulty, it must be said, is common to all theories of infant baptism, and results from the need to offer pastoral comfort to parents (and especially to bereaved ones) on the one hand and the need to accept that things do not always turn out as planned, on the other. In the end, Olevianus seems to have concluded, as anyone in his position must, that we walk in faith,

[181] Olevianus, *Der Gnadenbund Gottes*, 195.
[182] Olevianus, *De substantia*, 392.
[183] The text here is that of the current (1662) version; the original (1549) was slightly longer and more archaic in its language, but not substantially different.
[184] Olevianus, *De substantia*, 402. See Bierma, *German Calvinism*, 96–99.
[185] C. Olevianus, *Ad Romanos*, 574 (commenting on Rom. 11:17–18).

trusting in the promises of God but accepting that his sovereign will is beyond our understanding or control.

What did Olevianus have to say about the covenant concept outside the covenant of grace? This has been a controversial subject in modern times, with Karl Barth (1886–1968) insisting that he knew of no other covenant, while most other scholars have found up to five different covenants in his writings, above and beyond the centrally important covenant of grace.[186] The answer seems to be that the covenant of grace dominated Olevianus's thought but that he could (and sometimes did) use the term outside that context, though with less emphasis than has sometimes been attributed to him.

Olevianus very occasionally refers to a "covenant of creation," though more often he calls it something else—the "first covenant," the "natural covenant," or the "law (*ius*) of creation." What he meant by this was that Adam and Eve were created in perfect conformity to God's will, and that they were expected to maintain their relationship with him by constant obedience.[187] The fall took away the reality of perfection but not the obligation to maintain it, which is what has caused the present human dilemma. The covenant of grace restored the image of God that Adam had lost, but beyond that, Olevianus had little to say about it.[188] He did, however, state that the human conscience was the place where the law of nature made itself known, and the conscience played an important role in his understanding of the guilt of fallen man.[189] However, it is important to note that there is no sign in his writings that he regarded the natural law as a covenant of works that could be set against the covenant of grace, though it has often been claimed that he believed this.[190]

Of much greater importance in Olevianus's thinking was the "legal covenant" (*foedus legale*), which was revealed to Israel at Mount Sinai. The law of Moses bore the same relationship to the legal covenant that the conscience bore to the law of nature—it was the place where the demands of the legal covenant were made known and set the standard that the people of Israel were expected to keep.[191] But the law of Moses could be abrogated, as it was after the coming of Christ, without abolishing the legal covenant or its demands. The Gentiles, after all, had the law written on their hearts and were expected

[186] Karl Barth, *Church Dogmatics*, trans. G. W. Bromiley, 13 vols. in 4 (Edinburgh: T & T Clark, 1957–1988), IV/1:59. Originally published as *Kirchliche Dogmatik* (Zurich: Evangelisches Buchhandlung Zollingen, 1932–1967). See the discussion in Bierma, *German Calvinism*, 107–140.

[187] Olevianus, *De substantia*, 79–80.

[188] Ibid., 12.

[189] Ibid., 298.

[190] One particularly influential advocate of that idea was Philip Schaff. See his *The Creeds of Christendom*, 3 vols. (New York: Harper & Row, 1931), 1:773–774. For a refutation, see Bierma, *German Calvinism*, 117–118.

[191] Olevianus, *De substantia*, 12–13.

to keep it, even though they knew nothing of Moses.[192] In that sense, the legal covenant remains a living reality for every human being, teaching us the meaning of sin, convicting us of our guilt, and pointing us to our need of Christ. But once a person has received Christ, the legal covenant acquires a different meaning:

> The law is a part of the covenant of grace in that it is written on our hearts by the Spirit, and the preaching of repentance is the means or pen by which it is inscribed.[193]

Instead of being an instrument of condemnation, it is now a guide to the application of salvation—the so-called "third use of the law," as Reformed theology has traditionally understood it.

It remains only to note that Olevianus did not restrict this "third" or spiritual use of the law to believers in New Testament times. Just as the legal covenant could be separated from the law of Moses without losing its power or importance, so too could the law of grace transcend the Mosaic commandments even when they were still in force. It was thus possible for people before the coming of Christ to have a saving knowledge of him, even if this experience was less intense for them than it is for us.[194] The grace of God is, after all, the substance of the covenant—its administration varied from the old to the new dispensation, but fundamentally, like Jesus Christ, it was the same yesterday, today, and forever.[195]

With Olevianus, covenant theology may be said to have come to maturity. His teaching was passed on through the school at Herborn to the next generation of Reformed theologians in Germany and through them to its greatest seventeenth-century exponent, Johannes Cocceius (1603–1669). In the course of its transmission, the "covenant of creation" evolved into a "covenant of works," but the essential element of communion with God was maintained. Adam did not have to earn his salvation; his works were the outward manifestation of his response to the gracious calling of God.[196]

There is also considerable evidence that Olevianus was the major influence in the development of covenant theology in England, particularly in the works of William Perkins (1558–1602).[197] Perkins never mentioned Olevianus by name, but the parallels with his work are so striking that it seems very

192 Rom. 2:14–16. See Olevianus, *De substantia*, 252–253.
193 Ibid., 295.
194 Ibid., 229–230.
195 Heb. 13:8.
196 Johannes Cocceius, *Collationes de foedere et testamento Dei* (Franeker: J. Balck, 1648).
197 See Bierma, *German Calvinism*, 176–181.

unlikely that the Englishman could have come up with them independently.[198] As in Germany, there was a similar evolution, though it is hard to document it precisely, from the covenant of creation to the covenant of works, making it probable that this is the way that Olevianus was read in the next generation, even if he did not quite get to that point himself. Certainly the Westminster Confession, which was composed by men trained in the school of Perkins, if not of Olevianus, reflected a clear understanding of the Adamic covenant of works, which these men wrote into their statement of faith, thereby canonizing it as a fundamental aspect of classical Reformed theology.

Once we understand this background, the Westminster Confession's assertion of covenant theology falls naturally into place. It begins historically, as follows:

> The first covenant made with man was a covenant of works wherein life was promised to Adam, and in him to his posterity, upon condition of perfect and personal obedience.[199]

> God gave to Adam a law as a covenant of works, by which he bound him and all his posterity to personal, entire, exact, and perpetual obedience, promised life upon the fulfilling, and threatened death upon the breach of it, and endued him with power and ability to keep it.[200]

Apart from the mention of "works," these statements could have come straight out of Olevianus. Note in particular that the promise of "life" is not defined as "eternal life," perhaps because Reformed theology had not specified that but perhaps also because it made no sense in the context. God promised Adam that he would maintain him in the garden of Eden, but that cannot have been eternal life as we understand it because it was a life in time and space—he was told to be fruitful and multiply,[201] which would soon have led to vast overcrowding if everyone born in the Garden was to live forever! But apart from that, eternal life is something qualitatively different, which Adam could only have had by being united to Christ, and there was no mention of that in the creation account. The Confession is therefore silent, or at best ambiguous, on this point.

The next stage of the covenant is treated differently in different chapters of the Confession. In Chapter 8, which deals specifically with the covenant itself,

[198] See Victor L. Priebe, *The Covenant Theology of William Perkins* (unpublished PhD dissertation, Drew University, 1967).
[199] Westminster Confession, 8.2; see Bray, *Documents of the English Reformation*, 493.
[200] Westminster Confession, 19.1; see Bray, *Documents of the English Reformation*, 501.
[201] Gen. 1:28.

fallen man is offered the covenant of grace in Jesus Christ, which requires a faith that can be given only by the Holy Spirit, but that will be given to all those who are chosen for salvation. This covenant can also be called a testament (Olevianus again!) and was differently administered in the Old Testament. When Christ, the substance of the covenant, was exhibited, the old dispensation was wrapped up and replaced by something better, but the underlying unity of the dispensations is reaffirmed, because each in its own way manifests and depends on the work of Christ.[202]

In chapter 19, however, which deals with the law of God, we are told that, after Adam's fall, it

> . . . continued to be a perfect rule of righteousness and, as such, was delivered by God upon Mount Sinai in Ten Commandments and written in two tables, the first four commandments containing our duty toward God, and the other six our duty to man.[203]

This law reflected the natural moral conscience implanted in the first human beings, and was not abrogated by the coming of Christ. But in Israel it was supplemented by two further elements: a ceremonial law surrounding the priesthood and their sacrifices, and a judicial law designed for the political life of ancient Israel. In Christ the first of these has been totally fulfilled and made redundant, while the second was never meant to apply beyond its original context, although it may offer guidance to Christians as to how they should order their social life.[204] Above all, the law is of great benefit to the church as an indication of how we should live, what we should do to struggle against sin, and what blessings God has promised to his children. As the Confession sums this up,

> a man's doing good, and refraining from evil, because the law encourageth to the one, and deterreth from the other, is no evidence of his being under the law, and not under grace. Neither are the forementioned uses of the law contrary to the grace of the gospel, but do sweetly comply with it: the Spirit of Christ subduing and enabling the will of man to do that freely and cheerfully, which the will of God, revealed in the law, requireth to be done.[205]

Olevianus and Perkins would have recognized themselves in these statements without any problem, and although there have been further discussions

[202] Westminster Confession, 8.3–6; see Bray, *Documents of the English Reformation*, 493.
[203] Westminster Confession, 19.2; see Bray, *Documents of the English Reformation*, 501.
[204] Westminster Confession, 19.3–5; see Bray, *Documents of the English Reformation*, 501.
[205] Westminster Confession, 19.6–7; see Bray, *Documents of the English Reformation*, 502.

and modifications of what the Westminster Confession says in the centuries since it was composed—particularly with regard to the covenant of works, which is a concept less solidly grounded in Scripture than the covenant of grace is—the Reformed tradition continues to recognize it as the classical expression of how it understands the divine plan of salvation. Perhaps the most interesting thing about it is that by anchoring the work of Christ so firmly in the eternal purposes of God and stressing that it has not changed over time, the focus of divine activity in the world was subtly shifted away from the finished work of Christ to the work of the Holy Spirit, who has been sent to apply the Son's work in the hearts and lives of those who have been chosen for salvation. It is therefore to the way in which the church has understood the Holy Spirit and his work that we must now turn our attention.

PART SIX

The Person of the Holy Spirit

15

The Forgotten Person of the Trinity?

The Road Less Traveled

The classical centuries of Christian theological formation were preoccupied with defining the person and natures of Christ (Christology), which provided the framework for the medieval Western discussions relating to the work of Christ (soteriology). To this day, the centrality of the work of Christ is a marked feature of the Western tradition, whether we look at it in terms of worship, the doctrine of the church, or systematic theology. Every once in a while churches in the Western tradition are disturbed by an outbreak of enthusiasm, in which attention shifts away from the atoning work of Christ to the work of the Holy Spirit, but these occurrences are relatively rare and tend to be regarded as aberrations. The modern charismatic movement is an example of this, and the difficulty that the mainline churches have in incorporating it, along with the tendency of theologians to ignore or dismiss it altogether, demonstrates the nature of the problem. Pentecostal churches that emerged a century ago in a blaze of ecstatic activity have gradually "calmed down" and become more like other more traditional Protestant denominations, and there is no reason to doubt that the most recent charismatic wave will eventually take the same course.[1] No doubt, at some point another outburst will occur, and the pattern will repeat itself as it has countless times in the past. Like it or not, the Western tradition, both Protestant and Catholic, has never found it easy to accommodate the Holy Spirit as a person of the Trinity with his own distinct work that complements that of the Son without being subsumed by it.

[1] See Donald E. Miller and Tetsunao Yamamori, *Global Pentecostalism* (Berkeley: University of California Press, 2007); Allan H. Anderson and Walter J. Hollenweger, eds., *Pentecostals after a Century: Global Perspectives on a Movement in Transition* (Sheffield: Sheffield Academic Press, 1999); Walter J. Hollenweger, *The Pentecostals* (London: SCM, 1972). Originally published as *Enthusiastisches Christentum* (Wuppertal: Theologischer Verlag Brockhaus, 1969).

Was this development inevitable, or could another path have been taken? It is at this point that the difference between the Western and the Eastern ("Greek" or "Orthodox") churches becomes most visible and important. Of course, to some extent it had always been there. For a start, the West had only one major center—the city of Rome. Provincial writers from (North) Africa, Spain, and Gaul (now France) played an important part in the development of early Western theology, but Rome retained their allegiance to an extent that was unknown in the East, where Alexandria, Antioch, and Constantinople all vied with each other for supremacy. In the circumstances, it is hardly surprising that the West tended to emphasize unity over diversity in a way that the East did not.

Complementing this, there was also a different approach to language. In the East, Greek served as the main vehicle of government and of high culture, but it did not displace local tongues. After the legalization of Christianity, the Bible was translated into Coptic (Egyptian), Syriac, and Armenian, and a sizeable Christian literature in those languages soon appeared. Later on, when Greek missionaries went to the Slavs, they translated the Scriptures into Slavonic and established another literary tradition that continues to the present day. The West had nothing to compare with this. Latin was the only language of any real significance, and the use of local vernaculars was discouraged, if not actually suppressed. Attempts to translate the Bible into Celtic or Germanic tongues never got very far, and all public worship and theology was conducted in Latin, whether anyone understood it or not. Even where Latin had been the spoken tongue, it gradually became harder for ordinary people to follow it, but the church took little notice of that.[2] Italian, Spanish, Portuguese, and French took some centuries to emerge as potential rivals to their parent Latin, and when they finally did so, it was only in the secular sphere. After the Reformation, Protestants encouraged translation into the different vernaculars, but even they continued to use Latin for theological purposes until well into the eighteenth century and (in some cases) even later.

One effect of this was to preserve a sense of unity that overrode local variations, but it also inclined people to think that Pentecost had reversed the linguistic confusion of Babel by supplying the church with Latin—a sacred language that could be learned and interpreted by those with the gift of tongues. But this Latin was fossilized and anything but spontaneous; indeed, it was its very fixity that commended it to theologians and lawyers alike. Vernacular expressions could mean almost anything, but Latin phrases had

[2] The only real exception was that in 812, Charlemagne issued a decree ordering preachers to use the local vernaculars (*lingua rustica*) in their sermons, so as to be understood.

definitions that did not change.[3] This made it possible for the church to apply the gift of the Holy Spirit in a predictable and consistent way—the very thing against which "charismatic" groups have always protested. Theological debates followed a standard pattern that was immediately understood by those who knew its terminology, and even today it is much easier to speak of merit *de congruo* or *de condigno*, or of the efficacy of the sacraments *ex opere operato* or *ex opere operantis*, than it is to try to find vernacular equivalents for these phrases. Ordinary people have no idea what the theologians are talking about, but that does not bother the latter unduly, not least because they want others to think that their discipline is a specialized one that is best left to the experts.

The Eastern churches have not escaped the dangers of fossilization, and in some ways they have suffered from it more than the Western churches have, but its nature is different. In the East, standardization is the result of a tradition that cannot be changed because there is no one with the authority to change it. Before the Reformation in the West, the pope could impose a common policy on the churches under his jurisdiction, but there was no equivalent figure in the East. As a result, theological agreements between East and West, like those reached at Lyon in 1274 and Florence in 1439, could not be enforced in the East, where those who rejected them were able to block their acceptance. Later on, Protestantism complicated the picture by insisting on the unique authority of the Bible, coupled with freedom to do whatever seemed best on matters that were not clearly laid down in Scripture. This may be an untidy solution (as it certainly seems to Roman Catholics) but it works tolerably well in practice. Bible study has never been a denominational enterprise in the Protestant world, and although there is now a vast array of translations available, individual churches seldom insist on using one of them for theological reasons.[4] Both Catholics and Protestants have maintained a sense that they possess a *magisterium* (Latin, again!) which is readily available and to which they can appeal if they want to know what the mind of the Spirit is.

To this, the Eastern churches reply that their unity is grounded in the person and work of the Holy Spirit, who cannot be tied to earthly structures in

[3] A similar problem occurs today in many parts of Africa and Asia, where legal documents continue to be written in English or French, rather than in the local languages, because the latter do not possess the same stock of highly developed terminology.

[4] Some translations prefer to use (or to avoid) certain words because of their theological implications, but this is a relatively minor problem. For example, in the sixteenth and seventeenth centuries, conservatives wanted to translate *ekklêsia* as "church" whereas more radical people preferred to say "congregation." More recently, there has been a tendency among liberals to avoid words like "wrath" or "propitiation" and gender-specific words like "men" and "brethren," even though the original texts use them. Their choices are certainly theologically motivated, but when it is clear that they misrepresent what the Bible is saying, they can be criticized and amended accordingly.

the way that the Western churches have tried to do. Uniformity of practice, which is especially visible in public worship, is balanced by an unwillingness to define theological matters in ways that are more likely to divide the church than to unite it. An obvious example of this is the question of what happens to the bread and wine when they are consecrated in the Eucharist. The Western church has fallen apart over this, but the Eastern churches refuse to probe too deeply into the matter. Some Eastern theologians hold to a form of transubstantiation but others do not, and most of them have concluded that the matter cannot be resolved in human terms because it is a mystery. They say that in the Eucharist, the Holy Spirit takes the bread and wine and uses them for a spiritual purpose, which is to unite believers in the body of Christ. Beyond that, the Eastern churches say that it is both unwise and unnecessary to go. The liturgical forms are fixed, but this is in order to avoid confusion and to bear witness to the unity of the church in both time and space. As far as their theology is concerned, only the Holy Spirit can say what they really mean, because he alone understands the deep things of God.

The differences between East and West are rooted in different conceptions of who the Holy Spirit is and how he works in relation to the other persons of the Trinity. The West has gone to great lengths to define how the Spirit relates to the Son, because it is only in that context that the work of the Spirit can be understood. The East has resisted this tendency and to this day has refused to define the precise relationship between the second and third persons of the Godhead. As with the Eucharist, different theories compete for acceptance but none has ever been canonized. More important, the East has rejected the Western attempt to do this, and representatives of the Eastern churches have frequently classified this tendency as a major barrier (if not *the* major barrier) to the reunion of Christendom. It is therefore of the utmost importance in a history of theology that we should examine the different courses that East and West have followed over the centuries and try to understand why this is so.

As early as the fourth century, the resolution of the Christological problems thrown up by Arianism raised the question of the identity of the Holy Spirit. If the Father was fully God, which almost no one had ever doubted, and the Son was equally divine, what could be said about the third person of the Trinity? Was he also to be regarded as God, and if so, why was he not a second Son? The Niceno-Constantinopolitan Creed of 381, with its "expanded" section on the Holy Spirit, shows how the Cappadocian fathers grappled with these questions. Basil of Caesarea was the first person to write a major theological treatise (*De Spiritu Sancto*) devoted exclusively to the Holy Spirit. He followed the inductive method—starting from the evidence provided by the Spirit's work and building up a case for his divinity, rather than with the Trinity and deducing from there what might be said about the particular identity of the Spirit. This method was the exact opposite of the one used in Christology. When arguing about the divinity of the Son, theologians talked primarily about his person and nature(s), but when it came to the Holy Spirit, they concentrated on his work, which was taken to be the key to understanding his place in the Godhead. Because of that, the general agreement about the work of the Spirit that existed between East and West could produce theological unity only if it led to a corresponding agreement about his personal identity. If that did not happen, then the apparent agreement about his work was superficial. In the end, East and West developed different interpretations of the Holy Spirit's work because they could not agree about the identity of his person, though it took many centuries for that to become clear. Indeed, the failure of the two great branches of Christendom to come to a common mind on this question is still a mystery to many in the West, where the priority traditionally given to the work of the Holy Spirit makes differences over his personal identity seem arcane and relatively unimportant.

From the Western point of view, the Eastern tradition is the road less traveled, a fact that makes it attractive to some and repellent to others. It is no accident that those in the West who are most critical of their own tradition seek, and to some extent find, consolation in the East. But it has to be remembered that this attraction is the result of a reaction against certain aspects of Western theology rather than a disinterested embrace of a different theological tradition. As a result, Westerners who have converted to one of the Eastern churches often puzzle members of those churches who do not understand where they are coming from and are not sure whether they really share their theological outlook.

The Eastern churches have spent centuries defining themselves over against the West, and in doing so their theologians have had to engage in sometimes bitter polemic against members of their own communion who have been significantly influenced by Western ideas, and who have sometimes reproached their fellow Easterners for their refusal to accept them. Western converts to Eastern Orthodoxy are usually quite unaware of this phenomenon. Often they are emotionally inclined to adopt anything anti-Western, but they do so for the wrong reasons and show none of the sophistication that genuine theological debate demands. As a result, they can sometimes be more of an embarrassment than a help to the Eastern churches as they reflect on how they should understand the Trinity and relate to the Western tradition.

The Spirit of God in the Bible

The difficulties that Christians have had in coming to terms with the person and work of the Holy Spirit can be traced back to the Old Testament, where there are frequent references to the "Spirit of God." It is not always clear whether these passages refer to the being or nature of God, or whether they should be seen as allusions to the third person of the Trinity who had not yet been revealed as such. The ancient Israelites believed that God was "spirit" (*ruach*), and there seems to have been some connection between that spirit and the human soul, but Hebrew used a different word for the latter (*nephesh*), and Old Testament references to the "Spirit of God" make it clear that his presence in someone's life was the exception rather than the rule.[5]

In the creation narrative we are told that "the Spirit of God was hovering over the face of the waters,"[6] a statement that the early Christians did not hesitate to interpret in personal terms, but however obvious that may have seemed to them, theirs was a view from hindsight. The personhood of God's Spirit was never accepted by Jews as a legitimate interpretation of the biblical texts, and when Jesus taught his disciples about the coming of the Holy Spirit, he did not explicitly identify him with the Spirit of God in the Old Testament. In particular, he did not tell them that they would be filled with the Spirit in the way that Elijah and the other prophets had been. His disciples would certainly prophesy, as they themselves testified on the day of Pentecost, but although their experience was presented as the fulfillment of Old Testament prophecy,[7] it was not quite the same thing. For a start, the Holy Spirit would come upon all Christians, not just upon those called to be prophets, and there were many different spiritual gifts at work in the church.[8] The great men of ancient Israel had known powerful movements of the Spirit of God in and among them, but Christians were going to experience him in their lives on a permanent basis, whether that was manifested in extraordinary activities or not. To put it differently, in the Old Testament the Spirit of God was more of a force at work in specially chosen individuals who were charged with bringing the power of God to bear on our lives, whereas in the New Testament the Holy Spirit is more like a person who integrates believers into a relationship that embraces the Father and the Son in a way that was unknown before the coming of Christ. The difference was clearly expressed by Novatian (third century) as follows:

[5] Gen. 2:7. Compare Gen. 41:38; Ex. 31:3, etc.
[6] Gen. 1:2.
[7] Acts 2:17–21, quoting Joel 2:28–32.
[8] 1 Cor. 12:4–6.

> The Spirit is not new in the gospel, or even newly given. It was he who accused the people through the prophets, and who appealed to the Gentiles through the apostles. . . . The Spirit in the prophets and apostles was one and the same, except that in the prophets he was present on certain occasions whereas in the apostles he is always present. In former times he was not always in them, but in these last days, he is. In former times he distributed his gifts with reserve, but in these last days everything is poured out. In former times he was given sparingly, but in these last days he is bestowed liberally, although he was not shown before the Lord's resurrection.[9]

The early Christians had no problem in recognizing that God was by nature a spirit different from any of his creatures, and they assumed that the Spirit of God "hovering over the face of the waters" was a direct reference to the third person of the Godhead. Typical of their approach is the following remark by Ephrem the Syrian (fourth century):

> It was appropriate to reveal that the Spirit hovered, in order for us to learn that the work of creation was done in common by the Spirit, the Father, and the Son. The Father spoke. The Son created. And so it was right for the Spirit to offer his work, clearly revealed in his hovering, in order to demonstrate his unity with the other persons. Thus we learn that everything was perfected and accomplished by the Trinity.[10]

For Ephrem and his contemporaries, the creating work of the Holy Spirit was a foreshadowing of his re-creating work in baptism, in which "the waters made fertile by the hovering of that same divine Spirit might give birth to the children of God."[11] Today, most exegetes would dissent from the ancient Christian consensus and say that the reference to the "Spirit of God" in Genesis 1 is simply a way of referring to God himself and should not be taken to imply the existence of a distinct person called the Holy Spirit. That accords with traditional Jewish interpretation, of course, and in the absence of any detail that might suggest otherwise (such as a dialogue between the Spirit and God about how to proceed with the creation), it is probably the safest course to follow. However, there are still people today who are prepared to cite this verse as evidence that the Holy Spirit was active in creation, perhaps because they think that belief in a Creator Spirit would otherwise lack explicit biblical support. If so, that view would not have been shared by Irenaeus, who appealed to the Psalms as evidence of the Holy Spirit's work in creation:

---

[9] Novatian, *De Trinitate* 29.

[10] Ephrem Syrus, *Commentarium in Genesim* 1.

[11] Ibid. See also Jerome, *Homiliae* 10, who says the same thing.

> God is Spirit, and so he adorned all things by his Spirit, as the prophet also says: "By the Word of the Lord were the heavens established, and all their power by his Spirit."[12] Because the Word "establishes," which is to say, he works bodily and bestows existence [on things], while the Spirit arranges and forms the various "powers," the Son is rightly called the Word and the Spirit is called the Wisdom of God.[13]

Origen also found the presence of the Holy Spirit in Psalm 51:11 and even in Daniel 4:8, where King Nebuchadnezzar of Babylon is quoted as saying that the young Hebrew prophet was filled with "the spirit of the holy gods."[14]

These examples may be open to question, but there is evidence that the Holy Spirit (in the Christian sense of the term) was active in the Old Testament in a critically significant way. The New Testament tells us that "no prophecy was ever produced by the will of man, but men spoke from God as they were carried along by the Holy Spirit."[15] Taken by itself, this is a sweeping statement that could be interpreted to include even false prophecy, some of which we know was instigated by God in order to punish those who had disobeyed him.[16] But the context in which Peter was writing makes it clear that he was referring to the Bible, and his statement is backed up by the apostle Paul, who defined Scripture as "breathed out by God" (*theopneustos*), using the ambiguous word *pneuma* which can mean either "breath" or "spirit."[17] Either way, it seems to be indisputable that both Peter and Paul affirmed that the Holy Spirit inspired the Old Testament writers, and that was certainly the view held by the early church. There were different theories about the mechanics of divine inspiration, but the fact itself was never doubted, and it undergirds the use made of the Old Testament text by both Jesus and his disciples.

The theological importance of this is that if the Holy Spirit inspired the prophets to produce the Hebrew Bible, he must have been active in them before he was sent on the day of Pentecost, and so when Ezekiel (for example) wrote that "the Spirit lifted me up and brought me in the vision by the Spirit of God into Chaldea,"[18] we cannot exclude the possibility that he was referring to the third person of the Trinity, even though he did not recognize him as such. This does not prove that all Old Testament references to the "Spirit of God" can be read in the same way, but it does at least show us that there is some ambiguity

[12] Psalm 33:6.
[13] Irenaeus of Lyon, *De praedicatione apostolica* 1.5.
[14] Origen, *De principiis* 1.3.2.
[15] 2 Pet. 1:21.
[16] 1 Kings 22:22–23; 2 Chron. 18:21–22.
[17] 2 Pet. 1:20. See also 2 Tim. 3:16.
[18] Ezek. 11:24.

here and that the fathers of the church were not necessarily wrong in the way that they understood the text.

Readers of the New Testament sometimes remark that it seems to pay less attention to the Holy Spirit than to the other persons of the Trinity.[19] An obvious example of this is the fact that the apostle Paul greeted the churches he wrote to in the name of the Father and the Son, without mentioning the Spirit.[20] But whether that means that he paid less attention to the third person of the Godhead is more questionable. Paul spent a good deal of time telling his congregations about the work of the Holy Spirit, and some of the most famous chapters in his epistles (like Romans 8 and 1 Corinthians 12–14) are largely devoted to that theme. Sometimes it is hard to decide whether a particular passage is about the Son or the Spirit, as for example Galatians 4:6: "God has sent the Spirit of his Son into our hearts, crying 'Abba! Father!'" Is this about the Son, about the Holy Spirit, or about both? Here, and in similar instances elsewhere, such distinctions are unhelpful and misleading, because what Paul was saying is that our knowledge and experience of both the Father and the Son come in and through the indwelling presence of the Spirit. Origen recognized this and made it a fundamental principle of his own theological exposition:

> The apostles said that the Holy Spirit shared the honor and dignity of the Father and the Son. In his case, though, it is not clear whether he is begotten or unbegotten, or whether he is a Son of God or not.[21]

The divinity of the Holy Spirit was clearly affirmed by the early Christians, but precisely how his relationship to the Father and the Son should be described remained something of a mystery. To some extent it was spelled out by Jesus himself in the so-called "farewell discourses" in John 14–16. Those chapters contain the most sustained and detailed New Testament teaching about the Holy Spirit, and they make it plain that he cannot be pushed into the background without seriously distorting, and even destroying, the Christian message. The Holy Spirit is the "other Paraclete" (*allos Paraklêtos*), an unusual word that is normally translated as Comforter but may also be Counselor or Helper, and it was this definition that would be the starting point for theological reflection later on. What Jesus said is reinforced by the Acts of the Apostles, in particular the first two chapters, where the work of the Spirit is presented to us in graphic detail. The Holy Spirit was necessary for Christian baptism

[19] The best introduction to this subject remains Henry B. Swete, *The Holy Spirit in the New Testament* (London: Macmillan, 1909). It is still in print.

[20] The only exception is Colossians, where he mentioned the Father but not the Son in the initial greeting (but see Col. 1:3).

[21] Origen, *De principiis*, preface, 4.

to be complete, and as Origen noted, the dignity of the Spirit was such that although blasphemy against the Son could be forgiven, blasphemy against the Holy Spirit could not.[22]

Doubts about the exact meaning of the word "spirit" in the New Testament are basically the same as those we find in the Old Testament, arising as they do from the use of the word to refer to the nature of the divine being, the third person of the Trinity, and the human spirit. A classic example of the ambiguity that this could cause is John 4:24: "God is spirit, and those who worship him must worship in spirit and truth." To what does the word "spirit" refer in this verse? Most modern exegetes believe that it is best to think in generic terms and interpret it to refer mainly to the divine being, at least at the beginning of the verse. But what does it mean to say that the true worshiper must worship him in spirit? Is this to be understood even more generically, as if it means something like "sincerely," or "with the right attitude"? Or should we go further and say that true worship depends on the presence of the Holy Spirit in our hearts and therefore it must refer to that?

In interpreting this verse, the consensus of the early church was that "God is a spiritual being, and therefore those who worship him must worship him in the Holy Spirit and in truth." Origen made the case for interpreting "spirit" as a reference to the divine nature, and it seems that he was followed by almost everyone who came after him.[23] But Origen also mentioned the Holy Spirit when commenting on this verse, and that too was to find an echo later on.[24] The clearest exposition of this is found in Basil of Caesarea, who was expressing what had by the fourth century become the standard view:

> To worship in the Spirit implies that our intelligence has been enlightened. Consider the words spoken to the Samaritan woman. . . . By *truth* the Lord [Jesus] clearly meant himself. If we say that worship offered in the Son (the truth) is worship offered in the Father's image, we can say the same about worship offered in the Spirit, since the Spirit reveals in himself the divinity of the Lord. The Holy Spirit cannot be divided from the Father and the Son in worship. If you remain outside the Spirit, you cannot worship at all, and if you are in him you cannot separate him from God.[25]

We can therefore sum up the early Christian interpretation of the Bible's teaching about the Spirit of God by affirming that the fathers of the church

---

[22] Origen, *De principiis* 1.3.2. Origen was referring to Acts 8:17 and to Matt. 12:31.
[23] Origen, *De principiis* 1.1.4–5. See, for example, Didymus the Blind, *Fragmenta in Iohannem* 3, and Theodore of Mopsuestia, *Commentarium in Iohannis Evangelium* 4.23–24.
[24] Origen, *Commentarium in Iohannis Evangelium* 13.140.
[25] Basil of Caesarea, *De Spiritu Sancto* 26.64.

recognized the dual meaning of the word "spirit" and were happy to attribute personal actions of God's Spirit to the third person of the Trinity. They consistently ranked him along with the Son in relation to the Father, making it inevitable that when the relationship between the Father and the Son was defined, the question of how the Holy Spirit fitted in would be the next item on the agenda. Before that happened, though, the church was forced to come to terms with the personal character of the Spirit as the Paraclete (Comforter), a role prescribed for him in John 14:16 and subsequently given great prominence in the Montanist movement.[26]

The Paraclete and Personhood

The Montanists were a semi-charismatic movement that challenged the church to take the return of Christ seriously, even to the point of abandoning home and possessions in expectation of his imminent appearance. In this respect they were the forerunners of ecstatic sects that have emerged at different times and led their followers astray with this false hope.[27] Centuries of experience have taught us to be wary of such groups, but Tertullian embraced the Montanists as the surviving remnant of apostolic Christianity and gave them some credibility. How much he really knew about them is hard to say, and the traditional view that he left the mainline church to join them is debatable.[28] It is significant that we first come across their teaching in Tertullian's reaction to a man he called Praxeas,[29] who went to Rome sometime in the late second century to report on Montanist activities in Asia Minor and insist that they be condemned. According to Tertullian, Praxeas "expelled the Paraclete and crucified the Father,"[30] a typically laconic statement that implies that Praxeas was not only anti-Montanist in his sentiments but also anti-Trinitarian—a modalist with views similar to those attributed to Sabellius.

Modern research suggests that Montanus may have seen himself as the Paraclete, but the word is taken from John's Gospel, where it clearly refers to the Holy Spirit.[31] It is also clear that by the time Montanism came to the notice of Tertullian, the Paraclete was identified with the Spirit and not with

[26] The best general introduction is still Henry B. Swete, *The Holy Spirit in the Ancient Church* (London: Macmillan, 1912). See also the unique collection of sources in J. Elowsky, ed., *We Believe in the Holy Spirit*, vol. 4 of Thomas C. Oden, series ed., *Ancient Christian Doctrine* (Downers Grove, IL: InterVarsity Press, 2009).

[27] See Christine Trevett, *Montanism: Gender, Authority, and the New Prophecy* (Cambridge: Cambridge University Press, 1996).

[28] See Gerald L. Bray, *Holiness and the Will of God* (London: Marshall, Morgan & Scott, 1979). Trevett, *Montanism*, is similarly reluctant to use Tertullian's evidence as a guide to the sect and its beliefs.

[29] Praxeas might mean "busybody" and therefore be a derogatory epithet rather than the name of the person concerned.

[30] Tertullian, *Adversus Praxean* 1.

[31] See Trevett, *Montanism*, 92–95 for the arguments.

Montanus, which makes the latter attribution seem highly unlikely. Tertullian acknowledged that the Holy Spirit was fully God, deriving his origin from the Father through the Son, a phrase that was to recur many times in later Trinitarian controversies. In his own words,

> I do not deduce the Son from anywhere but from the substance of the Father. Nor do I think the Spirit comes from anywhere but from the Father through the Son. Be careful not to destroy the monarchy.[32]

Tertullian's principal concern, it would seem, was to make sure that the Christian experience of God, which was mediated through the indwelling presence of the Holy Spirit and which focused on Christ as Lord and Savior, did not lose sight of monotheism, which was represented by the Father but not confined to him. The "monarchy" of which he spoke was the single source of the Godhead, which embraced all three persons, even if it was expressed in terms of relationship to the Father.[33]

Tertullian did not use the word Paraclete in a non-Montanist context, but soon after his time we have the testimony of Novatian, who quite clearly did. In a lengthy passage defending the deity of Christ, Novatian argued that he must be God because the Holy Spirit derived his divine commission from him. He expressed this by making explicit reference to John 14–16 in these terms:

> The Paraclete has received from Christ what he may declare. Therefore . . . Christ is greater than the Paraclete, because the Paraclete would not receive from Christ unless he were inferior to him. But the very fact that the Paraclete receives from Christ proves that Christ must be God.[34]

About the same time as this, Origen was writing the first systematic exposition of Christian doctrine, in which he devoted a special chapter to the Holy Spirit that followed immediately after ones devoted to God the Father and to the Son. Like Tertullian and Novatian, Origen also used the word Paraclete but mainly in quotations from John's Gospel. He did not emphasize its importance but concentrated instead on the Spirit's being and on his place in the divine order. He noted that there is no indication that the Holy Spirit was ever created, and distinguished him clearly from the divine Wisdom.[35] Origen concluded that "it was not by ongoing advancement that he came to be the

---

[32] Tertullian, *Adversus Praxean* 4.1.

[33] The Greek word *archê* means both "source/origin/beginning" and "rule." We are more accustomed to thinking of it as the rule of a single person, but in the philosophical (and theological) vocabulary of Tertullian's time the emphasis was on single origin or source.

[34] Novatian, *De Trinitate* 16.

[35] Origen, *De principiis* 1.3.3. On the creation of Wisdom, see Prov. 8:22.

Holy Spirit. . . . If that had been the case, he would never be part of the unity of the Trinity, along with the Father and the Son."[36] The Holy Spirit was not to be preferred over the other persons of the Godhead, or accorded a dignity greater than theirs.[37] Instead,

> As the Son (who alone knows the Father) reveals him to those whom he chooses, so the Holy Spirit (who alone searches the deep things of God) reveals God to those whom he decides. . . . But we must not suppose that the Holy Spirit derives his knowledge from the Son.[38]

As far as Origen was concerned, the Holy Spirit did not need the Son to tell him about the Father, because he was just as much God as the Son was. Origen lived before the time when the word "person" was part of the recognized theological vocabulary, so it is anachronistic to ask whether he thought of the Holy Spirit in personal terms, but what he said about him is certainly compatible with a personal conception of his identity. In the fourth century, when the question was raised again, Origen's teaching was the basis for the development of what became the orthodox doctrine, and to that extent we can accept him as the forerunner of Trinitarian belief in later times.

But when speaking about the relationship of the Holy Spirit to the other members of the Trinity, Origen could say things that would surprise later generations. For example, he insisted that, "It is essential to accept that the Holy Spirit came into being (*egeneto*) by the Word, because the Word is older than he is."[39] Any denial of the Holy Spirit's *genesis* through the Son would lead to saying that he is "unbegotten" (*agennêton*), which is not possible because that is true only of the Father. His argument ran as follows:

> Persuaded as we are that there are three *hypostases*, the Father, the Son, and the Holy Spirit, and believing that nothing is unbegotten except the Father, we think it is better and more reverent to say that all things were made through the Word, and that the Holy Spirit is the most excellent and the first in order of everything that was made by the Father through the Son.[40]

In the fourth century, Epiphanius of Salamis would use this to accuse Origen of believing that the Holy Spirit was a creature, but this seems most unlikely, since elsewhere he explicitly denied that.[41] Instead, we should probably

---

[36] Origen, *De principiis* 1.3.4.
[37] Ibid., 1.3.7.
[38] Ibid., 1.3.4.
[39] Origen, *Commentarium in Iohannis Evangelium* 2.9–10.
[40] Ibid., 2.10.
[41] Epiphanius of Salamis, *Panarion* 64.5; Origen, *De principiis* 1.33.

take the *genesis* of the Spirit as referring to his procession, from the Father in the first instance and then through the Son. When speaking of how the Holy Spirit was related to the Son, Origen went so far as to say that "the Holy Spirit seems to have a need for the Son to minister to his *hypostasis*, not only for it to exist, but also for it to be wise, rational, just, and whatever else we ought to think of him as being by his participation in the attributes of Christ."[42]

The persistent belief that Origen thought of the Holy Spirit as "subordinate" to the Father and the Son in a divine hierarchy, rather along the lines of Novatian, is not really justified by the evidence.[43] Origen certainly believed that there was an order within the Godhead, but Christians have always confessed that, without subscribing to any kind of hierarchical subordinationism that would make one person inferior to another. Novatian can be read in that way, but not Origen, who (as so often) comes out sounding more sophisticated than his contemporaries or immediate successors. Most of the latter took what he said for granted, and it was only much later, in quite different circumstances, that the need to develop the doctrine further became pressing and Origen's formulations began to appear inadequate and misleading.

The Holy Spirit in the Ancient Creeds

The relative oblivion into which the doctrine of the Holy Spirit settled in the late third and early fourth centuries can best be measured by the creed of the First Council of Nicea (325), which contained only one short sentence on the subject: "We believe in the Holy Spirit."[44] Of course, the Holy Spirit did not disappear from view altogether, and interest in him and in his work may well have been stronger in the church than the surviving records testify, but even if that was true, there was nothing about him comparable to the interest shown in the person of the Son during the great fourth- and fifth-century debates. People like Alexander of Alexandria, Eustathius of Antioch, and Marcellus of Ancyra, who played such a prominent part in the Christological debates of the Nicene and post-Nicene era, mentioned the Holy Spirit only in passing, and it is impossible to say what their doctrine concerning him really was.[45]

The first writer to give us any detailed exposition of the Holy Spirit was

[42] Origen, *Commentarium in Iohannis Evangelium* 2.76.

[43] Even R. P. C. Hanson, *The Search for the Christian Doctrine of God* (Edinburgh: T & T Clark, 1988), 738–739, subscribes to this view, though without examining its foundation. The question is discussed in Johannes Quasten, *Patrology*, 3 vols. (Utrecht and Antwerp: Spectrum/Newman, 1950–1960), 2:76–79.

[44] See J. N. D. Kelly, *Early Christian Creeds*, 3rd ed. (London: Longman, 1972), 216. The so-called Apostles' Creed reflects the same stage of theological development, though its present form is much later in date.

[45] See Hanson, *Search for the Christian Doctrine of God*, 739–740. Hanson writes, "When we examine the creeds and confessions of faith which were so plentifully produced between the years 325 and 360, we gain the overwhelming impression that no school of thought during that period was particularly interested in the Holy Spirit" (741).

Eusebius of Caesarea, and he clearly promoted a subordinationism that made the Spirit less than fully God. In his words,

> The Spirit, the Paraclete, is neither God [the Father] nor the Son, since he has not received his origin from the Father in the same way as the Son has, but is one of the things that came into existence through the Son.[46]

Eusebius avoided saying that the Spirit was a creature but he came as close to that as he could, and other statements of his reinforce this impression. For example, when describing the three things the church believed in, Eusebius said that they were the Son's human nature, the presence of the divine Son of God in that nature, and the fact that God was the Father of this composite Son.[47] He did not mention the Holy Spirit at all. As far as we can tell, Eusebius's doctrine of the Spirit was without precedent, but it rapidly became standard Arian teaching. Father and Son were both divine and worthy of our worship, but not the Holy Spirit.[48] Even outside Arian circles, this approach went unchallenged for a generation, mainly because there was so little interest in the Holy Spirit in any quarter.

Cyril of Jerusalem may be regarded as a partial exception to this, in that his liturgical and catechetical concerns forced him to pay more attention to the Spirit, whose presence was deeply embedded in the baptismal formula.[49] Cyril said that the Holy Spirit had the same dignity of status as the Father and the Son, and that he spoke the Word of God through the prophets of both Old and New Testaments.[50] In particular, he insisted that the Spirit was higher than any angel and that what the Father has given to the Son, the latter shares with the Spirit.[51] On the other hand, Cyril avoided any discussion of the Spirit's nature or *hypostasis*, mainly because there is no mention of these things in Scripture.[52] Cyril was imprecise and was apparently trying to stay out of the controversies of his time, but within the constraints imposed by such diplomacy he came as close as he could to confessing the divine status of the Holy Spirit:

> The Holy Spirit lives and subsists distinctly alongside the Father and the Son, with whom he is always present. He does not speak from the mouth

[46] Eusebius of Caesarea, *Theologia ecclesiastica* 3.6.164.

[47] Ibid., 1.6.64–65.

[48] Eusebius of Caesarea, *De fide*, 2 (23).60. See Hanson, *Search for the Christian Doctrine of God*, 741–743, for a list of councils and statements in which this teaching is implied, even if it is seldom explicitly stated.

[49] Cyril of Jerusalem, *Catecheses* 16.4 (208).

[50] Ibid., 4.16 (106, 108).

[51] Ibid., 16.23–24 (234, 236).

[52] Ibid., 16.24 (236).

of the Father and the Son as a kind of breath that dissolves into the air, but has a distinct subsistence of his own in which he speaks, works, governs, and sanctifies. Yet there is a single, undivided, harmonious plan of salvation for us that comes from the Father, Son, and Holy Spirit.[53]

Also of interest is a letter attributed to George of Laodicea, who represented the homoeousian party of Basil of Ancyra at the Council of Nice in 359 and whose views were later reckoned to be virtually identical to those held by the pro-Nicene Athanasius and his supporters. Interestingly, the letter demonstrates a certain affinity with Tertullian:

> The Easterners confess that there is one Godhead embracing everything through the Son in the Spirit. They confess one Godhead, one sovereignty, and one rule, but nevertheless they recognize the persons in the properties of their *hypostases*. . . . They confess the Holy Spirit, whom the Scripture calls the Paraclete, recognizing that he subsists from the Father through the Son.[54]

In contrast to this, the homoean Arians did not hesitate to reduce the Holy Spirit to the level of the angels, a position which perhaps reflected that of Arius himself. As Germinius of Sirmium (d. 375?) put it in his debate with the otherwise unknown Heraclianus,

> The Holy Spirit is the chief of the angels and archangels. Just as the Son is not like the Father in everything, so the Holy Spirit is not like the Son in everything either.[55]

Particularly important in this connection is the confession of faith attributed to Wulfila (Ulfilas), which established what later Arianism would assume was the correct teaching on the subject of the Holy Spirit. While strong in his affirmation of the Spirit's work as God's agent, Wulfila was in no doubt that he could not be called God in himself:

> The Holy Spirit is neither Father nor Son, but was made by the Father through the Son. He is not first or second, but was placed by the second in third place. He is not ingenerate or generate, but was created by the ingenerate through the only begotten [Son]. . . . The Holy Spirit, the Paraclete, cannot be called either God or Lord, but received his existence from God [the Father] through the Lord [the Son]. He is not the originator or the creator, but the illuminator,

[53] Ibid., 17.5 (256).
[54] Epiphanius of Salamis, *Panarion* 73.14.3–4 (288–289). Nice, a city in Thrace, must not be confused with Nicea.
[55] *Altercatio Heracliani cum Germinio*, printed in PG Supp. 347.

> sanctifier, teacher, leader, helper, and intercessor . . . without whom nobody can say that Jesus is Lord.[56]

In the Western church it was the influence of Tertullian that set the tone for what followed in the fourth century. Hilary of Poitiers repeated his views almost exactly, though he incorporated the doctrine of the Holy Spirit into a vision of the eternal Trinity, and not merely into the Trinity as revealed in human history. This comes across most clearly in his famous phrase, *infinitas in aeterno, species in imagine, usus in munere*, by which he defined the three persons.[57] This pithy statement is hard to translate, but it can be broken down as follows:

1. *Infinitas in aeterno* ("infinity in the eternal"): this is the Father, and emphasizes his infinite and eternal nature, completely free from time and space.
2. *Species in imagine* ("the particular in the image"): this is the Son, and refers primarily to the particular manifestation of him, in whom the divine *species* appears in a defined image or form.
3. *Usus in munere* ("the experience in the gift"): this is the Holy Spirit, and emphasizes our experience or "use" of God in his gift (*munus*).

The three complement each other and must ultimately be the same thing, since otherwise the scheme elaborated by Hilary would not make sense. Each of the persons has his distinct identity, but this identity depends on the others, or at least the identity of the second and third persons depends on that of the first. The first person could presumably exist independently, but if he did so, we would have no knowledge or experience of him, and in that case the subject would not be discussed at all.

Other Western writers before Augustine are much the same as Hilary and made no original contribution to the doctrine of the Holy Spirit, with the possible exception of Marius Victorinus, who clearly recognized the Spirit's divinity and consubstantiality with the Father and the Son:

> God is spirit, Jesus is spirit and the Holy Spirit is spirit. The three share the same substance and are therefore *homoousion*. The Holy Spirit is from Christ as Christ is from God, and in him the One is Three.[58]

This formula would be taken up by Augustine and become the basis for his classic exposition of Western Trinitarianism, but in his own time, Marius was

[56] Quoted by Auxentius of Milan in Roger Gryson, *Scolies ariennes sur le concile d'Aquilée* (Paris: Cerf, 1980), 50–52.
[57] Hilary of Poitiers, *De Trinitate* 2.1.
[58] Marius Victorinus, *Adversus Arium* 1.14.

unread. Latin-speakers did not understand his subtlety, and the Greeks did not read Latin, making him a voice in the wilderness or, as it turned out, a prophet before his time.[59]

Before that happened, though, the question of the Holy Spirit's divinity erupted in the East in an unexpected way. Serapion, the bishop of Thmuis in Egypt, found himself having to deal with a group of people who acknowledged the divinity of the Son but denied that of the Holy Spirit. He wrote to Athanasius for advice, which prompted the latter to write back with the first detailed exposition of the Spirit's relationship to the other persons of the Trinity that we possess.[60] Athanasius's letters were probably written in or around 360, when he was in his third exile, but we cannot be certain of that. What is clear is that the people he was writing against believed in a divine Dyad (Father and Son), but denied the divinity of the Holy Spirit.[61] To counter this, Athanasius quoted the witness of Scripture, without fully realizing that the texts both he and his opponents appealed to in support of their arguments do not mean what they claimed they did.

The reason for this is that the Greek translation they were using was faulty. One of the texts that his opponents appealed to was Amos 4:13, which they read as, "I am establishing thunder and creating Spirit, and announcing to men his Christ," when in fact the Hebrew original reads, "He who forms the mountains and creates the wind, and declares to man what is his thought." The misreading of "thought" as "Christ" is an obvious error, but translating "wind" as "spirit" is more defensible, since the Greek word *pneuma* can bear both meanings. To his credit, Athanasius spotted that and accused his opponents of transforming the literal meaning of "wind" into the allegorical sense of "Spirit," which had the effect of making the Holy Spirit a creature when he was not.[62] It was this error that led them into heresy. Athanasius used the word *tropos* for "allegory," and so labeled these people *Tropici*, which is one of the names by which they are known to us. Later on they, or others who held the same ideas, would come to be known as "Spirit-fighters," or *Pneumatomachi*, which was to become the standard term for them, though they would also be associated with Macedonius, the bishop of Constantinople, who was deposed in 360, though there are no objective grounds for this association.

Athanasius did not want to press the biblical evidence beyond what it was

[59] For Latin writers like Lucifer of Cagliari, Phoebadius of Agen, and Gregory of Elvira, see the remarks of Hanson, *Search for the Christian Doctrine of God*, 747. All of them basically followed Tertullian and added nothing new to his teaching.
[60] C. R. B. Shapland, *Letters of St. Athanasius concerning the Holy Spirit* (London: Epworth, 1951).
[61] Athanasius, *Epistula ad Serapionem* 1.2.
[62] Ibid., 1.3–10.

able to bear, and so after discussing Amos 4:13 (and also 1 Timothy 5:21, another verse that does not mean what the Tropici claimed it did),[63] he concluded,

> It is enough to know that the Spirit is not a creature and is not listed along with created things, for nothing alien is associated with the Trinity, but is inseparable and consistent in itself. This doctrine is enough for believers. Anything beyond that, the cherubim cover with their wings.[64]

Having made that point to his satisfaction, Athanasius went on to develop his own understanding of Trinitarian relations, which he described by starting with the Son:

> Since the Son is one [with God] as the living *logos*, his perfect and fully sanctifying and illuminating energy (*energeia*) and gift must also be one [with him]. He proceeds from the Father because he is light, being sent and given from (*para*) the Son, whom we confess comes from (*ek*) the Father.[65]

This text has to be read very carefully, not just because of what it meant at the time but because of the way it was to be interpreted later on. It is not clear whether there is any real difference between the Greek prepositions *para* and *ek*, both of which are translated as "from," but perhaps the former means "from alongside of" and the latter "from inside of." If that is true, it would imply that the second and third persons have different origins and perhaps different natures also. The Son would share the Father's being fully because he came "out of" him, but whether the Holy Spirit came out of the Son in the same way would be less clear. It must also be noted that, for Athanasius, the Spirit was the Son's "energy," a concept of uncertain meaning in his time but one that would be developed in later centuries and given a very precise definition in retrospect. What is clear is that Athanasius believed that the Holy Spirit shared the same nature as the Father and the Son, but as with his predecessors, it is not certain that he regarded him as a *hypostasis* in the same way that the other two persons were. In particular, we do not know whether he saw any distinctive role for the Spirit in the work of salvation, which he seems to have attributed to the work of the Son alone.

What Athanasius did succeed in doing was to convince the church of his day that the doctrine of the Holy Spirit had to be developed further, and that by the way in which they defined the Trinity, the fathers of the First Council

[63] It says, "In the presence of God and of Christ Jesus and of the elect angels," which allowed the Tropici to claim that the Holy Spirit must be an angel, since otherwise he would not be included in the verse.
[64] Athanasius, *Epistula ad Serapionem* 1.14.
[65] Ibid., 1.20.

of Nicea had made that an essential part of Christian belief. As he put it, they "did not divorce the Holy Spirit from the Father and the Son, but glorified him along with them in the single faith of the Holy Trinity, because the deity of the Trinity is one."[66]

Athanasius laid a foundation that was then built on by his contemporary Epiphanius of Salamis, who made it his business to diagnose heresies and provide answers to them. Epiphanius did not hesitate to say that the Holy Spirit was not a creature, and described him as "proceeding from the Father and receiving from the Son," a formula that was to have a great future ahead of it.[67] But he also said that the Holy Spirit proceeded from both the Father and the Son, apparently without seeing any difference between that and the idea of proceeding from the former and receiving from the latter.[68] It is also to be noticed that Epiphanius sometimes observed the same distinction between *para* and *ek* that we find in Athanasius.[69] Athanasius twice said that the Spirit was *homoousion* with the Father and the Son, and Epiphanius had no hesitation on that score either.[70] In fact, he developed the idea in a way that Athanasius never did:

> The Trinity is always of the same *ousia*. There is no *ousia* apart from the Godhead, nor Godhead apart from the *ousia*, but the Godhead [Father], Son, and Holy Spirit all come from the same Godhead.[71]

One of the difficulties in interpreting Epiphanius and his contemporaries is that the theological terminology they used was not yet set in stone, so that it is not always clear what they meant. For example, in the text just quoted, Epiphanius went on to say that the Godhead had three persons (*prosôpa*) and a threefold *hypostasis*, but whether the latter is meant to be the equivalent of *prosôpon* or *ousia* is not clear—either is possible.[72] There is also the usual conflation of the Godhead with the Father, which in this context is particularly unfortunate. All this is a reminder to us that the doctrine of the Holy Spirit and of the Trinity was still developing its terminology, and we must be careful not to read later definitions back into sources like these unless there is good reason to do so.

Another theologian who contributed to this development was Didymus the

[66] Recorded by Theodoret of Cyrus, *Historia ecclesiastica* 4.3.14.

[67] Epiphanius of Salamis, *Ancoratus* 11.3, 73:1–2; *Panarion* 62.4.12, 69.18.4.

[68] Epiphanius of Salamis, *Ancoratus* 67.1, 70.7, 71.1.

[69] Ibid., 73.1.2.

[70] Compare Athanasius, *Epistula ad Serapionem* 1.27, 2.6, with Epiphanius of Salamis, *Panarion* 74.11.2.

[71] Epiphanius of Salamis, *Ancoratus* 6.10. Note that he uses the same word "Godhead" for the Father and for the divine nature.

[72] Epiphanius of Salamis, *Ancoratus* 67.7.

Blind of Alexandria, whose work survives in a translation made by Jerome. Didymus did not hesitate to call the Spirit a "substance" (*hypostasis*), adding for good measure that he comes from God the Father but is sent into the world by both the Father and the Son. This distinction would become important later on and helps us to understand the context in which Epiphanius spoke of the Spirit's procession from both of the other persons of the Trinity.[73] But it must also be remembered that Didymus was misinterpreted by Ambrose of Milan, who declared without ambiguity, "When the Holy Spirit proceeds from the Father and the Son, he is not separated from the Father, nor is he separated from the Son."[74] Presumably Ambrose did not notice that he had subtly misrepresented Didymus, but whether he realized that or not, it was his teaching, and not that of Didymus, that was to pass into the theology of Augustine and to become fixed in the Western tradition as a result.

The challenge of developing the doctrine of the Holy Spirit was taken up by Basil of Caesarea, who undertook the task mainly because the work of Athanasius and other pro-Nicene theologians had shown that there was a serious gap in Christian teaching that had to be filled if further heresy was to be avoided.[75] Basil's first foray into the field was an attack on the doctrine of a certain Eunomius, a homoean Arian whose views were almost identical to those of Wulfila.[76] Shortly after that, he came up against a group of Pneumatomachi who might best be characterized as homoeousian rather than as homoean in the way that Eunomius was. Their chief representative was Eustathius of Sebaste (300?–377?), originally a friend of Basil's but alienated from him because Basil felt there was a need to define the doctrine of the Holy Spirit more carefully, whereas Eustathius did not. Eustathius and his followers can be characterized as people who resisted theological systematization because it seemed to them to be going beyond the teaching of Scripture. Many of them were practically homoousian in their beliefs, and it was easy for them to assimilate into the pro-Nicene party when it became clear that the latter were in the ascendant. The fact that they were motivated more by a hesitant conservatism than by any defined belief of their own also made it hard for them to form a determined opposition to what was happening. The flavor of this diversity and the confusion

[73] Didymus of Alexandria, *De Spiritu Sancto* 23, 26.

[74] Ambrose of Milan, *De Spiritu Sancto* 1.11.120. It should be said that Jerome, who translated Didymus, was aware of Ambrose's work and commented unfavorably on it. See Hanson, *Search for the Christian Doctrine of God*, 756, n. 98.

[75] On Basil and his approach to theology, see Philip Rousseau, *Basil of Caesarea* (Berkeley: University of California Press, 1994); Bernard Sesboüé, *Saint Basile et la Trinité* (Paris: Desclée, 1998); Markos A. Orphanos, *Ho Hyios kai to Hagion Pneuma eis tên Triadologian tou Megalou Basileiou* (Athens: G. K. Parisianos, 1976); Geōrgios D. Martzelos, *Ousia kai energeiai tou Theou kata ton Megan Basileion* (Thessalonica: Pournaras, 1993).

[76] Basil of Caesarea, *Adversus Eunomium* 2.32 (645–648), 3.1 (653), 3.3.5 (665).

it could cause was captured shortly after Basil's death by his friend and erstwhile colleague Gregory of Nazianzus:

> Some assume that the Holy Spirit is an energy, some say that he is a creature, some that he is God, and some cannot decide which of these positions is true because they respect the Bible, which they claim does not clearly support any of them. . . . Some admit that there is a Trinity in God, but claim that its members are completely different from each other. One of them is infinite in being and energy, another is infinite in energy but not being, while the third is infinite in neither. Others give them titles like Creator, Co-operator, and Servant, believing that this dignity, order, or ranking corresponds to a hierarchy of realities which the names represent.[77]

What was common to the Pneumatomachi, and makes it possible for us to identify them as a group, was that they all agreed that the Holy Spirit was not God. He might be recognized as divine, eternal, and Lord, but not in the same way or to the same degree as the Father and the Son were. However they expressed it, the Holy Spirit was a lesser being who was not to be worshiped or even glorified, except perhaps with a lesser glory than the one accorded to the Father and the Son. In their eyes, the Spirit could not take part in creation (though whether he was himself a creature was a matter of dispute), he did not sit or reign with the Father and the Son in heaven, he was not omnipresent, and could not raise anyone from the dead, though he did have the power to convert the living to Christ.[78]

The Pneumatomachi derived their strength from their opponents' greatest weakness, which was the apparent inadequacy of the scriptural testimony used to support the assertions those opponents were making. Thus, for example, the Pneumatomachi wanted to know how the generation of the Son differed from the procession of the Spirit and argued that if the Holy Spirit was divine he must be either a second Son of the Father or a grandson, which they (rightly) thought was absurd.[79] Their opponents' constant appeal to the Trinitarian baptismal formula as proof of the equality of the three persons in God struck them as a cry of desperation, particularly as they could counter it with a number of biblical texts that seemed to prove the contrary.[80] In fact, the texts they quoted were not as clear as they thought, since they focused either on the Spirit's mis-

[77] Gregory of Nazianzus, *Orationes* 31.5.5.

[78] See Gregory of Nyssa, *Adversus Macedonianos de Spiritu Sancto*, 97–98.

[79] Epiphanius of Salamis, *Ancoratus* 71.1; *Panarion* 69.18.5; Gregory of Nazianzus, *Orationes* 31.7; and Basil of Caesarea, *Homiliae* 24.6.

[80] On the appeal to baptism, see Eusebius of Caesarea *Adversus Marcellum* 1.1.8; Athanasius, *Epistulae ad Serapionem* 1.28–30, 33; 3.6; 4.5; Basil of Caesarea, *De Spiritu Sancto* 10.26. Among the texts appealed to by the Pneumatomachi were Luke 10:22; John 1:3; 3:5; 6:46; 7:39; 14:26; 15:26; Acts 10:22; 1 Cor. 2:10; and Gal. 4:6.

sion in the world (which everyone agreed depended on the will of the Father and the Son) or else on the unproved assumption that any mention of an angel appearing to someone had to be taken as a reference to the Holy Spirit.

All of this left Basil in something of a dilemma. On the one hand, he agreed with much of what the Pneumatomachi were saying about the work of the Holy Spirit, including his dependence on the Father and the Son, but he wanted to go beyond what the Spirit *did* to a deeper understanding of who the Spirit *was*. Ultimately, he realized that these two things could not be separated, because it was the identity of the Holy Spirit as God that validated and guaranteed his work as something divine. He explained this as follows:

> We cannot conceive of the Holy Spirit as a finite nature subject to change or alteration like the creation. Rather, we must think of him as an intelligent essence (*ousia*), infinite in power, unlimited in greatness, immeasurable in time, and generous in the benefits that he has at his disposal. . . . He confers fulfillment on others but needs nothing himself. He cannot be increased by addition, but is full in himself. . . . He fills everything by his power but can be shared only by those who are worthy. Not everyone participates in him equally, because he distributes his power according to the proportion of faith. . . . The Spirit is present to each one who receives him in a unique one-to-one relationship. He gives everyone enough grace to enjoy him as far as they can, but no one can know him to the full extent of his power.[81]

This passage gives us a clear insight into the nature of Basil's doctrine of the Spirit. On the one hand, what he said makes it clear that the Spirit does things that only God can do, and that he does them not by delegation from the Father or the Son, but because he is intrinsically capable of acting in that way. On the other hand, the text does not actually say that the Spirit is God, and Basil was never that explicit in any of his writings. He nowhere claimed that the Spirit was *homoousion* with the Father and the Son, though it is hard to see how he could have denied it, and Basil did use the term when referring to the Trinity as a whole.[82] He also said that the Holy Spirit "shares the Father's nature, not created by his command but continually radiating from the substance," a convoluted form of expression that suggests he was trying to confess the *homoousion* without actually saying so.[83] In the end, Basil never clearly explained where the Spirit's power and authority came from, or how they were

[81] Basil of Caesarea, *De Spiritu Sancto* 9.22. There is a critical edition of this work in the series *Sources Chrétiennes*, along with an important introduction to it by B. Pruche, in Basile de Césarée, *Sur le Saint-Esprit* (Paris: Cerf, 1968).
[82] Basil of Caesarea, *De fide*, 4.
[83] Basil of Caesarea, *Homiliae* 15.2.

related to the power and authority of the other persons of the Godhead. The closest he came to that was in a letter he wrote to justify the position he took against Eustathius:

> We never divorce the Paraclete from his conjunction with the Father and the Son, for when our minds are lit up by the Spirit we look up to the Son, and in him we behold the Father as in an image.[84]

The same sense that there is an order in our experience of God and in his self-revelation to us also comes out in *De Spiritu Sancto*, though as usual it is a description rather than a definition of the process:

> Knowledge of God is from one Spirit through one Son to one Father. Conversely, essential goodness, sanctification, and royal dignity travel from the Father through the Only begotten to the Spirit.[85]

Basil's reluctance to define the Holy Spirit as a *hypostasis* comparable to the Son was due to his realization that the Bible is not that explicit. The baptismal formula was about as close to that as Scripture came, but important as that was, it was slim evidence on which to base such an important doctrine. As a result, Basil felt obliged to concentrate heavily on the Spirit's work, which was clearly that of God, and leave statements about the nature of his being to be culled from the somewhat nebulous deposit of tradition, which he claimed went back to the apostles.[86] That there was a long tradition of offering worship to the Holy Spirit was not in doubt, but no one could say for sure how far back it went. Its apparent absence from the New Testament, while not conclusive evidence that it was not of apostolic origin, was not encouraging. In the end, it must be said that Basil left the doctrine of the Holy Spirit in an unfinished state, and it would be the task of Gregory of Nazianzus to take matters further.

Gregory did that in his theological orations, which were delivered at Constantinople two years after Basil's death and in the run-up to the council that met there in 381. In the fifth and last of these orations he dealt with questions about the Holy Spirit, and it is there, more than anywhere else, that we find the fullest articulation of the doctrine before it was inserted into the so-called Nicene Creed.[87] Gregory began his discussion with a concise statement of who the persons of the Trinity were in relation to each other. As he saw them, the

---

[84] Basil of Caesarea, *Epistula* 226.3.
[85] Basil of Caesarea, *De Spiritu Sancto* 18.47.
[86] Basil of Caesarea, *Adversus Eunomium* 3.7; *De Spiritu Sancto* 9.22; *Epistulae* 54, 236.1, 258.2.
[87] The five theological orations are numbered 27–31 in Gregory's complete works, which is why the fifth of them is Oration 31. For an analysis of them, see Christopher A. Beeley, *Gregory of Nazianzus on the Trinity and the Knowledge of God* (Oxford: Oxford University Press, 2008).

Son was "light from the Father who is light," whom we see "in the Holy Spirit who is light."[88] Light defines the being of God, as many New Testament passages tell us, and so it was in relation to this that Gregory defined the persons, though there is no verse that explicitly refers to the Holy Spirit in that way.[89]

Gregory was not daunted by that, however, and went on to tackle the issues raised by the Pneumatomachi. When they claimed that if the Spirit was really God, he must be either begotten or unbegotten but since he was neither, he could not be God, Gregory retorted that sonship was an analogy drawn from human life and could not be made an objective criterion for deciding what the inner relations of the persons of the Godhead had to be. The fact that the relationship between the first and second persons is described in that way says nothing about how the third person relates to the others, and to extend the analogy to cover him was to go beyond the evidence of Scripture.[90] What the New Testament plainly states is that the Holy Spirit *proceeds* from the Father (John 15:26), and it is this concept that must determine how we understand his relationship to the other persons of the Trinity. Gregory had no idea what divine procession actually was—it was a mystery to him—but he was quite sure that it was different from divine generation, and that the Spirit was therefore not a second Son or grandson.[91] Similarly, when confronted with the argument that if everything was made through the Son, as John 1:2 claimed, the Holy Spirit must be one of the Son's creatures, Gregory simply replied that if the verse were to be taken that literally, the Son would have created the Father too, which was absurd![92]

Unlike Basil, Gregory had no hesitation in calling the Spirit God and in affirming that he was *homoousion* with the Father and the Son, because even if that was not explicitly stated in the Bible, it was an inference that was legitimately drawn from it. Gregory may be credited with the invention of the word *ekporeusis* ("procession") as a description of how the Holy Spirit revealed himself, but he was by no means tied to this as a technical term, and in other orations he was happy to use synonymous expressions such as *proodos* ("progression") and *ekpempsis* ('mission").[93] Later theological debates would refine this usage, without ceasing to appeal to Gregory as the authority for it, but he himself enjoyed the flexibility of a pioneer and did not have to bow to the weight of an already established tradition.

[88] Gregory of Nazianzus, *Orationes* 31.3.
[89] See John 8:12; James 1:17; 1 John 1:5.
[90] Gregory of Nazianzus, *Orationes* 31.7.
[91] Ibid., 31.8–9.
[92] Ibid., 31.12.
[93] Ibid., 30.19 and 25.16.

His freedom in this respect was particularly important in the way that he dealt with the biblical evidence and the problem of nonbiblical tradition, which had so troubled Basil. Gregory understood how weak Basil's appeal to unwritten "apostolic" tradition was, but he also knew why Basil had felt obliged to make it. In trying to resolve the dilemma posed by the incomplete nature of the New Testament data, Gregory came up with a much better solution. Rather than look to extraneous sources, he maintained that it was legitimate to draw conclusions from what Scripture actually says and use those conclusions as if they were divinely inspired. As examples, he gave the case of a man who says "twice five" or "twice seven," and argued that on the basis of statements like that, we can claim that he was talking about ten or fourteen, even if he never used those words.[94] Gregory applied this principle to the biblical self-revelation of God, which he said proceeded gradually by building on earlier self-manifestations and developing them one step at a time. As he put it,

> The Old Testament openly proclaimed the Father, but the Son is more blurred. The New Testament revealed the Son, but only sketched out the deity of the Spirit. The Spirit is now resident and active among us, giving us a clearer manifestation of himself. It was not a good idea to proclaim the Son openly as long as the deity of the Father was not universally acknowledged, nor was it good for us to be burdened with the Holy Spirit (if I may express the matter so crudely) as long as the Son's divinity was not fully accepted.[95]

In other words, we must take one thing at a time. Gregory even suggested that the divinity of the Holy Spirit was one of the things that the disciples could not bear as long as Jesus was still with them.[96] In this way, Gregory combined Scripture and tradition by interpreting the latter as the history of biblical interpretation. The theologians of the church were not relying on practices that had no known origin but on implications that could legitimately be drawn out from the biblical text and used to support their arguments. It was in this way, he claimed, that the full deity of the Holy Spirit could be affirmed on the basis of Scripture, even if that was not clearly stated in its pages.

Gregory of Nyssa, Basil's younger brother and the third of the great Cappadocian fathers, had little to add to what the others had already said. He did, however, have a gift for striking imagery, and he used it to get across the message that the Holy Spirit could proceed from the Father through the Son without being in any way inferior to them. One example he used was that of

[94] Ibid., 31.24–25.
[95] Ibid., 31.25.
[96] Ibid., 31.27. See John 16:12.

three torches, in which the flame of the first was used to light the second, and the flame of the second was used to light the third. This respected the order in which the persons of the Trinity came into being but did not compromise their equality, since all three torches burned with the same fire.[97] On the personal identity of the Holy Spirit, for example, he relied almost entirely on the baptismal formula and made little attempt to go beyond it.[98] But in one of his minor works he quoted what he said was a creed composed by Gregory Thaumaturgus, more than a hundred years before the great council of 381. It is unlikely that the creed went back that far because its language is too sophisticated and reflects the struggles of a later time, but it sums up where the Eastern church had got to with its doctrine of the Holy Spirit on the eve of the council, and the fact that it was readily endorsed by Gregory of Nyssa shows that it represented the mainstream of Greek theological thought in the late fourth century, if not earlier. In the form that it has come down to us, the creed reads,

> [We believe in] one Holy Spirit who possesses his existence (*hyparxis*) from God, and is manifested to men through the Son. He is the perfect image of the perfect Son, the cause of life for those who have life, a holy source and minister of sacred holiness. In him is manifested God the Father, who is above all and in all, and God the Son, who is through all, a perfect Trinity in glory, eternity, and sovereignty, neither divided nor differentiated.[99]

Whether Gregory ever went further than this in developing the idea of a double procession of the Holy Spirit is a matter of controversy. A letter attributed to Basil of Caesarea but now generally believed to be the work of Gregory of Nyssa makes it plain that everything in creation traces its origin to the Holy Spirit, who depends on the Son to whom he is inseparably joined, but at the same time the letter maintains a careful distinction between the procession of the Holy Spirit, which is said to be from the Father, and the close relationship that he has with the Son, who knows the Spirit "through himself and with himself," whatever that was supposed to imply.[100] Another key passage occurs in one of Gregory's sermons on the Lord's Prayer, where he said that "the Holy Spirit is said to be from the Father and is testified as being from the Son, . . . so the Holy Spirit who is from the Father is also the Spirit of Christ,"[101] but the authenticity of these words is disputed and the general consensus today is that

[97] Gregory of Nyssa, *De Spiritu Sancto adversus pneumatomachos Macedonianos* 3.
[98] Gregory of Nyssa, *Contra Eunomium* 2.1–2. See Hanson, *Search for the Christian Doctrine of God*, 787, for a general assessment of Gregory's teaching.
[99] Gregory of Nyssa, *Vita Gregorii Thaumaturgi*, in PG 46, coll. 912–913.
[100] Basil of Caesarea, *Epistula* 38.4.
[101] Gregory of Nyssa, *De oratione Dominica*, 3.

they were interpolated by a later hand desirous of making Gregory appear to support the double procession of the Spirit.[102] We must therefore conclude that Gregory of Nyssa was a typical Cappadocian in his Trinitarian doctrine, open to the desirability of establishing a link between the Son and the Holy Spirit but resistant to the suggestion that this could somehow be assimilated to the latter's procession from the Father.

It was at the Council of Constantinople that the labors of the Cappadocian fathers, and of Athanasius before them, bore fruit in the clause on the Holy Spirit that was added to the creed at that time. By 381 it was clearly impossible to rely on the terse statements of earlier times, and a more developed exposition was required, if only to counter the influence of the Pneumatomachi, who were present at the council in some numbers. The result is well known to us today because it is still regularly recited in the so-called Nicene Creed:

> We believe in the Holy Spirit, the Lord and giver of life
> Who proceeds from the Father
> Who together with the Father and Son is worshiped and glorified
> Who spoke by the prophets

This is essentially the doctrine of the Spirit that was taught by Basil of Caesarea. By 381 it had come to seem like a compromise between the moderate Pneumatomachi and Gregory of Nazianzus, who had gone considerably farther and was unhappy that the council was not prepared to follow him all the way.[103] The creed skirts around the question of the Holy Spirit's personal name, making no mention of the Paraclete, but points out that he is the Lord, basing this assertion on 2 Corinthians 3:17. In saying this, there is no doubt that the creed was equating the Spirit with the Father and the Son by using the word "Lord" in its traditional sense of Yahweh, the God of the Old Testament. The Holy Spirit is not Lord in relation to the Father and the Son, except insofar as they are also called Lord—it is in that sense a shared designation, just like "Holy" and "Spirit."

The procession from the Father came straight from John 15:26 and was already in theological use, though it may not have been widely known as early as 381. Even so, the clear biblical reference could not be doubted and would have been accepted by everyone at the council, however influenced by Pneumatomachian ideas they may have been. That the Spirit was worshiped and

---

[102] See Quasten, *Patrology*, 3:267–268. But Quasten's favorable view has been overturned by Werner Jaeger, "Eine dogmatische Interpolation im Text von Gregors Schrift *De oratione Dominica* und ihr kirchenpolitischer Hintergrund," in Hermann Dörries, ed., *Gregor von Nyssa's Lehre vom Heiligen Geist* (Leiden: Brill, 1966), 122–153. See especially 133.

[103] Gregory of Nazianzus, *De vita sua*, 1750–1758.

glorified along with the Father and the Son was probably a direct reference to the baptismal formula as found in Matthew 28:19, but there is no doubt that it was inserted into the creed in order to counteract Pneumatomachian claims to the contrary.

The last clause was taken directly from 2 Peter 1:21, which states that "no prophecy was ever produced by the will of man, but men spoke from God as they were carried along by the Holy Spirit." When combined with 2 Timothy 3:16, which says that "all Scripture is breathed out by God" it is as clear an indication of the Spirit's divinity as it is possible to get. Modern readers would probably say that this second verse refers more to the work of the Spirit than to his personal identity, but although that is understandable, it is not the emphasis that was originally intended. The men who composed the creed certainly believed in the divine inspiration of Scripture, but they were using this belief, and the fact that it was the Holy Spirit who inspired it, not to define the nature of the Bible but to identify the person of the Holy Spirit as fully divine. It certainly reflects Basil's tendency to move from what the Spirit does to who the Spirit is, but we must not lose sight of the aim that both he and the creed had in confessing that.

The most important question about the creed is its date of composition and the authority that it was originally given. The first unambiguous mention of it came only at the Council of Chalcedon in 451, when the archdeacon of Constantinople read it out as the creed of 381, apparently to general surprise.[104] The matter is complicated further by the fact that the Council of Ephesus in 431 re-promulgated the Creed of Nicea (325) and decreed that nothing should be added or taken away from it, which the creed of 381 obviously had done.[105] Were the fathers of Ephesus ignorant of the 381 creed, or did they not recognize its authority?

There is no clear answer to that question, but that it was a problem for some is indicated by an anonymous dialogue between a "Macedonian" (that is, a Pneumatomachus) and a pro-Nicene orthodox Christian, in which the former accused the latter of having expanded the Creed of Nicea and the latter admitted it.[106] The dialogue itself almost certainly predates Chalcedon by several years, and this part of it suggests that it may be picking up a discussion that followed the prohibition on additions made at the Council of Ephesus, since it would have little meaning otherwise. If that is so, then the creed of 381 must

---

[104] The standard work is J. N. D. Kelly, *Early Christian Creeds*, 296–367, from which these details are taken. See also Hanson, *Search for the Christian Doctrine of God*, 812–820, who accepts Kelly's conclusions and elaborates on them.

[105] *Conciliorum oecumenicorum decreta* (Bologna: Istituto per le Scienze Religiose, 1973), 65.

[106] *Second Macedonian dialogue*, in PG 28.1, col. 1204.

have been known and in fairly wide use before 451, although fears of violating the strictures of Ephesus may have led to its relative neglect in the years immediately preceding Chalcedon. What is certain is that after 451 it became the standard creedal text and replaced the earlier Nicene one to such an extent that it came to be regarded as the original creed of 325, with an addition or two made in 381. By then the Pneumatomachi were a distant memory and the church's teaching about the Holy Spirit had apparently settled down to a broad acceptance of the clauses composed by the First Council of Constantinople.

16

Spirit of the Father, Spirit of the Son

Double Procession?

In Trinitarian terms, the dispute with the Pneumatomachi was primarily about the relationship of the Holy Spirit to the Father. It seemed obvious to them that the Father was the Father of the Son, since the two terms are complementary. But does the Holy Spirit call the first person of the Trinity his Father, and if he does, why is he not a second son (or perhaps grandson)? As we have already seen, Athanasius and the Cappadocians struggled to point out that the names of the persons of the Godhead are not meant to be taken that literally. It was possible for the Holy Spirit to be fully God and equal to the other persons without being the Son's twin brother and without relating to the first person in precisely the same way that the Son does. It was to express this difference that the New Testament spoke of the generation of the Son but of the procession of the Holy Spirit, in both cases from the Father, who was universally recognized as the ultimate "Godhead" or source of divinity (*pêgê tês theotêtos* in Greek, *fons deitatis* in Latin).[1] To say that the Holy Spirit proceeds from the Father was to acknowledge that he is as fully God as the Son is, but in a different way and therefore with a different relationship to the other persons. But just as Gregory of Nazianzus found it impossible to say what the difference between generation and procession actually was, so (we may assume) he could not say precisely how the Spirit's relationship to the Father was different from that of the Son. Having said that, Gregory knew that there was some kind of difference between them and believed that if the two terms were synonymous, the two persons (Son and Spirit) would be interchangeable, which they are not. In other words, we

[1] It seems that the exact phrase does not occur until the sixth century, when we find it in Pseudo-Dionysius the Areopagite, *De divinis nomnibus* 2.5, but the idea was common long before then. See, for example, Hippolytus of Rome, *Contra Noetum* 11; Athanasius, *Contra Sabellianos* 11; Basil of Caesarea, *Contra Eunomium* 2.25; Theodoret of Cyrus, *Adversus haereses* 5.3.

are dealing here with a mystery, but also with a fact that cannot be ignored merely because we do not understand it.[2]

The relationship of the Holy Spirit to the Father was settled by the First Council of Constantinople in 381 and has never been seriously challenged since then. The relationship of the Spirit to the Son, however, remains a bone of contention between Eastern and Western Christians that is serious enough to prevent the reunion of the churches.[3] At first sight, it is hard to see why this should be so. That the Holy Spirit is in some sense the Spirit of the Son is clear from the New Testament—God has sent the Spirit of his Son into our hearts, crying "Abba, Father!"[4] That the Father and the Son often act together (as in creation) is also clear, so there would seem to be relatively little difficulty in saying that if the Holy Spirit proceeds from the Father, he might equally well proceed from the Son. It sounds simple and logical when put like that, but the evolution of the controversy has been very different. Even in 381, a statement like that one might easily have been misconstrued as a concession to the Pneumatomachi, who could have interpreted it as meaning that the Holy Spirit was a creature made by the Father and Son acting together! As it was, the Western church eventually came to accept a double procession of the Holy Spirit, but the Eastern churches have never agreed to that. Instead, they have developed their own understanding of the matter which is at odds with the West and have produced a kind of Trinitarian theology that now seems to be irreconcilable with both Roman Catholic and Protestant teaching on the subject. Why and how this happened is what we must now examine in greater detail.

We may begin with what was generally agreed on in 381, if not before. That was that if the *hypostasis* of the Father personifies the fount of deity, and if the Holy Spirit is God, then the Spirit must derive his existence from the Father. That is enough to establish that he is God, and there is no pressing need to refer to the Son at all. Would the Cappadocians have objected, as later defenders of their Trinitarian theology did, that if the Spirit proceeded from the Son as well as from the Father, the Son would automatically be the source of deity along with the Father, thereby blurring the Father's unique identity and establishing two sources of divinity? This is not certain, because no one asked them that question, but it is easy to see how a case could be argued along those lines.

[2] Gregory of Nazianzus, *Orationes* 31.12.

[3] It is certainly not the only question that divides the East from the West, and opinions differ as to how important it really is. It is not hard to imagine a situation in which other factors will prevent reunion even after agreement on the Spirit's procession has been reached, but it is safe to say that no reunion will occur without a common understanding on this subject.

[4] Gal. 4:6.

Some hesitation is called for, however, because Basil's contemporary, Epiphanius of Salamis, did discuss this and came up with a complex answer to it. Writing around 374 (several years before the First Council of Constantinople), Epiphanius said,

> I dare to say that . . . [no one knows] the Spirit except the Father and the Son, from whom he proceeds and from whom he receives. And [no one knows] the Father and the Son, except the Holy Spirit who is from (*para*) the Father and out of (*ek*) the Son.[5]

Unlike the Cappadocians, Epiphanius tried to define the relationship of the Son to the Holy Spirit, but what he said about it is not as clear as it might appear at first sight. Epiphanius seems to have said that the Spirit proceeds from the Father and the Son in slightly different (though, as Gregory of Nazianzus would later put it, undefinable) ways and receives (his divinity?) from both of them. Yet elsewhere, he expressed himself differently and with greater clarity, on this point in particular. He wrote,

> The Spirit is always with the Father and the Son. He is not the Father's sibling, nor is he begotten or created, nor is he the brother of the Son or the child of the Father. *He proceeds from the Father and receives from the Son.* He is not different from the Father and the Son but of the same being, of the same Godhead, of the Father and the Son, with the Father and the Son. The Spirit of Christ is the Spirit of the Father.[6]

Here Epiphanius clarified what he meant earlier when he said that the Spirit proceeds and receives from the Father and the Son. What he intended to say was that the Spirit proceeds from the former and receives from the latter, an assertion which chimes in more readily with the teaching of Basil.

Epiphanius also seems to have placed some weight on the use of the Greek prepositions *para* ("from") and *ek* ("out of"), which we have already noted elsewhere. Originally there was a genuine distinction between these prepositions, *para* meaning "from the side of" (as in "parallel") as opposed to *ek* ("from out of"), but this nuance was lost even before the composition of the New Testament. John 15:26 illustrates this very well because there the phrase "proceeds from the Father" is *ekporeuetai para to Patros*, where *ek* is part of the verb but *para* is the actual preposition. John clearly thought of them as synonymous, and the same must be true of Epiphanius, if only because had he made a

[5] Epiphanius of Salamis, *Ancoratus* 73.
[6] Epiphanius of Salamis, *Panarion* 62 (italics mine).

distinction between them, it would have been the wrong one. To have said that the Spirit came *out* of the Son but only from *alongside* the Father would have been the exact opposite of what he and his contemporaries understood by the distinction, as the above quotation of Athanasius (who used the prepositions "correctly") demonstrates.

That, however, is not all that we find in Epiphanius. Elsewhere he was prepared to accept that the Holy Spirit is "from both" the Father and the Son,[7] a phrase which apparently clarifies what he said at the end of the second quote given above and which has suggested to many Western interpreters that he believed that the Holy Spirit proceeds from both the Father and the Son. Unfortunately for them, however, Epiphanius's language is more subtle than this. What he said was that the Holy Spirit shares the common being (*ousia*) of the Father and the Son, a point that has never been in dispute. The question of the relationship between the Spirit and the Son is not a matter of the divine being which they share, but of the "cause" or origin of his *hypostasis*. The Spirit shares the Son's divine being because he proceeds from the Father, from whom both the Son and the Spirit receive their divinity, but this does not necessarily mean that Epiphanius believed that the Spirit relates to the Son in the same way as he relates to the Father.

This is what the debate is all about, and here the testimony of Epiphanius is of no help to the Western cause. Most probably, he came as close to the Western position as he did only because he knew nothing about it. Had he been aware of a debate about the possibility of a double procession of the Holy Spirit from both the Father and the Son, he would almost certainly have expressed himself differently and with far greater caution. We do not know that for sure, of course, but the logic of Epiphanius's overall argument suggests that he would have pulled back from the brink and recoiled from any "double procession" doctrine, if only because that would not really have corresponded with his overall thesis. As we have already noted, when he was being precise, Epiphanius said that the Spirit proceeds from the Father and receives from the Son, whatever that might imply:

> We believe in the Holy Spirit who spoke in the law, taught by the prophets, descended to the Jordan [in the baptism of Jesus], spoke by the apostles, and lives in the saints. This is how we believe in him: he is the Holy Spirit, the Spirit of God, the perfect Spirit, the Spirit Paraclete, uncreated, proceeding from (*ek*) the Father and receiving from (*ek*) the Son.[8]

[7] Epiphanius of Salamis, *Ancoratus* 67.
[8] Epiphanius of Salamis, *Symbolum fidei*, in Denzinger, *Enchiridion*, no. 44.

The Creed of Epiphanius is an elaboration of the one produced at Constantinople in 381 and for that reason it may not be authentic, though it seems to reflect his thought well enough. Suffice it to say that as far as the Spirit's ultimate origin was concerned, Epiphanius located it in his procession from the Father. Whatever he received from the Son he obtained as a result of that procession, but the two things were not the same. His procession from the Father gave him his hypostatic (or personal, as we would now say) identity, but his reception from the Son gave him his mission in the world. This distinction enabled Epiphanius and those after him to state that the Spirit is the Spirit of the Son as far as his mission is concerned, without being committed to saying that he is the Spirit of the Son with respect to his ultimate origin.

Western theologians have always questioned the validity of this distinction and insisted that what the Spirit does (in his mission) must reflect who the Spirit is (in his origin), but Eastern theologians who have followed Epiphanius do not interpret him that way and have insisted that, here as elsewhere, their Western counterparts have oversimplified a highly complex matter and failed to do justice to the teaching of Scripture on the subject. Some evidence for the Western tendency to simplify matters can be gleaned from Hilary of Poitiers, whose testimony is especially interesting in that he was one of the few Western theologians who had direct contact with the Greek-speaking world in the mid-fourth century. Exiled to Phrygia from 356 to 359, he was able to learn Eastern theology firsthand and later transmitted it to the Latin-speaking world. He knew how complicated Trinitarian theology could be, and in one of his prayers to the Father he said,

> I hold fast in my consciousness the truth that your Holy Spirit comes from you [Father] and through him [the Son], although I do not understand it, because I am slow when it comes to spiritual things.[9]

Nevertheless, there is no reason to doubt that he had understood where Epiphanius and the Cappadocians were coming from, whether he got it directly from them or not. In a very revealing passage he wrote,

> The Spirit of truth proceeds from the Father. He is sent by the Son and receives from the Son. But everything the Father has belongs to the Son, and it is for that reason that the one who receives from him is both the Spirit of God and the Spirit of Christ. The Spirit is a being who has the same nature as the Son, but he also has the nature of the Father. He is the Spirit of him

[9] Hilary of Poitiers, *De Trinitate* 12.56.

who raised Christ from the dead, but that was none other than the Spirit of the Christ who was so raised.[10]

Perhaps because he was translating Eastern theology into Latin as he went along, Hilary was more sensitive than most to the precise meaning of words, and he openly wondered whether the Spirit's procession from the Father and his receiving from the Son were just two different words for the same thing:

> Is receiving from the Son the same thing as proceeding from the Father? If we have to maintain that there is a difference between these two things, then at least we must admit that receiving from the Son is the same thing as receiving from the Father. The Lord declares: "He will take what is mine and declare it to you. All that the Father has is mine; therefore . . . he will take what is mine and declare it to you."[11] Whatever the Spirit receives, whether it is power, strength, or doctrine, the Son says will be taken from him. He lets it be understood that it will also be taken from the Father, because whatever the Father has is his.[12]

Hilary found Eastern theology difficult, but there is no reason to suppose that he misunderstood it. Even if he could see little real difference between the Spirit's procession and his mission, he would almost certainly have maintained that there is a distinction between procession from the Father and reception from the Son, because this distinction was biblical in origin.[13] Hilary can therefore be interpreted as someone who attempted to explain something that up to then had not been properly analyzed. In this he may be compared to Gregory of Nyssa, who did much the same thing but in a different way. Following the lead of Gregory of Nazianzus, Gregory of Nyssa interpreted both the generation of the Son and the procession of the Holy Spirit as abstract qualities that define the character of their respective *hypostases*. In this respect, he went beyond the Bible, which uses only the verbs "proceed" and "receive," and also beyond Basil, who stuck closely to biblical forms of expression.[14] Having done that, Gregory of Nyssa went on to argue that the Son's generation (*gennêsis*) was unique (as John 1:14 would suggest) and that it acted as a conduit for the

[10] Ibid., 8.26.
[11] John 16:14–15.
[12] Hilary of Poitiers, *De Trinitate* 8.20.
[13] See John 16:14.
[14] Gregory of Nazianzus, *Orationes* 25.16; Gregory of Nyssa, *Contra Eunomium* 12.2. Gregory of Nazianzus actually used the word *ekpempsis* ("mission") instead of *ekporeusis* ("procession"), which strengthens the case for Hilary's equation of the two terms. Gregory of Nyssa, however, reverted to *ekporeusis*, as did Caesarius of Nazianzus (*Dialogus*, 3).

procession of the Holy Spirit from the Father to the created order. In other words, Gregory of Nyssa claimed, as Tertullian (whose writings were unknown to Gregory) had already done, that the Holy Spirit proceeds from the Father through the Son, a formula that would be used in later times as an attempt to resolve the debate.[15]

It is difficult to summarize the Trinitarian theology of the Cappadocian fathers in a few words, but as it was to become the foundation of the classical theology of the Eastern church, a status that it retains to this day, we cannot ignore it. Between Basil and the two Gregorys there appears to have been a process of abstraction in which the biblical words "only begotten" and "proceeds" became "generation" and "procession," which were then defined as concepts that have properties of their own. If that is correct, Hilary probably did not realize it, since it was happening before his eyes in what seems to have been a more or less unconscious way. The logic of Cappadocian Trinitarianism is extremely subtle and is not easily grasped by those who have not been trained in Greek philosophical thought, so Hilary can hardly be blamed if he did not assimilate all its nuances. For example, Gregory of Nazianzus was careful to insist that "unbegottenness" (*agennêsia*) was not to be understood as a property of the divine being, but given that it was the thing that distinguished the *hypostasis* of the Father from those of the other two members of the Godhead, and given that the Father was the *hypostasis* of that divine being, this was a fine distinction to make![16] But fine though it was, it was still a distinction, and we must resist the Western tendency to level such things out for the sake of simplicity.

In the final analysis, Cappadocian Trinitarianism made it impossible for the Son to stand in the same relationship to the Holy Spirit as the Father does, because their respective *hypostases* are different. Hilary of Poitiers provided a bridge between the Greek East and the Latin West, but it was a bridge on which travel went in one direction only. Latin works were almost never translated into Greek, and so the Western tradition was largely unknown in the East for the better part of a thousand years. By the time it became available to the Eastern churches, battle lines had hardened to the point where it would prove impossible to undo or transcend them.[17]

[15] Gregory of Nyssa, *Epistula ad Ablabium*, in PG 45, col. 133.

[16] Gregory of Nazianzus, *Orationes* 39.12.

[17] For example, Augustine's *De Trinitate* was not translated into Greek until about 1282, when controversy between the two churches was at its height and Maximus Planudes, the Greek translator, thought that it would be useful if his fellow Greeks could understand where the Westerners were coming from. Planudes's translation has recently appeared in a critical edition with an introduction. See Manolis Papathômopoulos, Isavella Tsavari, and Gianpaolo Rigotti, eds., *Augoustinou* Peri Triados *biblia pentekaideka*, 2 vols. (Athens: Kentron Ekdoseôs Ergôn Hellênôn Syngrapheôn, 1995).

Augustine and the Holy Spirit

Augustine is undoubtedly the outstanding figure in Western Trinitarian thought, so much so that his great work *De Trinitate* (*On the Trinity*), which he wrote between 399 and 419, quickly became, and to a large extent still remains, the standard work on the subject in the Western tradition.[18] This is proof of his enduring influence, but it also creates difficulties for modern scholars and theologians. Defenders of the Western tradition naturally look back to Augustine and claim him for their own, even if that means taking what he wrote out of context and making him support positions of which he had never heard. Critics of the same tradition go to the other extreme and often reject his conclusions, with the same lack of attention to historical context that they accuse his defenders of. The result is that objectivity gets lost in polemic and it becomes almost impossible to evaluate Augustine fairly or to appreciate what his contribution to theological development really was.[19]

Augustine's ideas came from three main sources. First, he followed Tertullian in his fundamental monotheism, though he abandoned the ambiguous term *substantia* in favor of *essentia*, which was a more exact translation of the Greek *ousia* ("being"). He even accepted the Trinity of persons, despite his unhappiness with the term *persona*.[20] Augustine no doubt read Tertullian directly, but the latter's influence was also mediated to him through a number of Latin writers who had followed in his footsteps. Of these, by far the most important was Ambrose of Milan (339?–397), the man through whose ministry Augustine came to faith in Christ and who became his principal spiritual mentor. It would be fair to say that the later Augustine outgrew the tutelage of Ambrose, but the latter's legacy remained foundational, particularly where his doctrine of the Holy Spirit was concerned.

More clearly and unambiguously than anyone before him, Ambrose laid the theological foundations for a doctrine of the double procession of the Holy Spirit from both the Father and the Son. In doing so, he seems to have taken his cue from the words of the confession in the creed of 381, which says that the Holy Spirit is "the Lord, the giver of life," although it is unlikely that he was referring directly to that statement. His argument went like this:

---

[18] Augustine of Hippo, *The Trinity*, trans. Edmund Hill (Brooklyn, NY: New City, 1991). See also Lewis Ayres, *Augustine and the Trinity* (Cambridge: Cambridge University Press, 2010); and Oliver Du Roy, *L'intelligence de la foi en la Trinité selon Saint Augustin. Genèse de sa théologie trinitaire jusqu'en 391* (Paris: Etudes Augustiniennes, 1966).

[19] See Bradley G. Green, *Colin Gunton and the Failure of Augustine* (Eugene, OR: Pickwick, 2011) for an insightful critique of these tendencies.

[20] Augustine of Hippo, *De Trinitate* 5.8; 7.4–5.

> Just as the Father is the fount of life, so (as many have said) the Son is the fount of life also. . . . This means that he is the fount of the Holy Spirit, for the Spirit is life, as the Lord says: "The words that I have spoken to you are spirit and life."[21] For where the Spirit is there is also life, and where there is life, there is also the Holy Spirit. There are many, however, who think that this passage refers to the Father only as the fount, but they should pay more careful attention to what the Scripture says: "*With you* is the fountain of life."[22] In other words, the Son is with the Father, because the Word was with God in the beginning and was God.[23] But whether we understand the fountain in this text to be the Father or the Son, we certainly do not think of it in terms of created water, but as the fount of divine grace, the Holy Spirit, who is the living water. That is why the Lord said, "If you knew the gift of God and who it is that is saying to you, 'Give me a drink,' you would have asked him, and he would have given you living water."[24]

Ambrose did not mention the procession of the Holy Spirit, probably because he was unaware of the importance attached to it by Gregory of Nazianzus and the creed of 381, but the gist of his remarks is clear. On the basis of what he said above, it is very hard to see how Ambrose could have failed to advocate a double procession of the Holy Spirit had he been faced with the question. We may therefore attribute the fact that Augustine later took that step to his desire to integrate the latest theological expression coming from the East with the teaching of his master Ambrose. Augustine was aware that the Eastern church confessed that the Holy Spirit proceeds from the Father and that he was the Spirit of the Son, and so he asked himself the next question:

> If the Holy Spirit is the Spirit of the Son, why should we not believe that he proceeds from the Son? Indeed, if he did not proceed from the Son, Christ would not have breathed on his disciples after the resurrection and said, "Receive the Holy Spirit."[25] What else did such breathing mean than that the Holy Spirit also proceeds from the Son?[26]

In answer to the obvious objection that John 15:26 mentions only the Father, Augustine went on to add,

---

[21] John 6:63.
[22] Psalm 36:9.
[23] John 1:1.
[24] John 4:10. Ambrose of Milan, *De Spiritu Sancto* 1.15.172–174.
[25] John 20:22.
[26] Augustine of Hippo, *Tractatus in Iohannis Evangelium* 99.6.

> Jesus says this because it accords with his general practice of referring everything he has to the one from whom he is. Compare the place where he says, "My teaching is not mine but his that sent me."[27] If the teaching that he says was his Father's and not his own was actually his as well, how much more does the Holy Spirit proceed from him, just as he proceeds from the Father. The one from whom the Son receives his Godhead is the one from whom he can claim that the Holy Spirit proceeds.[28]

Augustine's appropriation of the Latin theological tradition was modified by two distinct, though related, influences from the Greek East. The first of these was the Neoplatonism of Porphyry, mediated through the converted philosopher Marius Victorinus.[29] The second was Cappadocian theology, mediated through Hilary of Poitiers. The Neoplatonism of Porphyry differed from that of Plotinus and Iamblichus, whose ideas had influenced the young Cappadocians. They regarded Being, Intelligence, and Soul as three separate *hypostases*, a belief that was not uncongenial to Cappadocian Trinitarianism, though it was by no means identical to it either. The Cappadocians had broken with Neoplatonism by declaring that the three *hypostases* constituted a single Being. Porphyry, however, thought that these three were all contained in a single *hypostasis*. Victorinus taught this kind of Neoplatonism, and after his conversion to Christianity he found that it fitted quite well into the traditional Trinitarianism of the Latin church.

Victorinus went on to account for the eternal generation of the Son and the eternal procession of the Holy Spirit by saying that to be is to move (*esse* = *moveri*), which means that there can be motion in the Being of God without involving change in that Being. On the specific question of the double procession of the Holy Spirit he had this to say:

> The Paraclete is from God and from Christ. . . . The Holy Spirit comes from the Son just as the Son comes from God, and as a logical consequence of that, the Holy Spirit also comes from the Father. . . . The Spirit has received from Christ, Christ has received from the Father, and for that reason the Spirit has also received from the Father. All three are therefore one, from the Father.[30]

---

[27] A free rendering of John 14:24.

[28] Augustine of Hippo, *Tractatus in Iohannis Evangelium* 99.7.

[29] On Neoplatonism and Christianity, see Richard T. Wallis, *Neoplatonism*, 2nd ed. (London: Duckworth, 1995); John M. Rist, *Plotinus: The Road to Reality* (Cambridge: Cambridge University Press, 1967); Dominic J. O'Meara, ed., *Neoplatonism and Christian Thought* (Norfolk, VA: International Society for Neoplatonic Studies, 1982); Etienne Gilson, *The Christian Philosophy of Saint Augustine* (London: Victor Gollancz, 1961); John M. Rist, *Augustine* (Cambridge: Cambridge University Press, 1994).

[30] Marius Victorinus *Adversus Arium*, 1A.13–14.

Augustine took this over and concluded that the persons of the Trinity were modes of being in God, who can manifest himself in different ways without ceasing to be the same as he always is. But whereas the Cappadocians recognized two levels in God, one of being (*ousia*) and one of existence (*hyparxis*), both of which were equally eternal, Augustine recognized only one, inside of which the persons or modes found their identity. However, this did not mean that the persons were no more than different names for the same thing. Still less were they to be regarded as distinct substances. Rather, the persons explained the pattern of motion within the one being of God. They were not objective realities in their own right, but expressions of real relations caused by the essential motion of the divine Being and subsistent in that Being.

It was at this point that Augustine's Trinitarianism became contradictory and confusing, because he wanted to avoid the suggestion that any of the persons was less than fully God, an error into which Tertullian's notion that the three persons were "portions" (*portiones*) of the divine being was liable to fall.[31] It was therefore necessary for him to tie the term "person" to the divine essence, with the result that, according to him, strictly speaking there could be only one person in God! A literalist might accuse Augustine of modalism at this point, but that would be unfair. In fact, he was edging toward a new understanding of God in which the two levels of objective reality, represented by the terms "person" and "substance," manifest each other. This was also the understanding of the Cappadocians, expressed by them in their doctrine of coinherence (*perichôrêsis*). What Augustine lacked was a sufficiently well-defined theological vocabulary that would have enabled him to escape contradiction in his use of the word "person." He recognized this himself:

> The only reason why we do not call all three together "one person" in the way that we call them one being and one God, but say that there are three persons, though we never say that there are three Gods or three beings, is that we want to keep at least one word for indicating what we mean by "Trinity," so that when we are asked what the three are that we confess, we are not reduced to complete silence.[32]

We see the problem more clearly when we realize that for Augustine, the names of the different persons were given to them in order to explain the nature of God's being to us. To him, the Father and the Son represented opposite poles of attraction, drawn to each other by the very contrast between them.

[31] See Tertullian, *Adversus Marcionem* 3.6.8, and the remarks by René Braun, Deus Christianorum. *Recherches sur le vocabulaire doctrinal de Tertullien*, 2nd ed. (Paris: Etudes Augustiniennes, 1977), 190.
[32] Augustine of Hippo, *De Trinitate* 7.11.

Because of his name, the Father was logically prior to the Son, but by the same token the Son must exist in order for the name Father to have any meaning. It was impossible for him to imagine one of them existing without the other. Augustine toyed with a number of different analogies that he believed would illustrate his position and confirm its validity, since the analogies were taken from human life. To be created in the image and likeness of God was to be created in the image and likeness of the Trinity, which Augustine illustrated by saying that memory, intellect, and will were the three essential modes of the single human mind.[33]

But the greatest single analogy, and the one that Augustine believed encapsulated the New Testament's teaching about God better than any other, was provided by the concept of love.[34] God is love, but love is not a thing. Love is the expression of a relationship and cannot exist if there is only one subject. Of course it is true that there is only one God, and it would be blasphemous to suggest that he made the world because he needed to have something to love. God's love must be perfect within himself because he is perfect, and his love for the creation can only be an extension of the love that subsists in him. God's love can therefore only be self-love. Human beings, who are created in his image, are also capable of self-love, which (rightly ordered) is a necessary part of a healthy human existence. But human beings are fallible and therefore our self-love is imperfect and corrupt. But God is perfect, and so his self-love is perfect too. What did that mean when it was worked out in Augustine's thought?

First, it meant that God must have a perfect conception of himself. Human beings usually have either an inflated view of themselves or suffer from low self-esteem, but neither of these things is possible with God. His self-awareness is accurate, which means that it is also complete and perfect. In his own mind he has formed an image of himself that corresponds in every way with who and what he really is. That image is his Son—the use of the word "conception" has a double value, since it can be used either of a mental or of a physical act, which further reinforces the link between the divine and the human, the spiritual and the material. The conception of the Son in the womb of the Virgin Mary was therefore only the physical manifestation on earth of an eternal generation of the same Son in heaven.

So much for the Father and the Son, but where did the Holy Spirit fit into this? Pursuing his analogy of love, Augustine said that the Father loves the image he has formed as he loves himself, which is only natural since the image

[33] Ibid., 7.12, 9.2. See John E. Sullivan, *The Image of God: The Doctrine of St. Augustine and Its Influence* (Dubuque, IA: Priory, 1963).
[34] Augustine of Hippo, *De Trinitate* 9.1–17.

is himself. The Father is therefore the lover and the Son is the one who is loved, or the beloved, as Scripture itself testifies. The Father's love for the Son must be perfect because it must correspond to who the Son is, but at the same time it is a reality distinct from the Son. Whereas the Son was generated (or begotten) in a single act, the love that the Father shows toward him is continuous—in other words, it proceeds on an ongoing basis, just as the Holy Spirit is said to proceed from the Father in the present tense and not in the past. Is the Holy Spirit therefore to be equated with the Father's love for the Son?

Not quite. Love, if it is to be perfect, must also be mutual. If the Father were to love the Son with his perfect love but that love were not returned by the Son, we would have what is known in human life as "unrequited love," which would be a tragedy rather than an expression of the perfection of the divine being. It is therefore impossible to imagine the Father's love for the Son without a corresponding love of the Son for the Father. The Son's love for the Father is secondary in the sense that it is a response to the Father's love for him, but it is in no way inferior. To be perfect, it must be equal to the Father's love for him, and therefore identical to it, because there is only one God. This means that if the Father's love for the Son is constantly proceeding from him, then the Son's love for the Father must be constantly proceeding from him as well. Furthermore, since each of these loves is perfect, they are in fact one love, and this one love is the Holy Spirit, who is the bond of love tying the Trinity together. Because the Holy Spirit is the mutual love of the Father and the Son, he stands in the same relationship to both. This relationship is expressed as "procession," and so he proceeds from both.[35] But because this double procession is essentially a single relation, it must be regarded as a single movement or operation, one that is common to both the Father and the Son.[36] Augustine summed all this up as follows:

> The Holy Spirit consists in the same unity of substance and in the same equality as the Father and the Son. Whether the Holy Spirit is the unity between them, the holiness they share, or their mutual love, or whether he is the unity because he is the love, and the love because he is the holiness, at least it is clear that he is not one of the other two. It is through him that the two are joined together, and through him that the begotten is loved by the begetter and loves the one who begot him. It is through him that they "keep the unity of the Spirit in the bond of peace."[37] They do not do this by participation in the Spirit but by their own essence. . . . Therefore the Holy

[35] Ibid., 15.27.
[36] Ibid., 5.15.
[37] Eph. 4:3.

> Spirit, whoever he is, is common to both the Father and the Son. That communion is consubstantial and coeternal. If it can rightly be called friendship, then so be it, but it is better to call it love. Love is a substance because God is a substance, and "God is love."[38] Since love is a substance along with the Father and the Son, it is just as great, good, holy and whatever else they are. . . . Therefore the Holy Spirit is equal to them. . . . And there are no more than three: one who loves him who is from himself, one who loves him from whom he is, and love itself.[39]

From this it will be obvious that the double procession of the Holy Spirit is essential, because if it is not agreed, the love of the Father for the Son would not be requited by any corresponding love of the Son for the Father, and the love that unites them would not exist. The end result is a Trinitarianism that is quite different from that of the Cappadocians. Yet it should not be forgotten that East and West were still moving in the same mental universe, and the traditions they developed independently of each other were not regarded by anyone as mutually exclusive, or even as very different. In particular, Augustine recognized that the Father's love took precedence over that of the Son, a view which could be regarded as compatible with the Cappadocian belief that he was the fount of deity:

> There must be a reason why, in the Trinity, only the Son is called the Word of God, only the Holy Spirit is called the Gift of God, and only the Father is the one from whom the Word is born and from whom the Holy Spirit principally proceeds. I have added the word "principally" because the Holy Spirit also proceeds from the Son. The Father gave this to the Son, not as if he were giving it to someone who did not yet have the Spirit, but as part of the very act of begetting him. The Father begat the Son in such a way that the common Gift proceeds from him also, making the Holy Spirit the Spirit of both.[40]

Furthermore, each side thought of relations as properties of a *hypostasis*. The difference was that in the Cappadocian case, each *hypostasis* of the Godhead was distinguished by a single relation, whereas for Augustine the one *substantia* (rebaptized as *essentia*) possessed three internal relations. This difference certainly had the potential to grow into genuine discord over time, but as long as a common universe of discourse survived, that did not happen. Only when that universe broke down was the mutual incompatibility of the two conceptions noticed, giving rise to a theological controversy that would

[38] 1 John 4:16.
[39] Augustine of Hippo, *De Trinitate* 6.7.
[40] Ibid., 15.29.

prove impossible to reconcile within the terms of the original development of the procession of the Holy Spirit within the Godhead.

The Origins of Controversy

One of the remarkable things about the double procession of the Holy Spirit is the amount of time it took for the controversy over it to get going in any serious way. The potential for discord may have been in place by 419, when Augustine finally published *De Trinitate*, but it went virtually unnoticed for nearly four hundred years, was not seriously debated until 1274, and did not reach some kind of resolution until 1439. In other words, it took 850 years for real controversy to erupt, and it then preoccupied theologians for a further 150 years, only to leave the church divided and still debating the question today—nearly six hundred years later still.[41] Compare this with the history of Christology, which first became controversial around 268, when the adoptianism of Paul of Samosata was condemned at Antioch, was then a major bone of contention from the First Council of Nicea in 325 until the Council of Chalcedon in 451, and was finally resolved (to the extent that it was) at the Third Council of Constantinople in 681. That is still a long time, but the main issues quickly came to the fore and most of the subsequent debates were attempts to resolve secondary points arising out of them. Dissenters emerged and continue to exist, but the non-Chalcedonian churches have always been marginal to the Christian world, and today it is generally agreed that the outstanding differences with them are more terminological than substantial.

Why was the personhood of the Holy Spirit so difficult to define, and why does it continue to be a barrier to Christian unity, with no apparent resolution in sight? Part of the explanation must lie in the political turmoil that engulfed the Roman empire in the fifth century, followed by the extraordinary rise and diffusion of Islam two hundred years later, when the Eastern and Western churches were cut off from each other for long periods of time and went their

[41] For a general overview of the controversy, see A. Edward Siecienski, *The* Filioque*: History of a Doctrinal Controversy* (Oxford: Oxford University Press, 2010); and Bernd Oberdorfer, *Filioque: Geschichte und Theologie eines ökumenischen Problems* (Göttingen: Vandenhoeck und Ruprecht, 2001). Older, but still valuable for the early period is Henry B. Swete, *On the History of the Doctrine of the Procession of the Holy Spirit from the Apostolic Age to the Death of Charlemagne* (Cambridge: Cambridge University Press, 1876; repr., 2012). For a detailed examination of the question from its origins to 1274, see Peter Gemeinhardt, *Die* Filioque*-Kontroverse zwischen Ost- und Westkirche im Frühmittelalter* (Berlin: Walter de Gruyter, 2002). For an overview from the standpoint of the Eastern church, see S. S. Bilalis, *Hê hairesis tou* Filioque, *I. Historikê kai kritikê theôrêsis tou* Filioque (Athens: Ekdoseis Orthodoxou Typou, 1972); Cyriaque Lampryllos, *La mystification fatale. Etude orthodoxe sur le* Filioque (Lausanne: L'âge d'homme, 1987); and Markos A. Orphanos, *The Procession of the Holy Spirit according to Certain Greek Fathers* (Athens: Apostoliki Diakonia, 1979). See also Stanley M. Burgess, *The Holy Spirit: Eastern Christian Traditions* (Peabody, MA: Hendrickson, 1989); Yves Congar, *I Believe in the Holy Spirit*, 3 vols. (New York: Seabury; and London: Geoffrey Chapman, 1983). Originally published as *Je crois en l'Esprit Saint* (Paris: Cerf, 1980); Jean-Miguel Garrigues, *L'Esprit qui dit Père et le problème du* Filioque (Paris: Téqui, 1981).

separate ways. The ongoing Christological controversies also inhibited serious discussion of the Holy Spirit, because until they were sorted out it was impossible to move on to anything else. Nevertheless, it must also be said that for a long time the problem was not recognized or understood, and this failure of perception also played an important part in delaying what to us seems like the inevitable.

Looking back at the historical record, we can say that for at least two centuries after Augustine, the potential problem of reconciling the different Trinitarian theologies of East and West was simply not recognized. This can be seen quite clearly in the work of Cyril of Alexandria, a major protagonist in the struggle against Nestorius and the Antiochene tradition of Christology, an ally of the Roman church, and a theologian who is revered equally by both the Chalcedonian and the non-Chalcedonian churches of the East.[42] Cyril was alive to the Pneumatomachian controversy, even though it was petering out in his day, and was keen to establish the natural divinity of the Holy Spirit based on his procession from the Father as the fount of deity. But he had no problem in extending this to the Son:

> The Spirit belongs properly to God the Father, and just as properly to the Son, not in the sense of two distinct substances, or of one [substance] conceived and existing separately in each of the two. Rather, it is because the Son is by nature from and in the Father, true fruit of his substance, that he takes the Spirit of his Father as a natural attribute [of his own].[43]

Even more striking is this:

> Since the Son is the fruit and the imprint of the *hypostasis* of the one who begot him, he possesses by its nature everything that belongs to the begetter. That is why he says, "Everything the Father has is mine; that is why I said to you that he will take what is mine to make it known to you"[44] He is obviously speaking of the Spirit who exists through him and in him.[45]

Cyril was even able to use John 20:22 in much the same way that Augustine did, though he did not draw the conclusion that Christ's breathing of the Spirit on his disciples after his resurrection proves that the latter proceeds from him.[46]

[42] See Marie-Odile Boulnois, "The Mystery of the Trinity according to Cyril of Alexandria: The Deployment of the Triad and Its Recapitulation into the Unity of Divinity," in Thomas G. Weinandy and Daniel A. Keating, eds., *The Theology of Saint Cyril of Alexandria: A Critical Appreciation* (London: T & T Clark, 2003), 75–111. See especially 103–108.
[43] Cyril of Alexandria, *Commentarium in Iohannis Evangelium* 17:18–19.
[44] John 16:15.
[45] Cyril of Alexandria, *Commentarium in Iohannis Evangelium* 16:15.
[46] Ibid., 14:16–17.

With statements like these, it is easy to see how Cyril was later co-opted by the Western church as a prime example of an Eastern father who confessed the double procession of the Holy Spirit.[47] Passages can be cited in which Cyril appeared to support such a conclusion, and he undoubtedly came closer to it than any other Greek theological writer before or since.[48] But these texts have to be held in tension with many others in which he spoke of the procession of the Holy Spirit from the Father through the Son, which was more typical of the Eastern tradition to which he naturally belonged.[49] Perhaps the fairest thing to say about Cyril's doctrine is that it was similar to that of Augustine and, had the two men ever met, they might have been able to reach agreement without serious difficulty.

But Cyril's teaching did not go uncontested in the East, as we can see from the comments made by Theodoret of Cyrus. Theodoret, it is true, represented the Antiochene school and was therefore no friend of Cyril's, so he would have been particularly keen to pick up anything Cyril said that might be used against him. Indeed, Theodoret seems to have thought that Cyril did affirm that the Holy Spirit had his existence from the Son, a doctrine that he then condemned as blasphemous.[50] Elsewhere, and in a less polemical context, Theodoret stated that the Holy Spirit is the Spirit of Christ because he is consubstantial with the Father and the Son, but not because he proceeds from both of them.[51] To him, the Holy Spirit was the Spirit of God [the Father] because of his origin and the Spirit of Christ because of his mission to the world, which he received from Christ, a view that would become a classic statement of the Eastern position on the matter in later times.[52]

While Theodoret was picking holes in Cyril's doctrine and making sure that it was not interpreted in a way that might suggest a double procession of the Spirit, the West was going a different way. On July 21, 447, Pope Leo I wrote a letter to Turibius, the bishop of Asturica (now Astorga) in Spain, in which he included the double procession of the Holy Spirit as part of the Catholic doctrine that he expected Turibius to uphold against the modalist tendencies of the Priscillianists and the Arianism of the Visigoths.[53] Barely

[47] See Bernard Meunier, "Cyrille d'Alexandrie au concile de Florence," *Annuarium Historiae Conciliorum* 21 (1989), 147–174; André de Halleux, "Cyrille, Théodoret et le *Filioque*," in *Revue d'Histoire Ecclésiastique* 74 (1979), 597–625.

[48] See, for example, Cyril of Alexandria, *Thesaurus de Trinitate* 34, 576ab, 585a; *Commentarium in Ioel* 2:28.

[49] See Cyril of Alexandria, *De adoratione in spiritu et veritate* 1.148a; *De Trinitate dialogi* 2, 423a; and above all, *Commentarium in Iohannis Evangelium* 14.20; 17.18–19; 20.22–23. Several other passages to the same effect are cited by Orphanos, *Procession* 41.

[50] *Apologeticus contra Theodoretum pro XII capitibus*, in PG 76, col. 432d.

[51] Theodoret of Cyrus, *Interpretatio Epistulae ad Romanos* 8.11.

[52] Ibid.

[53] Leo of Rome, *Epistula* 15.2. The text is in Denzinger, *Enchiridion*, no. 284. Leo intended the doctrine of the double procession to be proclaimed at a Council in Toledo, which was due to meet there in 447, but whether that

fifteen months later, the same Leo was writing to Flavian, the patriarch of Constantinople, who had solicited his help in the Christological controversy with Eutyches. Leo's reply, which was his now famous *Tome*, was read at the Council of Chalcedon on October 22, 451, where it was hailed as the authentic expression of orthodoxy. It did not say anything about the double procession of the Holy Spirit, but Leo's orthodoxy was accepted without question, which can only mean that no one knew or cared about his opinions on the subject of the Spirit's procession. On the other hand, the same council also authorized the creed of 381 in its definitive form, and it said nothing about the procession of the Spirit from the Son, so it cannot be claimed that Chalcedon supported the Augustinian view either.

A number of other Latin writers followed Augustine's lead more or less without comment.[54] The only one who took his ideas significantly further was Fulgentius of Ruspe (d. 533), who although he agreed with Augustine's teaching that the Spirit proceeded from the Father in the first instance, nevertheless argued that he proceeded from the common nature of the Father and the Son in such a way as to make his procession from both of them one of his own personal (hypostatic) properties.[55] Fulgentius based his teaching on the New Testament, claiming that the "Spirit of truth" (John 16:13) must be the Spirit of Christ because Christ is the truth (John 14:6). For him, therefore, the double procession was an apostolic teaching that was firmly grounded in the words of Jesus himself, taken (as it happens) from the very same farewell discourses in which the Spirit was said to proceed from the Father (John 15:26).[56]

Sometime around AD 500 the double procession appeared in the so-called Athanasian Creed, which was composed somewhere in southern Gaul and was first alluded to by Caesarius, bishop of Arles (502–542). That document had nothing to do with Athanasius, but the fact that it could be attributed to him without comment shows that no one in the Western church realized that Athanasius would not have included the double procession in it.[57] We next hear of the double procession in Spain, where it was added to the Nicene Creed at some

council was ever held is uncertain. The Priscillianists were followers of Priscillian of Avila (d. 385), who was put to death for heresy at Trier and whose body was later removed to his native Spain and buried (probably) at Santiago de Compostela—the route of its journey becoming the later trail of St. James. On this, see H. Chadwick, *Priscillian of Avila: The Occult and the Charismatic in the Early Church* (Oxford: Oxford University Press, 1975). The Visigoths were the Western branch of the Goths, who had been evangelized by the Arian Wulfila and who had occupied Spain in 409.

[54] These included Eucher of Lyon (d. 450), Gennadius of Marseilles (d. 495), Hormisdas of Rome (d. 453), and the great Boethius (480–526). See Siecienski, *Filioque*, 65–66 for the details.

[55] Fulgentius of Ruspe, *Epistula* 10.4; *De fide ad Petrum* 4.

[56] Fulgentius of Ruspe, *De fide ad Petrum* 11.54.

[57] See J. N. D. Kelly, *The Athanasian Creed* (London: A. & C. Black, 1964), 86–90. Kelly argued that Ambrose did not prepare the way for the Augustinian doctrine of the double procession, but (as we have seen) this view cannot be sustained from the evidence.

point, though we cannot say when. The traditional date given for this is 589, when the Spanish Visigoths finally gave up their Arianism at the Third Council of Toledo and submitted to the orthodoxy of Rome, and the double procession was part of the creed they were asked to profess.[58] Most scholars believe that the addition was made in order to counter Arianism, because if the Holy Spirit was said to proceed from the Father but not from the Son, the Arians could use this as an argument for claiming that the Father was God in a way that the Son was not. If that assumption is correct, then the doctrine may well have been added to the creed sometime *before* 589, in preparation for the abjuration of Arianism in that year or else shortly *afterwards*, in order to make the creed conform to what the Visigoths had confessed. Either way, it seems certain that the council itself did not make the alteration, though it had become standard teaching in the West by then.[59]

We do not know exactly what happened in Spain, but the addition to the creed that was made there would later have great historical significance. To the original text "who proceeds from the Father" was added "and [from] the Son," a phrase which in Latin is rendered by the single word *Filioque*, the name by which the controversy has been known ever since. It must be stressed that this addition to the creed occurred without reference to the Eastern position or prejudice against it, for the simple reason that it was unknown in Spain. In confessing the double procession of the Holy Spirit, the Spanish church was doing no more than shoring up its defenses against Arianism by rounding out the creed with what to them was a generally agreed Augustinian Trinitarianism. Whether anyone in the Eastern church at that time knew what was going on in the far West is uncertain, but if they did, they did not object and no more was heard of it.[60]

It was only in the middle of the seventh century that some awareness of the differences between East and West on this question began to appear. The first evidence that we have of this comes from Maximus the Confessor, who had been asked by his friend Marinus of Cyprus to explain whether the Western doctrine of the double procession of the Holy Spirit amounted to a denial that the Father was the first and only true cause (*aitia*) of divinity.[61] In reply to this,

[58] The text is in Denzinger, *Enchiridion*, no. 470.

[59] It was held by Agnellus of Ravenna (d. 569), Cassiodorus (d. 580), and Gregory of Tours (d. 594) among others. The only dissenting voice that we know of was that of Rusticus the Deacon, a sixth-century Roman writer and the nephew of Pope Vigilius (537–555). See Siecienski, *Filioque*, 66.

[60] The Eastern empire had reconquered part of southern Spain in the mid-sixth century and did not abandon it until about 626, so it is possible that word of what happened at Toledo in 589 did get back to Constantinople.

[61] Maximus the Confessor, *Opuscula theologica et polemica* 10, in PG 91, coll. 133–137; the date was probably 645 or 646. For the details, see Aidan Nichols, *Byzantine Gospel: Maximus the Confessor in Modern Scholarship* (Edinburgh: T & T Clark, 1993); Pierre Piret, *Le Christ et la Trinité selon Maxime le Confesseur* (Paris: Beauchesne, 1983).

Maximus said that the Westerners were merely following their church's ancient usage, which could also be found in Cyril of Alexandria.[62] In his own words,

> On that basis, they went on to show that they did not make the Son the cause of the Holy Spirit. They understood that the Father is the only cause (*mia aitia*) of the Son and of the Holy Spirit—of the Son by generation and of the Holy Spirit by procession. But they deliberately added that the Spirit proceeds through the Son in order to maintain the unity of the divine essence and avoid creating a hierarchy of being.[63]

Maximus pointed out that in Greek, the second "procession" of the Holy Spirit would be expressed differently—the biblical word *ekporeuesthai* would be reserved for the Spirit's procession from the Father, and *proienai* would be preferred for his "procession" from the Son, in order to make it clear that the two things are not identical. He obviously would have preferred it if the Westerners did the same, but he put their usage down to the poverty of the Latin language, which did not possess the same subtleties as Greek and was therefore forced to use one word ("procession") to express more than one concept.[64] This way of explaining the difference between the two traditions has had some appeal in modern times as a possible way of resolving the age-old conflict over the Spirit's procession, but it has met with resistance from some Eastern theologians who insist that Maximus was aware that the supposed deficiency of technical vocabulary in Latin was not the only problem.[65]

Although Maximus was aware of the differences between the Latin and Greek languages and regretted the difficulty that the Westerners had in assimilating the subtleties of Eastern thought, he was remarkably sympathetic to the Western position and did not believe that it was substantially different from his own.[66] In other contexts he could come very close to it, as the following extract shows:

---

[62] Cyril occasionally used the word *ekporeuesthai*, normally reserved for the procession of the Holy Spirit, for the generation of the Son. See his *Commentarium in Iohannis Evangelium* 10.15.

[63] Maximus the Confessor, *Opuscula* 10, in PG 91, col. 136.

[64] Maximus may not have known it, but Jerome had encouraged the broad use of *procedere* in Latin in his famous edition of the Bible (the Vulgate), where the word is found as a translation of several Greek equivalents. There is no reason to suppose, however, that Jerome was thinking about the procession of the Holy Spirit when making his translation. Difficulties of translation persist to the present day. Technically, "double procession" would be *dittê ekporeusis* in Greek, but this tends to be avoided in favor of other terms like *dittê proodos* ("double progression") which are less shocking to the Eastern Orthodox ear but also harder to pin down in terms of their precise meaning.

[65] Jean-Miguel Garrigues, *L'Esprit qui dit "Père" et le problème du* Filioque (Paris: Téqui, 1981) argues for this solution, but Jean-Claude Larchet, *Maxime le Confesseur, médiateur entre l'Orient et l'Occident* (Paris: Cerf, 1998) points out its inadequacies from the Eastern side. This scholarly battle has been continued in Jean-Claude Larchet, "La question du *Filioque*," *Le Messager Orthodoxe* 129 (1997), 3–58, and most recently in Jean-Miguel Garrigues, *Le Saint-Esprit, sceau de la Trinité. Le* Filioque *et l'originalité de l'Esprit dans sa personne et dans sa mission* (Paris: Cerf, 2011). This second volume includes the text (and an extended commentary on the meaning) of the Roman clarification of the *Filioque* which was published on June 29, 1995, and was largely the work of Jean-Miguel Garrigues himself.

[66] Maximus the Confessor, *Opuscula* 10, in PG 91, col. 136ab.

> Just as the Holy Spirit belongs to the nature of God the Father according to his essence, so he also belongs to the nature of the Son according to his essence, since he proceeds inexpressibly from the Father through his only begotten Son.[67]

Here and elsewhere, Maximus developed an understanding of the Holy Spirit that placed him firmly in the context of the Trinity as a whole. He recognized, to a degree that was (and still is) rare among Eastern theologians, that the way the Godhead is revealed to us in Christ must correspond to the pattern of relationships present inside God himself. In other words, if the Holy Spirit appears as the Spirit of Christ in his earthly mission, this must reflect some corresponding reality inside the being of God. The Son was eternally present with the Father and therefore cannot be excluded from the procession of the Spirit, in which he must have played a part. Similarly, the Holy Spirit bears witness not only to the Father but to the eternal relationship that exists between the Father and the Son, and in order to do that convincingly, he must have some eternal connection to both.

All of this would have been music to the ears of any disciple of Augustine, but Maximus clung stubbornly to the distinction between procession *from* the Father and procession *through* the Son and was not prepared to modify that in an Augustinian direction. Nor is there any sign that he knew about Augustine's Trinity of divine love. His understanding of the Western position came from Augustine's disciples and was probably mediated mostly through confessional formulas, like the one added to the creed in Spain. The underlying logic and theological framework that supported the double procession doctrine seems to have remained unknown to him; at least, it was not factored into his discussion of the question. In the final analysis, therefore, Maximus must be regarded as a sympathetic observer of the Western scene who did his best to explain it to his Eastern colleagues in a positive way, but he never really entered into it and so cannot be regarded as someone who managed to reconcile the two traditions. At best, his work was a plea to the Greeks to tolerate the Latins, not to embrace their position wholeheartedly and certainly not to accept their theological method as the right way forward.

An outright denial of the double procession of the Holy Spirit (if we except the polemical attack of Theodoret on Cyril of Alexandria) first occurs in the *Orthodox Faith* of John of Damascus, who was writing sometime in the early eighth century. There is nothing in what he says to suggest that he knew about the Spanish insertion in the creed, and his remarks show none of the signs of controversy. Most probably, he was simply trying to explain something that

[67] Maximus the Confessor, *Quaestiones ad Thalassium* 63.

occurred to him as he was trying to systematize the Trinitarian theology that he had inherited from the Cappadocians and the councils of the church. In a summary of Trinitarian relations he wrote,

> We say that the Holy Spirit is from the Father and call him the Spirit of the Father. We do not say that he is from the Son, but we call him the Spirit of the Son (for the divine apostle says: "If anyone does not have the Spirit of Christ")[68] and we confess that he appeared through the Son and is given to us (for he breathed on his disciples and said to them, "Receive the Holy Spirit").[69] Just as the ray and the illumination both come from the sun (which is the source of both), so the illumination is given to us by the ray. It is what enlightens us and is what we share in.[70]

What John taught about the Holy Spirit, and what was to become the standard Eastern interpretation of his being and his work, is clearly stated in the short chapter he devoted to the question. There he said,

> [The Holy Spirit is] a real power (*ousiôdês energeia*) that we perceive independently in his own *hypostasis*, coming out (*proerchomenê*) from the Father and resting (*anapauomenê*) in the Word, whose visible power he is. He cannot be separated from God, in whom he is, or from the Word, to whom he bears witness, nor can he fade away into nonexistence. Rather, like the Word, he is a *hypostasis* that is living, that takes decisions, that is self-moving and active, always desiring what is good and in every situation having power commensurate with his will, having neither beginning nor end.[71]

This passage confirms that John knew nothing of any controversy over the Holy Spirit, because if he had, he would have been more precise in his use of words. Where Maximus recommended using *ekporeuesthai* for the Spirit's procession from the Father and *proienai* for his relationship to the Son, John happily put *proerchesthai* (virtually the same as *proienai*) for the former and *anapauesthai* for the latter, a term that was probably taken from the baptism of Jesus, where the Spirit appeared in the form of a dove and "rested" on him, though the biblical word used for that is different.[72] John did use *ekporeuesthai* of the procession of the Holy Spirit from the Father, but only when alluding to (or quoting directly from) the creed, and it is interesting that when he cited the third article he did not hesitate to add his own gloss on it:

[68] Rom.8:9.
[69] John 20:22.
[70] John of Damascus, *De fide orthodoxa* 1.8.
[71] Ibid., 1.7.
[72] John 1:32. The word used there is *emeinen*, rather than *anêpauthê*, but it means the same thing.

> Likewise we believe also in one Holy Spirit, the Lord and giver of life, who proceeds from the Father *and rests on the Son*, who with the Father and the Son together is worshiped and glorified.[73]

It was not until a generation or more later that a note of controversy over the double procession was sounded for the first time, and then it came from an unexpected quarter. The rise of the Carolingian empire in Western Europe in the late eighth century, culminating in the coronation of Charlemagne as Holy Roman emperor by the pope on December 25, 800, provoked a diplomatic crisis because the Eastern emperors regarded themselves as the only legitimate successors to ancient Rome and were not prepared to countenance an independent revival of the Roman empire in the West. Unfortunately, there was no emperor in Constantinople at the time who could make good the claim, because the legitimate ruler, Constantine VI (780–797), had been blinded and deposed by his mother Irene (797–802), who ruled in her own name, something no woman had ever dared do before. This gave Charlemagne an excuse to have himself proclaimed emperor instead, and he took it.[74]

To support his actions, Charlemagne sought the help of his theologians, who justified this "usurpation" on two grounds. First, they argued that the pope had the right to make and unmake emperors—a dubious claim at best, and one that the Eastern church could easily refute. Second, they said that the Eastern emperors had been deposed in the West because of their fall into heresy. What heresy was that? Incredibly, the Carolingian divines claimed that the Eastern church had *deleted* the *Filioque* from the creed of 381![75] This extraordinary statement occurs in the so-called *Libri Carolini*, a collection of writings now generally attributed to Theodulf of Orléans (750?–821), which appeared sometime around 792.[76] Theodulf's argument was particularly interesting because he believed that to say that the Holy Spirit proceeds from the Father *through* the Son, rather than *from* him was wrong because the two things were not the same. What he wanted to see was a restoration of the primitive, apostolic teaching which (in his eyes) was that of the double procession.[77]

[73] John of Damascus, *De fide orthodoxa* 1.8. The interpolation is in *italics*.
[74] He did, however, offer to marry Irene!
[75] *Libri Carolini* 3.3.
[76] It is also called the *Opus Caroli regis contra synodum*. For a full discussion of this, see Richard Haugh, *Photius and the Carolingians* (Belmont, MA: Nordland, 1975), 45–53. For a view from the Eastern church, see Methodius G. Fouyas, *Hellênes kai Latinoi. Hê ekklêsiastikê antiparathesis Hellênon kai Latinôn apo tês epochês tou Megalou Phôtiou mechri tês synodou tês Flôrentias (858–1439)*, 2nd ed. (Athens: Apostoliki Diakonia, 1994).
[77] The complete wrongheadedness of this argument is breathtaking to modern readers, but of course, Theodulf had no historical perspective and no way of finding out the truth. One irony of his argument is that exactly the same thing would be said several centuries later by Greek opponents of the formula of union agreed on at the Council of Florence in 1439. The difference, of course, was that the Greeks used Theodulf's argument to prove the exact opposite—that the double procession had no place in a Christian confession.

The immediate upshot of this was a series of anti-Byzantine synods, held at Frankfurt (794), Friuli (797), and Aachen (Aix-la-Chapelle) (809). The first of these adopted the *Libri Carolini* as a recognized statement of faith, and of course the council affirmed the double procession of the Holy Spirit whenever it got the chance. It was at the Synod of Friuli that Paulinus of Aquileia (d. 802) delivered the first of what would become a long series of formal defenses of the *Filioque* clause and one that remained especially influential for centuries.[78] Paulinus knew that there had been additions to the creed in the past, most notably in 381, and saw nothing wrong with this, despite the prohibition made at the Council of Ephesus in 431, as long as the additions contemplated were in agreement with the intentions of the fathers who had composed the original documents.[79] According to Paulinus, this had become necessary in order to combat those heretics who were saying that the Holy Spirit proceeds from the Father *alone*. Those who added the words "and from the Son" (*Filioque*) were not altering the faith of the council of 381 but clarifying it.

Two things may be said about this. First, Paulinus obviously knew that Theodulf's argument in the *Libri Carolini* was misguided, and that the original creed had not contained any reference to a double procession of the Holy Spirit. The second is that events in Spain were having an impact on the thinking of the Western church in general. There had been a recrudescence of adoptianism there, associated with the names of Elipandus of Toledo (d. 802) and Felix of Urgel (d. 818). What brought that about is uncertain, though it may have had something to do with the Muslim conquest of the peninsula in the preceding century. Whatever the case, adoptianism threw traditional Trinitarian theology into a new crisis, one in which the divinity of the Son (in particular) came under fire. A procession of the Holy Spirit from the Father alone could only reinforce the idea that the Son was not God at all, and it was to combat that that the council wanted to take action. Spanish adoptianism had already been condemned at Frankfurt in 794, so the problem was clearly well known at the time. Neither Paulinus nor anyone else could have imagined that two generations later the formula which they judged to be heretical would become the battle cry of the Eastern church against the interpolation of the *Filioque* into the creed!

The *Libri Carolini* were by now recognized as being totally inadequate for their purpose, but in one particular, their influence was to linger to the pres-

[78] See Carl Giannoni, *Paulinus II, Patriarch von Aquileia. Ein Beitrag zum Kirchengeschichte Österreichs im Zeitalter Karls des Grossen* (Vienna: Mayer, 1896).

[79] His statement is printed in Albert Werminghoff, ed., *Concilia aevi Karolini* (Hanover: Hahnsche Buchhandlung, 1906), 182.

ent day. The notion that the *Filioque* clause was bound up with the doctrine of papal supremacy was taken up and embellished by a number of Eastern theologians, some of whom still make the connection today. As Timothy Ware has written,

> Orthodox writers also argue that . . . two consequences of the *Filioque*—subordination of the Holy Spirit, over-emphasis on the unity of God—have helped to bring about a distortion in the Roman Catholic doctrine of the church. Because the role of the Spirit has been neglected in the event, the church has come to be regarded too much as an institution of this world, governed in terms of earthly power and jurisdiction. And just as in the Western doctrine of God, unity was stressed at the expense of diversity, so in the Western conception of the church, unity has triumphed over diversity, and the result has been too great centralization and too great an emphasis on papal authority. Two different ways of thinking about God go hand in hand with two different ways of thinking about the church. The underlying causes of the schism between East and West—the *Filioque* and the papal claims—were not unconnected.[80]

It has to be said that this perception is not shared by most Western theologians. Protestants in particular have rejected papal claims without abandoning the *Filioque* and find it strange to think that there might be some inconsistency in this. In fairness, Orthodox participants in modern ecumenical dialogue seldom raise the issue, perhaps because they realize that the supposed connection is a bit far-fetched.

The *Libri Carolini* were soon superseded by two treatises of a much higher standard, one by Theodulf himself and the other by Alcuin of York (735?–804), an Englishman who was one of Charlemagne's most trusted advisers.[81] Alcuin's work was largely a collection of earlier sources, culled for the most part from Augustine and Fulgentius of Ruspe, but he nevertheless managed to structure his argument in a more systematic way than either of them had done.[82] He began with the underlying unity of substance that was common to the three persons of the Godhead, and argued that the property of being the "first principle" belonged to that unity rather than to the sole person of the Father.[83] He did not take it any further at that time, but his willingness to see the principle

[80] Timothy Ware, *The Orthodox Church* (London: Penguin, 1963), 222–223. See also Sergei Bulgakov, *Paraklet* (Paris: YMCA Press, 1936), 137.

[81] Alcuin of York, *De fide Sanctae et individuae Trinitatis*, in PL 101, coll. 1–63, and his *De processione Spiritus Sancti*, in PL 101, coll. 63–84.

[82] On the sources, see John Cavadini, "The Sources and Theology of Alcuin's *De fide Sanctae et individuae Trinitatis*," in *Traditio* 46 (1991), 123–146.

[83] This statement occurs in his *Commentarium in Iohannis Evangelium* 21 (on John 8:25), in PL 100, col. 864b–c.

of the Godhead as part of the divine being, and not as the particular property of the Father, would make it much easier for future generations of Western theologians to argue that Father and Son could (and did) act together as a single principle, something that the Greek East has always found incomprehensible. Alcuin also commented on John 15:26 as follows:

> It means that the Spirit proceeds equally from the Father and the Son and is sent equally from the Father and the Son, but on account of the distinction of persons, it is said here that he proceeds from the Father and is sent by the Son.[84]

This rather neatly sums up what the Western position was at that time. The Holy Spirit was said to proceed from both of the other two persons and to be sent by both of them as well, but when it came to interpreting the verse of Scripture on which the procession of the Holy Spirit was based, a distinction had to be made in order to protect the individual identity of the Father and the Son. At this level, Alcuin was on the same wavelength as the Eastern church, but in other ways he had moved on to a position where both actions applied equally to the Father and the Son. It was that aspect of his doctrine that would not, and could not, find any echo in the East, which thought it was illogical (as it undoubtedly was) and could never adopt it as its own.

By the time Alcuin was writing, the mounting tensions between East and West over the double procession were reaching Jerusalem, where Frankish and Greek monks clashed over the former's inclusion of the *Filioque* clause in the creed. Pope Leo III defended the Frankish monks and expressed his own support for the double procession in a letter he sent to the Eastern churches.[85] On the question of whether its addition to the creed was valid or not, the pope deferred to the judgment of Charlemagne and his theologians, which led Theodulf of Orléans to write a second learned work on the subject.[86] Its main purpose was the same as the one behind the *Libri Carolini*, but now Theodulf was considerably more sophisticated in his approach. Along with the usual batch of quotations from the Latin fathers, he reached out to the East and managed to find texts supporting his position in works written by (or attributed to) Didymus the Blind, Athanasius, and Cyril—all of them from Alexandria. The common characteristic in Theodulf's use of these sources is that he consistently equated the temporal mission of the Spirit with his eternal procession, allowing him to make free use of quotations proclaiming the former in support of the Western view of the latter.

---

[84] Alcuin of York, *Commentarium in Iohannis Evangelium* 37, in PL 100, col. 949c.
[85] Leo III, *Epistula* 15.
[86] Theodulf of Orléans, *Libellus de processione Spiritus Sancti*.

In response to the pope's request, Charlemagne convened another council at Aachen (809), where the main discussion revolved around a collection of patristic testimonies to the double procession of the Holy Spirit, similar to Theodulf's but compiled by Arn of Salzburg (d. 821).[87] The Council of Aachen not only pronounced that the *Filioque* was orthodox and could legitimately be added to the creed, but also that it was a fundamental teaching of the universal faith that must be firmly confessed by all orthodox believers.[88] For the first time, a council of the church declared that not only was the West right to add the clause, but the East was wrong to omit it—a different and much more dubious proposition. The precise sequence of events is unknown, but Charlemagne had long favored the creed of 381 and encouraged it to be used in worship. It seems likely that after the Synod of Aachen the *Filioque* was formally introduced into the liturgical form of the creed in Charlemagne's empire, with the result that its theology was soon being taken for granted everywhere in Western Europe.[89]

The Synod of Aachen appeared to settle the matter, but Leo III was not happy when he heard about it. After a meeting with Charlemagne's envoy, Smaragdus of St. Michiel, who went to Rome in 810 to explain the council's decisions, Leo III declared the *Filioque* to be orthodox but objected to putting it into the creed and (unsuccessfully) tried to get Charlemagne to change his policy.[90] Leo reinforced his decision by ordering the creed to be inscribed in both Greek and Latin on two silver plaques which he hung in St. Peter's basilica in Rome—without the *Filioque*, of course.[91]

After the time of Charlemagne, the *Filioque* controversy entered a new phase. Until then it had been largely a matter of politics, which many thought could be sorted out with a little good will on both sides, as Leo III tried to do. Only in the next generation did a serious theological investigation begin, and that led to real division of a kind that had not previously been experienced. In the West, there was a renewal of interest in the doctrine of the Spirit as part of the Trinitarianism developed by Gottschalk of Orbais and his great defender Ratramnus of Corbie.[92] The heart of Gottschalk's theology was the expression *trina deitas*, for which he is still known. Essentially, this meant that the distinction between the oneness of the divine being and the threeness of the divine

[87] Arn of Salzburg, *Testimonia ex sacris voluminibus collecta*, in Harald Willjung, ed., *Das Konzil von Aachen, 809* (Hanover: Hahnsche Buchhandlung, 1998).
[88] Harald Willjung, *Konzil von Aachen*, 237.
[89] See J. N. D. Kelly, *Early Christian Creeds*, 3rd ed. (London: Longman, 1972), 348–367.
[90] The relevant documentation is in Willjung, *Konzil von Aachen*, 289–312.
[91] Vittorio Peri, "Il simbolo epigrafico di San Leone III nelle basiliche Romane dei Santi Pietro e Paulo," in *Rivista di Archeologia Cristiana* 45 (1969), 191–221. They were still there in the thirteenth century and perhaps later.
[92] See Jean Jolivet, *Godescalc d'Orbais et la Trinité. La méthode de la théologie à l'époque carolingienne* (Paris: Vrin, 1958); and George H. Tavard, Trina deitas. *The Controversy between Hincmar and Gottschalk* (Milwaukee: Marquette University Press, 1996).

persons was artificial and untenable. According to Gottschalk, there is only one God, who manifests himself to us in a threefold manner. Everything we know about him has three dimensions to it, and we must interpret him in that way. We can easily understand why Gottschalk was accused of Sabellianism (modalism) and adoptianism, but that is not how he understood God. Far from thinking of a single being that is revealed to us in three different, but essentially superficial, forms that all point to an underlying unity, Gottschalk insisted that threeness was an integral part of that unity, which could not be perceived without it.

Furthermore, this seems to be what he believed that the Eastern tradition was saying. For example, he knew that the Greek liturgy praised God as *trishagion* ("thrice holy") but read this as *trina sanctitas* ("three-dimensional holiness") rather than as *ter sanctus* ("three times holy"), which was the standard interpretation. Gottschalk began his Trinitarian explorations with the persons, not with the one being of God, and in doing so he thought that he was standing in the patristic tradition of the East as well as of the West. Whether he realized it or not, there was more than a little reason for him to think that, because as far back as 557, Pope Pelagius I (556–561) had sent a confession of faith to the Frankish king Childebert I (d. 558) in which he said,

> [The Holy Spirit is] equal to the Father and the Son. . . . Proceeding from the Father outside time, he is the Spirit of the Father and of the Son, that is to say, three persons or subsistences of one essence or nature, of one strength, one operation, one blessedness, and one power, so that their unity may be trine and the Trinity may be one.[93]

Pelagius I had had no difficulty combining the adjective "trine" with the procession of the Holy Spirit from the Father, but by the ninth century it was no longer so easy to hold these two things together. The main reason for that seems to be that in the interval a more sophisticated concept of personhood had emerged. The beginnings of that can be traced to the Roman philosopher Boethius (480–526), who famously defined a "person" as "the individual substance of a rational nature."[94] This emphasis on individuality was absent from Augustine, who thought of personhood in more relational terms, as his teaching about the love of God demonstrates. Gottschalk, however, followed Boethius still further and insisted that the personal names of God are essential, or substantial, just as his natural attributes are.[95] Augustine had struggled

[93] Pelagius I, *Epistulae* 15, in PL 69, coll. 407–410.
[94] Boethius, *De personis et duabus naturis* 3.
[95] Hincmar of Reims, *De una et non trina deitate* 16. It should be noted that Hincmar was one of Gottschalk's greatest enemies and was quoting him here only to refute his teaching.

with the biblical evidence that God is Spirit and that God is Love, and only reluctantly concluded that the Spirit could be identified as Love.[96] But he never went so far as to identify the Love of God with his divine essence. Gottschalk, however, claimed that person and essence are the same thing in God, which was why he must be called both one and trine.

Gottschalk was condemned at the Council of Soissons in 853, but his theology was an indication of what was happening to Augustinian Trinitarianism and a portent of things to come. He assented to the double procession of the Holy Spirit, as did his accusers, but in reality that idea was superfluous to his theology, because all three persons were so intertwined with one another that no causal relations between them were conceivable. Each of them had always been there as part of the one divine being, and a theology in which one was begotten or proceeded from another was guilty of diminishing the eternal fullness of the Godhead. In other words, for Gottschalk, confessing the double procession of the Holy Spirit was a step in the right direction but it did not go far enough.

The traditional Western view, and that of the Eastern church, was very different from this, and John Scotus Eriugena was alive to the danger that the latter's theory entailed. Eriugena had a great advantage over his contemporaries in that he had a thorough knowledge of Greek, which he put to good use in translating Greek texts into Latin and in explaining the subtleties of Eastern theology to his intended readership. He fully understood that the being (*ousia*) and the persons (*hypostases*) of God were equally real in an objective sense but that they were also different and could not be homogenized in the way that Gottschalk was trying to do. He ascribed this apparent anomaly to the fact that all theology is transcendent and not definable in terms of human reason.[97] Gottschalk had tried to make sense of something that defied rational analysis, though it could be known by experience. In his analysis of the procession of the Holy Spirit, he said nothing that Maximus the Confessor would have objected to, even if the latter might have phrased it in a slightly different way:

> Although we believe and understand that the Holy Spirit proceeds from the Father through the Son, we must accept that this Spirit does not have two causes but only one—the Father, who is the cause of the Son who is born from him and of the Spirit who proceeds from him through the Son. . . . The Father, who is the principal and only cause of the procession of the Holy Spirit, is fully present in the Son as the Son is fully present in the Father, from

[96] Augustine of Hippo, *De Trinitate* 15.27.

[97] John Scotus Eriugena, *De divisione naturae* 2.31. See Deidre Carabine, *John Scottus Eriugena* (Oxford: Oxford University Press, 2000) for a general introduction to his thought.

> whom the Holy Spirit proceeds through the Son. . . . And the three are one in what is understood as Trinity in Unity.[98]

Eriugena took up the challenge posed by Gottschalk and answered him in a way that preserved the divine unity, but by a mutual interpenetration of the three persons, who retain their distinct identities and freedom of action, and not by a formula that effectively reduced them to three dimensions of a single reality.

In the East, further reflection on the procession of the Holy Spirit was spurred on by the Patriarch Photius (815?–897?), who is traditionally thought to have written two major treatises on the subject.[99] Photius is one of the most controversial figures in church history. In the East, he is regarded as a saint who defended the theological tradition when it was under serious threat, but in the West he has traditionally been seen as the man mainly responsible for splitting the church into its Eastern and Western halves.[100] What both sides agree on is that he was a brilliant scholar and a consummate politician who used his gifts for what he saw as the best interests of his church. Photius had to deal with Western attempts to evangelize Bulgaria, a Slavic country on the doorstep of Constantinople, where Frankish missionaries were naturally including the *Filioque* in the creed.[101] This gave him the opportunity to denounce the pope (and the West generally) as heretical. He was the first person to go that far, but in making his accusations he was careful to rest his case on the age-old teaching of the Roman pontiffs as well as that of the Greek fathers.[102]

Photius set out his argument with great thoroughness. He repeated the Cappadocian idea that the modes of existence in the Trinity are the properties of the *hypostases*, not of the divine essence (*ousia*), and he reinforced the contrast between these two levels of objective reality that the Western church found so hard to understand.[103] He then went on to say that, because the Father was

---

[98] John Scotus Eriugena, *De divisione naturae* 2.31.

[99] Photius, *De Spiritus Sancti mystagogia*, in PG 102, coll. 280–400, and *Epistula* 2, a letter circulated to the Eastern churches in 867, in PG 102, coll. 721–742. He also wrote a letter on the subject to the (Western) archbishop of Aquileia, who sympathized with his views (*Epistula* 291). The *Mystagogia* is almost certainly a composite work of some kind and may be at least partly the work of Metrophanes of Smyrna, a contemporary of Photius, but there is no way of knowing this for sure. In any case, it reflects the views of Photius quite closely and was usually regarded as his work by the controversialists of his and later times. See Tia Kolbaba, *Inventing Latin Heretics: Byzantines and the* Filioque *in the Ninth Century* (Kalamazoo, MI: Medieval Institute, 2008).

[100] For a general study and appreciation of him, see Francis Dvornik, *The Photian Schism* (Cambridge: Cambridge University Press, 1948).

[101] The mission to the Slavs created serious political problems. Constantine (Cyril) and Methodius had gone from Thessalonica to Moravia, where they established a church, only to find that Frankish pressure ensured that it would come under the jurisdiction of Rome, not Constantinople. Frankish incursions into Bulgaria, which was technically part of the Eastern empire, were a corresponding Western threat that Constantinople could not tolerate. See Alexis P. Vlasto, *The Entry of the Slavs into Christendom* (Cambridge: Cambridge University Press, 1970), and Dimitri Obolensky, *The Byzantine Commonwealth: Eastern Europe 500–1453* (London: Weidenfeld and Nicholson, 1971), for the details.

[102] Photius, *Mystagogia* 78–79.

[103] Ibid., 30. See Augustine of Hippo, *De Trinitate* 5.8.

the cause (*aition*) of the Godhead, he was different from the other two persons, both of whom were caused (*aitiata*) by the Father, albeit in different ways.[104] In particular, Photius insisted that the ability to generate other persons was a unique characteristic of the Father's *hypostasis* that could not be shared with any other without entailing his own loss of identity:

> If the Father is the cause of what is outside himself, not by reason of his nature but by reason of his *hypostasis*, it would be heretical to say that the identity of the Father's *hypostasis* includes the *hypostasis* of the Son. . . . The Son is in no way the cause of any of the [persons] in the Trinity.[105]

Photius then went on to argue that if the Holy Spirit proceeded from the Father's nature, rather than from his *hypostasis*, not only would he proceed from the Son, but he would also proceed from himself, because he shares the same nature as the others.[106] If there were a double procession of the Holy Spirit, the name "Father" would have no content because the property represented by it would no longer belong exclusively to him. The end result would be Sabellianism, or some newfangled version of it.[107] He even said that if the Son is begotten from the Father and the Holy Spirit proceeds from both, then there must be something else that comes out of the Spirit, since otherwise he would not have the reproductive capacity granted to the other two persons of the Trinity and would be inferior to them.[108] According to Photius, any involvement of the Son in the procession of the Holy Spirit would also imply that the procession from the Father was imperfect because otherwise the Son's participation would be superfluous. But since the Father is perfect, that cannot be the case, and so there is no need for the Son to be involved in the procession of the Spirit.[109]

In his argumentation, Photius harked back to Gregory of Nazianzus, with his inability to establish any clear distinction between the generation of the Son and the procession of the Holy Spirit, but he also showed the same tendency toward abstraction that we saw in Gottschalk's treatment of Augustine. Even as they moved farther apart in their conclusions, East and West were manifesting some of the same methods and tendencies in their respective theological methods.

Photius then went on to denounce the idea that the Holy Spirit proceeds from the Son. If that were to be accepted, he said, there would be two principles

---

104 Photius, *Mystagogia* 11.
105 Ibid., 15.
106 Ibid., 47.
107 Ibid., 9.
108 Ibid., 37; *Encyclica epistula ad archiepiscopales thronos per Orientem obtinentes* 19.
109 Photius, *Mystagogia* 7, 31, 44.

in the Godhead, one of which would be unoriginated (*anarchos*) and therefore superior to the other, which would have an origin outside himself.[110] That would in turn lead to an absurd imbalance, because the Holy Spirit would have two causes that were unequal to each other and as a result he would be internally divided.[111] Not only that, but the Trinity itself would be divided.[112] The argument that two persons of the Trinity cannot share a property that is denied to the third, Photius justified by saying that shared properties belong to the divine essence (*ousia*), despite the fact that this assertion seems to stand in contrast, if not quite in contradiction, to the statement that both the Son and the Spirit are "caused" (*aitiata*) in relation to the Father.

Furthermore, said Photius, if the Son were a cause of the Holy Spirit, then the Father would be both a direct and an indirect cause of his existence, by virtue of the fact that he is the cause of the Son as well.[113] To Photius, this suggested that the Spirit is the Father's grandson, an idea that seems a bit far-fetched, even for him, especially since he must have known that it was a charge that had been leveled against the orthodox pro-Nicenes of the fourth century by the Pneumatomachi![114] Finally, Photius took up the biblical evidence that the Spirit proceeds from the Father and receives from the Son, and argued that procession and reception were not the same thing.[115] Here, of course, he was on much firmer ground and could have claimed support from Western writers like Hilary of Poitiers, had he known about them.

Photius had to recognize that the Scriptures speak of the Holy Spirit as the Spirit of the Son and the Spirit of Christ, but he denied that these expressions had anything to do with the origin of the Spirit and actually distinguished them from each other. To Photius, the "Spirit of the Son" was no more than a confession of the *homoousion*, or shared essence of all three persons of the Trinity, while the "Spirit of Christ" referred to the anointing of his human nature at his conception and baptism, a wholly artificial distinction.[116]

On the positive side, Photius admitted that both the Father and the Son participate in the temporal mission of the Spirit in the world, though he drew a careful distinction between that and the Spirit's eternal procession.[117] When interpreting biblical passages that might be read differently, Photius was careful

[110] Ibid., 14.
[111] Ibid., 43.
[112] Photius, *Encyclica epistula* 17.
[113] Photius, *Mystagogia* 62.
[114] Photius, *Epistula ad archiepiscopum et metropolitanum Aquileiae* 9, in PG 102, col. 801.
[115] Photius, *Mystagogia* 21–23.
[116] Ibid., 51. Interestingly enough, a similar idea is found in Karl Barth, *Church Dogmatics*, trans. G. W. Bromiley, 13 vols. in 4 (Edinburgh: T & T Clark, 1936–1969), I/1:546–557. Originally published as *Kirchliche Dogmatik* (Zurich: Evangelisches Buchhandlung Zollingen, 1932–1967).
[117] Photius, *Mystagogia* 23.

to introduce this distinction into the way he read the texts. For example, when the apostle Paul said that God has sent the Spirit of his Son into our hearts (Gal. 4:6), he was not suggesting that the Son was the origin of the Spirit, but only that the Spirit shares the same nature as the Son.[118] When the Holy Spirit is called the Spirit of Christ, it is because he anointed Christ in his human nature, not because he proceeds from him.[119]

Somewhat oddly, given the Eastern church's objection to the addition of the word *Filioque* to the Latin version of the creed, Photius concluded his argument by making his own gloss on it, though of course he was careful not to add that to the actual text. To his mind, the words "who proceeds from the Father" implied "from the Father *alone*," and his argument from silence at this point is now universally accepted among the Eastern Orthodox. He had no idea that Paulinus of Aquileia had already rejected that idea as incompatible with the deity of the Son, and would probably have found it very hard to grasp the Western way of thinking if he had.

What estimation can be made of Photius? His logic is almost impeccable, but it is also completely self-contained. He did not know Augustine's arguments, nor did he reflect seriously on the Western tradition, which was a closed book to him. He allowed himself to be carried away by his own reasoning and came up with an analysis of the *Filioque* that his Latin contemporaries would not have recognized, even if they had been able to read his work. More seriously still, he never answered the positive challenge of the *Filioque*, which was to define how the Son and the Spirit were related. If the Spirit does not proceed from the Son, what is the nature of the connection between them? They must be related somehow, and the failure to grapple with this question was the great weakness of Photius's theology, as it still is of the Eastern tradition generally.

In the end, Photius's work must be regarded as an academic exercise more than anything else. It is true that it has always been the starting point for Orthodox arguments against the *Filioque*, and for that reason it must be taken seriously, but its use (and usefulness) in that respect came centuries after it was written. In his own time, his arguments were quickly forgotten. The Bulgarian crisis blew over, and by 880 the churches of East and West had patched up their differences and were once more in full communion with each other, with no mention being made of the *Filioque* one way or the other.[120]

Perhaps the saddest legacy of this episode is that the hostile tone that

---

[118] Ibid., 51.

[119] Ibid., 93. This was to become an important point later on.

[120] See Johan Meijer, *A Successful Council of Union: A Theological Analysis of the Photian Synod of 878–880* (Thessalonica: Patriarchikon Idryma Paterikôn Spoudôn, 1975), 184–186.

Photius occasionally adopted when dealing with Western Trinitarian ideas rubbed off on those who felt stung by the accusations he made. Even while he was still alive and writing, Pope Nicholas I issued a call for responses from the Western side, and soon one was produced by Aeneas of Paris (d. 870), which unfortunately echoes the same adversarial tone that Photius had used.[121]

There was also a certain tendency on the Eastern side to follow Photius's example, as can be seen in the *Syllogistic Chapters* composed by his contemporary, Nicetas of Byzantium.[122] Nicetas is chiefly known for his writings against Islam, and it may be that which influenced his approach to the *Filioque* dispute. To a man who had been preoccupied with defending the claims of Christian monotheism against Muslims who taunted them that the Trinity was a form of polytheism, it is likely that any suggestion that there might be more than a single principle of divinity in God would have been alarming.[123] Nicetas did not depend on Photius for his arguments against the double procession of the Holy Spirit, and claimed to have been the first Greek theologian to deal with the subject, which may mean that he was unaware of anything that Photius had written about it. But the fact that he reached the same conclusions is a reminder to us that Photius was not an eccentric individual with a grudge against the West—what he expressed was the latent view of the Eastern tradition as a whole.

Nicetas argued that there are some things that are unique to each *hypostasis* of the Trinity, some things that they all have in common, and some things that two of them share but not the third. What they all share belongs to the divine being (*ousia*), and what is unique to each of them defines their individual *hypostases*. What concerns us here is what is shared by two of them but not by the third. This is true of the "causedness" of the Son and the Holy Spirit, for example, which distinguishes both of them from the "uncaused" Father. Nicetas accepted that, but pointed out that when this happens, the "common" characteristic is a verbal construction, not a theological reality. To our minds, the Son and the Holy Spirit are both "caused" in relation to the Father, but this is only because we have combined two quite different things into a single overarching concept. The Son is caused by generation and the Holy Spirit is caused by procession, but generation and procession are not the same. Nicetas was open to the possibility that the Holy Spirit might proceed from the Son as

[121] Aeneas of Paris, *Liber adversus Graecos*, in PL 121, coll. 683–721.

[122] Nicetas of Byzantium, *Capita syllogistica*, in Joseph Hergenroether, ed., *Monumenta Graeca ad Photium eiusque historiam pertinentia* (Regensburg: G. J. Manz, 1869), 84–138. The Greek text is accompanied by a Latin translation made by the editor. There is also a modern edition with a German translation by Karl Förstel, *Schriften zum Islam/ Niketas von Byzanz* (Würzburg: Echter, 2000).

[123] This is the view taken by Kolbaba, *Inventing Latin Heretics*, 120–130.

well as from the Father, but only on the understanding that "procession" means something different in each case. This was an important clarification that was to become a standard assumption of Eastern theological thought on the subject. Of course, if that is the case, it is probably better to avoid confusion by using different words, and this is what the Easterners have generally done, by saying that the Holy Spirit proceeds from the Father and is manifested by (or through) the Son. In other words, the Father is the ultimate origin of the Spirit and the Son is merely the means by which he is revealed to us. This quickly became, and has remained, the only way in which the Eastern tradition can accommodate the idea that the Holy Spirit might "proceed" from or through the Son, and despite many attempts, it has proved impossible to reconcile their perception with the doctrine of the double procession as it was later developed in the West.[124]

Anselm and the Holy Spirit

After Photius and Nicetas passed from the scene, no more was heard of the *Filioque* until the eleventh century. It was finally added to the Roman version of the creed on February 14, 1014, as part of the reform of that church instigated by the German emperor Henry II and his advisers.[125] Forty years later, the pope and the patriarch of Constantinople excommunicated each other for jurisdictional reasons, but the Patriarch Michael Cerularius recalled the "blasphemous dogma" of the *Filioque*, which he added to his denunciations of the pope.[126] Cerularius was widely regarded as irascible, and would have been removed from office had he not died before his trial could take place, so his behavior should not be regarded as typical or definitive (although it subsequently became so). His more irenic successor, Constantine III Lichoudes (1059–1063), tried to patch things up with Rome by writing to the pope, asking for an explanation of the Latin doctrine of the double procession and hoping for a clarification.

An unsolicited reply was offered by Peter Damian (1007–1072) and may be taken as representing the Roman standpoint around 1060.[127] Peter began with a eulogy of the Roman see and its occupant, but did not rest his case for the double procession merely on the fact that it had received papal approval.

---

[124] The problem was less evident at the time because the *Filioque* was not accepted at Rome, and the popes were usually prepared to side with the East against the Frankish theologians, who were theoretically subject to their jurisdiction.

[125] Berno of Reichenau, *Libellus de quibusdam rebus ad missae officium pertinentibus*, in PL 142, coll. 1061–1061.

[126] PG 120, coll. 737–738. It should be said that the patriarch was excommunicated by the pope's legates, who were acting on their own authority, but their action was not repudiated by Rome.

[127] Peter Damian, *Contra errorem Graecorum de processione Spiritus Sancti* (*Opusculum* 38), in PL 145, coll. 633–642. An English translation can be found in James Likoudis, ed., *Ending the Byzantine Schism* (New Rochelle, NY: Catholics United for the Faith, 1992), 191–203.

Rather, he quoted Scripture at considerable length, pointing out that although John 15:26 says that the Holy Spirit proceeds from the Father (a belief that both sides naturally accepted), it does not deny that he also proceeds from the Son. To make that assumption on the basis of silence would be to misconstrue other sayings of Jesus, in which he told his disciples that his teaching was not his own and that anyone who believes in him does not believe in him, but in the one who sent him.[128] The correct interpretation of verses like these, said Peter, is not that Jesus' teaching was somehow alien to him but that belief in him entailed a relationship with the Father as well. It was in this perspective, argued Peter, that Jesus referred the procession of the Holy Spirit to the Father. In John 15:26 he was pointing out to his disciples that the Spirit proceeds from the Father *also*, so that they would not attribute his procession to the Son alone!

How Lichoudes reacted to this argument (if it ever reached him) we do not know. The schism of 1054 was never properly healed and is now taken to mark the definitive separation of East and West, though it was not perceived as such at the time. The two churches remained in communion with each other at the local level, and there is no indication that they regarded each other as schismatic. That awareness came only slowly, and was largely the result of the actions of the first crusaders, who in 1100 set up Latin bishops in Antioch and Jerusalem as rivals of their Greek counterparts. Most modern scholars believe that it was this provocative act, not the *Filioque* dispute, which was the real and lasting cause of the schism.[129]

The Crusades were the moment when East and West came face-to-face for the first time in a way that could not be finessed by diplomacy. When the Byzantine emperor appealed to the pope for help against the Turkish invaders who had recently deprived him of almost all of Asia Minor, the pope showed no hesitation in responding. There was no suggestion on his part that the Easterners were heretics who deserved what they were getting from the infidel. But the papacy could not raise troops in Western Europe unless there was a good spiritual reason for doing so. That was the chance to recapture the Holy Land, which had been lost to the Arabs as long ago as 638 and was of no interest to the Byzantines. From the start, therefore, the aims of West and East were different, a fact which the commanders in the field were quick to realize. To the knights of Western Europe who arrived in Constantinople, the Byzantines were effete and degenerate, scarcely different in many ways from the Muslims

[128] Peter quotes John 7:16 and 14:24.

[129] See Steven Runciman, *The Eastern Schism* (Oxford: Oxford University Press, 1955). The anathemas of 1054 were finally lifted in 1965. The most complete study of them and of the significance of their abolition is P. I. Boumis, *Ta anathemata Rômês—Kônstantinoupoleôs kai kanonikotês tês arseôs autôn* (Athens: Zôodochos Pêgê, 1980); and idem, *Synepeiai tês arseôs tôn anathematôn Rômês–Kônstantinoupoleôs* (Athens: Symmetria, 1994).

they were supposed to be conquering. To the Byzantines, on the other hand, the Westerners were uncouth barbarians whose zeal to conquer Jerusalem was pointless and politically unwise. The seeds of future discord were well and truly sown when the Byzantines stopped short at Antioch and let the crusaders go to Palestine on their own, an act that the latter regarded as treason to the sacred cause, for which the dubious theology of the Eastern church could be held responsible.

While all this was going on, the need to resolve the outstanding theological differences between the Eastern and Western churches was becoming acute. Much of southern Italy had been in Byzantine hands until the early eleventh century, and they had held onto Bari until 1071 when it finally surrendered to the Normans, cousins of the ones who had conquered England in 1066. There were still many Greeks there, and integrating their church with that of Rome was a pressing concern for the papacy. As it happened, when the first crusade was proclaimed, Anselm of Canterbury was in exile from his see and was taking refuge among the Normans of southern Italy.[130] In 1098 Pope Urban II asked him to expound the doctrine of the procession of the Holy Spirit in a way that would refute the claims originally made in the time of Photius and win the Greeks over to the Western position. The result was a discourse that Anselm later wrote up as a treatise.[131]

In response to the Greek arguments against the *Filioque*, Anselm took the standard position of Augustinian Trinitarianism but he was more precise, both in his dealing with the theses of the Photian era and in developing his own understanding of Trinitarian relations. Anselm denied the Photian contention that the two levels of objective reality in God (person and essence) were unconnected. On the contrary, he argued that the relations express to human minds how the three persons possess their common essence. The Father cannot come from the Son because, as their names tell us, it is the other way around. Likewise, the Father cannot come from the Holy Spirit, because the Spirit proceeds from him. The Son possesses the divine being because of his generation from the Father, in relation to whom his own identity is defined. Anselm argued that the Holy Spirit is free to proceed from the Father because there is nothing about his personal identity that would prevent that, but that if he does so (as John 15:26 says he does), he must proceed from the Son also, both because the

[130] Anselm was not a Norman himself, but lived and worked among them for most of his adult life.

[131] Anselm of Canterbury, *De processione Spiritus Sancti*, in PL 158, coll. 285–326. Translated by Richard Regan and published in *Anselm of Canterbury: The Major Works* (Oxford: Oxford University Press, 1998), 390–434, but with a different chapter division (noted here in parentheses). On Anselm and his medieval successors, see Dennis Ngien, *Apologetic for* Filioque *in Medieval Theology* (Milton Keynes: Paternoster, 2005), and Matthew Knell, *The Immanent Person of the Holy Spirit from Anselm to Lombard* (Milton Keynes: Paternoster, 2009).

identity of the Father is incomprehensible without the Son and because he is the Spirit of both. Anselm argued that if the Holy Spirit is fully God and consubstantial (*homoousion*) with the other two persons, he must proceed from the Son as well as from the Father:

> There is no relation of "father" apart from the relation of "son," just as there is no relation of "son" apart from the relation of "father." So, if one relation does not exist without the other, it is impossible to relate to one of them without the other. It therefore follows that if the Holy Spirit is from one of the relations he must be from both of them. . . . The Holy Spirit is from the Father because he is from God. But the Father is not more God than the Son is, and there is only one true God—the Father and the Son. So if the Holy Spirit is from the Father (since he is from God who is the Father), we cannot deny that he is also from the Son, since he is from God who is the Son [as well].[132]

To Anselm, the distinction that Photius made between the temporal mission of the Spirit from both the Father and the Son and his eternal procession from the Father alone was not a valid one, because in the being of God, the two processions of the Spirit, the one in time and the other in eternity, are parallel:

> I do not think that we can deny that there are two processions of the Holy Spirit, one when he originates from the Father and the other when he is given or sent, as long as we understand each procession in its own context. Of the second procession, the Lord [Jesus] has said, "The Spirit blows where he wishes. You hear the sound but you do not know where it comes from or where it goes."[133] . . . We can say of this procession that it is the same as being sent. Therefore, whether the Spirit proceeds only by originating from the Father, or only when he is given (or sent) and proceeds to sanctify creatures, or both ways, it follows that he proceeds from the Son.[134]

Nor was Anselm prepared to accept that the Holy Spirit could proceed from the Father through the Son, as both Tertullian and Gregory of Nyssa had suggested.[135] This was because, for him, the phrase "through the Son" was connected to the words of the creed, "by whom all things were made," and suggested that the Holy Spirit must be a creature. Anselm naturally rejected that and saw no difficulty in saying that the Son was the source of the Holy Spirit, because the Father had given the Son the ability to have life in himself.[136]

---

[132] Anselm of Canterbury, *De processione*, 2 (7).
[133] John 3:8, reading the Greek *pneuma* as "Spirit," not "wind."
[134] Anselm of Canterbury, *De processione* 6–7 (2).
[135] Ibid., 9 (4).
[136] Ibid., 20 (11). The allusion is to John 5:26.

The procession from the Son was the same as the procession from the Father, not because the two persons were confused or somehow merged into one, but because the Father had shared his distinctive life-giving property with the Son.

Most important for Anselm was his belief that the double procession of the Holy Spirit, far from dividing the Godhead in two, sealed the union between the Father and the Son and guaranteed their equality:

> Because God is both Father and Son, we say that the Holy Spirit is from both Father and Son. Since the Father is not before or after, greater or less than the Son, nor is one of them more or less God than the other, the Holy Spirit is not from the Father more than he is from the Son. . . . If that were the case, the Holy Spirit would not be from that in which the Father and the Son are one. It would then follow that the unity [of Father and Son] would be incomplete and relative, and that the different origin of the Holy Spirit in relation to them would be a sign of that diversity between them. But we cannot say that the Holy Spirit is not from what is common to the Father and the Son, since in that case, he would not be from God [who is both Father and Son].[137]

Anselm thus denied the Augustinian teaching that the Holy Spirit proceeds primarily (*principialiter*) from the Father, and posited the unity of Father and Son in their single spiration of the third person, rather than in the common Spirit that resulted from it:

> If the Greeks say that the Holy Spirit cannot be from two causes or two sources, we answer that we do not believe that on the ground that the Father and the Son are two [persons], but because they are one [God], so we do not say that there are two sources of the Spirit, but only one source.[138]

In saying this, Anselm moved away from locating the origin of the Holy Spirit in the divine essence that all three persons shared, to seeing it as inherent in the nature of their objective (or "real") relations. As he saw it, the Holy Spirit participates fully and equally in the mutual love of the Father and the Son and conveys both to the heart of the believer, not because of his *origin* from them but because of his permanent and ongoing *relationship* to them. This may seem like only a slight change from saying that the Holy Spirit is the fruit of the mutual love of the Father and the Son, but it made all the difference to Anselm. For that mutual love is the love of the atoning sacrifice of Calvary. On the cross, the divine self-offering and the divine forgiveness come together.

---

[137] Ibid., 14 (23).
[138] Ibid., 24 (14), 18 (10).

The Holy Spirit must be equally related to both, since otherwise he could not communicate the benefits of both to us. If he were the Spirit of the Father in a way that he is not the Spirit of the Son, our experience of God would be lopsided and incomplete.

We cannot forget that for Anselm, the procession of the Holy Spirit was intimately connected to his understanding of the incarnation and its purpose, but his Orthodox interlocutors may not have realized that.[139] There had been no corresponding discussion of the work of Christ in the Eastern church, and to them the doctrine of the procession of the Holy Spirit was not explicitly tied to that. They were moving along a trajectory that went directly from the person of Christ to the person of the Holy Spirit, without any intervening consideration of the work of Christ as a subject distinct from Christology. As a result, even if they could follow what Anselm was saying, they did not factor in the overall theological context that motivated him, and therefore missed something that was essential to his argument. Anselm did not say so explicitly, but for him a denial of the double procession of the Holy Spirit would have meant a denial of the Son's saving love in the life of the Christian, or at best, a relegation of that love to second place.

Anselm's contribution to the development of the doctrine of the double procession of the Holy Spirit is also significant at the level of New Testament exegesis. Unlike his Eastern counterparts, he did not confine himself to proof texts like John 14:26 and John 15:26, though he discussed those verses at length in chapter 9 of his treatise, arguing that the *quem ego mittam vobis a Patre* ("whom I shall send to you from the Father") of John 15:26 is the logical counterpart of the *mittet Pater in nomine meo* ("the Father will send in my name") of John 14:26. If the sending of the Spirit can be interchanged in this way, argued Anselm, the ontological basis for the sending must be identical. The Father sends the Spirit because the Spirit proceeds from him. If the Son also sends the Spirit, this must be because the Spirit also proceeds from the Son. If it were not so, it would not make sense for the Son to add that the Father sends the Spirit *in nomine meo* ("in my name"). The Father could, and therefore would, have sent him independently of the Son altogether.

But Anselm broadened the debate to include the whole compass of the farewell discourses of John 14–17. In chapter 11 of his treatise he took up John 16:13–14, verses that had been used to justify the language of reception when speaking of the Holy Spirit's relation to the Son. Anselm argued that because *quaecunque audiet, loquitur* ("whatever he hears, he speaks") is paralleled by

[139] Anselm referred explicitly to his "letter" *De incarnatione Verbi* in *De processione* 29 (16), where he repeats its argument.

de meo accipiet et annuntiabit vobis ("he will receive of mine and proclaim it to you"), the verbs *audire* ("hear") and *accipere* ("receive") must mean the same thing. The fact that the Holy Spirit does not speak by himself (*non loquitur de semetipso*) meant for Anselm that he could not speak on his own authority but only on behalf of the one from whom he hears and receives. Yet the Holy Spirit is not simply a mouthpiece; he is a person in his own right. Therefore, argued Anselm, the one from whom he hears and receives is the one from whom he is and proceeds.

Anselm broadened the scriptural argument still farther by demonstrating from other passages that the Father and the Son are one. Chapter 12 is taken up with a discussion of Matthew 11:27, which he used to support his earlier arguments. From there he extended his exegesis to the Psalms and beyond. Anselm's use of Scripture is certainly open to question, particularly when he gets into the Old Testament, but his basic assumption, which was that the *Filioque* clause does not stand or fall on the interpretation of John 15:26 in isolation, remains valid. That verse has to be read in context, and it was on that basis that Anselm claimed that the farewell discourses in John, the other Gospels, and Scripture as a whole, supported his argument in favor of the double procession of the Holy Spirit.

How can we assess Anselm nearly a thousand years later? On the one hand, we have to say that his arguments are theological, not political or historical. No doubt he must have been regarded in the East as an agent of the papacy, and his devotion to the Western position was certainly unquestioned, but he defended it by solid argumentation from Scripture and reason, not by relying on the tradition and supposed authority of his own church. The context in which he was working was polemical and potentially explosive, but it cannot be said that he added fuel to the fire. He regarded the Greeks as fellow Christians and sought only to instruct them in a way that would be acceptable to any reasonable person, not to score points in favor of the Latins. In this respect, his work stands in a class of its own and is superior to anything produced on either side before his time. On the other hand, like Photius, he was working within his own tradition and developing its inner logic, not listening to the arguments of the other side in a way that could be regarded as genuinely sympathetic to their concerns. That may not have been his fault, of course. Just as Photius could not read Latin, Anselm could not read Greek, and neither man had the breadth of education needed to appreciate where the other was coming from. Their expositions are therefore self-contained, making sense on their own premises but not really engaging seriously with the other side. That does not invalidate what Anselm had to say any more than it invalidates the contentions of Photius and his contemporaries, but it helps us to put them in their historical context and reminds us that we need to be cautious in the way we seek to use their arguments today.

The Course of the Controversy

Anselm belonged to the last generation of which it could fairly be said that it still thought in terms of a single Christian church embracing both East and West. By the time he died in 1109, the *de facto* separation of Christendom was well advanced. This is evident from the writings of Anselm of Havelberg (d. 1158), who went to Constantinople in 1135 and engaged in debate with Nicetas, the archbishop of Nicomedia, with the express intention of converting Nicetas to the Western position. We cannot be sure what really transpired in this encounter, but Anselm's account of it, which was written for home consumption, is clear and fair to the Greek side, which suggests that it is probably an accurate record of what happened.[140]

As a piece of theological writing, Anselm of Havelberg's *Dialogus* was the most technical to have appeared up to that time, though he lacked the depth of his earlier namesake. Nicetas presented the stock arguments of the Eastern tradition, which Anselm did his best to answer. The tone of the debate was cordial and it appears that both men were trying to reach agreement by consensus. They went over the Trinitarian ground carefully, demonstrating in the process just how much East and West had in common. Anselm was prepared to accept virtually everything Nicetas affirmed about the procession of the Holy Spirit from the Father, including his assertion that any procession from the Son must be different from that.[141] He even realized that if he had to choose between saying that the Holy Spirit proceeded from the common divine essence (*ousia*) or from the *hypostases* of the Father and/or the Son, he would end up either accepting the Eastern argument or turning the Holy Spirit into a kind of glorified creature that sprang from the divine being but was not a divine *hypostasis* in the true sense of the term.[142]

To avoid having to make such a choice, Anselm turned the question around by arguing that the Holy Spirit did not proceed from either the *hypostasis* or the essence of the Father and/or the Son, but from their mutual relation of love—the classic Augustinian position.[143] In what was perhaps the clearest

[140] Anselm of Havelberg, *Dialogus*, ed. Gaston Salet (Paris: Cerf, 1966). Also in PL 188, coll. 1163–1210. Anselm calls Nicetas "Nechites."
[141] Anselm of Havelberg, *Dialogus* 2.24.
[142] Ibid., 2.4.
[143] Ibid., 2.10.

statement to date of the function of the Holy Spirit as the "bond of love" that united the Father and the Son, Anselm wrote,

> By his breath, he [i.e., the Holy Spirit] joins both members of the Godhead and links them in one essence in himself—unity in Trinity and Trinity in unity, inexpressibly distinct yet wonderfully conjoined.[144]

Anselm left matters there, but his way of thinking was developed further in the next generation. One man who made a major (and generally underrated) contribution to it was William of St. Thierry (1070–1148), a companion of Bernard of Clairvaux and one of the greatest theologians of his age. William wrote,

> The Holy Spirit, who is the substantial will of the Father and the Son, so attaches the will of a man to himself that the soul, loving God and, by loving, sensing him, will be unexpectedly and entirely transformed—not into the nature of divinity certainly, but into a kind of blessedness beyond the human form yet short of the divine, in the joy of illuminating grace and the sense of an enlightened conscience.[145]

The same theme recurs in the writings of his younger contemporary, Richard of St. Victor (d. 1173), who analyzed Augustine's model of the Trinity and perfected it by modifying his idea that the Holy Spirit was the "bond of love" between the Father and the Son, an expression that seemed to make the Spirit something less than fully personal. In order to avoid that, Richard argued that for love to be perfect it must be shared by a community of persons. As he put it,

> If one person loves another and it goes no farther than that, there is love but it is not shared. If two persons love each other fully . . . there is love on both sides, but again it is not shared. Shared love only really exists when there is a third person who is loved by the other two in perfect harmony and community, because then the affection of the two persons is fused into one by the flame of love they have for the third. It is therefore clear that unless there were a third person in the Godhead, shared love would have no place in him.[146]

In developing his thought, Richard analyzed the concept of "person" to a degree that no one before him had done. He started with Boethius's definition of "person" as "the individual substance of a rational nature" and elaborated

---

[144] Ibid., 2.7.

[145] William of St. Thierry, *Speculum fidei*, 66. Edited by Marie-Madeleine Davy, *Deux traités sur la foi: le miroir de la foi, l'énigme de la foi* (Paris: J. Vrin, 1959), 72–73.

[146] Richard of St. Victor, *De Trinitate* 3.18. See also 3.15.

it by insisting on the individual and incommunicable *existence* of that rational nature in a community of relations.[147] In other words, a person was not just an object that could be observed and distinguished from other similar objects, but an agent that was active in relating to others—a "who" and not just a "what." This action and interaction defined personhood more than "origin," which could be understood only as a subsidiary concept. In other words, it was not the differences of origin that defined personal relations (which would then be unequal) but the similarity of those relations that pointed to the different origin of the individual persons that constituted them and made them perfect.

Richard argued that in God there must be three persons, one of whom was absolute in himself, one of whom owed his existence to that absolute person, and one of whom owed his existence to both of the others. That there could be only one absolute person was self-evident to him, because anything else would lead to chaos. If there were many self-existent persons, they would have no reason to acknowledge or relate to one another, nor could one self-existent person communicate that self-existence to anyone else, since communication implies relation and therefore some kind of dependence.[148] The one self-existent person (who is the Father, of course) can generate another person who is his equal, and must do so if his own personhood is to be fulfilled. The reason for this is that love cannot be entirely self-centered but must be directed to another being if it is to be truly itself. But it is only possible for the one self-existent person to generate one such other person, because if there were two or more, they would lack that individual and incommunicable essence that is needed to distinguish them from each other.[149] A third person, generated in the same way as the second, would not only be the second's twin but (in a perfect being) would merge with the second and be indistinguishable from him.

For that reason, a third person must be related to the other two in a different way. The logic of love between two persons suggests that a third person is necessary in order to prevent the mutual love of the two from becoming selfish and unproductive. Only when a third person appears, whom the other two love equally, is the perfection of their mutual love assured. But while that third person must share their perfection in order to be worthy of their perfect love, he must also be sufficiently different from them to be distinguishable and therefore lovable in his own right.[150] Richard rounded off his discussion by saying that there can be only one person who receives his identity from the others

[147] Ibid., 4.22–24.
[148] Ibid., 5.3–4.
[149] Ibid., 5.7.
[150] Ibid., 5.8.

but who is not the source of any other person's identity.[151] His whole scheme can be summarized as follows:

First Person (Father): The self-existent person who gives existence to others.
Second Person (Son): The person who receives existence from one and gives it to another.
Third Person (Holy Spirit): The person who receives existence from others.

Thus we find that in the perfection of the Godhead, there is one person who only gives, one person who only receives, and one person who both gives and receives. In this way, each of them is distinct from the others but retains his full divinity and therefore his participation in the unity of the one God. From there, Richard went on to argue that the Holy Spirit, as the mutual love of the Father and the Son, does not bear a fourth divine person but is sent to us instead, so that by being united to him we may share in the eternal love of God.[152] Within the context of Western theology, Richard's development of the personal relations in God must be regarded as one of the greatest achievements of the Augustinian tradition, whose compelling force is still felt today. But whether his elaborate Trinitarianism ever reached the Greeks is uncertain. If it did, it was not taken seriously by the Eastern churches and did not become the basis for any constructive dialogue between East and West.

Another important voice from this time was that of Gilbert de la Porrée (1075?–1154), who seemed to have solved the old problem of how the personal relations of the Trinity could be harmonized with the unity of the divine essence.[153] Gilbert said that it was necessary to distinguish the essence of a thing (*id quod est*) from the means whereby it had come to be (*id quo est*). Since the value of a thing could hardly be less than that of the means whereby it had come to be, the means also entered the realm of objective reality. In theological terms, it could therefore be said that the personal relations constituted the divine essence, because it was by them that the Father, the Son, and the Holy Spirit had acquired their identity. In other words, the relations were subsistent in God and constituted his substance.

Gilbert's philosophical outlook did not do justice to the persons of the Godhead, who in his view were constituted by the relations, which were logically prior to the persons they created. He was condemned for this, but his error would later be rectified by Thomas Aquinas (1226–1274), who said that

[151] Ibid., 5.12.
[152] Ibid., 6.14.
[153] On Gilbert, see Michael E. Williams, *The Teaching of Gilbert Porreta on the Trinity as Found in His Commentaries on Boethius* (Rome: Aedes Universitatis Gregorianae, 1951), and Etienne Gilson, *History of Christian Philosophy in the Middle Ages* (London: Sheed & Ward, 1955), 140–144, 620–621.

the persons are themselves the relations, making the question of priority redundant.[154] Gilbert was heavily dependent on the philosophical methods of Aristotle, which were being revived in the West even as they were fading from view in the East. From this time onward therefore, we are entitled to say that the two halves of Christendom were separated not only by political and cultural differences but also by theological methods that were not understood, let alone shared, by the other side.

At the time, no one could have predicted that these differences would be permanent. Richard's theology might have penetrated the East eventually, and the East might have produced a response to it based on its own traditions, but unforeseen political events conspired to make that impossible. In 1203, dynastic quarrels in Constantinople, combined with dissension and greed among the crusading armies that were trying to get to the Holy Land without the resources they needed to support them, led to a deal between a claimant to the Byzantine throne and the crusaders. In return for putting him in power, the renegade Alexius IV promised to fund the crusaders on their journey to Jerusalem. Grasping at this, the crusaders sailed to Constantinople, from which the reigning emperor Alexius III (1195–1203) fled. Alexius IV then took over the reins of power, only to find that there was no money to pay the crusaders. On April 13, 1204, they captured Constantinople and sacked it, amid scenes of appalling brutality and destruction. The Byzantine empire was officially Latinized, and the Eastern church was forcibly united to that of Rome. Pope Innocent III (1198–1216) privately deplored what had happened but took full advantage of the opportunity to extend his church's influence, and the circumstances that enabled him to do that have never been forgotten or forgiven in the East. The British historian Donald Nicol (1923–2003) wrote of it:

> . . . monasteries and churches were emptied of their wealth. Chalices, stripped of their jewels, became drinking-cups; icons became gaming-boards and tables; and nuns in their convents were raped and robbed. In St. Sophia the soldiers tore down the veil of the sanctuary and smashed the gold and silver carvings of the altar and the ambon[155] . . . a prostitute sat on the patriarch's throne singing bawdy French songs . . . the most horrifying account of all comes from the pen not of a Greek but of Innocent III, who was quick to condemn what he might have foreseen but had been powerless to prevent.[156]

---

[154] Thomas Aquinas, *Summa theologiae* I.40.2. See Gilles Emery, *The Trinitarian Theology of Saint Thomas Aquinas* (Oxford: Oxford University Press, 2007). Originally published as *La théologie trinitaire de saint Thomas d'Aquin* (Paris: Cerf, 2005).

[155] The lectern or pulpit.

[156] Donald Nicol, "The Fourth Crusade and the Greek and Latin Empires," in Joan M. Hussey, ed. *The Cambridge Medieval History IV: The Byzantine Empire*, 275–330. The quotation is on 286–287.

As a result of those events, the theological issues at stake could no longer be separated from political considerations. Even today, when dealing with the East, the Western churches must recognize that their ancestors were responsible for the most unspeakable crime ever committed by one group of Christians against another and try to understand what the consequences of that were for any hope of reunion. In the West, people often look back on the Crusades with a certain romanticized fondness and are happy to use the word for evangelistic campaigns and the like. But in the East, the Crusades were a catastrophe for the local Christians. Even under Muslim rule they had often been the majority population, but that changed as many were forcibly converted to Islam, so as not to give the West an excuse to "liberate" their religious brethren. The Byzantine empire was fatally weakened, even if remnants of it were able to survive for another 250 years, and in the end the whole of Eastern Europe succumbed to the domination of the Ottoman Turks, which was not alleviated until the nineteenth century. Even today, Constantinople (Istanbul) remains in Muslim hands, with little prospect that it will ever revert to Christian rule.

The psychological effect of this on the Eastern churches has been devastating, not least because it also signaled a permanent shift in the balance of power between the two halves of the Christian world.[157] Until the twelfth century there had been no question that the East was more advanced, theologically and culturally, than the West was. But after the Crusades, that began to change. For the first time, Western theological works were translated into Greek and circulated in the East, where they gained a number of highly educated and influential converts. These Westernizers, or "Latinophrones" as they were called, were an elite but they were well placed and did everything they could to bring their church closer to Western norms. Much of the story from 1204 to the final fall of Constantinople to the Turks in 1453 is a tale of the internal struggle in the Eastern church between the Latinophrones and their opponents. For that reason, the controversies of those years affected the Eastern churches far more than the Western one, and even today, members of those churches are more likely to be aware of theological issues like the double procession of the Holy Spirit than Roman Catholics or Protestants are.[158]

[157] For an understanding of how an educated modern Greek might perceive this, see Christos Yannaras, *Orthodoxy and the West*, trans. Peter Chamberas and Norman Russell (Boston, MA: Holy Cross Orthodox Press, 2006). The original text was published as *Orthodoxia kai Dysê stê neôterê Hellada* (Athens: Ekdoseis Domos, 1992). As the translators warn the reader, "the polemical tone—though not the passion—of the original has been modified" (xi).

[158] In recent years, the dominant trend in the Eastern churches has been to see the Latinophrones as heretics and deeply un-Orthodox, but although it is true that many of them eventually fled to the West and joined the Roman church, it is grossly unfair to characterize them in this way. For an alternative perspective that situates them in the long history of Byzantine humanism and defends the legitimacy of their position within the Eastern church, see Gerhard Podskalsky, *Von Photios zu Bessarion. Der Vorrang humanistisch geprägter Theologie in Byzanz und deren bleibenden Bedeutung* (Wiesbaden: Harrassowitz Verlag, 2003).

The Latin empire set up in Constantinople in 1204 was unable to take over all the former Byzantine territories, and was soon reduced to a small area around the city. Greek refugees established themselves in the provinces, especially in Nicea, which became the center of Greek resistance, and from there they worked steadily to recover the capital. Theological debate between East and West continued even in these inauspicious circumstances, but the tone was often polemical. It is therefore all the more remarkable that there were some theologians on the Eastern side who were still open to Western arguments and genuinely interested in the reunion of the churches. One of these was Nicephorus Blemmydes (d. 1272), who engaged in an unsuccessful debate with papal representatives who visited Nicea in 1234.[159] In 1250 Blemmydes found himself debating the double procession of the Holy Spirit with John of Parma, an experience that touched him deeply and led him to compile a collection of patristic references to the procession of the Spirit "through the Son."[160] That effort transformed his appreciation of the issues at stake and led him to criticize his fellow Greeks who could not rise above their anti-Western prejudices. He came to the conclusion that the Son did indeed participate in some way in the procession of the Holy Spirit, though it would be too much to say that he was converted to the Western position.[161] The most that can be said is that there were now significant differences of opinion on the Eastern side and a willingness on the part of some to consider the Western view, even if not to accept it outright.

The rulers of Nicea managed to recapture Constantinople in 1261, although they never expelled the crusaders from Greece entirely. The new emperor Michael VIII (1258–1282) promptly embarked on a diplomatic offensive designed to protect his gains from attack. A major element of his strategy was a formal and permanent reunion of the churches, which would relieve the West of any excuse to try to conquer his empire. Michael approached the papacy, and it was agreed to summon a council at Lyon in 1274, where church union would be the main item on the agenda. Michael may not have known it, but by then opinion in the West had hardened into opposition to the Eastern doctrine, which the Franciscan Bonaventure (1221–1274) was even able to condemn as

[159] On this debate, see Girolamo Golubovich, "Disputatio Latinorum et Graecorum," in *Archivum Franciscanum Historicum* 12 (1919), 428–470; Paul Canart, "Nicéphore Blemmyde et le mémoire adressé aux envoyés de Grégoire IX (Nicée, 1234)," in *Orientalia Christiana Periodica* 25 (1959), 310–325; and Joseph Munitiz, "A Reappraisal of Blemmydes' First Discussion with the Latins," in *Byzantinoslavica* 51 (1991), 20–26.

[160] The details are in *Nicephori Blemmydae autobiographia sive curriculum vitae*, ed. Joseph A. Munitiz (Turnhout: Brepols, 1984).

[161] See Nicephorus Blemmydes, *De processione Spiritus Sancti orationes duae*, in PG 142, coll. 553–584; and V. Grumel, "Nicéphore Blemmyde et la procession du Saint-Esprit," in *Revue des sciences philosophiques et théologiques* 18 (1929), 636–656. See also, V. I. Barvinok, *Nikifor Vlemmid i ego sočinenija* (Kiev: P. Barskij v Kieve, 1911); and Joseph Gill, *Byzantium and the Papacy 1198–1400* (New Brunswick, NJ: Rutgers University Press, 1979), 152–157.

unsophisticated and due to Greek ignorance, pride, and obstinacy.[162] Bonaventure's understanding of Trinitarian relations was heavily dependent on Richard of St. Victor and can be summed up in the following definition:

> The Spirit is properly called the bond of unity between the Father and the Son. Spirit, taken in the sense of spirituality, is common to the whole Trinity, but with respect to spiration, it is proper to the Holy Spirit. . . . The Holy Spirit proceeds from the Father and the Son, not because they are distinct persons but because in them there is one effect of their will, one active spiration.[163]

Bonaventure's contemporary, the Dominican Thomas Aquinas, wrote a treatise at the request of the pope, in which he defended the Western view of the *Filioque*, which he took with him to the Second Council of Lyon in 1274.[164]

Aquinas emphasized the problems of translating from Greek to Latin and vice versa, blaming this for most of the misunderstanding that had arisen. In particular, he was convinced that "from the Son" and "through the Son" meant the same thing and that the word "procession" was capable of a wide range of meanings. That was certainly true, but Aquinas was ignorant of Greek and therefore insensitive to its subtleties. Furthermore, about two-thirds of the quotations he made from Greek sources were either spurious or mistranslated, seriously reducing the value of his argument, but his authority as a theologian was such that in the West, his views became the semiofficial standard.[165] Agreement between the churches therefore came to mean acceptance of Thomas's position, warts and all, and it is only in recent times that this has been seriously questioned on the Roman Catholic side.[166]

Aquinas began his argument with the assertion that the New Testament speaks of the Spirit of the Son.[167] He then pointed out that Jesus told his disciples that he would send the Spirit to them after returning to the Father.[168] Next, he went on to say that the Holy Spirit takes what belongs to the Son and gives it to believers, and what belongs to the Son is his divinity.[169] He then claimed that various Greek sources taught that the Spirit was the image of the

---

[162] Bonaventure, *Commentarium in IV libros Sententiarum* 1.11.1.1.
[163] Ibid., I, d.10, a.1, q.1.
[164] Thomas Aquinas, *Contra errores Graecorum*, in *Opera omnia iussu Leonis XIII edita*, 40A, 67–105. There is an English translation in Likoudis, *Ending the Byzantine Schism*, 125–189. Only the second part of the work deals directly with the double procession of the Holy Spirit.
[165] In fairness to Aquinas, he did remark that many of the quotations from Greek sources seemed somewhat strange and out of character for their supposed authors!
[166] Protestants were not committed to Aquinas, of course, but their relative lack of interest in the doctrine allowed his views to dominate in their circles by default and usually without acknowledgment.
[167] Thomas Aquinas, *Contra errores Graecorum* 2.1, quoting Gal. 4:6.
[168] Ibid., 2.2, quoting John 15:26; 16:7.
[169] Ibid., 2.3, quoting John 16:14–15.

Son, basing this on Romans 8:29 and 1 Corinthians 15:49, though the "sources" are spurious.[170] Most importantly, Aquinas insisted that the Holy Spirit is a person who proceeds from the persons (*hypostases*) of the Father and the Son, and not merely an expression of their common essence, quoting Epiphanius of Salamis in his support.[171] He also claimed Cyril of Alexandria as evidence that the Eastern church believed that the Son was a personal spirator of the Holy Spirit along with the Father, but once again, the Greek sources he quoted are inauthentic.[172] However, we now know that in at least one instance he was able to show that Cyril's thought on the matter had been misinterpreted by Theodoret of Cyrus, whose "evidence" was wrongly used by the Eastern church to support its position.[173]

Most of Aquinas's arguments can be summed up by saying that they followed the lines already laid down by Anselm of Canterbury and Richard of St. Victor, both of whom he quoted; that they were rooted in the New Testament and in patristic sources (even if most of the latter are spurious); and that while he was trying to prove that the Holy Spirit proceeds from the Father and the Son as persons, he often conflated his evidence, using references to the divine essence, or expressions like "flow from" (taken to be synonymous with "proceed") to back up his argument. It is not difficult to see how a Greek opponent would pick holes in the treatise, and it is perhaps just as well that they never got the chance. In one particular, however, Aquinas made a move that was to have serious consequences for future dialogue between the estranged traditions of West and East. Concluding his remarks on the double procession, he said,

> The error of those who say that the vicar of Christ, the pontiff of the Roman church, does not have primacy over the universal church is just like the error of those who say that the Holy Spirit does not proceed from the Son. For Christ himself, the Son of God, consecrates and marks the church as his own with the Holy Spirit, his own character and seal . . .[174]

This link between the office and authority of the papacy on the one hand, and the double procession of the Holy Spirit on the other had ancient antecedents, as we have seen, but it would now become a major ingredient in the theological dispute and would complicate it in new and unforeseen ways. No longer

---

[170] Ibid., 2.5. We might add that the interpretation is also mistaken.

[171] Ibid., 2.12. Unfortunately, his text of Epiphanius (*Ancoratus* 81) was defective and the original does not corroborate what Aquinas was arguing.

[172] Ibid., 2.15–19.

[173] Thomas Aquinas, *De potentia*, 10.4.24. See André de Halleux, "Cyrille, Théodoret et le *Filioque*," in *Revue d'Histoire Ecclésiastique* LXXIV (1979), 597–625 for confirmation of this.

[174] Thomas Aquinas, *Contra errores Graecorum* 2.32.

would it be just a question of agreeing about the relationship between the Holy Spirit and the Son. From now on, acceptance of the Western position would also entail submission to the claims of the papacy—a very different matter.[175]

Like all his predecessors, Aquinas was essentially a disciple of Augustine, though he concentrated on aspects of his great *De Trinitate* that had not received the same attention in earlier times. In particular, he took the Augustinian analogy of mind, intellect, and will and applied it directly to the concept of "procession" within God:

> In God, procession corresponds only to an action inside the agent himself, and not to one that is directed to something external. In the spiritual world, the only actions of this kind are those of intellect and will. The procession of the Word corresponds to the action of the intellect. But there is another spiritual process following the action of the will, which is the emission of love, whereby what is loved is in the lover, just as what is expressed (or understood in the conception of an idea) is in the knower. For this reason there is another procession in God besides that of the Word, namely, the procession of love.[176]

More than anyone before him, Aquinas thought in terms of two processions from the Father, the procession we call "generation" that applies to the Son, and the one we call "procession" that applies to the Holy Spirit. This double use of the word "procession" is confusing to the uninitiated and points to a certain inadequacy in the vocabulary that Aquinas had at his disposal. This impression is confirmed by the fact that he insisted on a distinction between "cause" (which he rejected) and "principle" (which he preferred) as explanations of the origin of the persons of the Trinity, even though he occasionally used them as synonyms just as he accused the Greeks of mistakenly doing.[177]

Aquinas also defined "person" as "subsistent relation," though here again he made a distinction between human and divine persons that can be confusing. In human beings, the individual person is primary and his relations depend on that; but in God, persons and relations coincide, making it difficult to decide whether the former really precedes the latter. As an example of how a relation can condition the identity of a divine person, consider the following:

> The Father and the Son share a unity of essence and differ only in that the former is Father and the latter is Son. Anything other than that is common

[175] Aquinas believed that the *Filioque* had been added to the creed at a council called in the West under papal authority, but he did not say what council that was (*Summa theologiae* I.36.2.2.). He may have been thinking of one of the Councils of Toledo, perhaps the third, which met in 589 and has traditionally been credited with the addition.
[176] Thomas Aquinas, *Summa theologiae* Ia.27.3.
[177] Ibid., 1.36.3. Matters were not helped by the fact that Aquinas put the Greek denial of the *Filioque* down to ignorance and obstinacy on their part. See Thomas Aquinas, *Summa theologiae* I.36.2.

> to both of them. But the notions of paternity and sonship do not include the principle of the Holy Spirit. There is one relation by which the Father is Father and another by which he is the principle of the Holy Spirit. Therefore, being the principle of the Holy Spirit is something common to the Father and the Son.[178]

In other words, the procession of the Holy Spirit defines the persons of the Father and the Son in a way that overcomes their inherent opposition to each other and makes them a common principle of unity in the origin of the Holy Spirit. Seen in its own context, the Thomist synthesis is subtle and comprehensive, embracing different strands of Western Trinitarian theology and even reaching out to the East to some extent, particularly in the way that Thomas was willing to see the Spirit's procession from the Father as notionally prior to his procession from the Son. But the very sophistication of Aquinas's presentation distanced it from both the East and the world of the Western church fathers, who would not have been comfortable with his tendency toward philosophical abstraction, even if it helped to clarify some of the problems that had plagued earlier generations.

His equation of person with relation removed the Eastern complaint that in Western theology the persons are somehow dependent on their relations for their being, but it confirmed the Eastern suspicion that Western Trinitarianism sees nothing more than the relations in the persons of the Trinity, thereby compromising their hypostatic individuality. If the persons were no more than their relations, the Easterners argued, they would need each other to exist and they would therefore lack the self-sufficiency that is a fundamental attribute of God. In their view that could not be right, and such a doctrine merely confirmed the Eastern churches in their suspicion that the God of the West was no more than an impersonal essence and therefore intrinsically Sabellian (modalist).

Aquinas was very careful to assert that the Trinity and its relations within the being of God cannot be known by rational means because they belong to the sphere of divine revelation, but although he was clearer than his predecessors about the unbridgeable gap between this world and the next, he also found room for an analogy of continuity between the origin of the Son and the Holy Spirit on the one hand, and creation on the other. As he put it,

> Just as the Father speaks of himself and of every creature by his begotten Word, to the extent that the Word begotten adequately represents the Father and every creature, so he loves himself and every creature by the Holy Spirit,

[178] Thomas Aquinas, *Summa contra Gentiles* 4.24.

> in that the Holy Spirit proceeds as the love of the primal goodness by which the Father loves himself and every creature. It is therefore evident that a relation to the creature is implied both in the Word and in the Love that proceeds in a secondary way, insofar as the divine truth and goodness are the principle of understanding and loving all creatures.[179]

This link between the divine and the created would stir great unease in the Eastern world, where the absolute divide between the Creator and the creation was axiomatic and the fear of some covert return to Arianism or to Macedonianism was ever-present. What seemed unexceptional and even inspired to the West caused alarm in the East and may well explain why the doctrine of creation played such a large part in later Byzantine polemic around and against the double procession of the Holy Spirit.

In fairness to Aquinas, however, it must be said that within the confines of his own logical framework, his development of the double procession doctrine made good sense, and it is easy to see why he could not understand why the theologians of the Eastern church failed to see this.[180] For him, the double procession of the Holy Spirit was closely tied to the unity of the Father and the Son, and also with the unity of the person of Christ manifested in two natures.[181] To deny it would be to compromise the divine status of the Son.[182] Of particular importance to him was the fact that the salvation brought to mankind in and through the Holy Spirit was totally Christological in content, making it seem natural and obvious that the Spirit is the Son's "stamp" (*character*) and therefore that he proceeds from the Son as much as from the Father.[183]

It can also be said that Thomas paid more attention to the question of the double procession as time went on, even to the point where he might be said to have become obsessed with it.[184] His main claim was that the persons of the Godhead are distinguished from each other by "relative opposition."[185] The Father relates to the Son and the Holy Spirit in different ways, but this does not mean that he is two persons, because the different relations are not opposed to each other.[186] If there were no such relational opposition between the Son and the Spirit, he argued, they would be one and the same person, which would

[179] Thomas Aquinas, *Summa theologiae* I.36.2.
[180] See Gilles Emery, *Trinitarian Theology*, 269–297, for an exposition of Aquinas's position and his attitude toward the East.
[181] Thomas Aquinas, *Summa theologiae* I.36.2.3. See also Thomas Aquinas, *De potentia* 10.4.24.
[182] Thomas Aquinas, *Contra errores Graecorum* 2, prologue.
[183] Thomas Aquinas, *De potentia* 10.4; *Contra errores Graecorum* 2.6–7.
[184] See Gilles Emery, "La procession du Saint-Esprit chez Saint Thomas d'Aquin," in *Revue Thomiste* XCVI (1996), 559–569.
[185] Thomas Aquinas, *Summa theologiae* I.28.3–4; I.40.2–3.
[186] Ibid., 1.30.2; 1.36.2; *De potentia*, 10.5.

be a form of Sabellianism.[187] The Spirit's procession from the Son is therefore a safeguard against the loss of the Spirit's distinctive identity, and it was this, more than anything else, that drove Aquinas to conclude that a denial of the *Filioque* would expose the church to heresy. On the other hand, he understood that the Eastern church did in fact deny it without falling into Sabellianism, something that he regarded as an inconsistency in its thinking.[188]

Thomas was also driven to insist on the *Filioque* because of his identification of the Son with the Word and the Spirit with the Love of God. As he put it,

> It is necessary that Love should proceed from the Word. That is why we cannot love something unless we have first conceived of it in our mind. It is thus evident that the Holy Spirit proceeds from the Son.[189]

One last point was that the Holy Spirit proceeds from the Father and the Son insofar as they are one, but that this oneness must be understood not as describing the essence of the agent(s) but rather as the principle of their common action. As he put it,

> If "insofar as" means the condition of the one who acts or operates, the Holy Spirit proceeds from the Father and Son as two [*hypostases*], and insofar as they are distinct persons. . . . But if "insofar as" refers to the condition of the principle of the action, then . . . the Holy Spirit proceeds from them insofar as they are one. Since the operation comes from one single principle, there must be in the Father and the Son something that is singular and is the principle of the act of spiration, an act that is one and simple, by which the one and simple person of the Holy Spirit proceeds.[190]

This formula of two persons united in a single action called "spiration" would enter the common theology of the Western church and be used as the foundation of its understanding of the double procession at the Council of Florence in 1439, but it was not sufficiently current in Thomas's lifetime for it to have been used in discussions with the East at that time.

Thomas Aquinas never got to the Second Council of Lyon in 1274 because he died *en route*, but it made little difference. The Greeks were forced to accept the *Filioque* as fully orthodox and, although they were not formally committed to embracing the interpretations of Bonaventure and Aquinas, that must have been the Western understanding of what was intended by their agreement.

---

[187] Thomas Aquinas, *De potentia* 10.5.
[188] On this, see Gilles Emery, *Trinitarian Theology*, 294–297.
[189] Thomas Aquinas, *Summa theologiae* I.36.2.
[190] Thomas Aquinas, *Commentarium in libros Sententiarum*, 1.11.1.2.

What we can say for certain is that Western theology, whose influence in the East was already strong, was now free to penetrate to the heart of Eastern spirituality. The small but influential group of "Latinophrones" who surrounded the emperor undertook to spread the Western way of thinking among their coreligionists in the hope that it could be made to stick. No doubt some of them did this mainly for political reasons, but many of them were sincerely convinced that the Western position was right, and it is unfair to brand them as renegades. In spite of their efforts, however, there was a great deal of popular resistance in the East to a church union that amounted to surrender to the West. The counterattack was led by the monks of Constantinople and of Mount Athos, which now became the center of spiritual opposition to imperial Byzantine policy. The union was duly proclaimed in Constantinople on January 16, 1275, but it caused an immediate split in the church and lapsed when Michael VIII died on December 11, 1282. It was at that point that the sincerity of the Latinophrones was tested, and to their credit, most of them remained loyal to their cause and did not give up trying to convert the main body of the Eastern church to their view. Deprived of imperial support, they began to write in defense of their position and to translate the major Latin theological works that had shaped the Western tradition but that were virtually unknown in the Eastern world.[191]

When the Latinophrones sought to express the new Western theology in the context of their own Eastern tradition, they came up against two obstacles. First, the West did not distinguish between being (essence) and existence in the way that the Greeks did. Its theologians did not regard the Trinitarian relations as hypostatic properties distinct from the essence of God, but rather as hypostatic principles inherent in that essence. The practical consequence of this was that it was impossible for the Westerners to imagine how the Holy Spirit could have been sent into the world by the Father and the Son and acknowledged as the Spirit of both without having proceeded from each of them equally. This is why the West regarded the Eastern rejection of the *Filioque* as ignorant and obstinate—the Easterners could not see why there should be a necessary connection between the essence of God in himself and his revealed existence in the world.

Second, the West distinguished "principle" from "cause" in a way that the

[191] For the Second Council of Lyon and its aftermath, see Burkhard Roberg, *Das zweite Konzil von Lyon (1274)* (Paderborn: Ferdinand Schöningh, 1990); Joseph Gill, *Church Union: Rome and Byzantium (1204–1453)* (London: Variorum Reprints, 1979); Vitalien Laurent and Jean Darrouzès, *Dossier grec de l'union de Lyon (1273–1277)* (Paris: Institut Français d'Etudes Byzantines, 1976); Ch. A. Arambatzis, *Hê synodos tês Lyôn. Prosôpa kai theologia* (Thessalonica: Pournaras, 2002); G. P. Theodoroudis, *Hê ekporeusis tou Hagiou Pneumatos kata tous syngrapheis tou 13ou aiônos* (Thessalonica: Kourmanos, 1990).

East could not grasp, even though (as we saw in the case of Thomas Aquinas) the West did not always carry this distinction through in practice.[192] It was his inability to make this distinction meaningful to the Greek-speaking world that was to be the undoing of the Latinophrone patriarch John XI Beccus (1275–1282).[193]

Beccus began his career as an anti-Latin writer, but after the Second Council of Lyon he was converted to the Roman cause and was made patriarch of Constantinople in order to implement the church union agreed on at the council. Being an Easterner, he naturally tried to express the double procession of the Holy Spirit "as from a single principle" in terms of causality. This led him to claim that there was a "Sonly cause" of the Holy Spirit which leads up to and merges with the "Fatherly cause," so that in the end there is only one cause of the Holy Spirit.[194] But in the eyes of his fellow Easterners, this obscured the hypostatic individuality of the Father and the Son, whose distinct actions were folded into a single cause and therefore "confused." There is no way that this conflation can be avoided, if Beccus's interpretation of the Latin *principium* ("principle") as the equivalent of the Greek *aitia* ("cause") is adopted. The Greek term was simply not flexible enough to be able to accommodate the noncausal meaning attributed by Aquinas and others to *principium*.[195]

Beccus developed his argument by asking whether the Holy Spirit proceeded from the essence (*ousia*) of the Father or from his *hypostasis*. He answered by saying that if it was agreed that the Spirit proceeded from the Father's essence, it would also have to be said that that essence did not exist without its *hypostasis*. We would then have to conclude that the Spirit proceeds from both the essence and the *hypostasis* of the Father. But if that is true, it must also be agreed that the essence of the Father is the same as the essence of the Son, who cannot be distinguished from the Father at the level of their common *ousia*. It must also be agreed that, just as the essence of the Father does not exist without its corresponding *hypostasis*, the essence of the Son does not exist without his *hypostasis* either. Therefore, to proceed from the essence of the Father is to proceed from the essence of the Son, both of which are hypostatized as the distinct persons that we recognize in the Trinity. If this logic is accepted, then the Holy Spirit must proceed from the Father and the Son, and the *Filioque*

[192] See, for example, Thomas Aquinas, *Summa theologiae* I.33.1–2.

[193] On Beccus, see N. G. Xexakis, *Iôannês Bekkos kai hai theologikai antilêpseis autou* (Athens: Organismos Panepistimiou Athênôn, 1981).

[194] John Beccus, *De Spiritu Sancto*, in PG 146, coll. 196–614.

[195] *Principium* could more accurately have been translated as *archê*, but that would not have solved the problem. On the contrary, it would probably have made matters worse, because *archê* is the term used for the divine *monarchia*, which the Eastern fathers unanimously attributed to the Father alone.

doctrine is justified.[196] The problem of course was that in the Eastern tradition, the cause (*aitia*) of the Son and the Holy Spirit was not the essence of the Father but his *hypostasis* only, as John of Damascus had stated.[197]

It appears that Beccus followed Augustine as far as he understood him, but was unable to integrate the later Latin tradition into the framework of traditional Greek theological thought because of the latter's insistence on making a real distinction between the existence of the divine persons in God and the essence of the Godhead itself. Beccus also followed Aquinas's teaching that "from" and "through" were synonymous and applied this in a much more thorough way to his Greek sources, which he quoted accurately (unlike Aquinas, it must be said) but misinterpreted on this point, as on others.[198]

Beccus's most sophisticated opponent was Gregory II (George) of Cyprus (1241–1290), who was effectively his successor as patriarch of Constantinople from 1283 to 1289.[199] In his basic approach, Gregory followed the Photian tradition, arguing that the *hypostasis* of the Father is the source of divinity, and that he constitutes the "natural beginning and root of the Son and the Spirit."[200] Gregory freely admitted that the Holy Spirit shares the Son's divine essence (*ousia*), but as is the case with the Son, the Holy Spirit receives this from the Father's *hypostasis* alone. Therefore, even if the Holy Spirit can be described as coming from the Father and the Son according to his essence (this is the *homoousion*), as a divine *hypostasis* he does not proceed from both but only from the Father:

> Just as the Spirit is and is said to be consubstantial with the Son because both are consubstantial with the Father, we may certainly say that because of the identity of essence shared by the Father and the Son, the Spirit who comes from the essence of the Father may also rightly be said to come from the essence of the Son. But to say that he comes from the Son's *hypostasis* merely

196 John Beccus, *Peri tês henôseôs kai eirênês tôn tês Palaias kai Neas Rômês ekklêsiôn*, 29–30. The text can be found in PG 141, coll. 125d–128a, and in a critical edition by Hugo Laemmer, *Scriptorum Graeciae Orthodoxae: bibliotheca selecta*, 2 vols. (Freiburg-im-Breisgau, 1864–1866), 1:363–364.

197 John of Damascus, *De fide orthodoxa* 10.

198 See Xexakis, *Ioannês Bekkos*, 130–131.

199 Beccus was deposed on December 30, 1282, following the death of the emperor Michael VIII. His immediate successor was Joseph I, who had also been his predecessor (1266–1275), but Joseph died on March 23, 1283. On Gregory II, see Aristeides Papadakis, *Crisis in Byzantium: The* Filioque *Controversy in the Patriarchate of Gregory II of Cyprus (1283–1289)* (New York: Fordham University Press, 1983); Jean-Claude Larchet, ed., *La vie et l'oeuvre théologique de Georges/Grégoire II de Chypre (1241–1290) patriarche de Constantinople* (Paris: Cerf, 2012); Ch. N. Sabbatos, *Hê theologikê horologia kai problêmatikê tês pneumatologias Grêgoriou B' tou Kypriou* (Katerini: Ekdoseis Epektasê, 1997).

200 Gregory of Cyprus, *Logos antirrhêtikos tôn tou Bekkou blasphêmôn dogmatôn* (*A Discourse Denouncing the Blasphemous Doctrines of Beccus*). A critical edition with a parallel French translation can be found in Larchet, *La vie et l'oeuvre*, 166–257. An abbreviated version was published by Patriarch Dositheus of Jerusalem in his *Tomos agapês* (Iaşi, 1698), 387–404, and reproduced in PG 142, coll. 269–290 as *De processione Spiritus Sancti*. References to it here are given in both PG and Larchet. This statement is found in PG 142, col. 271 (Larchet, 5).

> because he comes from his essence, how can this reasonably be maintained—for my part, I do not see how it can—when the *hypostasis* of the Father is the single source of all divinity.[201]

Along with Photius, Gregory argued that a double procession of the Holy Spirit would introduce two principles or causes into the Trinity, but he added the additional twist that if the double procession were necessary, the Spirit's procession from the Father would be imperfect, which in turn would amount to saying that the Father is imperfect in himself.[202] It appears that Gregory rejected Beccus's position, which was that the "Sonly cause" of the Holy Spirit derived from the "Fatherly cause" on which the Son's hypostatic existence depended, by saying that not only was the Father the only cause of the Holy Spirit's existence, but that to say anything else was blasphemous.[203]

The second point that Gregory sought to establish was the eternal relation of the Son to the Holy Spirit, something that had not been defined in earlier Eastern theology and that had left an embarrassing gap in Eastern Trinitarianism. Gregory rejected Beccus's contention that the procession of the Holy Spirit "through the Son" was the same as a procession "from the Son" and argued that the temporal mission of the Spirit was an eternal manifestation (*ekphansis*) of the Spirit through the Son and not a consequence of his procession.[204] Gregory believed that the Holy Spirit could be called the Spirit of the Son and the Spirit of Christ because he held that the Holy Spirit came forth from the Son as the active power or energy of God. Having proceeded from the Father alone, the Spirit rests on the Son and "proceeds" from him into the world of men:

> The Spirit has his existence from the Son, but when we think of him as manifested, sent, given, breathed, coming to renew the creation, this is because by nature he has the Son as the giver and dispenser, while he is the one dispensed; the Son is his sender while he is the one who is sent.[205]

To back up the points he was making, Gregory quoted at length from the church fathers, particularly Athanasius, Cyril of Alexandria, Basil of Caesarea, and Gregory of Nyssa. He was particularly sensitive to the charge made by Beccus that Cyril of Alexandria had said that the Spirit has his being from the Son and that he belongs to the Son, and much of his treatise was spent in refuting

---

201 Gregory of Cyprus, *Logos antirrhêtikos*, in PG 142, col. 271 (Larchet, 5).
202 Gregory of Cyprus, *Scripta apologetica*, in PG 142, col. 254.
203 Gregory of Cyprus, *De processione*, PG 142, col. 295. This passage belongs to another document that is printed as an appendix to the *De processione* in Dositheus, *Tomos agapês*, 405–413, and reprinted in PG 142, coll. 290–300. Larchet does not include it in his edition.
204 Gregory of Cyprus, *Scripta apologetica*, in PG 142, col. 250.
205 Gregory of Cyprus, *De processione*, in PG 142, coll. 275 (Larchet, 32).

the Latinophrone interpretation of such statements. Where Gregory differed from the theologians who went before him was in saying that this manifestation of the Spirit through the Son was not something confined to the world of time and space, but was eternally present inside God.

In order to express this more precisely, Gregory developed a subtle distinction between "existing" (*hyparchei*) and "having existence" (*hyparxin echei*) which is key to understanding his thought:

> Those who affirm that the Paraclete, who is from the Father, has his existence (*hyparxin echei*) through the Son and from the Son . . . offer as proof the phrase that the Spirit exists (*hyparchei*) through the Son and from the Son. In some texts, the phrase denotes the Spirit's shining forth (*eklampsis*) and manifestation (*ekphansis*). . . . The Father is the foundation and source of both the Son and the Spirit, the only source of divinity and its only cause. If it is said by some of the saints that the Spirit proceeds through the Son, what is meant is the eternal manifestation of the Spirit by the Son, not the coming into being of the Spirit, who has his existence from the Father.[206]

According to Gregory, it was because the Holy Spirit exists and appears to us through the Son on whom he rests and in whom he abides, that Beccus and the Westerners he followed were able to talk of a double procession of the Spirit. But however true that might be at the level of his manifestation, in terms of his ultimate origin the Spirit derives his existence from the Father alone. Here we have come to one of the basic points of controversy between East and West. The West has always insisted that the way the persons of the Trinity manifest themselves to us reflects how they are related to one another inside the eternal being of God. The East, however, makes a distinction between our perception of the divine persons in time and space (the "economy" or "dispensation" of grace) and their mutual relationship inside God. As Gregory understood this, failure to make such a distinction would inevitably result in confusing the divine being with the created order in which the Trinity is manifested, and if that were to happen, the Holy Spirit might come to be regarded as a creature rather than as a person of the Godhead.

Gregory's understanding was that the Holy Spirit appears to us as the "energy" of the Son. Photius had thought of the gifts of the Holy Spirit as energies of God, but Gregory went further and identified the divine energy with the Holy Spirit himself, as he is manifested to us in and through the Son.[207] This had the

[206] Gregory of Cyprus, *Tomus fidei contra Beccum*, in PG 142, coll. 240, 242.

[207] Gregory of Cyprus, *De processione*, in PG 142, col. 288 (Larchet, 66). See Photius, *Amphilochia*, 75, in PG 101, col. 465.

great advantage of integrating the relationship of the Son to the Holy Spirit into the inner life of God without falling into the double procession doctrine, and although it has never been canonized as official Orthodox teaching, it has become the basis for all subsequent reflection on the subject in the Eastern church. Before leaving Gregory, it should be said that his polemic was directed entirely against John Beccus and his fellow Latinophrones, not against the Western church or its theologians, whom he never mentioned and almost certainly never read. The debate in which he was engaged was one that raged within the Eastern church, a fact that must be borne in mind if the history of the next century and a half is to be understood properly. In a very real sense, the argument over the double procession of the Holy Spirit divided the Eastern church as much as if not more than it separated the East from the West. The West, fortified by the arguments of Anselm of Canterbury, Peter Lombard, and Thomas Aquinas, was at one in its profession of the *Filioque*, but the East was disunited. Some accepted the Western position and sought only to domesticate it within the Greek tradition, while the opponents of the doctrine had different reasons for their resistance to it. If he did nothing else, Gregory of Cyprus consolidated opposition to the *Filioque* by giving it a solid base in the teachings of the Greek fathers, around which the entire church could rally and define its position.

The Parting of East and West

The distinctions of essence, energy, and existence made by Gregory of Cyprus were further refined by Gregory Palamas (1296?–1359), who became archbishop of Thessalonica in 1341.[208] He was undoubtedly the greatest of the later Byzantine theologians and in some respects may be regarded as the Greek answer to Thomas Aquinas.[209] More than anyone who went before him, Palamas

[208] His works have been edited by Panayotis Christou, *Grêgoriou tou Palama syngrammata*, 5 vols. (Thessalonica: Vasilikon Idryma Ereunôn [1–2], Ethnikon Idryma Ereunôn [3], Kyromanos [4–5], 1962–1992). A small selection in English has been published as *Gregory Palamas, The Triads*, trans. Nicholas Gendle (Mahwah, NY: Paulist, 1983), as well as *One Hundred and Fifty Chapters/St. Gregory Palamas*, ed. and trans. Robert E. Sinkewicz (Toronto: Pontifical Institute of Mediaeval Studies, 1988). See also John Meyendorff, *A Study of Gregory Palamas* (Leighton Buzzard: Faith Press, 1964). Originally published as *Introduction à l'étude de Grégoire Palamas* (Paris: Seuil, 1959); John Meyendorff, *St. Gregory Palamas and Orthodox Spirituality* (Crestwood, NY: St. Vladimir's Seminary Press, 1974). Originally published as *St. Grégoire Palamas et la mystique orthodoxe* (Paris: Seuil, 1959); Georgios I. Mantzaridis, *The Deification of Man* (Crestwood, NY: St. Vladimir's Seminary Press, 1984), also published in Greek, with additional material, as *Palamika* (Thessalonica: Pournaras, 1973); Jacques Lison, *L'Esprit répandu: la pneumatologie de Grégoire Palamas* (Paris: Cerf, 1994); S. Yagazoglou, *Koinônia theôseôs. Hê synthesê Christologias kai pneumatologias sto ergo tou Hagiou Grêgoriou tou Palama* (Athens: Domos, 2001). In Russian, there is K. Kern, *Antropologia Svjatogo Grigorija Palamy* (Paris: YMCA Press, 1950; repr., with a lengthy introduction, Moscow: Palomnik, 1996). Most of these studies assume that Palamas was opposed to the Western tradition. For a dissenting voice from the Greek side, see John Demetracopoulos, *Augoustinos kai Grêgorios Palamas. Ta problêmata tôn Aristotelikôn katêgoriôn kai tês triadikês psychotheologias* (Athens: Parousia, 1997), and in English, John Demetracopoulos, *Is Gregory Palamas an Existentialist? The Restoration of the True Meaning of His Comment on Exodus 3:14* (Athens: Parousia, 1996).

[209] See Anna N. Williams, *The Ground of Union: Deification in Aquinas and Palamas* (Oxford: Oxford University Press, 1999). See also Antoine Lévy, *Le créé et l'incréé. Maxime le Confesseur et Thomas d'Aquin* (Paris: Vrin,

systematized the doctrine of the Holy Spirit and related it to other branches of theology. In particular, he took up the distinction between the Father as the origin (*archê*) of the Son and the Spirit on the one hand, and the Trinity as the origin of the creation on the other, and claimed that the Western assertion that the Holy Spirit proceeds from the Father and the Son as from a single principle (*tanquam ab uno principio*) effectively made the Spirit a creature, because he was held to proceed from the divine essence rather than from the *hypostasis* of the Father. That criticism had already been present in Gregory of Cyprus, of course, but Palamas made it fundamental to his anti-Western polemic.[210]

Following the lead given by Gregory of Cyprus, Palamas shifted the traditional basis of Eastern Trinitarian theology away from an essence-existence duality to an energy-existence one instead. This meant that, whereas it had always been the custom to describe the three *hypostases* of the Trinity as possessing a common essence (*ousia*), Palamas defined our human knowledge of God in terms of his "energies" or actions. As he saw it, inside the Godhead, the Father produced both the Son and the Holy Spirit by his particular hypostatic energy, but outside the divine being, all three *hypostases* worked together to produce the created order by their common divine energy. The origin and nature of the second and third persons of the Trinity was therefore different from that of the creation, because they were the products of a single divine hypostasis and not of two or three *hypostases* acting together. It was this distinction between the essence of God and the divine energies that operated both inside God (as the energy of a single *hypostasis*) and outside him (as the energy of all three *hypostases* together) that formed the basis of Palamas's theology.

For example, it enabled Palamas to claim that as a divine energy the Holy Spirit proceeds from the Father through the Son, or even from the Father and Son together.[211] The reason for this is that we experience him as the Spirit of both the Father and the Son, but what we see of God relates only to the divine energies and not to his essence, which remains hidden from our eyes. At that level, we find ourselves attempting to describe the inner life of God, which is revealed to us in the Scriptures but is not directly experienced by us in our creaturely state. To claim that the Holy Spirit proceeds from the other two persons *inside* God would be to assimilate him to the creation, where it is the unity of the divine *hypostases* that makes itself felt, rather than their individuality. And

2006), who points out that since Palamas owed most of his basic theological principles to Maximus the Confessor, a comparison between him and Aquinas ought to start with Maximus. See Marcus Plested, *Orthodox Readings of Aquinas* (Oxford: Oxford University Press, 2012), 9–60.

210 Gregory Palamas, *Logoi apodeiktikoi dyo peri tês ekporeuseôs tou Hagiou Pneumatos*, 1.15. (Christou, 1:43–44). For a good overview of Palamas's doctrine and its relationship to the Eastern tradition in general, see the summary by Yagazoglou, *Koinônia theôseôs*, 171–197.

211 Gregory Palamas, *Logoi apodeiktikoi* 2.20 (Christou, 1:96–97).

of course, if the Spirit is assimilated to the creation he becomes in effect a creature himself—the ultimate blasphemy that Palamas was determined to avoid.

What is extraordinary about Palamas's Trinitarian theology is that he took up, for the first time in Greek theology, the Augustinian analogy of love, and applied it to the divine energy, on the ground that since the love of God can be known, it cannot belong to his incomprehensible essence. In Palamas's understanding, the Holy Spirit was the inexpressible love of the Father for the Son, which naturally proceeds from him and rests on the Son as the seal of his divine favor. The Son receives the Spirit from the Father and in this way the third person of the Godhead becomes the Son's Spirit as well—the Spirit of truth, wisdom, and the Word:

> The Spirit of the most high Word is the inexpressible love (*erôs*) of the Begetter toward him who is inexpressibly Begotten, the love which the Father's beloved Word and Son owes to his Begetter. But the Son has him from the Father, as one who emerged along with him and who rests in him [the Son] by their common nature (*symphyôs*). It is by this Word, speaking to us through the flesh, that we have been taught the name of the different existence of the Spirit from the Father, and that he is not from the Father alone, but from him also: "The Spirit of truth, who proceeds from the Father,"[212] he says, so that we might know that not only the Word but also the Spirit is from the Father, not begotten but proceeding, and that he is from the Son, having this from the Father, as the Spirit of truth, wisdom, and the Word.[213]

In this way, Palamas was able to make the brilliant deduction that the expression "God is love" is not identical to the phrase "God is Spirit," because love is a knowable energy while spirit is the unknowable essence of the divine. Palamas thus overcame a problem that had haunted Augustine, who eventually resolved it by concluding that love and spirit were the same thing in God.[214] In his incarnation, the Son shares his Spirit with us, which makes us think that the Spirit belongs to him, but this is true only insofar as the Spirit is the Son's energy. His hypostatic origin remains hidden from our eyes and incommunicable, as befits the perception of an Eastern theologian.[215]

---

[212] John 15:26.

[213] Gregory Palamas, *Capita physica, theologica, moralia et practica* (*Kephalaia 150*) 36, in PG 150, col. 1145 (Christou, 5:54–55).

[214] It should be said that Palamas's similarity to Augustine is almost certainly accidental. See Robert Sinkewicz, *One Hundred and Fifty Chapters*, 18; and Edmund E. Hussey, "The Palamite Trinitarian Models," in *St. Vladimir's Seminary Quarterly* 16 (1972), 83–89.

[215] See Jacques Lison, *L'Esprit répandu*, 94–97, who argues that for Palamas, the question of the Spirit's procession was secondary to his main purpose, and that while he defended the Eastern position, he was not dogmatically anti-Western on this point.

Palamas lived at a time of great intellectual ferment in the Byzantine world, and his theology was only one of a number of competing options that were doing the rounds at the time.[216] One of his younger contemporaries was Demetrius Cydones (1323?–1397), who translated much of Aquinas's work into Greek and was converted to the Western position in the process.[217] He entered into communion with Rome and spent his later years trying to persuade his fellow Greeks to abandon their hostility to the West and recognize that its theologians had examined the *Filioque* question with an intellectual rigor unknown in the East.[218] Cydones challenged the validity of the distinction his Greek colleagues were making between *ousia* and *hypostasis*, claiming that in God the two amounted to the same thing, so that it made no sense to claim that the Holy Spirit proceeded from the essence (*ousia*) of both the Father and the Son but from the *hypostasis* of the Father alone. The chief value of his work was that it gave the Greek-speaking world an authentic presentation of the most up-to-date Western position on the double procession of the Holy Spirit, though of course it failed to convince the opposition.

Cydones was an independent spirit who was not afraid to criticize his own compatriots for their narrow-minded and prejudiced approach to Western theology. He was particularly impressed by the strength and unity of the Roman church and by the independence of the popes with respect to secular rulers. He recognized that the patriarchs of Constantinople were in a very different position. They had to follow imperial policy, and that if they failed to do so, they would be deposed. He did not hesitate to blame the woes of the Byzantine world on this unsatisfactory state of affairs, and he seems to have believed quite genuinely that salvation could only come from acceptance of the West, which (as he liked to point out) was *Old* Rome, and therefore of superior authority to Constantinople (New Rome). It was a courageous position to take, but not one designed to win him friends in the East, as his fellow Latinophrones were also discovering.

At the other extreme to Cydones was Barlaam of Calabria (1295?–1348) who had no time for Palamas but did not like the *Filioque* either, even though, like Cydones, he ended his days in communion with Rome.[219] Ironically,

[216] It is important to remember this because, although many works of that period are now being edited and translated into Western European languages, the selection tends to be one-sided. Writings that support the *current* position of the Eastern Orthodox churches are much more likely to be printed than those of the Latinophrones who opposed them, giving a one-sided view of what was really going on at the time.

[217] Demetrius Cydones, *Apologia pro conversione sua*, ed. Giovanni Mercati, *Notizie di Procoro e Demetrio Cidone, Manuele Caleca e Teodoro Milteniota* (Vatican City: Editrice Vaticana, 1931), 359–403. An English translation is in Likoudis, *Ending the Byzantine Schism*, 22–70.

[218] Demetrius Cydones, *De processione Spiritus Sancti ad eos qui dicunt, Filium Dei non esse ex substantia Patris*, in PG 154, coll. 863–958.

[219] Barlaam of Calabria, *Opere contro i Latini*, ed. A. Frygios (Vatican City: Gregorian University Press, 1998), 244–666. In later life Barlaam wrote on the other side. See his *Probatio per Sacram Scripturam quod Spiritus Sanctus et ex Filio est quemadmodum ex Patre*, in PG 151, coll. 1313–1330.

Barlaam's writings against the Western view were absorbed by Nilus Cabasilas (1295?–1363), originally a great admirer of Thomas Aquinas and the teacher of Thomas's translator Demetrius Cydones, but used by him to refute everything Aquinas had taught on the subject.[220] More or less ignoring the controversial Photius, Cabasilas went back to Maximus the Confessor and argued that in his day East and West were agreed because at that time neither of them accepted the (erroneous) *Filioque* doctrine![221]

Unlike his predecessors, who debated with Western theology almost entirely through the Latinophrone interpretation of it, Cabasilas read Thomas Aquinas (in Cydones's translation) and countered his systematic theology directly. This is of special interest to us because Cabasilas put his finger on the difference between the essence and the *hypostases* of the Trinity that was so crucial to the debate between East and West. Where Aquinas saw nothing wrong in insisting that the Holy Spirit must proceed from both the Father and the Son because of their common essence, Cabasilas said that he was confusing the single act of spiration with the persons who performed it. An action cannot be divorced from the one who does it, and if there are two spirators (the Father and the Son) there must be two spirations. But since the Westerners admitted that there was only one spiration, they had to choose—either Father and Son were merged into one person, or the spiration came from only one of them, who (according to John 15:26) had to be the Father. As he put it,

> How would it not be absurd to say that the Father and the Son are two spirators, because of the number of subjects, and at the same time only one, because of their ability to produce a common spiration? How can it follow that the two spirators, Father and Son, are not two as they actually spirate? Actions have to depend on those who perform them, so if there are two spirators, those who actually spirate must also be two in number.[222]

As far as Cabasilas was concerned, the Western position made no sense, and it would be fair to say that his opinion has been shared by Orthodox theologians ever since, even if they have not always consciously attributed it to him.

Partisans of the Latinophrones[223] and of their opponents have gone back to this period and traced a line of "orthodoxy" that conforms to their own beliefs, but a more objective assessment compels us to say that Byzantine intel-

[220] A critical edition of Cabasilas's work with a French translation was published by Théophile Kislas, *Nil Cabasilas sur le Saint-Esprit* (Paris: Cerf, 2001). Nilus Cabasilas must be distinguished from his more famous nephew Nicholas Cabasilas, who is known today for his commentary on the liturgy and other spiritual works.

[221] Nilus Cabasilas, *Ek tou enantion pros to symperasma logoi* 5.4.

[222] Ibid., 1.18.

[223] Today they are almost all Westerners or members of Eastern churches in communion with Rome.

lectual life in the late fourteenth century was more varied and fluid than most later historians have been willing to admit. Individuals went back and forth in their opinions as they fought for the soul of the Greek church, but the West remained untroubled and largely ignorant of what was going on at Constantinople. Instead, there was developing at the grassroots level in Western Europe a mystical theology of the Trinity that assumed the *Filioque* and would have been impossible without it. The leading figure in this movement was Jan Van Ruysbroeck (or Ruusbroec) (1293–1381), who took the inherited Augustinian tradition and developed it along previously unknown lines.[224] While accepting that the Holy Spirit was the bond of love uniting the Father and the Son, Van Ruysbroeck went further and said that he was also the person who moves the others back into an enjoyment of their fundamental unity, out of which the dynamic process of generation and procession starts over again. This eternal movement within the Godhead was for him the perfection of the divine being because, thanks to the presence of the shared Holy Spirit, Father and Son fulfilled their own self-knowledge and love:

> . . . this noble nature that is the principal cause of all creatures is fruitful. Therefore it cannot rest in the unity of the Fatherhood, because of the stirrings of fruitfulness; but it must without cease give birth to the eternal Wisdom, that is, the Son of the Father. . . . Neither out of the fruitful nature, that is, Fatherhood, nor out of the Father's giving birth to his Son does love, that is, the Holy Spirit, flow; but out of the fact that the Son is born a person other than the Father. Where the Father beholds him as born, and everything one with him as the life of everything, and the Son, in turn, beholds the Father giving birth and fruitful, and himself, and all things, in the Father—this is seeing and seeing back in a fruitful nature—from this comes love, that is, the Holy Spirit, a bond from the Father to the Son and the Son to the Father. By this love, the persons are embraced and permeated and have flowed back into that unity out of which the Father without cease is giving birth. Now, even though they have flowed back into unity, there is no abiding, on account of nature's fruitfulness. This birth-giving and this flowing back into unity is the work of the Trinity. Thus, there is threeness of persons and oneness of nature.[225]

When the reunion of the churches returned to the theological agenda, the West presented a common front but the East was divided, a fact that would

[224] Jan Van Ruusbroec, *Opera omnia*, 11 vols. (Turnhout: Brepols, 1998–2005), which includes an English translation of the Middle Dutch and Latin texts. See also John Ruusbroec, *The Spiritual Espousals and Other Writings* (New York: Paulist, 1985) for a selection of his work. On his theology, see Rik Van Nieuwenhove, *Jan van Ruusbroec: Mystical Theologian of the Trinity* (Notre Dame, IN: University of Notre Dame Press, 2003).
[225] Van Ruusbroec, *Opera omnia*, vol. 4, *Dat Rijke der Ghelieven*, lines 1597–1624.

work against the traditional Greek view and almost guarantee that if any union were to take place, it would have to be on terms more or less dictated by Rome, a sure recipe for failure in the longer term.

There were still Greek theologians capable of upholding the Eastern tradition, as can be seen from the writings of Joseph Bryennius (1350?–1431?), who was one of those chosen to prepare the groundwork for the next attempt at holding a council of reunion. He wrote three lectures on the subject of the double procession and no fewer than twenty-one on the Trinity as a whole. The contents were not new, but the determination to maintain the Eastern tradition was undimmed and made it clear, for those with eyes to see, that the churches of the East would not merge quietly into that of Rome and the West.[226]

As in 1274, the impulse for reunion was more political than theological and came mainly from the desperate situation in which the Eastern empire found itself. By the 1430s the Muslim Turks were at the gates of Constantinople, and the emperor John VIII (1425–1448) knew that relief would not come from the West unless the churches were reunited. He therefore agreed to attend a council of the Western church that had begun at Basel, had moved to Ferrara, and would eventually be transferred to Florence. The emperor, the patriarch, and an impressive delegation of Greek theologians made their way to Italy, and serious discussion of the problems dividing the churches got under way.[227]

The first item of business was the addition of the *Filioque* to the Western version of the Niceno-Constantinopolitan Creed. According to the Eastern delegation, this contravened the seventh canon of the Council of Ephesus in 431, which had forbidden any addition to the "faith of Nicea," but the Westerners replied that it was not really an addition—just a clarification of what was implicitly there already. Later on, they got down to the more serious matter of the double procession itself, and it was not long before the key question came up: Did the Western church teach that the Holy Spirit proceeded from the *hypostases* of the Father and Son or from their common divine being? To this, the Western spokesman John of Montenero replied,

> The Spirit is from one principle because his procession is in common from the Father and is in the Son. . . . Whenever we say that he is "from the Father"

[226] See N. Ch. Ioannides, *Ho Iôsêph Bryennios. Bios, ergo, didaskalia* (Athens: HeptaLogos, 1985). His works have been edited and published by I. Delidimou, *Ta eurethenta*, 2 vols. (Thessalonica: Vasilios Rigopoulos, 1990–1991), and *Ta paraleipomena* (Thessalonica: Vasilios Rigopoulos, 1991). The twenty-one essays on the Trinity are in the first volume of the *Eurethenta*, 29–345, followed immediately by the three lectures on the double procession, 346–399.

[227] See Joseph Gill, *The Council of Florence* (Cambridge: Cambridge University Press, 1959) for the details. A summary can be found in A. Edward Siecienski, *Filioque*, 151–172.

> we mean that he is from his *hypostasis*, and whenever we say he is "from the Son" we mean that he is from his *hypostasis* [also]. Because the being of the Father and the Son is the same, and the Holy Spirit comes out of the Father, he comes out of the Son as well, and comes out as though from one.[228]

There followed a lengthy debate about Basil of Caesarea's doctrine of the Holy Spirit, to which both sides officially assented, though they interpreted him somewhat differently. The Easterners clung to their belief that any reference to the Holy Spirit being from or through the Son applied only to his earthly manifestation in his charismatic gifts, and not to his eternal origin inside God. When Montenero inquired as to whether the Greeks believed that the gifts of the Spirit were created or uncreated, the latter had the perfect opportunity to expound Gregory Palamas's teaching about the distinction between the essence and the energies of God, but the emperor intervened and forbade Mark Eugenicus, the chief Greek spokesman, from saying anything. No doubt this was because Palamas's teaching was controversial within the Eastern church and might have split their delegation, but it is hard not to think that an important opportunity to come to a common mind was missed.[229]

In the next phase of the debate, each side was given a chance to expound its position in a theologically rounded way, which gave John of Montenero the chance to reassure the Greeks that Rome affirmed that there was only one cause of the Son and the Holy Spirit, and that he was the Father.[230] This was welcomed by the Greeks, and for a brief moment it seemed as though John VIII would be able to get them to accept a reunion on the basis of that affirmation and the teaching of Maximus the Confessor in his letter to Marinus. It was certainly enough to persuade Bessarion of Nicea (1403–1472) and Isidore of Kiev (1385–1463), both of whom then became and remained staunch supporters of reunion.[231] It also persuaded George (Gennadius) Scholarius (1400?–1473?), although he would later go back on the decision and become the man who would preside over the final rejection of the council in the East. The Greek delegation was by now deeply divided, with Mark Eugenicus (1392?–1445), titular bishop of Ephesus (a city then in Turkish hands and rapidly decaying as

[228] Joseph Gill, *Quae supersunt actorum Graecorum concilii Florentini: Res Florentiae gestae* (Rome: Pontifical Oriental Institute, 1953), 260–261.

[229] This is the contention of Robert Haddad, "Stations of the *Filioque*," in *St. Vladimir's Seminary Quarterly* 46 (2002), 257–258.

[230] Joseph Gill, *Acta Graeca*, 390.

[231] Bessarion is sometimes known as Bessarion of Trebizond, his birthplace. He was appointed metropolitan of Nicea in 1437. Isidore was a Greek, the last one to become the head of the Russian church. On his return home in 1444, he was deposed from office for having signed the union of Florence. After that, Russia no longer accepted bishops from Constantinople on the ground that the patriarchate had fallen into heresy by accepting the double procession of the Holy Spirit.

a port), leading the opposition to any compromise.[232] Scholarius tried to bridge the gap by coming up with an ambiguous formula of his own:

> We Greeks confess that the Holy Spirit proceeds from the Father, belongs to the Son, and springs out from him; we affirm that he flows out substantially from both, that is to say, from the Father through the Son.[233]

This vague formula was rejected by all sides, but it is possible that Scholarius was trying to introduce a "third way" that represented the teaching of Gregory of Cyprus and Gregory Palamas, both of whom were otherwise ignored at Florence. It certainly seems that Palamas's admission that it was possible to speak of a procession "from the Son" or "through the Son" at the level of the divine energy allowed the Greek delegates to agree with the West that the two expressions were practically identical. It was on that basis that all but two of them consented to the formula of reunion that was proclaimed on July 6, 1439, in the following terms:

> The Holy Spirit is eternally from the Father and the Son, and has his essence and his subsistent being from the Father together with the Son, and proceeds from both eternally as from one principle and a single spiration. We declare that when the holy doctors and fathers say that the Holy Spirit proceeds from the Father through the Son, this bears the sense that hereby also the Son should be signified, according to the Greeks indeed as cause, and according to the Latins as principle of the subsistence of the Holy Spirit, just like the Father. We define also that the explanation of those words "and from the Son" [*Filioque*] was licitly and reasonably added to the creed for the sake of declaring the truth and from imminent need.[234]

Unfortunately, time would show that the two nonsignatories were to have the decisive voice in the longer term. One of them was the Patriarch Joseph, who died before the negotiations were completed, a fact that allowed later opponents of the union to claim that he had never given his consent to it. The other was Mark Eugenicus, who saw through the false compromise and dedicated the rest of his life to undoing the union that was based on it.

---

[232] Because of this, Mark Eugenicus is now revered as a saint by the Eastern Orthodox churches though he remains virtually unknown in the West. His works have been edited by René Graffin and François Nau, in *Patrologia Orientalis* [hereafter PO] (Paris: Firmin-Didot, 1907–), vols. 15 and 17. See N. P. Vasiliades, *Markos ho Eugenikos kai hê henôsis tôn ekklêsiôn*, 2nd ed. (Athens: Soter, 1973), and I. Bulović (Mpoulovits), *To mystêrion tês en têi Hagiai Triadi diakriseôs tês theias ousias kai energeias kata ton Hagion Markon Ephesou ton Eugenikon* (Thessalonica: Partiarchikon Idryma Paterikôn Spoudôn, 1983).

[233] Sylvester Syropoulos, *Memoirs* 8.40, in Vitalien Laurent, ed., *Les Mémoires du grand ecclésiarque de l'église de Constantinople Sylvestre Syropoulos sur le concile de Florence (1438–1439)*, 426.

[234] *Conciliorum Oecumenicorum Decreta*, 526.

Mark understood that the Greeks admitted the *Filioque* only at the level of the divine energy, while the West confessed it at the level of the Spirit's hypostatic existence.[235] In line with his immediate predecessors, but perhaps more clearly than they, Mark stated unequivocally that because the hypostatic qualities of each person were unique to that person and could not be shared with (or communicated to) any of the others, the Holy Spirit could proceed only from the Father.[236] A double procession from the *hypostases* of both the Father and the Son could only mean that there were two separate sources of divinity, whereas a procession from the common divine essence would make the Holy Spirit the subject of his own procession and tend to assimilate him to the created order—the familiar arguments of Gregory of Cyprus and Gregory Palamas.[237]

Mark went on to argue that because the Father was the cause of the Son and the Son was caused by the Father, the Son could not be the cause of the Holy Spirit, because that would make him both caused and a cause, both passive and active, which to his mind was an absurdity.[238] He even turned the Western tradition against itself by claiming that according to its logic, such a relation of opposition (i.e., cause-caused) produced a distinction of persons (Father-Son) and not a unity, which the doctrine of a double procession of the Holy Spirit presupposed.[239]

When confronted with the notion that the Holy Spirit might proceed from the Father through the Son, making the Father the ultimate source and the Son the means by which the Spirit comes into being, Mark replied that such a distinction was meaningless in practice. In order to demonstrate that, he took the analogy of a baby, who is born from his father through his mother but who has two principles of origin—male and female.[240] In saying this, Mark appeared to be agreeing with the Council of Florence's declaration that the prepositions "from" (*ek*) and "through" (*dia*) were synonymous, but he then went on to argue that this was not true. As he pointed out, the Greek theologians who had used the phrase "from the Father through the Son" understood two quite different things by it, making the Florentine compromise invalid.[241] Mark was undoubtedly right when he claimed that Florence had misunderstood the Greek tradition at this point, even if some of the evidence he used to support his contention can be questioned.

[235] Mark Eugenicus, *Confessio fidei* 1, in PG 160, coll. 1092–1096, and PO 17, 435–438; *Capita syllogistica* 10, in PO 17, 380–383.
[236] Mark Eugenicus, *Capita syllogistica* 1, in PO 17, 368–372.
[237] Ibid., 11 (PO 17, 383).
[238] Ibid., 34 (PO 17, 402–404).
[239] Ibid., 19 (PO 17, 388–389).
[240] Ibid., 40 (PO 17, 407–408).
[241] Ibid., 10 (PO 17, 380–383).

In dealing with the Western argument that there is an order in the Trinity and that the Spirit's place as the third person implied the preexistence and joint activity of the other two in the procession by which he came into being, Mark replied that there is no such sequence in God and that the tradition of naming them in that order was a matter of convenience, not a statement about the divine nature.[242] If it were, the Son and the Holy Spirit would be subordinate to the Father and not equal to him, which is clearly false, but in Mark's view that was a danger inherent in the Western position.[243] All these problems are solved, according to Mark, by saying that only the Father can bring another divine *hypostasis* into being. The fact that the Father has begotten the Son but breathes out the Holy Spirit ensures that while they are different both from each other and from their common source, they share the same divine nature.[244]

The mission of the Holy Spirit is a joint work, not only of the Father and the Son but of the Trinity as a whole, and belongs to the external (*ad extra*) acts of God in time and space. The Western tradition has confused this with the Trinitarian relations in the inner life of God, which remain above and beyond human understanding or experience.[245] Thus, when the risen Christ breathed his Holy Spirit onto the disciples, he did not give them the essence or the *hypostasis* of the Holy Spirit but only his energy, which is the most that we can know about him directly.[246] The same thing, of course, is true of the sending of the Spirit on the day of Pentecost.[247]

Mark's importance for the history of the *Filioque* controversy lies less in the originality of his thoughts than in his ability to marshal the traditional arguments of the Eastern churches and present them in the light of the reunion Council of Florence, to whose compromise decision he was implacably opposed. As long as the political need to preserve the union remained, his campaign against it was unsuccessful, but after the fall of Constantinople on May 29, 1453, the situation changed dramatically. On January 6, 1454, a synod of the reconstituted Eastern church formally abandoned the union of Florence, and with it went its spurious acceptance of the *Filioque*. In essence, the different positions of the Eastern and Western churches have remained unchanged since that time. There was a small group of Greeks who remained loyal to the union, most of them Latinophrones like Bessarion of Nicea who escaped to Italy, where they were influential in the revival of Greek learning that we call the

[242] Ibid., 6 (PO 17, 376–378).
[243] Ibid., 43 (PO 17, 409). Note that Mark did not accuse the West of confessing a latent subordinationism, but merely pointed out the danger of falling into it that was contained in its concept of Trinitarian order.
[244] Ibid., 26 (PO 17, 397).
[245] Ibid., 4 (PO 17, 373–376).
[246] Ibid., 8 (PO 17, 378–379). See John 20:22.
[247] Ibid., 4 (PO 17, 373–376). See Acts 2:2–4, which talks about the coming of the Spirit but not about who sent him.

Renaissance. Their exile was probably inevitable, especially as it was a political necessity for the survival of the Orthodox Church under Muslim rule. The church had to present a united front to its new and alien rulers, and it had to be anti-Western in order to escape suspicion. The other churches of the East followed suit, not least because Mark Eugenicus had taken the trouble to inform them of what was going on at Constantinople. In a circular letter to the patriarchs of Alexandria, Antioch, and Jerusalem, he wrote,

> So avoid them [the Latinophrones] and their fellowship. They are "false apostles, deceitful workmen, disguising themselves as apostles of Christ. And no wonder, for even Satan disguises himself as an angel of light. So it is no surprise if his servants also disguise themselves as servants of righteousness. Their end will correspond to their deeds."[248]

In such a climate, the *Filioque* stood no chance, and since then rejection of it has been a hallmark of allegiance to Eastern Orthodoxy, a badge of belonging that cannot be surrendered without incurring the charge of apostasy from the true faith.

Rome never repudiated the decisions agreed on at Florence and indeed extended them to a union with the Armenians (also in 1439), with the other monophysites (in 1442), and finally even with the Nestorians (in 1445). All of these churches were allowed to retain their historic liturgies and customs, but they were expected to acknowledge the orthodoxy of the *Filioque*. However, they were not obliged to include it in their version of the Niceno-Constantinopolitan Creed, and in that respect Rome was content to accept the decision made by Pope Leo III in 810. As with the Greek church, these unions were failures for the most part, though small groups remained loyal to Rome and continue to exist to this day as Uniates, or "Greek Catholics."

Needless to say, the existence of the Uniates was an added bone of contention between East and West, because they were regarded in the East as a Trojan horse designed to destroy the church from within. The fact that the Uniates were expected to believe the Western doctrine of the double procession of the Holy Spirit but were allowed not to confess it publicly only added to this feeling, which is still present today. Had only the original Uniates survived, this might not matter very much, but after the Reformation Rome made a great effort to win over as many Eastern Christians as it could. In Poland and Hungary, where the rulers were Catholic but large sections of the population were

[248] Mark Eugenicus, *Epistula encyclica contra Graeco-Latinos ad decretum synodi Florentinae*, 7 (PO 17, 458). The quotation is from 2 Cor. 11:13–15.

members of the Eastern church, they had considerable success, and today the vast majority of Uniates come from lands that once belonged to one or other of those medieval kingdoms. Subsequent boundary changes have placed them in Romania, Ukraine, and Belarus more than in modern Poland or Hungary, and because of emigration there are now considerable numbers of them in North America, Australia, and elsewhere. The compromise union of Florence therefore lives on and remains an important factor in the relations of the churches of East and West to the present day.

Having said that, the repudiation of the Council of Florence by the bulk of the Eastern churches effectively closed discussion of the double procession of the Holy Spirit. When Martin Luther broke with Rome he took little interest in the Greek church, and it was some decades before the Lutherans established effective contact with Constantinople. Eventually, however, they did manage to persuade the Patriarch Jeremias II to make a formal response to the Augsburg Confession of 1530. Jeremias's reply was not encouraging to the Lutherans, but he did not dwell on the *Filioque*. He argued that the text of the Nicene Creed ought to be the one officially approved by the ecumenical councils, which would have excluded the offending word, but he did not denounce the *Filioque* as such, nor did he mount a defense of Photian monopatrism.[249] The general impression we get is that, for Jeremias, the issue was not worth a lengthy argument, nor was it of great importance to the Lutherans, who took the traditional Western position for granted but did not reflect much on it.

Half a century later, some Protestants of a more Calvinist outlook once again tried to make contact with the Eastern church, and initially they had much greater success. Not the least of their triumphs was the conversion of Cyril Lucaris, patriarch of Alexandria from 1601 to 1621 and then (with interruptions) of Constantinople until his death in 1638.[250] But despite his attraction to Reformed theology, Lucaris remained a firm supporter of Gregory Palamas on the question of the *Filioque*, a position which he defended in a letter to the Dutch Remonstrant theologian Johannes Uytenbogaert (1557–1644) dated October 10, 1613, and again in a confession of faith published in Latin at Geneva in March 1629.[251] If a man like Lucaris felt unable to accept the Western view

[249] For a full discussion, see George Mastrantonis, *Augsburg and Constantinople: The Correspondence between the Tübingen Theologians and Patriarch Jeremiah II of Constantinople on the Augsburg Confession* (Brookline, MA: Holy Cross Orthodox Press, 1982); and Constantine N. Tsirpanlis, *The Historical and Ecumenical Significance of Jeremias II's Correspondence with the Lutherans (1573–1581)* (New York: EO Press, 1982).

[250] See George A. Hadjiantoniou, *Protestant Patriarch* (Richmond, VA: John Knox, 1961); and Steven Runciman, *The Great Church in Captivity* (Cambridge: Cambridge University Press, 1968), 259–288.

[251] Jean Aymon, *Monuments authentiques de la religion des Grecs et la fausseté de plusieurs confessions de foi des Chrétiens* (La Haye, 1708), 137–142. An English translation of the confession can be found in Hadjiantoniou, *Protestant Patriarch*, 141–145. Lucaris confessed that the Holy Spirit proceeds from the Father through the Son.

of the double procession of the Holy Spirit, we may confidently assume that the Eastern position on the matter had put down such deep roots in the Greek consciousness that even conversion to Protestantism could not disturb it.

The *Filioque* Question Today

Today the debates of the later Middle Ages seem remote and stale to many people. Little attention is paid to them, and when a theologian glances in that direction he is liable to conclude that much of the discussion was about abstractions that have little to do with living faith. This is not to deny that there is a committed band of dedicated medievalists who take a very different view, but they are definitely in a minority. Even in the Roman Catholic Church, the attempt to revive the theology of Thomas Aquinas that came to be known as Neo-Thomism has now largely run out of steam and been replaced by other approaches that are more or less hostile to it. The Protestant version of Neo-Scholasticism (as Thomism is often called) has fared little better, despite the impressive advocacy of Richard Muller and others, and it remains the preserve of a select few.[252] Theological discussion has moved on, and when an issue like the *Filioque* is raised today, it often meets with a mixture of incomprehension and impatience. Cannot such an obscure point be resolved or simply ignored?

From the Eastern side, which has always taken the matter more seriously, the most eloquent response to this skepticism has come from Vladimir Lossky (1903–1958):

> Whether we like it or not, the question of the Holy Spirit has been the sole dogmatic grounds for the separation of East and West. All the other divergences, which, historically, accompanied or followed the first dogmatic controversy about the *Filioque*, in the measure in which they too had some dogmatic importance, are more or less dependent upon that original issue. This is only too easy to understand, when we take into account the importance of the mystery of the Trinity and its place in the whole body of Christian teaching. Thus the polemical battle between the Greeks and the Latins was fought principally about the question of the Holy Spirit. If other questions have arisen and taken the first place in more recent inter-confessional debates, that is chiefly because the dogmatic plane on which the thought of theologians operates is no longer the same as it was in the medieval period. Ecclesiological problems increasingly determine the preoccupations of modern Christian thought. This is as it should be. However, the tendency to

[252] See Richard Muller, *Post-reformation Reformed Dogmatics*, 2nd ed., 4 vols. (Grand Rapids, MI: Baker Academic, 2003).

> underestimate and even to despise the pneumatological debates of the past which may be noticed among certain modern Orthodox theologians (and especially among Russians, who are too often ungrateful to Byzantium) suggests that these theologians, so ready to denounce their fathers, lack both dogmatic sense and reverence for the living tradition.[253]

Lossky was a Russian theologian in exile, who saw Western theology mainly in the light of the revival of Thomism which was then the dominant trend in France, where he lived and worked for most of his life, but he was not alone. The Romanian theologian Dumitru Stăniloae (1903–1993) pursued a similar line, though without the anti-Western animus that characterizes Lossky's writings.[254] Both men sought to revive the teaching of Gregory Palamas as the most authentic expression of Eastern Orthodox spirituality, and their impact has been considerable.

According to their way of thinking, the Holy Spirit rests on the Son as his energy. At the incarnation, the human nature of Christ received the Holy Spirit and, in so doing, it participated in the uncreated grace of God. This participation is a real one and forms the basis of the transformation of man which in Greek theology is known as *theôsis* ("deification"). At the same time, it is a participation in the divine realities by grace, not by nature. The argument put forward by the modern disciples of Palamas is that if the Holy Spirit proceeded from the Son at the level of his hypostatic existence, human participation in the life of God through that Spirit would have to be by nature, which is not possible. Therefore, either the Holy Spirit is reduced to the level of a creature, in whom we can participate as fellow creatures, or there is no genuine and immediate participation in him at all.[255] The grace that we receive from him would have to be a created grace, made by the Holy Spirit but not really a part of him. Since no one, even in the West, can accept this "solution" to the problem, the conclusion drawn by the neo-Palamites is that it must be wrong and that only the Eastern view of the question is tenable. In other words, we are back to the position taken by Nilus Cabasilas in the fourteenth century.

According to Lossky and Stăniloae, the Palamite combination of procession from the Father and manifestation by the Son was designed to overcome this problem. In his procession from the Father, the Holy Spirit remains inef-

[253] Vladimir Lossky, *In the Image and Likeness of God* (Crestwood, NY: St. Vladimir's Seminary Press, 1974), 71–72. Originally published as *A l'image et à la ressemblance de Dieu* (Paris: Aubier Montaigne, 1967).

[254] See, for example, Dumitru Stăniloae, "The Procession of the Holy Spirit from the Father and His Relation to the Son as the Basis of Our Deification and Adoption," in Lukas Vischer, ed., *Spirit of God, Spirit of Christ* (London: SPCK, 1981), 174–186. On Stăniloae, see Emil Bartoş, *Deification in Eastern Orthodox Theology: An Evaluation and Critique of the Theology of Dumitru Stăniloae* (Carlisle: Paternoster, 1999). Also published in Romanian as *Conceptul de îndumnezeire în teologia lui Dumitru Stăniloae* (Oradea: Editura Institutului Biblic Emanuel, 1999).

[255] Mark Eugenicus, *Capita syllogistica* 1.

fable in the hidden being of God. But in his manifestation by the Son, he becomes knowable and known as the divine energy at work in the world for the salvation of mankind. This is expressed by Stăniloae as follows:

> . . . this lack of interest [in the West] in the sending of the Spirit into the world, as uncreated energy, comes from the loss in the West of the doctrine of man's deification and adoption by God. In the West the relations between the divine Persons are seen almost exclusively as an inner-Trinitarian question, and thus as a question of speculative theology without consequences in practical life, or in the salvation of man understood as his transformation.
>
> In the East, the Trinitarian relations are seen as the basis for the relation of the Trinity to creation and for the salvation of creation. . . . In the West, on the other hand, one avoids drawing from the eternal relation of the Spirit to the Son, the conclusion that the Spirit is sent to men for a work which consists essentially in the deification and adoption of man.[256]

The nature of the Holy Spirit's relation to the Son is of particular importance in understanding the doctrine of the church, and especially the sacramental life. The Eastern Orthodox claim is that because of the *Filioque*, the Roman Catholic Church is obliged to regard every work of the Spirit as the work of Christ. From that perspective, the consecration of the sacramental elements is no longer a spiritual energizing of bread and wine by the invocation (*epiklêsis*) of the Holy Spirit to use created objects as the vehicle of this uncreated grace, but is a transformation, even a genuine transubstantiation of created objects, in what amounts to a reenactment of Christ's sacrifice at Calvary. These objects then become elements of created grace, which is physically infused into the recipient. As the Orthodox see it, in Roman Catholic theology this created grace is an extension of Christ's sacrifice at Calvary, not its Pentecostal fruit. The church is therefore the body of Christ whose earthly head (the pope) is the visible replica, or vicar, of Christ himself, rather than the kingdom of the Spirit in which all Christians share equally, even though they hold different positions in the government of that kingdom.[257] Palamas himself can be quoted in this antipapal sense, though how correctly is a matter of debate since the papacy in Palamas's day made fewer claims for itself than it does now.[258]

If Lossky and Stăniloae are right, Palamite theology can be said to have

---

[256] Dumitru Stăniloae, in Lukas Vischer, *Spirit of God*, 178.

[257] See Lossky, *In the Image*, 169–194.

[258] See Gregory Palamas, *Logoi apodeiktikoi* 1.4 (Christou, 1:32). The matter is discussed at some length by A. Radović, *Le mystère de la Sainte Trinité selon Saint Grégoire Palamas* (Paris: Cerf, 2012), 197–200. Originally published as *To mystêrion tou Hagiou Triados kata ton Hagion Grêgorion ton Palaman* (Thessalonica: Patriarchikon Idryma Paterikôn Spoudôn, 1973).

furthered the integration of Eastern spirituality in a way that has led to the development of a tradition that is opposed to Western (or at least to Roman Catholic) thinking at more than one point. Protestants reading what the Orthodox have to say about the sacraments and the papacy may be inclined to sympathize with them and wonder whether the Orthodox quarrel is with Rome alone. Can it be said, as it was by Archbishop Stylianos of Australia during the Anglican-Orthodox conversations held in Moscow on July 29, 1976, that the failure of Protestants to drop the *Filioque* clause when they broke with the papacy was an oversight and is inconsistent with their true theological position?[259]

Great caution is required here. Cyril Lucaris may not have been converted to the *Filioque*, but John Calvin had no doubts on the matter. Commenting on John 15:26, the traditional proof-text used by the Orthodox to defend their position, Calvin wrote,

> . . . it is Christ who sends the Spirit, but from the heavenly glory; that we may know that he is not a heavenly gift but a sure pledge of divine grace. From this it is clear how idle was the subtlety of the Greeks when, on the basis of these words, they denied that the Spirit proceeds from the Son. For Christ, according to his custom, names the Father here, to raise our eyes to the contemplation of his divinity.[260]

Admittedly, Calvin said almost nothing else on the subject, and his *Institutes* are remarkably barren on the matter. What little there is about it seems to follow Augustine almost word for word.[261] But although Calvin said little about the controversy, it does not follow that he thought the issue to be unimportant. On the contrary, set within the general framework of his theology, the doctrine of the *Filioque* is so obvious and fundamental that it is hardly worth arguing about. Without it there would have been no Reformed evangelical faith at all.[262]

Like Palamas, Calvin also rejected the framework of Thomistic philosophy. God cannot be contemplated as an abstract essence, but only in his existence as three persons.[263] Calvin also agreed with the Cappadocian fathers in saying that the persons are *hypostases* that are distinguished from one another by incommunicable properties.[264] Here we would expect Calvin to say that the properties are the relations, but he did not go that far. In fact, he did not say

---

[259] Kallistos Ware and Colin Davey, eds., *Anglican-Orthodox Dialogue: The Moscow Agreed Statement* (London: SPCK, 1977), 65.
[260] John Calvin, *The Gospel according to St. John 11–21* (Edinburgh: St. Andrew, 1961), 110.
[261] See Calvin, *Institutio* 1.13.18–19; 3.1.2–3.
[262] On Calvin's Trinitarianism, see Brannon Ellis, *Calvin, Classical Trinitarianism, and the Aseity of the Son* (Oxford: Oxford University Press, 2012).
[263] Calvin, *Institutio* 1.2.3; 1.13.2.
[264] Ibid., 1.13.6.

what the properties are, but he distinguished them quite clearly from the relations. Calvin did not think of the relations as objective categories in themselves but rather as the dispositions of the *hypostases*. They are not necessarily voluntary, although that is the prerogative of God's sovereign freedom, nor are they necessarily temporal, which in God's case would be an impossibility. God's internal relations are eternal but they are also free (i.e., not predetermined by his essence), so that the properties of the *hypostases*, whatever they are, do not limit God's relational capacities, either inside or outside of himself.

Calvin understood that the relationship that exists between man and God is possible because of the hypostatic character of human beings. Augustine believed that men were created in the image and likeness of the Trinity, with no special connection to any one of the divine persons.[265] But for Calvin, human beings are created in the image of the Son, who took on our humanity and died so that we might become his brethren and children of the same heavenly Father.[266] He also insisted that in the Son we see the fullness of God, as Paul declared in Colossians 2:9. Our relationship with the Son is secured by the Holy Spirit, who is the bond by which Christ effectually unites us to himself.[267] In language that might have been borrowed from Palamas, Calvin said that,

> . . . by means of him we become partakers of the divine nature, so as in a manner to feel his quickening energy within us.[268]

What else can this mean but that by the Holy Spirit we share in the uncreated grace of God? At this point Calvin was undoubtedly closer to the Eastern Orthodox than he was to the Thomist understanding of nature and grace, which is what may have attracted Cyril Lucaris to his thought.

But if that is the case, why did Calvin persist in upholding the *Filioque*? Was this just an inconsistency that he would have removed had he known anything of Palamas and his theology? That is unlikely. Calvin's spiritual development paralleled that of Palamas in many striking ways, but it took place in a different theological context. For Palamas, as for all Greek theology since Origen, the image of God in man was the human soul, an immaterial substance that shared the properties of the divine nature, though only to a finite degree. God became man in order to release the soul from the limitations imposed by its finitude and to transform the flesh by pouring out the divine energy of the Spirit upon it and making it divine.

[265] Augustine of Hippo, *Homiliae* 52.17–19; *De Trinitate* 11.1.
[266] Calvin, *Institutio* 1.15.3; *Commentary on Genesis* 1.26.
[267] Calvin, *Institutio* 3.1.1.
[268] Ibid., 1.13.14.

Not so with Calvin. For him, the image of God in man was the human *hypostasis* or person, the reflection of the person of the Son, implanted in us by a free act of God's grace.[269] This image was broken at the fall, which removed the relationship of obedience that had sustained it. At his incarnation, the Son restored the image by becoming a man, but he did not do this by himself. Jesus Christ was conceived by the Holy Spirit and baptized by him also, which shows that the Holy Spirit played an active part both in the Son's incarnation and in his earthly mission.

But now a curious fact emerges. Jesus was filled with the Spirit, but he did not pray in the Spirit or rely on the Spirit for illumination and comfort. On the contrary, he dispensed the Spirit and indicated that, after his departure, the Spirit would take his place in the life of the church. It may be possible to believe this within a Palamite framework, but Calvin clearly thought that the energy of the Holy Spirit was known by Christians, not because the Spirit was manifested as the energy of Christ, but by virtue of the hypostatic relationship which the Holy Spirit establishes with believers by dwelling in them. This indwelling presence of the Holy Spirit is a special gift from God, quite distinct from the work of the Spirit or of the divine energy in creation.[270]

The work of creation is external to the Trinity (and here Calvin would have agreed with Palamas) but the work of redemption is internal. This is why an unregenerate man can have some knowledge of God and even acknowledge that he is a personal being, but remain in ignorance of the Trinity. The work of the Holy Spirit is to remake us in the image of Christ, so that we may enjoy the benefits of the Son's relationship to the Father. We are not being transformed into God by nature but being raised into the fellowship of the Trinity as persons united with Christ by faith in him. If the Holy Spirit is the one who makes this possible, it must be because he has the ability to do so. If he were remaking us in the likeness of Christ's *nature*, as Palamas and his followers maintained, it would not be necessary for him to share in Christ's *hypostasis*. But according to Calvin, the Holy Spirit is remaking us in the likeness of Christ's *person*, so that we too may become sons of God by adoption. To be able to do this, the Spirit must share in the *hypostasis* of the Son, which means that he must proceed from him.

From this, the rest of the Reformed evangelical faith flows naturally, as Karl Barth did his best to show.[271] Barth was not particularly interested in ecumenical dialogue with the Eastern churches, and although he was certainly aware

[269] Ibid., 1.15.3.

[270] Ibid., 3.1.2.

[271] On this subject, see David Guretzki, *Karl Barth on the* Filioque (Farnham: Ashgate, 2009), especially 55–90.

that they rejected the doctrine, he never paid much attention to them or to their point of view. Nor was he trying to defend the traditional Western idea of the double procession, an expression that he found uncongenial, to say the least. What he did want to do was anchor the *Filioque* in a specifically Reformed hermeneutic, to which he regarded it as essential. In his early theological work, Barth attempted to incorporate the *Filioque* into his concept of the Word of God, which he believed came in three forms—as revelation, as Scripture, and as preaching, which he assimilated to Father, Son, and Holy Spirit. In his words,

> Scripture is not revelation, but from revelation. Preaching is not revelation or Scripture, but from both. But the Word of God is Scripture no less than it is revelation, and it is preaching no less than it is Scripture. Revelation is from God alone, Scripture is from revelation alone, and preaching is from revelation and Scripture. Yet there is no first or last, no greater or less. The first, the second, and the third are all God's Word in the same glory, unity in Trinity and Trinity in unity.[272]

Barth's primary focus was pastoral: how could a believer know that what he heard from his minister on Sunday was God's Word to him? If preaching was inspired by the Holy Spirit, but the Spirit flowed out from "revelation" without necessarily passing through Scripture, there was no way of knowing whether it was from God or not. But if preaching was the exposition of Scripture, then it could be judged by its faithfulness to the text, because we know that the text comes from God. Similarly, and by extrapolation, a spiritual experience unrelated to Christ would be of unknown origin, whereas one that was rooted and grounded in him would be from God. To say that the Holy Spirit is the Spirit of the Son was thus for Barth a guarantee of the authenticity of Christian experience, and his approach must be understood in that light.

Later on, Barth developed a more sophisticated approach to the question, but his early Christocentric and revelational emphases remained intact.[273] For example, he identified the Father with creation, the Son with history, and the Holy Spirit with creation history—a combination of both. He also argued that if God is a being (*Sein*) wholly unlike any other being, and that Father and Son were "modes" of that being (*Seinsweise*), there had to be a third "mode" for the other two to cohere properly. If there were not, they would be independent of each other, which is not possible within the one God. It may be argued whether it is really necessary to posit a third "mode" as the bond of unity between the

[272] Karl Barth, *Göttingen Dogmatics*, trans. G. W. Bromiley (Grand Rapids, MI: Eerdmans, 1991), 15.
[273] See Guretzki, *Karl Barth*, 91–178.

other two, but Barth argued that it was, because it was this third "mode"—the Holy Spirit—who not only bound the Father and the Son together inside their one being but also reached out to us and united us to God in Christ. In both cases, the Spirit was performing essentially the same function—joining together things that would otherwise fall apart.

There can be no denying that Barth's view of the *Filioque*, which he maintained through all the various other developments of his theology, can be questioned, as indeed it has been, both by his disciples and by others.[274] Not only was there no real engagement with the Eastern position, but there was no integration of sin and atonement into the picture either. It is all very well to say that the Spirit ties believers to Christ in the same way as he holds the Father and the Son together, but the nature of the relationship is different—the Son is not a sinner saved by grace! Barth did not live long enough to tackle that question, so it is impossible to say what he would have made of it, but at least one thing is clear. As far as he was concerned, the Reformed faith needed the *Filioque* doctrine for internal reasons of its own. Protestant ecumenists may be inclined to jettison it in the interests of ecumenical harmony, but this has not happened in practice and Barth would probably have explained this by saying that the Reformed subconscious knows that it cannot dispose of the doctrine without losing something fundamental to its own being.

Where Barth simply restated the traditional Western position on this and defended it against the East, Jürgen Moltmann (1926–) has taken a more conciliatory approach and has sought to find a way of combining both Eastern and Western traditions. He does not dispute that the Holy Spirit proceeds from the Father and suggests that the formula "through the Son" should be adopted to take account both of the Son's involvement in that procession and the Father's priority. He sees the relationship of the Father and the Son as primordial—the Spirit only proceeds from the Father because he is the Father of the Son (not the Father of the Spirit), so the Son's existence is presupposed even if only the procession from the Father is confessed. This has important consequences for our experience of divine suffering, because the Holy Spirit conveys to us the suffering of the Father in the death of his Son, making it impossible for us to be content with the notion that the Father is a distant and somewhat forbidding deity. In suggesting this, Moltmann has broken new ground and contributed to a deeper understanding of the mutual relations of the persons of the Godhead, something that is easily obscured when these are interpreted only in terms of

[274] See ibid., 123–134, for the views of Thomas Torrance on this question, as well as the extended discussion of modern reactions to his views in the first chapter, 5–53.

causation. Whether his attempted solution of the ancient dispute will bear fruit, however, remains to be seen.[275]

More generous still is the approach taken by Wolfhart Pannenberg (1928–), who has argued that the Augustinian doctrine of the *Filioque* is not in keeping with the witness of Scripture, and has gone on from there to add,

> We do not say this merely because John 15:26 tells us that the Spirit proceeds from the Father. . . . More difficult than this isolated saying is the fact that the Son . . . himself receives the Spirit. One may not ascribe this merely to his human nature, for it is as person that Jesus receives the Spirit. Hence we can say only that the Spirit proceeds from the Father and is received by the Son.[276]

Pannenberg speaks as a single individual, of course, and his logic is far from being watertight, but at least he shows that the Western church can afford to be flexible on the subject in a way that is not now possible in the East. But it would be a mistake to assume that the main Protestant churches are now ready to concede the Eastern position and abandon their traditional support for the *Filioque*. Bruce McCormack (1952–), for one, has reread Karl Barth on the subject and, after pointing out that Barth was concerned to affirm that the Father could only breathe out the Spirit as the Father of the Son, thus making Father and Son joint spirators of the third person, went on to say,

> What I would add to this thought is that the Holy Spirit is breathed forth to be the effective agent of all that is done by the Triune God in relation to the world, creation and redemption. It will not do to speak of the Spirit simply as the bond of love or the act of communion between Father and Son, though that also is true. But we can say much more than that. It is the Spirit who unites the man Jesus to the Word in the miraculous conception. It is the Spirit, poured out upon Jesus Christ which is the effective power by which he performs miracles, does his works of love, and suffers the passion of an impending withdrawal of the Father in his death. It is the Spirit who unites the man Jesus to the Word so that it may truly be said that God does what the man Jesus does. That is why being the effective agent of Father and Son in this world are personal properties of the Holy Spirit.[277]

[275] Jurgen Moltmann, *The Trinity and the Kingdom of God* (London: SCM, 1981), 178–187. Originally published as *Trinität und Reich Gottes* (Munich: Chr. Kaiser Verlag, 1980).

[276] Wolfhart Pannenberg, *Systematic Theology*, 3 vols. (Grand Rapids, MI: Eerdmans, 1991–1998), 1:317. Originally published as *Systematische Theologie*, 3 vols. (Göttingen: Vandenhoeck und Ruprecht, 1988–1993).

[277] Bruce L. McCormack, "The Lord and Giver of Life: A 'Barthian' Defense of the *Filioque*," in *Rethinking Trinitarian Theology: Disputed Questions and Contemporary Issues in Trinitarian Theology*, ed. Robert J. Woźniak and Giulio Maspero (London: T & T Clark, 2012), 250–251.

McCormack also points out that much the same view was held by the Puritan theologian John Owen (1616–1683), whom he quotes with approval as follows:

> The Holy Spirit is the Spirit of the Son no less than the Spirit of the Father. He proceedeth from Son as from the Father. . . . And hence he is the immediate operator of all divine acts of the Son himself, even on his human nature. Whatever the Son of God wrought in, by, or upon human nature, he did it by the Holy Ghost, who is his Spirit, as he is [also] the Spirit of the Father.[278]

Reformed theologians have not thrown in the towel yet, and neither, of course, have the Roman Catholics. A highly imaginative suggestion for resolving the question has come from the Catholic theologian Thomas Weinandy (1946–), who has proposed that the Father begets the Son in or by the Holy Spirit. In his words,

> The Son is begotten by the Father in the Spirit and thus the Spirit simultaneously proceeds from the Father as the one in whom the Son is begotten. The Son, being begotten in the Spirit, simultaneously loves the Father in the same Spirit by which he himself is begotten (is Loved).[279]

It is an ingenious solution, rooted in the Augustinian tradition but interpreting it in a way that manages to account for the relationship between the Holy Spirit and the Son that effectively bypasses the *Filioque* issue altogether. Whether it will find much support, however, is doubtful; it is too subtle and too little attested in the tradition for it to strike a chord on either side of the debate. But at least it shows that creative minds are still at work on the question, and as long as that is the case, we cannot abandon hope that an answer satisfactory to both East and West may someday be found.

The *Filioque* dispute did not split the church because the word's insertion in the Latin text of the Nicene Creed was canonically irregular. When the division between East and West finally hardened, it was because rival and mutually incompatible theologies had been constructed around it. In the East, the Holy Spirit was seen as the *energeia* of the Son, working in the world on his behalf but fully God, because the Son is fully God and his *energeia* reflects that. There is no unrealized potential (*dynamis*) in the divine being, which means that if God is present at all, he is present in the fullness of his power, which the Father bestows on the Holy Spirit so that he can become the Son's *energeia*.

---

[278] Ibid., 251, quoting from John Owen, *Pneumatologia*, in *The Works of John Owen*, 16 vols. (Edinburgh: Banner of Truth, 1965), 3:161.

[279] Thomas Weinandy, *The Father's Spirit of Sonship: Reconceiving the Trinity* (Edinburgh: T & T Clark, 1995), 17.

This way of thinking was unknown in the West, where the power (*potentia*) of God could not be understood in that way. *Potentia* would probably have to be translated into Greek as *dynamis*, not as *energeia*—or at least not usually as *energeia*—which to the Greek mind must suggest what Maximus the Confessor had long ago noted, which is that the Latin language is too poor to express theological concepts with sufficient precision and so had to use one word for two distinct concepts. But in compensation for that, the Western church increasingly recognized a distinction between God's absolute *potentia* and his ordained *potentia*, the former being hidden in the mystery of his essence and the latter revealed in the laws that govern the universe and mankind. The ability to keep the law of God was certainly seen as a gift of grace (i.e., the Holy Spirit) but this lacked the personal and relational character inherent in the *energeia* concept of the Spirit's presence. In Eastern theology, the beatific vision of God as seen by Jesus' disciples at the transfiguration became the model of spiritual experience, whereas in the West it was regarded as highly exceptional and not to be sought after in the ordinary course of life. Instead, believers were encouraged to keep the revealed law of God as this was interpreted by the authority of the church. Both the law and the authority to interpret it were gifts of the Holy Spirit, but the emphasis was on his work rather than on his personal presence. The two traditions were talking at cross-purposes, with neither side able to grasp the mind-set of the other, a problem that was made worse by the use of superficially similar vocabulary that concealed a real difference of thinking underneath.

The history of the *Filioque* dispute contains many sad episodes that everyone must regret, but we cannot overcome them by retreating into a vanished and irrecoverable past. Calvin and the Reformed faith achieved a higher synthesis than the medieval theologians had done because they moved from the level of nature to the level of faith, from the concept of incorporation into Christ to the concept of a personal relationship with him. In so doing, they achieved a depth of theological integration that the medieval controversialists failed to attain. The reunion of the churches, if it is to come, cannot take place by denying one side of the controversy in favor of the other. Evangelical spirituality has transcended both of them, incorporating elements of each but essentially going beyond them.[280] It may not be the definitive answer to the question, but it points a way forward and reminds the wider church that only by going deeper into the mystery of the inner life of God can we find the resolution that all parties to the dispute hope for but that has so far eluded us.

---

[280] See Oberdorfer, *Filioque*, 265–295.

PART SEVEN

The Work of the Holy Spirit

17

The Presence of God

From Glory to Glory

Many people will be surprised to discover that the work of the Holy Spirit was not developed as a doctrine until after the Protestant Reformation. Of course, Jesus taught his disciples about it, the letters of the apostles were filled with it, and if Pentecost means anything, the church could not have existed without it. People experienced the Spirit in their hearts, but when they talked about theology it was usually about something else—could the God of the Old Testament be equated with the Father of Jesus Christ? Was the Creator God also the Redeemer? How can Jesus Christ be divine when there is only one God who is transcendent and completely different from anything he has made? These were the questions that were debated, and it was only late in the day that attention turned to the work of the third person of the Trinity as distinct from that of the other two.

A key difference between the Son and the Holy Spirit is that the Spirit came into the world but without becoming incarnate. He was poured out on the church at Pentecost, but he had an elusive quality that was not true of the Son. As Jesus said, "The wind blows where it wishes, and you hear its sound, but you do not know where it comes from or where it goes. So it is with everyone who is born of the Spirit."[1] The only way anyone could know the Holy Spirit was through his work, but in the early church that knowledge was used mainly to prove that he was a divine person. We can see this in the Niceno-Constantinopolitan Creed, where he is described as "the giver of life." On the surface, this is a description of his work, but that is not what the creed is trying to say. Its emphasis is on the equality of the Spirit with the Father and the Son, of whom Jesus said, "As the Father has life in himself, so he has granted the Son also to have life in himself."[2] In other words, to confess that the Holy Spirit is a "giver of life" is to confess that he is equal to the other

[1] John 3:8. There is a play on words in this verse because the Greek word *pneuma* means both "wind" and "spirit."
[2] John 5:26.

persons of the Godhead; it is not intended to explain his work as something distinct from theirs.

This is not to say that the work of the Spirit was ignored, but it was discussed in other ways. Spiritual experience was always at the heart of the church's life, but for many centuries it tended to be regarded as something extraordinary that was enjoyed by an elite minority of its members. In the early days these were the martyrs, whose sacrifice gave them an air of holiness that ordinary mortals did not possess. Later on, this aura was transferred to monks and hermits, whose daily self-sacrifice was meant to bring them closer to God and gave them the reputation of being more spiritual than others. Even within the monastic tradition there were grades of sanctity, depending on the severity of the discipline to which the monks subjected themselves, and periodic renewals of the religious life invariably aimed for greater strictness in mortifying the flesh.

As time went on, asceticism combined with mystical experience to give an added dimension to the quest for holiness, and it was in this sphere, more than in any other, that women were to make a historic contribution to the development of Christian theology. The fathers of the early church were all men, though there were some notable female martyrs. But in the Middle Ages women like Hildegard of Bingen (1098–1179), Lady Julian of Norwich (1342?–1416?), and Margery Kempe (1373?–1438) left a corpus of devotional writing that is universally recognized as foundational to the Western mystical tradition. Only toward the end of the medieval period was there an attempt to translate the ideals of the monastic life into the humdrum world of everyday existence, and this began, as it probably had to, as the development of a new kind of monastery. Gilbert of Sempringham (1083?–1190) had led the way with the establishment of joint male and female religious houses, but it was left to Gerhard Groote (1340–1384) to develop the family convent, where complete communities strove to practice the spiritual principles thitherto reserved for the cloistered life. Groote's mission both reflected and encouraged a thirst among ordinary laypeople for a deeper experience of God, and this contributed in no small measure to the success of the Reformation 150 years after his time.[3]

It was the Reformation that provided the impetus for the development of a spirituality for the ordinary believer. Practices like daily prayer and Bible reading, that had always been regarded as monastic activities, now became the foundation of the Christian life for everyone. The concept of a vocation, which had previously been understood to mean a call to the priesthood or to

[3] For the definitive study of Groote and his movement, see Regnerus R. Post, *The Modern Devotion: Confrontation with Reformation and Humanism* (Leiden: Brill, 1968).

the monastic life, was now extended to cover every form of human activity. Men and women had a calling to serve God wherever they were placed and in whatever profession or activity in which they were engaged. The great divide between clergy and laity, between the religious and the secular, was broken down, partly by dismantling the features that had set the former apart (notably by the abolition of compulsory celibacy) but mostly by raising the dignity of occupations that had previously been thought of as profane and second-rate. In the Protestant kingdom of God, a carpenter or a gardener was just as holy as a priest or a monk, and more so if he was more faithful in the exercise of his calling than they were.

From there it was a short step to the view that only a Spirit-filled person could accomplish the will of God in the world, and that those who were not so blessed were not really Christians at all. The effects of that teaching were, and still are, revolutionary. For the first time, large numbers of people came to believe that academic achievement and ecclesiastical promotion meant nothing if the person so honored was not filled with the Holy Spirit—and it was obvious that many members of the church establishment were not. A poor and relatively uneducated man like John Bunyan (1628–1688) was a spiritual giant compared with the bishops who persecuted him, and the general recognition of this truth has left an indelible mark on the spirituality of the church ever since. The evangelical revival of the eighteenth century was the incarnation of that attitude, and in many ways it remains a counterculture to the institutional church(es) whose leaders understandably feel threatened by a movement that they cannot control and that tends not to accept their claims to authority. John Wesley (1703–1791) may have been one of the first to break the mold of church government by ignoring hostile bishops and ordaining his own men to the ministry, but he was certainly not the last, and the perception of what Christian service is has changed as a result. "Traditionalists" may regret this and react against it, as John Henry Newman (1801–1890) did, but they cannot put the clock back, and (as Newman discovered when he became a Roman Catholic) they are in reality as much the product of this change as those whom they oppose.

Today the doctrine of the Holy Spirit's personal divinity is seldom given much attention. Books about him tend to gloss over who he is and concentrate almost entirely on what he does. This is a pity, because the work of the Holy Spirit cannot be understood unless his divine personhood is acknowledged. If he were not a divine person, his work would be comparable to that of an angel, just as the work of the Son would be like that of a prophet. That would not make it unimportant, but it would be different and our relationship with

God would not be what it is. A glance at Islam and a deviant form of Christianity like Mormonism, both of which claim to be the revelation of a prophet and make great play of angels, shows us what this would be like. In these other religions, angels fill the void left by the absence of the Holy Spirit as the manifestation of God's presence in the world. Communication between God and man has to be explained somehow, and if God is transcendently inaccessible then it is logical that intermediate beings like angels should be called in to help. As spirits, angels can communicate with God, but as creatures they also speak to us. Christians recognize the existence of angels and do not deny their importance, but the work of the Holy Spirit cannot be reduced to their level. His indwelling presence in our hearts is not an episodic experience of the divine in the way that an angelic apparition is. On the contrary, it is the power of God at work in our lives and, as such, it gives our relationship with him a quality entirely different from and far superior to anything that a mere angel can provide.[4]

Whether we believe that the Holy Spirit proceeds from the Father alone, or from both the Father and the Son, also makes a difference to the way that we understand his work. If, as the Eastern tradition asserts, he proceeds from the Father alone, then his work is directly related to the Father and only indirectly (or secondarily) to the Son. But if he proceeds from both the Father and the Son as the Western churches confess, then his work is dependent on each of them equally and cannot reflect one without the other. Among other things, this means that we cannot think of the Holy Spirit as the one who renews or enhances creation without putting the Son's atoning sacrifice and death at the center of that process of renewal. One of the persistent criticisms made by Western theologians of Eastern Orthodoxy is that it tends to put too much emphasis on the limitations of creaturely finitude as the cause of mankind's alienation from God and not enough emphasis on sin and disobedience. This kind of imbalance is not possible if the Holy Spirit is thought to proceed from the Son as well as from the Father, because then the Son's redemptive work is just as important to the Spirit's mission as the original creation is.

Within the Western tradition itself, the mistaken tendency of some popular preachers to portray the Father as the supreme judge and the Son as our defender against that judgment is corrected by the double procession of the Holy Spirit, who brings both justice and mercy to bear in equal measure on the spiritual experience of the believer.

[4] Something of this is conveyed in Heb. 1:5–14, where the author brings out the stark contrast between angels and the Son. The Holy Spirit is not mentioned specifically, but since he is the Spirit of the Son, we may assume that what applies to the Son will apply to him also.

On the other hand, if we were to say that the Holy Spirit is the Spirit of the Son and not of the Father (or only indirectly of the Father), as was often the case in the early church, we might be tempted to see his work as giving us the power to suffer and die in imitation of Christ's suffering and death, as if the spirit of self-sacrifice were all that is needed to save us. That would open the door to a form of salvation by works which in the most extreme case might end up in a new kind of adoptianism.

It was only when the doctrine of the person and procession of the Holy Spirit was clarified—in different ways, as it turned out—that a detailed examination of his work could be carried out. In the Eastern church that examination was to be delayed for several centuries, and in some respects it has never really occurred. Discussion of the subject seems mainly to be in response to pressure from the West, which has sought to enlist (or reject) the Eastern tradition in the context of its own internal debates. In the Western church, however, disputes over the work of the Holy Spirit have determined what the main differences are between Roman Catholicism and Protestantism. They have also been the deciding factor in the many debates within the Protestant world that have produced not merely different churches but distinct theological traditions, which often coexist more or less uneasily within them.

In modern times we have been made aware of the doctrine's importance by the emergence of Pentecostal and charismatic movements that have made very specific claims about the Holy Spirit's work and have challenged the rest of the church to reconsider how we should interpret it. These movements have sometimes created new (Protestant) denominations but they have also penetrated the existing churches and transformed aspects of their preaching and worship, at least among those who have embraced it.[5] So strong has this been that today, if someone asks whether a person is "filled with the Spirit," he will probably be understood to be asking whether that person has had a charismatic spiritual experience.

Theologians may object to the narrowing of the concept of the indwelling presence of the Holy Spirit in this way, but it brings out as nothing else can how important it is for each individual Christian to have his own spiritual experience. It is not enough just to attend worship services or be counted as a nominal statistic on a church roll, and in our modern secular age, even the Eastern Orthodox churches, which have been most resistant to this trend, are

[5] Interestingly, the charismatic movement of recent times has found expression in the Roman Catholic Church but not among the Eastern Orthodox, who generally oppose it. On the other hand, some Protestant charismatics have converted to Eastern Orthodoxy, believing that they have found in it an institutional form of their own beliefs and experience of the Spirit.

being forced to recognize that not every baptized person is a true Christian. Something more than that is required for the label to have any meaning, and even the most traditional churches have seen the need to rethink their understanding of how the Spirit works among them. So it is usually those who are most aware of the challenges to the church that are posed by the strains of modern life who are most eager to abandon traditional ecclesiastical models and embrace some kind of Spirit-filled commitment, whether that involves ecstatic experiences (like speaking in tongues, for example) or not.[6]

The old picture of the church as the body of Christ on earth has thus been modified by a new emphasis on the transformed nature of that body. Like their Savior, believers are now expected to know what it means to be "risen, ascended and glorified" in the experience of the Spirit at work in their lives. It is a progression from outward expressions of belonging to inward conversion and commitment, a movement from glory to glory, of a kind that only the Holy Spirit can accomplish. As the apostle Paul told the Corinthians when they were quarreling over the validity of their baptism, "I planted, Apollos watered, but God gave the growth."[7] That this growth is now increasingly felt to be necessary shows just how important the Spirit's work has become for the life of the church, and why we must do our best to understand it in the light of what the Bible teaches and how it has been lived out in the ongoing life of God's people.

The Indwelling Power of God

The descent of the Holy Spirit on the day of Pentecost marks the beginning of the Christian church. Pentecost was the Jewish festival of the firstfruits, and those who were converted at that time were the founding members of the new kingdom of God. The Spirit's coming was marked by the miracle of speaking in tongues, a gift that enabled the apostles to preach the good news of salvation in Christ to people of many different cultures, each of whom heard them speaking in their own language.[8] But even at the time there were some who observed the phenomenon and concluded that the disciples of Jesus were drunk; they did not hear any message from God in what Peter and his companions were saying.[9] Speaking in tongues, or glossolalia (to give it its official name) continued to be a feature of the first Christian communities for at least a generation or so, but the ambiguity that surrounded it did not go away. When the apostle Paul wrote

[6] See, for example, George Weigel, *Evangelical Catholicism: Deep Reform in the Twenty-first Century Church* (Philadelphia: Basic Books, 2013). Weigel is a Roman Catholic who advocates that his church should adopt a number of features usually considered to be badges of evangelical and charismatic Protestantism.

[7] 1 Cor. 3:6.

[8] Acts 2:1–13.

[9] Acts 2:13.

to the Corinthians about it, he had to tell them to restrict its use in worship and ensure that anyone who did speak in a tongue was interpreted, so that everyone could understand what he was saying. The danger that uninformed onlookers would get the wrong idea was uppermost in his mind and was one of the main reasons why he discouraged the practice.[10]

Paul did not deny that tongues were a gift of the Holy Spirit, and he admitted that he spoke in them more than anyone.[11] What is remarkable about this is that, although he was usually anxious to encourage others to follow his example, in this case he did not. Paul did not want to spread glossolalia but to contain it, even though it was a work of the Holy Spirit. Why was this? The answer seems to be that speaking in tongues was a gift given to individuals primarily for their personal use and not for the benefit of the community as a whole. The work of the Holy Spirit was to build the church, and gifts that did not do that, even if they came from God, were of secondary importance. In fact, the disorder caused by unregulated speaking in tongues at Corinth gave Paul the opportunity to explain that there was a hierarchy of spiritual gifts that created a framework within which the Holy Spirit operated. The basic principle was that the church is the body of Christ and the indwelling Holy Spirit is its life force. The individual members of the congregation were compared to parts of the body—the eye, the ear, the hand, and so on—but none of these body parts could function on its own. It was the body as a whole that was filled with the Spirit, not its individual parts, which could only do what they were meant to by remaining attached to the wider fellowship.

At the top of Paul's list was the gift of apostleship, which was restricted by the requirement that an apostle was someone who had seen the risen Christ. Paul qualified only because he had received an extraordinary vision of Christ on the road to Damascus, almost as if he had been born too late.[12] Whether seeing the risen Christ was enough to make someone an apostle is hard to say. Paul gave the Corinthians a list of those who had done so, which included about five hundred people of whom we know nothing more than that by the time Paul was writing (about twenty-five years later) some of them had died.[13] The only ones he named were Peter and James, both of whom he had met shortly after his conversion and whom he knew personally. The election of Matthias to replace Judas tells us that there was a sense that the apostleship was confined to the inner core of twelve whom Jesus had chosen, and nothing Paul said to

[10] 1 Cor. 14:1–25.
[11] 1 Cor. 14:18.
[12] 1 Cor. 15:8.
[13] 1 Cor. 15:6.

the Corinthians contradicts that assumption.[14] Certainly the early church very quickly accepted that the Twelve were unique and that their ministerial commission did not extend to others.

This was important because the apostolic witness was the foundation of the teaching that was canonized in the New Testament. The apostles were inspired by the Holy Spirit to write down (or to get others to write down) what they had received from the Lord, and this deposit of faith had a unique authority attached to it. The authenticity of some of these writings was questioned in different parts of the church, but the issue at stake was always one of apostolic authorship. The classic case is the anonymous epistle to the Hebrews. Everyone knew that it was early in date and theologically rich in content, but uncertainty about who wrote it led a significant section of the church to resist its canonization. The force of this objection was such that it led many to attribute it to the apostle Paul, since that seemed to be the best way of ensuring that it would take its rightful place among the books of the New Testament. Today Pauline authorship of the epistle is generally discounted, but the reasoning that led to asserting it reminds us of the great importance that the church attached to apostolicity.[15]

For the later history of the church, the restriction of apostolicity to the first generation of Christians was to be of great significance, and at times it even became a bone of contention. It gave the church a criterion by which to judge when and how the process of scriptural revelation ceased.[16] Later prophets, like the Montanists, were rejected by the church because they lacked the necessary qualification of apostolicity, and to this day no Christian body has attempted to supplement the New Testament as it has been handed down from ancient times. Those who have produced their own holy books, like the Muslims in the Middle Ages or the Mormons in modern times, have been rejected for that reason as much as for any other. The all but universal confession of the church is that the Holy Spirit no longer works in that way and will not do so, because that aspect of his mission is now completed.

More subtle is the claim of the Roman church that the apostleship of Peter has been preserved in the succession of its bishops to the present day. In Roman Catholic theology, "apostolic succession" is not simply historical, because if it were, several churches in the Mediterranean world could claim it with equal

---

[14] Acts 1:23–26.

[15] For a recent discussion of the issues involved, see Gareth L. Cockerill, *The Epistle to the Hebrews* (Grand Rapids, MI: Eerdmans, 2012), 1–10. Cockerill suggests that Apollos was the most likely author of the epistle.

[16] See Bruce Metzger, *The Canon of the New Testament: Its Origin, Development, and Significance* (Oxford: Oxford University Press, 1987) for the full story; and C. F. D. Moule, *The Birth of the New Testament* (London: Adam & Charles Black, 1962).

validity. The pope claims to be Peter's successor as bishop of Rome, but he also claims to have Peter's apostolic authority, which makes the succession spiritual in nature. Apologists for this interpretation of apostolic succession naturally try to find whatever evidence for it that they can, and the history of the papacy has been distorted as a result. There is no doubt that the bishops of Rome have played a major role in the Christian world since ancient times, and the medieval popes did their best to gather as much power into their hands as they could. But in terms of doctrine, the belief that the bishop of Rome is a living apostle is of much more recent origin. In the fifteenth century it was still possible to argue that supreme power in the church lay in councils and not in a single individual, and it is really only since the Protestant Reformation that Rome has insisted on communion with the papacy as an essential part of the apostolic faith.

Confirmation that this doctrine was late in origin comes from the Protestant confessions, which were obviously antipapal in tone and intention but did not touch on any papal claim to apostolicity. The Thirty-nine Articles of the Church of England, for example, say no more than that the church of Rome has erred (as have the other ancient churches) and that the pope has no jurisdiction in England.[17] Even the Westminster Confession, composed nearly a century later when the divide between Protestants and Catholics had hardened, says only,

> There is no other head of the church but the Lord Jesus Christ. Nor can the pope of Rome in any sense be head thereof, but is that Antichrist, that man of sin and son of perdition that exalteth himself in the church, against Christ and all that is called God.[18]

Given this attitude, it is hard to believe that, had the Roman church been making the claims to papal apostolicity and infallibility that it makes today, the authors of the Westminster Confession would have said nothing about it. In truth, those papal claims were not formulated until the decree *Pastor aeternus* that was promulgated at the First Vatican Council on July 18, 1870. The decree quoted a number of ancient sources in support of its teaching, but these were taken out of context and almost all of them came from papal spokesmen, who were hardly neutral! The English translation of the decree reads,

> We teach and declare that by divine ordinance, the Roman church possesses a preeminence of ordinary power over every other church, and that this

[17] Articles 20 and 37.

[18] Westminster Confession, 25.6. See Gerald L. Bray, *Documents of the English Reformation* (Cambridge: James Clarke, 2004), 507.

> jurisdictional power of the Roman pontiff is both episcopal and immediate. Both clergy and faithful, of whatever rite and dignity, both singly and collectively, are bound to submit to this power by the duty of hierarchical subordination and true obedience, and this not only in matters concerning faith and morals, but also in those which regard the discipline and government of the church throughout the world. In this way, by unity with the Roman pontiff in communion and in profession of the same faith, the church of Christ becomes one flock under one supreme shepherd. This is the teaching of the Catholic truth, and no one can depart from it without endangering his faith and salvation.[19]

This same principle was reaffirmed and amplified in the constitution *Lumen gentium*, promulgated at the Second Vatican Council on November 21, 1964, though this time it was expressed in the context of the college of bishops:

> Just as, in accordance with the Lord's decree, St. Peter and the rest of the apostles constitute a unique apostolic college, so in like fashion the Roman pontiff, Peter's successor, and the bishops, the successors of the apostles, are related with and united to one another. . . . The Lord made Peter alone the rock-foundation and the holder of the keys of the church, and constituted him shepherd of his whole flock. . . . the bishops, whilst loyally respecting the primacy and preeminence of their head, exercise their own proper authority for the good of their faithful, indeed even for the good of the whole church, the organic structure and harmony of which are strengthened by the continued influence of the Holy Spirit.[20]

Needless to say, this assertion has been hotly contested by both Protestant and Eastern Orthodox Christians, neither of whom can accept the interpretation of Scripture and ancient tradition that these decrees presuppose. The disagreement is frequently expressed in terms of papal jurisdiction only, but as these texts demonstrate, the problem goes much deeper than that. What is really at stake here is the way in which the Holy Spirit works in the life of the church. Does he continue to bestow the gift of apostolicity on the bishops of Rome, or did that cease with the first generation? Do the popes have the authority to proclaim new doctrines, including that of their own infallibility, which Christians must receive and submit to as they would submit to the teaching of the New Testament? The historian can only say that before 1870 even the Roman church did not make such sweeping claims, and that, in this respect at

[19] *Conciliorum oecumenicorm decreta* 813–814; Denzinger, *Enchiridion*, no. 3060.

[20] *Lumen gentium* 3 (22). The text is in *Conciliorum oecumenicorum decreta* (Bologna: Istituto per le Scienze Religiose, 1973), 865–867; Denzinger, *Enchiridion*, no. 4147.

least, it has introduced something new under the guise of an old and venerable tradition that earlier generations interpreted quite differently.

When we come to prophets, whom the apostle Paul puts in second place, it is not immediately clear to whom he is referring. Prophecy in the Old Testament sense had disappeared centuries before, and the revival under John the Baptist was short-lived. It is possible that Paul was referring to the ancient prophets when he wrote that the church was "built on the foundation of the apostles and prophets," but this is not certain and the two words may be synonymous in this context.[21] However, there were prophets like Agabus, who appears twice in the Acts of the Apostles and who played a significant role in foretelling what would happen to Paul when he went up to Jerusalem for the last time.[22] There were also prophetesses, like the four unmarried daughters of the evangelist Philip, though what they actually did is unknown.[23] These people were allowed to speak in church services, but as with tongues, prophecy was to be controlled and carefully weighed by the hearers to see whether it was true or not.[24] How long this practice continued is impossible to say, but the commentators of the fourth and fifth centuries pass over it quickly and give the impression that it was something that no longer occurred in their day.

Prophecy as a phenomenon soon came to be associated with deviance, as we can see from the Montanist episode, and that tradition continued for centuries. Muhammad was a (self-proclaimed) prophet but the church did not believe him, and much the same can be said for the radical Anabaptists of the sixteenth century, the extreme Puritans of the seventeenth, and the periodic outbreaks of ecstatic preaching that recur from time to time. There has never been an office of "prophet" in the church comparable to that of an "apostle," nor has anyone ever spoken of a prophetic succession from one generation to the next.

At the time of the Reformation there was some attempt to find a role for prophecy that would do justice to the New Testament teaching on the subject without causing disorder in the congregations where it was manifested. The most popular "solution" to the question was to identify prophets with preachers who were called by God to proclaim his Word, even if the official church failed to recognize them. At a time when the clergy were often corrupt and lacking in spiritual gifts of any kind, such an interpretation carried conviction with people who longed for solid exposition of the Scriptures. John Calvin expressed it well:

---

21 Eph. 2:20.
22 Acts 11:28; 21:10.
23 Acts 21:9.
24 1 Cor. 14:29–33.

> I am certain in my own mind that he means by prophets, not those endowed with the gift of foretelling, but those who were blessed with the unique gift of dealing with Scripture, not only by interpreting it, but also by the wisdom they showed in making it meet the needs of the hour. My reason for thinking so is that Paul prefers prophecy to all the other gifts because it is a greater source of edification, a statement that can hardly be made to apply to the prediction of future events.[25]

Calvin's view was widely shared by the mainline Reformers and is still favored by some of their descendants today, though greater historical awareness has made it harder to make this equation without qualification. Perhaps the fairest thing to say is that most people today believe that preachers and preaching fulfill a significant part of the ancient role of the prophets and prophecy, without being exactly the same thing. At the same time, foretellers are treated with as much skepticism now as they were in the sixteenth century—with good reason, it must be said.

Third in Paul's list came the teachers, a category which he clearly distinguished from apostles and prophets but which it is hard for us to define with any precision. There have always been teachers of one kind or another in the church, ranging from mothers of young children to university professors of theology, but whether these can be put together as a recognizable category of people who had the spiritual gift of teaching is another question. Calvin thought that Paul was referring primarily to guardians of sound doctrine, and that may have been the case, especially since he was concerned to warn Timothy and Titus not to appoint men as teachers if they were incapable of doing that.[26] There were also false teachers, just as there were false apostles, so called (presumably) because they distorted the Word of God and emptied it of its power.[27] But as with prophets, there was no discernible continuity in the form of an ordained office in post-apostolic times, although the function was frequently assumed by monks and friars in the Middle Ages and was expected of the clergy, especially after the Reformation.

The other spiritually gifted people whom Paul mentions are a mixed bag of the supernatural and the mundane. Miracle workers and healers are placed next to administrators, a juxtaposition that seems strange to us. We may agree that administrators are often called upon to perform miracles, but this is surely not what Paul was talking about. Calvin's opinion here is typical of the general

---

[25] John Calvin, *The First Epistle of Paul to the Corinthians* 12:28, cited in the translation by J. W. Fraser (Edinburgh: Oliver & Boyd, 1960), 271.
[26] 1 Tim. 1:7; 2 Tim. 4:3; Titus 2:3.
[27] 2 Pet. 2:1.

reaction of the church through the ages: "It is difficult to make up one's mind about gifts and offices, of which the church has been deprived for so long, except for mere traces or shades of them, which are still to be found."[28] The general consensus of interpretation through the ages has been that the church must look for Spirit-filled people to exercise its ministries, whatever they may be, and that individual believers offering themselves for such service should aim to be as good and useful as possible. Particular job descriptions may be different over time and space, but the spiritual qualifications for them remain the same. Beyond that commonsense conclusion the church has never gone. The ways in which the Holy Spirit nourishes the church can vary, but his life-giving presence is the constant factor, which ensures that the body of Christ on earth will continue to grow and prosper.

[28] Calvin, *1 Corinthians* 12:28 (Fraser, 271).

18

The Inspiration of Holy Scripture

The Prophetic Word of God

The only mention of the work of the Holy Spirit in the Niceno-Constantinopolitan Creed credits him with the inspiration of the Bible, describing him as the one "who spoke by the prophets." This laconic statement was based on 2 Peter 1:21, which says, "No prophecy was ever produced by the will of man, but men spoke from God as they were carried along by the Holy Spirit." There was no doubt in Jewish minds that the Hebrew Bible (Old Testament) was inspired by God, and Jesus often referred to it as such, either directly or by implication, during his earthly ministry,[1] but only 2 Peter 1:21 states that this inspiration was the particular work of the Holy Spirit.[2] According to Peter, the third person of the Trinity was revealing God to his people centuries before the Son came into the world, but whether (or how far) the original recipients of his Word understood that is impossible to say.

No one in ancient Israel would have been surprised to be told that the Spirit of God inspired the prophets, but they would not have understood this in personal terms, as Peter did. Furthermore, for the early Christians, the Holy Spirit not only inspired the Scriptures but also interpreted them, something that the Jews had not experienced and that Jesus said would come to fruition only after his departure, when the Spirit would guide his disciples into all truth.[3] The same theme reappeared in the letters of Paul, where the Jewish people were portrayed as having the Word of God but not understanding it correctly, because they had been blinded to its real meaning.[4] In this way, the apostles and teachers of the early church were able to distinguish between the Spirit's act of

[1] See, for example, Matt. 4:4; 5:17–19; John 5:37–39.

[2] Compare 2 Tim. 3:16, which speaks of the Bible as "breathed out by God" but does not mention the Holy Spirit by name.

[3] John 5:39; 14:16–18; 16:13.

[4] Rom. 10:18–21; 11:25–32; 2 Cor. 3:13–16; Gal. 3:21–26.

revelation, which was an objective fact whether people understood the inspired text or not, and his work of interpretation, which was necessary if its meaning were to be properly appreciated. The problem of knowing what the Bible meant was not confined to unbelieving Jews, however. Christians could easily hear the gospel and respond to it without realizing what its full implications were, and even after the coming of Christ, some things remained mysterious, although they had been revealed to the church in principle.[5]

What the New Testament writers assumed about the divine inspiration of Scripture was taken for granted in post-apostolic times, and the implications of their statements were developed further. In the late second century Theophilus of Antioch wrote,

> Men of God carried in them the Holy Spirit and became prophets. They were inspired and made wise by God, becoming divinely taught, holy and righteous. That is why they were also considered worthy of receiving this reward, so that they might become God's instruments and bear the wisdom that comes from him. Through that wisdom they spoke about the creation of the world along with everything else, since they also predicted plagues, famines, and wars. They were not just one or two people, but many. . . . They all spoke consistently and in harmony with one another about the past, present, and future, the last of which we see being fulfilled in our own time.[6]

Somewhat later, Clement of Alexandria described the prophets as Hebrews who had been spiritually moved by the power and inspiration of God. He started with Adam, whom he claimed had spoken prophetically about Eve and about the naming of the creatures, and then went on through a list of Old Testament worthies, including women like Sarah, Deborah, and Huldah, concluding that there were no fewer than thirty-five inspired prophets named in the Hebrew Bible.[7] That this prophetic activity was fundamental to the origin of ancient Israel was also clear to Irenaeus, a contemporary of both Theophilus and Clement, who wrote,

> Abraham was a prophet who rejoiced greatly when, in the Spirit, he saw the day of the Lord's coming. In his own suffering he saw the One who would save him and all who followed his example of faith by trusting in God. The Lord [Christ] was not unknown to Abraham, whose day he desired to see.[8]

---

[5] The case of the "foolish Galatians" (Gal. 3:1) is an example of the former, and the mystery of the end of time is an example of the latter (1 Cor. 15:35–58; 1 Thess. 4:13–18). The entire book of Revelation also belongs in this category, and has frequently been misinterpreted for that reason.

[6] Theophilus of Antioch, *Ad Autolycum* 2.

[7] Clement of Alexandria, *Stromateis* 1.21.

[8] John 8:56.

> The Lord's Father also was not unknown, for Abraham had learned from the Word of the Lord and believed him. This is why it was accounted to him for righteousness, because it is faith in God that justifies us.[9]

From statements like these we can see that the Old Testament was important to the early Christians because it expounded the way of salvation that would eventually be fulfilled in Christ and gave examples of faithful men and women who believed the promises of God even when they did not see them worked out in their own lifetimes. By inspiring the prophets, the Holy Spirit was preparing the way for the coming of the Savior, who would fulfill what they had predicted and prove beyond any doubt that their words had come from God. As Origen put it,

> Before Christ came it was not always possible to prove that the ancient Scripture was divinely inspired. But when he came, he led those who might otherwise have suspected the law and prophets of not being divine to the clear conviction that they were composed with the aid of heavenly grace. Anyone who reads the words of the prophets with care and attention will feel the divinity that is in them and be led to believe that these are the words of God and not of mere men.[10]

The early Christians believed that, although the Hebrew Bible sometimes spoke of Christ openly, more often it did so in figures and allegories that concealed him from the spiritually blind but revealed his secret treasure to those who were able to receive it. Irenaeus did not hesitate to say that "the Son of God is embedded everywhere in Moses' writings,"[11] and Origen went even farther. Referring to the rock that Moses struck in the desert and echoing the words of the apostle Paul on that subject, he said,

> If any reader of Moses murmurs against him, and if the letter of the Law upsets him because so often it seems to be meaningless, [let him remember that] Moses shows him the rock that is Christ and leads him to it, so that he may drink from it and quench his thirst. This rock would not give water unless it had been struck, but once he was struck and crucified, he brought forth the streams of the New Testament.[12]

The qualifications needed for correctly interpreting the Bible formed the main theme of Tertullian's treatise *The Prescription of Heretics*, in which he maintained that only those illuminated by the Spirit of God by having been

[9] Irenaeus of Lyon, *Adversus omnes haereses* 4.5.5.
[10] Origen, *De principiis* 4.1.6.
[11] Irenaeus of Lyon, *Adversus omnes haereses* 4.10.1.
[12] Origen, *Homiliae in Exodum* 11.2. See 1 Cor. 10:4.

born again in Christ were able to read the Bible properly. Tertullian was in no doubt about what the Bible was—it was the "rule of faith" that determined the content of Christian belief and proclamation, and as far as he was concerned, its message was clear and coherent:

> This rule of faith . . . prescribes the belief that there is only one God, the Creator of the world, who made everything out of nothing by his Word, who was the first to be sent forth. This Word is his Son, and under the name of God, he was seen in different ways by the patriarchs, heard by the prophets, and at last brought down by the Spirit and power of the Father into the Virgin Mary. He became flesh in her womb and, being born of her, went out into the world as Jesus Christ. He preached the new law and promise of the kingdom of heaven and worked miracles. After he was crucified, he rose again on the third day. He then was taken up into the heavens and sat at the right hand of the Father. He sent in his place the Holy Spirit to guide those who believe. He will come again in glory to take the saints to the enjoyment of everlasting life. . . . This rule was taught by Christ and causes no problems except those introduced by heretics that lead people astray.[13]

Here we see the teaching and structure of the later creeds in embryonic form, a clear indication that they represented the checklist of doctrines that the early church considered were the core of the biblical message. Despite their variety in terms of authorship, age, and place of composition, the books of the Bible belonged together because they were the work of the one Holy Spirit, whose task was to proclaim the coming of the Savior into the world and to expound the consequences of that great event.

Before embarking on the study of the Bible, a new Christian had to learn what truth was and how God and created reality related to one another. The Scriptures were important because they provided access to true knowledge and explained the fundamental difference between the Creator and his creatures. The church had to be rooted and grounded in this truth, because without it the concept of salvation would be meaningless. As Irenaeus put it,

> The Spirit of God gives us knowledge of the truth and has established the dispensations of the Father and the Son by which he dwells with every generation, according to the will of the Father. True knowledge consists of the doctrine of the apostles, the ancient constitution of the worldwide church, and the distinctive manifestation of the body of Christ according to the succession of bishops. They have handed down the universal church to us, which

[13] Tertullian, *De praescriptione haereticorum* 12–13.

> is guarded and preserved without any distortion of the Scriptures, by a complete system of doctrine, with no additions or subtractions. . . . It consists of reading the Word of God without falsification and a legitimate and careful exposition of the same.[14]

In the ancient world it was commonly believed that poets, musicians, and even lawgivers were divinely inspired. Our word "music" comes from the Muses, pagan deities who were thought to bestow the gift of music-making on chosen individuals, so we should not be surprised that some early Christian writers drew on that belief to explain how the Scriptures had come into being. Athenagoras of Athens, for example, wrote,

> . . . the Spirit uttered the things with which the prophets like Moses, Isaiah, and Jeremiah were inspired. The Spirit used them as a flautist breathes into a flute . . . but it is up to you, when you encounter the books themselves, to examine carefully the prophecies they contain.[15]

But although Athenagoras was prepared to use a pagan image to describe the inspiration of the prophets, he insisted that the resulting message could (and should) be examined by rational minds to see whether it was true or not. The early Christians' faith in the authority of Scripture rested, not on an uncritical acceptance of divine inspiration, but on the conviction that the God who inspired the Bible was the God of truth, whose Word could be corroborated by testing it. Nor did the early Christians believe that the biblical writers were mere robots or automata who had no understanding of, or involvement with, the words that they wrote. Hippolytus of Rome (170?–235?) explained the process of inspiration like this:

> Just like musical instruments, the prophets had the Word, like the pick, united to them so that when they were moved by him, they proclaimed the will of God. They did not speak on their own authority—there should be no mistake about that—neither did they say whatever they liked. They were first endowed with wisdom by the Word, and then they were told the truth about the future by means of visions. When they were convinced, they proclaimed [to others] what God had revealed to them alone and had concealed from everyone else.[16]

Unlike the oracles of the Greek world and the secret documents of the mystery religions that competed with the early church for followers, the Hebrew

[14] Irenaeus of Lyon, *Adversus omnes haereses* 4.33.7–8.
[15] Athenagoras of Athens, *Libellus pro Christianis* 9.
[16] Hippolytus of Rome, *De Christo et Antichristo* 2.2.

Bible had long been available in the synagogues, and every Jewish boy was acquainted with its contents. Parts of it were hard to understand, and there were different schools of interpretation, but it was always possible to find someone who could guide the perplexed reader. The guidance thus offered might not be very good, and there were plenty of disputes about the true meaning of the text, but the books themselves were open to all, and individual teachers could put forward their own interpretation of them. Both Jesus and Paul demonstrated this by their ministry in the synagogues. Many of their hearers objected to what they had to say and tried to drive them out, but not before they had been allowed to deliver their message. From the career of Paul, we learn that open opposition was matched by genuine curiosity, and that there were some people in the synagogues who were ready to discuss his interpretation, and not simply reject it outright.[17]

This relative openness to different opinions carried over from the synagogue into the early church, though it was not without its problems. The true apostles had a clear message and insisted that theirs was the right interpretation of the Scriptures, but there were competing voices that preached something different, and it was hard to prevent them from spreading their own versions of the gospel. Paul referred to those people as "false apostles" who had wormed their way into the churches he had founded, but the fact that this was possible shows that the gospel message was freely available for comment. In at least one case, we know that there was an inadequately instructed teacher called Apollos, who had to be put right by Priscilla and Aquila after they had heard him expound the message of salvation incorrectly.[18] When we look at this in historical perspective, it is the openness of this process that strikes us most forcefully. In later times there would be centralized control mechanisms put in place to prevent individuals like Apollos from proclaiming their own independent (and potentially deviant) interpretations of the Bible, but that was a long time coming. Not until the church emerged as a legally recognized institution in the fourth century could it effectively control its preachers, and even then, different interpretations competed for acceptance. Only when one of these was canonized as "orthodox" and the others rejected as "heretical" were standards set in place that would help the church decide who was right and who was wrong.

Long before that, however, Irenaeus had defined heretics as those who refused to recognize the true Scripture and substituted their own compositions in its place. But oddly enough (from our perspective) he never tried to define

[17] For Jesus, see Luke 4:16–30; for Paul, see Acts 17:11.
[18] See Acts 18:24–26.

which books belonged in the Bible and which did not.[19] He recognized that there were two Testaments and presumably equated the older one with the Hebrew Scriptures, but he failed to provide a list of their contents.[20] This apparent reluctance to define the biblical canon is surprising to the modern mind, which looks for certainty and definition in such matters, but it is a fact. At the same time, it must be remembered that there was a large central core of writings that everyone accepted as being divinely inspired. This core included the books that Protestants now recognize as the Old Testament, the four Gospels, Acts, and the Pauline epistles (except Hebrews), and it was around that core that the canonical collection that we know today was built.

After the legalization of Christianity in the fourth century, it became a matter of some urgency to determine what was genuine Scripture and decide how it should be interpreted. Cyril of Jerusalem was very insistent on this in his instructions to new converts:

> Learn carefully, and from the church, what the books of the Old and New Testament are, and make sure that you do not read any spurious writings. Why should you trouble yourself about disputed books, when you do not know which ones are acknowledged by everyone? Read the divine Scriptures—the twenty-two books of the Old Testament that have been translated by the seventy-two interpreters.[21]

Cyril obviously had a definite body of literature in mind, but it is not certain what he meant by the "Old Testament." The twenty-two translated books would correspond to the text that Protestants now recognize as canonical, but the reference to the seventy-two translators is confusing, because they added several more books to the canon (the so-called Apocrypha) and we do not know whether Cyril meant to include them or not. He knew that there were books that not everyone accepted as genuine, but he did not appear to be greatly disturbed by that. Nor did his contemporary, Basil of Caesarea, seem to mind very much, even though he rejected the force of nonbiblical tradition and pleaded that the Scriptures were the only true judge between him and his opponents. He was convinced that an appeal to the sacred texts would decide whatever problem he was facing, but he never defined what those texts were.[22] This curious combination—consult the Bible but do not worry too much about what books are in it—was standard in ancient times despite the various attempts that were

[19] Irenaeus of Lyon, *Adversus omnes haereses* 3.11.9.
[20] Ibid., 4.32.2.
[21] Cyril of Jerusalem, *Catecheses* 4.33.
[22] Basil of Caesarea, *Epistula* 189.3.

made to establish the limits of the canon. That was effectively decided by the early fifth century at the latest, even though official definitions of it had to wait for another millennium or more.[23]

The most important, if not the earliest, list of the New Testament canonical books comes from the pen of Eusebius of Caesarea.[24] He divided them into three distinct categories—those that were universally accepted (*homologoumena*), those that were disputed (*antilegomena*), and those that were spurious or generally rejected (*notha*). In the first category came the four Gospels, the Acts of the Apostles, the Pauline epistles (apparently including Hebrews), 1 Peter and 1 John. In the second category were James, Jude, 2 Peter, 2 and 3 John. The third category consisted almost entirely of books that never made it into the canon, the one possible exception being the Apocalypse of John, or Book of Revelation, which Eusebius did not know what to do with. He recognized that some churches rejected it but that most acknowledged it to be genuine, but he left the question open and did not pronounce on it one way or the other. Cyril of Jerusalem, on the other hand, mentioned the four Gospels, the Acts of the Apostles, the fourteen epistles of Paul (including Hebrews), and the seven Catholic Epistles, but omitted Revelation entirely.[25] By chance it was Athanasius who first listed all the New Testament books that we now recognize, along with the Hebrew canon of the Old Testament. He said of them,

> These [books] are the fountains of salvation, so that those who are thirsty may be satisfied by the living words they contain. In these alone the teaching of godliness is proclaimed. Let no one add to these; let nothing be taken away from them.[26]

Despite Athanasius's clarity, the Eastern churches have never been able to agree on a fixed canon of New Testament books. On the whole, they tend to accept the twenty-seven books universally recognized elsewhere, but the Syrian churches, both monophysite and Nestorian, have found it hard to include the four shorter Catholic Epistles and the book of Revelation, which are often absent from their canonical lists. At the other end of the spectrum, the Ethiopian church (which is monophysite) sometimes adds eight additional books to

[23] See Bruce Metzger, *The Canon of the New Testament: Its Origin, Development, and Significance* (Oxford: Oxford University Press, 1987). For a less conservative approach covering both Testaments, see Lee M. McDonald and James A. Sanders, *The Canon Debate* (Peabody, MA: Hendrickson, 2002), and Lee M. McDonald, *The Biblical Canon: Its Origin, Transmission, and Authority* (Peabody, MA: Hendrickson, 2007).

[24] Eusebius of Caesarea, *Historia ecclesiastica* 3.25.1–7. There is a Latin text known today as the Muratorian fragment, named for Ludovico Antonio Muratori, who discovered it, which is probably older, but is of uncertain origin and authority.

[25] Cyril of Jerusalem, *Catecheses* 4.36.

[26] Athanasius of Alexandria, *Epistula festalis* 39 (AD 367). See Metzger, *Canon of the New Testament*, 211–212.

its New Testament. These books are supposed to be of Greek origin but are now known only in their Ethiopic versions.[27] In practice however, both of these exceptions are minor. They have had little or no impact on the doctrinal formulations of either church, and the other Eastern churches accept the standard twenty-seven books as their New Testament canon.

In the Western church, the debate about canonicity centered on the authorship of the epistle to the Hebrews, which was generally regarded as non-Pauline. Jerome, the leading biblical scholar of his day, dealt with this as follows:

> If the usage of the Latins does not receive it among the canonical Scriptures, neither (by the same liberty) do the Greek churches receive the Revelation of John. Yet we receive both of them, because we do not follow modern trends but the authority of ancient writers, who mostly quote each of them . . . as canonical.[28]

Augustine agreed with Jerome about this, and their joint authority was enough to establish the Western New Testament canon *de facto*, if not *de jure*.[29] That had to wait until the sixteenth century, when the twin pressures of the Renaissance and the Reformation reopened the question of the canon among both Roman Catholics and Protestants.[30] In the end, however, the traditional twenty-seven books were officially accepted by all sides, starting with the Roman Catholic decree *De canonicis Scripturis*, promulgated by the Council of Trent on April 8, 1546,[31] and followed by the French Confession of La Rochelle (1559), the Belgic Confession (1561), and Article 5 of the Thirty-nine Articles of the Church of England (1563).

The most important single qualification for admission to the New Testament canon was conformity to the semi-creedal "rule of faith," of which Tertullian's statements in his *Prescription of Heretics* are good examples. Any book that contained material incompatible with that "rule" would automatically be excluded from consideration as part of the canon. Another important qualification for acceptance was "apostolicity," a concept that was interpreted in a broad sense. A book was regarded as "apostolic" if it was written by an apostle, or if it had been composed by someone working with an apostle and writing more or less at his direction. The third main criterion was a book's continuous acceptance and use by the church at large. This can be determined by quotations in patristic writers, but above all by the existence of commentaries

[27] See Metzger, *Canon of the New Testament*, 225–228.
[28] Jerome, *Epistula* 129.
[29] Augustine of Hippo, *De doctrina Christiana* 2.13.
[30] See Metzger, *Canon of the New Testament*, 239–247.
[31] *Conciliorum oecumenicorum decreta* (Bologna: Istituto per le Scienze Religiose, 1973), 663–664.

for all twenty-seven canonical books of the New Testament, but for none of the disputed or spurious ones.[32]

Another matter of some importance was the form of the text that would be regarded as Spirit-inspired. Today most people assume that this must be the original Greek version, but this was not the view held by the Roman Catholic Church at the time of the Reformation. The Council of Trent, for example, specified that the entire Bible should be read in the Latin translation of Jerome, which was the only one the Roman church would accept as valid for doctrinal purposes.[33] The Reformers were largely dependent on the Byzantine ecclesiastical tradition, based on the texts read in the Greek church in the fifteenth century. These were brought by Greek scholars to the West at that time, and formed the basis for Erasmus's edition of the New Testament in 1516. Some fairly minor revisions followed, but in 1633 the Dutch printer Elsevier marketed a printed edition as the *Textus Receptus* ("received text"), which is how it is generally known today. In the nineteenth century a great many earlier manuscripts were discovered and New Testament textual criticism took on a different appearance. Today scholars use what is known as an "eclectic" text, based on a comparison of the best ancient authorities, out of which it has been reconstructed.[34] It is probably as close to the original as we are likely to get, and although there are many variant readings, few of them are of any real significance. Some verses that were once used to make doctrinal points have now been shown to be inauthentic, but this seldom if ever affects the doctrines themselves. The most famous example of this is in 1 John 5:7, which in some manuscripts contains a Trinitarian interpolation referring to the "three witnesses in heaven," who are named as the Father, the Son, and the Holy Spirit. That part of the verse is no longer printed or quoted as evidence for the Trinity in the New Testament, but this does not matter very much because there are other verses that support the doctrine equally well.

The Rule of Faith

In the early church period, the authority of Scripture for establishing Christian doctrine was significantly more important than the canonicity of particular books or the accuracy of the text. This seems strange to us today, but it makes

[32] This incidentally is also the main reason why the canon cannot be extended today. If a genuine letter of the apostle Paul were to turn up in the sands of Egypt, for example, there might be no question as to its conformity to the "rule of faith" or to its "apostolicity," but the fact that it has not been in continuous use down through the centuries would rule it out of consideration today.

[33] *Conciliorum oecumenicorum decreta*, 664–665.

[34] The latest printed edition is the twenty-eighth, popularly known as "Nestlé-Aland" in honor of its main editors. It is published as *Novum Testamentum Graece* (Stuttgart: Deutsche Bibelgesellschaft, 2012).

sense in the context of its time. Before the invention of printing it was impossible to ensure that everyone would be reading exactly the same thing. The ancients were skilled in the art of detecting scribal errors, but that was because they had to be. Mistakes crept in, but those who knew the "rule of faith" understood what the gist of the message was, and if the text did not conform to that, it would be altered on the assumption that a copyist had made a mistake. That was not always the case, of course, and there is evidence that scribes sometimes modified the true text, either because they did not understand it or because they felt that what it said was not consistent with the church's doctrine. This phenomenon is familiar to textual critics, who detect it in manuscript variants. Forced to decide what the original text said, these critics often prefer the "harder reading" (*lectio difficilior*) on the ground that the easier one probably represents a simplification made by people who did not understand (or did not like) the original.[35]

It was also true that, before printing made books affordable, few people possessed a complete Bible. Individual books or groups of books (like the twelve minor prophets or the Pauline epistles) circulated on scrolls in the synagogues and later in *codices* in the church.[36] It could easily happen that a particular individual or congregation had no access to parts of the Scriptures, and therefore operated with a shorter canon than the one we now have. It was also possible for *codices* to contain both canonical and noncanonical texts. There was no way of controlling this, and so the "rule of faith" came to play an essential part in helping people determine what was genuine and what was not. The invention of printing helped to reduce these problems by making it possible to circulate texts that were both complete and identical. Admittedly, they were seldom free of typographical errors, but these were usually easy to spot and readily corrected by readers, just as they are today.

Another important factor was that until the nineteenth century, most people functioned in an oral culture and heard the Bible read to them more often than they read it themselves. Reading was the occupation of an elite consisting mainly of priests, scribes, and academics. Everyone else listened to the Word of God being read and expounded orally, first in the synagogue and then in church.[37] The apostle Paul understood this instinctively when he wrote of his

[35] See Bart D. Ehrman, *The Orthodox Corruption of Scripture* (Oxford: Oxford University Press, 2011). It should be noted that the author's personal hostility to Christianity often causes him to overstate his case, but the existence of the underlying phenomenon is undeniable.

[36] The *codex* was a series of parchment sheets bound together rather like a modern book. The Christians made considerable use of this format, and some have even claimed that it was a Christian invention, though that seems unlikely. Even so, the church popularized it, and the most important ancient manuscripts are in *codex* form, e.g., the Codex Alexandrinus, the Codex Sinaiticus, and the Codex Vaticanus.

[37] Note that the English word "read" is cognate with the German *reden*, which means "make a speech."

fellow Jews, "How are they to believe in him [Jesus] of whom they have never heard? And how are they to hear without someone preaching?"[38] The Jews were famous as "people of the Book," but reading it (in our sense of the word) was not how most of them absorbed its contents. Some of them memorized large chunks, which they knew by heart and recognized when they heard it proclaimed, even though they might never have read it themselves.[39] Christians were much the same. It was only when universal primary education and cheap print editions of the Bible became widely available that the average churchgoer got his own copy and read it for himself. Until then most people accepted the authority of the Scriptures as mediated to them by preachers and teachers who were trained to handle them and who could correct (or gloss over) any errors or difficulties they found in the text.

Establishing the authority of the Bible in the church was therefore largely a matter of persuading the literate minority to accept it as the only source of spiritual truth and wisdom. In ancient times, Christian writers defended it against pagan competitors—Homer, for example, or the Greek philosophers. They based their arguments on such things as the antiquity of the Jewish law—Moses lived centuries before the Greek lawgivers and was therefore more authoritative than they were.[40] An anonymous writer of the third century put it succinctly:

> It is impossible to learn anything true about religion from your [pagan] teachers. By their mutual disagreement, they have given you enough proof of their ignorance. So I think it is reasonable for us to go back to our forefathers, who are greatly superior to your teachers. First, they are older. Second, they have taught us none of their private opinions. They do not differ from each other, nor have they tried to prove each other wrong. . . . [Our ancestors] submitted to the pure energy of the Divine Spirit, so that the divine plectrum could come down from heaven and use them as an instrument, like a harp or a lyre.[41]

Later on, the history of Israel was held up as a more accurate account of humanity's origins and development than any pagan myth. The supreme example of that kind of apologetic was Augustine's *City of God*, a massive defense of the biblical revelation that effectively overturned the traditional self-understanding

[38] Rom. 10:14.

[39] The Bereans mentioned in Acts 17:11 were exceptional in this respect—a point which the text of Acts does not hesitate to make.

[40] The argument from antiquity can be found in Justin Martyr, *Apologia I* 59.1; Theophilus of Antioch, *Ad Autolycum* 3.23; Tertullian, *De testimonio animae* 5; and Origen, *Contra Celsum* 6.43, and so may be regarded as a commonplace of early Christian apologetic.

[41] Pseudo-Justin, *Cohortatio ad Graecos* 8.

of the ancient Romans. Augustine argued that since the dawn of human history there has been a cosmic struggle between good and evil, represented by two "cities," one of which belongs to God and the other to Satan.[42]

These so-called "cities" were essentially spiritual realities that have manifested themselves in different forms on earth—Jerusalem and the church represented the city of God (without being identical to it), while Sodom, Babylon, Nineveh, and Rome stood for the city of Satan (again, without being identical to it). Every earthly city is a mixture of good and evil—Jerusalem was plagued by sin and rebellion against God, and Nineveh was capable of repentance, as the story of Jonah reminds us.[43] But these things were somehow extraordinary and even unnatural. Jerusalem was *supposed* to be free of sin in a way that the other cities were not, which made its corruption especially hard to bear. One day it would be rescued and cleansed from its transgressions, whereas Babylon, the city of Satan, would eventually be destroyed, however many good people there were in it, just as Sodom had been destroyed in the time of Abraham.[44] The Bible bears witness to this, and its history is the story of mankind. Augustine never thought to go to the Middle East and dig up the remains of Nineveh or Babylon in order to prove that the Bible was right. He saw no need to do that, because the truth of what it said was visible all around him, in the hearts and minds of the people to whom he preached and ministered. He did not care where the garden of Eden was, or what language the talking serpent spoke. What he knew was that the human race had fallen away from God, that the world is still in the grip of the power that tempted Adam and Eve, and that all men and women needed to hear and receive the gospel of Christ in order to be saved. The results of the fall were plain to everyone; how, when, and why it happened was important only to the extent that knowing the cause can help us understand the remedy. Beyond that, he was not really interested in the details.

This is not to say that the early Christians were indifferent to the historicity of the biblical stories. They were very insistent on the historical death and resurrection of Jesus in the time of Pontius Pilate, and Tertullian believed that the archives in Rome contained Pilate's account of the crucifixion and the empty tomb. There is no way of proving this today, of course, but he would hardly have made such a claim if it had not mattered to his contemporaries or if it could have been easily disproved.[45] His point was that the message of

[42] "City" is derived from Latin *civitas*, which corresponds to Greek *polis* and for which there is no real equivalent in modern culture. A *civitas/polis* was more than just a collection of dwellings—it was a community that had its own mini-civilization that was thought to be quite distinct from anything else.

[43] Jonah 3:6–10.

[44] Gen. 19:23–29.

[45] Tertullian, *Apologeticum* 21.19, 24.

the gospel was open to objective verification, which meant that what the Bible said must either be true or false. If it was true, its claims must be accepted; if it was false, Christianity was a sham and it ought to be rejected. Of course, Tertullian was a Christian himself, so he was trying to persuade his readers that what the Bible said was correct, but the principle that its message was open to possible falsification was understood and agreed by everyone. The Bible was examined according to the literary and historical standards of the time, and despite numerous objections from pagan philosophers and the like, it passed the test. It was this that made the Christian message quite different from pagan myths, and Christians seized on it as proof that what the Bible claimed was in fact true.

That said, there were limits to how literally the Bible could and should be read. Origen, for example, understood that the creation stories in Genesis 1–11 were stylized accounts of what had happened rather than straightforward narratives, but this did not mean that they were false, or even "unhistorical." They simply had to be read for what they were and interpreted accordingly. The same was true for the book of Revelation. Much of the Greek-speaking church had no idea how to read it and so tended to relegate it to the sidelines, even to the point of not including it in the canon. The Latin-speaking West was more positive about its canonicity, but even there, opinions differed widely as to how it should be understood. Those who took it literally concluded that the world would come to an end in the year 1000, which of course was still a long way off. Natural disasters and especially the fall of Rome to the barbarians in AD 410 were seen as signs of the coming end, and Revelation was interpreted accordingly. It fell to Augustine to see through this simplistic way of reading Revelation, and his *City of God* began as an essay of reinterpretation. As he saw it, the visions of Revelation could not be related directly to particular events in human history, and he concluded that there would be no end of the world in AD 1000. His sophisticated way of reading spiritual realities allowed him to claim that what we see and experience in our lives are "signs of the times" that remind us of the nature of the struggle between good and evil but not literal prophecies of future events.

Augustine's interpretation was so powerful that it became (and by and large has remained) the standard view of the mainline churches, though literalist alternatives continue to surface from time to time. In the ancient world, belief that Christ would return in AD 1000 was known as "chiliasm," while more recent occurrences of the phenomenon are called "millenarianism."[46]

[46] The Greek word for "thousand" is *chiliai* and the Latin is *mille*.

The difference between them is that whereas chiliasm could be regarded as mainstream Christian belief until it was refuted by Augustine, millenarianism has always been a counterculture that has flourished in times of turmoil and uncertainty. There was a revival of it in the Middle Ages and great debate about it among the sixteenth-century Reformers, though in both cases the Augustinian view eventually reasserted itself as the dominant one.[47]

In its modern form, millenarianism dates from the French Revolution, when the traditional European order was overthrown and many people thought that the end of the world was at hand. Thanks to the preaching of John Nelson Darby (1800–1882) and the wide dissemination of the Scofield Reference Bible, which reflected his ideas, a form of premillenarian dispensationalism became very popular in the nineteenth century, and several seminaries and colleges made it part of their core beliefs. This gave dispensationalism the status of "orthodox" teaching in many conservative evangelical circles and it soon developed a number of subcurrents, based on differing interpretations of what were assumed to be future historical events. Only in the late twentieth century did this kind of dispensationalism begin to break down, and although it still commands a considerable popular audience, it is no longer taken seriously by biblical scholars.[48] Theologically informed evangelicals now usually adopt something like the Augustinian position, and it seems fair to say that modern millenarianism is rapidly retreating into the countercultural undergrowth from which it emerged nearly two centuries ago.

It should be pointed out that denials of the "literal meaning" of the Bible gained widespread acceptance only when it was recognized that the passages concerned were never meant to be read in that way. For those who rejected such literalism, it was not a case of denying the authority of the Bible but of reading it as it was originally meant to be read. The classic example of this was the Song of Songs, which almost no one believed could be interpreted "literally." To the vast majority of those who read it before the nineteenth century, the Song was an allegory of divine love *and was intended to be so.* But allowing for exceptional cases like this one, the church generally clung to the view that the Bible was a historical record of God's dealing with his people, and that it was that fact which lay at the root of the authority that it claimed.

---

[47] See Richard K. Emmerson and Bernard McGinn, eds., *The Apocalypse in the Middle Ages* (Ithaca, NY: Cornell University Press, 1992); Irena Backus, *Reformation Readings of the Apocalypse: Geneva, Zurich and Wittenberg* (Oxford: Oxford University Press, 2000).

[48] The best modern study of this is Richard Bauckham, *The Theology of the Book of Revelation* (Cambridge: Cambridge University Press, 1993). It is particularly good because, rather than disparage alternative views, Bauckham demonstrates how they tend to be partial and inadequate interpretations of a text that has only become comprehensible now that the literary genre of "apocalyptic" has been rediscovered and analyzed.

The Handbook of the Christian Life

How the Scriptures should be interpreted quickly became a major concern of early Christian theologians, and especially of Origen, who devoted his life to the question. Origen was a noted textual critic who knew at least some Hebrew (an unusual accomplishment among Gentile Christians at that time) and was familiar with several Greek versions of the Old Testament. He compiled a comparative table of five different texts—four Greek, one Hebrew, and the Hebrew text in Greek letters, making a sixth column.[49] He also wrote commentaries and an important hermeneutical work called *De principiis* (*On First Principles*), in which he expounded his overall method of interpretation.

Origen began with the standard assumption that the Scriptures were a revelation from God and claimed that the reason so many people had misread them was that they had not absorbed the implications of that fact:

> The reason why those we have mentioned hold false opinions and make ungodly or ignorant statements about God seems to be just this, that Scripture is not understood in its spiritual sense, but is interpreted according to the letter only. For this reason, we must explain to those who believe that the sacred books are not the works of men, but that they were written and transmitted to us through the inspiration of the Holy Spirit by the will of the Father of the universe, through Jesus Christ, what methods of interpretation appear right to us, who keep to the rule of the heavenly church of Jesus Christ, through the succession of the apostles.[50]

In interpreting the Bible, Origen presupposed that it was a divine revelation to human beings in their created state, specifically designed to guide them in living the Christian life. It had three different senses, corresponding to the body, soul, and spirit of a man. Its literal sense spoke to the body, its moral sense to the soul, and its spiritual sense to the spirit. But which was which, and what sense should be considered primary in any given instance? To answer this question, Origen began with the overall purpose of the Holy Spirit in inspiring the Scriptures in the first place. As he saw it, the Spirit had two principal aims in view. The first was to instruct believers in the deep things of God, which only he knows.[51] The second was to help beginners in the faith, who need guidance and can be reached only when the deeper mysteries are expressed in the language and concepts of everyday life. This is why the creation narrative is presented in

[49] This is why it is known as the *Hexapla* ("six in one"). The text is now known only in fragments, but it apparently survived in Caesarea for many centuries and was consulted by people like Jerome (d. 420) and Procopius of Gaza (465?–528).

[50] Origen, *De principiis* 4.2.2.

[51] 1 Cor. 2:10. Origen, *De principiis* 4.2.10.

the way it is, and why the Bible contains so many examples of both righteous and unrighteous people. God did not want to lead anyone astray by concealing spiritual truths from them, but to reach out to the simple-minded and help them along the way to maturity. As Origen put it,

> The intention [of the Holy Spirit] was to make even the outer covering of the [underlying] spiritual truths, by which I mean the bodily part of the Scriptures, in many ways not useless but capable of improving the masses of the people as far as they are able to receive it.[52]

The bodily (or literal) sense of the Scriptures served an important purpose, and it would be wrong to suggest that Origen minimized or disparaged it. On the contrary, he believed that most of the time, what the Bible says is reliable history and must be treated with respect:

> We must state . . . that with regard to some things, we are well aware that the historical fact is true. For example, . . . Jerusalem is the capital of Judaea, where Solomon built a temple to God, and thousands of other such facts. The passages that are historically true are far more numerous than those which were composed with purely spiritual meanings.[53]

Nevertheless, there were texts that could not be taken in their literal sense. For example, in Joshua 5:2, God commanded Joshua to circumcise the sons of Israel "a second time," which is a physical impossibility. For that reason, Origen insisted that the text must be taken figuratively. What it really means is that Christ circumcises the sins of the soul by "the baptism of regeneration," which is necessary even for those who received the first one under the law of Moses.[54] Similarly, Origen rejected a literal interpretation of the Genesis account of creation in six twenty-four hour days on the ground that it was impossible.[55] Why did the Holy Spirit put such strange passages in his revelation? Origen explained this as follows:

> The Word of God has prepared stumbling-blocks, hindrances, and impossibilities that are inserted in the midst of the law and history, so that we might not be led astray by the sheer attractiveness of the language, and so either reject the true teachings completely (on the ground that we learn nothing

[52] Origen, *De principiis* 4.2.8.
[53] Ibid., 4.3.4.
[54] Origen, *Homiliae in Iesum Nave* 5.5–6. Of course, this connection was clearer to his readers than it is to us, because in both Hebrew and Greek the names *Joshua* and *Jesus* are identical. As for the second circumcision, modern exegetes usually assume that this refers to the generation that had been born in the desert and that had therefore not been circumcised the first time around.
[55] Origen, *De principiis* 4.3.1.

worthy of God from the Scriptures), or else never move away from the letter and so fail to learn anything of its more divine element.[56]

Origen accepted that the bodily sense was usually present in the literal meaning of the text, but not that that was always the case. Sometimes, he argued, there is no bodily sense at all—even the so-called "literal" meaning is self-evidently related directly to the soul and/or the spirit, and not to the body. To illustrate this, he developed an allegorical interpretation of John 2:6, where we read that at the wedding feast at Cana in Galilee there were six water jars reserved for the Jewish rites of purification, each of which contained two or three "measures."[57] As Origen interpreted this,

> The language refers to those whom the Apostle called Jews "inwardly,"[58] and it means that they are purified by the word of the Scriptures, which sometimes contain two measures (i.e., the soul and spirit levels of meaning) and in other cases three, since some passages also have a bodily sense that is capable of edifying the hearers.[59]

In other words, Origen believed that every text contains a soul and spirit level of meaning. The bodily sense, on the other hand, might be present, unsuitable, or even absent altogether. As an example of where the bodily meaning must be transcended for the text to have any real meaning, Origen quoted Paul's use of Deuteronomy 25:4 in 1 Corinthians 9:9–10. The Old Testament verse prohibited the muzzling of the ox that treads out the corn, but Paul challenged this literal interpretation by asking the Corinthians whether God was really that concerned about oxen. According to the apostle, the law was intended for our sake, because "the plowman should plow in hope and the thresher thresh in hope of sharing in the crop." The implication, which Paul drew out in the next verse, was that preachers ought to be paid and supported in their ministry by those who receive its benefits.[60] Origen took his cue from expositions like these, which had the authority of New Testament revelation behind them, and used them as examples of how to interpret other parts of the Mosaic Law that he thought were no longer applicable in their literal sense.

The muzzling of the ox is an example of what Origen regarded as the "soul" interpretation of the Scriptures, because it goes beyond the immediate

[56] Ibid., 4.2.9.
[57] The ESV translation modernizes this by putting "twenty or thirty gallons," on the ground that a "measure" was about ten gallons.
[58] Rom. 2:29.
[59] Origen, *De principiis* 4.2.5.
[60] 1 Cor. 9:11. Origen, *De principiis* 4.2.6.

needs of the body to enunciate a moral principle that should govern a particular kind of relationship. He did not think that it was a "spiritual" interpretation, because it does not take us beyond the practical application of the need to maintain pastors to a deeper understanding of the ways of God. In other words, it is commonsense kindness, but not saving truth. The spiritual sense, however, was the most meaningful one for Origen because it points us to heaven and eternal life. Unfortunately, the spiritual sense is often hard to understand and is therefore hidden from the eyes of those who are not mature enough to appreciate it. The spiritual sense tells us how past and future events are linked to the saving work of Christ, how they reflect God's eternal wisdom, and how the other two senses will be fulfilled in God's higher purpose for mankind and for his creation in general.[61] As with the "soul" sense, Origen turned to the teaching and example of the apostle Paul to justify this aspect of his hermeneutical method:

> In accordance with the apostolic promise, we have to seek after "a secret and hidden wisdom of God, which God decreed before the ages for our glory," which "none of the rulers of this age understood."[62] The same apostle also says elsewhere, after mentioning some narrative passages in Exodus and Numbers, that "these things happened to them as an example, but they were written down for our instruction, on whom the end of the ages has come."[63]

Later in the same passage, Origen quoted the famous example of Galatians 4:21–26, where Paul interpreted the two sons of Abraham, one born from a slave woman and the other from a free one, as two covenants symbolizing Israel (the slave) and the church (the freeborn).[64] This is not a "soul" reading of the text, because it has no practical application in this life but points directly to our eternal destiny—the free woman (Sarah) stands for the heavenly Jerusalem, which is the mother of us all.

This allegorical method of interpreting the Bible has come in for a lot of criticism over the years, on the ground that it takes the reader far away from any possible meaning and indulges in pure fantasy. In some respects, allegory can be compared to astrology in that both are psychological fantasies built on scientific fact. An astrologer needs to know his astronomy very well, but he uses that knowledge in order to engage in what we would now call pastoral counseling. There is nothing wrong with either of these things in themselves,

[61] Origen, *De principiis*, 4.2.9.
[62] 1 Cor. 2:7–8.
[63] 1 Cor. 10:11. Origen, *De principiis* 4.2.6.
[64] Origen, *De principiis* 4.2.6.

but they are not connected to one another in this way. Like a good astrologer, the allegorizer of Scripture needs to know the literal sense in order to be able to discern the clues he needs for his allegory to work properly, but the spiritual message that he constructs out of it is unrelated to the text on which it is based. It may be perfectly valid in itself, and a reasonable exposition of Christian doctrine, but it is not rooted in the source from which it claims to be derived.

How then should Origen's hermeneutic be judged? He may have taken some of his interpretations too far (and certainly many of his followers did), but the New Testament evidence that he claimed in support of his interpretation cannot be so easily dismissed, and it serves as a reminder to us that the "literal" sense of Scripture is a considerably more complex phenomenon than it appears to be at first sight. It may be fanciful to read the biblical text as if it were composed of literal, moral, and spiritual meanings corresponding to the tripartite nature of human beings, but we must not overlook the deeper truths that this somewhat naive approach contains. The Scriptures do have more than one level of meaning, and the Christian life is a complete experience, involving every aspect of human life. However we interpret the Bible, these principles remain fundamental, and if we forget them the text will lose its power to speak to us today. Origen may have been wrong in some ways, but his heart was in the right place, and in the end it is by the secrets of the heart that he, like we, will be judged.

The main problem that Origen and the early Christians faced concerned the right interpretation of the Old Testament. It was universally acknowledged as the Word of God but just as universally regarded as being in some sense inferior to the New Testament as a revelation of salvation in Christ. Christians accepted that the prophets of ancient Israel had been inspired by the Holy Spirit, but there was a clear difference between what happened to them and the way the Spirit works now. As John Chrysostom put it,

> In the case of the prophets, everyone admits that they had the gift of the Holy Spirit, but this grace was limited. It departed from the earth on the day that it was said, "Your house is left to you desolate"[65] Even before then, it had been in decline, for there was no longer any prophet in Israel, nor did grace visit their holy things. The Holy Spirit had been withheld, but he was to be poured forth abundantly in the future. That began after the crucifixion, not only in greater abundance but also in the increased greatness of the gifts.[66]

[65] Matt. 23:38.

[66] John Chrysostom, *Homiliae in Iohannis Evangelium* 51.2.

Undoubtedly the most sophisticated interpreter of Scripture in the early church was Augustine of Hippo, whose book *De doctrina Christiana* (*On Christian Doctrine*) is a classic that continues to be widely read and studied today. Augustine gave a detailed analysis of how the Bible is to be read and interpreted, beginning with the literal sense and moving from there to various kinds of spiritual interpretation. From beginning to end, his exposition was governed by the rule of faith and its consequences. The key to understanding the Bible was the same as the principle laid down by Tertullian two hundred years earlier. The interpreter must be filled with the Spirit, seek the will of the Father as revealed in Scripture, and find that will worked out in the life, death, and resurrection of Jesus Christ. Even if it is impossible for us to sound the depths of the Spirit's relationship to the first person of the Trinity, the practical effects of it are felt in the way we read the Word of God and apply it to our lives. If we do this in the way we should, we shall be formed into the image and likeness of Christ, which is the ultimate purpose for which the Father sent his Son into the world and the fruit of what his Spirit does when he gets to work in our lives.

Having said all that, Augustine nevertheless recognized that it was possible to make mistakes about the meaning of Scripture without betraying the essence of the gospel, even if he was not happy about the fact. As he wrote,

> Whoever understands Scripture in a way that the writer did not intend goes astray, but not because there is anything wrong in Scripture. But if his mistaken interpretation helps to build up love, which is the purpose of the commandment, he goes astray in much the same way as the man who leaves the highway but still gets to the place where the main road leads, even if he gets there by crossing the fields. But such a person is to be corrected and shown how much better it is not to go off the highway in the first place! If he gets into the habit of going astray, he may end up taking paths that lead elsewhere and end up going in the wrong direction altogether.[67]

Augustine knew nothing of what we would now call "systematic theology"; in his mind there was only the teaching of the Bible, which he expounded further (and at much greater length) in his classic work *The City of God*. For him, the Bible was the teaching given by Christ as part of his work as the Mediator between God and man:

> The Mediator spoke in former times through the prophets and later through his own mouth, and after that through the apostles, telling man all that he

[67] Augustine of Hippo, *De doctrina Christiana* 1.36 (41).

> decided was enough for man [to know]. He also instituted the Scriptures that we call canonical. These are the writings of outstanding authority in which we put our trust concerning those things that we need to know for our own good, but cannot discover by ourselves.[68]

Perhaps Augustine did not realize it, but his Christocentric approach to the Scriptures went further than had been the custom in the church before his time. Of course, it had always been accepted that Christ was the *theme* of the Scriptures, as Christ himself taught.[69] But when it came to *authorship*, most Christians would have attributed that to the Father, and/or the Holy Spirit, again following direct New Testament evidence.[70] Jesus nowhere claimed to have revealed the Old Testament, and he did not write anything himself, telling his disciples that the Holy Spirit would lead them into all truth after his departure.[71] Augustine obviously knew that, but in putting his own focus on the revealing work of the Mediator he was opening up a new dimension to our understanding of the Scriptures as the mind of Christ, which is also a New Testament principle.[72] It is in and through the Bible that we come to understand not only what Jesus said and did but what he thought and ordained from the beginning. Jesus did not fulfill them as if he were a kind of athlete facing a series of hurdles that he had to overcome, but as their author—what he had said all along that he would do, he actually did in his incarnate life and now continues to do in the life of his body, the church. The Bible was therefore not just a guide to what we should teach and confess to the world, but also a pattern of how we should think and live ourselves. In a word, it was the blueprint for a new civilization, which Augustine saw as a manifestation of the city of God on earth. It was the way, the truth, and the life because it was the word of Jesus, apart from whom no one could enter into the presence of God.[73]

Because he believed that the Bible was a revelation of the mind of Christ, Augustine assumed that it was coherent and that its message could be explained. Its basic structure was the history of God's dealings with his people, which reached a climax in the incarnation of the Son. But just as Jesus' actions usually conveyed more than was immediately apparent on the surface, so his words had hidden depths that only the spiritually mature could understand.[74] Augustine expressed it like this:

[68] Augustine of Hippo, *De civitate Dei* 11.3.
[69] John 5:39.
[70] For the Father, see Heb. 1:1; for the Holy Spirit, see 2 Pet. 1:21.
[71] John 16:13.
[72] See 1 Cor. 2:16.
[73] John 14:6. See Augustine of Hippo, *Confessiones* 7.18.24, for his statement of this.
[74] Augustine of Hippo, *De doctrina Christiana* 2.14–21. See Heb. 5:11–6:3, which expresses the same thing.

> Those who read [the Scriptures] in a frivolous spirit are liable to be misled by innumerable obscurities and ambiguities, and to mistake their meaning entirely. In some places they will not even be able to guess at a wrong meaning, so thick and dark is the fog that some passages are covered in. I have no doubt that this is due to divine providence, in order to break our pride with hard labor and save our intelligence from boredom, since we easily form a low opinion of things that are too obvious to need working out.[75]

For Augustine and his contemporaries, the relativity and limitations of human perception made it impossible to rely on reason alone as the criterion of truth.[76] The philosophers had tried that and had ended up with any number of different conceptions about the nature of reality, most of which could not possibly be correct. On the most charitable reading, they had grasped elements of the truth that might have led them to embrace Christianity if they had pooled their insights together. But because they did not, they contradicted one another, even when they belonged to the same school of philosophical thought. Augustine pointed this out when he contrasted what Plato had said about the human soul with what the Neoplatonist Porphyry was teaching some six centuries or more later:

> Plato and Porphyry each made certain statements which might have brought them both to become Christians if they had exchanged them with one another. Plato said that souls could not exist forever in a bodiless state, which is why he said that the souls of the wise would eventually return to bodies. . . . Porphyry, for his part, said that a completely purified soul will never return to the evils of this world once it has gone back to the Father. Had they communicated with each other . . . and shared their common beliefs, I think they would have seen that souls would return to bodies, but of a kind that would allow them to live in bliss and immortality.[77]

As Augustine saw it, the universe is bigger than we are, and so it is only to be expected that the mind of the Creator will be bigger than ours is. Access to the Creator's mind is impossible for ordinary human beings because of the great gulf that separates him from his creatures.[78] In the words of the apostle Paul, "Who are you, O man, to answer back to God? Will what is molded say to its molder, 'Why have you made me like this?'"[79] Human attempts to understand

[75] Augustine of Hippo, *De doctrina Christiana* 2.7.
[76] Ibid., 1.10–11.
[77] Augustine of Hippo, *De civitate Dei* 22.27. On Augustine's reckoning, Plato and Porphyry would have come to the conclusion outlined by Paul in 1 Cor. 15:42–55.
[78] Augustine of Hippo, *De doctrina Christiana* 1.5–7.
[79] Rom. 9:20.

the meaning of life are doomed to failure unless and until the Creator reveals himself to his creatures. This he has done, said Christians, in the word he spoke to Israel and in the sending of his Son as Jesus Christ.

Christians defended their position by using a number of arguments, some of which were more sound than others. One common assertion they made was that the Bible must be true because it is older than any work of Greek philosophy or history. In purely historical terms, Herodotus (fifth century BC) or Plato (fourth century BC) could have read Moses (fifteenth century BC?), but not the other way around.[80] To modern minds this is a curious argument to make, but in a world where antiquity was regarded as the hallmark of authenticity and where Christians were frequently accused of having invented a new religion (which was widely regarded as false because of its newness), it carried more weight than it would today. Augustine, however, was disinclined to believe this sort of thing, despite the evident similarities between some aspects of the Old Testament creation story and Plato's *Timaeus*. The most he was prepared to concede was that Plato "may have learned by word of mouth as much as he could understand of the contents of the Scriptures," and he preferred to think that whatever the Greek philosophers got right was due to the divine revelation given to the Gentiles in general and not to their reading of the Bible.[81]

More seriously, Christians also argued that the Hebrew Bible presented a coherent picture of the universe that was lacking in other systems of thought.[82] The Creator was a moral being, he was sovereign over his creatures and therefore not bound or limited by them, and his creation had a purpose that was being worked out in history and would be brought to fulfillment at some future time. This meant that everything that happens in the world has a meaning, even if we do not always understand what it is, and that we can have confidence in what we are doing because we know that it is serving the divine will. Even those who go against God's revealed will cannot alter this basic fact. They are what Paul called the vessels of wrath who are being prepared for destruction, whose fate serves to magnify the glory of God revealed in the vessels of mercy who have been spared that terrible fate.[83] Believers in Christ can rest assured that they are vessels of mercy, but they cannot explain why they are the ones who have been chosen for salvation and not others. All they know is that they

[80] See, for example, Justin Martyr, *Apologia I* 60; Clement of Alexandria, *Stromateis* 1.22; Origen, *Contra Celsum* 4.39; Eusebius of Caesarea, *Praeparatio evangelica* 11.9.2; Cyril of Alexandria, *Contra Iulianum* 29; Augustine of Hippo, *De doctrina Christiana* 2.43.

[81] Augustine of Hippo, *De civitate Dei* 8.11–12. See Rom. 1:19–20.

[82] See, for example, Augustine's description of paganism in *De civitate Dei* 4.10–11.

[83] Rom. 9:22.

have not deserved such favor, and this knowledge prevents them from becoming proud of their salvation.

The most telling argument the Christians used was that belief in Christ produced changed men and women. Those who believed in Christ shared in his mind, and this made them think in a way that was so different from the rest of the world that others could not understand them. They were prepared to abandon family, wealth, and career prospects for the sake of serving Christ, even if that meant dying for him on a cross or in the arena. Christians defied social taboos and traditional conventions. Those who had been strict Jews started to socialize with Gentiles. Those who had led immoral and unprofitable lives became honest and upright citizens. Of course this was an idealized picture—there were always plenty of failures and people who used the cover of the church in order to promote their own selfish interests—but there was enough truth in it to justify the point the apologists of the new faith were trying to make. Above all, those who opposed Christianity on intellectual grounds had nothing comparable to show for the practical consequences of their own beliefs. No one died for Platonism, and the pagan gods were anything but examples of moral rectitude. Compared with what else was on offer, the church could make a good case for the truth of what it preached.

Christians also relied heavily on historical facts to buttress their beliefs. The history of ancient Israel was taken as read, but more important to them was the life, death, and resurrection of Jesus Christ, which had happened in recent times under the noses of the Roman authorities themselves. Scoffers might deny the possibility of bodily resurrection from the dead on theoretical grounds, but no one had a convincing alternative explanation for the empty tomb of Jesus. The claim that he had appeared to his disciples afterwards was backed up by the experience of thousands of believers who had his Holy Spirit dwelling in their hearts. They had not seen Jesus in the flesh but they knew him in the Spirit. The distorting lens of history can easily magnify the quarrels that erupted between Christians, making us doubt their fundamental spiritual unity, but we must not forget that the memory of these disputes has been preserved because the church felt that they were problems that had to be resolved if that unity was to be maintained. The warm welcome given in the mid-fourth century to the exiled Athanasius in the West and to the exiled Hilary of Poitiers in the East is a reminder of this. At the human level these men were strangers and outcasts, but in spiritual terms they were heroes of the faith and were immediately recognized as brothers by people who could not understand a word they said.

Arians and Pelagians agreed with the members of the mainline church about the importance of the Bible and could even have argued that they paid more attention to its interpretation than their opponents did. The riposte of the orthodox was that heretics interpreted the Bible in a superficial way. Arius strung proof-texts together to support his case but understood nothing of their deeper meaning, which made his interpretation naive and unsound. Pelagius was accused of taking verses out of context and quoting them to prove something that the weight of the Bible as a whole would not support. In the end, as Tertullian had said in his book *On the Prescription of Heretics*, one had to be in tune with the Spirit who inspired the sacred texts in order to understand them properly. This was the conviction that united the proponents of orthodoxy and enabled it to win out in spite of the periodic condemnation of specific individuals and the deviant behavior of some church councils. Orthodoxy could be denied, it could be suppressed, it could even be legislated out of existence, but it could not be killed off. It always came back and triumphed because it carried conviction in a way that nothing else did.

The spiritual power of Christian orthodoxy was greater than any single individual or local church, but its eventual triumph was brought about by men who worked in and through the institutional structures that the apostles and their successors had created. It was not necessary for a man to hold office in the church in order to be heard, as the examples of Tertullian, Origen, and Jerome testify, but only those who were bishops of their local congregations took part in the councils that decided questions of Christian doctrine. The writings of learned individuals were highly respected but they were not canonized, nor were they necessarily copied or preserved. It is difficult to know for sure what has been lost, and in some cases "survival" is a relative term that can be misleading. For example, there are works by people like Melito of Sardis, Didymus the Blind of Alexandria, and Theodore of Mopsuestia that have been recovered in modern times, occasionally only in Armenian or Syriac translations. We know about them now, but how widely were they read in antiquity? That we cannot say, but the complete disappearance of their writings for many centuries must make us cautious about evaluating the influence that they may have exercised on the development of Christian doctrine.

What we do know is that the Bible was extensively copied, studied, and commented on by all sections of the church. For a long time scholars more or less ignored ancient biblical commentaries because their hermeneutical principles and conclusions are often quite different from what we would accept today and have therefore been felt to be of little relevance to us.[84] But whether

[84] This situation has changed dramatically in recent years. See, for example, Thomas C. Oden, gen. ed., *The Ancient Christian Commentary on Scripture*, 29 vols. (Downers Grove, IL: InterVarsity Press, 1998–2010); Charles Kannengiesser, *Handbook of Patristic Exegesis*, 2 vols. (Leiden: Brill, 2004).

that is true or not, the popularity of biblical commentary in the ancient world is of great historical importance because it helps us establish what the church's canon of sacred texts was and how it was read. It is particularly noticeable that for the Old Testament, there are commentaries on all the books found in the Hebrew Bible but not on those that have survived only in Greek translation. We can therefore say with some certainty that those books, which we now call the Apocrypha, were *not* used for preaching and teaching purposes in the early church, even if they were known and sometimes quoted. In the New Testament, there are commentaries on all the books we now recognize as canonical but not on other early Christian writings like the *Shepherd of Hermas*. In this way, the limits of the canon can be discerned by the survival of commentaries that were composed as aids to the church's ministry.

Apart from a few notes left by Clement of Alexandria, the first major commentator on the Bible was Origen, and the later Greek tradition was deeply indebted to him. Commentary writing became a serious business in the Greek-speaking world in the late fourth century and continued for about a hundred years. The most important names are those of Didymus the Blind, Theodore of Mopsuestia, and Theodoret of Cyrus, all of whom wrote extensively on the scriptural texts. Also important is John Chrysostom (d. 407), whose sermons were widely copied and used as practical commentaries for preachers. These sermons (or homilies) have come down to us, but many of the Greek commentaries have disappeared, at least in their original form. Origen's works survive to some extent mainly because they were translated into Latin by Rufinus, an associate of Jerome who was working around the year 400, and so do those of Theodoret of Cyrus (d. 466?), perhaps because he was never condemned for heresy.

The others are known mainly in fragments and quotations, the most important of which are found in the *Catenae* ("chains"), which are anthologies of different scriptural commentaries that were compiled in the sixth century.[85] Modern scholarship has been able to identify some of the sources that were used to make this anthology, which helps us to fill in the blanks in our knowledge of the early church's teaching and preaching activity. Who did this is unknown, but what is certain is that the medieval Greek church was still reading extracts from biblical commentaries that in some cases can be traced back to Origen. They had been selected and shaped into a canonical tradition which became the Eastern churches' authoritative guide to interpreting the Scriptures until modern times, and that is still being used as such in some places today.

[85] See John A. Cramer's five volumes of New Testament *Catenae* (Oxford: Oxford University Press, 1838–1841).

In the Latin world, commentary writing was slower to get off the ground. One of the earliest (and best) commentators on the Pauline epistles was an unknown writer who lived at Rome in the time of Pope Damasus I (366–384), whom we now call Ambrosiaster because his works were transmitted under the name of Ambrose of Milan (d. 397).[86] Jerome, the great translator of the Latin Bible, was also a prolific commentator and so was Pelagius, much to the embarrassment of later generations.[87] Augustine wrote a few commentaries, but apart from one on the Psalms and another on 1 John, they are relatively insignificant. On the other hand, he was fascinated by the creation narratives in Genesis 1–3 and wrote several times on them, and his deep knowledge of the Bible is clear in most of his other works, where he quotes freely from a wide range of texts to support his arguments.[88]

---

[86] An English translation is available in Gerald L. Bray, ed., *Ambrosiaster: Commentaries on Romans and 1–2 Corinthians*; and *Ambrosiaster: Commentaries on Galatians–Philemon* (Downers Grove, IL: InterVarsity Press, 2009). Ambrosiaster did not include Hebrews in his Pauline canon.

[87] His commentaries were preserved because they were recycled under the names of the fully orthodox Jerome and Cassiodorus.

[88] See Pamela Bright, ed., *Augustine and the Bible* (Notre Dame IN: University of Notre Dame Press, 1999).

The Preservation of the Church

The Mind of Christ

Of great significance for the life of the church was the series of councils summoned to resolve disputes and the regulations that they produced. Unlike the writings of individual theologians and scholars, these canons, as they are called, carried the authority of the church as a whole and in many cases became part of the laws by which it was governed.[1] It was generally believed that when the bishops met to seek God's will, the Holy Spirit would come down and reveal the mind of Christ to them. There would therefore be a consensus, as there was in the first synod recorded in the Acts of the Apostles.[2] In the words of Origen,

> If at any time a subject under investigation is unclear, let us go to Jesus with all unanimity in regard to the question in dispute, for he is present wherever two or three are gathered together in his name. He is ready by his presence with power to illuminate the hearts of those who truly desire to become his disciples.[3]

The theory sounds good but the reality, alas, was that when councils met, minority dissenters were driven out and their votes were not counted, though there were times when that technique did not work. At the Second Council of Ephesus in 449, for example, the opposition was strong enough to regroup and carry the day two years later at Chalcedon, where the party that had been dominant at Ephesus was alienated in its turn. The resulting schism has lasted to the present day, making it difficult to decide what the "will of the Spirit" really was!

For our purposes, the councils can be divided into two types. The first, and most common, was the local or provincial synod, which was summoned

[1] The Greek word "canon" (*kanôn*) came from legal usage; its Latin equivalent was *regula* ("rule").
[2] See Acts 15:1–29. "Synod" (Greek, *synodos*) and "council" (Latin, *concilium*) are synonymous in meaning, but today we usually distinguish them to some extent in practice. Ecumenical gatherings are always "councils," whereas "synods" tend to refer to meetings of a local or regional church, but usage is not consistent.
[3] Origen, *Commentarium in Matthaei Evangelium* 13.15.

to meet in some part of the Roman world. North Africa held a number of them from the mid-third to the early fifth centuries, and they were also held quite frequently in Gaul (modern France). The most famous of them were the seventeen Councils of Toledo, which met in Spain from the fifth to the seventh centuries and whose canons later became an important source of Western church legislation.[4]

Generally speaking, provincial councils met to decide organizational questions and dealt with doctrinal matters only in passing. This was because Christian doctrine affected the whole church, and only a council at which the entire Christian world was represented had the authority to decide what should be accepted as orthodox belief. Before the legalization of Christianity in 313 it was not possible to call such a council, but once the church was free from persecution it was not long before they began to meet. Those that were summoned by the emperors came to be called "ecumenical," and their decisions acquired an authority that to a large extent they still retain today.[5] In later centuries the power to convoke an ecumenical council would be claimed by the pope as the bishop of Rome, but no pope in ancient times attended one, and Rome's influence on their decision making, if not negligible, was certainly not decisive or more important than that of other churches. As long as the Eastern empire lasted, its emperors claimed the right to summon councils, and Protestants sometimes granted this privilege to secular rulers after the Reformation.[6]

If any local church dominated the ancient councils, it was Constantinople. This was not because of its historical importance, which was slight, but because it was where the emperor resided. Of the seven ancient councils now generally regarded as "ecumenical," no fewer than six took place in the capital or within a day's journey of it. The exception was the one held at Ephesus in 431, but even that was not all that far away from the center of imperial power.[7]

Taking them in order, the seven ecumenical councils were:

1. *The First Council of Nicea in 325*. This council condemned Arius and decreed that the Son of God was *homoousios* ("consubstantial") with the Father. Its acts have not survived, and all we have now are its confession of faith (which is *not* the Nicene Creed we know today), twenty disciplinary canons,

[4] One or two of these councils may never have taken place, but the number "seventeen" has stuck. The standard source for all conciliar documents is J. D. Mansi, I. B. Martin, and L. Petit, *Sacrorum conciliorum nova et amplissima collectio*, 55 vols. (Florence, Venice, Paris, Arnhem, Leipzig, 1759–1962).

[5] The word "ecumenical" comes from *oikoumenê*, the Greek word most often used to describe the Roman empire. (See Luke 2:1.)

[6] Article 22 of the 42 Articles of 1553 (revised as Article 21 of the 39 Articles of 1563/1571) says, "General councils may not be gathered together without the commandment and will of princes."

[7] For a brief introduction to the seven councils, see Leo D. Davis, *The First Seven Ecumenical Councils (325–787): Their History and Theology* (Collegeville, MN: Liturgical Press, 1983).

and a letter sent to the church of Alexandria that deals with particular problems that had arisen there. The canons and the letter are interesting because they give us a glimpse of what life must have been like in the years immediately following the end of the great persecution. The council found it necessary to legislate against the laxity and disorder that prevailed in certain places, and in the course of doing so, it laid down principles that in some cases are still widely observed today. For example, canon 9 states,

> As for those who have been ordained presbyters without examination, or if after having been interrogated and confessed their sins, someone has laid hands on them in defiance of the rule, the canon does not recognize persons so ordained. The church accepts only men of irreproachable character.[8]

Another canon that has survived the passage of time is number 16:

> Any presbyter or deacon who deserts his own church should not be received elsewhere but should be obliged to return to his own congregation or else be excommunicated. And if any bishop dares to ordain someone from another diocese without the consent of the bishop of that diocese, the ordination shall be annulled.[9]

Different churches have their own procedures for implementing these principles, but the concern expressed at Nicea for order and fairness is one that almost all Christian bodies continue to accept, not least because it is the practical application of the principle expressed by the apostle Paul that everything "should be done decently and in order."[10]

2. *The First Council of Constantinople in 381*. This council condemned Apollinarius and reaffirmed the humanity of the incarnate Christ. Its acts have not survived, and all that remains of it are a letter sent to Damasus I, the bishop of Rome, and seven canons, of which only the first four are certainly authentic.[11] Of these, by far the most important is the third, which states, "The bishop of Constantinople shall be next in honor to the bishop of Rome, because Constantinople is the new Rome."[12] This purely political decision upset Alexandria, which was demoted to third place in the hierarchy, and also Rome, which subsequently began to stress that it was the most important church,

---

[8] *Conciliorum oecumenicorum decreta* (Bologna: Istituto per le Scienze Religiose, 1973), 10.
[9] Ibid., 13–14.
[10] 1 Cor. 14:40.
[11] See Heinz Ohme, "Sources of the Greek Canon Law to the Quinisext Council (691/2)" in Wilfried Hartmann and Kenneth Pennington, eds., *The History of Byzantine and Eastern Canon Law to 1500* (Washington, DC: Catholic University of America Press, 2012), 49–53.
[12] *Conciliorum oecumenicorum decreta*, 32.

not because it was the capital of the empire but because Peter, the chief of the apostles, had been its first bishop. That clearly had carried no weight at the council, and Rome did not ratify this canon until 1215, but it is the basis on which the patriarch of Constantinople exercises a primacy of honor among the Eastern Orthodox churches to this day.

3. *The (First) Council of Ephesus in 431.* This council condemned Nestorius, who was subsequently deposed from the see of Constantinople. There are no conciliar acts in existence but we have the correspondence between Cyril of Alexandria and Nestorius, including the famous twelve anathemas appended to Cyril's third letter. The Eastern churches have managed to extract eight canons from this correspondence, but the council itself did not enact any such legislation. Apart from the condemnation of Nestorius, which was upheld by the Council of Chalcedon in 451, this third council is chiefly known today for having prohibited any additions to the "Creed of Nicea," which was probably that of 325 (no longer used), not that of 381 (our "Nicene Creed"), though this has been the subject of much controversy.

4. *The Council of Chalcedon in 451.* This council affirmed the doctrine that the incarnate Christ is one divine person in two natures which are neither merged nor separated. It reaffirmed the condemnation of Nestorius and denounced the monophysite teaching of Alexandria, while at the same time claiming the legacy of the great Cyril, who had died in 444. Chalcedon was immediately accepted in the West, where it soon became the touchstone of Christological orthodoxy, but its reception in the East was much patchier. In the end, the churches of Constantinople and Jerusalem agreed to it, but those of Alexandria and Antioch did not. The resulting schism between Chalcedonians and non-Chalcedonians split the church permanently, and even today, despite much friendlier contacts between the different groups, Chalcedon remains a barrier to the full reunion of the churches.[13]

The acts of the council survive in both Greek and Latin versions (which are not identical), as does the *Tome* of Leo I of Rome, which was read out and accepted as the definitive answer to the monophysitism of Eutyches.[14] The council also composed a definition of faith that remains the standard explanation of the two-natures Christology accepted in the West and by the church

[13] See Paulos Gregorios, William H. Lazareth, Nikos A. Nissiotis, eds., *Does Chalcedon Divide or Unite? Towards Convergence in Orthodox Christology* (Geneva: World Council of Churches, 1981). On the council itself, see Aloys Grillmeier and Heinrich Bacht, eds., *Das Konzil von Chalkedon*, 3 vols. (Würzburg: Echter Verlag, 1951–1954); and Robert V. Sellers, *The Council of Chalcedon: A Historical and Doctrinal Survey* (London: SPCK, 1961).

[14] Richard Price and Michael Gaddis, trans., *The Acts of the Council of Chalcedon*, 3 vols. (Liverpool: Liverpool University Press, 2007).

of Constantinople and those Eastern churches that are in communion with it. There are also thirty canons, of which the first twenty-seven are authentic and were universally agreed to at the time. Canon 28, which reaffirmed the position of Constantinople as the second see in the hierarchy, was sharply contested by the Roman delegation and so was omitted from the acts, even in the Eastern churches, which did not start including it until about a century later.[15]

5. *The Second Council of Constantinople in 553*. This council issued fourteen anathemas condemning the so-called "Three Chapters," theological works by Antiochene writers that were thought to be Nestorian, and also Origen. Origen had been a controversial figure for about 150 years and was condemned for his supposed belief in metempsychosis (a form of reincarnation). The three chapters were the complete works of Theodore of Mopsuestia, the writings of Theodoret of Cyrus against the First Council of Ephesus and Cyril of Alexandria, and the letter of Ibas of Edessa to Maris of Persia, in which he praised the works of Theodore of Mopsuestia. Condemning Theodoret and Ibas was tricky, because both men had been rehabilitated at the Council of Chalcedon, and the Roman church was particularly upset about that. There was also some disquiet about the propriety of condemning long-dead theologians, but those qualms were overcome and the council was eventually accepted by Chalcedonians everywhere, though not without considerable pressure applied by the emperor Justinian I (527–565), whose policies it reflected.[16]

6. *The Third Council of Constantinople in 680–681*. This council condemned monotheletism on the ground that it was not consonant with the church's previous doctrinal statements, but did little else. As with the fifth council, it was accepted by the Chalcedonians, whose teaching it upheld, but is relatively little known today.

Much more important for the life of the church was the Council *in Trullo*, sometimes called the Quinisext ("fifth-sixth") Council, in 692, which composed the disciplinary canons that were later attached to the previous two councils.[17] These were adopted by the Eastern Orthodox churches but not in the West, which has always had an ambiguous relationship to them and does not include them among the acts of the seven councils.[18]

[15] Rome did not recognize it until 1215. See Heinz Ohme, "Greek Canon Law," 57–66, for the details.

[16] The acts of the council have been published in translation by Richard Price, *The Acts of the Council of Constantinople of 553*, 2 vols. (Liverpool: Liverpool University Press, 2009; reissued in one volume with corrections, 2012). For a good account of it, see John Meyendorff, *Imperial Unity and Christian Divisions* (Crestwood, NY: St. Vladimir's Seminary Press, 1989), 207–250.

[17] The Trullum was the domed hall of the imperial palace in Constantinople.

[18] See George Nedungatt and Michael Featherstone, eds., *The Council in Trullo Revisited* (Rome: Pontificio Istituto Orientale, 1995). For those who read Greek, there is a detailed doctoral dissertation on the council that repays

The Council *in Trullo* enacted 102 canons, which were meant to cover every aspect of clerical life and public worship, and which are regarded today as the foundation of canon law in the East.[19] Many of its provisions were already commonly observed, but the council tried to impose uniformity based on the practice of the church at Constantinople. Customs that differed from that were forbidden, including some of those in use at Rome, which meant that the Roman church never ratified the council's decisions. In particular, the council established the rules for clerical marriage (rejecting the Roman preference for celibacy), decreeing that married men could be ordained as presbyters but not as bishops. It also rejected the Roman custom of using unleavened bread for Communion.

At the time, the emperor Justinian II (685–695; 705–711), at whose initiative the council was summoned, seems to have believed that Rome would eventually abandon its opposition, but it did not, and the council was quietly forgotten in the West. However, in the acrimonious atmosphere of 1054, when papal legates tried to force the patriarch of Constantinople to accept Roman supremacy and the patriarch replied in kind, the canons of the Council *in Trullo* were resurrected and used by both sides as an excuse to anathematize the other—the West complaining that the canons were invalid and depraved, the East insisting that Rome should accept them. After that, the council returned to the oblivion from which it had briefly been rescued in the West, but it was increasingly treated as ecumenical in the East, as it still is today.

7. *The Second Council of Nicea in 787*. This council issued twenty-two canons affirming that pictures of Christ were permitted in church and that they portrayed his divine person as well as his human nature. The council was the result of two generations of warfare in the East over iconoclasm, which it rejected, though the controversy was revived in the ninth century and was not finally settled until 843. Its decisions were almost immediately rejected in the West at a council held in Frankfurt in 794, and although that condemnation was later reversed, the council has never had much impact on Western theology. In sharp contrast to that, it has been very important in the East because it is the basis for the veneration of icons that forms such a central part of Orthodox worship.[20]

At the time of the Reformation, most Protestants rejected it because of its

careful reading. See G. Ch. Gavardinas, *Hê penthektê oikoumenikê synodos kai to nomothetiko tês ergo* (Katerini: Ekdoseis Epektasi, 1998).

[19] See Heinz Ohme, "Greek Canon Law," 77–84, for the details.

[20] Not for nothing is the final defeat of iconoclasm in 843 known in the Eastern churches as "the triumph of Orthodoxy."

promotion of the veneration of images. John Calvin wrote against it at some length, adducing the council of Frankfurt in his support before going on to say,

> When they discuss adoration, they lay great stress on the worship of Pharaoh, the staff of Joseph, and the inscription that Jacob erected. Not only do they pervert the meaning of Scripture, but in this last case, they quote what is nowhere to be found. Then verses like "Worship at his footstool,"[21] "Worship in his holy mountain,"[22] and "The rulers of the people will worship before your face"[23] seem to them to be solid proofs of their argument [in favor of the veneration of icons]. . . . Could they be made to utter greater and grosser absurdities than these? . . . Theodosius of Myra justified the practice by appealing to the dreams of his archdeacon, which he mentioned with as much seriousness as if he had received a message from heaven. . . . The fathers brought themselves into utter discredit by handling Scripture so childishly and wresting it so shamefully and profanely out of context.[24]

Somewhat later, and apparently independently of Calvin, the Anglican *Homily against Peril of Idolatry* issued its own condemnation of the council, saying that "a decree was made that images should be set up in all the churches of Greece, and that honor and worship also should be given unto the said images," adding for good measure that this was probably done because the two presidents of the council were the Roman bishop's legates, whose aim was to make "Constantinople within a short time, altogether like Rome itself."[25] This historical judgment is misguided, but there can be no doubt about the antipathy of the author toward the practice of venerating images, an antipathy which, it would be fair to say, has always characterized Protestantism.

Today the Eastern Orthodox churches accept all seven councils and regard them as the foundation of their official doctrine to which nothing can be added (except by another council, which has not yet been held). The Roman Catholic Church also accepts all seven, but puts less emphasis on the seventh and largely ignores the Council *in Trullo*. Most Protestant churches agree with the decisions of the first four councils, are ambivalent about the fifth and sixth, and tend to reject the seventh.[26] How much weight should now be given to the

[21] Psalm 99:5.
[22] Isa. 27:13.
[23] Perhaps a reference to Isa. 49:7.
[24] Calvin, *Institutio* 1.11.15. The discussion begins in the previous paragraph (1.11.14).
[25] The author of the *Homily* was probably John Jewel, the bishop of Salisbury. The quotations are from the second part of the homily and can be found in *The Homilies Appointed to Be Read in Churches* (Bishopstone: Brynmill, 2006), 147.
[26] The Nestorian church accepts only the first two, and the monophysite churches of the East only the first three.

disciplinary canons, as opposed to the doctrinal ones, is a matter of some debate. In the Eastern churches some argue that they have just as much authority as anything else the councils decided, but the Western churches, both Roman Catholic and Protestant, take a more liberal view. The ancient canons may sometimes be consulted and even applied if they are still thought to be relevant, but on the whole the Western churches recognize that they were intended for particular situations, most of which no longer obtain, and so they are not regarded as binding on the church today.

The councils of the early church gained in prestige over time, but how effective they were in establishing orthodox doctrinal and disciplinary norms is hard to say. It is clear that the fulminations against Arianism, Nestorianism, and so on had only limited effect, since these movements continued to exist regardless of what the ecumenical councils said about them. In North Africa there were many attempts to eradicate Donatism in a series of provincial synods, but they all failed. Only many centuries later, after the circumstances that had produced them had long been forgotten, were the canons of those synods collected and made authoritative for the medieval church. Furthermore, the fact that many of the disciplinary canons were frequently reenacted is a bad sign, because it indicates that the original regulations had been ignored so often that further legislation was required.

One of the problems the church had was that it lacked a central administration that could summon councils and then implement their decisions. It is true that after 381 there were five main centers (Rome, Constantinople, Alexandria, Antioch, and Jerusalem—in that order) that were granted particular prestige, but the defection of Alexandria and Antioch after Chalcedon and the division between East and West (which cut Rome off from the rest) sharply reduced their importance and ability to act.[27] Ecumenical councils could really be called only by the emperor, who resided in Constantinople but whose authority declined considerably after the rise of Islam in the seventh century and the growing importance of the Frankish kingdom in the West. It was still possible for an emperor to summon a council in 787, but as we have already seen, it was repudiated by the Franks, largely for political reasons. When the Frankish king Charlemagne was crowned emperor in Rome on Christmas Day in 800, the West acquired an independent secular authority to rival that of the East, and after that it was no longer certain, or even very likely, that a truly universal council could be summoned at all. A council held in Constantinople in 870 was later regarded as "ecumenical" in the West because it deposed Photius, the capital's

[27] Orthodox patriarchs in communion with Constantinople were still appointed, but they ministered to tiny flocks and cannot be regarded as representative of these great sees.

bishop (patriarch), but the Eastern churches never ratified this. Ten years later a further council was held in Constantinople that reinstated Photius, and there is an ongoing debate as to whether that second council should be recognized as "ecumenical" instead of the earlier one.[28]

Either way, it hardly matters, because the age of truly ecumenical councils was clearly over by then. The revived Western empire fell apart, only to be reconstituted in a diminished form in the late tenth century. As the "Holy Roman Empire of the German Nation," it would survive until 1806, but its emperors never assumed the kind of ecclesiastical role to which their Eastern counterparts were accustomed. Instead, the vacuum was filled by the bishop of Rome, who steadily emerged as a secular ruler in his own right, and took upon himself the authority to summon "universal" church councils. The problem, of course, was that those councils were attended only by those who accepted papal jurisdiction and so (despite their name) they were not really "ecumenical" at all. Their decisions would be accepted *within* the Roman church, but those outside of it rejected them—as is still the case today. As a result, although their theological decisions and disciplinary canons played a formative role in shaping what we now call the Roman Catholic Church, they seldom had any wider impact, and as time went on they were increasingly used to attack and condemn those who opposed the universal jurisdiction of the papacy.[29]

The gap in understanding between East and West to which these developments bore witness was most clearly seen at the two councils that attempted to reunite what had by then become the separated churches of Rome and Constantinople. Both of them were jointly chaired by the pope and the Eastern emperor, but it was clear where the weight of authority lay. At the Second Council of Lyon (1274) and again at the Council of Florence (1439), the emperor ended up submitting to the pope—only to discover on his return to the East that his people would not follow him. The fall of Constantinople to the Turks in 1453 put an end to such ventures, but the sad result was that many on the Eastern

[28] See Johan Meijer, *A Successful Council of Reunion: A Theological Analysis of the Photian Synod of 879–880* (Thessalonica: Patriarchikon Idryma Paterikôn Spoudôn, 1975). See also Francis Dvornik, *The Photian Schism* (Cambridge: Cambridge University Press, 1948); Richard Haugh, *Photius and the Carolingians: The Trinitarian Controversy* (Belmont, MA: Nordland, 1975); and *Monumenta Graeca ad Photium eiusque historiam pertinentia*, ed. Joseph Hergenröther (Regensburg: G. J. Manz, 1869; repr., with an introduction by Joan M. Hussey, Farnborough: Gregg International, 1969).

[29] There were seven councils in the Middle Ages that were primarily dedicated to the internal reform of the church. These were the four Lateran Councils (1123, 1139, 1173, and 1215), two councils held at Lyon (1245 and 1274), and one at Vienne (1313). Most of their decisions were incorporated into the church's canon law. Following those, there were four "reformation" councils dealing mainly with heresy and indiscipline: Constance (1413–1417), Basel-Florence (1436–1444), Lateran V (1512–1517), and Trent (1545–1563). There have also been two modern councils that are hard to classify in these traditional terms: Vatican I (1870) and Vatican II (1962–1965). Vatican II was distinguished by significant participation from non–Roman Catholic churches, but its decisions were not applicable to them.

side preferred to live under Muslim rule (where they were given substantial autonomy) than to submit to the Western church, which would have done its best to assimilate them to its own customs and traditions.[30]

The disappearance of the Eastern empire and the absence of any secular authority that could call an ecumenical council today makes it difficult for the Eastern Orthodox churches to decide how to call one if it were necessary. The patriarch of Constantinople, as honorary head of the Eastern churches, would probably be expected to summon such a gathering, but he has never done that before and has no canonical power to do so. With Rome, of course, things are very different. As recently as the Second Vatican Council (1962–1965) its position was made crystal clear:

> The Roman pontiff, by reason of his office as the vicar of Christ, and as pastor of the entire church, has full, supreme and universal power over the whole church, a power which he can always exercise unhindered. The order of bishops is the successor to the college of the apostles. . . . The supreme authority over the whole church which this college possesses, is exercised in a solemn way in an ecumenical council. There never is an ecumenical council which is not confirmed or at least recognized as such by Peter's successor, and it is the prerogative of the Roman pontiff to convoke such councils, to preside over them and to confirm them.[31]

Unfortunately, the practical effect of statements like this is to make calling a genuinely universal council of the Christian church today impossible. Non-Roman churches would never accept that the pope has the unique authority given to him by God to summon such a council and preside over it, and any council called by him (as the Second Vatican Council was) will affect only those who are in communion with Rome. Interdenominational bodies like the World Council of Churches contain only Protestant and Eastern Orthodox members because the Roman church cannot belong to any organization that it does not control and whose decisions are not subject to what is in effect a papal veto. In other words, the papacy, meant to be the universal symbol of Christian unity,

[30] The literature on this subject is vast, and much of it concentrates on the political complications of the attempted reunions. For more purely theological treatments, see Martin Jugie, *Le schisme byzantin* (Paris: Lethielleux, 1941); Joseph Gill, *Church Union: Rome and Byzantium (1204–1453)* (London: Variorum Reprints, 1979); Burkhard Roberg, *Das zweite Konzil von Lyon (1274)* (Paderborn: Ferdinand Schöningh, 1990); *Dossier grec de l'union de Lyon (1273–1277)*, ed. Vitalien Laurent and Jean Darrouzès (Paris: Institut Français d'Etudes Byzantines, 1976); and Joseph Gill, *The Council of Florence* (Cambridge: Cambridge University Press, 1959). It should be said that most of these works are written from the Western point of view and can be quite polemical at times. Unfortunately, the corresponding literature from the East is often even worse in this respect! See, for example, Methodius G. Fouyas, *Hê ekklêsiastikê antiparathesis Hellênôn kai Latinôn apo tês epochês tou Megalou Phôtiou mechri tês synodou tês Flôrentias (858–1439)*, 2nd ed. (Athens: Apostoliki Diakonia, 1994). A more balanced Eastern view can be found in Ch. A. Arampatzês, *Hê synodos tês Lyôn. Prosôpa kai theologia* (Thessalonica: Pournaras, 2002).

[31] *Lumen gentium* 3.23, in *Conciliorum oecumenicorum decreta*, 818.

has become one of the greatest barriers to it—an irony which (it must be said) has occasionally been remarked on by the popes themselves.

This is not to say that the unity of the church is an impossible dream, but only that it cannot be brought about within the existing structures because of the internal conflict that those structures manifest. It is not for human beings to say that what is impossible for us is impossible for God, but it seems to be the case that if the Holy Spirit is moving the churches closer together (and in many ways that does seem to be happening), the form and substance of that newfound unity will have to be different from what prevailed in the past and what is still, on paper at least, the official doctrine of the main historic Christian communions.

The Wisdom of the Ages

Of all the concepts associated with Christian theology, none is more elastic than that of tradition, which in its broadest sense can cover virtually everything. Even on the most conservative reading of the Pentateuch, for example, the book of Genesis (on which the rest depends) must be regarded as oral tradition, handed on over many centuries until Moses finally wrote it down. Judaism developed traditions of its own, some of which were incorporated in what we now recognize as the Old Testament, but many of which were not. By the time of Jesus, the written canon had established itself as the supreme authority in matters of faith, and the teachings of the priests and rabbis that were designed to supplement and interpret it were coming under criticism. This was a basic theme of the ministry of Jesus, who never tired of pointing out that the Jewish establishment had nullified the sense of the Scriptures by overlaying them with traditions of their own making.[32] The scribes and Pharisees were not impressed by this argument, and their descendants set about codifying these traditions into what we now know as the Mishnah and the Talmud. In that way, Rabbinic tradition, even more than the Hebrew Bible, became (and has remained) the foundation stone of modern Judaism, giving it a different feel from anything that could be found in ancient Israel.

In the New Testament, the Gospels are records of sayings and events that had occurred some years earlier, and it is generally assumed that the Evangelists were using sources that scholars qualify as "tradition," whether oral or written. The early church undoubtedly had a number of customs and practices that had been handed down from earliest times, some of which varied from place to place, perhaps because the apostles or their associates had made special

[32] Matt. 15:3–9; Mark 7:9–13. See also 1 Pet. 1:18.

arrangements for them or because they took over different elements from the synagogue and created their own form of worship and discipline. The evidence of the New Testament suggests that as long as there was an overall pattern of decent order, the precise details did not matter very much.[33] Certainly no one seemed to think that what was done in one congregation ought to be followed everywhere else, and there is no sign that the customs of Jerusalem took precedence over those of Antioch or Rome.[34]

As the church established itself, these inherited practices took on an authority of their own. Religious observance is usually conservative, and people get attached to what they are used to, so we should not be surprised by this. It is easy to imagine the reaction when something was questioned: "But we have always done it like this!" And of course, it would have been natural to assume that "always" meant "since the time of the apostles." As the first generations died and faded from living memory, assertions of that kind could not easily be checked. Modern research has cast doubt on a number of things, and we now know that once-revered texts like the so-called *Apostolic Constitutions*[35] and the Apostles' Creed were later compositions with little or no connection to the apostles, but that knowledge is of limited usefulness in trying to work out what was handed down from the beginning and what was not.

What we can say, though, is that whatever the early Christians believed about the origin of their particular patterns of worship and devotion, the primary authority they turned to for guidance was the New Testament, to whose teaching every congregation had to submit. Even though there were some books that were not accepted everywhere, the core of the present canon was universally agreed upon and could not be challenged.[36] When the fathers of the church thought about apostolic "tradition," it was to the New Testament that they instinctively appealed, regarding it as the deposit of faith that had been handed down to them. This is clear from Irenaeus, who wrote,

> When [the Gnostics] are rebutted from the Scriptures [i.e., the Old Testament], they turn around and accuse those Scriptures of being incorrect, . . . but when we appeal to the tradition that comes from the apostles [i.e., the New Testament], which is preserved by the succession of presbyters in the churches, they object to tradition, saying that they are wiser not only than the presbyters but also than the very apostles.[37]

[33] See 1 Cor. 14:40.
[34] If anything, it was the reverse! See Gal. 2:11–14.
[35] Printed in Philip Schaff, ed., *Library of the Ante-Nicene Fathers* (Peabody, MA: Hendrickson, 1994), 7:385–505.
[36] Hebrews was doubted by some in the Western church, and 2 and 3 John and 2 Peter were not received in the Syriac churches, but these were exceptions that were eventually overcome.
[37] Irenaeus of Lyon, *Adversus omnes haereses* 3.2.1.

Tertullian, writing slightly later, said much the same thing, and so did Origen.[38] Nevertheless, they were aware that the church had rules that could not to be found in the Scriptures but that must be observed because they had the authority of precedent and antiquity behind them. Tertullian wrote,

> If you insist on having a positive scriptural injunction for these and other such rules, you will not find any. Tradition is presented as their origin. Custom is their validator, and faith is their observer. . . . You can justify keeping even unwritten tradition if it is established by custom. The proper witness for it is that it has proved its worth by continuous observance over a long time.[39]

Other traditions could be observed in addition to Scripture, but not if they contradicted it. This was made clear by Cyprian, who paid special attention to matters of church order. After telling his flock that they "must diligently observe and keep the practice delivered from divine tradition and apostolic observance," he went on to add,

> How presumptuous it is to prefer human tradition to divine ordinance! How can we not see that God is indignant and angry whenever a human tradition relaxes the divine commandments and ignores them. . . . Custom without truth is simply the antiquity of error.[40]

It was not for many centuries that any extrabiblical rules or customs were officially recognized as authorities in their own right. The opinions of men like Tertullian and Origen were highly influential, but that did not prevent them from being condemned, though in both cases that did not happen until long after their deaths, and the condemnations were only partially effective. The important point is that, despite their renown and the fact that almost all their successors borrowed freely from them, their teachings were not canonized. Later generations felt free to object to what they said, particularly if it appeared to be insufficiently biblical. Thus, Tertullian's approval of the Montanists was rejected, as was Origen's Platonism, even if there was considerable sympathy in the church for the teachings that their appeal to such sources was meant to support. What was acceptable and what was not was eventually outlined in the so-called *Decretum Gelasianum de libris recipiendis et non recipiendis* (*Decree of Gelasius Concerning Those Books That Are to Be Accepted and Those That Are Not*), attributed to Pope Gelasius I (492–496) but

[38] Tertullian, *De praescriptione haereticorum* 6; Origen, *De principiis*, preface, 2.
[39] Tertullian, *De corona* 4.
[40] Cyprian of Carthage, *Epistula* 67.5; 73.3, 9.

most probably composed somewhat later by an anonymous writer in southern Gaul (France).[41]

The emergence of tradition as an independent theological authority can probably be dated to the Council *in Trullo*. Rather than simply take what they thought would be most convenient for the church of their day, the fathers of that council took care to examine traditional practices with a view to deciding which of them should be regarded as the norm for the future. A good example of this was the question of the celibacy to be required of the clergy.[42] It could be argued that the apostle Paul preferred the celibate life for those called to a ministry like his, and of course Jesus was celibate, though nothing was made of this in the New Testament.[43] It seems to have been assumed that bishops and presbyters would normally be married and have families, though high standards of behavior were imposed on them from the beginning.[44]

After the legalization of the church, however, the dramatic influx of new "converts" created fresh problems. Many people were distressed by what they saw as increasing worldliness and sought a remedy for what they saw as the growing corruption of the church establishment. All over the Roman world there were individuals who sought to get closer to God by going off to the desert in imitation of Moses, Elijah, Paul, and even Jesus himself. There they thought they could escape the "world" and do battle with the Devil in a purely spiritual way. Initially they lived on their own as hermits,[45] but gradually many of them came together to form the communities we now call convents or monasteries.[46] These were the "monks," and they saw their way of life as a purer, more authentic form of Christianity than the one generally on offer in the churches. The monks were not a threat to the organized church in the way that the Donatists were, but they were a challenge to the slackness and indiscipline that had crept in once persecution ceased and large numbers of people flocked to join it for reasons that were not always tied to belief in Christ.

In sharp contrast to the Donatists, the monks attracted the admiration

[41] The authority of the *Decretum Gelasianum* was greatly enhanced when important parts of it were included in Gratian's *Decretum* (see below), D. 15.3.1–29. Interestingly, it says quite a bit about Origen and mentions Montanus (in section 29), but there is not a word about Tertullian, whose writings may have been unknown to the author.
[42] For a full discussion of this, see C. G. Pitsakis, "Clergé marié et célibat dans la législation du Concile *in Trullo*: le point de vue oriental," in Nedungatt and Featherstone, *Council in Trullo Revisited*, 263–306. The widespread idea that the council was somehow "anti-Roman" in its decrees is refuted by Heinz Ohme, "Die sogennanten 'anti-römischen Kanones' des Concilium Quinisextum (692)—Vereinheitlichung als Gefahr für die Einheit der Kirche," in the same volume, 307–321.
[43] See 1 Cor. 7:7.
[44] See 1 Tim. 3:1–5.
[45] The word comes from the Greek *erêmitês*, a "desert-dweller," from *erêmos* ("desert").
[46] The word *conventus* just means a "gathering" and was used for both male and female communities, though in modern English it is normally reserved for female ones only. *Monastêrion* is a Greek word meaning the home of the *monachoi* ("solitaries"), from which the English word "monk" is derived.

and support of important church leaders like Athanasius of Alexandria and Basil of Caesarea, who did all they could to foster their example among the serious-minded. Athanasius wrote the biography of Anthony (250?–356), a desert hermit who is often considered to have been the founder of Christian monasticism.[47] We can see the results of this a century later, when Augustine was converted to Christianity. Instead of marrying his mistress and settling down to the life of a Roman gentleman, as his mother wanted him to do,[48] he gave everything up, sent his mistress away, and became a monk. The same story could be repeated dozens of times over, and almost all the prominent Christians we read about in these centuries followed a similar path. By the end of the sixth century, Pope Gregory I the Great (590–604) was trying to make monasticism compulsory for the ordained ministers of the church, so beneficial did he believe it to be. He failed, but the ideal remained and was finally implemented by Rome in 1123.[49] It was repudiated by the Protestant Reformers (four hundred years later!) but despite many difficulties, it is still the rule in the Roman Catholic Church to the present day.

The long-term effect of monasticism was that it created two distinct types of Christians. The vast majority constituted the *laos* ("people"), who attended services, made a profession of faith, and tried to live their lives as best they could in the light of what they understood of the gospel.[50] The minority was a spiritual elite, set apart by various degrees of asceticism that were gradually codified into rules of "religion," and living in protected environments—the desert or the monastery.[51] There were few points of contact between the two groups, except that those who conducted worship in local congregations were increasingly drawn to (and from) monastic communities.

What effect did such a division have on the life of the church? Was it possible to believe that the Holy Spirit had willed there to be a kind of two-speed Christianity, one for ordinary people and a fast track to heaven for those prepared to pay the price of ascetic self-discipline? No one really asked that question, though it must have been obvious which way the wind was blowing, and that serious believers would almost have to become monks (or nuns; monasticism was open to women as well as to men) to demonstrate that they really

[47] Anthanasius, *Vita Sancti Antonii*. An English translation can be found in Robert C. Gregg, ed., *The Life of Antony and the Letter to Marcellinus* (New York: Paulist, 1980). On early desert monasticism in general, see Derwas Chitty, *The Desert a City*, 2nd ed. (London: Mowbrays, 1977).
[48] It should be said for clarification that his mother wanted him to marry and settle down—but not with his mistress. She had a more respectable young lady in mind for him!
[49] It had been compulsory for bishops since 692, at least in the Eastern church.
[50] A member of the *laos* was a *laikos*, from which derive the English words "lay" and "laity," as opposed to the clergy.
[51] Note that the word "religion" was used to refer to a monastic order, whose members were the "religious," a usage that is still common in the Roman Catholic Church today.

meant it. After AD 500, prominent lay Christians became increasingly hard to find. Everyone was baptized, but apart from the spiritual elite, few took their faith all that seriously, nor were they really expected to. If you wanted to read the Bible and pray you could certainly do so—by joining a monastery. Anything else came to be seen as odd, as inappropriate, and finally as virtually impossible.

It must be emphasized that this movement toward monasticism and the creation of a spiritual elite was largely voluntary. There are stories of how individuals were forced into a monastery for political and other social reasons, but that was relatively rare. In the early days at least, most monks and nuns were deeply sincere and active in the promotion of their faith—without them, northern Europe might never have been evangelized. Furthermore, it did not take much to convince anyone that a growing and expanding church should be led by enthusiasts who would be free from corruption. The vast wealth that was now coming into the church through bequests and gifts from grateful donors could easily have become an irresistible temptation for people more concerned to advance the standing of their own families than to spread the kingdom of God. Having this wealth in the hands of men who were devoted to poverty and celibacy was no bad thing, because it gave some assurance that the funds would be used for the purpose for which they had been given. It was not a perfect system, of course, but in the circumstances one can understand its attraction, and it would be wrong to hold up particular cases of abuse as if they were typical. On the whole, the institutional church survived the transition from persecution to power remarkably well, and as long as the methods used to achieve this worked there was no need to question them.

From the church's point of view there were obvious advantages in having a body of men at hand who could be used to further its mission without having to worry about families and other worldly ties. Paul had said that it was better to be single for the sake of ministry,[52] and as he was writing under the guidance of the Holy Spirit, who could question that? Nevertheless, as Pope Gregory I discovered, a policy to that effect could not easily be implemented, and so another kind of hierarchy developed within the church. Bishops were the first to be selected on the basis of their celibacy, which was fairly easy, as there were relatively few of them. Lower down the scale, celibacy was much harder to enforce, especially in villages where a single minister would be in a socially awkward, if not altogether untenable position. Even after celibacy was imposed on the parish clergy, concubinage was often tolerated among them and it was

[52] 1 Cor. 7:1–38.

that abuse, rather than the practice of "celibacy" in the strict sense, that the Reformers felt they had to correct.

Today clerical celibacy is not highly regarded even among Roman Catholics, so it is especially important for us to understand why it was so widely promoted in earlier times. The fact is that in a society where there was little social mobility and sons were often expected to follow in their father's footsteps, the office of bishop was somewhat problematic. If it was held by a married man with a family, a substantial portion of the church's revenues would have to be used to support them, not least by the provision of a dowry for the bishop's daughters. It might also happen that a bishop's son would claim the church, or a substantial proportion of its revenues, as his legitimate inheritance. In order to prevent such abuses, the emperor Justinian I issued a series of laws that effectively required bishops to be celibate and to have no offspring of any kind.[53] The Council *in Trullo* adopted this legislation, but "liberalized" it somewhat, by allowing married men with families to be elected as bishops—provided that, if elected, they should separate from the wives and not recognize their children as legitimate heirs of church property.[54]

Whether (and how far) the rule of celibacy should be extended to cover presbyters, deacons, and others who were ordained in the service of the church, was left somewhat vague. Married men could be admitted to these offices and keep their wives, but if they were widowed they could not remarry.[55] Was this a recognition that the imposition of celibacy on bishops was a novelty, or was it a concession to the weakness of the flesh that a more consistent approach to the question would have ruled out? This has been a matter of considerable controversy over the years, with "liberals" inclining to the former view and "conservatives" to the latter.[56]

The most fascinating thing about this legislation is that the canonists who approved it recognized that it contradicted not only the New Testament but a number of earlier councils that had allowed for married clergy and bishops. They did not openly repudiate this earlier testimony, but explained why they were moving away from it:

> We say this [that bishops should be celibate] not for the abolition and overthrowing of apostolic ordinances, but in order to provide for the salvation

[53] *Codex iuris civilis* 1.3.41–47.
[54] Synod *in Trullo*, canon 12.
[55] Ibid., canon 13.
[56] See Roman Cholij, *Clerical Celibacy in East and West* (Leominster: Fowler Wright, 1988), who makes a thorough study of the Council *in Trullo* and comes down firmly on the conservative side. It should be noted that Cholij (1956–) was a priest of the Ukrainian Catholic Church, a body which follows the Eastern rite but is in communion with Rome. He has since left the priesthood, married, and become a commercial lawyer.

> and progress of the people toward better things, and that no reproach may attach to the priestly state, for the divine apostle says, "Do all to the glory of God. Give no offense to Jews or to Greeks or to the church of God, just as I try to please everyone in everything I do, not seeking my own advantage, but that of many, that they may be saved. Be imitators of me, as I am of Christ."[57]

Here we see how the canonists could invoke a biblical principle to overturn a biblical precedent that did not agree with what they were advocating. This practice was to become common and would later be used to justify many departures from ancient models. A famous example of it was the case of Michael Cerularius, patriarch of Constantinople from 1043 to 1059, who, in a dispute with the pope over the nature and extent of the latter's jurisdiction, argued that the use of unleavened bread or wafers (known as "azymes") in the Lord's Supper was a Judaistic practice and therefore unlawful. His own church had abandoned the practice in the distant past, even though Jesus had undoubtedly used unleavened bread at the Last Supper and the Roman church continued to do so. For Cerularius, the tradition of his church was enough to warrant a declaration of heresy against anyone who did not follow its customs, and the azymes controversy dragged on for centuries. It was not officially laid to rest until the Council of Florence in 1439, but divergent practices still continue and are now often a mark of distinction between Protestant and Roman Catholic churches, as well as between the latter and the Eastern Orthodox.[58]

Between the time of Cerularius and the Council of Florence there had been a significant development of canon law in the Eastern church, though it was less pronounced and less influential than in the West.[59] One reason for this is that the imperial government did not collapse, and so a great deal of ecclesiastical legislation was written into the law of the state, not that of the church. The canon lawyers spent much of their time integrating sacred and secular legal norms, with an eye to practical application of the regulations governing church life. The greatest of them were John Zonaras (1090?–1150?), Alexius Aristenos (1100?–1170?), and Theodore Balsamon (1138?–1198?). Zonaras wrote to a higher literary standard than the others, but Balsamon was more aware of the need to harmonize seemingly contradictory laws, rather in the manner of the

[57] Synod *in Trullo*, canon 13. The quotation is from 1 Cor. 10:31–11:1.

[58] For the decree saying that the use of azymes was a matter of indifference, see *Conciliorum oecumenicorum decreta*, 527, ll. 23–29.

[59] It is also much less well known. See Hartmann and Pennington, *Byzantine Canon Law*, and the brief introduction by John A. McGuckin, *The Ascent of Christian Law: Patristic and Byzantine Formulations of a New Civilization* (Yonkers, NY: St. Vladimir's Seminary Press, 2012).

Western canonist Gratian, whose work appeared in the lifetime of Zonaras but was unknown in the East until much later. Aristenos was less prolific but equally influential in the Eastern churches, and regarded by them as being on a par with the other two.

The most important collection of Byzantine ecclesiastical and civil laws, however, was the one made by Constantine Harmenopoulos (1320?–1385), which appeared in six volumes and hence is known as the *Hexabiblos*.[60] As it came out only a few years before the Ottoman Turks overran the Balkans and subjected most of their Christian population to Muslim rule, the *Hexabiblos* was to play an important role as the chief legal resource of the Orthodox Church until the nineteenth century, when it was gradually replaced by modern civil codes.[61] It carried on the Eastern tradition of a mixed civil-ecclesiastical legal system, which still influences the life and standing of the church in Eastern Orthodox countries today.

When we turn to the Western church, we find that the elevation of tradition to the status of an independent authority was underway by the mid-ninth century, driven by men who were supporters of the Roman claim to primacy. We do not know who those men were, but their legacy was the so-called *Donation of Constantine*, a forged document that purported to be a grant from the first Christian emperor to the bishop of Rome, giving him jurisdiction over the whole Western empire. It was frequently used by later popes to support their claims, not least in the quarrel with Cerularius. The *Donation* was followed in about 850 by a compilation of papal pronouncements now known as the *False Decretals*, put together by an unknown monk who was trying to bolster papal authority, which he wanted to see invoked against the secular rulers and local ecclesiastics of his day.

It is easy for modern observers to be critical of medieval Christendom and to emphasize the limitations that eventually led to its demise. This, however, is a view from hindsight that overlooks the enormous achievement of those who erected the scaffolding on which European civilization would be built and whose influence persists to this day in innumerable ways. It was the medieval church that created our legal systems, our parliamentary institutions, and our universities. Without them the world we live in now would be inconceivable. It is therefore essential for us to understand that the development of these things was at root theological, an application of the kingly reign of Christ to the circumstances in which the church found itself.

[60] Konstantinos Armenopoulos, *Procheiron nomôn ê hexabiblos* (Athens: Dodoni, 1971).

[61] In Greece, this was a long, drawn-out process, beginning in 1835 but not completed until 1946, when the *Hexabiblos* finally passed into history.

The collapse of the Roman empire in the West and the conversion of the barbarian tribes of the north could not have been foreseen before the time of Augustine and was still far from certain two centuries later, when Pope Gregory I sent another Augustine to evangelize the Anglo-Saxons in what had been Roman Britain but was now England. The subsequent emergence of Islam and its conquest of North Africa and Spain would also have been unimaginable in Gregory's time. It would be a further two centuries before Western Europe started to acquire its own identity in the empire of Charlemagne, which turned out to be a loose confederation of semi-independent principalities that expressed its unity and coherence in spiritual terms. In such a world the church was bound to play a central role, and the head of that church would be its most important single individual. That this should be the bishop of Rome was inevitable, because Rome was the only place in Western Europe that had a direct link with the New Testament, and it had always been the recognized capital of the Latin world.

By the Middle Ages, the empire was long gone and Rome was on the periphery of a culture whose center of gravity had shifted to the northwest (roughly the area between Paris and the Rhineland), but its bishop was portable. He could travel in a way that buildings and monuments could not, and over time his personal authority rose above the limitations of his geographical position. By the eleventh century, the restored empire of Charlemagne and his successors was in decline and the church was losing its sense of unity and universality. Roman bishops were elected by competing factions in the city, and some lasted only a few days in office before they were removed by more powerful rivals. This situation could not endure, and in 1046 the emperor Henry III (1039–1056) felt obliged to act. He forced the Romans to let him decide who should be pope, and over the next ten years appointed four men who were dedicated to the cause of reform. One of them was Leo IX (1049–1054), who was responsible for stirring up the trouble with Michael Cerularius that led to permanent schism between Rome and the Eastern churches.

After Henry III's death there was a brief attempt on the part of the Roman nobility to regain their right to elect the pope, but this was forestalled by Pope Nicholas II (1058–1061), who in 1059 issued a decree saying that, in the future, all popes would be elected by the college of cardinals, a group of senior clerics who assisted the pope with his administrative duties.[62] This was the beginning of a massive increase in the authority of the Roman

[62] The name comes from the Latin word *cardo* ("hinge"). The cardinals were so called because they were the hinges on which the door that gave access to the presence of God (the pope himself) swung.

papacy, which for the next 250 years would be the most powerful institution in Western Europe.[63]

By themselves, the *False Decretals* might have quietly disappeared, but they acquired a new lease on life when they were integrated into a much more sophisticated defense of papal primacy and power. This was the work of Gratian, an Italian monk and canon lawyer of the mid-twelfth century, who undertook to compile an encyclopedic work of church law with the express intention of systematizing it. It was he, more than anyone else, who established the nature of papal primacy, the authority and jurisdiction of the see of Rome, and the rights and duties belonging to the other orders of ministry that flowed from it. As he tried to demonstrate, Jesus had chosen Peter to be the head of the church after his departure, and Peter was the first bishop of Rome. Everything else flowed from that. The New Testament was authoritative because it was recognized by the apostolic see. The ecumenical councils were received in the church to the extent that Rome had given them her stamp of approval. When doubts arose about how something was to be interpreted or applied, members of the church could appeal to Rome for a decision. Gratian did not claim that the pope was infallible—that came much later—but he did believe that the Holy Spirit preserved the church in truth, and that the means which he normally used for that purpose were the papacy and its courts and councils. Individuals might go wrong, but the institutional framework had been given by God and would always be preserved from error.

Gratian was not the first person to attempt to bring judicial order out of canonical chaos, but he was more successful than his predecessors and his work was more enduring. His efforts culminated in what he called the *Concordantia discordantium canonum* ("*Concordance of Discordant Canons*") but which is usually referred to today simply as the *Decretum Gratiani*. Arranged thematically, with considerable space given to the outworking of case law in particular circumstances, the *Decretum* became the foundation of all subsequent ecclesiastical legislation. It appeared in about 1140 and was supplemented by the *Liber extra* of Pope Gregory IX, which was published in 1234 and focused on papal decretals. Other such collections came along in due course—the *Liber sextus* of Pope Boniface VIII in 1298, the *Clementinae* of Pope Clement V in 1313, and the *Extravagantes* of Pope John XXII in 1327. A few more additions appeared in the later Middle Ages until the entire collection was published as the *Corpus iuris canonici* in 1503.[64] Those who were called to shape and

[63] See Ullmann, *Short History of the Papacy*.

[64] The first edition of the collection, made by Jean Chappuis, appeared in 1500, but it was the second one that became definitive. It was edited by Emil Friedberg and published in two volumes in 1879. There is an English trans-

administer this body of law were in no doubt that it had been inspired by God in order to meet the needs of the times. In the words of Othobon, the papal legate to the British Isles, in his preamble to the constitutions he delivered to the English church in 1268,

> The commandments of God and the law of the Most High were given in ancient times so that the creature who had broken the yoke by turning away from the peace of his God, might live under the observance of the law and commandment as his lamp and light (having been given hope like a shadow in the promises made to the patriarchs) while waiting for the coming of the King of Peace, the high priest who would reconcile the world and restore all things. In the same way, it is the privilege of the adopted children of the bride, and the glory of the sons of holy mother church, to hear from her the commandments of life, so that they may keep their hearts in the beauty of peace, in the purity of chastity, and in the discipline of modesty, suppressing their harmful desires by the judgment of reason. In furtherance of this aim, the decrees of the holy fathers, divinely promulgated by their own mouths and containing the principles of justice and the doctrines of fairness, flowed out like broad rivers, and the sacred constitutions of the supreme pontiffs, the legates of his apostolic see, and the other prelates of the church, have been circulated to the entire world like tributaries from the breadth of those rivers. These [canons] have been issued because of the needs of different times and appear as new remedies [corresponding to] the new diseases that have been generated by human frailty.[65]

The message could hardly be clearer. What God gave to his people in ancient times through the mouths of the prophets was now being communicated to them by the leaders of the church, who drew their inspiration from the "broad rivers" of Holy Scripture but devised laws that were needed to deal with current problems. The pope and his bishops stood in the tradition of the prophets and apostles and exercised an authority that was not only comparable to theirs but more immediately relevant as well.

The *Liber extra* was published in five books, with each volume being dedicated to a particular subject. This pattern subsequently imposed itself as the standard for all medieval canons and was subdivided as follows:

---

lation of the first twenty (out of 101) "distinctions" published as Gratian, *The Treatise on Laws with the Ordinary Gloss* (Washington, DC: Catholic University of America Press, 1993).

[65] Othobon, as he is known in English, was Cardinal Ottobuono Fieschi (1205?–1276), who spent three years (1265–1268) in England as papal legate and issued a set of constitutions for the church that (in principle at least) are still recognized as valid today. He was elected pope as Hadrian V in 1276 but died after only a month in office. The Latin text of the above is in Frederick M. Powicke and Christopher R. Cheney, eds., *Councils and Synods with Other Documents Relating to the English Church II (1205–1313)*, 2 vols. (Oxford: Oxford University Press, 1964), 2:747.

1. *Iudex* (Judge)	This dealt with the constitution and organization of the church.
2. *Iudicium* (Judgment)	This covered jurisdictional and procedural rules.
3. *Clerus* (Clergy)	This outlined the offices and duties of the ordained clergy.
4. *Connubium* (Matrimony)	This dealt with marriage, divorce, and domestic relations.
5. *Crimen* (Crime)	This outlined the penal law of the church.

The structure was clear and was meant to be comprehensive.[66] The church embraced everyone, so its nature and government naturally came first, followed by the rules that governed them. Next came the clergy and the laity—matrimony being confined to the latter—and the final summation in the punishments that were to be meted out for particular offenses. The law was administered through ecclesiastical courts, which claimed sovereign immunity over their procedures. A layperson could be convicted in a church court, but a "spiritual person" (that is, someone who was in holy orders or who had taken monastic vows) might at least try to escape secular jurisdiction because of his special status. The boundary between secular and ecclesiastical jurisdiction was not always clear, though there were laws like the *Articuli cleri* of 1316 in England, which granted the church courts particular areas of competence. These included what we would normally call "family law" today, but defamation of character and usury were also considered to be spiritual offenses punishable by the church courts. In this way the church acquired sole jurisdiction over matrimony, which enabled it to abolish divorce altogether, and the probate of wills. Divorce was replaced by separation from bed and board and by annulment, the first of which retained the marriage formally in being and the second of which denied that it had ever taken place.

On the other hand, ownership of a church was treated as part of property law and so was adjudicated in the secular courts. A "spiritual person" who was accused of a secular crime (like murder) could petition for "benefit of clergy," a privilege that was granted to anyone who could sign his (or even her) name. This entitled the beneficiary to special treatment and reinforced the sense that the clergy were not like other people.

The *Corpus iuris canonici* was the repository of medieval canon law, which constituted "tradition" as this was understood by Martin Luther and his fel-

[66] See James A. Brundage, *Medieval Canon Law* (London: Longman, 1995) for a popular and accessible introduction to the subject. For more detailed treatments, see Harold J. Berman, *Law and Revolution: The Formation of the Western Legal Tradition* (Cambridge, MA: Harvard University Press, 1983); and Richard H. Helmholz, *The Spirit of Classical Canon Law* (Athens, GA: University of Georgia Press, 1996).

low Reformers. It was so closely connected to the papacy that when Luther repudiated Roman jurisdiction he staged a public burning of the *Corpus* as evidence of what he had done. Somewhat later, Henry VIII did much the same thing when he broke with Rome, a move which (not coincidentally) was largely occasioned by disagreements over the application of canon law to questions of matrimony and annulment.[67] But whereas most Protestant countries restructured their church laws and (usually) integrated them into the secular legal system, England and Ireland did not, giving Anglicanism the peculiar feel of being a "bridge church" between Rome and the Reformation. It was not until the nineteenth century that the Anglican system was reformed, but the ecclesiastical courts of the Church of England, greatly reduced in scope though they may be, still retain complete independence from the secular law.[68]

The legacy of this era is felt today mostly in the sphere of matrimony, which many people still think of as a basically religious rite. The New Testament church married no one, however. It was only in the Middle Ages that a marriage ceremony in the presence of the church (*in facie ecclesiae*) became the norm, but so powerful has this association become that it is now difficult to re-secularize it. In many countries people must marry before a state official and then (if they wish) they can add a religious ceremony of blessing, but in the English-speaking world (including the United States, in spite of the formal separation of church and state) churches are still generally permitted to perform and register marriages. This can cause problems when it comes to the remarriage of divorced people or the acceptance of homosexual "marriage," neither of which is consistent with Christian principles. The result is that there is now a divide between those churches (like the Church of England) which stick to the principles and send those who do not measure up to their standards to the civil authorities, and those churches (like most mainline Protestant denominations in the USA) which ignore traditional Christian values in favor of keeping in step with the march of secular "progress." What started as a division of labor between the church and the state courts has become a theological issue separating those who are faithful to the Word of God from those who have declared it outdated and moved on, led (as they always claim) by the "Spirit"!

[67] Henry VIII "froze" the canon law in 1535, pending the establishment of a commission that would draft a new constitution for the church. Henry also closed the canon law faculties at both Oxford and Cambridge. As things turned out, though, the commission's work was rejected by the English parliament, so the "frozen" canon law of 1535 continues to have a residual authority in England to this day. See Gerald L. Bray, ed., *Tudor Church Reform: The Henrician Canons and the* Reformatio legum ecclesiasticarum (Woodbridge: Boydell & Brewer, 2000). The Roman Catholic Church replaced it in 1917 and again in 1983!

[68] In England, benefit of clergy was removed in 1827, civil matrimony was introduced in 1837, defamation of character became a fully civil offense in 1855, and civil divorce and the secular probate of wills date from 1858. None of this had anything to do with Protestantism or the Reformation; the reforms were due entirely to the secularizing spirit of the age.

It is impossible to understand the differences between Eastern and Western Christendom without a proper grasp of the way in which the canon law developed differently in each of them. In the East there was a fusion of church and state which its apologists call *symphônia*, but in the West, secular government fell apart and the church was forced to step into the void. By the time the states of Western Europe were strong enough to reassert their rights, the church had a grip on society that it was unwilling to relinquish. Canon law had become an instrument of papal power, quoting ancient sources in order to justify contemporary practice. The effects of this can be seen in Distinction 10 of the *Decretum Gratiani*, which establishes the relationship between ecclesiastical and secular authorities:

> Imperial ordinances are not to be followed in any ecclesiastical dispute. . . . They are not above the ordinance of God, but below it. Ecclesiastical laws may not be abrogated by an imperial judgment. . . . We do not say that imperial ordinances (which the church often invokes against heretics and tyrants, and which defend it against evildoers) should be completely rejected, but we do affirm that they may not be applied to the prejudice of evangelical, apostolic, or canonical decrees (to which they should be subordinate).[69]

Gratian's immediate source for this was a letter written by Pope Nicholas I (858–867) but quoting Pope Innocent I (401–417) and Pope Gregory I (590–604) in support of what he had to say. The original contexts were ignored, but the cumulative effect of such quotations was to demonstrate the antiquity and perennity of the principle that the church is independent of the state and (in case of conflict between them) superior to it. Here we see not only a medieval power play between rival institutions but an affirmation of the rights of the Christian conscience over secular authority, which lies at the root of modern concepts of "human rights." For good measure, Gratian quoted the same Pope Nicholas I in a letter he sent to the Eastern emperor Michael III (842–867), pointing out that this order of things was the will of Christ himself:

> Because the Mediator between God and men, the man Christ Jesus,[70] wanted human hearts to be raised up by the medicine of humility and not thrown down into hell by human pride, he divided the offices of both powers according to the activities and distinct dignities that are proper to them. Christian emperors need the popes for eternal life, and popes follow imperial ordinances exclusively in temporal affairs. Thus, spiritual activity is kept free

[69] Gratian, *Decretum* D. 10.1.1–3.
[70] See 1 Tim. 2:5.

> from fleshly incursions, and just as no soldier of God gets entangled in civilian pursuits, so someone who is entangled in civilian pursuits is not seen to preside over divine matters.[71]

Note that Nicholas I and Gratian, although they lived three centuries apart, both believed that the legal system they were administering was part of the work of Christ as the Mediator between God and man. It was the church, as Christ's body on earth, that gave expression to this mediatorial work, thereby justifying and affirming its central place in the divine plan of salvation.

Obviously the popes could not exercise the ministry to which they believed they were called without an army of supporters behind them. The pope was himself a bishop, which meant that all other bishops shared to some extent in his tasks. They were his representatives in the different local churches and were therefore expected to imitate his consecration to the celibate life. The situation of presbyters and other clergy was not so clear, and Gratian (at least) believed that the practice of the Eastern church should be regarded as the norm.[72] Gratian's attitude is interesting because he was writing at the very moment that clerical celibacy was being made compulsory in the Western church. Canon 6 of the Second Lateran Council, held under the aegis of Pope Innocent II (1130–1143), declared,

> We decree that if those who are in the order of subdeacon or above marry or have concubines, they should forfeit their office and ecclesiastical benefice. For since they ought to be and be called the temple of God, the vessels of the Lord, the sacred dwelling place (*sacrarium*) of the Holy Spirit, it is beneath their dignity for them to be involved in marriage and impurity.[73]

Strictly speaking, this could be interpreted in the same sense as the canons of the Council *in Trullo*, that is, as applying only to clergy who were already ordained and not to candidates for ordination who might already be married. This interpretation has prevailed in the case of orders below that of presbyter (priest), but it has always been understood as forbidding the ordination to the priesthood of any non-celibate man.

Justification for this prohibition was sought in biblical injunctions to God's

---

[71] Gratian, *Decretum* D. 10.8. Note the allusion to 2 Tim. 2:4, and the way in which Nicholas I applied it. In his commentary on this, Gratian argued that the word "exclusively" applies to "temporal affairs" and not to "follow," from which he concludes that spiritual matters (like matrimony) do not fall under secular jurisdiction, whereas secular ones, like those involving the shedding of blood, do not fall under the jurisdiction of the church.

[72] See Roman Cholij, *Clerical Celibacy in East and West*, 63–68. Cholij argues that Gratian's position was wrong and that he should have plumped for more consistent clerical celibacy.

[73] *Conciliorum oecumenicorum decreta*, 198. Quoted by Gratian in D. 28.2, this canon reflects earlier ones like canon 21 of the First Lateran Council (1123), also quoted by Gratian (D. 27.8), canon 4 of the Council of Clermont (1130), and canon 4 of the Council of Reims (1131).

people not to engage in sexual intercourse in times of special communion with God.[74] Since it was a presbyter's duty to be in a constant state of such special communion, celibacy for him was the obvious consequence. Christian ministry was being increasingly modeled on that of the Old Testament priesthood, a link that is preserved in the Roman ordinal to this day.[75] To the standard objection that Jewish priests were married and were drawn from a hereditary caste of Levites, the answer was that the old law had been superseded by the new dispensation of Christ. On the one hand, the Christian priesthood was in principle open to any man, but on the other hand it was restricted in a different way—by celibacy. The end result was the emergence of a class of priests that was unknown in the New Testament but that became so dominant that it virtually claimed the "church" for itself.[76]

The creation of a professional celibate priesthood was the ultimate triumph of tradition over Scripture, and helps to explain why it was such a target for the Protestant Reformers in the sixteenth century. What is perhaps less well appreciated is that the priest so consecrated was believed to stand in the place of Christ in the church, performing a ministry analogous to his:

> The ministerial priesthood has the task not only of representing Christ—Head of the Church—before the assembly of the faithful, but also of acting in the name of the whole Church when presenting to God the prayer of the Church, and above all when offering the Eucharistic sacrifice.[77]

Priest and sacrifice went together, first on the cross of Calvary and then in the re-presentation of that divine self-offering in the worship of the universal church.

The Source of Truth

By 1415, Western Europe was starting to recover a sense of its classical past. The ancient Roman world was present in its ruins, but it was something of a mystery and no one knew much about classical Greece. Plato and Aristotle were read to some extent in Latin translations, and ancient Greek science was being transmitted to the Latin world by way of the Muslim Arabs and Jews of Spain, but such influences could always be dismissed as anti-Christian. It was a different matter when classical Greek culture began to reach the West from

[74] Ex. 19:15; 1 Sam. 21:4–5; see also 1 Cor. 7:5–6.
[75] See the *Catechism of the Catholic Church* (London: Geoffrey Chapman, 1994; and New York: Doubleday, 1995), ss. 1541–1543.
[76] Even today, ordination to ministry is sometimes described as "going into the church," as if the church were an organization comparable to the military or the diplomatic service.
[77] *Catechism of the Catholic Church*, s. 1552.

Constantinople, where it had long been integrated into, or at least tolerated alongside, the official Judeo-Christian belief system. The Byzantines distinguished between the inner wisdom, which came from the Bible and theology, and the outer wisdom, where their pagan ancestors led the way, though for most of them the former was far more important than the latter. Even so, every cultured Greek-speaker knew the classics and was aware that, in the early days of the church, the Holy Spirit had revealed God's truth to the world in their language.

Educated people in the West had always known that their Latin Bible was a translation, but few of them thought that this mattered. Even Wyclif used the Latin, and his followers translated the Bible into English from it, not from the original texts. But the rediscovery of Eastern Christianity, and the need to enter into dialogue with it, changed all this. For example, the papacy claimed that, when the emperor Constantine left Rome to found his new city on the site of ancient Byzantium, he had given the pope jurisdiction over what was then the Western Roman empire. The Eastern church knew nothing of that, of course, and, by searching through the Roman archives, Lorenzo Valla was able to show that the so-called *Donation of Constantine* was a ninth-century forgery. At the Council of Florence, the Western church had tried to use the Athanasian Creed as an example of the acceptance of the *Filioque* by a leading Greek father, but as that was a false attribution, the Eastern church knew nothing about it either. Embarrassments of this kind made people aware that things were often not what they seemed, and showed that it was imperative for the Roman church to rethink its claims in the light of these emerging facts.

More seriously, the Eastern church was able to question the accuracy of the Latin translation of the Bible, which the papacy used to bolster its authority. It was not merely a difference of language but one of content as well—the Greeks had preserved a different textual tradition, and many of their readings were at variance with what was generally accepted at Rome. Who was right? Modern scholars know that this is not a simple question, because the Latin Bible was based on manuscripts earlier in date than the Greek texts available to the Byzantines and is therefore sometimes more accurate than they are, but this subtlety was not appreciated at the time. Instead, the cry went up that the Latin Bible was in danger of being wrong because it was a translation, and suddenly scholars had to learn the original Greek and Hebrew if they wanted to be sure of getting it right.

Given that the Bible was the ultimate source of Christian doctrine, the consternation this caused can only be imagined. What if someone were to discover that the American Constitution was originally written in French or German and that the English version that everyone uses was faulty in many places? How would people react if it was demonstrated that some famous constitutional judgments were fundamentally flawed because they were based on a wrong translation? Would the law be changed to reflect that new discovery, or would people simply be advised to accept what had been done in ignorance and move on? In that case, what authority would the original text have? We have to appreciate the nature of the dilemma the fifteenth-century church faced if we are to understand how the advance of scholarship undermined its authority without ever intending to do so. The courts that got away with condemning Hus to death in 1415 could do nothing against Erasmus of Rotterdam (1466–1536) less than a century later, even though Erasmus's advocacy of "back to the sources" was potentially far more damaging to the existing order than anything Hus could have imagined.

Erasmus and the academic establishment of his time had no trouble accepting the principle that translations of the Bible ought to be based on the original languages. The Reformers were naturally part of this new wave, but even today it is almost impossible to distinguish them from other humanist scholars who did not break with the Roman church. An example of that is the work of Jacques Lefèvre d'Etaples (1460?–1536), whose critical methods were virtually identical to those later used by John Calvin but who never became a "Protestant" in any formal sense. At the level of pure scholarship, the differences caused by the Reformation were slow to take root, and for a generation academics on both sides continued to share ideas and work together more or less harmoniously. Erasmus himself never abandoned the Roman church, but he took refuge in and died in Protestant Basel, where he was deeply respected regardless of his ecclesiastical allegiance.

Lines were not formally drawn until the fourth session of the Council of Trent (April 8, 1546), when the list of biblical books originally drawn up by Augustine of Hippo was canonized.[78] Augustine favored the Greek Septuagint translation over the Hebrew Old Testament, partly because he believed that it had been divinely inspired and partly because he thought that the Jews had tried to prevent their Scriptures from reaching a wider audience. As he put it,

> Even if things are found in Hebrew codices that differ from what the Septuagint says, in my judgment they should give way to what divine providence has achieved through these translators; and that is that the books which the Jewish people were unwilling to share with others, whether out of a religious sense or out of envy, were made available by the Lord . . . to the nations that

[78] *Conciliorum oecumenicorum decreta*, 663–664. Augustine's list is in *De doctrina Christiana* 2.13.

> were going to believe. It may well be the case that the Seventy translated the Hebrew in such a way as the Holy Spirit, who was guiding them and gave them all one voice, judged would be most suitable for the Gentiles.[79]

The Tridentine decree made no mention of Augustine, however, perhaps because it was accompanied by a second one that ignored both the Hebrew and the Septuagint and proclaimed that,

> the old and popular (*vulgata*) edition, that has proved its worth in the church by its long use over many centuries, should be taken as the authentic text in public readings, disputations, sermons and expositions, and no one should dare or presume to reject it for any reason whatsoever.[80]

This decree, which was an embarrassment to Catholic scholars at the time and is now all but forgotten (despite its official status as a conciliar document), effectively handed serious biblical scholarship over to the Reformers. Would Erasmus have remained loyal to the papacy if he had lived to see this? It is hard to believe that he would have done so, but it is also hard to believe that the Protestants did not immediately take advantage of the situation. John Calvin, for example, despite his renown as a biblical commentator, had nothing to say about the canon and even accepted that the Greek translation of the Hebrew Bible was providentially ordered by God because, "the Hebrew language was in no estimation and almost unknown; and assuredly, had God not provided for religion, it would have utterly perished."[81]

Somewhat surprisingly, the first Protestant canonical list did not appear until 1563, when it was given in Article 6 of the Thirty-nine Articles of the Church of England. As for the extra books that are found only in the Septuagint, the Article added, "the church doth read [them] for example of life and instruction of manners; but yet doth it not apply them to establish any doctrine," citing Jerome as the authority for this position.[82] This rather benign approach to the extra books, or Apocrypha as they are generally known, did not last. The Westminster Confession of Faith, which the English parliament approved on December 4, 1646, and which was published on April 29, 1647, was the first confessional document to attempt a thorough analysis of the character and

---

[79] Augustine of Hippo, *De doctrina Christiana* 2.22.

[80] *Conciliorum oecumenicorum decreta*, 664. See also the preface to the Reims New Testament (1582), the first Roman Catholic translation into English, where the reasons for basing the text on the Latin are set out in full; see Gerald L. Bray, ed., *Documents of the English Reformation* (Cambridge: James Clarke, 2004), 380–381.

[81] Calvin, *Institutio* 1.8.10.

[82] Jerome, *Epistula* 53.8. For a careful study of Jerome's somewhat ambiguous attitude toward the Hebrew and Greek versions of the Old Testament, see Dennis Brown, Vir trilinguus: *A Study in the Biblical Exegesis of Saint Jerome* (Kampen: Kok Pharos, 1992), 55–86. A shorter account can be found in J. N. D. Kelly, *Jerome* (London: Duckworth, 1975), 153–167.

authority of the canonical Scriptures, and its position has remained authoritative among most English-speaking Protestants to the present day.[83] In revising the Thirty-nine Articles it had this to say:

> The books commonly called Apocrypha, not being of divine inspiration, are no part of the canon of Scripture, and therefore are of no authority in the church of God, nor to be any otherwise approved or made use of, than other human writings.[84]

It was not until well after the Reformation that Protestants began to develop the theological framework and significance of biblical authority for the life of the church. It was inevitable that they would do this sooner or later, because by recognizing the Bible not just as the supreme authority for establishing faith and doctrine—that had always been agreed by everyone—but as the *only* authority for such things, deciding what the nature of that authority was became essential. The germ of what would become standard Protestant teaching was already present in Luther, who wrote,

> The holy Christian people are recognized by their possession of the holy Word of God. . . . The Holy Spirit administers it and anoints or sanctifies the Christian church with it.[85]

The first generation of Reformers was concerned to establish the principle of *sola Scriptura* ("Scripture alone"), by which they meant that whatever could not be proved from the biblical text must not be made a requirement of Christian belief.[86] Perhaps the best statement of this position is the summary given by Archbishop Thomas Cranmer in his Forty-two Articles of 1553:

> Holy Scripture containeth all things necessary to salvation: so that whatsoever is neither read therein, nor may be proved thereby, although it be sometime received of the faithful, as godly and profitable for an order and

[83] It is the (or an) official confession of most Presbyterian churches, but variants of it were adopted by Congregationalists and Baptists, and equivalent statements can often be found in non-English-speaking countries. It also forms the historical basis of most modern interdenominational statements on Scripture, particularly among evangelicals. See Bray, *Documents of the English Reformation*, 486–520, for the complete original text.

[84] Westminster Confession, 1.3; see Bray, *Documents of the English Reformation*, 488. It may be noted in passing that the Confession also included Lamentations in the list of Old Testament books. It had been left out in Article 6 (as well as in the Tridentine and Augustinian lists), probably because it was regarded as an appendix to Jeremiah and included under his name.

[85] Martin Luther, *On the Councils and the Church*, 3, in Jaroslav Pelikan and Helmut T. Lehmann, eds., *Luther's Works*, 55 vols. (St. Louis: Concordia, vols. 1–30; and Philadelphia: Fortress, vols. 31–55, 1955–1986), 41:148–149. It is clear from the context that Luther was referring to the Bible when he spoke about the "Word of God," and later on in his argument he makes the equation explicit (see 151).

[86] Richard A. Muller, *Post-Reformation Reformed Dogmatics: The Rise and Development of Reformed Orthodoxy, ca. 1520 to ca. 1725*, 2nd ed., 4 vols. (Grand Rapids, MI: Baker, 2003). See especially vol. 2, *Holy Scripture: The Cognitive Foundation of Theology*.

comeliness: yet no man ought to be constrained to believe it as an article of the faith, or repute it requisite to the necessity of salvation.[87]

John Calvin went further than his predecessors and gave an extended exposition of the character of Holy Scripture that became, and to a large extent has remained, the standard Reformed teaching on the subject. In Calvin's mind, the Bible was authoritative for two (related) reasons. First, it is the Word of God, as the prophets and apostles who wrote it attested:

> The prophets and apostles boast not their own acuteness, or any qualities which win credit to speakers, nor do they dwell on reasons; but they appeal to the sacred name of God, in order that the whole world may be compelled to submission.[88]

But Calvin also recognized that the truth of this would not register with people unless or until God bore witness to his own words by sealing them in the hearts of the hearers through the inward testimony of the Holy Spirit:

> Let it therefore be held as fixed, that those who are inwardly taught by the Holy Spirit acquiesce implicitly in Scripture; that Scripture, carrying its own evidence along with it, does not submit to proofs and arguments, but owes the full conviction with which we ought to receive it to the testimony of the Spirit. Enlightened by him, we no longer believe, either on our own judgment or that of others, that the Scriptures are from God, but in a way superior to human judgment, feel perfectly assured—as much as if we beheld the image of God visibly impressed on it—that it came to us, by the instrumentality of men, from the very mouth of God.[89]

When it came to textual criticism, Calvin was largely untroubled by the doubts and objections that we are familiar with today. As far as he was concerned, the evidence not only that Moses wrote the Pentateuch but that the miracles and other extraordinary events recorded in it were a true and accurate reporting of the facts was simply that "he published all these things in the assembly of the people."[90] Prophecies of things that did not take place until several centuries afterwards were authenticated by comparing them with

[87] Article 5; see Bray, *Documents of the English Reformation*, 287. In the revised Thirty-nine Articles of 1563, the article reappeared as Article 6, and the phrase "although it be sometime received of the faithful, as godly and profitable for an order and comeliness; yet no man ought to be constrained to believe it" was taken out and replaced by, "is not to be required of any man, that it should be believed." The revision represented a hardening of attitudes against nonscriptural church traditions, which were no longer recognized as having served a useful purpose in their day.
[88] Calvin, *Institutio* 1.7.4.
[89] Ibid., 1.7.5.
[90] Ibid., 1.8.5.

other events where there could be no doubt about the prophetic nature of the Old Testament witness. For example, if someone were to object that Moses' prophecy that Judah would obtain the preeminent position in Israel was not a genuine foretelling of events but a gloss (or insertion) added later, after it had happened, what about the prophecy that one day the Gentiles would be admitted to the Israelite covenant, which was clearly not fulfilled until long after it was first given?[91] To get a flavor of Calvin's arguments, consider what he said about the Isaianic prophecy of the coming of Cyrus:

> After the prophet thus spoke, more than a hundred years elapsed before Cyrus was born. . . . It was impossible at that time to guess that some Cyrus would arise to make war on the Babylonians. . . . Does not this simple, unadorned narrative plainly demonstrate that what Isaiah spoke was not the conjecture of man, but the undoubted oracle of God?[92]

Here we are light years away from modern textual criticism, whose exponents either take it for granted that the "prophecy" was composed after the event or else that the reference to Cyrus was interpolated after his identity became known. Calvin had no sense of anything like that and knew nothing of archaeology or its many subdisciplines (like epigraphy). No doubt if someone had gone to Mount Ararat and come back with reports of having seen the remains of Noah's ark he would have been prepared to believe it, but no one did—or even thought about doing so. In this respect, Calvin and his contemporaries were no different from the New Testament writers, Augustine, and all the generations in between. Their authorities were literary (Josephus, for example), not archaeological, and in that way, their "return to the sources" was really an appeal to tradition—not that of the medieval church, but that of the ancient Israelites and their contemporaries in the Greco-Roman world. As long as those witnesses were regarded as credible, Calvin's arguments could hold their own. It would only be when they came to be doubted, and when other means of discovering "what really happened" came on the scene, that his line of argument, whatever validity it might have in some respects, would have to be supplemented by something else.[93]

When dealing with questions of canon and of textual accuracy, the Reformers were not really breaking new ground but only taking sides in a

[91] Ibid., 1.8.7. The prophecy regarding Judah is in Gen. 49:10; that of the eventual inclusion of the Gentiles can be found scattered throughout the Old Testament, beginning with Gen. 12:3.

[92] Calvin, *Institutio* 1.8.8. The reference is to Isa. 44:28; 45:1.

[93] This is one reason why modern defenders of biblical authority find it so hard to appeal to the Reformers, despite their sympathy with what Calvin and others were trying to say. Like it or not, the world has moved on, and appeals to antiquity of the kind Calvin made are no longer persuasive in the way that they once were.

debate that had begun more than a millennium before their time but had never been properly resolved. In dealing with the wider questions of systematic theology, Luther and Calvin had little to add to what had gone before; the *Institutes*, for example, follow a generally conservative approach modeled on the Apostles' Creed and influenced to some extent by Peter Lombard's *Sentences*, which they came to replace in most Protestant seminaries. But the following generation of Reformers, motivated by the appeal to "Scripture alone" (*sola Scriptura*), which had marked the Reformation from the beginning, moved toward a different conception of what theology should look like. In the Second Helvetic [Swiss] Confession of 1566, the doctrine of Scripture was made the first chapter of theological exposition, because Scripture was the source from which all other Christian doctrines flowed.[94] The (perhaps unintended) consequence of this was that the doctrine of God, which had always come first, was now relegated to second place.

Where a man like Tertullian would have said that conversion to Christ opened up the meaning of the Bible, the sixteenth-century Reformers tended to think that it was the other way around: conviction of the reliability of Scripture would lead people to Christ. If that were so, then any error found in the Bible would cast doubt on the gospel message and might lead to a loss of faith, which is precisely what occurred in many parts of the Protestant world when the literal accuracy of the Bible was questioned and/or denied from the late seventeenth century onward. Before that time, the proponents of what we now call Protestant (or Reformed) Orthodoxy avoided this problem by clinging to Calvin's doctrine that it was by the inner witness of the Holy Spirit that a person would come both to the conviction of the absolute trustworthiness of his inspired Word and to faith in the Christ of whom that Word bore witness. That the Bible contains many things that are obscure to unaided human reason was not denied, but this caused no problem for those whose minds had been enlightened by the Spirit. The seventeenth-century English Puritan John Lightfoot (1602–1675), who was one of the greatest Hebrew scholars of his time, explained this as follows:

> There are not points, in all the mysteries of divinity, contrary to reason, if we resolve them into the right principle; that is, if we resolve them into the power, will and working of God. That this vast universe should be created of nothing, in a moment; that God should become man; that dead bodies should

[94] For the text of the confession, see Emidio Campi, *Confessio Helvetica posterior*, in Andreas Mühling and Peter Opitz, eds., *Reformierte Bekenntnisschriften*, 3 vols. (Neukirchen-Vluyn: Neukirchener Verlag, 2002–2014), 2/2:243–345. An English translation is available in Philip Schaff, *The Creeds of Christendom*, 3 vols. (New York: Harper & Row, 1931), 3:831–909. There is also an analysis of the text in Schaff, *Creeds of Christendom*, 1:390–420.

> be raised again; that this mortal should put on immortality—are high mysteries, many regions above natural reason—but not a whit contrary to reason, if you resolve them, as I said before, into the power, will and working of God.[95]

Like the Second Helvetic Confession of 1566 and the Irish Articles of 1615,[96] which seem to have been its more immediate inspiration, the Westminster Confession started off with a full chapter on Scripture, which it placed before the doctrine of God and the Trinity. That chapter consists of ten sections, which may be summarized as follows:[97]

1. Natural theology (i.e., the works of creation) can tell us that there is a God but not about what is needed for salvation. That is why God revealed himself to his church, and in order to protect that revelation from corruption, it was subsequently committed to writing. Since direct revelation has now ceased, Holy Scripture is the only means we have of knowing the will of God.[98]
2. The canonical books are listed in order, with the names we now give them.
3. The deuterocanonical books ("Apocrypha") are rejected, but not listed by name.
4. The authority of Scripture does not depend on human testimony but on God, who is its true author and the source of all truth.
5. The church can point us toward the Scriptures, and their form and content may excite our reverence, but in the end, the only way that we shall be persuaded of their truth and authority is by the inner working of the Holy Spirit in our hearts.
6. Everything necessary for salvation is set out in Scripture, either directly or by implication, and it needs no further additions to it. Even so, its message can be understood only by the inner illumination of the Holy Spirit, and there are some things (such as the pattern of Christian worship) which are not spelled out in the Bible but have been left to the godly determination of the church. In one sense this was not an original statement but a repetition of Article 20 of the Thirty-nine Articles of the Church of England (1563), which reads,

---

95 *The Whole Works of Rev. John Lightfoot*, ed. John R. Pitman, 13 vols. (London: Dove, 1822–1825), 6:53, in a sermon entitled, "The Great Assize." See Jace R. Broadhurst, *What Is the Literal Sense? Considering the Hermeneutic of John Lightfoot* (Eugene, OR: Pickwick, 2012).

96 See Bray, *Documents of the English Reformation*, 437–452 for the text of these.

97 See ibid., 487–489.

98 Note that the Confession does *not* say that the Bible was directly revealed by God; it was given to the "church," by which both ancient Israel and the Christian church were meant, and the church committed it to writing—a position closer to that of Roman Catholicism than many modern Protestants realize. On the question of divine revelation apart from Scripture, see Garnet H. Milne, *The Westminster Confession of Faith and the Cessation of Special Revelation: The Majority Puritan Viewpoint on Whether Extra-Biblical Prophecy Is Still Possible* (Milton Keynes: Paternoster, 2007), who concludes that most of the divines at the assembly did accept that God still spoke to people, but not in a canonically authoritative way.

> The church hath power to decree rites or ceremonies, and authority in controversies of faith, and yet it is not lawful for the church to ordain anything that is contrary to God's Word written, neither may it so expound one place of Scripture, that it be repugnant to another. Wherefore, although the church be a witness and a keeper of Holy Writ, yet, as it ought not to decree anything against the same, so besides the same ought it not to enforce anything to be believed for necessity of salvation.

But note that, unlike Article 20, the Westminster Confession follows Calvin by also acknowledging "the inward illumination of the Spirit of God to be necessary for the saving understanding of such things as are revealed in the Word." This addition is of vital importance because it is a recognition that mental persuasion of the literal truth of the Bible is not enough for a living faith. The book that was inspired by the Holy Spirit must also be interpreted by that same Spirit, without whom salvation would be impossible.

7. Not everything in Scripture is clear, or equally obvious to everyone, but the essential message is plain enough and can be understood by every normal human being. This too had already been stated a century before by Thomas Cranmer, in "A Fruitful Exhortation to the Reading and Knowledge of Holy Scripture," which appeared as the first homily in the *Book of Homilies* that was published in 1547:

> Although many things in the Scripture be spoken in obscure mysteries, yet there is nothing spoken under dark mysteries in one place but the selfsame thing, in other places, is spoken more familiarly and plainly, to the capacity both of learned and unlearned.[99]

8. The Old Testament in Hebrew and the New Testament in Greek are the original texts that were inspired by God, and all theological controversies must be settled by referring to them. However, for everyday use in the church, translations are necessary and authorized.

9. The difficult parts of Scripture are to be interpreted by the clearer ones. There is no need to appeal to any external authority.

10. The ultimate authority in matters of interpretation is the Holy Spirit, speaking through the Scriptures themselves, and it is to his authority that the church must defer.

Apart from the list of canonical books, there is little here that could not also be found in Calvin's *Institutes*, and the dependence of the Confession on

[99] *The Homilies Appointed to Be Read in Churches*, ed. John Griffiths (revised) (Bishopstone, Hertfordshire: Brynmill, 2006), 9.

them is obvious. The most interesting thing about it is the emphasis on the work of the Holy Spirit as the one who bears witness to the divine origin of Scripture, who convinces us of its truth, and who interprets it for us by pointing us to clearer passages by which we can explain difficulties. This too was the emphasis of Calvin, and we can see here, as clearly as anywhere, how strong his influence remained nearly a century after his death. For some curious reason, the Confession does not say that the Holy Spirit was the inspirer of the prophets, even though 2 Peter 1:21 is cited three times among the "proof-texts" that parliament ordered should be attached to it. The composers of the Confession no doubt believed it, but perhaps they thought it was too obvious to mention, or were wary of drawing attention to only one of the divine persons when all three were involved in the process.[100]

While all this was going on, the study of Hebrew and Greek was making steady advances. The Greek text of the New Testament was not seriously challenged at this stage because all the best manuscripts available came from the same Byzantine ecclesiastical tradition that had formed the basis of Erasmus's edition of 1516. The Hebrew text was also stable, largely because there was only a single manuscript tradition, which included marginal alternative readings (the so-called *Qere*) and the vowel points that had been inserted by the Masoretic scribes in late antiquity. Unfortunately, neither of these things was at all clear to the Hebraists of the sixteenth century, who assumed that both the marginal alternatives and the vowel points were part of the original, divinely inspired text. That this was not so was demonstrated by Louis Cappel (1585–1658). A French Protestant, Cappel wrote a tract to prove that the vowel points were later additions, but although he eventually managed to get it published, it was not well received.[101] He then went on to ascribe the different readings to ancient copyists' errors, which again he found extremely difficult to get published. He finished the work in 1634, but it was only after his son, Jean Cappel, had converted to Catholicism and obtained a royal warrant for its publication, that it finally appeared in print.[102] Once again, this caused a storm, and the defenders of Protestant orthodoxy felt obliged to protest. The only official document that reflects this reaction, however, is the *Formula consensus Helvetica*, composed in 1675 and largely confined to Switzerland. Generally

[100] Unfortunately, the minutes of the Westminster Assembly are too thin at this point to be able to tell us much about what was going through the minds of those who composed the Confession. See Chad Van Dixhoorn, ed., *The Minutes and Papers of the Westminster Assembly 1643–1652*, 5 vols. (Oxford: Oxford University Press, 2012), 3:636–638 (sessions 471–475, from July 17–25, 1645).

[101] Louis Cappel, *Arcanum punctationis revelatum* (Leiden: Erpenius, 1624).

[102] Louis Cappel, *Critica sacra, sive de variis quae in sacris Veteris Testamenti libris occurrunt lectionibus libri sex* (Paris: Cramoisy, 1650).

recognized today as the last of the Reformed confessions, the *Formula* stated in no uncertain terms,

> Concerning the Hebrew text of the Old Testament, which we have received from the tradition of the Jewish church, to which the oracles of God were long ago committed,[103] and still retain, is *theopneustos* ("divinely inspired") with respect to its consonants, its vowels (whether the points themselves or only the force of the points), as well as to its matter and its words, so that along with the text of the New Testament, it is the unique and error-free canon of our faith and life.[104]

The main body of the Reformed churches never went that far, at least not officially, and it can be argued that the phrase "the force of the points" allowed the defenders of the *Formula* to escape the charge that the points themselves were part of the original text.[105] Today, it is fair to say, no one would go as far as the *Formula* in defending the inspiration of the Hebrew vowel points, and its claim marks the extreme limit of the dogmatic assertion of the biblical text's verbal inerrancy before the rise of modern historical and textual criticism.[106]

The big difference between the way the fathers of the church understood the work of the Holy Spirit in the interpretation of Scripture and the approach of Protestant Orthodoxy can be seen most clearly in the way that the difficulties of the literal text were treated. In ancient and medieval times, problems of chronology, grammar, and so on were thought to have been placed there deliberately, as a reminder from God that the Bible is about spiritual things that cannot be understood by rational means alone. The scholars of Protestant Orthodoxy agreed with them on this but did not resort to allegory in order to explain textual difficulties. Instead, they believed that solutions could be found by rational means—a deeper study of the original languages, closer attention to chronology, and so on. This opened them up to the possibility, and eventually to the probability, that the texts had been redacted by a succession of unknown people, who had been empowered by the Holy Spirit to do that. In that way

[103] A reference to Rom. 3:2.

[104] *Formula consensus Helvetica*, 2. Text in Hermann A. Niemeyer, ed. *Collectio confessionum in Ecclesiis Reformatis publicatarum* (Leipzig: J. Kilnkhardt, 1840), 731.

[105] This makes sense, in that no word in the Hebrew text was pronounced without vowels. The problem was to know what those vowels were, and (as modern textual criticism has demonstrated) there are a number of places where the Masoretic pointing is probably best read differently. The most famous example in the New Testament occurs in Heb. 11:21, where the reading is that the dying Jacob bowed in worship over the head of his staff (*rabdos*, which in Hebrew would be *matteh*), which follows the Septuagint reading. The Masoretic pointing, however, points *mtth* as *mitteh* ("bed"), which appears to make more sense. Jerome, incidentally, translated "bed" in Gen. 47:31 but "staff" in Heb. 11:21, as does the ESV.

[106] See Richard Muller, "The Debate over the Vowel Points and the Crisis in Orthodox Hermeneutics," in *After Calvin: Studies in the Development of a Theological Tradition* (Oxford: Oxford University Press, 2003), 146–155.

they tried to maintain an essential unity between the human and the divine elements that had gone into the production of the Bible as we now have it.

Those who understood the historical process of the text's development (guided by the Spirit) would interpret it correctly, and so there was no need to go beyond what was written to look for some hidden spiritual meaning. Protestant Orthodoxy thus broke with the church's ancient hermeneutical tradition without abandoning its conviction that the Scriptures were inspired by the Holy Spirit. But at the same time, by emphasizing the importance of rational analysis of its literal sense as the way to understand its true meaning, Protestant Orthodoxy also prepared the way for modern critical study of the Bible, in which the appeal to its divine inspiration would cease to have any practical application.

20

The Pathway to Heaven

Angels and Archangels

Is it possible for human beings to have an experience of heaven before death? The Old Testament says little or nothing about this. The closest it comes is the mention of Moses, who saw God face-to-face, but that was unique and its meaning is unclear.[1] Later on, Elijah was taken up to heaven in a chariot of fire, but as he did not return, that can hardly be regarded as a mystical experience.[2] Beyond that, we have dreams and visions, but those who had them did not claim to have gone up to heaven themselves.[3] It is only in the New Testament that there is any suggestion that people could have an out-of-body experience of God. The apostle Paul told the Corinthians,

> I know a man in Christ who fourteen years ago was caught up to the third heaven—whether in the body or out of the body I do not know, God knows. And I know that this man was caught up into paradise—whether in the body or out of the body I do not know, God knows—and he heard things that cannot be told, which man may not utter.[4]

The only other mention of anything like this comes in the book of Revelation, where John heard a voice telling him to come up to heaven and mentions that he did so, "in the Spirit."[5] Unlike the man mentioned by Paul, John was not reduced to silence—on the contrary, it was his ascent into heaven that provided the backdrop to his subsequent vision, which he described at great length. The difficulty is that, while we know the details of what John *saw*, we have no explanation of what his vision *meant*, and the church has lived through two millennia of doubt on this score.[6]

---

[1] Ex. 33:11; Num. 12:8; Deut. 34:10.
[2] 2 Kings 2:11–12.
[3] See, for example, Isa. 6:1–7; Dan. 7:1–14.
[4] 2 Cor. 12:2–4.
[5] Rev. 4:1–2.
[6] This is true of the church as a whole, though of course, particular individuals have often been only too ready to explain the meaning of John's vision—and invariably they have been wrong.

What is important for later theology is that the New Testament accepts the possibility of such ecstatic experiences. Paul did not say whom he had in mind, though there is a long tradition that says that he was speaking about himself in the third person.[7] John was an eyewitness, but the purpose for which he was taken up to heaven was unique to him and there was no suggestion that anyone else would be given a comparable vision. The attitude of the church to it is perhaps best seen in the fact that the canonicity of Revelation was long in doubt, especially in the Eastern church. There was never any suggestion that such experiences were normal occurrences or that believers should be encouraged to seek them. Even in the lists of spiritual gifts, nothing of this kind is ever mentioned, and had Paul not brought the subject up on his own initiative, it is unlikely that the church would ever have known about it.

This ambiguity has always puzzled commentators. On the one hand, it is impossible to deny the reality of such experiences, or even their desirability, since Paul was clearly prepared to boast about the man who had had one. On the other hand, there was no indication of why such an experience was given or how it could be obtained, if indeed it could be. Paul himself did not know what exactly had transpired, and there is no mention of any message or lesson to be drawn from it. The "third heaven" was a mystery in itself—did it represent the third in a series of heavens, and if so, was it the highest of them or merely one of seven? Was it the same as paradise or different?[8] There was no obvious answer to questions like these and no suggestion that anyone should try to solve the problem. A mystery it was and a mystery it ought to remain, remarked Gregory of Nazianzus, whose opinion seems to have carried the day.[9]

It was only later, and in somewhat obscure circumstances, that extraordinary spiritual experiences became the object of direct inquiry, with a view to repeating them. Credit for this is usually given to an unknown writer of the late fifth or early sixth century who is known to the theological tradition as Dionysius (or Denys) the Areopagite. The historical Dionysius was one of Paul's rare converts at Athens, which gave these writings immense authority for those who believed that he was their author.[10] The choice of pseudonym can hardly be accidental, since Athens was the center of the Greek philosophical world and the Pseudo-Dionysius was clearly well versed in late Neoplatonism. Ironically, it is that fact which caused a number of medieval scholars, and virtually all modern

[7] This was the standard view in the early church, which seemed to think that Paul had been given this experience in order to reassure him that he was not inferior to the other apostles. See Gerald L. Bray, ed., *1–2 Corinthians*, vol. 7 in *The Ancient Christian Commentary on Scripture, New Testament*, Thomas C. Oden, gen. ed. (Downers Grove, IL: InterVarsity Press, 1999), 298–299, for a selection of examples.

[8] Ambrosiaster thought that paradise was higher than the third heaven and that Paul had gone to both.

[9] Gregory of Nazianzus, *Oratio* 22.14.

[10] Acts 17:34.

ones, to question the authenticity of his writings, since the historical Dionysius could hardly have been expected to be familiar with philosophical concepts that did not exist in his day. But who he was is impossible to say, and modern research has established no more than that he may have lived in Antioch around AD 500.[11] His influence spread quickly, however, thanks not least to the enthusiasm of Maximus the Confessor, and he was one of the very few Greek authors to have been translated into Latin in the early Middle Ages. That was the work of John Scotus Eriugena (815?–877?), who believed that he was the historical Dionysius and therefore attributed great authority to his writings. As a result, there is both an Eastern and a Western tradition of mysticism associated with the Areopagite, and it is instructive to see how they differ from one another.

The degree to which the Pseudo-Dionysius was influenced by Neoplatonism is controversial, and in modern times it has shaped the way he has been viewed, especially by those theologians who deplore the impact of Platonic thinking on the early Christians. There is no doubt that he borrowed a good deal from Proclus (412–485), one of the last and greatest heads of Plato's Academy at Athens, but as Proclus had also been influenced by Christian thinking, this relationship is more complex than it might appear. Nevertheless, it is clear from reading his works that the Pseudo-Dionysius was a Christian first and a Neoplatonist second. Perhaps the fairest estimation of him is that he was trying to solve problems that confronted the Neoplatonists in their search for an integrated view of reality. That was what the church had to offer the pagan world in its divine revelation, and the Pseudo-Dionysius made achieving that integration the goal of his intellectual endeavors.

In this, he succeeded brilliantly. Neoplatonism believed in the underlying unity of all things but could not explain how what was originally one had become many and varied. Somehow, the supreme being had produced lesser beings by a process of emanation from itself. These lesser beings differed from it in all kinds of ways, but each difference was a mark of inferiority to the original perfection. The goal of philosophy was to work out how far human beings had fallen away from the ideal and what steps could (and should) be taken to achieve reintegration with it.

The Christian answer to this theory of emanation was twofold. First, Christians explained the origin of the universe as the creative act of God outside himself. The world is not a product of the divine being, sharing its nature to a lesser

[11] The *Corpus Areopagiticum* (or *Dionysiacum*) has been translated into English by Colm Luibheid and Paul Rorem, *Pseudo-Dionysius: The Complete Works* (Mahwah, NJ: Paulist, 1987). For a good introduction to his work, see that volume and also Andrew Louth, *Denys the Areopagite* (London: Geoffrey Chapman, 1989). The classical modern study of his thought is René Roques, *L'univers dionysien. Structure hiérarchique du monde selon le Pseudo-Denys* (Paris: Montaigne, 1954; repr., Paris: Cerf, 1983).

degree, but something totally different. This made it possible for Christians to argue that the creation is perfect in itself—not by comparison with the incomparable divine being, but by exhibiting the nature that had been given to it by the Creator. Second, the world was made by a personal God who entered into a relationship with his creatures, and especially with mankind. Knowledge of God did not come from rising higher on the scale of being, but from illumination. God is light. Moreover, not only does that light shine in the darkness; it gives its light to everyone.[12] The first act of the Creator was to order the appearance of light, which does not seem to have been something he made, but something that in a mysterious way emanated from him and reflected his being.[13] In this way, the Platonic concept of emanation was reinterpreted and applied to divine revelation, both in creation and in Christ, the light of the world.[14]

But not only is God light; he is also love. For Neoplatonists, love (*erôs*) was a form of desire, a god in its own right that was rooted in the material universe but that had the capacity to raise those who surrendered to it to a higher plane of consciousness. The Pseudo-Dionysius rejected that completely. For him, love was not a desire for self-satisfaction, however nobly that might be conceived, but a form of self-denial that came as close to imitating the divine perfection as it was possible to get. God had set the example of this by creating the world. He was not obliged to do that, nor could the created order be regarded as an extension of himself. It was something different, that only came into being because God stepped out of himself, as it were, and made it.

The difference can be seen in the meaning of the Greek word *ekstasis* ("stepping out"), from which we get our word "ecstasy." To the Platonist, "ecstasy" was the experience of a higher level of being, but to the Pseudo-Dionysius it was an act of self-sacrificing love. As he put it,

> The Source of all things, in his wonderful and good love for them, by the overflow of his loving goodness, is carried outside himself in his providential care for everything that exists, so enchanted is he in goodness, love, and longing. Removed from his position above and beyond all, he condescends to be present in all, according to an ecstatic and transcendent power that is inseparable from himself.[15]

When God stepped out of himself, he put his own interests aside for the sake of what he was making, and so for a Christian, the experience of true "ec-

[12] John 1:4–9.
[13] Gen. 1:3; 1 John 1:5.
[14] John 8:12. See also Luke 2:32.
[15] Pseudo-Dionysius, *De divinis nominibus* 4.13 (712 A–B).

stasy" had to be analogous, if not identical. This was why suffering, death, and resurrection—concepts that to the Platonic mind were disgusting and shameful because of their materialist overtones—were at the very heart of the Christian life. The world was not merely the work of the Creator; it was also a manifestation of him, not as he is in himself, because that is unknowable, but as he is in relation to others. In a word, the entire creation is a theophany, and it is this concept, more than any other, that explains the vision of the Areopagite.[16]

It is when we understand this that we can see that the Pseudo-Dionysius was not copying Neoplatonism but supplanting it by reinterpreting its legitimate aims. Neoplatonists and Christians both wanted to escape the world of sin and death and enter into communion with the divine source of all being, but (as the Pseudo-Dionysius was intent on demonstrating) only Christians could actually achieve this. This was because Christians had a relationship to Jesus Christ, himself the Creator of all things, that made such transcendence possible. The early church had always wondered why the sinless Son of God had been baptized in his human flesh, but the Pseudo-Dionysius believed he had found the answer:

> In being initiated into that sacred rite of the divine birth, the perfecting anointing of the ointment gives us a visitation of the thearchic Spirit. What this symbolism signifies, I think, is that the one who received the sanctification of the thearchic Spirit for us, while at the same time remaining unchanged in his own divinity, arranges now for the thearchic Spirit to be given to us.[17]

It is in the power of the Spirit that the Christian can receive the illumination that comes from the divine light. The experience of this is twofold. It may be mediated through the hierarchies that the Creator has built into his creation, in order to give it a necessary structure and sense of purpose, but it may also be immediate, if the creature comes into direct contact with his Creator. Here, too, we see both the similarities with Neoplatonism and the differences. The Neoplatonists believed in hierarchy, but thought it was necessary because they could not have immediate access to the supreme being. Furthermore, the Pseudo-Dionysius believed that there were two contrasting hierarchies, a celestial one composed of angelic beings, and an earthly one, manifested in the life and rituals of the church. The celestial hierarchy pointed downwards from God to the material world but the ecclesiastical hierarchy went in the other direction, taking man up to God. The two hierarchies were complementary, meeting in the intersection

[16] The point was made by Andrew Louth, *Denys*, 85, and fully developed by Eric D. Perl, *Theophany: The Neoplatonic Philosophy of Dionysius the Areopagite* (Albany: State University of New York Press, 2007).

[17] Pseudo-Dionysius, *De hierarchia ecclesiastica* 4.3.11 (484 C). The word "thearchic" is a transcription of the Greek *thearchikon*, which is often (somewhat inadequately) translated as "divine." "Thearchic" implies that the Spirit is not merely divine but God, the source and ruler of all things.

of spirit and matter that produced divine revelation, but neither was essential to the spiritual experience of the believer, for whom there was always the possibility of direct access to God himself. Nevertheless, the hierarchical order served an important purpose, which the Pseudo-Dionysius explained as follows:

> The goal of a hierarchy is to enable beings to be as similar to God as possible, and to be united with him. A hierarchy has God as its source of all understanding and action. It is forever looking directly at the beauty of God. A hierarchy bears in itself the mark of God. Hierarchy causes its members to be images of God in all respects, to be clear and spotless mirrors reflecting the glow of primordial light, and of God himself. It ensures that when its members have received this full and divine splendor they can pass on this light generously, and in accordance with God's will, to beings who are lower down the scale.[18]

To participate in the hierarchy was therefore to share in the love of God, since what the believer received from him, he was called to pass on to others. It was given to mankind, because there were three stages that had to be covered before a full experience of God was obtainable. These stages were those of purification (*katharsis*), illumination (*phôtismos*), and union with God (*henôsis*), and the hierarchies were designed to cater to each of these in turn. The best way to appreciate this is to consider table 20.1:

Table 20.1

	Celestial[A]	**Ecclesiastical**
Union [with God]	Seraphim	Unction
	Cherubim	Eucharist
	Thrones	Baptism
Illumination	Dominions	Bishops
	Powers	Priests
	Authorities	Deacons
Purification	Principalities	Monks
	Archangels	Laymen
	Angels	Catechumens[B]

Notes: [A]The names of the celestial hierarchy can all be found in the New Testament, but without the arrangement found here. See Eph. 1:21; Col. 1:16; 1 Thess. 4:16; Jude 9. [B]This also included those who had been excluded from the body of the church for whatever reason—penitents, for example, and those who were demon-possessed.

[18] Pseudo-Dionysius, *De hierarchia caelesti* 3.2 (165 A).

There was a further correspondence within the ecclesiastical hierarchy, between the sacred rites of union and their ministers on the one hand, and between the ministers and those ministered to on the other. Table 20.2 will help to clarify this:

Table 20.2

	Rite	**Ministers**	**Recipients**
Union [with God]	Unction	Bishops	Monks
Illumination	Eucharist	Priests	Laymen
Purification	Baptism	Deacons	Catechumens

A careful study of these diagrams will reveal a great deal about the way the structures of the church and its ministry were perceived and developed by those who came under the influence of the Pseudo-Dionysius. At the bottom were those who were in need of cleansing from sin and instruction in the faith. There were a good many of these in the early sixth century, but with the spread of infant baptism catechumens died out. The Eastern Orthodox churches still preserve the memory of them in their liturgies, which contain a "departure of the catechumens" just before the consecration of the Eucharistic elements is about to begin, but this is now residual. In the Western churches the memory of them has survived better, with the rite of confirmation replacing that of baptism in churches that baptize infants but also with the presence of a bias in favor of rejecting infant baptism altogether.[19] Laymen receiving the Eucharist from a priest may be regarded as the "normal" state of affairs, even at the present time, in virtually every church, whether the same terminology is used or not.[20]

It is the link between monks, bishops, and unction that seems most surprising today, but it was of great importance to the Pseudo-Dionysius. Monks were not necessarily in holy orders, but they were not ordinary laymen either. They had set themselves apart by a spiritual self-discipline that brought them closer to God, and therefore they stood in relation to the other members of their order as the bishops stood in relation to priests and deacons. The Pseudo-Dionysius put it like this:

[19] Another residual reminder of this can be found in the Anglican Ordinal (1550), where deacons are permitted to baptize infants in the absence of a priest.

[20] It may be noted here that the Pseudo-Dionysius used different words for the things and people he was describing, perhaps because there was no fixed terminology in his time. He was among the first, if not the first, to use the term *hiereus* for a Christian *presbyteros*, but apparently he did so without any connotation of Eucharistic sacrifice.

> The sacred rank of the monks has been purified from all stain and possesses full power and complete holiness in its own activities. To the extent that is permissible, it has entered upon sacred contemplative activity and has achieved intellectual contemplation and communion. This order is entrusted to the perfecting power of those men of God, the bishops, whose enlightening activities and hierarchical traditions have introduced it, according to ability, to the holy operations of the sacred rites it has beheld.[21]

It would not be until the Council *in Trullo* in 692 that bishops would be obliged to be celibate (in effect, monks), but the origins of that can clearly be traced to the Dionysian ecclesiastical hierarchy. It can also be said that the Pseudo-Dionysius introduced another concept, and one that has echoed down through the ages in almost every church. This was that the holder of a church office should exhibit the degree of holiness in his personal life that attached to that office. How could a priest, for example, administer the sacred rite of the Eucharist if he were not holy enough to do so? This notion has been frequently combated in the Western world, where as the title of Article 26 of the Church of England puts it, "the unworthiness of the ministers . . . hinders not the effect of the sacrament," but it has to be said that this flies in the face of popular expectation. On this point at least, even the average Protestant is likely to side with the Pseudo-Dionysius in expecting his pastor to be a holier man than he is, whatever theological theory (and practical reality) might say to the contrary.

The unction with holy oil (*myron*) is another puzzle. There was no such rite in the church of Pseudo-Dionysius's day, except in Syria, which is one reason why scholars think that he must have come from there. There was a certain linkage between anointing and completion or perfection, in the sense that chrismation was regarded as the completion of baptism, and extreme unction (the last rites) the end of human life, and Christ himself was the Anointed One, but this seems to have been something different. In fact, it is probable that in the Areopagite's mind, the rite was purely secondary, even if one existed in the Syrian church. The true anointing was (and could only be) a spiritual gift, hidden from public view, as the Syrian rite apparently was, and given solely by the grace of God. Those familiar with the great tradition of Welsh preaching exemplified by men like Martyn Lloyd-Jones (1899–1981) will recognize it as the *hwyl*, a Welsh word that Lloyd-Jones and others would often translate as "unction." Once again, we find that spiritual traditions which on the surface

[21] Pseudo-Dionysius, *De hierarchia ecclesiastica* 6.1.3 (532 D). The Pseudo-Dionysius usually referred to bishops as "hierarchs," as was the case here.

appear to be at opposite ends of the theological spectrum can sometimes be closer to one another than anyone would have suspected.

Above and beyond the hierarchies there was the presence of God himself. Because he was the Creator of everything that exists, all his creatures reflect his glory and, if he so chooses, can be admitted into his presence. This was an important consideration, because it allowed individuals to transcend the hierarchical structure in which they were placed and enter into direct communion with God. In the Neoplatonism of the Pseudo-Dionysius's time, great importance was attached to Plato's *Parmenides*, which posited the existence of distinct hypotheses—first the One, of which nothing could be said, and then the others, which could be described in detail. The One could be mentioned only in terms of what it was not, a procedure that was called "negative" or "apophatic" reasoning. The others could be approached "positively" or "cataphatically."[22] In the Neoplatonic scheme of things, apophatic and cataphatic discourse were quite separate from one another and could not be used of the same being.

Here again, the Pseudo-Dionysius broke the Neoplatonic mold. For him, the One was the God of the Bible, who could be approached both cataphatically and apophatically. The revealed hierarchies were essentially cataphatic, telling us what God is like and explaining where we fit in his overall scheme of things. But to know him personally, we must go beyond the cataphatic dimension to the apophatic, because in himself, God is above and beyond both his creation and his self-revelation, which is adapted to the parameters of the created order. To give an example of this, we are accustomed to saying that God is "good." But what does that mean? Goodness is comprehensible only in relative terms; we cannot define it except in relation to its opposites. But God is what he is without reference to anything else. Therefore, in him, "goodness" is a meaningless concept. The same goes for everything else we say about him. He is invisible, but only to us who have created eyes. He is eternal, but only to those who are conditioned by time. And so on. Yet in spite of the fact that God is totally different from anything we can know or conceive, it is still possible to relate to him because he relates to us, not in philosophical categories but in love.

For us to love God as he has loved us is to empty ourselves of all pride and knowledge, and submit our minds to the controlling power of his Holy Spirit, who will allow us to see what is hidden from both men and angels. As the Pseudo-Dionysius put it,

> I pray that we might come to that darkness which is so far above light! If only we lacked sight and knowledge so that we might see and know, without seeing

[22] The Greek words *kataphasis* and *apophasis* mean "affirmation" and "negation" respectively.

> or knowing, all that lies beyond vision and knowledge. To really see and know would be to praise the transcendent One in a transcending way. . . . When we made assertions we began with the first things, moved down through intermediate terms and finally reached the last things. But now as we climb back up from the lowest to the highest, we deny all things in order to know unhiddenly that unknowing which is hidden from all beings who possess knowledge, so that we may see, beyond being, that darkness that is concealed from all the light among beings.[23]

Here we have reached the heart of apophatic theology, the intellectual counterculture that has informed Christian mysticism down through the ages and that remains an ever-challenging alternative to the cerebral academic exercises that so often pass as "theology" in our universities, divinity schools, and theological colleges. In the end, there is no substitute for a humble and a contrite heart, which alone will see the glory of God.

The influence of the Pseudo-Dionysius was felt almost immediately in the Greek-speaking world, thanks to the efforts of John of Scythopolis (d. 550) and of Maximus the Confessor, both of whom wrote annotations on his work. A Syriac translation was also made about the same time, or even earlier, which is a reminder to us that by straddling the growing divide between Chalcedonians and monophysites in the East, the Pseudo-Dionysius was able to help the spiritual traditions of the diverging churches stay closer together than they might have done otherwise. In the West, the *Corpus Areopagiticum* exercised its main influence from the twelfth century onward, but in a very different context. In the Eastern church, the emphasis was always on the liturgical elements in his writings, which were central both to them and to the Pseudo-Dionysius's own interests. In the West, however, it was the growing awareness of the desirability of an individual spirituality that attracted people to him, and his influence was felt mainly in the area of private mystical experience. Because of that, although his impact was profound, it was also less obvious and direct, and it never touched the public theology of the Western church to any significant extent.

In the East, however, things were very different. The Pseudo-Dionysius cannot be credited with having developed Eastern liturgical spirituality, which was already formed when he began to write, but his work certainly played its part in preventing the Westernization of that theology in the later Middle Ages. This can be seen most clearly in the nonexistence in the East of anything comparable to the sacramental theology of the Western Middle Ages. The

[23] Pseudo-Dionysius, *De theologia mystica* 2 (1025 A–B).

Pseudo-Dionysius had said a great deal about baptism and the Eucharist, but he called them *teletai* ("rites") and linked them to unction and to the burial service, which for him symbolized resurrection to a new life in Christ.[24] It is therefore misleading to think of his treatment of baptism and the Eucharist in sacramental terms. The Greek word normally used to translate "sacrament" is *mystêrion*, but although the Pseudo-Dionysius was familiar with it and used it regularly, he did not equate it with any *teletês*. Instead, he retained the New Testament sense of the word, using it to mean the fellowship of love that we have with God.[25] That love had been a secret hidden from the beginning of time but was revealed in Christ and proclaimed to the world by the church. It did not matter to the Pseudo-Dionysius precisely *how* it was proclaimed, since everything the church said and did was part of the revelation of this "mystery." Later on, pressure from the West persuaded many Orthodox churches to agree that there were seven *mystêria* corresponding to the seven sacraments, but this artificial categorization never caught on and today it is largely downplayed, if not altogether abandoned.

The Western churches have never understood this difference, and to this day their arguments over the sacraments go unheard in the East because their nature is not properly understood. But the Pseudo-Dionysius can claim to have had at least one significant impact on Western liturgy. Those familiar with the Anglican *Book of Common Prayer* will recognize it immediately in the approach to Holy Communion where "with angels and archangels, and all the company of heaven, we laud and magnify thy glorious Name, evermore praising thee and saying: 'Holy, holy, holy, Lord God of hosts, heaven and earth are full of thy glory. Glory be to thee, O Lord most high.'" The spirit of the Areopagite lives on in the fellowship of the saints with the celestial hierarchy gathered before the throne of grace.

The Peace That Passes Understanding

One of the many things that the Pseudo-Dionysius said about the difference between Neoplatonism and Christianity was the obvious one that the Neoplatonists accepted polytheism whereas Christians did not. The Pseudo-Dionysius recognized that the pagan gods stood for something that genuinely existed, even though it was completely misunderstood before the coming of Christ. The pagans were trying to make contact with the world of the divine and knew that it was possible to do so, but their understanding was faulty. What they were

[24] In this sense, the word survives in Greek to this day, where a funeral home is a *grapheion teletôn*.
[25] See Eph. 3:9; Col. 3:3.

doing was confusing God's work in the world, which is highly varied, with God himself, who is one. As a result, they believed in many gods, because they were counting his operations as if they were divine beings in their own right. Christians did not make that mistake because the one God had revealed himself to them in Jesus Christ, and so they were able to make the right distinction between who God is and what he does. As he put it,

> "Being itself," "life itself," "divinity itself"—these are names honoring source, divinity, and cause, and they are applied to the one transcendent cause and source [who dwells] beyond the source of all things. But we also use the same terms in a derivative way, and apply them to the provident acts of power that come forth from the God in whom nothing at all participates.[26]

Here we see the traces of what was to become a significant element of Eastern Christian theology. The essence of God remains hidden from our eyes, but we perceive him—and can enter into communion with him—in his operations, or "energies" as they came to be called.

This distinction is fundamental because without it, it would have been impossible for the Eastern church to develop its particular understanding of how the believer relates to God. The term often used today to describe this is *theôsis*, a Greek word that is usually, if somewhat unhappily, translated as "deification." In recent years there has been a tremendous revival of interest in this subject, sparked off mainly by the publication of two seminal works by the Russian Orthodox theologian in exile Vladimir Lossky.[27] Since then there has been a renaissance of interest in the subject, often motivated by enthusiasts whose attachment to the idea has a tendency to lead them into taking extreme positions in favor of it. It is by no means uncommon for studies of *theôsis* to trace its origins back, not only to the New Testament, but to pre-Christian Judaism and even to pagan Hellenism, something which the fathers of the church would certainly have repudiated had they known about it.[28]

---

[26] Pseudo-Dionysus, *De divinis nominibus* 11.6 (953 D–956 A).

[27] Vladimir Lossky, *The Mystical Theology of the Eastern Church* (Cambridge: James Clarke, 1957). Originally published as *Essai sur la théologie mystique de l'Eglise d'Orient* (Paris: Aubier, 1944); idem, *In the Image and Likeness of God* (Crestwood, NY: St. Vladimir's Seminary Press, 1974). Originally published as *A l'image et à la ressemblance de Dieu* (Paris: Aubier Montaigne, 1967).

[28] The most thorough recent study is by Norman Russell, *The Doctrine of Deification in the Greek Patristic Tradition* (Oxford: Oxford University Press, 2004), which is generally balanced in its conclusions. See also Jules Gross, *The Divinization of the Christian according to the Greek Fathers* (Anaheim, CA: A & C, 2002). Originally published as *La divinisation du Chrétien d'après les Pères grecs: contribution historique de la doctrine de la grâce* (Paris: Gabalda, 1938); Stephen Thomas, *Deification in the Eastern Orthodox Tradition: A Biblical Perspective* (Piscataway, NJ: Gorgias, 2007), Michael J. Christensen and Jeffery A. Wittung, eds., *Partakers of the Divine Nature: The History and Development of Deification in the Christian Traditions* (Grand Rapids, MI: Baker, 2007); Stephen Finlan and Vladimir Kharlamov, eds., *Theôsis: Deification in Christian Theology* (Eugene, OR: Pickwick, 2006); Vladimir Kharlamov, *Theôsis: Deification in Christian Theology II* (Eugene, OR: Pickwick, 2011); Norman Russell, *Fellow Workers with God: Orthodox Thinking on Theosis* (Crestwood, NY: St. Vladimir's Seminary Press,

The biblical text most often cited in support of the apostolic origin of *theôsis* is 2 Peter 1:3–4, which reads,

> His divine power has granted to us all things that pertain to life and godliness, through the knowledge of him who called us to his own glory and excellence, by which he has granted to us his precious and very great promises, so that through them you may become *partakers of the divine nature*, having escaped from the corruption that is in the world because of sinful desire.

The interpretation of these verses is controversial, not least because many modern scholars deny the apostolic origin of 2 Peter. It is relatively easy to read *theôsis* back into this passage if we assume that it was written, not by Peter, but by a second-century convert to Christianity who was deeply influenced by Middle Platonism, but this interpretation is uncertain at best and probably ought to be rejected.[29] Origen seems to have equated participation in the divine nature with the "fellowship of the Holy Spirit," which Paul mentions in 2 Corinthians 13:14, and other early church writers are similarly ambiguous.[30] For Hilary of Poitiers, it meant that Christians must not measure God's nature by ours, but evaluate his truth in accordance with the grandeur of his witness concerning himself.[31] It is only when we come to Bede (673–735) that we get an interpretation that seems to point in the direction of what we would now call *theôsis*:

> The greater your knowledge of God becomes, the more you will realize the magnitude of his promises. When God blesses us, he changes our very being so that whatever we were by nature is transformed by the gift of his Holy Spirit, so that we may truly become partakers of his nature.[32]

This similarity to *theôsis* is probably not accidental, since Bede lived at a time when the doctrine had already been developed in the East, and had connections with that world which might have informed him of those developments.[33]

2009); Paul M. Collins, *Partaking in Divine Nature: Deification and Communion* (London: T & T Clark, 2010); Daniel Keating, *Deification and Grace* (Naples, FL: Sapientia, 2007); and Panayiotis Nellas, *Deification in Christ: Orthodox Perspectives on the Nature of the Human Person* (Crestwood, NY: St. Vladimir's Seminary Press, 1987), originally published in Greek as *Zôon theoumenon. Prooptikes gia mia Orthodoxê katanoêsê tou anthrôpou*, 2nd ed. (Athens: Synaxi, 1981).

[29] For a study in favor of that position, see Stephen Finlan, "Second Peter's Notion of Divine Participation," in Finlan and Kharlamov, *Theôsis*, 32–50; for an opposing view, see James Starr, "Does 2 Peter 1:4 Speak of Deification?" in Christensen and Wittung, *Partakers of the Divine Nature*, 81–92.

[30] Origen, *Homiliae in Leviticum* 4.4.2.

[31] Hilary of Poitiers, *De Trinitate* 1.18.

[32] Bede, *Commentarium in secundam Beati Petri epistulam* 1:4.

[33] Theodore of Tarsus, a Greek, had been archbishop of Canterbury (668–690) in Bede's youth and was greatly revered by him as one of the main promoters of theological learning in England.

In fact, most of the discussion surrounding 2 Peter 1:3–4 and other texts like it seems to have focused on the eschatological fulfillment of the promises made to believers in Christ. As Paul said: "now we see in a mirror dimly, but then face to face. Now I know in part; then I shall know fully, even as I have been fully known."[34] If that is what is understood by *theôsis*, then obviously the New Testament is full of that idea, but here the enthusiasts for the doctrine are faced with enormous difficulties in attempting to impose their interpretation of theological developments. First, the word *theôsis* in nowhere found in the Scriptures, nor is its near-synonym *theopoiêsis*, which was more frequently used in the early church period to describe the concept. Second, even when *theôsis* came into Christian use, as it did (apparently for the first time) in the orations of Gregory of Nazianzus, it was used in many different senses and cannot be regarded as a technical theological term before the time of Maximus the Confessor, at the earliest.[35] Third, *theôsis* implies a transformation of our human nature by an indwelling presence of the divine that its advocates insist is quite different from the traditional (Western) understanding of sanctification, but the patristic quotes they use to support their position make no distinction between deification and sanctification, and can just as easily—and probably more naturally—be interpreted in favor of the latter.[36] It certainly seems hard to believe that *theôsis*, as it is now understood, could have formed part of the teaching of Augustine of Hippo, let alone of Martin Luther or John Calvin, without anyone (including them) having noticed it until just a few years ago.[37]

Recent enthusiasm for *theôsis* notwithstanding, it seems most reasonable to suggest that the doctrine of a direct experience of God in this life, and not just in the next, owes its development to Maximus the Confessor, who was inspired mainly by the Pseudo-Dionysius.[38] Of course neither Maximus nor

---

[34] 1 Cor. 13:12.

[35] On this, see Russell, *Doctrine of Deification*, 214–215.

[36] This is admitted, at least with respect to Irenaeus, by Jeffrey Finch, "Irenaeus on the Christological Basis of Human Divinization," in Finlan and Kharlamov, ed, *Theôsis*, 86–103. See especially his conclusions on 103.

[37] For these claims, see Robert Puchniak, "Augustine's Conception of Deification Revisited," in Finlan and Kharlamov, *Theôsis*, 122–133; and Myk Habets, "Reforming *Theôsis*," in the same volume, 146–167, and his *Theosis in the Theology of Thomas Torrance* (Farnham: Ashgate, 2009). Habets bases much of what he says about the Protestant Reformers on theories developed by Thomas Torrance (1913–2007), who might be described as the original Western enthusiast for this aspect of the Eastern tradition. See, for example, Thomas F. Torrance, ed., *Theological Dialogue between Orthodox and Reformed Churches*, 2 vols. (Edinburgh: Scottish Academic Press, 1985–1993). On Luther in particular, see Reinhard Flogaus, *Theosis bei Palamas und Luther. Ein Beitrag zum ökumenischen Gespräch* (Göttingen: Vandenhoeck und Ruprecht, 1997); and Tuomo Mannermaa, *Der im Glauben gegenwärtige Christus: Rechtfertigung und Vergottung zum ökumenischen Dialog* (Hannover: Lutherisches Verlagshaus, 1989); and on an attempt to see Calvin as a latter-day disciple of the Pseudo-Dionysius, see Carl A. Keller, *Calvin mystique. Au coeur de la pensée du Réformateur* (Geneva: Labor et Fides, 2001).

[38] See, for example, Vladimir Kharlamov, *The Beauty of the Unity and the Harmony of the Whole: The Concept of Theosis in the Theology of Pseudo-Dionysius the Areopagite* (Eugene, OR: Wipf & Stock, 2009); and Ivan V. Popov, "Ideja obozhenija v drevne-vostochnoj tserkvi" in *Voprosy filosofii i psikhologii* 97 (1906), 165–213, translated into

the Pseudo-Dionysius believed that they were innovators; each of them thought that he was doing no more than clarifying the ancient tradition of the church. That may be true, but it is in their writings that something like what we would recognize as *theôsis* becomes clear for the first time, and it is them, rather than Irenaeus or the Cappadocians, that we can speak of as specifically Eastern, as opposed to Western, theologians.[39]

As we have already seen in our discussion of the person of Christ, Maximus the Confessor has long been known for the courageous part he played in defeating monothelitism in the seventh century, but until relatively recently his wider theological interests were little studied, at least in the West. Things began to change when Hans Urs von Balthasar (1905–1988) published *Die kosmische Liturgie* (1941) and, more important, a French translation of the same, *La liturgie cosmique* (1947).[40] That led to a wave of research on his writings, especially in France, that has given the scholarly world a fresh appreciation of his achievements and their importance. Maximus had an ability to synthesize different strands of theology into a coherent whole that was firmly grounded, not only in the incarnation of the Son but, more significantly, in the way his disciples are transformed by it.

For Maximus, the key event in the earthly life of Jesus was his transfiguration, when the divine nature of his humanity was revealed and his decisive place in the divine plan of salvation, previously communicated through the law (Moses) and the prophets (Elijah), was confirmed. But then Maximus went on to describe what happened to Peter, James, and John, the disciples who witnessed this great event:

> They passed over from flesh to spirit before they had put aside this fleshly life, by the change in their powers of sense that the Spirit worked in them, lifting the veils of the passions from the intellectual activity that was in them. Then, when both their bodily and spiritual senses had been purified, they were taught the spiritual meanings of the mysteries that were shown to them.[41]

Among the mysteries revealed to them was the significance of the clothing that Jesus was wearing. It too was transfigured, because,

---

English and published as "The Idea of Deification in the Early Eastern Church," in Kharlamov, ed. *Theôsis II*, 42–82. For a good summary of both the Pseudo-Dionysius and Maximus, see Russell, *Doctrine of Deification*, 248–295.

[39] For the relationship of the Cappadocians to the later development of *theôsis* and the essence-energies distinction in God, see Vladimir Kharlamov, "Basil of Caesarea and the Cappadocians on the Distinction between the Essence and Energies in God and Its Relevance to the Deification Theme," in Vladimir Kharlamov, ed., *Theôsis II*, 100–145.

[40] Typically, it was not until 2003 that an English translation appeared as *Cosmic Liturgy* (San Francisco: Ignatius, 2003).

[41] Maximus the Confessor, *Ambigua*, 10.17 (1128 A). The English translation is in Andrew Louth, ed., *Maximus the Confessor* (London: Routledge, 1996), 109.

> The whitened garments conveyed a symbol of the words of Holy Scripture, which in this case became shining, clear, and limpid to them, and were grasped by the mind without any riddling puzzle or symbolic shadow, revealing the meaning that lay hidden within them. Thus they arrived at a clear and correct understanding concerning God, and were set free from every attachment to the world and the flesh.[42]

But that was not all. The clothes could also stand for creation, which, like a garment, can be understood as the power of the creative Word who wears it. There was no contradiction between these two possible interpretations, because,

> In both cases, what is said is accommodated to the meaning, because in both cases that meaning can be veiled from us because of its obscurity, in case we should dare to apply it unworthily to what is beyond our comprehension—in the case of the written Holy Scripture, to the One revealed as the Word, or in the case of creation, to the One revealed as Creator.[43]

In these short excerpts from a single passage in his writings, we catch a glimpse of how Maximus was able to integrate a wide range of things in a single image—the incarnation, the Bible, the creation, and the spiritual experience of the believer who had access to them all because he was illuminated by the power of the Holy Spirit. To us, it may seem that Maximus was reading too much into the story of the transfiguration, but his vision for the coherence of the Christian revelation is one that believers in every age can share.

Maximus was quite open in acknowledging the debt he owed to the Pseudo-Dionysius, but although he insisted that he had nothing to add to what the Areopagite had said, in fact his exposition of the meaning of the church's liturgy is both more subtle and more profound than anything found in his supposed mentor. Both men began with what by their time had become a fundamental reality of public worship: the sanctuary, where the sacred elements of Communion were consecrated, had been separated off from the main body (nave) of the church. The Pseudo-Dionysius spoke of the bishop as coming from the sanctuary into the nave, where he exhibited the elements to the people, and then returning to the sanctuary from which he had come. It was an essentially circular movement that corresponded to the cyclical view of time that he shared with the Neoplatonists and with Origen before them.

Maximus took this imagery and transformed it to correspond to a linear

[42] Maximus the Confessor, *Ambigua* 10.17 (1128 B).
[43] Ibid., 10.17 (1128 C).

view of time. The bishop does not wait until after the consecration of the sacred elements to emerge from the sanctuary, but does so right at the beginning of the service, as a reminder that it was while we were still sinners that Christ came into the world. The development of the liturgy from that point symbolized the sense of transformation from the earthly to the heavenly that was so central to Maximus's understanding of the message of the gospel. For Maximus, the church was first and foremost the visible manifestation of God in his oneness:

> The holy church is an image of God because it accomplishes the same unity among believers as God does. However different [believers] are, they find themselves united in the church by faith. This unity has been accomplished by God in regard to the essence of beings without confusion, in bringing into silence and oneness what differences there were . . . through their leaning toward him and their unification with him as their cause, foundation, and goal.[44]

But in addition to being an image of God, the church is also an image of the world, because it is there that God and his creation meet and embrace one another. It is a microcosm of reality in the same way that the human being, as a composite of spirit and matter, is also a microcosm (on a different scale) of that same reality. The life of the believing community and the life of the individual believer thus merge into one. The church is like an outsized man, possessing its own mind (*nous*) and practical application of knowledge by its power of reasoning (*logos*).[45] Because of this, the consecration of the elements of bread and wine in the liturgy is both symbolic and real. The liturgy participates in the reality of God as a secret mystery that the believing mind is called upon to interpret. As it does so, it is raised to that higher level of contemplation and deified by its own participation in the liturgical movement of divine grace. The hidden sanctuary (where the elements are consecrated) and the open nave (where they are consumed) are not foreign to one another but interact, each in its appointed sphere. The circular movement of the bishop who comes from the sanctuary to the nave and goes back again is not abolished, but it is subordinated to a deeper purpose, which is the goal of bringing every believer into the sanctuary—first in his own spirit, and then in the body of the church. What appears on the surface to be a division between clergy and laity is in fact a creative tension that leads ever onward and upward to the final goal:

---

[44] Maximus the Confessor, *Mystagogia* 1 (668 B-C).
[45] Ibid., 5 (681 C).

> By Holy Communion in the spotless and life-giving mysteries we are given fellowship and identity with Christ by participation in his likeness, by which man is considered worthy to become God. For we believe that in this present life we already have a share in these gifts of the Holy Spirit through the love that comes by faith, and in the future age (after we have kept the commandments to the best of our ability) we believe that we shall really share in them in their concrete reality. . . . Then we shall pass from the grace of faith to the grace of sight, when our God and Savior Jesus Christ will transform us into himself by taking away the marks of our corruption, and bestow on us the originals of the mysteries that have been represented to us in this life in material symbols [of bread and wine].[46]

It will be observed here that the questions that would agitate Western theology and divide the church at the time of the Reformation have no place in Maximus's vision. He did not ask, and he did not care, whether the priests had been validly ordained or whether the consecrated elements had been transubstantiated into the body and blood of Christ. Such questions would probably have struck him as grossly materialistic and unworthy of a true worshiper of God. Those who had been transfigured by the Holy Spirit could combine the word of Scripture with the substance of material objects and through them behold the incarnate Lord. Being united with him, they were lifted above such mundane considerations and set apart to enjoy the firstfruits of the eternal kingdom of heavenly light.

After Maximus there was little further development of the *theôsis* theme for many centuries. Echoes of it can be found in John of Damascus, but considering John's great importance for later theology, they are few and far between.[47] Not until we come to Symeon the New Theologian (949–1022) do we encounter someone whose thought reached the heights of Maximus and the Pseudo-Dionysius.[48] Like his predecessors, Symeon was a controversial figure in his own time, and there were many who felt threatened by his desire for an ever-deeper communion with God. In one of his hymns, he wrote that not only do we become members of Christ—he enters into us and becomes each of our members, leaving no part of our human nature untouched by divine light. To those accustomed to thinking of the body as somehow sinful or lacking in dignity, this could be shocking, particularly since Symeon did not hesitate

[46] Ibid., 24 (704 D–705 A).

[47] See Russell, *Doctrine of Deification*, 299–300.

[48] He was called the "New Theologian" because later generations recognized that his mystical understanding of the divine was on a par with the other two "theologians" of the Greek church—John the Divine, the author of the book of Revelation; and Gregory of Nazianzus.

to include our sexual organs along with everything else.[49] The intensity of his appeal to a personal experience of this was also felt to be something new and strange, though it was to form the basis of the subsequent development of the doctrine. In his own words,

> The man who is inwardly illuminated by the light of the Holy Spirit cannot endure the sight of it, but falls face down on the earth and cries out in great fear and amazement, since he has seen and experienced something beyond nature, thought, or conception. . . . He is utterly incapable of controlling himself, and even though he pours out incessant tears that bring him some relief, the flame of his desire kindles all the more. Then his tears flow even more copiously and, washed by their flow, he becomes even more radiant.[50]

It was this emphasis on participation in the divine light, with every part of the human body, that was to dominate monastic spirituality in the East from then on. During Symeon's lifetime, monks began to colonize Mount Athos, where they established a semi-independent state that survives to this day. It was there, more than anywhere else, that the practice of *theôsis* was encouraged and developed, and from there that the last and greatest spiritual movement associated with it would arise.

We cannot say for sure when the contemplative practices now known as "hesychasm," from the Greek word *hêsychia* ("peace," "tranquillity") arose, but they were already widespread when the young Gregory Palamas went to Athos in 1318. Turkish raids on the mountain forced him to take refuge elsewhere for a while, but by 1331 at the latest, he was back in the Athonite monastery of St. Savva (Sabbas). There he got word of the impact that the newly arrived philosopher Barlaam of Calabria was having in Constantinople. Barlaam maintained that the Western position on the *Filioque* was wrong because the nature of the Holy Spirit's procession within the Godhead was beyond human understanding. While not unsympathetic to Barlaam's view of the *Filioque*, Palamas nevertheless realized that if Barlaam were right, then the Eastern position was just as untenable as the Western one was, since nothing could be said about what was essentially unknowable.[51]

To get around this difficulty, Palamas said that while God's essence (*ousia*) is beyond our understanding, he could be known in his energies (*energeiai*). In

[49] Symeon the New Theologian, *Hymni* 15, 141–157.

[50] Symeon the New Theologian, *Capitula* (*Kephalaia*) 68.

[51] For a brief summary of the controversy between Palamas and Barlaam, see John Meyendorff, *St. Gregory Palamas and Orthodox Spirituality* (Crestwood, NY: St. Vladimir's Seminary Press, 1974), 86–106. For a more detailed analysis, see Ch. G. Sotiropoulos, *Themata theologias tou 14 aiônos* (Athens: Hellênikê Lithographia Gerakas Attikês, 1987).

that way it was possible for mortal men to participate in the divine light, and therefore in the reality of God himself. Barlaam was shocked by this claim, and accused Palamas of heresy in suggesting that the infinite God could somehow be perceived by finite human minds. That led Palamas to reply in 1341 with his treatise *On theôsis*, the first ever to be written in explicit defense of this teaching.

As Palamas understood it, knowledge of God must always be fundamentally apophatic because God cannot be reduced to human categories of thought, but that did not mean that it was impossible to have a direct experience of him. The monastic contemplation of the divine light was contemplation of God's glory, which is not the essence of God, to be sure, but which is nevertheless divine because it transforms the body as well as the soul of man by communicating its own splendor to them.[52] This experience went beyond the sensual and could not be explained in words, but that it occurred was beyond doubt.[53]

Barlaam countered this by saying that the divine grace experienced by the monks was something created. It was a symbol of divinity, perhaps, but in fact it was no more than the perfecting of rational human nature and not to be confused with God.[54] Palamas rejected this, saying that the light was not a substance or a thing as such, but a relationship with God in which he united himself with man while remaining completely different from his creatures in his own uncreated essence.[55]

Palamas agreed with Barlaam that the divine transformation of human nature was realized in the incarnation of the Son, but he went further than this by insisting that it was not enough simply to contemplate him in his human state. Believers were expected to appropriate Christ's incarnation by their own baptism, in which they received the grace of adoption and the deifying gift of the Holy Spirit. This grace of adoption is identical with

> . . . the light of ineffable glory seen by the saints, the enhypostatic, uncreated light, eternally issuing from the eternal in a manner beyond our understanding. Now it is seen only in part, but in the life to come it will be revealed to the worthy more perfectly.[56]

Following Maximus the Confessor, Palamas went on to explain that the light that the contemplatives saw was the light that shone on the transfigured Christ. Gregory called this light "enhypostatic" because it was not an inde-

---

[52] Gregory Palamas, *Triades* 1.3.5.
[53] Ibid., 2.3.8.
[54] Ibid., 3.1.5; 3.3.11–13.
[55] Ibid., 3.1.29.
[56] Ibid., 3.1.6.

pendent reality. Its *hypostasis* was Christ, who was himself the deifying light.[57] It could not be reduced to the level of human perfection, because in that case the creature would not be born again of God.[58] *Theôsis* is therefore not moral excellence or rational infallibility but a supernatural gift that transforms the recipient and makes divinity visible in him.[59] What Christ the Son is by nature, the Christian can become by the grace of adoption:

> When the saints contemplate this divine light within themselves, seeing it by the divinizing communion of the Holy Spirit . . . then they behold the garment of their deification, their mind being glorified and filled by the grace of the Word. It is beautiful beyond measure in its splendor, just as the divinity of the Word on the mountain glorified the body attached to it with its divine light. For as the Gospel says, he gave the glory which the Father had given him to those who were obedient to him, and willed that they should be one with him and contemplate his glory.[60]

Palamas was supported by the monks of Mount Athos, and in 1341 the home (i.e., standing) synod of Constantinople gave its approval to his teaching.[61] Barlaam thereupon departed for Italy, where he had come from, but the controversy continued, animated now by Gregory Akindynos (1300?–1438), a monk who had tried to mediate between Palamas and Barlaam, but who after 1341 found himself attacking what he thought were the excesses of the victor. Akindynos could not understand the supposed difference between the essence and the energies of God, and seemed to think that the desire for *theôsis* was more akin to the fall of Lucifer than to any genuine spiritual life:

> It is the madness from which the first apostate from God suffered, and though he was the morning star, he became darkness. . . . He then transmitted it to our forefather [Adam] in return for that wondrous hope of divinity by which he had enticed him, thereby depriving him of the immortality that he had received from his Creator. Just as the present apostates [i.e., the hesychasts] do to those who put their trust in them, boasting that they have become uncreated gods themselves and promising that they will make those who obey them become the same as they are.[62]

---

[57] Ibid., 3.1.16–17.
[58] Ibid., 3.1.30.
[59] Ibid., 3.1.33.
[60] Ibid., 1.3.5. The biblical allusion is to John 17:22–24.
[61] On the details of this and the subsequent hesychast synods, see D. G. Koutsouris, *Synodoi kai theologia gia ton hêsychasmo* (Athens: Ekdosis Hieras Mêtropoleôs Thêbôn kai Lebadeias, 1997). The details of the 1341 synods (there was one held in June and another in July) are on 31–113.
[62] Gregory Akindynos, *Epistula* 49.45–52.

Palamas realized that he had not communicated his thought properly and made an effort to respond with the assurance that the saints are gods only by participation in that aspect of the divine that was available to them to participate in, that is, the divine energy. No one could know the essence of God, and it was a mistake to interpret *theôsis* in that way.[63] Another two synods were held in Constantinople in 1347, which vindicated Palamas once again, and shortly after that he became archbishop of Thessalonica.[64] The decisions taken there were ratified and made a formal part of church teaching at a further synod held in 1351, which the Eastern Orthodox churches now regard as definitive.[65] That should have been the end of the matter, but opposition continued, led now by Nicephorus Gregoras (1295?–1360), a prominent layman in Constantinople, and by Prochorus Cydones (1330?–1369?), brother of Demetrius and, like him, deeply influenced by contemporary Latin theology. They basically took up the objections made by Barlaam, and Cydones wrote at length against the synod of 1351, but they did not succeed. Palamas died in 1359, and in 1368 the home synod of Constantinople not only upheld his teaching but canonized him as a saint, an act that finally brought the controversy to an end.[66]

How should Palamas be judged? His learned contemporaries who could not accept his radical rethinking of the ancient Eastern tradition believed that he was changing the church's doctrine, while he himself always insisted that he was doing no more than looking at it from a fresh perspective. At the present time, it seems that most modern scholars side with him on this point against his detractors, but that may be largely because of the general sympathy that Palamas attracts nowadays.[67] What seems certain is that his opposition to Barlaam and those who thought like him did not derive from any deep antipathy toward Western theology. Theirs was a quarrel within the Byzantine world and can only be properly understood in that context. On the other hand, there seems to be no doubt that some of those who were defeated in the hesychast controversy were driven into the Western camp and became Latinophrones, whether they wanted to or not.[68] As a result, by the fifteenth century, denial of the *Filioque* and affirmation of hesychasm were two of the fundamental identity markers of the Eastern Orthodox churches, something that has more or less remained the case until the present day.[69]

---

[63] Gregory Palamas, *Capitula* (*Kephalaia*) 105.

[64] On the synods of February and August 1347, see Koutsouris, *Synodoi*, 151–199.

[65] See Koutsouris, *Synodoi*, 201–264 for the details.

[66] See ibid., 265–297.

[67] See, for example, Thomas L. Anastos, "Gregory Palamas's Radicalization of the Essence, Energies, and Hypostasis Model of God," *Greek Orthodox Theological Review* 38 (1993): 335–349; and David Bradshaw, *Aristotle East and West: Metaphysics and the Division of Christendom* (Cambridge: Cambridge University Press, 2004).

[68] See Plested, *Orthodox Responses*, 63–107, for some examples.

[69] It is, however, much easier for an Orthodox to distance himself from hesychasm than it would be for him to affirm the *Filioque*.

For better or for worse, it is impossible for us to read the Eastern Orthodox tradition without taking Palamas into account. What went before him is now interpreted through his eyes, and almost everything that has happened since has been touched by his influence. Modern ecumenical discussions can agree on any number of points of detail, but if they cannot reach agreement on the theology of Palamas they are using the same language to talk past one another. That is why so many Western theologians have bent over backwards to find *theôsis* in their own tradition, an enterprise that (it must be said) forces them to simplify the Eastern doctrine and distort their own heritage to make them both fit each other. To understand this properly, we must now turn to contemporary developments in the West and the great reformation of the church to which they gave rise.

The Imitation of Christ

A generation after the death of Gregory Palamas, a certain Thomas Hemerken (or Hemerlein) was born at Kempen, in the lower Rhineland, sometime around 1380. In 1392 he went to nearby Deventer to study, and remained there for seven years. During that time he came into contact with the Brethren of the Common Life, a new kind of semimonastic order started by Gerhard Groote and known for its espousal of the so-called *devotio moderna*, or new devotion. Groote wanted families to live together in community and practice the monastic virtues as much as they could. Celibacy was replaced by chastity within marriage, but otherwise much of the monastic round of prayer and work was taken over and adapted for community use. Thomas did not join the Brethren but remained a devoted follower of their principles, and his work was inspired by their ideals and example. He wrote a biography of Groote and another of Groote's colleague Florentius Radewijns (1350?–1400), which shows how deeply attached to them he was.

On leaving Deventer in 1399, Thomas went to Zwolle, where he took his vows as a monk in 1406 and remained until his death in 1471. He wrote a number of short books on the subject of devotion to Christ, but none attained the fame or the popularity of *The Imitation of Christ*, which remains a spiritual classic and is still widely read today. It is undoubtedly the most widely read medieval book and has been translated into any number of languages, but it has not often been commented on or studied, and there has been relatively little scholarly research on Thomas as a person. He remains a shadowy figure, and the uneventfulness of his life makes it difficult to write a substantial biography of him. Nevertheless, his influence on generations of Christians has been profound, and despite the changes in theological emphasis that have occurred over the centuries, his little treatise has never gone out of fashion or out of print.

The Imitation of Christ is in three books, which may have been written separately and even by different authors, but if so, they were collected and published as one. The third book can be conveniently subdivided into two, because the discourse on Holy Communion that concludes it forms a distinct unit of its own, and that practice is followed in some modern editions. The first book is a series of meditations on different aspects of the Christian life. Thomas begins by telling us that if we want to be truly enlightened and free from ignorance, we must study the life of Christ and do our best to imitate him. Studying theology for its own sake is pointless if we do not have the love of God in our hearts and do not model our life after his. To seek the kingdom of heaven by turning our backs on the desires of this world is the greatest wisdom there is. As he puts it,

> The teaching of Christ is more excellent than all the advice of the saints, and he who has his spirit will find in it a hidden manna. Now, there are many who hear the Gospel often but care little for it because they have not the spirit of Christ. . . . It is not learning that makes a man holy and just, but a virtuous life. . . . For what would it profit us to know the whole Bible by heart and the principles of all the philosophers, if we live without grace and the love of God?[70]

Thomas then reminds us that even the most learned person is ignorant of most things, and so we must approach all knowledge in humility. Our senses often deceive us, and theorizing about what we think we can see is liable to lead us astray. He who is the Truth must reveal himself to us if we are to understand him, and it is only by being reconciled to God that we shall have the simplicity of heart that we need for real understanding.

According to Thomas, everything in this life is a mixture of perfection and imperfection. If we spent as much time trying to get rid of our vices and pursue virtue as we do in solving the world's problems, we would be much happier and more content with our lives. God is not interested in what we know, but in how we apply our knowledge to the business of living. Famous teachers come and go, but the love of Christ is with us forever. In Thomas's words,

> How many there are who perish because of vain worldly knowledge and too little care for serving God. . . . He is truly great who has great charity. He is truly great who is little in his own eyes and makes nothing of the highest

[70] Thomas à Kempis, *The Imitation of Christ* 1.1. The quotations are taken from the translation by Aloysius Croft and Harold Bolton (Peabody, MA: Hendrickson, 2004).

honor. He is truly wise who looks upon all earthly things as folly that he may gain Christ. He who does God's will and renounces his own is truly very learned.[71]

In Thomas's opinion, the wise man will not yield to his impulses but will ponder things carefully in the light of God's will. Too often we are more prepared to criticize other people than we are to help them, and we must resist this temptation. We are too eager to listen to wicked gossip, and that too we must avoid. It is living a good life that makes us wise, and that wisdom will put our minds at rest.

Thomas then tells us that truth and wisdom are to be found in reading Holy Scripture. In addition to that, we should read godly literature, not because of who wrote it but because of what it contains. The identity of the author is a secondary consideration, because truth is the same wherever it comes from. In reading the Bible we should submit to its teaching in humility and not get lost in arguments about minor points of interpretation. If we approach it with the right attitude, we shall be fed by its teaching and grow in the knowledge and love of God:

> Our curiosity often impedes our reading of the Scriptures, when we wish to understand and mull over what we ought simply to read and pass by. If you would profit from it, therefore, read with humility, simplicity, and faith, and never seek a reputation for being learned. Seek willingly and listen attentively to the words of the saints; do not be displeased with the sayings of the ancients, for they were not made without purpose.[72]

Thomas reminds his readers that there are many temptations that will ensnare us if we are not careful. First, we must learn to control our desires, which can easily distort our perception of things. Second, we must learn to trust in God and not in our own possessions or achievements. The riches and beauty of this world will pass away and can be easily destroyed, and we must remember that, however good we are, we are never good enough for God. Rather than boast of ourselves, we should look for the good in others and realize how far short we come in many things.

Thomas warns us not to become overly familiar with other people, because our faults are liable to be all too evident, and those close to us will despise us for them. True intimacy should be reserved for our relationship with God, who knows our heart and sees everything that we do. In human affairs, we should

[71] Ibid., 1.3.
[72] Ibid., 1.5.

seek to be obedient to the authorities placed over us. We all prefer our own opinions to those of others, but sometimes we must sacrifice them for the sake of peace. It is always safer to seek advice and listen to it than it is to give it.

Human conversation all too often degenerates into idle chatter and should be avoided for that reason. When we have occasion to speak, we should use it to edify others so that we may all grow in grace together. Above all, we should turn away from our own whims and fancies, and seek to root out the vices that encumber us one at a time. External religious observance is not enough; we must look into our heart and pray for its cleansing. If we are hard on ourselves, then we shall be blessed with a good life. From time to time we shall encounter trouble and adversity, but that is good for the soul because it reminds us that our greatest need is for God.

Temptation is a fact of life, and we need to develop our skills in resisting it. Many people try to run away from temptation but succeed only in falling more deeply into it. We are called by God to stand up to it and fight back. It is particularly important to squash it at the beginning, because the longer we let it go on, the more easily we shall fall into its clutches. Some people are tempted more at the beginning of their Christian life, and others feel it more toward the end. For many, temptation comes and goes throughout their lives. Individuals differ in this respect, but we must never despair when we are tempted, because God knows what we are capable of, and he is preparing us for life in heaven with him. Our duty is to resist, and he will reward us with his strength:

> In temptations and trials, the progress of a man is measured; in them opportunity for merit and virtue is made more manifest. When a man is not troubled it is not hard for him to be fervent and devout, but if he bears up patiently in time of adversity, there is hope for great progress.[73]

Thomas warns us not to pass judgment on others. Many people are happy only when things go according to their plans, and they are not prepared to give way to the opinions of others. Old habits are hard to break, and no one wants to be led into the unknown. This is why we must not rely on our own intelligence but put our trust in Jesus Christ, who will draw us to himself and give us wisdom greater than any human can attain by his own efforts.

Everything we do should be done in a spirit of love. If it is not, then it is of no value, however good it may be in itself. Love for others seeks the glory of God and not self-worth. The person who is full of love will have no interest in the things of this world, but will cherish the mind and will of God above

[73] Ibid., 1.13.

all things. The faults of others are easy to see, but we must learn to bear with them, remembering that others have to put up with us. No one is perfect, which is why God tells us to bear one another's burdens and help build them up rather than tear them down.

The monastic life is a wonderful opportunity for setting the cares of the world aside and for growing in grace, but it is not easy and should not be undertaken lightly. The saints of old were frequently attacked by spiritual enemies, especially when they were alone in contemplation. A monk is exposed to the dangers of self-deception even more than most people, and must always be on guard against the attacks of Satan. Time must be set aside for prayer and devotion, and in the presence of God we must always be humble and repentant. The tears of godly sorrow will lead us to deeper communion with Christ, who alone will give us peace and contentment.

Living in solitude may cut us off from the honor and glory of this world, but this should not disturb us. Thinking of an early death is more likely to lead us to repentance than hoping for a long life. Our time on earth is short and full of trouble one way or another. We shall never be free from sin in this life, and we depend for everything on the grace of God. Death is the greatest challenge we face, and it is in the light of it that we must remember that we have been given this life in order to seek our salvation. We shall all stand before the great judgment seat of God, and then we shall understand what the privations and disciplines of this life really mean.

Thomas concludes the first book by reminding us that the time is short, and that what is past will never return. We must keep our eyes firmly fixed on where we are going, and remember that, before we know it, we shall stand in the presence of God. It is that which must guide our steps and form our understanding of what we are doing in this world. In sum,

> A fervent and diligent man is ready for all things. It is greater work to resist vices and passions than to sweat in physical toil. He who does not overcome small faults, shall fall little by little into greater ones. If you have spent the day profitably, you will always be happy at eventide. Watch over yourself, arouse yourself, warn yourself, and regardless of what becomes of others, do not neglect yourself. The more violence you do to yourself, the more progress you will make.[74]

The second book is much shorter than the first and concentrates on pursuing the inner life of the soul. Thomas begins by telling us to turn to God with

[74] Ibid., 1.25.

all our heart. When we do so, we shall find that Christ will come to us and dwell with us, because we have prepared a place for him in our lives. We must remember that he is the only guest who should be admitted into our souls, because he alone can bring us healing and reconciliation with God. The person who loves Jesus is free from the affections of this life and can rise above them to enjoy perfect peace with God.

Humility must be our watchword in all things. If other people rebuke us for our faults we should be glad, because it will teach us to be more humble. God speaks to those who are lowly of heart, and we have not made any progress in this life until we accept that we are inferior to everyone else.

It is far better to be peaceful than to be learned. If we have a desire to change the world, let us start with ourselves. We are all good at excusing our own faults but seldom find it in our heart to excuse others in the same way. We all want to live with nice people who are just like us, but find it hard to put up with those whom we dislike or find difficult. Some people live at peace with themselves and with others, and some people do not. But the child of God will be at peace with himself and try to bring it to others, because like Christ he will go out to find those who need it most.

To rise above earthly passions, it is necessary to be straightforward in our intentions and pure in our desires. Only if we are free from human passions and full of the love of God will we enjoy the inner freedom that will make it possible for us to live the Christian life as we should. Just as an iron cast into the fire loses its rust and glows with new life, so the Christian who turns completely to God will be stripped of his old nature and become a new creation in Christ.

We must not trust in ourselves or rely on our own judgment, but examine our motives carefully and do our utmost to mortify the sins of our own flesh. If we do that, we shall have no time to brood on the failings of others, but will be guided in all things by what pleases God. The essential quality of the spiritual man is a good conscience, which we can obtain only if we love and fear God with all our heart. If we do that, we shall not be disturbed by the blame we receive from others, nor shall we glory in their approval. What matters is that we are right in the sight of God, because then we shall be truly free and happy:

> He who minds neither praise nor blame possesses great peace of heart and, if his conscience is good, he will easily be contented and at peace. Praise adds nothing to your holiness, nor does blame take anything from it. You are what you are, and you cannot be said to be better than you are in God's sight. If

> you consider well what you are within, you will not care what men say about you. They look to appearances, but God looks to the heart.[75]

The person who knows what it means to love Jesus and who despises himself for the sake of the Lord is truly blessed. If we cultivate his friendship, he will never desert us but will keep us close to him even when everyone else turns away from us. If we think we have friends in this world, we are likely to be quickly deceived, but God will never let us down, and we must trust in him for everything.

If Jesus is near to us we are safe, whatever happens to us in this life. Without him we are dry and hard. Knowing how to talk to him is a great art that we have to learn very carefully. We must always be humble in his presence and obedient to what he tells us. If we are, he will love us and help us in our difficulties. When the grace of God comes into our lives we can do all things, but if it leaves us we are powerless. If we feel abandoned, then we must seek him once more, and he will turn our sorrow into joy.

It is a great thing to be able to live without human consolation, but an even greater one to endure without divine comfort either. Many great saints have had to suffer the loss of all things in this life, and they have not always felt the power of God in their lives at that time. God's comfort is a gift and does not come automatically to us when we think we need it. Sometimes we have to endure our suffering longer than we expect because God is teaching us to wait for him. He will come to us at the right time and restore us, if we have the faith to trust in him. No one is so holy that he has never felt abandoned by God at some time in his life. God subjects us to these periods of dryness so that we shall welcome his coming and draw closer to him.

To appreciate God's grace, we need patience more than comfort. God's consolation is a great thing, but too often we are ungrateful and do not give ourselves entirely to him in response. The greatest people are those who think the least of themselves. The way to keep the grace of God is to be grateful when it is given and patient when it is not, because then God will restore us to his favor and keep us humble.

Thomas goes on to say that there are always many people who love Jesus, but few who are willing to bear his cross. We are willing to follow him when times are good, but turn away when the going gets tough. Yet we are called to abandon everything for his sake, to take up our cross and follow him. It is in the cross that we find salvation and life, in the cross that we are given protection from our enemies, and in the cross that we are blessed with the strength

---

[75] Ibid., 2.6.

of mind that we need in order to attain to perfect holiness. It is only as we are crucified with Christ that we shall live, only by his life that our lives will be changed. It was in love that he was crucified for us, and in love that we must bear our cross for him. If we suffer with him, we shall also reign with him in glory, and no one who has not suffered is worthy of that eternal reward. If there were something better than suffering for our eternal salvation, Christ would have told us what it is, but this is the way he has taken and the way that he expects us to follow in order to dwell with him in his heavenly kingdom. As Thomas put it,

> No man is fit to enjoy heaven unless he has resigned himself to suffer hardship for Christ. Nothing is more acceptable to God, nothing more helpful to you on this earth than to suffer willingly for Christ. If you had to make a choice, you ought to wish rather to suffer for Christ than to enjoy many consolations, for thus you would be more like Christ and more like all the saints. Our merit and progress consist not in many pleasures and comforts but rather in enduring great afflictions and sufferings.[76]

The third book of *The Imitation of Christ* is by far the longest and comprises about two-thirds of the entire work. It takes up the theme of interior consolation and examines how God brings that to us. It repeats the main themes of the previous books and applies them directly to our lives by taking the form of a dialogue between Christ and his disciple whom he leads into an ever deeper understanding of his ways. Thomas begins with the blessedness of the soul that hears the Lord speaking to it and that receives consolation directly from him. There can be no greater consolation than listening to the voice of God speaking to us, and no greater joy than responding to that voice and going forward in sincerity and truth.

The truth speaks to us in ways that go beyond words, but when we hear it, it gives life to the word revealed to the prophets and apostles in Scripture. When Christ comes to us, he reveals himself as the one who inspired the holy men of old and shows us what the true meaning of their testimony is. When we understand that, we must write his words on our heart and meditate on them, so that we shall be prepared for the struggle against temptation that we shall soon be called to face.

Our life with God must be lived in humility and truth, if we are to experience his love as we should. Thomas takes his cue here from 1 Corinthians 13, emphasizing the need for patient endurance. At all times we must remember

[76] Ibid., 2.12.

the importance of humility and never presume on the grace of God. The less we think of ourselves and the more we think of him, the better it will be. Everything that happens to us is ultimately for our good, and if we put God first in our lives we shall never be disappointed or distracted from our love. Our own desires merely get in the way of God's love for us, and we must do all we can to suppress them.

The child of God will obey the voice of Christ, whether he understands its purpose or not. God's plan is often hidden from our eyes, and we must trust him to know what he is doing. We should seek comfort in God alone and cast all our cares on him, because he knows what is best for us and will bring it to pass in his good time. When we are called to suffer in this world, we should bear it patiently and remember that it is given to us so that we may learn to be patient. Above all, we must recognize that we cannot live in our own strength alone, but must rely on him for everything. There is nothing in the world greater than Christ, and we must keep him always in the forefront of our thoughts.

We must also learn to count our blessings, which are always very great, even when we are called to suffer. If we are humble and put others before ourselves, we shall have peace of mind and be greatly blessed. Rather than worry needlessly about things that do not matter, we must put our trust in God and find true peace of mind in him. Prayer, not study, is the way to true liberation, and self-love is the greatest barrier to fellowship with God.

Those who live as God wants them to will be slandered by others and subjected to trouble in this life, but when that happens we must call on him for assistance and he will hear us. Sometimes these things are sent for precisely that purpose. We must look for the Creator by letting go of all created things. Self-denial and renunciation are the keys to true happiness. If our souls are restless, they will find their rest in him and nowhere else. Those who love God will find all their desires fulfilled in him.

Temptations are inevitable in this life, and attacks from other people are common. Only by dying to ourselves can we be free of such things. We must manage our affairs as best we can, but ultimately trust in God for protection. We should not spend too much time worrying about our business on earth, because there is no good in us and we have nothing to boast about in ourselves. We must learn to despise the honors of this life and not to trust in worldly knowledge or outward things. God looks on the heart, and he will take care of us. We should not believe what other people say because they may easily be mistaken, and when we are abused we must trust in God.

We shall be called to endure many things in this life, but for the sake of eternity we must bear them all. Everything will be revealed in the light of eternity, and then we shall understand God's purposes for us. There is nothing to compare with eternal life, and that is what we should strive for. If we are deserted and left alone, we should put our trust in God, who will save us. If we cannot do great things, then we should do little ones and be content with the privilege of being able to serve in a humble capacity.

The disciple of Christ must not claim divine consolation as a right, but consider himself worthy only of punishment. God's grace is not given to those whose focus is on earthly things, but to those who look toward heaven. Nature and grace pull us in opposite directions; nature is corrupt, but God's grace is able to overcome it. We must therefore deny ourselves and take up the cross of Christ, but not be too worried if we fail to follow him as we ought to. God sees the intentions of our heart, and his judgments are beyond our understanding. Our duty is to put our trust in him, and he will reward us as he has promised to do. The voice of the disciple concludes with a prayer:

> My God, the Father of mercies, to you I look, in you I trust. Bless and sanctify my soul with heavenly benediction, so that it may become your holy dwelling and the seat of your eternal glory. And in this temple of your dignity let nothing be found that might offend your majesty. In your great goodness, and in the multitude of your mercies, look upon me and listen to the prayer of your poor servant exiled from you in the region of the shadow of death. Protect and preserve the soul of your poor servant among the many dangers of this corruptible life, and direct him by your accompanying grace, through the ways of peace, to the land of everlasting light.[77]

The last eighteen chapters, which may be separated into a fourth book, are still in dialogue form, and constitute an extended meditation on Holy Communion. To approach the Lord's Table, the first requirement is reverence. In the sacrament of Holy Communion, God shows how great his goodness and love toward us are, and it is in gratitude for that that we should approach the feast. Furthermore, we should come to the Table often, because many great blessings are given to those who receive the gifts of Christ worthily.

The sacrament is a gift of God to his people, and those called to administer it must show themselves to be worthy of their high calling. Before approaching the Lord's Supper we must examine our consciences and determine to amend our lives. We must remember that Christ's offering of himself for us is also our offering; it is in and through him that we are saved. We should

[77] Ibid., 3.59.

therefore offer ourselves and all that we have to God, praying for others as we do so.

We should not abstain from Holy Communion without good reason, because to do so is to neglect the grace of God. We must prepare ourselves with great care before receiving the sacrament, and desire to be united with Christ in it. To do this rightly, humility and self-denial are essential. We must not be afraid to reveal our needs to Christ and to seek his grace. If we have a burning desire to receive him, he will come to us as he has promised. Finally, we should not spend our time examining what the sacrament is or trying to define it precisely, but imitate Christ in humility and submit our own understanding to him in faith. Human reason is weak and can be deceived, but the believer will never be abandoned and will enjoy the wonder of things that are beyond the power of human words to explain. In the words of the disciple,

> When I think how some devout persons come to your holy sacrament with the greatest devotion and love, I am frequently ashamed and confused that I approach your altar and the table of Holy Communion so coldly and indifferently; that I remain so dry and devoid of heartfelt affection; that I am not completely inflamed in your presence, O my God, nor so strongly drawn and attracted as many devout persons who, in their great desire for communion and intense heart love, could not restrain their tears but longed from the depths of their souls and bodies to embrace you, the fountain of life.[78]

Here more clearly than anywhere else we see how souls on fire with the Spirit of God were seeking comfort in the ministrations of a church that in many respects was cold and indifferent to their needs. Priests who said Mass by rote or wanted money for their services, bishops who were absent from their sees and saw no need to exercise spiritual discipline, let alone practice it themselves—men like that were asking for trouble from those who felt cheated by an institution that was supposed to bring them closer to God rather than drive them further away from him. Theologians were tied up in knots about the precise nature of the consecrated elements, a debate that Thomas evidently regarded as a waste of time. The Protestant Reformation had many causes, but the greatest and most enduring of them was the desire to know Christ and to make him known, a desire that burned nowhere more brightly than in the writings attributed to the humble monk Thomas à Kempis and his longing to imitate Christ in every aspect of his life.

[78] Ibid., 4.14 (3.73).

21

The Mystical Body of Christ

The Gift of Righteousness

How central to the thinking of the Protestant Reformers was the work of the Holy Spirit? It is one of the oddities of modern theology that this question has seldom been asked, let alone answered, in any direct or comprehensive way. So obscure had it become by the mid-twentieth century that the Danish theologian Regin Prenter (1907–1990) felt obliged to write a book to explain Luther's teaching on the subject because (as he put it in his introduction) no one knew what to say about it![1] Prenter pointed out that although Luther used traditional Augustinian terminology to express his ideas, his own experience of God led him to modify its content considerably. Where Augustine had conceived of the work of the Spirit in terms of an infusion of divine love (*caritas*) that elicits a corresponding human affection, which the Spirit then leads upward until the believer achieves a perfect union with God, Luther saw the Holy Spirit as the life-giver who enters the believer in order to put the old man to death and give him the indwelling presence of the risen Christ in his heart. In his own words,

> The Spirit, the divine grace, grants strength and power to the heart; indeed, he creates a new man who takes pleasure in God's commandments and who does everything he should do with joy. The [indwelling] spirit can never be contained in any letter. It cannot be written like the law, with ink, on stone or in books. Instead, it is inscribed only in the heart as a living writing of the Holy Spirit. . . . all who believe in Christ receive God's grace and the Holy Spirit, whereby all sins are forgiven, all laws fulfilled, and they become God's children and are eternally blessed.[2]

[1] Regin Prenter, *Spiritus Creator: Luther's Concept of the Holy Spirit* (Philadelphia: Muhlenberg, 1953). Originally published as *Spiritus Creator. Studier i Luthers teologi* (Copenhagen: Samlerens Forlag, 1946). There is also a German translation by Walter Thiemann, *Spiritus Creator. Studien zu Luthers Theologie* (Munich: Kaiser Verlag, 1954), that contains notes and references to Luther and to modern Lutheran theologians that were left out in the English translation.

[2] Martin Luther, *Concerning the Letter and the Spirit*, in in Jaroslav Pelikan and Helmut T. Lehmann, eds., *Luther's Works*, 55 vols. (St. Louis: Concordia, vols. 1–30; and Philadelphia: Fortress, vols. 31–55, 1955–1986), 39:182–183. The work dates from 1521.

Prenter's thesis has been criticized within the Lutheran world because he preferred a systematic approach that neglected the historical development of Luther's thought, and it has to be said that Prenter's work has not made much of an impression on Luther studies in general. But when it has been pursued, Prenter's view has been confirmed and developed further.[3] One of the benefits of the recent attempts to find a concept of *theôsis* in the Reformers has been to revive an awareness that they were deeply concerned with the third person of the Trinity and that the relative neglect of the subject in the past two hundred years is an aberration that has distorted subsequent appreciation of their theology.[4]

Today it is generally agreed that justification by faith alone was the point on which Luther said the church stands if it preaches the doctrine, or falls if it does not.[5] But although this was a prominent theme of his as early as his first series of lectures on Galatians (1519), it did not become the center of his teaching until some time later. In the Augsburg Confession of 1530, for example, which became the defining statement of what a (Lutheran) Protestant was, the doctrine of justification was treated somewhat cursorily:

> . . . men cannot be justified before God by their own strength, merits, or works, but are justified freely by faith on account of Christ, when they believe that they have been received into grace and that their sins have been forgiven on account of Christ, who by his death has made satisfaction for our sins. God reckons this faith as righteousness in his sight (Rom. 3:4).[6]

There is no further elaboration of the theme and, in particular, no discussion of the place of good works *after* justification. It was only in Luther's magisterial second series of lectures on Galatians, in 1535, that the subject would get a full airing, after which it would occupy a more significant place in the confessions of the Protestant churches. This can be seen from the confession of faith that resulted from the negotiations between the Wittenberg theologians

[3] See, for example, Pekka Kärkkäinen, *Luthers trinitarische Theologie des Heiligen Geistes* (Mainz: Verlag Philipp von Zabern, 2005).

[4] The so-called "Finnish school" of Lutheranism is a good example of this neglect. See Carl E. Braaten and Robert W. Jenson, eds., *Union with Christ: The New Finnish Interpretation of Luther* (Grand Rapids, MI: Eerdmans, 1998) for a selection of their writings.

[5] Luther is usually quoted as having spoken of the *articulus stantis aut cadentis ecclesiae*, but this is a seventeenth-century paraphrase of his actual words, which were *isto articulo stante, stat ecclesia; ruente, ruit ecclesia*, written in a commentary on Psalm 130:4. See the Latin text in his *Commentarium in XV Psalmos graduum*, in *Gesammelte Werke* 40/3.352.3.

[6] *Augsburg Confession* 4. Text in Gerald L. Bray, ed., *Documents of the English Reformation*, 2nd ed. (Cambridge: James Clarke, 2004), 607. For a good introduction to this and other Lutheran confessional documents, see Charles P. Arand, Robert Kolb and James A. Nestingen, eds., *The Lutheran Confessions: History and Theology of the Book of Concord* (Minneapolis: Fortress, 2012).

and the ambassadors of King Henry VIII of England in 1535–1536, where it was treated at much greater length than it had been before.[7]

In the Wittenberg Articles, justification by faith was placed in the context of penitence, which was analyzed into three consecutive parts: contrition, faith, and (new) obedience. Contrition was defined as a conviction of sin so deep that it drives the sinner to despair of finding salvation by his own efforts. It is at that point that the message of the gospel comes to rescue and restore him:

> By this faith [in Christ] terrified consciences are lifted up and hearts are made peaceful and set free from the terrors of sin and death, as Paul says, "Being justified by faith we have peace with God."[8] For if, to God's judgment against sin, we were to oppose our worthiness and our merits as a satisfaction for sin, the promise of reconciliation would become uncertain for us and our consciences would be driven to despair, as Paul says, "The law works wrath."[9] What ought to be offered for sin is Christ's merit and the free promise of mercy which is given for his sake . . .[10]

The Articles then go on to add,

> This faith, which comforts terrified hearts, is engendered and strengthened by the gospel and by absolution, which applies the promises of grace to individuals. . . . Therefore justification, which comes about through faith in the manner described, is renewal and regeneration.[11]

Having dealt with the first two parts of penitence, the Wittenberg Articles then expound what Luther called the "new obedience" of the Christian, that is to say, the place and value of good works in the life of the believer. After stating at great length that not even the most devout saints can earn God's favor by their behavior, the Articles continue in this vein:

> Since renewal occurs in justification, this new life is obedience to God. Therefore justification cannot be retained unless this incipient obedience is retained. . . . The value of this incipient obedience is great, for although it is imperfect, nevertheless, because the people concerned are in Christ, this obedience is reckoned to be a kind of fulfillment of the law and is righteous-

[7] See *The Wittenberg Articles of 1536*, 4–5, in Bray, *Documents of the English Reformation*, 123–137. These Articles were probably written by Philipp Melanchthon and approved by Luther, but what happened to them after that is unclear. Most of them disappeared from view and were not rediscovered until 1905, so their witness is seldom brought to bear in discussion of the subject.

[8] Rom. 5:1.

[9] Rom. 4:15.

[10] *Wittenberg Articles* 4. Text in Bray, *Documents of the English Reformation*, 125.

[11] Ibid., 126.

> ness, as Scripture often calls it. . . . This should not be understood as if we obtain remission of sins and reconciliation on account of our works, but the meaning is that both righteousnesses are necessary. First, faith is necessary, for by it we are justified before God, . . . and then another righteousness is necessary and owed, the righteousness of works and of a good conscience.[12]

Here we find another theme that was prominent in Luther's teaching—the existence of two kinds of "righteousness," which Luther distinguished by calling them "passive" and "active." Passive righteousness could be received only by faith in Christ, and was therefore unique to believers. Active righteousness came from human works, and by its nature was restricted to the affairs of this world. It could also be obtained by unbelievers, who would inevitably use it to justify themselves. As Luther expressed it in his preface to his second series of lectures on Galatians, which he wrote at about the same time as the Wittenberg Articles were being composed:

> My teaching is that there is a clear distinction between two kinds of righteousness, the active and the passive, so that morality must not be confused with faith, works must not take the place of grace, and secular society must not prevail over religion. Both kinds of righteousness are necessary, but each of them has its limits. Christian righteousness applies to the new man and the righteousness of the law applies to the old man, who is born of flesh and blood. . . . In a Christian, the law should rule only over the flesh and not over the conscience. Give the law its due, but do not let it exceed its jurisdiction.[13]

It was the passive righteousness that validated the active equivalent, because only a righteousness received from Christ could have justifying power. From beginning to end, Luther's constant refrain was that we can do nothing to save ourselves, but must be united to Christ so that his righteousness can be extended ("imputed") to us. Active righteousness is valid only insofar as we are united to Christ, with his righteousness at work in us, because even after we have been justified we are still sinners.

This much has been generally agreed by Luther scholars of all persuasions, but it was precisely at this point that Prenter reminded his colleagues that Luther had taught that union with Christ, and the active righteousness that resulted from it, was the work of the Holy Spirit and not that of the regenerate believer. To ignore the work of the Spirit was to turn the gospel into a new

[12] *Wittenberg Articles* 5. Text in Bray, *Documents of the English Reformation*, 135.

[13] Martin Luther, *Second Lectures on Galatians*, the preface. The text is in Pelikan and Lehmann, *Luther's Works*, 26:7.

law, which Prenter believed many of his colleagues had inadvertently done. Evidence to support Prenter's contention can be found in the Wittenberg Articles, which state,

> Since the Holy Spirit is effective, he also creates new promptings in our hearts, which assent to God's law, *viz.*, faith, the love of God, the fear of God, hatred of sin, the determination not to sin, and other good fruits, in accordance with the passage: "I will put my law in their hearts."[14]

This was taken up and repeated in the Ten Articles of 1536, which the English ambassadors to Wittenberg composed on their return home, and which became the first confessional statement of the reformed Church of England:

> God necessarily requireth of us to do good works commanded by him; and that not only outward and civil works, but also the inward and spiritual motions and graces of the Holy Ghost; that is to say, to dread and fear God, to love God, to have firm confidence and trust in God, to invocate and call upon God, to have patience in all adversities, to hate sin, and to have certain purpose and will not to sin again, and such other like motions and virtues. . . . We must not only do outward and civil good works, but also we must have these foresaid inward spiritual motions, consenting and agreeable to the law of God.[15]

These statements prove that by 1536 the work of the Holy Spirit in justification was not only being clearly articulated but had become an important point of Protestant doctrine. The testimony of the Ten Articles is especially significant because the English theologians who drafted them diluted or omitted those parts of the Wittenberg Articles which would not have been acceptable to the very conservative King Henry VIII. Justification by faith alone was one of the few Lutheran teachings that they clung to without modification, and their willingness to emphasize the inner work of the Holy Spirit in achieving it is impressive testimony to its importance. The significance of this is even greater when we reflect that subsequent Anglican statements of faith either glossed it over or omitted it entirely. *The First Book of Homilies*, which was produced in 1547 as an extended explanation of Protestant doctrine, says nothing about it, nor do the Articles of Religion, apart from a backhanded reference in the article on works before justification, which tells us that "works done before the grace of Christ, and the inspiration of his Spirit, are not pleasant to God . . ."[16]

[14] Article 4; see Bray, *Documents of the English Reformation*, 126. The biblical quotation is from Jer. 31:33.
[15] Article 5; see Bray, *Documents of the English Reformation*, 171.
[16] Article 12 of 1552 and 13 of 1563/1571; see Bray, *Documents of the English Reformation*, 292.

Given that in most respects the later Anglican confessions are greatly expanded versions of the Ten Articles, it is surprising to see that there was a retreat from the bold statement about the work of the Holy Spirit that appeared in 1536, even though it was never denied or withdrawn. This relative deemphasizing of the Spirit may have been due to the growing influence of spiritualizing antinomians, who rejected the boundaries set by the Word of God and proclaimed a freedom of the Spirit that all too easily slipped into disorder and heresy, but it may also have been the effect of the relatively strong influence of Erasmus, which operated as a counterweight to Luther in the minds of the English reformers. Whatever the case, it has to be said that there was a noticeable lack of attention paid to the Holy Spirit in the classical Anglican formularies, which stands in sharp contrast to their Lutheran and Reformed equivalents elsewhere.

The importance of the work of the Holy Spirit in justification becomes clearer when we realize that, for Luther, the Christian is not someone who has ceased from sinning, which is impossible in this life, but someone who has been made to realize what his true spiritual state is. Luther made that point forcefully in his comments on Galatians 3:6, which summarize his teaching nicely:

> The Christian is righteous and a sinner at the same time (*simul iustus et peccator*), holy and profane, an enemy of God and a child of God. Only those who understand the true meaning of justification will understand this apparent paradox.[17]

"The true meaning of justification" was now to be the battleground and the cause of irreparable division between the followers of Luther and those who remained loyal to Rome. Protestants came in different shapes and sizes, but on this point they were all agreed. When the Roman authorities finally got together to decide what to do about them, justification was one of the first subjects to which they turned their attention, thereby lending additional credibility to Luther's claim that it was this doctrine that would make or break the church. In 1545 the pope summoned a council to meet at Trent, an Italian city in the domains of the Holy Roman emperor, and so felt to be "neutral" territory.[18] At its sixth session (January 13, 1547), nearly a year after Luther's death, the council issued a long statement on justification, making its position vis-à-vis the Protestants abundantly clear.[19]

[17] Luther, *Second Lectures on Galatians*, in Pelikan and Lehmann, *Luther's Works*, 26:94.
[18] Trent remained Austrian until 1919, when it was given to Italy following the collapse of the Austro-Hungarian empire in the First World War.
[19] The decree on justification, with its accompanying canons, is in *Conciliorum oecumenicorum decreta* (Bologna: Istituto per le Scienze Religiose, 1973), 671–681.

In some respects, the Council of Trent agreed with Luther. It anathematized anyone who said that it was possible to be justified by his own works, or that people could choose to be saved or to love God without the help of God's grace.[20] But having said that, it then denied the key elements of Luther's teaching. It claimed that God's grace was given to enable a person to exercise his free will by cooperating with him in order to obtain his justification, and it specifically rejected the concept of "passive" righteousness.[21] It went on from there to reject Luther's concept of the bondage of the will and the Protestant belief that good works done before justification are by nature sinful.[22] The idea that faith alone justified the wicked was condemned, as was Luther's assertion that it is only by Christ's righteousness that we can be justified.[23] Trent further denied that anyone could have assurance of salvation based on justification by faith alone, and rejected Luther's contention that even those who are justified and in a state of grace cannot fulfill the commandments of God.[24]

On occasion, it is clear that the fathers of the council misunderstood Protestant teaching, as when they gave the impression that Luther had taught that the Ten Commandments do not apply to Christians, which was manifestly false.[25] They seem to have had no idea of the new obedience, or of its importance in Protestant teaching, because many of the remaining canons were directed against those who thought that good works performed *after* justification were unnecessary or harmful.[26] The gist of Trent's teaching is summed up in the following canon:

> If anyone says that the good works of a justified person are the gifts of God in such a way that they are not also the good merits of the one justified; or that the justified person does not, by the good works done by him through the grace of God and the merit of Jesus Christ (whose living member he is), truly merit an increase in grace, eternal life, and (so long as he dies in grace) the acquisition of his own eternal life and also an increase in glory: let him be anathema.[27]

From the standpoint of the Council of Trent, to be united to Christ was to be set free to cooperate with him, not least in working off the penalties incurred for sin both before and after the reception of grace. Trent validated and

[20] Canons of Trent 1–3.
[21] Ibid., 4.
[22] Ibid., 5, 7.
[23] Ibid., 9–14.
[24] Ibid., 15–18.
[25] Ibid., 19.
[26] Ibid., 21–26.
[27] Ibid., 32.

reinforced the penitential system that had come under such strong attack from the Protestants; it closed the door to any reform of the church that would have taken it in a Lutheran direction. Luther understood that to change the doctrine would be to change the church along with it, which at first he did not want to do and did not think was necessary. He continued to believe that the church was the body of Christ, who worked in and through it only, and it was only slowly that he and his followers came to realize that Christ's body was not to be found in the church of Rome as it then existed.

Luther died just as the Council of Trent was starting, and so he never had the chance to respond to it. It was a different matter with the next generation, though, and in John Calvin's works we find the whole question set out in a clear, concise, and logical way. Calvin made a clear distinction between the work of Christ, accomplished for the salvation of the elect by the sacrifice that he presented to the Father, and the work of the Holy Spirit, by whom believers are united to Christ. In particular, Calvin stressed that the Holy Spirit comes to believers in and through Christ, to whom he has been given in his office as Mediator of the new covenant. In other words, the Holy Spirit comes to believers not just as the Spirit of the Son of God but also as the Spirit of the man Jesus Christ, in whom he dwells "in a special way, so that he might separate us from the world and unite us to him in the hope of an eternal inheritance."[28] Calvin stated this quite explicitly when he wrote,

> The Spirit is called the Spirit of Christ, not only because the eternal Word of God is united with the Father and the Spirit, but also because of his office of Mediator, because if he had not been endued with the energy of the Spirit, he would have come to us in vain.[29]

Next, Calvin went on to say that giving faith to believers was the Spirit's first and most important work. Quoting a number of New Testament passages that support this view, he culminated his exposition by a short discussion of Christ's words to his disciples before his crucifixion, when he promised to send them "the Spirit of truth, whom the world cannot receive."[30] As Calvin explained,

> Christ assigned to the Spirit, as his proper work, to bring to remembrance the things which he had taught in words, for it would be pointless to offer light to the blind if the Spirit of knowledge did not open the intellectual eye.

[28] Calvin, *Institutio* 3.1.2. On this subject, see Mark A. Garcia, *Life in Christ: Union with Christ and Twofold Grace in Calvin's Theology* (Milton Keynes: Paternoster, 2008).
[29] Calvin, *Institutio* 3.1.2.
[30] John 14:17.

> Thus he himself may properly be called the key by which the treasures of the kingdom of heaven are unlocked, and his illumination is the eye of the mind that allows us to see . . .[31]

After discoursing at great length on the nature of faith as a divine gift, and refuting a number of errors that had crept into the teaching of the medieval church, Calvin finally came to the central question of justification, for which the chapters on faith were an obvious preparation. In eight substantial chapters, followed by a further one on Christian liberty, Calvin expounded the doctrine of justification by faith alone, ignoring the objections raised against Luther's teaching by the Council of Trent, but giving full rein to his opposition to Andreas Osiander, a Lutheran theologian who, in Calvin's words, taught "that we are not justified by the mere grace of the Mediator, and that righteousness is not simply or entirely offered to us in his person, but that we are made partakers of divine righteousness when God is united to us in his essence."[32] Calvin, along with Melanchthon and other Lutheran theologians, opposed this teaching on the ground that it misrepresented what the New Testament taught about the work of the Holy Spirit in the life of the believer. Using the image of the sun, which is both light and heat, Calvin argued that just as we cannot say that the earth is warmed by the sun's light or illuminated by its heat, so we cannot confuse the two aspects of God's grace at work in our lives. Justification and sanctification are inseparable, but they are not identical. The Father accepts us into his presence thanks to the intercession of the Son our Mediator, but he gives us his Spirit of adoption so that we may be re-formed in his image.[33]

This distinction is often referred to as the "double grace" that comes from the union of the believer with Christ. As long as Luther was alive, controversy over this was avoided, but after his death (on February 18, 1546) his followers advanced different interpretations of Luther's teaching on the subject of justification and sanctification. Osiander was one of the first to take a public position on the matter, and was perceived by most of his fellow Lutherans as an extremist who regarded justification by faith alone as a declaration by the Father that the elect have been accepted in and by the sacrifice of the Son for their sins. Sanctification was the logical result of that, and was signified espe-

[31] Calvin, *Institutio* 3.1.4.

[32] Ibid., 3.11.5. See Garcia, *Life in Christ*, 43–45, 198–252. On the Osiandrist controversy, see Timothy J. Wengert, *Defending Faith: Lutheran Response to Andreas Osiander's Doctrine of Justification 1551–1559* (Tübingen: Mohr Siebeck, 2012).

[33] Calvin, *Institutio* 3.11.6. Philipp Melanchthon used the same metaphor in the same context. See his postil on John 16:5, intended for the fourth Sunday after Easter, in *Corpus Reformatorum*, ed. G. Baum, E. Cunitz, and E. Reuss (Braunschweig: C. A. Schwetschke und Sohn, 1863–1900), XXIV:815.

cially in the Eucharist, where the believer partook of the body and blood of Christ that were present "in, with, and under" the forms of bread and wine. Luther's teaching that the body of Christ was "ubiquitous" made this interpretation possible, because the ascended and glorified Christ could be present, along with his human nature, wherever he chose.

Osiander took that view to its logical conclusion, and to the consternation of his fellow Lutherans taught that in the Eucharist (and more generally in union with Christ) the believer is essentially one with him, partaking of his nature in a real and direct way. Ironically, Calvin was perceived to be very close to Osiander in his teaching, because he too proclaimed a real union with Christ that was not just a forensic declaration of righteousness but a genuine transformation of the believer. The difference was that Calvin insisted that this transformation did not come about by a union of natures or essences, but by the indwelling of the Holy Spirit, who made the believer a child of God and opened up the way to his receiving all the benefits that accompanied that status. For that reason it was not Christ who was present "in, with, and under" the species of bread and wine, but the Holy Spirit who used those material things to enter into spiritual communion with those who received them by faith.[34]

The confusion, as Calvin saw it, came about because of a wrong understanding of faith, which is the designated means to an end which is union with Christ, but not the end in itself. Calvin compared faith to a jar of clay in which gold (justification) is deposited: it is not the faith, which is always weak and inadequate, that counts, but the gift that it brings which is our real treasure and salvation.[35] The clay jar in which this treasure is enclosed stands, first of all, for the human nature of the incarnate Son, and second, for us who share that human nature. Jesus was made righteous for us not because of his divinity, but because his human nature was transformed by the indwelling presence of God. If he were righteous by virtue of his divine nature he would not be our Savior, because we would be incapable of sharing that righteousness in any way. But just as the divine righteousness was imputed to his human nature, so it is also imputed to us by the indwelling presence of the Holy Spirit. We remain jars of clay and can never be anything other than that, but the divine Spirit inside those jars works his regenerating power in us so that we become by grace something that we could never be (or

[34] Garcia, *Life in Christ*, 208–252, has a full discussion of this subject and points out that it was in the controversies with Osiander and other Lutherans during the 1550s that Calvin developed his teaching about the "double grace" to the fullest. Garcia also maintains that Calvin's sense of distinctiveness from the Lutherans was shared (and probably inspired) by Peter Martyr Vermigli (1499–1562), with whom he corresponded on the subject. According to Garcia, the Osiander conflict was symptomatic of a deeper difference between Calvin and Vermigli (on the one hand) and the Lutherans (on the other) which soon led to a parting of the ways between the two main Protestant groups.

[35] Calvin, *Institutio* 3.11.7.

become) by nature. After a lengthy discussion of the subject, Calvin summed it all up as follows:

> When God reconciles us to himself by the intervention of the righteousness of Christ, and bestowing on us the free pardon of sins, regards us as righteous, his goodness is simultaneously conjoined with mercy, so that he dwells in us by his Holy Spirit, by whose work the lusts of our flesh are daily mortified and we are sanctified, which means that we are consecrated to the Lord for purity of life and our hearts are trained to obey the law.[36]

Calvin contrasted this with the teaching of the medieval Scholastics, whom he groups together as one. He began by saying that there was no difference at all between them and the Reformed as far as the basic principle was concerned, since they both agreed that sinners are freely delivered from condemnation and receive justification by the forgiveness of their sins. But he went on to point out that,

> under the term "justification" the Scholastics include the renovation by which the Spirit forms us anew for obedience to the law, and in describing the righteousness of the regenerate man, they maintain that once he is reconciled to God in Christ, he is considered righteous because of his good works, and is accepted [by God] on that basis.[37]

In that subtle way, the Scholastics transferred the work of Christ seated at the right hand of the Father (as our Mediator) to the work of the Holy Spirit dwelling in our hearts by faith, thereby making our salvation depend not on Christ's perfect mediation but on our imperfect reception of spiritual power. This was nothing less than saying that we have lost our salvation altogether, since our inadequate response could never satisfy the demands of God's righteousness.[38] Calvin rounded off his discussion of justification with a chapter on Christian liberty, which he admitted was implicit in everything he had already said on the subject, but he felt that it was based on particular principles that he ought to bring together for the sake of clarity. Oddly enough, he never mentioned the Holy Spirit by name in this summary, but it is clear from reading it that the whole chapter presupposed the indwelling presence of the Spirit in the heart of the believer. As Calvin stated the matter,

> It must be carefully observed that Christian liberty is in every respect a spiritual matter, which consists of giving peace to trembling consciences, whether

[36] Ibid., 3.14.9.
[37] Ibid., 3.14.11.
[38] Ibid., 3.11.12–13.

> they are anxious and upset about whether they have obtained the forgiveness of sins, or whether their imperfect works . . . are pleasing to God, or whether they are worried about doing things that do not matter one way or the other.[39]

Here we see what for Calvin was central: the role of the conscience in forming the Christian life. In spiritual matters, the conscience is set free from the need to obey the external pattern of the law, because it is impossible to earn salvation by works. But in temporal things, the believer is bound by his conscience to obey the laws of the state because the state has been established by God for the purpose of civil government. No Christian has the right to appeal to his spiritual freedom as an excuse for breaking the laws that promote peace, order, and good government on earth.[40]

Calvin defined the conscience as knowledge fortified by conviction. A believer is one who knows what is right in intellectual terms (which Calvin called "science") but who is also persuaded by the Spirit of God that he must do what is right and seek forgiveness for his sin if he fails. Since even the most law-abiding person will fail to achieve perfection in this, the conscience acts as a spiritual watchdog that polices the believer's behavior, accuses him of falling short, and drives him to Christ for reconciliation and justification. It is the ultimate work of the Holy Spirit, who bears witness with our spirit that we are children of God.[41] It was also the foundation on which the next generation of Reformed theologians, and in particular the Puritans, were to build their own distinctive teaching about assurance of salvation and having peace with God.

The True Church

The Reformers and their Catholic counterparts both believed that the church was the body of Christ in and through which he now works in the world. That was why they were so disturbed by the corrupt state in which they found it and were determined to purify it as much as they could. Only gradually did they realize that the incarnational theology that undergirded the medieval doctrine of the church was inadequate and had to be supplemented, if not replaced, by an understanding of the church as the creation of the Holy Spirit. That led them to put more weight on the "invisible" church and less on the visible institution as the authentic manifestation of God at work in the world, although this shift in

[39] Ibid., 3.19.9. This passage was carried over from the first edition of the *Institutio* in 1536, which shows how fundamental it was to Calvin's thought. See Peter Barth, ed., *Ioannis Calvini opera selecta*, 5 vols. (Munich: Chr. Kaiser Verlag, 1926), 1:228. For a discussion of Calvin's view of Christian liberty, see George H. Tavard, *The Starting Point of Calvin's Theology* (Grand Rapids, MI: Eerdmans, 2000), 154–167.

[40] Calvin, *Institutio* 3.19.15.

[41] Rom. 8:16.

emphasis was a slow process and was imperfectly realized. But Luther did not hesitate to state the principle that the true church was made holy, not by being in communion with Rome, but by being filled with the Spirit:

> Christian holiness, or the holiness common to Christendom, is found where the Holy Spirit gives people faith in Christ and thus sanctifies them,[42] that is, he renews heart, soul, body, work, and conduct, inscribing the commandments of God not on tables of stone, but in hearts of flesh.[43] Or if I may speak plainly, he imparts true knowledge of God . . . so that those whom he enlightens with true faith can resist all heresies, overcome all false ideas and errors, and thus remain pure in faith. . . . He also bestows strength and comforts timid, despondent, weak consciences against the accusation and turmoil of sin. . . . He also imparts true fear and love of God . . .[44]

How new was this perspective? The identification of the visible church with the kingdom of God on earth had certainly not gone unchallenged in medieval times. Perhaps the first person to call it into question, if somewhat inadvertently, was Joachim da Fiore (1135?–1202), an Italian monk known for his mystical writings and apocalyptic predictions.[45] Joachim believed that the existing order was so thoroughly corrupt that only a miracle could save it. To his mind, the problem was that the secular rulers of his time, and notably Emperor Frederick II (1194–1250), were the Antichrist foretold in Scripture. To combat this menace, Joachim prophesied that a great pope would arise, cleanse the church of its sins, and repel the Antichrist once and for all.

In Joachim's day it was still possible to believe that the papacy would be the agent of renewal, but a century after his death things appeared very different. The corruption and the Antichrist were still there, but by the mid-fourteenth century it was the pope who was in the dock. The "Babylonian captivity" of the papacy in Avignon (1305–1377) was seen by many as an abuse of the institution, and the high-handed behavior of Pope John XXII (1316–1334) was especially resented. The apocalyptic stream had gone underground but it was still around and greatly feared, because no one could tell when it might erupt or what harm that would cause. Would-be reformers of the church like John Wyclif and Jan Hus were dogged by this. They preached the need for spiritual change only to discover that others interpreted their message as a call to overturn the established order in both church and state.

---

[42] Acts 15:9.
[43] 2 Cor. 3:3.
[44] Luther, *On the Councils and the Church*, 3, in Pelikan and Lehmann, *Luther's Works*, 41:145–146.
[45] See Marjorie Reeves, *Joachim of Fiore and the Prophetic Future* (London: SPCK, 1976).

On the eve of the Reformation and among the first generation of Protestants, Joachim's visions were not only known but were often cited as evidence that the pope was the Antichrist. It so happened that when King Richard I (1189–1199) went on crusade he wintered at Messina in 1190–1191, during which time he met Joachim personally. Joachim apparently discoursed at great length about the future of the world, and concluded that the seventh beast, who would be the last and greatest Antichrist, had already been born at Rome.[46] Joachim thought of him as a secular ruler, but of course it was easy for the Reformers to adapt his remarks to the later development of the Antichrist tradition, which they did not hesitate to read back into the founder of the myth. John Bale (1495–1563) had this to say:

> When King Richard was yet in the land of Palestine, he sent to the isle of Calabria for Abbas Ioachim, of whose famous learning and wonderful prophecies he had heard much. Among other demands he asked him of Antichrist, what time and in what place he should chiefly appear. Antichrist (saith he) is already born in the city of Rome and will set himself yet higher in the seat apostolic. I thought (said the king) that he should have been born in Antioch or in Babylon. . . . Not so, saith Joachim . . .[47]

Peasants' revolts, apocalyptic prophecies, and general social breakdown became a feature of most movements for reform down to the Reformation and even later. Seventeenth-century England, for example, saw not only an epic struggle for power between the conservative establishment and the Puritans, but a series of outbreaks of radicalism that offered visions of alternative societies.

The Reformation had scarcely broken out when different people started proclaiming their own vision of what the church of Christ should be. Some, like Thomas Müntzer (1489?–1525)[48] and Jan of Leiden (1509–1536) started out as idealists but soon found themselves succumbing to the worst excesses of immorality. Like cult leaders in any age, they had a hypnotic power over their followers, whom they did not hesitate to lead to destruction, giving radicalism a bad name from which it took more than four centuries to escape. There is some evidence that Müntzer, at least, was influenced by Joachim, whom he regarded highly, but it is difficult to determine just how important that influence was.[49]

Others were less incendiary but in their own way just as subversive. In

[46] See ibid., 22–24, 136–139.
[47] Johan Bale, *The First Two Partes of the Actes or Unchast Examples of the English Votaryes Gathered out of Their Own Legendes and Chronicles* (London: A. Vele and R. Jugge, 1551), fo. 108v (spelling modernized). Quoted with the original spelling in Reeves, *Joachim of Fiore*, 136.
[48] Hans-Jürgen Goertz, *Thomas Müntzer, Apocalyptic Mystic and Revolutionary* (Edinburgh: T & T Clark, 1993).
[49] See Reeves, *Joachim of Fiore*, 141–142.

Zurich, for example, first Balthasar Hubmaier (1480?–1526)[50] and then Pilgram Marpeck (1495?–1556)[51] challenged the authority of Huldrych Zwingli and the city council by advocating believers' baptism only—and then by rebaptizing themselves and their followers. Martin Luther attacked these Anabaptists ("rebaptizers"), as they came to be called, on theological grounds and made it clear that they could have no part of his Reformation.[52]

For the most part, these radical movements were crushed, though the Anabaptists managed to survive in a modified form. Most of them were simply too idealistic to be able to succeed and their followers were often rightly accused of an unrealistic fanaticism. But for all their shortcomings, the radical movements reasserted the basic Christian principle that the kingdom of Christ is not of this world. No human organization, however well-conceived, organized, and faithful to its principles it may be, can hope to measure up to the glories of heaven, and people who pretend that they can are almost invariably going to draw attention to their failings rather than to their good points. In that respect, radicalism of the Anabaptist kind became and has remained a witness to the transcendent nature of the body and the work of Christ. The church would not truly become itself until it met the challenge that the radicals posed and adapted its self-understanding accordingly.

Did Luther worry about this? Not unduly, it would seem. Attempts were certainly made to link him (both positively and negatively) to the prophecies of Joachim da Fiore, but although he was aware of them, he does not seem to have taken them very seriously.[53] To him, the church was an invisible body of believers, united to Jesus Christ, who had ascended from earth to heaven and taken us with him, at least in spirit. As he put it,

> Christ has gone to the Father and is now invisible. He sits in heaven at the right hand of the Father, not as a judge but as one who has been made for us wisdom, righteousness, sanctification, and redemption from God;[54] in short, he is our High Priest, interceding for us and reigning over us and in us through grace. In his presence we notice no sin and feel no terror or remorse of conscience. Sin cannot happen in this [state of] Christian righteousness, for where there is no law, there can be no transgression.[55]

---

[50] See Eddie Mabry, *Balthasar Hubmaier's Doctrine of the Church* (Lanham, MD: University Press of America, 1994); H. Wayne Pipkin and John H. Yoder, eds., *Balthasar Hubmaier, Theologian of Anabaptism* (Scottdale, PA: Herald, 1989); John D. Rempel, *The Lord's Supper in Anabaptism: A Study in the Christology of Balthasar Hubmaier, Pilgram Marpeck, and Dirk Philips* (Waterloo, ON: Herald, 1993).

[51] William Klaassen and Walter Klaassen, eds., *The Writings of Pilgram Marpeck* (Kitchener, ON: Herald, 1978); idem, *Pilgram Marpeck: A Life of Dissent and Conformity* (Waterloo, ON: Herald, 2008).

[52] Martin Luther, *Concerning Rebaptism* (1528). The text is in Pelikan and Lehmann, *Luther's Works*, 40:229–262.

[53] See Reeves, *Joachim of Fiore*, 138.

[54] 1 Cor. 1:30.

[55] Rom. 4:15. Luther, *Second Lectures on Galatians*, preface. See Pelikan and Lehmann, *Luther's Works*, 26:8.

The work of the Son was complete, and those who believe are united to him in his eternal glory. The question now was to work out how believers on earth relate to the king in heaven; the form of the institutions by and through which that communion would take place was important only insofar as it facilitated the purpose for which those institutions were designed. And that was less to do with the work of the Son than with the work of the Holy Spirit, whom the Son had promised his disciples that he would send after his departure, and who would lead them into all truth.[56] Luther himself was very clear about this:

> Because God has now allowed his holy gospel to go forth, he deals with us in two ways—first outwardly, and then inwardly. Outwardly, he deals with us through the preached Word, or the gospel, and through the visible signs of baptism and the Lord's Supper. Inwardly, he deals with us through the Holy Spirit and faith. But this is always in such a way and in this order that the outward means must precede the inward means, and the inward means follow after, through the outward means. God has willed that he will not give anyone the inward gifts other than through the outward means.[57]

In saying this, Luther was denouncing the radical wing of the Reformation that wanted to dispense with anything that smacked of institutionalism and reminding his hearers of the central importance of the church and its ministry.[58] But the distinction he made between the outward signs and the inward reality that they represented was important because it implicitly denied the medieval church's claim that its sacraments operated automatically (*ex opere operato*). Luther recognized that even if the Word was duly preached and the sacraments rightly administered, only the Holy Spirit could effect what these outward things proclaimed. In an ideal world, outward and inward would go together, but as Luther knew from his own experience, that did not often happen in practice. He lived in a world where virtually everyone was baptized in infancy and where many people went to Communion fairly regularly, but where the gospel message was by no means always heard or received. In other words, the application of the outward signs was much broader than the inward change that they stood for, and this was perhaps the most serious pastoral problem that he faced. People thought they were Christians because they had done all the right things, but many of them did not know the gospel and some were openly opposed to it. How could this discrepancy be explained?

---

[56] John 16:7–15.

[57] Martin Luther, *Against the Heavenly Prophets in the Matter of Images and Sacraments*, in Pelikan and Lehmann, *Luther's Works*, 40:83.

[58] See Luther, *Concerning Rebaptism*, in Pelikan and Lehmann, *Luther's Works*, 40:231, where he said precisely this.

For the radicals, the answer was simple. The church had gone wrong by not exercising the discipline needed to keep the faithful in line, and they proposed to restore it. One of their leaders, Michael Sattler (1490?–1527), was banished from Zurich in 1525 and ministered for a time in Strasbourg before moving on into central Germany. He and a number of his fellow radicals held a conference on February 24, 1527, at Schleitheim (near Schaffhausen, in northern Switzerland). There, under Sattler's leadership, they produced a series of seven articles that came to define the Anabaptist movement. All seven dealt with the nature of the church, but it was the first one, on baptism, that immediately attracted most attention.[59] They were as follows:

1. Baptism shall be given to those who have learned repentance, who believe that their sins have been taken away by Christ, who want to be buried and to rise again with him, and who (on the basis of these beliefs) ask to be baptized. Infant baptism is excluded, being the highest and most important of the pope's abominations.

2. Those who have been rightly baptized but who have fallen into sin will be admonished twice, and on the third offense, they shall be banned from the fellowship. This banning will take place immediately before the breaking of bread. (It was, in essence, excommunication, though that word was not used.)

3. Only the duly baptized can partake of the breaking of bread.

4. Those who have not been properly baptized are unbelievers, and it is the duty of the baptized to separate themselves from them, because they are evil and an abomination to the Lord.

5. Pastors will be appointed to lead worship, to teach the congregation(s), to preside at the breaking of bread, and to exercise discipline. If a pastor requires disciplining himself, two or three witnesses must give evidence and the discipline must be exercised in public, as a warning to others. Pastors who are banished or martyred will be replaced by others whom the congregation will ordain.

6. The "sword" (i.e., secular power) has no place in the church and no Christian should serve as a magistrate or in any position where he would be compelled to use worldly force.

7. No oaths may be sworn under any circumstances.

It is obvious from these that the church should consist only of baptized believers who must protect themselves from corruption, both within (by discipline)

[59] The articles were written in German and translated into Latin. They survive in both manuscript and printed form. The English translation by John C. Wenger first appeared in the *Mennonite Quarterly Review* 19 (1945): 247–253, and was reprinted in William J. Lumpkin, *Baptist Confessions of Faith*, 2nd ed. (Valley Forge, PA: Judson, 1969), 23–31.

and without (by separation from the world). In some respects, the Anabaptists were a kind of monastic movement, and the rules governing their separation from others have a clear monastic pedigree behind them. They could probably have established themselves as a religious community, but the requirement of believer's baptism, which in their case invariably meant rebaptism, since they had all been baptized as infants, put them beyond the pale. In the eyes of most people in the early sixteenth century, to renounce baptism was to abandon not only the institutional church but the faith which that church was called to proclaim, however imperfectly it succeeded in doing so. It is not surprising therefore that the weight of opposition to them centered on infant baptism and the spiritual state of those who had received it, whether they were professing believers or not.

In the New Testament people were baptized on profession of faith as a sign that they had repented of their sins and been born again into a new life in Christ, and that continued to be the norm for several centuries afterwards.[60] No one can say for sure when the practice of baptizing infants began or how widespread it was in the centuries of persecution, though it was certainly in existence by AD 200 because it was about then that Tertullian wrote against it.[61] The first person to defend infant baptism and to offer a theological justification for it was Origen, who wrote,

> Little children are baptized for the forgiveness of sins. Whose sins are they? When did they sin? How can this explanation of the baptismal washing be upheld in the case of small children . . . ? "No man is clean of stain, not even if his life on earth lasted but a single day."[62] Through the mystery of baptism, the stains of birth are put aside, which is why even small children are baptized. For "unless one is born of water and the Spirit, he cannot see the kingdom of God."[63]

Commenting on this and similar passages in Origen, Everett Ferguson has warned us not to read the necessity for baptismal cleansing in terms of original sin, as would later be the case with Augustine, but rather to see it as a continuation of Jewish purification rites performed after childbirth.[64] But even if Ferguson is right about this, there is no doubt that Origen linked infant baptism to some kind of cleansing, and it is not difficult to see how his argumentation could be adapted to the removal of original sin.

---

[60] See Everett Ferguson, *Baptism in the Early Church: History, Theology, and Liturgy in the First Five Centuries* (Grand Rapids, MI: Eerdmans, 2009) for the most detailed study of the subject to date.

[61] Tertullian, *De baptismo* 18.

[62] Job 14:4–5 (LXX).

[63] John 3:5. Origen, *Homiliae in Lucae Evangelium* 14.5 (on Luke 2:22).

[64] Ferguson, *Baptism*, 367–370.

Origen's contemporary, Cyprian of Carthage, seems to have been the first to link baptism with circumcision and therefore to recommend that it be administered on the eighth day after birth, as circumcision was. As for the connection with sin, Cyprian thought that if an adult could be baptized for forgiveness of the sins he had committed, a child ought to be that much easier to forgive, since he had committed no sins of his own:

> If forgiveness of sins is granted even to the worst transgressors and to those who have sinned greatly against God, and if no one is held back from baptism and grace, how much less should an infant be held back. Having just been born, he has not sinned at all, except that by being born physically according to Adam, he has contracted the contagion of death by that. . . . An infant can be much more easily forgiven because the sins remitted to him are not his own but those of others.[65]

Augustine picked this up in his debates against the Pelagians, who denied the existence of original (or birth) sin, and argued that just as descent from Adam brings damnation to all who are born in the flesh, so rebirth by the Holy Spirit in baptism brings justification and rebirth to all those who have been predestined and born again in that way.[66] To the objection that little children did not understand what was happening, he replied,

> Even if that faith that is found in the will of believers does not turn an infant into a believer, the sacrament of that faith does so. Just as the response is given [by the parents and godparents] that the child believes, he is also called a believer, not because he assents to the reality with his mind but because he receives the sacrament of that reality. When he comes to the age of reason he will not repeat the sacrament, but will understand it and submit to its truth by the agreement of his will.[67]

By the sixteenth century, and for at least a millennium before that, infant baptism was the almost universal norm, especially for the children of baptized Christians. But as Luther said, who knows whether a person being baptized has faith or not? To base baptism on a profession of faith would lead to endless rebaptizings, since faith is always imperfect and fluctuates from one day to the next.[68] We do not know whether children have faith or not. The fact that they cannot express it does not mean that it is not there; after all, they cannot say

[65] Cyprian of Carthage, *Epistulae* 64.5.

[66] Augustine of Hippo, *De peccatorum meritis et remissione et de baptismo parvulorum ad Marcellinum libri tres* 2.27.43.

[67] Augustine of Hippo, *Epistulae* 98.10.

[68] Luther, *Concerning Rebaptism*, in Pelikan and Lehmann, *Luther's Works*, 40:240–241.

that they are human beings either, even though it is obvious to everyone else that they are.[69]

Interestingly, Luther based his belief in infant baptism on the covenant promises of God, an idea that modern theologians generally associate not with him but with the Reformed tradition going back to Calvin. Yet Luther was quite adamant on this point, saying that Jesus commanded his disciples to go and baptize all nations without mentioning a word about their faith.[70] In fairness, Luther did say that faith should be added to baptism, but,

> We are not to base baptism on faith. There is quite a difference between having faith . . . and making baptism depend on faith. . . . Whoever allows himself to be baptized on the strength of his faith is not only uncertain, but an idolater who denies Christ. For he trusts in and builds on something of his own, namely, on a gift he has received from God, and not on God's Word alone.[71]

On one point, Luther was prepared to concede that those who opposed the practice of infant baptism were correct, and that was that there is no evidence in Scripture to support it. But he countered this argument by saying that there is no evidence in Scripture that forbids it either, and added that the evidence of its universal practice since ancient times tipped the scales in its favor. As he put it,

> If infant baptism were not right, it would follow that for more than a thousand years there was no baptism or any Christendom, which is impossible. In that case, the article of the creed, "I believe in one holy, Christian church" would be false. . . . If infant baptism is wrong, then for more than a thousand years Christendom would have been without baptism, and if it were without baptism, it would not have been Christendom. For the Christian church is the bride of Christ, subject and obedient to him. It has his Spirit, his Word, his baptism, his sacrament, and all that Christ has. If infant baptism were not the universal norm but were accepted only by some (like the papacy), then the Anabaptists might have a case . . . but the fact that it has spread throughout the Christian world makes it highly improbable that it is wrong and gives instead a strong indication that it is right.[72]

Luther did not base his defense of infant baptism on the need to eradicate original sin by the so-called "prevenient grace" that the sacrament was meant

[69] Ibid., 40:241–242.
[70] Matt. 28:19; ibid., 40:252.
[71] Ibid., 40:252.
[72] Ibid., 40:256–257.

to provide. This was not because he did not believe in original sin but because he rejected the sacramental structure of grace that claimed that baptism was just the first step in a lifelong process that would finally culminate in salvation. Instead of that, he believed that anyone who received in faith the promise given to him in baptism was saved, whereas the sacrament would have no effect on those who failed to believe when they were given the chance. Baptism was a promise that had to be claimed by faith; it was not an accomplished fact that operated whether the person who received it believed or not. At the same time, although the faith that received baptism was always weak and inadequate, baptism itself rested on the guarantee that God would keep his promise and took effect in spite of the believer's inability to grasp it fully. Luther explained this as follows:

> If an adult wants to be baptized . . . he will not blurt out and say: "I want to move mountains by my faith." Instead, he will say: "I believe, but I do not ground this belief on my faith, which may be too weak or uncertain. I want to be baptized because it is God's command. . . . if I am baptized because of his command, I know for certain that I have been baptized. If I were to be baptized on the strength of my own faith, I might be unbaptized tomorrow, if my faith failed me or I started to worry that yesterday my faith was not quite right. But now that does not affect me. God and his command may be attacked, but I know for sure that I have been baptized on his Word. . . . If I believe, this baptism is of value to me. If I do not believe, it is of no value. But baptism itself is not wrong or uncertain because of that. It is not a matter of chance, but is as sure as the Word and command of God.[73]

Given the importance of Anabaptism in the 1520s, it is surprising to discover that the Augsburg Confession (1530) said almost nothing about it. The Anabaptists were condemned, of course, but without any explanation of the reasons for that.[74] This lacuna was filled to some extent in the Wittenberg Articles (1536), which state,

> . . . through baptism, remission of sins and the grace of Christ are offered to children as well as adults, that baptism should not be repeated, that children should be baptized and that through baptism, children obtain remission of sins and grace, and become sons of God, because the promise of grace and of eternal life belongs not only to adults but also to children.

[73] Ibid., 40:253.

[74] *Confessio Augustana* 9.

> Because children are born with original sin, they need remission of that sin, and it is forgiven in such a way that guilt is removed, but the matter of sin, viz., corruption of nature or concupiscence, still remains in this life, although it begins to be healed, because the Holy Spirit is efficacious in children. . . . Therefore we approve the statement of the Church which condemned the Pelagians who denied that children possess original sin, and we also condemn the Anabaptists who deny that children are to be baptized.[75]

Most of this was taken over and included in the English Ten Articles (1536), and it can also be found in the unpublished Thirteen Articles (1538), which were found among the papers of Archbishop Thomas Cranmer, showing how significant this statement was.[76] Yet by the time we get to the Forty-two Articles (1553) most of this material has disappeared once more, with no mention of either the Pelagians or the Anabaptists, though the baptism of children is of course recommended.[77]

It seems that the threat of Anabaptism and the worry about Pelagianism were both in decline in the 1530s, despite the warnings given in the Wittenberg Articles. The Smalcald Articles of 1537, for example, said nothing about either of them, though they explicitly rejected both the Dominican (Thomist) and Franciscan (Scotist) views of the subject. The Dominicans held that God placed a spiritual power in the water of baptism that washed away sin, whereas the Franciscans maintained that sin was washed away only by the will of God, and not by the Word or the water.[78] For his part, Luther insisted on the primacy of the Word, which alone made the sacrament effective.[79]

At bottom, Luther's doctrine of baptism reflected his understanding of the church as the hospital of sinners depending entirely on the grace of God for their salvation rather than as a company of the saved who boasted of their faith and achievements. The former was the kingdom of the Spirit over which Christ ruled; the latter was a company of heathen who gloried in their own pride and rejected Christ. Seen in that light, the difference over baptism was not a trivial matter of personal opinion but a fundamental marker that distinguished those who belonged to the true church of God from those who remained strangers to it.

When we turn to the teaching of John Calvin on the subject of baptism, we find that, in the main, he followed Luther's approach and developed it more

[75] Wittenberg Articles, 3; see Bray, *Documents of the English Reformation*, 121–122.
[76] Ten Articles 2 (See Bray, *Documents of the English Reformation*, 165–166); Thirteen Articles 6 (See Bray, *Documents of the English Reformation*, 191–192).
[77] Forty-two Articles 28; see Bray, *Documents of the English Reformation*, 301. Repeated with slight variations as Article 27 of the Thirty-nine Articles (1563).
[78] For the Dominican view, see Thomas Aquinas, *Summa theologiae* III.62.4; for the Franciscan view, see John Duns Scotus, *Commentarium in libros Sententiarum* 4.1.2.
[79] Martin Luther, *The Schmalkald Articles*, trans. William R. Russell (Minneapolis: Fortress, 1995), 3.5.1–3.

systematically.[80] In particular, he took over Luther's assertion that baptism is like circumcision—part of the covenant that God has made with his people. There was no question that infant boys were circumcised in the Old Testament, nor was there much doubt that the New Testament broadened the bounds of the covenant to include both women and Gentiles. It therefore seemed strange for the covenant sign to be withdrawn from infants when in every other respect the covenant was being extended. Calvin went beyond Luther, however, in examining the arguments of the Anabaptists in detail. As he saw it, they were these:

1. Baptism and circumcision are not equivalents. Circumcision was given for the mortification of the flesh, not for the regeneration of the spirit. To this, Calvin answered that baptism was also given for mortification of the flesh and quotes the words of Paul, who wrote, "You were circumcised with a circumcision made without hands, by putting off the body of the flesh, by the circumcision of Christ, having been buried with him in baptism . . ."[81]

2. The old covenant was carnal, but the new covenant is spiritual. Under the old covenant, Abraham's children were his physical descendants, but under the new covenant, they are the people who share his faith. Calvin admitted that there was some truth in this observation, but insisted that the old covenant was *also* spiritual. Circumcision had been given to Abraham as a sign of his faith, which proves that it was a spiritual, and not merely a physical sign.[82]

3. The old covenant people of God contained unbelievers who were physically descended from Abraham, which is why it was corrupt. The new covenant embraces only believers. Calvin both agreed and disagreed with this assessment. He agreed that the covenant properly applied only to believers (the elect) but insisted that the promise of it was given more widely in both the old and the new dispensation. The visible church is therefore a mixed company of believers and unbelievers, just as ancient Israel was.[83]

4. Children cannot understand what is happening to them. They are therefore to be regarded as sons of Adam until they are old enough to understand and receive the new birth in Christ. Calvin countered this argument by saying that to leave a child unbaptized was to consign him to damnation and that God can (and does) sanctify infants, who must be born again by his action before they can be saved. Age and physical incapacity are not barriers to the power of the Holy Spirit, as the sanctification of John the Baptist in his mother's womb demonstrates.[84]

---

[80] Calvin, *Institutio* 4.16.1–32.
[81] Col. 2:11–12. Calvin, *Institutio* 4.16.10–11.
[82] Calvin, *Institutio* 4.16.13. See Rom. 4:9–12.
[83] Calvin, *Institutio* 4.16.14–15.
[84] Luke 1:15. Calvin, *Institutio* 4.16.17.

5. Baptism is given for the forgiveness of sins, but infants have not sinned and so do not need to be forgiven. Calvin rebutted this argument by pointing out that every human being is conceived and born in sin. If God has promised to show mercy to children, he argued, why should we withhold from them the covenant sign of that mercy, seeing that it is so much less than the actual mercy itself?[85]

6. The apostles baptized only on profession of faith and repentance. Calvin replied that this applies to Gentiles who are outside the covenant and therefore unable to receive baptism for their children. The children of Christian parents, however, are immediately received as members of the covenant, just as the children of Jews were.[86]

7. Baptism is indissolubly linked with being born again, as John 3:5 implies when it says, "Unless one is born of water and the Spirit, he cannot enter the kingdom of God." A child cannot be born of the Spirit, and so ought not to be baptized with water. Calvin replied to this by denying that John 3:5 has anything to do with baptism. He claimed that "water and Spirit" must be taken together to mean "the power of the Spirit," which has the same effect on the soul as water has on the body.[87]

It is from this last point that Calvin went on to develop his understanding of water baptism, which essentially paralleled that of Luther. Water by itself cannot save anyone, and those who rushed to have their newborn babies baptized out of fear that they might otherwise go to eternal damnation were victims of superstition. Jesus himself taught that anyone who heard his word and believed that the Father had sent him had passed from death to life, and he never condemned anyone merely for not being baptized.[88] The sacrament was an extension of the preaching of the Word, but just as the Word is not heard or understood by everyone, so too, the promise of baptism is not realized in all who receive it. But that is no reason not to give it, just as the knowledge that not everyone will hear the Word is any reason not to preach it. The children of believers are the heirs of salvation, and although what they do with their inheritance can be known and determined only by the Spirit of God, the church has no power or authority to withhold it from them.[89]

What Calvin had to say about baptism was entirely consistent with his view of the relationship between the visible and the invisible church. While

[85] Ibid., 4.16.22.
[86] Ibid., 4.16.23.
[87] Ibid., 4.16.25.
[88] Ibid., 4.16.26.
[89] Ibid., 4.16.28–32.

granting that the latter is the only "true" church, he never despised or rejected the former. As he put it,

> After the Lord had made his covenant with the Jews, it was preserved not so much by them as by its own strength, by which it resisted their ungodliness. Such is the certainty and constancy of God's goodness that the Lord's covenant continued there. His faithfulness could not be obliterated by their perfidy, nor could circumcision be so profaned at their hands as to no longer be a true sign and sacrament of his covenant. . . . Likewise, having deposited his covenant in France, Italy, Germany, Spain, and England, when those countries were oppressed by the Antichrist [the Pope], he preserved baptism there as evidence that his covenant is inviolable. Baptism, consecrated by his lips, retains its power in spite of human depravity . . .[90]

Here we see the logical outworking of what both Luther and Calvin taught about the nature of the sacrament and its relationship to the church. Baptism is and remains a witness, not to the faith of those who receive it, but to the faithfulness of the one who has given it. The covenant people may go astray and lose the blessing of the promise that baptism offers, but the witness remains unchanged and will be rediscovered by those whom the Holy Spirit enlightens. These are the elect, who have been chosen for salvation, and it is they—and they alone—who enjoy the benefits of God's declared will and promise.

If theological outrage could kill a movement, the Anabaptists would have disappeared very quickly, but that did not happen. The early communities multiplied, in spite of persecution, and diversified—or divided—over what came to be seen by some as secondary points, notably those articles of the Schleitheim Confession that advocated separation from the world. Their radicalism had led them into trouble, especially after a group claiming their beliefs seized the city of Münster in 1535 and proceeded to turn it into a "paradise," when in fact it was an immoral tyranny. Münster was recaptured by forces loyal to the established authorities, and Anabaptism was effectively outlawed, though a semblance of it managed to survive and regroup under the leadership of Menno Simons (1496–1561). At first, Menno (a former Catholic priest) was fairly tolerant, but over time he became stricter in his views and as a result his movement split into three divergent strands. One of these was even stricter than he was, another followed his line more or less to the letter, and a third was somewhat more lax. These last lived in a Dutch region known as Waterland (near Amsterdam), and in 1555 they fell out with the others over the issue of

[90] Ibid., 4.1.11.

excommunication. Menno and his supporters insisted that offenders should be banned from the fellowship after their first offense, whereas the Waterlanders stuck with the original pattern agreed at Schleitheim—two admonitions first, and then exclusion on the third infraction.

This marked the Waterlanders out as "liberals," and before long they were being courted by other Anabaptists who had gone to Poland, where they had been seduced into a form of unitarianism. Faced with this threat, two Waterlander ministers, Hans de Ries (1553–1638) and Lubbert Gerritz (1534–1612), drew up a confession of faith, now known as the Second Mennonite or Waterland Confession, which they published in 1580 (or 1581).[91] This confession is a theological world away from the Schleitheim articles. It was composed as a complete statement of belief and organized thematically in a way that would be immediately understood by non-Mennonites. To the uninitiated, it looks very much like a Reformed statement of faith, with its emphasis on the covenant and on the three offices of Christ as prophet, priest, and king. In line with Calvin, there is considerable emphasis on the spiritual nature of the church, including especially Article 19, which asserts that it is necessary to know Christ not only intellectually, but according to the Spirit.[92]

Article 24 on the church is especially interesting because it accepts Calvin's distinction between the "true" church, which is invisible, and the visible community, which is a mixed body of the faithful and the reprobate. This was a commonplace of Reformed teaching, of course, but for Anabaptists it was a denial of everything their forebears had stood for. There had been no such thing as a mixed church at Schleitheim—anyone suspected of unbelief back then was simply driven out of the fellowship. Article 30 on the sacraments is equally compatible with a Reformed interpretation:

> The sacraments are external and visible actions, and signs of the immense goodness of God toward us; placing before our eyes, on the part of God, the internal and spiritual action which God accomplishes through Christ (the Holy Spirit co-operating) by regenerating, justifying, spiritually nourishing and sustaining the souls which repent and believe; we on our part, by the same means, confess religion, repentance, faith and our obedience by earnestly directing our conscience to the service (or worship) of God.[93]

---

[91] There was supposedly a "first" confession produced in 1577, but all trace of it has vanished, unless it was just an earlier version of the second one. See Lumpkin, *Baptist Confessions*, 43. The English translation of the original Latin is published in Lumpkin, *Baptist Confessions*, 44–66.

[92] Lumpkin, *Baptist Confessions*, 54.

[93] Lumpkin, *Baptist Confessions*, 60.

Even the articles on baptism (31–32) could be accepted by a Reformed theologian, with the single (though obvious) exception of the stricture at the end of Article 31, which says that baptism is effective for all who receive it with a penitent heart "but by no means infants."[94] There is a similar Reformed feel to the articles on the Lord's Supper (33–34), and it is especially noticeable that excommunication, though reaffirmed, is made clearly subject to the Word of God.[95] The validity of the civil magistrate is also accepted, though in faithfulness to their tradition, the prohibition on oaths is maintained.[96] All in all, the Waterland Confession must be regarded as a domestication of the Anabaptist tradition within the mainstream of Reformed Protestant orthodoxy. Certain distinctives of that tradition are maintained—as they would have to be if the name "Anabaptist" was to have any meaning—but they have been significantly deemphasized. In particular, there is no suggestion that those who reject Anabaptism are necessarily evil and that they must therefore be shunned. Believer's baptism is confessed, but in a purely positive sense, with no fulminations against those who disagreed with it.

This "virtual Calvinism" and rejection of sectarianism was to be of great importance in the extension of Anabaptist principles to the English-speaking world. The frustrations felt by many Puritans in England at not being allowed to reform the national church as they would like were beginning to spill over into separate conventicles that met more or less clandestinely in the 1590s. The English government could not tolerate such potential subversion, but although they persecuted the separatists (as the more extreme exponents of radical Puritanism are known), they preferred to exile them. Most went to Holland, where they regrouped and formed a church in Amsterdam, which composed a statement of its principles in 1596. Known from its opening line as "A True Confession of the Faith," it became the charter of English congregationalism, though it had not yet been affected by any significant contact with Anabaptists.[97]

Meanwhile, separatist tendencies continued to manifest themselves in England, and sometime around 1607 a new fellowship was set up by those who rejected what they saw as the compromises of the state church. Forced into exile, they made their way to the Netherlands in 1608, where they met the already established congregationalists. Some of the new exiles joined it without further ado, but others decamped with one of their leaders, a certain John Rob-

[94] Lumpkin, *Baptist Confessions*, 60.
[95] Article 35. Lumpkin, *Baptist Confessions*, 62. It should be remembered that Article 33 of the Church of England's Thirty-nine Articles says much the same thing. Excommunication was by no means an Anabaptist peculiarity!
[96] In Articles 37 and 38. See Lumpkin, *Baptist Confessions*, 63–64.
[97] For the text, see Lumpkin, *Baptist Confessions*, 82–97. Much as he wanted to claim them as Proto-Baptists, even Lumpkin had to admit that their views had not advanced that far as early as 1596.

inson (1576–1625), to Leiden, from where (in 1620) many of them emigrated to America on the *Mayflower*. Others followed John Smyth (1570?–1612), who had been a licensed preacher (lecturer) at Lincoln. Smyth soon found himself criticizing the Amsterdam congregationalists who, in his view, had not gone far enough with their radicalism, and about the same time he met a group of Waterlanders, who acquainted him with believer's baptism. Whether he took it over from them or came to the same conclusion himself is disputed, but it hardly matters. Either way, he rejected infant baptism and set about founding a new church.

Interestingly enough, Smyth refused to join the Waterlanders because he objected to some of their doctrines, which he thought were heretical. So instead of being baptized by them, he baptized himself and then proceeded to baptize his followers as well. Soon afterwards, his growing knowledge of the Waterlanders persuaded him that his earlier opinion of them had been wrong, and in 1610 he and his congregation applied to join their fellowship. Not everyone concurred with this, however, and a small group under the leadership of Thomas Helwys (1575?–1616?) broke away to form their own church. In some respects the dispute between Smyth and Helwys may seem quite comical. Helwys broke with Smyth because he continued to recognize Smyth's baptism even after Smyth himself had repudiated it, and after disapproving of Smyth's attempts to join the Waterlanders, he did so himself as soon as he had started his own congregation! But at a deeper level, as the confessions of the two men illustrate, their disagreement mirrored a division in the Dutch Reformed church that was to be of major significance after their deaths. Helwys devised a confession that was almost identical to that of the Waterlanders, but without Article 19 (on the necessity of knowing Christ according to the Spirit) or Article 22 (on regeneration), odd though those omissions must appear to be. Smyth's confession, on the other hand, was a bold repudiation of Calvinism. He even denied that there were people condemned to eternal damnation or that there was such a thing as original sin.[98]

In 1611, Helwys produced another confession that stressed the reality of original sin and rejected any idea of free will. He also retracted his earlier willingness to support the Waterlanders' refusal to take an oath.[99] In fact, the English Baptists had never shown any enthusiasm for the Anabaptists' pacifism or for their unwillingness to take part in civil affairs. The Helwys congregation left Holland in 1612 and returned to England, where they were persecuted but managed to establish a Baptist church. The Smyth congregation, left without

[98] For the text, see Lumpkin, *Baptist Confessions*, 100–101.
[99] For the text, see ibid., 117–123.

a leader after Smyth died in August 1612, was finally integrated with the Waterlanders in 1615 after issuing another confession that repudiated the doctrine of original sin and affirmed,

> That infants are conceived and born in innocency without sin, and that so dying are undoubtedly saved, and that this is to be understood of all infants under heaven, for where there is no law there is no transgression . . . the law was not given to infants, but to them that could understand.[100]

In all of these confessions infant baptism was openly or silently repudiated, but the main dispute lay elsewhere. It was the question that was wracking the Netherlands at the time: What was the true nature of the Reformed faith? Were human beings chosen for salvation or condemned to destruction before they were born, or did they play some part in shaping their own destiny? The Baptist confessions give us a precious insight into the way this controversy was perceived in the second decade of the seventeenth century, when it was becoming of key political importance in the Dutch Reformed world. At the same time, they are also evidence that purely Anabaptist issues were now taking a backseat—not that they were repudiated, but they were no longer the central concern even of those who subscribed to them and defined their churches accordingly.

Life in the Spirit

One of the features of the Anabaptist movement that is often overlooked is the strong emphasis it placed on the fellowship of the church as the place where the individual believer would be strengthened and would grow in faith and obedience. Of course, Christians had always believed that in theory, but the exercise of discipline that many believed had been the norm in the early centuries was impossible when virtually the entire population was considered to belong to the church. The authorities did what they could to ensure that the basic rules were observed, especially with regard to matrimony, but often their major preoccupation was with the collection of tithes, which every church member was expected to pay for the maintenance of the clergy and the upkeep of church property. Church courts existed, but they spent most of their time settling family disputes, and excommunication was increasingly reserved for those who failed to pay their tithes. Anything more spiritual than that was usually beyond their ability to cope with. No one checked to see whether laypeople went to

[100] Article 20 of the propositions and conclusions adopted in 1612. See Lumpkin, *Baptist Confessions*, 127. The entire text is on 124–142.

church or understood what was going on there when they did, and superstitious practices were rife. Heresy was dealt with if it affected the clergy or the universities, but beyond that, it was only the followers of academics like John Wyclif who were likely to be questioned. The truth was that most people did not know enough to know whether they were heretics or not, and asking ordinary people theological questions was a waste of time. People were occasionally arrested, tried, and put to death for things like witchcraft, but these proceedings were often highly suspect because the victims seldom knew what they were talking about and so incriminated themselves through ignorance.

Educated people and would-be reformers knew all this, of course, but had no idea how the problem could be tackled, let alone resolved. The Anabaptists succeeded (to the extent that they did) only by radically redefining the church so as to exclude all but a tiny minority of the population, over whom they could keep a constant eye. They managed to maintain a high level of church discipline within their own circles, but being shunned by an Anabaptist group was hardly a social handicap—quite the reverse, one suspects, at least in most places. Certainly leaving an Anabaptist community was far easier than leaving a state church, and once a person had broken his ties with the Anabaptists, there was little they could do to pursue him any further. As a result, spiritual discipline was effectively voluntary; only those who wanted to submit to it actually did so, unless of course they were wives or dependents of church members who were subject to discipline and therefore had no choice in the matter.

The Reformers—Lutheran, Calvinist, and even Anabaptist—knew that raising the standards of church members and thus of the general spiritual life of the church depended largely on effective oversight, which in practice meant the creation of a body of ministers big enough, and theologically well educated enough, to make it work. This is why they all gave such prominence to the ordained ministry, which was central to every project of reform among Protestants and Catholics alike.

One complication with this was the rapid spread of a married clergy among Protestants of all kinds. Allowing the clergy to marry seems like an obvious reform to us now, but it was one of the most difficult pills for people in the sixteenth century to swallow. For all the abuse caused by widespread concubinage and sexual sin, there was still a sense that the priest was a man set apart who ought to make a sacrifice worthy of his office and be free to exercise it without the ties of family and property that marriage would inevitably bring. Like it or not, the marriage of the clergy was a change brought about by the clergy themselves. It was they who were clamoring for it, not the laypeople, many of whom were quite happy to continue with the traditional arrangements. In England, for example, clerical marriage did not become legal until 1549—fifteen years after the break with Rome, when parliament, at the request of Thomas Cranmer, the archbishop of Canterbury, reluctantly agreed to permit it.[101]

Four years later, when the Catholic Mary I ascended the throne, the act was rescinded and all married priests (up to a third of the total in some places) were deposed. At the restoration of Protestantism in 1559, clerical marriage was once again permitted, but only by royal injunction and with due regard to the fact that "there hath grown offence and some slander to the church by lack of discreet and sober behavior in many ministers of the church, both in choosing of their wives and in indiscreet living with them."[102] The remedy proposed was that no clergyman should take a wife without the prior approval of his bishop and two justices of the peace, who were expected to examine the woman in question to make sure that she was suitable. Moreover, anyone who was a master, dean, or fellow of a college was not allowed to marry at all—a prohibition that was not lifted in Oxford and Cambridge until 1882. The 1549 act was reinstated in 1603, after the death of Queen Elizabeth I, and gradually the restrictions on clerical marriage were eased in practice, if not in theory, but what impresses us most today is the extreme reluctance shown by the lay authorities in allowing this change.

Clerical marriage was theologically significant in that it destroyed a pillar of the medieval sacramental system, in which the clergy had been set apart from the laity and "mysticized" into a separate category of human being. Martin Luther and his contemporaries deeply resented this, regarding it as a prime example of what Luther called "the Babylonian captivity of the church" by the papacy.[103] Luther recognized that the ministry of teaching the gospel and administering the sacraments had been given by God, and the Augsburg Confession stated that no one should take on the office of doing so unless he was "rightly called" to it, but what that right calling was supposed to be was left unexplained.[104]

In a treatise sent to Bohemia in 1523, Luther warned his followers there not to submit to papal ordinations, but to follow their own path, which he described as getting the elders of the congregation together, praying for wisdom in making the right choice of ministers, and then laying hands on them,

---

[101] An Act to Take Away All Positive Laws against the Marriage of Priests, 2–3 Edward VI, c. 21 (1549). The text is in Bray, *Documents of the English Reformation*, 279–280. The preamble to the act makes it quite clear that clerical celibacy is preferable to clerical marriage, but that the latter had become necessary because the former had led to "uncleanness of living and other great inconveniences not meet to be rehearsed."

[102] The Elizabethan Injunctions (1559) 29; see Bray, *Documents of the English Reformation*, 342.

[103] Martin Luther, *The Babylonian Captivity of the Church*, I, in Pelikan and Lehmann, *Luther's Works*, 36:27–28.

[104] *Confessio Augustana* 14. Compare this with Article 5 of the same Confession, which affirms the divine origin of the ministry of Word and sacrament.

without recourse to any higher or more traditional authority. He recognized that this was an innovation and understood that it would not be universally popular, but gave the following advice:

> None should be forced to believe. We must give freedom and honor to the Holy Spirit that he may move wherever he will. . . . We cannot hope that these things will be acceptable to all, especially right away. . . . It is enough if at first, a few set the example.[105]

Later on, when he was describing the nature of the church, Luther had this to say:

> The church is recognized externally by the fact that it consecrates or calls ministers, or has offices that it is to administer. There must be bishops, pastors, or preachers, who publicly and privately give, administer and use the aforementioned . . . holy possessions on behalf of the church and in its name. . . . The people as a whole cannot do these things, but must entrust or have them entrusted to one person.[106]

Who should supervise this, he did not say. He seemed to assume that whoever was in charge of church affairs would see to it that ministers would be appointed, using the criteria laid down in the New Testament. On this he was quite clear:

> The Holy Spirit has excepted women, children, and incompetent people from this function, but chooses (except in emergencies) only competent males to fill this office.[107]

In other words, it was the work of the Holy Spirit to raise up men to perform the tasks of the ordained ministry, and it was the duty of the church to recognize those who had been so called by God. Luther did, however, accept that mistakes could be made, and in that case, church members should overlook the unsatisfactory character of the minister and remember that the Word and sacraments have their own validity, quite independent of those who have the calling to administer them.[108]

The inadequacy of this position was realized by Thomas Cranmer, who revised the Augsburg Confession by expanding it to say that "rightly called" meant "called by those in the church who, according to the Word of God and

[105] Martin Luther, *Concerning the Ministry*, in Pelikan and Lehmann, *Luther's Works*, 40:40–41.
[106] Luther, *On the Councils and the Church*, in Pelikan and Lehmann, *Luther's Works*, 41:154.
[107] Ibid., 41:154.
[108] Ibid., 41:156.

the laws and customs of each country, have the right to call and ordain." The emphasis here was on law and order, rather than on qualifications or competence, and this was later repeated in the Forty-two Articles (1553).[109] In a typically English touch, he added,

> No one called to the ministry, including the Roman or any other bishop, can claim for himself, as by divine right, the power to teach publicly, to administer the sacraments, or exercise any ecclesiastical function in another diocese or parish—i.e., neither a bishop in another diocese nor a parish priest in another parish.[110]

This addition never made it into the Forty-two Articles, but its spirit is clear and it was immediately recognized as the canonical norm for the conduct of ministers, which (in England at least) it still is.[111] It is not hard to see why a state church would find it necessary to control its ministry by legal means, but it is more surprising to discover that the first Anabaptists were equally strict. The Schleitheim Confession, for example, makes it clear that a minister must be a man who is highly respected by those *outside* the church (not only by those within), that he must be disciplined if he goes astray, and that he must be immediately replaced if he is exiled or martyred for his faith.[112] The Confession does not say who should do the ordaining, though it may be assumed that if a replacement minister was to be appointed "immediately" it must have been by and with the consent of the congregation. That was subsequently laid down specifically in the Waterland Confession of 1580 (1581) in two distinct articles:

> 27. Calling or election to the aforesaid ministries is accomplished through the ministers of the church and its members conjointly, and by invocation of the name of God; for God alone knows hearts, walks in the midst of the believers who are congregated in his name, and through his Holy Spirit directs their intellects and minds so that through them he manifests and calls forth such as he knows will be useful to his church.
>
> 28. But although the election and call aforesaid are accomplished in the method [aforesaid], yet confirmation in the ministry itself is performed by

[109] Article 24; see Bray, *Documents of the English Reformation*, 297–298. It was subsequently taken over (unchanged) as Article 23 of the Thirty-nine Articles (1563).

[110] The Thirteen Articles, 10; see Bray, *Documents of the English Reformation*, 200. The Wittenberg Articles of 1536 had taken over the Augsburg Confession's statement on this point without alteration (Article 9; Bray, *Documents of the English Reformation*, 141) but the Ten Articles that were subsequently extracted from them did not mention the ministry at all.

[111] Canons 49–50 of the canons of 1603 (1604). See Gerald L. Bray, *The Anglican Canons 1529–1947* (Woodbridge: Boydell & Brewer, 1998), 336–339, for the text. These particular canons were rescinded in 1969 and not replaced, but the same principle is enshrined in the Extra-parochial Ministry Measure (1967), and so the canons are no longer needed.

[112] Lumpkin, *Baptist Confessions*, 27.

the elders of the people in the presence of the church, and that (for the most part) by the laying on of hands.[113]

It is remarkable that the Waterland Confession pays more attention to the calling of ministers than it does to baptism, but also that its teaching so closely parallels the advice Luther gave to the Bohemians but filtered through the analysis of John Calvin, who, in his customary manner, was systematic and thorough in his treatment of the subject. Calvin agreed with Luther that Christ alone was head of the church and that all ministries and functions within it were the gifts of his Spirit, but he also believed that there was a specific order that had to be followed in choosing and appointing ministers for the church. Drawing on the teaching of the apostle Paul in Ephesians 4, he noted that when Christ ascended to his heavenly glory he gave gifts to men, which included making some of them apostles, prophets, evangelists, pastors, and teachers.[114] In his comments on this, Calvin remarked that the ministry of particular men was one of the main ways in which God's people were kept together in a single body. As he put it,

> By the ministers to whom Christ has committed this office and given grace to discharge it, he dispenses and distributes his gifts to the church, and thus exhibits himself as in a manner actually present by exerting the energy of his Spirit in this institution, so as to prevent it from being vain or fruitless. In this way, the renewal of the saints is accomplished and the body of Christ is edified.[115]

Because of this, Calvin concluded that whoever tries to subvert the ministry is guilty of plotting the destruction of the church. At the same time, he also recognized that there is a difference between ordinary and extraordinary forms of ministry that must be respected. In the list given by Paul, apostles, prophets, and evangelists were classified by Calvin as "extraordinary" in the sense that they had been given at the beginning of the church but subsequently withdrawn, except in unusual circumstances. Pastors and teachers, however, were "ordinary" ministers whose functions had continued without interruption since apostolic times.[116] At the same time, he also claimed that modern pastors were more or less the equivalent of the ancient apostles and evangelists, while teachers corresponded to the ancient prophets, so that their functions had not been lost even though their offices had disappeared.[117] Many people today will question the

---

[113] Lumpkin, *Baptist Confessions*, 58–59.
[114] Eph. 4:8–11. Calvin, *Institutio* 4.3.1.
[115] Calvin, *Institutio* 4.3.2.
[116] Ibid., 4.3.4.
[117] Ibid., 4.3.5.

validity of this interpretation, but Calvin's purpose was not to discourse on the continuance (or disappearance) of spiritual gifts. His concern was to reassure his contemporaries that nothing of importance had been lost to the church and that its ministry could still function as it had in New Testament times.

An important part of that ministry was pastoral teaching and guidance, which was to be given not just publicly to the whole church, but also privately to individual believers, as an extension of the public ministry that he believed was grounded in the practice of the apostles themselves.[118] Like Cranmer, Calvin also insisted that ministers should remain in the place to which they had been assigned so that decency and order might be preserved, though he did not exclude the possibility that, in exceptional circumstances, a pastor might be required to intervene elsewhere. In that sense, his office was a universal ministry of the church and not just the function assigned to him by a single congregation.[119] Calvin was indifferent to the titles such ministers should have because he knew that the words "bishop," "presbyter," and "pastor" were used synonymously in the New Testament. In this, he was quite different from Cranmer, who thought that the ancient church had three orders—bishops, presbyters (priests), and deacons; but when it came to the training and preparation of such ministers, the two men were agreed. Cranmer wrote,

> It is evident unto all men diligently reading Holy Scripture and ancient authors, that from the apostles' time there have been these orders of ministers in Christ's church; bishops, priests and deacons. Which offices were evermore had in such reverend estimation that no man might presume to execute any of them, except he were first called, tried, examined, and known to have such qualities as are requisite for the same; and also by public prayer, with imposition of hands, were approved and admitted thereunto by lawful authority.[120]

Here we see the same appeal to lawful authority as was evident in Cranmer's revision of the Augsburg Confession, but with the added element of training and examination that brought him much closer to Calvin than it might otherwise appear. Calvin concluded his exposition of the calling of a minister by outlining the procedures that were to be followed.[121] These may be listed as follows:

1. An outward call by the church ought to be preceded by an inward call from God. No one can be a successful minister if he does not have this inward

[118] Ibid., 4.3.6, quoting Acts 20:20, 31.
[119] Calvin, *Institutio* 4.3.7.
[120] The preface to the Ordinal of 1550 (appended to the Book of Common Prayer).
[121] What follows is a digest of Calvin, *Institutio* 4.3.11–16.

calling. On the other hand, there are some people who are called outwardly but who do not have the inner conviction that goes with it. In that case, the man in question will either be given the conviction he needs or else will have an unsuccessful ministry.

2. Only those who are of sound doctrine and holy life should be chosen. Anyone unfit or inadequate for the task must be rejected, although it is understood that everyone will need the grace of the Holy Spirit if he is to succeed in his office.

3. The apostles were called directly by God, but this was exceptional and is not repeated for the other offices. A bishop, for example, should be chosen by other men, set apart for the ministry, and then ordained by the laying on of hands, as the Holy Spirit commanded the church to do in the case of Paul and Barnabas.[122]

4. The leaders of the church should select candidates they think are suitable for ordination and then let the people decide by vote which one(s) they want. This was the practice of the early church, attested in the New Testament and as late as the third century.[123]

5. A man chosen for ministry is to have hands laid on him by other pastors, not by the whole congregation. In exceptional cases, one other pastor may suffice, but normally there should be at least two and if possible more.

In expounding the choice and ordination of ministers in such detail, Calvin was establishing a pattern that he believed was necessary to maintain the purity of the church. As far as possible, individual responsibility for ordination was to be avoided, because the opinion of only one person was not an adequate guide to the suitability of a candidate. But at the same time, it took a pastor to know a pastor—the untrained eyes of ordinary church members were not to be allowed free rein in the selection process. Only when all the candidates were suitable were they to be allowed a choice, a procedure that was as much about maintaining good relations with the congregation as it was about upholding the standards of the ministry.

It is clear from the above that although the Reformers were broadly agreed about how the ministry should be ordered, there were significant differences of detail that over time came to characterize distinct ecclesiastical traditions. The Lutherans and Anglicans generally thought of the ministry of Word and sacraments as settled and objective in character. They wanted ministers who were adequate for their appointed tasks, but they were alive to the problem of

---

[122] Acts 13:2–3.

[123] Acts 6:3; Cyprian, *Epistula* 3.

finding them and so had to allow for a certain amount of failure. The Anabaptists and the Reformed, on the other hand, placed greater emphasis on the right choice of ministers and cast doubt on the validity of ministries where this was not the case. As an example, the medieval church had permitted laypeople to administer baptism, a practice that both Lutherans and Anglicans continued. The main practical reason for this was the high rate of infant mortality. It was not always possible to find a minister able to baptize at short notice, and so it was quite common for midwives (in particular) to do it if necessary. The Anabaptists obviously rejected this, but so did Calvin, on the ground that it was a superstition based on the false assumption that baptism was necessary for salvation. Faced with having to choose, Calvin preferred that infants should be baptized by ministers in the church and not by private individuals, even if that meant that the infant would die unbaptized. Christians had nothing to fear from that, because the promise of God was to them and to their children, and the promise would not be cancelled for want of baptismal water.[124]

On another front, the difference between the Lutheran and the Reformed approach was one of the chief causes of English Puritanism. The Puritans were Reformed in their thinking, and believed that worthy ministers were required if a valid ministry was to be maintained. They roundly criticized the established church for tolerating inadequately trained pastors, many of whom were so ignorant that they could not even obtain a license to preach. Many people agreed with them in principle, but it was practically impossible to convert an entire body of clergy, who may have numbered up to twenty thousand men, into preaching pastors overnight. Although efforts were made to improve matters, it took about two generations before it could be said that the average clergyman had at least the formal qualifications for his appointment.[125]

How can we assess the attempts made by the Reformers to provide an adequate ministry for the church? First, we have to realize that permitting the clergy to marry was part of a wider program that was designed to abolish the spiritual estate as a distinct category of people in church and society. Monasteries were dissolved, and both monks and nuns were encouraged to return to the lay state and marry if they were still young enough to do so. Clergy families soon became the norm, and because wives and children were not ordained, ministers were much more integrated into ordinary life than they had been before. Even so, a married clergy had its own problems. The demand for an educated ministry meant that they were a new elite, set apart no longer by their celibacy but by their university degrees. People of that class tended to marry

[124] Calvin, *Institutio* 4.15.20.

[125] See Canon 46 of 1603 (1604) for evidence of this (Bray, *Anglican Canons*, 334–335).

women from similar backgrounds and bring up children capable of following in their footsteps, which ensured that the clerical order, while no longer cut off from the rest of society by celibacy, would nevertheless be an identifiably middle-class social phenomenon—too poor for the aristocracy, too rich for the peasantry, and too academic for either. As a result, Protestant pastors were often not much more integrated into the wider world than their Catholic counterparts were, despite the strenuous efforts of the Reformers to make them so.

It was also the case that those who could not afford to go to a university (the vast majority of the population) had no hope of being ordained, which made it difficult to believe that the Holy Spirit had chosen the church's ministers. This became a real problem when gifted preachers appeared who had not had the proper education. John Bunyan is an outstanding example of this phenomenon. Lacking the right credentials, he could not be ordained and remained an outsider to the church establishment, but how many of those who had gone through the correct procedures could hold a candle to him as a preacher and teacher of the Word? In the eighteenth century, John Wesley (1703–1791) found himself trapped in the same predicament when he tried to appoint men to minister to his Methodist congregations. Like Bunyan, they had the right spiritual fervor but lacked the formal qualifications, which meant that Wesley had to "ordain" them outside the system, a move which eventually led to the formation of a new denomination. In America, the same problem appeared and became acute. Colleges and seminaries could not turn out men fast enough to fill the pulpits of a rapidly expanding country, and their graduates generally did not want to go to the frontier. Inevitably a kind of "do it yourself" ministry appeared, the effects of which linger to the present day.

It is only in modern times, with the spread of higher education, that the clergy are no longer seen to be an anomalous class of their own, though the church generally remains solidly middle-class and an ordained ministry that requires a university education is still often effectively closed to people of humbler social backgrounds. If you are not a regular reader, you are unlikely to be at home in the average Protestant church, whatever the official doctrine might be. The same is true, it must be said, if you want to be a minister but are not married. Very few congregations are happy to have single people as their pastors, which is a great change from the sixteenth century—in this case, the permission given to marry has almost become an obligation, which, like all obligations imposed without biblical warrant, carries with it its own set of problems. As the Anglicans of Queen Elizabeth I's time realized, encouraging a clergyman to marry the wrong person could be just as bad (or even worse) in its effects as imposing celibacy.

How ministers are chosen, paid, and organized varies from denomination to denomination, but these are secondary details. Although the medieval priest has been replaced by a pastor or minister, his actual functions have not changed that much. It is the pastor who is normally expected to preach, to lead worship, and to look after the spiritual needs of his congregation. He will probably have a church council to help him, and perhaps also lay elders and/or deacons. These offices have the appearance of being biblical, but it is not clear to what extent they really correspond to the elders and deacons we read about in the New Testament. What is almost always the case is that lay elders and deacons are theologically untrained and unpaid volunteers who support themselves with other, secular work. Because of that, they often have limited amounts of time to devote to the church, leaving the full-time pastor effectively in charge. Denominational theories of ministry may differ, but that is how it almost always works out in practice, making the Reformers' plans for collective leadership and responsibility almost as hard to implement today as they were then.

In one important respect, though, the role of the Protestant clergy has changed. It has been diminished, in comparison with Roman Catholic clergy, by the admission of the laity to the councils of the church. This was a basic feature of the Reformation, when "lay involvement" took the form of state intervention. It is not well enough understood today that in sixteenth-century Europe, virtually everyone (except the Jews) belonged to the church. Because there was no democracy as we know it today, the voice of the laity was communicated through its appointed rulers—the kings, nobles, and occasionally parliamentarians who legislated for religion. In Protestant countries it was these people who ultimately determined what the church's worship and doctrine would be, a point that we must never forget. It is often claimed that John Calvin acted like a dictator in Geneva, but this is not true. Calvin had to do what the city council told him to do, and he was not even granted citizenship there until 1559, only five years before his death. In one famous case, the burning of Michael Servetus (1509?–1553) for heresy, Calvin pleaded for a lesser sentence but the council insisted on applying what had always been the standard punishment for that crime, and so Servetus perished. Today Calvin gets blamed for his death, when in fact he opposed it, because people do not understand that, in line with his own beliefs about the ministry, he was the servant of the Genevan church and not its master.[126]

Ministers were called first and foremost to preach and teach the Word of God, which meant expounding Holy Scripture to their congregations and

[126] See the detailed discussion of this incident in Bruce Gordon, *Calvin* (New Haven, CT: Yale University Press, 2009), 217–232.

urging them to take its message to heart. All the Reformers did this, but as we might expect, no one did it quite as thoroughly as John Calvin, who set out with a deliberate program intended to cover the entire Bible. He did not live long enough to complete the project, but he managed to comment on the New Testament (up to and including 1 John) and a good portion of the Old Testament before he died. He also preached sermons on most of these texts, though many of them remain unedited and a good number have been lost. The most important thing is that he set a model for preaching and teaching that was copied all over Protestant Europe and that has continued to be influential to the present day. He demonstrated how exposition must be based on exegesis of the text, and then how the message must be applied to the lives of ordinary congregations. It is always possible to disagree with particular interpretations that he gives, but the overall pattern is one that still characterizes Protestant ministry and continues to give Reformed theology a solid anchoring in the Bible.

In at least one case, a set of sermons became part of the theological framework of the local church. This was in England, where *The First Book of Homilies* came out in 1547 as a way of helping ignorant priests preach the Reformed message to their people. There were twelve sermons in all. The first six covered theological topics like Scripture, the fall of mankind, salvation, faith, good works, and love, while the last six dealt with more practical pastoral matters—swearing, backsliding, fear of death, obedience, fornication, and brawling. This pattern was typical of the time—the Ten Articles were similarly divided, as was the Augsburg Confession—and it shows us how the Reformers perceived their task. On the one hand they had to inculcate doctrinal principles, while on the other hand they had to encourage godly behavior in the light of those principles. The fact that these homilies were meant to be read in sequence was supposed to ensure a balanced teaching diet and give laypeople, for the first time, a serious course of theological instruction so as to enable them to participate more intelligently in worship and in the life of the church.

In 1562 there appeared *The Second Book of Homilies*, which is about three times the length of the first book but has quite a different orientation. Basic doctrine now gave way to practical admonitions about things like the dangers of idolatry and drunkenness, followed by a series of sermons related to the Prayer Book and the liturgical year. England was the only country to take printed sermons as seriously as this, but it is safe to say that in all Protestant churches a tradition was established whereby preaching became the chief means by which doctrine and a knowledge of Scripture was communicated to the people.

There was also a considerable outpouring of other devotional literature—

primers, catechisms, and so on—that were meant to inculcate the faith and that (in some cases) can be regarded as sources of church teaching comparable to official confessions of faith. These were studied and often memorized in the new schools that were established to educate boys (more rarely girls), and over time they created a theologically literate laity that could understand the sermons preached in church and apply them to their lives. The clergy were the engine that drove this—they preached on Sundays and very often acted as schoolmasters during the week.

The importance of this cannot be overestimated. Professional theologians could not ignore the demands of ordinary people, and the clergy found it difficult to live in an isolated theological world of their own. Doctrinal disputes became the stuff of everyday life and politics, while in turn, everyday life and politics helped to shape the agenda, if not the content, of theological discourse. Mysticism, so prominent in the Middle Ages and among Catholics who resisted the Reformation (especially in Spain), practically disappeared from Protestant theological discourse, because it was inherently elitist, and instead a democratized, and often formulaic, kind of theology took its place. Lay participation was the key to everything, and if that meant that sometimes artistic standards were lowered to accommodate more plebeian tastes (as in hymn singing, for example), it also meant that moral and spiritual standards among the laity were immeasurably raised.

At the heart of Protestant schemes for spiritual discipline was the celebration of the Eucharist, which they usually preferred to call the Lord's Supper, following the custom of the early church.[127] Luther and the first generation of Reformers were preoccupied with undoing the medieval doctrine of transubstantiation and abolishing the various ritual and devotional practices that had grown up around it.[128] This gave them little opportunity to develop a more positive approach to the subject. In the Smalcald Articles, for example, the section dealing with what it called "the sacrament of the altar" had three paragraphs—one upholding the ubiquity of the body of Christ, one attacking the practice of giving Communion in one kind only, and one denouncing transubstantiation.[129]

[127] The names given to this have (somewhat oddly) become indicative of the theological position adopted by those who use them. Thus, "Lord's Supper" is now common only among Reformed Protestants. Anglicans and Lutherans usually say "Holy Communion" (though both designations are found in the Book of Common Prayer, with preference being given to the "Lord's Supper"), while Catholics cling to the Mass, a term that was anathema to Calvin because of its theological associations (see *Institutio* 4.18.1). The Eastern Orthodox churches often use the word "Liturgy," somewhat inaccurately, while some Protestant groups say "the breaking of bread." In this context, "Eucharist" is intended to be a neutral, ecumenical word—not claimed by anyone in particular, and for that reason more or less acceptable to all!

[128] For the increasing importance of these in the fifteenth century, see Miri Rubin, *Corpus Christi: The Eucharist in Late Medieval Culture* (Cambridge: Cambridge University Press, 1991).

[129] Article 3.6, in Luther, *Schmalkald Articles*, 27–28.

Article 28 of the Thirty-nine Articles of the Church of England does somewhat better, but not much, and the influence of medieval debates is clearly apparent both in it and in the articles immediately following, which cover the same ground as the Smalcald Articles, though with a different take on the question of the ubiquity of Christ's body.[130]

Given this context, it is interesting to note that the Anabaptist Schleitheim Confession takes a different approach. Ignoring the medieval debates, it says,

> Whoever has not been called by one God to one faith, to one baptism, to one Spirit, to one body, with all the children of God's church, cannot be made one bread with them, as indeed must be done if one is truly to break bread according to the command of Christ.[131]

As ever, it was John Calvin who undertook the systematic exposition of the Lord's Supper, and his closeness to the Anabaptist position on this can be seen from the way he refuted the Anabaptist argument that infant baptism was no more valid that infant Communion, of which Calvin (and the rest of the church) disapproved. In answer to this, Calvin insisted that baptism and the Lord's Supper were quite different from each other, and that the common designation of "sacrament" did not mean that what applied to the one could be transferred automatically to the other.[132] He appealed to the teaching of the apostle Paul, who said, "Let a person examine himself, then, and so eat of the bread and drink of the cup. For anyone who eats and drinks without discerning the body eats and drinks judgment on himself."[133] He also claimed that under the old covenant, circumcision had been given to infants, but they had not partaken of the Passover meal until they were old enough to understand what it was about. For these reasons, therefore, infant Communion was wrong, even though Calvin admitted that it had been practiced in the early church.[134]

At the same time, Calvin readily agreed that the Lord's Supper followed on from baptism as feeding followed on from natural human birth. In his words,

> Just as God, having regenerated us in baptism, ingrafts us into the fellowship of his church and makes us his by adoption, so we have said that he performs the role of a provident parent, in continually supplying the food by which he may sustain and preserve us in the life to which he has begotten us by his Word. Christ is the only food of our soul, and so our heavenly Father invites

[130] Articles 28–31.
[131] Lumpkin, *Baptist Confessions*, 26.
[132] Calvin, *Institutio* 4.16.30.
[133] 1 Cor. 11:28–29.
[134] Calvin accepted the somewhat ambiguous evidence of Cyprian of Carthage, *De lapsis* 25, and of Augustine of Hippo, *Ad Bonifacium* I, 40 (22).

> us to him, so that when we have been refreshed by communion with him, we may gather new strength until such time as we reach heavenly immortality. But as this mystery of the secret union of Christ with believers is incomprehensible by nature, he exhibits its figure and image in visible signs adapted to our capacity.[135]

It was in the Lord's Supper that the deep meaning of the gospel was most fully revealed and experienced. Calvin's words on this subject are worth quoting at length:

> We can confidently assure ourselves that eternal life . . . is ours, and that the kingdom of heaven . . . can no more be taken from us than from him. On the other hand, we cannot be condemned for our sins, from the guilt of which he absolves us, seeing that he has been pleased that these should be imputed to himself as if they were his own. This is the wonderful exchange made by his boundless goodness. Having become one of us as the Son of Man, he has made us one with him as sons of God. By his own descent to the earth he has prepared our ascent into heaven. . . . Having taken upon himself the burden of unrighteousness that oppressed us, he has clothed us with his righteousness.[136]

The theology is that of Martin Luther, but the context is communion in the Lord's Supper, which Calvin believed was the work of the Holy Spirit. To those who found it hard to imagine how the body and blood of Christ could be the spiritual food that unites us to him when they are so far away from us in time and space—Calvin opposed the Lutheran doctrine of ubiquity—he had this to say:

> Let us remember how far the secret virtue of the Holy Spirit surpasses all our conceptions, and how foolish it is to want to measure its immensity by our feeble capacity. Therefore, what our mind does not comprehend, let faith conceive—namely, that the Spirit truly unites things that are separated by space.[137]

Like the other Reformers before him, Calvin did not hesitate to condemn the Roman doctrine of transubstantiation, nor did he mince his words when it came to the Lutheran teaching about ubiquity. But these debates were couched in the context of a real participation in the sacrifice of Christ, a participation

[135] Calvin, *Institutio* 4.17.1.
[136] Ibid., 4.17.2.
[137] Ibid., 4.17.10.

that was possible and meaningful only when it was informed and applied by the work of the Holy Spirit in the heart of the believer.

This becomes clear when we examine the so-called *Consensus Tigurinus*, an agreement drawn up between Calvin and Heinrich Bullinger, which was soon accepted by most of the Swiss Protestant churches (though Bern held out for many years) and had considerable influence elsewhere, notably in England and in Germany, where Melanchthon expressed his satisfaction with it.[138] The *Consensus* begins by asserting that the sacraments are dependent on the gospel and only benefit those who are united to Christ.[139] Having expiated our sins in his human nature, Christ is now to be considered as a "repairer" (*reparator*), who reforms whatever is corrupt in us by the power of his Holy Spirit, so that we may no longer live for the world and the flesh, and that God may dwell in us.[140] This he does in the person of his Holy Spirit.[141] As for the relationship between the signs of bread and wine and the things signified by them,

> Because these things that the Lord has given as witnesses and seals of his grace are true, there is no doubt that he performs inwardly by his Spirit that which the sacraments figure to our eyes and other senses. . . . We should look not to the signs themselves, but to the promise attached to them. It is as far as our faith in the promise there offered prevails that the benefits of which we speak will display themselves.[142]

A major concern for both Calvin and Bullinger was that the celebration of Holy Communion should not be surrounded by devotional practices reminiscent of Roman Catholicism, and for that reason they went out of their way to insist that the elements of bread and wine contained nothing supernatural in themselves. As they said, "though the sacraments are sometimes called seals . . . of faith, yet the Spirit alone is the true seal,"[143] an affirmation that made it possible for them to state that people could receive the elements without getting any spiritual benefit from them, and conversely, they could also commune with Christ apart from the sacrament.[144] They were also determined to avoid any suggestion of the "ubiquity" of Christ's bodily presence:

[138] The text has been edited with a commentary and bibliography by Eberhard Busch in *Reformierte Bekenntnisschriften I/2 (1535–1549)* (Neukirchen-Vlyun: Neukirchener Verlag, 2006), 467–490. *Tiguricum* is the Latin form of "Zurich."

[139] *Consensus Tigurinus* 2–3.

[140] Ibid., 4.

[141] Ibid., 6.

[142] Ibid., 8, 10.

[143] Ibid., 15.

[144] Ibid., 16–20.

> We must guard particularly against any idea of a local presence. For while the signs are present in this world . . . Christ, regarded as man, must be sought nowhere else than in heaven, and in no other way than with the mind and eye of faith. Therefore it is a perverse and impious superstition to inclose him under the elements of this world.[145]

A careful reading of the *Consensus* will show that in most respects it can be reconciled with Luther's teaching on the subject, and perhaps if he had lived to see it, he would have accepted it as a true statement of his beliefs, as Melanchthon did. But Luther had never warmed to the Swiss, and some of his followers interpreted the *Consensus* as a rejection of his teaching. They naturally focused on the question of "ubiquity," which the *Consensus* clearly did reject, and the division between what would become the Lutheran and the Reformed traditions grew deeper in consequence. The impact of the *Consensus* is, however, clearly visible in the Forty-two Articles of the Church of England (1553), which states,

> Forasmuch as the truth of man's nature requireth, that the body of one and the selfsame man cannot be at one time in diverse places, but must needs be in one certain place; therefore the body of Christ cannot be present at one time in many and diverse places. And because, as Holy Scripture doth teach, Christ was taken up into heaven, and there shall continue until the end of the world, a faithful man ought not either to believe or openly to confess the real and bodily presence, as they term it, of Christ's flesh and blood, in the sacrament of the Lord's Supper.[146]

One way or another, the *Consensus Tigurinus* became foundational to the Reformed understanding of the Lord's Supper and remains so to this day, even if its influence is seldom acknowledged.[147]

As for the other sacraments of the medieval system, Calvin insisted that they belonged in a different category. He rejected the idea that confirmation was a sacrament in its own right and deplored the way in which it had been elevated above baptism by restricting it to a chrismation (anointing with oil) that could be given only by the bishop.[148] What he wanted to see was a com-

[145] Ibid., 21. See also 25.
[146] Article 29; see Bray, *Documents of the English Reformation*, 302. This was rewritten and considerably shortened in 1563 as Article 28. The concluding paragraph, which states that unbelievers do not partake of Christ when they eat and drink the sacrament, was omitted at that time at the request of Queen Elizabeth I, probably out of deference to the Lutherans, but was reinstated as Article 29 in 1571.
[147] See, for example, the Westminster Confession, 29.5–8 (1647), which says the same things but in a slightly different way.
[148] Calvin, *Institutio* 4.19.5–11.

plete transformation of the rite into something quite distinct from baptism but to his mind equally necessary in the life of the church. In his words, it would be "catechizing by which those in childhood, or immediately beyond it, would give an account of the faith in front of the church."[149] He wanted to see a form drawn up for this purpose, which even a ten-year-old could recite publicly and be corrected, if there was any point of the faith that he did not grasp correctly. Calvin saw this as an excellent way of encouraging parents to teach their children properly, and of reminding the rest of the church what it was that they were expected to believe. What a child could understand, anyone could understand, and by hearing it publicly recited, the faith of the whole community could be built up.

Penance and Extreme Unction were both rejected by Calvin because there was no scriptural warrant for them. The New Testament certainly spoke about repentance, but associated it with baptism, and in Calvin's view, to add a sacrament of penance on top of that was to call into question the reality of regeneration.[150] Extreme Unction claimed biblical support from James 5:14, which advises the elders to pray over the sick and anoint them with oil so that they may be healed. Calvin admitted that oil was used in Scripture as a sign of the Holy Spirit and his gifts, but claimed that the church had inverted this by attributing spiritual powers to the oil itself:

> Just as the apostles, not without cause, openly declared (by using the symbol of oil) that the gift of healing that had been committed to them was not their own, but the power of the Holy Spirit, so these men [the papists] insult the Holy Spirit by making his power consist of a filthy oil of no efficacy. It is just like saying that all oil is the power of the Holy Spirit . . . and that every dove is the Holy Spirit, because he appeared in that form.[151]

Modern readers will note that Calvin avoided any discussion of spiritual healing as such, but the tone of his remarks strongly suggests that he believed that it was a gift that no longer functioned in the life of the church. When talking about the details, he remarked that if Extreme Unction followed the New Testament precept, it would be administered to every sick person by a group of elders, and not just to the dying, by a priest. But he never suggested that this practice should be restored, and there is no evidence that any Protestant church did so at the time.[152]

---

[149] Ibid., 4.19.13.
[150] Ibid., 4.19.17.
[151] Ibid., 4.19.20.
[152] Ibid., 4.19.21. Healing rites have been revived to some extent in modern times, but hardly anyone now does what James recommended, even if they believe in spiritual healing and practice it.

This leaves only Matrimony, a subject on which the Reformers had a good deal to say, though Calvin was noticeably more reticent than most. We have already seen how keen they were to allow clerical marriage, but that was a specialized interest, even though it was obviously dear to the hearts of men who were themselves mostly ex-priests or ex-monks. As a social institution, matrimony could be said to have been the will of God from the time of Adam and Eve, but it was not specifically Christian and could hardly be regarded as a sacrament of the gospel. Confusion had arisen because the apostle Paul had called marriage a "mystery," and in the Middle Ages, the Greek word *mystêrion* was generally regarded as the equivalent of the Latin *sacramentum*.[153]

In ancient times, matrimony had been a largely secular affair, though Christians were advised not to marry outside the faith.[154] The New Testament church did not perform weddings, and church marriages did not become common until after the year 1000. By the time of the Reformation, though, they had become universal, which meant that there was no divorce. This caused some hardship in cases where couples simply did not get along, and there were many cases of unofficial separations and cohabitation with other partners, often with children being born out of wedlock. The snag was that these arrangements were not recognized and, when a man died, his possessions would go to his legal wife and children, even if he had not seen them for years, while those he lived with were disinherited. This situation was both complicated and productive of considerable misery, and the Reformers wanted to straighten it out—by legalizing divorce! That, of course, meant that they could not recognize matrimony as a sacrament, since the grace of God could not be withdrawn or denied, though they allowed that it was a holy ordinance. There were a number of attempts to secularize marriage in the sixteenth and seventeenth centuries, but few of them were successful. Popular feeling was against it, and there was a genuine fear of divorce, especially among women who could find themselves destitute because of it.

For obvious reasons, the question of divorce was particularly discussed in England, where the matrimonial misadventures of King Henry VIII had led to the break with Rome in 1534. Henry never got divorced in the modern sense of the word—three of his marriages were annulled, a procedure that differed from divorce in that the marriage was declared never to have taken place, and any children born from it were automatically bastardized. This was inconvenient for Henry, who had to have special legislation passed in order to legitimize his daughters and give them the right to succeed to the throne, but the question

[153] See Eph. 5:32.
[154] 2 Cor. 6:14.

had wider implications for society as a whole. Should divorce, understood as the dissolution of a valid marriage (and therefore without prejudice to the inheritance rights of the children), be accepted?[155]

The New Testament had theoretically allowed for divorce in cases of adultery,[156] but this had been overlooked by medieval canonical legislation, which simply banned it altogether. It was therefore relatively easy for the Reformers to argue for introducing divorce after adultery, but could they go any further than that on the basis of Scripture? One man who tried to do so was Martin Bucer, who wrote a remarkable treatise called *De regno Christi* (*The Kingdom of Christ*) which outlined the way he thought a Christian society ought to be governed and which he dedicated to King Edward VI of England.[157] Bucer developed his argument in favor of divorce by citing precedents from the early church allowing divorce and remarriage in cases of desertion, and even for people who had taken a vow of celibacy.[158] He even cited Old Testament texts such as Deuteronomy 24:1–4 as evidence that God had not only tolerated divorce in ancient times but commanded it in certain cases, and argued that what was permitted in Israel was also permissible for Christians, despite Jesus' own words to the contrary.[159] By these and other hermeneutical sleights of hand Bucer convinced himself that the Scriptures did not forbid divorce in the way that a simple reading of Matthew 19 might suggest. It was not that he wanted to be lenient to adulterers, of course. In fact, he thought that they should be put to death, which to his mind was yet another reason for saying that mere divorce must apply to other circumstances.[160]

The influence of Bucer's argument can perhaps be detected in the proposed reform of the English canon law known to us as the *Reformatio legum ecclesiasticarum*, which was compiled by Thomas Cranmer and his associates in 1553 but never received parliamentary sanction.[161] The *Reformatio* enjoined "the

[155] There is a considerable body of scholarly writing on this subject. See, for example, Lawrence Stone, *Road to Divorce: England 1530–1987* (Oxford: Oxford University Press, 1990); Eric J. Carlson, *Marriage and the English Reformation* (Oxford: Blackwell, 1994); Martin Ingram, *Church Courts, Sex, and Marriage in England, 1570–1640* (Cambridge: Cambridge University Press, 1987); David Cressy, *Birth, Marriage, and Death: Ritual, Religion, and the Life-cycle in Tudor and Stuart England* (Oxford: Oxford University Press, 1997).

[156] Matt. 19:3–9.

[157] Francois Wendel, ed., *Martini Buceri opera Latina XV: De regno Christi* (Paris: Presses Universitaires de France; and Gütersloh: C. Bertelsmann Verlag, 1955). An English translation is available in Wilhelm Pauck, ed., *Melanchthon and Bucer* (Philadelphia: Westminster, 1969), 174–394), but unfortunately the chapters on divorce (2.22–46) were omitted because the editor found them tedious and because they had already been translated and published by John Milton in the seventeenth century. They must therefore be read in John Milton, *The Judgment of Martin Bucer concerning Divorce* (London: Matthew Simmons, 1644). On Bucer's views, see Herman J. Selderhuis, *Marriage and Divorce in the Thought of Martin Bucer* (Kirksville, MO: Thomas Jefferson University Press, 1999). Originally published as *Huwelijk en echtscheiding bij Martin Bucer* (Leiden: Uitgeverij J. J. Groen en Zoon, 1994).

[158] Bucer, *De regno* 2.22–24.

[159] Ibid., 2.26–27.

[160] Ibid., 2.32–33.

[161] For the Latin text and English translation, see Bray, *Tudor Church Reform*. The relevant chapter is 10 (264–279).

most severe punishment" for adulterers, but it stopped short of the death penalty, preferring exile or life imprisonment instead.[162] The innocent party, male or female, was then free to remarry.[163] Divorce on the ground of desertion was more problematic, but it was allowed in cases of prolonged absence, though it was not specified how long "prolonged" was.[164] The assumption was that it would almost always be the man who deserted his wife, not the other way around, probably because men had much greater social freedom and were often called away on business or to fight in war. In the latter case, if a husband failed to return and his whereabouts were unknown, he could be declared legally dead, allowing his "widow" to remarry. But if he should happen to turn up again, even after many years, she would have to take him back (and presumably the second marriage would be automatically annulled, though the *Reformatio* did not say that.)[165]

Beyond that, the *Reformatio* allowed divorce in cases of "deadly hostility" between the partners, appealing in this instance to the teaching of the apostle Paul, even though he never addressed the matter.[166] Cruelty was also accepted as grounds for divorce, but not minor disagreements or incurable disease.[167] For a spouse to incite his or her partner to commit adultery (so as to obtain a divorce) was regarded as a crime, as was aiding and abetting such behavior.[168] But (to the modern mind at least) the most extraordinary provision must surely be the one relating to cases of double adultery, i.e., where each party to the marriage was guilty:

> If the person who has been convicted of adultery is able to prove the same crime against the other marriage partner, and does so before that party has proceeded to a new marriage, the equal guilt of each party shall incur equal punishment, and the former marriage between them shall remain valid.[169]

Perhaps exile or life imprisonment were not such bad options after all! What the modern reader has to understand is that the provisions of the *Reformatio* were very liberal for their time, and they did not represent popular opinion. The *Reformatio* never received official sanction and so never became law, though by an odd quirk of history, some of its provisions were incorporated

[162] *Reformatio legum ecclesiasticarum* 10.2–3.
[163] Ibid., 10.5.
[164] Ibid., 10.7–8.
[165] Ibid., 10.9.
[166] Ibid., 10.10. The biblical text referred to was probably 1 Cor. 7:15, where Paul allowed a Christian to remarry if he or she was deserted by an unbelieving spouse.
[167] *Reformatio legum ecclesiasticarum* 10.11–13.
[168] Ibid., 10.16, 18.
[169] Ibid., 10.17.

in Bishop Edmund Gibson's *Codex iuris Ecclesiae Anglicanae*, which first appeared in 1713 and was subsequently regarded as authoritative.[170] As a result, it was widely believed that the English Reformers had permitted divorce, and that the Church of England had subsequently gone back to medieval practice. That argument, false though it was, was used in the 1850s to facilitate the introduction of civil divorce, and it was not finally disproved until the early twentieth century, by which time the church had lost control of divorce proceedings.[171]

It is one of the oddities of church history that the Puritans, who were normally quite strict in disciplinary matters, nevertheless found themselves arguing for the legalization of divorce, as John Milton did in the 1640s. But whatever the rights and wrongs of that campaign may have been, social custom was too strong and biblical support too weak for them to succeed, and divorce reform never became a feature of Protestantism in the way that Martin Bucer had wanted it to be.

By the end of the sixteenth century, it was becoming clear that the Protestant countries of northern Europe were developing a different kind of society than the one that had existed before the Reformation and that continued to exist in those lands that remained loyal to the papacy.[172] For at least two generations after Martin Luther, the theological agenda of Western Christendom was set by Protestants, and the Roman Catholic Church could do little but defend its positions against further erosion. In this it was remarkably successful. After a slow start, the pope managed to convene the Council of Trent that sat in twenty-five sessions spread over eighteen years (1545–1563) and enacted a series of decrees that were to define the church for the next four centuries.[173]

The council was not in continuous operation but met in three distinct phases. The first of these comprised ten sessions and lasted through 1546 and the first half of 1547. In these sessions, the council reiterated the ancient Nicene Creed, defined the canon of Scripture, and ventured into matters of theological controversy such as original sin, justification by faith, and the meaning of the sacraments. Interspersed among these decrees were injunctions ordering bishops, priests, and monks to obtain copies of the Scriptures and to preach

[170] See Bray, *Tudor Church Reform*, 773–782, for the evidence from Gibson's *Codex*.

[171] For the details, see Lewis Dibdin, *English Church Law and Divorce*, part 1 (London: John Murray, 1912), 1–79. Dibdin cites a number of English Protestant divines on the subject, none of whom was as accommodating as the *Reformatio* would have been, which shows that its provisions were not generally accepted as church policy.

[172] See, for example, Philip Benedict, *Christ's Churches Purely Reformed: A Social History of Calvinism* (New Haven, CT: Yale University Press, 2002) for developments on the European continent; and Patrick Collinson, *The Religion of Protestants: The Church in English Society* (Oxford: Oxford University Press, 1982).

[173] On the Council of Trent, see John W. O'Malley, *Trent: What Happened at the Council* (Cambridge, MA: Belknap of Harvard University, 2013). The definitive study is Olivier de La Brosse, Joseph Lecler, and Henri Holstein, eds., *Les conciles de Latran V et de Trente: 1512–1517 et 1545–1548* (Paris: Fayard, 2007); and J. Lecler and H. Holstein, eds., *Le concile de Trente 1551–1563* (Paris: Fayard, 2005). Both volumes are published in the series *Histoire des conciles oecuméniques*, 10–11.

from them in order to combat the spread of "heresy" (i.e., Protestantism).[174] To do this effectively, they were also ordered to reside in the places to which they had been officially appointed, which too few of them were doing, and to put into operation the provisions that had been made centuries before in a number of papal decretals, but which had been neglected over the years.[175] In effect, it amounted to a tightening of the traditional discipline on the assumption that it was laxity and corruption that had provoked the Protestant revolt.

The second group of sessions (11–16) met in 1551–1552. In addition to decrees concerning the Eucharist, Penance, and Extreme Unction, they also issued a number of injunctions for practical reformation of the church's practices, concentrating now on the application of discipline by establishing effective procedures for its implementation.[176] Finally, there was a third group of nine sessions in 1562–1563, which issued decrees concerning the celebration of the Mass and the administration of Holy Communion, as well as regulations for Holy Orders and Matrimony. In these sessions there were further injunctions for the reformation of discipline, concentrating now mainly on the quality and numbers of the clergy along with the administration of cathedral and parish churches.

The upshot of all this was that, in the future, the clergy would be more strictly supervised, the pattern of worship would be more closely regulated, and uniformity (as decided by the pope) would be imposed as much as was practicable. The aim was to ensure that every Catholic could go into a church anywhere in the world and feel at home. The Tridentine Mass (approved in 1570) said or sung in Latin would be the same everywhere, the clergy would receive the same spiritual and pastoral formation, and the religious orders would be more closely supervised by the bishops, and especially by the pope himself. In such a system, innovation was not welcome, and although it would be wrong to say that there was no theological development at all, what did occur was minor compared to what was going on in Protestant churches at the same time, and Protestant influence was apparent (or suspected) whenever anyone sought to break the established mold.

A classic case of that was the emergence of Jansenism, named after its chief proponent, Cornelius Jansen (1585–1638). It was no coincidence that Jansen was a professor of theology at Utrecht, in the heart of the mainly Protestant Netherlands, nor that his chief theological inspiration was Augustine of Hippo, from whom he got such Protestant-sounding ideas as predestination,

---

[174] *Conciliorum oecumenicorum decreta*, 667–670.
[175] Ibid., 681–683; 686–689.
[176] Ibid., 698–701; 714–718.

total depravity, and salvation by grace alone. These similarities to Calvinism did not go unnoticed, of course, and the Jansenists were attacked by the followers of Luis de Molina (1535–1600), who gave much greater scope to human free will than Jansen did. The debate rumbled on for the rest of the seventeenth century. Jansenism was condemned by Pope Innocent X in his bull *Cum occasione*, issued in 1653, but it found a supporter in Blaise Pascal (1623–1662), whose *Provincial Letters* and *Pensées* were to become classics of French and Christian literature that are still read today by Protestants as much as by Catholics. Jansenism was not finally extinguished until 1713, when Pope Clement XI issued his bull *Unigenitus*, which obliged the remaining Jansenists to submit or suffer the consequences. Of course most of them submitted, at least formally, but their ideas continued to circulate underground and were an important factor in bringing about the French Revolution in 1789, when the structures that had persecuted them were finally destroyed forever.[177]

The great loser in all of this was almost certainly the papacy. On the surface, its authority was strengthened by the centralizing measures taken at the Council of Trent, but in reality its real power and influence were in steady, long-term decline. Three incidents mark the stages of this decline:

1. In 1494, the pope was asked to adjudicate between Spain and Portugal, each of which was starting to explore the world beyond Europe. In the treaty of Tordesillas (supplemented in 1529 by a further treaty of Zaragoza), the entire world was divided between the two countries. Spain got North America and the western half of South America, while Portugal got what is now Brazil and Africa. In 1529 the line was extended to the far east, giving Portugal India and China, and Spain the Philippines. No one questioned the validity of this award, and to this day its effects can be seen in Latin America and to some extent in Africa and Asia, where Portuguese colonies continued to exist into the late twentieth century.[178]

2. In 1582, after the Reformation, Pope Gregory XIII reformed the ancient Roman calendar to bring it into greater conformity with the solar year. The remaining Catholic countries accepted it almost immediately, though they did so of their own free will, and not because the pope told them to. The Protestant countries refused, because even though the reform was a good one, agreeing to it would look like submission to the papacy. Only very gradually did they

[177] On this subject, see Dale K. Van Kley, *The Religious Origins of the French Revolution: From Calvin to the Civil Constitution, 1560–1791* (New Haven, CT: Yale University Press, 1996).

[178] Angola and Mozambique in Africa, for example, and Goa (India), Macau (China), and East Timor in Asia. The Portuguese were driven out of Goa in 1961, left Africa and Timor in 1975, and handed Macau back to the Chinese in 1999.

change their minds, with the majority going over by 1700, though the British Isles held out against it until 1752. Orthodox Russia never accepted it at all. After the revolution there, the Bolsheviks introduced it in 1918, but the church refused to change and still uses the old calendar. Other Orthodox countries and churches (like that of Greece) adopted the reform in the 1920s, but even today the entire Orthodox world still celebrates Easter according to the traditional date, which puts it out of line with the Western churches.

3. In 1648, the European powers ended the Thirty Years' War in Germany, which had been fought between Protestants and Catholics, without any reference to the papacy at all. The Peace of Westphalia, as this treaty is known, is now generally reckoned to have been the beginning of the modern state system in which politics was effectively separated from religion, even if individual states continued to maintain an exclusive church establishment, as most of them did.

By the time of the French Revolution, it was possible for Napoleon to dream of abolishing the papacy altogether, but although that failed, its temporal power was finally extinguished in 1870, just as the First Vatican Council was proclaiming the pope's infallibility![179] His canonical authority grew in inverse relation to his real power and influence, so that today Catholics decide for themselves whether to listen to what he says or not, and many Protestants find him quite congenial—attitudes that would have been unthinkable on either side in the sixteenth century. On balance, this has to be seen as a victory for Protestantism, because whatever the official documents say, the pope's standing now rests, not on his claims to doctrinal infallibility, but on his credibility as a voice of the Holy Spirit speaking to the church. When what he says accords with what most Christians recognize as spiritual truth, he is listened to; when it does not (as, for example, in the prohibition of artificial means of birth control), he is largely ignored. Martin Luther would have been glad.

The Scope of the Covenant

The basic principles of covenant theology were election and predestination. Today these are often lumped together and regarded as virtually the same thing, but they were not understood like that in the sixteenth century. Election was the foreordination of God, determined outside time and space and therefore "before" the creation of the world. Predestination, as the name suggests, pointed to where the elect were headed, which was toward eternal fellowship

[179] *Conciliorum oecumenicorum decreta*, 815–816. A semblance of that power was restored in 1929, when the current Vatican City State was created by Benito Mussolini, as a way of gaining popularity with Catholics at that time.

with God in heaven. The individual believer could therefore look back to his election and forward to his predestined goal.

How this theoretical pattern is applied in practice is the work of the Holy Spirit. It is he who calls the elect out of the world, he who empowers them to live the Christian life and to fight the spiritual battles that go with it, and he who will lead believers into glory at the end. Covenant theology did not triumph without a battle, however, and it was the outcome of that struggle that would determine the character of "Calvinism" as it has been understood ever since. The second generation of Reformed theologians, represented by men like Theodore de Bèze, or Beza (1519–1605), and William Perkins (1558–1602), said that Christ's atoning sacrifice coincides with his saving work.[180] This means that everyone whose sins Jesus atoned for is saved. But since we know that in fact not everyone is saved, it follows that he has atoned for the sins of only those who are. Furthermore, since Christ was the Lamb of God who was slain before the foundation of the world, the number of those chosen for salvation must have been known to God before they were created, and certainly before the fall of Adam. This is the doctrine known as "supralapsarianism" ("before the fall") and was taught by both Beza and Perkins:

> God's will is twofold—general and special. God's general will is to permit that which is evil, not simply, but because with God evil hath some respect of good, and in this respect we say that God decreed Adam's fall. God's special will is his approving will, whereby he taketh pleasure and delight in that which is good; and in this regard God nilled [i.e., did not will] Adam's fall and man's sins and yet in some respect he may be said to will them. A magistrate, though he take no comfort or delight in the death and execution of a malefactor, yet he decreeth and appointeth it, and so may be said to will it.[181]

Perkins elaborated on this further when he said,

> God before all worlds did purpose to hate some creatures, and that justly, so far forth as his hating of them will serve for the manifestation of his justice, but he neither hates them indeed . . . before they are; and therefore, actual hatred comes not in till after the creation. Whom God hath

[180] See Richard Muller, *Christ and the Decree: Christology and Predestination in Reformed Theology from Calvin to Perkins*, 2nd ed. (Grand Rapids, MI: Baker, 1988). For a good discussion of Beza's role and an assessment of the current state of scholarly opinion about it, see Shawn D. Wright, *Our Sovereign Refuge: The Pastoral Theology of Theodore Beza* (Milton Keynes: Paternoster, 2004).

[181] William Perkins, *The Workes of That Famous and Worthy Minister of Christ in the Universitie of Cambridge, Mr William Perkins*, 3 vols. (London: John Legatt & Cantrell Legge, 1616–1618), 3.2:298 (spelling and punctuation modernized).

> decreed . . . to hate, them being once created, he hates in Adam with actual hatred.[182]

He also claimed that,

> The supreme end of God's counsel is not damnation but the declaration of his justice in the just destruction of the creature; neither doth God decree man's damnation as it is damnation, that is, the ruin of man and the putting of him forth to punishment, but as it is a real execution of justice.[183]

Modern readers may be inclined to think that Perkins's views were extreme, but in his day they were not, nor were they especially Puritan. John Whitgift (1530?–1604), who was archbishop of Canterbury from 1583 and a notorious anti-Puritan, nevertheless approved a series of nine articles on predestination, originally drawn up by William Whitaker (1548–1595), regius professor of divinity at Cambridge and a leading Puritan in the university during Perkins's time. These so-called Lambeth Articles (1595) were not ratified by the queen, who would not authorize anything that might upset her settlement of religion at the start of her reign, but they were widely approved of and incorporated unamended into the Irish Articles in 1615. They affirm the salvation of the elect, but also the predestination of the non-elect to eternal damnation:

> Saving grace is not granted, communicated or given to all men, so that they might be saved by it if they wished to be. No one can come to Christ unless it is given to him, and unless the Father draws him. And not all men are drawn by the Father to come to the Son. It is not placed in the will or power of any and every man to be saved.[184]

The system worked out by these men was concise and logical, but it provoked opposition from those who did not accept Reformed theology and disquiet among some of those who did.[185] The main reason for this was that there are many passages of Scripture that say that Christ died for the sins of the whole world and that God desires the salvation of everyone. Not even Beza or Perkins believed that God was responsible for the damnation of those who were not chosen for salvation (the "reprobate"), and so it is not surprising that, before very long, there was pressure put on Reformed theologians to modify

[182] Perkins, *Workes*, 1:287.
[183] Ibid.
[184] Lambeth Articles, 7–9; see Bray, *Documents of the English Reformation*, 399–400 for the complete text. In the Irish Articles, the above statement is no. 32 (Bray, *Documents of the English Reformation*, 442). See also Victoria C. Miller, *The Lambeth Articles* (Oxford: Latimer, 1994).
[185] See Nicholas Tyacke, *Anti-Calvinists: The Rise of English Arminianism, c.1590–1640* (Oxford: Oxford University Press, 1987).

their teaching in a way that would accommodate the universal dimension of Christ's saving work.

The most serious challenge to this emerging orthodoxy came from Jacob Arminius (1560–1609), who believed that he was a true exponent of Calvin's teachings and that those who were moving in the direction of covenant theology had misinterpreted them.[186] In 1602 he wrote an "examination" of Perkins's pamphlet on the order and mode of predestination as a contribution to a debate that was already going on in England, though in a somewhat fitful way.[187] It is now known that opposition to the doctrine of predestination among English Protestants was present as far back as the reign of Mary I (1553–1558).[188] More recently, there had been a controversy in Cambridge in 1595 following a sermon preached by William Barrett in which he denounced the prevailing predestinarian theology of Perkins and William Whitaker (1548?–1595), then Regius Professor of Divinity.[189] It was generally assumed that Barrett was influenced by Peter Baro (1534–1599), a Frenchman who was then the Lady Margaret Professor of Divinity, and Baro was soon put under investigation. After the publication of the Lambeth Articles he was ordered to ensure that his teaching conformed to them, but after initially appearing to submit, he launched a broadside attack on them in 1596 and as a result was not reelected to his professorial chair. The Baro affair divided English opinion and won him sympathy that his ideas alone might not have earned him, but for the time being at least, his anti-predestinarian views were effectively suppressed.[190]

Following this incident, Perkins wrote his *De praedestinationis modo et*

---

[186] The classic biography of Arminius is Carl Bangs, *Arminius: A Study in the Dutch Reformation* (Nashville: Abingdon, 1971; repr., Eugene, OR: Wipf & Stock, 1998). Among more recent works on his theology, see in particular Richard Muller, *God, Creation, and Providence in the Theology of Jacob Arminius: Sources and Directions of Scholastic Protestantism in the Era of Early Orthodoxy* (Grand Rapids, MI: Baker, 1991); F. Stuart Clarke, *The Ground of Election: Jacobus Arminius' Doctrine of the Work and Person of Christ* (Milton Keynes: Paternoster, 2006); Keith D. Stanglin and Thomas H. McCall, *Jacob Arminius: Theologian of Grace* (Oxford: Oxford University Press, 2012). Most of his works can be found in English translation in *The Works of James Arminius*, trans. James Nichols, 2 vols. (London: Longman, Hurst, Rees, Orme, Brown, & Green, 1825–1828); and vol. 3, trans. William Nichols (London: Thomas Baker, 1875). All three volumes, edited by William R. Bagnall, are now published together with a new introduction by Carl Bangs (Grand Rapids, MI: Baker, 1986). For other works, not included in this translation, see the bibliography in Stanglin and McCall, *Jacob Arminius*, 211–212.

[187] Jacobus Arminius, *Examen modestum libelli quem Dominus Gulielmus Perkinsius edidit de praedestinationis modo et ordine, itemque de amplitudine divinae gratiae* (Leiden: Godefridus Basson, 1612). An English translation is available in *Works of James Arminius*, 3:249–484.

[188] Carl Bangs, *Arminius*, cites the example of John Trewe, an obscure clergyman who wrote against predestination at that time, but whose work was not published for nearly three centuries. See *Authentic Documents Relative to the Predestinarian Controversy Which Took Place among Those Who Were Imprisoned for Their Adherence to the Doctrines of the Reformation by Queen Mary*, ed. Richard Laurence (Oxford: W. Baxter, 1819). Trewe belonged to a group known as the "free-willers," whose acknowledged leader was a certain Henry Harte. They are best known from the writings of their leading opponent, John Bradford (d. 1555). See Aubrey Townsend, ed., *The Writings of John Bradford* (Cambridge: Cambridge University Press, 1853; repr., Edinburgh: Banner of Truth, 1979).

[189] It was this incident that led to the publication of the Lambeth Articles later in the year.

[190] See Nicholas Tyacke, *Anti-Calvinists*, 29–40.

ordine, which was published at Cambridge in 1598 and a year later at Basel.[191] Arminius sat down to write a lengthy reply and sent it to Perkins for comment before publishing it. Unfortunately Perkins died before he could read what Arminius had to say, and the book was not published for a decade, when Arminius himself was dead. Nevertheless, Arminius's views had become widely known before his death, and the delayed publication of his reply to Perkins only confirmed them.[192]

By then, however, the situation in the Netherlands had moved on. Shortly after Arminius died, his followers drew up a series of five articles, which they subsequently published as a *Remonstrance* to the Dutch Reformed Church.[193] The gist of these articles, with the Bible verses quoted in support of them, was as follows:

1. God determined by an unchangeable decree, made from before the foundation of the world, that he would save, in, for and through Christ and by the grace of the Holy Spirit, those who believed in him and who persevered in their faith to the end. Those who refused to believe he would condemn.[194]
2. Jesus died for everyone and has obtained redemption and forgiveness for the entire human race, but only those who believe in him enjoy the benefits of this.[195]
3. Fallen man has no good in himself but must be born again in Christ, through his Holy Spirit, and renewed in his mind, in order to think straight and do what is pleasing to God.[196]
4. The grace of God is the beginning and end of all good works, so that without the prevenient and cooperating grace of God the regenerate man can do nothing. But God's grace is not irresistible.[197]
5. Those who are united to Christ and who have his life-giving Spirit have the power to resist the world, the flesh, and the Devil. Jesus Christ helps them by the grace of his Holy Spirit as they struggle, and he guarantees them the victory.[198] Whether such people can fall away again is unclear, and Scripture must be examined more carefully before we can teach this.

[191] William Perkins, *De praedestinationis modo et ordine* (Cambridge: John Legat, 1598; Basel: C. Waldkirch, 1599). It was this second printing that Arminius used in his refutation.
[192] For a detailed exposition of Arminius's reply to Perkins, see Bangs, *Arminius*, 206–221.
[193] The original text in Dutch and Latin, along with an English translation, can be found in Schaff, *Creeds of Christendom*, 3:545–549.
[194] John 3:36.
[195] John 3:16; 1 John 2:2.
[196] John 15:5.
[197] Acts 7:51.
[198] John 10:28.

The publication of the *Remonstrance* caused a storm of controversy that threatened to tear the fabric of the Dutch Republic apart, and so in 1618 the Dutch Reformed Church convened a synod at Dordrecht (Dort) in order to sort out the theological issues that it raised. Representatives from all the Reformed churches, including the British, were invited, and their conclusions represented what would subsequently become standard teaching in their churches.[199]

The Synod of Dort composed a five-point reply to the *Remonstrance* which became the standard definition of "Calvinism" as this is now understood.[200] The first of its canons concerned the freedom of God's election.[201] Could God choose anyone he liked, or was there some chance of influencing his decision? Were some types of people more likely to be preferred over others? This question was a spin-off from the idea of free will, because it suggested that some people might put extra effort into being saved and be rewarded accordingly. But even if God did pay attention to human efforts of this kind, no one could say that he was bound to honor them or that he demanded them as a precondition for showing people his favor. His absolute sovereignty, and therefore his complete freedom, had to be safeguarded, and so the synod declared in favor of *unconditional election*:

> Election is the unchangeable purpose of God whereby, before the foundation of the world, he hath out of mere grace, according to the sovereign good pleasure of his own will, chosen . . . a certain number of persons to redemption in Christ, whom he from eternity appointed the Mediator and head of the elect,

[199] A good account of these events from a theologically neutral perspective can be found in Jonathan I. Israel, *The Dutch Republic: Its Rise, Greatness, and Fall, 1477–1806* (Oxford: Oxford University Press, 1995), 450–477. See also Anthony Milton, ed., *The British Delegation and the Synod of Dort (1618–1619)* (Woodbridge: Boydell & Brewer, 2005). Note that although England and Scotland were separate kingdoms with their own churches, they sent a single delegation to Dort because they shared a common ruler, James I of England (1603–1625) and VI of Scotland (1567–1625).

[200] The relationship between this Calvinism and what went before it is a matter of considerable debate. On one side are those who believe that Dort and its apologists narrowed the teaching of Calvin to the point of serious distortion. See Robert T. Kendall, *Calvin and English Calvinism to 1649* (Oxford: Oxford University Press, 1979), and the response by Paul Helm, *Calvin and the Calvinists* (Edinburgh: Banner of Truth, 1982). See also Paul Helm, *Calvin at the Centre* (Oxford: Oxford University Press, 2010) for a fuller exposition of Calvin's links with later Calvinism. For an intermediate position, see Alan Sell, *The Great Debate: Calvinism, Arminianism, and Salvation* (Worthing: Walter, 1982). At the present time, it seems that the weight of scholarly opinion favors Paul Helm's contention that there was an essential continuity between Calvin and those who claimed his legacy at Dort and later, though it is generally accepted that the latter clarified and tightened up some of the "loose ends" in Calvin's own writings. On Calvin's position, see Jonathan H. Rainbow, *The Will of God and the Cross: An Historical and Theological Study of John Calvin's Doctrine of Limited Redemption* (Allison Park, PA: Pickwick, 1990) for the evidence that Calvin did hold a doctrine of limited atonement. See also Richard Muller, *After Calvin: Studies in the Development of a Theological Tradition* (Oxford: Oxford University Press, 2003), 63–102); and Lee Gatiss, *For Us and for Our Salvation: "Limited Atonement" in the Bible, Doctrine, History, and Ministry* (London: Latimer Trust, 2012). The Latin text of the canons of Dort is in Schaff, *The Creeds of Christendom*, 3 vols. (New York: Harper & Row, 1931), 3:550–580, followed by an abbreviated English translation (581–597). A fuller English translation is in Bray, *Documents of the English Reformation*, 453–478.

[201] In English-speaking countries the order of the canons has usually been made to conform to the acronym TULIP, thereby putting "total depravity" first, when in fact it came third in the original text. In other words, TULIP should more accurately be ULTIP!

> and the foundation of salvation. This elect number, though by nature neither better nor more deserving than others . . . God hath decreed to give to Christ to be saved by him and effectually to call and draw them to his communion by his Word and Spirit.[202]

The second issue was to prove the most controversial, even after the synod pronounced its verdict on it. Did Christ die for everyone or merely for the elect? There was of course no problem where the elect were concerned, because in their case everything had worked out as planned. But what about the others? Could Christ have died for people who were not saved? Would this mean that his power to save was limited, that his sacrifice was to some extent wasted, or that sinners could defy God and get away with it? None of these things made sense to the men of Dort. As the high priest of the new covenant, Christ had come to sacrifice himself for those who belonged to that covenant, just as the ancient Jewish high priest had sacrificed the lamb of atonement for those who belonged to Israel. Christ united sinners to himself and then paid for their sins; he did not die for "sins" in the abstract and then let anyone who so chose subscribe to the benefits that his atoning death had brought. So the delegates voted for *limited atonement* as the only solution that did full justice to all the issues involved. Nevertheless, given the objections that have been frequently raised against this, it is important to recall what the synod affirmed about the efficacy of Christ's saving death:

> The death of the Son of God is the only and most perfect sacrifice and satisfaction for sin; is of infinite worth and value, abundantly sufficient to expiate the sins of the whole world. . . . Moreover, the promise of the Gospel is that whosoever believeth in Christ crucified shall not perish, but have everlasting life. This promise . . . ought to be declared and published to all nations, and to all persons . . . without distinction.[203]

The synod clearly affirmed that those who perished died, not because the sacrifice of Christ was inadequate to save them but because they refused to believe in him.[204] In Anselm's scheme, which the Synod of Dort endorsed in principle, the Son's sacrifice was sufficient for the sins of the whole world, and no one could commit a sin too great for his blood to be able to cover it. In modern language we might say that the death of Christ is a comprehensive insurance policy that has no small print and no exclusions attached to it. It is

[202] Canons of Dort, 1.7; see Bray, *Documents of the English Reformation*, 458.
[203] Canons of Dort, 2.3, 5; see Bray, *Documents of the English Reformation*, 463–464.
[204] Canons of Dort, 2.6; see Bray, *Documents of the English Reformation*, 464.

universal coverage, and for that reason it can (and must) be preached to the whole world as the answer to the problem of sin and alienation from God. But if Jesus came to his own and died for them, the question of the efficacy of his atoning sacrifice is reopened. There is no doubt that his coverage of the chosen ones (the "elect") is complete, but what about those who have not been chosen for salvation? Several answers can be (and have been) given to this:

1. First, there are those who say that the language of election is figurative. In Christ, everyone has been chosen, whether they know that or not. This view, or variations of it, has been popular in modern times, when it has become associated with Karl Barth and his followers, but there are at least two problems with it.[205] The first one is that the Bible never says anything like this. From the beginning to the end, it is clear that God has chosen some people and not others.[206] We do not know the reasons for his choice, but that it is there is beyond question. The second one is that it denies human freedom, even as it claims to be asserting the worth of every human being. What if I do not want to go to heaven? There are plenty of people who have no interest in spiritual things and do not believe in them. Should they be coerced against their will? That is what social improvement schemes like communism try to do. They may mean well and even do some good in purely objective terms, but the end result is tyranny, not freedom. A heaven full of people who do not want to be there would be a kind of hell, and that is not what the Christian gospel promises us.

2. Second, there are those who think that Christ died for everyone but that we are free to accept or reject him as we choose. That was essentially the argument of the Remonstrants. It sounds good, but there are several flaws in it. One obvious flaw is that not everyone has heard the gospel. Can a choice be made in ignorance? To this the usual answer is that people are saved according to the light that has been given to them, but if that is the case, why preach the gospel? What if someone follows the light given to him but rejects Christ, as is the case with any number of people? Are they saved because they are true to their own convictions, or lost because they have rejected Christ? Modern liberals will opt for the former conclusion, but what would they say about someone like Caiaphas? He sent Jesus to his death because he thought it was better to let one man die than to see the entire nation put in danger, which from his point of view

[205] See David Gibson, *Reading the Decree: Exegesis, Election, and Christology in Calvin and Barth* (London: T & T Clark, 2009). Defenses of the "Barthian" view have also appeared, but in the words of Mark Garcia, they "have done little more than repeat the heavily criticized [Barthian] model in a reorganized and re-presented form" (Garcia, *Life in Christ*, 192). For examples of that approach, see Kevin D. Kennedy, *Union with Christ and the Extent of the Atonement in Calvin* (New York: Peter Lang, 2002); Graham Redding, *Prayer and the Priesthood of Christ in the Reformed Tradition* (Edinburgh: T & T Clark, 2003).

[206] See, for example, Paul's analysis of Esau and Jacob, Rom. 9:11–13, cited by the canons of Dort (1.10).

could be justified as an understandable, even as a responsible, thing to do.[207] Can we believe that he was saved for helping to crucify Christ in the way he did?

3. Third, there are those who conclude from the evidence that Jesus Christ died for those whom he has chosen for salvation. His death, like that of the sacrificial lamb offered in the temple on the Jewish Day of Atonement, is efficacious in its context, but not outside of it. The lamb's blood paid for the sins of Israel because that is what it was intended to do. No doubt it could have paid for the sins of others as well, since their sins would not have been any more serious than Israel's and possibly less so, but it had no such effect because that was not the intention. Similarly, Jesus came to his own and died for them. His death is sufficient to pay for the sins of others as well, but it does not do so because that was never its intention. To say otherwise is to say that God's saving purpose has been thwarted, which cannot be true. God is sovereign, and his purposes cannot be overthrown by anyone else. He has created us and can dispose of us as he chooses. The New Testament states clearly that he came to his own, to redeem the lost sheep of the house of Israel.[208] Nothing about his mission was accidental, and no part of it can be undone by human or demonic opposition. If it could be, we would have no assurance of salvation and our faith would be fatally undermined. It was this third option that the Synod of Dort endorsed:

> It was the will of God that Christ, by the blood of the cross whereby he confirmed the new covenant, should effectually redeem out of every people, tribe, nation and language, all those and those only, who were from eternity chosen for salvation and given to him by the Father; that he should confer upon them faith, which together with all the other saving gifts of the Holy Spirit, he purchased for them by his death.[209]

Shifting the weight of the atonement from sins to sinners had an important consequence that was not immediately perceived at the time. The doctrine of limited (or as it is sometimes called, "definite") atonement has met with considerable resistance from those who think that it abolishes human freedom and makes preaching the gospel unnecessary. Nothing could be further from the truth. God's choice gives freedom to those who would not otherwise have it, because human beings in their natural state are in bondage to Satan. What we think of as "freedom" is an illusion because in reality it is nothing but a license to destroy ourselves by being cut off from God. Preaching the gospel can

[207] John 11:50; 18:14.
[208] John 1:11; Matt. 15:24.
[209] Canons of Dort, 2.8; see Bray, *Documents of the English Reformation*, 464.

be compared to calling the sheep to order. If the sheep hear nothing, they will not respond even though they are sheep. It is not for those who are told to do the calling to question whether God might find some other way to gather his flock. He has commanded them to do it and has told them that his people will respond when they hear the message. What the doctrine does do is free them from anxiety. Some of those they preach to will not respond, and it is easy to think that the fault must lie with the preachers and their methods. When they realize that it is God who calls and appoints his sheep and that preachers are called to preach to all, whether they are sheep or not, the preachers can leave the judgment to him and not worry about it. In the end, preachers are just unworthy servants,[210] but they are called to be servants all the same. To be allowed to participate in God's saving work is an immense privilege, and it is not for them to start telling God what to do. Neither Luther nor Calvin worked this out in a systematic way, but as the Synod of Dort saw it, it is where the logic of justification by faith alone naturally takes us.

The third article concerned the state of fallen man. Was there a residue of his created nature that had somehow resisted the impact of sin and could therefore respond to the grace of God of its own free will? It was not difficult for the men of Dort to conclude that this could not be the case. Augustine had condemned the same view more than a thousand years earlier, and it went against the logic of the New Testament. To be saved, the old Adam had to die and be born again, which in itself tells us that there was no healthy part of him left that could begin the work of healing and restoration. Without much difficulty, therefore, the synod declared for the *total depravity* of fallen man (which the Remonstrants had themselves recognized), but they did not interpret this to mean that human beings have been deprived of all knowledge of what is right:

> There remain in man since the fall the glimmerings of natural light, whereby he retains some knowledge of God, of natural things, and of the difference between good and evil, and discovers some regard for virtue, good order in society, and for maintaining an orderly external deportment. But . . . this light, such as it is, man in various ways renders wholly polluted, and holds it back in unrighteousness, by doing which he becomes inexcusable before God.[211]

The fourth question concerned the nature of grace, which in practice meant the work of the Holy Spirit in the human heart. If the Spirit comes to dwell in our hearts by faith, can we tell him to go away? Do we have the power to reject

[210] Luke 17:10.
[211] Canons of Dort, 3/4.4; see Bray, *Documents of the English Reformation*, 466–467.

the will of God for our lives? To understand this properly, we may be helped by using the analogy of soap powders. Some of these advertise themselves as being able to remove the deepest stains and the hardest dirt. Shoppers are expected to know that there are some stains that are very stubborn and will not go away by using weaker detergents, and experience tells us that even the strongest ones are not always effective. Are there sins like that? Is it possible that we may be so contaminated by our wrongdoing that no cleansing is possible? No doubt the Holy Spirit has his work cut out for him in many cases, but does this mean that he cannot do it? Faced with this question, the men of Dort answered in favor of *irresistible grace*, proclaiming thereby that God can overcome the opposition of the most hardened sinner:

> When God accomplishes his good pleasure in the elect, or works in them true conversion, he not only causes the Gospel to be externally preached to them and powerfully illuminates their minds by his Holy Spirit, that they may rightly understand and discern the things of the Spirit of God, but by the efficacy of the same regenerating Spirit he pervades the inmost recesses of the man; he opens the closed and softens the hardened heart, and circumcises that which was uncircumcised; infuses new qualities into the will, which, though heretofore dead, he quickens.[212]

Finally, there was the question of eternal salvation. Granted that my sins can be forgiven, what assurance can I have that I shall not fall away a second time? The believer is not sinless, so can it be that sins committed after conversion might cancel out the benefits of salvation and lead to eternal damnation? Here the Synod of Dort appealed to the words of Paul, when he said that the Holy Spirit "bears witness with our spirit that we are children of God."[213] Once saved, always saved. They therefore concluded that the Bible teaches the *perseverance of the saints*, however much they may be tempted to sin and turn away from God. He will not let his people go, and if once we have tasted the blessing of salvation, we can rest assured that it will never again be taken away from us:

> God, who is rich in mercy, according to his unchangeable purpose of election, does not wholly withdraw the Holy Spirit from his own people, even in their melancholy falls; nor suffer them to proceed so far as to lose the grace of adoption and forfeit the state of justification. . . . he preserves in them the incorruptible seed of regeneration from perishing or being totally lost; and

[212] Canons of Dort, 3/4.11; see Bray, *Documents of the English Reformation*, 468.
[213] Rom. 8:16.

> again, by his Word and Spirit, he certainly and effectually renews them to repentance.[214]

Settling these questions was not without its price, and there have always been some who have not been able to subscribe to the canons of Dort, or at least not fully. They may even call themselves "three-point" or "four-point" Calvinists, failing to see that such a pick-and-choose approach is inconsistent and ultimately impossible. The work of the Holy Spirit is of a piece—either it is the work of the sovereign God or it is not. If one or more of the canons of Dort is rejected, sooner or later the effects of that will be felt in a weakened theology that cannot bear the weight of the biblical revelation that it is expected to carry. This was the conviction, and the fear, of those who found themselves embroiled in the next phase of controversy, which focused primarily on the extent and application of Christ's atonement.

The Extent of Christ's Atonement

Surprising as it will seem to some, the doctrine of the atonement did not figure as prominently in Reformation debates as it did in subsequent Protestant theology. The main reason for this is that at first it seemed that its main outlines were agreed on by all sides. As Anselm had taught, everyone believed that Jesus Christ had died for the sins of the whole world and that his sacrifice was sufficient to satisfy the demands of God's justice. Jesus Christ had taken that sacrifice up to heaven with him at the ascension, and now, seated at the right hand of the Father, he pleads for us on that basis. In the Mass, the priest claimed to bring Christ's sacrifice back down to earth, so that those who believed could receive it for themselves when they took Communion. Those who received the sacrament received Christ efficaciously, regardless of their personal faith. Those who did not take the sacrament did not receive him, and were subject to condemnation for their unbelief.[215] The shed blood of Christ was sufficient to cover every sin committed, but very few people were able to confess or receive the sacrament often enough to be sure of obtaining eternal salvation when they died. In other words, although the blood of Christ present in the Mass was sufficient to pay the price for every sin, it was effective only for those sins which were actually confessed. The sacrament was a kind of medicine, that would work if taken in the proper dosage at the right intervals, but not otherwise. Peter Damian (1007–1072) had expressed this very clearly in a statement that was to become classic:

---

[214] Canons of Dort, 5.6–7; see Bray, *Documents of the English Reformation*, 473.

[215] Note that the *Consensus Tigurinus* of 1549 expressly disowned this belief (Article 19).

> The cup of immortality that is the product of our infirmity and the power of God, possesses the quality of profiting all men; but if one does not drink from it, he will not be cured.[216]

That phrase would resurface after the Reformation and be used to support the doctrine of universal atonement, though in a way that concealed its origins in medieval sacramental theology.

The theological differences that dominated the Reformation debates centered on the doctrine of justification, which took the atoning work of Christ as a given and concentrated on how we appropriate its benefits. To be justified by faith alone meant that the saving work of Christ on the cross was fully and immediately applied to every believer, whether he was a notorious sinner or a paragon of moral rectitude in the eyes of the world. The Reformers taught that justifying faith is not to be equated with a human act of belief, because that would make it no more than a different kind of work. True faith is a gift of God, and only those to whom it is given are justified by it. The Reformers knew that the gospel had been preached to some nations but not to others, and also that where it had been proclaimed, the response to it had been far from uniformly positive. Some people understood the message, repented, and believed, but others rejected it, and there were many who did not much care one way or the other. Why was this so? If God was in control, there had to be some explanation other than human freedom of choice, because those who had never heard the message or else failed to understand it had not deliberately chosen their own damnation. Free choice would also have compromised the sovereignty of God over his creation by giving human beings a decision-making power that could act independently of his will and even thwart it.

The Bible made it clear that those who were saved were chosen by God, starting with ancient Israel and continuing through the apostles and the men and women of the early church. In the New Testament, people came to Christ by hearing the gospel preached and by responding to it, but did they have a real choice in the matter? The most famous convert of them all, the apostle Paul, did not choose Christ as his Savior.[217] People who wanted to follow Jesus without having been called by him were usually challenged about the authenticity of their apparent "faith," and when the truth became apparent, they were turned away.[218] Those who received justification and the promised forgiveness of sins were those who had been called and chosen by

---

[216] Peter Damian, *Epistula* 180.3 See Owen J. Blum and Irven M. Resnick, eds., *The Letters of Peter Damian*, 6 vols. (Washington, DC: Catholic University of America Press, 1989–2005), 6:296.

[217] Acts 9:4–6, 15. See also Gal. 1:12–16.

[218] Matt. 8:18–22; 19:16–22.

God, not people who had decided to try it out for themselves to see what would happen.

Given this, the question of the extent of the atonement was certain to become a pressing issue sooner or later. If it is faith in Christ's atoning work that justifies us, and we can only be justified when the grace of God convicts us of that, we are bound to ask what the connection between these things is. The teaching of Arminius on the subject was quickly refuted by the Synod of Dort, but elsewhere many Reformed theologians responded to the challenge he had presented by seeking to shore up what many perceived to be a weakness in the supralapsarian theology of Beza and Perkins. The story of what would eventually become known as Amyraldianism is essentially a chronicle of these attempts, made by men who were determined to find a way of maintaining a form of limited atonement that did justice to the universalistic passages of Scripture and satisfied the complaints raised by the Arminians, but without succumbing to their doctrine.

It seems that the first move in the direction of accommodating objections to the doctrine of Beza and Perkins was made by James Ussher (1581–1656), who was certainly being given the credit for it by the time he died.[219] Ussher is sometimes thought to have "softened" Beza's teaching, which had become the standard orthodoxy of the Reformed churches, but it might be better to say that he expanded it to take into account considerations that had previously been overlooked or discounted.[220] The first and most important of these had to do with the *sufficiency* of Christ's atoning death. The Christian church had always taught that Christ's death was adequate to pay for the sins of the whole world and that anyone who turned to him for forgiveness would be saved. If Beza's doctrine were to be interpreted to mean that Christ had died only for the elect and had therefore *not* paid the price for the sins of the whole world, his atoning work could be presented as inadequate. It might even be possible to say that, while Christ's atonement was sufficient for those who benefited from it, others might find their salvation by some other means, a danger that had already been foreseen by Article 18 of the Thirty-nine Articles of the Church of England, which anathematized such an idea.[221]

[219] On Ussher, see Alan Ford, *James Ussher: Theology, History, and Politics in Early-modern Ireland and England* (Oxford: Oxford University Press, 2007); R. Buick Knox, *James Ussher, Archbishop of Armagh* (Cardiff: University of Wales Press, 1967). Richard Baxter, another believer in universal atonement, made the same claim on several occasions. See Jonathan D. Moore, *English Hypothetical Universalism: John Preston and the Softening of Reformed Theology* (Grand Rapids, MI: Eerdmans, 2007), 173–175.

[220] It should also be remembered that Ussher was often credited with having authored the Irish Articles of 1615, which incorporated the Lambeth Articles. Although he probably did not do so, he certainly stood by the Irish Articles when their authority in the Church of Ireland was questioned in the 1630s. See Ford, *James Ussher*, 85–103, 185–192.

[221] See Bray, *Documents of the English Reformation*, 295.

In order to protect the uniqueness and finality of Christ's saving work, Ussher felt it necessary to stress that Christ, as the second Adam, had paid the price of the first Adam's sin and by doing so had covered the entire human race. This was intended to be a clarification of Reformed teaching, not a denial of it, and although there were some who were reluctant to accept his position, most theologians of the time agreed that, in this sense at least, Christ's atoning work was indeed universal. A hidden implication of Ussher's teaching, however, was that if Christ paid the price for Adam's sin, he could not have done this until after Adam's sin had been committed. This led him to abandon Beza's supralapsarianism in favor of what we now know as "infralapsarianism" ("after the fall"), a doctrine that states that Christ's atoning death was a direct response to the fall of Adam and its consequences, not a foreordained sacrifice for the salvation of the eternally predestined elect. Ussher's position was undoubtedly a modification of the accepted Reformed orthodoxy of his time, but it was not a rejection of it. He was still able to believe in limited atonement because, although Christ's death was a sufficient response to Adam's sin, its effects were not applied to everyone equally. Only those chosen for salvation were actually covered by Christ's work, and that limitation had been God's intention from the beginning.

As Ussher himself recognized, his doctrine created a distinction in Christ's atoning work that had not been present in the teaching of Beza or Perkins, to whom it was all of a piece. Ussher distinguished between two different aspects of the atonement, one of which was universal and the other particular. In its universal aspect, Christ's death had paid the price for every sin ever committed by any human being, so that no one had to look elsewhere for forgiveness because of some inadequacy in Christ's saving work. But according to its particular aspect, only the elect received the benefit of that work, rendering the universalism of Christ's atonement purely hypothetical in practice. A reprobate could not be saved in any way other than by the shed blood of Christ, which was sufficient to pay the price for his sins, but this did not happen, because as a reprobate he was not chosen for salvation. Ussher believed that his teaching was an improvement on that of Beza and Perkins because it did not exclude reprobates from the atonement, even if they did not benefit from it either. Christ's work was intended for their salvation as well as that of the elect, but the fact that they rejected it meant that what was meant to save them condemned them instead. This was essentially what the apostle Paul said of those who ate and drank the Lord's Supper unworthily: they used what was meant to further their salvation for their own damnation.[222]

[222] 1 Cor. 11:27.

Ussher was critical of the Reformed orthodoxy of Beza and Perkins, even to the point of saying that to believe that Christ died only for the elect and that his death had no impact at all on the reprobate was absurd. He was convinced that Christ's atoning work was the medicine every sinner needed to be healed, and even quoted Peter Damian on this subject, apparently under the misapprehension that he was the fifth-century Augustinian church father, Prosper of Aquitaine (c. 400–455):

> All Adam's sons have taken a mortal sickness from their father, which, if it be not remedied, will, without fail, bring them to the second death: no medicine under heaven can heal this disease, but only a potion confected of the blood of the Lamb of God, who came "to take away the sins of the world"; which as Prosper truly notes: "*Habet in se quod omnibus prosit, sed si non bibitur non medetur.* (The virtue thereof is such, that if all did take it, all without doubt should be recovered, but without taking it there is no recovery.)"[223]

Ussher regarded this as the teaching of the universal church, to which he fully subscribed. Did he understand the sacramental context of the quotation? The language is certainly suggestive, but if he really believed that it came from the fifth century and not the eleventh, there would have been no reason to connect it with transubstantiation or the Mass, which he could have dismissed as a misinterpretation of the original meaning. But the resonance with medieval sacramentalism is striking, and the lingering popular devotion to it, which the Reformers were trying so hard to stamp out, may well account for the readiness of John Preston (1587–1628), for example, to repeat the quotation (and the attribution to Prosper) with surprising regularity.[224]

To Ussher, proclaiming the universality of Christ's atoning work had the great advantage that it made every sin pardonable. By fully satisfying the Father's wrath against sin, the Son had made it possible for him to show mercy to anyone at any time, since he was no longer constrained by the unsatisfied demands of his own justice. This also explains why the offer of the gospel is universal, going out to all human beings regardless of their spiritual condition in the sight of God (a point on which all were agreed). The practical effect of this can best be seen in Ussher's interpretation of John 1:29, ". . . the Lamb of God, who takes away the sin of the world." Where earlier generations of Reformed theologians had tended to interpret this by restricting the word

[223] *The Whole Works of the Most Reverend James Ussher, D. D., Lord Archbishop of Armagh and Primate of All Ireland: With the Life of the Author and an Account of His Writings*, ed. Charles R. Elrington, 17 vols. (Dublin: Hodges & Smith, 1847–1848), 12:570.

[224] See Moore, *English Hypothetical Universalism*, 163, n. 111.

"world" to mean something like "some people drawn from every race and nation" rather than everyone who ever lived, Ussher preferred to modify the phrase "take away" instead. In his words,

> [The death of Christ] doth not actually take away all the sins of the world, but virtually. It hath power to do it if it be rightly applied, the sacrifice hath such virtue in it, that if all the world would take it, and apply it, it would expiate, and remove the sins of the whole world.[225]

Furthermore, although Ussher did not deny the standard Reformed interpretation of John 17:9, according to which Jesus did not intercede for the whole world but only for his own sheep (the elect), he did not let this deter him from saying that even so, Christ had still paid the price for the sins of the whole world without exception.

In spite of Ussher's criticisms of the position taken by Beza and Perkins and his proposed alternatives, it is hard to see how his view can be regarded as a "softening" of the classical Reformed position. Certainly Ussher himself would not have thought that he was weakening it in any way. On the contrary, where the earlier teaching had simply ignored the reprobate, Ussher claimed to have accounted for them by making Christ's sacrifice applicable to them too, though to contrary effect. In his eyes, he had closed the door to any alternative form of salvation, had upheld the universality of God's sovereign power, and had shown how something originally intended for salvation had ended up condemning those who did not receive it—and in a way that put the blame for this firmly on the condemned and not on God, who had withheld nothing of his love from them. The weakness in Ussher's theology was that it could not avoid separating the extent of the atonement's sufficiency from the extent of its efficacy, thus allowing that Christ died for the reprobate in vain. The root of Ussher's difficulty may have been that he found it impossible to distinguish with sufficient clarity between acts of sin and the sinners who committed them. Revealingly, he never said whether paying the price for Adam's sin meant that Adam himself was one of the elect or not. Presumably Adam could have been saved as an individual, but as the "federal head" of the fallen human race, to have elected him would have meant electing the whole of mankind—in other words, the universality of the atonement would have become universalism. Ussher never wanted to say anything like that, which is why he was careful to separate sufficiency from efficacy, but if others were to apply the logic of Beza and Perkins to his scheme, they might easily end up

---

[225] Ussher, *Whole Works*, 13:160–161.

with a doctrine far removed from the Reformed orthodoxy that he was trying so hard to defend.

At the time, Ussher's gloss on classical Reformed orthodoxy was brilliant and persuasive. In particular, it seems to have influenced the divines who met at Dordrecht (Dort) in the winter of 1618–1619 to settle the Arminian question, and through them to have passed into the mainstream of Reformed orthodoxy. Along the way, Ussher acquired disciples, whom he persuaded to adopt his hypothetical universalism, though as often happens with ideas that are not formally defined, those who accepted his position modified it in different ways, with the result that "hypothetical universalism" was not a single doctrine but a family of closely related ideas that were capable of further mutation.[226] At some point, one of those mutations might cross the line from orthodoxy to heresy, but Ussher could not have known that, although it is possible to see how a trajectory could develop from (or in line with) his teaching and move off in a direction that he did not foresee.

One of Ussher's admirers was John Davenant (1572–1641), who had a brilliant career at Cambridge before becoming bishop of Salisbury in 1621. He was one of the delegates to the Synod of Dort, where he presented a paper on the atonement that outlines views clearly similar to and probably derived from Ussher's, though Ussher is not mentioned by name. We do not know when Davenant first expressed such opinions, but it is plain that he held them sometime before he went to Dort, where he was the main influence behind the proposals put forward by the British delegation on the question of the atonement.[227] Davenant began by asserting two propositions which were evidently designed to show his adherence to the classical Reformed orthodoxy of Beza and Perkins, and which he claimed received the assent of the other delegations at Dort:

1. Out of the special love and intention of both God the Father and Christ himself, Christ died for the elect, in order to obtain for them automatically, and confer on them infallibly, the forgiveness of sins and eternal salvation.
2. Out of this same love, through and on account of the merit and intercession of Christ, faith, perseverance, and all other things by which the condition of the covenant is fulfilled and the promised benefit, i.e. eternal life, is infallibly obtained, are given to these same elect.

[226] Unfortunately, we are reliant on Richard Baxter's testimony for our understanding of Ussher's role here, and Baxter was not a disinterested party. It may be no coincidence that Baxter revealed this a year after Ussher's death, when the latter was no longer available for comment. See Moore, *English Hypothetical Universalism*, 173–175, for the details.

[227] That text survives and has been edited and printed in Milton, *British Delegation and the Synod of Dort*, 218–222.

But Davenant then went on to say that the British delegation proposed three further statements, which also received general approval at the synod:

1. God took pity on the fallen human race and sent his Son, who gave himself as the price of redemption for the sins of the whole world.
2. The universal Gospel promise is founded on this merit of the death of Christ, so that all who believe in Christ automatically receive the forgiveness of sins and eternal life.
3. Just as in the church salvation is offered to everyone according to the promise of the Gospel, so the administration of its grace is sufficient to convict all those who do not repent and believe that they will perish by their own voluntary fault, either by ignoring or disdaining the Gospel, and will not receive the benefits it offers.

When we look at the canons as they were eventually agreed upon by the synod, we can easily see how influential these three further propositions had been. Among other things, the canons of Dort state,

> 2.3. The death of the Son of God is the only and most perfect sacrifice and satisfaction for sin; is of infinite worth and value, abundantly sufficient to expiate the sins of the whole world.
> 2.5. Moreover the promise of the Gospel is that whosoever believeth in Christ crucified shall not perish, but have everlasting life. This promise, together with the command to repent and believe, ought to be declared and published to all nations, and to all persons promiscuously and without distinction, to whom God out of his good pleasure sends the Gospel.
> 2.6. And whereas many who are called by the Gospel do not repent nor believe in Christ, but perish in unbelief; this is not owing to any defect or insufficiency in the sacrifice offered by Christ upon the cross, but is wholly to be imputed to themselves.
> 2.7. But as many as truly believe and are delivered and saved from sin and destruction through the death of Christ, are indebted for this benefit solely to the grace of God given them in Christ from everlasting, and not to any merit of their own.[228]

Davenant's draft proposals regarding "hypothetical universalism" were thus fully accommodated by the synod. Not only was the complete sufficiency of Christ's death explicitly acknowledged, but the promise of the gospel was declared to be for all people everywhere, and the hope of eternal salvation

[228] See Bray, *Documents of the English Reformation*, 463–464.

for those who repent and believe was to be preached to everyone. Failure to respond to that preaching was ascribed not to God's predetermined choice but to the fault of the hearers, but at the same time, those who did respond and believe could attribute this only to the grace of God, who had eternally chosen them for salvation.

What was left here of Beza's doctrine of limited atonement? It is clear that the Synod of Dort did not endorse the strict view that Christ had died for the elect in a way that made his sacrifice irrelevant to everyone else. The benefits of salvation were predetermined not by the extent of the atonement's efficacy but by the gift of justifying faith in Christ's saving death. The limitation of the atonement was therefore due to the fixed number of those who were called and chosen to believe and not to any inadequacy in the mercy of God. To put it a different way, the reprobate were excluded from the kingdom of heaven because of their unbelief, not because there was not enough saving grace to go around!

Thanks to the decision of the Synod of Dort, it is fair to say that "hypothetical universalism" became the received orthodoxy of the Reformed churches in a way that it had not been before. Whether this represented an expansion of the teaching of Beza and Perkins, designed to deal with objections that they had not considered, or whether it was a softening of classical Reformed orthodoxy is largely a matter of perspective. The important thing to remember is that eternal election was not lost sight of or abandoned, however much the sufficiency of Christ's saving work for all mankind was affirmed. The fathers of Dort could congratulate themselves on having found a formula that did justice to the universalist language of Scripture without compromising its equally strong particularist emphasis on election and reprobation. By expressing these doctrines within the framework of the covenant of grace, they allowed for the presence of a significant number of non-elect within the wider covenant community of the visible church, and it was this aspect of their decisions that would have the longest-lasting impact on subsequent Reformed theology.

It is when we come to look at what happened *after* the Synod of Dort that we begin to see the problems inherent in hypothetical universalism as it had developed up to that time. To put it simply, how hypothetical was it? Granted that the death of Christ was sufficient to pay for the sins of the whole world, was there any chance that it would ever do so in practice? Or was this universalism merely theoretical, with no practical application either in fact or in intention?

This was the question that John Davenant had to grapple with in the years after the synod, as he tried to get its canons accepted by the Church of England. In pursuit of this aim, he bent over backwards to make the universalism of Christ's atonement as real as possible, an effort that forced him to postulate a double will, or double love, in Christ. In support of this, he argued that Christ showed a general love for the whole of mankind by dying for our sins on the cross, but that he also showed (and still shows) a more particular love for the elect, by conferring the benefits of that atoning work exclusively on them. To the objection that such a doctrine made the first kind of love a mere pretense, Davenant answered that, on the contrary, Christ's death had made every human being potentially salvable and therefore showed God's deep love for all humankind without exception. God, Davenant claimed, is actually predisposed to save everyone, and in the death of Christ, all human beings (and perhaps even fallen angels, though he did not press this point) had what he called a "common right" to salvation and were therefore theoretically able to receive it.

Leaving aside the situation of the elect, who would be saved in any case, what effect did this have on the reprobate? Davenant replied that they too were better off in many ways because of Christ's death. For a start, they benefited from the presence of the elect among them. By becoming incarnate and paying the price of Adam's sin, the Son of God brought advantages to the whole of mankind, advantages that were denied to the fallen angels, for example.[229] Furthermore, the sacrifice of Christ was as wide in its effects as the preaching of the gospel. Just as it was possible for non-elect people to respond to the gospel and show the fruits of repentance in their lives without being called to eternal salvation, so it could be said that the blood of Christ was at work in their lives, though not to saving effect. This was the case of those (and they were many) who came under the influence of the gospel and responded by changing their lives, at least for a time, though they lacked the assurance of justifying faith.

Davenant also developed an elaborate theory of a two-stage reconciliation which he believed would resolve the difficulties that a theory of double grace inevitably created. In the first stage, God's wrath was appeased and he was made well-disposed to a reconciliation with fallen man. That is what Christ's death on the cross accomplished. In the second stage, that reconciliation would be sealed by the faith of those who had been called to receive it. This was the sticking point. The elect were given the grace to believe whether they wanted it or not; in their case, election was unconditional. The non-elect, however, were presented with the condition of faith, which would open up the reality of salvation to them as well, if only they could meet it. The snag was that since faith is a gift of God and not a work of man, the non-elect had no hope of obtaining it

[229] Davenant's view of the fallen angels is curious. On the one hand, he believed that Christ's sacrifice was sufficient to pay for their sin as well as for Adam's, but on the other hand, he also believed that the incarnation showed a divine preference for saving humans rather than angels, and so he effectively ruled them out as potential recipients of divine grace.

and were therefore cut off from salvation. In other words, the covenant of grace by which we are saved comes in two forms: an unconditional one that saves the elect, and a conditional one that is offered to everyone but saves no one. Its real purpose was to seal the love of the Father for the Son by demonstrating that the latter's work of mediation was and is fully accepted by the former. To cap it all off, God does not harden the hearts of the reprobate, according to Davenant, but simply leaves them as they are, with their hearts already hardened! Even so, the fact that salvation is conditional on faith makes it a real possibility, and the refusal of reprobates to take advantage of it is entirely their own fault, although there is no chance that they can ever have the faith of the elect.

What Davenant ended up with was a convoluted doctrinal system that, if anything, made it harder to defend Reformed orthodoxy than it had been before. For example, although he saw the weakness in Ussher's division of the priestly work of Christ into a universal satisfaction and a particular intercession (for the elect only) and avoided it, he did so by claiming that Christ not only paid the price for the sins of all human beings but also interceded for them with the Father. Did he do this in the full knowledge that his prayers would not be heard? Did the Father reject the Son's intercession, and if he did, does that imply that the elect for whom Christ also intercedes might be in jeopardy, as the Father might conceivably refuse to listen to Christ's pleas on their behalf as well? In trying to satisfy the complaints of those who did not like the doctrine of reprobation and its implications, Davenant ended up skating on some very thin ice. Much as he may have protested to the contrary, his views of what happened to the non-elect were (and remained) purely hypothetical, not real, and it was this that kept him on the side of Reformed orthodoxy. But sooner or later, someone was bound to ask whether it was possible to go as far as he did without any consequences. If what Davenant claimed for universality was true, then surely salvation for the "non-elect" must be not only a possibility but a reality, at least in some cases. That Davenant was moving in that direction can scarcely be doubted, and it would not be long before the focus of attention would shift from the extent of the atonement to the extent of election, and the whole Reformed paradigm would be called into question.

Another man who was deeply influenced by the hypothetical universalism of Ussher and Davenant was John Preston, whose life and theology have recently been the subject of an extended monograph.[230] Preston was not at the Synod of Dort, and the brevity of his life (1587–1628) undoubtedly curtailed both the development of his thought and the extent of his personal influence,

[230] J. D. Moore, *English Hypothetical Universalism: John Preston and the Softening of Reformed Theology* (Grand Rapids, MI: Eerdmans, 2007). The book was originally a doctoral thesis (2000) and subsequently revised.

but he was deeply respected by his contemporaries and highly regarded by the next generation, which looked back to him as the paragon of Reformed orthodoxy in Jacobean England. He was a close associate of Davenant and an admirer of Ussher, and it is possible that both of those men learned as much from Preston as he did from them. At the very least, it seems probable that Davenant's more developed post-Dort ideas were developed at Preston's instigation, and in some cases borrowed from him outright, making Preston as much an author of later "hypothetical universalism" as he was a proponent of the earlier, Ussherian variety.

Interestingly, Preston never said that Christ had died for the elect, though he often used language that makes sense only in a particularist framework, and he has frequently been called a "high Calvinist" in the Perkins mold.[231] However, on reading his works it soon becomes clear that he is usually closer to Davenant than to Perkins on the issues that separated the two of them, though in some respects he may be said to have adopted a mediating position. For example, Preston believed (as did Davenant) that the meaning of Christ's death was not restricted to the elect, but he also believed (like Perkins) that Christ interceded only for those who were predestined to salvation and not for the reprobate. To the charge that this would make the sufficiency of Christ's satisfaction for sin more extensive than its effectiveness, his rather unusual reply was that Christ "over-bought" us by paying a price for our salvation that was far higher than we are worth! That there should be something "left over" and technically unnecessary is therefore not surprising, but a further sign of the great love that he has for us.

The suggestion that Christ's atoning work may have involved a form of excess payment inevitably raises the question of whether, or to what extent, it can be said that Christ died in vain, a possibility mentioned by the apostle Paul, though only to be immediately rejected (Gal. 2:21; 1 Cor. 1:17). Preston's answer to this question was ambiguous. On the one hand, he claimed that Christ's death would indeed have been "in vain" if there were no subsequent gospel call, no conversions, and no assurance of salvation provided by the sacraments. In other words, in trying to explain why Christ's death was not wasted, Preston appealed to precisely those things that were most often cited by opponents of the classical view of limited atonement as reasons for rejecting it. On the other hand, he also said that Christ's death is "in vain" when believers are not as godly as they should be, when the gospel call is rejected by those to whom

[231] Preston's preferred term was "believers," a word which leaves open the question of whether they were elect or not, though the context of his remarks usually makes it clear that they were, since faith was a gift of God bestowed on his elect only.

it is issued, and when we do not apply Christ's pardon to ourselves. In other words, it is when the elect fail to live up to their calling that Christ's sacrifice is rendered void, not when it fails to convert the reprobate.

What we see here is a sure pastoral instinct that holds the two aspects of Christ's atoning work together in a way that a more abstract theological theory would find hard to do. In Preston's mind, the incarnation of the Son of God must have a saving significance, which by its nature extends to the entire human race.[232] But in practical terms, it is the elect who struggle with the call of Christ, of which they know themselves to be unworthy. By sending his Son to die for the sins of the world, God has demonstrated his willingness for every human being to repent and be saved, but for reasons known only to him, justifying faith is given only to a few, and even *they* find it hard to apply as they should. Those who do not receive this gift may die in ignorance of it, but if they hear the promise of the gospel, they will not respond to it, because their innate capacity to do so has been impaired. Just as a blind man has eyes, so a reprobate one has a will, but in each case the natural human faculty is unable to perform its designated function. In the end, the more a reprobate understands of the gospel, the more he is likely to reject it and the greater his condemnation will be. Here, perhaps more than anywhere else, Preston came down firmly on the side of traditional Reformed orthodoxy. The visible church was the expression of the general covenant made with all sorts and conditions of men (in England, with what was effectively the entire population), and within it the gospel promises and the sacramental assurances were routinely given to those who attended public worship. But within this visible church there was a secret company of the elect, known only to God, for whom the outward signs were a means of conversion. They were a spiritual elite, but not in the sense that the world knows such things. To be godly was not to gloat over the fate of the reprobate, but to know one's unworthiness of the gift of salvation and therefore to live a life of constant repentance and self-humiliation before God—the very opposite of the sense of spiritual superiority of which they were so often accused. Godliness went against the inclinations of human nature, and for that reason it could not be earned, even by those who might seek after it. Death to self was the ultimate form of participation in the death of Christ, and the only reliable sign that his atoning sacrifice had taken effect in a believer's life.

In that sense, Preston upheld the doctrine of limited atonement as understood by the Synod of Dort. Had he lived longer, he might well have been pressured to expand his horizons in the way that Davenant evidently did, but

[232] But it did not include the fallen angels, toward whom the Son extended no similar compassion. Preston saw more clearly than Davenant on this point, it would appear.

his early death spared him that. Preston has therefore come down to us as an ambiguous figure, claimed by all sides but not fitting into any particular mold, which is perhaps a more faithful picture of his age than the ones that have come down to us through the biographies of those who lived longer but who for that reason also became more committed to one fixed position or another.

Whatever differences there were among the Reformed in the British Isles when it came to the question of the extent of the atonement, room was found to accommodate them. They all subscribed to the canons of Dort, which they wanted to see ratified by the king, though they never were. They were also quite clear that their theology was in no sense "Arminian," because they insisted on both the primacy and the limitations of divine election in the work of salvation. Christ's atoning work was fully applied only to those who had been chosen from before the foundation of the world, and they alone were the recipients of justifying faith. In the final analysis, their universalist tendencies were (as they themselves were keen to stress) purely hypothetical, and used only to extricate themselves from theologically unacceptable alternatives, like having to blame God for the condemnation of the reprobate.

In France, however, events took a different turn. This was not because the French Reformed Church was uninfluenced by British theologians. On the contrary, it was agreed by everyone that the question of hypothetical universalism arose in France because of the teaching of one man, the Scot, John Cameron (1579–1625). Born to a middle-class Glaswegian family, Cameron left his native Scotland for France in 1600 and trained for the ministry in that country. He became known as a brilliant controversialist, but also as a troublemaker in Bordeaux, which he left in 1618, in order to take up a chair in theology at the Protestant academy of Saumur. However, he remained there for less than three years, because civil unrest forced him to leave in haste, this time for London. As a supporter of King James VI (I of England), Cameron was appointed Principal and Professor of Theology at Glasgow, where he spent the academic year 1622–1623. Once again he was soon embroiled in controversy and left for London, but by mid-1623 he was back in Paris. He tried to get Louis XIII to return his Saumur post to him, but the king was wary of foreign Protestants and eventually Cameron went to Montauban instead. Unable to steer clear of trouble, he tried to intervene in a dispute among local Huguenots over the propriety of using violence to defend their rights. In May 1625 he was seriously injured in a riot and never fully recovered, dying six months later. Cameron's memory was revered at Saumur, where his theology (or what was believed to be his theology) soon took root, but elsewhere in France there was much less enthusiasm for his ideas. He was never formally condemned, and during his lifetime protested his loyalty to the Synod of Dort, but before long his legacy was being severely criticized, not least because of the conclusions that some of his disciples were drawing from it.

What Cameron actually taught and where he got his ideas from is somewhat unclear.[233] As far as we can tell, his Scottish education was conventional and unlikely to have encouraged opposition to Beza of the kind that was to characterize him later on. It may have been his naturally combative nature that caused him to rebel against the accepted orthodoxy of his time, or his originality as a thinker in his own right. We know that he embraced the idea that God's covenants form the basis of Reformed theology as this had been developed at Heidelberg by Caspar Olevianus and Zachary Ursinus, but we also know that he developed his own, apparently unique, interpretation of this idea. At Heidelberg in 1608, he defended the previously unheard-of thesis that God had made a triple covenant with man. According to this theory, there was a covenant of works made with Adam before the fall, which was replaced by a covenant of grace afterwards, but this covenant of grace was in fact supplemented by a third covenant, in which God's promise of salvation was made to depend on faith in the sufficiency of Christ's sacrifice. Cameron actually called this third covenant a *foedus hypotheticum*. As Brian Armstrong has expressed it,

> In this hypothetical covenant God does what he has promised because the creature fulfils the requirement annexed thereto. Yet though God's action is in this way made dependent upon man's response, this response itself proceeds from his antecedent love which produces whatever good there may be in that man. It is this *foedus hypotheticum* which has to do with God's redemptive activity.[234]

Two years after the Heidelberg disputation, Cameron entered into a private correspondence with one of his students, the famous Hebraist Louis Cappel, in which he argued that Christ had died for all men, even though only the elect were ultimately saved. These letters were not published until after Cameron's death, so they had no influence at the time, although they make it clear that he was already opposed to Beza and advocating a doctrine of hypothetical universalism. As far as we can tell, he came to this position independently, and his theory of a triple covenant was not identical with the double covenant promoted by Davenant and others after Cameron's death. Nor is there any evidence that he influenced Ussher or other British divines, though he may

[233] For a discussion of the links and possibilities, see Brian G. Armstrong, *Calvinism and the Amyraut Heresy* (Madison: University of Wisconsin Press, 1969), 42–70.
[234] Ibid., 49–50.

have. Had he settled back in England or Scotland in 1622, it is possible, and perhaps probable, that he would have allied himself with men like Ussher, Davenant, and Preston, and that his theology would have been regarded as no more than a variant of theirs. But because he was in France and died young, his ideas were developed outside the British context and without the fellowship that like minds would have produced. Instead of being modified and matured by ongoing debate, Cameron's hypothetical universalism was canonized and defended by his former pupils at Saumur, and then by their students in the next generation. His most famous pupil and the standard-bearer of his thought was Moïse Amyraut (1596–1664), who published his views on the subject in 1634–1638 and attributed his main ideas to Cameron. For this reason, the theology attributed to Amyraut might more properly be assigned to Cameron, but as it was Amyraut who expressed it and propagated it, he is the one who takes both the credit and the blame for the ideas it expressed.

An important characteristic of Cameron's theology that carried over into Amyraut's teaching was the way in which he subsumed natural theology into the overall covenant scheme. In doing this he went beyond Calvin, who spoke only of a "sense of the divine" (*sensus divinitatis*) given to Adam, that has not been completely obscured by the fall, although the evidence suggests that Cameron never developed the implications of his terminology beyond what Calvin would have said. Nevertheless, by absorbing mankind's natural awareness of God into a covenant pattern, Cameron created a framework that would demand that the covenant of grace should correspond to it in some way. In other words, it would become important for later theologians to demonstrate that God's plan of redemption should cover all those who benefited from the original covenant of nature (the term which Cameron used instead of "works"), since if it did not, the coherence of God's saving activity would be compromised. It was this necessity that led to theories of how God's saving grace affected the reprobate, a question that might never have arisen had Adam's "sense of the divine" not been regarded as a form of covenant.[235]

The basic text of Amyraldianism is the short treatise on predestination that Amyraut published in 1634.[236] This was soon followed by a study of Calvin's predestinarian teaching, in which he tried to show that his views were identical to those of his Genevan master, and a much longer answer to a certain Mon-

[235] It should be pointed out that this tendency has become endemic to Reformed theology. Neither the Bible nor Calvin says anything about a covenant of nature or works made with Adam and preceding the covenant of grace made with Abraham, but this pattern of thinking has persisted, with consequences that at times are only dubiously "biblical."

[236] Moïse Amyraut, *Brief traité de la prédestination et de ses principales dépendances* (Saumur: J. Lesnier et I. Desbordes, 1634).

sieur de la Milletière, in which he defended what he believed was the Reformed doctrine of grace.[237] As with other proponents of hypothetical universalism, the twin pillars of Amyraut's doctrine were the universal sufficiency of Christ's atoning work and God's election of those who were destined for salvation. The opening chapters of the *Brief traité* outlined the creation of the universe according to a plan and order that reflect the perfection of God's own being. The big difference between the Creator and the creation was that the former is eternal whereas the latter is temporal and destined eventually to perish. Man is the crown of the created order, but he does not escape its inherent corruptibility. It was the existence of this constitutional weakness that led Adam into sin and caused him to fail to fulfill the purpose for which he had been created. God determined to put this right, but the only way he could do so was by overcoming the essential weakness of human nature. This was achieved by the incarnation of the Son of God, who brought his perfect divinity to bear on the weak flesh of mankind, and through his death and resurrection transformed human nature into something spiritual rather than material, and therefore capable of becoming and remaining perfect.

From this perspective, the death and resurrection of Christ dealt with Adam's sin as if it were a congenital defect in the human race. Christ's work was of universal import because human nature is itself universal.[238] In Amyraut's scheme, Christ could not have died exclusively for the elect, because that would have made the elect a special kind of creature, distinct from the mass of humanity. This was clearly false and, if it had been accepted, it would have made any notion of redemption nonsensical. In fact, Amyraut's understanding of the atonement was such that it was not necessarily connected with redemption at all. Theoretically at least, it would have been possible for Christ to have died and paid the price for Adam's sin without anyone being elected for salvation as a result, though admittedly there would have been little point in that. The death of Christ was designed to make the salvation of the human race possible and it was applied to that end, but there was no preexisting company of the elect who would need Christ's sacrifice in order to make their election sure. In other words, Christ's atoning work was not particular or limited because it could not be; at the time it was decided in the mind of God, there were no elect creatures waiting to benefit from it. Election, which Amyraut (it must be remembered) believed was a necessary

[237] Moïse Amyraut, *Eschantillon de la doctrine de Calvin touchant la prédestination* (Saumur: J. Lesnier et I. Desbordes, 1636); Moïse Amyraut, *Du mérite des oeuvres, contre les opinions de Monsieur de la Milletière* (Saumur: J. Lesnier et I. Desbordes, 1638).

[238] It is clear that this belief owes more to ancient Greek philosophical ideas than it does to biblical religion, though Amyraut never realized or admitted that.

precondition for salvation, occurred only *after* the sacrifice had been made, and in the light of it.

To Amyraut himself this must have seemed eminently logical, because it is hard to imagine justifying faith being given to anyone when there was nothing to believe in. But in the logic of Reformed atonement theology, it was the other way around. There could be no meaningful atonement if there was nothing to be atoned for, and the existence of sin could not be abstracted from the sinners who committed it. Amyraut's understanding of the fall of man was also open to the objection that he did not take the supernatural origin and nature of evil seriously enough. To argue that Adam fell because he was a weak, material creature and not a strong, spiritual being sounds plausible until mention is made of Satan, a spiritual being who had sinned, presumably without the excuse of having a nature that could do nothing else.

It is when we understand how Amyraut conceived of sin—as a corruption of human nature rather than as personal disobedience—that we can appreciate why he was so concerned to affirm a universal redemption. In that sense, God has provided in Christ an unlimited atonement for sin, which may be applied to anyone and everyone at his behest. It is not true, however, to say that Amyraut was led into universalism because of this. In his own words,

> And yet these words, *God desires the salvation of all men*, necessarily receive this limitation, *provided that they believe*. If they do not believe, he does not desire it.[239]

At first sight, this appears to make the will of God dependent on human choice, but that is not what Amyraut believed either. He asserted that God chose people for faith in a way that takes no account of any human virtues or works, and he adds that without this, our election and predestination as believers would not have been possible. In other words, God is the author of faith, and if he does not give it to some people, then they are not saved. Indeed, said Amyraut, it is by refusing to grant his saving grace to all men indiscriminately that God demonstrates his severity toward sin and his determination to punish it.

Why does God not punish everyone equally? This would certainly be justified by the nature of human sin, said Amyraut, but some people are chosen for salvation so that the Son's sacrifice will not be left fruitless. Christ's willingness to die on the cross for the sins of the world must also be acknowledged,

[239] Amyraut, *Brief traité*, ch. 7. His original words were, "Et partant ces paroles, *Dieu veut le salut de tous les hommes*, reçoivent nécessairement cette limitation, *pourvu qu'ils croient*. S'ils ne croient pas, il ne le veut pas" (italics his).

and therefore a certain number of people must be saved. As Amyraut put it, the grace of atonement is universal, but God's mercy in pardoning particular individuals is restricted by the nature of his election.[240] Those who perish do so because, although they have been shown grace, they have not obtained mercy. They are not expressly condemned, but simply overlooked, rather in the way that the sun sheds its light on some places and leaves others in darkness, not intentionally but by oversight.

Amyraut's scheme was rounded out by saying that God brings his elect to faith by the preaching of the gospel and by the way in which he puts a "right spirit" in us so that we can respond to the gospel in faith. This perspective had the effect of making the preaching of the gospel, and therefore the ministry of the church, essential. If the elect had been chosen in advance, it would not ultimately matter whether they ever heard the gospel preached or not, because their salvation would have been secured already. But if election is made to depend on the preaching of the gospel, then that becomes all-important, and the role of the church in salvation, which had been essential to medieval theology, is retained, the only difference being that preaching replaces the sacraments as the chief means of grace. Furthermore, in Amyraut's scheme, predestination did not rule out the place of the will in conversion. God prepares our understanding so that our will is ready to receive him, but it is only when we do so that our election and predestination are secured. It is certainly true that God approaches us first and prepares us to receive him; we cannot come to this point on our own. But at the same time, he engages our hearts and minds in such a way as to make us responsible for our own faith (or lack of it), so that the condition imposed for the reception of salvation is a real one.

Not surprisingly, Amyraut's opponents were quick to perceive inconsistencies in his scheme of things and to insist that he had strayed from the true path of Reformed theology. Amyraut understood that they found the separation between the sufficiency of Christ's atonement and the limitation of its application inconsistent, and that they thought he was opening the door to universalism, if not actually preaching it. According to them, if Christ had died for everyone on condition that they had faith, then the Holy Spirit was responsible for giving that faith to everyone Christ died for, in other words, to the entire human race:

> Mr Cameron says [or "said"] that Jesus Christ died for all men on condition of faith, from that you conclude that it is therefore necessary for the cause of faith, that is, according to you, the illumination of the Spirit, should be common to all men. And [you] add this reason, that Christ would not really

[240] Rom. 9:15.

> have died for them if he had not also earned for them the grace of which the cause of faith consists. You say that Jesus Christ died for all men on condition of faith, for which reason he has also made the illumination which is the cause of faith, common [to all men].[241]

Amyraut never admitted this charge and did his utmost to try to convince people that he was a faithful follower of Calvin and his sixteenth-century associates. In doing so, he made it clear that he had followed John Cameron, whose ideas he regarded as identical with his own:

> I am surprised how you attribute only to me and to Mr Cameron the opinion that the external grace which is offered to all those who are called, is sufficient for the salvation of those who are called, seeing that in the sense in which it is proposed, this is the doctrine of Calvin, Hyperius, Musculus, Bullinger, Pellican, Aretius and so many other excellent persons, and that it is the distinction commonly received in our schools, that Christ died *sufficiently for all and efficaciously for the elect alone*. For if Christ died sufficiently for all, the death of Christ is a grace sufficient for all, and the manifestation of that death a grace equally sufficient, at least in a way that is consonant with its nature.[242]

Here we can see, perhaps more clearly than anywhere else, the problem of reconciling the sufficiency of Christ's atonement for *sins*, and the efficacy of his atonement for saving *sinners*. When this distinction is not properly made, sufficiency for sins is bound to become sufficiency for sinners and thus open the door to Arminianism or even universalism, since otherwise there is the virtual certainty that there will be leftover grace that is not used. How much of that there will be depends entirely on the decision of God, who dispenses it as he chooses, but why would he make his Son suffer needlessly? If it is really true that men are saved in order to guarantee that the death of the Son of God should not be fruitless, how can it be that not everyone is saved, since his death would then bear its maximum fruit? By what logic can it really be restricted? Do not the concepts of "election" and "predestination" become words to describe

[241] "M. Cameron dit que Jésus Christ est mort pour tous les hommes sous la condition de la foi. De là vous concluez qu'il faut donc que la cause de la foi, c'est-à-dire, selon vous, l'illumination de l'Esprit, soit commune à tous hommes. Et [vous] en ajoutez cette raison, que Christ ne serait pas véritablement mort pour eux, s'il ne leur avait aussi acquis la grâce en laquelle consiste la cause de la foi. Vous dites que Jésus Christ est mort pour tous les hommes sous la condition de la foi, à raison de quoi il leur a aussi rendu l'illumination qui est la cause de la foi, commune" (Amyraut, *Réplique à M. de la Milletière*, 325).

[242] "Je m'étonne comment vous faites particulière à M. Cameron et moi cette opinion, que la grâce extérieure qui est offerte à tous ceux qu'on appelle; vu qu'au sens qu'il l'a proposée, c'est la doctrine de Calvin, de Hyperius, de Musculus, de Bullinger, de Pellicanus, d'Aretius et de tant d'autres excellents personnages, et que c'est la distinction communément reçue en nos écoles, que Christ est mort *suffisament pour tous, et efficacieusement pour les seuls élus*. Car si Christ est mort suffisament pour tous, la mort du Christ est une grâce suffisante à tous, et la manifestation de cette mort une grâce suffisante de même, au moins d'une suffisance convenable à sa nature" (Amyraut, *Réplique à M. de la Milletière*, 329).

the life of the believer *after* his profession of faith and not before, opening up at least the possibility that that profession of faith is a meritorious work of its own? Amyraut's scheme came as close to universalism as it was possible to get within the framework of traditional Reformed theology, much as he denied it. It may have been an extreme reaction for the French Protestant church to have condemned him for heresy, especially considering what he wanted to affirm about divine election and predestination, but it is hard not to conclude that his way of trying to explain this was built on faulty premises and was therefore condemned to reach erroneous conclusions, even as he was doing his utmost to avoid misunderstandings and to preserve at least the limited efficacy of the atoning work of Christ intact.

Did Amyraut really deny limited atonement? If the theology of Beza or Perkins is taken as the standard, the answer would probably have to be yes, but hypothetical universalism had long since modified that, and Amyraut could claim to stand within the canons of Dort, which became the standard for determining what limited atonement would mean in subsequent Reformed theology. It is essential to bear this in mind, because so much modern debate on this question fails to take it into consideration. Brian Armstrong's extensive study of Amyraut's theology comes down in his favor over against Beza, but as this can be claimed of the canons of Dort as well, it is of little real significance.[243] A similar misunderstanding can be seen in the short article by David Broughton Knox (1916–1994), who seemed to think that hypothetical universalism, of the kind espoused by Ussher, Davenant, and Cameron, was "Arminianism" as opposed to the Beza-Perkins doctrine, which he labeled "Calvinism."[244] Knox rejected limited atonement of the Beza-Perkins variety, but in fact the substance of his doctrine is virtually identical to that propounded by the Synod of Dort and is fully consonant with Reformed orthodoxy, or "Calvinism" as this has been understood since 1619.

Amyraut's weakness was in his reordering of the divine decrees in such a way as to separate the atoning work of Christ from election and predestination. To argue that Christ's death was of universal efficacy at one level but not at another was to introduce a duality in the plan of God that is ultimately untenable and must be rejected. Hypothetical universalism began as a reaction to the one-sided approach of Beza, and its contribution to understanding the true teaching of the Bible was fully integrated into Reformed theology by the

243 Brian G. Armstrong, *Calvinism and the Amyraut Heresy* (Madison: University of Wisconsin Press, 1969). Armstrong is agenda-driven and predisposed to accept Amyraldianism because of his antipathy to Reformed orthodoxy, a prejudice that should not be confused with Amyraut's own intentions.

244 *D. Broughton Knox: Selected Works I: The Doctrine of God* (Kingsford, NSW: Matthias Media, 2000), 260–266.

canons of Dort. Then as now, every Reformed theologian agrees that it is essential to maintain that Christ's atoning death is sufficient for the sins of the whole world and that the gospel must be proclaimed to every creature. But these beliefs do not represent any form of universalism. On the contrary, they reflect the teaching of Jesus, that it is the duty of the church to go out and find the lost sheep of the house of Israel, not to attract goats on the assumption that with enough faith they can be transformed into sheep and be saved too. To be sure, we cannot tell them apart, and the visible church includes a good number of goats (the "reprobate") who benefit from their association with the sheep but who will not share the same inheritance in heaven. To apply this analogy to Amyraut's teaching, he believed that the distinction between sheep and goats was a moral and spiritual one, which appeared only when God picked out certain goats and changed them into sheep, so that the Shepherd who had given his life for them would not be left without a flock. In saying this, Amyraut was not trying to deviate from the Reformed faith, and it is probably unjust to regard him as a heretic, because in the end he did believe that the sheep were created by God and that only they were saved. But having said that, Amyraut opened the door to deviations that appeared in the late seventeenth century and claimed his teaching as their inspiration. In the words of Roger Nicole, who has made an extensive survey of this process,

> The doctrine of hypothetical universalism acted as a corrosive factor in the French Reformed Church. Tolerated at first because it was felt that an outright condemnation would lead to schism, it slowly undermined respect for the confessional standards and disrupted internal unity and cohesion. As far as can be seen, it did not in fact help to promote any basic union with the Lutherans, nor did it materially assist in preventing abjurations to the Roman Catholic faith. On the other hand, it did provide a bridge toward Arminianism and perhaps toward the semi-Pelagian tendencies of the Church of Rome. The advantages that Amyraut had envisaged failed to materialize, and the dangers against which his opponents had warned did in fact eventuate.[245]

The Assurance of Salvation

John Calvin's belief that union with Christ was sealed by the indwelling presence of the Holy Spirit in the hearts of believers meant that the work of that Spirit must be located in those hearts. Whatever the Spirit does beyond that, he does primarily through those whom he has chosen and prepared for salvation. As the apostle Paul taught, the elect are called to work out their salvation in fear

[245] Roger Nicole, *Standing Forth* (Fearn: Christian Focus, 2002), 326.

and trembling, knowing who it is who has called them and what the purpose of their calling is.[246] The medieval church had assumed that someone called by God would head for a monastery and/or seek ordination in the church, but the Reformers thought differently. To their minds, God's call was for everyone, but not everyone was meant to be an ordained minister. God also called people to be farmers, tradesmen, politicians, housewives, and maids. Protestant preachers accordingly insisted that it was the duty of every believer to discover what God's calling for him or her was and to take responsibility for that. Christians might find that they were being called to do something that was uncongenial to them, just as Jonah was called to preach to the Ninevites when he did not want to, but if so, God would overrule their rebelliousness, as the story of Jonah made clear. If the people concerned were truly elect and predestined, God would get his way and they would eventually come around and accept his will for them. On the other hand, if their recalcitrance was allowed to go unchecked they would suffer the consequences and be destroyed, a sure sign that they were not among the elect to begin with. The danger in this was that worldly success could be made to seem like proof of divine election, and Protestantism has often been caricatured in this way by people who disagree with its underlying theology. But to think like that is to misunderstand the fundamental premise of Reformed theology, which rests on belief in the indwelling presence and work of the Holy Spirit. Worldly success proves nothing—what matters is the inward disposition of the heart, which is much harder to discern.

Thus we see how Reformed theology led inexorably from the public to the private domain. Election and predestination could not be regarded as community affairs, applicable to the Netherlands or to Great Britain as societies but not necessarily to the individuals within them. Nor was it good enough to say, as Christians had long been accustomed to doing, that while only the elect will be saved in the end, no one can know for sure who the elect are, or be confident of his or her own salvation. That there would always be uncertainty in human minds over the total number of the elect was relatively easy to accept, because no individual can know the mind of God in its fullness. But that the individual believer could not know whether he would go to heaven when he died was intolerable. To put it bluntly, was it really possible for someone to follow Christ all his life in complete sincerity and yet go to hell when he died? The Catholic church answered this question by saying that such a person would probably go to purgatory on the basis of his merits, which (if they were sufficient) might even allow him into heaven straightaway, as one of the "saints." That option

[246] See Phil. 2:12–13.

was not available to the Reformers. Merits were of no value to them and purgatory did not exist, so the person in question was left unsure about what would happen to him when he died. The English Ten Articles of 1536 dealt with the problem as follows:

> It standeth with the very due order of charity [for] a Christian man to pray for souls departed, and to commit them in our prayers to God's mercy . . . whereby they may be relieved . . . of some part of their pain; but forasmuch as the place where they be, the name thereof, and the kinds of pains there, also be to us uncertain by Scripture; therefore this with other things we remit to Almighty God, unto whose mercy it is meet and convenient for us to commend them, trusting that God accepteth our prayers for them, referring the rest wholly to God, to whom is known their estate and condition.[247]

Not surprisingly, many ordinary believers were not happy with this uncertainty and wanted to be reassured that their faith was not in vain. Some may even have been tempted to go on believing in purgatory as the lesser of two evils. If they did not know that they would be going to heaven, at least they could have some assurance that they would not be consigned to eternal damnation in hell either.[248] So Protestant theologians turned their attention to the work of the Holy Spirit in the heart of the believer, which they proceeded to analyze in great detail, to see whether and to what extent this question could be answered.

What we now call "assurance of salvation" was usually termed "security" in pre-Reformation times, and was regarded as both impossible in principle and undesirable in practice, since security was associated with pride. There was a fear that if someone was convinced that he had nothing to worry about, he would not bother trying to live a morally upright life and so would not only ruin himself in this world but would deprive himself of bliss in the next as well. Gregory the Great's assessment was taken as authoritative:

> But none of the elect, as long as they are in this life, claim any confidence of security for themselves. At all times they are wary of being tempted and afraid of the attacks of the hidden enemy. Even when there are no temptations at work, they are still deeply troubled by their wariness. For often an imprudent sense of security has been a grave danger to many, with the result

[247] Ten Articles, 10; see Bray, *Documents of the English Reformation*, 173–174.

[248] It is hard to find any direct evidence of this from the sixteenth century, unless we can take relapse into Catholicism (which was fairly common) as a sign of it. But in modern times, there have been Protestants who have lacked (or discounted) assurance and have turned either to Catholicism (as John Henry Newman did) or to a reconsideration of the desirability of purgatory. For an example of the latter tendency, see Jerry L. Walls, *Purgatory: The Logic of Total Transformation* (Oxford: Oxford University Press, 2012).

> that they have experienced the attacks of the wily enemy, not because they have been tempted but because they have already surrendered to him. We must therefore be always on guard, so that the mind, which is constantly being attacked, is never lulled to sleep by some higher intention. In this way it will not desert its laborious duty and, wallowing in conflicting feelings as if it were lying in quicksand, determine to prostitute itself to the Devil who is coming to corrupt it.[249]

This attitude of Gregory's has to be appreciated, because it is over the question of assurance that modern Protestants and Catholics fail to understand each other. Catholics tend to believe that when Protestants say that they know they are going to heaven when they die they are being arrogant and presumptuous. Only good people can get to heaven, they think, and how can Protestants claim to be good? Protestants, for their part, know that Catholics do not believe in assurance of salvation as they do, but often fail to realize that, if they had the same perception of eternal security that Catholics have, they would not believe it either. No Protestant thinks that he can do whatever he likes and go to heaven regardless! Believers are not good people—they are sinners saved by grace—but the Holy Spirit who dwells in their hearts assures them that they are united to Christ and so are saved by his righteousness, not by anything they have (or have not) done themselves.

The basic outline of this theology was established by Martin Luther, who made it a cornerstone of his own preaching and teaching. In his preface to Paul's epistle to the Romans he wrote,

> Faith is a living, daring confidence in God's grace, so sure and certain that the believer would stake his life on it a thousand times. This knowledge and confidence in God's grace makes men glad, bold and happy in dealing with God.[250]

But as Luther constantly reiterated in his writings against the Anabaptists, "faith," understood as a human feeling or conviction, was unstable and could not be relied on. True assurance did not rest on that but on the Word of God as proclaimed by the church:

> He who prays for the forgiveness of his sins and hears the absolution of Christ, should be certain that truly, just as the Word declares, his sins are forgiven;

[249] Gregory the Great, *Moralia in Iob* (29:24), 20.3.8 (PL 76, co. 139). See also his letter to Gregoria, a lady of Constantinople, in which he tells her: "You must not feel safe against your sins, because if you do you will not be able to weep for those same sins on the last day of your life. Whenever that day comes, you must be always vigilant, always on guard and afraid of your transgressions, and wash them away every day with your tears" (*Epistulae*, VII, 25 [PL 77, col. 878]).

[250] Martin Luther, *Preface to Romans*, in Pelikan and Lehmann, *Luther's Works*, 35:370–371.

> and he should be assured that this is in no sense man's work, but God's work. Whatever, therefore, is done in the church must rest on certainty.[251]

For this reason, it was perfectly possible, indeed the normal state of the Christian in this life, to have "certainty" without "security." "Certainty" was the assurance that God would keep his promises to us, whatever our subjective thoughts, feelings, or behavior might be at any given moment, whereas "security" was the sense that we have been set free from spiritual struggle altogether. A Christian might have fleeting glimpses of that in this life, but spiritual warfare was the common condition of believers, and to rest on one's laurels (as it were) was dangerous in the extreme. This view became the standard teaching of the Reformed churches and was reflected in the canons of the Synod of Dort, which stated,

> Of the preservation of the elect to salvation, and of their perseverance in the faith, true believers may and do obtain assurance according to the measure of their faith. . . . This certainty of perseverance however, is so far from exciting in believers a spirit of pride, or of rendering them carnally secure, that (on the contrary) it is the real source of humility . . . and of solid rejoicing in God.[252]

In his fundamental approach to the question, Huldrych Zwingli was very similar to Luther. For example, he wrote,

> Faith is nothing else than certain assurance by which man relies on the merit of Christ. . . . That man himself contributes nothing, but believes that all things are directed and ordered by God's providence, and this comes only from giving himself to God and trusting in him completely; that he understands in faith that God does everything, even though we cannot perceive it.[253]

But where Luther stressed the objectivity of Word and sacrament in the life of the church, Zwingli placed more emphasis on the inner witness of the Holy Spirit in the heart of the believer:

> For the Spirit cannot deceive. If he tells us that God is our Father, and we with certainty and confidence call him Father, assured of our eternal inheritance, it is certain that God's Spirit had been poured out in our hearts. It is therefore

[251] Martin Luther, *Exposition of the Psalms*, 90:17, in Pelikan and Lehmann, *Luther's Works*, 13:140.
[252] Canons of Dort, 5.9, 12; see Bray, *Documents of the English Reformation*, 473–474.
[253] Huldrych Zwingli, *Auslegung des 20. Artkels*, in *Hudereich Zwinglis sämtliche Werke*, ed. E. Egli, G. Finsler et al., 14 vols. (Zurich: Verlag Berichthaus, 1905–1968), 2:182. The date was January 29, 1523. These volumes are also part of the *Corpus Reformatorum* (LXXXVIII–CI).

> certain that the one who is thus secure and safe is elect, for those who believe are ordained to eternal life.[254]

The evidence of this is a life of good works that flow naturally from faith and that can be claimed as evidence of salvation, though of course they cannot be used to obtain it.[255] Zwingli's successor at Zurich, Heinrich Bullinger, took his predecessor's teaching still further along the same lines. As far as Bullinger was concerned, faith was a gift of God given only to the elect, so that anyone who believed could claim assurance of salvation on that account:

> Faith therefore is a most assured sign that thou art elected; and whiles thou art called to the communion of Christ, and art taught faith, the most loving God declareth towards thee his election and good-will. . . . God's predestination is not stayed or stirred with any worthiness or unworthiness of ours; but of the mere grace and mercy of God the Father, it respecteth Christ alone. And because our salvation doth stay only upon him, it cannot but be most certain.[256]

There seem to be some grounds for saying that in later years Bullinger retreated from his earlier equation of faith with assurance, regarding the latter as something that faith produces as time goes on, rather than as a conviction that cannot be distinguished from it. Like the other Reformers, Bullinger had to account for the fact that, as Luther perceived and as the Bible itself testifies from the lives of people as prominent as Abraham, Moses, Elijah, and Peter, faith goes up and down, making "assurance" somewhat problematic if it is too closely tied to that.[257] But too much should not be made of this. Bullinger may avoid using the word "assurance" but it is hard to escape that conclusion from something like the following:

> Faith is a certain knowledge of the truth, and a constant, firm and undoubted trust and assent of the human mind to the Word of God, originating from the Holy Spirit, by which it believes all truth, principally the promises of God and in them Christ himself, in whom is set forth all fullness of life and salvation: which, since it receives all good things, has him indwelling and living. Or, faith is a certain knowledge, a firm trust and an undoubted assent to the Word of God: which, inspired in our soul by the Spirit of God, believes

---

[254] Huldrych Zwingli, *Fidei ratio*, in, *Werke*, 6:2, 800. The date was July 3, 1530.
[255] Huldrych Zwingli, *Adversus Hieronymum Emserum antibolon*, in *Werke*, 3:257. The date was August 20, 1524.
[256] Henry Bullinger, *The Decades of Henry Bullinger*, ed. Thomas Harding, 5 vols. in 4 (Cambridge: Cambridge University Press, 1849–1851), 4:185–188. The English translation was done by "H. I." and originally published in 1577, so it would have been well known in late sixteenth-century England.
[257] For the arguments and the evidence, see J. R. Beeke, *The Quest for Full Assurance: The Legacy of Calvin and His Successors* (Edinburgh: Banner of Truth, 1999), 31–35.

> piously all truth that is to be believed, receives Christ himself, and possesses in him life, righteousness and all good things.[258]

By the time Bullinger got going, the Council of Trent was considering the question, and in 1547 it defined the Roman Catholic doctrine in the following terms, which clearly echo the teaching of Pope Gregory I nearly a millennium before:

> No one, so long as he is in this mortal life, ought to be presumptuous about the secret mystery of divine predestination, so as to claim that he is certainly one of the number of the predestined as if it were true that he is justified and either cannot sin any more, or if he does sin, that he can promise himself an assured repentance, for apart from a special revelation, it is impossible to know whom God has chosen for everlasting life.[259]

When we turn to the teaching of John Calvin, we find that in all essentials it was virtually identical to that of Luther, Zwingli, and Bullinger. If anything, Calvin put even greater emphasis on the work of the Holy Spirit than they did:

> The Spirit of revelation which we receive . . . is from God, and so is above all the heavens, is of genuine and unchangeable truth, and beyond every possibility of doubt . . . the elect have been given the Spirit by whose witness they know for a certainty that they have been adopted to the hope of eternal salvation.[260]

Elsewhere he went as far as they did, or even further, in condemning those who lacked the assurance that faith brought to the elect:

> [Paul] declares that those who doubt their possession of Christ and their membership in his body are reprobates. Let us therefore understand that the only true faith is that which allows us to rest in God's grace, not with a dubious opinion but with firm and steadfast assurance.[261]

But Calvin was well aware, following Luther, that in practice assurance of faith is often lacking in believers because their faith is weak, and he devoted several paragraphs in his *Institutes* to solving what he clearly saw as a problem.[262] Several commentators have detected a contradiction here between the Calvin of his com-

---

[258] Heinrich Bullinger, *De gratia Dei iustificante nos propter Christum* (Zurich: Froschauer, 1554), 43.

[259] *Conciliorum oecumenicorum decreta*, 676. (This is the decree on justification, chapter 12, promulgated in the sixth session on January 13, 1547).

[260] Calvin, *The First Epistle of Paul to the Corinthians*, trans. John W. Fraser (Edinburgh: Oliver & Boyd, 1960), 59 (on 1 Cor. 2:12).

[261] Calvin, *The Second Epistle of Paul to the Corinthians*, trans. T. A. Smail (Edinburgh: Oliver & Boyd, 1964), 173 (on 2 Cor. 13:5).

[262] Calvin, *Institutio* 3.2.17–43.

mentaries, where he preaches Pauline assurance, and the Calvin of the *Institutes*, where he seems to backtrack and admit that no such assurance is possible in this life. But in an extended discussion of the question, Joel Beeke has demonstrated that this is a superficial analysis.[263] In Calvin's view, faith and the assurance that comes with it were gifts of the Holy Spirit that could never be taken away, just as the Spirit himself never departs from the heart of a believer. But assurance could not be merely intellectual assent to the truth of the gospel, important though that was. It also had to be lived out in experience, and here the Christian was engaged in a lifelong struggle against the world, the flesh, and the Devil. Lack of assurance could not be ascribed to any deficiency on God's part; rather it was the inevitable consequence of the continuing power of the "old Adam" over believers. The best way to deal with it was to claim the promises of God as he has told us to do. This was especially evident in Calvin's teaching on the power and necessity of prayer:

> The confidence of which I speak is not something that frees the mind of all anxiety. . . . The best stimulus which the saints have to prayer is when, because of their own necessities, they feel most upset and are all but driven to despair until faith comes to their aid at just the right time. It is then that the goodness of God shines on them, so that even though they are weighed down by distress and tormented by the fear of worse still to come, they still trust in his goodness and so both lighten the burden of endurance and take comfort in the hope of final deliverance.[264]

Calvin was in no doubt that this spiritual warfare would have only one outcome, and that that would be the confirmation of the validity of the faith given to believers. As he put it,

> The pious mind, however agitated and torn it may be, in the end overcomes all difficulties and does not allow its confidence in the divine mercy to be destroyed. On the contrary, the struggles that exercise and disturb it tend to establish this confidence. . . . Faith remains fixed in the believer's breast and can never be eradicated from it. However shaken it may seem to be in one way or another, its flame is never quenched to the point that it no longer lurks somewhere under the embers.[265]

Calvin was also alive to the importance of good works as confirmation of the reality of a believer's faith, though like all the Reformers, he was adamant that they could not be relied on as a justification or proof of salvation:

---

263 Beeke, *Quest for Full Assurance*, 44–72.
264 Calvin, *Institutio* 3.20.11.
265 Ibid., 3.2.21.

> Works . . . are proof of God's dwelling and reigning in us. This confidence in works has no place unless you have already put your whole trust in the mercy of God. . . . The Christian mind must not turn back to the merit of works as an aid to salvation, but must dwell entirely on the free promise of justification. But we forbid no believer from confirming and supporting his faith by the signs of God's favor toward him. When we recall the gifts that God has bestowed on us, they are like rays of the divine countenance by which we can behold the highest light of his goodness; much more is this the case with the gift of good works, which shows that we have received the Spirit of adoption.[266]

The position of Calvin would therefore seem to be clear, and in line with that of his Protestant contemporaries. It is when we come to his successor, Theodore Beza, that questions arise, as we have already seen.[267] That Beza developed Calvin's teaching further is universally agreed, but in which direction did he go and to what effect? Beza was more analytical and systematic than Calvin, but that does not mean that the two men disagreed or that Beza distorted Calvin's thought in any significant way. For example, Calvin believed that faith brought knowledge and assurance with it, whereas Beza separated out faith as mere knowledge (*notitia*) from acceptance (*assensus*) and trust (*fiducia*). But although he made these distinctions, he did not disagree with Calvin's view that only all three together would bring assurance to the believer. Whether, or to what extent, it was possible to have only one or two of the three elements was another question, and here perhaps Beza was more accommodating than Calvin had been, but if so, this should be understood as a clarification of the latter's thought and not as a distortion of it.

There does seem to be some ground for saying that Beza spent more time discussing the problem of weak faith than Calvin did. Without disagreeing with Calvin as to the "big picture" of how faith and assurance go together, Beza was apparently more prepared to allow that a man of weak faith might look to the works of sanctification in his life as evidence for the indwelling presence of the Holy Spirit. In his words,

> When Satan putteth us in doubt of our election, we may not search first the resolution in the eternal counsel of God, whose majesty we cannot compre-

---

[266] Ibid., 3.14.18.

[267] See Wright, *Our Sovereign Refuge*, 71–81, for an examination of the controversy over Beza's doctrine of assurance and its relationship to Calvin's teaching. After looking at the different viewpoints commonly expressed in modern scholarship, Wright concludes that Beza was much closer to Calvin than is often recognized, though there are signs that toward the end of his life he was moving toward a more abstract understanding of the doctrine. See also Beeke, *Quest for Full Assurance*, 72–81.

> hend, but on the contrary we must begin at the sanctification which we feel in ourselves to ascend up more higher, for as much as our sanctification, from whence proceedeth good works, is a certain effect of the faith, or rather of Jesus Christ dwelling in us by faith. . . . Sanctification, with the fruits thereof, is the first step or degree whereby we begin to ascend up to the first and true cause of our salvation, to wit, of our free eternal election.[268]

At the same time, Beza also insisted that pointing to the subjective evidence of works as evidence of election was possible only because works were part of a package that had to be received as a whole. For weak believers, works might be the best way to begin, but as they grew in assurance they would move on to higher things. As he put it,

> Seeing that good works are for us the certain evidences of our faith, they also bring to us afterwards the certainty of our eternal election. Faith lays hold of Christ, by which, being justified and sanctified, we have the enjoyment of the glory to which we have been destined before the foundation of the world. . . . All that we have said of faith and its effects would be useless if we would not add this point of eternal election as the sole foundation and support of all the assurance of Christians.[269]

Taking all this into consideration, we have to conclude that Beza did not depart from Calvin in any major way, even if his analysis left the door open for later theologians to focus more particularly on one aspect of his teaching—in this case, the validity of appealing to the evidence of works of sanctification—and then take it out of the original context in a way that would fundamentally distort its original significance.[270]

In a wide-ranging study of Beza's works, Shawn Wright has shown that for Beza there were seven factors that had to be taken into account when discussing assurance.[271] The first of these was God's character and the nature of his promises. God has pledged to save his elect, and he does not lie—therefore, the Christian can rest assured that he will do what he has said he will do, even if it is not immediately clear to the believer how he will do it.[272] The second factor

---

268 Theodore Beza, *A Briefe and Pithie Summe of Christian Faith Made in the Forme of a Confession, with a Confutation of Al Such Superstitious Errors, as Are Contrarie Therunto*, trans. Robert Fyll (London: Roger Ward, 1639), 71–72. There is also a modern translation called *The Christian Faith*, by J. Clark (Lewes: Focus Christian Ministries Trust, 1992). The original Latin text was published as *Confessio Christianae fidei, et eiusdem collatio cum papisticis haeresibus* (Geneva: Eustathius Vignon, 1587).

269 Beza, *Briefe and Pithie Summe*, 19.

270 See Robert Letham, "Theodore Beza: A Reassessment" in *Scottish Journal of Theology* 40 (1987): 25–40.

271 Wright, *Our Sovereign Refuge*, 204–217.

272 Wright supports this assertion mainly by quoting from Beza's prayers and other devotional works in which he showed a particular desire to speak to ordinary people about trusting God for their salvation. See especially

was the life, death, and resurrection of Jesus Christ for the salvation of God's people. Human feelings and earthly tragedies cannot alter that fact, which remains the ground on which we plead our salvation.[273]

The third factor was faith, by which the believer comes to understand the work of Christ on his behalf and to trust in him.[274] The fourth factor was the indwelling presence of the Holy Spirit in the heart of the Christian. The Spirit applies the work of Christ to the lives of the elect, not least by making them aware of how desperately they need him. Thus the believer may feel himself to be very far from God, but that very feeling will make him cling all the more to Christ as his only hope, and that hope is his assurance of salvation.[275] The fifth factor was the church, the blessed company of all those who have had the same experience and whose example is there to comfort individuals who may think that they have been abandoned by God.[276] The sixth factor was prayer, by which believers develop their relationship with God and grow in grace.[277] The seventh and final factor was heaven, the knowledge and expectation of which increases in the life of the Christian until he comes to the point where his whole life is focused on attaining it.[278]

Modern observers may find some of the elements in this list somewhat strange, particularly the emphasis on heaven, which to most people seems more of a hope than a reality. But even if we might be tempted to shorten the list somewhat, it is clear that reliance on the works of sanctification is nowhere to be found. For Beza, such works were evidence of the indwelling presence of the Holy Spirit and their only useful purpose was to point beyond themselves to him. Assurance of salvation was therefore not based on introspection but on trust in a higher reality who makes himself known in us, and it is only as we come to understand that and to trust more fully in him that the promise given by God works itself out in our lives.

Theodore Beza lived an unusually long life (1519–1605) and became a living legend in his own time. His renown in England can be gauged from the fact that the Roman Catholic translators of the New Testament were forced to treat him with respect, even though they disagreed with him on many points.[279]

Maister Bezaes Houshold Prayers, trans. John Barnes (London: J. Barnes, 1603), fo. O3r-v., and the prayer "for the morning" (fo. N3v-N10r).

[273] Again, Wright quotes from *Houshold Prayers* (fo. M1v-M3r; Q2r-Q3v) and from *Christian Meditations upon Eight Psalmes of the Prophet David* (London: Christopher Barker, 1582), fo. G4r-v. The original French text, published in the same year, has been edited by Mario Richter and reissued as *Chrestiennes méditations* (Geneva: Droz, 1964).

[274] Again, Wright quotes the *Houshold Prayers*, fo. E3v-E4r.

[275] See the discussion above. Wright quotes *Briefe and Pithie Summe*, 246–247, etc.

[276] Again, Wright quotes the *Houshold Prayers*, particularly the one "that we may not depart from the church" (fo. F8v-G2v).

[277] Wright quotes the *Houshold Prayers*, fo. B1v-B2r to support this.

[278] Wright supports his contention by further quotes from the *Houshold Prayers* and from *Christian Meditations*.

[279] See Bray, *Documents of the English Reformation*, 376–383. The Reims translation, as it is called, appeared in 1582.

More significantly, his most important works were translated into English from 1577 onward, and some of his Latin treatises even appeared in English but not in his native French![280] Calvin's commentaries and *Institutes* were being translated into English at the same time, along with many of his sermons. These were eagerly read and imitated by many, not least by William Perkins. Perkins analyzed the traditional teaching about assurance that he had taken over from Calvin and Beza into even finer details, with the key distinction being the all-important difference between objective assurance, rooted in the work of Christ, and subjective assurance, based on the work of the Holy Spirit in the heart of the believer.[281]

Of particular importance was the way in which he understood weak and strong faith. For Perkins, weak faith was intellectual assent to the truth of the gospel, which was the common possession of all Christians. Strong faith, by contrast, was the personal conviction that came by the inner working of the Spirit. Much of Perkins's ministry was spent reassuring those of weak faith that there was no need for them to despair, and encouraging them to seek the deeper experience of God that strong faith would bring. In 1596 Perkins wrote three books entitled *Of the Cases of Conscience*, in which he discussed at length the relationship between conscience, faith, and assurance. In answer to the question as to how a man could be sure of his own election, Perkins wrote,

> Election, vocation, faith, adoption, justification, sanctification and eternal glorification are never separated in the faith of any man, but like inseparable companions, go hand in hand; so as he that can be assured of one of them, may infallibly conclude in his own heart, that he hath and shall have interest in all the other in his due time. . . . In a chain, the two extremes are knit together by the middle links, and in the order of causes of happiness and salvation, faith hath a middle place, and by it hath the child of God assured hold of his election, and effectual vocation, and consequently of his glorification in the kingdom of heaven.[282]

Like his predecessors, Perkins was primarily concerned to get believers to this point in their spiritual experience, but he was constantly confronted by cases of people who claimed to believe in Christ but who had no sense of assurance at all. To them, Perkins recommended a spiritual program that focused

280 See Wright, *Our Sovereign Refuge*, 235–242, for a complete list.

281 For a detailed presentation of Perkins's beliefs, see Beeke, *Quest for Full Assurance*, 83–98.

282 In Thomas F. Merrill, ed., *William Perkins, 1558–1602, English Puritanist; His Pioneer Works on Casuistry: "A Discourse of Conscience" and "The Whole Treatise of Cases of Conscience"* (Nieuwkoop: B. De Graaf, 1966), 111–112 (spelling modernized). The original text is in William Perkins, *The First Booke of the Cases of Conscience, Concerning Man Simply Considered in Himselfe without Relation to Another*, 6, in *Works*, 2:18.

on making use of the means of grace provided by the church and its ministry. In his customarily methodical way, he even listed the steps to be taken, which may be paraphrased as follows:[283]

1. Feel your need and in bitterness of heart, bewail the offense every sin of yours gives to God.
2. Strive against the flesh and its lusts.
3. Desire the grace of God and the merit of Christ, in order to obtain eternal life.
4. When you receive grace, be grateful for it and treat it as a precious jewel.
5. Love the minister of God's Word and follow his guidance.
6. Call on God earnestly, even with tears.
7. Desire and love the return of Christ and the day of judgment, when sin will be finally removed.
8. Flee every opportunity given to sin, and do all you can to come to a new life.
9. Persevere in these things as long as you live.

Perkins's Reformed credentials are perhaps nowhere more on display than in the way he viewed the sacraments. Fully confident of the power of the ministry of the Word, Perkins had this to say about a sacrament:

> [A sacrament is] a prop and stay for faith to lean upon. For it cannot entitle us into the inheritance of the sons of God, as the covenant doth, but only by reason of faith going before, it doth seal that which before was bestowed upon us.[284]

The most important result of Perkins's teaching on assurance was that it laid the foundation for what the Westminster Confession of Faith decreed on the subject, and that in turn has become the benchmark for all subsequent Reformed theology.[285] The Confession started by admitting that there were some people who claim assurance of salvation wrongly, but that that abuse did not take away the hope of true believers:

> Although hypocrites and other unregenerate men may vainly deceive themselves with false hopes and carnal presumptions of being in the favor of God

[283] The original list is in Perkins, *Golden Chaine*, 58, in *Works*, 1:115.
[284] Perkins, *Golden Chaine*, 32, in *Works*, 1:73 (spelling modernized).
[285] Considering its importance, there was remarkably little debate about it in the Westminster assembly, which approved it in a single session (707), held on the morning of September 15, 1646. See Chad Van Dixhoorn, ed., *Minutes and Papers of the Westminster Assembly*, 5 vols. (Oxford: Oxford University Press, 2012), 4:278–279. More time was devoted to finding scriptural proofs for the doctrine (sessions 794–795, February 17–18, 1647), see Van Dixhoorn, *Minutes and Papers*, 4:432–435. For a full discussion, see Beeke, *Quest for Full Assurance*, 111–164.

> and estate of salvation, . . . yet such as truly believe in the Lord Jesus and love him in sincerity, endeavoring to walk in all good conscience before him, may in this life be certainly assured that they are in the state of grace.[286]

The Confession then went on to say that this assurance was infallible for three specific reasons. It was founded on,

1. The divine truth of the promises of salvation.
2. The inward evidence of the grace contained in those promises.
3. The witness of the Spirit of adoption in the hearts of believers.[287]

Next, the Confession asserts what Perkins and others had already said about weak faith. A true believer might have to wait for a long time and go through many doubts before obtaining full assurance, but this is possible without any miraculous intervention. Those in doubt must do all they can to "make [their] calling and election sure" by a strict pattern of spiritual self-discipline.[288] But most tellingly of all, the Confession admits that,

> True believers may have the assurance of their salvation diverse ways shaken, diminished and intermitted, as by negligence in preserving of it, by falling into some special sin which woundeth the conscience and grieveth the Spirit, by some sudden or vehement temptation, by God's withdrawing the light of his countenance and suffering even such as fear him to walk in darkness and to have no light . . .[289]

Yet even in such a dreadful state, they should not despair, because,

> . . . they [are] never utterly destitute of that seed of God and life of faith, that love of Christ and the brethren, that sincerity of heart and conscience of duty out of which by the operation of the Spirit, this assurance may in due time be revived, and by the which in the meantime, they are supported [i.e., protected] from utter despair.[290]

To anyone accustomed to reading official statements of faith, what comes across most clearly here is the deep pastoral tone of the chapter, which reflects the spirit in which Beza and Perkins wrote. To accuse them, as some modern scholars have done, of a cerebral and heartless approach to the Christian life is completely false. However rationalistic some of their expositions may seem to

---

[286] Westminster Confession, 18.1; see Bray, *Documents of the English Reformation*, 500.
[287] Ibid., 18.2; see Bray, *Documents of the English Reformation*, 500.
[288] Ibid., 18.3; see Bray, *Documents of the English Reformation*, 500–501.
[289] Ibid., 18.4; see Bray, *Documents of the English Reformation*, 501.
[290] Ibid., 18.4; see Bray, ibid.

be, they never lost sight of the spiritual heart of their theology, as this chapter eloquently reminds us. The same was true of those who, in the next generation, were charged with the task of expounding and developing the doctrine still further.

Chief among them was John Owen, who had played a major role at the Westminster assembly and would naturally be expected to have defended its theology afterwards.[291] Owen was to be the author of perhaps the greatest book on the Holy Spirit ever written, though it says relatively little about the work of the Spirit in assurance.[292] In principle, like all his Reformed predecessors, Owen believed that the purposes of God are fixed and unchangeable, which gives believers hope and confidence in him and his promises:

> His purpose, which is "according unto election," is unchangeable; and therefore, the final perseverance and salvation of those concerned in it are everlastingly secured. . . . And there is no greater encouragement to grow and persist in holiness than what is administered by this assurance of a blessed end and issue of it.[293]

Like others before him, and many of his contemporaries, Owen was preoccupied with the problem of weak faith, which was being held up to him as evidence that there is no real assurance in this life. To this, Owen replied,

> I no way doubt but many thousands of believers, whose apprehensions of the nature, properties, and conditions of things, as they are in themselves, are low, weak, and confused, yet, having received the Spirit of adoption, bearing witness with their spirits that they are children of God . . . have been taken up into as high a degree of comforting and cheering assurance, and that upon the most infallible foundation imaginable . . .[294]

There is some evidence that Owen was more precise than the Westminster Confession in his understanding of the way assurance was given to the believer, because the Savoy Declaration of Faith and Order, which he largely drafted, changes some of the wording in the original Confession, to include "the blood and righteousness of Christ, revealed in the Gospel" and "the immediate witness of the Holy Spirit," whose witness to our adoption leaves our hearts "more humble and holy."[295] These alterations do not change the sub-

[291] For Owen and the development of his doctrine of assurance, see Beeke, *Quest for Full Assurance*, 165–213.

[292] This was *Pneumatologia: A Discourse on the Holy Spirit*, most of which was published in 1674 but parts of which did not appear until 1693, a decade after his death. The complete text is in *The Works of John Owen*, ed. William H. Goold, 16 vols. (Edinburgh: Banner of Truth, 1965), where it is vols. 3–4.

[293] Owen, *Pneumatologia*, book 5, ch. 2, in *Works*, 3:601–602.

[294] Owen, *Doctrine of the Saints' Perseverance*, ch. 1, in *Works*, 11:83.

[295] Savoy Declaration, 18.2. See J. R. Beeke, *Quest for Full Assurance*, 187–188.

stance of the Westminster Confession, but they may reflect Owen's considered understanding of its deeper meaning. Certainly he later went beyond the last section of the Confession in the way he dealt with adversity in this life:

> This life is not a season to be always taking wages in; our work is not yet done; we are not always to abide in this mount; we must down again into the battle—fight again, cry again, complain again. Shall the soul be thought now to have lost its assurance? Not at all. It had before assurance with joy, triumph and exaltation; it hath it now, or may have, with wrestling, cries, tears and supplications. And a man's assurance may be as good, as true, when he lies on the earth with a sense of sin, as when he is carried up to the third heaven with a sense of love and foretaste of glory.[296]

Having been ejected from his position at Oxford and forced to lie low after the restoration of the king in 1660, Owen knew what he was talking about, and there is much in his writing about assurance that reflects his own struggles and his somewhat tumultuous life. Nevertheless, Owen believed that it was possible to attain to full assurance of faith, which he saw as a guarantee of ultimate victory over all the assaults of the enemy, rather than as a state of moral and spiritual perfection:

> This "full assurance" is not of the nature or essence of [hope], but an especial degree of it in its own improvement. A weak, imperfect hope, will give but weak and imperfect relief under trouble; but that which riseth up unto the full assurance will complete our relief. Wherefore, as hope itself is necessary, so is this degree of it, especially where trials do abound. Yet neither is hope in this degree absolute, or absolutely perfect. Our minds in this world are not capable of such a degree of assurance in spiritual things as to free us from assaults to the contrary, and impressions of fear sometimes from those assaults: but there is such a degree attainable as is always victorious; which will give the soul peace at all times, and sometimes fill it with joy.[297]

Where Owen did differ from many of his contemporaries was in his rejection of the idea that "full assurance" was equivalent to a sealing of the Spirit distinct from what occurred on profession of faith. Like Calvin before him, Owen equated the sealing with conversion, and was not afraid to rebuke his colleagues who thought otherwise:

[296] Owen, *An Exposition upon Psalm CXXX*, v. 4, in *Works*, 6:551.

[297] Owen, *An Exposition of the Epistle to the Hebrews*, William H. Goold, ed., 7 vols. (Grand Rapids, MI: Baker, 1980), 5:200 (on Heb. 6:11).

> It hath been generally conceived that this sealing with the Spirit is that which gives assurance unto believers—and so indeed it doth, although the way whereby it doth it hath not been rightly apprehended; and therefore, none have been able to declare the especial nature of that act of the Spirit whereby he seals us, whence such assurance should ensue. . . . That God abideth in us and we in him is the subject-matter of our assurance. . . . The Spirit himself . . . is the great evidence, the great ground of assurance, which we have that God hath taken us into a near and dear relation unto himself, "because he hath given us of his Spirit."[298]

As Owen himself admitted, this was at odds with what others had been saying for quite some time. Richard Sibbes (1577–1635), for example, taught that there was a once-for-all sealing that occurred at the time of conversion, but also that there was a second sealing that occurred as one matured in the Christian life.[299] Thomas Goodwin (1600–1679), a friend and close associate of Owen's, also held this doctrine. As he put it,

> Look what difference there is between that way, when we know God's love to us but by signs only: this is knowing and gathering his love *ex alio*, by effect, collecting it from another thing, and so is but discursive; as when the cause is known by the effects, though the Spirit secretly joins a testimony in the conclusion; and that other which comes from an immediate light of the Spirit's sealing up that light, and the taste of it, and revealing God's heart and mind in itself towards us. This is so transcendent, as it works joy unspeakable and glorious; it is intuitive; not so the other.[300]

This idea of a second, "intuitive" sealing with the Spirit became typical of later Puritan thought and was to have a great future, though one, it must be said, that did not always stay within the bounds of Reformed orthodoxy in the way that Goodwin did.[301]

In the next generation, another perspective was put forward by the Scottish divine Ebenezer Erskine (1680–1754), who distinguished between what he called the assurance of faith and the assurance of sense. In his words,

---

[298] Owen, *Pneumatologia*, book 8, ch. 6 in *Works*, 4:405.

[299] Richard Sibbes, *Commentary on 2 Corinthians* 1, v. 22, in Alexander B. Grosart, ed., *The Complete Works of Richard Sibbes*, 7 vols. (Edinburgh: James Nichol, 1862; repr., Edinburgh: Banner of Truth, 1973–1982), 3:453. See Mark E. Dever, *Richard Sibbes: Puritanism and Calvinism in Late Elizabethan and Early Stuart England* (Macon, GA: Mercer University Press, 2000), 161–210.

[300] Thomas Goodwin, *Of the Creatures and the Condition of Their State by Creation*, 7, in John C. Miller, ed., *The Works of Thomas Goodwin, D. D.*, 12 vols. (Edinburgh: James Nichol, 1861–1867; repr., Eureka, CA: Tanski, 1996), 7:66. On Goodwin, see Beeke, *Quest for Full Assurance*, 245–268. Note that volume 6 has also been reprinted separately as *The Work of the Holy Spirit* (Edinburgh: Banner of Truth, 1979).

[301] On the subject of the Holy Spirit in Puritan teaching, see Geoffrey F. Nuttall, *The Holy Spirit in Puritan Faith and Experience* (Oxford: Blackwell, 1946); reprinted with an introduction by Peter Lake (Chicago: University of Chicago Press, 1992). The additional introduction is particularly valuable as a survey of research into Puritanism from 1945 to about 1990.

> There is a great difference betwixt the assurance of faith and the assurance of sense, which follows upon faith. The assurance of faith is a direct, but the assurance of sense is a reflex act of the soul. The assurance of faith hath its object and foundation from without, but that of sense has them within. The object of the assurance of faith is a Christ revealed, promised and offered in the Word; the object of an assurance of sense is a Christ formed within us by the Holy Spirit. The assurance of faith is the cause, that of sense is the effect; the first is the root, and the other is the fruit. The assurance of faith eyes the promise in its stability, flowing from the veracity of the promiser; the assurance of sense, it eyes the promise in its actual accomplishment. By the assurance of faith, Abraham believed that he should have a son in his old age, because God who cannot lie had promised; but by the assurance of sense, he believed it when he got Isaac in his arms.[302]

The doctrine of assurance was characteristic of the English Puritans, but it was by no means their exclusive property. It was widely shared by Dutch theologians of the period, whose witness is generally called the *Nadere Reformatie*, or "deeper" Reformation.[303] Connections between the Netherlands and Great Britain in the seventeenth century were so close that in theological terms, at least, they can be regarded as a single country. British theologians like William Ames (1576–1633) and Alexander Comrie (1705–1774) spent a large part of their lives and ministries in the Netherlands, and the translation of theological works in both directions was a major industry. On the question of assurance, it has sometimes been suggested that the Dutch were more cerebral and intellectual, the British more applied and practical in their thinking, but this is a broad generalization that does not really stand up when the works of individual people are examined.

What is true is that the Dutch Reformed theologians were more closely knit than their British counterparts, with little temptation to hive off in a sectarian direction. They were also more inclined to develop systematic theologies and remain loyal to them, even when they were capable of falling out on other matters. This can be seen in the relationship between the followers of Gisbertius Voetius (1589–1676) and those of Johannes Cocceius (1603–1669). The former were more inclined toward a straitlaced view of personal spiritual discipline, while the latter ate, drank, and were merry—not least on the Sabbath day! But when it came to doctrinal matters, it was hard to tell them apart, the only real

[302] Erskine, *Assurance of Faith, Open and Applied*, Sermon 11, 6 (on Heb. 10:22), in *The Whole Works of Ebenezer Erskine*, 3 vols. (London: W. Baynes, 1810), 1:254.

[303] There is no generally agreed translation for this term in English. See Beeke, *Quest for Full Assurance*, 286–309, where he discusses it at length.

difference being that Cocceius was credited with having developed the final version of covenant theology, in which Adam had been given a covenant of works and those following him (Noah, Abraham, Moses, and David), had received a covenant of grace. But the roots of that doctrine were already deeply embedded in Reformed thinking and, in that respect, Cocceius was a synthesizer rather than a true innovator.[304]

The Dutchmen of the *Nadere Reformatie* were not Puritans, but this was partly because their political situation did not force them to oppose the state's religious policies. They could afford to concentrate more exclusively on spiritual issues because they had the freedom to do so, whereas their British counterparts were usually in opposition to the government and the leaders of the church. That obliged them to mix theology with politics, which seldom did either of them much good. But both the Dutch and the British were deeply involved in mainstream church affairs and wanted to use their spiritual insights to effect a long-lasting change in society. In this, they were too idealistic to be able to succeed as much as they originally hoped, but there can be no doubt that they made an impact that would change their respective countries forever and give them a sense of the presence of God in public life that to this day has not completely faded from view.

The Fellowship of the Spirit

The experience of the Holy Spirit, combined with a strong belief in election and predestination, was bound to have serious repercussions for the understanding of what constituted the true church of Christ. Oddly enough, this question does not seem to have troubled the first two generations of Reformers very much. Luther and Calvin understood that there were many in the church who were not true believers, but they believed that it was their duty to teach them the truth and persuade them to accept it. Only later, as the Protestant churches settled down and it became clear that the true teaching was not producing the kind of spiritual renewal that those who were conscious of the indwelling Spirit in their hearts believed ought to be occurring, nor was there much hope of reforming their ecclesiastical institutions in the direction they desired, did some groups start to withdraw into "conventicles" or fellowships of their own. In England, for example, such "separatism" was almost unknown before the 1590s but by 1640 it had become a major component of the religious scene and its advocates were vying with establishment Puritans (like Richard Sibbes) for influence—and eventually for power.

[304] See William J. Van Asselt, *The Federal Theology of J. Coccejus* (Leiden: Brill, 2001).

At the heart of this new tendency lay the place of Scripture in the Christian life. For the mainline Reformers, the Holy Spirit spoke through the written Word, which he had inspired and given to the church, a belief which meant that only ministers trained in biblical studies and theology had the ability or the right to interpret it—that was their spiritual gift, to be used for the upbuilding of the church as a whole. Anything else was potentially dangerous and ought to be avoided. Richard Baxter (1615–1691) put it like this:

> Interpret Scripture well, and you may interpret the Spirit's motions easily. If any new duty be motioned to you, which Scripture commandeth not, take such motions as not from God (unless it were by extraordinary, confirmed revelation).[305]

The message was fairly clear, unless, of course, a person felt that he had access to extraordinary revelation, which many seventeenth-century radicals did. John Howe (1630–1705) was another Puritan minister who said much the same thing, though he was more willing than Baxter was to allow for the possibility of some form of extrabiblical revelation:

> The supreme power binds not its own hands. We may be sure that the inward testimony of the Spirit never is opposite to the outward testimony of his Gospel which is the Spirit's testimony also. . . . But we cannot be sure he never speaks nor suggests things to the spirits of men but by the external testimony. . . . Nor do I believe that it can ever be proved that he *never* doth immediately testify his own special love to holy souls without the intervention of some part of his external word . . . or that he *always* doth it in the way of methodical reasoning therefrom . . . [although] he never says anything in this matter by his Spirit to the hearts of men repugnant to what the same Spirit hath said in his word . . .[306]

The principle was thus firmly established that if the Holy Spirit speaks outside the Scriptures, what he says will agree with them, even if they do not simply contain the same material in another form. The need to discern whether a claimed revelation from God could be accepted as such was therefore dependent on reason and on logical deduction from the Scriptures, which Richard Sibbes had no problem with:

> The Spirit of God is so wise an agent that he works upon the soul, preserving the principles of a man. It alters the judgment by presenting greater reasons, and further light than it saw before. . . . When the Spirit of God sets the will

[305] Richard Baxter, *The Christian Directory*, in William Orme, ed., *The Practical Works of the Reverend Richard Baxter*, 23 vols. (London: James Duncan, 1830), 2:198.

[306] John Howe, *A Treatise of Delighting in God*, I, in Henry Rogers, ed., *The Works of John Howe, M. A., Sometime Fellow of Magdalen College, Oxon*, 2 vols. (London: The Religious Tract Society, 1862), 2:85–86.

> at liberty, a man doth that he doth with full advisement of reason; for though God work upon the will, it is with enlightening of the understanding at the same time. . . . The judgment of man enlightened by reason is above any creature; for reason is a beam of God. . . . judgment is the spark of God. Nature is but God's candle. It is a light of the same light that grace is of, but inferior.[307]

The modern reader is liable to understand Sibbes as a forerunner of the rationalism that was to dominate theological thinking in the late seventeenth and early eighteenth centuries, and to some extent this perception is valid. It is certainly true that the rationalists of a later generation believed that they were following men like Sibbes in their pursuit of truth, but whether Sibbes would have acknowledged them as his progeny is much less certain. Sibbes believed in the validity of human reasoning, but he knew that it could never be dissociated from personal experience:

> How do you know the word to be the word? It carrieth proof and evidence in itself. It is an evidence that the fire is hot to him that feeleth it, and that the sun shineth to him that looks on it; how much more doth the word. . . . I am sure I felt it, it warmed my heart, and converted me.[308]

This was stated with even greater clarity in the next generation. Peter Sterry (1613–1672) was very forthright about this, and may even have had Sibbes in his sights:

> Some say that all truths which come by revelation of the Spirit may also be demonstrated by reason. But if they be, they are then no more divine, but human truths. They lose their certainty, beauty, efficacy. . . . Spiritual truths discovered by demonstrations of reason are like the mistress in her cookmaid's clothes . . .[309]

John Owen, the great synthesizer of Puritan thought, called this work of the Spirit an illumination, and taught that it was necessary if spiritual things were to be understood correctly:

> The true nature of saving illumination consists in this, that it gives the mind such a direct intuitive insight and prospect into spiritual things, as that in their own spiritual nature they suit, please and satisfy it.[310]

[307] Sibbes, *Excellency of the Gospel above the Law*, in *Complete Works*, 4:225, 234.
[308] Sibbes, *Commentary on 2 Corinthians 4*, v. 7, in *Complete Works*, 4:363.
[309] Peter Sterry, *The Spirits Conviction of Sinne* (London: Matthew Simmons, 1645), 26–27. This was originally a sermon preached before the House of Commons on November 26, 1645.
[310] Owen, *Pneumatologia*, book 1, ch. 1, in *Works*, 3:16.

As for the authority of the institutional church as the privileged interpreter of the Bible, few Protestants had much time for that, though not all went as far as Peter Sterry in proposing an alternative:

> The Papists . . . persuade us to receive the testimony, not of the Spirit but of the church, for a touchstone of truth. . . . but we need no visible judge on earth to determine upon our consciences what is Scripture, what is the essence of Scripture. We have an invisible judge and witness in our own breasts.[311]

Most of the mainline Puritans continued to hold that line against any form of Spirit-driven activity that was not closely tied to (and dependent on) the written Word of God, but even among them there were signs that the appeal to the inner witness of the Spirit was hard to resist. Toward the end of his life, Richard Baxter wrote,

> [I am] much more apprehensive than heretofore of the necessity of well grounding men in their religion, and especially of the witness of the indwelling Spirit, for I more sensibly perceive that the Spirit is the great witness of Christ and Christianity to the world, and though the folly of fanatics tempted me long to overlook the strength of this testimony of the Spirit, . . . yet now I see that the Holy Ghost in another manner is the witness of Christ and his agent in the world.[312]

This feeling can be compared with what George Fox (1624–1691), the founder of the Quakers, said. Baxter was deeply opposed to the Quakers because to his mind they went far beyond anything the Scriptures encouraged, but Fox did not see matters that way.[313] To his mind, the illumination of the Spirit might come independently of biblical revelation, but he could either find it there later or, by looking to Christ, could come to the conviction that what he had grasped was something given by the same Spirit who had inspired the written Word:

> This I saw in the pure openings of the light, without the help of any man; neither did I then know where to find it in the Scriptures, though afterwards, searching the Scriptures, I found it. . . . These things I did not see by the help of man nor by the letter, though they are written in the letter, but I saw them in the light of the Lord Jesus Christ, and by his immediate

[311] Sterry, *Spirits Conviction*, 28.

[312] Richard Baxter, *Reliquiae Baxterianae*, ed. M. Sylvester, 3 vols. (London: T. Parkhurst, J. Robinson, J. Lawrence, J. Dunton, 1696), 1:213 (4).

[313] For evidence of Baxter's opposition to the Quakers, see, for example, his *Practical Works*, 12:500.

> Spirit and power, as did the holy men of God, by whom the Holy Scriptures were written.[314]

As long as these observations remained the private property of those who made (or observed) them, there was little problem. But soon a question arose that followed logically on the belief that individuals were given special revelations from God, related to the Scriptures but not necessarily dependent on them. Could such people be allowed to preach? Samuel Petto and his friends were in no doubt about this:

> Every man . . . to whomsoever the Spirit hath afforded a gift, either wisely to speak and apply Gospel truths to the souls of others . . . or understandingly to give an exposition of the Scriptures, every man that hath such gifts, it belongeth to his place and calling, to use those gifts . . . else he crosseth the end of the Spirit.[315]

When the Puritan parliament decreed that no one was to preach unless he had been ordained, John Saltmarsh (d. 1647) objected:

> The infinitely abounding Spirit of God, which blows when and where it listeth, and ministers in Christians according to the gift, and prophesies according to the will of Almighty God, is made subject to the laws and ordinances of men . . . to outward ceremonies, as ordination, etc. God must not speak until man give him leave, nor teach, nor preach, but whom man allows, and approves, and ordains.[316]

This sentiment was widely shared, not least by Oliver Cromwell (1599–1658), who was in a strong position to permit lay preaching during the commonwealth period in England.[317] George Fox was even prepared to let women preach, but although his position on this was regarded as extreme, it became one of the hallmarks of the Quakers.[318]

Openness to a do-it-yourself ministry went hand in hand with a relativization of the importance of the sacraments, the administration of which (on the whole) was entrusted to ordained ministers. John Bunyan, for example, though

---

[314] George Fox, *A Journal or Historical Account of the Life, Travels, Sufferings, Christian Experience, and Labour of Love in the Work of the Ministry of That Ancient, Eminent, and Faithful Servant of Christ, George Fox*, ed. Thomas Ellwood, 2 vols. (London: Thomas Northcott, 1694), 1:34–36.

[315] Samuel Petto, John Martin, and Frederick Woodal, *The Preacher Sent, or a Vindication of the Liberty of Publick Preaching by Some Men Not Ordained* (London: J. T. Livewell Chapman, 1659), 48.

[316] John Saltmarsh, *Sparkles of Glory* (London: Giles Calvert, 1647), 5.

[317] On Cromwell's support for this, see Nuttall, *Holy Spirit in Puritan Faith*, 85–86.

[318] George Fox, *A Collection of Many Select Epistles, Letters, and Testimonies*, ed. George Whitehead (London: T. Sowle, 1698), 244. See Nuttall, *Holy Spirit in Puritan Faith*, 87–89.

he preached and practiced believers' baptism, did not hesitate to criticize those who made too much of the ordinance:

> I do not plead for a despising of baptism, but a bearing with our brother that cannot do with it for want of light. . . . the best of baptism he hath . . . he is baptized by that one Spirit, he hath the heart of water baptism, the signification thereof; he wanteth only the outward show, which if he had, would not prove him a truly visible saint; it would not tell me he had grace in his heart.[319]

A similar attitude can be found with respect to the Lord's Supper. No less a person than John Milton (1608–1674) said,

> We nowhere read in Scripture of the Lord's Supper being distributed to the first Christians by an appointed minister. . . . I know no reason therefore why ministers refuse to permit the celebration of the Lord's Supper, except where they themselves are allowed to minister it.[320]

William Erbury (1604–1654) noted that the gifts of the Spirit outlined in 1 Corinthians had disappeared, and thought that the sacraments should have gone with them:

> Why should ordinances continue, and not the gifts? Why should baptism and breaking of bread abide more then than the baptism of the Spirit, and all those gifts, seeing the Spirit was given to abide with them forever?[321]

From there it was a short step to abandoning the sacraments altogether, which is what George Fox and the Quakers eventually did. Their logic seems to have been that "when the perfect comes, the partial will pass away."[322] The visible sacraments were only shadows of the spiritual reality, and those who knew the latter could easily dispense with the former:

> Dear friends, mind the steadfast guide in the Lord, where we do all meet in the eternal Spirit, in oneness, all being baptized by it into one body, having one food, the eternal bread of life, which the immortal feed upon, and all made to drink into one Spirit, which is the cup of the communion of the blood of our Lord Jesus Christ, which makes perfect and redeems from all

---

[319] John Bunyan, *A Confession of My Faith and a Reason of My Practice*, in *The Entire Works of John Bunyan*, ed. Henry Stebbing, 4 vols. (London: James S. Virtue, 1859–1660), 1:430. A slightly different version can be found in Roger Sharrock, ed., *The Miscellaneous Works of John Bunyan*, 13 vols. (Oxford: Oxford University Press, 1976–1994), 4:172.

[320] *The Prose Works of John Milton*, ed. James A. St. John, 5 vols. (London: Bohn, 1848–1853), 4:417–418.

[321] William Erbury, *The Testimony of William Erbery, Left upon Records for the Saints of Succeeding Ages* (London: Giles Calvert, 1658), 303.

[322] 1 Cor. 13:10.

> that is vain, fleshly and earthly, up to God, who is holy, pure, spiritual and eternal.[323]

What Fox had in mind is of a piece with the kind of dispensationalism that was being preached by John Saltmarsh and William Erbury at much the same time. They were convinced that in the Old Testament, God had revealed himself as the Father, but in terms that were quite material, with food laws, animal sacrifices, and the like. The coming of the Son was the occasion for a more spiritual approach, and the third age, that of the Spirit,

> . . . will be more spiritual yet; for though Christ was in the days of his flesh, yet he was not full come, till the Spirit was sent; therefore this second coming will be more in the Spirit . . .[324]

The pattern is strangely reminiscent of Joachim da Fiore, but there is unlikely to have been any direct connection with medieval apocalyptic dispensationalism.[325] The Puritans lived in an apocalyptic age, and their victory in the civil war against the king made it seem possible that Christ would soon return and take up his kingdom on earth.[326] But something of it had been present in the Puritan project for a long time, as we can see from the famous farewell speech of John Robinson, the founder of the Plymouth colony in Massachusetts, which may be dated to 1620:

> . . . the Lutherans, they could not be drawn to go beyond what Luther saw; . . . and so also, saith he, you see the Calvinists, they stick where he left them, a misery much to be lamented, for though they were precious shining lights in their times, yet God had not revealed his whole will to them; and were they now living . . . they would be as ready and willing to embrace further light, as that they had received . . . it is not possible that the Christian world should come so lately out of such thick anti-Christian darkness, and that perfection of knowledge should break forth at once.[327]

A generation later, those who believed that the Spirit had indeed given them further light were often inclined to be tolerant—or at least to recommend toler-

---

[323] Fox, *Epistles*, 26.
[324] Erbury, *Testimony*, 248.
[325] See Geoffrey F. Nuttall, *Holy Spirit in Puritan Theology*, 102–105, for a discussion of this possibility.
[326] This theme has been studied most thoroughly by Christopher Hill, *The World Turned Upside Down: Radical Ideas during the English Revolution* (London: Temple Smith, 1972). See also, J. F. McGregor and Barry Reay, eds., *Radical Religion in the English Revolution* (Oxford: Oxford University Press, 1984); and Mark R. Bell, *Apocalypse How? Baptist Movements during the English Revolution* (Macon, GA: Mercer University Press, 2000). See also Nuttall, *Holy Spirit in Puritan Theology*, 109–117.
[327] *The Works of John Robinson, Pastor of the Pilgrim Fathers*, ed. Robert Ashton, 3 vols. (London: John Snow, 1851), 1:xliv-xlv.

ance—toward those who disagreed with them on the finer points of Christian doctrine. Francis Rous (1579–1659), for example, wrote,

> When Christ speaks to thee to follow him one way, thou mayst not with Peter make quarrels and questions concerning John's other way; for so mayst thou receive Peter's answer from the Master: "What is that to thee? Follow thou me!" It is the Master's part to allot the way and work of his disciples, and therefore let both Peter and John walk that different way, to which their Master hath differently directed them.[328]

Oliver Cromwell shared the same vision and breadth of tolerance, born largely out of his experience in the army, where men of many different views had worshiped and fought together:

> Presbyterians, Independents, all have here the same spirit of faith and prayer, the same presence and answer; they agree here, have no names of difference; pity it is it should be otherwise anywhere! All that believe have the real unity, which is most glorious, because inward and spiritual, in the body, and to the head.[329]

But as Cromwell may have known—and if he did not yet know it, he would soon find out—his views were not shared by all, certainly not by those in the Westminster assembly, which was meeting at the same time as he was writing. About a year before Cromwell penned the above, one of the Scottish delegates at Westminster, Samuel Rutherford (1600?–1661), wrote to Lady Boyd:

> Thomas Goodwin, Jeremiah Burroughs and some others, four or five who are for the Independent way, stand in our way and are mighty opposites to Presbyterian government. . . . the truth is, we have many and grieved spirits with the work, and for my part, I often despair of the reformation of this land, which saw never anything but the high places of their fathers, and the remnant of Babylon's pollutions. . . . Multitudes of Anabaptists, Antinomians, Familists,[330] Separatists, are here; the best of the people are of the Independent way. As for myself, I know no more if there be a sound

---

[328] Francis Rous, *Treatises and Meditations Dedicated to the Saints, and to the Excellent throughout These Three Nations* (London: Robert White, 1657), 645. The allusion is to John 21:22.

[329] Oliver Cromwell, *Letters and Speeches*, ed. Thomas Carlyle, 2 vols. (London: Chapman & Hall, 1845), Letter XV (September 14, 1645), 1:185; *Letters and Speeches*, 3rd ed., 3 vols. (London: J. M. Dent, 1908), 1:230. On Cromwell's religious policy, see Blair Worden, *God's Instruments: Political Conduct in the England of Oliver Cromwell* (Oxford: Oxford University Press, 2012).

[330] These were members of the sect known as the Family of Love. See Christopher W. Marsh, *The Family of Love in English Society, 1550–1630* (Cambridge: Cambridge University Press, 1994).

> Christian . . . at London (though I doubt not but there are many) than if I were in Spain.[331]

A very different spirit was that of John Milton, who in the same year that Rutherford was complaining of the remnant of Babylon's pollutions, was bold enough to tell the parliament that the entire English nation was specially chosen by God:

> Lords and Commons of England, consider what nation it is whereof ye are, and whereof ye are the governors. . . . God is decreeing to begin some new and great period in his church, even to the reforming of Reformation itself; what does he then but reveal himself to his servants, and as his manner is, first to his Englishmen?[332]

Milton and Rutherford were rubbing shoulders in London in 1644, but although they were supposedly on the same side in the civil war, theologically speaking they were on different planets. Cromwell responded to the Scottish Presbyterians, of whom Rutherford was one of the chief, by dismissing their concerns out of hand:

> Your pretended fear lest error should step in is like the man who would keep all the wine out of the country lest men should be drunk.[333]

And Milton echoed him, proclaiming to all the world that no force could ever defeat the truth:

> And though all the winds of doctrine were let loose to play upon the earth, so truth be in the field, we do injuriously, by licensing and prohibiting, to misdoubt her strength. Let her and falsehood grapple; who ever knew truth put to the worse, in a free and open encounter? Her confuting is the best and surest suppressing. He who hears what praying there is for light and clearer knowledge to be sent down among us, would think of other matters to be constituted beyond the discipline of Geneva [i.e., Presbyterianism], framed and fabricked already to our hands.[334]

These men were convinced that the Holy Spirit was at work in their hearts,

---

[331] Samuel Rutherford, *The Letters of Samuel Rutherford*, ed. Thomas Smith (Edinburgh: Oliphant, Anderson & Ferrier, 1881), part 3, letter 53 (542–543). The date was May 25, 1644.

[332] John Milton, *Areopagitica*, in *Milton's Selected Poetry and Prose*, ed. Jason P. Rosenblatt (New York: W. W. Norton, 2011), 370.

[333] Cromwell, *Letters and Speeches*, Letter XCVII (September 12, 1650), 2:64 (1st ed., 1845); Letter CVLVIII, 2:195 (3rd. ed., 1908).

[334] Milton, *Areopagitica*, in Rosenblatt, *Milton's Selected Poetry and Prose*, 375.

and claimed to have no difficulty in telling who the true saints were. Thomas Goodwin, for example, said,

> Now, if you ask me what it is the saints know, which another man knows not, I answer you fully. He himself cannot tell you, for it is certain, as to that impression which the Holy Ghost leaves upon the heart of a man, that man can never make the like impression on another; he may describe it to you, but he cannot convey the same image and impression upon the heart of any man else.[335]

Or as Peter Sterry put it,

> I can no more convey a sense of the difference between reason and Spirit into any soul that hath not seen these two lights shining in itself, than I can convey the difference between salt and sugar to him who hath never tasted sweet or sharp.[336]

Those who had the Spirit knew it; those who did not could be told about it, but they would never really understand what was being said to them. Even Richard Baxter felt the same way, as he wrote in a letter to Barbara Lambe, whose husband had become a Baptist but was wondering whether he ought to return to the Presbyterians:

> There is a connaturality of Spirit in the saints that will work by sympathy, and by closing uniting inclinations, through greater differences and impediments than the external act of baptism, as a lodestone will exercise its attractive force through a stone wall. I have an inward sense in my soul . . . that your husband, and you, and I are one in our dear Lord, that if all the self-conceited dividers in the world should contradict it on the account of baptism, I could not believe them.[337]

But by far the most mystical of all the Puritan writers was Morgan Llwyd (1619–1659), who wrote,

> No church but the spiritual, no spirit but the second Adam, no temple of God but the pure thought of man, no enduring temple for man but the Almighty, and the Lamb, no unity but the unity of the everlasting Spirit, no singing, no communion, no union, no praying, no membership in any church, but when the Spirit of the head rules in might.[338]

[335] Goodwin, *A Discourse of the Glory of the Gospel*, ch. 4. in *Works*, 4:297.
[336] Sterry, *Spirits Conviction*, 24.
[337] Baxter, *Reliquiae Baxterianae*, appendix, 3:54. The year was 1658.
[338] Morgan Llwyd, *Llyfr y tri aderyn*, in *Gweithiau*, ed. Thomas E. Ellis and John H. Davies, 2 vols (Bangor: Jarvis & Foster, 1899–1908), 1:207. The translation follows that in Nuttall, *Holy Spirit in Puritan Theology*, 149. The *Llyfr* has been reedited by T. M. Wynn (Cardiff: University of Wales Press, 1988).

Summing up these conflicting voices is not easy, but it would be fair to say that virtually everyone who was touched by Puritanism was convinced that he (or she) was filled with the Spirit of God and therefore entitled to live out the implications of that in a society free of petty restrictions imposed by state and church authorities that were often little more than relics of an ungodly past. In theory, those who had the Spirit would recognize each other as brethren and fellow heirs of the kingdom of God, which many thought would appear at any minute. Differences, they believed, could be ignored or forgiven, as Oliver Cromwell said:

> If men will profess—if they be under Baptism,[339] be they those of the Independent judgment simply, or of the Presbyterian judgment—in the name of God, encourage them, countenance them; so long as they do plainly continue to be thankful to God, and to make use of the liberty given them to enjoy their own consciences. For, as it was said today, this is the peculiar interest all this while contended for.[340]

The fellowship of the Spirit was all about freedom of conscience for the godly. Roman Catholics were excluded because they were both wrong and intolerant (the two things were seen to be interconnected), Anglicans were officially persecuted but usually tolerated as long as they kept their heads down, and some of the more extreme radical sects had to be suppressed in the interests of public order. But although there were obvious limits to toleration, the principle had been established, and those who were willing to tolerate others who disagreed with them were generally welcomed (or at least left alone).

But disagreements there were, and eventually they would overwhelm the fellowship of the Spirit that Cromwell and his associates believed they had been able to create. In a perceptive analysis, Geoffrey Nuttall (1911–2007) defined the main points at issue as follows:[341]

1. *The relation between the Holy Spirit and reason.* To mainstream moderates like Sibbes and Baxter, these two things went together—the Holy Spirit worked in and through human reason in order to turn right faith (orthodoxy) into right practice. The more radical Puritans repudiated this, believing that the Spirit was far superior to reason and almost by definition in conflict with it.

2. *The relation between the Holy Spirit and the Word of God in Scripture.* Again, men like Sibbes and Baxter saw the church as being under the Word—

[339] In other words, if they were Baptists.

[340] Cromwell, *Letters and Speeches*, Speech 5 (September 17, 1656), 2:444 (1st ed., 1845); 3:167–168 (3rd. ed., 1908).

[341] Nuttall, *Holy Spirit and Puritan Theology*, 155.

the living voice of the Spirit confirmed and illuminated the written Word. The radicals increasingly made the living Spirit a parallel (and in effect, superior) force on the understanding that only a man filled with the Spirit could preach the Word with conviction. From there it was but a short step to saying that anyone filled with the Spirit could preach, and traditional church order went by the board.

3. *The cessation of spiritual gifts.* Once more, Sibbes and Baxter assumed that this had occurred and that, in the contemporary church, the Spirit operated almost exclusively through well-established channels of ministry and church order. The radicals dissented from this, often claiming that the gifts had continued over time, or if evidence for that was hard to come by, had returned to mark the end times, in which they believed they were living.

4. *The intellectual and moral perfectibility of those who were filled with the Spirit.* The mainstream Puritans denied the possibility of this, but the radicals were more inclined to treat regeneration as a complete package; a man who had been set free from sin was just that—sinless.

It was on this last point that the Quakers parted company with the main body of the Puritans and ended up being persecuted, in spite of Cromwell's personal sympathy for George Fox. The Quakers came to believe that every human being had the "light" or "seed" of the divine Spirit within them. Basing themselves on John 1:9 ("The true light, which gives light to everyone, was coming into the world"), they argued that no human being was deprived of the Spirit of God in some measure. When George Fox wrote to Quaker prisoners who had been captured by the Turks, he told them,

> Get the Turk's and Moor's language, that you might be the more enabled to direct them to the grace and Spirit of God in them, which they have from God in their hearts.[342]

The "heathen" were not reprobates condemned to hell, but unenlightened brethren, who needed only that the divine gift should be stirred up in them. If that was true of Muslims, how much more must it be true of those born in a Christian society who had not made any public profession of faith? Richard Baxter agreed that God enlightened every human being with the light of nature, but that was not to be confused with the light of salvation, which was given only to the elect. George Fox was so appalled by this that he thought that Baxter was unfit to teach the Scriptures, of which (in Fox's view) he was

---

[342] Fox, *Epistles*, 493.

so ignorant.[343] Between these two radically opposed viewpoints there could be no compromise and no fellowship of the Spirit. The two went their separate ways—Baxter into a reason-based theology that ultimately verged on pure rationalism, and Fox into a mysticism that to all practical purposes became a universalism that discounted the power and seriousness of sin. The former view, inadequate though it was, was largely contained within the church; the latter one was not. But as time would show, the practical universalism of the Quakers, shorn of its religious overtones, was to have a much greater impact than mere numbers would suggest, and the traditional orthodoxy of the Protestant (and more broadly Christian) tradition would fight for its life and finally be excluded from the public square as the fellowship of the Spirit was secularized into the common bond uniting all citizens, whatever their particular religious beliefs might be.

To these four points may be added a fifth, which was the attitude taken toward apocalypticism and the nearness of the coming millennium. In revolutionary Britain there were many who believed that the end was nigh, and some who wanted to hasten it by any means they could. One curious result of this was that in 1656 the commonwealth government readmitted the Jews to England (they had been banished in 1290) on the understanding that their conversion was imminent and that once it occurred, Christ would come again. If all (or most of) the Jews were gathered together in one place, the likelihood was that the Messiah would come there first—hence the encouragement given to Jews to settle in Britain![344]

By the end of the seventeenth century it was clear that this scenario was not going to occur, and Richard Baxter had given up on millenarian dreams some years before his death.[345] But that did not deter others, and especially not those Puritans who had emigrated to the American colonies. There, some people managed to persuade themselves that the native American Indians were the ten lost tribes of Israel, and that when they were converted, the end would finally come. This extraordinary idea was supported by an appeal to a certain kind of fairness—other continents had been blessed by God in the past, and now perhaps it would be America's turn:

> Asia, Africa and Europe have, each of them, had a glorious Gospel-day; none therefore will be grieved at anyone's pleading that America may be made a

[343] Richard Baxter, *The Quakers Catechism* (London: A. M. for Thomas Hill, 1656), 7; George Fox, *The Great Mistery of the Great Whore Unfolded* (London: Thomas Simmons, 1659), 28.
[344] See David S. Katz, *Philo-Semitism and the Readmission of the Jews to England 1603–1655* (Oxford: Clarendon, 1982).
[345] See William M. Lamont, *Richard Baxter and the Millennium* (London: Croom Helm, 1979).

> co-partner with her sisters in the free and sovereign grace of God. . . . And when the Messiah shall have gathered his sheep belonging to this his American fold, his church's music being then complete in harmony, the whole universe shall ring again with seraphical acclamations: ONE FLOCK! ONE SHEPHERD![346]

Apocalypticism with an American tinge became a staple of the New England Puritan diet, and was to play a significant role in the rise of revivalism there in the eighteenth century. Jonathan Edwards, for example, believed that the second coming of Christ would take place in Northampton (Massachusetts) and that the renewal of the world would probably begin in America.[347] It never became an official doctrine, and in later years many church leaders tried to distance themselves from it, but it survived at the popular level and (in different permutations) continues to affect American religious life today to a degree unknown elsewhere.[348]

The Devoted Life

The student of Reformation attitudes toward devotional life and commitment is almost bound to concentrate on the church, the ministry, and the sacraments—the public face of the Christian community rather than the private spirituality of its individual members. Apart from the obvious fact that public worship is much easier to trace than private devotions are, there is a reasonable degree of certainty that what was done in the church was common to a variety of people and not a personal eccentricity of which some record happens to have survived. But beyond the nature and limitations of the evidence available, it is also true that the Reformers were more preoccupied with the church as a whole than with particular believers, unless the latter were causing trouble for some reason. Much of their time was spent organizing the common life of the church by producing forms of worship, catechisms, and even schools where children were taught exactly the same thing. In any given country where a local church had a monopoly, there was more religious uniformity after the Reformation than there had been before. England offers a classic example of this. Not only did the church impose a Book of *Common* Prayer on its congregations, which was to become a hallmark of classical Anglicanism, but Thomas Cranmer, the

---

[346] Samuel Sewall, *Phaenomena quaedam apocalyptica ad aspectum novi orbis configurata* (Boston, MA: Bartholomew Green & John Allen, 1697), dedication.

[347] In a letter to William McCulloch, dated March 5, 1744. See Jonathan Edwards, *Apocalyptic Writings*, in *The Works of Jonathan Edwards*, ed. Perry Miller et al., 73 vols. (New Haven, CT: Yale University Press, 1957–), 5:29; and *The Freedom of the Will*, 4.7, in *Works*, 1:381–383.

[348] For the details, see W. R. Ward, *Early Evangelicalism: A Global Intellectual History, 1670–1789* (Cambridge: Cambridge University Press, 2006), 85–98.

original architect of the whole project, actually justified this to those required to use the book he produced for them:

> Whereas heretofore there hath been great diversity in saying and singing in churches within this realm; some following Salisbury use, some Hereford use, and some the use of Bangor, some of York, some of Lincoln; now from henceforth all the whole realm shall have but one use.[349]

Religious orders that promoted their own forms of spirituality were dissolved, and itinerant preaching like that of the medieval friars was forbidden. The worship of God was understood to be a corporate activity, not merely in each congregation but across the church as a whole. It was assumed that if the words were right, the Holy Spirit would be at work, even if it could be surmised that many people would be drifting off during the prayers, some would not understand them, and a few might even be quietly objecting to them as they were read. The Reformers naturally deplored such things, but individual laxity or recalcitrance did not affect the validity of the prayers themselves, because they did not depend on the subjective attitudes of the worshipers. Even those who wanted change, as the Puritans did, usually thought in corporate terms—they wanted each congregation to decide how it would worship, not each member of it. What might happen if people were left to their own devices was recorded with some exasperation by Richard Baxter:

> Old Mr Ashe hath often told us that this was the mind of the old Nonconformists, and that he hath often heard some weak ministers so disorderly in prayer, especially in baptism and the Lord's Supper, that he could have wished that they would rather use the Common Prayer.[350]

Having said that, there was something about Protestant worship that demanded individual commitment. The worshiper could not just sit or stand quietly while the minister recited prayers, even if they were no longer in a foreign language. He was expected to participate by joining in the responses at least, and sometimes there might even be opportunities to sing along with the choir. The service was conducted in the language of the people, and the all-important sermon was meant to instruct and challenge everyone present. Church services were like school lessons, and the forms adopted for conducting them were intended for popular instruction. What the Reformers wanted was

[349] *Concerning the Service of the Church*, prefixed to the *Book of Common Prayer* in 1549 and reprinted in subsequent editions.

[350] Baxter, *Reliquiae Baxterianae*, 2:174. He was referring to Simeon Ashe (1595?–1662), a well-known Puritan minister. Nonconformists were those who refused to use the Prayer Book.

not individual expression in the modern sense but personal commitment to a common faith and pattern of worship.

Private devotion was not forbidden, but it was not much encouraged either. Before the Reformation, private masses had been common, and had often been celebrated in people's houses. Side chapels had altars and facilities for private prayer, and people were encouraged to light candles before statues and so on. All that was swept away by the Reformation. Family devotions were encouraged, but they too were corporate, led by the head of the house with everyone else joining in as appropriate. Private Bible study was not high on anyone's agenda, the main reason being the fear of heresy. If people were allowed to read the Scriptures for themselves, without the proper pastoral guidance, there was no telling what they might come up with, and it must be said that the appearance of outlandish sects in the sixteenth and seventeenth centuries lends credence to this fear. There was also a strong conviction that the Holy Spirit would speak only in and through the Scriptures, and their interpretation was (of course) in the hands of the ministers of the Word. Richard Sibbes put it well when he wrote,

> There must be a Spirit in me, as there is a Spirit in the Scripture, before I can see anything. . . .
>
> The breath of the Spirit in us is suitable to the Spirit's breathing in the Scriptures; the same Spirit doth not breathe contrary motions. . . .
>
> As the spirits in the arteries quicken the blood in the veins, so the Spirit of God goes along with the Word, and makes it work.[351]

An anonymous "A. M." also wrote,

> I did wonderfully esteem and value the Scriptures; and my heart was wonderfully set against those that pretend to revelations without, or not agreeable to or against the Scriptures.[352]

Individuals were encouraged to meditate on the biblical text that had formed the substance of the week's sermon and apply it to their lives, but that was the private extension of an essentially public activity and quite unlike what we think of as Bible study today.

This pattern did not begin to change until the later seventeenth century, when several factors combined to make greater concentration on the individual

[351] The three paragraphs cited are from, respectively, Sibbes, *Commentary on 2 Corinthians 1*, v. 21, in *Complete Works*, 3:434; *A Fountain Sealed*, in *Complete Works*, 5:427; *Divine Meditations and Holy Contemplations*, 80, in *Complete Works*, 7:193.

[352] Cited by Samuel Petto, *Roses from Sharon* (London: Livewell Chapman, 1654), 18.

Christian's devotional life more attractive. One of them was political. The Reformers and their opponents were prominent figures in church and society, whose views influenced secular rulers and led to revolts and wars that were more or less endemic in much of central Europe until 1648. In that year, the great powers finally agreed to take religion out of international politics and to let each state decide its own form of confession and worship. The result was that most countries ended up with a carefully regulated state church that was supposed to embrace the entire population. Where that was not possible, one of two things happened. Either the state excluded its minorities (as in France, where Protestants were eventually forced to convert to Catholicism or go into exile), or the state broke up into smaller units, which is what happened in Germany.

The British Isles presented a more complex picture, in that following a civil war between "Anglicans" who supported the king and "Puritans" who backed parliament (1642–1649) and the failure of a Puritan based "commonwealth" (1649–1660), the restored monarchy tried to impose a settlement according to which everyone would be comprehended in a broad Anglican church.[353] The result was that a substantial number of English Puritans left the established church and became "Dissenters," Scotland went into low-level but fairly constant revolt, and Ireland contained so many disparate elements that it scarcely knew which way to turn.[354] One imaginative solution to the problem of Dissent in England was to export it, which the government actually did, albeit on a limited scale. William Penn (1644–1718), a Quaker, was given land in what became Pennsylvania, where he was allowed to offer religious toleration to anyone who wanted it. John Locke (1632–1704) was commissioned to draw up a constitution for the Carolinas, in which religious toleration was made a fundamental principle for the first time, though it did not last long in practice. Other American colonies were already in Puritan hands, with the curious result that what was considered Dissent in the mother country was actually the state church in Massachusetts and Connecticut.

In 1688, there occurred an event known today as the "glorious revolution," in which the English parliament ejected the Catholic King James II (1685–1688) and claimed supremacy for itself in government. It then settled the Anglican

---

[353] The literature on this subject is vast. For books that cover the religious and theological dimension, see Peter Lake, *Anglicans and Puritans?* (London: Unwin Hyman, 1988); Conrad Russell, *The Fall of the British Monarchies 1637–1642* (Oxford: Oxford University Press, 1991); Hugh Trevor-Roper, *Catholics, Anglicans, and Puritans* (London: Martin Secker & Warburg, 1987); William Lamont, *Puritanism and Historical Controversy* (London: University College London Press, 1996); John Spurr, *English Puritanism 1603–1689* (Basingstoke: Macmillan, 1998); and idem, *The Restoration Church of England, 1646–1689* (New Haven, CT: Yale University Press, 1991).

[354] For an overview of the complex Irish situation, see Sean Connolly, *Divided Kingdom: Ireland 1630–1800* (Oxford: Oxford University Press, 2008).

(episcopal) church in England, persuaded the Irish parliament to do the same in Ireland, and allowed the Scottish parliament to establish a Presbyterian church in that country. In England, a limited toleration was granted to Dissenters but not to Catholics, and the same applied to Ireland, though Catholics (who formed the vast majority of the population there) were tolerated more often than not. As long as people paid lip service to the state church, no one enquired too deeply about their private beliefs. Officially, however, the established churches were expected to stick to the theology of the Thirty-nine Articles of Religion (in England and Ireland) and the Westminster Confession (in Scotland). Theology as taught in the universities became the exposition of these and other classic texts (like the ancient creeds), to which everyone who held office in church, state, or education had to subscribe.

This was a clear victory for the state, which had long been trying to achieve something of this kind. As far back as December 1628, when theological disputes were raging in England, King Charles I had issued a declaration demanding assent to the Thirty-nine Articles and had this to say about any speculation beyond them:

> We will, that all further curious search be laid aside, and these disputes shut up in God's promises, as they be generally set forth to us in the Holy Scriptures, and the general meaning of the Articles of the Church of England according to them. And . . . if any public reader in either of our universities, or any head or master of a college, or any other person respectively in either of them, shall affix any new sense to any Article, or shall publicly read, determine, or hold any public disputation, or . . . shall preach or print anything either way, other than is already established . . . he, or they the offenders, shall be liable to our displeasure . . . and we will see there shall be due execution upon them.[355]

What had been impossible for the king to maintain in the 1630s, when theological questions dominated political discourse, became the norm thirty years later, when such questions had been effectively removed from the public arena. Many people went along with this development quite sincerely, particularly in England, where opposition to the Puritans had been strong in Oxford, and among the upper classes there was a flowering of what became known as "latitudinarianism." This was a kind of liberalism that allowed a wide range of theological interpretations (something that the ambiguities of many of the Articles of Religion did little to discourage) and tended to foster moralism instead

[355] The King's Declaration, affixed to the Articles in the Book of Common Prayer (1662), where it still remains. See Bray, *Documents of the English Reformation*, 481–482.

of spirituality in the Puritan sense.[356] Two men who represented the new mood were Jeremy Taylor (1613–1667) and William Law (1686–1761), whose books of spiritual devotion have survived the test of time and are still in print today.

Taylor was a long-standing opponent of Puritanism and had been imprisoned during the commonwealth period, when his most famous works were written.[357] After the restoration, he became a bishop in Ireland and a pillar of the new establishment. William Law was less fortunate. Having started off as a supporter of the king, he found himself unable to accept the succession of the Protestant George I (1714–1727) to the throne instead of the Stuart pretender, and so had to leave his university post and live in semi-seclusion for the rest of his life. It was then that he wrote his greatest works, including *A Serious Call to a Devout and Holy Life*, which was to have a great impact on John and Charles Wesley.[358] The fact that both of these men were able to publish freely although they were open opponents of the regime in power shows how far things had changed since the sixteenth century, when neither would have been allowed such liberty and both might easily have been put to death for their opinions. What they recommended was a pattern of spiritual discipline not unlike that of medieval Catholicism, though modified and updated to meet later circumstances. Neither showed any inclination to convert to Rome, but both believed that something important was missing in the spiritual life of their times and they sought to supply what was lacking. The result was perilously close to legalism, into which those who took their advice often fell, but it should be remembered that their original intentions were quite different. What they wanted was a revival of individual piety, an application of spiritual principles to daily life, and it was this, more than the particular form that it took, that appealed to a generation that wanted the consolations of religion that neither the arid theological disputes of the universities nor the enthusiastic disorder (as they saw it) of the Puritans could give them.

A similar situation and the feelings that it engendered could be found all over Protestant Europe and to a large extent in Catholic France also at this time.[359] Mysticism had formed a powerful component of sixteenth-century Catholicism, especially in Spain, where it produced such towering figures as John of

[356] See Christopher F. Allison, *The Rise of Moralism: The Proclamation of the Gospel from Hooker to Baxter* (London: SPCK, 1966).

[357] Jeremy Taylor, *The Rule and Exercises of Holy Living* (London: Richard Royston, 1650); idem, *The Rule and Exercises of Holy Dying* (London: Richard Royston, 1651).

[358] William Law, *A Serious Call to a Devout and Holy Life* (London: William Innys, 1729).

[359] French Catholicism was always more independent and less "Roman" than its Spanish or Italian equivalents, making private initiatives easier. The standard study in English is John McManners, *Church and Society in Eighteenth-century France*, 2 vols. (Oxford: Oxford University Press, 1998). For the tensions between Rome and Paris this independence could cause, see Pierre Blet, *Les nonces du pape à la cour de Louis XIV* (Paris: Perrin, 2002).

the Cross (1542–1591) and Teresa of Avila (1515–1582), who together founded a religious order, the Discalced ("shoeless") Carmelites, and whose writings continue to be widely read both within and beyond the Hispanic world.[360] Less well-known but equally influential was Miguel de Molinos (1628–1696), whose *Spiritual Guide*, first published in 1675, became a runaway best seller in his own lifetime and is still being reprinted.[361] Molinos fell afoul of the Inquisition, and in 1687 he was imprisoned for life, but by then he had attracted a large number of followers, who became known as "Quietists" because of their preference for silent contemplation as the main form of their devotion.

Quietism's most famous exponent was Jeanne Marie Bouvier de la Motte (1648–1717), better known under her married name as Madame Guyon. After dedicating her life to Christ, which in her case meant contracting a "spiritual marriage" with Jesus when she was only twenty-four and still married to her earthly husband (who died in 1676), she became a sensation at the French court, where she attracted the support of François Fénelon (1651–1715), tutor to the king's grandsons and a leading Catholic churchman of his day. The condemnation of Molinos unfortunately thrust Madame Guyon into the spotlight, and there followed a brief but bitter controversy over her views, in which her chief accuser was Jacques-Bénigne Bossuet (1627–1704), another leading French churchman and, until the Guyon affair blew up, a friend of Fénelon.[362] Bossuet won the battle, but Madame Guyon's writings were widely circulated across Europe, and in Protestant eyes she became a martyr for her faith.[363] Her commentary on the Song of Songs was especially influential.[364] In it, she proposed three stages of spiritual advancement, beginning with a strict discipline of devotion and dedication to works of piety. From there, some would rise to a second stage, which was the recognition and enjoyment of the Spirit of God in their hearts. The third and final achievement, reserved for the elect few, was a vision of God in which he revealed how far the believer was from him in one sense but how near in another, because he was present in the innermost recesses of the heart.

---

[360] See Colin P. Thompson, *Saint John of the Cross: Songs in the Night* (London: SPCK, 2008); E. Carrera, *Teresa of Avila's Autobiography: Authority, Power, and the Self in Mid-sixteenth Century Spain* (London: Legenda/Modern Humanities Research Association and Maney Publications, 2005). Each of these studies contains an extensive bibliography on its subject.

[361] Miguel de Molinos, *The Spiritual Guide*, ed. Robert P. Baird (Mahwah, NJ: Paulist, 2010).

[362] The whole story is recounted in detail in Paul Hazard, *The European Mind, 1680–1715* (London: Pelican, 1964), 477–490. The book was originally published as *La crise de la conscience européenne (1680–1715)* (Paris: Boivin, 1935). See also Nancy C. James, *The Conflict over "Pure Love" in Seventeenth-century France: The Tumult over the Mysticism of Madame Guyon* (Lewiston, NY: Mellen, 2008).

[363] See Phyllis Thompson, *Madame Guyon: Martyr of the Holy Spirit* (London: Hodder & Stoughton, 1986).

[364] Jeanne Guyon, *Le Cantique des Cantiques de Salomon interprété selon le sens mistique et la vraie représentation des états intérieurs* (Lyon: A. Briasson, 1688); known in English as *Spiritual Torrents*: Annie W. Marston, trans., *A Short Method of Prayer and Spiritual Torrents* (London: Sampson Low, Marston, Low & Searle, 1875).

Another influential French voice was that of Pierre Poiret (1646–1719), a Huguenot refugee who made it his life's work to trace mystics and their writings, and get as many of them published as he could. It was thanks to him that Madame Guyon reached an international public, and he was also largely responsible for reawakening interest in Jakob Boehme (1575–1624), a Silesian mystic who during his lifetime had fallen foul of Lutheran, Reformed, and Catholic alike.[365] Boehme was considerably more unorthodox than Madame Guyon, but in the atmosphere of the late seventeenth and early eighteenth centuries Poiret was able to market them both under the attractive and catch-all label of "spiritual experience." His prestige was enormous, and his patronage of odd people like Madame Guyon and the even odder Antoinette Bourignon (1616–1680), a deeply disturbed woman whom he regarded as a saint, convinced even John Wesley of her legitimacy and led to her ideas being propagated in pietistic circles.[366]

Poiret based himself in the Netherlands, but it was in Germany, where the multiplicity and proximity of rival church establishments was most acute, that the desire to go beyond the official "orthodoxies" was to take the most concrete and long-lasting form. In the late seventeenth century, groups of German Protestants experienced a spiritual revival known by the somewhat pejorative term "pietism," that was to spread and exert considerable influence all over Europe and beyond. The emphasis of the early pietists was on private (or semi-private, small-group) Bible study, prayer, and hymn singing, all of them designed with personal edification in mind. These activities were not intended to supplant the institutional church but to supplement the somewhat meager spiritual diet on offer there. In many places, preaching had become too academic and unrelated to people's lives, with no devotional component to worship services that might have made it more palatable.[367] There was also a distressing tendency in some quarters to engage in polemic against other churches rather than expound the Word of God for its own sake. By concentrating on the essentials, the pietists were able to reach large numbers of ordinary people and minister to their personal spiritual needs.[368]

Pietism is usually said to have begun in 1675, when Philipp Jakob Spener (1635–1705), head of the local church in Frankfurt, wrote an introduction to

[365] For a sample of his writings, see *Jacob Boehme: Essential Readings*, ed. Robin Waterfield (Wellingborough: Crucible, 1989).

[366] Ward, *Early Evangelicalism*, 53–54. On Antoinette Bourignon, see Marthe van der Does, *Antoinette Bourignon 1616–1680: la vie et l'oeuvre d'une mystique chrétienne* (Amsterdam: Holland University Press, 1974).

[367] Astonishing though it must seem today, the Anglican Book of Common Prayer (1662) made no provision for hymn-singing at all.

[368] For an introduction to pietism and a selection of pietist writings, see Peter C. Erb, ed., *Pietists: Selected Writings* (Mahwah, NJ: Paulist, 1983); and Carter Lindberg, *The Pietist Theologians* (Oxford: Blackwell, 2005).

the postil of Johann Arndt (1555–1621), a Lutheran devotional writer of the previous century, which he entitled *Pia desideria*.[369] Arndt had stressed personal piety at a time when the Protestant churches were hardening their confessional stances, and his message, encapsulated in his best-selling *Wahres Christentum* (*True Christianity*), was especially welcome in a Germany that had been through a generation of devastating religious warfare.[370] The pietists opposed the defenders of doctrinal "orthodoxy," whether Lutheran or Calvinist, not because they disagreed with the fundamental theology that they proclaimed but because they thought that they had become too dry and too focused on secondary issues that divided the church, instead of on the liberating message of the gospel, which Spener and others believed would unite it. As Spener put it,

> . . . disputing is not enough either to maintain the truth among ourselves or to impart it to the erring. The holy love of God is necessary. If only we evangelicals would make it our serious business to offer God the fruits of his truth in fervent love, conduct ourselves in a manner worthy of our calling, and show this in recognizable and unalloyed love of our neighbors, including those who are heretics, by practicing the duties mentioned above! If only the erring, even if they cannot yet grasp the truth which we bear witness to, would make an effort (and we ourselves should point them in this direction) to begin to serve God, in love of God and fellow man, at least to the extent of the knowledge which they may still have from Christian instruction! There is no doubt that God would then allow us to grow more and more in our knowledge of the truth, and also give us the pleasure of seeing others, whose error we now lament, alongside us in the same faith.[371]

What Spener proposed was a program that he believed the Holy Spirit would use to illuminate the minds of all genuine believers and bring them together in spite of their theological differences. He concentrated more on the Christian's subjective experience of redemption than on the objective facts of Christ's saving work in history, though he never denied the latter, and told his opponents that Luther himself would have approved of what he was doing, because he had also been deeply influenced by medieval mystical theology.[372] Spener's "orthodox" opponents, however, thought that his emphasis on personal experience replaced a belief in justification by faith alone with one

369 Philipp J. Spener, *Pia desideria*, trans. Theodore G. Tappert (Philadelphia: Fortress, 1964).

370 See John Arndt, *True Christianity*, trans. Peter Erb (London: SPCK, 1979).

371 Spener, *Pia desideria*, 3.4, 102.

372 Philipp J. Spener, *On Hindrances to Theological Studies*, in Erb, *Pietists*, 67–68. Spener said, "I doubt if Luther owed as much to any scholastic as he did to Tauler and similar writers," referring to the impact that the medieval mystic Johannes Tauler (1300?–1361) is known to have had on the young Luther.

grounded in works of pious devotion. The fact that Spener advocated forming small groups to develop these practices was also used against him, because the "orthodox" saw this as a form of secession from the state church, something that had been outlawed by the peace of Westphalia in 1648.[373] Spener also alienated the "orthodox" by the way he appeared to downgrade academic learning, which they regarded as essential:

> It is certain that a young man who fervently loves God, although adorned with limited gifts, will be more useful to the church of God with his meager talent and academic achievement than a vain and worldly fool with double doctor's degrees who is very clever but has not been taught by God. The work of the former is blessed, and he is aided by the Holy Spirit. The latter has only a carnal knowledge, with which he can easily do more harm than good.[374]

But what really attracted the ire of Spener's opponents was the way he appeared to sit loose to the ordinances of the established church, whose efficacy he attributed to the inner working of the Holy Spirit and not to any form of "right administration" by a minister ordained for that purpose. In his words,

> . . . the divine means of Word and sacrament are concerned with the inner man. Hence it is not enough that we hear the Word with our outward ear, but we must let it penetrate our heart, so that we may hear the Holy Spirit speak there. . . . Nor is it enough to be baptized, but the inner man, where we have put on Christ in baptism, must also keep Christ on and bear witness to him in our outward life. Nor is it enough to have received the Lord's Supper externally, but the inner man must truly be fed with that blessed food. . . . Nor, again, is it enough to worship God in an external temple, but the inner man worships God best in his own temple, whether or not he is in an external temple at the time.[375]

Spener had his detractors, but he had many supporters as well. One of them was August Hermann Francke (1663–1727), who was converted in 1687 and appointed to the new university of Halle in 1692. Under Francke's influence, Halle became a center of pietism that developed a social welfare program, a foreign missionary outreach, and a printing press—three ingredients that would continue to characterize the movement as it spread across Germany and around the world. Francke developed a theory of conversion that he regarded as normative,

---

[373] Only Roman Catholics, Lutherans, and Calvinists enjoyed the free exercise of religion in the Holy Roman Empire at that time, and the emergence of pietism was thought by some to imply the creation of a fourth religious stream that was unrecognized by the state.

[374] Spener, *Pia desideria*, 3.5, 108.

[375] Spener, *Pia desideria*, 3.6, 117.

as it too came to characterize pietism. Conversion was a new birth, brought about by a spiritual struggle that led through an experience of deep sorrow for sin, a desire for repentance, and a ready acceptance of the offer of divine grace, which alone could deliver the sinful soul. Once received, that grace completely transformed the believer, giving him the foundation he needed to grow into a new life, lived in imitation of Christ.

Perhaps the most important long-term result of Halle pietism was the way in which its representatives redefined the nature of heresy, to make the term applicable only to those who rejected the basic truths of Christianity. In that way, the pietists were able to break free from the constraints of Lutheran confessionalism and recognize not only the Reformed but also Anabaptists and Roman Catholics as fellow Christians.

There had always been a certain affinity for mysticism among the early pietists, but this was developed further by Gottfried Arnold (1666–1714), who interpreted the new birth in terms of a mystical union with God. For Arnold, the inner voice of the Spirit was the most important factor in the Christian life, much to be preferred over the "dead letter" of formal orthodoxy, though he was careful not to go beyond (or away from) the Scriptures. Nevertheless, for him the indwelling presence of the Holy Spirit meant that the believer was participating in the nature of God himself, rising to the level of the angels and achieving perfect communion with the divine and the spiritual perfection that went with that. Of course, Arnold understood that this process would be complete only in heaven, but he still believed that it was possible to have such ecstatic experiences in this life, which served as a foretaste of the glory still to come.

Of particular interest was his belief, derived ultimately from Boehme, that the redeemed soul was united with the divine Wisdom (Sophia), which was God's gift to believers and gave them the power to realize the new creation that they were in Christ.[376] Of Sophia he wrote,

> . . . every spirit created according to God's image may find the divine virgin in himself and in his being. She is given once again after the fall to all men in a secret spiritual way and wishes to bring each person once again to his former life in her. . . . Adam should have been satisfied with this and willing to live with this pure bride in paradise; he ought also to have remained desirous only for God. However, after he turned outward with doubt and desire toward creatures and became earthly, the divine Sophia turned away from him and from the whole of the earth, and instead of a heavenly bride he received an

[376] Gottfried Arnold, *Das Geheimniss der göttlichen Sophia oder Weissheit* (Leipzig: T. Fritsch, 1700).

> earthly carnal Eve which God created for him in his sleep (which was already an indication of his weakening) . . .[377]

By this means, Arnold was able to apply the traditional teaching of the mystics to the life of the average Christian—what had previously been the preserve of a select few (monks, hermits, and the like) now became not only available, but compulsory, for everyone who seriously wanted to follow Christ. As he understood it,

> When a fervid lover of his spiritual mother-bride, given to him by the Father, has begun, then the Holy Spirit who teaches truly will open one thing after another to him if he does not tire in prayer and obedience. . . . He who learns to know wisdom will first see and note that she is good and loving, an image of the goodness of God himself. . . . The first and most necessary thing for such a soul is to duly hold to the Father and crawl to him in prayer. . . . In such prayer the Holy Spirit will teach the soul to grasp and to draw nearer to the most gracious guide to the throne herself.[378]

Needless to say, there was a great gulf between this vision of the Christian life and the established church in which Arnold lived, and before long he had worked out a theory of church history according to which progressive institutionalization had led to a loss of true faith and to domination by a clerical caste that knew little or nothing of the Spirit of God.[379] The Roman church may have been the worst offender, but the Lutherans and other mainline Protestants were not much better. Arnold was a separatist in spirit, and used his influence to found or to encourage radical pietist groups all over Germany and Scandinavia, as well as in Pennsylvania, where they were welcomed with open arms. He also developed links with Pierre Poiret and Madame Guyon, both of whom influenced Gerhard Tersteegen (1697–1769), who came from the Reformed church in the Rhineland and helped spread pietism among those of a Calvinist, as well as those from a Lutheran, background.

Another branch of pietism, quite different from the one that flourished at Halle, soon appeared in southwestern Germany, in the duchy of Württemberg. Its chief representatives were the biblical scholar Johann Albrecht Bengel (1687–1752) and Friedrich Christoph Oetinger (1702–1782). Like the Lutherans

[377] Gottfried Arnold, *On the Arrival and First Voice of Sophia in Man*, in Erb, *Pietists*, 219–220. This idea was later to become very popular in Russia, where Dostoevsky called many of his heroines Sophia (or Sonia) and portrayed them as saving figures. It also formed the basis of the sophiology of Sergei Bulgakov (1871–1944), for which he was condemned by the Russian church abroad in 1935. See Sergei Bulgakov, *Sophia, the Wisdom of God: An Outline of Sophiology* (Hudson, NY: Lindisfarne, 1993).
[378] Arnold, *On the Arrival*, in Erb, *Pietists*, 221–222.
[379] Gottfried Arnold, *Unparteiische Kirche- und Ketzerhistorie* (Frankfurt-am-Main: T. Fritsch, 1699).

at Halle, Bengel was attracted to Reformed theology and especially to serious biblical study, of which he became the greatest master since Beza. He spent years trying to harmonize the variant readings of the New Testament manuscripts he had access to, and in the process greatly advanced the science of textual criticism.[380] Unfortunately, he also speculated about the return of Christ, which he predicted would occur in 1836.[381] Nothing happened, of course, but such was his prestige as a biblical scholar that this error did not damage his reputation, and his commentary on the Bible remained required reading in the Protestant world.

Oetinger followed a rather different path, turning away from theological study to pure mysticism. He thought that he could uncover the secret behind the various philosophical systems of his time and thereby find the key to understanding the universe. He came to believe that man was being guided toward the creation of a new spiritual body in which the oppositions of this world, between spirit and matter and between mind and the objects of its perception, would be overcome by being absorbed into a unifying middle ground that represented wisdom and ultimate truth. As he expressed it,

> I seek to deal with principles in a nonsectarian way if I can, and to explain Holy Scripture, but not without the works of God [in nature]. With regard to chemistry, it belongs to the true knowledge of God of that which is necessary, simple, and useful for understanding. Not gold or silver, but the true way, wisdom in Holy Scripture, brought me to this. In holy things there must be a harmony of all—in nature also. . . . In so skeptical a time, the truth of God in nature and Scripture is my basis. I am in trouble if I am abandoned before God, if I desire something other than God's eternal purpose, if I attend to any leader other than the Holy Spirit.[382]

Yet another kind of pietism was the form associated with Nikolaus Ludwig, Count von Zinzendorf (1700–1760). As a young man, Zinzendorf had heard that the Moravians, an offshoot of the Hussite movement in what is now the Czech Republic, and Protestant in a non-confessional way, were being persecuted in their homeland and had to flee. Zinzendorf offered them land on his estate, which was just across the border in southeastern Germany, and there they built Herrnhut, a communal settlement that was to become their future

[380] Johann A. Bengel, *Gnomon Novi Testamenti* (Tübingen: Johann Heinrich Philipp Schramm, 1742). Translated into English as *Gnomon of the New Testament*, trans. Andrew R. Fausset, 5 vols. (Edinburgh: T & T Clark, 1857–1858).

[381] Johann A. Bengel, *Bengelius's Introduction to His Exposition of the Apocalypse* (London: J. Ryall and R. Withy, 1757).

[382] Friedrich C. Oetinger, *A Confession of Thought*, in Erb, *Pietists*, 277 (modified). Translated from Karl C. E. Ehmann, *Oetingers Leben und Briefe* (Stuttgart: J. F. Steinkopf, 1859), 563–564.

base. At first it was difficult to establish harmony in the community, especially as it included a number of non-Moravians who were attracted by their ideals but lacked their background and spiritual perspective. Nevertheless, Zinzendorf persevered in trying to bring them together, and on August 13, 1727, the entire group experienced a collective spiritual renewal. Central to this was their conviction that,

> . . . whoever does not daily prove by his conversation that it is his full determination to be delivered from sin through the merits of Jesus, and to follow daily more after holiness, to grow in the likeness of his Lord, to be cleansed from all spiritual idolatry, vanity and self-will, to walk as Jesus did, and to bear his reproach and shame—such a one is not a genuine brother. But whoever has this disposition of heart, though he maintain sectarian, fanatical, or at least defective opinions, shall not on that account be despised among us, nor in case of his even separating himself from us will we immediately forsake him, but we will rather follow him in his wanderings and spare him, and bear with him in the spirit of love, patience and meekness.[383]

After that, they became evangelists for the new birth, and within a decade they had established churches and settlements all over Germany, in England, and in the American colonies. The theology that these born-again Moravians took with them was largely the work of Zinzendorf, and it excited great opposition from other pietists, notably from Bengel, who wrote a long book against it, but also more widely.[384] In this theology, the redemptive work of Christ was central because Christ was the only way that the hidden God of the Bible revealed himself to the world. This had little or nothing to do with reason or academic achievement:

> Religion can be grasped without the conclusions of reason; otherwise no one could have religion except the person with intelligence. As a result, the best theologians would be those who have the greatest reason. This cannot be believed and is opposed by experience.[385]

According to Zinzendorf, faith in Christ led to an experience of love for him that could only be compared to the life between a bride and her bridegroom. Unlike other pietists, Zinzendorf saw the marriage bond as central to human understanding of spiritual experience, even to the point where he was

383 From Article 3 of the *Brotherly Union and Agreement at Herrnhut*, in *The Memorial Days of the Renewed Church of the Brethren* (Ashton-under-Lyne: T. Cunningham, 1822), 106–107.

384 Johann A. Bengel, *Abriss der sogenannten Brüdergemeinde* (Stuttgart: Metzler, 1751). See also Gottfried Mälzer, *Bengel und Zinzendorf* (Witten: Luther-Verlag, 1968).

385 Nicolaus L. von Zinzendorf, *Der Teutsche Socrates* (Leipzig: Walther, 1732), 289.

prepared to regard the Holy Spirit as the divine mother, who in union with the Father gave birth to the Son in the heart of the believer. He was also unhappy with Francke's emphasis on sorrow for sin and repentance, preferring to see the new birth as a joyous experience that brought assurance of salvation with it. Typical of his approach is this:

> . . . when you have once caught sight of the beauty of his suffering, so that in all your life you will not be able to get rid of that sight, then he conducts you with his eyes wherever he will have you; then with his eyes he teaches you what good and evil is. Your knowledge of good and evil lies in his eyes, not in the tree from which Adam poisoned himself, . . . but rather in the eyes of the tortured Lamb. . . . As far as this image looks on you, into the inner recesses of your mortal bodies, so far will you be changed, pervaded and captivated by the person of Jesus, that your brethren will no longer perceive you as a man . . . and brother of the same persuasion only, but as a consort, as a playmate for the marriage bed of the blessed Creator and eternal husband of the human soul.[386]

Zinzendorf was perhaps the first Christian leader to have what we would now recognize as a truly "ecumenical" vision. His aim was not to win converts to Moravianism but to foster an appreciation of the presence of the true church in a wide variety of denominations, and by doing that to bring them together. As might be expected, he was perceived by many of his contemporaries as an ecclesiastical imperialist who was using this vision as a means of subverting existing churches and bringing them into a union that he would ultimately control. For that reason among others, objections to him grew apace and he had little success, but in a way that he could not have foreseen, his influence was to be monumental for Protestant Christianity.

This was because Zinzendorf was indirectly instrumental in the conversion of John Wesley (1703–1791).[387] Wesley came from a family that had rejected the Calvinism of the seventeenth century for a rather dry, ritualistic religion. His father had been a leading exponent of "high church" establishment Anglicanism, but was well aware that England was a long way from reflecting the kind of Christian society that he thought it ought to be.[388] He also had links with

[386] Nicolaus L. von Zinzendorf, *Nine Public Lectures on Important Subjects in Religion*, trans. and ed., George W. Forrell (Iowa City: University of Iowa Press, 1973), 86 (slightly modified).

[387] For the works of John Wesley, the standard edition is Thomas Jackson, ed., *The Works of the Reverend John Wesley*, 3rd ed., 14 vols. (London: John Mason, 1829–1831), reprinted in 7 vols. (Grand Rapids, MI: Baker, 1996). A new critical edition is in preparation, edited by Albert C. Outler et al., *The Works of John Wesley*, 25 vols. (Nashville: Abingdon, 1984–). An assessment of Wesley and Methodism can be found in Kenneth Wilson, *Methodist Theology* (London: T & T Clark, 2011).

[388] Samuel Wesley (1662–1735) was the chief author of a report submitted to the Convocation of Canterbury on March 21, 1711, called *A Representation of the Present State of Religion among Us, with Regard to the Late*

Thomas Bray (1658–1730), who had been sent to Maryland in 1696 to organize the Church of England there, and out of whose missionary efforts grew the Society for Promoting Christian Knowledge (1699) and the Society for the Propagation of the Gospel (1701), both of which still exist.[389] The young Wesley therefore grew up in an environment where the need for Christian education and for missionary work, especially in the colonies, was taken more seriously than was common at that time. As a student at Oxford, he tried to reform the morals of his fellow students and gathered around him a "holy club" that encouraged strict self-discipline and regular spiritual exercises similar to those encouraged by William Law. He later offered himself for ordination and in 1735 went to the newly founded colony of Georgia, hoping to propagate his ideals in a place that he thought had not been settled long enough to have acquired the bad habits of England or of the other colonies.

Wesley had a hard time in Georgia, but on his way there he had met August Gottlieb Spangenberg (1704–1792), a Moravian missionary second in importance only to Zinzendorf himself. After his return to London, Wesley made contact with the Moravians, and on May 24, 1738, went (apparently against his will) to one of their meetings in Aldersgate Street. As he later told the story,

> In the evening I went very unwillingly to a society in Aldersgate Street, where one was reading Luther's preface to the Epistle to the Romans. About a quarter before nine, while he was describing the change which God works in the heart through faith in Christ, I felt my heart strangely warmed. I felt I did trust in Christ, in Christ alone, for salvation; and an assurance was given me that he had taken away my sins, even mine, and saved me from the law of sin and death.[390]

Soon after this, Wesley went to Germany for three months, where he met a number of leading pietists and imbibed their fundamental principles. Wesley's conversion brought his formal religion to life and gave him an outlook that was much more sympathetic to the Reformers and the Puritans than it had previously been, but it did not make him a Calvinist. On the contrary, he repudiated the doctrines of election and predestination because he thought they were a bar to evangelism—as far as he was concerned, the gospel was meant for everyone. He also retained a deep interest in personal holiness that he had inherited from his parents and family friends. The result was Methodism, a form of enthusi-

Excessive Growth of Infidelity, Heresy, and Profaneness. The text is in Gerald L. Bray, ed., *Records of Convocation*, 20 vols. (Woodbridge: Boydell & Brewer, 2005–2006), 10:280–291.

[389] The former is better known by its initials as the SPCK, and the latter has merged with other organizations to become the USPG, or "United Society, etc."

[390] John Wesley, *The Journal of John Wesley*, ed. Nehemiah Curnock, 8 vols. (London: Peter Culley), 1:475–477.

astic, pietistic Christianity that laid great stress on evangelism and on personal morality, but had little time for the intricacies of doctrine and instinctively recoiled from anything that smacked of predestination or limited atonement.[391]

Banned from most pulpits because of his unorthodox enthusiasm, Wesley went out into the streets, where his preaching had dramatic effects. People fell down and wept when they had their sins brought home to them. All over England there were mass conversions, sometimes amid scenes of considerable hysteria. The revival soon split into Calvinist and Arminian wings, because there was a considerable body of Anglicans who took to Wesley's evangelistic zeal without adopting his theology. Reformed theology had not died out in the Anglican world, even if it had to keep its head down much of the time, and its followers were quick to take advantage of the new mood that swept over the country in the 1730s.[392] Chief among them was George Whitefield (1714–1770), who had been part of Wesley's "holy club" at Oxford and who was initially a strong supporter of Wesley's revivalism, but who fell out with him over theological issues related to the divide between Calvinism and Arminianism.[393] Whitefield clung to the former, particularly as it was presented in the Thirty-nine Articles, and after 1740 he and Wesley went their separate ways. Much the same can be said for Howell Harris (1714–1773), one of the great leaders of the Methodist movement in Wales, which subsequently came to be called "Calvinistic Methodism," and for those who were touched by revivalism in Scotland, almost all of whom remained staunch Presbyterians, even if they were unimpressed with the officially presbyterian Church of Scotland, which was by then dominated by "moderates" who did their best to stamp them out.[394]

In general terms, it can be said that the Calvinists stayed within the Church of England, where they later formed an evangelical party (as they also did in the

---

[391] In fairness, it must be said that Wesley was reacting more against the debased form of Calvinism that he encountered in his contemporaries, who refused to evangelize on the ground that God in his sovereignty would gather the elect and that human involvement in the process was neither necessary nor permissible.

[392] On the survival of Reformed theology in the restoration Church of England, see Stephen Hampton, *Anti-Arminians: The Anglican Reformed Tradition from Charles II to George I* (Oxford: Oxford University Press, 2008).

[393] *The Works of the Reverend George Whitefield*, 6 vols. (London: Edward and Charles Dilly, 1771–1772; repr., Oswestry: Quinta, 2000). See also Ian J. Maddock, *Men of One Book: A Comparison of Two Methodist Preachers, John Wesley and George Whitefield* (Eugene, OR: Pickwick, 2011); Jerome D. Mahaffey, *The Accidental Revolutionary: George Whitefield and the Creation of America* (Waco, TX: Baylor University Press, 2011); and Frank Lambert, *"Pedlar in Divinity": George Whitefield and the Transatlantic Revivals 1737–1770* (Princeton, NJ: Princeton University Press, 2003).

[394] This was the unfortunate fate of the so-called "marrow men," who supported a form of neo-Puritan pietism in the early eighteenth century, inspired by Edward Fisher's book, *The Marrow of Modern Divinity* (London: R. W. for G. Calvert, 1645); 7th ed. (London: G. Dawson for G. Calvert, 1650, reset and repr., Fearn: Christian Focus, 2009). Fisher (1612?–1656?) was a leading Puritan controversialist in his lifetime. The "marrow men" were Scottish admirers of his work, who wanted to implement his principles in the Church of Scotland, but who were persecuted and hounded out by the "Moderates" in 1723. See David C. Lachman, *The Marrow Controversy: An Historical and Theological Analysis* (Edinburgh: Rutherford House, 1988).

Church of Scotland), while the Arminians gradually drifted away and—despite Wesley's objections—eventually created their own Methodist denomination. This occurred first in America, where after the war of independence (which Wesley strongly opposed), the Methodists regrouped and formed their own denomination. Wesley eventually accepted the situation and in 1784 he issued twenty-four Articles of Religion which were intended to be the doctrinal basis of the new church. These were an abridgment of the standard Thirty-nine Articles of the Church of England that omitted all the Calvinist material and anything specific to the English church (like the supremacy of the monarch in church affairs).[395]

Whitefield was equally influential in America, and although his followers never established a church of their own, they helped to transform many Baptist and Presbyterian churches out of all recognition.[396] Equally important was the work of Jonathan Edwards (1703–1758), who by common consent was the greatest theologian that colonial America produced and whose achievement has scarcely been equaled since. Like Whitefield, Edwards was a Calvinist, but his roots lay in Puritan New England, not in the Anglican church, and it was in that context that he ministered for most of his life. In his early years, Edwards was strongly influenced by the rationalism of John Locke and Isaac Newton (1642–1727), and he retained an interest in the natural sciences all his life, becoming a strong advocate of smallpox vaccination, for example, from which he unfortunately died after having himself inoculated.[397]

But far from becoming a rationalist himself, Edwards attributed the order in creation to the providential hand of God and regarded it as further proof that God had made the world for the enjoyment of his elect. After being ordained to the ministry, Edwards served in Northampton (Massachusetts), where he soon found himself caught up in a religious revival. For a few years (1733–1735),

[395] In 1804 the American Methodists added another article (no. 23) and made minor changes to the wording of some of the others. The Anglican Articles that Wesley dropped were 3, 8, 13, 15, 17–18, 20–21, 26, 29, 31, 33–34 and 36–37. The text is in Schaff, *Creeds of Christendom*, 3:807–813.

[396] Whitefield himself remained an Anglican, like Wesley, but the Church of England was decimated (in America) by the American Revolution, and many of its former members either emigrated or went to other denominations. Even so, the Protestant Episcopal Church, which was organized in 1786, contained a significant proportion of evangelicals who had been influenced by Whitefield and who remained a significant force in the church until 1873, when many of them seceded to form the Reformed Episcopal Church. In 1875 that denomination also adopted a revised form of the Thirty-nine Articles (reduced to thirty-five), which was more Calvinist in flavor than the Methodist equivalent had been. See Schaff, *Creeds of Christendom*, 3:814–826.

[397] The standard biography of Edwards is George M. Marsden, *Jonathan Edwards: A Life* (New Haven, CT: Yale University Press, 2003), and his theology is outlined in detail by Michael J. McClymond and Gerald R. McDermott, *The Theology of Jonathan Edwards* (Oxford: Oxford University Press, 2012). A complete online critical edition of his works is available through the Jonathan Edwards Center at Yale University. For a comparative study of Edwards, Wesley, and Whitefield, see Mark A. Noll, *The Rise of Evangelicalism: The Age of Edwards, Whitefield, and the Wesleys* (Leicester: Apollos, 2004). See also the perceptive essay by Douglas A. Sweeney and Brandon G. Withrow, "Jonathan Edwards: Continuator or Pioneer of Evangelical History?" in Michael A. G. Haykin and Kenneth J. Steward, eds., *The Emergence of Evangelicalism* (Nottingham: Apollos, 2008), 278–301.

much of New England was affected by this, but what had begun as an outbreak of pious joy turned sour when a number of people were convicted of their sinfulness without coming to a personal knowledge of Christ as their Savior. This led to a wave of despair that resulted in some suicides, and the revival petered out. Later on, Edwards met George Whitefield, and the two men became allies, though not close friends. Whitefield was more emotional than Edwards and emphasized religious experience more than rational thought, whereas Edwards tried to keep the two things in balance. But although this difference of outlook was significant to them personally, it scarcely affected the wider movement of revival that spread through the colonies in the 1740s. Even in Britain, despite the fact that he was still young and had never been there, Edwards was quickly recognized as an important theologian and spiritual writer, and his fame soon spread to the pietists of continental Europe.

There can be no doubt that Edwards was, or at least wanted to be, a Reformed theologian in the classical mold. He was educated on John Owen, Johannes Cocceius, and above all François Turretini (1623–1687) and his son Jean-Alphonse Turretini (1671–1737), whose works became the standard defenses of Reformed orthodoxy until the early nineteenth century.[398] He was accordingly a supralapsarian in believing that the redemption of mankind had been planned long before the fall of Adam:

> Some things were done before the world was created, yea from eternity. The persons of the Trinity were, as it were, confederated in a design, and a covenant of redemption. . . . There were things done at the creation of the world, in order to that work, for the world itself seems to have been created in order to it. . . . The creation of heaven was in order to the work of redemption, [as] a habitation for the redeemed. . . . This lower world . . . was doubtless created to be a stage upon which this great and wonderful work of redemption should be transacted.[399]

On the other hand, he said some things that are very hard to square with traditional Reformed orthodoxy. For example, he believed that the elect came to a recognition of God's beauty in himself before they felt his love for them, which makes one wonder how that was possible, unless we posit some form of natural theology or common grace, available (at least in principle) to everyone, and not merely to the elect:

---

[398] The main text was Francisco Turretini, *Institutio theologiae elencticae, in qua status controversiae perspicue exponitur, praecipua orthodoxorum argumenta proponuntur, et fontes solutionum aperiuntur*, 3 vols. (Geneva: Samuel de Tournes, 1686–1688). See J. Mark Beach, *Christ and the Covenant: Francis Turretin's Federal Theology as a Defense of the Doctrine of Grace* (Göttingen: Vandenhoeck and Ruprecht, 2007). To this was later added Jean A. Turretini, *Historiae ecclesiasticae; compendium a Christo nato usque ad annum MDCC* (Geneva: Fabri et Barrillot, 1734).

[399] Edwards, *The Work of Redemption*, in *Works*, 1:534.

> They do not first see that God loves them, and then see that he is lovely; but they first see that God is lovely, and that Christ is excellent and glorious; their hearts are first captivated with this view, and the exercises of their love are wont, from time to time, to begin here, and to arise primarily from these views; and then, consequentially, they see God's love and great favor to them.[400]

Here Edwards was moving into the realm of experiential theology in a way that subtly distanced him from strict Calvinism but that made him a child of his age. He doubted the reality of his own conversion because he had not experienced "conversion in those particular steps, wherein the people of New England, and anciently the Dissenters of Old England, used to experience it."[401] Instead of the standard narrative of conviction leading to self-abasement and repentance, Edwards had "a new kind of apprehensions and ideas of Christ, and the work of redemption, and the glorious way of salvation by him."[402] It was this experience that led him to place great emphasis on feelings, or as he called them, "affections," in the process of conversion, though he understood that not all emotions were of God. In response to the critics of revivalist enthusiasm Edwards said,

> There must be light in the understanding, as well as an affected, fervent heart; where there is heat without light there can be nothing divine or heavenly in that heart. True religion, in great part, consists in holy affections, so on the other hand, where there is a kind of light without heat, a head stored with notions and speculations, with a cold and unaffected heart, there can be nothing divine in that light—that knowledge is no true spiritual knowledge of divine things.[403]

Nor was there any doubt in Edwards's mind about what effect conversion would have on the soul of the believer:

> Holiness, which is as it were the beauty of sweetness of the divine nature, is as much the proper nature of the Holy Spirit, as heat is the nature of fire, or sweetness was the nature of that holy anointing oil, which was the principal type of the Holy Ghost in the Mosaic dispensation.[404]

Armed with spiritual fervor, intellectual conviction, and personal holiness, the preachers of revival were ready to undertake their task. That they were not

---

[400] Edwards, *Works*, 1:276.
[401] Edwards, *Works*, 16:779.
[402] Ibid., 16:793.
[403] Edwards, *A Treatise Concerning the Religious Affections*, in *Works*, 2:120.
[404] Ibid., 2:201.

always as balanced or as successful as Edwards wanted them to be was hardly his fault, especially since neither he nor anyone else had any means of controlling them. Revival was by definition independent of human authority—any suggestion that it could be manipulated or laid on to order would have been a contradiction in terms. What Edwards did was provide a theological framework within which the work of revival could be tested and its true fruits be integrated into the life of the church. He also had an answer to those of a "Calvinist" persuasion who had corrupted the doctrine of predestination into a fatalism that precluded evangelistic effort of any kind. The faithful evangelist would see hearts melt at the preaching of the Word, but he would also see other hearts harden, because it was only the elect who would be saved. The reprobate would hear the words but not the Word, because their spirit could not accept the Spirit of Christ.

To Edwards, that was true Calvinism, and he happily identified himself with it. But for all their differences, both Calvinist and Arminian evangelicals stood out from others as people who had had a personal experience of the Holy Spirit at work in their lives. A definite conversion narrative developed and was repeated in the form of personal testimonies at virtually every meeting. Hymns were composed in large numbers and became a staple of public worship, something that had never been true before. Most of these hymns were heavily doctrinal in content and conveyed the theology of the authors to the congregations who sang them. Initially, some of them were used as propaganda in favor of Calvinism or Arminianism, but how effective that was is hard to say. Augustus Toplady (1740–1778), for example, was a prominent hymn-writer who was a major opponent of John Wesley, and both Wesley and his younger brother Charles (1707–1788) replied in kind.[405] But although the controversy was intense at the time, it is a measure of how it was transcended by the spirit of revival that few people today are aware that "O for a Thousand Tongues to Sing" and "And Can It Be" are Wesleyan and therefore Arminian in inspiration, while "Rock of Ages" and "Amazing Grace" are Calvinist.[406] A common evangelical faith, rooted in a conversion experience, succeeded in pushing such theological niceties into the background, even in Wesley's own lifetime. The Cambridge preacher Charles Simeon (1759–1836), for example, went to visit Wesley in the latter's old age and quizzed him on his theology. It turned out that on the fundamentals of sin, forgiveness, grace, and new life in Christ the two men were agreed, making whatever differences they had over election and predestination seem unimportant by

[405] See Lee Gatiss, *The True Profession of the Gospel: Augustus Toplady and Reclaiming Our Reformed Foundations* (London: Latimer Trust, 2010).

[406] The former was written by Toplady and the latter by John Newton (1725–1807).

comparison.[407] This was a long way from the Synod of Dort, and no doubt it reflects the fact that Wesley was not an Arminian in the original sense any more than Simeon was a Calvinist, whatever labels they may have adopted (or been given). There were real differences between the two men to be sure, and they went their separate ways, but the ability to strike a balance between Calvinism and Arminianism was characteristic of evangelicalism and has remained so.[408]

Central to the evangelical experience was the power of the Holy Spirit to transform lives.[409] Even if some of the stories told were exaggerated, there was nevertheless a strong sense that when a person was taken over by the Spirit of God he would become a new creation in Christ. Drunkards gave up drink, adulterers became good family men, slave traders became abolitionists. For the first time in living memory, religion was seen to be making a difference to the way men thought and behaved. People not only became more aware of the social evils they had been tolerating, but were persuaded that something could be done to end them. Movements of social reform, stretching from child care to prisons, were the product of the evangelical revival, and in two generations the face of both Europe and America was changed out of recognition. Not only that, the evangelicals believed that they were riding the crest of a great wave of spiritual outpouring that was stretching around the world. Missionaries began to volunteer for service in countries like India and China, which to most Europeans were unknown territory. Their aim was to preach the gospel and transform every human society in the same way that they were transforming their own at home.

It was on the foreign mission field that missionaries were forced to reexamine their theological assumptions and priorities. Their inherited denominationalism had some importance in Europe and North America, but meant little in places where Protestant Christianity had previously been unknown. Conflicts between Presbyterians, Lutherans, and Episcopalians were luxuries that missionaries in pagan environments could not afford. While remaining loyal to their origins, many of them soon mellowed in this respect and preferred not to compete with one another, even if that meant allowing another tribe to become Baptists or Anglicans. Getting unbelievers converted to Christ was the main

---

[407] For Simeon's account of the meeting (sometime in the mid-1780s), see Charles Simeon, *Horae homileticae*, 11 vols. (London: Richard Watts, 1819–1820), 1:xvii-xviii.

[408] Evangelicalism is under-researched, and there is no definitive history of it. For its multiple origins, see Haykin and Steward, *Emergence of Evangelicalism*; and Ward, *Early Evangelicalism*, which is particularly good on the complex prehistory of pietism. The standard history is David W. Bebbington, *Evangelicalism in Modern Britain: A History from the 1730s to the 1980s* (London: Unwin Hyman, 1989). See also Donald M. Lewis, *The Blackwell Dictionary of Evangelical Biography* (Oxford: Blackwell, 1995).

[409] See Bruce Hindmarsh, *The Evangelical Conversion Narrative* (Oxford: Oxford University Press, 2005).

thing, and there was plenty of work for everyone to do. There were exceptions to this spirit of cooperation, but on the whole a generic kind of evangelical Protestantism became the norm in what we now call the developing world, and in some places, like sub-Saharan Africa, it spread rapidly.

By the late nineteenth century many Protestants had come to believe that Christianity, progress, and Western civilization were essentially different aspects of the same thing, and they looked forward to a time when they would take over the world, fulfilling the gospel commission begun by the outpouring of the Holy Spirit at Pentecost. Interdenominational organizations like the Young Men's Christian Association (YMCA) and the Student Christian Movement (SCM) were spreading this message, and in 1910 a great missionary conference was held at Edinburgh—an event that is generally thought to mark the beginning of the modern ecumenical movement.[410] Events were to prove the optimists wrong, and as it would turn out, more people would die for their Christian faith in the twentieth century than in the rest of the church's history combined. Countries that in 1910 were still officially Christian would be secularized, sometimes with openly (and even militantly) atheist governments, and believers would suffer discrimination even in Europe and North America if they insisted on maintaining their convictions in the public arena. Ecumenical organizations like the World Council of Churches (founded in 1948) would succumb to theological liberalism and left-wing politics, with the result that a century after the ecumenical movement began, most observers had become deeply disenchanted with it, at least in its institutional forms.

On the other hand, over the past two generations practical cooperation between different denominations has grown immensely, the traditional barriers that divided Protestant churches from one another have largely broken down, and even bodies that have traditionally been hostile to those outside their ranks, like the Roman Catholic and Eastern Orthodox churches, have been drawn into dialogue with other Christians. In the academic world, theological studies are now an ecumenical enterprise at every level, and those who hold to a particular confessional outlook cannot ignore what is going on elsewhere in the Christian world. Denominationalism has certainly not disappeared, and new divisions have arisen that seem more likely to reshape them than to make them obsolete, but Christians of all kinds are now aware of one another to a degree that they never were before, and very often they cooperate (especially at the local level) in a way that would have been unthinkable before the rise of the ecumenical movement. It is still too early to say what all this will lead to, but however we

[410] For the history of this movement, see Michael Kinnamon and Brian E. Cope, *The Ecumenical Movement: An Anthology of Key Texts and Voices* (Grand Rapids, MI: Eerdmans, 1997).

interpret it, most people would agree that the Holy Spirit is still at work among the people of God, bringing them together (and separating the wheat from the chaff) in ways that will undoubtedly open up a new chapter in the history of the church here on earth.

The Pentecostal Mission

One of the characteristic emphases of John Wesley's ministry that was to make a long-lasting impact was his belief in what he called "Christian perfection," understood as a state of religious attainment that was characterized by a sudden outpouring of the Holy Spirit, which he often called a "second blessing."[411] The theory was that conversion to Christ was an essential first step on the road to heaven, but although it was undoubtedly a work of the Spirit, it did not remove the believer's propensity to sin. Temptation remained an ever-present reality, and there was a real danger of falling into it. As Paul said,

> I do not understand my own actions. For I do not do what I want, but I do the very thing I hate. . . . I have the desire to do what is right, but not the ability to carry it out. For I do not do the good I want, but the evil I do not want is what I keep on doing.[412]

Taken at face value, this is the common experience of every Christian, and Paul uses it to make it plain just how much we are in need of the grace of God. Yet many people would argue that this is not the experience of a Christian at all, but of an unbeliever before he comes to faith. According to that interpretation, what Paul is saying here is what had once been true of him but was true no longer. As he said earlier in the same chapter,

> Now we are released from the law, having died to that which held us captive, so that we serve in the new way of the Spirit and not in the old way of the written code.[413]

There we have it, say those who adopt this second interpretation—the new life of the Spirit! Once the Spirit of God gets to work in a person's heart, the old struggle with sin is overcome and a new life of spiritual perfection becomes possible. If this interpretation is correct, the apostle Paul would presumably have believed that he had received the fullness of the Spirit's new life at the

[411] Surprisingly little has been written about this. For the best modern account, see William E. Sangster, *The Path to Perfection: An Examination and Restatement of John Wesley's Doctrine of Christian Perfection* (London: Hodder & Stoughton, 1943; repr., London: Epworth, 1964).
[412] Rom. 7:15, 18–19.
[413] Rom. 7:6.

time of his conversion—there is certainly no mention in his writings of any post-conversion experience that might be called a "second blessing." But in the Wesleyan scheme of things, people who came to Christ were expected to put sin behind them, as the apostle John had taught:

> If we say we have not sinned, we make him a liar . . . but now he cleanses us "from all unrighteousness" that we may "go and sin no more."[414]

Wesley never claimed to have had such an experience himself, but he knew many hundreds of people who had. He would not have said that he was no longer a sinner, but only that his sinful tendencies had been permanently overcome by the indwelling power of the Holy Spirit. Fortunately, he has left us an account of how he reached this conviction, which enables us to retrace its origins:

> In the year 1725 . . . I met with Bishop [Jeremy] Taylor's *Rules and exercises of holy living and holy dying*. In reading several parts of this book, I was exceedingly affected: that part in particular which relates to purity of intention. Instantly I resolved to dedicate all my life to God. . . . In the year 1726 I met with [Thomas à] Kempis' *Christian pattern*.[415] The nature and extent of inward religion, the religion of the heart, now appeared to me in a stronger light than ever it had done before. . . . A year or two after, Mr [William] Law's *Christian perfection* and *Serious call* were put into my hands. These convinced me more than ever of the absolute impossibility of being half a Christian. And I determined, through his grace (the absolute necessity of which I was deeply sensible of) to be all devoted to God—to give him all my soul, my body and my substance.[416]

It will be immediately clear from this that Wesley was thinking along these lines more than a decade before his famous conversion experience, which (in this respect at least) merely reinforced thoughts that he had long nursed. How indebted he was to the Protestant Reformers is much harder to say. In one sense, of course, he was brought up on them, and as far as the Anglican Reformation is concerned, there is no sign that he ever departed from it. He was converted by hearing Luther's preface to Romans being read, which ought to settle the matter, but it does not. In later life, he distanced himself both from Luther and from the Moravians through whom he had come to faith. After reading Luther's second set of lectures on Galatians, he had this to say:

[414] John Wesley, *A Plain Account of Christian Perfection* (London: R. Hawes, 1777), 16, 22; in Jackson, *Works*, 11:384.

[415] Now known as *The Imitation of Christ*.

[416] Wesley, *Plain Account*, 2–4, 5–6, in Jackson, *Works*, 11:366–367.

> How blasphemously does he [Luther] speak of good works and of the law of God—constantly coupling the law with sin, death, hell or the devil; and teaching that Christ delivers us from them all alike. Whereas it can no more be proved by Scripture that Christ delivers us from the law of God than that he delivers us from holiness or from heaven. Here (I apprehend) is the real spring of the grand error of the Moravians. They follow Luther, for better, for worse. Hence their: "No works; no law; no commandments."[417]

Of Calvin, Wesley had little good to say, but as his views were colored by the "Calvinists" of his own time, we should perhaps not pay too much attention to his expressed opinions. It is, however, noticeable that in his *Christian Library*, a compilation of spiritual writings that he made in order to familiarize the public with the great devotional treasures of the past, he included works by Roman Catholics and pietist sectaries, but not a word of either Luther or Calvin.

To understand Wesley properly, we must first consider what he meant by the word "sin," which he defined as "a voluntary transgression of a known law."[418] Perfection, to his mind, was therefore a matter of the will—it was, in effect, voluntary obedience to the law. When he talked about "Christian perfection," therefore, he meant doing what God has commanded us to do in Scripture, and not about some state of absolute sinlessness that no human being (apart from the incarnate Christ) can ever achieve. Wesley knew that there were people who objected to using the term "perfection" to describe what he had in mind, but he justified it by saying,

> As to the word, it is Scriptural; therefore neither you nor I can in conscience object against it, unless we would send the Holy Ghost to school and teach him to speak who made the tongue.[419]

That this was a second blessing that might not come until many years after initial conversion, Wesley affirmed with equal clarity. He even thought that it was unnecessary to speak about it at all until there were signs that a believer was ready to receive the teaching:

> Certainly till persons experience something of the second awakening, till they are feeling convinced of inbred sin so as to earnestly groan for deliverance from it, we need not speak to them of present sanctification.[420]

[417] Wesley, *Journal*, 2:467. The date was June 15, 1741.
[418] John Wesley, *The Letters of the Reverend John Wesley*, ed. John Telford, 8 vols. (London: Epworth, 1931), 5:322 (to Mrs. Bennis, June 16, 1772).
[419] Wesley, *Letters*, 4:212–223 (to Mrs. Maitland, May 12, 1763).
[420] Wesley, *Letters*, 6:144–145 (to Ann Bolton, March 15, 1775).

Nor was Wesley convinced that the second blessing was properly described as "receiving the Holy Spirit," although he was aware that some people were using that expression and (against his better judgment, it must be said) he did not feel able to repudiate it. As he saw the matter,

> With all zeal and diligence confirm the brethren, 1. in holding fast that whereto they have attained—namely, the remission of all their sins by faith in a bleeding Lord; 2. in expecting a second change, whereby they shall be saved from all sin and perfected in love. If they like to call this "receiving the Holy Ghost" they may; only the phrase in that sense is not Scriptural and not quite proper; for they all "received the Holy Ghost" when they were justified. God then "sent forth the Spirit of his Son into their hearts, crying: 'Abba, Father'."[421]

Nevertheless it seems clear that Wesley made a sharp distinction between justification, which he equated with initial conversion, and sanctification, which to him was the second blessing. He acknowledged that in each case there was a time of preparation for the experience, but insisted that this was not to be confused with the experience itself:

> A gradual work of grace constantly precedes the instantaneous work both of justification and sanctification. But the work itself (of sanctification as well as of justification) is undoubtedly instantaneous. As after a gradual conviction of the guilt and power of sin you was [*sic*] justified in a moment, so after a gradually increasing conviction of inbred sin you will be sanctified in a moment. And who knows how soon? Why not now?[422]

Here we are brought face-to-face with another of Wesley's convictions: spiritual experience, including that of "perfection," was meant to be part and parcel of a living relationship with Jesus Christ. Sanctification was not a transformed state of being that would be achieved after a long period of spiritual self-discipline but a reality that was constantly present and challenging the commitment of the believer. In that sense, it is misleading to say that it could be either "gained" or "lost" because it was not an objective possession. It could only be measured by the believer's faithfulness within the relationship that God had granted him by the grace of union with Christ; outside or beyond that context, the concept had no meaning. But at the same time, relationships are real and can be permanent. To those who thought that

[421] John Wesley, *Letters*, 5:214–215 (to Joseph Benson, December 28, 1770). The biblical quotation is from Gal. 4:6, and the allusion is probably to John 20:22 rather than to Acts 2:4.

[422] Wesley, *Letters*, 7:222 (to Arthur Keene, June 21, 1784).

believers who proclaimed that they had been sanctified were deceiving themselves, Wesley had this to say:

> If a man be deeply and fully convinced, after justification, of inbred sin; if he then experience a gradual mortification of sin, and afterwards an entire renewal in the image of God; if to this change, immensely greater than that wrought before he was justified, be added a clear, direct witness of the renewal; I judge it is as impossible this man should be deceived therein, as that God should lie. And if one whom I know to be a man of veracity testify these things to me, I ought not, without some sufficient reason, to reject his testimony.[423]

It was this belief that gave rise to the so-called "holiness" movements that flourished from the late eighteenth to the early twentieth centuries, and which are best understood as a development within and out of Methodism. The basic idea was that it is possible to attain to a higher spiritual state. In a curious way, this might be compared to the traditional sacramental link between baptism and confirmation. Just as baptism was a new birth in Christ and confirmation was the sealing of the Spirit that accompanied that new birth, either at the time or several years later, so conversion put people into a new relationship with Christ, but one that also had to be sealed with the Spirit.

Testimonies to the power of God at work in the lives of individuals abound. Writing in June 1779, John Oliver testified to his own experience, which went back as far as 1762. After agonizing over his sin and begging to be released from its grip, Oliver and a friend had the following experience:

> The Lord was conquered by our instant prayer and we had the petition we asked of him. I was baptized with the Holy Ghost and with fire, and felt that perfect love casteth out fear. . . .[424] If ever I had access to the throne of grace, it was on this memorable day. Our Lord was inexpressibly near; it seemed we might ask and have whatever we wanted. . . . From this time I went forth in the power and spirit of love. I felt nothing but love, and desired nothing more than love. . . . from that day to this, I have not lost my sight of, nor my affection for, Christian perfection.[425]

John Manners had the same experience, though in his case he wanted assurance from God that his conversion had not been a form of self-deception:

[423] Wesley, *Plain Account*, 19, in Jackson, *Works*, 11:401–402.
[424] An allusion to 1 John 4:18.
[425] *The Arminian Magazine*, II (1779), 427–428.

> I desired the Lord not to let me deceive myself, but give me a witness if I was saved from sin. And in about a week he gave me my desire, the full, clear witness of his Spirit. It has not left me one moment since. I am now always happy in God. I always feel his love, and all my tempers, and desires, and words, and actions, flow from it.[426]

The perennity of this experience of God is well illustrated by the experience of George Skinner, which must have taken place sometime in the late nineteenth or early twentieth century:

> Never had the devil so tempted me to doubt God as when he gave me grace to trust him to sanctify me wholly according to his promise in 1 Thessalonians 5:23–24. . . . every time, God enabled me to hurl that promise that he had given me at the devil, and every time he left me, defeated by the Word. And then in God's own time came his deep inward assurance that he had cleansed my heart from all sin and filled me with his Holy Spirit, and that inward assurance has remained with me through the years as a very precious possession.[427]

It should be said that this phenomenon appeared in a context where virtually everyone had been baptized and made some profession of faith. By the early nineteenth century conversion was no longer an outlandish experience reserved for a few enthusiasts but had become a mainstream expectation, at least in Protestant Christianity. The reality, however, was that the pastoral needs of the converted were as great as they had ever been. It soon became clear that even consciously active Christians had times of depression and doubt. They might have to suffer defeat and disappointment in their lives, deal with unexpected diseases or other crises, and face a multitude of challenges for which they had no special preparation. The poet William Cowper (1731–1800) expressed it very well in the *Olney Hymns* of 1779:

> Where is the blessedness I knew
> When first I saw the Lord?
> Where is the soul-refreshing view
> Of Jesus and his Word? . . .
>
> Return, O holy dove, return,
> Sweet messenger of rest!
> I hate the sins that made thee mourn
> And drove thee from my breast.

[426] *The Arminian Magazine*, III (1780), 276.
[427] George S. Ingram, *The Fulness of the Holy Spirit* (London: Thynne, 1934), 23.

Cowper himself was a chronic depressive, and it has to be said that there was a certain incidence of that character type in the circles most attracted by his kind of theology, though the desire to recapture the heady days of conversion was a common one and proved attractive to many. The notion that a second blessing could solve every problem lurked beneath the surface and helped to influence the way people thought about the work of the Spirit in their lives.

Revivalism became very popular and was characterized by the same need to demonstrate the reality of a transformed life as had marked the earlier calls for conversion. But how were already converted people supposed to demonstrate that they had been revived? One way was to go on doing the same things they had done before but with greater intensity. All-night prayer vigils, for example, could demonstrate a level of commitment well above the ordinary, and indeed, well beyond what was possible for most people most of the time. Revivalism was individualistic on the whole, and concentrated on eradicating the temptations offered by alcohol and gambling rather than on dealing with social issues in the way that an earlier generation of converts had done. The spirit that had led men like William Wilberforce (1759–1833) and John Newton (1725–1807) to campaign against slavery did not seem to lead their revived grandchildren to deal with racial segregation or the problems of the urban working class, which either were ignored or were tackled by others.[428]

It was probably inevitable that revivalism and the holiness movement would eventually move into the supernatural realm, and looking back on it now, the surprise is that it took them so long. Be that as it may, in the early years of the twentieth century a new phenomenon began to appear in those circles—widespread speaking in tongues, regarded by those who practiced it as a new Pentecost. For a long time this was essentially a working-class movement led by relatively uneducated preachers, and it was severely criticized by the establishment, not least by prominent conservatives like Benjamin Warfield (1851–1921), who argued that the so-called "Pentecostal gifts" had ceased in the days of the apostles.[429] Yet in spite of this opposition, and perhaps to some extent because of it, Pentecostalism spread and soon created new denominations to reflect its particular view of the Holy Spirit.

As with most such revival movements, it eventually settled down, and many Pentecostals became virtually indistinguishable from other Protestants, though they continued to insist that the Holy Spirit can and does work in miraculous ways today. In the 1960s this belief spilled over into parts of the mainline

[428] William Booth (1829–1912), for example, originally a Methodist preacher, started the Salvation Army because he thought that Methodism had become too respectable and insufficiently concerned with the poor.
[429] Benjamin B. Warfield, *Counterfeit Miracles* (Decatur, GA: Columbia Theological Seminary, 1918).

churches, where it took root as the "charismatic movement." Charismatics are hard to define precisely, though everyone recognizes them when they see them. They invariably believe that the Holy Spirit is a living and transforming presence in their lives, and for most of them the evidence of this tends to be found in extraordinary manifestations of one kind or another. Speaking in tongues is still very common, but it has been supplemented by other things, including claimed gifts of healing, prophecy, and so on. The difficulty of course is demonstrating that there is any objective validity in the claims that charismatics make. Are their prophecies genuine? How can we tell? What lies behind claims of spiritual healing?

These and other questions have troubled many observers but they seldom dampen the enthusiasm of those directly involved. Charismatics do not deny the divine inspiration of Scripture, but often they go beyond it. They are less concerned with the inspiration of the biblical text than with its power to inspire them. If it succeeds in doing that, then fine, but if not they will look elsewhere. The word of a charismatic prophet, for example, will often carry as much weight as any verse from the Bible, and there is seldom much desire among them to examine such revelations for their credibility. It is here that non-charismatic Christians, and particularly those who share their generally conservative approach to the Scriptures, have the greatest reservations and find themselves unable to be as supportive of charismatic tendencies as those who advocate them might wish they were.[430]

An attempt to answer some of the criticisms and to construct a biblical and systematic theology from a charismatic perspective was made by J[ohn] Rodman Williams (1918–2008) in a major work that is so far the most serious study of the charismatic phenomenon.[431] Williams essentially confirmed the roots of the movement in the Wesleyan and holiness traditions and admitted that some of the criticisms made by others had a degree of validity. But in the end, he insisted that the spiritual gifts "alone are *the* manifestation of the Spirit."[432] It is that insistence which continues to separate charismatics from others, and which will have to be resolved if the movement is to take its place within the broader Christian world.

Whatever the rights and wrongs of the charismatic movement's view of the work of the Holy Spirit may be, there can be little doubt that it has had the ability to raise the profile of this doctrine in the consciousness of many Christians

[430] See Daniel B. Wallace and M. James Sawyer, *Who's Afraid of the Holy Spirit? An Investigation into the Ministry of the Spirit of God Today* (Dallas, TX: Biblical Studies Press, 2005).
[431] J. Rodman Williams, *Renewal Theology*, 3 vols. (Grand Rapids, MI: Zondervan, 1988–1992).
[432] Williams, *Renewal Theology*, 2:331.

and shape the way we use our theological vocabulary. Today, if someone speaks about being "filled with the Spirit" or talks about spiritual gifts, a charismatic context will probably be assumed. Relatively few people will connect the term to a conversion experience, and far fewer to anything sacramental, such as being filled with the Spirit at or by baptism. That may be regretted or it may be welcomed, but either way it is a fact that now has to be reckoned with, whatever view of the matter a particular individual or church may hold.

PART EIGHT

One God in Three Persons

22

The Classical Doctrine of God

The Patristic Synthesis

In one sense, Christian theology has always been about God, but surprising though it may seem, the "doctrine of God" as we now understand it was not developed until the Middle Ages, and did not become a serious theological problem until modern times. The main reason for this is that the early Christians simply adopted the contemporary Jewish understanding of God and integrated their experience of Jesus Christ into that. When they came up against ancient Greek philosophy, they expressed their faith in Greek philosophical terms but always remained rooted in the God of the Bible, whose objective existence and self-revelation determined what they could say about him. For example, the Old Testament makes it quite clear that God cannot be seen or limited in any way; the sin of idolatry was one of the worst that an Israelite could commit. We are told that the heavens cannot contain God, that even if we descend to the depths of hell he is there, and that he is not bound by human limitations.[1] The philosophical mind said that he was therefore invisible, incomprehensible, and omnipresent—technical terms that the Hebrew language did not possess but that seemed appropriate to use when describing what the Bible assumes must be true about the being and nature of God.

Preaching the gospel to the Gentile world certainly involved some adaptation to Greek ways of thinking, but to argue, as Adolf von Harnack (1851–1930) did, that the early Christians "Hellenized" their faith (thereby distorting it in the process) is going too far. To them, invisibility was not a concept to be defined in the abstract but only a word that could be used to describe the nature of the God whom they worshiped. We can see this from the fact that the nouns we use today either did not exist in Greek or were very rare and seldom (if ever) used in reference to God. Thus we find that God was defined as "invisible" (*aoratos*), but there is no readily available Greek word for the abstract "invisibility." The same is true for incomprehensibility, immutability,

[1] Among numerous references, see especially Psalm 139:7–10; Isa. 66:1.

omnipresence, omniscience, omnipotence, and so on. The adjectives were in common use, but not the corresponding nouns that we are so familiar with today. For the church fathers, philosophy was a tool for evangelism, or (as their medieval successors liked to say) it was the handmaid of theology. The God of Abraham, Isaac, and Jacob was not made to conform to some preconceived set of theoretical principles, but the reverse: abstract philosophical terms were interpreted to suit the requirements of the biblical revelation. This led the early Christians to confess that God was by nature "impassible" (free of suffering) but that in the incarnate Son he had suffered and died on the cross. Christian impassibility was therefore not the same thing as the classical Greek *apatheia*, even though the Christians used that word to describe it. Similarly, the invisible God had become visible in Jesus Christ, making it necessary to redefine divine "invisibility" in a way that could accommodate the incarnation of the Son.

It was the need to explain how God could become a man in Jesus Christ that shaped the theology of the early church more than anything else. In dealing with the Jews, Christians had to defend the idea that there was a plurality in the one God that made it possible to experience him as the Son (and as the Holy Spirit) without denying his essential oneness. In preaching to the Gentile world, they had to defend the unique transcendence of a divine being who was nevertheless personal (and therefore relational) in a way that the "supreme being" of the philosophers was not. The difference between these two concepts was well expressed in the way they used the present participle of the verb "to be." Philosophers talked of ultimate reality as *to on*, using the impersonal neuter for "the being," or "that which is." Christians, on the other hand, used the biblical masculine form—*ho ôn*, "he who is," not because God was male as opposed to female, but because he was personal rather than abstract.[2]

Systematization, when it came, concentrated on how the three divine persons could be defined as a Trinity. The earliest phase of this was modalistic, attempting to explain how the one God could appear to be three without ceasing to be one. According to this way of thinking, either the Son and the Holy Spirit were parts of God's being that had acquired a distinct existence of their own, or they were different forms that he took under certain conditions. Thus, there were people who said that the Son was the mind (*logos*) of God and that the third person was the divine spirit. But it was nonsensical to suggest that the Father had somehow been separated from his mind and his spirit, so that idea never got very far. More tenacious was the view that God was a single substance that appeared in different forms—the root, the shoot, and the fruit (of a

[2] This form appears in Rev. 1:8.

plant) for instance, or the source, the river, and the canal, or even the sun, its heat, and its rays of light. These pictures were in regular use as sermon illustrations, as they still are today. The trouble with them was that although a source, a river, and a canal contain the same substance (water), they do not interact in a personal way. Given that personal interaction within the Godhead was the only way the gospel could be understood, this was a fatal weakness, and so images drawn from nature, sometimes referred to as "vestiges of the Trinity" (*vestigia Trinitatis*), eventually disappeared from serious theological discourse.

In recent times it has been widely assumed that the Eastern church expounded the Trinity by starting with the individual persons—putting their mutual relationship at the center of their reflection on the unity of the divine being. The Western church supposedly did the opposite, beginning with the oneness of God and looking for the Trinity inside that, exposing itself to the charge of modalism in the process. This theory has been traced back to Théodore de Régnon (1831–1893), a French Jesuit who developed it toward the end of the nineteenth century.[3] In recent years his picture has been questioned, and today most scholars recognize that it is too schematic to do justice to a more complex reality. But in one respect at least, what he said remains true. This is that writing treatises on the Trinity was largely (if not entirely) confined to the Latin tradition. The Greeks spoke about the three *hypostases* of the one God, but only in the West did books with the title *De Trinitate* actually appear.

The first one that we know of was written by Novatian of Rome (mid-third century), and he was followed a hundred years later by Marius Victorinus, Hilary of Poitiers, and Augustine of Hippo. Of these, Hilary is perhaps the most instructive because, unlike the others, he was personally familiar with Eastern thought. Exiled to Asia Minor, he met the Cappadocians on their home territory and translated their theology into Latin. But it is characteristic of the two halves of the Christian world at that time that whereas the Cappadocians dealt with the divine persons individually, Hilary grouped them together under the heading of "Trinity" and interpreted them within that systematic framework. It was Augustine who brought that approach to full fruition in his magisterial *De Trinitate*, which remains the starting point for any serious discussion of the subject in the Western church.

But even in the West, it is hard to say how far this systematic approach penetrated the consciousness of the church as a whole. If we look at the creeds, for example, we find that they have a clear Trinitarian structure, with separate sections devoted to the Father, Son, and Holy Spirit, but the Trinity itself is

[3] Théodore de Régnon, *Etudes de théologie positive sur la Sainte Trinité* (Paris: Retaux, 1892).

never mentioned. That did not happen until the appearance of the *Quicunque vult*, or so-called Athanasian Creed, sometime around AD 500. There we find a developed and even somewhat abstract presentation of the doctrine of God that deals in turn with both the unity of his nature and the distinction of the three persons. On the first point, we are told that the Father, the Son, and the Holy Spirit are all uncreated, "incomprehensible," and eternal. The logic of this may not be immediately apparent, but it has to do with the nature of creation, whose two great determining factors are space and time. In relation to that, the uncreated God is by deduction unlimited by either space or time.[4] The persons are then distinguished by their so-called "relations of origin," which have no objective existence in themselves but only describe how they are connected to each other, following the standard patristic pattern. This is summed up in table 22.1:

Table 22.1

	Father	**Son**	**Holy Spirit**
Divine nature			
Uncreated	yes	yes	yes
Incomprehensible	yes	yes	yes
Eternal	yes	yes	yes
Divine persons			
Unbegotten	yes	no	no
Begotten	no	yes	no
Proceeding	no	no	yes

The limitations of this schematization are most apparent in the definitions of the divine persons. The Holy Spirit is not "begotten" in the way that the Son is, but he is not "unbegotten" either—such terminology does not apply to him but only to the Father-Son relationship. The generation of the Son might also be described as a kind of procession, although this term is normally reserved for the Holy Spirit, whose procession from both the Father and the Son was affirmed by the *Quicunque vult* in a way that was still uncommon, even in the West.

[4] The word "incomprehensible," which appears in the standard translations, is somewhat misleading today because we tend to interpret it intellectually rather than physically. The Latin word is *immensus* ("without measure"), which gives a better idea of what is meant. Of course we must not translate it as "immense," which just means "very big" in modern English!

The next move toward systematization came in the *Exposition of the Orthodox Faith*, by John of Damascus, which remains the classic exposition of the subject in the Eastern churches.[5] Using the standard categories of ancient physics, he described God as shown in table 22.2:

Table 22.2

Time (beginning):	without beginning, uncreated, unbegotten
Time (end):	imperishable, immortal, everlasting
Space:	infinite, uncircumscribed, boundless, of infinite power
Matter:	simple, uncompound, incorporeal, without flux
Quality:	passionless, unchangeable, unalterable, unseen

Most of these words are negatives, because that is the only way that God can be properly described in philosophical terms. John's work was translated into Latin in the twelfth century, and used by Peter Lombard as a model for his own attempts at systematization, but there is reason to think that his logical presentation of the divine attributes was not properly understood. The West had not had the same philosophical or rhetorical training that John had received and was therefore not so attuned to his way of thinking. This was not necessarily a bad thing, but it did mean that God's attributes would be presented in a very different way in the Western tradition, as we shall see.

Peter Lombard devoted only one section of his *Sentences* to the nature of God.[6] Apart from a fairly substantial quotation from Jerome near the beginning and passing references to Hilary of Poitiers, Boethius, and Isidore of Seville, his sources are all from Augustine of Hippo, and more than two thirds of them are from his *De Trinitate*.[7] Peter's presentation is thoroughly Augustinian in origin but it is essentially eclectic, since even his selections from *De Trinitate* are for the most part unconnected to each other.[8]

Peter began by explaining that God is an unchanging essence, an assertion that he derived from Augustine's and Jerome's interpretation of the biblical use of "I am" and "he is" to describe him. Next, he expounded God's immutability by quoting Augustine as follows:

[5] John of Damascus, *De fide orthodoxa* 1.8.

[6] Peter Lombard, *Sententiae* 1.8.1–8. In the Silano translation it takes up only a few pages (vol. 1, 44–51).

[7] There are twelve quotations from Augustine's *De Trinitate*, five from other works of his, two from Hilary, and one each from Jerome, Boethius, and Isidore.

[8] Of the fifteen books of Augustine's *De Trinitate*, the Lombard quotes from the first book twice, the fifth book three times, the sixth book five times, and the seventh and the fifteenth books once each. The rest is overlooked.

> Other essences or substances are subject to accidents which produce in them changes, whether great or small. In God, nothing like this can occur, and so only the substance or essence which is God is unchangeable. . . . For whatever is changed does not preserve its own being, and whatever can be changed (even if it is not) can still cease to be what it was. Only that which is not only not changed, but also incapable of being changed is most truly said to be.[9]

Immutability implies immortality, a point that the Lombard went on to make by further quotations from Augustine and from the New Testament.[10] Peter then considered the divine simplicity and contrasted it with the complexity of bodily creatures. After pointing out (by copious quotations from Augustine) that both material and spiritual creatures have attributes and parts that make it possible to analyze and dissect their compound beings, he added,

> But God, although he is called in many ways, yet is truly and most highly simple. Thus, he is called great, good, wise, blessed, true, and so on. . . . But his goodness is the same as his wisdom, greatness, and truth, and in him it is not one thing to be blessed and another to be great, wise, true, good, or simply to be.[11]

In the last two chapters devoted to the subject of the divine nature, Peter went on to show that, according to Augustine, it is wrong to refer to God as a "substance," because,

> . . . if God subsists in such a way that he may properly be called a substance, then there is something in him as if he were a subject, and he would not be simple. But it is deeply ungodly to say that God subsists and is the subject of his own goodness and that this goodness is not a substance (or rather an essence), and that God is not the same as his goodness, which is rather to be found in him as in a subject. It is therefore wrong to call God a substance.[12]

Peter rounded off his presentation by appealing to Hilary, Boethius, and Isidore in support of Augustine's doctrine of the simplicity of the divine being, concluding with the equally Augustinian thought that this simplicity is possessed equally by each of the three divine persons, who therefore cannot be

[9] Peter Lombard, *Sententiae* 1.8.2, quoting Augustine of Hippo, *De Trinitate* 5.3.

[10] 1 Tim. 6:16. He also referred to other biblical passages to support God's unchangeableness (James 1:17; Psalm 102:27–28; Mal. 3:6).

[11] Peter Lombard, *Sententiae* 1.8.4.3, quoting Augustine of Hippo, *De Trinitate* 6.7.

[12] Peter Lombard, *Sententiae* 1.8.7, quoting Augustine of Hippo, *De Trinitate* 7.9–10.

identified with one part or aspect of God, as the Sabellians (modalists) had tried to do.[13]

Peter's main concern was for the simplicity of God's essence, an attribute that John of Damascus had mentioned, but only as one among others. The reason for this seems to have been the need he felt to reject all forms of modalism, which had to be done before a doctrine of the Trinity could be constructed. For him, talk of the nature of God's being was basically an introduction to the Trinity rather than a theological subject in itself. In that respect, Peter faithfully summarized and reflected the patristic synthesis, but did so in a way that would go far beyond anything the fathers of the church ever contemplated. Furthermore, and perhaps somewhat ominously, it was a way that was to remain alien to the Eastern tradition, despite the attempts of some Greek theologians to come to terms with it in the later Middle Ages.

The God of the Philosophers

Peter Lombard's work quickly became the fundamental theological textbook of the Western church. In the century after his death there was a vast increase of speculation about the knowability of God, beginning with the evidence for his existence and proceeding from there to a detailed analysis of his attributes. The supreme master of this was Thomas Aquinas, whose *Summa contra Gentiles* and his magisterial (if uncompleted) *Summa theologiae* still largely define what we mean today when we talk about the "doctrine of God."

Aquinas began his exposition of God's oneness by establishing a fundamental distinction that had always been known but had never been stated with such clarity before. In his words,

> There is a twofold mode of truth in what we profess about God. Some truths about God exceed all the ability of human reason. Such is the truth that God is triune. But there are some truths which the natural reason also is able to reach. Such are that God exists, that he is one, and the like. In fact, such truths have been proved demonstrably by the philosophers, guided by the light of natural reason.[14]

That paragraph neatly summarizes the entire Western tradition of philosophical theology. According to Aquinas, the Trinity is a revealed mystery that cannot be known otherwise, but the divine unity is a proper subject for logical analysis. Because of this, the doctrine of God had to be expounded under two

[13] Peter Lombard, *Sententiae* 1.8.8, quoting Augustine of Hippo, *De civitate Dei* 11.10.
[14] Thomas Aquinas, *Summa contra Gentiles* 1.3.2.

separate headings, which are usually known by their Latin names as *de Deo uno* ("the one God") and *de Deo trino* ("the threefold God"). It soon became customary for theologians to deal with the one God first and then move on to the Trinity. The two "modes of truth" would often be given equal weight (something that Peter Lombard and his predecessors would have found incomprehensible) and, following the logic inherent in Aquinas's distinction, they would be treated in quite different ways.

The first treatise would essentially be a philosophical exercise, but the second might take different forms. Aquinas himself preferred a biblical exposition backed up by patristic quotations, especially from Augustine, but after his time it tended to become another philosophical exploration, undertaken as a way of tying the two kinds of theology together. The danger in this was that the Trinity would be sidelined or reduced to a kind of modalism, simply because—as Aquinas himself clearly understood—it was not susceptible to philosophical analysis in the first place. To pursue the "one God" theme to its logical conclusion would therefore tend to exclude the Trinity altogether, making a kind of generic "monotheism," similar to that of Judaism and Islam, plausible in a way that it had not been before. It would take many centuries for that kind of monotheism to establish itself, but the seeds were sown (however unwittingly) by Thomas, and it was against the backdrop of his analysis of the divine being that modern interfaith monotheism eventually developed.

One thing that is striking about Thomas Aquinas is his widespread and openly recognized dependence on the philosophy of Aristotle, whose thought reached him mainly through Muslim intermediaries like the Persian Avicenna (980–1037) and the Spanish Averroes (1126–1198).[15] There had long been a close connection between Christian theology and various forms of ancient philosophy, especially Neoplatonism, but however important pagan philosophical influences on Christianity were, no one had ever tried to construct a synthesis of them. Aquinas's division of theology changed that significantly. Despite a good deal of resistance from traditionalist forces in the church, Aristotelian thought entered Western theology and remained a significant force within it for centuries. This development was paralleled in other disciplines, which did not break free of it until the seventeenth century. The Protestant Reformers had tried to reject Aristotelian categories in their theology but without success, because those categories were still felt to be necessary for conveying theological ideas. Unfortunately, by the time they were giving way in the natural sciences, they had become so entrenched in both Protestant and Roman Catholic

[15] Avicenna is the Latinized form of Abu Ali al-Husayn ibn Abd Allah ibn Sina, and Averroes is the Latinized form of Abu I-Walid Muhammad bin Ahmad Ibn Rushd.

"orthodoxies" that they could no longer be dispensed with without calling Orthodoxy itself into question. As a result, much of the history of theology since the eighteenth century can be written in terms of a struggle between those who wanted to preserve traditional doctrines (whether in an Aristotelian guise or not) and those who wanted to jettison them on the ground that they were no longer tenable.

Aquinas did not believe that God had revealed only truths that human reason could not work out for itself. He knew that there were things that the mind could discover on its own but that were so complicated that it would take a long time to do so and would give those with greater intelligence an unfair advantage. Therefore, God had provided a Scripture that contained a revelation of things knowable as well as things unknowable by reason alone. This combination allowed believers to proceed from the one to the other in a natural and consistent way, because even what the human mind can work out for itself is part of God's truth.[16] Human reason is meant to give us a basis for understanding what lies beyond it as well as a thirst for finding out more than we are able to discover on our own. As Aquinas saw it, this was designed to inculcate intellectual humility in the enquirer, which was the essential prerequisite for true understanding.[17]

Aquinas was ready to use miracles as proof of the existence of a higher wisdom than that which can be known by rational investigation alone. As he put it,

> . . . [the divine wisdom] gives visible manifestation to works that surpass the ability of nature. There are wonderful cures of illnesses, . . . the raising of the dead; . . . the inspiration given to human minds, so that simple and unlearned people, [who are] filled with the gift of the Holy Spirit, suddenly come to possess the highest wisdom and the readiest eloquence. When these arguments were examined, . . . an innumerable throng of people, both simple and learned, flocked to the Christian faith.[18]

Lest anyone think that miracles have now ceased, he added: "It is also a fact that, even in our own time God does not cease to work miracles through his saints for the confirmation of the faith."[19] He was well aware of the competition the church faced from Islam, which he denounced on the ground that in this respect it was the exact opposite of Christianity, which offered miraculous proofs for its beliefs. In his words,

---

[16] Thomas Aquinas, *Summa contra Gentiles* 1.4.6.
[17] Ibid., 1.5.4.
[18] Ibid., 1.6.1.
[19] Ibid., 1.6.3.

> Muhammad seduced the people by promises of carnal pleasure. . . . his teachings also contained precepts that were in conformity with this. . . . As for proofs of the truth of his doctrine, he produced only things that could be grasped by the natural ability of anyone with a very modest brain. The truths that he taught, he mingled with fables and completely false teachings. He did not produce any miracles, which is the only sure way of bearing witness to divine inspiration, because a visible action that can only be divine reveals that the one who does it is an inspired teacher of truth.[20]

Aquinas accepted that a religion like Islam contained many elements of truth, but without miracles to back it up, there was no reason to suppose that it is divinely inspired. In contrast to this, Christianity offered evidence of things like the resurrection of the body that went beyond human ability to produce, but that were not irrational or incomprehensible. As Aquinas put it, "No opinion or belief is implanted in man by God which is contrary to man's natural knowledge."[21] A man may come back from the dead, but he is still a man and can be perceived as such by ordinary human means.

Having established what he understood by reason and its relationship to faith, Aquinas went on to examine the so-called "proofs" for the existence of God. He agreed in principle with those who claimed that God's existence was self-evident and therefore did not need to be proved, on the ground that the existence of anything implies that there must be an ultimate being that makes sense of it all. But although he accepted that argument in theory, he went on to say that what is true in the abstract is not true in practice:

> . . . because we are not able to conceive in our minds what God is, so he remains unknown in relation to us. That every whole is greater than one of its parts is self-evident in absolute terms, but it is unknown to those who cannot conceive what the nature of the whole is.[22]

God's absolute being is too big for the human mind to grasp, and so we must approach him by indirect means, starting with his works and detecting in them signs of what he must be like in himself. This is not a futile exercise, because God has created material things in and through which his presence can be sensed, as the apostle Paul himself said.[23] From there, Aquinas went on to say that there are five ways in which God's existence can be demonstrated from the forces of nature.[24] These can be summed up as follows:

---

[20] Ibid., 1.6.4.
[21] Ibid., 1.7.4.
[22] Ibid., 1.11.2.
[23] Ibid., 1.12.9; *Summa theologiae* I.2.2, quoting Rom. 1:20.
[24] Ibid., 1.2.3.

1. God is the first (or "prime") mover of all things.[25]
2. God is the first (or uncaused) cause of all effects.
3. God is the necessary being that has to exist in order for everything else to exist.
4. God is the most perfect being.
5. God is the mind that orders all things.

Basic to these arguments is the belief that the universe is inherently logical. Everything that exists must have some rational explanation, even if our human minds are unable to understand what that is. If that is admitted, the rest follows on naturally, or so Aquinas thought. The five ways listed above are not "proofs" in the usual modern sense of the word, but means by which God's existence can be justified. Aquinas did not think that such "proofs" would convince unbelievers, but saw them as a reassurance for Christians who wanted to have a firm ground for their faith.[26] Nor were these propositions the only ones that could be used to defend belief in the existence of God. Anselm of Canterbury had already advanced the so-called "ontological" argument, which asserts that there must be a being greater than any other, and that is what we call "God." Later on, there would be more arguments put forward as ways of defending God's existence, some of which are still used today, but common to them all is the assumption that the existence of God can be demonstrated from what he has made, as Romans 1:20 states.[27] That belief is what constitutes the basis of all so-called "natural theology."

Once Aquinas had demonstrated the necessity of God's existence, he went on to consider God's nature. Before examining it in detail, however, he pointed out that it is difficult to make positive statements about God, because his being is beyond anything that we can conceive. Therefore, the best way to think of him is often not by what he is, but by what he is not, an approach that parallels the apophatic theology of the Pseudo-Dionysius and the Eastern mystical tradition:

> In considering the divine substance, we should especially make use of the way of negation. For by its incomprehensibility, the divine substance surpasses every form that our intellect reaches. Thus we are unable to apprehend it by knowing what it is. Yet we are able to have some knowledge of it by knowing what it is not. The nearer we get to God, the more we are able to discount particular concepts of him.[28]

[25] For a detailed discussion of this idea, which is derived almost entirely from Aristotle, see Thomas Aquinas, *Summa contra Gentiles* 1.13.1–35.

[26] Ibid., 1.9.2–3.

[27] For a brief summary of what they are and who holds (or has held) them, see Peter Kreeft, *Summa of the* Summa (San Francisco: Ignatius, 1990), 63–64.

[28] Thomas Aquinas, *Summa contra Gentiles* 1.14.2. For the evidence that Aquinas was influenced by Pseudo-Dionysius the Areopagite, see Brian Davies, *The Thought of Thomas Aquinas* (Oxford: Clarendon, 1992), 40–43.

For Aquinas, the basic truth about God was the fact that he is immutable. This is what lies behind the concepts of the first mover and the uncaused cause—other things have come from somewhere, but God is where he has always been and always will be. He is outside of time and space, dwelling in an eternal dimension which we are forced to express as unending time but which is actually quite different. God has no unrealized potential still waiting to be developed, since that would also imply time and space. Everything he does is done in eternity, or as the philosophers would say, his being is pure act. That means that he cannot be an object that can be circumscribed or defined. Like Peter Lombard before him, Thomas was deeply concerned to emphasize the simplicity of the divine being, which he analyzed in even greater detail than his predecessor had done. His logic was as follows:

> Every compound is potentially dissoluble. This arises from the nature of composition, even though in some compounds there is an element that resists dissolution. But what can be dissolved can also cease to be. This does not apply to God, because he is in himself the necessary being. So there is no composition in God.[29]

From there, Aquinas went on to say that there can be nothing violent or unnatural in God, nor can he be any sort of body. Since God is absolute being, his essence must be identical to it, which is why there is no room for anything else in him. God cannot have "accidents," the word he used to mean what we would call "properties" or "characteristics." His logic is clear:

> Being cannot share in anything that does not belong to its essence, even though what is can participate in something else. The reason for this is that there is nothing more formal or more simple than [absolute] being, which therefore participates in nothing, but the divine substance is being itself, and therefore has nothing that does not belong to its substance. So no accident can reside in it.[30]

Having established that, Aquinas went on to explain how nothing can be added to God, how he cannot belong to a species of beings because he is unique. He then tackled the question of pantheism—the belief that God is the fundamental being of all existing things. Drawing on the evidence of Scripture and even of the Pseudo-Dionysius, Thomas pointed out that if that were true, the world would have to be just as eternal and unchanging as God is, which

[29] Thomas Aquinas, *Summa contra Gentiles* 1.18.4.
[30] Ibid., 1.23.5.

is clearly false.[31] Finally, he pointed out that God's simplicity means that he is also perfect, though not in the human sense of the word. "Perfect" literally means "fully made," which implies that there has been a process at work, and that cannot apply to God.[32]

But how can a simple, perfect, eternal being have any point of contact with his creatures when they are so different from him? This question is answered by Scripture itself, where we are told that human beings have been made in his image and likeness, even though there is nothing on earth or in heaven that can be compared to him.[33] Aquinas described the connection between God and his creation like this:

> The heat generated by the sun must bear some likeness to its active power, . . . and because of this heat the sun also is said to be hot, even though not in the same way. Thus the sun bears some resemblance to the things in which it produces its effects, . . . but it is also unlike them insofar as the effects do not possess heat and so on in the same way as they are found in the sun. In the same way, God gave everything their perfections and is therefore both like and unlike all of them.[34]

From this example of two different kinds of heat, Aquinas went on to say that the words we use to designate some virtue in us—like goodness, wisdom, or being—can also be used of God, but only by analogy or metaphor. All human words have something imperfect about them, and are unable to do full justice to God. A word like "goodness" cannot describe him properly because, unlike God, goodness is an abstraction that does not exist in reality. Calling God "good" is wrong also because it implies that God can be measured in relation to something else. But the virtue that those words refer to is found in God, who is the archetypal example and source of what they mean. Aquinas endorsed the teaching of the Pseudo-Dionysius on this point, agreeing with him that such terms can be used of God because of what they intend to say but at the same time they cannot be used of him in their literal sense, because they are inadequate to do justice to the reality of his being.[35]

But although what we say about God is inadequate because it can only be expressed in relation to our own lives and experience, it does not follow that the words we use are arbitrary. It is a natural part of a creature's existence to want to fulfill its potential, on the assumption that what it was made for is

[31] Ibid., 1.26.1–13.
[32] Ibid., 1.28.10.
[33] Compare Gen. 1:26–27 with Isa. 40:18 and Psalm 86:8.
[34] Thomas Aquinas, *Summa contra Gentiles* 1.29.2.
[35] Ibid., 1.30.3; see Pseudo-Dionysius the Areopagite, *De divinis nominibus* 1.5; *De caelesti hierarchia* 2.3.

what constitutes its good. If a creature succeeds in this, it will become perfect and therefore as good as it can be. God is perfect already, and so he must be regarded as good. For the same reason, God must also be entirely good (because of his simplicity), the highest good (because of his sovereignty), and the ultimate source of all goodness (because he is the Creator of all things).[36] The same logic can be extended to any other virtue, of which God will by definition be the greatest example and ultimate source. Furthermore, the divine simplicity also means that in him all the virtues are rolled into one, even though we can make a theoretical distinction between them. Thus (for example) because God is supremely good and supremely wise, his wisdom is perfectly good and his goodness is entirely rational. Not only that, but his virtues, like his being, are eternal and infinite, and therefore incapable of being improved upon (or diminished) in any way.

Human beings can describe God only by way of analogy, because even if what we say about him resembles our experience, that similarity is conditioned by the nature of our respective beings.[37] Because he is absolute being, his attributes are absolute and coextensive with that being, whereas our attributes are refracted through our limitations. We have a notion of goodness that impels us to desire it above everything else, and so does God. But in his case, he attains his desire in the perfection of his own being, which we can never do because we can never be perfect. Nevertheless, the fact that we have a desire to be like God gives us some point of contact with his being, and that makes what we say about him meaningful and coherent.

The equation of God's being with absolute goodness means that there can be no evil in him, and that evil is really "nonbeing."[38] At this point Aquinas was relying more on Aristotle than on Scripture, as he himself admitted:

> If the good is "that which is sought by all,"[39] it follows that every nature flees evil as such. Whatever is contrary to the natural appetite of a thing is violent and unnatural, so evil is violent and unnatural in that thing. In a compound substance, evil may be natural insofar as it is related to something in that substance, but God is not compound, nor can there be anything violent or unnatural in him.[40]

Logically, a being that must necessarily exist can have no accidents, because accidents are variable and therefore not strictly necessary in themselves. What

[36] Thomas Aquinas, *Summa contra Gentiles* 1.37–41; *Summa theologiae* I.6.3.
[37] Thomas Aquinas, *Summa contra Gentiles* 1.34.
[38] Ibid., 1.39.
[39] Aristotle, *Ethica Nicomachea* 1.1 (1094a, 3).
[40] Thomas Aquinas, *Summa contra Gentiles* 1.39.7.

God is, though, must be necessary, and there can be nothing superfluous in him. It also follows from this principle that there can be only one God, since necessary being can be only one thing.[41] It is here that problems arise for a doctrine of the Trinity, because how is it possible for differentiation to subsist in the one necessary being? Aquinas skirted around this question by appealing to the mystery of revelation, which goes beyond the limitations of human reason, but it is not hard to see how those who wanted to reconcile the two kinds of theology would find this intolerable. God cannot be coherent at one level and incoherent at another, and in the long term philosophical theology was almost bound to be unitarian rather than Trinitarian in character.

Of the remaining divine attributes Aquinas had relatively little to say. He naturally insisted that God is infinite and intelligent, since both of those things are necessary to his perfection and to his role as Creator. As he put it,

> Whoever knows something perfectly knows what can be said of it truly and what fits its nature. It fits God's nature to be the cause of other things, and since God knows himself perfectly, he knows that he is such a cause. This cannot be unless he knows what he causes and what he causes is something outside himself, since nothing can be its own cause. For this reason, God knows things other than himself.[42]

The expressions are somewhat convoluted but the underlying logic is clear. A perfect being who is also the Creator must know everything perfectly, and that includes the purpose and destiny of the creation.[43] God even knows what evil is because he knows every conceivable good, and since evil is defined as the opposite of good, he must know that too, since otherwise he would not be able to define what is good.[44] In this way, Aquinas could develop a complete system of predestination and reprobation that was rooted in the necessity of divine omniscience. God can even exhibit some "passions" like joy and delight, because such things are good and are therefore a necessary element of his being.[45] Finally, and in some ways most important of all, Aquinas believed that God is love because he wills his own good, and willing the good is what love is:

> The nature of love is that the lover wills the good of the one he loves. Since God wills the good of others as well as his own, he loves himself along with other things.[46]

[41] Ibid., 1.42.8.
[42] Ibid., 1.49.4.
[43] Ibid., 1.68.
[44] Ibid., 1.71.
[45] Ibid., 1.90.
[46] Ibid., 1.91.2.

Here, perhaps better than anywhere else, we can measure the distance between Aquinas and his mentor Augustine. For the latter, God is love because he is a relational Trinity of persons—"love" is a term not applicable to the nature of his substance. But for Aquinas, love is a quality in God that is knowable and is therefore part of his divine unity. That does not exclude the possibility that it belongs to his hidden Trinity as well, but in that case the two must be connected, and it is love that will form the bridge from one level of the divine being to the other. Furthermore, love is a personal thing, which makes us ask whether God can be described as one person as well as (or instead of) three. Aquinas never asked that question, but later generations did, and they were to answer it in a way that he would certainly have repudiated.

The Reformation Breakthrough

The Thomist synthesis of philosophy and theology was not universally accepted in his lifetime, and in the fourteenth century it was severely challenged by William of Ockham and others, who developed what we now call "nominalism," a radical critique of Thomist scholasticism that competed with it for influence for the next two hundred years. Martin Luther was closer to Ockham than he was to Thomas, and many of his contemporaries were Neoplatonists. The humanist world of Erasmus was not bound to any one philosophical system, but it tended to regard Thomistic Aristotelianism as old-fashioned. It was this, more than any outright rejection of his approach, that accounts for the fact that Aquinas was little read or cited by the main Protestant Reformers. Luther and Calvin did not particularly disagree with (most of) what Thomas said, but they approached theological questions from a different perspective. They were less interested in explaining why God had to be perfect, good, invisible, omnipotent, and so on, and more concerned with applying those truths to the work of salvation in and through Jesus Christ.

This change of focus was brought about by a new emphasis on the Bible alone (*sola Scriptura*) as the source of Christian doctrine. What God did in Christ was more important than what he was in himself, even if the former ultimately depended on the latter. A book like Calvin's *Institutes* did not follow the Thomist distinction between God as one and God as three, but was more like Peter Lombard's *Sentences*, with which Calvin interacted far more than he did with Aquinas.[47] Nevertheless, Calvin's masterpiece breathes a very

[47] Scholars argue over whether Calvin ever read Aquinas, but there is no doubt that he was familiar with the man he normally refers to as the "Master of the Sentences," Peter Lombard. This can be easily explained, since it was the Lombard, and not Aquinas, whose work remained the standard theological textbook until the sixteenth century. In the Reformed world, Calvin's *Institutes* replaced it, not the *Summa theologiae* of Aquinas.

different spirit from either the *Sentences* or the *Summa theologiae*. Like those who went before him, Calvin accepted that there was a close connection between the knowledge of God and human self-knowledge, and that the latter was imperfect. But instead of developing the theory of how we can rise to an understanding of the divine by analogy, Calvin started with the need for men to recognize their own sinfulness. As he put it,

> Each of us must be stung by an awareness of our own unhappiness in order to attain at least some knowledge of God. It is from the feeling of our own ignorance, vanity, poverty, infirmity, and (what is more) depravity and corruption that we recognize that the true light of wisdom, virtue, the abundance of every good, and purity of righteousness rest in the Lord alone. To this extent, we are prompted by our own ills to contemplate the good things of God, and we cannot seriously aspire to him before we begin to become displeased with ourselves.[48]

From there, Calvin went on to argue that true knowledge of God depends on "piety," by which he meant the desire to know the truth and the humility to accept it.[49] He believed that every human being is endowed with a natural knowledge of the divine, which manifests itself in the religions of the world, even if those religions have often been corrupted by unscrupulous people wanting to dominate others.[50] We do everything we can to suppress and corrupt the truth, but it shines forth in the creation as a reminder of who made us and what he wants from us.[51] The witness is there, but we cannot embrace it because of our innate rebelliousness, which even uses the things of God's world as means of concealing the truth about him. That is the nature of idolatry, which is as universal in the human race as the awareness of the existence of divinity is.

The only way out of this is to be confronted with the truth about God that comes to us in Holy Scripture, a theme that occupies the main portion of the first book of the *Institutes*.[52] Calvin thus accepts the classical distinction between the knowledge of God that is available to the human mind and that which can be known only by Scripture, but he denies that it is possible to build on so-called "natural theology" in any constructive way. The reason for that was not the inadequacy of nature so much as the corruption of the human mind, which meant that independent study of God's creation would inevitably be misdirected, and not just insufficient to give man a knowledge of God.

---

[48] Calvin, *Institutio* 1.1.1.
[49] Ibid., 1.2.1.
[50] Ibid., 1.3.1.
[51] Ibid., 1.4–5.
[52] Ibid., 1.6–14.

Calvin's insistence on the necessity of Scripture for the true knowledge of God was essentially pragmatic, in the sense that he recognized that the revelation was first given to men like Adam, Noah, and Abraham, none of whom had a written text to guide them.[53] That came only later, in order to ensure that the content of God's personal revelation to the patriarchs was preserved and disseminated correctly:

> Whether God became known to the patriarchs through oracles and visions, or by the work and ministry of men, he put into their minds what they should pass on to later generations. There is no doubt that a firm certainty of their teaching was engraved on their hearts, so that they were convinced that what they knew came from God. By his Word, God made faith forever unambiguous . . .[54]

Calvin did not deny that Scripture taught the unity of God in all his divine perfections, but he never developed the theme beyond saying that the revelation of God's nature was a warning against any tendency toward idolatry.[55] To his mind, that tendency was disturbingly present in the church, which had fallen into the temptation of venerating icons and statutes as representations of the living God and had even justified this by specious appeals to the Bible.[56]

It was at this point that Calvin introduced his discussion of the Trinity.[57] He was in no doubt that Scripture taught that there are three persons in the one being (essence or substance) of God, and fully accepted traditional orthodox teaching. But he also knew that that had been questioned in his own time by men who rejected it as unbiblical. One of the most important of these was Michael Servetus (1509?–1553), who as a young man had written a notorious treatise against it.[58] Servetus rested his case on the belief that, because the vocabulary used to describe the Trinity was nowhere to be found in Scripture, it did not teach the doctrine. If Servetus was right, anyone who claimed to base his faith on a doctrine of *sola Scriptura* would have to reject the Trinity as a corruption of it, or at the very least discount it as an unnecessary addition to the body of revealed truth. Calvin could hardly dispute Servetus's basic contention, which was that words like "person" and "Trinity" were not to be found in

---

[53] Ibid., 1.6.1.
[54] Ibid., 1.6.2.
[55] Ibid., 1.11.1–4.
[56] Ibid., 1.11.5–15.
[57] Ibid., 1.13. This was the position adopted in the fifth and final edition of the *Institutio* (1559), but in all the earlier editions it had been preceded by an exposition of Christ as the sole object of faith, which in the final edition was put in *Institutio* 3.2, where it forms part of the work of the Holy Spirit.
[58] Michael Servetus, *De Trinitatis erroribus* (Haguenau: Setzer, 1531); Earl M. Wilbur, trans., "On the Errors of the Trinity," in *Two Treatises on the Trinity* (Cambridge, MA: Harvard University Press, 1932).

the New Testament, but he denied that this was enough to prove that Scripture did not teach the doctrine those words were used to express. As he put it,

> Although heretics rail against the word "person," and some squeamish people object to using a term fashioned by the human mind, they cannot shake our conviction that there are three who are spoken of, each of which is fully God, yet that there is only one God. What wickedness it is to disapprove of words that are doing no more than explain what is attested and sealed by Scripture.[59]

Calvin rehearsed the standard arguments for the divinity of the Son and the Holy Spirit in order to establish that there were three divine persons before going on to examine how they were related to one another inside the one God. Rather than follow ancient analogies, he looked at the way the Bible presented each of them and concluded as follows:

1. The Father initiates and plans the divine activity.
2. The Son arranges the divine activity in a particular order.
3. The Holy Spirit puts the divine activity into practice.[60]

Divine activity is one, but it cannot exist without an agent or agents, and this is how Calvin saw the three persons working together in the one God. Whether (or to what extent) this Trinity was revealed in the Old Testament was a more difficult question, and here we must admit that Calvin's answer was unsatisfactory. Basing himself on Paul's prayer to "the Lord" in 2 Corinthians 12:8, whom he correctly identified as Christ, Calvin extrapolated to *YHWH* (Yahweh), the Old Testament name of God which was normally rendered as "Lord" in Greek translation and in the New Testament. On that basis, he was prepared to accept the idea that the Son of God had appeared to the patriarchs and that most, if not all mentions of *YHWH* in the Old Testament were Christological.[61] The church fathers had long ago "discovered" Christ in the Old Testament, of course, and the idea was a commonplace of Christian biblical interpretation, but it seems that Calvin was the first person to make such a direct and comprehensive link with the name of *YHWH*.

This interpretation of the Old Testament name of God would not be accepted today, but its theological importance for Calvin was that it made the Son (and by implication the Holy Spirit) *autotheos* ("God-in-himself")

[59] Calvin, *Institutio* 1.13.3.
[60] Ibid., 1.13.18.
[61] Ibid., 1.13.9, 20.

in the same way as the Father.[62] This doctrine became typical of him and was followed by what would later be considered to be mainstream Reformed theology, but it was strongly opposed by Roman Catholics, by Lutherans, and even by a number of Reformed theologians, particularly among the Arminians and Remonstrants of the seventeenth century.[63] Yet Calvin himself was convinced that he was doing no more than following the teaching of Augustine, which he believed was based on the clear testimony of Scripture. Augustine had stated that "Christ with respect to himself is called God, but with respect to the Father, he is called the Son."[64] Calvin echoed this as follows:

> When we speak simply of the Son without regard to the Father, we well and properly declare him to be of himself, and for this reason we call him the sole beginning. But when we mark the relation that he has with the Father, we rightly make the Father the beginning of the Son. The whole fifth book of Augustine's *De Trinitate* is concerned with explaining this. It is much safer to stop with that relation that Augustine sets forth than to wander into many ephemeral speculations by trying to penetrate the divine mystery too subtly.[65]

Calvin backed up his argument by the logical assertion that if only the Father is *autotheos*, then any divine attribute possessed by the other persons must derive from him and not be held by the Son and the Holy Spirit in their own right. In that case, their attributes would necessarily be inferior to those of the Father, since they would not possess the absolute quality inherent in divinity. Valentino Gentile (1520?–1566) had tried to moderate Servetus's views by saying that the Father was the *essentiator* ("essence-giver") who bestowed his being on the Son and on the Holy Spirit, but Calvin pointed out that this was a false solution that solved nothing.[66] The divine essence is either absolute or else it is not divine—whatever is communicated to another person is by definition inferior to it.

One of the difficulties that Calvin had to face was that his insistence on the idea that the Son and the Holy Spirit were *autotheos* in the same way as the Father left others with the impression that he was denying the Son's eternal

[62] This point was brought out by Benjamin B. Warfield, "Calvin's Doctrine of the Trinity" in *Princeton Theological Review* 7/4 (1909): 553–652; reprinted in Samuel G. Craig, ed., *Calvin and Augustine* (Philadelphia: Presbyterian & Reformed, 1956), 189–284. For a recent reassessment of Warfield, see Brannon Ellis, *Calvin, Classical Trinitarianism, and the Aseity of the Son* (Oxford: Oxford University Press, 2012), 4–11.

[63] See Ellis, *Calvin*, 37–196, for a detailed discussion of the different options.

[64] Augustine of Hippo, *Enarrationes in Psalmos* 109 (110): 13 (PL 37, col. 1457), quoted in Calvin, *Institutio* 1.13.19.

[65] Calvin, *Institutio* 1.13.19.

[66] Ibid., 1.13.23. For Gentile's confession of faith, see *Calvini opera*, IX, in *Corpus Reformatorum*, ed. G. Baum, E. Cunitz, and E. Reuss (Braunschweig: C. A. Schwetschke und Sohn, 1863–1900), XXXVII:393.

generation (and by implication, the Holy Spirit's eternal procession too).[67] This misunderstanding was based on a fundamental inability to distinguish the two modes of discourse in God—the one personal and the other essential. Classical Trinitarian orthodoxy had always said that the Son was eternally generated from the Father as a person, but that as a substance or being he was fully God. It was not that distinction that caused the problem, but Calvin's insistence that the Son's personal generation had nothing to do with his possession of the divine essence. Most people had always assumed that when the Father begat the Son he communicated the divine essence to him, just as happens in human birth. A child's human nature is the same as that of his parents, but it is also derived from them, and this is how "eternal generation" was most naturally understood.

Calvin denied that. As he believed, the Son was fully and eternally in possession of the divine essence in his own right, or *a se ipso* ("from himself"), as this was expressed in Latin. He argued that this "aseity" of the Son was not only biblical, but that it was also the only way that an essential subordination of the Son to the Father could be avoided. What Calvin was trying to say was that the language of generation and procession described personal relationship and not essential origin. In eternity, neither generation nor procession could have any temporal meaning, so these words described a permanent state of affairs and not a process by which the Father somehow extended his being to the Son and the Holy Spirit. It was a logical deduction from existing orthodoxy, but Calvin's clear separation of essence from personal relation was a development of earlier tradition that many of his contemporaries interpreted as a departure from it.

Calvin's originality in this respect was strongly influenced by his battles against the anti-Trinitarians of his time. In his view, for the traditionally orthodox to say that the Father alone was *autotheos* was to play into the hands of these heretics, because they said exactly the same thing. Indeed, on their own terms, the heretics would be justified if such a view were to be adopted by the orthodox, because if the Son and the Holy Spirit were not *autotheos*, they could not be God at all. It would then matter very little whether the heretics were neo-Arians, neo-Sabellians (modalists), or whatever, because the fundamental point that held Trinitarian orthodoxy together would have been conceded in advance.

These disputes seem somewhat arcane to us today, but they are of great importance because they reveal how men like Servetus and Gentile were fashioning

[67] See Ellis, *Calvin*, 39–50, with respect to Calvin's dispute with Pierre Caroli (1480–1545?) over this point.

a peculiarly modern view of God as the Father alone. Such a doctrine, if accepted, would mean that the Son was essentially no different from any believer, particularly if it were agreed that he had become a man in Jesus Christ. The end result would have been a neo-adoptianism, which Calvin was determined to avoid. What Calvin did was reveal a weakness in classical orthodoxy as it was generally understood in his time. This is clear from the way he was criticized by Robert Bellarmine (1542–1621), a strong defender of Roman Catholicism who was nevertheless usually fair to his Protestant opponents and willing to regard them as orthodox as far as he could. Bellarmine thought that Calvin had taught that "Christ is God of himself (*a se ipso*) and not from the Father."[68]

This was a half-truth that revealed Bellarmine's difficulty in understanding what Calvin meant. For Bellarmine, it was inconceivable that Christ could be *both* God in himself *and* God from the Father also, because he thought that belief in the eternal generation of the Son necessitated belief in a derived divine essence. But at the same time, Bellarmine recognized that Calvin confessed that there was only one divine being and so, whatever he meant by Christ being God in himself, it did not imply that there were three distinct gods. His conclusion was that Calvin was orthodox in intention but that his way of expressing this was unfortunate and open to misunderstanding.

Bellarmine's moderate response stands in contrast to the teaching of Jacob Arminius, who not only dissented from Calvin but said so in no uncertain terms:

> The Son of God is not called by the ancient fathers "God from himself" and this is a dangerous expression. For *autotheos* properly signifies that the Son does not have the divine essence from another person. But it is by a catachresis [i.e., improperly] that the essence which the Son has is not from another. . . . The divine essence is communicated to the Son by the Father, and this properly and truly. So it is wrongly asserted "that the divine essence is indeed properly said to be common to the Son and to the Father, but is improperly said to be communicated."[69] For it is not common to both except in reference to its being communicated.[70]

Denial of the Son's aseity became a hallmark of Arminianism, and in its own time it was probably even more important than the questions about predestination and salvation that were so famously disputed at the Synod of Dort.

[68] R. Bellarmine, "*De Christo*" 2.19, in *Disputationes . . . de controversiis Christianae fidei adversus huius temporis haereticos*, 3 vols. (Ingolstadt: D. Sartorius, 1586–1593), 1:217.

[69] A quotation from Lucas Trelcatius, *Scholastica et methodica locorum communium sacrae theologiae institutio* (London: J. Bill, 1604), II, fo. 18r. Trelcatius (1573–1607) was a prominent defender of Calvin's doctrine of the Son's aseity. For a discussion of his position, see Ellis, *Calvin*, 176–183.

[70] Jacobus Arminius, *Certain Articles to Be Diligently Examined and Weighed*, 3.1–2, in *Works*, 2:707–708.

As evidence for this, we may quote Simon Episcopius (1583–1643), a disciple of Arminius who led the Remonstrants at the Synod. As he put it,

> The Father alone possesses the divine nature and those divine attributes of himself (or of no one else) but the Son and the Holy Spirit [possess them] of the Father, and so the Father is the source and origin of the whole divinity that is in the Son and the Holy Spirit. This is brought out not merely in the terms themselves, or in the words "Son" and "Holy Spirit," which convey subordination (by generation and spiration) in their most basic meaning, but also constantly in the expressions used in Holy Scripture.[71]

What Episcopius feared was that any denial that the divine nature was communicated by the Father to the other persons would inevitably lead to tritheism, which Bellarmine had acknowledged was not what Calvin taught. In Episcopius's words,

> Those who argue that the divine nature is common to the Son and the Holy Spirit, along with the Father, and is not communicated [to them by the Father], seem to me to err dangerously, for not only does their view take away the essential property of the generation of the Son and of the procession of the Holy Spirit, but it also introduces a collaterality of the persons, which makes it necessary for them to be recognized as three gods.[72]

The alternative to this was worked out by Herman Alexander Röell (1653–1718), a Dutch theologian who represented the last phase of Reformed orthodoxy and showed what could happen to it when it tried to come to terms with contemporary philosophical developments. Röell rejected the Remonstrants' latent subordinationism in favor of Calvin's doctrine of aseity, but unlike Calvin, he denied the existence of any personal relations in God. For him, the divine persons were simply there as part of God's eternal being and could not be distinguished from one another except in the context of their temporal mission. In other words, God the Son was revealed in Jesus Christ but had no distinct existence apart from that. Röell insisted that he remained a Trinitarian, but if personal distinctions did not count for anything, it is hard to see what that might mean. At the very least, his followers were being prepared to accept a practical if not a theoretical unitarianism, and it is to that development that we must now turn.

[71] Simon Episcopius, *Institutiones theologicae*, in *Opera theologica*, 2 vols. (Amsterdam: J. Blaeu, 1650–1665), 1:4.2.32.
[72] Ibid., 1:4.2.32.

The Emergence of Unitarianism

Among the radical thinkers who appeared in the wake of the Reformation were the Socinians, named for two Italians, Lelio Sozzini (1525–1562) and his nephew Fausto (1539–1604), whose doctrines formed the basis of their beliefs. Coming from a long line of jurists, the Sozzinis tackled theological questions from the standpoint of Roman law as opposed to the mixed traditions of Neoplatonic and Aristotelian philosophy that had largely shaped the medieval Western tradition. Taking a pragmatic approach to questions of justice, they rejected the idea that Adam had been created righteous and immortal, and had fallen because of his disobedience to the command of God. On the contrary, they thought that he had been created mortal and with no natural virtue, since (in their eyes) virtue could only be the result of a voluntary choice. What Adam had was reason and a will to make the right decisions if he chose to do so, but he also possessed desires that led him in a purely self-seeking direction. The "fall" was therefore his decision to follow his desires rather than choose the path of virtuous self-sacrifice. Left to his own devices, Adam's choice was understandable because he had no innate knowledge of God. That could come only from divine revelation, which was not given at creation, was only partially communicated in the Old Testament, and was not fully manifested until the coming of Jesus Christ.[73] But even as this revelation was not innate in created man, so it was not forced on him by God—it was always a matter of human choice, and therefore virtuous. This choice was an act of the rational will, and therefore what was chosen was subject to the dictates of reason, which excluded irrational concepts like the Trinity.

To people who relied on the Roman legal tradition as the Sozzinis did, the notion that there were three persons in the one God made no sense. As an intelligent agent, God could certainly be described as a "person" (as defined by Roman law), but only as one, not three, because he is a single being. The so-called "natural law" was not morally perfect, because such perfection depended on virtuous living and was not a direct gift from God to Adam. The laws of nature had nothing to do with divine revelation, and so human justice, including the rule of the secular state, lay outside the competence of any religious authority. In a world where it was universally believed that public morality depended on religious belief and that atheism was the root of crime, these opinions were deeply subversive, but at a time when religious belief was a sub-

[73] Faustus Socinus, *De statu primi hominis ante lapsum disputatio* (Raków: Sternaciani, 1610), also in *Fausti Socini Senensis opera omnia*, 2 vols. (Amsterdam: Irenicus Philalethius, 1666–1668), 2:253–369. The best modern study, which contains a valuable overview of recent scholarship, is S. Mortimer, *Reason and Religion in the English Revolution: The Challenge of Socinianism* (Cambridge: Cambridge University Press, 2010).

ject of controversy resulting in deep social and political division, the conviction that it must be true was inevitably weakened. What the Sozzinis offered was a basis for human society based not on revealed truth but on the findings of a supposedly objective reason with which men of all faiths and none could agree.

In pursuing their aim, the Sozzinis were aided by the Renaissance insistence on careful exegesis of the original Hebrew and Greek texts of the Bible, unencumbered by later accretions. The doctrine of the Trinity, elaborated as it had been at the ecumenical councils of the fourth and fifth centuries and canonized in the Athanasian Creed, was a prime candidate for deconstruction. Traditional commentators had focused on John's Gospel as biblical proof for the deity of the three persons of the Godhead, interpreting such phrases as "in the beginning was the Word"[74] as referring to the eternal generation of the Son. But in his commentary on this passage, Fausto Sozzini said,

> Those who in this place want to have the word "beginning" designate the eternity of Christ stand convicted of the most egregious error from the mere fact that their opinion is supported by no authority in either the New Testament or the Old. As a matter of fact, you will not find "beginning" used for eternity anywhere in the Scriptures. On this account, we maintain that the word "beginning" in this passage refers not to eternity, but to the order of the thing that John is writing about—Jesus Christ as the beloved son of God; in this matter imitating Moses, who when writing his history, made the word "beginning" the opening of Genesis 1:1.[75]

The Socinians were persecuted for their unorthodox beliefs, but they were able to find refuge in Transylvania and Poland, where a mixed religious population and weak local governments allowed a sect like theirs to flourish.[76] Working from Raków in Poland, they produced the so-called *Racovian Catechism*, which outlined their views and was soon translated from the original Polish into Latin, and from there into all the major languages of Europe.[77] The *Catechism* was almost universally censured, but the vehemence of the attacks against it revealed the insecurity that so many of its readers felt when they read it. In spite of themselves, leading thinkers were attracted to at least some of its

[74] John 1:1.

[75] F. Socinus, *Explicatio primae partis primi capitis Iohannis, in est usquae ad versum 15*, in *Opera omnia*, 1:77–78.

[76] Transylvania was a semi-independent principality under Ottoman Turkish (and therefore Muslim) suzerainty, which allowed Unitarians to acquire legal standing. Poland was an aristocratic republic with an elected king and no overall religious majority population. For sources relating to Socinianism in Poland, see *Myśl ariańska w Polsce XVII wieku: antologia tekstów*, ed. Zbigniew Ogonowski (Wroclaw: Zakład Narodowy im. Ossolińskich, 1991).

[77] The first English translation was dedicated to King James I (VI), who ordered it to be burned. It was retranslated and published as *The Racovian cathechisme* (Amsterdam: B. Janz, 1652). The most widely used version today is the translation by Thomas Rees, published as *The Racovian Cathechism* (London: Longman, Hurst, Rees, Orme, & Brown, 1818). The denial of the Trinity is found in section 3.1.

ideas, and it exercised an influence out of all proportion to the actual numbers of Socinians. In the Netherlands, it was admired by the Remonstrants, who were attracted to its advocacy of free will in religious matters. Even the jurist Hugo Grotius (1583–1645), though an opponent of Socinianism, was affected by the Socinian argument that the natural law was not morally perfect and could be developed and adapted to meet different needs.[78]

The relationship between Arminius, his followers, and the Socinians was a complex one. At one level, they had little in common, not least because Arminius believed in a covenant of grace that could be traced all the way back to Adam, whereas Fausto Sozzini saw nothing of grace in the Old Testament and believed that only those who put their faith in Christ's new covenant could be saved.[79] But both Simon Episcopius and Hugo Grotius, who as Remonstrants were widely regarded as heirs of Arminius, tended to discount the historical covenant and place great weight on the teaching of Christ as something entirely new. They also tended to think in terms of historical development in a way that had not been true before. Instead of a natural moral law that existed in eternity, even if it was applied (and broken) in different ways because of human sinfulness, Grotius came to believe that all law had evolved over time and that Christ had played a key role in this. Not only had he introduced new (and higher) principles of moral conduct, he had also established a particular form of church government (episcopalianism, as it happened), which gave it divine sanction. It was therefore not possible, as he had previously thought and as Reformed theology had generally taught, for the church to be ordered by the civil authorities according to whatever form best suited them. In other words, the government of the church lay outside the control of the state, just as the affairs of the state had no connection with the church.

This theoretical separation between the temporal and the spiritual was particularly noticeable in the way that Grotius read the Bible. Christ had come to bring moral and spiritual principles that were of eternal worth and therefore essentially independent of time and space, but the Bible was a historical record, not so much of divine revelation itself (which was timeless) but of the ways in which it had been given over the centuries. This meant that it was necessary to study the human author of each book of the Bible and his historical circumstances, in order to gain the perspective needed to discover the Word of God in the text. Grotius followed this idea up by writing commentaries that started from the human point of view and sought to explain believers' contact with (and relationship to) God, rather than with God and his declarations to

78 On Grotius, see Mortimer, *Reason and Religion*, 26–33.
79 See Mortimer, *Reason and Religion*, 120–123.

man. It was the beginning of historical, as opposed to purely theological, commentary writing, though of course Grotius did not make that distinction—to him, history *was* theology, and vice versa.[80] Regarded as a curiosity at the time, Grotius's approach was to become standard in modern commentary writing, which, in this respect at least, owes more to the Sozzinis than it does to Luther or Calvin.

The defeat of the Remonstrants in the Netherlands struck a blow at Socinian influence there, but it proved to be only temporary, as the later works of Grotius showed. It was probably because of the complex relationship between Socinianism and the Arminian heritage that the two were often conflated in the popular mind, especially in England, where the opponents of the reigning Calvinist ideology were often branded "Arminian" even though they had little in common with the historical Arminius and were more like the much-reviled Socinians.

By the 1630s Socinian ideas were starting to penetrate England, where they would be given a good airing in the theologically charged climate that would eventually lead to civil war. As in the Netherlands, we are once again faced with a picture of all but universal rejection of Socinian ideas, combined with an appropriation of those elements of Socinian thought that seemed to be most congenial and useful in the circumstances. This became clear in the work of William Chillingworth (1602–1644), whose search for religious certainty led him from Calvinism to Roman Catholicism and back to faith in the Bible alone as "the religion of Protestants."[81] Chillingworth wrote in answer to the Jesuit Edward Knott (1582–1656), a polemicist who had recently published a book asserting that there could be no salvation outside the Roman communion.[82] This gave it a prestige and an audience that it would otherwise not have obtained and inadvertently helped to spread Socinian principles on which Chillingworth's arguments were often based.[83]

Chillingworth was not a Socinian himself, but like them he believed that everything necessary to Christian faith was contained in Scripture, which revealed a law of Christ higher than that of nature, that men were free to accept or reject as they chose. This made him anti-Puritan as well as anti-Catholic, and in the circumstances of approaching civil war, that was much more important. Chillingworth worked under the patronage of Lord Falkland, whose

[80] Hugo Grotius, *Annotationes in libros Evangeliorum* (Amsterdam: J. & C. Blaeu, 1641); *Hugonis Grotii annotata in Vetus Testamentum*, 3 vols. (Paris: Sébastien Cramoisy, 1644).
[81] William Chillingworth, *The Religion of Protestants a Safe Way to Salvation* (Oxford: Leonard Lichfield, 1638).
[82] Eward Knott, *Mercy and Truth: Or Charity Maintayned by Catholiques* (Saint Omer: English College Press, 1634).
[83] See Mortimer, *Reason and Religion*, 63–82, for an extended discussion of Chillingworth's relationship to (and dependence on) Socinian ideas.

home at Great Tew became the center of a "reasoned" approach to the social and religious questions that threatened to tear England apart. The Great Tew circle imagined that it was above the fray, and some historians have interpreted them that way, but in reality they came down on the royalist (anti-Puritan) side when war finally broke out. Their social status probably made that inevitable, but their religious and political opinions also determined their decision. The Puritans wanted what they called a "godly commonwealth," one in which the law of Christ and the law of the land would merge into one, whereas their opponents wanted to keep Christ's commandments separate (and on a higher plane) from the law of the state. Great Tew was just outside Oxford, and when the king was forced to move to the city in 1642, it was easy for the ideas of the one to merge with the cause of the other. Its great spokesman was Henry Hammond (1605–1660), an Anglican clergyman whose books and tracts, and especially his *Practicall Catechisme*, in which he put his main ideas into practice, were extremely popular and went through many editions in the 1640s.[84]

According to Hammond, Jesus Christ had come as a moral teacher who led Israel toward a higher understanding of God. The old law was in no sense a message of salvation, which meant that Christ's death was not an atoning sacrifice. Mankind was not guilty of having broken the commands of God—only ignorant and imperfect. The new law of Christ gave believers an opportunity to improve themselves by following it. The result was that the anti-Puritan party adopted a Socinian view of the world, which, in the eyes of those who adopted it, made room for virtuous living and its rewards—the Protestant equivalent of salvation by works. That in turn was meant to encourage social responsibility and civic order, both of which were breaking down in the crucible of war and theological pluralism (that is, anarchy) that Puritanism brought in its wake. The belief that Christ had established a new law, including a church with its own hierarchy, enabled Hammond to argue that the bishops of his day were divinely appointed ministers of God, thereby reinforcing the traditional form of church government even as its doctrine of salvation by grace through faith (and not by works) was being eviscerated. In this respect, Hammond and his followers were not at all Socinian and could escape that charge by pointing to their devotion to the established order. The ancient forms were preserved but their substance was abandoned, a combination that allowed new and unorthodox ideas to creep into the Church of England without serious opposition.

Once this way of thinking established itself, it was only a short step toward theological relativism, even though many in the royalist camp would have been

[84] The *Practicall Catechisme* appeared first at Oxford in 1644 or 1645, but the standard edition was the one issued in 1646 as *Large Additions to the Practical Catechisme* (London: M. F. for R. Royston, 1646).

horrified at the thought. Hammond himself remained formally orthodox, but others saw where his teaching would lead and accused him of Socinianism.[85] If the Bible did not teach a developed doctrine of the Trinity (of the kind found in the ancient creeds), then even if there was some truth in it, it was of little practical importance and could not be imposed on Christians as an essential mark of faith. The fact that it made no logical sense was an additional reason to ignore it, and before long, "Protestantism" was no longer being defined in traditional theological terms. More than that, the Bible was being used as evidence *against* theology rather than as support *for* it, driving a wedge between God's Word and man's interpretation of it that would lead truly pious minds to choose the former and reject the latter. Calvin could not have imagined a profession of *sola Scriptura* that did not affirm the Trinity, but a century later that had become possible, and perhaps even desirable, if not absolutely necessary.

Seen in the context of the evolving theology of the seventeenth century, Henry Hammond appears to have been torn by contradictory impulses. On the one hand, he wanted to believe that Christianity was a freely chosen pathway to self-improvement, but at the same time he upheld the claims of the established church and insisted that salvation could be obtained only by belonging to it. In spite of himself, he clung to the doctrine of original sin (and therefore to the universal need for redemption), although this left him with no explanation for the fact that the gospel had not been revealed to every human being, so that free choice was not a practical option for them. Neither was it an option for babies who died in infancy.

These anomalies were quickly spotted by Jeremy Taylor, who ironed them out by rejecting original sin and adopting a more consistent free-will approach. This brought him closer to Socinianism, but he never went all the way. Whereas the Sozzinis had drawn a firm line between natural law, which they regarded as inferior and expendable, and the law of Christ, Taylor combined the two into one—to him, what Christ taught was the natural law and no more. What was different about Jesus was not what he taught about the law but what he had to say about the next life. Those who did good would be rewarded, but those who did not would be punished—a doctrine that Taylor thought would provide sufficient incentive for doing good works here on earth.[86] In this form, a modified Socinianism would exert a strong appeal among post-Puritan English divines and form the basis of what would come to be known as "latitudinarianism," or "broad-mindedness."[87]

---

[85] See Mortimer, *Reason and Religion*, 123–128.

[86] See ibid., 137–146.

[87] See Isabel Rivers, *Reason, Grace, and Sentiment: A Study of the Language of Religion, Grace, and Ethics in England 1660–1780*, 2 vols. (Cambridge: Cambridge University Press, 1991–2000), 1:66–77.

For all the attractiveness of Socinian ideas, however, the mainline churches could not embrace them wholeheartedly. Quite apart from the opposition of the orthodox, the weight of liturgical tradition was too strong to be overturned. This obstacle to change was particularly evident in the case of the Trinity, which logically should have been abandoned but was not. For the Socinians, anti-Trinitarianism lay at the root of their theological system. This had been pointed out by Johan Crell (1590–1633), an early convert to Socinianism from Lutheranism, whose major work, *De Deo uno Patre* (*The One God the Father*), appeared in 1631.[88] Crell argued that it was impossible to separate a person from its being (essence), which made the doctrine of the Trinity inconceivable. Jesus Christ was for him no more than a human being to whom God had delegated magisterial authority, but not his divine essence. Crell's assertions provoked a number of refutations, but some of these did little more than reveal the weakness of the Trinitarian case. Johannes Bisterfeld (1605–1655), for example, was among the earliest of Crell's opponents, but his argument that the world was inherently Trinitarian in nature was based on a peculiar form of Neoplatonism, not on the Bible, and it soon provoked equally stringent opposition from orthodox theologians like Abraham Calovius (1612–1686).[89]

The attempt to defend the Trinity on the basis of philosophy rather than Scripture played into the hands of the Socinians, and before long there were theologians who were advocating that the doctrine should be dropped because it was unscriptural and divisive. That was the position taken by the Remonstrant Stephanus Curcellaeus (1586–1659), who was supported by Hugo Grotius, at least as far as biblical interpretation was concerned. Matters were not made easier by Roman Catholic apologists who, sensing the embarrassment of Protestants who were trying to argue for the Trinity on the basis of Scripture alone, insisted that the doctrine could be maintained only by appealing to the authority of the church, which had formulated it.[90] Perhaps the oddest Trinitarian defense of all was that of Thomas Hobbes (1588–1679), who rejected the language of Aristotelian metaphysics and redefined "person" to mean a role that could be adopted (or delegated) by an individual in order to serve a particular purpose. As Hobbes saw it, God had done this three times—in Moses, in Christ, and in the apostles—thereby making him

[88] Jan Crell, *De Deo uno Patre*, 2 vols. (Raków: Sternaciani, 1631).

[89] Johannes Bisterfeld, *De uno Deo, Patre, Filio et Spiritu Sancto, mysterium pietatis* (Leiden: Elsevier, 1639). Calovius's refutation is found in a letter he wrote to the Socinian Martin Ruar. It can be found in P. Tannery and Cornelis De Waard, eds., *Correspondance du Père Marin Mersenne*, 17 vols. (Paris: Presses Universitaires de France, 1932–1988), 10:742–743.

[90] That was the line taken by the Jesuit Denis Petau, or Petavius (1583–1652), and followed by many subsequent Roman Catholic apologists. See Sarah Mortimer, *Reason and Religion*, 149–157, for the evidence.

a Trinity of "persons."[91] This was really a form of modalism, which reveals the extremities in which even defenders of the Trinity found themselves when attacked by men like Crell.

It should be said, however, that not all defenders of the Trinity argued for their position on rational or philosophical lines that would sooner or later get them into embarrassing difficulty. John Owen, for example, who was perhaps the greatest exponent of the doctrine in seventeenth-century England, appealed to personal experience in a way that recalled the Greek fathers of the church, with whose writings he and many of his contemporaries were deeply familiar. As Owen explained,

> When we bring our prayers to God the Father and end them in the name of Jesus Christ, yet the Son is no less invocated and worshiped in the beginning than the Father, though he be peculiarly mentioned as *Mediator* in the close, not as Son to himself but as Mediator of the whole Trinity, or God in Trinity. . . . For the Son and the Holy Ghost are no less worshiped in our access to God than the Father himself. . . . So that when, by the distinct dispensation of the Trinity, and every person, . . . by what name soever, of Father, Son, or Holy Ghost, we invocate him.[92]

Owen's apologetic was closely connected with traditional Christian spirituality, which is one reason why it has survived the test of time. Socinianism's appeal to his contemporaries was that it combined reliance on the power of reason with an affirmation of the supreme authority of Scripture, which it thought was entirely reasonable. To their minds, there was no need to indulge in mystical contemplation that went beyond scientific evidence and "proof," because as they understood it, that made a nonsense of the whole concept of revelation. From a purely rational standpoint, it made no sense to say that God should be thought of as three distinct persons, and so we should not do so. The Bible did not use the term "person," so clear-headed people who accepted the principle of *sola Scriptura* were free to follow the dictates of logic. In the words of John Biddle (1615–1662), who was probably the translator of the Racovian catechism in its 1652 edition,

[91] Thomas Hobbes, *Leviathan*, ed. Richard Tuck (Cambridge: Cambridge University Press, 1991), 338–342. The first edition appeared in 1651.

[92] John Owen, *Of Communion with God the Father, Sonne, and Holy Ghost, Each Person Distinctly, in Love, Grace, and Consolation* (Oxford: A. Lichfield, 1657), 3.8, 343; also in *The Works of John Owen*, 16 vols. (Edinburgh: Banner of Truth, 1965), 2:3.8, 269. Compare this with Gregory of Nazianzus, *Orato de sancto baptismati*, 40.41: "No sooner do I conceive of the One than I am illumined by the splendor of the three; no sooner do I distinguish them than I am carried back to the One. When I think of any one of the three I think of him as the whole. . . . I cannot grasp the greatness of that one so as to attribute a greater greatness to the rest. When I contemplate the three together I see but one torch, and cannot divide or measure the undivided light."

> By "person," I understand, as philosophers do, *suppositum intelligens*, that is, an intellectual substance complete, and not a mood or subsistence; which are fantastical and senseless terms, brought in to cozen the simple.[93]

Biddle was not a Socinian, as is clear from the fact that his notion of "person" was rooted in philosophy rather than in law, but it made little difference in practice. Like the Socinians, he was convinced that the idea of the Trinity was a medieval corruption of the true faith of Christ. In his words,

> For though Luther and Calvin deserve much praise for the pains they took in cleansing our religion from sundry idolatrous pollutions of the Roman Anti-Christ, yet are the dregs still left behind—I mean the crass opinion touching three persons in God. Which error not only made way for those pollutions, but lying at the bottom, corrupteth almost the whole religion.[94]

According to Biddle, God was a single divine person, Christ was a single human person who did the will of God and was rewarded by being raised from the dead, and the Holy Spirit was a force, not a person at all. None of this was meant to discount the reality of salvation. On the contrary, Biddle and others like him thought they were affirming the gospel with a clarity that had become obscured by speculation about a Trinity of persons. Biddle's thought reflected not only the influence of Socinianism but also the growing tendency to think of a "person" in individual rather than in relational terms. The word was increasingly being used to refer to the mental, moral, and spiritual capacities of each human being, and not in the communal way that had characterized earlier usage. To put it differently, in classical Christian theology it was impossible for only one person to exist, because persons by definition have relations with other persons. But in Biddle's scheme of things, if God were truly one and sovereign over all existing things, he could only be a single person, since anything else would destroy his uniqueness. In Biddle's mental universe, the absolute could not be relative at the same time, even within itself.

In the early seventeenth century, Socinianism became an almost mythical threat and was constantly attacked by the leading theologians of the time, even when it was hard to detect. That gave it a status and a hearing that it might not otherwise have had and made it attractive to people who were unhappy with the

[93] John Biddle, *XII Arguments Drawn out of the Scripture*, in *The Apostolical and True Opinion concerning the Holy Trinity* (London: J. C., 1653). On the reedition of the *Catechism* and the problems it caused, see Mortimer, *Reason and Religion*, 165–167. On Biddle and his fellow Unitarians, see Paul C. H. Lim, *Mystery Unveiled: The Crisis of the Trinity in Early Modern England* (Oxford: Oxford University Press, 2012).

[94] John Biddle, *A Confession of Faith Touching the Holy Trinity, according to the Scripture* (London: publisher unknown, 1648), preface, 2–3.

constant quarreling (as they saw it) among men who all supposedly accepted the same infallible Bible. The strength of the Sozzinis was their belief in the power and authority of human reason, which they claimed was objective and supported their views. Unencumbered by the dubious claims of revelation, and basing themselves on reason alone (or so they thought), the Socinians believed that they could create a viable religion that combined spiritual experience with moral behavior. To them, Jesus was a model of this—not God in human flesh, but an insightful man who led the way toward a higher and purer form of morality. They also benefited from the discomfiture of their opponents, who found it difficult to explain a doctrine that they regarded as a mystery beyond human comprehension. In the form professed by the church, the doctrine of the Trinity could not be traced back beyond the fourth century, making it difficult to defend in the context of a *sola Scriptura* approach to theology and almost impossible to impose as a belief that was necessary for salvation. As a result, the orthodox were defeated as much by the weaknesses inherent in their own argument as by any arguments from Socinian or crypto-Socinian positions.[95]

In its original form, Socinianism had largely disappeared by the mid-seventeenth century, but its theological legacy was inherited by freethinkers, who became the first modern Unitarians. There were many reasons why rationalistic thinking triumphed over the various "orthodoxies" that dominated late-seventeenth-century theology, but one of them that should not be overlooked was that many theologians were attracted to rationalism and were prepared to use its methods in defense of their own beliefs. Richard Baxter, for example, had this to say about the Trinity:

> The essential immanent acts of God are three: 1. *Sibi vivere*, or to be essential active life in himself; 2. *Se intelligere*, to know himself; 3. *Se amare*, or to be *amor sui*. . . . I have elsewhere showed that many of them, and other divines, do take the last named immanent acts in God to be the same with the three persons or subsistences, even the three divine principles. . . . All that I say here is that, seeing the Trinity of divine principles (or formal essentialities) and the threefold act are so certainly evident to natural reason itself that no understanding person can deny them, we have no reason to think the Trinity of eternal subsistences incredible and a thing that the Christian faith is to be suspected for, but quite the contrary, though they are mysteries above our reach (as all of God is . . .).[96]

[95] See, for example, Francis Cheynell, *The Divine Triunity of the Father, Son, and Holy Spirit* (London: T. R & E. M., 1650). Cheynell wrote a spirited defense of the Trinity but it failed to persuade his opponents or attract much support from those who shared his concerns.

[96] Richard Baxter, *Catholick Theologie* (London: Robert White for Nevill Simmons, 1675), 1.3.25, 27. Carl Trueman attributes this incipient rationalism to the influence of the Italian radical thinker Tommaso Campanella (1568–

Socinianism, or rather its Unitarian offspring, gained the hearing it did and almost destroyed Trinitarian orthodoxy in late seventeenth-century England, not because of its intrinsic merits (which were few) but because the mind-set that it reflected was already present and growing in the leading theologians of the time.[97] As Thomas Aquinas had realized, a purely philosophical theology would have to focus on the oneness of God and would therefore probably end up as unitarian by default, but by 1700 any theological formulation that could not be justified by reason was regarded as untenable, not just because it was thought to be "obscurantist" but because it was also thought to be incompatible with Scripture, which made its appeal to the human mind and was therefore thought to be eminently rational.

Ironic though it must seem, Unitarians and Trinitarians held the same high view of the Bible and agreed about how it was to be interpreted—both were advocates of the Reformation principle of *sola Scriptura*. Where they differed was that Unitarians read the biblical text superficially—there was no explicit mention of the Trinity in it, therefore it did not teach such a doctrine. Trinitarians, on the other hand, appealed to Scripture's deeper sense, arguing that although the words themselves were not to be found in the text, it could not be coherently interpreted without recourse to such terminology. The traditional terms were not obligatory (because they were not strictly "scriptural"), but failing a better alternative, they were the best thing available.

Nevertheless, there was more to the push toward a rationalistic theology in the late seventeenth century than mere philosophical abstraction. Equally important, particularly in the longer term, was the developing notion of the "person" as a conscious subject. This can be traced back to René Descartes (1596–1650), whose famous "I think, therefore I am" (*cogito, ergo sum*) became the slogan of the new way of thinking, and within a generation it had become almost a standard definition of the term "person."[98] The measure of its success came in 1690, when William Sherlock (1641?–1707) used it in an attempt to defend Trinitarian orthodoxy against contemporary detractors of the doctrine. The result was a disaster, because Sherlock effectively conceded the case to his opponents.[99] There could not be three centers of consciousness in

1639). See "A Small Step towards Rationalism: The Impact of the Metaphysics of Tommaso Campanella on the Theology of Richard Baxter," in Carl R. Trueman and R. Scott Clark, eds., *Protestant Scholasticism: Essays in Reassessment* (Carlisle: Paternoster, 1999), 181–195.

[97] See Philip Dixon, *Nice and Hot Disputes: The Doctrine of the Trinity in the Seventeenth Century* (London: T & T Clark, 2003).

[98] Ibid., 109–116.

[99] William Sherlock, *A Vindication of the Doctrine of the Holy and Ever-blessed Trinity and the Incarnation of the Son of God: Occasioned by the Brief Notes on the Creed of St. Athanasius and the Brief History of the Unitarians, or Socinians, as Containing an Answer to Both* (London: W. Rogers, 1690).

the one God, and if that is what a "person" was supposed to be, then he could be only one person and not three. Sherlock never intended it, but the triumph of his definition ruined his argument. Moreover, it was a definition that was to prove very enduring and is still used today by people who want to demonstrate that the classical doctrine of the Trinity can no longer be defended by using a vocabulary that has changed its meaning.

Allied with this was the growing conviction among many that the differences between orthodox Trinitarians and Unitarians were overblown. Since Trinitarian language could not be found in Scripture, it was difficult to insist that it must be used as the only permissible interpretation of it. As Stephen Nye (1648–1719) wrote in the midst of a heated dispute in the 1690s,

> I am persuaded that the questions concerning the Trinity, the divinity of our Savior and the incarnation, so long controverted between the church and the Unitarians, are a strife, mostly about words and terms, not of things and realities.[100]

This view was contested by the defenders of traditional orthodoxy, but its attractiveness was increasingly appreciated, especially in university circles, where the persecution of new ideas was especially unwelcome. Some, like Isaac Newton (1642–1727) and John Locke (1632–1704), responded to this challenge by saying little or nothing about the Trinity. Newton wrote against the doctrine but then suppressed his book and did not allow it to be published.[101] Locke defended Christianity on the grounds of reason but ignored the Trinity completely—an eloquent statement at a time when the doctrine was at the center of theological controversy.[102]

Not everyone was able to escape so lightly, though. William Whiston (1667–1752), Lucasian Professor of Mathematics at Cambridge, was censured for his latent Arianism and deprived of his position in 1710, after which he published a lengthy defense of his views, which he claimed were those of the early church.[103] Samuel Clarke (1675–1729) was even less lucky. After publishing *The Scripture Doctrine of the Trinity* in 1712, he was put on trial and condemned for heresy. He lost his teaching post but was spared any further punishment by the intervention of the archbishop of Canterbury, who protected him.[104] His repudiation of traditional orthodoxy was perfectly clear:

---

[100] Stephen Nye, *The Agreement of the Unitarians with the Catholic Church* (London?: publisher unknown, 1697).
[101] See J. Force and Richard Popkin, *Essays on the Context, Nature, and Influence of Isaac Newton's Theology* (Dordrecht: Kluwer, 1990).
[102] John Locke, *The Reasonableness of Christianity* (London: Awnsham & John Churchill, 1695).
[103] William Whiston, *Primitive Christianity Revived*, 4 vols. (London: privately printed, 1711).
[104] S. Clarke, *The Scripture Doctrine of the Trinity* (London: James Knapton, 1712). See Dixon, *Nice and Hot Disputes*, 183–196, for the story.

> What the proper metaphysical nature, essence or substance of any of the divine persons is, the Scripture has nowhere at all declared, but describes and distinguishes them always by their personal characters, offices, powers and attributes. . . . All reasonings therefore (beyond what is strictly demonstrable by the most evident and undeniable light of nature) deduced from their supposed metaphysical nature, essence or substance, instead of their personal characters, offices, powers and attributes delivered in Scripture, are uncertain, and at best probably hypotheses.[105]

Following the general drift of his time, Clarke defined a "person" not as a substance but as an agent, making Trinitarianism just as untenable as Sherlock's idea of consciousness had done, but in this case, quite deliberately. But Clarke did not deny the saving work of Christ, nor did he discount the divine inspiration of Scripture. On the contrary, like the others who had gone before him, he believed that his own skepticism about Trinitarian language could only make these truths more important.

In 1719 the English Presbyterian church took the fateful decision to allow ministers to dissent from Trinitarianism on the ground that the doctrine was not absolutely clear from Scripture, and by the end of the eighteenth century it had dissolved into Unitarianism.[106] The Church of England was prevented from following suit by its status as the church established by law, but a growing number of its ministers had "mental reservations" about the Trinity and the matter was not pressed. Before long the doctrine of the Trinity appeared as something of an embarrassing anachronism, and the attempts of men like Daniel Waterland (1683–1740) to defend it, though competently argued, fell on deaf ears.[107] A new spirit was in the air, and although Unitarianism would not be officially tolerated within the established church, there would be no more persecutions for it either, and a *de facto* toleration soon became the order of the day.

---

[105] Clarke, *Scripture Doctrine*, 122–123.

[106] The standard history of Unitarianism is Earl M. Wilbur, *A History of Unitarianism in Transylvania, England, and America* (Boston: Beacon, 1952).

[107] Daniel Waterland, *A Vindication of Christ's Divinity* (Cambridge: Corn. Crownfield, 1719).

23

The Eclipse of Theology

The Cult of Reason

In the years around 1700, the Christian civilization of Western Europe was giving way to "secularization," meaning that the different churches and their theologies were no longer the determining factor in politics and society. In their place a new culture was emerging, one that tried to transcend the divisions brought about by the Reformation by ignoring them. State churches continued to exist, confessional orthodoxies remained compulsory in the universities and in government service, and dissenting minorities were still discriminated against, but in the intellectual salons that met in London, Amsterdam, and Paris, these things were increasingly discounted and derided as relics of an ignorant and superstitious past. Members of the privileged élite could say whatever they pleased and even get their work published, though often under assumed names and in books whose publishers were hard to trace. In the nature of things, these people were dissidents, and it soon became almost *de rigueur* for them to denounce everything the establishment represented. Orthodox religion was ridiculed, theology was condemned as nonsensical, and the clergy were either mocked for their corruption and hypocrisy or won over to these ideas. It must not be forgotten that a significant number of those who opposed the reigning piety of their time were themselves churchmen who were theoretically sworn to uphold it. Attacks on the system from without were often matched by covert sympathy from within, a problem that only encouraged the skeptics to denounce the churches as filled with power-hungry clerics who did not believe what they were expected to confess and teach to others.

The great historian of the European Enlightenment was the Frenchman Paul Hazard (1878–1944), who claimed that it was between 1680 and 1715 that the seismic shift in mentalities took place.[1] He has been followed more recently by Peter Gay (1923–) and above all by Jonathan Israel (1946–), whose

[1] Paul Hazard, *The European Mind (1680–1715)* (Cleveland: World, 1963). Originally published as *La crise de la conscience européenne (1680–1715)* (Paris: Boivin, 1935).

magisterial three-volume work on the subject is unlikely to be surpassed anytime soon.[2] They all agree that an intellectual revolution occurred in the years around 1700 that was to create the modern world and that the hegemonic status of Christianity in European culture was seriously weakened, if not completely displaced. The failure of the churches to produce an adequate response to the challenges of Enlightenment thinking, despite many attempts to do so, ensured the latter's long-term triumph, despite the persistence of widespread popular devotion and the remnants of an earlier Christendom that occasionally survived as vestiges of the "age of faith."

Modern historians generally agree that Enlightenment thought originated in the English-speaking world during the seventeenth century, but that it did not make a wider impact until it was embraced in France and later on in Germany. To this day, most English-speaking people are surprised to hear that the Enlightenment originated with them—the word itself is a translation of the German *Aufklärung*, which suggests a foreign provenance—which may be because it developed naturally out of the peculiar circumstances of the British Isles. The English Reformation had been a kind of compromise between Catholic and Protestant tendencies that allowed for a wide range of theological opinion. After the Puritan interlude (1640–1660), Britain settled down to a situation in which the established Church of England was rigid in episcopal and liturgical form but much more tolerant of different ideas, while from 1690 onward the equally established Church of Scotland was presbyterian. In Ireland the established church was Anglican, but Presbyterians were given a special status, and both groups had to face an overwhelming Roman Catholic majority. The overseas colonies were mostly Anglican, but as there were no bishops there, this meant relatively little. Moreover, some of the most important colonies were congregationalist (Massachusetts and Connecticut, for example) or even Quaker (Pennsylvania), while others had no religious establishment (New York, Rhode Island). All this variety coexisted under a single crown, the wearer of which from 1685 onward might be Roman Catholic (James II), Dutch Reformed (William III), or Lutheran (George I) as well as Anglican (Mary II and Anne). Even when it was eventually decided (in 1701) that the monarch must be a Prot-

[2] Peter Gay, *The Enlightenment: An Interpretation*, 2 vols. (London: Weidenfeld & Nicolson, 1967); Jonathan I. Israel, *Radical Enlightenment: Philosophy and the Making of Modernity 1650–1750* (Oxford: Oxford University Press, 2001); idem, *Enlightenment Contested: Philosophy, Modernity and the Emancipation of Man 1670–1752* (Oxford: Oxford University Press, 2006); *Democratic Enlightenment: Philosophy, Revolution and Human Rights 1750–1790* (Oxford: Oxford University Press, 2012). For a comprehensive survey of Enlightenment and post-Enlightenment theology, see James C. Livingston et al., *Modern Christian Thought*, 2nd ed., 2 vols. (Minneapolis: Fortress, 2006). The first volume is subtitled *The Enlightenment and the Nineteenth Century*; the second is subtitled *The Twentieth Century* and contains additional sections written by Francis S. Fiorenza, Sarah Coakley, and James H. Evans, Jr.

estant, the only stipulation was that he or she should enter into communion with the Church of England, which George I and his Hanoverian successors duly did, even though they were not Anglican in the doctrinal sense.[3]

A political system that could incorporate such variety was not going to be very diligent (or successful) at persecuting dissenting minorities, which flourished in spite of the disabilities imposed on them, but neither was its established church going to provoke much open hostility. Many people moved from one world to the other according to circumstances—joining the established church was called "conforming" (not "converting") to it, which clearly suggests that all that was required was outward assent, with few questions asked about inner conviction. Only the very unlucky—like Irish Catholics at times of threatened French invasion—were likely to suffer any form of persecution. Participation in political life was restricted to Anglicans (or to Presbyterians in Scotland), but the property qualifications required for that were so restrictive that only a small minority of the population was eligible in any case, so few people thought of this restriction as an injustice.[4] British flexibility in religious matters was appreciated and greatly admired by people who were forced to live in countries where it did not exist—especially France. There, the toleration that had been granted to the Protestant (Huguenot) minority by the Edict of Nantes in 1598 was whittled down and finally revoked in 1685, leading to an outflow of refugees but also to a spate of superficial conversions to Roman Catholicism. The injustice of the expulsions, combined with the insincerity of many of the "conversions" and the immoral hypocrisy of some of the leading Catholic persecutors, notably King Louis XIV (1643–1715) himself, alienated many French intellectuals. As Pierre Bayle (1647–1707) wrote at the time,

> If people only knew the force and present significance of the expression, no one would ever envy France the distinction of being "wholly Catholic" under Louis the Great. It is now a long time since those who arrogate to themselves the name of Catholic *par excellence*, have been perpetrating deeds that excite such horror in every human heart that any decent person must regard it as an insult to be called a Catholic. . . . It is evident that to speak of the Catholic religion and the religion of the unrighteous is one and the same thing.[5]

The moral advantage gained by the Huguenots as they suffered for their faith reignited anti-Catholic prejudice in Britain and the Netherlands, where

[3] In Scotland, the monarch was—and still is—a presbyterian, even though he or she is also the supreme governor of the (episcopal) Church of England, which is not in communion with the Church of Scotland.

[4] In Ireland, for example, it was not unknown for one member of the family to conform to the established church (and therefore be eligible to own land and hold public office) while the rest remained Roman Catholics.

[5] Pierre Bayle, *Lettre écrite de Londres à M. l'abbé de . . . , chanoine de N. D. de. . . . ce que c'est que la France toute catholique sous le règne de Louis le Grand* (Saint Omer: Jean Pierre Lami, 1686). "Louis the Great" was Louis XIV.

many of the exiles found refuge and from where they continued to campaign against the injustice inflicted on them. Almost anything subversive of France could be published in Holland, and it made little difference where it came from. Jacques-Bénigne Bossuet, one of the leading defenders of Louis XIV and his Catholic establishment, bore witness to this:

> Not long ago we received a book from Holland entitled *Critical History of the Principal Commentators on the New Testament*. Its author was Mr. Simon, a priest.[6] It is one of those books which have been refused the church's *imprimatur* and therefore cannot be printed here. It can only be circulated in a country where there are no restrictions, and among the enemies of the faith. But despite all the precautions and vigilance of the authorities, such books do manage to creep in. They do the rounds and pass from one reader to another. They are all the more eagerly devoured because they are not easy to come by, because they are rare, because they excite curiosity—in a word, because they are forbidden.[7]

The Protestants may have been the heroes of the hour among French radicals, but they were far from being tolerant themselves. Their synods were just as condemning of dissent as their Catholic counterparts were, the only difference being that their sentences could not be carried out. Worse still, Protestant pastors were often infected by heresy. In 1670, for example, Isaac d'Huisseau (d. 1672) of the Protestant academy of Saumur published a book on the reunion of the churches in which he proposed that nothing should be demanded of anyone that was not clearly stated in the Bible. It sounded good, but in the circumstances, it was a plea for Socinianism.[8] Richard Simon saw this clearly. Commenting on the condemnation of d'Huisseau, he said,

> The little herd, by treating the minister d'Huisseau with such conspicuous severity, hoped to intimidate the many other ministers who hold similar ideas. They confided their intentions to a number of ministers in the provinces, who signified their approval; and we may take it that, if they had not thus shown a firm hand, it would have been all over with Calvinism in France. The leading men of that sect would have openly proclaimed themselves Arminians, if not downright Socinians. As it is, they have contented themselves with being so inwardly, letting only their most intimate friends into their secret.

[6] Richard Simon (1638–1712), a convert from Protestantism to Catholicism who remained a radical critic of traditional Christianity. The book appeared as *Histoire critique des principaux commentateurs du Nouveau Testament* (Rotterdam: Reinier Leers, 1693).

[7] Jacques B. Bossuet, *Défense de la tradition et des Saints Pères* (Paris: J. T. Hérissant, 1763), preface, 8.

[8] Isidore d'Huisseau, *La réunion du christianisme* (Saumur: René Pean, 1670).

It was because they were afraid of losing their posts that they acted as they did. They subscribe to the confession of faith purely and simply for reasons of policy, holding (as they do) that Calvin and the other early Reformers left their work only half done.[9]

As in England and elsewhere, the charge of Socinianism was not one to be taken lightly. Pierre Bayle rejected it, but he did so in a way that made it plain that he was even more radical than they were:

God forbid that I should wish to go as far . . . as the Socinians. But if limits are to be assigned to speculative truths, I think there ought to be none in respect of the ordinary practical principles which have to do with morals. What I mean is that we ought always and without exception to refer moral laws to that natural conception of equity which, no less than the metaphysical light, illumines every man that comes into the world.[10] That is the conclusion we are bound to come to . . . that any particular dogma, whatever it may be, whether it is advanced on the authority of the Scriptures, or whatever else may be its origin, is to be regarded as false if it clashes with the clear and definite conclusions of the natural understanding, and that more particularly in the domain of ethics.[11]

Bayle was not a man to be trifled with. His great *Dictionnaire historique et critique* was presented as an encyclopedic reference work of human knowledge, but alongside the undisputed facts it contains are innumerable criticisms of famous figures and past events, many of them craftily concealed in footnotes so as to escape the detection of the censors.[12] Nothing like it had ever appeared before, and within a few years it was the quintessential reference document of a whole new intellectual movement, the heart of which was adherence to the principles of "reason."[13]

Appeal to human reason as the measure of truth did not begin with Bayle, to be sure. It had already raised its head in the work of René Descartes, who in the judgment of many was its true originator. But Descartes was dead before his ideas were widely received, and had no one else thought like him they might have been ignored. Consider the following:

Whereas for some years past an obscure person, who goes by the name of Reason, has been trying to force his way into the schools of our university,

[9] Richard Simon, *Lettres choisies*, 4 vols. (Amsterdam: Pierre Mortier, 1730), 3:3.
[10] A reference to John 1:9.
[11] Pierre Bayle, *Commentaire philosophique sur ces paroles de Jésus-Christ: "Contrains-les d'entrer"* (Canterbury: Thomas Litwel, but in reality Amsterdam: Abraham Wolfgang, 1686), 1.1.1.
[12] Pierre Bayle, *Dictionnaire historique et critique* (Rotterdam: R. Leers, 1697).
[13] On the extent of Bayle's influence, see Gay, *Enlightenment*, 1:2.5.2.4; and Israel, *Radical Enlightenment*, 331–341.

> and whereas the said person, aided and abetted by certain comical charlatans calling themselves Gassendists, Cartesians, Malebranchistes—vagabonds all of them—designs to accuse and then to expel Aristotle . . .[14]

Another thinker of the period who was to gain a great reputation later on was Benedict Spinoza (1632–1677), the first Jew to become a major figure on the European intellectual scene during his own lifetime. Spinoza taught that the pursuit of happiness was the pursuit not of pleasure but of truth, but that finding truth was not necessarily a renunciation of pleasure, as the great religions all taught. Conforming one's will to the truth was the way to finding peace of mind, a goal that was within the grasp of human striving:

> . . . we act only through the will of God, we share in the divine nature, and this participation increases as our actions approach perfection and our knowledge of God grows more complete. Such a doctrine, in addition to bringing us perfect peace of mind, has the further advantage of showing us what our sovereign happiness consists of—the knowledge of God, which leads us to act only as love and our duty towards God may direct.[15]

But Spinoza owed much of his fame and influence to Pierre Bayle, who commented on him in his *Dictionnaire* as follows:

> Very few people are suspected of sharing his doctrines, and of those, few have seriously studied them, and of those who have, fewer still have grasped his meaning. . . . But the truth of the matter is that by and large, everyone who has little religion in him, or none at all, and does not much care who knows it, is dubbed a Spinozist.[16]

This comment is typical of Bayle's cryptic style. He actually approved of Spinoza, but did not want anyone to accuse him of saying so, and so he phrased his remarks as if to say that no one really understood him. Yet clearly there were a number of people around who were regarded as Spinoza's followers, and they were all people of little or no religious belief! Much the same thing can be found in Richard Simon:

> Do not accuse me of using the same language as the impious Spinoza, who states his complete disbelief in the miracles recorded in the Scriptures. This

[14] Francois Bernier and Nicholas Boileau Despréaux, *Requeste des maistres ès arts, professeurs et régens de l'Université de Paris, présentée à la cour souveraine de Parnasse* (Delphi [Paris]: Société des imprimeurs de la Cour de Parnasse, 1671). Pierre Gassendi (1592–1655) and Nicolas de Malebranche (1638–1715) were just as famous as Descartes in the late seventeenth century, but they failed to carry conviction in the same way and are now mostly forgotten.

[15] Benedict Spinoza, *Ethics*, ed. Edwin Curley, 2 vols. (London: Penguin, 1996), 2:4A.

[16] Bayle, *Dictionnaire*, "Spinoza."

idea, which does me wrong, is widely held, and I beg you to dismiss it from your minds. It is right and proper to condemn the impious conclusions that Spinoza draws from some of the axioms he lays down, but those axioms are not always false in themselves, nor always to be rejected.[17]

In other words, Spinoza's conclusions may sometimes have been wrong but his rationalistic principles were quite all right and ought to be accepted! Bayle followed through on his devotion to the power of human reason by taking every opportunity he could to denounce popular superstitions. In his day it was common for even educated people to believe in astrology, and to regard comets (in particular) as portents of evil. To Bayle, this belief was a form of pride, as if to say that God was so bothered about what might happen to us that he ordered the universe accordingly. As he put it,

> The more we study the ways of man, the more we are forced to recognize that pride is his ruling passion. . . . He persuades himself that when it is time for him to die, the whole of nature is stirred to its depths and heaven itself goes out of its way to add some splendor to his funeral rites. Foolish, ridiculous vanity! If we looked at the universe correctly, we would soon realize that the birth or death of a king is a very small matter when set against the background of universal order—far too small for heaven to be concerned about. . . . It is true that Providence is concerned about us, but although we have our allotted place in the general scheme of things, the heavenly purpose is directed toward something much greater than our particular preservation, and while we derive great benefit from the movements of the heavenly bodies, it is not merely for the sake of this earth that they are set in motion.[18]

To the clergy who typically appealed to "mystery" and "miracle" when confronted by something they did not understand, Bayle had this to say:

> . . . why do you follow what the crowd thinks, instead of consulting the oracle of Reason? It is because you believe that there is something divinely inspired about it, . . . because you imagine that the common consent of so many people down through the ages can only be the result of some kind of inspiration—*vox populi, vox Dei*; it is because, as a theologian, you are accustomed to stop thinking when you are in the presence of a "mystery."[19]

[17] R. Simon, *Lettres choisies*, 2nd ed., 4 vols. (Amsterdam: Pierre Mortier, 1730), 4:12.

[18] Pierre Bayle, *Pensées diverses, écrites à un docteur de la Sorbonne à l'occasion de la comète qui parut au mois de décembre 1680* (Rotterdam: R. Leers, 1683), 83.

[19] Bayle, *Pensées diverses*, 8.

When it came to the interpretation of the Bible, Spinoza was no less revolutionary in his ideas, which can only be compared to those of Hugo Grotius a generation earlier. Far from seeing the Bible as the divinely inspired Word of God that must be taken at face value, Spinoza outlined what he saw as the fundamental principles of textual criticism:

> . . . the history of the Scriptures . . . should teach us to understand the various ups and downs that may have befallen the prophetic books whose tradition has been handed down to us—the life, character, and aim of the author of each book; the part which he played; at what period, on what occasion, for whom and in what language he composed his writings. Nor is that enough. We need to know what happened to each particular book, the circumstances in which it was originally composed, into whose hands it subsequently fell, the various lessons it has been thought to convey, by whom it was included in the sacred canon, and finally, how all these books came to be embodied in a single collection.[20]

With this we have reached the point at which revelation ceased to be enough. Spinoza did not say that the Bible was not divinely inspired, but even if it was, it still had to be read as if it were a text susceptible to the ordinary critique of natural human reason. If it contained things (as it undoubtedly did) that the rational mind could not accept, because they were either physically impossible or morally repugnant (and therefore unworthy of God), those things had to be rejected. Simon resolved this problem (at least to his own satisfaction) by appealing to the tradition of the church, which was there to explain passages of Scripture that would otherwise be impossible to understand. This device was typical of Roman Catholic apologists, especially in their debates with Protestants, but Simon understood it differently. Traditional Catholics had always assumed that the mysteries of Scripture were divinely inspired, needing the church only to expound them correctly, but Simon was hinting that the church was there to give a meaning to something that would otherwise be nonsensical.[21] It is hardly surprising that he was condemned for heresy!

While this was going on in France, the English scene was dominated by men who were rationalists in one sense but not in another. John Tillotson (1630–1694), for example, who became archbishop of Canterbury in 1691, took a line very similar to that of Thomas Aquinas centuries before. For him, two things were necessary for any teaching to be accepted as genuinely divine. The first of these was that it should contain nothing that contradicted the nature

[20] Benedict Spinoza, *Tractatus theologico-politicus* (Hamburg: H. Künrath, 1670), 7.
[21] Richard Simon, *Histoire critique du Vieux Testament* (Paris: Veuve Billaine, 1678), preface.

of God. That would have been generally agreed by everyone at the time, but the second criterion was more unusual. This was that the teaching should be supported by a miracle, as proof that it came from God. In Tillotson's words,

> Though a doctrine be never so reasonable in itself, this is no certain argument that it is from God if no testimony from heaven be given to it; because it may be the result and issue of human reason and discourse; and though a doctrine be attested by miracles, yet the matter of it may be so unreasonable and absurd . . . that no miracles can be sufficient to give confirmation to it.[22]

John Locke followed Tillotson, at least as far as the biblical revelation was concerned. As he said,

> The holy men of old who had revelations from God had something else besides that internal light of assurance in their own minds to testify to them that it was from God. They were not left to their own persuasions alone, that those persuasions were from God, but had outward signs to convince them of the Author of those revelations.[23]

Five years later Locke wrote again on the reasonableness of Christianity, and argued that a man who had no access to divine revelation could nevertheless find his way to God:

> God had, by the light of reason, revealed to all mankind who would make use of that light, that he was good and merciful. The same spark of the divine nature and knowledge of man . . . showed him the law he was under as a man; showed him also the way of atoning the merciful, kind, compassionate Author and Father of him and his being, when he had transgressed that law. He that made use of that candle of the Lord . . . could not miss . . . the way to reconciliation and forgiveness when he had failed his duty.[24]

Unlike the Socinians, Locke clung to orthodox Christian teaching, but he argued that it was possible for someone who lacked access to divine revelation to reach the same conclusion by the right use of his natural reason. This obviously raised the question of whether revelation was necessary, and Locke had no real answer to give. At the most basic level it was superfluous, but given that many people are unclear about how to use their minds and may be distracted

[22] John Tillotson, *Works*, 3 vols. (London: J and R. Tonson, 1752), 3:493–494.
[23] John Locke, *An Essay concerning Human Understanding* (Oxford: Oxford University Press, 1956), 363. The book was first published in 1690.
[24] John Locke, *The Reasonableness of Christianity* (Palo Alto, CA: Stanford University Press, 1958), 55. The book was first published in 1695.

from doing so, it served the purpose of focusing their attention on something that they lacked the time or the inclination (though not the ability) to find out for themselves. Locke may not have realized it, but in saying that, he surrendered the claim of traditional orthodoxy, which was that divine revelation was essential for a true knowledge of God and that without it, even a well-disposed individual would go wrong and perish.

In England, censorship was abolished in 1695, the same year that Locke published his great work, and before long there was an outpouring of scandalous literature, much of which denounced not only the church but Christianity itself. So bad did this become that in 1698 parliament was forced to pass a Blasphemy Act in a vain attempt to stem the tide.[25] The classic work in this genre, and a major factor leading to the Blasphemy Act, was a book called *Christianity Not Mysterious*, by John Toland (1670–1722). Toland was an Irishman, perhaps the illegitimate son of a Roman Catholic priest, who became the archetypal freethinker of his age. He was immensely popular in intellectual circles, not least because he presented himself as a "trophy of grace," having been saved from the evils of Roman Catholicism by his embrace of reason. Most of his hearers were viscerally anti-Catholic and rejoiced at his "conversion," even if it was to a Protestantism that was nothing more than pure rationalism. As Toland explained,

> . . . there is nothing in the Gospel contrary to reason, nor above it; and . . . no Christian doctrine can properly be called a mystery.[26]

Toland's arguments were naive, and much of what he said was designed to shock his readers rather than to inform them, but his opponents soon realized that much of it was derived from the ideas of John Locke, although Locke himself had no particular affinity with him. This dependence was brought out by Edward Stillingfleet (1635–1699), bishop of Worcester and a leading representative of the moderate, or "latitudinarian" party in the Church of England. Stillingfleet was no enemy of reason; in fact, as a latitudinarian, he believed that Trinitarianism could be defended on rational grounds and wrote against those who denied that claim. He argued that the main difference between him and men like Locke and Toland was that he believed that reason could (and should) be used to support revealed truth, whereas the latter thought that it should replace any supposed "revelation." He was a moderate in the sense that

[25] 9 William III, c. 35. It was amended in 1813 (53 George III, c. 160) to protect Unitarians by removing the Trinitarian clause in the original act, and was finally repealed on July 21, 1967. No prosecutions were ever brought under the act.

[26] John Toland, *Christianity Not Mysterious* (London: Sam Buckley, 1696), 6.

he denied Calvin's doctrine of aseity and clung to the idea that the generation of the Son involved a communication to him of the Father's divine essence, though he was careful to stress that this was a very complicated matter and could not easily be explained. That (he thought) was the reason why Trinitarians disagreed among each other—they believed the same thing but could not find a common form of words that would satisfy everyone.

Stillingfleet was particularly scathing in his criticism of what he saw as simplistic definitions of the word "person" that excluded the possibility of having three of them in one substance. He argued that just as God is not a creature, so divine personhood could not be equated with the human variety, which was conditioned by the limitations of human nature. What he did not realize was that by seeking to extend the meaning of the term to cover a divine reality that had no human counterpart, he was making it unintelligible—at least to people like Locke. It was in this way that theology and philosophy parted company, with each side insisting that it was employing the gift of reason, but doing this in different and (ultimately) mutually incompatible ways.[27]

It was this cleavage, rather than any crude triumph of "reason" over "revelation," that signaled the beginning of the so-called "Enlightenment." Like the Renaissance before it, the Enlightenment was promoted by people who saw their work as a deliverance from what they believed was the obscurantism the church promoted as "theology." Both these words are propagandistic—in the first instance, European society was supposedly "reborn"; in the second, it was theoretically given light and understanding. But whereas the Renaissance had led to a renewal of theology based on the rediscovery of ancient texts that had been unknown or little read, the Enlightenment did not. The main reason for this was that the Renaissance was a rediscovery of lost documents that undermined existing beliefs by appealing to more ancient (and therefore more authoritative) sources. The Enlightenment, on the other hand, rejected the traditions of the past and thought that the older they were the more unacceptable they were likely to be. We can see the effect of this by considering how the meaning of the word "primitive" changed from one context to the other. In the literary tradition of the Renaissance it meant "authentic" and was therefore good, but in the scientific culture of the Enlightenment it came to mean "unsophisticated" and was therefore bad. The fact that it is the latter meaning

[27] Edward Stillingfleet, *A Discourse in Vindication of the Doctrine of the Trinity, with an Answer to the Late Socinian Objections against It from Scripture, Antiquity, and Reason, and a Preface concerning the Different Explications of the Trinity, and the Tendency of the Present Socinian Controversie*, in *The Works of That Eminent and Most Learned Prelate, Late Lord Bishop of Worcester, Together with His Life and Character*, 6 vols. (London: J. Heptinstall, 1710), 3:455.

that predominates in modern discourse shows just how effective Enlightenment propaganda has been![28]

The ultimate reconciliation between reason and revelation was offered by Matthew Tindal (1655–1733), who shortly before his death published the first volume of his main work, *Christianity as Old as the Creation*.[29] His argument was that because God is eternally perfect, his law must be the same in every time and place. Any contact with him will tell the same story, and special revelation cannot add anything further to it. In his words,

> If all own that God at no time could have any motive to give laws to mankind but for their good, and that he is at all times equally good, and at all times acts upon the same motives, must they not own with me, except they are inconsistent with themselves, that his laws at all times must be the same?[30]

He followed this up with observations on the relationship between natural and revealed religion, which he regarded as identical in substance, though different in the way they were communicated:

> I think too great a stress cannot be laid on natural religion which, as I take it, differs not from revealed but in the manner of its being communicated. The one being the internal, as the other the external revelation of the same unchangeable will of a being, who is alike at all times infinitely wise and good.[31]

Whether it was because of the crude way in which he stated his case, or because it came after so many other statements of a similar kind from other people, Tindal's book lit a fuse among English theologians, who seem to have risen up in a body to oppose him. William Law (1686–1761), George Berkeley (1685–1753), and Joseph Butler (1692–1752) all refuted him at length, thereby inadvertently producing a golden age of Anglican apologetic.[32]

By the early eighteenth century, fashionable religion, both Protestant and Roman Catholic, was libertine in both theology and morals. Belief in miracles was widely laughed at, and those who tried to live holy lives were often derided in upper-class intellectual circles. Their superficial skepticism was represented by men like Anthony Collins (1676–1729), whose *Discourse of Free-thinking*

[28] For example, although theologians still talk about "primitive Christianity," by which they mean the earliest form(s) of it, to the nonspecialist the term sounds negative and unappealing.
[29] Matthew Tindal, *Christianity as Old as the Creation* (London: publisher unknown, 1730).
[30] Ibid., 34.
[31] Ibid., 32.
[32] William Law, *The Case of Reason* (London: W. Innys, 1731); George Berkeley, *Alciphron* (London: J. Tonson, 1732); Joseph Butler, *The Analogy of Religion* (London: John and Paul Knapton, 1736).

became the basic text of the new intelligentsia.[33] Collins saw the new movement he was promoting as a kind of anti-church in which the "deity" was worshiped according to the lights of reason but (as time went on) with the aid of a mishmash of arcane and basically absurd rituals that formed the basis of modern freemasonry.[34]

Deism, as this new movement or pseudo-religion was called, soon became the theology of choice in intellectual circles, not only in England but also in France, from where it spread across Europe. In France, men like François-Marie Arouet, better known as Voltaire (1694–1778), and Jean-Jacques Rousseau (1712–1778) were increasingly bold in their attacks on what they saw as a decadent Catholic church and state. Modern scholarship has questioned the validity of that assessment, pointing out that eighteenth-century French Catholicism was much more vigorous than its critics have allowed. But be that as it may, it was the voice of its enemies that would carry the day, first in the salons of Paris and then in the French Revolution.[35]

Voltaire was a particularly influential and enigmatic figure. Brought up to be a loyal Roman Catholic, he maintained a love-hate relationship with that spiritual inheritance throughout his life. He came to hate institutional and dogmatic Catholicism, which he regarded as "infamous" (*l'infâme*, as he called it), and wanted to see stamped out, but he maintained a deep reverence for the order of the universe, which he attributed to the beneficence of a wise and loving Creator. Combining Thomas Aquinas and Descartes, he defended belief in God on the ground that there had to be a first cause of all things:

> I exist, so something exists. If something exists, then something must have existed from all eternity, because whatever exists either exists by itself or else has received its existence from something else. If it exists by itself, it exists of necessity and has always done so—it is God. . . . Intelligence is not essential to matter, for a rock or grain do not think. Where then have the material particles that think and feel got those things from? . . . Since thought and sensation do not belong to the essence of matter, they must have received them as gifts from a Supreme Being, the intelligent, infinite, and original cause of all beings.[36]

---

[33] Anthony Collins, *A Discourse of Free-Thinking, Occasioned by the Rise and Growth of a Sect Called Free-Thinkers* (London [The Hague]: printer unknown, 1713).

[34] See John Lawrence, *Freemasonry—A Religion?* (Eastbourne: Kingsway, 1987); and J. Ridley, *A Brief History of the Freemasons* (London: Robinson, 2008).

[35] See, for example, John McManners, *Church and Society in Eighteenth-century France*, 2 vols. (Oxford: Oxford University Press, 1998); and Ségolène de Dainville-Barbiche, *Devenir curé à Paris. Institutions et carrières ecclésiastiques (1695–1789)* (Paris: Presses Universitaires de France, 2005). See also Dale K. Van Kley, *The Religious Origins of the French Revolution: From Calvin to the Civil Constitution, 1560–1791* (New Haven, CT: Yale University Press, 1996).

[36] Voltaire, *Traité de métaphysique*, 2, in *Oeuvres complètes de Voltaire*, 145 vols. (Oxford: Taylor Foundation, 1968–), 14:427–428.

Immediately before that he gave his other main reason for believing in the existence of God, which was what we now call the argument from design. The way in which everything seemed to be so precisely adapted to meet particular ends convinced him that it must be the work of an intelligent designer in the same way that a watch was:

> When I see a watch whose hands mark the hours, I conclude that an intelligent being has arranged the springs of this machine. . . . When I see the springs of the human body, I conclude that an intelligent being has arranged these organs. . . . but from this argument I cannot conclude anything further than that it is probable that an intelligent and superior being has skillfully prepared and fashioned the matter.[37]

Voltaire distanced himself from deists of the Tindal variety by insisting that God played an active role in the world in punishing injustice and rewarding virtue, though he did not presume to know how he did so and admitted that some events were beyond human ability to comprehend. In his definition of a theist, he had this to say:

> The theist does not know how God punishes, how he rewards, how he pardons; for he is not presumptuous enough to flatter himself that he understands how God acts; but he knows that God does act and that he is just. The difficulties opposed to a providence do not stagger him in his faith, because they are only great difficulties, not proofs; he submits himself to that providence, although he only perceives some of its effects and some appearances; and judging of the things he does not see from those he does see, he thinks that this providence pervades all places and all ages.[38]

This lofty vision, which Voltaire ascribed to "reason" but that might equally well be called wishful thinking, stands in sharp contrast to his opinion of Christianity, a religion whose gory details he regarded with extreme distaste. As he put it,

> May the great God who hears me—a God who certainly could not be born of a girl, nor die on a gibbet, nor be eaten in a morsel of paste, nor have inspired this book [the Bible] with its contradictions, follies and horrors—may this God have pity on the sect of Christians who blaspheme him![39]

---

[37] Voltaire, *Traité de métaphysique*, 2, in *Oeuvres complètes*, 14:426. This analogy was made famous by William Paley (1743–1805) in his *Natural Theology* (London: R. Faulder, 1802), but Paley got it from Voltaire.
[38] Voltaire, *Dictionnaire philosophique*, article "*théiste*," in *Oeuvres complètes*, 36:546–547.
[39] Voltaire, *Sermon of the Fifty* (Jersey City, NJ: Ross Paxton, 1963), 28. The original French text is in *Oeuvres complètes*, 49a:69–139.

With an attitude like that, we can hardly expect Voltaire to have had a high view of the Trinity, a doctrine that he attacked with particular vehemence. He could not understand why people had fought so hard over what to him was intellectual nonsense. After cataloguing the various components of the orthodox doctrine, he wrote,

> I do not understand any of this; no one has ever understood any of this, and this is the reason for which people have slaughtered one another.[40]

It was a simplistic assessment, but one that was rooted in a moral indignation born of the undoubted fact that Christians had persecuted one another over matters of doctrine and that the Roman church of his own day was still claiming the right to do so. The so-called *affaire Calas*, which erupted in 1762 when a Protestant father was falsely accused of having killed his son in order to prevent the latter's conversion to Catholicism, disgusted not only Voltaire but a wide section of French opinion, and it was in reaction to events like those that his sarcasm—and his appeal to the Christian conscience—must be judged.[41]

Jean-Jacques Rousseau was a deist of a different flavor than Voltaire. He was born and brought up as a Protestant in Geneva, converting (if that is the word) to Catholicism when he left the city in 1728 but reverting to Protestantism when he went back home in 1754. Rousseau's ideas were shaped by a search for truth that crossed denominational lines and led him to regard the barriers between different forms of Christianity as relative and to some extent unreal. As he saw it, most theological arguments rested on assumptions that could not be proved, and so were of dubious value. Far better, he thought, to concentrate on what was demonstrably true. The result was "reverent doubt" with respect to specific religious claims combined with genuine devotion to the universal principles that they represented:

> I call to witness the God of Peace whom I adore, and whom I proclaim to you, that my inquiries were honestly made, but when I discovered that they were and always would be unsuccessful, and that I embarked upon a boundless ocean, I turned back and restricted my faith within the limits of my primitive ideas. . . . I closed all my books. There is one book that is open to everyone—the book of nature. In this good and great volume I learn to serve and adore its Author. If I use my reason, if I cultivate it, if I employ rightly the innate faculties which God bestows upon me, I shall learn by myself to

[40] Voltaire, *Dictionnaire philosophique*, article "Arius," in *Oeuvres complètes*, 35:370.
[41] See Patrick Cabanel, *Histoire du protestantisme*, 894–900.

> know and love him, to love his works, to will what he wills and to fulfill all my duties upon earth.[42]

Whereas Voltaire believed in the progress of civilization and science, tools that would chase away the remains of primitive superstition, Rousseau preferred the image of the "noble savage," the native of the jungle or of the American forest who had been untouched by the corruption of human development and so manifested the purity of mankind in its original state. Needless to say, Rousseau knew nothing about such people—they were a product of his imagination. But then, his readers knew nothing about them either, and it was pleasant for them to suppose that a return to the simplicity of a long-lost past would solve all the problems of the present. Rousseau's naive approach to life extended to his view of providence, where he actually clashed with Voltaire. Following the Lisbon earthquake in 1755, Voltaire had written a poem in which his lament for the undeserved suffering it had caused led him to question the divine ordering of the universe. But Rousseau had no doubts, and in reply to Voltaire, he wrote,

> All the subtleties of metaphysics will not make me doubt for a moment the immortality of the soul or a beneficent Providence. I feel it, I believe it, I want it, I hope for it, and I shall defend it to my last breath.[43]

What was clear about Rousseau was that his faith was not rational in the sense that Voltaire's was. On the contrary, it was grounded in feeling and morality. Rousseau clearly thought that the one should lead to the other, a progression that was guaranteed by the working of conscience:

> Conscience! Conscience! Divine instinct, immortal voice from heaven, sure guide for a creature ignorant and finite indeed, yet intelligent and free; infallible judge of good and evil, making man like God! In thee consists the excellence of man's nature and the morality of his actions; apart from thee I find nothing in myself to raise me above the beast.[44]

As for the existence of God, Rousseau sometimes gave the impression that he was on some kind of life-support machine that was dependent on the human will. As his Savoyard vicar advised Emile,

---

[42] Jean-Jacques Rousseau, *Emile* (London: Dent, 1993), 270–271. Originally published in 1762. The words are those of the Savoyard vicar who makes his confession to Emile.
[43] Jean-Jacques Rousseau, *Correspondance générale*, ed. Theophile Dufour and P. P. Plan, 20 vols. (Paris: Armand Colin, 1924–1934), 2:324. The letter was dated August 18, 1756.
[44] Rousseau, *Emile*, 254.

> My son, keep your soul in such a state that you always desire that there should be a God and you will never doubt it. Moreover, whatever decision you come to, remember that the real duties of religion are independent of human institutions, that a righteous heart is the true temple of the Godhead.[45]

If Enlightenment deism originated in England and became the unofficial religion of the French intelligentsia, it was in Germany that its deepest impact would be felt. Eighteenth-century Germany was not a nation state but a conglomeration of principalities great and small joined together in the Holy Roman Empire, which existed under the aegis of the Catholic Habsburgs in Vienna but tolerated different confessions according to the preferences of the microstates concerned. One result of this was a proliferation of universities, sponsored by individual rulers for the support of their particular religious option and for the prestige of their family and principality. Whereas England had only two universities—Oxford and Cambridge—Germany had more than twenty, which gave much greater scope for the development of every kind of advanced study.[46] Furthermore, what was banned in one university might be tolerated, even encouraged, in another, making the censorship of ideas more difficult than it was elsewhere. Professors who were dismissed in one place might easily be hired somewhere else and so continue to spread their message, which of course was almost impossible to censor effectively once it appeared in print.

The German Enlightenment had native roots, but in the European market of ideas it is fair to say that the French read the English and the Germans read the French (and sometimes also the English), rather than the other way around, giving the impression that the new way of thinking flowed mainly in one direction. By the time that changed in the nineteenth century, the British had forgotten where deistic ideas had originally come from and associated "liberal" theology with Germany, a misapprehension that German scholars are occasionally anxious to dispel.[47] In Germany the Enlightenment may be said to have begun with Gottfried Leibniz (1646–1716), for whom the path to deism had passed through what we would now call ecumenism. Leibniz was

---

[45] Ibid., 275.

[46] To Oxford and Cambridge might be added the four Scottish universities (St. Andrews, Glasgow, Aberdeen, and Edinburgh), the University of Dublin (Trinity College) and perhaps Harvard and Yale colleges in the colonies, but the grand total was still less than half of what was found in Germany. One of the great patrons of learning at this time was George II (1727–1760), king of Great Britain and ruler of Hanover as well. He founded the British Library in London, the Cambridge University Library and the University of Göttingen, which soon became the main repository of British learning in Germany. He also left his mark on America, where the colony of Georgia and George Washington (1732–1799) were both named after him.

[47] This is true, for example, of Henning G. von Reventlow, *The Authority of the Bible and the Rise of the Modern World* (London: SCM, 1984). Originally published as *Bibelautorität und Geist der Moderne. Die Bedeutung des Bibelverständnisses für die geistesgeschichtliche und politische Entwicklung in England von der Reformation bis zur Aufklärung* (Göttingen: Vandenhoeck und Ruprecht, 1980).

a Lutheran who was strongly attracted to Roman Catholicism and who even spent time in Rome, where he was offered the post of Vatican librarian.[48] He knew from experience that his fellow Lutherans were somewhat blinkered in their understanding of Catholicism, but when he tried to effect a *rapprochement* between the two great wings of Western Christendom he discovered that his Catholic counterparts were equally intransigent and dogmatic, to the point of insisting on the need to subscribe to every last detail of the great church councils. Leibniz preferred to concentrate on the things that Protestants and Catholics held in common, which to his mind were sufficiently great as to make the reunion of the churches relatively simple. All that was needed was to get rid of unnecessary dogma, which to those who upheld it seemed like a plea to dispense with truth altogether.

Leibniz's kind of "basic Christianity" fitted in well with the spirit of the time, which held that any doctrine that was contrary to reason must be rejected. That was the message of Christian Wolff (1679–1754), who taught philosophy at the formerly pietist university of Halle, though Wolff was careful to say that almost everything a person ought to confess was contained in the Bible.[49] This was a new version of *sola Scriptura*—not everything contained in the Bible was required for Christian belief, but everything that formed a necessary part of that belief could be found in the Bible! That principle became the guiding light of German deism and helps to explain its Bible-centeredness, which distinguished it from contemporary thought in Britain and France. It also explains why German biblical criticism acquired the volume and prominence that it did in the late eighteenth and nineteenth centuries. Far from being an objective attempt to uncover the true nature of Scripture, it was from the beginning an ideologically driven enterprise, designed to show that the Bible was not what the church thought it was.

By far the most radical exponent of this line of thinking was Hermann Samuel Reimarus (1694–1768), professor of oriental languages at Hamburg, who is often regarded as the founder of modern biblical criticism.[50] Reimarus's views were so radical that he felt unable to share them with anyone else. After his death, Gotthold Ephraim Lessing (1729–1781) obtained his daughter's permission to publish them, but anonymously. A selection of his writings came out as the *Wolfenbüttel Fragments*, named for the library where Lessing worked,

---

[48] For the whole story, see Hazard, *European Mind*, 253–274.

[49] C. Wolff, *Theologia naturalis*, 2 vols. (Frankfurt: Renger, 1736–1737).

[50] Albert Schweitzer's classic demolition of nineteenth-century German biblical scholarship, published in English as *The Quest for the Historical Jesus: A Critical Study of Its Progress from Reimarus to Wrede* (London: A. & C. Black, 1910), was originally published in German simply as *Von Reimarus zu Wrede. Eine Geschichte der Leben-Jesu-Forschung* (Tübingen: J. C. Mohr, 1906).

and it was in that form that they became known (and influential) all over Germany.[51] Lessing obviously agreed with most (if not all) of what Reimarus had written, and in his edition of the "fragments" he appended his own observations on them. He made it clear that as far as he was concerned, the Bible was not the final authority for Christian faith:

> The letter is not the spirit, and the Bible is not religion. Consequently, objections to the letter and to the Bible are not also objections to the spirit and to religion. . . . religion was there before the Bible existed. Christianity was there before the evangelists and apostles wrote. A long period elapsed before the first of them wrote, and a very considerable time before the entire canon was complete. . . . The written traditions must be interpreted by their inward truth and no written traditions can give the religion any inward truth if it has none.[52]

The question of truth was one that exercised Lessing throughout his career. He agreed with orthodox theologians that the miracles and fulfillments of prophecy recorded in the Bible would have to be believed if they were witnessed, or if comparable events still occurred. But the fact is that there are no miracles nowadays, and so we must rely entirely on the trustworthiness of the historical record. How do we know whether it is correct? Here we have to use our judgment, which can never be objectively verified or disproved. A miracle recorded in the Bible can therefore not claim the same kind of authority as an event witnessed today, and for that reason we should not be asked to believe it with the same degree of confidence. In his words,

> If no historical truth can be demonstrated, then nothing can be demonstrated by means of historical truths. That is: accidental truths of history can never become the proof of necessary truths of reason.[53]

But Lessing took the argument further than this. Even if he was prepared to believe that Jesus performed miracles, did that make it necessary to believe that he was the Son of God? In other words, did historical truths, debatable though they might be, lead to theological truths, which by definition were of a different order entirely, since they lay outside the realm of time and space? For this reason, Lessing claimed that the proof of religious truth does not (and cannot) lie in the empirical verification of events described in the Bible. It can only

[51] Gotthold E. Lessing, *Fragmente des wolfenbüttelschen Ungenannten* (Berlin: A. Wever, 1784).
[52] Gotthold E. Lessing, quoted in Henry Chadwick, *Lessing's Theological Writings* (London: A. & C. Black, 1956), 18.
[53] Gotthold E. Lessing, *On the Proof of the Spirit and of Power* (1777), in Chadwick, *Lessing*, 53.

be justified by its correspondence with personal experience, and that would almost certainly be moral in nature. We know that it is a good thing to love other people, so when Jesus taught his disciples to do that, we can demonstrate the truth of his words by doing the same thing ourselves and seeing the results.

In a curious way, Lessing was more "orthodox" than most of his fellow deists, and some would say that he was not really a deist at all, because he insisted that Christianity was not just a theory about eternal truth but also a faith rooted in historical experience. As he would have put it, we believe what the first Christians believed because we experience the same things in our lives today. That the tale has grown in the telling can be cheerfully admitted, but when these accretions are stripped away there still remains a hard core of historical fact. Christianity is therefore not to be understood as the Western manifestation of universal ideas about the nature of reality which might equally well be shared by Muslims, Hindus, or others. On the contrary, it was inescapably tied to the historical figure of Jesus Christ, whose teaching was proper to him and must be recognized as such.

Even in Britain's American colonies rationalism gained a foothold, despite the impact of religious revival there. Benjamin Franklin (1706–1790), for example, went to hear George Whitefield preach and was greatly impressed by his style and delivery, but he was not converted and remained attached to his version of deism. Neither was Thomas Jefferson (1743–1826), who even tried to rewrite the Gospels by removing their unacceptably supernatural bits, including the accounts of the resurrection.[54] It was these men, and not the revivalists, who led the drive for American political independence and established the Western world's first officially secular state. Organized religion was made an optional extra, but notions of God and spirituality could not be dismissed so easily. What emerged was a civic religion that paid honor to the "deity" and positively reveled in the "spirit," which was regarded as a religious impulse that was vital to human life and progress. What was resisted was definition—Jesus might have been the greatest man who ever lived and an example for subsequent generations to follow, but to claim that he was the Son of God who suffered and died for the sins of the world was to be sectarian and dogmatic.

Opposition to deistic rationalism was by no means unknown, but it was uneven and often unlucky. A case in point is Joseph Butler, whose *Analogy of Religion* was the most celebrated and long-lasting defense of traditional theism and remained a classic in the English-speaking world for the better part of a century. Butler realized that the deists' appeal to nature was simplistic. In their

[54] *The Jefferson Bible: The Life and Morals of Jesus of Nazareth Extracted Textually from the Gospels in Greek, Latin, French, and English* (Washington, DC: Smithsonian Books, 2011).

eyes, the natural world was simple and perfect, self-evident in its charms. The reality, of course, is more complicated than that. There is pain and suffering in nature, there are natural phenomena which are less than perfect (physically abnormal animals and people, for example), and not everything works out for the best in the best of all possible worlds. So to use nature as a standard by which to judge the alleged imperfections of revelation seemed to Butler to miss the target completely. He thought that both the natural and the supernatural worlds exhibited the same phenomena, and that the "imperfections" of the Bible were paralleled by the imperfections of the natural world, because apart from God himself, nothing is entirely perfect.

Butler argued that just as natural things go through a process of growth and decay without changing their essential being, the human soul could do the same. The death of the body was by no means to be regarded as the end of our existence, and was just as likely to be the beginning of a higher state of experience.[55] Furthermore, the existence of our moral sense, and the general belief that it is right to reward the good and punish the bad, was seen by Butler as an argument for a higher religious truth. Why, he asked, would we have such sentiments if there was nothing more to them than what we observe in this life, where so often the good go unrewarded and the wicked prosper? If there is justice at all, an afterlife is necessary in order to make sense of what we observe and experience here and now:

> The fact of our case, which we find by experience, is that [God] exercises dominion or government over us at present, by rewarding and punishing us for our actions. . . . And thus the whole analogy of nature . . . most fully shows that there is nothing incredible in the general doctrine of religion, that God will reward and punish men for their actions hereafter.[56]

As for miracles, Butler claimed that they could not be denied simply because their cause was unknown. There are many things in the natural world that cannot be explained, and "mystery" is simply the name given to natural processes that are beyond our comprehension.[57] Butler succeeded in demonstrating that the deists were naive in assuming the perfection of nature, but his argument that both reason and revelation were faulty was not likely to win him many friends. Traditional Christianity had always insisted that revelation was perfect, and those in the Thomist fold argued that its purpose was to perfect the inadequacies of nature. However one looked at it, reason and revelation

[55] Butler, *Analogy of Religion*, 9.
[56] Ibid., 54–55.
[57] Ibid., 248–249.

were not parallel—the latter was either superior to the former (as Christians claimed) or the opposite (as the deists and others thought). So despite his good intentions, Bishop Butler failed to convince his opponents, and in some respects he may even have strengthened their skepticism.

The real weakness of the deists, and of rationalists like Butler who tried to answer them on their own ground, was that they paid insufficient attention to the supernatural element of Christianity—that part of revelation that could not be demonstrated by reason but demanded faith if it was to be experienced at all. This was pointed out by none other than Pierre Bayle, in a note appended to his dictionary article on Antoinette Bourignon. According to Bayle, Mme Bourignon used to tell philosophers,

> . . . that their problem arose from trying to understand things in the light of human reason without preparing for the illumination of divine faith which required that we should abrogate our reason, our intellect, our feeble understanding so that God might kindle and diffuse his divine light within us. Unless this is done, not only is God imperfectly recognized, but he and his truth are excluded from the soul by this activity of our reason and the workings of our corrupt intelligence—and that, in itself, is a kind of atheism and denial of God.[58]

The Reconstruction of Theology

Atheism seems like a strange subject for a history of theology, but the modern world cannot be understood without taking it into consideration. In one sense, of course, atheists had been around for a long time. Socrates was put to death because he did not believe in the gods of ancient Athens and was therefore guilty of "atheism." The early Christians were accused of it for essentially the same reason.[59] Even today, Christians might be regarded as "atheists" by Hindus, because we reject their pantheon of gods and goddesses. But this definition of atheism seems strange to us, because in the modern world an atheist is not someone who denies the existence of pagan or Hindu gods, but someone who thinks that the God of the Bible does not exist. In this respect, it might be said that Christianity has triumphed over its rivals because it is now assumed that by "God" what is meant is the Father of Jesus Christ. Atheists themselves seldom bother to refute the claims of Islam or even of Judaism, much as they must logically disagree with them. Their target is Christianity, which they often confuse with "religion" to a degree that Christians themselves would hesitate

[58] Bayle, *Dictionnaire*, article "Bourignon," note K.
[59] Justin Martyr, *Apologia I* 6.

to do. Indeed, it is not too much to say that modern atheism has furthered the evangelization of the world by lumping all supernatural beliefs together as Christian and objecting to them accordingly!

The rise and spread of atheism as we know it today is of recent origin. There were always people who rejected God for one reason or another, but to call them "atheists" is problematic. More often it was a word applied to those who rejected the established order of things, or who led immoral lives. People like that were certainly not Christians in any positive sense, but whether they rejected the existence of God on philosophical grounds is hard to say. All discourse in the sixteenth and seventeenth centuries was permeated by theological assumptions that even those who disagreed with them found impossible to escape. When we add to that the fact that religious belief was compulsory by law, so that those who did not have it were forced to dissemble their skepticism, we are left with evidence that is hard to interpret and almost impossible to use as proof of genuine atheism.[60]

As a social and political force, modern atheism exists only within the Christian world, or as an extension of it. The great theoretical atheists—Marx, Nietzsche, Freud, and so on—all worked in a Christian context, and their opposition to "religion" would be incomprehensible otherwise. Atheistic political regimes have prospered mainly in the Christian world—Russia and Eastern Europe, for example. It is true that it has spread to China and to a few peripheral countries like North Korea and Vietnam, but even there, Christians are their chief rivals and opponents. To the extent that atheism has penetrated the Islamic world, it has done so on the back of Russian imperialism—only in Central Asia (Uzbekistan, etc.) and the Caucasus (Azerbaijan) has it had any success, and there it is clearly a foreign import that is now being rejected along with the other remnants of Soviet communism.

Atheism as we know it is therefore a Christian, or perhaps better, an anti-Christian phenomenon that can only be understood as a reaction to a certain type of Christian theology. From one point of view, its existence may be the logical outcome of evangelization, because if the light has shone in the darkness and the darkness has not accepted it,[61] "atheism" would seem to be the inevitable consequence. Michael Buckley has summed up the current situation very well:

> Unlike any civilization or intellectual culture that has preceded it in the past or accompanies it today, Western philosophical and theological reflection

[60] For an appreciation of the problems involved, see Lucien Febvre, *The Problem of Unbelief in the Sixteenth Century: The Religion of Rabelais* (Cambridge, MA: Harvard University Press, 1982). Originally published as *Le problème de l'incroyance au XVIe siècle: la religion de Rabelais* (Paris: Albin Michel, 1942; 2nd ed., 1968).
[61] See John 1:9–11.

> now confront the denial of God no longer as a random option or as an idiosyncratic philosophy, but as a heritage of two centuries. Atheism exists now in the West with a length of lineage and with a comprehensiveness of human commitments unlike anything which it has enjoyed before.[62]

Quite how the deism of the eighteenth century Enlightenment evolved into open atheism is a matter of controversy. By and large, the philosophers of the early Enlightenment rejected atheism as a viable option, though they turned away from the churches and their dogmatism even more emphatically. Indeed, it was not unusual for them to blame the confessionalism of the post-Reformation churches and the zeal with which each branch of Christendom persecuted the others for having created the spirit of atheism in the first place. Thomas Jefferson put it like this:

> I can never join Calvin in addressing his god. He was indeed an atheist, which I can never be; or rather his religion was daemonism. If ever man worshiped a false god, he did. The being described in his five points, is not the god whom you and I acknowledge and adore, the creator and benevolent governor of the world; but a daemon of malignant spirit. It would be more pardonable to believe in no god at all than to blaspheme him by the atrocious attributes of Calvin.[63]

What Jefferson wrote about Calvin could have been said about any theologian or theological system that was competing for influence in the eighteenth century. When dogmaticians of different schools all claimed an exclusive hold on truth, which one of them was to be believed? How could the honest enquirer choose between them without adopting a neutral standpoint from which to compare them? Once that was attempted, of course, the "neutral" standpoint—reason—took over and displaced the competing systems that (in varying degrees) departed from it. When theologians tried to shore up their beliefs by making their own appeal to reason they simply fell into a trap, allowing their opponents to set the criteria by which their propositions would be assessed. Once that happened, Calvinism, Thomism, and Lutheranism would all dissolve into rationalism and either disappear completely, or (as happened in most of the churches) remain merely as symbolic and traditional expressions of a common belief that for historical reasons had developed into what appeared to be mutually antagonistic theologies. As long as one of these confessions was

[62] Michael J. Buckley, *At the Origins of Modern Atheism* (New Haven, CT: Yale University Press, 1987), 36.
[63] In a letter to John Adams, April 11, 1823. Printed in Albert Bergh, ed., *The Writings of Thomas Jefferson*, 20 vols. (Washington, DC: Thomas Jefferson Memorial Association, 1903), 15:425. Jefferson apparently did not know that the "five points of Calvinism" came from the Synod of Dort and had nothing to do with Calvin himself.

enforced by law, it was expedient for the philosophical skeptic to adopt it—Rousseau, for example, was a Catholic in France but a Calvinist in Geneva—but it made no difference in practice. Once that happened, it would be only a matter of time before the hold of the religious establishments would weaken, and people would be free to express their belief or unbelief in any way they might choose. In this climate, atheism, with its rejection of all religious belief systems, could present itself as the rational alternative, built on a foundation that did not need God to justify it and therefore did not run the risk of falling into the potentially censorious hands of any particular church.

When this line was crossed is hard to say, because (as with all such developments) it happened almost without anyone noticing it at the time. But three figures stand out—one from Britain, one from France, and one from Germany, as befits a movement that had roots in all three countries. The first British thinker who must be described as an atheist in the modern sense was David Hume (1711–1776). Brought up in a Scottish Calvinist environment, Hume retained its legacy of private virtue and public uprightness but never showed any sign of appreciating or sharing its religious foundation. In *The Natural History of Religion*, he stated that anyone who examined the religions of the world would have to conclude that their ideas were nothing but "sick men's dreams."[64]

Hume did not call himself an atheist, and he was horrified by his French contemporaries who so readily mocked the religious establishment. He was on good terms with many leading churchmen of his day and had no desire to alienate them by debunking their beliefs. Yet despite his politeness, he did not hesitate to reject what for many was the core evidence for the truth of Christianity—the occurrence of miracles. He argued that because a miracle is by definition a violation of the laws of nature, and that those laws have been established by universal experience, there is really no place for one. If universal experience were overturned it would no longer be universal, and the law of nature would have to be revised accordingly. But if that happened, the phenomenon that caused the revision would no longer be seen as miraculous, and the concept of "miracle" would give way to one of "problem solved" instead:

> There must . . . be a uniform experience against every miraculous act, otherwise the event would not merit that appellation. And as a uniform experience amounts to a proof, there is here a direct and full proof, from the nature of the fact, against the existence of any miracle.[65]

[64] David Hume, *The Natural History of Religion* (London: A. & H. Bradlaugh Bonner, 1889), 15, 74. The book was first published in 1757.

[65] David Hume, *An Enquiry concerning Human Understanding*, ed. Peter Millican (Oxford: Oxford University Press, 2008), 10/1.12. The book was first published in 1748.

Unexplained phenomena were for Hume a stimulus to further research into their causes and not an invitation to credulity in the name of religion. In fact, he rejected reason altogether as a means of proving the truth of the Christian faith:

> I am the better pleased with the method of reasoning here delivered, as I think it may serve to confound those dangerous friends or disguised enemies of the Christian religion who have undertaken to defend it by the principles of human reason. Our most holy religion is founded on faith, not on reason; and it is a sure method of exposing it to put it to such a trial as it is by no means fitted to endure.[66]

To Hume, the real miracle (if there was one) was that anyone believed in Christianity at all. As he put it,

> Whoever is moved by faith to assent to it is conscious of a continued miracle in his own person which subverts all the principles of his understanding and gives him a determination to believe what is most contrary to custom and experience.[67]

What forces us to conclude that Hume was an atheist is not the fact that he separated faith from reason and regarded them as mutually incompatible. That view has been held by many Christians, both in ancient times and today, who have recognized that "we walk by faith, not by sight."[68] Hume's atheism rests on his conviction that faith has no validity—only reason can be used to measure all things, and reason does not naturally conclude that the world has been made by a good and all-powerful Creator. In that respect, he was more penetrating in his analysis than the deists, because he understood that the natural world was not the paradise they made it out to be:

> Look round this universe. What an immense profusion of beings. . . . You admire this prodigious variety and fecundity. But inspect a little more narrowly these living existences. . . . How hostile and destructive to each other. . . . The whole presents nothing but the idea of a blind nature, impregnated by a great vivifying principle, and pouring forth from her lap, without discernment or parental care, her maimed and abortive children.[69]

Hume's counterpart in France was his contemporary, Denis Diderot (1713–1784).[70] After a religious upbringing during which he almost became a Jesuit,

[66] Ibid., 10/2.40.
[67] Ibid., 10/2.41.
[68] 2 Cor. 5:7.
[69] David Hume, *Dialogues concerning Natural Religion*, ed. Norman K. Smith (London: T. Nelson, 1947), 211.
[70] On Diderot and his influence, see Israel, *Enlightenment Contested*, 781–862.

Diderot abandoned religion for the pleasures of philosophy. He was deeply attracted to the ideas of René Descartes and Isaac Newton but could not understand why their rationally based thinking should have led them to a "leap of faith," occasioned by a commitment to metaphysics that he found baffling and unnecessary. As Diderot saw it, the inner workings of the physical universe justified themselves. Matter was not an inert substance that had to be fashioned by some intelligent designer but a self-generating force that was able to evolve by itself into the many forms of it that we see today. Whether God existed or not was beside the point—he was not needed as an explanation of the way the world worked.[71] The "force of nature" was not moral in the traditional sense, but this did not worry Diderot. He was convinced that religions suppressed natural desires and thought that they should be set free. He saw nothing wrong with sexual experimentation of a kind that most people would regard as "pornographic," and in this he was followed by the notorious Marquis de Sade (1740–1814), who gave his name to "sadism." It was an extreme that few were prepared to follow, but it must be admitted that the modern world suggests that there is indeed a strong link between atheism and sexual profligacy, with the latter replacing the former as the ultimate source of satisfaction. Like it or not, Diderot has as much claim to be the patron philosopher of modernity as David Hume, and the practical results of his atheism are there for all to see.

In Germany, atheism emerged in a different way and to a large extent against the will of those who propagated it. This can be seen from the life and work of Immanuel Kant (1724–1804), who did not think of himself as an atheist and is usually not regarded as one, but whose system of thought inevitably pointed in that direction. One reason why Kant has escaped the charge of atheism is that he rejected the sharp contrast between faith and reason made by David Hume. Kant did not reject faith as superfluous to human requirements but saw it as one aspect, along with knowledge, that could legitimately claim to be rational. Kant had been brought up in a pietistic atmosphere, but he rejected what he saw as the hypocritical practices of the pietists and kept himself at arm's length from the established church. Nevertheless, pietism had left him with a religious feeling that was lacking in Hume and with a desire to establish some sort of existential commitment to his intellectual belief system.

One way in which Kant was different from Hume was in his approach to the question of the mind. Hume, like Locke before him, had regarded the human mind as a passive receptacle of ideas that shape it and give it the criteria for establishing meaning. Kant, on the other hand, believed that the mind was an

[71] See Buckley, *Origins of Atheism*, 194–250, for a detailed examination of Diderot's thought.

active agent in its own right, that could take the data provided by experience and shape them to its understanding of reality—mind over matter, instead of the other way around. The mind, however, is limited by its nature and cannot form an understanding of anything that goes beyond sensory experience in time and space. For that reason, it cannot conceive of God because when it tries to do so, it is forced into a kind of idolatry by turning something knowable in the created order into a deity to be worshiped. On the basis of that belief, Kant demolished the traditional "proofs" for the existence of God because, even if we can see such things as "being" and "causality" within the created order, we have no way of going beyond them to some principle that lies outside our experience and therefore cannot be defined by it.

When it came to religion, Kant asserted that the impulse for religious belief came not from any external divine revelation but from an internal moral impulse that owes its primary origin to reason. "Doing the right thing" is something that everyone believes, but we have to admit that we seldom achieve it and that there are plenty of examples of good people who suffer unjustly. However, we can hold those ideas only if we accept that there is a standard of morality that goes beyond them, and it is here that religion enters the picture. Mankind has no empirical evidence for the existence of God, but there is a moral imperative pushing us in that direction. In Kant's words,

> [It is] a duty for us to promote the *summum bonum* [supreme good]; consequently it is not merely allowable but it is a necessity connected with duty as a requisite, that we should presuppose the possibility of this *summum bonum*; and as it is possible only on condition of the existence of God, it inseparably connects the supposition of this with duty; that is, it is morally necessary to assume the existence of God.[72]

Kant recognized, however, that human efforts by themselves cannot make us better, and that for that we need the assistance of a higher power. At this point reason fails us, because it cannot go beyond the world of sense perception, which is necessary if we are to obtain the help that we need to live a moral life. Kant insisted that this help was available, since if it were not, we would have no knowledge of our own inadequacy and would not be driven to seek it. But his belief that the mind is an active participant in the knowledge of things impelled him to adopt what traditional Christianity would call a doctrine of salvation by works:

[72] Immanuel Kant, *The Critique of Practical Reason*, in Thomas K. Abbott, *Kant's Theory of Ethics* (London: Longmans, Green, 1879), 218.

> Where shall we start . . . with a faith in what God has done on our behalf, or with what we are to do to become worthy of God's assistance? In answering this question we cannot hesitate in deciding for the second alternative . . . we can certainly hope to partake in the appropriation of another's atoning merit, and so of salvation, only by qualifying for it through our own efforts to fulfill every human duty—and this obedience must be the effect of our own action and not, once again, of a foreign influence in the presence of whom we are passive.[73]

Given that Kant was officially a Lutheran, this rejection of justification by faith alone amounted to a denial of the faith altogether, an impression that is only strengthened by the following:

> With all our strength we must strive after the holy disposition of a course of life well-pleasing to God, in order to believe that the love of God toward man (already assured us through reason), so far as man does endeavor with all his power to do the will of God, will make good, in consideration of his upright disposition, the deficiency of the deed, whatever this deficiency may be.[74]

In other words, Kant decided on the basis of reason that there is a good and loving God who will honor our efforts to do our best, but the definition of what is right, good, and divine ultimately depends on what we think it ought to be. To be fair to him, he was prepared to accept that Jesus Christ provided an example of how this was possible in practice, and not just in theory, but although Jesus' earthly life offers us a useful lesson in this respect, it is not absolutely necessary. It is rather like a diagram telling the purchaser how to assemble the product he has just bought—the true handyman should be able to do without it and figure it out for himself.[75] At the same time, Kant did not believe that salvation was a purely individual matter. On the contrary, he thought that it could be realized only in a community of faith, because morality by definition involves other people. The church as we see it on earth is the institutional symbol of what that community should be, and it has the duty to point us toward it, but the two things should not be confused. Moral perfection is not possible in any existing human society, and especially not in the established church, which is weighed down by its own inadequacies. Yet gradually, Kant believed, it would give way to a universal religion of reason, whose advent would be the coming of the kingdom of God on earth.[76]

---

[73] Immanuel Kant, *Religion within the Limits of Reason Alone* (Lasalle, IL: Open Court, 1960), 43. Originally published as *Religion innerhalb der Grenzen der blossen Vernunft* (Konigsberg: Bey F. Nicolovius, 1794).
[74] Ibid., 110.
[75] Ibid., 55–57.
[76] Ibid., 113.

Kant was working within the Protestant world of Prussia, where any sign of unorthodoxy was liable to lead to a loss of his professorial chair. He was genuinely conflicted by the claims of the moral conscience and sought to find a way to accommodate it that would have seemed quite foreign to someone like Diderot, though not to Hume. We should therefore not be surprised to discover that he expressed his beliefs in language that would resonate with that of traditional Christianity, a fact that made them more acceptable to his contemporaries. But at the same time, we must not ignore where he was coming from. In the end, Kant's moral religion was a work of man, not of God, who was a concept called in to play its/his part, not the sovereign Lord of the universe in whose hands we tremble. In Christian terms, therefore, Kant was an atheist, and as succeeding generations stripped away his theology (as he had also stripped away the theology of his medieval and Reformation predecessors), the idea that one could be moral and atheist gradually took hold. The struggle to achieve goodness ceased to be impossible and became instead the glory of man—but of a man without any knowledge of, or relationship with, God.

If debates about the work of the Holy Spirit were central to the divisions of the Western church at the time of the Reformation, we should not be surprised to discover that, although the eighteenth-century deists rejected the Trinitarian framework of those debates, they were often attracted by the thought that there was a universal spirit that created and upheld the universe. This idea had the great advantage that the concept of a divine spirit was common to both "civilized" and "uncivilized" people whether they had received a special revelation or not, and could therefore be regarded as innate to human nature. Belief in such a divine spirit was a useful way of accommodating religious experience within a rational framework, and it provided a basis for morality that, as Kant showed, could not easily be dispensed with. Its very indefinability worked to its advantage. There had to be some underlying principle holding the universe together, and whether one called it the supreme being, the divine mind, or the Spirit of God made little difference. Detached from its moorings in the Trinity, the Christian doctrine of the Holy Spirit could be adapted to meet this new way of thinking—and it was.

The concept of a universal world spirit was not particularly prominent in the early days of the Enlightenment, when reason was held to be sufficient for human understanding and materialism appeared attractive to many. But as the weaknesses of this position became more apparent, attitudes started to change. Pietism had produced large groups of people who claimed to have had a personal experience of God, and the evidence for his existence was there to see in scores of lives that had been transformed for the better as a result. The philosophers might laugh at the absurdities of official religion, but it was hard to deny that it was something more than superstition that held society together and controlled the hearts and minds of people who in many ways were just as thoughtful and well educated as themselves. There was something about human life that rationality could not explain or account for, and that something was the province of religion. The emotions, the senses, and the higher thoughts of man were all bound up with religious systems that had produced what the enlightenment called civilization. In progressing from the primeval forest to the plains of Mesopotamia and Egypt, the noble savages of antiquity had developed a religious awareness that bound them together and allowed them to advance to higher things.

Change came partly through the efforts of Johann Georg Hamann (1730–1788), a native of East Prussia who was brought up as a pietist and had a life-changing conversion experience while still a young man. Some of his friends tried to shake him out of that, and even appealed to Kant for support, but Hamann was not to be persuaded. On the contrary, he came to think of the Enlightenment as a kind of idolatry in which reason had become a god (or better still, a goddess), as indeed she did at one stage in the French Revolution.[77] But before that, Hamann had already attacked the philosophers of his time, including Kant, for their intellectual presumption:

> Do not be against the truth with your vainglorious knowledge of God. . . . For all the propositions of your so-called general, healthy and expert reason are lies—more incomprehensible, contradictory, and barren than all the mysteries, miracles and signs of the most holy faith. . . . The object of your reflections and devotion is not God, but a mere word-image, like your universal human reason, which by a more than poetic license you deify as a real person.[78]

Hamann knew that rationalism was ultimately self-destructive because, when pushed to the extreme, it caused everyone to doubt everything and encouraged no one to believe anything. But human life had survived for centuries by finding meaning in the mind that it expressed in language—not necessarily rational or logical language, but the tongue of poetry, metaphor, and myth. It was in response to this innate desire that God had spoken to the patriarchs and that he had sent his Son to fulfill the potential in human nature and the promises of his own prophetic Word:

[77] In 1794 the cathedral church of Notre-Dame in Paris was transformed into a temple of "reason," and a statue of the "goddess" was erected inside it.

[78] J. G. Hamann, "The Letter H by Itself," in Ronald G. Smith, *J. G. Hamann 1730–1788: A Study in Christian Existence* (London: Collins, 1960), 203–204.

> The mustard-seed of anthropomorphosis and apotheosis, which is hidden in the heart and mouth of every religion, appears here [in the Bible] in the greatness of a tree of knowledge and of life in the midst of the garden—all philosophical contradictions, and the whole historical riddle of our existence . . . are resolved by the primal message of the Word become flesh.[79]

One of the people most deeply influenced by Hamann was Johann Gottfried Herder (1744–1803). Herder picked up Hamann's interest in language and developed it further. He did not believe that human language was a gift of divine origin, because he thought that if it were, it would have to be perfect and one, which it obviously was not. But neither did he think that it was a human invention, developed by imitating animal sounds. Instead of that, he thought that human language was a capacity innate in man and exclusive to the human race that permitted the expression of imagination, reason, and culture. The diversity of language over time and space was a sign for Herder that all human perceptions are relative. This does not make them false, but it imposes on the critic the duty to put himself in the shoes of the speaker he is trying to interpret in order to make sense of what he is saying. A Hebrew prophet could not be judged by the standards of an eighteenth-century philosopher, but must be read in the context of the time in which he lived.

Herder's view seems obvious to us today, but it was hard for his contemporaries to come to terms with. The orthodox believed that God's Word was eternal and therefore that it could not change or be different from one historical context to another, while the rationalists were convinced that, since truth is the same everywhere, different expressions of it must be mutually compatible. Herder challenged these assumptions by arguing that each nation and society had its own ways of expressing the truth known to it, and that it was the duty of researchers to discover what that truth was. But at the same time, he also believed that Christianity stood above the different national and cultural expressions of truth and that it was able to help them grow into a higher unity. Missionaries should therefore try to understand the religions of the people they went to, find out what was good in them, and preach the gospel in a way that would build on that:

> Every nation blossoms like a tree from its own roots. Christianity, which is the true conviction about God and human beings, is nothing but the pure dew of heaven for all nations that does not change any tree's character or fruit, or strip any human beings of their own nature. . . . I do not need to tell you that

[79] J. G. Hamann, *Zweifel und Einfälle*, in Smith, *J. G. Hamann*, 259.

> the so-called propagation and expansion of Christianity would look quite different [if this approach were taken.][80]

Herder believed that the Bible was a book written by men for men, because God could not speak to them or to us in any other way. As the early church fathers would have put it, he had to accommodate himself to our limitations in order to communicate his truth to us, but because of that, it is now necessary for us to discover what the particular limitations of the ancient writers were, so that we can decipher the meaning of their words for us today. For example, it might be true that the stories of the Old Testament are fables, but that does not make them unimportant or untrue. As he put it,

> Perhaps Joshua did believe that the sun stood still or sat in the sky. Why should this bother me? He was able to believe this in accordance with his own historical context, and God found it beneath his dignity . . . to prove himself to be a professor of astrology and to explain to Joshua whether the sun or the earth moved.[81]

Herder thus has a fair claim to be the first truly modern interpreter of the Bible. He was not disturbed by the way in which the sacred text blended historical fact with narrative metaphorical language, such as that used in the story of creation, because that kind of mixture was natural for those who wrote the text and for whom it was written. It only causes problems when a different (in this case, modern rationalist) mind-set is applied to it and it no longer makes sense. Herder can be criticized for being naive, and there were certainly many details of interpretation that he had neither the time nor the inclination to work out, but that should not detract from his greatness. Without realizing it, he had rediscovered the hermeneutic of the early church—Origen would have been stunned to learn that Herder had to explain the obvious to his contemporaries—and over time his approach was accepted by almost everyone engaged in biblical studies. The details might be debated, but the basic method became and still remains the bedrock of biblical interpretation today.

The legacy of Kant and Hamann might have followed Herder into the developing disciplines of linguistics and hermeneutics, leaving theology behind, but that did not happen, largely thanks to the genius of two men of very different character. Georg Wilhelm Friedrich Hegel (1770–1831) was a man of many parts whose life spanned one of the most turbulent periods in European

[80] Johann G. Herder, *First Dialogue concerning National Religions*, in Marcia Bunge, ed., *Against Pure Reason: Writings on Religion, Language, and History* (Minneapolis: Fortress, 1993), 102, 105–106.
[81] Johann G. Herder, *Concerning the Divinity and Use of the Bible*, in Bunge, *Against Pure Reason*, 210.

history.[82] The French Revolution, which broke out in 1789, hit Germany in full force a few years later and transformed the country in ways that would not be fully apparent until it was finally united in 1871. But long before that it was clear that the old regime was gone beyond recall and that a new world was dawning. Lacking a centralized state, the Germans were free to speculate about what this might be like, with little danger that anyone would try to stop them—or put their ideas into practice! As a result, German philosophy and theology enjoyed a renaissance at a time when France was in turmoil and other European countries were too afraid to experiment with new ideas.

Hegel began where Herder left off, with a deeply rooted idea of folk religion and its virtues. Unlike Herder, though, he concentrated on ancient Greece and Rome as his models, finding in them the elements of a religious culture governed by the principle of human freedom. Hegel's understanding of the ancient world was highly romanticized and quite inaccurate, but it was widely shared by his contemporaries, who looked to them as models of how a country should be governed.[83] The trouble with Christianity, as the young Hegel saw it, was that it was *not* a folk religion, but an alien message of salvation that had been imposed on native beliefs in an attempt to wipe them out. He soon realized that that view was too simplistic, and he spent many years wrestling with the subject in the light of Kant's distinction between theoretical and practical religion, but his view was typical of the age he lived in.

Kant had accepted that the moral perfection that the soul ought to attain in theory could not be realized in this life, which demanded practical action. "Love your neighbor," for example, was a noble ideal, but if it was to mean anything it would have to have practical consequences, and those might be contradictory. What if a man gave all his possessions to feed the poor but then had nothing left to take care of his own family? Dilemmas of this kind could be resolved only by instituting laws to govern behavior in particular circumstances, complete with a system of punishments and forgiveness for those who failed in their duty, as everyone sooner or later would. This explained how the law of Moses had come into being and why the death of Jesus was interpreted as an atoning sacrifice for sin. By studying the life and teaching of Jesus, Hegel came to see the matter very differently.

---

[82] The standard modern work on Hegel is Charles Taylor, *Hegel* (Cambridge: Cambridge University Press, 1975).

[83] Consider, for example, the monumental history of Edward Gibbon, *The History of the Decline and Fall of the Roman Empire*, 6 vols. (London: W. Strahan, 1776–1788); Gibbon blamed the empire's demise on a combination of "barbarism and religion," i.e., Christianity. The United States, which came into being even as Gibbon was writing, modeled itself on ancient Rome, with its Capitol and senate, and everyone loved the Greeks—so much so, in fact, that Lord Byron and other Philhellenes were able to muster enough support for Greek rebels against Turkish rule that the country became independent just as Hegel was dying. Only later did people find out (the hard way) that the modern Greeks were much more like the Turks than like their ancient forebears.

In Hegel's view, Hebrew religion was an expression of alienation. Abraham was prepared to leave his country and even to sacrifice his son because he could see nothing in nature that would link him in any way to God:

> The whole world Abraham regarded as simply his opposite; if he did not take it to be a nullity, he looked on it as sustained by the God who was alien to it. Nothing in nature was supposed to have any part in God; everything was simply under God's mastery.[84]

In later years Hegel came to think that this was the great genius of Hebraic religion, because it had preached the alienation of man from nature that was the result of his acquisition of knowledge:

> Man, created in the image of God, lost, it is said, his state of absolute contentment, by eating of the tree of the knowledge of good and evil. Sin consists here only in knowledge—this is the sinful element, and by it, man is stated to have trifled away his natural happiness. This is a deep truth, that evil lies in consciousness, for the brute beasts are neither evil nor good; the natural man quite as little. Consciousness occasions the separation of the ego . . . from the pure essence of the will, i.e., from the good. Knowledge, as the disannulling of the unity of mere nature, is the fall, which is no casual conception, but the eternal history of Spirit.[85]

The loss of innocence and the acquisition of knowledge was evil because of the alienation that it produced inside the human consciousness, but it was also necessary because without separation there could be no reconciliation, and reconciliation was what the Spirit was essentially all about. Given his Hebraic inheritance, Jesus had little choice but to present his message as coming from a transcendent God, since only such a being could escape the tyranny of the bondage imposed by the "fall." It was Jesus' mission to reconcile the estranged consciousness of man to the natural state from which it had departed, and this could be done only by love. In his early days, Hegel saw this as well-meaning but ineffective because it could not achieve the synthesis that he thought was necessary:

> Love is a divine spirit but it falls short of religion. To become religion, it must manifest itself in an objective form. A feeling, something subjective, it must be fused with the universal, with something represented in idea. . . . The need

[84] Georg W. F. Hegel, "The Spirit of Christianity and Its Fate," in *Hegel's Early Theological Writings*, ed. T. M. Knox (Chicago: University of Chicago Press, 1961), 185.

[85] Georg W. F. Hegel, *The Philosophy of History* (New York: Dover, 1956), 321. The series of lectures was given in 1830–1831 and first published in 1837.

> to unite subject with object, to unite feeling and feeling's demand for objects, with the intellect, to unite them in something beautiful, in a god, by means of fantasy, is the supreme need of the human spirit and the urge to religion.[86]

Somewhat oddly, Hegel's negative attitude toward Christianity mellowed when he gave up trying to be a theologian and concentrated on philosophy instead. His understanding of the faith went through a process of *Aufhebung* or "transformation," which is to say that it was erased at the lower level and reborn on a higher plane. He came to realize that men had not fought and died for centuries over nothing, and that Christianity must contain some valid truth. He concluded that in fact it had attained to a level of perfect unity between the divine and the human which produced the Absolute Spirit.

Hegel saw the Trinity as the theological expression of a reality that permeates human life. According to him, everything that exists seeks to identify its opposite in order to interact with it and produce a higher combination of the two. That combination will then in turn seek its opposite and repeat the process, which is how the world advances from one stage of development to the next. In God, the transcendent Father naturally seeks to create the incarnate Son in opposition to himself, but he then combines with the Son to produce the Holy Spirit, who is a higher synthesis of them both. Finally, the Holy Spirit comes into the world seeking its opposite, the material universe and in particular the human race, and by combining with it produces a still higher degree of awareness. This pattern is intrinsic to the Christian vision of the Godhead because it is fundamental to reality. Hegel did not bother much about the historical details of Jesus' life, which were secondary to his concerns, though he did insist that the universal had to be actualized in the particular, and so the incarnation of Christ was the central event around which all the rest had to be understood:

> Considered only in respect of his talents, character and morality—as a teacher and so forth—we place him [Jesus] in the same category as Socrates and others. . . . But if Christ is to be looked upon only as an excellent, even sinless individual and nothing more, the concept of . . . Absolute Truth is ignored. But this is the desideratum, the point from which we have to start. Make of Christ what you will, exegetically, critically, historically—demonstrate as you please, how the doctrines of the church were established by councils, attained currency as a result of this or that episcopal passion—let all such circumstances have been what they might—the only concerning question is: "What is the idea or the truth in and for itself?"[87]

[86] Georg W. F. Hegel, "On Christianity," in *Early Theological Writings*, 289.
[87] Hegel, *Philosophy of History*, 326.

The incarnation of Christ was for Hegel the historical manifestation of an eternal idea that was necessary for the reconciliation of mind and matter, of thought and sense-perception. It was all very well for the philosophers to posit the existence of Absolute Truth, but unless that Truth were concretized in human experience it would remain an abstraction of limited value. This is what occurred, said Hegel, in the life of Jesus:

> Christ has appeared—a man who is God—God who is man, and thereby peace and reconciliation have accrued to the world. . . . The appearance of the Christian God . . . [is] unique in its kind; it can occur only once, for God is realized as a subject, and as manifested subjectivity, [he] is only one individual.[88]

Central to the meaning of the incarnation is the crucifixion and death of Jesus, which Hegel interpreted in a uniquely imaginative way. For him, this was the infinite Spirit embracing the finite world, which included taking on human alienation and death. If this had not happened, the Spirit would not have embraced human finitude to its fullest extent, and no real reconciliation of the finite and the infinite would have taken place. In the death of Christ, the eternal Spirit died in its adopted finitude, thereby putting an end to everything that alienates man from God. The crucifixion could not be the end of the story, however, because by losing its finitude the Absolute Spirit was once again free to realize its own potential. God is no longer a heavenly being standing over and against the human race but one of us who has taken on our life in order to achieve *Aufhebung*—the destruction of this life by its transformation into something higher.

The ascension into heaven completes this process, as the crucified finite is reunited with the eternal Spirit, but it is with a difference. The crucifixion of the finite body of Christ was not just the fate of a single individual but the beginning of a new phase in human life generally. Everyone who is united to Christ in his death and resurrection is transformed in the same way, and made part of a new spiritual community. As Hegel put it,

> The sensuous existence in which Spirit is embodied is only a transitional phase. Christ dies; only as dead is he exalted to heaven and sits at the right hand of God; only thus is he Spirit. He himself says: "When I am no longer with you, the Spirit will guide you into all truth."[89] Not till the feast of Pentecost were the apostles filled with the Holy Spirit. To the apostles, Christ

[88] Ibid., 325–325.
[89] A paraphrase of John 16:10–13.

> as a living [human being] was not the same as he was to them later on as the Spirit of the church, in which he became to them for the first time an object for their truly spiritual consciousness.[90]

Hegel then went on to draw the conclusion that with Pentecost the kingdom of the Spirit has arrived, bringing with it the reconciliation of God and man that was implicit from the beginning of creation. The practical consequences of this were enormous. Set free from the restrictions imposed by his finitude and alienation, man could now achieve his highest potential by surrendering to pure self-consciousness, which was the only way of attaining the truth. Christ appears as the example we are called to follow:

> Christ—man as man—in whom the unity of God and man has appeared, has in his death, and his history generally, himself presented the eternal history of Spirit—a history which every man has to accomplish in himself in order to exist as Spirit or to become a child of God, a citizen of his kingdom. The followers of Christ, who join together on [the basis of] this principle and live in the spiritual life as their aim, form the church, which is the kingdom of God.[91]

For Hegel, the Spirit was not a person in the traditional Christian sense but the life-force that determines what persons are and what they can do. The Holy Spirit is the only one of the Trinity who manifests the reality of God, having combined in himself (itself?) and thereby overcome the partial truths contained in the realms of the Father and the Son. Because the Spirit is embodied in the church, God is inside us, making the absolute known in our finitude, whose limitations have been set aside. But even this is not the last word. Christianity is a historical actualization of eternal truth, but is not eternal truth itself. For that we must rise to the level of philosophy, where the particulars of history are merged into the universals of eternity. The glory of Christianity is that it makes that further move possible in a way that no other religion does. It contains within itself the seeds of its own *Aufhebung*, or "transformation through self-destruction," which is its ultimate destiny and its glory.

Assessing Hegel's thought is extremely difficult, and no one should be surprised to discover that his legacy has been varied and controversial. Some have said that he used Christian language as a foil for his own purposes, which were quite different, and have felt free to abandon what they see as his theological jargon in order to concentrate on the real meaning underneath. But to say that is to miss the point that, for Hegel, truth was attained by a coincidence

[90] Hegel, *Philosophy of History*, 325.
[91] Ibid., 328.

of opposites, not by unmasking a false framework that conceals the reality underneath it. The Christian gospel was therefore a real factor in the search for Absolute Spirit and could not be dismissed as mere metaphor or myth. At the same time, Hegel clearly did not feel bound by historical facts, which he interpreted as a revelation of spiritual principles that might not always be fully understood. He could therefore live quite happily with the idea that the miracles Jesus was reputed to have performed never actually happened, because they symbolized a spiritual truth that was valid in spite of the facts. Miracle-stories reinforced the principle that the spiritual must be manifested in the material in order to reconcile the two, but they were supportive illustrations of it and not the principle itself. Christians were therefore wrong to rely on miracles as evidence for the truth of their faith, because that truth was eternally present in the nature of reality and was worked out by the reconciliation of opposing forces within it.

The protean nature of Hegel's thought can best be measured by what happened to it after he died. Two quite different schools of thought emerged from it, which scholars call "right" and "left." The "right" school emphasized the theological character of Hegel's work and sought to reconstruct Christian doctrine in the light of it. Most of these theologians have now been forgotten, although the idea that the life of Christ is more symbol than fact still resurfaces from time to time.[92] But tellingly, it is the so-called "left" wing of the Hegelian school that really left its mark, in the work of David Strauss (1808–1874), Bruno Bauer (1809–1882), who actually denied the existence of the historical Jesus, Ludwig Feuerbach (1804–1872), and above all, Karl Marx (1818–1883), whose Hegelianism would change the face of the world in the twentieth century.

To the casual observer, Hegel's thought appears as an eclectic fantasy based on a set of ideas that he presupposes but does not justify by serious critique or investigation. But it was a fantasy that had considerable appeal to an age beset by revolution and uncertainty. By combining good and evil, instead of merely opposing one to the other, Hegel enabled his contemporaries to accept the horrific destruction they were witnessing around them as part of a necessary evolution. He provided them with a sense of purpose to what was otherwise senseless violence and allowed people to see that even death had a higher goal, not in heaven but in a transformed humanity. Absurd and idolatrous as this must seem to Christians, it nevertheless captured the imagination of generations and is still a powerful intellectual force in the world today.

[92] For an overview of this, see Livingston, *Modern Christian Thought*, 1:129–138.

Very different from Hegel was his contemporary Friedrich Schleiermacher (1768–1834). Both men taught at the university of Berlin, Schleiermacher from its foundation in 1811 and Hegel from 1818, but they were poles apart intellectually and did not like each other. This is somewhat ironic today, when we tend to lump both men together as representatives of the liberal German school of thought in the early nineteenth century, but this is the result of historical reassessment and was less obvious at the time. Schleiermacher is now credited with having been the first modern liberal theologian in Germany because this is the judgment that Karl Barth passed on him two generations after his death, but when set next to Hegel, he appears to be quite conservative. The reason for that, no doubt, is that by the time Barth was writing, Schleiermacher was still regarded as recognizably Christian in a way that Hegel was not, and so it is not surprising that Barth concentrated on him as the archetypal "liberal" within the wider Christian fold.

Like many others before him, Schleiermacher came from a pietistic background and only met the cultured atheism of his time when he went to university. It shocked him profoundly, but when he went to Berlin in 1796 he was drawn into the emerging Romantic movement and fell under the influence of Friedrich Schlegel (1772–1829), who was one of its leading exponents. Schlegel and his associates taught the young Schleiermacher the importance of feelings, especially for religion. In 1799 Schleiermacher published his first book, *On Religion: Speeches to Its Cultured Despisers.*[93] In five speeches, he outlined first a defense of his approach and then (in order) the nature of religion, the cultivation of religion, association in religion, and the various religions that exist in the world. He began by taking on the antireligious prejudices of the cultured intelligentsia of his time, whom he described as follows:

> The life of cultivated persons is removed from anything that would in the least way resemble religion. I know that you worship the deity in holy silence just as little as you visit the forsaken temples, that in your tasteful dwellings, there are no other household gods than the maxims of the sages and the songs of the poets, and that humanity and fatherland, art and science (for you imagine yourselves capable of all of this) have taken possession of your minds so completely that no room is left over for the eternal and holy being that for you lies beyond the world, and that you have no feelings for and with it.

[93] Friedrich Schleiermacher, *Über die Religion: Reden an die Gebildeten unter ihren Verächtern* (Berlin: J. F. Unger, 1799), trans. Richard Crouter, 2nd ed. (Cambridge: Cambridge University Press, 1996). The third edition (1831) was translated by John Oman, *On Religion: Speeches to Its Cultured Despisers* (London: K. Paul, Trench, Trübner, 1893; republished New York: Harper & Row, 1958).

> You have succeeded in making your earthly lives so rich and many-sided, that you no longer need the eternal.[94]

The thought world he was addressing sounds very much like the world of Hegel, which reminds us that Hegel was also a child of his time and not nearly as original as his later disciples believed him to be. Schleiermacher described the forces of civilization like this:

> You know that the deity, by an immutable law, has compelled itself to divide its great work endlessly, to fuse together each definite being only out of two opposing forces, and to realize each of its eternal thoughts in twin forms that are hostile to each other and yet exist inseparably only through each other. This whole corporeal world . . . appears to the best informed and most thoughtful among you only as an eternally prolonged play of opposing forces.[95]

In human life, Schleiermacher divided these opposing forces into people who were basically materialistic and either unable or unwilling to consider spiritual truths, and people who were interested only in abstract concepts and regarded visible reality as both too complex and corrupt. However, Schleiermacher did not give up on mankind completely. On the contrary, he said that,

> At all times the deity sends people here and there, in whom both tendencies are combined in a more fruitful manner, equips them with wondrous gifts, prepares their way with an all-powerful word, and employs them as translators of its will and its works and as mediators of what would otherwise remain eternally separated.[96]

Such gifted people form a "higher priesthood that proclaims the inner meaning of all spiritual secrets, and speaks down from the kingdom of God."[97] The cultured men of Schleiermacher's time thought that religion sprang from fear of an eternal being who determines the events of this life by what theologians call "providence," and from expectation of a future life, conceived of as "immortality." Seen from the outside, these impulses appear in the form of dogmas and rituals that vary in sophistication from one context to another, but that are all essentially the same and equally absurd. But, asked Schleiermacher, was that the right way to look at the question of religion? In sharp contrast to Hegel, he answered that religion is "by its whole nature . . . just as far removed

[94] Schleiermacher, *On Religion*, 1 (Oman, 1–2).
[95] Ibid., 5 (Oman, 3–4).
[96] Ibid., 6 (Oman, 6).
[97] Ibid., 7 (Oman, 7).

from all that is systematic as philosophy is by its nature inclined toward it."[98] In other words, rationalism would never unlock the key to an understanding of religion. The true student of the phenomenon must learn to look at it from the inside, to see what gives it its coherence and makes it tick, and not rest content with vague and superficial conclusions derived from outward effects, such as its usefulness in maintaining justice and order in the world. Neither morality nor justice lies at the heart of religion, said Schleiermacher; but what does, if they are excluded?

The answer to that question formed the bulk of his second speech on the subject, which he revised for the third edition of *On Religion*, which appeared in 1831. Hegel identified religion with philosophy, and Kant thought it was morality, but in both cases the result was to define religion as something other than what it really is and therefore to make it unnecessary. "Belief," said Schleiermacher, "must be something different from a mixture of opinions about God and the world, and of precepts for one life or two."[99] Religion cannot be equated with knowledge, which varies far too much and is too uncertain to form a basis for eternal life. Nor can it be morality, which is concerned only with right behavior in this world. What it is, is feeling—not in the sense of mere emotion, but in the sense of intuition. It is essentially contemplative, but not in a scientific sense, as if it were searching for a first cause of all things. Rather,

> The contemplation of the pious [person] is the immediate consciousness of the universal existence of all finite things, in and through the infinite, and of all temporal things in and through the eternal. Religion is to seek this and find it in all that lives and moves, in all growth and change, in all doing and suffering. It is to have life and to know life in immediate feeling, only as such an existence in the infinite and eternal. Where this is found, religion is satisfied.[100]

Contemplation is by definition the activity of individuals, but it is directed outwardly. A person who has discovered the nature of things within himself will want to share this with others, because no man is an island. As Schleiermacher expressed it in his fourth speech,

> We see that even from childhood on, man is primarily concerned to communicate these intuitions and feelings. He willingly lets his concepts, about whose origins no doubts can in any case arise, rest in themselves. But he

[98] Ibid., 14 (Oman, 17).
[99] Ibid., 31 (Oman).
[100] Ibid., 36 (Oman).

> wants to have witnesses for and participants in that which enters his senses and arouses his feelings. How should he keep to himself the influences of the universe that appear to him as greatest and most irresistible? How should he wish to retain within himself that which most strongly forces him out of himself and which, like nothing else, impresses him with the fact that he cannot know himself in and of himself alone? Rather, his first endeavor, when a religious view has become clear to him, or a pious feeling penetrates his soul, is also to direct others to the object, and if possible, to communicate the vibrations of his mind to him.[101]

Every religious person, according to Schleiermacher, will seek and find the truth for himself. In his attempts to preserve it and communicate it to others, he may develop or attach himself to rituals and forms of expression that others have used in the past—this is how doctrines, liturgies, and churches have come into being. But these things are not the essence of religion, nor is the Bible to be revered as its source. Speaking once more to the cultured despisers of religion, Schleiermacher assures them,

> You are right to despise the paltry imitators who derive their religion wholly from someone else or cling to a dead document by which they swear and from which they draw proof. Every holy writing is merely a mausoleum of religion, a monument that a great spirit was there that no longer exists; for if it still lived and were active, why would it attach such great importance to the dead letter that can only be a weak reproduction of it? It is not the person who believes in a holy writing who has religion, but only the one who needs none and probably could make one for himself.[102]

What Schleiermacher valued was "piety"—a devotional commitment that reflected the presence of the deity in one's life, whatever ideas it might express. Such a religion cannot be taught, but others may see the pious man's way of life and be moved to imitate it themselves. The precise way it was expressed was secondary to him, but he was quite convinced that it must have some concrete manifestation and not be just an abstract idea in the mind. Schleiermacher believed that existing religions were such manifestations, but that one way or another they had been corrupted by dogmatists who tried to tie everything down, or else by nominal adherents who went through the external motions but had little or no appreciation of their inner meaning.[103] Such distortions, of which Christianity had its fair share, must be recognized for what they were

[101] Ibid., 73 (Oman, 149).
[102] Ibid., 50 (Oman, 91).
[103] Ibid., 113 (Oman, 238).

and not used to pass judgment on the deeper content of what the religion was trying to express. Schleiermacher had no intention of excusing believers from their duty to avoid such things, but he was writing for the cultured despisers of religion, and it was here that the latter tended to misrepresent what they were rejecting, and going wrong in the process.

When looking at the different religions of the world, Schleiermacher classified them in what we might call a hierarchy of worth. The lowest form of religion was what he called "natural"—the kind of religion that philosophers like Rousseau wanted to put in the place of Christianity. After considering it briefly, he summed it up like this:

> This natural religion . . . has no unity of a specific view for its religious intuition. It is therefore no determinate form, no truly individual presentation of religion; and those who confess only it have no specific dwelling in its realm, but are strangers whose home, if they have one (which I doubt) must lie elsewhere. . . . I cannot grant more to the adherents of natural religion than the dim intimations that precede that living intuition that opens the religious life to a person.[104]

Next on the evolutionary scale came the religions of antiquity and of faraway peoples, though Schleiermacher did not specify what he meant by that. He said nothing about Islam, of which his knowledge was probably not great, nor about Hinduism and Buddhism, which must have been a closed book to him. In any case, he passed them over in a few short lines:

> However fortunate you may be at deciphering the crude and individual religions of distant peoples or at sorting out the many types of individual religions that lie enclosed in the beautiful mythology of the Greeks and Romans is all the same to me; may their gods guide you. But when you approach the most holy, where the universe is intuited in its highest unity, when you want to contemplate the different forms of systematic religions—not the exotic and strange but those that are still more or less present among us—then it cannot be a matter of indifference to me whether you find the right point from which you must view them.[105]

Judaism was in a category of its own, and we cannot be surprised that Schleiermacher devoted much more attention to it than he did to the others. It is also more important for our purposes, because what he said about it was of great significance for his understanding of the Christian heritage and also

[104] Ibid., 109–110 (Oman, 232–233).
[105] Ibid., 113 (Oman, 238).

for the fate of the Jews in Germany later on. Surprisingly (from our point of view), he began by saying that Judaism was a dead religion. This opinion was widespread among his Prussian contemporaries, but its obvious falsehood is all the more disturbing because of that. As for the fact that Judaism was somehow the forerunner of Christianity, Schleiermacher had no time for such assertions, however self-evident they may seem to us. As he rather bluntly said, "I hate that type of historical reference in religion."[106] His appreciation of Judaism, such as it was, was extremely odd. In his estimation,

> Judaism has such a beautiful childlike character, and this is so completely buried, and the whole constitutes such a remarkable example of the corruption and total disappearance of religion from a great body in which it was formerly found.[107]

What Schleiermacher claimed was that even when political and cultural factors were discounted, Judaism remained a religion of retribution, "of the infinite's own reaction against every individual finite form that proceeds from free choice by acting through another finite element that is not viewed as proceeding from free choice."[108] He went on to add,

> All other attributes of God that are also intuited express themselves according to this principle and are always seen in connection with this. The deity is thus portrayed throughout as rewarding, chastising, and punishing what is singled out in the individual person.[109]

But according to Schleiermacher, the more Jews moved out of their original tribal culture and interacted with the rest of the world, the less their religious inheritance was suited to their new circumstances. They struggled on for a time, but,

> [Judaism] died when its holy books were closed; then the conversation of Jehovah with his people was viewed as ended; the political association that was linked to it dragged on in an ailing existence, and its external parts were preserved even longer still, the unpleasant appearance of a mechanical movement after the life and spirit had long since departed.[110]

Christianity, in Schleiermacher's opinion, was completely different from this. Not a local manifestation of religion like Judaism, nor restricted to the single

---

[106] Ibid., 114 (Oman, 238).
[107] Ibid., 114 (Oman, 238–239).
[108] Ibid., 114 (Oman, 239).
[109] Ibid., 114 (Oman, 239).
[110] Ibid., 115 (Oman, 240–241).

theme of retribution, Christianity was free to take in the heights and depths of human spiritual experience. At its heart lay the intuition that everything finite was straining against the unity of the whole and that, in response to that, the deity was reconciling the hostility it had to face and shaping a higher synthesis out of it. The fact that it takes a global approach to the separation of man from God, and fights on all fronts to contain and reverse that process, means that Christianity is forever fighting its enemies. As Schleiermacher explained it,

> In order to make clear its innermost nature it must everywhere disclose all corruption, be it in morals or in the manner of thinking, and above all in the irreligious principle itself. Without mercy it therefore unmasks every false morality, every inferior religion, every unfortunate mixture of the two whereby their mutual nakedness is supposed to be covered. . . . Christianity destroyed . . . the last expectation of its closest brothers and contemporaries and called it irreligious and godless to wish for or to expect some other restoration than the hope for a better religion, for a higher view of things, and for eternal life in God.[111]

When it came to the person of Jesus, Schleiermacher could not explain how it was that he had come to think of himself as the one who would reconcile the finite and the infinite, but somehow he possessed a deeper insight into the nature of reality than anyone else. When the supreme test of his faith came, he sacrificed himself, but not before planning ahead by telling his disciples how they were to remember him after he had gone. But however close Jesus was to God, he never claimed to be the sole mediator, and anyone who follows him can (and should) have the same spiritual experience that he had and even develop it further:

> Never did he pass off the intuitions and the feelings he himself could communicate as the whole compass of religion that was to proceed from his basic intuition; he always pointed to the truth that would come after him.[112] Thus his disciples also never set limits to the Holy Spirit; its unlimited freedom and the thorough unity of its revelations were universally acknowledged by them.[113]

Schleiermacher redefined religion as a self-consciousness that expressed itself in doctrines, rituals, and liturgies but that was never bound or determined by them. Such fixed forms represented a particular stage in the evolution of humanity toward a greater (and higher) awareness of the Spirit, which in turn

[111] Ibid., 117 (Oman, 242–243).
[112] As in John 16:13, for example.
[113] Schleiermacher, *On Religion*, 121 (Oman, 248).

produced a deeper sense of relational dependence on it. In this sense, feeling and piety were at the heart of religious experience; doctrine and the church were merely the outward forms it took.

Schleiermacher developed his ideas further in his masterpiece, *The Christian Faith*, which appeared in two volumes in 1821–1822, and in a second, revised edition in 1830–1831, which is now the standard text.[114] Its basic premise is that Christians become aware of the absolute power of God over time and space by their experience of sin and redemption. The fact that we ascribe our deliverance from the former and our enjoyment of the latter entirely to divine activity on our behalf is the universal given that is present in the Christian consciousness. The main divine attributes involved in this are holiness and righteousness, and it is as we apprehend the meaning and implications of these that we come to a knowledge of God that transforms our lives. Our awareness of sin does not come from an external law or condemnation, but from an inner self-awareness that causes us to repent and seek reconciliation with the deity from whom we have been alienated. Jesus was sinless because in him there was no such alienation and his consciousness was perfectly aligned with the divine. He is there to show us the way to achieve such reconciling harmony with the infinite, but does not take our place or do it for us. In that sense, he is our example and not our substitute, but Schleiermacher did not believe that we can achieve our own reconciliation by following Jesus. Instead, he insisted that because Jesus was the only man who was perfectly reconciled to God, he was the channel through whom reconciliation is conveyed to us. He is therefore a genuine mediator of salvation, the only one capable of retuning our souls so that they are consonant with the being and will of God.

In reconstructing Christian doctrine the way he did, Schleiermacher did not know what to do with the Trinity, which was not in the New Testament and did not form part of the original teaching of Jesus. Nor did it reflect any of the divine attributes associated with personal self-consciousness, and yet there was no denying its centrality for Christian faith and experience. Schleiermacher "solved" the problem of what to do about it by putting it in an appendix to his theology and then investigating how it could be fitted in with the rest. He began by asserting that the divine essence is united with human nature in the personality of Christ and in the common Spirit of the church, two basic doctrines on which the church's interpretation of Christianity stands or falls.[115] It

[114] Friedrich Schleiermacher, *Der christliche Glaube nach der Grundsätzen der Evangelischen Kirche im Zusammenhange dargestellt*, 2 vols. (Berlin: G. Reimer, 1830–1831); English translation, *The Christian Faith* (Edinburgh: T & T Clark, 1928).

[115] Schleiermacher, *Christian Faith*, 170.1.

was to defend this double truth, he claimed, that the doctrine of the Trinity was originally developed.

The equality of the Father and the Son was a necessary deduction from the fact that our sense of the need for redemption must be met and matched by a redemption that brings us into fellowship with God. To put this in traditional language, if we had offended the Father but the Son was not capable of overcoming that offense, we would not have any relationship with God and would not be saved. This is why it is perfectly understandable that all forms of subordination within the Godhead have been consistently rejected by the church.[116] On the other hand, Schleiermacher found it virtually impossible to explain how the single divine essence can manifest itself equally in three persons who are related to one another in modes of dependence—the Son being begotten from the Father and the Holy Spirit proceeding from both. He wrote,

> The pre-eminence given to the Father . . . proves that he is after all conceived as standing in a different relation to the unity of the essence; so that those who feel it to be superfluous to prove that divine attributes and activities belong to the Father, while they insist on proof for the Son and the Spirit, are all of them far from being strict Trinitarians; for they identify the Father with the unity of the divine essence, but not the Son or the Spirit. This can be traced right back to the idea of Origen, that the Father is God absolutely [*autotheos*], while the Son and Spirit are God only by participation in the divine essence—an idea which is positively rejected by orthodox church teachers but secretly underlies their whole procedure.[117]

Schleiermacher resolved his difficulties with the doctrine by historicizing it. He claimed that it was understandable that the complexities of unity in Trinity would have to be carefully worked out at a time when the majority of Christians were converts from paganism, but that as that situation passed into history, the formulas canonized by the great councils of the early church became dated and lost their relevance. As a result,

> It is natural that people who cannot reconcile themselves to the difficulties and imperfections that cling to the formulae current in Trinitarian doctrine should say that they repudiate everything connected with it, whereas in point of fact their piety is by no means lacking in the specifically Christian stamp. This is the case often enough at the present moment not only in the Unitarian

[116] Ibid., 171.1.
[117] Ibid., 171.5.

> societies of England and America, but also among the scattered opponents of the doctrine of the Trinity in our own country.[118]

Here we see how Schleiermacher's understanding of the Trinity could embrace Unitarianism without undue difficulty, a clear indication that he did not really grasp the inner workings of the doctrine, despite his claim to having expounded it correctly. He concluded his remarks by suggesting that there were two difficulties that still needed to be ironed out. The first of these was the relation between the unity of the divine essence and the Trinity of persons, and the second was the meaning of the term "Father" and the relation of the first to the second and third persons. He left these issues hanging, claiming that he was unable to complete the task of resolving problems that went back to the beginnings of Christian theology. It was an apparently humble approach to take, but of course it was really a rejection of the ancient orthodox tradition, with nothing to put in its place.

The theories of Schleiermacher and especially of Hegel caught the mood of the age and became foundational to the development of much nineteenth-century thought. Jesus was very popular as a romantic figure, and men like David Strauss (1808–1874) and Ernest Renan (1823–1892) popularized their romantic idealism by attempting to write biographies of him, explaining who he "really" was.[119] Neither of them took the Gospels at face value, and both lent their weight to the increasingly common view that the Evangelists had doctored their material for their own religious purposes. Stripped of their additions and fantasies, the "real" Jesus came across as an inspiring figure whose life and teaching revealed the power of the divine spirit at work in a truly good man. Here was the "gentle Jesus, meek and mild" of contemporary hymnody that did so much to turn the Gospels into a middle-class morality play. If the Trinity figured at all in this, it was that Jesus looked up to God as his Father, identified himself as a Son, and shared his Spirit with his followers, whom he invited to claim their own adoption as children of God. Strauss wrote a generation before Renan and was a theologian in a way that Renan was not, so his views were both more shocking and more influential when they appeared. He defended his critical approach to the Gospels by asserting that the truth of the Christian faith had nothing to do with historical facts. There had already been some historians who had doubted whether the New Testament writers were eyewitnesses of what they described, and who suspected that the stories

[118] Ibid., 172.2.

[119] David F. Strauss, *Das Leben Jesu, kritisch berabeitet* (Stuttgart: P. Balz'sche Buchhandlung, 1836); English translation by George Eliot, *Life of Jesus Critically Examined* (London: Chapman Brothers, 1846); E. Renan, *La vie de Jésus* (Paris: Michel Lévy, 1863); English translation, *The Life of Jesus* (London: Trübner, 1864).

surrounding Jesus had been embroidered by legendary pious accretions, but none had taken these suspicions to their logical conclusion. Strauss derided what he called their "eclecticism"—picking and choosing what to regard as historical and what not—and set out his own approach as follows:

> The proceedings of these eclectics is most arbitrary, since they decide what belongs to history and what to myth almost entirely on subjective grounds. Such distinctions are equally foreign to the evangelists, to logical reasoning and to historical criticism. In consistency with these opinions, this writer applies the notion of myth to the entire history of the life of Jesus, recognizes myths or mythical embellishments in every portion, and ranges under the category of myth not merely the miraculous occurrences during the infancy of Jesus, but also those of his public life, not merely miracles operated on Jesus, but those done by him.[120]

Strauss argued that myth was the natural category used by premodern people to describe their beliefs, and did not think that the Gospel writers were trying to deceive anyone in this respect. In fact, he claimed that the mythical dimension was innate to religion, and that if it was missing, the religion in question would be defective.[121] To his mind, what the early Christians had done was to take the existing Jewish expectations of the Messiah and apply them to Jesus, whether they were historically accurate or not. As Strauss put it,

> It could not have been easier for the person who first added any new feature to the description of Jesus to believe in its genuineness, since his argument would be: Such things must have happened to the Messiah, Jesus was the Messiah, therefore such things happened to him.[122]

Strauss attributed his critical stance to Hegel, but in reaction to the latter's belief that historical occurrences reflected philosophical truths. According to Strauss, there was no connection between the two whatsoever. History had to be judged according to its own criteria, and any attempt to impose philosophical ideas on it would inevitably end up in myth, which is precisely what the religious mind does (and did) with the stories of Jesus.[123]

Strauss and Renan had a considerable influence in literary circles—Strauss's English translator was the novelist George Eliot—but much less among professional theologians. In the academic world, the most powerful single influence

[120] Strauss, *Life of Jesus*, 64–65.
[121] Ibid., 80.
[122] Ibid., 84. (Eliot's English translation is slightly modified.)
[123] Strauss argued this in his *Streitschriften zur Vertheidingung miener Schrift über das Leben Jesu*, 3 parts in 1 vol. (Tübingen: C. F. Osiander, 1841), 3:57–126.

was that of Ferdinand Christian Baur (1792–1860) and the so-called "Tübingen school" that surrounded him and propagated his ideas.[124] Baur rewrote the history of the early church along Hegelian lines. He argued that the church had a history of development that could not be separated from parallel events in the secular world, and that the doctrines it formulated over time reflected the clash of ideas that went into what became the orthodox synthesis. This process began in the New Testament, which according to Baur contains both Jewish and Gentile elements that were fused together into what he called "early Catholicism." This was the tendency to create structures and impose a particular "orthodoxy" on the primitive Christian communities, and it went without saying that Baur regarded this as a corruption of the original teaching of Jesus, however understandable (and even necessary) that might have been at the time. Those parts of the New Testament that reflected this evolution were then naturally regarded as late in date—Luke/Acts and the Pastoral Epistles in particular. Baur also interpreted the creeds and councils of the patristic era in this light, as a synthesis of Judeo-Christian and Hellenistic cultures that would eventually produce a new European civilization.

Baur did not believe that there was such a thing as objective history—to him, it was all an ideological construction based on the presuppositions of the historian but, if done properly, connected through him to the mind of the eternal Spirit. As he explained,

> Whether one calls the speculative method "Hegelian" or something else, the nature of speculation is and remains the reasoning consideration of the object with which one is concerned; it is the posture of the consciousness in relation to the object. . . . Without speculation, every historical investigation . . . is a mere tarrying on the superfluous and external side of the subject matter. The more important and comprehensive the object is with which historical investigation is concerned . . . the more such investigation approaches not merely reproducing in itself what the individual thought and did but a thinking in itself of the eternal thoughts of the eternal Spirit, whose work history is.[125]

Baur's thesis was to set the agenda for theological and historical research for the next 150 years and is still the dominant position today. It has been contested many times, of course, and there are signs that it may finally be disintegrating,

[124] See Donald J. Dietrich and Michael J. Himes, *The Legacy of the Tübingen School: The Relevance of Nineteenth Century Theology for the Twenty-first Century* (New York: Crossroad, 1997); Horton Harris, *The Tübingen School: A Historical and Theological Investigation of the School of F. C. Baur* (Leicester: Apollos, 1990).

[125] Ferdinand C. Baur, *Die christliche Lehre von der Dreieinigkeit und Menschwerdung Gottes in ihrer geschichtlichen Entwicklung*, 3 vols. (Tübingen: C. F. Osiander, 1841–1843), 1:xviii-xix.

but its influence has been enormous and is usually what is reflected in modern textbooks and reference works, even those written or compiled by people who are unsympathetic to the Tübingen school itself.

The influence of Hegel and Schleiermacher on Baur is beyond dispute, but his concentration on history led him in a somewhat different direction, as can be seen from his approach to the relationship between the historical Jesus of Nazareth and the Christ who is worshiped by the church. For Hegel (and basically for Schleiermacher also) what really mattered was the Christ of faith—the historical details of the earthly life of Jesus were of little interest to them and could easily be romanticized, as Strauss and Renan did. This was not good enough for Baur. He believed that there was an essential connection between the Jesus of history and the Christ of faith. Although he accepted that the two were not identical, there nevertheless had to be something in the former that led to the latter. No other failed prophet had succeeded in becoming a divine figure worshiped as God in a worldwide religious organization, and it was hard to see how that could have happened to Jesus without some cause that could be traced back to him. The historical Jesus was therefore important in his own right, and to that extent at least, Baur must be seen as a conservative figure when compared to his academic contemporaries and models.[126]

Romantic idealism swept across the German Protestant world in the first half of the nineteenth century, but it left its mark elsewhere as well, especially in France. The collapse of the Catholic monarchy in the French Revolution created a spiritual vacuum that had to be filled, and a window of opportunity opened up for a nonclerical form of Catholicism to emerge. The most prominent representative of that was François René de Chateaubriand (1768–1848), whose classic work *Le génie du Christianisme* became the chief inspiration of the revived Catholicism of the early nineteenth century.[127] Chateaubriand was a romantic and somewhat dubious convert to Catholicism in the wake of the revolution, and his appeal was more to the tradition of European culture than to the Bible or the origins of the church. As he put it, there was "no disgrace in being believers with Newton and Bossuet, with Pascal and Racine."[128] It was a strange approach, at least from a theologian's point of view, but it was effective in restoring the credit of Christianity in France at a time when the church had to rebuild itself from the ruins of the previous decade.

[126] See Robert Morgan, "Ferdinand Christian Baur," in Ninian Smart, John Clayton, Patrick Sherry, and Steven T. Katz, eds., *Nineteenth-century Religious Thought in the West*, 3 vols. (Cambridge: Cambridge University Press, 1985), 1:261–284, especially 279ff.

[127] François-René de Chateaubriand, *Le génie du Christianisme ou beautés de la religion chrétienne* (Paris: Migneret, 1802); reissued with a commentary by Emmanuel Godo (Paris: Cerf, 2011). English translation by Charles I. White, *The Genius of Christianity* (Baltimore: J. Murphy, 1856; reissued New York: H. Fertig, 1976).

[128] de Chateaubriand, *Genius*, 49.

The closest any French Catholic was to come to German romanticism can be seen in the life and work of Hugues-Félicité Robert de LaMennais (1782–1854), another child of the revolution who turned against it and sought refuge in the age-old authority of the Catholic church:

> Since [the time of] Jesus Christ, what authority dare anyone compare to that of the Catholic church, the heir of all primordial traditions, of the first revelation and the Mosaic revelation, of all the truths known in antiquity, of which its teaching is only the development? Going back as it does to the origin of the world, it unites all the authorities in its authority.[129]

LaMennais detected three kinds of religious indifference that he regarded as destructive and against which he aimed his work. The first was the attitude of the atheist, who rejects religion but thinks that it is useful as a means of controlling the masses. The second was the approach of the deists, who recognize that some form of natural religion is necessary but reject all claims to revelation and find it impossible to settle on any one form of religion as definitive. The third—and most interesting—form of indifference was that of Protestants, who pointed to the Bible as their authority but could not agree about what the Bible said. In the end, argued LaMennais, their approach was just as rationalistic as that of the deists and the atheists because, despite its professed acceptance of the principle of revealed truth, it was their human minds that decided what that divine truth was.

LaMennais was hailed as a hero when his book appeared, and at one point it seemed as though he might be made a cardinal, but that was not to be. Instead of joining the hierarchy of the established church, he turned his attention to the plight of the working man and became what would later be called a "socialist." He became an ardent supporter of freedom of conscience, education, and the press—all ideas that were anathema to the church authorities in Rome. In 1834 he was condemned for supposed heresy, and after that he gradually drifted out of the official church. Even so, he continued to inspire a small group of Catholic thinkers who adopted and adapted his ideas as time went on, and today he is widely hailed as one of the architects of "modern" Catholic thought.[130]

The nineteenth century was a time when secularization and religious "feeling" went hand in hand. Faith in the power of reason and natural science was

[129] Hugues-Felicite R. de LaMennais, *Essai sur l'indifférence en matière de religion*, 4 vols. (Paris: Tournachon-Molin et H. Séguin, 1817–1823); English translation of vol. 1, *Essay on Indifference in Matters of Religion* (London: J. Macqueen, 1895), 293.

[130] See B. M. G. Reardon, *Liberalism and Tradition: Aspects of Catholic Thought in Nineteenth-century France* (Cambridge: Cambridge University Press, 1975).

almost unbounded, and though the churches put up stiff resistance when rationalism was applied to theology, they could not buck the general trend. Instead, they found themselves under increasing attack from even more sinister forces that would make idealists like Hegel seem like staunch defenders of the traditional faith by comparison.

The most important figure in this respect was Ludwig Feuerbach (1804–1872), who studied under Hegel and absorbed his ideas but then turned them on their head. Hegel had posited a world of ideas that then manifested themselves in concrete reality. In Feuerbach's view,

> Hegel's philosophy is the last ambitious attempt to reestablish lost, defeated Christianity by means of philosophy, by following the universal modern procedure and identifying the negation of Christianity with Christianity itself. The much lauded speculative identity of spirit and matter, infinite and finite, divine and human, is nothing more than the accursed paradox of the modern age: the identity of belief and unbelief, theology and philosophy, religion and atheism, Christianity and paganism, at the very summit—the summit of metaphysics. Hegel conceals this contradiction by making of atheism, the negation, an objective component of God—God as a process, and atheism as one component of this process.[131]

Hegel thought of man as God in his self-alienation, but Feuerbach retorted that the exact opposite was the truth: man had created God by projecting his dissatisfaction with himself onto a higher being. In other words, it is man who is God and not the other way around. Christianity reveals humanity's own self-consciousness, including its hopes and fears, its ideals and its failures:

> Consciousness of God is self-consciousness, knowledge of God is self-knowledge. By his God you know the man, and by the man his God—the two are identical. Whatever is God to a man, that is his heart and soul; and conversely, God is the manifested inward nature, the expressed self of a man—religion the solemn unveiling of a man's hidden treasures, the revelation of his intimate thoughts . . .[132]

To Feuerbach, the resurrection of Christ was nothing more than a projection of the human desire for immortality, which can be attested in every religion

[131] Ludwig Feuerbach, "Zur Kritik der Hegelschen Philosophie," in *Sämtliche Werke*, 2nd ed., 12 vols. (Stuttgart: F. Frommann, 1959–1960), 2:257.

[132] Ludwig Feuerbach, *The Essence of Christianity*, trans. M. Evans (George Eliot) (London: J. Chapman, 1854; reissued New York: Harper, 1957), 13. The original was *Das Wesen des Christentums* (Leipzig: O. Wigand, 1843).

and philosophy.[133] The Trinity, in particular, is just a projection of the human desire for community:

> In a solitary God the essential need for duality, for love, for community, for the real, complete self-consciousness, for the *alter ego*, is excluded. This lack is therefore satisfied by religion in this way: in the still solitude of the divine being is placed another, a second, different from God according to his person but identical with him in his essence—God the Son as opposed to God the Father. God the Father is *I*, God the Son is *Thou*. . . . The third person of the Trinity expresses nothing more than the love of the two divine persons for each other, the unity of the Son and the Father, the idea of community . . .[134]

When human love fails, there is a divine substitute at hand, ready to fulfill the needs that have been disappointed in this life. Christian theology was full of meaning for Feuerbach, but it had to be interpreted in a purely human way, as a projection of our psychology that expresses our desires and makes up for what we fail to achieve. Feuerbach believed that such a projection was necessary, and so concluded that an irreligious person was someone who had no reason for living:

> Every man must place before himself a God, i.e., an aim, a purpose. . . . He who has no aim has no home, no sanctuary; aimlessness is the greatest unhappiness. . . . He who has an aim has, *eo ipso*, a religion, if not in the narrow sense of common pietism, yet—and this is the only sense to be considered—in the sense of reason, in the sense of the universal, the only true love.[135]

Feuerbach's inversion of Christian theology and his picture of it as human self-alienation is easily refuted by the facts. Granted that there have been some Christians who have used their religion as a psychological crutch, this cannot be said of them all, and certainly not of the great artists, writers, musicians, and others who have found great inspiration and liberation in its teachings. Nor does it make much sense to deny the existence of God on the ground that there are no metaphysical abstractions, but then to create a generic "man," who (on that assumption) ought not to exist either. Whether or not there is a God is a question that cannot be answered in purely human terms, but we can say for certain that there is no "generic" man—we are all individuals, but how can such a diverse multitude project belief in the same God? In the end, Feuerbach's critique of Christianity collapsed under the weight of its own inner

133 Feuerbach, *The Essence of Christianity*, 135.
134 Ibid., 67.
135 Ibid., 64.

contradictions, but that has not prevented it from having a major—and possibly *the* major—impact on modern thinking. Whether we are talking about religious thinkers like Søren Kierkegaard (1813–1855), atheists like Friedrich Nietzsche (1844–1900), psychologists like Sigmund Freud (1856–1939), philosophers like Karl Marx (1818–1883) and Martin Heidegger (1889–1976), or even Jewish thinkers like Martin Buber (1878–1965), all have been deeply influenced by Feuerbach, who through them has become the true intellectual father of the modern world.

The clearest turning point in nineteenth-century theology came in 1859, when Charles Darwin (1809–1882) published his seminal work on the origin of species.[136] It was immediately denounced by prominent churchmen as a denial of biblical revelation and the basic principles of Christianity, but within a few years its main thesis had been integrated into the spirit of the age and had become for many a new dogma.[137] Darwin grew up in an intellectual atmosphere dominated by the natural theology of William Paley (1743–1805).[138] Paley had taken over the view of Voltaire, who believed that there could not be design in the universe without a designer, and he made that the basis of his thinking. Science studied the design and theology expounded the character of the designer—the two disciplines went hand in hand. Paley's view was seldom directly challenged, but it was progressively undermined by new biological discoveries and thinking. It did not take long for paleontologists to work out that the world could not have been created in six days and that a much longer period of time was demanded by the fossil and geological evidence.

What exactly happened, though, remained unclear. To some, the six days of Genesis represented six epochs, each of which was separated by a natural catastrophe that paved the way for the next one. That idea was overturned by Charles Lyell (1797–1875), who argued "that all former changes of the organic and inorganic creation are referable to one uninterrupted succession of physical events governed by the laws now in operation."[139] If Lyell was correct, then some form of evolution was necessary to explain how and why life on earth had changed from one geological epoch to the next. Furthermore, these changes had to be global in order to account for the fact that whole species disappeared and new ones came into being—it was not a matter of individual survival here and there. If one dinosaur vanished, they all did, just as the emergence of one

[136] Charles Darwin, *On the Origin of Species by Means of Natural Selection* (London: John Murray, 1859).

[137] The story is well told by G. Himmelfarb, *Darwin and the Darwinian Revolution* (Chicago: Ivan R. Dee, 1996), a reprint of the first edition (Garden City, NY: Doubleday, 1959).

[138] William Paley, *Natural Theology, or Evidence of the Existence and Attributes of the Deity* (London: R. Faulder, 1802).

[139] Charles Lyell, *Principles of Geology, Being an Attempt to Explain the Former Changes of the Earth's Surface by Reference to Causes Now in Operation*, 3 vols. (London: John Murray, 1830–1833), 1:144.

human being presaged the appearance of a vast multitude. No one said it specifically, but there was little room in such a vision for intervention by specific people—in this scenario, the idea that Adam could have engendered the fall of the entire human race was no more plausible than that Christ could have saved it.

None of this necessarily challenged the view that the world had been made by a Creator who in some mysterious way supervised its development—what theologians called "providence"—and as long as no one could explain how particular species originated, this was a perfectly respectable view to hold. Paley's natural theology had been modified but not disproved. It was here that Darwin entered the picture. His examination of the evidence led him to conclude that a process of natural selection was more credible than one of providential intervention:

> If you say that God ordained that at some time and place a dozen slight variations should arise, and that one of them alone should be preserved in the struggle for life and the other eleven should perish in the first or few generations, then the saying seems to me to be verbiage. It comes to merely saying that everything that is, is ordained. . . . Why should you or I speak of variation as having been . . . "ordained and guided without doubt by an intelligent cause on a preconceived and definite plan"? Would you not call this theological pedantry or display?[140]

For Darwin, the discovery of natural selection was the final nail in Paley's coffin, since natural selection was a chance process in which many elements were progressively discarded and many false starts were made. If there were an intelligent designer, why would there be such apparent wastage? The survival of the fittest, as Darwin's theory came to be known, was an unpleasant business, but it seemed to accord with what actually occurred much better than the theory that everything was made by a beneficent Creator for a positive and noble purpose.[141]

Opposition to Darwin was widespread but of greatly varying quality. A number of scientists opposed his views on scientific grounds—like everything else, Darwin's theory was a mental construction applied to the facts, and while there were many phenomena that appeared to corroborate his theory, there were others that did not. Others refused to abandon Paley's teleological argument, even if they acknowledged that it had to be modified to some degree. Still others retreated into a biblical literalism that condemned Darwin outright. The

140 Francis Darwin and Alfred C. Seward, *More Letters of Charles Darwin*, 2 vols. (London: J. Murray, 1903), 1:194.
141 Charles Darwin, *Autobiography: With Original Omissions Restored*, ed. N. Barlow (London: Collins, 1958), 87.

most perceptive of Darwin's Christian critics was undoubtedly Charles Hodge (1797–1878), who argued that Darwin's denial of providence put him at odds with biblical Christianity:

> The conclusion of the whole matter is that the denial of design in nature is virtually the denial of God. Mr Darwin's theory does deny all design in nature, therefore his theory is virtually atheistical; his theory, not he himself. He believes in a Creator. But when that Creator . . . called matter and living germ into existence and then abandoned the universe to itself, to be controlled by chance and necessity, without any purpose on his part as to the result, or any intervention or guidance, then he is virtually consigned, so far as we are concerned, to non-existence. . . . Mr Darwin's admirers adopt and laud his theory, for the special reason that it banishes God from the world.[142]

Hodge's critique can be faulted because it relied on the assumption that it would never be possible to close the gap between the material evidence and the question of the ultimate creation of life, which has now been shown to be untrue, but modern apologists for a Christian view of human origins generally adopt a modified form of his apologetic, insisting that however complex the process may have been, there is ultimately no contradiction between scientific discoveries and the providential ordering of the universe by a wise and loving God.[143]

Unfortunately, Hodge's measured approach was not emulated by most of the others who entered the fray on one side or the other. It is hard to decide whether the greater damage was done by those who rejected Darwin in favor of a simplistic reading of the Bible, as did Philip Henry Gosse (1810–1888),[144] a scientist who clung tenaciously to belief in a six-day creation, or by those like Lyman Abbott (1835–1922), who embraced Darwinism and was even able to claim that, "The divinity of man is not different in kind from the divinity of Christ, because it is not different in kind from the divinity of God."[145] Those who adopted Gosse's position alienated not only the scientific community

[142] Charles Hodge, *What Is Darwinism?* (London: T. Nelson and Sons, 1874), 173–174.

[143] For recent statements of this position from a scientific point of view, see Francis Collins, *The Language of God* (New York: Free Press, 2006); David J. Bartholomew, *God, Chance, and Purpose: Can God Have It Both Ways?* (Cambridge: Cambridge University Press, 2008). On the controversy generally, see David Hull, *Darwin and His Critics: The Reception of Darwin's Theory of Evolution by the Scientific Community* (Cambridge, MA: Harvard University Press, 1973); James R. Moore, *The Post-Darwinian Controversies: A Study of the Protestant Struggle to Come to Terms with Darwin in Great Britain and America 1870–1900* (Cambridge: Cambridge University Press, 1979); David N. Livingstone, *Darwin's Forgotten Defenders: The Encounter between Evangelical Theology and Evolutionary Thought* (Grand Rapids, MI: Eerdmans, 1987); Jon H. Roberts, *Darwinism and the Divine in America: Protestant Intellectuals and Organic Evolution 1859–1900* (Madison: University of Wisconsin Press, 1988); Jonathan Wells, *Charles Hodge's Critique of Darwinism* (Lewiston, NY: Edwin Mellon, 1988).

[144] See Edmund Gosse, *The Life of Philip Henry Gosse* (London: K. Paul, Trench, Trübner, 1890).

[145] Lyman Abbott, *The Theology of an Evolutionist* (London:, 1897), 73.

but also many of their own potential supporters in conservative Protestant churches who thought that the facts ought to be accounted for rather than dismissed in favor of a narrow view of biblical "truth," but those who followed Abbott often ended up leaving the church and Christianity behind, since what he was saying appeared to be little more than Feuerbach adapted to the pulpit.

The link between Feuerbach and Darwin was made by Karl Marx, a disciple of the former who welcomed the discoveries of the latter as evidence that the materialistic view of the universe was the correct one. Marx accepted Feuerbach's view that religion was a projection of human thoughts and desires, but he went further:

> Feuerbach resolves the religious essence into the human essence. But human essence is no abstraction inherent in each single individual. In its reality it is the ensemble of social relations. . . . Feuerbach, consequently, does not see that the "religious sentiment" is itself a social product, and that the abstract individual whom he analyzes belongs in reality to a particular form of society.[146]

Marx was unfair to Feuerbach, but that was because he saw him, as he saw all philosophers, as theoreticians who came up with a picture of life and then sat back to contemplate it. Marx, on the other hand, believed that such visions should be used (if they were usable at all) to change the world. He regarded religion, and especially Christianity, as an integral part of the capitalist order that had to be overthrown if human progress was to be achieved, and it is in that way that his opinions on the subject must be understood. As he put it,

> The religious world is but the reflex of the real world. And for a society based upon the production of commodities, in which the producers in general enter into social relations with one another by treating their products as commodities and values, whereby they reduce their individual private labor to the standard of homogeneous human labor—for such a society, Christianity, with its *cultus* of abstract man . . . is the most fitting form of religion.[147]

From there, everything else flowed logically. Class conflict, motivated by economics, would be resolved by the survival of the fittest, but they were not randomly selected—the fittest were the working class for whose benefit human history was tending. Religion, and especially Christianity, had its uses, but it was a bulwark of the ruling class that would have to be displaced. Hence,

[146] Karl Marx and Friedrich Engels, *On Religion* (Moscow: Foreign Languages Publishing House, 1979), 71.
[147] Ibid., 135.

there would be no place for it in the socialist utopia, and those who clung to it would inevitably be regarded as enemies of progress. Marx's ideology was to have enormous, and in his lifetime unforeseeable, success in the twentieth century, but it was also hollowed out from within and eventually collapsed of its own weight, at least in those countries where it was officially put into practice. Its theoretical basis has also been challenged and successfully discredited from a Christian point of view.[148] But Marxism as an ideology survives, not least in some major American universities, so the struggle against it cannot be regarded as over.

The subsequent history of liberal Protestant theology in the nineteenth century can be written fairly briefly. Its leading figure after 1870 was Albrecht Ritschl (1822–1889), who studied under F. C. Baur at Tübingen but who later rejected his theories of the historical origins of Christianity.[149] He taught at Bonn from 1846 and at Göttingen from 1864 until his death. It was there that he wrote what was to become his major work, a three-volume study of the doctrine of justification and reconciliation.[150] It was rapidly attacked in orthodox and pietist circles, for neither of which Ritschl had any sympathy, and it is clear that he was closer to Feuerbach than would normally be expected from a Christian theologian. As he said,

> In every religion, what is sought, with the help of the superhuman spiritual power reverenced by man, is a solution of the contradiction in which man finds himself, as both a part of the world of nature and a spiritual personality claiming to dominate nature. For in the former *role* he is a part of nature, dependent on her, subject to and confined by other things; but as spirit he is moved by the impulse to maintain his independence against them. In this juncture, religion springs up as faith in superhuman spiritual powers, by whose help the power which man possesses of himself is in some way supplemented, and elevated into a unity of its own kind which is a match for the pressure of the natural world.[151]

The main difference between Ritschl and Feuerbach is that Ritschl believed that God was really there, and not just a projection of human longings, but

[148] Leszek Kołakowski, *Main Currents of Marxism: Its Origins, Growth and Dissolution*, 3 vols. (Oxford: Oxford University Press, 1978). Originally published as *Glowne nurty Marksizmu—powstanie, rozwój, rozkład*, 3 vols. (Paris: Instytut Literacki, 1976–1978). See also Alistair Kee, *Marx and the Failure of Liberation Theology* (London: SCM, 1990); Nicholas Lash, *A Matter of Hope: A Theologian's Reflections on the Thought of Karl Marx* (Notre Dame, IN: University of Notre Dame Press, 1982); Karl Popper, *The Open Society and Its Enemies*, 2 vols. (London: Routledge and Kegan Paul, 1945).

[149] On Ritschl, see Darrell Jodock, ed., *Ritschl in Retrospect: History, Community, and Science* (Minneapolis: Fortress, 1995); David Lotz, *Ritschl and Luther* (Nashville: Abingdon, 1974); David L. Mueller, *An Introduction to the Theology of Albrecht Ritschl* (Philadelphia: Westminster, 1969).

[150] Albrecht Ritschl, *A Critical History of the Christian Doctrine of Justification and Reconciliation*, 3 vols. (vols. 1–2: Edinburgh: Edmiston & Douglas, 1872; vol. 3: Edinburgh: T & T Clark, 1900). Originally published as *Die christliche Lehre der Rechtfertigung und Versöhnung*, 3 vols. (Bonn: A. Marcus, 1870–1874).

[151] Ritschl, *Critical History*, 3:199.

there can be no doubt that, for him too, religion began as an earthly quest and not as a divine revelation. Ritschl opposed the biographical approach of Strauss, but what he offered instead was not much better. As he put it,

> It is no mere accident that the subversion of Jesus' religious importance has been undertaken under the guise of writing his life, for this very undertaking implies the surrender of the conviction that Jesus, as the founder of the perfect moral and spiritual religion, belongs to a higher order than all other men. But for that reason, it is likewise vain to attempt to re-establish the importance of Christ by the same biographical expedient. We can discover the full compass of his historical actuality solely from the faith of the Christian community.[152]

Ritschl was not indifferent to history and insisted that it be studied with the greatest rigor and responsibility, but he did not believe that it was possible to come to any objective judgment about the meaning of Jesus' life and death. In the end, that had to be a matter of faith, not of historical knowledge, and faith was the sphere of the church. But at the same time, Ritschl doubted whether the church had got it right—the miracles and resurrection stories were not historical, in his opinion, and so that aspect of the church's faith had to be discounted. It was a thin basis for making any assessment of Jesus, but that did not deter Ritschl, who insisted that he held the same convictions as Martin Luther:

> . . . while assuming the formula of the two natures, Luther really connects the religious estimate of Christ as God with the significance which Christ's work has for the Christian community. . . . According to Luther, the Godhead of Christ is not exhausted by maintaining the existence in Christ of the divine nature; the chief point is that in his exertions as man his Godhead is manifest and savingly effective.[153]

This was a most peculiar reading of Luther, but may be regarded as typical of the liberal school at this time, which claimed the great Reformer as their own. As a result, many non-Lutherans came to believe that Protestantism was, and had always been, a man-centered religion, quite alien to the Christianity of the Bible or of the Catholic church.

Ritschl believed that Christ's humanity was demonstrated by his ability to communicate his moral attributes to his followers, but that at the same time, he remained unique:

---

152 Ibid., 3:3.
153 Ibid., 3:393.

> . . . being the first to realize in his own personal life the final purpose of the kingdom of God, [Christ] is therefore alone of his kind, for should any other fulfill the same task as perfectly as he, yet he would be unlike him because dependent on him. Therefore, as the original type of the humanity to be united into the kingdom of God, he is the original object of the love of God, so that the love of God for the members of his kingdom also is *only* mediated through him.[154]

Here we are in the realm of pure fantasy. Christ is supposedly the best and greatest man who ever lived, and if anyone were to equal him in that respect, he would still be dependent on him because he got there first! Christ's divinity was a courtesy designation accorded to him by the Christian community in recognition of his saving work, nothing more.[155] Ritschl thought that the church came to this conclusion only after careful investigation—Jesus was thoroughly vetted before being given such a high honor! But whether he really deserved it is hard to say, since in dying for others, Jesus was also working toward the fulfillment of his own existence:

> The fundamental condition of the ethical apprehension of Jesus is contained in the statement, that what Jesus actually was and accomplished, that he is in the first place for himself. Every intelligent life moves within the lines of a personal self-end. This the old theologians could not bring themselves to see.[156]

So, at bottom, Jesus was human because he was selfish after all, just like the rest of us! This naturally affected what happened in the work of justification. According to Ritschl, the Christian community had imputed to it "his position towards the love of God, in which he maintained himself by his obedience."[157] The result was a curious doctrine of salvation by works, because instead of being reconciled to God by the shed blood of Christ in his substitutionary atonement for our sins, we have been reconciled to him in his atoning work, which means that we must work along with him in order to bring what he is doing to perfection. Furthermore, this reconciliation is not individual, but can be understood only in the context of a community:

> Religion is always social. Christ did not aim at any action upon men which would merely be amoral instruction of individuals. On the contrary, his pur-

---

[154] Albrecht Ritschl, *Instruction in the Christian Religion*, in Albert T. Swing, ed., *The Theology of Albrecht Ritschl* (London: Longmans, Green, 1901), 200. The *Instruction* was originally published as *Unterricht in der christlichen Religion* (Bonn: A. Marcus, 1875).

[155] Ritschl, *Critical History*, 3:400.

[156] Ibid., 3:442.

[157] Ibid., 3:547.

> pose in the latter direction was subordinated to the creation of a new religion. The individual believer, therefore, can rightly understand his position relative to God only as meaning that he is reconciled by God through Christ in the community founded by Christ.[158]

The concrete individual is thus subjected to the abstract community, whose identity is not clear. It must be the church, but is it a local congregation, a national church, or the universal body of believers, and how do we know which of these to choose? Ritschl did not worry too much about that sort of thing, because to him the church in all its forms was a manifestation of the coming kingdom of God. His outlook was positive and forward-looking; even pain and suffering were part of a higher good that had to be understood and embraced.[159] It was a rosy picture that chimed in well with the upbeat mood of the late nineteenth century, but it was going to suffer a cruel blow in the next generation. Ritschl was fortunate indeed that he did not live to see that.

One of Ritschl's disciples who did live to see it was Wilhelm Herrmann (1846–1922), who had been educated in the pietism of Halle but later sat at Ritschl's feet in order, as he put it, to escape its suffocating influence. From 1879 to 1917 he taught at Marburg, and numbered among his pupils such future luminaries as Karl Barth (1886–1968) and Rudolf Bultmann (1884–1976). Herrmann believed that scientific knowledge was valid in its own sphere, but that there was a world of moral freedom that only religion could address. Without that, human moral freedom would become anarchy and lead to self-destruction instead of self-fulfillment as it was meant to do. To Herrmann, Christian doctrine and the literal reading of Scripture were the great enemies of faith because they allowed people to think that knowledge about God was the same as communion with him, which it was not. The historical Jesus was important to him, not because Jesus was God but because his historicity made it possible for us to understand and enter into his inner life, whose liberating power constituted the faith of believers. Once the inner life of Jesus takes hold of our inner life, the question of his historicity ceases to matter because its meaning is revealed to us in our experience of him.

This rather odd way of thinking led to a debate with Martin Kähler (1835–1912), who drew a sharp distinction between the Jesus of history and the Christ of faith and said that the former is knowable because it is the latter—the risen, ascended, and glorified Christ—who is the author of

[158] Ritschl, *Instruction*, 233.
[159] Ibid., 174–175.

the New Testament picture of him.[160] There is therefore no historical Jesus at all in the strict sense of the word, because the Gospel portrait(s) of him are those of men who had met the risen Christ and whose understanding had been shaped by that. The crucial distinction between *Historie* (facts and events) and *Geschichte* (meaning), which was to play such a big part in twentieth-century Gospel criticism, was thus born and brought to center stage for the first time.

The other disciple of Ritschl who would live to see another day and whose influence was to be at least as great as Herrmann's, if not greater, was Adolf von Harnack (1851–1930).[161] Born and brought up in a strict pietist home in Estonia, where his father lectured at the then German-language university of Dorpat (now Tartu), Harnack held chairs at both Giessen and Marburg before being called to Berlin in 1888. By then, however, he was already the subject of controversy for his views, and he could take the Berlin post only after the emperor Wilhelm II (1888–1918) intervened on his behalf. Harnack would remain loyal to the emperor for the rest of his life and was knighted for his support for the German war effort in 1914.

The reason for the trouble was that Harnack had already published the first volume of his great history of dogma, in which he attempted to show that Christian doctrine was of late and dubious origin, and that the church should rid itself of it once and for all.[162] He said much the same thing in a series of sixteen lectures that he gave in Berlin in the winter of 1899–1900 and subsequently published.[163] At one level, Harnack's thesis was a development of the Early Catholicism of the Tübingen School of F. C. Baur, but Harnack took it much further. Three fundamental themes guided his work.[164] The first of these was the idea of the kingdom of God and its coming. Harnack interpreted this as,

> . . . the rule of the holy God in the hearts of individuals; it is God himself in his power. From this point of view everything that is dramatic in the external sense has vanished and gone. . . . It is not a question of angels and devils, thrones and principalities, but of God and the soul, the soul and its God.[165]

---

[160] Kähler's view of Herrmann's position is found in the second edition of his book, *The So-called Historical Jesus and the Historic Biblical Christ*, trans. and ed. Carl E. Braaten (Philadelphia: Fortress, 1964). Originally published as *Der sogenannte historische Jesus und der geschichtliche, biblische Christus*, 2nd ed. (Leipzig: A. Deichert, 1896).

[161] On Harnack, see Wayne Glick, *The Reality of Christianity: A Study of Adolf von Harnack as Historian and Theologian* (New York: Harper & Row, 1967).

[162] Adolf Harnack, *Lehrbuch der Dogmengeschichte*, 3 vols (Freiburg-im-Breisgau: Akademische Verlagsbuchhandlung von J. C. B. Mohr, 1886–1890). The third edition was translated into English as *The History of Dogma*, 7 vols. (London: Williams & Norgate, 1894–1899).

[163] Adolf Harnack, *Das Wesen des Christentums* (Leipzig: Hinrichs, 1900); English translation, *What Is Christianity?* (London: Williams & Norgate, 1901).

[164] See Harnack, *History of Dogma*, 1:58–59.

[165] Harnack, *What Is Christianity?* 56.

The second theme of Jesus' teaching was about God the Father and the infinite value of the human soul. Following in the steps of Ritschl, Harnack wrote,

> The man who can say "My Father" to the being who rules heaven and earth, is thereby raised above heaven and earth and has a value which is higher than all the matter of this world.[166]

Finally, Jesus taught a higher righteousness, in which any link between ethics and external observances is finally broken, and the commandment of love, which was the motivating force behind the moral life of the believer:

> It was in this sense that Jesus combined religion and morality, and in this sense religion may be called the soul of morality and morality the body of religion. We can thus understand how it was that Jesus could place the love of God and the love of one's neighbor side by side; the love of one's neighbor is the only practical proof on earth of that love of God which is strong in humility.[167]

What provoked a storm of opposition to this kind of teaching was Harnack's assertion that the gospel was about the Father, not about the Son. As far as he was concerned, Jesus' sonship resided in the degree of his knowledge of God, which far surpassed that of any other human being. Here again, we are in the realm of fantasy. What persuaded Harnack that Jesus knew more about God than anyone else? How was it possible to make such a judgment? To these questions, his answer was,

> Fire is kindled only by fire; personal life only by personal forces. Let us rid ourselves of all dogmatic sophistry, and leave others to pass verdicts of exclusion. The Gospel nowhere says that God's mercy is limited to Jesus' mission. But history shows us that he is the one who brings the weary and heavy laden to God, and again, that it is he who raised mankind to the new level, and his teaching is still the touchstone, in that it brings men to bliss and brings them to judgment.[168]

So in the end it was history and the experience it brought that ratified what the Gospels had to say about Jesus, and it was lives lived in the light of that, not dogmas formed to express or explain it, that were the true proofs of their truth.

The last great representative of the nineteenth-century liberal school was

[166] Ibid., 67.
[167] Ibid., 73.
[168] Ibid., 145.

Ernst Troeltsch (1865–1923).[169] As a young man he came under the influence of Albrecht Ritschl and absorbed his understanding of religion as a historical phenomenon, but felt that Ritschl had not gone far enough in applying his methods to Christianity. Ritschl had clung stubbornly to a dogmatic framework, as if Christianity could be taken out of its history and expounded as a complete set of fully formed ideas, but Troeltsch argued that such an approach was wrong. He thought that Jesus and his followers should be studied as products of their own time and context, without any appeal to divine revelation or supernatural intervention. He became a leading participant in what was known as the "history of religions school" (*die religionsgeschichtliche Schule*), whose interests ranged far and wide, from biblical studies to contemporary politics.

Troeltsch saw clearly that the Reformation era was drawing to a close and had effectively been replaced by a different kind of Protestantism after the French Revolution, though he also knew that the influence of the institutional church on wider society had all but disappeared. He deplored the reaction of many of his colleagues, who (in his opinion) had retreated into a kind of parallel universe, inventing a nonhistorical "history of salvation" (*Heilsgeschichte*) that interpreted events as the outworking of a divine plan centered on the appearance of Christ rather than as organic developments within a universal human culture. Troeltsch recognized that such an approach depended on the acceptance of a natural theology, a concept which he rejected. As he put it,

> Instead of constructing a natural theology we now conduct a general investigation into the phenomena and essence of religion; and where an exclusive, supernatural authority was once claimed, we now assess the place of Christianity in the history of religions with reference to the philosophy of history. Hence the Bible is now viewed as a human document, an artifact of Christianity [and not as a divine revelation].[170]

Troeltsch's historicism was inevitably based on a kind of relativism, but this did not mean that Christianity was to be regarded just as one religion among

[169] See Hans G. Drescher, *Ernst Troeltsch: His Life and Work*, trans. John Bowden (London: SCM, 1992). Originally published as *Ernst Troeltsch* (Göttingen: Vandenhoeck und Ruprecht, 1991); John P. Clayton, ed., *Ernst Troeltsch and the Future of Theology* (Cambridge: Cambridge University Press, 1976); Toshimasa Yasukata, *Ernst Troeltsch: Systematic Theologian of Radical Historicality* (Atlanta: Scholars Press, 1986); Walter E. Wyman, *The Concept of* Glaubenslehre*: Ernst Troeltsch and the Theological Heritage of Schleiermacher* (Chico, CA: Scholars Press, 1983); Mark D. Chapman, *Ernst Troeltsch and Liberal Theology: Religion and Cultural Synthesis in Wilhelmine Germany* (Oxford: Oxford University Press, 2001); Sarah Coakley, *Christ without Absolutes: A Study of the Christology of Ernst Troeltsch* (Oxford: Clarendon, 1988). His writings have been collected and published as *Gesammelte Schriften*, 4 vols. (Tübingen: J. C. B. Mohr, 1912–1925). In English, there is a collection of his essays, Robert Morgan and Michael Pye, trans. and ed., *Ernst Troeltsch: Writings on Theology and Religion* (Atlanta: John Knox, 1977).
[170] Ernst Troeltsch, *The Christian Faith* (Minneapolis: Fortress, 1991), 9. Originally published (posthumously) as *Die Glaubenslehre* (Munich: Duncker & Humblot, 1925).

many. Though he rejected the methods of Hegel and Ritschl, he nevertheless clung to the belief that the Christian faith was the highest form of religion that had yet evolved, a view that would have seemed obvious in his time, when the Christian societies of Europe and America were clearly more advanced in scientific terms than any others. Like his predecessors, he believed that all religions had certain goals and that these could be analyzed and ranked according to a scale of values which, though ultimately subjective and based on personal conviction rather than on hard evidence, was nevertheless most likely to commend itself to thinking people everywhere. As he put it,

> It is necessary to make a choice between redemption through meditation on a transcendent being (or non-being) and redemption through faithful, trusting participation in the person-like character of God, the ground of all life and of all genuine value. This is a choice that depends on religious conviction, not scientific demonstration. The higher goal and the greater profundity of life are found on the side of personalistic religion.[171]

Of course, even Troeltsch could see the flaws in his argument, and as he probed more deeply into the history of Christianity and the nature of other religions, he came to understand that matters were more complex than a straightforward evolution of religious thought over time was able to explain. Not only were there many different and competing forms of Christianity, but other religions turned out to be more sophisticated than Troeltsch had previously imagined, and the carnage of the First World War showed that Europe did not have the superior civilization that many had previously taken for granted. This awareness drove him back to a more spiritual conception of Christianity, and even to an acceptance of the concept of revelation:

> [Christianity] is God's countenance revealed to us; it is the way in which, being what we are, we receive and react to the revelation of God. It is binding upon us and brings us deliverance. It is final and unconditional for us, because we have nothing else, and because in what we have we can recognize the accents of the divine voice. But this does not preclude the possibility that other racial groups living under entirely different cultural conditions may experience their contact with the divine life in quite a different way.[172]

[171] Ernst Troeltsch, *The Absoluteness of Christianity and the History of Religions*, 2nd ed. (Richmond, VA: John Knox, 1971), 51. Originally published as *Die Absolutheit des Christentums und die Religionsgeschichte* (Tübingen: J. C. B. Mohr, 1912). The first edition was published by the same press in 1902.

[172] Ernst Troeltsch, "The Place of Christianity among the World Religions," in *Christian Thought; Its History and Application*, ed. Friedrich von Hügel (London: University of London Press, 1923), 55–56. The lecture was intended for delivery in Oxford, but Troeltsch died before he could give it. The original German was published subsequently as *Der Historismus und seine Überwindung; Fünf Vorträge* (Berlin: Pan Verlag R. Heise, 1924).

Troeltsch even came to insist that the historical Jesus was a real figure who had transformed the religious culture of his day, even if the details we find in the Gospels have been "enriched" (as he put it):

> . . . it is not a question of individual details but of the factuality of the total historical phenomenon of Jesus and the basic outline of his teaching and his religious personality. This must be capable of being established by means of historical criticism as historical reality if the "symbol of Christ" is to have a firm and strong inner basis in the "fact" of Jesus.[173]

In the end, the most radical critic of the traditional emphasis in Christian theology on revealed truth and systematic doctrine came through his historical investigation to a reassertion of some of the basic elements of that position, even though he continued to reject its methods of inquiry. In his words,

> Someone who sees in Christianity the permanent, utmost plateau of man's religion will naturally also see and seek in its founding personality deeper forces than someone who sees in it nothing but a passing phase of religious formation.[174]

The liberal theology of the nineteenth century eventually collapsed, theoretically because of its own inner contradictions and practically because its idealism was blown to bits in the First World War, though it survived longest where the effects of the war were felt least—in the United States. Long before then, however, its intellectual underpinnings were being demolished in the lands of its origin, even if it took a major catastrophe for that to become apparent to all.

One man who heralded the eventual eclipse of rationalistic liberalism was Søren Kierkegaard (1813–1855).[175] Kierkegaard was writing at the height of the liberal advance in mid-century and he died young, so that many of his ideas never matured as they might have done later. Much of what he wrote was pseudonymous and deliberately enigmatic. He lived for many years as a virtual recluse and suffered from depression, which makes his work even harder to interpret. Because he wrote as a layman, his books were not considered to

[173] Ernst Troeltsch, "The Significance of the Historical Existence of Jesus for Faith," in Morgan and Pye, *Writings on Theology and Religion*, 198. Originally published as *Die Bedeutung der Geschichtlichkeit Jesu für den Glauben* (Tübingen: J. C. B. Mohr, 1911).

[174] Ernst Troeltsch, "Half a Century of Theology: A Review," in Morgan and Pye, *Writings*, 72. Originally published as "Rückblick über ein halbes Jahrhundert der theologischen Wissenschaft," in *Zeitschrift für wissenschaftliche Theologie* LI (1908), 97–135 (*Gesammelte Schriften*, 2:193–226).

[175] On Kierkegaard, see John Lippitt and George Pattison, eds., *The Oxford Handbook on Kierkegaard* (Oxford: Oxford University Press, 2013), which contains a full study of the man and his works and provides the most up-to-date bibliography.

be "theology," and were never studied in Lutheran seminaries, even in Scandinavia. He was a strong critic of the state church in Denmark, which meant that the church did nothing to encourage people to read his books, even if it did not actually censor them. Finally, he wrote in Danish, a language that was not widely known outside his homeland and that effectively prevented his work from circulating internationally for half a century after his death.

It seems that in the last years of his life Kierkegaard came to a deep religious faith of his own, but also to a realization that it was something quite different from what the vast majority of his fellow citizens experienced. Jesus had said that the gate into the kingdom of heaven was narrow and that there were few who found it, but the Danish church simply assumed that everyone was headed that way and that all it had to do was make their passage as comfortable as possible. The result, of course, was that no one cared one way or the other, and so biblical Christianity went by default.[176]

In Kierkegaard's view, true faith could come only by passing through a dark night of the soul, a period of despair in which a person starts to look seriously for eternal values. That despair had to be rooted in concepts of sin and guilt, because without them neither repentance nor true self-knowledge would be possible. On the contrary, a person who sought to excuse himself or who failed to penetrate to the depths of his inner alienation from God would never know spiritual peace:

> The person who turns toward himself with the absolute criterion will of course not be able to go on living in the bliss that if he keeps the commandments and has received no sentence for anything and is regarded by the clique of revivalists as a really sincere person he then is a good fellow, who, if he does not die soon, will in a short time become all too perfect for this world. He will, on the contrary, again and again discover guilt and in turn discover it within the totality-category: guilt.[177]

For Kierkegaard, ethical systems that paid no attention to sin and guilt were worthless. Original sin was not something to be discussed in dogmatics but a reality to be assumed as fundamental. Abraham was called out from the common mass of humanity and told to worship God, whatever the cost, even if that meant sacrificing his own son. Knowledge of the living God meant that a man's ethical relations to others were determined by his primary (and prior)

[176] See the correspondence and articles by Kierkegaard concerning Bishop Mynster in *Kierkegaard's Writings*, 26 vols. (Princeton, NJ: Princeton University Press, 1978–2000), 23:498–509.

[177] Søren Kierkegaard, *Concluding Unscientific Postscript*, in *Kierkegaard's Writings*, 12/1:549.

relationship to God, not the other way around, as so many of Kierkegaard's contemporaries seemed to think.[178]

To Kierkegaard, the greatest miracle in history was that the eternal and infinite God chose to become a man, an act which in itself meant that he accepted the role of a humble servant. Humility is therefore the only spiritual condition in which it is possible to experience God, because it is the only state that corresponds to his self-revelation.[179] Furthermore, if the divine self-revelation is a miracle, so is human acceptance of and submission to it in faith. Faith is not something that can be inherited, nor is it historical—it is an existential encounter with God that is both individual and timeless.[180]

Kierkegaard was not interested in exploring the origins of Christianity in order to dissect them. For him, the faith was a given to which each individual is called to respond by taking it on himself. Someone who fails to do this may know a great deal about the subject in purely objective terms, but will have no experience of it in the only way that matters; he will not discover the truth that he is seeking by purely rational and scientific means.[181] Kierkegaard has often been interpreted as opening the door to pure subjectivism, in which no certainty is possible, but this is probably a misunderstanding of his position. He lived at a time when it was still possible to assume that the Gospels and the general content of Christianity were objectively true—questions of biblical criticism did not arise for him. What he wanted was personal participation in that objective reality, and it is in that sense that he should be understood. Faith for him was not a leap into the dark but an acceptance of the true light, without which even the most intelligent person is blind.

Another key figure in the dissolution of the liberal consensus was Friedrich Nietzsche, a declared enemy of Christianity, which he viewed in terms not unlike those of Kierkegaard.[182] Nietzsche suffered from persistent ill health and had to resign his teaching post at Basel in 1879. For the next ten years he wandered Europe and wrote his most significant works, but in 1889 he was declared insane and spent the rest of his life in seclusion, unable to do anything. But by then he had plumbed the depths of the spiritual crisis of his age, and had already committed his thoughts to writing. Looking at Christianity in

[178] Søren Kierkegaard, *Fear and Trembling*, in *Kierkegaard's Writings*, 6:15–23.

[179] Søren Kierkegaard, *Philosophical Fragments*, in *Kierkegaard's Writings*, 7/1:64.

[180] Ibid., 7/1:100.

[181] Kierkegaard, *Concluding Unscientific Postscript*, in *Kierkegaard's Writings*, 12/1:21.

[182] The literature on Nietzsche is vast. Among recent works, see Didier Franck, *Nietzsche and the Shadow of God* (Evanston, IL: Northwestern University Press, 2012). Originally published as *Nietzsche et l'ombre de Dieu* (Paris: Preses Universitaires de France, 1998); Robert R. Williams, *Tragedy, Recognition, and the Death of God: Studies in Hegel and Nietzsche* (Oxford: Oxford University Press, 2012); Ashley Woodward, ed., *Interpreting Nietzsche: Reception and Influence* (London: Continuum, 2011).

particular, he claimed that it had committed suicide by pursuing its own goal of seeking the truth, which it could not contain:

> What, strictly speaking, has actually conquered the Christian God. . . . Christian morality itself, the concept of truthfulness which was taken more and more seriously, the confessional punctiliousness of Christian conscience, translated and sublimated into scientific conscience, into intellectual purity at any price. Regarding nature as though it were a proof of God's goodness and providence, interpreting history in honor of divine reason, as a constant testimonial to an ethical world order. . . . Now all that is over, it has conscience against it, every sensitive conscience sees it as indecent, as a pack of lies.[183]

Nietzsche accepted that there had been an evolution of the human species, but he saw this in negative terms. According to him, the survival of the "fittest" was only the survival of the most powerful, whose lust for further domination exposes it to extinction. There is no upward progress, but only the downward spiral that will lead to final catastrophe.[184] Nietzsche's acid criticism of everything and everyone stopped short when he came to the person of Jesus, who exhibited a perfect tranquillity in the face of suffering and death, and therefore triumphed over his tormentors:

> This "bringer of glad tidings" died as he had lived, as he had taught—not to redeem men but to show how one must live. This practice is his legacy to mankind: his behavior before the judges, before the catchpoles, before the accusers and all kinds of slander and scorn—his behavior on the cross. He does not resist, he does not defend his right, he takes no step which might ward off the worst; on the contrary, he provokes it. And he begs, he suffers, he loves with those, in those, who do him evil. Not to resist, not to be angry, not to hold responsible—but to resist not even the evil one—to love him.[185]

Nietzsche was a tragic figure, but his legacy to the Christian church was profound. His understanding of Christianity was that of a nineteenth-century liberal moralist, and that was why he rejected it. He saw its hypocrisy and its inner contradictions only too well. Liberal Christianity had killed God in the traditional sense and was trying to make a new "superman" (*Übermensch*) to take his place. It might succeed, but if it did, it would produce a creature who

[183] Friedrich Nietzsche, *On the Genealogy of Morality*, ed. Keith Ansell-Pearson (Cambridge: Cambridge University Press, 1994), 126–127. The work was originally published as *Zur Genealogie der Moral. Eine Streitschrift* (Leipzig: Naumann, 1887).

[184] Friedrich Nietzsche, *The Will to Power*, trans. Walter Kaufmann and R. J. Hollingdale (New York: Random House, 1967), 358. Originally published as *Die Wille zur Macht* (Leipzig: Naumann, 1901).

[185] Friedrich Nietzsche, *The Antichrist*, trans. H. L. Mencken (New York: A. A. Knopf, 1920), 35. Originally published as *Der Antichrist* (Leipzig: Naumann, 1888).

was neither man nor God. Whether this creature would turn out to be a monster or a higher form of life—or both—only time would tell, but Nietzsche, of course, feared the worst. In any case, the God that confronted him in the theology of his day was dead, the pretensions of the churches were worthless, and man was left to stand alone before his fate. If he was to be rescued from that, an entirely new theology would be required.

The last word on classical liberal theology belongs to Albert Schweitzer (1875–1965). Schweitzer believed, along with Johannes Weiss (1863–1914) and Alfred Loisy, that Jesus' teaching and self-understanding were fundamentally eschatological.[186] But Schweitzer went beyond his contemporaries by demonstrating that this truth could be used to judge the whole of nineteenth-century Jesus research, and therefore the whole of that century's theology as well. After a lengthy survey of the many "lives of Jesus" that his age had produced, Schweitzer concluded,

> Jesus means something to our world because a mighty spiritual force streams forth from him and flows through our time also. This fact can neither be shaken nor confirmed by any historical discovery. It is the solid foundation of Christianity. The mistake was to suppose that Jesus could come to mean more to our time by entering into it as a man like ourselves. That is not possible. First, because such a Jesus never existed. Secondly, because, although historical knowledge can no doubt introduce greater clearness into an existing spiritual life, it cannot call spiritual life into existence. History can destroy the present; it can reconcile the present with the past; can even to a certain extent transport the present into the past; but to contribute to the making of the present is not given unto it.[187]

Liberal theology had tried to make Jesus a man of its time and had failed. What might replace it and carry conviction remained to be seen.

The Crisis of Authority: Roman Catholicism

The eighteenth and early nineteenth centuries were a difficult time for the traditionally orthodox. One of their biggest problems was that they were the official establishment in almost every Christian country. Orthodoxy took different forms, which reflected the legacy of the Reformation and post-Reformation

---

[186] The idea seems to have originated with Weiss, who developed it in his book *Die Predigt Jesu vom Reiche Gottes* (Göttingen: Vandenhoeck und Ruprecht, 1892); English trans., *Jesus' Proclamation of the Kingdom of God* (London: SCM, 1971).

[187] Albert Schweitzer, *The Quest of the Historical Jesus: A Critical Study of Its Progress from Reimarus to Wrede*, ch. 20 (London: SCM, 1981; a reissue of the 3rd ed., London: A. & C. Black, 1954), 397. Originally published as *Von Reimarus zu Wrede. Eine Geschichte der Leben-Jesu-Forschung* (Tübingen: J. C. B. Mohr, 1906).

disputes, but on the core doctrines of the Christian faith they were generally agreed. A movement like pietism could transcend many of the differences while remaining faithful to the Bible and to the creedal tradition of the early church, and it reached out across the Christian world, though with varying degrees of success. Enlightenment rationalism also went beyond confessional boundaries, and men like Voltaire felt that they were attacking all official Christianity, not just Roman Catholicism, though undoubtedly his audience was larger in Protestant countries than it might otherwise have been because the Roman church was his main target.

The revolutions of the late eighteenth century effectively brought the confessional era to an end. In the United States, and later in France and the Netherlands, the old religious establishments were dismantled and all beliefs (or none) were put on an equal footing. This was subsequently reversed in France, at least to some degree, but Roman Catholicism was on the defensive there in the nineteenth century and until the final separation between church and state in 1905.[188] Elsewhere, church establishments were retained but their powers were constantly being diluted by the grant of civil rights to those who did not belong to the state church. They were also hobbled by the imposition of doctrinal and liturgical norms that they had themselves developed in the seventeenth century or earlier but were no longer free to modify or expand. The Church of England, for example, was tied to the Thirty-nine Articles of Religion (1571) and the Book of Common Prayer (1662), neither of which it could amend or supplement. The Church of Scotland was similarly bound to the Westminster Confession (1646) and its subsidiary documents, which it could do nothing to change. That suited the conservative mentality, of course, but it meant that orthodoxy would be associated with social and political reaction and would find it difficult to express its theology in a creative way. As a result, it was very hard for the orthodox to engage new intellectual currents in a constructive way, and they tended to promote a return to the past that was unrealistic and ultimately impossible to achieve.

Perceptive observers of modern orthodoxy in the different Christian churches have noticed that, whatever they may claim, its defenders have been influenced by Enlightenment (and often by romantic) tendencies almost as much as their opponents who openly embraced and supported them. For example, even in conservative theological circles, the doctrine of the Trinity did not fare

[188] In 1802 Napoleon signed a concordat with the Vatican, granting Roman Catholicism many of the privileges of a state church, but the same privileges were also given to Protestants. The concordat system was subsequently extended to other Catholic countries, both in Europe and in Latin America, and in some of them it remains in force (though usually in a modified form) to the present time.

too well in the nineteenth century. In the Protestant world, it often seemed as though the orthodox practiced a kind of serial monotheism. Sometimes they concentrated on God the Father, seeing him as a beneficent Creator and/or as the Judge of the world who would punish the wicked and bring justice to bear on all mankind at the end of time. At other times they concentrated on Jesus, the Savior of the world who died for our sins and rose again to give us eternal life. Against the rationalists, they insisted that Jesus was far more than just a moral example, but all that was necessary for salvation was to trust in him—the rest of the theological package could be relegated to a secondary level and was of little real interest. Occasionally the Holy Spirit took center stage, but that was less common, and on the whole the third person of the Godhead was not emphasized in theologically conservative circles, perhaps because of a fear that it might encourage the sort of extremism that was commonly observed in popular "revivals." This attitude was all the easier because expository preaching of the Scriptures seldom demanded the sort of systematic thought that the doctrine of the Trinity required, and when it did, it was usually possible to skirt around it by concentrating either on Jesus or on the spiritual experience of the believer. The personal interaction present within the Trinity thus went by default, and even the soundest ministers of the Word were often at a loss to know what to say about it.

In the Roman Catholic Church the situation was not very different. The fate of LaMennais highlighted the biggest problem that the church faced in the nineteenth century. How was it to come to terms with the postrevolutionary world? Its enemies could hardly forget that it had been a pillar of the old regime, and no one expected the papacy to change its ways to any significant extent. Internally, at least, Rome had been less affected by enlightenment principles than the Protestant churches, and it clung more tenaciously to traditional doctrinal formulas, but it could not escape the fundamental question of ecclesiology. Granted that it was the true church, the body of Christ on earth that claimed the allegiance of all baptized Christians everywhere, how was this going to be put into practice in an intellectual climate that had replaced the authority of religious dogmatism with the sovereignty of human reason?

One way of doing this was to deemphasize the humanity of Jesus. To the rationalist mind, Jesus was no more than a Galilean prophet who had been elevated to divinity by his more enthusiastic followers. Later on, under the influence of Kant and others, he was exalted as the most perfect moral teacher who had ever lived, but this was still less than a resounding affirmation of his divinity, and only that would suffice. Like all the traditionally orthodox, Roman Catholic theologians were bound by the creeds and the definitions of the ancient ecumenical councils—whatever they said, Jesus Christ would still have to be one divine person manifested in two natures, one of which was fully divine but the other of which was fully human. Was that second affirmation going to become the means by which the doctrine of Christ's divinity would be subtly eroded?

The Catholic church thought that the best way to avoid that danger was to concentrate on the source of Christ's humanity, the Virgin Mary. Mary had been honored in the Christian world for many centuries, but this had never caused much of a theological problem and was not an issue at the time of the Reformation. It is certainly true that the Reformers cut back on the more extravagant forms of Marian devotion, but they did not single out her cult for special condemnation. A good gauge of their attitude can be found in the holy days set aside for special commemoration in the Anglican *Book of Common Prayer*. The English Reformers were determined to limit such devotions to things and people that could be found in the New Testament. Saints' days were accordingly restricted to the apostles and a few others, like John the Baptist and the archangel Michael. But Mary was remembered both on the feast of the Annunciation (March 25) and on the day she went to the temple to be purified after the birth of Jesus (February 2), two events in her life that were recorded in Scripture.[189] No one ever complained about the degree of attention given to Mary, as far as we know. The Puritans wanted to abolish all such commemorations, including Christmas, but they never singled out inordinate devotion to Mary as a reason for their attitude. We can only conclude that although the veneration of Mary existed in the pre-Reformation church, it did not make any particular impression and was not perceived as a theological problem in its own right.

Devotion to the Virgin Mary was especially popular in Mediterranean countries, and it seems that it increased greatly in southern Italy, and later in Spain and Portugal, in the sixteenth and seventeenth centuries. Later on, it was one of the most important weapons used by the Jesuits in the re-Catholicizing of Poland.[190] But this was popular piety and not official church teaching. The Council of Trent, for example, had said very little on the subject, contenting itself with a reaffirmation of the decree of Pope Sixtus IV (1471–1484) governing the celebration of the feast of Mary's immaculate conception and

[189] The dates were calculated on the basis that Christ was born on December 25. This placed the Annunciation nine months earlier, and until 1752 it was celebrated in England as New Year's Day. The Purification was forty days after Christmas. Oddly enough, it is still widely celebrated in the United States, but in the secularized form of "Groundhog Day."

[190] See William R. Ward, *Christianity under the* Ancien Régime, *1648–1789* (Cambridge: Cambridge University Press, 1999), 51–52, 213–214.

a reassertion of the traditional belief that she had been preserved by God's grace from committing actual sin during her lifetime.[191] Those statements fell short of making the belief that Mary had been born without original sin an obligatory part of Catholic doctrine, though they recognized that belief in her immaculate conception was widespread, and to that extent they left the door open for further development.[192]

That came in the nineteenth century, and the circumstances make it clear that it was part of a wider program aimed against the revolutionary movements of the time. In 1846 Pius IX (1846–1878) was elected pope—the longest-serving holder of the papal office to date. One of his first acts was to denounce rationalism:

> By a preposterous and extremely fallacious mode of argumentation, they [the rationalists] never stop appealing to the power and excellence of human reason, exalting it against the most holy faith of Christ, and with extreme boldness they keep saying that that faith is opposed to human reason. It is scarcely possible to imagine or to think of anything more foolish, more ungodly or more contrary to reason itself. For even if the faith goes beyond reason, there can never be any real conflict or disagreement between them, because they both spring from one and the same source of unchangeable and eternal truth, the most good and most high God, and they assist each other, so that right reason demonstrates, protects and defends the truth of faith, whereas faith delivers reason from all error, and by the understanding it has of divine things, it enlightens, confirms and perfects reason in a wonderful way.[193]

Initially, Pius IX favored a form of moderate liberalism, but in 1848 he was chased out of Rome by insurgent nationalists who proclaimed a republic and wanted a united Italy. He was soon restored to his throne, but after that experience his attitude hardened. The modern world in all its forms became the declared enemy. Eventually he would produce his notorious *Syllabus of Errors*, in which he denounced the view that the pope "can or should reconcile himself to, or agree with progress, liberalism and modern culture."[194] Ten years before

[191] See the decree on original sin (6), promulgated at the fifth session on June 17, 1546, in *Conciliorum oecumenicorum decreta* (Bologna: Istituto per le Scienze Religiose, 1973), 667, and the canons on justification (23), promulgated at the sixth session on January 13, 1547, in *Conciliorum oecumenicorum decreta*, 680. The decree of Sixtus IV, dated February 28, 1476, is in the *Extravagantes communes* 3.12.1, in Emil Friedberg, *Corpus iuris canonici*, 2 vols. (Leipzig: B. Tauchnitz, 1879; repr., Graz: Akademische Druck- und Verlagsanstalt, 1955, 1995), 2:col. 1285.

[192] On the Marian tradition, see Jaroslav Pelikan, *Mary through the Centuries: Her Place in the History of Culture* (New Haven, CT: Yale University Press, 1996).

[193] In the encyclical *Qui pluribus* of November 9, 1846. (Denzinger, *Enchiridion*, no. 2776).

[194] Error 80 in *Syllabus errorum*, published on the feast of the immaculate conception of Mary, December 8, 1864 (Denzinger, *Enchiridion*, no. 2980).

that, however, he had already proclaimed the immaculate conception of Mary in the following terms:

> We declare, pronounce and define that the doctrine which holds that the blessed Virgin Mary was, from the first moment of her conception, by a singular grace and favor of Almighty God, with regard to the merits of Jesus Christ, Savior of the human race, preserved intact from any stain of original sin, is a doctrine revealed by God, and that therefore it must be firmly and constantly believed by all the faithful.[195]

For good measure, Pius IX went on to say that anyone who denied the doctrine of Mary's immaculate conception condemned himself, made shipwreck of his faith, and separated himself from the only true church—a condemnation that embraced not only Protestants and many Eastern Orthodox, but even such Catholic luminaries as Thomas Aquinas, though this was never acknowledged. It was a high price to pay for attacking the liberalism of the age, and it was not long before theological criticism of it was being voiced. One of the most serious charges was that Mary, whose womb had been the first and primary locus of the work of the Holy Spirit on earth, somehow took the place of the Holy Spirit in the life of the church. She was venerated as the first Christian, the mother of all who submit to the will of God so that Christ may be born in them and they in him. This criticism had of course been rejected by competent Roman Catholic theologians, but the fact that it could be made at all shows how problematic the person and work of Mary had become for many.[196] She had in fact been detached from the rest of the human race in order to become the mother of Jesus, a curious maneuver and one that was bound to call his humanity, as well as hers, into question.

The second way in which Pius IX sought to counter the effects of liberalism was in his efforts to define the ministry of the pope. Obviously it was not possible for him to say that the popes were immaculately conceived or sinless, but he did the next best thing—he summoned a council of the church and got it to declare that whenever he spoke officially (*ex cathedra*) on a matter of faith and morals, he was infallible, an attribute which up to then had never been applied to anyone except God himself.[197]

Like the cult of the Virgin Mary, papal power over the church had been

---

[195] In the encyclical *Ineffabilis Deus*, published on December 8, 1854 (Denzinger, *Enchiridion*, no. 2803).

[196] See Yves Congar, *I Believe in the Holy Spirit*, 3 vols. (New York: Seabury, 1983), 1:2.9.3. Originally published as *Je crois en l'Esprit-Saint*, 3 vols. (Paris: Cerf, 1979–1980).

[197] See Derek Holmes, *The Triumph of the Holy See* (London: Burns & Oates, 1978; and Shepherdstown, WV: Patmos, 1978). For a modern reassessment from a Roman Catholic point of view, see Jean M. Tillard, *The Bishop of Rome* (London: SPCK, 1983). Originally published as *L'évêque de Rome* (Paris: Cerf, 1982).

growing for centuries, but it was never regarded as absolute, and even the Protestant Reformers had not been as opposed to it as their followers later became.[198] Although they uniformly repudiated the pope's claim to exercise spiritual jurisdiction without consultation, and many of them regarded his "dictatorship" over the church as the rule of the Antichrist, they might have accepted him as a kind of president of the Western church if he had been prepared to subscribe to their basic theological principles. The Reformation had been more about justification by faith and the authority of the Scriptures than about the papacy, though negative attitudes toward it hardened as time went on. Roman Catholics naturally had a more positive view of it, but the Catholic countries of Europe were never inclined to submit to papal dictation, and in the eighteenth century they had even managed to force Rome to disband the Jesuit order, which had been founded at the time of the Reformation with the specific purpose of defending the pope. Napoleon Bonaparte, himself a Catholic of sorts, even seized Pius VII and forced him to go to France, giving many the impression that he was about to abolish the institution just as he abolished the Holy Roman Empire in 1806.

A major influence on postrevolutionary Catholic thinking was Joseph de Maistre (1753–1821), whose early inclinations toward liberalism were cut short by the revolution. He fled to Italy and became the Sardinian ambassador to Russia, where he lived for fifteen years (1802–1817) and where he wrote his most important works.[199] Those experiences persuaded him that human life is plagued by a lust for power. He was deeply critical of the deistic love of "nature" and thought that the romantic vision of society was naive in the extreme. For him, the guiding principle of politics was not reason but original sin, a reality that demanded clear and firm government. In the secular world, that was provided by kings, whose sovereignty was absolute and who represented God to the people. But in the church, it devolved on the pope, whose authority was supreme and infallible. De Maistre expressed all this in a book about the pope, which was widely circulated and persuaded many of the need to declare him infallible, though ironically, when it was first published it was coolly received in Rome.[200] He saw the church in the mirror image of *ancien régime* France. The ancient councils were comparable to the States General (*Etats généraux*) or parliament, which had eventually given way to absolute monarchy, and in the same way, there was no more need for church councils either. It did not

[198] For the history, see Klaus Schatz, *Papal Primacy from Its Origins to the Present* (Collegeville, MN: Liturgical Press, 1996). Originally published as *Der päpstliche Primat: seine Geschichte von den Ursprungen bis zur Gegenwart* (Würzburg: Echter Verlag, 1990).
[199] *The Works of Joseph de Maistre*, 2nd ed., ed. and trans. Jack Lively (New York: Schocken, 1971).
[200] Joseph de Maistre, *Du pape*, 2 vols. (Lyon: Rusand, 1819). English translation, *The Pope* (London: C. Dolman, 1850).

seem to occur to him that it was the suspension of the *Etats généraux* that had ultimately produced the crisis that brought down the French kingdom and that the same might happen to the papacy if his ideas were to be followed! What was clear to everyone, though, was that de Maistre was deeply opposed to anything that smacked of democracy, and it was that which appealed to Pius IX. In his eyes, as in de Maistre's, the only way to ensure the preservation of the church, and thus of the truth of the gospel, was by having an earthly authority who could pronounce what that truth was and impose his decisions on everyone who called himself a Catholic Christian.

The immediate circumstances in which papal infallibility was proclaimed were full of danger for the papacy. In 1861, most of the Papal States had been incorporated into the newly formed Kingdom of Italy, and the pope was left with only the "patrimony of St. Peter"—Rome and its immediate vicinity. Everyone knew that this was a temporary arrangement, and it continued only because it was being supported by the French emperor, Napoleon III (1852–1870). That support could be withdrawn at any moment and then the Italians would invade, probably with the support of the great majority of the population. Aware of this, and intent on preserving his spiritual if not his temporal authority, Pius IX summoned the First Vatican Council, which met in Rome in 1869–1870.[201] There were only four sessions in all, and it was clear from the start what the agenda was. After a fairly standard profession of faith at the second session (January 6, 1870), there followed a more extensive affirmation of the Catholic faith. This was basically an attack on contemporary rationalism and had four chapters—one each on God the Creator, revelation, faith, and the relationship between faith and reason. None of that was in any way surprising, and most of it could have been affirmed by any theologically orthodox Christian, even by those whom Pius IX castigated for their "heretical depravity" in the canons appended to it.[202]

However this was all a warm-up for the real business of the council in its fourth and final session (July 18, 1870), which promulgated "the first dogmatic constitution on the church of Christ." It contained four chapters, the first on the institution of the primacy of Peter, the second on the succession of that primacy through his successors, the third on the power and extent of the Roman pontiff's primacy, and the last on the infallibility of his teaching office (*magisterium*).[203] The first two chapters purport to ground the office of the Roman bishop in the life and apostolic commission of the apostle Peter, based

[201] It opened on the feast of the immaculate conception (December 8, 1869), Pius IX's favorite day.
[202] Canon 4.3, in *Conciliorum oecumenicorum decreta* 811.
[203] The full text of the constitution, known as *Pastor aeternus*, is in *Conciliorum oeucmenicorum decreta* 811–816.

on specific New Testament texts.[204] It is fair to say that modern biblical scholars read these passages very differently, and it is hard to imagine anyone today using them for this purpose.[205] The second chapter asserts that Peter's somewhat questionable authority was handed down through his supposed successors at Rome in an unbroken line from the first century to the present, another proposition that virtually no one (including the majority of Roman Catholic scholars) would now want to assert and that is almost certainly untenable in the light of the known facts.[206] The third chapter is a defense of papal jurisdiction over the whole church and corresponds quite closely to what the popes had claimed at least from the time of the Reformation onward and in many respects since the great reforms of the eleventh century.[207] But it was the fourth chapter that brought something new to the discussion and that has caused the greatest controversy, both then and since. Citing the precedents of the past and the dangers from liberals in the present, the chapter stated quite clearly,

> We teach that it is a dogma revealed by God that when the Roman pontiff speaks *ex cathedra*, that is to say, when in the course of fulfilling his charge as pastor and teacher of all Christians, he defines, by virtue of his supreme apostolic authority, that a doctrine in some matter of faith or morals must be held by the whole church, he enjoys, by virtue of the divine assistance which was promised to him in the person of Saint Peter, that infallibility which the divine Redeemer wanted his church to be provided with when it defines doctrine concerning faith or morals. In consequence, these definitions of the Roman pontiff are irreformable in themselves, and not because the church has agreed to them.[208]

It is true that this infallibility was hedged about with *caveats* and precautions. It was only when speaking *ex cathedra*, and then only when pronouncing the mind of the church on a matter of faith and morals, that the pope was to be considered infallible. But of course lines were easily blurred. No one really knew (or knows) which of his statements were infallible and which were not. Someone who is capable of infallibility in certain circumstances is bound to be regarded as a being apart, and his words are likely to carry an authority they

[204] Matt. 16:16–19 and John 21:15–17.

[205] See Markus Bockmuehl, *Simon Peter in Scripture and Memory* (Grand Rapids, MI: Baker Academic, 2012).

[206] One of the problems is that so few of the facts are known. The earliest succession list is found in Irenaeus of Lyon, *Adversus haereses* 3.3.3, and contains twelve names, but the first eight are shadowy figures whose real role at Rome remains uncertain. See J. N. D. Kelly, *The Oxford Dictionary of Popes*, 2nd ed., revised by Michael J. Walsh (Oxford: Oxford University Press, 2010) for the details.

[207] The chapter quoted the confession of the Byzantine Emperor Michael VIII that had been read at the Second Council of Lyon in 1274, and also the "agreement" about papal primacy reached between East and West at Florence in 1439.

[208] *Conciliorum oecumenicorum decreta* 816 (Denzinger, *Enchiridion*, no. 3074).

might not otherwise have. Papal infallibility was a way of stressing the work of the Holy Spirit in and through the vicar of Christ on earth, but it was focused on the church and not on God or the Trinity, whatever the official texts might say. The communion of the church in the inner life of God did not come into the discussion; rather, attention was focused on how God communicated his will through an intermediary, whose existence served to keep a respectable distance between him and the members of the church. For practical purposes, ordinary Christians had to do what the pope told them to do and assume that what he said was God's will for them.

By no means everyone at the council accepted this, and for the first time since the Reformation there was a major breakaway from the Roman church, led mainly by German theologians who could not accept such an unhistorical doctrine. They had been shaped in the school of Johann Sebastian von Drey (1777–1853), who had founded a Catholic school at Tübingen and who had done much to interpret the ideas of Baur and his colleagues in a way that Catholics could accept. Another powerful voice had been that of Johann Adam Möhler (1796–1838), who had managed to combine belief in the necessity of a monarchical papacy with a more flexible view of how the church's doctrine had grown over time and how it should be implemented in the life of the church. For Möhler, as for Drey, the pope could not act without the bishops, nor the bishops without the pope—together they formed a creative tension that served to support the infallible truth that was the gift of Christ to the church, and not just to a single individual (however exalted) within it.[209] The group that broke away was led by the German Catholic professor Johann Joseph Ignaz von Döllinger (1799–1890), and formed what is now called the Old Catholic church, a small body that includes a number of dissident national Catholic churches and is strongest in the Netherlands, Switzerland, and Poland. It has good relations with many Protestant and Eastern Orthodox churches but has (so far) failed to produce a distinctive theology of its own.[210]

Those who accepted the new doctrine, willingly or otherwise, soon found themselves having to accept a revival of medieval scholasticism, which had been going on in Catholic circles for a generation but became the official teaching of the church only under Pius IX's successor, Pope Leo XIII (1878–1893). Soon after taking office, Leo issued an encyclical, *Aeterni Patris*, in which he declared,

[209] On this, see, for example Alexander Dru, *The Contribution of German Catholicism* (New York: Hawthorn, 1963); Gerald A. McCool, *Catholic Theology in the Nineteenth Century: The Quest for a Unitary Method* (New York: Seabury, 1977); Thomas F. O'Meara, *Romantic Idealism and Roman Catholicism: Schelling and the Theologians* (Notre Dame, IN: University of Notre Dame Press, 1982).

[210] See Johann Döllinger, *The Pope and the Council* (London: Rivingtons, 1869). Originally published as *Der Papst und das Concil* (Leipzig: J. F. Steinacker, 1869).

> Assuredly we do not attribute to human philosophy a power and authority such that we might think it capable of refuting or destroying every error. . . . Nevertheless, we must not despise or neglect the natural aids that have been placed at the disposition of men by the blessing of divine wisdom, . . . and of all these aids, the carefully controlled use of philosophy is certainly one that is prominent. Indeed, it is not in vain that God has planted in the human spirit the light of reason, and in no sense does the added light of faith extinguish or dim the vigor of the [human] mind. On the contrary, it brings it to perfection, and by increasing its strength, it makes it capable of even greater things. . . . Among all the scholastic doctors, the most outstanding by far is Thomas Aquinas. . . . Thomas collected the teachings of the others and organized them as if they were different parts of a body. He placed them in an order so admirable, and gave them such a boost, that he is rightly considered the special defender and the glory of the Catholic Church . . .[211]

Leo XIII was not a reactionary hankering after a lost Middle Ages, however. He genuinely believed that Thomas possessed the key to a revival of Catholic philosophy and theology that could hold its own in the modern world, but he insisted that his work should be taken as an inspiration, not slavishly followed:

> . . . if there is something that was taken too far by the scholastic doctors or taught in a way that was not sufficiently prudent, if there is something in them that is not in agreement with the doctrines worked out in later times, or finally, if there is something in them that seems most improbable, we do not want it offered for the consideration of our present age.[212]

The intentions of Leo XIII were of course interpreted in different ways. Some took his words to mean that they should adhere strictly to Thomas, while others stretched the liberty granted to them in the final paragraph so far that they almost ignored him. To bring order out of such chaos, Pope Pius X (1903–1914) issued a decree on June 19, 1914 (*Doctoris angelici*), ordering all Catholic seminaries to teach the *Summa theologiae* and examine it—in Latin! This was followed up by a list of twenty-four theses which purported to explain what Thomism was, so as to avoid any possible misunderstanding (or subtle failure to comply with the decree).[213] On March 19, 1917, Pope Benedict XV (1914–1922) clarified this still further by explaining that it was not necessary to follow Thomas in every detail. As Leo XIII had intended, Thomas was meant to serve as a model in general terms, and it was his method, not his conclu-

[211] *Aeterni Patris*, issued August 4, 1879. (Denzinger, *Enchiridion*, nos. 3135, 3139).
[212] Ibid., no. 3140.
[213] Issued by the Sacred Congregation of Studies on July 27, 1914 (Denzinger, *Enchiridion*, nos. 3601–3624).

sions, that counted most.[214] This so-called neo-Thomism was to remain the only permitted teaching in the Roman Catholic Church until the pontificate of John XXIII (1958–1963) who relaxed the requirement, and the Second Vatican Council (1962–1965), which virtually abandoned neo-Thomism altogether.[215] It still exists, but has become only one school of Catholic thought among many, and its innate conservatism has often led to its being marginalized by more "progressive" Catholics in recent years. However it is still capable of attracting followers, not least among converts from Protestantism, who often seem to be more attracted to it than native Roman Catholics are.[216]

Even in its heyday, however, neo-Thomism was not without its opponents, most of whom were silenced at the time but whose spiritual heirs resurfaced to claim what they believed was their rightful place at and after the Second Vatican Council. A large number of them were French, perhaps because the French Catholic church had always been more independent of Rome than most of the others, and because after the revolution it was there that the battle between traditional Catholicism and modern liberalism was most fiercely fought. While the majority of Catholics sided with the traditionalists, there was always an important minority that dissented from their view and sought a reconciliation between the church and modern thought.

The spiritual father of dissident French Catholicism was Louis Bautain (1796–1867), who went through a period of doubt in his youth and was attracted to the study of German idealism. Eventually he returned to the Catholic church, having been disillusioned by his study of Kant in particular, and after being ordained as a priest in 1828, he began to teach at the little seminary (*Petit Séminaire*) in Strasbourg. From the beginning, he was opposed to neo-Scholasticism, which at that time was the dominant trend at the large seminary (*Grand Séminaire*) in Strasbourg and was therefore something that Bautain was unable to avoid. The publication of his important book, *La philosophie du*

[214] *Quod de fovenda*, a letter sent by Benedict XV to the Jesuit general, Wladimir Ledochowski. Printed in *Acta Romana* S. I, IX (1917), 318–319, and in *Zeitschrift für Katholische Theologie* XLII (1918), 206.

[215] The acts of the Second Vatican Council (Vatican II) are in *Conciliorum oecumenicorum decreta*, 817–1135. The most common English translation and commentary on them is Austin Flannery, *Vatican Council II: The Conciliar and Post-conciliar Documents* (Dublin: Dominican, 1975). The conciliar documents should now be read alongside the *Catechism of the Catholic Church* (London: Geoffrey Chapman, 1994; and New York: Doubleday, 1995). The original text was drawn up in French and published as *Catéchisme de l'Eglise Catholique* (Paris: Mame-Plon, 1992) and then translated into Latin and published as *Catechismus Catholicae Ecclesiae* (Rome: Libreria Editrice Vaticana, 1997). It is the Latin text that is considered to be authoritative. Also important for interpreting the council is the revised code of canon law, published as *Codex iuris canonici* (Rome: Libreria Editrice Vaticana, 1983). The Latin text, with parallel English translation and extensive notes, is available in Ernest Caparros, Michel Thériault, and Jean Thorn, eds., *Code of Canon Law Annotated* (Montreal: Wilson & Lafleur Limitée, 1993).

[216] See Etienne Gilson, *The Christian Philosophy of Thomas Aquinas* (New York: Random House, 1956), and the works of Gerald A. McCool, *Nineteenth-century Scholasticism: The Quest for a Unitary Method* (New York: Fordham University Press, 1989); *From Unity to Pluralism: The Internal Evolution of Thomism* (New York: Fordham University Press, 1992); and *The Neo-Thomists* (Milwaukee: Marquette University Press, 1994). As an example of current neo-Thomism, see Peter Kreeft, *Summa of the* Summa (San Francisco: Ignatius, 1990).

christianisme, in 1835, threw down the gauntlet and began a controversy that led to his recantation in 1840 and the rapid disintegration of his following.[217]

Bautain dissented from classical scholasticism in his belief that faith was not merely the precondition for knowledge, but a form of knowledge in itself, though one that was a dim light that needed further illumination:

> The superior light which must produce it, descends into the depths of the soul and it is absorbed there; and thus cannot be reflected in the intelligence, still insufficiently developed, and therefore incapable of conceiving the idea and embracing knowledge. There results what is called *faith*, which is the root of the idea. . . . But let no one be deceived. Faith, as obscure as it is on account of its depth, is intelligent; it is an intelligence penetrated by the action of truth, but which is not yet conscious of itself and that which penetrates it; it is an unreflected and hence less brilliant light.[218]

Bautain was clearly influenced by romanticism, but although he certainly inclined to think that men of genius, whether Christians or not, had received a special illumination from on high, he nevertheless made a clear distinction between them and the biblical prophets and apostles. Writing to some Jewish disciples of his, he said,

> O my friends, do you not realize that between a true Israelite and a deist there is the same difference as between a civilized man and a child growing up in savagery? The god of the deist is force, nature, fate, destiny; it is a general cause, assumed to exist because the reason demands a cause . . . [or it is] a rational entity, an abstraction, an idol of the mind. . . . And that is what you would substitute for the God of Israel and of Moses, the living God who created man in his image, animated him with his Spirit, and preserves him with his Providence?[219]

Bautain was in some ways too much like a Protestant to suit contemporary Catholic tastes, and it is not surprising that he was condemned for "fideism"—relying too much on faith alone!

The next stage in the development of a left-wing Catholic theology came with the publication of Renan's *Life of Jesus*, an event that some have seen as the beginning of Catholic "modernism."[220] Other important influences were

---

[217] Louis Bautain, *La philosophie du christianisme*, 2 vols. (Paris: Dérivaux, 1835). For studies of Bautain in English, see William M. Horton, *The Philosophy of the Abbé Bautin* (New York: New York University Press, 1926); Reardon, *Liberalism and Tradition*, 113–137; Gerald A. McCool, *Catholic Theology in the Nineteenth Century* (New York: Seabury, 1977), 37–58.

[218] Louis Bautain, *Psychologie expérimentale*, 2 vols. (Strasbourg: Dérivaux, 1839), 2:376–377.

[219] Ibid., 1:19–21.

[220] See Claude Tresmontant, *La crise moderniste* (Paris: Seuil, 1979), 14–35.

Maurice Blondel (1861–1949), a Catholic layman, Lucien Laberthonnière (1860–1932), a priest, and Henri Bergson (1859–1941), a Jew with a strong sympathy for Roman Catholicism. In their different ways, all three of these philosophers turned away from rationalism, including its neo-Scholastic variety, and emphasized the importance of things like faith and intuition for our understanding of spiritual things.[221] But the man who made the greatest impact in theological circles was Alfred Loisy (1857–1940), a Catholic priest who was excommunicated as a dangerous heretic in 1908.[222]

Loisy began to teach at the Institut Catholique in Paris in 1881, and at the same time he attended Renan's lectures at the Collège de France. Although he rejected Renan's rationalism, he was attracted by his passion for historical study and resolved to apply critical methods to both the Old and New Testaments.[223] As a result, he was dismissed from his teaching post and was forced to become a chaplain to a girls' school. But when his opinions on the religion of Israel were condemned by the archbishop of Paris, François-Marie-Benjamin Cardinal Richard (1886–1908), in 1900, he was appointed a lecturer at the Ecole Pratique des Hautes-Etudes, which was a section of the University of Paris (Sorbonne). The timing was significant. France had been embroiled in an increasingly bitter conflict between the Catholic church and the state, where left-wing anticlericalism was gaining ground. Those opposed to the church used the educational system to propagate their beliefs, so Loisy's appointment to the Sorbonne was in its own way an attack on Catholicism.[224] Safely ensconced in his chair in Paris, Loisy was free to embark on his most controversial work so far: *The Gospel and the Church*.[225]

Loisy was clearly inspired by Harnack, but he differed from his German contemporary in some important respects. As a Protestant, Harnack gave a special place to the Scriptures and tended to discount the evidence of extra-canonical writings, but Loisy argued that such an approach was too narrow. In his opinion, the tradition of the church was essential for our understanding of Jesus, since it was the only way we could have access to him. There was no "pure gospel" accessible to the clever student of the New Testament, because it was all tradition, one way or another. The canon of the Bible was just officially

[221] Maurice Blondel, *L'action* (Paris: F. Alcan, 1893); Lucien Laberthonnière, *Essais de philosophie religieuse* (Paris: P. Lethielleux, 1903); Henri Bergson, *L'énergie spirituelle* (Paris: Presses Universitaires de France, 1946); idem, *Les deux sources de la morale et la religion* (Paris: Presses Universitaires de France, 1946).

[222] See Reardon, *Liberalism and Tradition*, 249–281; Tresmontant, *Crise moderniste*, 35–66.

[223] Alfred Loisy, *Histoire du canon de l'Ancien Testament* (Paris: Letouzey et Ané, 1890); *Histoire du canon du Nouveau Testament* (Paris: J. Maisonneuve, 1891).

[224] Church and state were finally separated in France at the end of 1905.

[225] A. Loisy, *L'Evangile et l'église* (Paris: Emile Nourry, 1902); English translation, *The Gospel and the Church* (London: Isbister, 1903).

authorized tradition, not a separate source distinguishable from the rest as "divine revelation." In his words,

> Whatever we think, theologically, of tradition, whether we trust it or regard it with suspicion, we know Christ only by tradition, across the tradition, and in the tradition of the primitive Christians. This is as much as to say that Christ is inseparable from his work, and that the attempt to define the essence of Christianity according to the pure Gospel of Jesus, apart from the tradition, cannot succeed, for the mere idea of the Gospel without tradition is in flagrant contradiction with the facts submitted to criticism.[226]

Loisy was a brilliant analyst of the Gospels and perceived, earlier than Albert Schweitzer (1875–1965) did, that they were deeply eschatological in nature, couched in the language and thought forms of Jewish apocalyptic to a degree that was completely foreign to men like Ritschl. Harnack knew that too, but he thought that Jewish apocalyptic could simply be discarded for the "real" message of individual salvation. Loisy rejected this. To him, Harnack's distinction between the outward form of the message and its inner substance was a false one. Jesus came to preach the kingdom of God, not the forgiveness of the sins of particular individuals, even if that was part of it. Where Baur had interpreted the emergence of Christianity as a decline from the freedom of the original proclamation to the institutionalization that he called "early Catholicism," Loisy turned this on its head—Jesus had foretold the coming of the kingdom, and that prophecy was realized in the appearance of the Catholic church:

> It is certain that Jesus did not systematize beforehand the constitution of the church. . . . Jesus foretold the kingdom and it is the church that came, enlarging the form of the Gospel, which it was impossible to preserve as it was. . . . The preservation of its primitive state was impossible, its restoration now is equally out of the question, because the conditions under which the Gospel was produced have disappeared for ever. . . . It is easy today to see in the Catholic church what stands today for the idea of the heavenly kingdom, for the idea of the Messiah . . . and for the idea of the apostolate. . . . The tradition of the church keeps them, interpreting and adapting them to the varying conditions of humanity.[227]

The church was still the same as it had been in New Testament times and yet it had grown and developed over the centuries, as the proclamation of

[226] Loisy, *Gospel and Church*, 13.
[227] Ibid., 210–211.

papal infallibility had demonstrated. The same is true of its doctrines, which have evolved over time, even if their substance has remained much the same. As Loisy explained it,

> The conceptions that the church presents as revealed dogmas are not truths fallen from heaven and preserved by religious tradition in the precise form in which they first appeared. . . . Though the dogmas may be divine in origin and substance, they are human in structure and composition. It is inconceivable that their future should not correspond to their past. Reason never ceases to put questions to faith, and traditional formulas are submitted to a constant work of interpretation.[228]

This explained why dogmatic definitions were always contingent upon the circumstances in which they were made, and might therefore have to be restated when those conditions were altered. Loisy concluded,

> The church does not exact belief in its formulas as the adequate expression of absolute truth, but presents them as the least imperfect expression that is morally possible. . . . The ecclesiastical formula is the auxiliary of faith, the guiding line of religious thought: it cannot be the integral object of that thought, seeing that object is God himself, Christ and his work; each man lays hold of the object as he can, with the aid of the formula. As all souls and all intelligences differ one from the other, the gradations of belief are also of infinite variety, under the sole direction of the church and in the unity of her creed. The incessant evolution of doctrine is made by the work of individuals, as their activity reacts on the general activity, and these individuals are they who think for the church while thinking with her.[229]

Loisy was condemned for his views because the Roman church of his time could not accept his concept of development and change. As far as it was concerned, the truth of the faith had been revealed intact from the beginning, and to question that was to desert the cause of Christ. But there were many Catholic intellectuals at the time who sided with him, and whose voice would not be silenced forever. What Loisy retained was belief in the authority of the church, and in Roman Catholic terms, that was what really mattered. The Bible could be interpreted in different ways and particular traditions could be adopted or ignored, but the important thing was that decisions on such matters were taken by the supreme pontiff who sat in the same chair of St. Peter that had existed in Rome from New Testament times onward. In that respect, Loisy was not only a

228 Ibid., 210–211.
229 Ibid., 224–225.

conservative but a defender of the papal claims enunciated at the First Vatican Council, little though it was appreciated at the time.

A different kind of Catholic modernism was that of George Tyrrell (1861–1909), an Irish Anglican who was attracted to Anglo-Catholicism but moved on into the Roman church in 1877.[230] However, he never lost his Irish love of combat, nor (if the truth be told) his independent Protestant spirit. Initially a devotee of Thomas Aquinas and the new Scholasticism, Tyrrell began to move in more liberal Catholic circles, and by 1899 he was openly calling for a revision of traditional Catholic doctrines. He was forced to stop teaching, and for the last decade of his life was involved in an increasingly bitter dispute with the church, which led him to call for a root and branch reform of virtually everything in it. When Catholic modernism was officially condemned and proscribed in 1907, Tyrrell took up the cudgels in defense of those accused, and was excommunicated as a result.[231] Tyrrell believed with Loisy that the biblical picture of Jesus was that of an apocalyptic prophet, and like Loisy, he contrasted this with the bourgeois Christ of liberal Protestantism—the infamous "gentle Jesus, meek and mild." To those who thought that this apocalyptic Jesus was no closer to the Christ of the Catholic church than he was to liberal Protestantism, Tyrrell replied that it was necessary to see the transcendental idea that was present in Jesus and safeguarded by the teaching and practice of the Catholic church. Jesus was wrong about the imminent end of the world, but his basic spiritual message survived the limitations imposed by his historical circumstances and remains valid for us today:

> This contempt of the world preached by Jesus was not Buddhistic in its motive. It was a contempt for a lower and transitory form of existence in favor of a higher—a proximate pessimism but an ultimate optimism. That the world was thought to be in its death agony made it doubly contemptible. But when this thought was dropped by the church, the world still remained contemptible. It was but a preparation and a purgatory, the theater of the great conflict between the forces of good and evil—a conflict that could be decided in favor of Good only by the coming of the Son of Man. . . . The emphatic Persian dualism of good and evil, of the Kingdom of God and of Satan, is common to the idea of Jesus and the idea of Catholicism. . . . It is not between Jesus and Catholicism but between Jesus and liberal Protestantism that no bridge, but only a great gulf, is fixed.[232]

[230] See Ellen Leonard, *George Tyrrell and the Catholic Tradition* (London: Darton, Longman & Todd, 1982).
[231] The detailed condemnation was in a papal encyclical, *Pascendi Domini gregis*, issued by Pope Pius X on September 8, 1907, the feast of the birth of the Virgin Mary (Denzinger, *Enchiridion*, nos. 3475–3500).
[232] George Tyrrell, *Christianity at the Crossroads* (London: Longmans, 1909), 69–73. It is tempting to think that only an Irish Protestant like Tyrrell would equate Catholicism with Zoroastrian dualism and see nothing wrong with it.

Tyrrell was indifferent to questions of historicity and tended to see events like Jesus' ascension into heaven as more like parables of spiritual truth than facts to be ascertained by the usual historical criteria. It was inevitable that he would be condemned for his cavalier attitude toward the Bible, as was Loisy for the same reason. Catholic modernism, far from changing the church in its direction, had the opposite effect, at least in the short term. On July 3, 1907, shortly before condemning the modernists by name, Pope Pius X catalogued their distinctive teachings and condemned them one by one (there were sixty-five in all). His censure touched on the doctrine of Christ and the sacraments, but the weight of his attack was directed toward their doctrine of Scripture, whose inspiration and inerrancy they denied.[233] Perhaps unknown to Pius X, his censure could have been written by the conservative Protestants at Princeton Theological Seminary and (with a few changes here and there, mostly relating to the church), it would be readily adopted by the Evangelical Theological Society in the United States today.

The Crisis of Authority: Protestantism

When we turn to the Protestant world, the situation was more complex, partly because of the great variety of Protestant churches and partly because Enlightenment rationalism and later romanticism found it easier to establish a foothold there than it did in the Roman Catholic Church. This is not to say that there were not a number of radical theologians who lost their university posts because they rejected the official orthodoxy of their churches—there were. But as the nineteenth century wore on, that kind of discipline either broke down or else ceased to matter very much, because a professor who lost his chair in one university could usually go somewhere else and be greeted with open arms. By 1900, heresy trials were increasingly a thing of the past, though conservative groups were well established and active in churches which had by then become noticeably more pluralistic in their theology than they had been a hundred years earlier.

Taking the main Protestant denominations one by one, confessionalism was probably strongest among the Lutherans, despite the fact that pietism and rationalism were also prominent, at least in parts of Germany. Lutheran orthodoxy stuck rigidly to the *Formula of Concord* and cannot be called creative in any real sense, but it had a strong following in some places. In 1817 the Prussian king Frederick William III, who was Reformed, decided to unite the Lutheran and the Reformed churches of his kingdom. He devised a new liturgy

233 *Lamentabili*, issued on July 3, 1907 (Denzinger, *Enchiridion*, nos. 3401–3466).

and issued regulations for the united church, which he believed would overcome an ancient but unnecessary division between two different kinds of Protestants. Initially there was little trouble, but as the union took hold, more and more aspects of church life were combined in a way that was neither purely Lutheran nor purely Reformed. In 1830 the three-hundredth anniversary of the Augsburg Confession produced an outpouring of devotion to the Lutheran cause, and before long there was an organized group of "Old Lutherans" demanding the right to secede and form a distinctively Lutheran church.[234]

Permission for this was not granted until 1845, but by then a number of confessionally minded Lutherans had left Germany for the United States and Australia, where they set up independent churches of their own. Today the largest and best known of these is the Missouri Synod, which remains loyal to the stance of its founders and has produced a number of important scholars and church historians. It is, however, a sectarian form of Lutheranism and keeps its distance from other Christians, including other Lutherans. It excels in the production of historical studies and expositions of traditional Lutheranism, but has not generated much in the way of creative theology, and members of the church who engage seriously with other traditions often end up by leaving it for more tolerant pastures elsewhere.

In Germany, confessional Lutheranism was kept alive by men like Ernst Wilhelm Hengstenberg (1802–1869), who stressed the centrality of the atoning work of Christ, an emphasis that led him to place a high value on the Old Testament and its accounts of the temple laws and sacrifices. His great book, *The Christology of the Old Testament*, first appeared in 1829 and is still widely read today.[235] Also in this group were Johann Karl Friedrich Keil (1807–1888) and Franz Delitzsch (1813–1890), whose biblical commentaries were a model of careful exegesis that has never been surpassed. The Scandinavian countries also had some very conservative theological movements, mostly connected with pietism, which helped to shape the churches there, especially in Norway and Finland, but which did not produce a distinctive theological school of their own.

The Anglican churches followed a somewhat similar path. Having been regarded as Reformed for most of the seventeenth and eighteenth centuries, Anglicans began to move off in different directions in the years after 1800. Deism and other forms of rationalism, which might be said to have had Anglican roots, had by then emigrated to other churches, leaving the field to the

[234] See Christopher Clark, *Iron Kingdom: The Rise and Downfall of Prussia 1600–1947* (London: Penguin, 2006), 412–424.

[235] Ernst W. Hengstenberg, *Christologie des Alten Testaments und Commentar über die messianischen Weissagungen der Propheten*, 3 vols. (Berlin: L. Oehmigke, 1829–1835); English translation, *The Christology of the Old Testament and a Commentary on the Messianic Predictions of the Prophets* (London: F. & J. Rivington, 1847).

apologetic tradition of men like Berkeley, Butler, and Paley. The evangelical movement was strong but internally divided, with the Wesleyans on the point of forming a new denomination and the "Calvinists" intent on remaining within the establishment and loyal to its doctrine and liturgy. There was also a high church party, whose theology was more latitudinarian but who were determined to hang onto the status of a national church, which they claimed owed its origin and ultimate allegiance to the apostles of Jesus and not to more recent confessions, whether Protestant or Catholic.

It was from this group that a theologically conservative movement would emerge and even claim the word "Anglican" for itself. Its basic belief was that Anglicanism was a third branch of Christianity that could be put alongside Rome and the Eastern churches and traced back to apostolic times. With more romance than reason, it claimed the heritage of the Celtic church and even the legends of ancient Britain, which included such fantasies as the migration of Joseph of Arimathea to Glastonbury in the first century.[236] The branch theory was promoted by William Palmer (1811–1879), an eccentric Englishman who tried to establish communion between the Anglican and Eastern Orthodox churches and who spent his last days in Rome.[237] Palmer never got very far with his ecumenical projects, and most Anglicans were puzzled by him, but he was a close associate of John Henry Newman (1801–1890) and it is there that his historical importance lies. It was Palmer who persuaded Newman that the Thirty-nine Articles of the Church of England could be read in a Roman Catholic way, a curious belief that was to have serious consequences for Newman.

Newman was an extraordinary figure whose legacy remains controversial in both the Roman and the Anglican churches.[238] At the age of fifteen he experienced an evangelical conversion that shaped him for the rest of his life, but when he went up to Oxford a few years later he fell in with the high church party in the university. At that time, their main preoccupation was the defense of the national establishment of religion, which was under threat from liberalizing tendencies. In 1833 the British parliament decided to suppress ten Irish bishoprics in defiance of church opinion.[239] John Keble (1792–1866), one of

[236] The standard source book for this was David Wilkins, *Concilia Magnae Britanniae et Hiberniae a synodo Verulamensi AD CCCCXLVI ad Londinensem AD MDCCXVII*, 4 vols. (London: R. Gosling, F. Gyles, T. Woodward, and C. Davis, 1737). Wilkins put the legendary material in an appendix at the end of his collection, but it was available nonetheless.

[237] This was ironic, because Pope Pius IX had taken the trouble to condemn the branch theory in a letter to the (Roman Catholic) bishops of England, dated September 16, 1864. (Denzinger, *Enchiridion*, no. 2885).

[238] For a full biography, written by one of his Roman Catholic admirers, see Ian Ker, *John Henry Newman: A Biography* (Oxford: Oxford University Press, 1988). For a more critical assessment, see Frank M. Turner, *John Henry Newman: The Challenge to Evangelical Religion* (New Haven, CT: Yale University Press, 2002).

[239] The bishoprics were part of the (Anglican) Church of Ireland, which was officially established although only about ten percent of the population belonged to it.

Newman's colleagues at Oxford, preached against this in the annual assize sermon, which coincidentally fell on Bastille Day, July 14, 1833. In it he said,

> The legislature of England and Ireland (the members of which are not even bound to profess belief in the atonement), this body has virtually usurped the commission of those whom our Savior entrusted with at least one voice in making ecclesiastical laws, on matters wholly or partly spiritual. The same legislature has also ratified, to its full extent, this principle—that the apostolical church in this realm is henceforth only to stand, in the eye of the state, as one sect among many.[240]

Following this clarion call, a number of sympathizers gathered in Oxford to decide how to combat the wave of secularism that they saw threatening what was then the United Church of England and Ireland, and the so-called Oxford Movement was born.[241] Its founders decided to publish a series of tracts, the theme of which would be to uphold the apostolic succession of the church, meaning by that term that the church derived its authority and commission not from the state but from God. Newman wrote the first of them, in which he stated,

> We have been born not of blood, nor of the will of the flesh, nor of the will of man, but of God. The Lord Jesus Christ gave his Spirit to his apostles; they in turn laid their hands on those who should succeed them; and these again on others; and so the sacred gift has been handed down to our present bishops, who have appointed us as their assistants, and in some sense representatives.[242]

Within a few years the Tractarians (as they were then called) had established themselves as a major force within the Anglican church and were attracting widespread sympathy, but then things started to go wrong. When one of their number, Richard Hurrell Froude (1803–1836), died, Newman and Keble published his journal, which contained shockingly anti-Protestant statements, blaming the Reformation for all the ills of the present.[243] Froude harked back to the Middle Ages and longed for a restoration of Catholic Christendom, which

[240] John Keble, *National Apostasy, Considered in a Sermon Preached in St. Mary's Church, Oxford before His Majesty's Judges of Assize on Sunday, July 14th, 1833* (Steventon, Abingdon: Rocket, 1983).

[241] On the movement and its history, see the classic account by one of its members, Richard W. Church, *The Oxford Movement: Twelve Years, 1833–1845* (Chicago: University of Chicago Press, 1970); Geoffrey Faber, *Oxford Apostles: A Character Study of the Oxford Movement* (London: Faber & Faber, 1933); and Owen Chadwick, *The Mind of the Oxford Movement* (London: Adam & Chales Black, 1960).

[242] John H. Newman, *Thoughts on the Ministerial Commission Respectfully Addressed to the Clergy*, in *Tracts for the Times*, 6 vols. (London: J. G. and F. Rivington, 1833–1841), tract 1.

[243] John H. Newman and John Keble, *Remains of the Late Richard Hurrell Froude, MA, Fellow of Oriel College, Oxford*, 2 vols. (London: J. G. and F. Rivington: 1838).

he saw as the only sure bulwark against modern irreligion, but the publication of his views alienated many and opened up a chasm between the Tractarians and the rest of the church.[244] By the time Newman published his reinterpretation of the Articles in *Tract XC*, he was already on the way to leaving the Church of England for Rome, and the furious reaction to his exposition of the Catholic nature of Anglicanism merely drove him further down that road.

In 1845 he finally made the leap, and the last half of his life he spent as a Roman Catholic. It was not a comfortable journey, because Newman soon discovered that the Rome he had admired from a distance was quite different from the one that eventually embraced him. He discovered that it was not only traditionalist but obscurantist, not only authoritative but authoritarian. When papal infallibility was proclaimed in 1870 he privately dissented, but it was too late for him to return to the Church of England, and joining the Old Catholics would have meant repudiating everything he had done since 1833. His final years were sad ones as he saw his projects for regenerating the church fail and the world become even more secularized than it had been in his youth. He wrote a number of important books in which he outlined his religious philosophy, but it is generally agreed today that they are more interesting for their theories than for any practical application they may have.[245] Theologically speaking, Newman's most important work remains his *Essay on the Development of Christian Doctrine*, written in the years immediately preceding his conversion to Roman Catholicism and published shortly afterwards. In it he argued that an idea planted in the mind takes time to grow and mature. The early Christians had an experience of God that they accepted, and only after that did they reflect more deeply on it. In his words,

> The mind which is habituated to the thought of God, of Christ, of the Holy Spirit, naturally turns with a devout curiosity to the contemplation of the object of its adoration, and begins to form statements concerning it, before it knows whither, or how far, it will be carried. One proposition necessarily leads to another. . . . This process is its development, and results in a series, or rather body, of dogmatic statements, till what was an impression on the imagination has become a system or creed in the reason.[246]

---

[244] See Peter B. Nockles, *The Oxford Movement in Context: Anglican High Churchmanship 1760–1857* (Cambridge: Cambridge University Press, 1994).

[245] Newman was asked to become the first rector of the proposed Catholic University of Dublin, a post that he held from 1851 to 1858. The experiment was a failure, but it led Newman to write *The Idea of a University*, first published as two separate sections in 1853 and 1858, but still in print (London: Routledge/Thoemmes, 2001). Other books that are still in print are *An Essay in Aid of a Grammar of Assent* (London: Burns, Oates, 1870), and *Apologia pro vita sua* (London: Longman, Green, Longman, Roberts & Green, 1864).

[246] John H. Newman, *An Essay on the Development of Christian Doctrine* (London: James Toovey, 1845), 1.2.9.

This logic enabled him to reconcile the origins of Christianity as described in the New Testament with a doctrinal framework that did not emerge until several centuries later, and of course it also led him to project that development down to the present time, always assuming that it took place under the aegis of the church founded by the apostles. For Newman, the development of doctrine was valid only to the extent that it was tied in with the apostolic succession—the two things went together and (to his mind) found their full expression only in the Church of Rome.

The effect of Newman's conversion on the Oxford Movement was traumatic. Some of its members followed him to Rome, others became agnostics, but the majority remained within the Anglican church, where they formed what would come to be called Anglo-Catholicism. Apart from Keble, who remained faithful to the church of his birth, its chief spokesman was Edward Bouverie Pusey (1800–1882), who became Regius Professor of Hebrew in the University of Oxford in 1828 and spent the rest of his life battling against all forms of Enlightenment rationalism, whether in the criticism of the Bible or in the modernization of the church.[247] He combined an ultraconservative reading of the Old Testament with ritualism, a movement for the re-Catholicizing of the Anglican church, but he had more success with the latter than with the former. By the time he died, he was fighting a losing battle against the radical criticism of the Bible that was pouring out of Germany, although more and more churches were adopting vestments, formal liturgy, and various Catholic devotional practices that had been abandoned at the time of the Reformation.

After Pusey's death, Anglo-Catholicism diverged into a conservative wing that kept the Roman connection alive, and a liberal wing that might best be described as modern unbelief in medieval dress. This liberal Catholicism was less at home in Rome and more adapted to the liberal trends in wider society, so it is not surprising that it came to dominate the movement and to establish itself as the Anglican "norm."[248] That is still the case today, although the historical underpinnings of Anglo-Catholicism as a development of true Anglicanism have been shot to pieces by modern scholarship.[249] The Oxford Movement and later Anglo-Catholicism looked for spiritual authority in the legacy of the early church, assuming that it could be justified by the historical succession from the apostles to the present. They produced a number of excellent patristic scholars,

[247] See Perry Butler, ed., *Pusey Rediscovered* (London: SPCK, 1983).
[248] For its development and theology, see Arthur M. Ramsey, *From Gore to Temple: The Development of Anglican Theology between* Lux Mundi *and the Second World War 1889–1939* (London: Longmans, Green, 1960). See also Kenneth Leech and Rowan Williams, *Essays Catholic and Radical: A Jubilee Group Symposium for the 150th Anniversary of the Beginning of the Oxford Movement 1833–1983* (London: Bowerdean, 1983).
[249] For a good summary of this, see Mark D. Chapman, *Anglican Theology* (London: T & T Clark, 2012).

but their general understanding of history was naive and they could defend their position only by rewriting the story of the Church of England to suit their ideology. Newman realized this and went to Rome, and there has been a steady trickle of similar conversions since his time. A romantic and pseudo-traditionalist attachment to rituals and symbolism has kept Anglo-Catholicism alive, but it has now been marginalized in the Anglican Communion and is no longer theologically productive in any meaningful sense.

A very different approach to Anglican tradition was the confessionalism of the evangelicals, who opposed the Tractarians by appealing to the foundational documents of the Church of England, especially its Articles of Religion and the Book of Common Prayer.[250] Their chief spokesman was John Charles Ryle (1816–1900), who became the first bishop of Liverpool in 1880, but their chief theologian was William Henry Griffith Thomas (1861–1924), whose books *The Principles of Theology*, an exposition of the Thirty-nine Articles, and *The Catholic Faith* are the definitive statements of their position.[251] They served to instruct Anglican evangelicals in the main issues involved in combating Anglo-Catholicism, and as historical studies they are superior to anything the latter produced. But they had little or nothing to say about the challenges of modern theology, and when a new generation of evangelicals emerged in the 1960s they went out of fashion and are now seldom seen. Once again, the search for authority in ancient tradition turned out to have limited appeal and proved to be inadequate to answer the questions of a new and less traditionalist age.

In between Anglo-Catholicism and evangelicalism was a third strand of Anglicanism, usually known today as the "broad church." By its nature it is hard to define and nowadays is often equated with liberalism, though this is inexact. In the nineteenth century it could often be very conservative, though in ways that did not fit either of the other two schools of thought. This was particularly evident in the field of biblical studies, where the challenge of German radicalism was met, not by another ideology, but by an emphasis on close and painstaking research. The outstanding scholar in this field was Joseph Barber Lightfoot (1828–1889), whose extensive and detailed studies, not only of the Pauline epistles but also of post-apostolic letters attributed to Clement of Rome and Ignatius of Antioch, have been of lasting importance. Lightfoot

[250] For the history of this much-neglected aspect of Anglicanism, see Peter Toon, *Evangelical Theology 1833–1856: A Response to Tractarianism* (London: Marshall, Morgan & Scott, 1979); James C. Whisenant, *A Fragile Unity: Anti-ritualism and the Division of Anglican Evangelicalism in the Nineteenth Century* (Milton Keynes: Paternoster, 2003); Martin Wellings, *Evangelicals Embattled: Responses of Evangelicals in the Church of England to Ritualism, Darwinism, and Theological Liberalism 1890–1930* (Milton Keynes: Paternoster, 2003).

[251] William H. Griffith Thomas, *The Principles of Theology* (London: Longmans, Green, 1930); *The Catholic Faith* (London: Hodder & Stoughton, 1905). To them should be added *The Tutorial Prayer Book*, ed. Charles Neil and J. M. Willoughby (London: Harrison Trust, 1912).

was able to show that seven of the Ignatian epistles were genuine and therefore that the "Catholic" developments in the early church were much earlier than the Tübingen School had imagined.[252]

One long-term result of this was that biblical studies in the United Kingdom and the rest of the English-speaking world have traditionally been relatively conservative and largely free of dogmatic assumptions. Much more attention has been paid to the discoveries of archaeology than has been the case in Germany, and it is still common for Anglo-American scholars to use such evidence in support of their (usually conservative) conclusions about the meaning of the biblical text. This method has contributed to the resistance among English-speaking theologians to the more philosophical theories of the Germans and other continental Europeans, and that has allowed traditional orthodox forms of Protestantism to remain vigorous and competitive to a degree that is not true elsewhere.

Anglicanism is best viewed as a somewhat eccentric expression of the Reformed theological tradition, which in any case is more varied than any of the other main branches of Christendom. It embraces not only the heritage of the English Puritans and the (mainly Scottish) Presbyterians, but also the Protestant churches of the Netherlands, Switzerland, the Rhineland in Germany, and outposts in other places like France and Hungary, where they have always been a minority, though not an insignificant one. In the eighteenth century, Enlightenment rationalism made perhaps its greatest impact among them, if only because they were more open to new ideas and to further developments in theology and philosophy than most other churches were. The result, however, was far from being a success. In England, the Presbyterians almost all became Unitarians. In Scotland and the Netherlands, they settled into a nondogmatic establishmentarianism that was deadly conservative and quite unfit to deal with the challenges posed by the new ideas of the rationalists. In New England many of them also became Unitarians, and as the frontier of the United States expanded westward, they found it hard to compete with revivalism and the creative anarchy that so often prevailed in church life there.[253] Heretical movements like Seventh-Day Adventism and the Latter-Day Saints (Mormons) betray a strong Old Testament streak that is almost certainly due to the Reformed emphasis on covenant theology, but there was no central authority to control or suppress them.

[252] See J. B. Lightfoot and J. R. Harmer, *The Apostolic Fathers*, 2nd ed., ed. and revised by Michael W. Holmes (Grand Rapids, MI: Baker, 1989). The first edition was published as *The Apostolic Fathers* (London: Macmillan, 1891).

[253] On American Unitarianism and its effects, see Gary Dorrien, *The Making of American Liberal Theology: Imagining Progressive Religion 1805–1900* (Louisville: Westminster John Knox, 2001).

It was the need to create a coherent Reformed tradition in America, as much as anything else, that led to the formation of an orthodox school that would maintain, defend, and promote its theology in what was effectively an open marketplace for ideas. In 1812 the Presbyterian Church opened a seminary at Princeton, and named Archibald Alexander (1772–1851) as its first president. Alexander came from a Scots-Irish background, in which the Westminster Confession and the covenanting tradition were highly valued. But he had to work with Presbyterians whose heritage was English and Puritan, like the disciples of Jonathan Edwards and the founders of Princeton. He was also very indebted to European Calvinism, especially as that had developed in Switzerland. As a result, the writings of François Turretin and the Second Helvetic Confession (1566) were just as important at Princeton as the more obvious legacy from the British Isles. The Dutch heritage was less in evidence, apart from the canons of the Synod of Dort (1619) which were the common possession of all the Reformed.[254] The importance of finding the right balance among the different influences clamoring for attention was brought out very clearly by Alexander, who used it as a justification for founding the seminary in the first place:

> It is curious to observe how nearly extremes sometimes approach each other in their ultimate effects. No two things appear more opposite in their origin and operation than Unitarianism and enthusiasm—the one proceeding from the pride of reason, the other from the exuberance of the imagination—the one renouncing all pretensions to divine assistance, the other professing to be guided by inspiration at every step: yet in this they agree, that they equally tend to discredit and set aside the authority of the Scriptures of truth. The rationalist will not receive many of the doctrines of revelation because they do not accord with his preconceived notions, which he calls the dictates of reason. The enthusiast will not submit to the authority of Scripture because he imagines that he is under the direction of a superior guide. The one makes his own reason the judge of what he will receive as true from the volume of revelation; the other determines everything, whether it relate to opinion or practice, by the suggestions of his fancied inspiration.[255]

Alexander wanted to preserve the union of thought and experience that he felt had been upset by both rationalism and "enthusiasm," and he believed that the best way to do this was to adhere to the teaching of the Bible. If asked what that teaching was, he would have replied that, essentially, it was Calvinism. In

[254] See Mark A. Noll, *The Princeton Theology 1812–1921*, 2nd ed. (Grand Rapids, MI: Baker, 2001).

[255] Archibald Alexander, *A Sermon Delivered at the Opening of the General Assembly of the Presbyterian Church in the United States* (Philadelphia: Hopkins & Earle, 1808), quoted in Noll, *Princeton Theology*, 53.

other words, follow the teachings of the Reformed confessions and you will understand the meaning of the Scriptures on which you can then base your life. In intellectual terms this was an application of Scottish commonsense philosophy, which had been developed by Thomas Reid (1710–1796) in answer to both the rationalism of the deists and the skepticism of David Hume. Once again, we see that balance is the overriding concern—the extremes must be avoided so that each element of human knowledge and experience can be allotted its proper place. This, for Alexander and the Princeton theologians who followed him, was the ultimate basis of assurance and therefore of authority in the Christian life.

In their view, we are meant to start with convictions taught us by divine revelation and tested by experience. They followed the principles developed by Francis Bacon (1561–1626) and Isaac Newton. These were based on an inductive method that started with the known facts and built on them in order to attain a deeper knowledge of reality. Essentially, there was no difference between the material and the spiritual realms. Material reality offers itself to us for our investigation, and spiritual reality does the same. The biblical revelation is just as objectively real as rocks and trees are, and it can be investigated by using the same techniques of experiment and reason. The laws of nature and the law of God are thus equally "scientific" and can be accepted on the same basis. If there is any difference between them, it is only that human intuition may be enough to guide us in material matters, but only the inner witness of the Holy Spirit (as Calvin said) can do the same for the realm of the spirit.

Alexander was the first president of Princeton seminary, but the man who really made it a going concern was his pupil, colleague, and finally successor, Charles Hodge, whose *Systematic Theology* became and still remains the greatest single monument to the school's outlook.[256] Hodge famously said that no original idea in theology was to be found in his writings, a statement that, taken out of context, has often been used to discredit him and his approach.[257] In fact, of course, nothing could be further from the truth. Hodge was not trying to invent new doctrines or alter the nature of Christianity, and in that sense it is right to say that his works contained nothing "new." But he did aim to put theological study on a firmer foundation than any that it had previously enjoyed, and it was the challenge of the liberalism of his time that drove him to this. In arguing that theology was a science like any other science, Hodge added two essential principles:

[256] Charles Hodge, *Systematic Theology*, 3 vols. (vols. 1–2: New York: Charles Scribner, 1871; vol. 3: New York: Scribner, Armstrong, 1872). See John W. Stewart and James H. Moorhead, *Charles Hodge Revisited: A Critical Appraisal of His Life and Work* (Grand Rapids, MI: Eerdmans, 2002).

[257] A. A. Hodge, *The Life of Charles Hodge* (New York: Charles Scribner's Sons, 1880), 256–257.

1. Science is not just collecting facts; it is arranging those facts in a way that makes sense and allows the scientist to go on to acquire further knowledge and deeper understanding of his subject.
2. Every particular science follows its own method. If a wrong or inadequate method is adopted, the results will be falsified.

Hodge used the first of these principles to go beyond simple biblicism. It was not enough, he claimed, for people to learn Bible verses and repeat them mechanically as the "Word of God." They had to understand what the verses meant and how they held together in the overarching whole that was revelation. In this respect, Hodge distanced himself from the popular religion of uneducated preachers that was all too common in his America.

He adopted the second principle when examining the work of the great theologians of the past and present. Many of them had been essentially rationalists, starting with certain axioms like "There is a supreme being who is infinitely good" and then adapting the biblical evidence to suit the proposition already enunciated. In more recent times there had sprung up a mystical theology, rooted in pietism but brought to full flower in the work of Schleiermacher and his followers, which made truth dependent on the subjective feelings of each individual, thereby removing any possibility of acquiring objective truth or reliable authority for belief. Instead of these, the inductive method common to all the sciences offered a certainty that nothing else could provide:

> The Bible is to the theologian what nature is to the man of science. It is his store-house of facts; and his method of ascertaining what the Bible teaches, is the same as that which the natural philosopher adopts to ascertain what nature teaches.[258]

Systematic theology was not a framework to be imposed on the Bible, but a set of conclusions that emerges from the Scriptures in the course of investigating them in the same way that scientific theories are the result of experiment. The real issue then became the nature of the Bible. The church had always believed that it was the divinely inspired Word of God, as Hodge himself stated:

> All Christians in every age and every name have regarded the Bible in all its parts as in such a sense the Word of God as to be infallible and of divine authority. . . . Greeks [i.e., Eastern Orthodox], Romans [i.e., Catholics] and Protestants all agree in saying that everything in the Bible which purports to

[258] Charles Hodge, *Systematic Theology*, 1:10.

be the Word of God . . . is to be received with the same faith and submission, as though spoken by the lips of God himself.[259]

This theological principle was universal and ecumenical, and not the preserve of the Reformed tradition. What distinguished the latter and made it superior to the others was the consistency with which it applied the principle and employed it as the only source of all true spiritual knowledge. In Hodge's view, it was necessary to distinguish three different types of divine communication before embarking on a systematic study of the Bible. These were,

1. *Revelation*. This is God's communication of knowledge to human beings, who may or may not understand it and may or may not be authorized to share it with others. The boy Samuel, for example, received a revelation from God but did not understand it until he asked Eli the high priest to explain it to him.[260]

2. *Inspiration*. This is God's communication of infallible truth, whether by revelation or not. The authors of the historical books of the Old Testament, and indeed of the Gospels, may not have had any special revelation from God, but they were nevertheless inspired by him to tell the truth.

3. *Illumination*. This is God's communication of understanding to all faithful Christians, so that they will discern the Word of truth and learn to apply it in their own lives. Those so illumined do not (and cannot) add to the objective content of the divinely inspired Word, but by their lives they reveal its truth to others and thereby confirm its authority.

Hodge's understanding of inspiration was very different from that of contemporary romantics like Schleiermacher. Far from being a mystical experience of an indwelling oracular voice that would inevitably lead to private interpretations of varying worth, inspiration for Hodge was objective communication of divine truth in ordinary human language that was (in principle) accessible to everyone. Such a view left him open to the charge that the human authors of Scripture were nothing more than machines taking dictation from the Holy Spirit, but Hodge strenuously repudiated that view:

> It is a mere popular misconception with which, however, even scholars are often chargeable, which supposes that verbal inspiration implies such a dictation as supersedes the free selection of his words on the part of the sacred writer. It is a fundamental principle of Scriptural theology that a man may be

[259] Charles Hodge, "Inspiration," *Biblical Repertory and Princeton Review* 29 (October 1857): 660–687. This quotation is on 664.
[260] 1 Sam. 3:4–9.

> infallibly guided in his free acts. . . . Verbal inspiration therefore, or that influence of the Spirit which controlled the sacred writers in the selection of their words, allowed them perfect freedom within the limits of truth. They were kept from error and guided to the use of words which expressed the mind of the Spirit, but within these limits they were free to use such language and to narrate such circumstances as suited their own taste or purpose.[261]

Hodge was aware that there were many difficulties in the biblical texts that could not be explained, but this did not bother him unduly. He thought they were mostly trivial details that did not affect the main message that the texts were trying to convey, and that they could therefore be overlooked or relegated to a secondary level of interpretation. As he put it,

> With regard to those [difficulties] which cannot be satisfactorily explained it is rational to confess our ignorance, but irrational to assume that what we cannot explain is inexplicable. There are so many errors of transcription in the text of Scripture, such obscurity as to matters necessary to elucidate these ancient records, so little is known of contemporary history, that a man's faith in the divinity of the Bible must be small indeed if it be shaken because he cannot harmonize the conflicting dates and numbers in Kings and Chronicles. We are perfectly willing to let these difficulties remain and to allow the objectors to make the most of them. They can no more shake the faith of a Christian than the unsolved perturbations of the orbit of a comet shake the astronomer's confidence in the law of gravitation.[262]

Biblical scholars who do not share Hodge's understanding of inspiration have found it easy to ridicule his position, but careful examination will show that it makes good sense. There is no reason to suppose that the Bible was incomprehensible to those who wrote it, and it is perfectly true that many apparent difficulties can be (and some actually have been) resolved by further knowledge. No true scientist (or criminal investigator!) will neglect apparently inexplicable pieces of evidence, the meaning of which may well fall into place in due course. In this respect it was Hodge, and not his critics, who was the superior interpreter of the biblical text.

More questionable is the way in which he distinguishes "inspiration" from both revelation and illumination. Is "inspiration" really meant to confer the gift of infallibility? Here we find an astonishing parallel with the contemporary Roman Catholic dogma of papal infallibility. An attribute properly belonging

[261] Hodge, "Inspiration," 677.
[262] Ibid., 686–687.

only to God is somehow conferred on human beings, either because they are the head of the church or because they have been appointed to write a part of the Bible. It is not a permanent gift—neither the pope nor the biblical writers are held to be infallible all the time—but is limited to a specific context. Nevertheless, the claim raises a deeper question: is this possible? Is it what God has promised to his apostles and their successors? And even if what they say is infallible, how can we know whether our interpretation of it is equally certain? Is it not more likely that, as fallible beings ourselves, we shall not be able to grasp the meaning of an infallible text or pronouncement? Of course, the intention in both cases is good: to give believers the assurance that they can have certainty and authority in spiritual things. But whether this can be done by communicating an otherwise incommunicable divine attribute to human recipients must remain at least questionable. Those who assert that it not only can be, but has been done, must accept that their view will be open to doubt by people who think that it crosses the line between what is human and what is divine.

Hodge's defense of the inspiration of the biblical writers and the consequent infallibility of what they wrote was continued and developed further by his son, Archibald Alexander Hodge (1823–1886), who succeeded his father but outlived him by only eight years, and more especially by Benjamin Breckenridge Warfield (1851–1921), who was by common consent the greatest and most intellectual of the orthodox Princeton theologians. In an essay written together with A. A. Hodge and published in 1881, Warfield laid down the basic principles that were to guide their interpretation of the doctrine of biblical inspiration. Remarkably, the two men insisted that it was not the starting point but the culmination of theological inquiry, which had to establish a number of other propositions first, before the inspiration of Scripture could be discussed:

> Very many religious and historical truths must be established before we come to the question of inspiration; as for instance, the being and moral government of God, the fallen condition of man, the fact of a redemptive scheme, the general historical truth of the Scriptures and the validity and authority of the revelation of God's will which they contain—i.e., the general truth of Christianity and its doctrines. Hence it follows that while the inspiration of the Scriptures is true, and, being true, is a principle fundamental to the adequate interpretation of Scripture, it nevertheless is not in the first instance a principle fundamental to the truth of the Christian religion.[263]

[263] A. A. Hodge and B. B. Warfield, "Inspiration," *Presbyterian Review* 2 (April 1881): 225–260; quoted here from Noll, *Princeton Theology*, 222.

This statement is of great importance because it put the doctrine of inspiration within a wider theological framework and insisted that it was only in that context that it could be properly understood. Later generations would try to dissociate the doctrine of inspiration (with its corollaries of infallibility and inerrancy) from any confessional stance, with catastrophic results that Hodge and Warfield would certainly have repudiated.

When it came to the origin of the biblical text, Hodge and Warfield gave full credit to the human agency of the writers chosen for the task, and affirmed that the texts we have reflect their specific gifts and backgrounds. Interestingly, they were prepared to grant spiritual illumination a bigger role in this process than Charles Hodge had contemplated:

> The Bible moreover, being a work of the Spirit for spiritual ends, each writer was prepared precisely for his part in the work by the personal dealings of the Holy Spirit with his soul. Spiritual illumination is very different from either revelation or inspiration, and yet it had, under the providence of God, a large share in the genesis of Scripture, contributing to it a portion of that divine element which makes it the Word of God.[264]

Apart from a few words of prophecy which were given directly by God, the entire text of Scripture was composed according to the above process and may thus be regarded as fully human as well as fully divine. That, of course, made it easier to accept the faults and errors in the extant texts, since infallible inspiration pertained only to the original (autograph) versions, which are now all lost. In fact, Hodge and Warfield were not especially concerned with that aspect of the matter, since their main preoccupation was with the practical application of the teaching that the Bible contained. As they put it,

> . . . the great design and effect of inspiration is to render the Sacred Scriptures in all their parts a divinely infallible and authoritative rule of faith and practice, and hence that in all their elements of thought and expression, concerned in the great purpose of conveying to men a revelation of spiritual doctrine or duty, the Scriptures are absolutely infallible.[265]

Warfield spent most of his long career defending and elucidating his doctrine of the divine inspiration of Scripture, taking on the critics who claimed that his assertions flew in the face of the evidence (or lack of it) and continuing to insist that nothing of any significance had been lost or distorted in the

[264] Hodge and Warfield, "Inspiration," 224 (Noll).
[265] Ibid., 228 (Noll).

course of the transmission of the original texts to us today. His views provoked considerable controversy within the Presbyterian church, though for a while it seemed that his side was winning the battle against their liberal and modernist opponents. In 1910 the General Assembly of the church adopted a five-point checklist of "fundamental" doctrines that had to be maintained at all costs. First among them was the inerrancy of Scripture, followed by the virgin birth of Christ, the substitutionary atonement of Christ, the bodily resurrection of Christ, and the historical authenticity of the biblical miracles. It may be noted that nothing was said about Darwinism or any form of creationism, because that was not an issue. Charles Hodge had found it difficult to accept biological evolution, but Warfield had come to terms with it, and while he thought it was unproved, he did not regard it as a threat to Christian belief or to the interpretation of the Bible.

Unfortunately, it proved impossible to stem the tide of liberalism, and by the time Warfield died in 1921, the integrity of Princeton Theological Seminary was under attack. Further disputes over the next decade led to a reorganization of the Seminary in 1929, which forced John Gresham Machen (1881–1937), Warfield's spiritual successor, to leave and form his own seminary in nearby Philadelphia (Westminster Theological Seminary), which continues to uphold the traditional Princetonian position. Princeton itself continues as a relatively conservative seminary, but it is no longer committed to the Warfield doctrine of inspiration and has lost its reputation as the greatest theological seminary in the Reformed Christian world.

Very different from the conservative bastion of Princeton was the experience of the orthodox Reformed churchmen in the Netherlands. The old Dutch Reformed Church (*Hervormde Kerk*) had been disestablished during the French Revolution, and its former privileges were not restored when the new Kingdom of the Netherlands was created in 1815. After a rocky start, which saw the secession of the Belgian provinces in 1830, the kingdom settled down to an increasingly democratic system of government. The Netherlands had always been the most pluralistic country in Europe, but this was not because its people were indifferent in matters of religion. Some were, of course, and they formed the freethinking, or liberal element in the population. But there were many Roman Catholics, especially in the south, and conservative Protestants who felt that they had been dispossessed of their country.

It was not possible for the Dutch to return to the church establishment of the eighteenth century, nor did the more convinced Protestants desire that. Instead, what they wanted was the freedom to develop their own theology and way of life without interference, and they were prepared to grant the same rights to others. The result was an experiment in social organization that was (and is) without parallel elsewhere. Different confessional and non-confessional groups were encouraged to develop their own mini-societies, with schools, universities, political parties, and cultural organizations that reflected their beliefs. On matters of common concern they would compromise and work together, but in everything else they would go their separate ways. This process came to be called *verzuiling* ("pillarization") from the Dutch word *zuil* ("pillar") and was largely the brainchild of Abraham Kuyper (1837–1920), an extraordinarily gifted man who founded his own church, his own political party, and his own university, all with the intention of promoting his version of a conservative Reformed (Calvinist) theology and worldview.[266]

Kuyper came from a thought-world that was very different from that of the American Presbyterians, even if they shared the same fundamental Calvinism. The Americans had generally supported their revolution and usually downplayed the differences between themselves and the secular rationalism of the new United States, which they interpreted along fundamentally Christian lines. Kuyper, on the other hand, rejected the French Revolution completely and was devoted to the House of Orange, the family that had led the Calvinist revolt in the sixteenth century and had become the royal family of the new kingdom in 1815. The Princetonians sought to claim the whole of American culture for themselves, whereas Kuyper was more modest and realistic, demanding only a share of social influence and not seeking to dominate the national culture entirely.

These differences were the product of differing beliefs about the relationship of the church to wider society. The Princetonians believed that rational evidence, applied in a scientifically inductive manner, would lead to an objective truth that no rational person could deny—and that truth would be Calvinism. Kuyper, while he agreed that Calvinism was the ultimate truth, did not believe that it could be acquired by empirical thought. On the contrary, he insisted that only a supernatural conversion could produce the mind-set needed to embrace the Calvinist worldview, which was incomprehensible to anyone who was not born again of the Holy Spirit. To put it bluntly, the Americans thought that honest scientific investigation would lead to faith, whereas Kuyper maintained that faith would lead to honest scientific investigation. In other words, he was

[266] See James D. Bratt, *Abraham Kuyper: Modern Calvinist, Christian Democrat* (Grand Rapids, MI: Eerdmans, 2013); John H. Wood, *Going Dutch in the Modern Age: Abraham Kuyper's Struggle for a Free Church in the Nineteenth-century Netherlands* (Oxford: Oxford University Press, 2013). There is very little in English that covers Dutch neo-Calvinism satisfactorily, or relates it to comparable movements in the English-speaking world. See Harriet A. Harris, *Fundamentalism and Evangelicals* (Oxford: Oxford University Press, 1998), 205–277, for good coverage of the topics of specific interest to us here. Also of interest is James D. Bratt, *Dutch Calvinism in Modern America: A History of a Conservative Subculture* (Grand Rapids, MI: Eerdmans, 1984).

more interested in the presuppositions with which theologians began than in the evidence that their investigations produced. The Americans also believed that, because their investigative method in theology was applicable to any discipline, they had no need to expand into areas unfamiliar to them as theologians. Kuyper, on the other hand, was forced by his presuppositions to extend his theological principles to cover the whole of life—every scientific discipline had to be brought under the Word of God.

In this he was supported by Herman Bavinck (1854–1921), the greatest theologian that Dutch neo-Calvinism produced. Bavinck was fully conversant with the intellectual trends of his time and understood the need to counteract the effects of Darwinism and Marxism, in particular.[267] Kuyper and Bavinck were in contact with both Charles Hodge and Warfield, and both sides were well aware of the differences that separated them. But at the same time they respected one another and cooperated when they could. In October 1898 Kuyper was invited to Princeton to give the Stone Lectures, which were soon published and are still in print today.[268] In those lectures and elsewhere he strongly emphasized the importance of what he called *palingenesis*, being born again, as the necessary key to all understanding, including of Scripture itself:

> If by palingenesis you stand vitally related to the Christ as "the head of the body," the relation between your consciousness and the Holy Scripture is born from this of itself. But if that relation of the palingenesis does not bind you to the Christ of God as head of the body of the new humanity, you cannot kneel before him in worship, neither can the Scripture be to you a Holy Scripture.[269]

Bavinck was invited to give the same lectures in 1908–1909, and these were subsequently published as *The Philosophy of Revelation*.[270] While accepting the divine revelation of Holy Scripture, Bavinck went much further than that. As he explained,

> Revelation, while having its center in the Person of Christ, in its periphery extends to the uttermost ends of creation. It does not stand isolated in nature

[267] Bavinck's greatness is universally recognized, but his influence has been less than it should have been because most of his writings have until recently been available only in his native Dutch and have not circulated widely outside the Netherlands, South Africa, and the Dutch emigrant community in the United States. His *Reformed Dogmatics* (4 vols., Grand Rapids, MI: Baker, 2008) are now available, as is a handy collection of his writings, edited by John Bolt, James D. Bratt and Paul J. Visser, *The J. H. Bavinck Reader* (Grand Rapids, MI: Eerdmans, 2013).

[268] Abraham Kuyper, *Calvinism; Six Stone Lectures* (Edinburgh: T & T Clark, 1899); reprinted as *Lectures on Calvinism* (Peabody, MA: Hendrickson, 2008).

[269] Abraham Kuyper, *Principles of Sacred Theology*, trans. John Hendrik de Vries (Grand Rapids, MI: Eerdmans, 1968), 459.

[270] Herman Bavinck, *The Philosophy of Revelation* (New York: Longmans, Green, 1909). The book was simultaneously published in Dutch and German, and the English version has since been reprinted (Grand Rapids, MI: Baker, 1979).

> and history. . . . The world itself rests on revelation; revelation is the presupposition, the foundation, the secret of all that exists in all its forms. The deeper science pushes its investigations, the more clearly will it discover that revelation underlies all created being. . . . that special revelation which comes to us in the Person of Christ is built on these presuppositions. The foundations of creation and redemption are the same.[271]

Bavinck made revelation the fundamental principle of all human thought, and in doing so he tied philosophy to theology in a way that recalls the great struggles of the early church against gnosticism, a connection of which he was fully aware and a tradition in which he willingly placed himself.[272] Here was a vision that was capable of providing a serious answer to the rationalism of the age, and perhaps it will continue to do so, though inevitably in a modified and updated form.

The differences between the Dutch Calvinists and the Princetonians were obvious to those who studied both traditions in depth, but such people were few in number. Dutch immigration to America brought Kuyperian principles to the English-speaking world, but they were also modified by their contact with a new environment. A hybrid theology developed in the work of men like Cornelius Van Til (1895–1987), in which the apologetical concerns of the Princetonians merged with the presuppositionalism of the Kuyperians. The result was a doctrine that demanded complete submission to the authority of the divine revelation found in Scripture as a precondition for demonstrating its truth and infallibility:

> . . . the only way in which Warfield's view of the Bible and its inspiration can be defended is by pointing out that it is and has to be presupposed in order that there be any intelligible human predication. . . . When men argue about the phenomena of Scripture as though these phenomena were intelligible in terms of themselves, apart from the revelation of God, . . . then their attack or defense is nothing but a beating in the air. To assume autonomous self-interpretation is to negate the necessity of special revelation.[273]

The Dutch influence on Reformed theology in America, and to some extent also in the wider English-speaking world, has been considerable, not least because of the intense publishing activity that has emanated from its center

[271] Bavinck, *Philosophy of Revelation*, 27.
[272] Ibid., 242–269.
[273] Cornelius Van Til, *In Defense of the Faith*, 3 vols. (Phillipsburg, NJ: Presbyterian & Reformed, 1967), 1:26.

in Grand Rapids, Michigan.[274] But although its contribution is well known, it has been less influential than might be supposed. One of the reasons for this is that it is a foreign import, not just linguistically but conceptually as well. Americans are pragmatic in the British tradition and not ideological, a fact that makes any appeal to presuppositions, as opposed to the inductive method of following evidence open to every honest mind, something alien to them. Kuyperian Calvinism was also inherently sectarian, claiming that it alone possessed the fullness of truth and that all non-Calvinists were intellectually unregenerate. In the pluralistic atmosphere of the English-speaking world, that blanket judgment could never be accepted, even by those who otherwise shared the Calvinist vision. The practice of *verzuiling* was also unexportable, the one exception being South Africa, where the local Afrikaners, descendants of seventeenth-century Dutch settlers, adapted it to produce the policy of racial *apartheid*, which attracted the condemnation of the entire world before it was abandoned in the 1990s.

But perhaps most significantly, Kuyperians were intellectual elitists in the European tradition who had no time for popular revivalism or even for pietism. The Princetonians, on the other hand, had roots in the evangelical tradition, and they had to stay in touch with the grassroots of the church on which they were often financially dependent. As a result, men like Warfield were much kinder to popularizers like Reuben Archer Torrey (1856–1928) than the Dutch would have been, and in the early twentieth century they found themselves increasingly allied with them against the liberal modernists in all denominations.[275] Added to that was a feature common to both sides—their inherent fissiparousness, which led to the creation of any number of denominations and sub-denominations following splits over points of principle that were obscure to all but those involved. This tendency was only accentuated by attempts to merge the two traditions into one, an operation that almost inevitably led to a suppression of differences that produced an incoherent synthesis. Like the conservative Roman and Anglo-Catholics, the conservative Reformed groups knew what they were against but found it harder to agree about what they were for, and in the struggles for influence of the 1920s and later, they inevitably lost ground as a result.

In another way, though, the Reformed response to liberalism had an unintended effect. Its emphasis on biblical infallibility (and later, inerrancy) spread

[274] Eerdmans, Baker, Zondervan, and Kregel are all based there, and all publish high-quality theological books from many different traditions.

[275] See, for example, Warfield's review of Torrey's rather simplistic book, *What the Bible Teaches* (Chicago: Fleming H. Revell, 1898), *Presbyterian and Reformed Review* 39 (July 1899): 562–564; reprinted in Noll, *Princeton Theology*, 299–301.

beyond the confines of confessional Presbyterianism to become a hallmark of "evangelical" churches that may be found in any Protestant denomination or none. In many cases, biblical infallibility (or inerrancy) has been detached from any systematic theology and sometimes even elevated into the one doctrine that all preachers and teachers must profess, however much they may disagree on other things. This has produced a curious situation, in that a belief that has ancient roots but that until recently was never formulated in precise terms has now managed to sideline, if not actually displace, the rest of traditional Christian teaching to become the touchstone by which orthodoxy is decided.

The Crisis of Authority: Eastern Orthodoxy

The Eastern Orthodox theological tradition, as we might expect, responded to the challenges posed by Enlightenment rationalism in its own way, borrowing from the Western churches (usually without acknowledgment and sometimes even in conscious opposition to them) but at the same time drawing on its own resources. Orthodox theology did not disappear after the fall of Constantinople in 1453, but it was under threat from different quarters and to a large extent it retreated into itself.[276] Most Orthodox countries fell into the hands of the Ottoman Turks, who tolerated their faith but discouraged any attempt to propagate or develop it. Those Orthodox who were able to maintain contact with Western countries found themselves pressured by both Protestants and Catholics to adopt their respective expressions of the Western tradition, and some of them did so. Generally speaking, the Protestants were content to let the Eastern churches continue as they were, but wanted their agreement on the points of theological controversy that set them apart from Rome. They knew that anti-Romanism was alive and well in the East, and thought that this common factor would be enough to spread Protestant doctrines and principles in the Eastern churches.

The main difficulty, as they soon discovered, was that the Eastern tradition had never absorbed the scholasticism of the medieval West and therefore lacked the theological categories in which the Reformation debates were expressed. They also had an aversion to defining their beliefs more precisely than they felt was necessary and did not want to go beyond what the ancient ecumenical councils had decreed. As a result, though relations were often friendly, there was no real meeting of minds, and reconciliation between Protestants and Orthodox proved to be chimerical.[277] The closest anyone came to it was Cyril Lucaris (1572–1638),

[276] For the history of this period, see Steven Runciman, *The Great Church in Captivity* (Cambridge: Cambridge University Press, 1968); George A. Maloney, *A History of Orthodox Theology since 1453* (Belmont, MA: Nordland, 1976); G. Podskalsky, *Griechische Theologie in der Zeit der Türkenherrschaft* (München: C. H. Beck, 1988).

[277] Steven Runciman, *Great Church*, tells the whole story, 226–319. For the details of dialogue with the Lutherans, see George Mastrantonis, *Augsburg and Constantinople* (Brookline, MA: Holy Cross Orthodox Press, 1982); and

Greek patriarch of Alexandria and then of Constantinople, who adopted a form of Calvinism and tried to get his church to accept it. He might have succeeded, at least to some extent, but he was thwarted by opposition stirred up by the Jesuits and was eventually murdered by the Turks, probably with Jesuit collusion.[278]

The Roman Catholics were more successful in purely theological terms, though they never concealed their proselytizing intentions. The Greeks had long had contacts with Italy and the western Mediterranean, and there were many Western Catholics living in the Ottoman empire and on the Greek islands, some of which remained in Venetian hands until the surrender of Venice to revolutionary France in 1797. There was also the important fact that Rome and the Eastern patriarchates recognized each other as churches, even though they were in schism. This gave them a framework for dialogue that was lacking in their dealings with the Protestants. As far as outright conversion was concerned, Rome's efforts had limited success. The Greeks were generally resistant, and it was only in a few marginal cases that the Latin church managed to implant itself in the Ottoman empire. In Bulgaria, a small surviving group of so-called Paulicians, or Bogomils, whose doctrines were dualistic and heretical, was absorbed into the Catholic church in 1650. In the Lebanon, the Maronites, another ancient sect of uncertain origin and doctrine, was reconciled to Rome in the sixteenth century, with a college for training their priests being opened there in 1584.

The real prize, however, lay further north, in the Ukrainian lands that had become part of the Polish Commonwealth during the Middle Ages. The Poles were originally tolerant of Orthodox worship, but in the struggle against Protestantism attitudes toward non–Roman Catholics hardened and the pressure to convert increased. This resulted in the Union of Brest, which took place in 1596 and was consolidated in the following generation. The Orthodox were allowed to keep their traditions, but they had to submit to the pope as the head of the church. On the vexed question of the *Filioque* they were forced to confess the truth of the doctrine but were not obliged to add the offending clause to their version of the Nicene Creed.[279] Known as Uniates or "Greek Catholics," these converts were never accepted as genuine by the remaining Orthodox, who periodically suppressed the church whenever it fell under Russian rule.[280]

Partly under this influence, and partly to protect themselves against further

Constantine Tsirpanlis, *The Historical and Ecumenical Significance of Jeremias II's Correspondence with the Lutherans (1573–1581)* (New York: American Institute for Patristic and Byzantine Studies, 1982).

[278] See George A. Hadjiantoniou, *Protestant Patriarch* (Richmond, VA: John Knox, 1961).

[279] The most detailed study of this movement is Ambroise Jobert, *De Luther a Mohila. La Pologne dans la crise de la Chrétienté 1517–1648* (Paris: Institut d'Etudes Slaves, 1974).

[280] This happened in 1839 and again—under communism—in 1946.

losses, the Orthodox of central and eastern Europe began to organize their own seminaries, conceived on Roman lines and even using Latin as the medium of instruction, but retaining at least the semblance of traditional Orthodox theology. Prominent in this movement was Peter Mogila (1597–1646), a remarkable man who studied Latin theology in both Poland and France before returning to Kiev, where he founded a theological academy. There he composed a confession of faith that was adopted at an Orthodox synod held in 1642 at Iaşi (Jassy) in Moldavia, which was then under nominal Turkish control but effectively run by Greek deputies appointed by the sultan. The following year it was approved by Patriarch Parthenius I of Constantinople (1639–1644), since when it has been regarded as authoritative in the Orthodox world, though only insofar as it accords with the teaching of the ecumenical councils.[281] The effect of Mogila's efforts was to Latinize the Orthodox church in the Ukraine and subsequently in Russia, as the latter expanded southward and many Kievan theologians migrated to Moscow. Mogila's influence also penetrated the Greek-speaking world, where it came to fruition in another confession of faith, written by Patriarch Dositheus II of Jerusalem (1669–1707) and published by him in 1672.[282] Today the Confession of Dositheus also enjoys widespread acceptance in the Orthodox world, but like Mogila's, its authority is circumscribed by the seven ecumenical councils and cannot be regarded as definitive.

The overall effect of these seventeenth-century efforts was to excise any trace of Lucaris's Calvinism from the Orthodox world and to reconstruct its theology along essentially Roman Catholic lines, though without the distinctive doctrines of the Catholic church. This tradition was to continue as the dominant one in the Orthodox churches until the twentieth century, when a younger generation of theologians, disturbed by the secularization of the Orthodox world, sought to return to the earlier traditions of Byzantium.[283]

After the fall of the empire of Trebizond to the Ottoman Turks in 1461, the only independent Orthodox states were far to the north, on the steppes of Russia. But they were just beginning to recover from the Tatar invasions of the previous two centuries and had not yet united into a single polity. The Russian church had developed under the guidance of Greek bishops sent from

[281] See Maloney, *History*, 33–38 for the details. The confession itself can be found in Ernest J. Kimmel, *Monumenta fidei ecclesiae orientalis*, 2 vols. (Jena: F. Mauke, 1850), 1:52–55. It should be noted that the original text was in Latin but that it was an amended Greek translation that was approved by the patriarch in 1643. Both versions are in Philip Schaff, *The Creeds of Christendom*, 3 vols. (New York: Harper & Row, 1931), 2:275–400.

[282] The Confession of Dositheus is in Ernest J. Kimmel, *Libri symbolici ecclesiae orientalis* (Jena: C. Hochhausenium, 1843), 325–488. It has also been published separately as *Dositheou homologia* (Thessalonica: Ekdoseis Vas. Rêgopoulou, 1983). The Greek text, with parallel Latin translation, is in Schaff, *Creeds of Christendom*, 2:401–444.

[283] For a modern example of Latinizing Orthodox theology, see Panagiotis N. Trembelas, *Dogmatikê tês Orthodoxou Katholikês Ekklêsias*, 3 vols. (Athens: vols. 1–2, Zôê, 1959; vol. 3, Sôtêr, 1961).

Constantinople, but after Isidore of Kiev signed the union with Rome at Florence in 1439 he was no longer welcome and was forced out in 1441. After some years of confusion, the Russians finally appointed their own metropolitan (bishop) of Moscow in 1448 and the link with Constantinople was severed. It took nearly 150 years for the Greeks to recognize this, but with the Roman Catholics rapidly making inroads from Poland, they realized that something had to be done, and in 1589 the first patriarch of "all the Russias" was consecrated in Moscow.[284]

For the next hundred years, the patriarch played a major role in the Russian state, helping to hold it together in the "time of troubles" that followed the extinction of the Muscovite dynasty in 1598. When Mikhail Romanov took the throne in 1613, he made his father (who had taken monastic vows after the death of his wife) patriarch, cementing the link between church and state even further. By far the most important patriarch of the seventeenth century was Nikita Minin (1605–1681), better known by his canonical name of Nikon, whose reign lasted from 1652 to 1658 but whose deposition in that year was not confirmed until 1666. Nikon became famous, not to say notorious, for the liturgical reforms that he wanted to introduce into the Russian church in order to bring it into line with Constantinople and the wider Orthodox world. Over the centuries, the Russian service books had been corrupted by faulty copying, and in some respects the church had lagged behind developments elsewhere. It should have been a straightforward reform, but it was not. The opposition was led by the archpriest ("protopope") Avvakum (1620?–1682), a saintly man who thought that any change to the liturgy would compromise the church's standing before God. There was also a nationalistic element, in the sense that Avvakum and his followers saw no reason that the Slavs should defer to the Greeks, especially since it was the latter who had fallen into heresy at Florence in 1439 and who had tried to drag the Russians down with them.[285]

The result was a schism (*raskol*) in the Russian church that has lasted to the present day. Avvakum's followers were known as the "old ritualists" (*staroobr'adtsi*), or "Old Believers" as they are more often called in English. Their concerns seem strange and somewhat trivial to outsiders, but they were prepared to suffer for their beliefs and were widely respected in a church that paid great attention to external rites and ceremonies. This must be borne in mind when studying Russian Orthodoxy, because its extreme conservatism in

[284] For the early history of the Russian church and the split with Constantinople, see John Fennell, *A History of the Russian Church to 1448* (London: Longman, 1995); and John Meyendorff, *Byzantium and the Rise of Russia* (Crestwood, NY: Saint Vladimir's Seminary Press, 1989). For the story of Russian Christianity and its culture, see James H. Billington, *The Icon and the Axe: An Interpretive History of Russian Culture* (New York: Vintage, 1966).
[285] See Paul Meyendorff, *Russia, Ritual, and Reform* (Crestwood, NY: Saint Vladimir's Seminary Press, 1987).

such matters has always made any reform, however desirable, very difficult to achieve. In the end, Nikon was deprived of his office but his reforms were kept in place—a compromise that satisfied no one. This was the state of the church when Peter I (1682–1725), known as "the Great," became czar. He was still underage and for many years could do nothing, but he passed the time traveling abroad, studying the world and biding his time. When he finally got the opportunity to act, he did so. Peter had seen the Protestant societies of Western Europe at first hand, and thought he could turn Russia into something similar. When Patriarch Adrian (1690–1700) died, he was not replaced and Peter began to plan his own reorganization of the church.[286]

It took him two decades to complete, but in 1721 Peter issued an Ecclesiastical Regulation that remained the constitution of the Russian state church until the 1917 revolution. The patriarchate was abolished and the monasteries were dissolved, a serious matter in the Orthodox world because its bishops had to be celibate and were therefore mostly drawn from among the monks. Outside the church, Peter ordered his nobles to shave their beards and to dress like Westerners, which cut them off from both the church and Russian tradition. Instead, he encouraged them to learn French, which inevitably led to the penetration of Enlightenment ideas. In this somewhat curious way, Russia was more affected by the Enlightenment than any other European state, even though it was among the least able to absorb it. It was during this time of enforced Westernization that Païsy Velichkovsky (1722–1794), a Ukrainian who spent much of his life in Moldavia, went to Mount Athos in the hope of gaining access to ancient Greek sources of monastic life which he could use to plan a revival back home.[287]

Païsy found that Athos was in a bad state, and that the manuscripts he thought would be readily available there were not accessible to him. Instead, he was attacked by guardians of the Athonite status quo, who felt threatened by his enthusiasm. In 1764 he was recalled to Moldavia and charged with the restoration of monasticism there, a task to which he brought his love of patristic sources that spoke of prayer and the spiritual life. Aided by a team of Romanian monks, he supervised the translation of the original Greek texts at his disposal into Romanian and Church Slavonic, doing most of the latter himself. This activity was in full swing when there suddenly appeared a rich collection of material that had been put together by Macarius of Corinth (1731–1805) and Nicodemus of the Holy Mountain ("the Hagiorite") (1749–1809) and

[286] See James Cracraft, *The Church Reform of Peter the Great* (Stanford, CA: Stanford University Press, 1971) for the details.

[287] See John A. McGuckin, "The Making of the *Philokalia*: A Tale of Monks and Manuscripts," in Brock Bingaman and Bradley Nassif, eds., *The* Philokalia*: A Classic Text of Orthodox Spirituality* (Oxford: Oxford University Press, 2012), 36–49.

published at Venice in 1782.[288] Païsy immediately began to translate the book into Slavonic and published it in four volumes as the *Dobrotol'ubie* in 1793.[289] The Greek version almost disappeared from view, but the Slavonic one became very popular and was eventually translated into Russian and expanded still further by Theophan the Recluse (1815–1894). It was published in five volumes between 1877 and 1905 and is now regarded as the classic text.[290]

The importance of the *Philokalia*, as it is generally known in English, is that it was an attempt by two Greek scholars to counteract the growing influence of the Enlightenment among their compatriots. In the eighteenth century, many Greeks went abroad to Italy or France for study and imbibed the new ideas that were circulating freely there. The first one to make a mark in his homeland was Eugenius Voulgaris (1716–1806), who was born on the then Venetian island of Corfu and studied in Venice before returning to take up a number of posts in Greece. In 1753 he became the head of the academy on Mount Athos, and in 1760 he was appointed to the patriarchal school in Constantinople, where he remained until 1763. His espousal of Western rationalist thinking and his unfounded criticisms of pro-union Byzantines like Bessarion made him unwelcome and he soon left for Leipzig, where he was free to say what he liked. He attracted the notice of Catherine II of Russia, who invited him to go there, and in 1775 she made him bishop of Cherson and Slavyansk. He soon tired of that, however, and returned to St. Petersburg, where he continued to write up to his death. Voulgaris was reliably anti-Roman and edited or composed a number of works against the Catholic church. While on a visit to Berlin in 1769 he met Voltaire and translated some of his polemical works into Greek, including one on the desirability of religious tolerance. Voulgaris made it clear, however, that he did not share Voltaire's skeptical outlook and that by "tolerance" he meant freedom of worship for the Orthodox who lived in Catholic countries—not the other way around.[291]

But despite his eclectic and inconsistent views, Voulgaris contributed substantially toward the education of a new generation of Greeks, who were much more radical than he was. The best-known of these was Adamantios Koraês (1748–1833), widely honored in Greece today as the founder of the Modern Greek literary language, who promoted critical biblical studies among the

[288] *Phliokalia tôn hierôn nêptikôn* (Venice: A. Bortoli, 1782).

[289] A facsimile edition has been published as *Dobrotl'ubie* (Bucharest: R. Vînturilor, 1990).

[290] *Dobrotol'ubie*, 5 vols. (Moscow: I. Efimov, 1883–1889). A facsimile copy of the original Russian edition has been published (Paris: YMCA Press, 1988), and it is from that that the English translation is being prepared. So far, four volumes of it have appeared in print, translated by G. E. H. Palmer, Philip Sherrard, and Kallistos Ware (London: Faber & Faber, 1979–). There is also a modern Romanian version, prepared by Dumitru Stăniloae, which contains even more texts.

[291] See Gerhard Podskalsky, *Griechische Theologie*, 344–353.

Orthodox and began the movement for translating the Bible into the vernacular tongue. This was seen as an attack on church authority, and to some extent Koraês may be regarded as a latter-day Erasmus in this respect. He never returned to Greece, which perhaps was just as well in the circumstances. More radical still was Theophilus Kaïrês (1784–1853), who as a monk went to Pisa to study and then on to Paris, where he met freethinkers like Auguste Comte (1798–1857) and was persuaded to abandon Christianity for a vague form of positivistic deism. When he tried to bring that back to Greece, however, he was jailed for his apostasy and died in prison.

The independent Greek state that emerged from the war of independence (1821–1829) was a curious mixture of the radical and the traditional. It appealed to ancient Greece and its heroes for its national inspiration—a radical and anti-Christian stance that mimicked contemporary rationalist values in the West—but at the same time it defended the traditional Orthodoxy to which the vast majority of the population remained attached. This duality continues to influence Greece to this day, and has provided ample material for Orthodox polemicists to vent their spleen against both the West and the failings of their own country.[292] The fact that the patriarchate remained under Turkish control, and that until 1913 the majority of Greeks still lived in the Ottoman empire, made it difficult for either side to control the church, since the risk of one falling out with the other to the detriment of the nation was too great. As a result, Greek theology stagnated in the nineteenth century, while the intellectual leadership of the Orthodox world passed to Russia.[293]

The revival of Orthodoxy in Russia was a slow process that was hindered by the alienation of the aristocracy from the church and by the suffocating power of the state bureaucracy over it. Czar Alexander I (1801–1825) was a mystic who allowed Protestant evangelical groups like the British and Foreign Bible Society to work in the country, but such initiatives were short-lived and bore little fruit at the time. One of the men most influenced by this tendency was Filaret Drozdov (1782–1867), who became metropolitan of Moscow in 1821. His apparent sympathies with Protestantism caused alarm in more conservative circles, however, and in 1823 he was ordered to write a catechism that would hopefully bring him back to true Orthodoxy. It is a measure of the sad condition of the church at the time that his work caused a scandal, not because it revealed any Protestant tendencies but because he had translated the Nicene

[292] Christos Yannaras, *Orthodoxy and the West* (Brookline, MA: Holy Cross Orthodox Press, 2006). Originally published as *Orthodoxia kai Dysê stê neôterê Hellada* (Athens: Ekdoseis Domos, 1992).

[293] On modern Russian theology, see Georges Florovsky, *Ways of Russian Theology*, 2 vols. (Belmont, MA: Nordland, 1979–1987). Originally published as *Puti russkogo bogoslovija* (Paris: YMCA Press, 1937).

Creed and the Lord's Prayer from Slavonic into Russian! Filaret had to redo his catechism, and in 1827 a more conservative edition appeared. That, too, was felt to need further revising, but the third edition in 1839 proved to be definitive. It was translated into a number of other Orthodox languages and widely used as a school text, but like all such works it never received any official authority. Orthodoxy remained wedded to the seven ancient councils and could not adapt to the changing times in any way that went beyond them.[294] This reactionary attitude reached its apogee in the work of Mikhail Petrovich (Makary) Bulgakov (1816–1883), the most influential Russian theologian of the nineteenth century, whose work showed no originality and was to a great extent reliant on Roman Catholic and Protestant sources that usually were not acknowledged.[295] As in the Greek world, the representatives of the official church were incapable of truly creative thought, and theological renewal would have to come from elsewhere.

Victory over Napoleon had led to a resurgence of nationalism and a correspondingly anti-French attitude, but this tied in with the prevailing romanticism in the rest of Europe at the same time and so was not really a reaction against the West, whatever its proponents may have thought. In an effort to stave off liberalism and promote unity in their empire, the Russian authorities began to stress the ideological trinity of autocracy, nationality, and Orthodoxy as the three pillars of national identity. It was a combination that contained hidden dangers, since the church was commandeered for the service of an ultraconservative state and inevitably became associated with all its failures and corruption. Russian Westernizers were almost all against the prevailing church establishment, and as time went on, more and more of them became freethinkers and atheists, in line with prevailing attitudes elsewhere. As we now know, it was from this tendency that revolutionary impulses would stir and eventually take over the country, destroying the old order and purging the church in a way that few people in the nineteenth century could have imagined.

History is written by the victors, and so for most of the twentieth century the opposition to the Westernizers in Russia was portrayed as reactionary and obscurantist, if it was taken seriously at all. But the collapse of Soviet communism and the revival of Russian nationalism has altered the picture. It is no longer clear that the Westernizers really won, and the views of their op-

[294] *Prostrannyj khristianskij katikhizis Filareta, mitropolita Moskovskogo* (Moscow: Izdatel'stvo Svjatogo Sinoda, 1839). There is an English translation of it in Schaff, *Creeds of Christendom*, 2:445–542.

[295] His great writings were, "An Introduction to Orthodox Theology," or *Vvedenije v pravoslavnoje bogoslovije* (St. Petersburg: Tipograpfija vojenno-uchebnykh zavedenij, 1847); "Orthodox Dogmatic Theology," or *Pravoslavnoje dogmaticheskoje bogoslovije*, 4 vols. (St. Petersburg: Tipografija vojenno-uchebnykh zavedenij,1849–1853); and his "Guide to the Study of Christian Orthodox Dogmatic Theology" or *Rukovodstvo k izucheniju khristianskogo pravoslavno-dogmaticheskogo bogoslovija* (St. Petersburg: Tipografija vojenno-uchebnykh zavedenij,1869).

ponents can now be aired once more. Under the umbrella of the official czarist ideology, but initially independent of it, was a current of thought known as Slavophilism.[296] Slavophilism was a form of romanticism that owed more than its proponents were prepared to admit to the thought of rationalists like John Locke and Catholic reactionaries like Joseph de Maistre. But fundamental to its outlook was the belief that Russia was a unique nation with a special destiny. It was not meant to conquer the world but to show by its own suffering a path of redemption for a lost humanity—to become, in other words, a kind of new incarnation of God on earth. This was expressed by Pyotr Chaadaev (1794–1856), himself a Westernizer who had come to terms with Russia as a special case, as follows:

> We shall not throw off the influence of alien ideas until we have fully understood the path along which we have traveled, until an involuntary confession of all our errors has escaped our lips, until a cry of pain and repentance that will echo throughout the world has burst from our breast. Only then, in the natural course of events, shall we take our place amongst those nations that are destined to act on behalf of humanity, not only as battering-rams or truncheons, but also as bearers of ideas.[297]

What those "alien ideas" were was not so obvious and had to be decided by each individual. Chaadaev did not sympathize with either the Westernizers or the reactionary nationalists, but the Slavophiles gave a clear answer: the salvation of Russia lay in Orthodoxy, which alone expressed the historical vocation of the nation. Chaadaev's teaching on this point was taken up by Ivan Kireevsky (1806–1856). Like Chaadaev, Kireevsky had been educated in Enlightenment thought, but in later life he grew disenchanted with the limitations of its rationalism and looked elsewhere for the certainty of authoritative truth. He found it, or so he thought, in the simple faith of the Russian peasantry, which he turned into a philosophy of his own. As he saw it, the Orthodox church was not just one branch of Christendom but the temporal bearer of an eternal message. Whereas Roman Catholicism and Protestantism were

[296] See Andrzej Walicki, *The Slavophile Controversy: History of a Conservative Utopia in Nineteenth-century Russian Thought* (Oxford: Oxford University Press, 1975; repr., Notre Dame, IN: University of Notre Dame Press, 1989). Originally published as *W kregu konserwatywnej utopii. Struktura i przemiany rosyjskiego slowianofilstwa* (Warsaw: Państwowe Wydawnictwo Naukowe, 1964). It may perhaps be noted that the concept of Utopia was by no means alien to the Westernizers either. The communist regime was in fact described as such by Mikhail Heller and Aleksandr M. Nekrich, *Utopia in Power: The History of the Soviet Union from 1917 to the Present* (New York: Summit, 1986). Originally published as *Utopija u vlasti* (New York: Overseas Publications Interchange, 1982).

[297] Peter Chaadaev, *Sochinenija i pis'ma*, 2 vols. (Moscow: Tipografija A. I. Mamontova, 1913–1914), 1:274. English translations of Chaadaev's works are available in Raymond T. McNally, *The Major Works of Peter Chaadaev* (Notre Dame, IN: University of Notre Dame Press, 1969); and Raymond T. McNally and Richard Tempest, eds., *Philosophical Works of Peter Chaadaev* (Dordrecht: Kluwer Academic Publishers, 1991).

compromised by their close association with the material world, the Orthodox church was different. In his words,

> The Orthodox church does not limit its self-consciousness to any particular epoch, however much this epoch might consider itself wiser than any former. The sum total of all Christians of all ages, past and present, comprises one indivisible, eternal, living assembly of the faithful, held together just as much by the unity of consciousness as through the communion of prayer.[298]

For Kireevsky, the dynamics of community were just as important as any theological considerations, and for that reason many Orthodox thinkers have refused to accept him as one of their own. But the idea that the church is a microcosm on earth of a heavenly reality, and that it is manifested in the fellowship of believers, was an insight that would not disappear so easily. If the church is a communion, then God must be one too, and from there it is but a short step to affirming the fundamental place of the Trinity in any doctrine of the Christian life.

Full-blown religious Slavophilism, however, came only with the work of Aleksei Khomyakov (1804–1860), who everyone agrees was the principal founder of the movement, even if the exact nature of the relationship between him and Kireevsky is disputed.[299] Khomyakov was more interested in the nature of the church than in other aspects of Christian doctrine, and he corresponded with William Palmer. As Andrzej Walicki (1930–) has put it,

> Khomyakov's theology was not directly influenced by Tractarianism, but on the other hand his general aims were very similar; he, too, was motivated by an anti-intellectual conception of faith, by distrust of individualism and isolationism, and by the quest for a pure and undefiled church tradition.[300]

Khomyakov took over Kireevsky's criticism of both Roman Catholicism and Protestantism and developed it on more purely theological lines. According to him, the true church was an expression of corporate unity that preserved individual freedom, a unique combination that is created and preserved by spiritual love. But when Rome added the *Filioque* clause to the Nicene Creed, it broke the law of love and chose unity at the expense of freedom. The Protestant revolt against this, which is perfectly understandable in the context, went the

---

[298] Ivan N. Kireevsky, *Polnoje sobranije sochinenij*, 2 vols. (Moscow: Tipographija Imperatorskogo Moskovskogo Universiteta, 1911; repr., in facsimile, Farnborough: Gregg, 1970), 1:248.
[299] See Walicki, *Slavophile Movement*, 179–180. On Khomyakov's ideas, see Serge Bolshakoff, *The Doctrine of the Unity of the Church in the Works of Khomyakov and Moehler* (London: SPCK, 1946).
[300] Walicki, *Slavophile Movement*, 189.

other way, preferring freedom over unity. In his view, both Western traditions were rationalistic—the Catholic in a materialistic way and the Protestant in an idealistic one. What was needed was a return to the primitive church that Orthodoxy alone had preserved intact:

> Christianity is nothing other than freedom in Christ. . . . I consider the [Orthodox] church to have greater freedom than the Protestants. For Protestantism holds the Scriptures to be an infallible and at the same time *external* authority, while to the church the Scriptures are evidence of herself; she regards them as an inner fact of her own existence. It is therefore quite erroneous to suppose that the church demands enforced unity or enforced obedience; on the contrary, the church abhors both the former and the latter, for in matters of faith enforced unity is falsehood and enforced obedience is death.[301]

The term Khomyakov chose to express this voluntary but organic fellowship was *sobornost'*, a Slavonic term based on *sobor* ("council"). It is used to mean what in the Western church is usually described as "catholicity," but it might equally well be rendered as "conciliarity." The key point was that *sobornost'* was not a creation of some ecclesiastical organization but a gift of the Holy Spirit. More than that, even, it was the *presence* of the Spirit himself in the life of the church, giving it a divine unity that would otherwise be inconceivable. Khomyakov's spiritual vision of Orthodoxy stood in sharp contrast to the reality of the Russian Orthodox Church, a sad fact that even he had to recognize. For a long time, his writings could only be published abroad and he was frequently criticized for ignoring the importance of the church's doctrines and canons. To many in the church's hierarchy, Khomyakov came across as a typical Protestant, because he was a layman who dared to pronounce on church affairs and claim the indwelling presence of the Holy Spirit as his justification for doing so. At the same time, his ideas were deeply attractive to many educated Russians who were looking for spiritual renewal in the church, and it would be fair to say that he inspired a whole generation of theologians who were to come to prominence during and after the revolution. But whether his ideas are condemned or adored, it is fair to say that they bear little or no relation to any perceived reality—especially not in the Orthodox church! Khomyakov realized that, but it did not bother him, because in his view, the ideal should not be judged by the way it was corrupted by human sin and failure.

[301] Alexsei S. Khomyakov, *Polnoje sobranije sochinenij*, 8 vols. in 4 (Moscow: Universitetskaja Tipografija, 1900–1914), 2:198–199. His essay, *The Church Is One*, has been translated into English and published, with an introduction by N. Zernov (London: Fellowship of St. Alban and St. Sergius, 1968).

Sobornost' became, and has remained, a goal to strive for, and it is still capable of winning supporters today.[302]

Slavophilism was full of contradictions. It was an intellectual movement that condemned intellectualism in favor of peasant simplicity. It was chauvinistically Russian and Orthodox, yet dependent on Western models to such an extent that it is scarcely intelligible without them. It interpreted the Orthodox church as the manifestation of the Holy Spirit, the bond that reconciled the principles of unity and freedom that had been sundered in the West, yet it ferociously rejected the *Filioque*, which was the consummate expression of that bond in theological terms. Its profoundest critic was also one of its deepest admirers—Fyodor Dostoevsky (1821–1881).[303] Dostoevsky believed that humanity, and especially Russian humanity, had lost its soul by succumbing to individualism—the antihero of his novel *Crime and Punishment* is called Raskol'nikov, the Russian word for "schismatic." But Dostoevsky also doubted that any of the solutions proposed by the Slavophiles would work, because he understood the nature of the demonic forces that had trapped mankind. In *The Devils* (*The Possessed*) the antihero is Stavrogin, a word composed of the Greek for "cross" (*stauros*) and the Russian for "horn" (*rog*), a combination of Christ and the Devil who in the end commits suicide in order to achieve the freedom and unity with nature that he craved.

Dostoevsky did not live to see the eclipse of Slavophilism as a viable religious philosophy, but it was to occur only a few years after his death. The main actor in that drama was the young Vladimir Solovyov (1853–1900),[304] who broke with his Slavophile mentors in 1883 and embarked on a different path toward the reconciliation of God and man. Instead of setting the West against the East as the Slavophiles (and Dostoevsky) had done, Solovyov preferred the

[302] For example, it is the name of the journal of the Fellowship of St. Alban and St. Sergius, a society primarily dedicated to fostering unity between Anglicans and Orthodox but that has in recent years extended its mission to embrace other Christian bodies as well.

[303] The literature on Dostoevsky is enormous and written from every point of view. For a good recent study, with a lengthy bibliography, see Rowan Williams, *Dostoevsky: Language, Faith, and Fiction* (Waco, TX: Baylor University Press, 2008; London: Continuum, 2009).

[304] Often written as "Soloviev," which leads to a false pronunciation. (The stress is on the final syllable, in a position where "ye" or "ie" is sounded as "yo.") His collected works are published as Vladimir S. Solovyov, *Sobranije sochinenij*, 9 vols. (St. Petersburg: Obshchestvennaja pol'za, 1901–1907). A tenth volume was published by the same publisher in 1914, and a twelve-volume edition (in six) has also been published, containing two volumes (in one) of additional material (Brussels: Foyer Oriental Chrétien, 1966–1969). It is this edition that is cited below as *Works*. At the present time, a new edition of his writings and letters is in course of preparation as *Polnoje sobranije sochinenij i pisem*, 20 vols. (Moscow: Nauka, 2000–). English translations of some of his works are available, notably, S. L. Frank, ed., *A Solovyov Anthology*, 2nd ed. (London: Saint Austin, 2001); Peter P. Zouboff, trans., *Lectures on Godmanhood* (London: D. Dobson, 1948); H. Rees, trans., *Russia and the Universal Church* (London: G. Bles, 1948). Of the many studies available, see especially Frederick C. Copleston, *Russian Religious Philosophy: Selected Aspects* (Notre Dame, IN: Search, 1988); Judith D. Kornblatt and Richard F. Gustafson, *Russian Religious Thought* (Madison: University of Wisconsin Press, 1996), 27–87; B. M. G. Reardon, *Religious Thought in the Nineteenth Century* (Cambridge: Cambridge University Press, 1966), 218–236.

ecumenical vision of William Palmer, which he interpreted in biblical terms: Rome was the church of Peter, Protestantism was the movement of Paul, and the Eastern church was the embodiment of the spiritual theology of John. Like the Trinity, all three had their place in the Christian canon, and their unity had to be sought in reconciling their differences, not in preferring one to the exclusion of the others. This was a view that was very uncongenial to the Russian church, which was not at all impressed by Solovyov's favorable attitude toward Roman Catholicism in particular.[305] Solovyov was not deterred by this, however, and he ended his days in Rome, a "convert" to Catholicism who never abandoned his Eastern roots but who, like William Palmer before him, sought to unite the different Christian traditions in his own personal practice, even when he knew that the institutions that embodied them were a long way from coming to terms with each other.

Solovyov's ecumenical efforts were matched by a religious philosophy that was essentially Hegelian in conception but moved beyond the oppositions of Hegel to posit a different kind of synthesis. Whereas Hegel had believed that competing forces struggled with each other to shape a higher reality that was different from either of them, Solovyov saw those forces as valid in themselves, combining with each other to produce a synthesis that was indeed higher but not "different," in the sense that what was there from the beginning was still fully present, but manifested in a new context which gave it its true meaning.

At the heart of his theology was the person of Christ, because Christianity was first and foremost a message of salvation—that much he got from his reading of Dostoevsky. That salvation comes to us in Jesus Christ, who is the self-expression of God the Father, made from the union of the Logos (the Father's energy) and Sophia (wisdom, the world's soul). In a vision that recalls the second-century Gnostics, Solovyov maintained that Sophia used her freedom to break the union she had with the Logos and in this act what we know as Creation emerges.[306] Christ, the original union of the Logos and Sophia, is best understood as the idea of Creation, and salvation is a restoration of that idea by a reunion of Sophia with the Logos.

All of this consciously picked up the theology of Origen, who coined the term *theanthrôpos* ("Godman"), but it was reworked in the light of the idealistic philosophy of Friedrich Schelling (1775–1854), with whom Solovyov felt a particular bond of spiritual kinship. What he did in effect was rewrite Schelling

---

[305] He expressed these views in (among other places) his lectures on Godmanhood, *Chtenija o bogochelovechestve*, 2, in *Works*, 3:15–18.

[306] The Gnostic dimension to Solovyov's thought was explored by Maria Carlson, "Gnostic Elements in the Cosmogony of Vladimir Soloviev," in Kornblatt and Gustafson, *Russian Religious Thought*, 49–67.

in Christian terms, using Origenistic language as the means to do so. In the incarnation, the Son of God made room for humanity in his divinity, thereby giving it the chance to submit itself fully to the divine will. This is the heart of what he called *bogochelovechestvo*, or "Godmanhood." Solovyov did not ignore the transcendental character of God (the Father), and maintained that it was only the Logos that became incarnate, even though the Logos was fully divine. It was the relationship between the Son (Logos) and the Father that gave the incarnation its special character:

> In Christ his humanity—his rational will—was subordinated completely in everything to the Father's will, and through this feat of self-renunciation he subordinated his material nature, healing, transfiguring, and resurrecting it in a new spiritual form. Likewise in the church the divine holiness, received by the will and reason of humanity, must be extended through a feat of self-renunciation by people and nations to all of mankind, to all its natural life, and through that to the life of the whole world for its recovery, transfiguration, and resurrection.[307]

The incarnation is thus the key to everything, in Solovyov's view. Christ brought salvation to the world by joining human nature to himself and perfecting it through the course of his earthly life. Similarly, the church is a trinity of spirit (the invisible church), soul (the visible church), and flesh (its external, material nature), the reunion of which is its goal. Triune in every aspect of its makeup, the restored body of Christ will be "the true and full image and likeness of the triune God, his true kingdom, the expression of his power and glory."[308] The sacraments are the chief instruments of this transformation because they "embrace and sanctify not only the moral and spiritual life of man, but also his physical life and reunite . . . with divinity the originating principles of the material nature of the whole visible world."[309]

Solovyov knew that there were Jewish and pagan writers in ancient times who held ideas very similar to those of the Christians, and that this fact was held up as evidence that Christianity was neither original nor true, but he disputed such claims vigorously. When talking about the *hypostases* of the Godhead, for example, he said,

> It is totally impossible to deny the connection between the doctrine of Philo and Neoplatonism on the one hand and Christianity, i.e., the Christian doc-

[307] Solovyov, *Velikij spor i khristianskaja politika*, 4, in *Works*, 4:51.
[308] Solovyov, *Dukhovnyje osnovy zhizni*, 2, in *Works*, 3:381.
[309] Ibid., 2, in *Works*, 3:399.

> trine of the Holy Trinity or of the Triune God on the other. If the essence of the divine life was defined by the thinkers of Alexandria in a purely apperceptive way on the basis of a theoretical idea of a divinity, in Christianity, the *same* all-one divine life appeared as a fact, as a historical reality, in the living individuality of a historical person.[310]

Solovyov believed that the goal of salvation was a "deified mankind" that had appeared in embryonic form in many different places, but that began in earnest in a single individual (Jesus Christ) and can only be brought to completion by the participation of the whole of humanity. When that is achieved, God will be all in all and we will be one with him.[311] When that happens, Logos will once more be united with Sophia and the kingdom of God will reign on earth. The church is not just the messenger of this future kingdom but the means by which it is gradually being brought into being right now. What the ancient monastic tradition had confined to the spiritual experience of the individual monk who was called out of the world in order to attain it, Solovyov turned into the universal progress of mankind that is continually taking place in each one of us, individually but also, and more importantly, collectively too. He turned the idea of *sobornost'* from being a description of God's people gathered together to being an active principle of salvation. As he put it:

> The church is not just a gathering together of people (believers), but mainly that which gathers them together, i.e., the essential form of union given to people from above by means of which they can become partakers of the divine nature.[312]

It is obvious that Solovyov was deeply attracted to the Greek patristic tradition, and particularly to the thought of Maximus the Confessor, which he did much to bring back into currency among modern theologians.[313] It should be equally clear that Solovyov's vision is a long way from the narrative of redemption usually heard in the Western church, with its emphasis on atonement for sin and salvation through the shed blood of Christ, a perspective that Solovyov rejected, although he admitted that it did have some good points about it.[314] But whatever those points were, they could not replace what for him was fundamental: "Christ subordinates and harmonizes his human will with the divine

---

310 Solovyov, *Chtenija o bogochelovechestve*, 6, in *Works*, 3:81.
311 Solovyov, *Dukhovnyje osnovy zhizni*, 1, in *Works*, 3:318–319.
312 Ibid., 2, in *Works*, 3:384. There is an important reference here to 2 Peter 1:4, which recurs as a constant refrain in modern Orthodox theology.
313 See Hans Urs von Balthasar, *The Glory of the Lord*, 7 vols. (Edinburgh: T & T Clark, 1982–1991), 3:279–352, especially his remarks on pages 287–288.
314 Solovyov, *Chtenija o bogochelovechestve*, 11–12, in *Works*, 3:163.

will, divinizing his humanity after his divinity became man."[315] For him, it was this *obozhenie*, as Solovyov called it, or *theôsis*, inadequately rendered in English as "deification," that lay at the heart of his gospel message and that has had such an influence on modern Orthodox thinking. Deification uses language drawn from the fathers of the church and was intended to be a repristination of their message for the modern age, but in fact it seems to be something different from what they taught. Solovyov's man is an imperfect creature on his way to perfection by being reunited with the elements of creation that have been separated by a false quest for freedom, but attractive though that idea has proved to many, it must be doubted whether it can really be harmonized with the church's traditional teaching of salvation by grace through faith. In the end, Solovyov was an idealist with a vision of what ought to be, not a preacher of what really was, or what needs to be done about it.

Solovyov's answer to the human dilemma may have been more romantic than realistic, but it was very influential and helped turn a generation of younger thinkers away from the materialism and atheism that dominated the Russian intelligentsia in the years around 1900. There was a kind of spiritual revival in the reign of Nicholas II (1894–1917), the last czar of Russia, in which he to some extent participated. Nicholas was not an intellectual, of course, but he was a religious man to a degree that most of his predecessors had not been, and he may be compared in that respect to the other two royal martyrs in modern European history—Charles I of England (1625–1649) and Louis XVI of France (1774–1793). The czar made Orthodoxy and old pre-Petrine Russia fashionable in a way that they had not been for two centuries, but while that merely persuaded the revolutionaries that Christianity was an evil that had to be abolished along with the absolute monarchy it was tied up with, others were prepared to take a second look. Once they did so, the attractiveness of the Christian vision, especially as Solovyov had articulated it, was enough to convince some that it, and not the doctrine of atheistic materialism, was the way of salvation for Russia and for the world.[316]

Evidence of this new wave of thought appeared for the first time in a collection of essays called *Vekhi* (*Landmarks*), written by seven men who had themselves recently converted from militant atheism to Christianity.[317] *Vekhi*

[315] Ibid., 11–12, in *Works*, 3:170.

[316] It cannot be stressed too often that, in the Russian mind, the salvation of Russia was meant to be the firstfruits of the salvation of mankind; it was Russia's destiny to lead the way for others. That aspect, at least, was retained by the Communists when they took power—the Soviet Union was always seen as the vanguard of human progress and universal transformation.

[317] N. A. Berdyaev et al., *Vekhi. Sbornik statei o rysskoj intelligentsii* (Moscow: Tipografija V. M. Sablina, 1909). Translated into English by Marian Schwartz and published as Boris Shragin and Albert Todd, eds., *Landmarks: A Collection of Essays on the Russian Intelligentsia—1909* (New York: Karz Howard, 1977). On its importance for the modern intelligentsia, see E. S. Elbakian, *Religija v soznanii rossijskoj intelligentsii XIX-nachala XX vv. Filosofsko-istoricheskij analiz* (Moscow: Rosspen, 1996).

was such a threat to the revolutionaries that Lenin wrote a tract against it, thereby preserving a memory of it among his followers long after the authors had died or gone into exile.[318] Its witness was long dormant and suppressed, but when communism finally started to crack, it was rediscovered and became once again an important landmark for a new generation.

There were seven contributors to *Vekhi*, all of them Orthodox laymen, though one (Sergei Bulgakov) was later ordained to the priesthood. No fewer than three of them came from a Jewish background and one was Ukrainian.[319] They were a diverse group, but their intellectual journeys had been similar—having passed through rationalism and (often) Marxism, they had turned to Christianity because of the hollowness of such ideologies. Nikolai Berdyaev (1874–1948) expressed this clearly when he wrote,

> It turns out that a falsely directed love for one's fellow man can kill one's love for God, since the love of truth, like the love of beauty or any other absolute value, is an expression of love for the divine being. This love for one's fellow man was false since it was not founded on genuine respect for man as an equal and kindred soul through one Father. On the one hand, it was compassion and pity for the man of the "people"; on the other, it turned into the worship of man and the people. Genuine love of the people is love, not against truth and God, but in truth and God, not pity that denies man's dignity, but the recognition of God's own image in each person.[320]

Sergei Bulgakov (1871–1944) pointed out, with an accuracy that still applies to many people today, how the Russian intelligentsia derived its good traits from its ancestral Christian heritage, a legacy that slipped away in the second and third generations of those who first turned away from it:

> . . . spiritual habits instilled by the church account for more than one of the better traits of the Russian intelligentsia, which it loses the more it departs from the church: for example, a certain puritanism, a rigorous morality, a unique asceticism, and a strictness with regard to personal life. Leaders of the Russian intelligentsia, such as Dobrolyubov[321] and Chernyshevsky[322] (both

[318] "Concerning *Vekhi*," originally published by Vladimir Ilyin (as he called himself) in *Novyj Den'* XV, December 13, 1909, and reprinted in *Lenin: collected works*, 45 vols. (Moscow: Progress Publishers, 1974), 16:123–131.

[319] The three Jews were Mikhail Osipovich Gershenzon (1869–1925), Aleksander Solomonovich Izgoev (1872–1935), and Semyon Lyudvigovich Frank (1877–1950). The Ukrainian was Bogdan Aleksandrovich Kistyakovsky (1869–1920). The other three were Nikolai Aleksandrovich Berdyaev (1874–1948), Sergei Nikolaevich Bulgakov (1871–1944), and Pyotr Berngardovich Struve (1870–1944), all of whom were prominent in the emigration after 1917.

[320] Nikolai A. Berdyaev, in *Landmarks*, 10 (*Vekhi*, 8–9).

[321] Nikolai Aleksandrovich Dobrolyubov (1836–1861) was a literary critic and revolutionary agitator who died of tuberculosis when only twenty-five years old.

[322] Nikolai Gavrilovich Chernyshevsky was a left-wing social reformer who wrote a famous book called *Chto delat'?* (*What Is to Be Done?*), which became a handbook of the future revolutionaries.

> seminarians, both raised in religious families of clergymen), preserve almost intact their earlier moral traits, which, however, their historical children and grandchildren gradually lose.[323]

Bulgakov continued for several more pages in the same vein, pointing out how the ideals of the intelligentsia were a shadow of the realities that they affected to ignore and despise, and arguing, with Dostoevsky for support, that Russia (and by extension the modern world) was not lapsing into "atheism" in the pure sense, but rather fighting a titanic spiritual battle between God and the Devil that the latter could never win.

The other contributors wrote in a similar vein. Mikhail Gershenzon (1869–1925) even quoted John Bunyan, in a passage where he described his miserable spiritual state before he was converted.[324] These men were neither simpletons nor fanatics. They had lived through the revolution of 1905 and believed that a new day was dawning in Russia, as indeed it was. Gone was the chauvinism of the Slavophiles, to be replaced by a positive vision bequeathed to them by Solovyov and Dostoevsky, both of whom they repeatedly quoted or alluded to. Five of them would subsequently be exiled, with only the Ukrainian Kistyakovsky dying at home in 1920 and Gershenzon, who was allowed to stay in Russia, in 1925. But their collective voice did not die, and it was they, more than anyone, who launched what Nicolas Zernov (properly Nikolai Zyornov, 1898–1980) was to call "the Russian religious renaissance" of the twentieth century.[325]

---

[323] Sergei N. Bulgakov, in *Landmarks*, 28 (*Vekhi*, 29).

[324] Mikhail O. Gershenzon, in *Landmarks*, 68 (*Vekhi*, 75). The quote is from John Bunyan, *Grace Abounding to the Chief of Sinners*, ed. Roger Sharrock (Oxford: Oxford University Press, 1962), 58–59.

[325] See Nicolas Zernov, *The Russian Religious Renaissance of the Twentieth Century* (London: Darton, Longman & Todd, 1963). A Russian translation appeared in 1974 and a second edition of it in 1991 (Paris: YMCA Press).

24

The Trinitarian Revival

The Protestant World

The First World War marked a watershed in the history of Western civilization. Before it, the belief that the nominally Christian countries of the world would go on being the vanguard of civilization and progress was unchallenged. European empires were in control of most of Africa and Asia, and even the United States had gained a foothold in the Pacific and the Caribbean. The Western hemisphere was largely outside these imperial systems, but the countries there were of European origin and so not really an exception to the general pattern of universal European domination. No one seriously believed that places like China or the handful of Muslim states like Persia (Iran) and Afghanistan that had escaped direct colonization (though not indirect economic subordination), would ever amount to much, and they were regarded as barbarous and exotic by most people in the West. Japan was a partial exception to the rule, but until it defeated Russia in 1905 no one took it very seriously, and even then, its claims to be treated as a world power were often disregarded by white Europeans and Americans who took it for granted that other races were inferior to them.

The events of 1914–1918 shattered these illusions. The most civilized "Christian" countries in the world tore each other apart and, when it was all over, four great empires collapsed—Protestant Germany, Catholic Austria-Hungary, Orthodox Russia, and Islamic Ottoman Turkey. Germany was not dismembered or incapacitated to the extent that the other three were, but psychologically it was particularly hard-hit because it was there, more than anywhere else, that Enlightenment theories of progress had taken root and become almost universally accepted. That the world's most scientifically advanced country could be defeated seemed incredible, and as the history of the next generation was to show, it was not accepted by those most directly affected.[1] Something had clearly gone wrong, but what was it?

[1] One of the key factors that allowed Adolf Hitler (1889–1945) to come to power in Germany was the widespread feeling that the country had been stabbed in the back in 1918 and unfairly treated in the subsequent peace

When the war broke out, a young pastor named Karl Barth was shocked to discover that his former professors in Berlin were supporting Germany's war aims.[2] He had gone to a working-class parish in his native Switzerland only two years before, but had discovered that he could not communicate with the local people who did not understand or appreciate the kind of theology he was preaching to them. These two events combined to provoke a spiritual crisis in him, and he began to reread the New Testament, in particular Paul's epistle to the Romans. By the time the war ended he had written a commentary on it, which he published in 1919.[3] It made little impact at the time, but it propelled Barth on a quest for a way out of the impasse that German cultural Christianity had found itself in. He began to immerse himself in the writings of Fyodor Dostoevsky and Søren Kierkegaard, which had only recently been translated into German and become widely available. From them he learned about the depths of human sinfulness and the immense gulf that separates man from God. Speaking to a student conference at Aarau (Switzerland) on April 17, 1920, Barth said,

> The Bible has only one theological interest, and this interest is purely objective: the interest in God himself. It is this that I would like to call the otherworldliness, the non-historicity, the worldly objectivity of the Biblical lines. It is a new, incomparable, unachievable, not only heavenly but supra-heavenly line: God has caught the attention of these humans for himself. God demands their full attention, their complete obedience. For God wants to remain faithful to himself. God is holy and remains so. God does not want to be seized, put into operation, and utilized. . . . God does not want to be something next to other things but wants to be Wholly Other. . . . God does not want to establish a history of religions. He wants to be the Lord of our lives, the eternal Lord of the world. This is what the Bible is about.[4]

---

negotiations. The former theory is groundless, but there is substance to the view that the country was punished too severely by the victors, who were by no means innocent. The best histories of the period are by Golo Mann, *The History of Germany since 1789* (London: Chatto & Windus, 1968). Originally published as *Deutsche Geschichte des neunzehnten und zwanzigsten Jahrhunderts* (Frankfurt am Main: S. Fischer Verlag, 1958); and Michael Burleigh, *The Third Reich: A New History* (London: Macmillan, 2000).

[2] The literature on Barth is immense and constantly growing. His writings are now being published in *Karl Barth Gesamtausgabe* (Zurich: Theologischer Verlag, 1973–). To date nearly fifty volumes have appeared. The standard biography is Eberhard Busch, *Karl Barth: His Life from Letters and Autobiographical Texts*, trans. John Bowden (London: SCM, 1976). Originally published as *Karl Barths Lebenslauf: nach seined Briefen und autobiographischen Texten*, 2nd ed. (Munich: Chr. Kaiser Verlag, 1976). An interesting study by one of his former students is Thomas F. Torrance, *Karl Barth: An Introduction to His Early Theology 1910–1931*, 2nd ed. (Edinburgh: T & T Clark, 2000; 1st ed., London: SCM, 1962). Among the many studies of his theological method that are available, special attention should be drawn to Stephen W. Sykes, ed., *Karl Barth—Studies of His Theological Methods* (Oxford: Clarendon, 1979); Colin Brown, *Karl Barth and the Christian Message* (London: Tyndale Press, 1967); Bruce L. McCormack, *Karl Barth's Critically Realistic Dialectical Theology: Its Genesis and Development 1909–1936* (Oxford: Clarendon, 1995).

[3] Karl Barth, *Der Römerbrief* (Bern: Bäschlin, 1919).

[4] Karl Barth, "Biblical Questions, Insights, and Vistas," in *The Word of God and Theology*, trans. Amy Marga (London: T & T Clark, 2011), 86–87. Published in German as *Das Wort Gottes und die Theologie* (Munich: Chr.

Barth immediately incurred the wrath of the leading theologians of his time, not least of all Adolf von Harnack, who thought that he was a radical in the tradition of the sixteenth-century Anabaptists, who would overturn all order in church and state. They complained that Barth was talking about such things as the divine sonship of Christ, atonement by his blood, Paul's use of the Old Testament, and so on, as if these were viable concepts for the present and not just mythical hangovers from an earlier time.[5] Barth mulled over these criticisms for a while and then produced his second, much altered, edition of the Romans commentary, in which he replied as follows:

> In contrast with this comfortable dismissal of uncomfortable points it has been my "Biblicism" which has compelled me to wrestle with these "scandals of modern thought" until I have found myself able to undertake the interpretation of them. . . . I have, moreover, no desire to conceal the fact that my "Biblicist" method—which means in the end no more than "consider well"—is applicable also to the study of Lao-Tze and of Goethe. . . . When I am called a "Biblicist," all that can rightly be proved against me is that I hold it profitable for men to take [the Bible's] conceptions at least as seriously as they take their own.[6]

By this time Barth's views were becoming better known, and the second edition struck the German world like a bombshell. It was not so much a commentary in the usual sense, as a theological manifesto calling for a return to the orthodoxy of an earlier age. That, however, would be too simple an interpretation of what Barth was advocating. Barth did not reject what he saw as the genuine advances of historical criticism, but to his mind what it had done was to remind us that the biblical witness is just that—a witness by men living in time and space to an event that went beyond those limitations. We no longer have direct access to what they saw and touched with their hands, concerning the word of life,[7] but we have their testimony and are invited to accept it in faith. By submitting ourselves to the human word that we read in Scripture, we bear witness to God's Word addressed to us and at work in our lives. Direct access to revealed truth is impossible, but it comes to us in the way that God has appointed—by the testimony of those who first saw and believed.

Kaiser Verlag, 1924). The lecture was first published separately as *Biblische Fragen, Einsichten und Ausblicke* (Munich: Chr. Kaiser Verlag, 1920).

[5] For a good overview of this controversy, see James C. Livingston et al., *Modern Christian Thought*, 2nd ed., 2 vols. (Minneapolis: Fortress, 2006), 2:63–71. Livingston brings out the support that Barth received at this time from Emil Brunner and Rudolf Bultmann, both of whom would diverge from him in later years.

[6] Karl Barth, *The Epistle to the Romans*, 2nd ed. (London: Oxford University Press, H. Milford, 1933), 12. Originally published as *Der Römerbrief* (Munich: Chr. Kaiser Verlag, 1922).

[7] 1 John 1:1.

This interaction between eternity and time, the infinite and the finite, Barth and his colleagues called "dialectical." It was not like the old Hegelian dialectic, where opposites engaged each other in order to arrive at a higher truth, but a tension between two worlds of being that can never be finally resolved in this life. Our words can be only approximative attempts to convey what is beyond our understanding. To attempt to overcome this either by bringing heaven down to earth (dogmatism) or by taking earth up to heaven (mysticism) will inevitably fail because it is trying to do the impossible. This was the problem with liberal theology, as Barth understood it. It had wanted to have an immediate experience of God, to abolish the tension between heaven and earth, not by the old dogmatism which had purported to say what the divine revelation was, but by a new form of it, which identified "God" with man and claimed that our own psychological experiences or self-consciousness was an expression of the divine. As Barth expressed it,

> . . . what is clearly seen to be indisputable reality is the invisibility of God. . . . And what does this mean but that we can know nothing of God, that we are not God, that the Lord is to be feared? Herein lies his pre-eminence over all gods; and here is that which marks him out as God, as Creator and Redeemer.[8]

Man cannot ascend to God, but God can come down to man and reveal himself, which is what he has done in Jesus Christ. The paradox of this, however, is that God reveals himself as a hidden God. Christ does not come on the clouds of heaven, but as a meek and lowly servant. To know him as he really is, is possible only by faith, which is a gift of grace:

> He takes the form of a slave; he moves to the cross and to death; his greatest achievement is a negative achievement. He is not a genius; . . . he is not a hero or a leader of men. He is neither poet nor thinker: "My God, my God, why hast thou forsaken me?"[9] . . . In Jesus revelation is a paradox. . . . Therefore it is not accessible to our perception. . . . He becomes a scandal to the Jews and to the Greeks foolishness.[10] In Jesus the communication of God begins with a rebuff, with the exposure of a vast chasm, with the clear revelation of a great stumbling-block . . .[11]

Barth had no time for the so-called quest for the historical Jesus, not just because that Jesus would never be found but because even if he could be, he

[8] Barth, *Epistle to the Romans*, 47.
[9] Matt. 27:46; Mark 15:34, quoted from Psalm 22:1.
[10] Cf. 1 Cor. 1:23.
[11] Barth, *Epistle to the Romans*, 97–99.

would not be the object of our faith. The historical Jesus of Nazareth has been transformed by the miracle of his resurrection from the dead, and it is that which forms the basis for our faith:

> Jesus has been . . . declared to be the Son of God with power, according to the Holy Spirit, through his resurrection from the dead. In this declaration and appointment—which are beyond historical definition—lies the true significance of Jesus. As Christ, Jesus is the plane which lies beyond our comprehension. . . . In the resurrection the new world of the Holy Spirit touches the old world of the flesh. . . . Even though we have known Christ after the flesh yet now we know him so no longer.[12]

One of the biggest problems we face when reading Scripture, argued Barth, is that we go to it asking our questions in the expectation that we shall be given answers that suit us. That may well happen, but if it does, the danger is that we shall misinterpret the message by applying it in a naive and superficial way to address situations that it does not have in view. Barth expressed his convictions on this subject very clearly in a lecture that he gave on February 6, 1917:

> When we come to the Bible with our questions of "How should I think of God and the world? How do I get to the divine? What kind of attitude shall I take?" it answers us with something like: "My dear friend, That is your affair, which you must not ask me about. . . ." The Bible does not tell us how we are supposed to talk with God, but rather what God says to us. It does not say how we are to find our way to him, but how God has sought and found the way to us. It does not show the right relationship into which we must place ourselves with him, but the covenant which God has made with all those who are the children of Abraham in faith, and which God has sealed in Jesus Christ once and for all. This is what stands in the Bible. The Word of God stands in the Bible.[13]

Barth was always firmly Protestant in his outlook, but he appreciated medieval theology, especially that of Anselm, whose theological approach he regarded as a model for his own work.[14] Anselm had argued that we must start with the faith of the church and test whether it was true, not with some independent philosophical presupposition that we must then align with the faith of the church. As Barth explained it,

---

[12] Ibid., 29–30. Cf. 2 Cor. 5:16.

[13] Karl Barth, "The New World in the Bible," in *Word of God and Theology*, 25.

[14] Karl Barth, *Anselm:* fides quaerens intellectum: *Anselm's Proof of the Existence of God in the Context of His Theological Scheme* (London: SCM, 1960; reissued Pittsburgh, PA: Pickwick, 1975). Translated from the second German edition, Fides quaerens intellectum. *Anselms Beweis der Existenz Gottes in Zusammenhang seines theologischen Programms* (Zurich: Evangelischer Verlag, 1958). The first edition was published in 1931 (Munich: Chr. Kaiser Verlag, 1931).

> Faith is related to the *Credo* of the church into which we are baptized. Thus the knowledge that is sought cannot be anything but an extension and explication of that acceptance of the *Credo* of the church, which faith itself already implied. The man who asks for Christian knowledge asks: To what extent is it thus?", on the basis of a presupposition that is never for a moment questioned, namely that it is as he, a Christian, believes. That and that alone. A science of faith, which denied or even questioned the Faith (the *Credo* of the church), would *ipso facto* cease to be either "faithful" or "scientific." . . . *Intelligere* comes about by reflection on the *Credo* that has already been spoken and affirmed.[15]

Whether his study of Anselm marked a fundamental change in Barth's thinking, or whether it merely confirmed the direction in which he had been heading all along, is disputed, but it hardly matters. Whatever the case, he was to spend the rest of his life developing the ideas he found in Anselm and producing his monumental *Church Dogmatics*, which by common consent is the greatest theological work of the twentieth century.[16] But within months of the publication of the first volume, Adolf Hitler came to power in Germany and Barth faced an entirely new challenge. As a Swiss national he had greater freedom to speak out against the anti-Christian policies of the new regime, and he did so without hesitation. In July 1934 he wrote the text of what became known as the Barmen Declaration, a confession in six articles adopted by the Confessing Synod of the German Evangelical Church. It stated,

> Jesus Christ, as he is attested to us in Holy Scripture, is the one Word of God whom we have to hear, and whom we have to trust and obey in life and death. We reject the false doctrine that the church could or should recognize as a source of its proclamation, beyond and besides this one Word of God, yet other events, powers, historic figures, and truths as God's revelation.[17]

It might be thought that the Barmen Declaration would have been unanimously assented to by all Christians, but that was not the case. Almost immediately, Emil Brunner attacked it, as did a number of Roman Catholic theologians, because it denied the validity of natural theology. Conservative Lutherans also complained because it ignored traditional Lutheran teaching

[15] Barth, *Anselm*, 26–27.

[16] Karl Barth, *Church Dogmatics* (study edition), 31 vols. (London: T & T Clark, 2009. Originally trans. G. W. Bromiley, 13 vols. in 4 (Edinburgh: T & T Clark, 1956–1975). Originally published as *Kirchliche Dogmatik* (Zollikon-Zurich: Evangelische Buchhandlung, 1932–1967).

[17] *Die Barmer theologische Erklärung*, in *Das eine Wort für alle: Einführung und Dokumentation*, ed. Alfred Burgsmüller and Rudolf Weth (Neukirchen-Vluyn: Neukirchener Verlag, 1993). English text in Rolf Ahlers, *The Barmen Theological Declaration of 1934: The Archaeology of a Confessional Text* (Lewiston, NY: Edwin Mellen, 1986), 39–42.

on the relationship between church and state. It was a Reformed document, in spite of the fact that the Barmen synod was meant to embrace all Protestant Christians, and the squabbling over it shows how divided and out of touch with reality many people in the German churches were at that time.[18] Unfortunately, it must be said that Barth himself was inconsistent in his application of biblical principles to the political sphere, because he refused to condemn Communism in the same way as he denounced Nazism.[19] He did, however, campaign against nuclear weapons, though without much success.[20]

It was, however, with the *Church Dogmatics* that Barth was chiefly preoccupied for the last thirty years of his life. He was expelled from Germany in 1935 and returned to his native Switzerland, where he subsequently remained. There he gave himself over to massive theological construction (or reconstruction), centered on a few cardinal principles but embracing the whole scope of Christian faith and practice. His intention was to take the orthodox theology of the past—the great creeds and, in his case, the confessions of the Reformed church—and repristinate them for modern use. It is for this reason that he and his followers have been called "neo-orthodox," a term that recalls the "neo-Thomism" of contemporary Roman Catholicism and the "neo-Calvinism" of the Dutch Reformed, both of which he opposed (and whose representatives opposed him.) But, different though his approach was to theirs, they all had one thing in common: they were looking back to an earlier time in the history of theology and seeking to revivify it, conscious that the historical development that had actually occurred had led to a dead end.

In the first volume, Barth developed his doctrine of the Word of God, which assumed three distinct but closely related forms:

1. The Word as revealed in Jesus Christ.
2. The Word as written in Holy Scripture.
3. The Word as proclaimed by the church.

According to Barth, there is no substantial difference among these three—they are all different forms of the same eternal Word. Jesus Christ is absolute and fundamental, since without him there would be no Word to hear or proclaim at all. The Bible is the Word of God insofar as it speaks about Christ. It

[18] People in other countries were no better, of course, but they did not have to face the issues as starkly as Germans did at that time, and many were unaware of the Declaration until after 1945, when the story of Christian resistance to the Nazi regime could be told.

[19] Karl Barth, *Against the Stream: Shorter Post-war Writings 1946–1952* (New York: Philosophical Library, 1954), 106–118. The relevant text was originally published as *Christliche Gemeinde im Wechsel der Staatsordnungen: Dokumente einer Ungarnreise* (Zollikon-Zurich: Evangelischer Verlag, 1948).

[20] See John H. Yoder, *Karl Barth and the Problem of War* (Nashville: Abingdon, 1970), for a full discussion of this and other matters relating to Barth's views on war and peace.

is open to other interpretations because it is ultimately a human word, given in time and space, but such interpretations are ultimately false. The true reader of the text will come to it with theological presuppositions, determined by his faith in Christ, and so will hear the text speaking about him. To understand the text rightly, we must subordinate our own thoughts to its authority, because it has been given to teach us and not to be criticized by us as we might choose. In Barth's words,

> Subordination must concern the purpose and meaning indicated in the ideas, thoughts and convictions of the prophets and apostles, that is, the testimony which, by what they say as human beings like ourselves, they wish to bear. To this testimony of their words we must subordinate ourselves.[21]

Barth's words here are ambiguous. To the believing Christian they might mean that we must submit ourselves to the authority of God speaking to us in and through his Holy Spirit, but they might also mean something considerably less than that—submitting to the witness of the prophets and apostles and trusting that they got it right. Nor is it at all clear whether such a stance can escape the impact of philosophical and other assumptions that readers inevitably bring to the text beforehand. It is all very well to criticize the fathers of the church for having been influenced in their reading by Neoplatonism, but can modern interpreters avoid a similar dependence on current patterns of thought? Taken to its logical conclusion, such a suggestion would imply that the true reader of Scripture must go out of the world entirely and have nothing to say to it—or that what he might want to say would be incomprehensible, because it would be grounded in concepts unknown (and unknowable) to the general public. That Barth did not want to say that is clear from the third aspect of the Word, which is proclamation. More than most theologians of his time he stressed the importance of preaching as the means by which God communicates his Word to others and legitimates its authority in their lives. It is not enough to read the text—we must be convicted by it. Barth did not invent the word *kêrygma* ("preaching" or "proclamation"), but his emphasis on it did much to make it a household word in theological circles, something that had never been true before.

The second focal point of the *Church Dogmatics* is Christology. This is closely tied to the Word, of course, but as Barth developed his thinking it became more central to his concerns and went far beyond the task of preaching, important though that was. Having begun early in his career with the statement

[21] Barth, *Church Dogmatics*, I/2, 2.3.21.2, 718.

that God was "Wholly Other" and not in any way to be confused with the immanentist thinking of nineteenth-century liberalism, Barth moved toward a more balanced approach as time went on. God remained totally transcendent, but in Christ he made himself known, not just as a message or idea but as a human being. In Barth's words,

> We must not refer to the second "person" of the Trinity as such, to the eternal Son or the eternal Word of God *in abstracto*. . . . According to the free and gracious will of God the eternal Son of God is Jesus Christ. . . . He is the decision of God in time, and yet according to what took place in time the decision which was made from all eternity.[22]

Barth went so far as to see even the creation itself as a prefiguration of Christ, who is its ultimate goal and fulfillment. Christ is the prototype of humanity, the final work of creation, the one against whom everything else must be measured and judged. The created order is imperfect and falls short of Christ, but that is the reason why he came—to put back in place what had gone wrong:

> In his relation to God a man may become a sinner and thus distort and corrupt his own nature, but he cannot revoke what was decided in Jesus apart from him concerning the true nature of man. . . . And if Jesus forgives his sins and restores his spoiled relation to God, this means that Jesus again controls what originally belongs to him. . . . He has the freedom and power to do this. . . . And he does just that by making himself our Savior.[23]

Like Augustine before him, Barth was thus forced to regard sin and evil as nonexistent, as negations of true being that have no meaning in themselves. As he put it,

> [Sin and evil] is that which is excluded from all present and future existence, i.e., chaos, the world fashioned otherwise than according to the divine purpose, and therefore formless and intrinsically impossible. . . . That which is ungodly and anti-godly can have reality only as that by which God's decision and operation has been rejected and disappeared, and therefore only as a frontier of that which is and will be according to God's decision and action.[24]

As Barth saw it, God had intended to save the creation in Christ, and man's rebellion cannot thwart that divine purpose. For him, this was the essence of

[22] Ibid., IV/1, 13.57.2, 52.
[23] Ibid., III/2, 10.43.2, 50–51.
[24] Ibid., III/1, 9.41.2, 102.

God's election: by creating man, God had chosen him to dwell with him in eternity. It is here, more obviously than anywhere else, that Barth parted company, not only with the Reformed tradition but (more important) with the teaching of Scripture itself. In the Bible, election pertains to Abraham and Israel; even Christians are incorporated into this election and not redeemed by some other arrangement. The underlying assumption is that it is a work of divine grace and has nothing to do with any kind of entitlement on man's part. The vast majority of the human race gets what it deserves: death, which is the reward for sin. But a minority is rescued from this fate, not because it is any better than the others, but because God has chosen to show his glory in this way. Those who are elect have not chosen their status, and may not even want it, as the history of the ever-rebellious Israel demonstrates only too clearly. But like Saul of Tarsus on the road to Damascus, they get it in spite of their desires or deserts because the sovereign God has determined that it should be so.

Barth took elements of this doctrine but turned them into something quite different. He agreed with the Reformers that salvation is entirely of grace, that those who are saved do not deserve it and that in many cases they rebel against it. The difference was that what the Bible applies to one nation—the physical, but more important, the spiritual descendants of Abraham (who include many who are not physically descended from him)—Barth applied to the entire human race. This was the logical and necessary outcome of his doctrine that Christ is the crown and ultimate goal of the created order, because if that is so, then all things must come together in him and universal redemption becomes inevitable.

Barth went further than this, however, and claimed that in Christ, God chose himself for rejection. By dying on the cross, Christ paid the price of human alienation from God, thereby overcoming all that is wrong in us and opening the door for our salvation in and through him. It is because he has been crucified for us that we live, because the whole of human nature has been redeemed:

> What we have to consider in the elected man Jesus is, then, the destiny of human nature, its exaltation to fellowship with God. . . . It is in this man that the exaltation itself is revealed and proclaimed. For with his decree concerning this man, God decreed too that this man should be the cause and instrument of our exaltation.[25]

From the very beginning, Barth had his passionate detractors as well as his devoted followers, a feature that has continued since his death and makes any

[25] Ibid., II/2, 7.33.1, 118.

consensus about the lasting value of his work impossible to achieve at the present time.[26] But whether we like his work or loathe it, there can be no doubt that Barth set a theological agenda that continues to bear fruit in our time, and we cannot understand the modern church without taking that influence into account.

At the heart of Barth's theology was his doctrine of the Trinity, and here he made an undoubted contribution to the development of modern thought.[27] Christian theology is a revelation—but a revelation of what? The answer to this has to be "God," but in what way is God revealed to us? Standard Reformed dogmatics had always assumed that the primary locus of God's revelation was in Scripture, his Word to his people. By reading the Bible and appreciating its divine character, Christians would come to understand who its author was and what he was like. This approach can be traced back to the Second Helvetic Confession of 1566, which, for the first time, put the doctrine of Scripture ahead of the doctrine of God in its order of things to be confessed by the church. Before that time, however, it had been customary to begin the study of systematic theology with the doctrine of God. The medieval Scholastics had broken this down into the one God, who was treated first, and then the Trinity, but in the earliest phase of Scholasticism this division had not been rigorously observed. Peter Lombard, for example, began his *Sentences* with the Trinity and subsumed the attributes of God's unity under that heading. Insofar as he drew on church tradition, it was the approach of the Lombard, and not that of the later Scholastics, wither pre- or post-Reformation, on which Barth primarily drew. But as with everything else, he went his own way when it came to interpreting the doctrine he inherited.

Barth knew, of course, that the Trinity was not to be found in a developed form in the New Testament:

---

[26] From the standpoint of his admirers, see Thomas F. Torrance, *Karl Barth, Biblical and Evangelical Theologian* (Edinburgh: T & T Clark, 1990), and the account of his chief English translator, G. W. Bromiley, *Introduction to the Theology of Karl Barth* (Grand Rapids, MI: Eerdmans, 1979), and George Hunsinger, *How to Read Karl Barth: The Shape of His Theology* (Oxford: Oxford University Press, 1991). Among his neo-Calvinist detractors, see the comprehensive work by Cornelius Van Til, and the highly critical book by Cornelius Van Til, *Christianity and Barthianism* (Philadelphia: Presbyterian & Reformed, 1962), and also G. C. Berkouwer, *The Triumph of Grace in the Theology of Karl Barth* (London: Paternoster, 1956). A recent publication that covers many major aspects of Barth's thought, from a critical evangelical standpoint, is David Gibson and Daniel Strange, eds., *Engaging with Barth: Contemporary Evangelical Critiques* (Nottingham: Apollos, 2008). For an evaluation of his Roman Catholic critics, see John Machen, *The Autonomy Theme in the* Church Dogmatics*: Karl Barth and His Critics* (Cambridge: Cambridge University Press, 1990). It should be said that, despite Barth's own anti-Catholicism, some astute Roman Catholic critics have found much to admire and appreciate in his work. See, for example, Hans Urs von Balthasar, *The Theology of Karl Barth: Exposition and Interpretation* (San Francisco: Communio, 1992). Originally published as *Karl Barth: Darstellung und Deutung seiner Theologie* (Cologne: J. Hegner, 1951; reissued Einsiedeln: Johannes Verlag, 1976). Another fascinated critic is Rowan Williams, "Barth on the Triune God," in Stephen Sykes, ed., *Karl Barth*, 147–193.

[27] See Emmanuel Durand and Vincent Holzer, eds., *Les sources du renouveau de la théologie trinitaire au XXe siècle* (Paris: Cerf, 2008); and *Les réalisations du renouveau trinitaire au XXe siècle* (Paris: Cerf, 2010); Stephen Holmes, *The Quest for the Trinity: The Doctrine of God in Scripture, History, and Modernity* (Downers Grove, IL: InterVarsity Press, 2012).

> . . . this doctrine is not to be found in the texts of the Old and New Testament witness to God's revelation. It did not arise out of the historical situations to which these texts belong. It is the exegesis of these texts in the language, which means also in the light, of the questions arising out of a later situation. It belongs to the church. It is a *theologoumenon*. It is a dogma.[28]

Barth, however, puts the doctrine at the center of his dogmatics because he says that it is the Trinity that distinguishes Christian faith from any other kind of revealed monotheism:

> The doctrine of the Trinity is what basically distinguishes the Christian doctrine of God as Christian, and therefore what already distinguishes the Christian concept of revelation as Christian, in contrast to all other possible doctrines of God or concepts of revelation.[29]

In revising his theological perspective, Barth was working in conscious opposition to Schleiermacher, whose whole approach he regarded as fundamentally flawed. Schleiermacher had put the Trinity at the end of his dogmatics as a tentative appendix as to how one might conceive of Christian theology, and in so doing he had inverted the gospel message—putting the cart before the horse in a very big way. Schleiermacher's approach was consistent with the evolution of traditional Western dogmatics, which had reduced God to an object of speculation and implicitly denied revelation, even when they confessed it as a theological principle. The lengthy theological treatises that had appeared on the oneness of God, outlining his attributes in great detail, were (in Barth's view) a waste of time, especially as those who wrote them agreed with him that God was "Wholly Other." That was why his attributes could only be expressed negatively, but the end result is that we can say nothing about him unless we retreat into a mystical or apophatic theology, which was the exact opposite of dogmatics.

Barth was not prepared to follow that logic, and argued that the Bible implied the existence of a Trinitarian God, even if it did not explicitly say so:

> . . . in the Bible revelation signifies the self-unveiling, imparted to men, of a God who according to his essence cannot be unveiled to man. This content

[28] Barth, *Church Dogmatics*, I/1, 2.1.9.4, 431. Barth knew that a *theologoumenon* was just a theological opinion, whereas a dogma was a settled decision of the church that had to be believed, but unlike theologians who did not take historical development into consideration, he believed that, in the case of the Trinity at least, the former had become the latter as a result of centuries of theological argument. His own approach was to retrace this process, not so much as it occurred in the early church (although he mentioned that) but as it must occur in any responsible reflection on the biblical witness.

[29] Ibid., I/1, 1.7.1, 301.

> according to the Biblical witness is of such a nature, that in view of the three elements of the veiling, unveiling, and impartation of God, we have cause to speak of a threefold otherness of the one God, who according to the witness of the Bible has revealed himself. The Biblical witness to God's revelation faces us with the possibility of interpreting the one proposition "God reveals himself as the Lord" three times in a different sense. This possibility is the Biblical root of the doctrine of the Trinity.[30]

The early Christians had taken up the challenge of further definition, partly because it was latent in the text and partly because it was necessary if their proclamation of God's self-revelation was to make sense. Modern Christians might have to proclaim the message in a different way, but it behooved theologians to have a proper respect for their forebears and not to dismiss their insights out of hand:

> . . . theologians have always lived by some sort of philosophy, and in that respect they always will. But instead of getting into a Pharisaic froth about it and consigning whole periods to the Hades of a philosophy accused of denying the Gospel—only because one's own philosophy is different!—it were better to canvass the question, and in strictness, that question alone, as to what the theologians of the early period really meant to assert in the language of their philosophy. . . . Who gives us the right to consider our own "piety"—even if its agreement with the Reformation and the New Testament did appear ever so impeccable—the only one possible in the church, and to exalt it to a standard by which to measure the attainments of past periods?[31]

As Barth saw the matter, it was Jesus who revealed to us that God is a Trinity of divine persons. The Jews had some notion of God at work in many different ways, but although they used terms like "Spirit of the Lord" that were later taken up by Christians to refer to persons of the Trinity, they never went that far themselves. They could not have done so, because Jesus Christ was not revealed to them in the Old Testament period. It is only Jesus who has told us that God is our Father, that he himself is the Son (who is also God), and that he sends the Holy Spirit to dwell in the hearts of his followers as God's self-revealing presence in the world:

> . . . if we mean by the word "revelation" [that] "the Word became flesh and dwelt among us,"[32] then we are asserting something that is to be grounded

[30] Ibid., I/1, 2.1.9.4, 431.
[31] Ibid., I/1, 2.1.9.4, 434.
[32] John 1:14.

> only within the Trinity; namely, by the will of the Father, by the mission of the Son and of the Holy Spirit, by the eternal decree of the triune God, i.e. not otherwise than as the knowledge of God from God, as knowledge of the Light in the Light.[33]

The incarnation of the Word in Christ is therefore the context in which the doctrine of the Trinity can be—but also must be—formulated. To fail to do this would be to fail to hear the Word proclaimed in Christ, which would be a denial of the Christian faith itself. In saying this, Barth was accused by his detractors of what they called "Christomonism," that is to say, a concentration on Christ so exclusive that there was no room for anything else, but this charge is unfair. Barth's focus on Jesus Christ was typical of nineteenth-century thought, which saw Jesus as the model human being and thought of Christianity as an attempt to follow his example. Barth rejected that facile interpretation, but by keeping Jesus firmly at the center of his thinking he at least connected with that approach and could correct it by insisting that Jesus was not just a remarkable human teacher, but the earthly revelation of the hidden God. As he put it,

> We mean by the doctrine of the Trinity . . . the proposition that he whom the Christian church calls God and proclaims as God—therefore the God who has revealed himself according to the witness of Scripture—is the same in unimpaired unity, yet also the same in unimpaired variety, thrice in a different way.[34]

Barth's approach to the Trinity is remarkable because it opened up a line of thought that had never been developed in Christian thinking before. In the early church it had generally been assumed that the Father was the link person in the Godhead. The Son and the Holy Spirit were thought of as deriving from him in some way, and that is how they were defined—the Son was begotten of the Father and the Holy Spirit proceeds from him. After Augustine, the Western tradition came to see the Holy Spirit as the link person in the Godhead, the bond of unity between the Father and the Son that made them one and communicated that divine reality to us by dwelling in our hearts by faith. That approach naturally involved a confession of the double procession of the Holy Spirit (*Filioque*), which eventually caused a split between the Eastern and the Western theological traditions.

Barth acknowledged these traditions and defended them, but he went further.[35] No one had ever constructed a Trinitarian theology based on the person of

[33] Barth, *Church Dogmatics*, I/1, 1.4.3, 134.
[34] Ibid., I/1, 2.1.8.2, 353.
[35] For his acceptance of Augustine's position, see ibid., I/1, 2.1.11.1, 470, where he mentions it explicitly.

the Son, despite the fact that it is in and through Jesus Christ that we have come to a knowledge of the Trinity in the first place. This was Barth's great achievement. In imitation of the basic Augustinian structure, which started with the concept of love and explained the persons of the Trinity as the Lover, the Beloved, and Love, Barth began with the idea of revelation and explained how the Father was the Revealer, the Son was the Revealed and the Holy Spirit was Revelation itself:

> . . . it is God who reveals himself in a like manner as the Father in his self-veiling and holiness, as he does as the Son in his self-unveiling and mercy, and as the Spirit in his self-impartation and love. Father, Son and Spirit are the one, single and equal God.[36]

Nor could it be otherwise. Barth effectively interprets the unity of God, not in terms of abstract absolute attributes that he supposedly possesses as part of his being, but as essentially threefold. The classical distinction between God as One and God as Three is therefore invalid, because God as One is also God as Three—his threeness is part of his oneness, which cannot exist in any other way:

> The name of Father, Son and Spirit means that God is the one God in threefold repetition; and that in such a way, that this repetition itself is grounded in his Godhead; hence in such a way that it signifies no alteration in his Godhead; but also in such a way that only in this repetition is he the one God; in such a way that his Godhead stands or falls with the fact that in this repetition he is God; but precisely for the reason that in each repetition he is the one God.[37]

How God can be the same and yet different at the same time is a mystery, but it is that mystery that lies at the core of his being. In him, singularity and plurality are reconciled, so that each one is perfect in itself and yet dwells in equally perfect harmony with the other:

> Here . . . we have to do with a unity of identity and non-identity. Here God lives his divine life, which may be brought neither under the denominator of simplicity nor under that of multiplicity, but includes within itself both simplicity and multiplicity. . . . Here God himself is really distinguished from himself: God, and God again and differently, and God a third time. . . . Note that the divine being draws from this not only its inner perfection . . . but

[36] Ibid., I/1, 2.1.9.4, 438. Elsewhere, he speaks of the Son as "Revelation" and of the Spirit as "Revealedness," but these are no more than different words for the same thing. See Barth, *Church Dogmatics*, I/1, 1.7.1, 295.
[37] Ibid., I/1, 2.1.9.1, 402.

> from it also draws the outer perfection of its form, its thorough-going distinctiveness, as the unity of identity and non-identity. . . . This is inevitable if God is triune.[38]

On Barth's model, the one who is the Revealed (or Revelation, understood in historic, objective terms) has to be the central figure in the Trinity, because only in him do we see who the other persons are. Barth did not like the term "person" and preferred to speak about "modes of being" (*Seinsweise*), an unfortunate expression that inevitably raised the specter of modalism. But Barth rejected that because, in classical modalism, the revealed forms of God were not all that there was to know:

> Modalism in the last resort means the denial of God. Our God, and only our God, that is, who makes himself ours in his revelation, is God. To relativize this God, as is done in the doctrine of the real God beyond this manifest God, is to relativize, i.e. to deny, the one real God.[39]

Barth disliked the term "person" because in modern times it has come to mean "a subject of consciousness," which, if applied to the Trinity, would mean that there must be three Gods.[40] It was also a way of making God in man's image instead of the other way around, which Barth was always determined to avoid:

> . . . when we speak today of person, involuntarily and almost irresistibly the idea arises of something rather like the way in which we men are persons. And actually this idea is as ill-suited as possible to describe what God the Father, the Son and the Holy Spirit is. . . . when the Christian church speaks of the triune God, it means that God is not just in one way, but that he is the Father and the Son and the Holy Spirit. Three times the one and the same, threefold, but above all triune, he, the Father, the Son and the Holy Spirit, in himself and in the highest and in his revelation.[41]

Disputes over the appropriateness of using the traditional terminology today should not obscure the fact that Barth thought of the three divine "persons" in a way that preserved their essential distinctiveness and was therefore not modalist in the classical sense. Yet, as always with Barth, things are never that straightforward. Of the Father he said,

[38] Ibid., II/1, 6.31.3, 659–660.
[39] Ibid., I/1, 2.1.9.4, 439.
[40] Ibid., I/1, 2.1.8.2, 351.
[41] Karl Barth, *Dogmatics in Outline* (London: SCM, 1949), 42–43. Originally published as *Die christliche Dogmatik im Entwurf* (Munich: Chr. Kasier Verlag, 1927).

> He is what he reveals himself as being, namely, the Father of Jesus Christ his Son, who as such is himself God. He can be so, because he is himself the Father in himself, because Fatherhood is an eternal mode of existence of the divine essence.[42]

Link this to the concept of revelation, and the result is,

> Revelation has eternal content and eternal validity. Throughout all the depths of Deity, not as the penultimate but as the ultimate thing to be said about God, God is God the Son just as he is God the Father.[43]

As Barth understood it, the Father-Creator presents himself to us by emptying himself in the Son-Reconciler, which is why the two are one and we see the fullness of God in the Son. This self-emptying is the supreme manifestation of the divine love, which is communicated to us by the Spirit-Redeemer, who transcends the opposition inherent in the Father-Son relationship:

> Knowledge of revelation, as it may arise on the witness of Scripture, means . . . knowledge of the Lord as him who meets us and unites us to himself. And this Lord can be our God, he can meet us and unite us to himself, because he is God in these three modes of existence as Father, Son and Spirit, because creation, reconciliation, redemption, the entire being, language and action in which he wills to be our God, is grounded and typified in his own essence, in his Godness itself.[44]

A fundamental aspect of Barth's Trinitarian doctrine is that it opens the way for us to have a personal relationship with God, what Feuerbach had characterized as an "I-Thou" dialogue between the Father and the Son, extended to include us because of our union with Christ.[45] This is the link between God and man, and without the Trinity it would not be possible, since our communication with God proceeds in and through his self-revelation to us, and is not the projection of our own thoughts onto a hidden and unknown deity.

The link between the Son and believers encouraged Barth to develop his understanding of the relationship between the Father and the Son even further. Barth came to believe that there was something inherent in the person of the Son that made it inevitable that it would be he, and not the Father or the Holy Spirit, who would come into the world to redeem fallen man. As he expressed it, ". . . humility is not alien to the nature of the true God, but supremely proper

---

[42] Barth, *Church Dogmatics*, I/1, 2.1.10.2, 448.
[43] Ibid., I/1, 2.1.11.2, 474.
[44] Ibid., I/1, 2.1.9.4, 440.
[45] Ibid., III/2, 10.45.1, 203. This section develops this theme at some length.

to him in his mode of being as the Son."[46] In other words, humility is a personal property of the Son. This means that although the Son freely accepted his role as the Redeemer of mankind and was not forced into it by the Father, there was nevertheless something in him that ensured that he would be the one who would do his Father's will and not the other way around. Barth did not go on to develop this idea with respect to the Holy Spirit, but as Bruce McCormack has pointed out, the logic of his argument would suggest that the Spirit is also constitutionally predisposed to being the agent of the Father and the Son in the divine work of salvation.[47] If that interpretation is correct, then Barth has truly broken through to a deeper understanding of inner-Trinitarian relations that has still to exercise its potential influence on the development of our understanding of God the Holy Trinity.

How can we sum up the work of a theological giant like Barth? Perhaps the best way is to start by suggesting that, for him, the orthodox Christian tradition was a historical fact, a reality that needed to be appropriated and defended. He was in no sense a liberal who wanted to reject the past as of no value and create a new understanding of ultimate reality based on scientifically observed facts as opposed to psychological myths. Nor was he a traditionalist, if by that is meant someone whose principal concern is to maintain or restore something inherited from the past. Barth wanted to make the revelation that had been given in the past speak to the present (and by implication to the future) in a way that was faithful to its content but that could also communicate to people today. We must never forget the proclamatory aspect of his theology: what could not be preached should not be taught or confessed. When it came time for confession, as it did in Germany after Hitler came to power, it is noticeable how Barth defaulted to the standard Christian forms of doctrinal statement; there is nothing in the Barmen Declaration to suggest an impractical, airy-fairy theology, nor was he ever an ivory tower academic. Whether he succeeded in his aims may be questioned, but we ought at least to recognize what those aims were and to accept that his intentions were fully orthodox and in line with the Reformed tradition.[48]

At the same time, we must also recognize that Barth's critics have been too numerous and too varied for us to be able to dismiss them as misguided, in the way that some of his supporters have tried to do. It is not just traditionalism

[46] Ibid., IV/2, 15.64.2, 42.

[47] See Bruce L. McCormack, "The Lord and Giver of Life: A 'Barthian' Defense of the *Filioque*," in *Rethinking Trinitarian Theology: Disputed Questions and Contemporary Issues in Trinitarian Theology*, ed. Robert J. Woźniak and Giulio Maspero (London: T & T Clark, 2012), 248–250.

[48] See Michael S. Horton, "A Stony Jar: The Legacy of Karl Barth for Evangelical Theology," in Gibson and Strange, *Engaging with Barth*, 346–381, who attempts to do just this, while maintaining a critical stance toward the outcome.

or an inability to appreciate the grandeur of Barth's theological vision that have provoked unease in so many circles, but a genuine perception that there are many loose ends in his thinking that often make it difficult to determine what he was really saying or to construct a coherent whole out of it. This is not necessarily fatal, of course, and may even be a mark of greatness, as it was in Martin Luther, whose thought is often equally difficult to pin down. But it may also be in part due to Barth's own project and the methods that he adopted to further it. Anyone who takes an existing body of tradition and who attempts to give it a comprehensive makeover is almost bound to come unstuck sooner or later. Barth's legacy will survive to the extent that it can be incorporated into that tradition and passed on to future generations. Most likely it will be his thoughts on the Trinity that will prove to be the most long-lasting and fruitful, but even that remains to be seen. The jury is still out, and it looks as though it will be some time yet before we can say with assurance not only that Barth was a great theologian but also in what precisely that greatness consisted.

To date, Barth's influence on succeeding generations of Protestant theologians has been considerable. Relatively few of them have followed his approach, but they have been challenged by him to recast their theology in a mold that will do justice both to the biblical revelation and to secular thought. If there is some truth in the charge that Barth failed to address the latter adequately because of his repudiation of natural theology, there is more truth in the fact that it would be much harder for post-Barthian theologians to develop a philosophical theology that failed to take either the Bible or the concept of divine revelation into account. The belief that religion is essentially an expression of human self-consciousness did not disappear, as Barth would have wished, but it was being challenged by the claims of one who was Wholly Other, and theologians could not avoid taking that into account.

The effects of Barth's clarion call for a new departure in theology can be seen most clearly in the way it caused erstwhile colleagues like Emil Brunner (1889–1966) and Rudolf Bultmann (1884–1976) to dissent from it and take different paths—different not only from Barth but from each other. Brunner initially followed Barth in his dialectical approach to theological questions, believing that a new equilibrium had to be established between God and man, theology and anthropology. But as Barth leaned more to the side of pure theology, Brunner went the other way, or (as he saw it) tried to maintain the earlier balance that he thought Barth had lost. Like Barth, his focus was Christological, but it was typical of his outlook that his great book on the subject was called *The Mediator*, a title that reflected the vision he had of

Jesus as the link between the two worlds that he was trying to hold together.[49] That was followed by *Nature and Grace* and *Man in Revolt*, two works that developed his theological anthropology, the first of which led Barth to pen a blistering reply, accusing him of having abandoned the theological task altogether.[50] Unbowed by Barth's reaction, Brunner went on to publish *The Divine-human Encounter*, a major work in which he outlined the contrast (as he saw it) between the rationalist conception of truth inherited from the ancient Greeks with the biblical emphasis on personal relationships and communication.[51] After that he began work on his own dogmatics, which appeared between 1946 and 1960.[52]

Brunner's basic approach was that the closer we get to questions of existence and the meaning of the human person in relation to God, the more we are affected by sin and alienation from him. Conversely, the further away we are from these questions, the less we have to do with existential problems and the more closely connected we are with the world around us:

> The nearer anything lies to the center of existence where we are concerned with the whole, that is, with man's relation to God and the being of the person, the greater is the disturbance of rational knowledge by sin; the further away anything lies from the center, the less the disturbance is felt, and the less difference there is between knowing as a believer or as an unbeliever. This disturbance reaches its maximum in theology and its minimum in the exact sciences, and zero in the sphere of the formal. Hence it is meaningless to speak of a "Christian mathematics."[53]

For Brunner, the question of truth was above all the province of the encounter between God and man, the famous "I and Thou" as opposed to the rationalistic "I and It" to which he contrasted it.[54] Unfortunately it was the latter that had dominated theology in the modern period, with catastrophic results:

---

[49] Emil Brunner, *The Mediator* (London: Lutterworth, 1934), translated from the second German edition of *Der Mittler* (Tübingen: J. C. B. Mohr, 1st ed. 1927; 2nd ed., 1930).

[50] Emil Brunner, *Natur und Gnade* (Tübingen, J. C. B. Mohr, 1st ed., 1934; 2nd ed. 1935); Karl Barth, *Nein! Antwort an Emil Brunner* (Munich: Chr. Kaiser Verlag, 1934). Brunner's second edition was greatly expanded and contained a reply to Barth's accusations. Both works were translated into English and published in one volume as *Natural Theology* (London: Geoffrey Bles, 1946); Emil Brunner, *Der Mensch im Widerspruch* (Berlin: Furche Verlag, 1937), English trans., *Man in Revolt* (London: R. T. S.—Lutterworth, 1939).

[51] Emil Brunner, *Wahrheit als Begegnung* (Tübingen: J. C. B. Mohr, 1937); English trans., *The Divine-human Encounter* (London: SCM, 1944).

[52] See Emil Brunner, *Offenbarung und Vernunft* (Zurich: Zwingli Verlag, 1941), translated into English as *Revelation and Reason: The Christian Doctrine of Faith and Knowledge* (London: SCM, 1947), a prolegomenon to *Dogmatik*, 3 vols. (Zurich: Zwingli Verlag, 1946–1960); trans. *Dogmatics*, 3 vols. (London: Lutterworth, 1949–1962).

[53] Brunner, *Revelation and Reason*, 383.

[54] Brunner was deeply influenced by the Jewish philosopher Martin Buber, who published his famous *Ich und Du* in 1936 (Berlin: Schocken Verlag, 1936); English trans., *I and Thou* (Edinburgh: T & T Clark, 1937). Buber had got his idea mainly from Kierkegaard, but as we have already seen, it went back ultimately to Feuerbach.

> This shows us the confusion that is created when the doctrine of God, instead of starting from this disclosure of his personal being as subject, starts from any kind of neutral definition of being, such as that of the theology determined by Platonism, Aristotelianism and Neo-Platonism.[55]

Faith in Jesus Christ, the unique way by which we encounter the personal being of God, does not come from human knowledge, however exalted, but only by the work of the Holy Spirit, who comes to us through the witness of those who encountered Jesus in the flesh and proclaimed his message to the world:

> Faith in Jesus Christ is not based upon a previous faith in the Bible, but is based solely upon the witness of the Holy Spirit; this witness, however, does not come to us save through the witness of the Apostles. . . . [Scripture] is a "word" inspired by the Spirit of God, yet at the same time it is a human message; its "human character" means that it is colored by the frailty and imperfection of all that is human.[56]

Here we can see that for all his many differences with Barth, Brunner came down in the end on the side of the need for a personal relationship with God in Christ, which was only possible by the power of the Holy Spirit and was mediated through the Bible, whose human character merely reinforced Brunner's conviction that God speaks to man in the latter's context, warts and all.

Very different from this was the reaction of Rudolf Bultmann, who was also an admirer of Barth in their early days. Bultmann spent most of his career at Marburg, where he taught from 1921 to 1951, but it was only after he retired that his work became widely known outside German theological circles and that he became notorious for his belief in the need to "demythologize" the Christian faith. Unlike many of his contemporaries, Bultmann has left us a personal memoir in which he explained his theological development:

> It seemed to me that . . . the new theology [of Barth] correctly saw that Christian faith is the answer to the Word of the transcendent God which encounters man, and that theology has to deal with this Word and the man who has been encountered by it. This judgment, however, has never led me to a simple condemnation of "liberal" theology; on the contrary, I have endeavored throughout my entire work to carry farther the tradition of historical-critical research as it was practiced in "liberal" theology. . . . In doing so, the work of existential philosophy, which I came to know through my discussions

[55] Brunner, *Dogmatics*, I (*The Christian Doctrine of God*), 141.
[56] Ibid., 34.

> with Martin Heidegger, became of decisive significance for me. . . . In my efforts to make philosophy fruitful for theology, I have come more and more into opposition to Karl Barth. I remain grateful to him, however, for the decisive things I have learned from him.[57]

Bultmann was preoccupied with what he saw as the need to reconceive the relationship between divine activity and human understanding so that it might fit the worldview of the modern, scientific age. In earlier times, people readily attributed events to the work of angels, demons, and so on, but this is no longer the case. Today we reject such things as "mythological," but the mistake has been to throw God out along with the mythology surrounding him. It was this missing sense of God that Bultmann sought to recover:

> In mythological thinking the action of God, whether in nature, history, human fortune, or the inner life of the soul, is understood as an action that intervenes between the natural, or historical or psychological course of events; it breaks and links them at the same time. The divine causality is inserted as a link in the chain of the events which follow one another according to the causal nexus. This is meant by the popular notion that a miraculous event cannot be understood except as a miracle, that is, as the effect of a supernatural cause. In such thinking, the action of God is indeed conceived in the same way as secular actions or events are conceived, for the divine power which effects miracles is considered as a natural power.[58]

In contrast to this, Bultmann insisted that divine action in the world can only be perceived by the believer who interprets events as works of God. Such an interpretation is possible only for those who have faith; others will see the same events differently because they do not share the same presuppositions. At the same time, Bultmann rejected the idea of a sovereign divine providence, which to him was nothing other than pantheism. Instead, he believed that God works through specific events in the world, of which the coming of Jesus Christ was far and away the most important:

> Pantheism is a conviction given in advance, a general world-view, which affirms that every event in the world is the work of God because God is immanent in the world. Christian faith, by contrast, holds that God acts on me, speaks to me here and now. The Christian believes this because he knows that

[57] Charles W. Kegley, ed., *The Theology of Rudolf Bultmann* (New York: Harper & Row; and London: SCM, 1966), xxiv.

[58] Rudolf Bultmann, *Jesus Christ and Mythology* (London: SCM, 1958; reissued 2012), 61. The German original was published subsequently as *Jesus Christus und die Mythologie* (Hamburg: Furche Verlag, 1964).

> he is addressed by the grace of God which meets him in the Word of God, in Jesus Christ. God's grace opens his eyes to see that "in everything God works for good with those who love him"[59] This faith is not a knowledge possessed once and for all; it is not a general world-view. It can be realized only here and now.[60]

This realization was the special province of the *kêrygma*, or proclamation, which brought the living Word into the world and made Christ real. In its own way, Bultmann's understanding of this is paralleled in the Roman Catholic teaching of the "real presence" of Christ in the sacrament—God comes into the world in a form that men can understand and absorb. The need for preaching to speak to our situation became for Bultmann the main justification for his work of demythologizing—the Bible, and in particular, the New Testament, had to be stripped of its ancient cultural baggage and restated for modern consumption. It was at this point that alarm bells began to ring in the wider theological world. Who determined what constituted "myth"? If there were no angels, why was there a God? What was it that made Jesus Christ special for us today, when he lived and taught in a context with which we have no affinity? Should real demythologization not lead to an abandonment of Christianity altogether, and its replacement by some kind of world-philosophy that is unencumbered by such embarrassments as the resurrection of Jesus from the dead, which (in Bultmann's view) was clearly unhistorical?

In trying to make the gospel intelligible to "modern man," Bultmann had evacuated it of any link to historical fact, and therefore of any connection to empirical reality. The problem was that Christianity could not be rewritten in this way without ceasing to be itself, a conclusion that Bultmann resisted but that was evident to those who read his work. Those who followed him soon left the church, or (if they remained in it) ceased to believe what it taught. Matters came to a head when Bultmann's ideas reached a wider public and had to be refuted by those who realized that the alternative was the dissolution of theology altogether.[61]

Yet for all his faults, Bultmann remained, as he himself confessed, deeply indebted to Karl Barth. His kerygmatic approach was Barthian, as was his focus on the "Christ-event" and its central importance for our knowledge of God. In some ways, it may be said that he took Barth's theology to its logical

[59] Rom. 8:28.
[60] Bultmann, *Jesus Christ and Mythology*, 63–64.
[61] See, for example, John Hick, ed., *The Myth of God Incarnate* (London: SCM, 1977), which caused a furor when it was published. It was soon answered by Michael Green, ed., *The Truth of God Incarnate* (London: Hodder & Stoughton, 1977), but the damage had been done. Since then, it may be said, Bultmann's theology has gone into steep decline and is no longer influential.

conclusion by divorcing it from the created order and making it indeed "wholly other." But although Bultmann spoke of Christ and the Spirit, he had no Trinitarian theology to speak of, and no conception that a relationship with God was a union with him in his inner divine life, not a communication from some inaccessible universe that we must accept purely on faith in the one who proclaimed it. In that sense, Bultmann can be regarded as someone who ushered in the most recent phase of theological development, not in the way he intended, but in reaction to it, and that reaction, like his own initial impulse toward "demythologization," is ultimately traceable to the pervasive influence of Karl Barth on his thinking.

Another theological trajectory that owed its origin to Barth was that of Dietrich Bonhoeffer (1906–1945), a man whose political involvement in opposition to Hitler landed him in prison and cost him his life in the closing days of the Second World War. His status as a martyr gave him a postwar prominence that he would otherwise not have had, but his connection with Barth was a real one and lends added interest to his reaction to the man he regarded as a mentor until the very end. Bonhoeffer responded positively to Barth's emphasis on the sovereign majesty of the transcendent God, but came to believe that Barth had developed this in a one-sided way. For Bonhoeffer, God not only revealed himself to mankind in Jesus Christ, but by becoming a man himself, he also identified with the human race in all its complex ambiguity. This came out clearly in the Christian confession that Christ was "sinless." In what respect was this true? As Bonhoeffer expressed it,

> Simply stated, the sinlessness of Jesus fails if it is based upon the observable acts of Jesus. . . . They are not sinless, but ambiguous. . . . The assertion of the sinlessness of Jesus in his deeds is not an evident moral judgment, but an assertion of faith that it is he who performs these ambiguous deeds, he it is who is in eternity without sin.[62]

For Bonhoeffer, the imitation of Christ could not be a striving to attain to a heavenly reality that is beyond human achievement or understanding, but rather a seeking to be united with him in his earthly life, which shattered the conventional morality of his time and challenged the powers that be with a new and (to them) alien way of life:

> Ethical thinking in terms of spheres, then, is invalidated by faith in the revelation of the ultimate reality in Jesus Christ, and this means that there is no

[62] Dietrich Bonhoeffer, *Christology* (London: Collins, 1966; reissued, 1978), 113. Originally published as D. Bonhoeffer, *Gesammelte Schriften*, 6 vols. (Munich: Chr. Kaiser Verlag, 1958–1974), vol. 3.

> real possibility of being a Christian outside the reality of the world and that there is no real worldly existence outside the reality of Jesus Christ. There is no place to which the Christian can withdraw from the world, whether it be outwardly or in the sphere of the inner life. . . . His worldliness does not divide him from the world. Belonging wholly to Christ, he stands at the same time wholly in the world.[63]

The ultimate effect of this was a complete inversion of Christianity, as can be seen from his interpretation of the atonement. Far from taking away the sins of the world, Christ, according to Bonhoeffer, makes everyone who believes in him guilty, and therefore bound to sacrifice himself in a way that is analogous to his own death on the cross:

> Jesus took upon himself the guilt of all men, and for that reason every man who acts responsibly becomes guilty. If any man tries to escape guilt in responsibility he detaches himself from the ultimate reality of human existence . . .[64]

From there it was but a short step to the "religionless Christianity" that Bonhoeffer has become famous for. A man who has to take Christ on himself, to become a little Christ in his own circumstances, is not someone who has been saved but someone who has been condemned. Of course, Bonhoeffer saw this condemnation as salvation—deliverance from the selfishness and meaningless existence that modern man has been forced into—and it is understandable how people who are tired of the spiritual emptiness of the consumer society would find his spiritual call to arms attractive. Only later (and perhaps too late) is it likely to dawn on them that, in the process, God has been lost, not found. Bonhoeffer commands our respect because he put his principles into practice and paid the highest price for them, but like Bultmann's theology, if in a different way, his answer to the problem of man's communication with God ended up by cutting it off altogether.

Another admirer of Barth's who went a different way was Paul Tillich (1886–1965). Dismissed from his university chair in Frankfurt because of his open opposition to Hitler, he emigrated to the United States and taught at Union Theological Seminary in New York (1933–1955). For that reason, his thought became widely known in the English-speaking world and his later works were written in English. Tillich dissented from Barth because he felt that

---

[63] Dietrich Bonhoeffer, *Ethics* (London: SCM, 1955), 66–67. Originally published as *Ethik* (Munich: Chr. Kaiser Verlag, 1949).

[64] Bonhoeffer, *Ethics*, 10.

the latter was too "supernaturalistic" in his orientation—a complaint common to Brunner, Bultmann, and Bonhoeffer as well. Tillich chose to adopt a purely anthropocentric approach, claiming that people are concerned primarily with their own lives and what they might mean. In his view, whatever was most important to an individual was that individual's god, and so the real question was what value our own "ultimate concern" had. To commit oneself to something that was merely transient, like a political program, was to invite disappointment, although to engage with something that could only be accepted on faith was an act of courage that might entail sacrifice of a different kind:

> If faith is understood as belief that something is true, doubt is incompatible with the act of faith. If faith is understood as being ultimately concerned, doubt is a necessary element in it. It is a consequence of the risk of faith. . . . It does not reject every concrete truth, but it is aware of the element of insecurity in every existential truth. At the same time, the doubt which is implied in faith accepts this insecurity and takes it into itself as an act of courage. Faith includes courage. Therefore, it can include the doubt about itself.[65]

The biblical picture of creation, in which Adam and Eve are made to live with God but then fall away from their state of innocence, had to be rejected as a myth, said Tillich, because in his view, the primal state of man could only be one of unrealized potential—and therefore it was open to the possibility of going wrong (as it did). In his words,

> Orthodox theologians have heaped perfection after perfection upon Adam before the fall, making him equal with the picture of the Christ. This procedure is not only absurd; it makes the fall completely unintelligible. Mere potentiality or dreaming innocence is not perfection. Only the conscious union of existence and essence is perfection. . . . The symbol "Adam before the fall" must be understood as the dreaming innocence of undecided potentialities.[66]

Man's decision to take charge of his own life was the end of innocence, but it was also the departure from essence to existence, a tragic and dangerous situation that comes about as the result of claiming personal freedom. Sin is not disobedience to the law of God but alienation from the ground of our being. In the midst of all this, however, Tillich retained his Barthian belief that God is "wholly other." He is not a "being" in the normal sense of the word, because to call him that would be to define him and therefore limit him. Nor is he "life"

[65] Paul Tillich, *The Dynamics of Faith* (New York: Harper, 1956), 18–20.

[66] Paul Tillich, *Systematic Theology*, 3 vols. (Chicago: University of Chicago Press, 1951–1963), 2:34.

as we understand it, because if he were, he would not be both the source of our life and completely different from us. What links us to God, said Tillich, is not our "essence" but our personhood:

> The symbol "personal God" is absolutely fundamental because an existential relation is a person-to-person relation. Man cannot be ultimately concerned about anything that is less than personal, but since personality includes individuality, the question arises in what sense God can be called an individual. . . . "Personal God" does not mean that God is a person. It means that God is the ground of everything personal and that he carries within himself the ontological power of personality.[67]

Tillich believed that in Jesus Christ the eternal connection between God and man that had been broken by man's desire for personal freedom was overcome. Jesus had a God-consciousness that overcame his alienation and anxiety, making it possible for him to live the life of a new being, one who was totally in harmony with both God and his fellow man. He was a real, historical figure, but it was not in that that his importance lay. Rather, it was in Peter's confession of him as the Christ, because Peter saw what Jesus really was: God in human flesh. It is this that we must see today, but in ways that fit our own contexts. Jesus may appear to us as an African-American or as a woman, not because that is what he was historically but because that is what he is now, for those who need to see him in that way. This reality is multifaceted, but it is always historical—present in the experience of living, breathing human beings. Transcendence is completely rejected, and in this respect, Tillich was far removed from Barth. His vision of the kingdom of God expresses this well:

> It is not a victory of the kingdom of God in history if the individual tries to take himself out of participation in history in the name of the transcendent kingdom of God. . . . For the transcendent is actual within the inner-historical. . . . The more one's destiny is directly determined by one's active participation, the more historical sacrifice is demanded. Where such sacrifice is maturely accepted, a victory of the kingdom of God has occurred.[68]

Tillich's theology is curiously apophatic and mystical. God's essence is hidden from our eyes, and our only contact with him is personal. The difference between him and the great mystics is that for Tillich the personal dimension is not Trinitarian. As with his other twentieth-century colleagues, the "I-Thou"

---

[67] Ibid., 1:244–245.
[68] Ibid., 3:392.

relationship between God and man is a one-on-one, not one in the fellowship of the three. There is no divine life above and beyond human life in which we are called to participate. Tillich's insistence that we cannot leave this world behind in order to find peace with God in some transcendental "kingdom" is an important corrective to the kind of popular piety that justifies noninvolvement in human affairs and the toleration of rank injustice (for others, of course) by a kind of "pie-in-the-sky-when-you-die" philosophy, but it does so at the cost of abandoning the transcendent altogether. As Barth would have been the first to notice, that is not the Christian message, and so it has proved. Tillich is remembered as an important theologian in his day, but he has not been widely followed and this situation seems unlikely to change in the foreseeable future.

By the middle of the twentieth century it was becoming clear that there was a problem with the doctrine of God arising from the way in which he was perceived to interact with human beings. No one could doubt that in this world "change and decay in all around I see," and that if God were truly active in human history, then he must somehow be capable of sharing in the evolution of his creation.[69] This concern underlay much of the reaction against the theology of Karl Barth, who seemed to many to be positing a God so "wholly other" that he could never be thought of in that way. In ancient times there had been philosophies that said that the universe was in a constant state of flux—in their different ways, Heraclitus (540?–480? BC), Democritus (460–370 BC), and Epicurus (341–270 BC) all thought so. But by the time Christianity developed a systematic theology, it was generally agreed that the "supreme being" was unchanging, and therefore presumably "static," since if he were not, his being would be contingent on events and therefore not truly supreme.

This worldview, which was shared by theologians and scientists alike, came under severe strain when physicists started to question whether there is such a thing as "substance" or "being" at all, and preferred to speak about "energy" instead. Energy is by definition active and moving all the time, and it is the ultimate reality. If there is a God, he must therefore share this characteristic, something that had not previously been properly understood, let alone confessed, even though the Bible clearly presents him as an active force in human affairs. That God contained inner movement was also implicit in Hegel's understanding of the Trinity, since if two opposite "persons" combined to produce a third, something must have been going on, even if our finite minds find it hard to conceive what it was. The revival of the idea that ultimate reality was dynamic, not static, and the increasing desire to involve God in the affairs of

[69] The quotation is a line from the well-known hymn *Abide with Me*, written by Henry F. Lyte in 1847. Lyte's message, of course, was that while the world changes, God does not.

the world combined to encourage, if not actually produce, a new development that is known today as "Process Theology."

Process Theology can be traced back to Alfred North Whitehead (1861–1947), the son of an Anglican clergyman but not himself a theologian or even a Christian.[70] Whitehead believed that the world is constantly engaged in a process of creation in which things interact with one another, changing, developing, and combining as they go along. This development is complex, but is the work of actually existing entities that mutate and eventually perish over time, but out of them come new forms of being that manifest the same basic characteristics, which are in themselves unchanging. These constant factors have real potential, and in their various manifestations they are all heading toward a goal of self-realization. This is a constant factor in their makeup and is a sign of their immortality, even if the forms in which they appear "change and decay" over time. Such a vision of the universe demands the existence of a fixed, eternal reality because otherwise there would be nothing to aim for, no standard by which development could be measured. The ancient Greeks thought that the eternal flux was essentially cyclical—what goes around comes around and, in the end, nothing really changes at all. But Whitehead could not accept that. He believed in linear, not cyclical, time and therefore in a goal to which everything was headed. That goal was God.

God was the one, Whitehead argued, who made sense of the process, who started it off, who assured its orderly development toward its goals—and who exemplified it supremely in himself. This apparent paradox was possible because God was dipolar. At one pole, he was a constant—ordering and adjusting the eternal things that he then prepared for entry into the temporal world. Colors, for example, can fade away and change, but red is always red, blue is always blue, and so on. They reappear in different circumstances but always look the same, or so Whitehead believed. The problem was that this God had no "reality" within the time and space framework because he was above and beyond it. This was where his other pole came into play. His primordial nature entered into the flow of the universe and took the consequences—mutual engagement with other entities that were also in a state of flux. This interaction meant that while one pole of his being was unchanging, the other was constantly growing

[70] See Charles Hartshorne and W. Creighton Peden, *Whitehead's View of Reality* (Newcastle: Cambridge Scholars, 2010); Roland Faber, *God as Poet of the World: Exploring Process Theologies* (Louisville: Westminster John Knox, 2008); Murray Code, *Process, Reality, and the Power of Symbols: Thinking with A. N. Whitehead* (Basingstoke: Palgrave Macmillan, 2007); David R. Griffin, *Whitehead's Radically Different Postmodern Philosophy: An Argument for Its Contemporary Relevance* (Albany: State University of New York Press, 2007). On Process Theology in general, see Bruce G. Epperly, *Process Theology: A Guide for the Perplexed* (London: T & T Clark, 2011); George W. Shields, *Process and Analysis: Whitehead, Hartshorne, and the Analytic Tradition* (Albany: State University of New York Press, 2003).

and developing by its contact with other things, to which it related in a state of mutual interdependence:

> God, as well as being primordial, is also consequent. He is the beginning and the end. . . . Thus, by reason of the relativity of all things, there is a reaction of the world on God. . . . God's conceptual nature is unchanged, by reason of its final completeness. But his derivative nature is consequent upon the creative advance of the world.[71]

Whitehead's doctrine of God was truly radical. He broke with nearly two thousand years of Christian tradition by claiming that God has potential (*dynamis*) and not merely power (*energeia*), or "realized potential." In the latter vision, which had been standard in Christian tradition, God was an unmoved and unmovable sovereign whose will had to be obeyed, and there was no room for love, dialogue, or what we would now call personal interaction. A dynamic God, on the other hand, was capable of growth and development, which did not really constitute "change" because it was part of his nature. God would only "change" if he stood still, which is what classical Christian theism insisted he did!

Whether Whitehead could think of God as the Creator of the world rather depends on what is meant by the term "creation." At one pole of his being, he was definitely the initiator, so perhaps in that sense the word "creator" is not inappropriate. But at the other pole he was constantly changing and developing himself by interacting with other things. This concept was a brilliant answer to the problem of human freedom and the existence of evil, since interaction of the kind Whitehead envisaged could take place only among equals, allowing for the possibility that God's will might be thwarted in some way by the will of others. But can Christian theology accept that God is not sovereign over creation and that he can be defeated by evil (if "evil" means something contrary to his will)? This was the possibility that Whitehead left hanging, and is one of the reasons why his theistic vision of the universe cannot really be called "Christian."

Whitehead's philosophical ideas might have died an early death had they not been taken up and developed by Charles Hartshorne (1897–2000), who is the true originator of Process Theology.[72] Like Whitehead, Hartshorne was the

[71] Alfred N. Whitehead, *Process and Reality: An Essay in Cosmology* (Cambridge: Cambridge University Press, 1929), 523–524. This book was the published version of his Gifford Lectures, delivered in Edinburgh in 1927–1928. The Gifford Lectures were established to promote the claims of religion based on the evidence of natural science.

[72] See Alan Gragg, *Charles Hartshorne* (Waco, TX: Word, 1973); Robert Kane and Stephen H. Phillips, *Hartshorne, Process Philosophy and Theology* (Albany: State University of New York Press, 1997); Donald W. Viney, *Charles Hartshorne and the Existence of God* (Albany: State University of New York Press, 1985).

son of an Anglican minister. He studied at Harvard after the First World War and spent nearly three years in Germany sitting at the feet of eminent philosophers like Edmund Husserl (1859–1938) and Martin Heidegger (1889–1976), whose influence on Rudolf Bultmann we have already seen. He then returned to Harvard, where for a short time he was Whitehead's teaching and research assistant. After that he taught philosophy and theology in Chicago (1938–1955) before moving to Atlanta (Emory University) and eventually to Texas. He lived to an extreme old age and was active almost to the very end, allowing him to develop his ideas over a long period of time and even to outlive some of them.

Hartshorne believed that classical Christian theism had become untenable in the modern world, but rejected the common assumption that atheism was the only alternative. Instead of that, he proposed the idea of *panentheism*, a term that was apparently invented by Karl Christian Friedrich Krause (1781–1832), one of Hegel's pupils and disciples. This was the belief that the universe is part of God's being and that they interact with one another, but that God is bigger than the universe. It also means that God cannot interfere with human freedom, and because he is involved in time, he cannot know the future either. In this view, God is not absolutely perfect (the idea of classical theism), nor is he completely lacking in perfection. Instead, he is partially perfect, that is to say, in some respects he manifests absolute perfection but in other respects he has not reached that goal—at least not yet. Whether he can (or will) is not yet known—that is the hidden future.[73]

Hartshorne's belief allowed him to redefine what classical theism had always understood by the "love" of God. Instead of seeing this as a superhuman benevolence reaching down from on high, he thought of it as empathy—God coming into our lives and sharing our pain and suffering.[74] Hartshorne did not think of God as a person or as a Trinity of persons in the classical sense, but he did believe that Jesus Christ was the supreme historical manifestation of divine love. Unlike many others in the Protestant world, Hartshorne made no attempt to downplay the historical reality of Christ's death and resurrection, both of which fitted into Hartshorne's scheme of eternal growth and development. Nor was he interested in mythology as a theological concept, for much the same reason. In fact, he was quite forthright in his challenge to the Christian world:

> I can only say that if it is Jesus as literally divine who loves men, really loves them, then my point, so far as I can see, is granted. . . . Instead of simply

[73] Charles Hartshorne, *Man's Vision of God and the Logic of Theism* (Chicago, IL and New York: Willet, Clark, 1941), 11–12.

[74] Charles Hartshorne, *Reality as Social Process: Studies in Metaphysics and Religion* (Glencoe, IL: Free Press, 1953), 147.

> adding Jesus to an unreconstructed idea of a non-loving God, should we not take him as proof that God really is love—just that, without equivocation?[75]

Hartshorne was prepared to believe that in Christ we see the work of a man who was so closely in tune with the spirit of the universe that he fully manifested the reality of God, but why it should have been Jesus of Nazareth who deserved this exalted status, rather than anyone else, is unclear. In Hartshorne's case it probably reflects the lingering power that religious tradition has over the minds of those who have been brought up in a Christian society. Hartshorne's Jesus was a myth constructed by his own mind, but it was no less powerful or attractive for that. For what Hartshorne attributed to Jesus and claimed had been brought to perfection in him is a reality that we can all share in. The doctrine of the Trinity, which Christians constructed to explain Jesus and his meaning for them expresses that experience very clearly. The cosmic force that we call God is a creative source of existence and may be defined as our innate potential as human beings. This creative source cannot remain quiescent because that is not its nature, and it must express itself. It has done this most fully in Jesus, who represents the supreme achievement of human fulfillment. But that is not enough, since what flows together in Christ must then flow out again into the world, inviting a responsive movement on the part of all who come into contact with it. This is what Christians call the work of the Holy Spirit, the burst of energy that creates a new man and a new society.

It is hard for an uncommitted observer not to conclude that this is a lot of wishful thinking, but beyond that, Process Theology raises a number of questions that seem to be virtually impossible to answer. Are human beings superior to other created things because of their personhood? In a world of energy, if human persons are agents because otherwise they would not be able to participate in the flow of reality, is this not true of other beings as well? And what about "reactionaries" who resist the tide of history or thwart the will of God, as Hartshorne believed was possible? If progress and development are part of ultimate reality itself, is resistance to them even conceivable? What about those who do not realize their potential? Are such people to be condemned for having turned away from God? How can anyone know what his or her potential is in the first place? As a system of thought, Process Theology leaves a lot of loose ends, but that does not worry its advocates, because in a world of constant motion, "loose ends" are what one would expect to find. Freedom is bought at the cost of coherence, but while this may appeal to particular individuals, it is hardly adequate as an explanation of the universe, which must hold together

[75] Ibid., 24.

somehow. Divine providence may have its difficulties, but if it is removed from the equation the danger is that everything will fall apart, which is surely worse.

Process Theology is very difficult for most people to understand because its advocates go in for complex technical vocabulary that means little or nothing to the uninitiated. Even so, it has been defended by its devotees as a truly creative and transforming kind of Christian theology, as the following testimony indicates:

> . . . I have learned that theology, at its best, seeks to transform people's lives by providing an insightful vision of reality that enables persons [*sic*] to find meaning, inspiration, and challenge. I have found this connection between theological vision and spiritual and ethical practices especially to be true for the movement in contemporary theology described as Process Theology. Once persons [*sic*] begin to understand Process Theology's innovative ways of describing God's relationship with the world, the problem of evil, human creativity, and freedom, and the ethical and spiritual significance of [the] non-human world, they recognize the unique contribution that Process Theology makes to understand[ing] religious life, social transformation, and ethical behavior. They also discover how different Process Theology is from more traditional theologies . . .[76]

A major problem for Process Theology is the moral question of good and evil. If everything is in constant flux and individuals are able to participate in creating their own future, and if this creativity is inextricably linked to God, it is hard to see what place there can be for the concept of evil. How would anyone recognize it, especially if it is what one person actively desires? To take an extreme example, Adolf Hitler was purposeful and creative, and few people did as much as he did to achieve his vision, but no one believes that this was a good thing. Process Theology resolves this problem by denying the nature of God. As Whitehead put it, "The limitation of God is his goodness. . . . it is not true that God is in all respects infinite."[77] To put limits like this on God compromises his sovereignty, and that raises all kinds of other difficulties that Process Theology has no way of dealing with. The Christian tradition has always had to grapple with the problem of evil, and it would be foolish to pretend that it has found a ready answer to the sin and suffering that plague human existence. But to deny the sovereignty of God is to deny his absolute power to save, and that Christians cannot accept. In the final analysis, it is hard not to conclude that, although Process Theology offers us freedom, in fact it

[76] Epperly, *Process Theology*, 3.

[77] Alfred N. Whitehead, *Religion in the Making* (New York: Meridian, 1972), 147.

leads us into uncertainty and fear because of the limits that it places on the infinite power of God.

Process Theology is a diffuse concept that has seldom been adopted in its entirely, or perhaps it would be better to say that different versions of it have been proposed, with varying results.[78] But the underlying idea that God is dynamic and not static has had a much broader influence. Perhaps the most substantial contribution along these lines has been made by Eberhard Jüngel (1934–), whose main idea may be expressed as "God's being is in becoming."[79] Like so many other Protestant theologians in Germany, Jüngel saw himself as a disciple of Karl Barth, and it was in that capacity that he first entered the theological fray, claiming to represent Barth's "true" teaching in contrast to Helmut Gollwitzer (1908–1993), another follower of Barth, who, in Jüngel's opinion, had misrepresented the master's teaching.[80] In what purported to be a reply to Gollwitzer, Jüngel chose selected passages of Barth, mostly from the *Church Dogmatics*, to demonstrate that Gollwitzer was wrong on at least two counts.[81] One is that Gollwitzer had said that God was not a being in the usual sense of the word, but that in his historical dealings with us he was effectively a being, because otherwise he could not communicate with us. This left him stating that God was a being and nonbeing at the same time. In Jüngel's estimation, that would mean that God once was, but "is" no longer, since his revelation to mankind is now complete and ended with the death of Christ on the cross. The second problem that Jüngel saw with Gollwitzer is that the latter claimed that God was a "being in and for itself," though how that could be the case when he was nonbeing in himself and only became a being in relation to others, he did not explain. In response to this, Jüngel wrote,

> If we want to think of God's being "in and for itself," as postulated by Gollwitzer, in a Christian manner, i.e., in conformity with revelation, *must* we not then think of this being as being which, in a certain way, is already in advance of history, in that God as Father, Son and Spirit is already so to speak "ours in advance"?[82] The historical power of God's revelation which stooped

[78] See the discussion in Livingston, *Modern Christian Thought*, 2:309–339.

[79] The title of his book on the Trinity. Eberhard Jüngel, *Gottes Sein ist im Werden: verantwortliche Rede vom Sein Gottes bei Karl Barth*, 2nd ed. (Tübingen: J. C. B. Mohr, 1966), translated as *The Doctrine of the Trinity: God's Being Is in Becoming* (Edinburgh: Scottish Academic Press, 1976). See also Eberhard Jüngel, *Gott als Geheimnis der Welt*, 3rd ed. (Tübingen: J. C. B. Mohr, 1977), translated as *God as the Mystery of the World: On the Foundation of the Theology of the Crucified One in the Dispute between Theism and Atheism* (Edinburgh: T & T Clark, 1983). On Jüngel's theology, see John B. Webster, *Eberhard Jüngel: An Introduction to His Theology* (Cambridge: Cambridge University Press, 1986); John B. Webster, ed., *The Possibilities of Theology: Studies in the Theology of Eberhard Jüngel in His Sixtieth Year* (Edinburgh: T & T Clark, 1994).

[80] Helmut Gollwitzer, *Die Existenz Gottes im Bekenntnis des Glaubens* (Munich: Chr. Kaiser Verlag, 1963), translated as *The Existence of God as Confessed by Faith* (London: SCM, 1965).

[81] Jüngel, *Trinity*, xii-xvii.

[82] Here Jüngel referred to Barth, *Church Dogmatics*, I/1, 383, and I/2, 34, to support his case.

down even to the acceptance of the utter weakness of death—*estaurôthê ex astheneias*, he was crucified through weakness[83]—must have already been grounded in the pre-historical power (*Potenz*) of the being of God as Father, Son and Holy Spirit.[84]

Jüngel next went on to explain why this matters. According to him (and therefore, as he would claim, according to Barth also), the question of God's being or existence—Gollwitzer used the two words interchangeably, which was another source of potential confusion—was fundamental to theology:

> The being of God is the hermeneutical problem of theology. More exactly: the fact that the being of God *proceeds* is precisely the hermeneutical problem. For only because the being of God proceeds is there an encounter between God and man. And the hermeneutical problem is grounded precisely in this encounter between God and man which owes its origin to the movement of God's being. This encounter [is] . . . first and above all the encounter between the electing God and the elected man which is fulfilled in Jesus Christ. Thus the existence of the man Jesus confronts us with the hermeneutical problem . . .[85]

How can this hermeneutical problem be resolved? The answer, according to Barth (which Jüngel takes as a given), is through God's revelation, which is the self-interpretation of God.[86] He then goes on to add,

> But revelation as the *self-interpretation of God* is the root of the doctrine of the Trinity. The doctrine of the Trinity is then consequently the interpretation of revelation and therewith the interpretation of the being of God made possible by revelation as the self-interpretation of God.[87]

Furthermore, because God's revelation to us is a revelation of himself, there is an exact correspondence between what he is and what he says he is, between his inner being (*ad intra*) and his expression of it (*ad extra*). This formula, which is usually attributed to Karl Rahner (1904–1984), Jüngel claims to have found in Barth's *Church Dogmatics*.[88] Jüngel then went on to say that God in

---

[83] See 2 Cor. 13:4.
[84] Jüngel, *Trinity*, xvii. *Potenz* is of course "potential," or *dynamis* in Greek, not *energeia*.
[85] Ibid., xx-xxi.
[86] Jüngel quotes this phrase from Barth, *Church Dogmatics*, I/1, 311.
[87] Jüngel, *Trinity*, 15.
[88] Ibid., 23–24. See Barth, *Church Dogmatics*, II/1, 657 and 660, where the form of the perfect being of God is defined as the "wonderful unity of identity and non-identity, of simplicity and multiplicity, inward and outward." Rahner's formula is, "The economic Trinity is the immanent Trinity and the immanent Trinity is the economic Trinity" (Karl Rahner, *The Trinity* [London: Burns & Oates; New York: Herder & Herder, 1970], 22). It was originally published in 1967 as "Der dreifaltige Gott als transzendenter Urgrund der Heilsgeschichte," in Johannes Feiner and Magnus

his being is a subject, but he is an *active* subject.[89] Therefore God must be motion in himself:

> God's independent being must thus be understood from the event of revelation as an event granting this event of revelation. God's being as subsistence is self-movement. As self-movement God's independent being makes revelation possible. Revelation as God's interpretation of himself is the expression of this self-movement of the being of God.[90]

God's being as self-movement is therefore a constant state of becoming, which is worked out in the pattern of self-relatedness that we call the Trinity:

> God's self-relatedness thus springs from the becoming in which God's being is. The becoming in which God's being is is a becoming out of the word in which God says Yes to himself. But to God's affirmation of himself there corresponds the affirmation of the creature through God. . . . in that God in Jesus Christ *became* man, he is as creature exposed to perishing. . . . God's "being in becoming" was swallowed up in perishing, the perishing was swallowed up in the becoming. Therewith it was settled that God's being *remains* a being in becoming. With his Yes to man God remains, in the event of the death of Jesus Christ, true to himself as the Triune God.[91]

Thus we see that Jüngel does not draw a clear distinction between the being and the persons of the Godhead but merges them into a single concept that is the divine self-movement. The persons are united in eternity, but in their movement they are constantly drawing closer to one another and so perfecting their unity. As they do this, they (somewhat paradoxically) become more distinct from each other because they do not dissolve into each other. Therefore, the closer they get the more apparent the uniqueness of each one of them is and the easier it becomes to see how they relate to one another.

This intrinsic relatedness of the Trinity is the basis of their relationship to us because by an act of their common will we have been invited to share in their inner life. The "primal decision" of God to be a Trinity of persons is a mystery to us, but it certainly included the Son of Man. The work of Christ is central to the Trinitarian being of God because it is in it that we see the ultimate purpose and nature of the divine self-movement. Jüngel's premise is that the more we sacrifice of ourselves, the more we grow in conscious possession of ourselves

Löhrer, eds., *Mysterium salutis. Grundriss heilsgeschichtlicher Dogmatik*, 5 vols. (Einsiedeln: Benzinger Verlag, 1965–1976), 2:317–401.

[89] Jüngel, *Trinity*, 68.

[90] Ibid., 93.

[91] Ibid., 107–108.

as well. Sacrifice is the key to success, and in this God has set us the example by becoming a man in Christ and dying for the sins of the world. God did not need the universe in order to exist or to be himself, but creation and redemption have contributed to his self-growth as a community of love. That is why our salvation matters to God and helps to explain how it affects him without changing his fundamental nature. Jüngel's is a profound and absorbing vision that seeks to do full justice to the persons of God and their relationships, both in himself and with us, and difficult though it may be to grasp, it seems likely that it will survive and bear fruit for some time to come.

In conclusion, modern Protestant thought on the Trinity is as diverse as Protestantism itself, but it is fair to say that most of it labors in the shadow of Karl Barth, whose work remains the touchstone for the thinking of others. Barth's followers have sought to extend and interpret his thought in order to respond to new challenges as they arise, while those who are unhappy with some aspect of his achievement have tried to produce an alternative. Broadly speaking, the latter can be divided into those conservatives who have rejected his understanding of the Bible as a fallible record of human response to divine revelation, and those who have tried to find some way to accommodate natural theology in their doctrine of God.

Some of the more interesting contributions to theology in recent times have come from Protestants who have questioned the way in which the Western tradition has developed and who have sought to return to earlier models. Colin Gunton (1941–2003), for example, saw Augustine and Augustinianism as the chief problem and wrote at length against it, though his approach has recently been questioned and may not survive serious criticism.[92] Less focused on a single target but equally concerned to renew theological thought in a traditional but fresh way is Robert Jenson (1930–).[93]

Also creative and productive are philosophical theologians like Richard Swinburne (1934–), who has produced new arguments for the existence of God on the basis of probability rather than certainty. His basic argument is that while none of the traditional "proofs" for God's existence is definitive, when they are all taken together, the weight of probability is on their side.[94]

[92] Colin E. Gunton, *The Promise of Trinitarian Theology* (Edinburgh: T & T Clark, 1991); *The Triune Creator: A Historical and Systematic Study* (Edinburgh: Edinburgh University Press, 1998); *Father, Son, and Holy Spirit: Toward a Fully Trinitarian Theology* (London: T & T Clark, 2003). For a critical assessment, see Bradley G. Green, *Colin Gunton and the Failure of Augustine: The Theology of Colin Gunton in Light of Augustine* (Eugene, OR: Pickwick, 2011).

[93] Robert W. Jenson, *The Triune Identity* (Philadelphia: Fortress, 1982); *Systematic Theology*, 2 vols. (New York: Oxford University Press, 1997–1999).

[94] Richard Swinburne, *The Coherence of Theism* (Oxford: Clarendon, 1977); *The Existence of God* (Oxford: Clarendon, 1979); *The Existence of God* (Oxford: Clarendon, 1981); *The Christian God* (Oxford: Clarendon, 1994).

Widely published and highly respected too are neo-Calvinists like Alvin Plantinga (1932–), Nicholas Wolterstorff (1932–), and Paul Helm (1940–), who have maintained a conservative Reformed philosophical approach to theology at the highest academic level.[95] It is still too soon to say whether their work will last or be influential in the longer term, but they have at least demonstrated that neo-Calvinism is still a going concern in the marketplace of theological ideas.

It is inevitable that creative theological thinking will move beyond Barth one way or another; the real question is to discern how great his influence on those future developments will be. At the present time we cannot make a definitive judgment about this, but it safe to say that so far, no thinker of Barth's stature has emerged to replace him as the benchmark for Protestant theology, which remains indebted to him in much the same way as pre-Barthian theologians were indebted to Schleiermacher.

The Roman Catholic Church

Paralleling the renewal of interest in Trinitarian theology in the Protestant world and interacting with it at various points has been a corresponding revival of the doctrine among Roman Catholics. Given the nature of the Roman church, it is to be expected that discussion within it has been more unified and interactive than in the Protestant world, where theologians have sometimes worked not only independently but in ignorance of one another, but that is only partially true. Isolation of the Protestant kind is not really possible in the Roman church, but mutual awareness has not led to uniformity of approach or to general agreement among its theologians. Indeed, one might almost take Jüngel's vision of the Trinity and say that in the Roman Catholic Church, the more theologians have interacted with one another the more distinct they have become, and, being only human, the more likely those distinctions have been to produce conflict and give rise to competing schools of thought.

In the early part of the twentieth century, Rome was still preoccupied with the fallout from the modernist controversy associated with Alfred Loisy and George Tyrrell, and its theological watchdogs were on the alert for anything that might be interpreted as a deviation from their version of orthodoxy. It would be wrong to say that theologians who worked in that atmosphere were

His views have recently been criticized by Herman Philipse, *God in the Age of Science? A Critique of Religious Reason* (Oxford: Oxford University Press, 2012), who recognizes how serious and worthy of refutation they are.

[95] Alvin Plantinga, *Where the Conflict Really Lies* (New York: Oxford University Press, 2011); Kelly J. Clark and Michael Rea, eds., *Reason, Metaphysics, and Mind: New Essays on the Philosophy of Alvin Plantinga* (New York: Oxford University Press, 2012); Nicholas Wolterstorff, *Divine Discourse: Philosophical Reflections on the Claim That God Speaks* (Cambridge; Cambridge University Press, 1995); Paul Helm, *The Providence of God* (Leicester: InterVarsity Press, 1993); *Eternal God* (Oxford: Oxford University Press, 1988, 2nd ed., 2010); *Calvin at the Centre* (Oxford: Oxford University Press, 2010).

uniformly derivative in their thinking and afraid to embark on new lines of thought for fear of condemnation, although after the lifting of the censorship at the time of the Second Vatican Council (1962–1965), that impression of them was certainly given by younger scholars who felt constrained by (or who disagreed with) the approaches taken in the previous generation.

One prominent voice that managed to bridge the pre- and post-Vatican II worlds was that of Bernard Lonergan (1904–1984), an Irish-Canadian theologian who taught for many years at the Gregorian University in Rome.[96] Unfortunately, his major works on the Trinity and Christology were in Latin and were not translated into English until many years after his death, which greatly restricted their influence.[97] Lonergan stood firmly in the Neo-Thomist natural theology tradition, which lost its dominant position in Roman Catholic theology after the council, but he was by no means antiquarian in his thinking. He wanted to achieve a balance between accepting the witness of the theological tradition and the need to express it in ways that would speak to the theologian's own generation:

> If one is to harken to the word, one must also bear witness to it. If one engages in *lectio divina*, there come to mind *quaestiones*. If one assimilates tradition, one learns that one should pass it on. If one encounters the past, one also has to take one's stand toward the future. In brief, there is a theology *in oratione obliqua* that tells what Paul and John, Augustine and Aquinas, and anyone else had to say about God and the economy of salvation. But there is also a theology *in oratione recta* in which the theologian, enlightened by the past, confronts the problems of his own day.[98]

Lonergan's basic thesis was that the New Testament is a divine revelation given to the "whole person," as he put it, whereas the Nicene Creed is an intellectual analysis of the Gospel data:

> . . . it is not hard to see that what corresponds to the Gospels is undifferentiated consciousness, whereas what corresponds to dogma is differentiated

[96] *The Collected Works of Bernard Lonergan*, Frederick E. Crowe and Robert M. Doran, eds., 22 vols. (Toronto: University of Toronto Press, 1988–2014).

[97] Bernard Lonergan, *De Deo Trino*, 2 vols. (Rome: Gregorian University Press, 1964); English translation with facing Latin original, *The Triune God*, 2 vols. (Toronto: University of Toronto Press, 2007–2009), which are vols. 11–12 of the *Collected Works*. The first part of *De Deo Trino* (*Pars dogmatica*, 7–112) was translated and published during Lonergan's lifetime as *The Way to Nicea* (London: Darton, Longman & Todd, 1976). Studies of Lonergan include David Tracy, *The Achievement of Bernard Lonergan* (New York: Herder & Herder, 1970); Hugo Meynell, *The Theology of Bernard Lonergan* (Chico, CA: Scholars Press, 1986); Frederick E. Crowe, *Appropriating the Lonergan Idea* (Washington, DC: Catholic University of America Press, 1989); Craig S. Boly, *The Road to Lonergan's Method in Theology: The Order of Theological Ideas* (Lanham, MD: University Press of America, 1991); William A. Stewart, *Introduction to Lonergan's Insight: An Invitation to Philosophize* (Lewiston, NY: Edwin Mellen, 1996); Gerard Walmsley, *Lonergan on Philosophic Pluralism: The Polymorphism of Consciousness as the Key to Philosophy* (Toronto: University of Toronto Press, 2008).

[98] Bernard Lonergan, *Method in Theology* (London: Darton, Longman & Todd, 1972), 133.

> consciousness. For the Gospels are addressed to the whole person, on all levels of operation. The dogmas, on the contrary, demand a subject who can focus attention on the aspect of truth alone, so that other powers are under the sway of intellect, or else are somehow stilled.[99]

What forced the church to move from the Gospels to the creeds was an evolution from a nonanalytical to an analytical approach to philosophical and theological questions. Whereas earlier generations had been content to record impressions of their experiences, as time went on people wanted to categorize them and arrange them in systems that required a more precise definition of concepts and vocabulary. The creeds of the church represent this later phase of its intellectual development, but they were not concessions to a Hellenistic way of thinking. On the contrary, whereas the ancient Greeks had been content to think in abstract terms, the Gospels forced Christians to abandon talk about "essences" and concentrate instead on what actually existed in a concrete form. Dogma is the proclamation of what is already present in the Scriptures as the Word of God—it is not an alternative philosophy. As Lonergan expressed it,

> The emergence of the very notion of dogma, grounded in the Word of God as true, was a movement from obscurity to clarity; on the other hand, the doctrine of the Christian church concerning Jesus Christ advanced not from obscurity to clarity but from one kind of clarity to another. What Mark, Paul and John thought about Christ was neither confused nor obscure, but quite clear and distinct; yet their teaching acquired a new kind of clarity and distinctness through the definition of Nicea. But further dogmas had to follow, and then the historical investigation of dogmas, before the fact and the nature of dogmatic development itself could be clearly established.[100]

Later still there were further movements, first to an even more abstract philosophical level, represented at its height by Thomas Aquinas, and then in modern times to the realm of feeling and psychology, which take us even deeper into the mystery of human and divine existence. Aquinas had concluded (correctly) that in God there are two processions, which produce four relations and three persons, but his way of understanding the Trinity had to be adapted for modern use. It was at this point that Lonergan came into conflict with the standard-bearers of neo-Thomism, in particular with Etienne Gilson (1884–1978), who had expressed the conviction that classical Thomist realism

[99] Bernard Lonergan, *The Way to Nicea*, 3 (*Collected Works*, 11:33).
[100] Lonergan, *Way to Nicea*, 13 (*Collected Works*, 11:49).

was valid for modern as well as for medieval thought.[101] Lonergan disputed this, not so much because he thought that Thomas was wrong but because Thomas was constrained by his worldview, or "horizon," which forced him to think in a way that is no longer viable. For Thomas, perception was the basis of factual knowledge, an approach that every subsequent generation, including that of the Enlightenment, had shared with him, but that had now been replaced by something else, which Lonergan called "insight," i.e., the ability to make value judgments and so get beyond superficial perceptions to the heart of the matter in question.[102]

Less interested than some of his contemporaries in whether God is an immutable substance or not, Lonergan was well aware of the psychological issues that secular writers like Freud and Jung were raising in connection with personal identity, and he sought to interpret Trinitarian personhood in light of them. To his mind, the classical persons of the Godhead must now be understood as three subjects of a single consciousness, which is what the divine "substance" amounts to in modern parlance.[103] In his scheme of things, what Thomas had called the first procession in God produced two relations, as follows:

1. Understanding (the Father) forming conception (the Son). This is generation, or begetting.
2. Conception formed. This is the reciprocal action of the Son recognizing his begottenness.

Following on from that, the second procession also produced two relations, which are,

1. Evincing love in accordance with conception. This is the Father bringing forth or "spirating" the Holy Spirit, having already generated the Son.
2. Love evinced. This is the Holy Spirit recognizing his spiration in his reciprocal relationship with the Father, and presumably also with the Son, though Lonergan did not say that explicitly.

In essence, Lonergan's doctrine was very similar to that of Augustine, though it had clearly passed through a scholastic phase on its way to being psychologized—a clear example of how, in Lonergan's view, doctrine develops along with human culture without changing in any fundamental way.

[101] Etienne Gilson, *Réalisme thomiste et critique de la connaissance* (Paris: J. Vrin, 1939).
[102] Lonergan developed this idea in his major philosophical treatise, *Insight: A Study of Human Understanding* (London: Longmans, Green, 1957).
[103] What follows here was expounded by Lonergan in *De Deo Trino*, vol. 2 (*Collected Works*, vol. 12), 145–189; 235–261.

Following the standard Western approach, Lonergan next said that the temporal missions of the persons of the Trinity flow naturally from their eternal processions, but added that the missions are not intrinsic to the processions, which can and do exist independently of them. In other words, Lonergan rejected the idea that the Trinity and the world are somehow interdependent. Here he demonstrated his loyalty to the ancient tradition of the church in an intellectual climate where the notion of Trinitarian dynamism was being developed in order to establish such an interconnection, which many modern theologians in the Thomist tradition insisted was necessary.

Lonergan's Trinitarianism is interesting and important for the way it tried to integrate modern ways of thinking with traditional Christian doctrine, which was the essence of the neo-Thomist approach. It is open to serious criticism, however, in its fundamental premise. Was there really an evolution from a pre-analytical to an analytical intellectual climate that took place between the New Testament period and the First Council of Nicea in 325? What evidence is there for saying that? Everything we know about the early church suggests that the creeds developed out of baptismal formulas that were used to admit new converts into the church, and that they were never intended to supplant, or even to interpret, the New Testament, where intellectual assent to doctrinal statements is also required of believers.[104] This connection highlights a weakness of Roman Catholic theology generally, which is that it is inadequately grounded in the Scriptures. All too often, it has produced an impressive philosophical edifice that has insufficient biblical support and is therefore open to serious question. Lonergan lived long enough to see a revival of biblically centered theological thinking within his own church, but he never really adjusted to it, and that remained the great weakness of his overall approach.

Another theologian who made a great impact on twentieth-century Roman Catholic theology was Karl Rahner (1904–1984), who was Lonergan's exact contemporary but a very different scholar and theologian.[105] Like Lonergan he was a Jesuit, but unlike him he was very much on the outside of the church establishment in the years before the Second Vatican Council. Lonergan taught at the Gregorian University in Rome from 1953 to 1965, whereas Rahner was closely associated with Yves Congar (1904–1995), Henri de Lubac (1896–1991), and Marie-Dominique Chenu (1895–1990), all of whom were in reaction to the Neo-Thomism of their youth and more concerned to develop a new style of theology that was deeply suspect in Rome. In particular, they were unhappy

[104] See, for example, 1 John 4:1–3.

[105] For a comprehensive bibliography of Rahner's works and also of major studies on him, see Vincent Holzer, *Le Dieu Trinité dans l'histoire. Le différend théologique Balthasar-Rahner* (Paris: Cerf, 1995), 460–472.

with the way in which theological themes had become stylized and even fossilized in their vocabulary and expression, and they wanted to reinterpret the inherited tradition in new categories.[106] Where Lonergan was content to take the traditional terms and rework them to suit modern understandings of reality, Rahner wanted an approach to theological questions that would replace all forms of Thomism with a new philosophical outlook. One of the reasons he gave for this was the fact that very few ordinary Christians had a genuinely Trinitarian faith, because the doctrine made no sense to them:

> . . . despite their orthodox confession of the Trinity, Christians are, in their practical life, almost mere "monotheists." We must be willing to admit that, should the doctrine of the Trinity have to be dropped as false, the major part of religious literature could well remain virtually unchanged. . . . One has the feeling that, for the catechism of head and heart (as contrasted with the printed catechism), the Christian's idea of the incarnation would not have to change at all if there were no Trinity. For God would still, as (the one) person, have become man, which is in fact about all the average Christian explicitly grasps when he confesses the incarnation.[107]

In criticizing the theological tradition that had produced this state of affairs, Rahner was careful not to condemn it outright. As he put it, the Augustinian and Thomist systems were fine for those who thought like that, but as not many people do, those concepts are increasingly alien to the modern world. In his words,

> The hints given in Scripture show that the two divine processions [of scholastic theology], whose reality is assured by revelation, have certainly something to do with the two basic spiritual activities of knowing and loving. Thus the starting point of an Augustinian theology of the Trinity is undeniable. Yet if, unlike scholastic theology, we wish to avoid an artificial "eisegesis" into Scriptural theology, we shall have to remember that this inner conception is indicated in Scripture only insofar as, in the economy of salvation, this intra-divine knowledge is seen as self-revealing, and this intra-divine love as self-communicating.[108]

From this we can see that Rahner wanted his theology to be more clearly based on the Bible, and in that way he came closer to Protestantism than most

[106] See Martin Lenk, *Von der Gotteserkenntnis: natürliche Theologie im Werk Henri de Lubac* (Frankfurt am Main: Knecht, 1993).
[107] Rahner, *Trinity*, 10–11.
[108] Ibid., 19.

of his fellow Catholic theologians would have done at that time. He recognized this himself, but was careful to distinguish the two positions and to insist that the Catholic one remained superior:

> He who does biblical theology wishes to say exactly what the Scripture says, yet he cannot simply repeat the words of Scripture. In this respect, it seems to me, the only but essential difference between Protestant and Catholic theology is this: that for the Catholic theologian the logical explanation of the words of Scripture by the church can definitely become a statement of faith, whereas for the Protestant theologian it remains basically theology, and it may always be revised and reversed.[109]

Rahner several times referred to this Catholic assurance of faith as the reason why he clung to traditional terms like "person" and "substance" when discussing the Trinity, but it is clear from the way his argument developed that he was chafing at this restriction and would much rather have replaced the official wording with something else. Indeed, the last part of his treatise is actually devoted to that theme, as we shall see.

Rahner did not write extensively on the Trinity, but what he did say was of fundamental importance and has been deeply influential in the Roman Catholic Church since Vatican II. Some even credit him with having begun the revival of interest in Trinitarian theology, but that is too narrow a view and ignores the fact that not only did Karl Barth get there first but Rahner was influenced by him. Perhaps the fairest thing to say is that Rahner made the Trinitarian revival a reality for Catholic theologians, thereby ensuring that it did not remain an exclusively Protestant phenomenon.

Rahner started from the proposition that the economic Trinity and the immanent Trinity are identical, but insisted that it is only through the former that we can have access to the latter or any understanding of it.[110] In other words, what God has done in history tells us who he is in eternity, and beyond that we can know nothing about him. As we see in the divine drama of salvation, the three persons of the Trinity have their own identity that is grounded in an inner necessity that makes them what they are and ensures that they are not interchangeable. The Father did not become a man and die on the cross, because he could not do so: the inner logic of his personal identity made that not merely inappropriate but impossible. The same is true of the Holy Spirit. Why this is so is revealed by their functions, to which their personal identity

[109] Ibid., 54.

[110] See, for example, Ibid., 48: ". . . it is a fact of salvation history that we know about the Trinity because the Father's Word has entered our history and has given us his Spirit."

is closely connected. In essence, the Father is the archetypal divine person, the one who is called "God" without qualification and the one to whom the others must relate in order to define themselves. This does not make him more truly divine than the other persons, but the Father must first be who and what he is in order for them to be who and what they are:

> . . . the self-communication of the persons occurs according to their personal peculiarity, that is, also according to and in virtue of their mutual relations. Should a divine person communicate himself otherwise than in and through his relations to the other persons, so as to have his own relation to the justified (and the other way around), this would presuppose that each single divine person, even as such, as mentally distinct from the one and same essence, would be something absolute and not merely relative. We would no longer be speaking of the Trinity. . . . The Father gives himself to us as Father, that is, precisely because and insofar as he himself, being essentially with himself, utters himself and in this way communicates the Son as his own, personal self-manifestation, and because and insofar as the Father and the Son (receiving from the Father), welcoming each other in love, drawn and returning to each other, communicate themselves in this way, as received in mutual love, that is, as Holy Spirit.[111]

The Son, whom Rahner preferred to call the Logos, is the Father's self-expression in truth. Here Rahner picked up the well-known Johannine theme, which he regarded as essential to the whole process of revelation. If what we have received is not the truth, then we can have no assurance that we know anything about God at all. The Holy Spirit is the bond of love between the Father and the Son (a well-worn Augustinian theme) and therefore also the bond of love between us and God. Once again, Rahner showed that he was rooted in biblical thinking, especially that of Paul.[112] The practical importance of this for Rahner was that it meant that God relates to us in both truth and love. The two belong inseparably together, and one cannot exist without the other. According to the biblical revelation, I am meant to love the truth and submit to it as the highest authority. If I fail to love the truth, or if what I love is false, my existence is inauthentic and I will suffer accordingly.

Where Rahner's theology becomes problematic is in the difficulty he had with the idea of "person." In this he was similar to Barth, because he too regarded the word "person" as referring to an independent subject of consciousness, and therefore inappropriate as a term to use in modern theology. He did

[111] Ibid., 35.
[112] See, for example, Gal. 4:6.

not agree with Lonergan that a person can share consciousness with others, and therefore he was forced back into a kind of modalism that allows for the existence of only one person in God. Rahner rejected the charge of modalism, just as Barth did, and for the same reason. The revelation of God was not a façade that concealed his true nature, but a self-manifestation that produced a real experience of God:

> The Trinity is not for us a reality which can only be expressed as a doctrine. The Trinity itself is with us, it is not merely given to us because revelation offers us statements about it. Rather these statements are made to us because the reality of which they speak is bestowed upon us. They are not made in order to test our faith in something to which we have no real relation.[113]

As with Barth, this rejection of modalism is largely a matter of definition. Rahner insisted that there is only one self-utterance in God ("I am") and no mutual love between the Father and the Son, because that would require two separate acts, which would suggest that the persons can function independently of each other, even if it is only to establish their mutual relationship.[114]

Rahner was convinced that the immanent and the economic Trinity are identical, but there is a problem here because, while he thought that interpersonal relations are possible between human beings and also between God and man, he could not find room for them within God himself. But if that were so, what are we to make of the relationship between Christ and his Father, which is amply attested in the Gospels? Is this the human Jesus talking to God? It might seem so in some cases, but the so-called "high priestly prayer" of Jesus in John 17 would surely rule that interpretation out, especially when Jesus starts talking about the glory he had with the Father in eternity! In the end, Rahner depersonalized the Trinity by arguing that the word "person" ought to be understood as a "distinctive manner of subsistence":

> . . . the one God subsists in three distinct manners of subsisting. "Distinct manner of subsisting" would then be the explanatory concept, not for person, which refers to that which subsists as distinct, but for the "personality" which makes God's concrete reality, as it meets us in different ways, into precisely this one who meets us thus. . . . The single "person" in God would then be: God as existing and meeting us in this determined distinct manner of subsisting.[115]

[113] Rahner, *Trinity*, 39.
[114] Ibid., 106.
[115] Ibid., 109–110.

Very different from both Rahner and Lonergan was Hans Urs von Balthasar (1905–1988).[116] Like them he was also trained as a Jesuit, but he left the order in 1950 because he felt called to work for the sanctification of the world from within, and became a secular priest. That decision was not popular at the time, but Balthasar survived both the criticism and the opposition he received and at the end of his life was nominated to become a cardinal, though he died two days before the ceremony of induction was due to take place. He was a man of immense erudition and wide sympathies, being the first Catholic theologian to write a detailed study of Karl Barth, for example, for which he was much praised by his subject. Unlike both Lonergan and Rahner, who were clearly identified with a particular theological tradition, Balthasar was more eclectic in his sympathies, and his theology is therefore harder to pin down. He had a deep pastoral concern and was strongly attracted to all forms of Christian mysticism, which gave him a sympathy with the Eastern Orthodox tradition that was unusual among theologians of his generation. In Basel, where he spent most of his adult life, Balthasar set up a religious community of laypeople, and from there he began an active publishing ministry. He never occupied an academic chair, but spent his time reflecting and publishing on a wide range of spiritual writers, whose legacy he wanted to claim for a genuinely alternative theology.

Balthasar was close to Karl Barth in many ways, but he disagreed sharply with Barth over the question of the appropriate use of analogy in theology. Barth insisted that all language about God is based on what he called the analogy of faith, by which God establishes a relationship with his human creatures. He rejected what he regarded as the Roman Catholic analogy of being (*analogia entis*), which went back to the scholastic theology of the Middle Ages and was in his view a kind of idolatry. Balthasar challenged this, defending the analogy of being as a fuller understanding of God's presence in the world than a mere analogy of faith. What he meant was that the personal relationship of faith that exists between the believer and God must be grounded in a deeper relationship between the creation and the Creator, which forms the context in which the relationship based on faith can emerge and develop.

[116] For a comprehensive bibliography of Balthasar's works and also of major studies on him, see Holzer, *Le Dieu Trinité*, 455–460, or Cornelia Capol, *Hans Urs von Balthasar: Bibliographie* (Fribourg: Johannes Verlag, 1990). Studies on him include John Riches, ed., *The Analogy of Beauty: The Theology of Hans Urs von Balthasar* (Edinburgh: T & T Clark, 1986); John J. O'Donnell, *Hans Urs von Balthasar* (London: Geoffrey Chapman, 1991); B. McGregor and T. Norris, eds., *The Beauty of Christ: An Introduction to the Theology of Hans Urs von Balthasar* (Edinburgh: T & T Clark, 1994); William T. Dickens, *Hans Urs von Balthasar's Theological Aesthetics: A Model for Biblical Interpretation* (Notre Dame, IN: University of Notre Dame Press, 2003); David C. Schindler, *Hans Urs von Balthasar and the Dramatic Structure of Truth: A Philosophical Investigation* (New York: Fordham University Press, 2004); Aidan Nichols, *Divine Fruitfulness: A Guide to Balthasar's Theology beyond the Trilogy* (London: T & T Clark, 2007); R. Howsare, *Balthasar: A Guide for the Perplexed* (London: T & T Clark, 2009), Aidan Nichols, *A Key to Balthasar: Hans Urs von Balthasar on Beauty, Goodness, and Truth* (London: Darton, Longman & Todd, 2011).

This led Balthasar to elaborate a theological program in which beauty, goodness, and truth were the ways in which God manifests himself in the world and binds it to himself. Working this out progressively, he produced a massive trilogy of works in which he dealt with each of them in turn. The first of these was devoted to the aesthetics of beauty, which Balthasar regarded as fundamental for any appreciation of God and his works.[117] He was strongly critical of Protestant theology for having ignored this dimension of reality and thereby impoverished its understanding of the divine. From there he moved on to dramatics, because he believed that the form of beauty had to be manifested in the goodness of action for it to be authentic (and not deceptive).[118] Finally, he wrote at length on logic and the nature of truth, which to him was the outcome of the coincidence between the beauty of form and dramatic action.[119] As he concluded his great work, he explained it as follows:

> Our trilogy of aesthetics, dramatics and logic is built upon the mutual enlightenment existing between theological categories and the philosophical transcendentals. What one identifies as the qualities of being encompassing each and every existent (the transcendentals), seem to open up the most appropriate access to the mysteries of Christian theology.[120]

At the heart of everything lies the Trinitarian being of God, who reveals himself supremely in the theological drama of salvation. As Balthasar put it,

> Jesus experiences his human consciousness entirely in terms of mission. The Father has commissioned him, in the Holy Spirit, to reveal God's nature and his disposition toward man. . . . He is the revelation of man as he ought to be, as he is and as he is once more to become (through Christ's action on man's behalf). . . . Jesus does not live in order to exhibit himself as the highest example of the human species but solely to fulfill the Father's will.[121]

In this great act of self-giving, Jesus Christ reveals himself to be the Son of God, and in him we see the beauty of the divine being, which is lived entirely in self-sacrificial love:

---

[117] Hans Urs von Balthasar, *Herrlichkeit. Eine theologische Ästhetik*, 3 vols. (Einsiedeln: Johannes Verlag, 1960–1967); English trans., *The Glory of the Lord*, 7 vols. (Edinburgh: T & T Clark, 1982–1991).

[118] Hans Urs von Balthasar, *Theodramatik*, 4 vols. (Einsiedeln: Johannes Verlag, 1973–1983); English trans., *Theo-drama: Theological Dramatic Theory*, 5 vols. (San Francisco: Ignatius, 1988–1998).

[119] Hans Urs von Balthasar, *Theologik*, 3 vols. (Einsiedeln: Johannes Verlag, 1985–1987); English trans., *Theo-logic: Theological Logical Theory*, 3 vols. (San Francisco: Ignatius, 2000–2005).

[120] Hans Urs von Balthasar, *Theologik*, 2nd ed., 3 vols. (Einsiedeln: Johannes Verlag, 1988), 1:vii-xxi (*Epilog*, 37). This addition to the original text is not in the English translation but was quoted by Thomas Norris, "The Symphonic Unity of His Theology: An Overview," in McGregor and Norris, *Beauty of Christ*, 226.

[121] Balthasar, *Theo-drama*, 3:224–225.

> . . . the Father strips himself, without remainder, of his Godhead and hands it over to the Son; he imparts to the Son all that is his. . . . The Father must not be thought to exist prior to this self-surrender (in an Arian sense): he *is* this movement of self-giving that holds nothing back. . . . Inherent in the Father's love is an absolute renunciation: he will not be God for himself alone. He lets go of his divinity and, in this sense, manifests a (divine) Godlessness (of love, of course). The latter must not be confused with the godlessness that is found within the world, although it undergirds it, renders it possible and goes beyond it. The Son's answer to the gift of Godhead . . . can only be eternal thanksgiving (*eucharistia*) to the Father, the Source—a thanksgiving as selfless and unreserved as the Father's original self-surrender. Proceeding from both . . . there breathes the "Spirit" who is common to both: as the essence of love, he maintains the infinite difference between them, seals it, and, since he is the one Spirit of them both, bridges it.[122]

This is a complex vision that perhaps only a mind like Balthasar's was capable of creating and sustaining. As the latent Augustinianism of this passage shows, it maintained the broad outlines of the Western tradition but played with them in ways that help us see that rigid categorization is impossible when we are talking about God. In sharp contrast to the theologians with whom he came into conflict (Rahner especially), who seemed to Balthasar to have erred too far in the direction of history and contingency in describing the self-revelation of God, Balthasar developed a mystical picture of the Trinity that he regarded as more suggestive than definitive.[123] In that sense he provided a much-needed corrective to the overly dry and abstract approach of the more philosophically inclined theologians of his time, but whether his construction can stand on its own may be doubted. His concepts of beauty, goodness, and truth are never clearly defined, and although he insisted that they were objective, they come across to most people as the opposite—the subjective creations of an imaginative mind more than an analysis of divine realities. Balthasar's theology is best viewed as a challenging critique of the dominant trend in modern Western thought, rather than as a viable replacement for it. There is much to be learned from it, but it must also be anchored in the historical events of the gospel and not theologized away as some kind of cosmic drama whose plot is never-ending.[124]

122 Ibid., 4:323–324.

123 On the conflict between Balthasar and Rahner, see Holzer, *Le Dieu Trinité*, which is devoted to the subject.

124 Cf. what Balthasar himself said about this: "The drama of the Trinity lasts forever: the Father was never without the Son, nor were Father and Son ever without the Spirit. Everything temporal takes place within the embrace of the eternal action and as its consequence" (*Theo-drama*, vol. 4).

The Eastern Orthodox Tradition

Perhaps the most surprising and potentially promising development of twentieth-century theology was the reemergence of the Eastern Orthodox churches as serious participants in ecumenical dialogue. The Eastern churches had long been accustomed to receiving new ideas from the West, which they absorbed or rejected according to their own particular outlook. For centuries Constantinople in the Ottoman empire and Moscow in Russia had been the poles to which all the Orthodox looked, and as the former went into decline, the latter took on increasing prominence. This situation changed dramatically after 1917, when the Communists came to power in Russia and the Orthodox church was persecuted. Its leading intellectuals were forced to flee to exile in the West, where they established seminaries and theological schools that exported the fruits of the nineteenth-century revival and began to publish their views in Western languages, making them more accessible.[125]

At the same time, large-scale emigration from traditionally Orthodox countries, greatly increased by the exchange of populations between Greece and Turkey in 1923, produced ethnic communities in the United States and elsewhere, who also helped to open lines of contact between East and West.[126] The full impact of this would not be felt for another generation, but from the 1960s onward the Orthodox have played a significant part in ecumenical discussions of all kinds and their views can no longer be ignored as they once were. For the first time in centuries, the Eastern church is meeting its Western counterparts as an equal, and Western theologians are seriously asking whether that tradition has important insights to contribute to the development of theology in Protestant and Catholic circles.

In the first phase of the Russian emigration, one of the most influential voices was that of Vladimir Lossky (1903–1958), son of the philosopher Nikolai Lossky, who was expelled from Russia with his family in 1922. They settled in Paris, where Lossky taught and interacted with the leading Catholic theologians of his time. His writings reflect the chauvinism of late

[125] Initially, most of them went to Berlin and Paris, but later many made their way to New York as well. Today, the Institut Saint-Serge in Paris and St. Vladimir's Theological Seminary in Crestwood, NY, are their principal theological centers. Holy Cross Orthodox Seminary in Boston, MA, is of Greek origin.

[126] The collapse of the Ottoman empire led to a Greek invasion of Asia Minor which was repelled by resurgent Turkish nationalists. When hostilities ended, the Muslim minority in Greece (with the exception of Western Thrace) was exchanged for the Christian minority in the new Republic of Turkey (apart from those in Constantinople). As there were far more Greeks in Turkey than the other way around, and Greece was a much smaller and poorer country, the impact on it was dramatic and destabilizing, leading to substantial emigration. Christian minorities in other parts of the Middle East (Lebanon, Armenia and Egypt) followed suit in due course, emigrating in successive waves as the pressure on them from Islamic extremists grew harder to resist.

nineteenth-century Russia, strengthened by the bitter experience of revolution and exile, but Lossky was much more than a disappointed Russian nationalist. He directed the Orthodox world not to pan-Slavism but to Byzantium and urged its theologians to reconsider and rejuvenate the ancient Greek theological tradition. This gave him an audience in places like Romania and Greece that he would not otherwise have had, and contributed greatly to the emergence of the neo-Byzantine theology that is so characteristic of modern Orthodoxy.[127]

Lossky started with the principle enunciated by the Russian theologian Vasily Bolotov (1853–1900), which was that the Trinity is at the center of all spirituality.[128] Because that is so, said Lossky, the differences between the East and West are all ultimately connected to the *Filioque* clause. It is not possible to say whether the dispute over that preceded or followed the separation of the two traditions, but whatever happened in the past, today it is the disagreement about the procession of the Holy Spirit, not any liturgical or ritual differences, that continues to prevent a reunion of the churches.

Lossky naturally took the Eastern view of the *Filioque* question, and argued that the addition to the creed represents a theological regression rather than a legitimate development of the biblical tradition.[129] To his mind, the Holy Spirit cannot be the personification of the common substance of the Father and the Son, because if he were, he would not be a *hypostasis* at all:

> If this were admitted, personal diversity in the Trinity in effect would be relativized; inasmuch as the Holy Spirit is one *hypostasis*, the Holy Spirit only represents the unity of the two in their identical nature. Here the logical impossibility of any opposition between *three* terms intervenes, and the clarity of this triadological system shows itself to be extremely superficial. Indeed, on these lines, we cannot reach a mode of distinguishing the three *hypostases* from each other without confounding them in one way or another with the essence. In fact, the absolute diversity of the Three cannot be based on their relations of opposition without admitting, implicitly or explicitly, the primacy of the essence over the *hypostases*, by assuming a relative (and therefore secondary) basis for personal diversity

[127] Lossky's most important works are *The Mystical Theology of the Eastern Church* (Cambridge and London: James Clarke, 1957). Originally published as *Essai sur la théologie mystique de l'église d'Orient* (Paris: Aubier, 1944); *The Vision of God* (Leighton Buzzard: Faith Press, 1963). Originally published as *La vision de Dieu* (Neuchâtel and Paris: Delachaux et Niestlé, 1962); *In the Image and Likeness of God* (London and Oxford: Mowbrays, 1975). Originally published as *A l'image et à la ressemblance de Dieu* (Paris: Aubier Montaigne, 1967).

[128] Vasilay Bolotov, "Thesen über das *Filioque* (von einem russischen Theologen)," in *Revue internationale de théologie*, VI (1898), 681–712. The review was published by the Old Catholics, with whom Bolotov was in dialogue at the time.

[129] Vladimir Lossky, "The Procession of the Holy Spirit in Orthodox Trinitarian Doctrine," in *Image and Likeness*, 71–96.

in contrast to natural identity. But that is exactly what Orthodox theology cannot admit.[130]

Here Lossky used the objectivity of the Greek concept to counterbalance the relationality inherent in Western ideas of personhood, and put his finger on a genuine weakness of the Western approach. From the time of Augustine onward, it has always been difficult for Western theology to think of the Holy Spirit as a person in his own right, and the tendency to depersonalize him altogether by turning him into a cosmic spiritual force was certainly well advanced by the time Lossky got to grips with Western Trinitarianism. His observation was a useful and indeed necessary corrective to this, but only in recent years has it been taken seriously by Western theologians.

Lossky then went on to say that the individual identity of the persons of the Trinity is not determined by their relations of origin. Those relations express a latent diversity in the Godhead that determines what the relations will be like. In other words, the relations of the persons of the Trinity to each other testify to their inherent diversity as persons and are not to be categorized as relations of opposition, as the Western tradition has usually thought, especially in its Thomist form.[131]

Lossky also maintained that all three persons of the Trinity possess one and the same essence (*ousia*). They do this in dependence on the Father as persons, but that is not the reason why they are consubstantial with him. They do not derive their essence from the Father but possess it in their own right, their "dependence" on him being a matter of personal relation to him, not of essential origin from him:

> The one nature and the three *hypostases* are presented simultaneously to our understanding, with neither prior to the other. The origin of the *hypostases* is not impersonal, since it is referred to the person of the Father, but it is unthinkable apart from their common possession of the same essence, the "divinity in division undivided."[132] Otherwise we should have three divine individuals, three Gods bound together by an abstract idea of Godhead. On the other hand, since consubstantiality is the non-hypostatic identity of the three, in that they have (or rather *are*) a common essence, the unity of the three *hypostases* is inconceivable apart from the monarchy of the Father, who is the *principle* of the common possession of the same

[130] Ibid., 77–78.
[131] Ibid., 79–80.
[132] Gregory of Nazianzus, *Oratio* XXXI, 14.

> one essence. Otherwise we should be concerned with a simple essence, differentiated by relationships.[133]

In saying this, Lossky naturally believed that he was following the Cappadocian fathers, but it seems that he was interpreting them in a rather tendentious way. They spoke quite happily about causation, and even if this should not be interpreted literally, it is surely going too far to suggest that causation has no bearing on the identity of the Trinitarian persons in Cappadocian theology.

In dealing with Augustine, Lossky asserted that his psychological and other analogies of the Trinity are really external qualities that Augustine has introduced into the Godhead.[134] Here we see the mystical streak in Lossky's theology, which he regarded as typical of Eastern thought and which he emphasized in his critique of the Western tradition. According to Lossky, concepts like "mind," "will," and "love" do not really apply to the inner life of God because he is above such things. A mind needs something to contemplate, but what does this mean when there is nothing but itself? A will has to make decisions, but how can it when there is nothing to decide? And of course, love needs someone or something to love, but if there is nothing there, how can it be manifested? Augustine of course answered such questions by saying that God contemplated himself, but it is arguable, as Lossky pointed out, that in doing this he reduced the persons of the Godhead to inner movements in God which, taken on their own, divide and diminish his being. Once again we see how he put his finger on the difficulty that Western theologians have always had in properly hypostatizing the persons of the Trinity, and in doing so challenged the West to rethink its approach.

Lossky himself tried to resolve the problem by reviving the Palamite distinction between the essence and energies of God, regarding the latter as uncreated operations of the divine being in the world which do not necessarily reflect that being itself.[135] In this way, Lossky denied that the economic Trinity has to be an exact reflection of the immanent one, without divorcing one from the other. It is therefore possible, as Orthodox theology has always asserted, that the Holy Spirit can be the Spirit of the Son in his temporal mission, because then he is acting as the divine energy of the Son, without having proceeded from him to begin with:

> . . . the personal advent of the Holy Spirit does not have the character of a work that is subordinate, and in some sort functional, in relation to that of

[133] Lossky, *Image and Likeness*, 81.
[134] Lossky, *Mystical Theology*, 95–96.
[135] Ibid., 67–90; *Vision of God*, 124–137.

> the Son. Pentecost is not a "continuation" of the incarnation. It is its sequel, its result. The creature has become fit to receive the Holy Spirit and he descends into the world and fills with his presence the church which has been redeemed, washed and purified by the blood of Christ.[136]

Like others who have adopted this view, Lossky appealed to the baptism of Jesus as evidence that the Holy Spirit proceeds from the Father and rests on the Son, giving him that radiance that we see when we contemplate his transfigured glory.[137] In the mystical theology of the Eastern church, the transfiguration of Christ plays a central role because it reveals the Son in his heavenly glory, but (typically) the Western tradition has usually downplayed and even ignored it altogether. Here we see how it is possible for people who have been shaped by alternative theological traditions to read the same Gospels with completely different eyes. Lossky challenged his Western counterparts, not least those who rely on a doctrine of *sola Scriptura* for their theology, to take seriously an event that most of them have preferred to pass over in silence.

Lossky's theology, it would be fair to say, has appealed most to those who for one reason or another have been unhappy with the way the Western tradition has developed. This includes Orthodox who regret (or resent) the influence that Western theology has exerted on Eastern thinking in modern times, but it also includes a number of Westerners who have questioned the validity of their own tradition. Some of these have become Orthodox in the hope of recovering the "authentic" Christian tradition, and Lossky's partisan and sometimes bitterly anti-Western approach appeals to them. This is unfortunate, because the issues Lossky raised are too serious to be trivialized by such polemics. East and West have to reconsider each other's positions and try to come to a common mind, but it is idle to suppose that this will be achieved by the victory of one over the other. Banishing Augustine in order to exalt the Cappadocians or Gregory Palamas is a pointless exercise and is most unlikely to move the church forward into the deeper unity that proponents of such theories claim to want. The Western tradition has its weaknesses, and it is good for it to be challenged in the way that Lossky has done, but it is naive to think that a simple "return" to Lossky's version of the Eastern tradition is all that is required. The truth is that Lossky did not simply repeat the standard view of the Eastern church—in many ways he took the tradition as he saw it and shaped it in ways that had not previously been known. For example, he developed an "economy of the Holy Spirit" quite different from that of the Son because of his concern to make

[136] Lossky, *Mystical Theology*, 159.
[137] Ibid., 149.

the Son and the Spirit as independent of each other as possible.[138] He did not succeed in persuading his fellow Orthodox that he was right, so admirers of his approach should realize that following his interpretations might not be as "Orthodox" as they suppose.[139]

Another Orthodox theologian who has been very influential in the West is Jean (or John) Zizioulas (properly Iôannês Zêzioulas,1931–), who taught theology for many years in both London and Glasgow.[140] Like Lossky, Zizioulas based himself firmly in the Cappadocian tradition, which he wanted to revive for modern use, but he lacked Lossky's polemical spirit and was generally more pastoral and less philosophical in his approach. Zizioulas's main contention was that there occurred a revolution in patristic theology in which the concept of person/*hypostasis* displaced that of substance/nature as the starting point for serious theological reflection. Until the fourth century, words like "God" and "man," as they are used of the incarnate Son in the Nicene Creed, for example, referred primarily to the substance of divinity and humanity, not to a person or a *hypostasis*. Today, of course, we would normally think of "God" and "man" in personal terms *first*, moving on perhaps to their substance or nature but not starting from there. This is the effect of the patristic theological revolution, and it has altered our perception of God ever since. In particular, it makes it impossible to claim that patristic theology was unduly influenced by contemporary philosophy, and especially by Neoplatonism, because that philosophy had no concept of the person as an agent in control of his being, as opposed to the person or *hypostasis* as a manifestation of an underlying (and ultimately controlling) substance.[141]

That such a shift had taken place by the mid-fifth century is clear from the decrees of the Council of Chalcedon, in which the incarnate Christ is defined as a single (divine) person in two natures. At the time, this was a new idea and hard to absorb. This is amply testified by what happened afterwards, as the Eastern church split into warring camps because too few people really understood what was going on. That much seems to be clear, and it is fair to say that most informed people today would agree with it. What Zizioulas wanted to argue, though, is that this theological revolution took place not at Chalcedon (where it could be attributed to the intervention of Pope Leo I of Rome, whose *Tome* broke the logjam and allowed the council to come to a decision), but in

138 Ibid., 156–173.

139 One person who openly repudiated his interpretation of the work of the Holy Spirit was John Zizioulas, *Being as Communion* (London: Darton, Longman & Todd, 1985), 124–125.

140 He is also bishop, or metropolitan of the New Testament church of Pergamum, a see that effectively ceased to exist in 1923 when the exchange of populations between Greece and Turkey took place. See Rev. 2:12–17.

141 Zizioulas, *Being as Communion*, 27–50.

the work of the Cappadocian fathers a century before. According to him, they were the ones who not only distinguished the concept of *hypostasis* from that of being or substance (*ousia*) but made the former primary over the latter:

> Among the Greek fathers [Zizioulas has the Cappadocians in mind] the unity of God, the one God, and the ontological "principle" or "cause" of the being and life of God does not consist in the one substance of God but in the *hypostasis*, that is, *the person of the Father*. The one God is not the one substance but the Father, who is the "cause" both of the generation of the Son and of the procession of the Spirit. Consequently, the ontological "principle" of God is traced back . . . to the person. Thus when we say that God "is," we do not bind the personal freedom of God—the being of God is not an ontological "necessity" or a simple "reality" for God—but we ascribe the being of God to his personal freedom. In a more analytical way this means that God, as Father and not as substance, perpetually confirms through "being" his *free* will to exist.[142]

Most Western theologians would assent to the first part of this proposition, but the second part is more controversial. What the Cappadocians said is undoubtedly compatible with what happened at Chalcedon, but did they go as far in their thinking as the Chalcedonians did? If they did, why was it that no one in the Eastern church, either in Alexandria or at Antioch, picked it up? It is hard to believe, if Zizioulas is right and the Eastern church understood it at the time, that there would have been any Christological controversy at all, or that the decision of Chalcedon would have been opposed as strongly (and for as long) as it was. The truth is that all branches of the Eastern church, Chalcedonian and non-Chalcedonian, see themselves as heirs of the Cappadocians and of Cyril of Alexandria, but they have been unable to agree about the conclusions of the Council of Chalcedon in 451. Zizioulas may have been right in his contention, but if so there is more work to be done before it can be said that his theory has won the day.

Oddly enough, Zizioulas weakened his case by saying that for the Cappadocians the substance of God *is* the person of the Father. Certainly they believed that the Father was the hypostatization of the divine substance, but is that the same thing as claiming that the two are identical? Lossky would certainly not have agreed with that, as we have just seen. Because the person of the Father and the substance of God are the same, said Zizioulas, all the divine attributes must be derived from the person of the Father. This means

[142] Ibid., 40–41.

that, strictly speaking, personhood is a quality that as a matter of absolute right belongs exclusively to the Father. He alone is *autotheos*, God-in-himself, another assertion that goes against what Lossky was arguing on the basis of the same patristic sources.

In Zizioulas's thinking, the Son and the Holy Spirit are equal to the Father because that is the Father's gift to them; it is not something that they possess in their own right. Zizioulas said that this is necessary because persons cannot exhibit a mutually reciprocal form of causality. In other words, if the Son is truly the Son, it must be because he has been begotten by the Father. The Father cannot be who he is only because the Son has independently decided to submit to his authority and recognize him as his Father. Of course, this assertion also makes it impossible to accept the *Filioque*—always an underlying concern of any Orthodox theologian—because the Holy Spirit cannot proceed from more than one other person. On the other hand, Zizioulas was quite prepared to accept that, although both the Son and the Holy Spirit have been constituted by the Father as the "fountainhead of deity," the Father is also in some sense *conditioned* by the existence of the Son and the Holy Spirit—he cannot exist without either of them. That has always been understood in the context of the Father-Son relationship, but Zizioulas may have added something new by extending this relational necessity to cover the Holy Spirit as well.

One point to bear in mind when trying to assess Zizioulas's theology is that his writings were produced in the West and have made their greatest impact outside Orthodox circles. This unfortunately typifies much of what passes for dialogue with the Eastern tradition today. Western readers are acquainted with what has been published in the West and have seldom bothered to inquire how far this really represents the mind of the Eastern church. They have been insufficiently attuned to the important distinction that the East makes between *dogma*, which is the officially sanctioned teaching that all Orthodox must accept, and *theologoumena*, which are theological opinions uttered by those who reflect on the church's dogma but which carry no comparable authority.

The *theologoumena* of Lossky and Zizioulas are unlikely to be rejected by the Orthodox churches in any formal sense, but they are equally unlikely to be canonized as authoritative interpretations of the Eastern tradition, and it would be most unwise for their Western admirers to fall into that trap. Dialogue with the Eastern tradition is important and stimulating, but it is also much more subtle than most Westerners realize. The Eastern church lacks a *magisterium* comparable to that of Rome, but it is also bound to its tradition in a way that few Westerners (and especially Protestants) can appreciate. All that can be said with reasonable certainty is that reunion with the East will not come about as the result of ecumenical discussions between theologians, however fruitful those may be in other ways.[143] What we are dealing with here is a mystery that goes beyond the ability of the human intellect to fathom, and only when we can agree to keep silence about those depths in God that we shall never penetrate is there any real chance that we may come to a common mind and find ourselves in a reunited Christendom.

[143] For a good presentation of the Eastern position without the polemics, see Boris Bobrinskoy, *The Mystery of the Trinity: Trinitarian Experience and Vision in the Biblical and Patristic Tradition* (Crestwood, NY: St. Vladimir's Seminary Press, 1999). Originally published as *Le mystère de la Trinité. Cours de théologie orthodoxe* (Paris: Cerf, 1996).

25

The Challenge of God Today

A Suffering God?

> There is but one living and true God, everlasting, without body, parts, or passions; of infinite power, wisdom, and goodness; the Maker and Preserver of all things both visible and invisible.[1]

The opening sentence of the first of the Thirty-nine Articles of Religion states the classical doctrine of God with admirable succinctness. It was taken almost word for word from the Augsburg Confession of 1530, but not quite, because Thomas Cranmer made a small but significant addition to it. The Augsburg article says that "there is only one living and true God, everlasting, without body or parts."[2] Cranmer reworked this by interpreting "everlasting" as the third attribute of the one living and true God, and creating a new triad of body, parts, *and passions*. Yet what to him was probably just a cosmetic addition has since become the most prominent and controversial issue being debated in modern theology.[3]

The reason for this is that a generation ago the traditional doctrine of divine impassibility, as transmitted in the above Article, was almost universally rejected by theologians who had lived through the horrors of the Second World War. In a phrase made famous by Jürgen Moltmann (1926–), they wondered where God was in Auschwitz.[4] To answer this question they reshaped the classical picture of an impassible God. Taking the crucifixion of Jesus as their model, they focused on his cry of dereliction, "My God, my God, why hast thou forsaken me?"[5] and saw in this the ultimate identification of God with human pain. The atoning purpose of Christ's sacrifice was nudged out of the picture and replaced by suffering, which became an end in itself. Only by seeing

[1] Article 1, *Thirty-nine Articles of the Church of England.*

[2] *Confessio Augustana*, 1.

[3] For a comprehensive summary of the problems and debates, see James F. Keating and Thomas J. White, eds., *Divine Impassibility and the Mystery of Human Suffering* (Grand Rapids, MI: Eerdmans, 2009). See also Christopher W. Morgan and Robert A. Peterson, eds., *Suffering and the Goodness of God* (Wheaton, IL: Crossway, 2008).

[4] See Richard Bauckham, *Moltmann: Messianic Theology in the Making* (Basingstoke: Marshall Pickering, 1987).

[5] Matt. 27:46; Mark 15:34. The quotation is from Ps. 22:1 (KJV).

that there is a cross at the heart of God could Moltmann and his colleagues come to terms with what they themselves had lived through, but what they saw in that cross was solidarity with the plight of humanity more than redemption from human sin:

> The Christ event on the cross is a God event. And conversely, the God event takes place on the cross of the risen Christ. Here God has not just acted externally, in his unattainable glory and eternity. Here he has acted in himself and has gone on to suffer in himself. Here he himself is love with all his being. . . . Jesus' death cannot be understood "as the death of God," but only as death *in* God. . . . If one uses the phrase, it is advisable to abandon the concept of God and to speak of the relationships of the Son and the Father and the Spirit at the point at which "God" might be expected to be mentioned. From the life of these three, which has within it the death of Jesus, there then emerges who God is and what his Godhead means. Most previous statements about the specifically Christian understanding of talk about "the death of God" have lacked a dimension, the Trinitarian dimension.[6]

It is largely for this reason that their answer, while very understandable in the circumstances, was inadequate. We now know that the horror of Nazi genocide was not an isolated aberration but the harbinger of a new form of human behavior made possible by the invention of the means of mass destruction. Auschwitz, it turned out, was not unique, but the beginning of a trend. At the same time, great technological advances were occurring that were applied not only (or even mainly) to mass destruction. They could also be used for good, and the great advances in the control of disease and the cure of scourges like cancer, along with growing international cooperation in dealing with crises caused by natural disasters and failed states, gave people a new hope that human suffering can be overcome. Horrible as Auschwitz was, it was not and cannot be the last word on the subject of suffering. The potential curability of pain, which was never a practical possibility before, thus became an added factor in the equation. If weak human beings can solve this problem, why did the all-powerful God not do so long ago? Moltmann addressed this issue directly:

> It is in suffering that the whole human question about God arises; for incomprehensible suffering calls the God of men and women in question. The suffering of a single innocent child is an irrefutable rebuttal of the notion of

[6] Jürgen Moltmann, *The Crucified God* (London: SCM, 1974), 205, 207. Originally published as *Der gekreuzigte Gott* (Munich: Chr. Kaiser Verlag, 1973).

> the almighty and kindly God in heaven. For a God who lets the innocent suffer and who permits senseless death is not worthy to be called God at all. . . . Suffering as punishment for sin is an explanation that has a very limited value. . . . The history of Christ's sufferings belongs to the history of the sufferings of mankind, by virtue of the passionate love which Christ manifests and reveals. . . . The interpretation of Christ's death on the cross as an atoning event in the framework of the question of human guilt is the central part of universal significance, but it is not the whole of it, or all its fullness.[7]

Moltmann made his greatest impact on twentieth-century theology by raising the question of God's impassibility and asking whether the traditional doctrine makes sense in the modern context. In the early church, God's impassibility was seen as a natural consequence of his sovereignty. A God who could be harmed or even affected by an external power was not fully in control of the universe, and that the early Christians could not allow. Furthermore, many of the emotions that we today see in a more positive light, the ancients thought were dangerous. Falling in love, for example, could cause severe problems in a society where marriages were usually arranged for financial or dynastic reasons. To say that "God is love" therefore had to mean that love was something other than a passion that could be stirred at the wrong moment and for the wrong reasons. In saying that God is impassible, the ancients were not trying to distance him from the cares and concerns of ordinary human life, but to set him free to be able to deal with human problems in a rational way.

In a brilliant monograph on the subject, Thomas Weinandy (1946–) has pointed out that a suffering God would be of no help to us, not simply because he would cease to be the transcendent Deity whose very noninvolvement with human suffering makes it possible for him to intervene effectively to deal with it, but also—and most interestingly—because a suffering God would have to suffer in his own divine way and not in ours. In other words, his divine suffering would be no more like ours than his divine being is, and we would be just as unable to relate to it. Far from drawing us nearer to him, it would reveal even more clearly the depth of the chasm that separates him from his creatures:

> Many contemporary theologians . . . argue that God must be passible if his groaning, suffering and love are to be actual and genuine. . . . What makes Yahweh's thoughts so different from our own and what makes his ways so different from our own is that he is so different from us. . . . Yahweh is passionate but it is the passion of the Wholly Other, and he is able to express

[7] Jürgen Moltmann, *The Trinity and the Kingdom of God* (London: SCM, 1981), 47, 52. Originally published as *Trinität und Reich Gottes* (Munich: Chr. Kaiser Verlag, 1980).

> such depth of passion only because he is the Wholly Other. . . . if one were to conceive of God's love, suffering and groaning in such a manner as to undermine his complete otherness, then his love, suffering and groaning would be diminished, and thus the significance [of them] . . . would be completely lost.[8]

Furthermore, says Weinandy, God did not create evil, which has no objective existence in its own right. Evil is not inherent in particular things but is a state of rebellion against God, something which he is obviously incapable of. To imagine anything else is both incoherent and disastrous for our understanding of God, sin, and salvation:

> . . . if the persons of the Trinity were infected with suffering, it would mean that they were deprived of some good, and so enmeshed in sin and evil. Thus they would no longer be subsistent relations fully in act possessing fully actualized love and goodness, but would now be in potency to obtaining or re-obtaining the good they did not possess. However, this loss would render them impotent to create, and thus to relate creatures to themselves in the fullness of their love and goodness in an immediate, dynamic, intimate, and unbreakable manner. While a suffering God may have some intellectual and emotional appeal (often more emotional than intellectual), such an understanding of God is philosophically and theologically disastrous in its consequences. It may give the appearance of providing consolation to the innocent victims of sin and evil, but ultimately it throws into complete disarray the whole philosophical and theological structure upon which an authentic biblical understanding of God and of his loving relationship to creation and humankind is based.[9]

Weinandy also points out that an important distinction must be made between the kind of suffering that is inflicted from without and that which is generated from within. A man who is flogged and crucified, as Jesus was, suffers in his human nature because that nature is susceptible to attacks inflicted by other material forces, but this kind of suffering cannot affect God (or the divine nature of Jesus) in the same way, because the divine nature is not susceptible to physical torment.

Nevertheless, Weinandy admits that Jesus of Nazareth suffered as a person, and his person is divine, not human. The classical expression of this, which has been confessed by the church since ancient times, is that, on the cross, the divine person of the Son of God suffered and died in his human nature,

---

[8] Thomas G. Weinandy, *Does God Suffer?* (Edinburgh: T & T Clark, 2000), 59.
[9] Ibid., 158.

having acquired the latter expressly for that purpose. What is new is that now theologians are asking, If the divine person of the Son genuinely suffered, what does that say about the other divine persons? The traditional emphasis has always been on the relationship between the Son and the human race, citing the prophet Isaiah's famous words, "Surely he has borne our griefs and carried our sorrows" in support of their contention.[10] But because the focus has always been on human healing, not on divine suffering, the question of how the passion of the Son might affect the Father and the Holy Spirit has not received much attention from theologians. Popular piety, expressed particularly in hymns, may occasionally refer to the Father's grief at seeing his Son die on the cross, and it is possible that devotion to Mary has become as prominent as it has because she could (and did) display grief over this in a way that the Father could not or did not, but on the whole this question did not surface in serious theological debate until Moltmann brought it up.

This relative neglect of the effect of the Son's suffering on the other persons of the Trinity is surprising in view of the fact that, in the Bible, God is frequently portrayed as one who reacts to his people's plight in ways that can only be described as emotional. Weinandy analyzes this and points out that such statements are made in the context of God's personal relationship with his people and not with reference to the divine being in itself. If God grieves for his people it is because he has a link with them that stirs him to such feeling, not because he is physically or emotionally weak and liable to burst into tears:

> . . . since God does not suffer, his love becomes absolutely free in its expression and supremely pure in its purpose. If God did suffer, it would mean that God would need not only to alleviate the suffering of others, but also his own suffering, and thus there would be an inbuilt self-interest in God's love and consolation. However, since God does not suffer, his care for those who do suffer is freely given and not evoked by some need on his part. His love is freely expressed, entirely for the sake of those he loves.[11]

If the divine person of the Son suffered on our behalf, it is inconceivable, because of their intimate relationship with him, that the Father and the Holy Spirit would not have shared in that suffering. They did not undergo the pain of the cross, of course, and they certainly did not die, because their divine nature is incapable of death. But to the extent that they are related to the Son, they participated in his suffering and were affected by it. This, of course, is

[10] Isa. 53:4, quoted also in Matt. 8:17.

[11] Weinandy, *Does God Suffer?* 160–161.

essentially what the Christian tradition has always claimed when it says that the Father pardons sinners on the basis of the Son's sacrifice. It is that sacrifice that moves the Father to pity and to forgive those who do not deserve to be forgiven.

What Weinandy reminds us of, and where his view is an important corrective to Moltmann, is that God's relational feelings toward us have a purpose, which is not merely empathy with our plight but healing and salvation from it. Suffering is not an end in itself, and we must not be trapped into thinking that there is no escape. If Christians want to talk about a God who feels our pain, then they ought to add that he brings that pain to an end by triumphing over it and allowing us to inherit a new life, where pain and suffering no longer exist. If we do that, we can address the fears of earlier generations—that if God were to suffer, he would be deprived of the ability to be himself—and can begin to explore the depths of his relationship to us and what that means for our understanding of him. People have been doing this experientially for centuries, of course, but now it is time for theologians to do justice to their witness by giving it a proper theological framework within which it can be understood and honored. In sum, Weinandy recognizes that Moltmann and his followers had the best intentions, but shows that their attempts to deepen our understanding of how God relates to the world have actually had the opposite effect, and that a corrective is needed to their one-sided approach.

In the sixteenth century, and for most (if not all) of Christian history before that, it was taken for granted that God has no body, and that since parts and passions are properties of a body, it follows logically that he does not have them either. This belief was inherited from Judaism. The well-known anthropomorphisms of the Old Testament, according to which God was said to have an eye, a hand, and so on, were regarded as figures of speech rather than as literal descriptions of a finite heavenly being. In a world where almost everyone else portrayed their deities in human terms, the Mosaic prohibition against idolatry was enough to prove that the God of Israel could not be reduced to bodily dimensions. Whether he had parts or not became something of an issue when the doctrine of the Trinity was first elaborated, because there were some naive individuals who thought that the *logos*, or mind, of God and the Spirit were detachable parts of the divine being, but this notion was easily refuted. Everyone realized that God did not lose his mind when the Son became a man, nor did he cease to be a spirit on the day of Pentecost, so it was not difficult to conclude that, whatever the members of the Trinity were, they were not parts of a finite divine body.

The question of divine passions, however, caused much greater difficulty. It may be true that theological discussion in the early church reflected the concerns of men formed in the schools of ancient Greek philosophy, but that is not the only reason they had a problem. To the ancients, passion was a sensation inflicted by an external power, and not a self-generated feeling. Three attributes of God, each of them amply attested in the Hebrew Bible, made it seem incompatible with his being and forced the early Christians to conclude that God must be impassible.

The first, and in some ways most important, of these was his transcendence. As the Creator, God dwelt above and beyond his creation. His being was unlike anything he had made, and suffering was therefore just as inapplicable to him as anything else in the created order was. The second divine attribute that made impassibility seem necessary was his perfection, which implied immutability.[12] Suffering would involve some form of change and was therefore ruled out as impossible in God's case, because for a perfect being, change would necessarily involve a loss of that perfection. The third attribute that suffering called into question, as we have already remarked, was God's sovereignty. If he could be attacked and harmed by an external force, that force would be more powerful than he is and would compromise his sovereignty over his creation, something that the early church could never have accepted.

All these things argued in favor of a doctrine of divine impassibility, but there was another side to the Old Testament witness that also had to be accounted for. There God is portrayed as loving his children, as being angry with their disobedience, and even as hating people or things that he has rejected.[13] From our modern point of view there is some ambiguity in these verses, because it is often not clear whether the mention of God's love or hate is a revelation of his inner feelings or just the human perception of God's actions, which vary according to our obedience or disobedience but which do not reflect any real change in him. But there are also several places where he is described as a God of compassion, whose love for his people overrides their disobedience and encourages him to show them mercy and forgiveness, even though they clearly do not deserve it.[14] Some of these texts emphasize that God shows compassion because of the covenant he established with Abraham, which makes it clear that the Bible is not simply using human language to explain divine actions that in themselves have nothing to do with feelings. God is portrayed throughout the Old Testament as a God who has established what we would call a personal

[12] Immutability had already been an issue in the nineteenth century, when the emergence of a kenotic Christology called it into question. It was defended most notably by Isaak August Dorner (1809–1884), whose articles on the subject have been only fairly recently translated into English for the first time and published as *Divine Immutability: A Critical Reconsideration* (Minneapolis: Fortress, 1994). They originally appeared in the *Jahrbücher für deutsche Theologie*, 1/2:361–416; 2/3 (1857):440–500; 3/4 (1858):579–660.

[13] See Deut. 1:27; Hos. 9:15; Mal. 1:3.

[14] 2 Kings 13:23; 2 Chron. 36:15; Ps. 78:38; 86:15; 111:4; 112:4; 145:8; Jer. 12:15; Lam. 3:32; Mic. 7:19.

relationship with his creatures, and especially with the nation with which he has entered into covenant. We have to recognize that, underlying all talk about divine emotions, there lies this deeper question of how an infinite, transcendent God can have a meaningful relationship with beings that are finite and have been created by him.

It is also important to note that suffering and feeling are not identical. Even if we confine ourselves to external sensation, it is clear that the suffering one would endure from being shot by an arrow is not the same as the feeling one would get by simply touching it. This distinction was recognized by the ancients, who used different words to describe the two things. Suffering in this sense was *pathos* and feeling was *aisthêsis*, a word that could be applied to any form of sense perception. Today we think of *aisthêsis* primarily in relation to sight or sound, as when we say that a work of art or music is aesthetically pleasing. The more material meaning survives, but mainly in the negative, so that when our bodily feelings are numbed we say we have been anaesthetized, precisely in order to avoid the pain of suffering. In the New Testament, *aisthêsis* plays a role in the healing touch of Jesus, as it also does in the case of the woman who touched his garment and was cured of her illness.[15] In at least one case, the healing of the two blind men at Jericho, we are told that Jesus took pity on them, so it is clear that his emotions sometimes played a part in his healing ministry, although it was his physical touch and not his inner reaction that produced the cure.[16]

Did Jesus suffer on our behalf because of his compassion for us? Hebrews 4:15 says that "we do not have a high priest who is unable to sympathize with our weaknesses," but this is a mistranslation. The Greek word is *sympathêsai*, which implies physical suffering in a way that the English word that derives from it does not. The Jewish high priest could not be "sympathetic," not because he was emotionally challenged, but because he did not suffer for the sins of the people. The modern reader is liable to think primarily in terms of an emotional bond and wonder how the high priest could have been so hard-hearted. Perhaps he was not. Given that he was sacrificing for his own sins as well as for those of the people, he may have been extremely sympathetic to them in our sense of the word, but because he could not be their substitute, the writer to the Hebrews argued that he could not feel their pain. That is what Hebrews 4:15 means, not that the temple priests lacked normal human feelings. This is a good example of how changing perceptions of what *pathos* and *sympatheia* are can affect the way

[15] Matt. 8:15; 9:20.
[16] Matt. 20:34.

in which we read and interpret ancient texts, and modify our theological understanding based on them.

The importance of this change in perception must not be underestimated. Pursuing this analogy further, the Jesuit theologian Jean Galot (1919–2008) agreed with Moltmann that the Father suffered along with the Son when the latter died on the cross, but in a way that is best described as "compassion" and not actual suffering:

> Only the Son suffers on the cross, but the Father, a distinct divine person and intimately united to the Son, suffers with him. The Father's is a suffering of compassion, of exceptional intensity because of their complete oneness. . . . In the suffering face of the Savior we must also see the suffering face of the Father. Jesus' human suffering enables us to enter into the mystery of the Father's divine suffering.[17]

Galot used two Old Testament examples of a father-son relationship as evidence that God the Father must also have felt for the suffering of his Son.[18] The first example he chose was Abraham, who was called to sacrifice his son Isaac, and the second was David and his son Absalom.[19] Unfortunately, there are difficulties with both of these cases if we try to use them as models for God's behavior. How Abraham felt when he was told to sacrifice Isaac we do not know. The order came from God, but Isaac was the child of God's promise and Abraham's reaction must be understood in that light. Faced with the choice between obeying God or saving his son, Abraham obeyed God and was rewarded by seeing his son being spared at the last minute. If his personal feelings came into it, we are not told, and it is hard to know what they would have been. Abraham put his duty to God before any feelings he may have had for his son, and the Bible implies that this was the right thing for him to do. Consider the alternative. If Abraham had refused God's command, he would have lost the covenant promises, and would have ended up feeling far worse than he did. Instead, Abraham trusted God and told Isaac to do the same. The emphasis of the story is on the triumph of faith over natural feeling, which makes it wrong to interpret it in the way that Galot did.

As for the case of David and Absalom, David's grief over his son's death was an unmistakable display of fatherly feeling, but it was also inappropriate. As Joab had to remind the king, Absalom deserved what he got and David's

[17] Jean Galot, *Abba, Father* (New York: Alba House, 1992), 138–139. Originally published as *Découvrir le père* (Louvain: Sintal, 1985).

[18] Jean Galot, *Dieu souffre-t-il?* (Paris: P. Lethielleux, 1976), 92–97, 114–118.

[19] Gen. 22:1–18; 2 Sam. 18:31–19:7.

reaction would be taken as a sign of his weakness, not admired as the proper reaction of a caring father. It should also be said that Absalom's death does not parallel that of Jesus. Unlike Absalom, Jesus died voluntarily in obedience to his Father. The New Testament says nothing about the Father's reaction to his Son's death, but tells us that on the third day he raised him from the dead in confirmation of his perfect obedience. We also know that Jesus never asked the Father to pity him. On the contrary, when his hour came, Jesus asked the Father to glorify himself in his Son's sufferings, which is a rather different thing.[20]

It should be clear by now that a large part of the problem we have with the idea of divine impassibility is that when we ask whether God has feelings, we want an answer to a question that would not have been put that way in the past and we find it hard to grasp the kind of response that would most likely have been given back then. People have not changed, of course, and neither has God, but we must adjust our perceptions and our vocabulary if we are going to discover what the Bible and the theological tradition have to say about this, if we are not to end up talking at cross-purposes. To put it succinctly, what to them was primarily an issue of how God acts, to us is primarily an issue of how God relates to his creatures and especially to his own people, whether that involves action on his part or not.

For Christians, discussion about feelings in God must also take the incarnation of the Son into account. No one doubts that Jesus of Nazareth was fully human, with all the senses and emotions that any man would have. The Gospels tell us of his reactions to different events, and especially to the news that Lazarus had died before he arrived to heal him. The shortest verse of the Bible says it all: "Jesus wept."[21] He shared fully in the joys of the wedding feast at Cana and in the sorrows of those who sought him out for healing and restoration. What he felt about Judas's betrayal or Peter's denial is not recorded, but we can imagine that he reacted in much the same way as any of us would. It is not the humanity of Jesus which raises difficulties, but his divinity, and it is on that aspect of the matter that the Christian theological tradition until very recently always focused its attention.

Nowadays we have moved into a different kind of discussion. Our affluent societies are plagued not with physical suffering, though there is still plenty of that about, but with self-doubt, frustration, and loneliness. Our psychological unease is not new by any means, but it has become more pressing in an age when happiness and self-fulfillment have replaced survival as the priority for most people. We also live in a world where relationships are in crisis. The

[20] John 17:4–5.
[21] John 11:35.

breakdown of the traditional family unit has reached epidemic proportions, and the full consequences have yet to be felt. With greater freedom has come greater self-centeredness, and in such a climate, feelings are bound to take on an importance they never previously had.

It is considerations like these that feed into the modern desire to find feelings in God. We cannot imagine having a relationship with an emotionally inert person. Images and memories of distant parents and formal relationships between children and adults, which we often associate with the Victorian era, disturb the modern mind and seem unnatural to us. If God is our Father, we do not want him to resemble the distant Victorian *paterfamilias* but to be more like an adult friend and mentor in whom we can confide. It is true, of course, that adults conceal things from children and parents' emotional responses are almost bound to be more measured and guarded than their children's are, but for parents not to have any empathy with their offspring seems bizarre. Surely, therefore, there must be room for emotion in God?

This in brief is the case for saying that God has feelings. Relationships demand them, and if we are in a relationship with God our Father, there must be something in him that can connect with us at the emotional level if the analogy with human relationships is to have any meaning. The differences between God's nature and ours will put his feelings for us in their proper perspective but they will not eliminate them altogether, because they are eternally present in the Trinity and were not created, but only manifested to us in the incarnation of the Son.

How valid is this modern demand for feelings in God? Do we have to revise or abandon the traditional understanding of his immutability in order to accommodate them, or should we instead aim our criticism at current perceptions of human desires on the ground that they are illegitimate and demean both God in himself and our relationship with him? Let us try to get the problem in focus.

Classical Christian theism would say that if there are feelings in God at all, they must be present at the level of the divine persons, because the divine nature is beyond our comprehension and experience, so even if he did have feelings, they would be unknowable and irrelevant to us. This is Weinandy's argument against Moltmann. Second, the modern question of whether God has feelings must be distinguished from the traditional doctrine of his impassibility, because feelings are internal and can be self-generated, which was not true of suffering as that was understood in the past. If human beings can have feelings without necessarily experiencing pain caused by an external influence, then surely the same must be true of God, because we have been created in his image and likeness. Third, do the feelings of Jesus, experienced by his divine person in his human nature, extend to the other persons of the Trinity, or are they unique to him? If they involve the other members of the Godhead, did Jesus have feelings as God as well as feelings as man, and if he did, were these two types of feeling distinct from each other?

No one doubts that, in his human nature, the Son of God had the feelings of a man. He took that nature back into heaven with him at his ascension, so presumably his human feelings continue to exist along with his glorified human body and the wounds that it bore for our salvation. In our relationship with the glorified Son, it should therefore be possible for us to express our feelings and receive a sympathetic response from him. Of course, the feelings of the glorified humanity of Christ are purified and perfected in a way that ours cannot be, because they are freed from the limitations that he was subject to during his earthly life. To that extent, his heavenly feelings must be different from ours, but they are human feelings nonetheless. To take the clearest example of this, our love for God is imperfect while his love for us is perfect, but our relationship is still one of mutual love and we relate to him on that basis.

That much is agreed by everyone. The question is whether, or how, the feelings experienced by the divine person of the Son in his human nature affect his relationship to the Father and the Holy Spirit. In other words, how does his personal relationship with us affect his personal relationship with them? Within the Trinity, we know that the Father relates to the incarnate Son in his human finitude, which the Son shares with us, but not in his sinfulness, because even as a human being he was not sinful. Only when the Son voluntarily became sin for us did the Father's wrath fall on him, but this was not because the relationship between them was broken. On the contrary, the wrath of God could fall on the Son in the way that it did precisely because the relationship of love between the Father and the Son was strong enough to bear it. The Father did not punish the Son because he turned against him in anger, but because the Son voluntarily took our place on the cross and accepted our punishment. His suffering was an act of obedience, and that obedience was a mark of his love for the Father.

That love is eternal inside the Trinity, which is why the Father and the Holy Spirit were not cut off from the Son's human suffering on our behalf, nor were they unaffected by it. Their love for the Son and his love for them meant that they were deeply involved in his agony, even if they did not feel it themselves. That involvement did not change or diminish them, but revealed the depth and power of the love that binds them together. But at the same time, there are compelling reasons for saying that that love is (and must be) both impassible and immutable. It is impassible, because if it were to suffer it would be harmed and made less effective; it is immutable, because if it changed it would cease to be what it is and our salvation would be compromised, if not lost altogether. These, then, are the parameters of the current debate. On the one hand, we want to say that God relates to us as a compassionate Father, but on the other hand, we want him to be strong to save, and not overwhelmed by the burden of bearing our griefs. How these two things can be accommodated in a single theological confession, without compromising either one or producing internal contradictions in our understanding of God, is the task that modern theology faces. What the final answer will be is not yet clear, but whatever it is, we can be certain that only a solution that respects the existing tradition while finding a way of expressing what we now want to say will stand the test of time and become an enduring part of our theological inheritance in the years to come.

The Credibility of Theology

The prominence of the doctrine of the Trinity in recent theology has gone hand in hand with the development of an ecumenical approach that would have seemed unlikely at the beginning of the twentieth century. It is hard to know whether, or to what extent, the two phenomena are connected. Those who initiated the Trinitarian revival were not particularly ecumenical in their outlook, but it is apparent from hindsight that theological interests were converging and those from different parts of the church were talking about the same things, even if not always in the same language.

The ecumenical movement began on the mission field and is usually said to have begun in earnest at the World Missions Conference held in Edinburgh in 1910. It got going in a serious way after the Second World War, with the founding of the World Council of Churches (WCC) in 1948. In its early years, the WCC did a good deal of useful work and some of its subsidiary commissions made real progress toward genuine understanding among the different branches of Christendom. As time went on, however, hopes for increasing convergence began to fade. The WCC became quite political and liberal in its theology, losing both support and credibility in many parts of the world. Church unions occurred in one or two places, but on the whole the record was poor. The claim that church division was a "scandal" did not go down well with those who were proud of their own traditions, and the admission of the Eastern Orthodox churches in 1961 made hopes of organic reunion seem quite utopian. The Roman Catholic Church never joined at all, and without it the WCC's claim to represent worldwide Christianity was bound to be hollow.

Having said that, there were some areas in which ecumenism was a great success. In the academic world, faculties of theology, seminaries, and theological colleges gradually opened their doors to professors and students of other denominations and, as time went on, many of them merged or shared their teaching with those of different backgrounds. Institutions took time to change, but the world of theological discourse opened up very quickly. It rapidly ceased to matter what a theologian's own confessional stance might be; his work was read and commented on across the board. Protestants and Roman Catholics were reading each other's books, attending conferences together, and exchanging ideas as if they belonged to a single guild of professional theologians for whom denominational labels were secondary. Before long, even the Eastern Orthodox were joining in, and although official conversations between the different churches seldom got very far, contacts at the academic level became frequent and are now accepted as normal.

The effects of this were manifold. For a start, there was a growing interest in, and emphasis on, the common inheritance of the patristic era. All Christians acknowledge their debt to the fathers of the Greek and Latin churches, and studying them was a way to find common ground and debate differences within an agreed framework. That in turn led to a renewed concentration on the subject matter of patristic theology, which was deeply rooted in the Trinity and in Christology. The disruption caused by the Council of Chalcedon in the Eastern churches, which had been largely ignored in the West for centuries, resurfaced and became the object of renewed theological interest.[22] Some of this was admittedly due to liberalizing pressures in the West that wanted to overturn the decisions made at Chalcedon, but it was also an occasion to reaffirm the fundamental orthodoxy of those decisions and to reexamine the reasons why some of the churches of the East could not agree to them. Gradually, a consensus emerged that said that the differences were largely ones of terminology, not of doctrinal substance, and the ancient non-Chalcedonian churches were welcomed back into the main body of Christendom.

The *Filioque* dispute was also reopened, though with greater trepidation because in some places tensions between the Western and the Eastern churches were still raw, though largely for political rather than theological reasons. Here again, some progress was made, culminating in the *Clarification* issued by the Vatican on September 8, 1995, which affirmed the validity of each tradition when considered on its own terms and opened a possible way forward for future agreement. No one pretended that a substantial breakthrough had occurred at

[22] See, for example, Paulos Gregorios, William H. Lazareth, Nikos A. Nissiotis, eds., *Does Chalcedon Divide or Unite? Towards Convergence in Orthodox Christology* (Geneva: WCC, 1981).

the ecclesiastical level, but the atmosphere in which differences were discussed had been transformed.[23]

Other dialogues, such as the ones between the Roman Catholic Church and different Protestant bodies about justification by faith and other distinctively Protestant or Catholic doctrines, have tended to claim more and deliver less than Catholic-Orthodox dialogue has done, but the reasons for this are not hard to see. Protestant churches are divided both among and within themselves, often over matters that have little to do with Roman Catholicism, and in recent times the Roman church has seldom made the issues of the Reformation a priority. Thus, a truly ecumenical discussion of justification by faith would have to be held among Protestants first, then between Protestants and Roman Catholics, and finally with the Eastern Orthodox, many of whom have never heard of it and do not know where to place it in their own theological systems. This is not an easy thing to do, whereas concentration on the Trinity is both understandable and of universal interest. Indeed, as this history of theology has tried to show, studying the Trinity in logical sequence may be the best way to tackle subjects that at first sight seem obscure or of secondary importance to those who are not immediately familiar with them.

Concentration on the doctrine of the Trinity has had the beneficial effect of showing how the different aspects of Christian theology can and must be held together in one overarching doctrine of God.[24] In the end, everything relates to him in some way or other, and it is noticeable how recent theological work has often tended to make room for the Trinitarian dimension of whatever it is that is being discussed. Sometimes this can seem a bit forced, but at least it shows a desire to think both systematically and Christianly.

This last aspect is of special importance today because we live in a secular world where religion of any kind is often seen as anomalous and where the top priority of governments and other social agencies is to keep the peace. The potential of religious differences to create civil disorder are too well known for most states to turn a blind eye to them, and religious leaders of all persuasions

[23] The *Clarification* was published in *L'Osservatore Romano* on September 13, 1995, with an English translation following on September 20, 1995, 3, 6. A French translation can be found in Jean-Miguel Garrigues, *Le Saint-Esprit, sceau de la Trinité. Le* Filioque *et l'originalité trinitaire de l'Esprit dans sa personne et dans sa mission* (Paris: Cerf, 2011), 233–242. For a critique of the *Clarification* from the Orthodox side, see Jean-Claude Larchet, *Personne et nature: la Trinité, le Christ, l'homme: contributions aux dialogues interorthodoxe et interchrétien* (Paris: Cerf, 2011). A Roman Catholic response to this and other criticisms can be found in J. Y. Brachet and Emmanuel Durand, "La réception de la *Clarification* de 1995 sur le *Filioque*," *Irénikon* 78 (2005): 47–109; and in Lucas F. Mateo Seco, *Teología Trinitaria: Dios Espíritu Santo* (Madrid: Rialp, 2005), 146–203.

[24] See Gilles Emery and Matthew Levering, eds., *The Oxford Handbook of the Trinity* (Oxford: Oxford University Press, 2011); Stephen R. Holmes, *The Quest for the Trinity: The Doctrine of God in Scripture, History, and Modernity* (Downers Grove, IL: InterVarsity Press, 2012); Robert J. Woźniak and Giulio Maspero, eds., *Rethinking Trinitarian Theology: Disputed Questions and Contemporary Issues in Trinitarian Theology* (London: T & T Clark, 2012).

are under pressure to get along with one another as much as they can. From a civil perspective that makes good sense, but it can cause problems for those who are committed to a particular religion, especially if that religion includes the demand that its followers should actively seek to convert others, as both Christianity and Islam do.

In this atmosphere, the assertion that the three great monotheistic religions, or "faiths of Abraham," have enough in common to be able to make common cause with one another has a special appeal to many.[25] The doctrine of the Trinity stands as a reminder to us that this way of thinking makes no sense. Christianity is not monotheistic in the way that Judaism and Islam are, because the belief that there are three persons in the one God is anathema to them. The rediscovery of the centrality of that belief for Christians and the way it has been developed and celebrated in recent years demonstrate that interfaith dialogue is of very limited value and quite unlikely to lead to the tripartite alliance that its advocates seem to want. Christians have not developed their Trinitarian theology in a deliberate attempt to counteract the impact of other religions, but it is bound to have that effect, and for this we can only be grateful. We do not want to encourage religious warfare, but neither can we allow our faith to be homogenized into a generic monotheism that would falsify its basic premise and remove the gospel message of salvation in and through Jesus Christ alone.

The renewed emphasis on Trinitarian theology has another salutary effect in that it acts as a check on the modern tendency to downgrade "theology" to the level of social action, or even of psychology. We see this in the proliferation of such things as "feminist theology," "queer theology," "black theology," and even "water buffalo theology."[26] Theology is about God, not about human beings, and however important the matters raised by these different "theologies" may be to those affected by them, none of them can claim to be saying anything of significance about God. Focusing on the Trinity turns us away from ourselves and makes us concentrate on him. It is certainly true that attempts have been made to commandeer Trinitarian thought for more secular purposes, but the nature of the subject makes it hard to carry this through with any conviction. The incarnation of the Son reminds us that the material world is not ignored when we turn our minds to God, but it is also kept in its proper place, and for this too we may be grateful.

Trinitarian theology can also provide a helpful model for interpreting the

[25] See, for example, Anton Wessels, *The Torah, the Gospel, and the Qur'an: Three Books, Two Cities, One Tale* (Grand Rapids, MI: Eerdmans, 2013). Originally published as *Thora, Evangelie en Koran: 3 boeken, 2 steden, 1 verhall* (Kampen: Kok, 2010).

[26] Kōsuke Koyama, *Water Buffalo Theology* (Maryknoll, NY: Orbis, 1974; 2nd ed., 1999).

Bible. Just as the Word and the Spirit stand in equal, but different, relationships to God the Father, who initiated the divine plan of salvation and to whom the Word and the Spirit report back, so we can say that the Word of Scripture and the Spirit of its interpretation have equal, but also different, relationships to the Truth that they represent. The Word has taken on written form and become subject to all the limitations of the material world. It can be mutilated, abridged, misunderstood, and even lost (as it was in ancient Judah),[27] but it remains the Word of God that is sharper than any two-edged sword, and it does not lose its ability to cut between the mind of man and the Spirit of God.[28] Its credibility can be attacked and its relevance denied, but in spite of all the attempts that are made to silence it, it continues to speak with power to those who have ears to hear.[29]

The Word exists on its own, but it is not recognized or understood without the Spirit, just as Jesus was not recognized or understood without divine revelation of who he really was.[30] Without the guidance of the Holy Spirit, it is possible to see, taste, and handle the Word of life,[31] without understanding a thing about it. This can easily be seen from the world of biblical studies today, where thousands of scholars come up with theories about the biblical text that bear little or no relation to what it is really about. It can also be seen in any number of sermons that lack the power to convict their hearers because they are not in tune with the Spirit of the text they are supposed to be expounding. At the other extreme, there are those who say that they are filled with the Spirit and have a great deal of enthusiasm to back up their claim but whose message is a far cry from anything to be found in the Word. They may indeed be filled with a spirit, but it is not the Spirit of God if what they say is not faithful to what he has revealed.[32] Here Trinitarian theology offers us a model of relationships that can and should be applied to the way we interpret the Bible.

Finally, and perhaps most important of all, an emphasis on the Trinity helps us to keep the right balance between equality and difference, on which all human life depends. The tension between these two things is an old one and goes right through our culture at every level. On the one hand, we want to proclaim that everyone is equal, that no one should be able to receive special privileges because of an accident of birth, financial resources, family connections, and so on. Even if these factors can never be eliminated, we feel that they

[27] See 2 Kings 22:8–10.
[28] Heb. 4:12.
[29] See Matt. 11:15; 13:9, 43.
[30] Matt. 16:13–17.
[31] See 1 John 1:1.
[32] 1 John 4:2–6.

should be minimized and counteracted as far as possible in order to provide a level playing field for all. At the same time, we all want to be different. No one wants his or her identity to be ignored, derided, or reshaped to fit a mold invented by someone else. We think of others as being "typical" of something but we are not like that—we are unique! People who do not recognize that do not understand us—a common complaint, it has to be said.

The doctrine of the Trinity provides us with the perfect model of how equality and difference can be reconciled in a single being. The three persons of the Godhead are different from one another at one level yet exactly the same at another. In their differences they have established a hierarchy of order that they respect—the Son does the will of his Father, not the other way around. But in their equality they are all alike, so that the will of the Father is shared by the Son and by the Holy Spirit because it is common to them. This balance is extremely difficult to achieve in human affairs, but the divine archetype is there to make us realize that it is possible for those who have been made in his image. At the present time, the prophets of equality appear to be in the ascendant, and anything that might restrict or deny this is attacked and if possible removed. But this is a one-sided approach that sooner or later will have to come to terms with the legitimate claims of diversity, which is also promoted in many places today. It is in mutual self-giving that the equality of difference is most clearly and properly manifested, and here the Trinity comes to our aid by providing us with the supreme example:

> Have this mind among yourselves, which is yours in Christ Jesus, who, though he was in the form of God, did not count equality with God a thing to be grasped, but emptied himself, by taking the form of a servant . . .[33]

There can be few counsels more appropriate for the needs of the modern world than this one, and it is the pattern set by God himself that shows us the way we should go.

Where Are We Now?

It is said that prophecy is a dangerous business, especially when it involves the future, and historians have to be particularly careful not to predict what might happen on the basis of past events alone. We can perceive (or construct) patterns from what we already know, but to assume that these will continue without interruption would be hazardous indeed. What we can do, however, is survey the current state of Christian theology and point out matters that

[33] Phil. 2:5–7.

sooner or later will have to be dealt with, even if we cannot say how or when that will be. First, it seems clear that the Christian world will have to work out a new Trinitarian synthesis, and to some extent that is already happening. We can no longer simply fall back on Augustine or the Cappadocians, but must try to integrate the insights of both in a higher synthesis. On the one hand, we must do all we can to avoid falling into the trap of accidentally depersonalizing the Holy Spirit, as the post-Augustinian Western tradition has often been accused of doing, not without some justification. On the other hand, we must also work out a satisfactory way of describing the relationship between the Son and the Holy Spirit, recognizing that this is unfinished business left over from the councils of the early church and that merely abandoning the *Filioque* clause in the interests of ecumenical harmony is not enough. Reconciling East and West to the general satisfaction of both sides will not be easy, but there is at least a chance that we now have sufficient historical knowledge and enough good will on both sides to make a solution to this problem conceivable, which is the first step on the way to making it possible as well.

It will also be necessary to come to terms with how we define the being or substance of God. This concept has to be liberated from notions of being that were current in earlier times and that envisage a "static" deity who is totally removed from his creation and essentially incompatible with it. Without going to the opposite extreme (as embodied in Process Theology, for example), it is now necessary to work out more clearly how God relates to his creatures, and especially to human beings, whom he has made in his own image and likeness, without ceasing to be himself. In particular, we have to examine how an essentially impassible God can relate to us, as the Bible says he does, in love as well as in anger and pain. In what way can we say that he has "feelings" without compromising his sovereign perfection?

We also have to reconsider what it means to be human, and how human beings should relate to God and to each other. In particular, this will mean a deeper investigation into the notion of personhood, and how this is affected by our natures, as well as by death and resurrection to a new life with Christ. What changes after our physical death and what stays the same must be more closely examined in order to achieve the equilibrium that alone can do justice to the biblical revelation.

In addition to that, we also have to rethink the relationship between the finite and the infinite, especially as this affects the character and content of revelation. How much of God's infinite being can we know, and does it make sense to say that we can know it, but only partially? Is the knowledge we have "true," and if so, in what sense? This is a much deeper question than simply examining whether statements in the Bible are historically accurate or not. That is important, but what we are talking about here is the nature of our knowledge, which has not been adequately analyzed in the light of modern understandings. We do not have to accept current secular theories without question, but we do have to consider what they are saying and try to come up with a response that is both faithful to our inherited tradition and comprehensible to the modern mind.

It is obvious that the center of gravity in the Christian world is rapidly shifting from its traditional European base to what we now call the developing world or the "global south," but what this means for the future of theology is impossible to say. The main lines of theological tradition have already been laid down, and whatever contribution these newly evangelized areas will make to it, they will not be able to change or undo the past. The idea that a Chinese or African theology will emerge and be quite different from what we have known for hundreds of years is attractive to some but it is not a realistic possibility. Such a theology, if it were ever to appear, would lack universality and would be suspected of being unorthodox, not only in the old European world but also in the newer countries, which do not want to be cut off from the ancient roots of Christianity. Whatever insights theologians from the so-called "majority world" may bring to the discussion, they will have to connect with what is already there. Most likely, the theologians who succeed in doing this will not be perceived as coming from (or as being bound to) a particular place, but will be recognized as belonging to a global conversation in which ethnicity and regional identity do not matter very much.

Whether, or in what way, ecclesiological questions will feature in future theological debates is as yet unclear. The ecumenical movement has shown what the possibilities and limitations of this approach are, and it seems unlikely that any serious advance will be made in the foreseeable future. Some Protestant bodies may merge with one another, but the threefold division of Protestant, Catholic, and Orthodox is likely to remain in place for a long time to come. At another level, however, new alliances will be formed across these divides, and indeed have been formed already. Today we think especially of "liberal" and "conservative" approaches and recognize that these tendencies are usually more meaningful than denominational labels. Nor is this surprising. An Anglican who believes in the bodily resurrection of Jesus Christ is bound to have more in common with a Baptist, Catholic, or Orthodox person who believes the same thing than he is with a member of his own church who does not, and the same is true across the board. Alliances are already forming that unite people of a broadly similar outlook, and over time that is bound to have an impact on traditional denominational divisions.

What the lasting effects of that will be is hard to say. Perhaps, in the short term at least, it is more likely to lead to the disintegration of existing denominational structures and a realignment along more meaningful theological lines than to any wider push for unity. That process is already underway in some Protestant churches, and it may accelerate in the years ahead if current theological divisions grow deeper. On the other hand, it may be that the liberal wing of the various churches will atrophy to the point where it no longer counts. But people have predicted the imminent demise of liberalism before and it has not happened; instead, the ground of debate has shifted and a new type of liberal has appeared to take the place of the old.

Whatever else happens, we can be sure that the existing theological traditions will endure. Two hundred years from now theologians will still be arguing their case from the Bible, the fathers of the church, and the universally acknowledged theological giants of later times—men like Thomas Aquinas, Martin Luther, and John Calvin. Many of the trends and theories that we are familiar with today will fade away, some of them into the deepest oblivion, but the classics will remain and future generations will continue to cut their theological teeth on them. The real question is whether, and in what way, the currently received tradition will expand and add new works to its canon. Where they might come from, and what the exact nature of their contribution may be, are questions that we cannot now answer—we can only wait and see what the Lord has in store for us in the years ahead. What we can say for certain is that as long as the Christian church continues to exist there will be theological reflection, because without theology the Bible and its message cannot be preached or understood, let alone applied, as it must be if the gospel is to be securely implanted in the hearts and minds of believers. Here there really is no choice. God the Father has spoken to us in his Word; God the Son calls for us to hear and respond to that Word, which is found only and fully in him; and God the Holy Spirit gives us the understanding and the will to accept that Word and allow it to transform our lives by uniting us to Christ, in whom we dwell in the heavenly places and have fellowship with all three persons of the Godhead. Amen.

Chronological List of Persons

(The list includes only those persons mentioned by their dates in this work. Dates for persons identified as church or governmental officials are for their years of rule.)

Heraclitus	540?–480? BC
Herodotus	5th century BC
Democritus	460–370 BC
Plato	429–347 BC
Socrates	d. 399 BC
Aristotle	384–322 BC
Epicurus	341–270 BC
Alcinous	150? BC
Vergil	70–19 BC
Cicero	d. 43 BC
Augustus (emperor)	27 BC–AD 14
Philo of Alexandria	d. 50
Seneca	d. 65
Polycarp	69?–155
Clement of Rome	c. 95
Trajan (emperor)	98–117
Justin Martyr	100?–165
Pliny the Younger	111–112
Irenaeus of Lyon	130?–200
Marcion of Pontus	fl. c. 144
Tatian	c. 150
Valentinus	c. 150
Clement of Alexandria	150?–215?
Tertullian	160?–220?
Melito of Sardis	c. 160
Celsus	c. 160–180
Montanus	c. 170?
Hippolytus of Rome	170?–235?
Origen	185?–254?
Cyprian of Carthage	200?–258
Plotinus	200?–270
Porphyry	234?–303?
Iamblichus	242?–327
Novatian	c. 250
Theognostus	fl. c. 250–280
Anthony (desert monk)	250–356
Arius	256?–336
Dionysius of Alexandria	c. 260
Eusebius of Caesarea	264?–339
Gregory Thaumaturgus of Pontus	d. 270?
Aurelian (emperor)	270–275
Victorinus, Marius	275–363
Pierius	fl. c. 280–300
Marcellus	280?–370?
Diocletian (emperor)	285–305
Athanasius	296?–373
Eusebius of Emesa	300?–359?
George of Laodicea	300?–361
Eustathius of Sebaste	300?–377?
Wulfila (Ulfilas)	310?–383
Apollinarius of Laodicea	310?–390?
Cyril of Jerusalem	313?–386
Didymus the Blind	313?–398
Hilary of Poitiers	315?–368?

Eustathius of Antioch	fl. 320–337
Epiphanius of Salamis	315?–403
Alexander of Alexandria	d. 328
Basil of Caesarea	329?–379
Arnobius of Sicca	d. 330?
Gregory of Nazianzus	330?–390
Eunomius of Cyzicus	330?–390?
Gregory of Nyssa	330?–395?
Ambrose of Milan	339?–397
Constantine I (emperor)	d. 337
Constantius II (emperor)	337–361
Jerome	340?–420
Eusebius of Nicomedia	d. 341
Asterius the Sophist	d. 341?
Liberius (bishop of Rome)	352–366
Augustine of Hippo	354–430
Donatus	d. 355?
Eudoxius	d. 360
Optatus of Milevis	c. 360–390
Cassian, John	360?–435?
Julian the Apostate (emperor)	361–363
Acacius of Caesarea	d. 365?
Damasus I (pope)	366–384
Aetius	d. 367
Synesius of Cyrene	373?–414?
Germinius of Sirmium	d. 375?
Theodosius I (emperor)	378–395
Nestorius	381?–451?
Theophilus of Alexandria	385–412
Innocent I (pope)	401–417
Chrysostom, John	d. 407
Theodosius II (emperor)	408–450
Proclus	412–485
Celestine I	422–432
Theodore of Mopsuestia	d. 428
Sabas	439–533
Leo (bishop of Rome)	440–461
Marcian	450–457
Dioscorus of Alexandria	d. 454
Severus of Antioch	456?–538
Leo I (emperor)	457–474
Timothy III Salophakiolos	460–475
Theodoret of Cyrus	d. 466?
Acacius (bishop of Constantinople)	472–489
Zeno	476–491
Timothy II Aelurus	d. 477
Boethius	480–526
Benedict of Nursia	480?–543
Cassiodorus	485?–585?
Anastasius I (emperor)	491–518
Gelasius I (pope)	492–496
Dionysius (Denys) the Areopagite (Pseudo-Dionysius)	c. 500
Caesarius (bishop of Arles)	502–542
Hormisdas (bishop of Rome)	514–523
Justin I (emperor)	518–527
Justinian I (emperor)	527–565
Agapetus I (bishop of Rome)	535–536
Pelagius I (pope)	556–561
Childebert I (Frankish king)	d. 558
Justin II (emperor)	565–578
Maximus the Confessor	580–662
Maurice (emperor)	584–602
Gregory I the Great (pope)	590–604
Chosroes (Khusraw) II (Persian king)	590–628
Sergius (bishop of Constantinople)	610–638
Heraclius (emperor)	610–641
Muhammad	d. 632
Constans II (emperor)	641–668
Martin I (bishop of Rome)	649–655
Bede	673–735
John of Damascus	675?–749?

Justinian II (emperor)	685–695; 705–711
Gregory II (pope)	715–731
Leo III (emperor)	717–741
Alcuin of York	735?–804
Constantine V (emperor)	741–775
Theodulf of Orléans	750?–821
Charles the Great ("Charlemagne"; emperor)	772–814
Maurus, Rabanus	776?–856
Constantine VI (emperor)	780–797
Radbertus	785?–865?
Paulinus of Aquileia	d. 802
Eriugena, John Scotus (Scottus)	815?–877?
Photius (patriarch)	815?–897?
Arn of Salzburg	d. 821
Charles II ("the Bald") (king of France)	840–877
Michael III (emperor)	842–867
Haimo of Auxerre	d. 855?
Nicholas I (pope)	858–867
Ratramnus	d. 870?
Symeon the New Theologian	949–1022
Avicenna	980–1037
Berengar of Tours	999?–1088
Peter Damian	1007–1072
Bruno of Cologne	1030?–1101
Anselm of Canterbury	1033–1109
Henry III (emperor)	1039–1056
Ivo of Chartres	1040?–1115
Leo IX (pope)	1049–1054
Hildebert of Tours	1055?–1133
Henry IV of Germany (emperor)	1056–1105
Nicholas II (pope)	1058–1061
Constantine III Lichoudes (patriarch)	1059–1063
William of St. Thierry	1070–1148
Gregory VII (pope)	1073–1085
de la Porrée, Gilbert	1075?–1154
Abelard, Peter	1079?–1142
de Bourg-Dieu, Hervé	1080?–1150
Gilbert of Sempringham	1083–1190
Urban II (pope)	1088–1099
Zonaras, John	1090?–1150?
Bernard of Clairvaux	1090–1153
Peter Lombard	1090?–1160
Hugh of St. Victor	1096?–1141
Hildegard of Bingen	1098–1179
Aristenos, Alexius	1100?–1170?
Andrew of St. Victor	1110?–1175
Baldwin of Forde	1125?–1190
Averroes	1126–1198
Innocent II (pope)	1130–1143
da Fiore, Joachim	1135?–1202
Balsamon, Theodore	1138?–1198?
Pullen, Robert	d. 1146
William of Auxerre	1160?–1231
Thomas of Chobham	1160?–1236?
Dominic	1170–1221
Richard of St. Victor	d. 1173
William of Auvergne	1180?–1249
Francis	1181–1226
Alexander of Hales	1185?–1245
Richard I (king of England)	1189–1199
Frederick II (emperor)	1194–1250
Alexius III (emperor)	1195–1203
Innocent III (pope)	1198–1216
Albert the Great	1206?–1280
Bonaventure	1221–1274
Thomas Aquinas	1226–1274
Gregory II (George) of Cyprus	1241–1290
Innocent IV (pope)	1243–1254
Olivi, Petrus Iohannes	1248?–1298?
Michael VIII (emperor)	1258–1282

Dante Alighieri	1265?–1321
Scotus, John Duns	1266–1308
Gregory X (pope)	1271–1276
Blemmydes, Nicephorus	d. 1272
Beccus, John XI (patriarch)	1275–1282
Marsilius of Padua	1275?–1342?
Gregory II (George) of Cyprus (patriarch)	1283–1289
Philip IV (king of France)	1285–1314
William of Ockham	1288?–1348?
Holcot, Robert	1290?–1349
Van Ruysbroeck (Ruusbroec), Jan	1293–1381
Barlaam of Calabria	1295?–1348
Gregoras, Nicephorus	1295?–1360
Cabasilas, Nilus	1295?–1363
Palamas, Gregory	1296?–1359
Akindynos, Gregory	1300?–1438
Benedict XI (pope)	1303–1304
Clement V (pope)	1305–1314
John XXII (pope)	1316–1334
Harmenopoulos, Constantine	1320?–1385
Cabasilas, Nicholas	1322?–1391?
Cydones, Demetrius	1323?–1397
Wyclif (Wycliffe), John	1328–1384
Cydones, Prochorus	1330?–1369?
Groote, Gerhard	1340–1384
Lady Julian of Norwich	1342?–1416?
Radewijns, Florentius	1350?–1400
Bryennius, Joseph	1350?–1431?
Plethon, George Gemistos	1360?–1452
Hus, Jan	1371?–1415
Kempe, Margery	1373?–1438
Thomas à Kempis	1380–1471
Isidore of Kiev	1385–1463
Eugenicus, Mark	1392?–1445
Gutenberg, Johann	1398–1468
Scholarius, George (Gennadius)	1400?–1473?
Bessarion of Nicaea	1403–1472
Valla, Lorenzo	1407–1457
Martin V (pope)	1417–1431
Biel, Gabriel	1420?–1495
John VIII (emperor)	1425–1448
Eugenius IV (pope)	1431–1447
d'Etaples, Jacques Lefèvre	1460?–1536
Erasmus of Rotterdam	1466–1536
Sixtus IV (pope)	1471–1484
Hubmaier, Balthasar	1480?–1526
Luther, Martin	1483–1546
Zwingli, Huldrych	1484–1531
Frederick III of Saxony	1486–1525
Müntzer, Thomas	1489?–1525
Farel, Guillaume	1489–1565
Sattler, Michael	1490?–1527
Albrecht of Hohenzollern	1490–1545
Bucer, Martin	1491–1551
Alexander VI (pope)	1492–1503
Marpeck, Pilgram	1495?–1556
Bale, John	1495–1563
Menno Simons	1496–1561
Melanchthon, Philipp	1497–1560
Musculus, Wolfgang	1497–1563
Osiander, Andreas	1498–1552
Julius II (pope)	1503–1513
Bullinger, Heinrich	1504–1575
Jan of Leiden	1509–1536
Servetus, Michael	1509?–1553
Calvin, John	1509–1564
Leo X (pope)	1513–1521
François I (king of France)	1515–1547
Teresa of Avila	1515–1582
Beza, Theodore	1519–1605
Gentile, Valentino	1520?–1566

Sozzini, Lelio	1525–1562
Whitgift, John	1530?–1604
Ursinus, Zacharias	1534–1583
Baro, Peter	1534–1599
Gerritz, Lubbert	1534–1612
de Molina, Luis	1535–1600
Olevianus, Caspar	1536–1587
Fausto, nephew of Lelio Sozzini	1539–1604
John of the Cross	1542–1591
Bellarmine, Robert	1542–1621
Whitaker, William	1548–1595
Mary I (queen of England)	1553–1558
de Ries, Hans	1553–1638
Arndt, Johann	1555–1621
Hooker, Richard	1556?–1600
Uytenbogaert, Johannes	1557–1644
Perkins, William	1558–1602
Elizabeth I	1558–1603
Arminius, Jacob	1560–1609
Bacon, Francis	1561–1626
Smyth, John	1570?–1612
Lucaris, Cyril	1572–1638
Davenant, John	1572–1641
Helwys, Thomas	1575?–1616?
Boehme, Jakob	1575–1624
Robinson, John	1576–1625
Ames, William	1576–1633
Sibbes, Richard	1577–1635
Cameron, John	1579–1625
Rous, Francis	1579–1659
Ussher, James	1581–1656
Knott, Edward	1582–1656
Episcopius, Simon	1583–1643
Grotius, Hugo	1583–1645
Jansen, Cornelius	1585–1638
Cappel, Louis	1585–1658
Curcellaeus, Stephanus	1586–1659
Preston, John	1587–1628
Hobbes, Thomas	1588–1679
Voetius, Gisbertius	1589–1676
Crell, Johan	1590–1633
Descartes, René	1596–1650
Amyraut, Moïse	1596–1664
Mogila, Peter	1597–1646
Cromwell, Oliver	1599–1658
Rutherford, Samuel	1600?–1661
Goodwin, Thomas	1600–1679
Chillingworth, William	1602–1644
Lightfoot, John	1602–1675
James I of England (VI of Scotland)	1603–1625
Cocceius, Johannes	1603–1669
Erbury, William	1604–1654
Bisterfeld, Johannes	1605–1655
Hammond, Henry	1605–1660
Minin, Nikita	1605–1681
Milton, John	1608–1674
Calovius, Abraham	1612–1686
Taylor, Jeremy	1613–1667
Sterry, Peter	1613–1672
Biddle, John	1615–1662
Baxter, Richard	1615–1691
Bourignon, Antoinette	1616–1680
Owen, John	1616–1683
Llwyd, Morgan	1619–1659
Avvakum	1620?–1682
Pascal, Blaise	1623–1662
Turretini, François	1623–1687
Fox, George	1624–1691
Charles I (king of England)	1625–1649
Bossuet, Jacques-Bénigne	1627–1704
Bunyan, John	1628–1688
de Molinos, Miguel	1628–1696

Tillotson, John	1630–1694
Howe, John	1630–1705
Spinoza, Benedict	1632–1677
Locke, John	1632–1704
Stillingfleet, Edward	1635–1699
Spener, Philipp Jakob	1635–1705
Parthenius I (patriarch)	1639–1644
Sherlock, William	1641?–1707
Newton, Isaac	1642–1727
Louis XIV (king of France)	1643–1715
Penn, William	1644–1718
Leibniz, Gottfried	1646–1716
Poiret, Pierre	1646–1719
Bayle, Pierre	1647–1707
de la Motte, Jeanne Marie Bouvier (Madame Guyon)	1648–1717
Madame Guyon	1648–1717
Nye, Stephen	1648–1719
Fénelon, François	1651–1715
Röell, Herman Alexander	1653–1718
Tindal, Matthew	1655–1733
Bray, Thomas	1658–1730
Francke, August Hermann	1663–1727
Arnold, Gottfried	1666–1714
Whiston, William	1667–1752
Dositheus II (patriarch)	1669–1707
Toland, John	1670–1722
Turretini, Jean-Alphonse	1671–1737
Clarke, Samuel	1675–1729
Collins, Anthony	1676–1729
Wolff, Christian	1679–1754
Erskine, Ebenezer	1680–1754
Peter I (czar)	1682–1725
Waterland, Daniel	1683–1740
James II of England (VII of Scotland)	1685–1688
Berkeley, George	1685–1753
Law, William	1686–1761
Bengel, Johann Albrecht	1687–1752
Adrian (patriarch)	1690–1700
Butler, Joseph	1692–1752
Reimarus, Hermann Samuel	1694–1768
Voltaire (François-Marie Arouet)	1694–1778
Tersteegen, Gerhard	1697–1769
von Zinzendorf, Nikolaus Ludwig	1700–1760
Oetinger, Friedrich Christoph	1702–1782
Edwards, Jonathan	1703–1758
Wesley, John	1703–1791
Spangenberg, August Gottlieb	1704–1792
Comrie, Alexander	1705–1774
Franklin, Benjamin	1706–1790
Wesley, Charles	1707–1788
Reid, Thomas	1710–1796
Hume, David	1711–1776
Rousseau, Jean-Jacques	1712–1778
Diderot, Denis	1713–1784
George I (king of Great Britain)	1714–1727
Whitefield, George	1714–1770
Harris, Howell	1714–1773
Voulgaris, Eugenius	1716–1806
Velichkovsky, Païsy	1722–1794
Kant, Immanuel	1724–1804
Newton, John	1725–1807
Lessing, Gotthold Ephraim	1729–1781
Hamann, Johann Georg	1730–1788
Cowper, William	1731–1800
Macarius of Corinth	1731–1805
Toplady, Augustus	1740–1778
Marquis de Sade	1740–1814
Paley, William	1743–1805
Jefferson, Thomas	1743–1826
Herder, Johann Gottfried	1744–1803
Koraês, Adamantios	1748–1833

Nicodemus of the Holy Mountain	1749–1809
de Maistre, Joseph	1753–1821
Wilberforce, William	1759–1833
Simeon, Charles	1759–1836
Schleiermacher, Friedrich	1768–1834
de Chateaubriand, François René	1768–1848
Hegel, Georg Wilhelm Friedrich	1770–1831
Schlegel, Friedrich	1772–1829
Alexander, Archibald	1772–1851
Louis XVI (king of France)	1774–1793
Schelling, Friedrich	1775–1854
von Drey, Johann Sebastian	1777–1853
Krause, Karl Christian Friedrich	1781–1832
de LaMennais, Hugues-Félicité Robert	1782–1854
Drozdov, Filaret	1782–1867
Kaïrês, Theophilus	1784–1853
Baur, Ferdinand Christian	1792–1860
Keble, John	1792–1866
Chaadaev, Pyotr	1794–1856
Möhler, Johann Adam	1796–1838
Bautain, Louis	1796–1867
Lyell, Charles	1797–1875
Hodge, Charles	1797–1878
Comte, Auguste	1798–1857
von Döllinger, Johann Joseph Ignaz	1799–1890
Darby, John Nelson	1800–1882
Pusey, Edward Bouverie	1800–1882
Alexander I (czar)	1801–1825
Newman, John Henry	1801–1890
Hengstenberg, Ernst Wilhelm	1802–1869
Froude, Richard Hurrell	1803–1836
Khomyakov, Aleksei	1804–1860
Feuerbach, Ludwig	1804–1872
Kireevsky, Ivan	1806–1856
Keil, Johann Karl Friedrich	1807–1888
Strauss, David	1808–1874
Bauer, Bruno	1809–1882
Darwin, Charles	1809–1882
Gosse, Philip Henry	1810–1888
Palmer, William	1811–1879
Kierkegaard, Søren	1813–1855
Delitzsch, Franz	1813–1890
Theophan the Recluse	1815–1894
Bulgakov, Mikhail Petrovich (Makary)	1816–1883
Ryle, John Charles	1816–1900
Marx, Karl	1818–1883
Dostoevsky, Fyodor	1821–1881
Ritschl, Albrecht	1822–1889
Hodge, Archibald Alexander	1823–1886
Renan, Ernest	1823–1892
Lightfoot, Joseph Barber	1828–1889
de Régnon, Théodore	1831–1893
Kähler, Martin	1835–1912
Abbott, Lyman	1835–1922
Kuyper, Abraham	1837–1920
Nietzsche, Friedrich	1844–1900
Pius IX (pope)	1846–1878
Herrmann, Wilhelm	1846–1922
Warfield, Benjamin B.	1851–1921
von Harnack, Adolf	1851–1930
Napoleon III (emperor)	1852–1870
Bolotov, Vasily	1853–1900
Solovyov, Vladimir	1853–1900
Bavinck, Herman	1854–1921
Torrey, Reuben Archer	1856–1928
Loisy, Alfred	1857–1940
Husserl, Edmund	1859–1938
Bergson, Henri	1859–1941
Laberthonnière, Lucien	1860–1932

Tyrrell, George	1861–1909
Thomas, William Henry Griffith	1861–1924
Whitehead, Alfred North	1861–1947
Blondel, Maurice	1861–1949
Weiss, Johannes	1863–1914
Troeltsch, Ernst	1865–1923
Gershenzon, Mikhail	1869–1925
Bulgakov, Sergei	1871–1944
Berdyaev, Nikolai	1874–1948
Schweitzer, Albert	1875–1965
Leo XIII (pope)	1878–1893
Hazard, Paul	1878–1944
Buber, Martin	1878–1965
Aulén, Gustaf	1879–1977
Machen, John Gresham	1881–1937
Bultmann, Rudolf	1884–1976
Gilson, Etienne	1884–1978
Richard, François-Marie-Benjamin (cardinal)	1886–1908
Tillich, Paul	1886–1965
Barth, Karl	1886–1968
Wilhelm II (emperor)	1888–1918
Brunner, Emil	1889–1966
Heidegger, Martin	1889–1976
Nicholas II (czar)	1894–1917
Van Til, Cornelius	1895–1987
Chenu, Marie-Dominique	1895–1990
Knowles, David	1896–1974
de Lubac, Henri	1896–1991
Hartshorne, Charles	1897–2000
Lloyd-Jones, Martyn	1899–1981
Pius X (pope)	1903–1914
Lossky, Vladimir	1903–1958
Stăniloae, Dumitru	1903–1993
Lonergan, Bernard	1904–1984
Rahner, Karl	1904–1984
Congar, Yves	1904–1995
von Balthasar, Hans Urs	1905–1988
Bonhoeffer, Dietrich	1906–1945
Prenter, Regin	1907–1990
Gollwitzer, Helmut	1908–1993
Grillmeier, Aloys	1910–1998
Nuttall, Geoffrey	1911–2007
Benedict XV (pope)	1914–1922
Hanson, Richard	1916–1988
Knox, David Broughton	1916–1994
Williams, J. Rodman	1918–2008
Galot, Jean	1919–2008
Gay, Peter	1923–
LeGoff, Jacques	1924–2014
Moltmann, Jürgen	1926–
Pannenberg, Wolfhart	1928–
Walicki, Andrzej	1930–
Oberman, Heiko	1930–2001
Plantinga, Alvin	1932–
Wolterstorff, Nicholas	1932–
Jüngel, Eberhard	1934–
Swinburne, Richard	1934–
Helm, Paul	1940–
Gunton, Colin	1941–2003
Israel, Jonathan	1946–
Weinandy, Thomas	1946–
McCormack, Bruce	1952–
John XXIII (pope)	1958–1963

Chronological List of Events

(The list includes only those events mentioned by their dates in this work.)

Constantine I legalizes Christianity	313
Council of Nicea	325
Constantine moves capital from Rome to Byzantium (Constantinople)	330
Fourth Creed of Antioch	341
Council of Serdica	343
Antiochene Council	344
Council at Sirmium	351
Goths invade Roman empire	376
Constantinian dynasty ends	378
Theodosius declares Christianity official religion of Roman empire	380
First Council of Constantinople	381
Goths establish semi-independent kingdom in Spain	409
Fall of Rome	410
Council of Carthage	411
Goths establish semi-independent kingdom in North Africa	430
Council of Ephesus	431
Council of Chalcedon	451
Goths establish semi-independent kingdom in Italy	476
Last Western emperor deposed, imperial regalia sent to Constantinople	476
Chalcedonian Definition	487
Athanasian Creed	500?
Great Synod in Antioch	513
Second Council of Constantinople	533
Visigoths in Spain converted to Catholicism	589
Persia invades Eastern empire, takes most of Syria, Palestine, Egypt	590–628
Constantinople besieged by Avars	626
Muslim Arabs invade Syria, Palestine, Egypt	632–642
Third Council of Constantinople	680–681
Council *in Trullo* in Constantinople	692

Muslim conquest of North Africa	698
Arabic becomes dominant language in eastern Roman empire	706
Arabs invade Spain	711
Franks repulse Arabs at Poitiers	732
Ravenna falls to Lombards	751
Second Council of Nicaea	787
Anti-Byzantine synods at Frankfurt	794
Anti-Byzantine synods at Friuli	797
Charlemagne crowned by pope as Holy Roman Emperor	800
Anti-Byzantine synods at Aachen (Aix-la-Chapelle)	809
First Crusade	1095
Constantinople sacked	1204
Fourth Lateran Council	1215
Frederick II leads crusade to Holy Land, retakes Jerusalem	1229
Rulers of Nicea recapture Constantinople	1261
Second Council of Lyon	1274
Papacy in Avignon ("Babylonian captivity")	1305–1377
Papacy returns from Avignon to Rome	1377
Council of Constance	1414–1417
Council of Basel	1438
Pragmatic sanction of Bourges	1438–1516
Council of Florence	1439
Constantinople falls to the Turks	1453
Gutenberg prints New Testament	1456
Treaty of Tordesillas	1494
Martin Luther's Ninety-five Theses	1517
Treaty of Zaragoza	1529
Augsburg Confession	1530
Church of England breaks with Rome	1534
Wittenberg Articles	1535–1536
English Ten Articles	1536
Smalcald Articles	1537
Council of Trent	1545–1563
Forty-two Articles of Church of England	1553
Peace of Augsburg	1555
Final edition of Calvin's *Institutes of the Christian Religion*	1559
French Confession of La Rochelle	1559

Belgic Confession	1561
Second Helvetic Confession	1566
Elizabeth I excommunicated	1570
Thirty-nine Articles of Church of England	1571
Thomas Wilcox and supporters called "Puritans"	1572
Formula of Concord	1577
Second Mennonite (Waterland) Confession	1580(81)
Lambeth Articles	1595
Edict of Nantes	1598
James VI of Scotland to English throne as James I	1603
Irish Articles	1615
Synod of Dort	1619
Westminster Confession	1646
Peace of Westphalia	1648
Book of Common Prayer	1662
Edict of Nantes revoked	1685
"Glorious Revolution" (English parliament ejects Catholic King James II)	1688
First Vatican Council	1869–1870
Dead Sea scrolls discovered at Qumran	1947
Second Vatican Council	1962–1965

General Index

Abbott, Lyman, 1078
Abel, 53, 508, 544
Abelard, Peter, 452–453, 479
Abraham, 46, 57, 58–59, 60, 67, 89, 93, 101, 127, 435, 495, 588, 589, 1002, 1055, 1213
Absalom, 1213–1214
Acacius (bishop of Constantinople), 374, 376–377
Acacius of Caesarea, 261, 262, 270
Achamoth, 129–130
Adam, 51–53, 82, 84, 86–87, 88, 101, 167, 168, 178, 184, 431, 438, 490, 599, 601, 882, 1002, 1172
Admonition to the Parliament (Wilcox), 579
adoption/adoptianism, 227–231, 323, 660, 822
Aeterni Patris (encyclical of Leo XIII), 1101–1102
Aetius, 262
affaire Calas, the, 1035
Afrikaners, 1128
Agabus, 733
Against Celsus (Origen), 213–214
"Against Peril of Idolatry" (Jewel), 397
Agapetus I, 377
Agrippa, 294
Akathistos (Greek: not seated) hymn, 393
Akindynos, Gregory, 823
Alaric the Goth, 423
Albert the Great, 503, 504, 516
Albrecht of Hohenzollern, 526
Alcinous, 106
Alcuin of York, 514, 661
Alexander, Archibald, 1117, 1118
Alexander I, 1135
Alexander VI, 570
Alexander of Alexandria, 116, 234, 235, 237, 247–248, 249, 256, 620
Alexander the Great, 295
Alexander of Hales, 480, 501, 516
Alexandria, 348, 361, 364, 416, 608, 767
Alexius III, 682
Alexius IV, 682
Alighieri, Dante, 500
allegory, 47, 50, 145, 461, 560, 624
Amalekites, 75
Ambrose of Milan, 41, 287, 460, 469, 477–478, 545, 627, 644–645, 763
Ames, William, 937
Amish, the, 578
Amyraldianism, 901
Amyraut, Moïse, 914–920
Anabaptists, 578, 733, 850, 852–853, 858, 860, 864, 865, 872, 945, 1149
Analogy of Religion (Butler), 1040
Anatolius, 360
Andrew of St. Victor, 560–561
angels/archangels, 55, 79, 83, 84, 86, 123, 124, 125, 126, 129, 135, 172, 180, 195, 225, 291, 366, 436, 448, 450, 451, 629, 803–813, 908, 911, 961, 1084, 1168, 1169
Anglican Reformation, 975
Anglicanism/Anglicans, 871–872, 873, 954, 965, 967, 1022, 1023, 1110–1116. *See also* Anglo-Catholicism/Anglo-Catholics
Anglo-Catholicism/Anglo-Catholics, 1114–1115
Anglo-Saxons, 783
Anselm of Canterbury, 439, 443–452, 527, 532, 671–678, 686, 696, 894, 899, 995, 1151, 1152
Anselm of Havelberg, 678
Anthony the hermit, 255, 778
anthrôpotokos (Greek: man-bearer), 342
Antichrist, 64, 572, 573, 581, 731, 848–849, 860, 1098
Antinomians, 945
Antioch, 240, 348, 364, 608, 767
aphthartodocetism, 378
Apocrypha, the, 29, 40–41, 742, 762, 793, 798
Apollinarians, 327
Apollinarius of Laodicea, 281, 287, 326–327, 327–329, 330, 332, 342, 343, 344, 358, 370, 377, 766

Apollos, 741
Apostles' Creed, 399, 775, 797
apostleship/apostolicity, 729–733
Apostolic Constitutions, 775
apostolic succession, 730–733
Apostolic Tradition (anonymous; credited to Hippolytus of Rome), 458
Aquila, 38–39, 44, 741
Aquinas, Thomas, 471–472, 474, 503, 516, 518, 536–537, 553, 555, 567, 681–682, 685–690, 693, 696, 991–1000, 1018, 1033, 1097, 1102, 1186, 1225
Arabic language, 295
Arabs, 386–387, 393, 553, 672, 790
Aramaic, 294, 295
Aratus, 104
Arianism, 233–246, 259, 272, 273, 399, 610, 621, 653, 689
Arians, 154, 239, 244, 245, 246, 267, 273, 323–324, 327, 329–330, 373, 622, 655
Aristenos, Alexius, 781
Aristotelianism, 243
Aristotle, 197, 467–468, 470, 553, 682, 790, 992
Arius, 153, 232, 233–234, 234–237, 242, 247, 250, 251, 255, 256, 257, 323–324, 340, 761, 765
Armenia/Armenians, 386, 707, 1004
Armenian language, 295
Arminianism, 1006–1007
Arminius, Jacob, 891, 892, 901, 1006
Armstrong, Brian, 913, 919
Arn of Salzburg, 663
Arndt, Johann, 959
Arnobius, 132
Arnold, Gottfried, 961–962
Articles of Religion (J. Wesley), 968
Articuli cleri laws (1316), 786
Asia Minor, 211, 617, 672
Asterius the Sophist, 240–242, 250, 256
Athanasian Creed (Latin title: *Quicunque vult*), 117, 119, 272, 364, 390, 654, 791, 988
Athanasius of Alexandria, 205, 228, 229, 254–255, 257, 263, 265–272, 274, 278, 281, 282, 289, 312, 324–326, 327, 332, 333, 335, 344, 364, 370, 416, 622, 624, 627, 637, 694, 743, 760, 778
atheism, 21, 1008, 1042–1050, 1060, 1074, 1144, 1146, 1177
Athenagoras of Athens, 194, 195, 740
atonement, 439, 442, 1171; extent of, 899–920 passim; limited atonement, 896
Augsburg Confession (1530), 708, 837, 856, 866, 867–878, 875, 1110, 1205
Augustine of Hippo, 40, 164, 181–182, 200, 278, 287, 288, 291, 321–322, 359–360, 417–420, 431, 432, 442, 460–461, 469, 479, 497–498, 512–514, 536, 545, 551, 562, 583, 623, 627, 657, 661, 687, 693, 698, 712, 713, 747–748, 749, 763, 778, 792–793, 796, 836, 853, 854, 897, 987, 989, 992, 1004, 1155, 1183, 1187, 1199; on the Holy Spirit, 644–651; on the interpretation of Scripture, 756–759; and the Pelagian controversy, 423–430, 432–433; on the personhood of God, 664–665
Augustus, 211
Aulén, Gustaf, 439–440
Aurelian, 215–216
Auschwitz, 1206
authority, crisis of, 553–570 passim
Avars, the, 393
Averroes, 553, 992
Avicenna, 553, 992
Avignon, 556, 848
Avvakum, 1132

Babel, 55–56
Babylonian Captivity of the Church, The (Luther), 530
Bacon, Francis, 1118
Bale, John, 849
Balsamon, Theodore, 781
baptism, 186, 410–421, 422–423, 514, 597–599, 615, 728, 810, 852–860, 858–860; infant baptism, 414, 429, 586, 587, 598–599, 853–857, 960. *See also* sacraments (the seven specific sacraments)
Bardanes, George, 505
Barlaam of Calabria, 699–700, 821–823, 824
Barmen Declaration (1934), 1152–1153, 1164
Barnabas, 80, 157
Baro, Peter, 891
Barrett, William, 891
Barth, Karl, 599, 714–716, 895, 1060, 1083, 1148–1165 passim, 1168, 1169–1170, 1171–1172, 1174, 1180, 1181, 1183, 1190, 1192, 1193
Bartholomew, 505
Basil of Ancyra, 260, 261, 263, 265, 270, 278
Basil of Caesarea, 278, 279, 281, 285, 287, 320, 333, 335, 378, 381, 400–401, 459, 545, 616, 627, 629–630, 632, 634, 694, 703, 742, 778
Basilides of Alexandria, 124–126
Basiliscus, 374
Bauer, Bruno, 1059
Baur, Ferdinand Christian, 1071–1072, 1080, 1084, 1101, 1106
Bautain, Louis, 1103–1104
Bavinck, Herman, 1126–1127
Baxter, Richard, 901, 905, 939, 941, 947, 948–949, 950, 952, 1017
Bayle, Pierre, 1023, 1025, 1026–1027, 1042

Bede, 41, 815
Beeke, Joel, 927
Bellarmine, Robert, 1006
Benedict XI, 555–556
Benedict XV, 1102
Benedict of Nursia, 545
Bengal, Johann Albrecht, 962–963
Berdyaev, Nikolai, 1145
Berengar of Tours, 466–467
Bergson, Henri, 1105
Berkeley, George, 1032
Bernard of Clairvaux, 452, 498, 508, 550
Bessarion of Nicea, 703, 706
Beza, Theodore, 889, 890, 901, 904, 907, 913, 919, 928–931, 933
Bible, the, 745, 749, 761–762, 791–792, 798, 800–801, 1009, 1038, 1053; allegorical method for the interpretation of, 754–755, 1028; biblical revelation, 1028, 1029–1030, 1123; as the divinely inspired Word of God, 1119–1120; and God's revelation, 1158–1159; the Hebrew Bible, 740–741; translations of after the legalization of Christianity, 608. *See also* Vulgate, the
biblicism, 1119
Biddle, John, 1015–1016
Biel, Gabriel, 519, 521
Bisterfeld, Johannes, 1014
Blasphemy Act (1698), 1030
Blemmydes, Nicephorus, 684
Blondel, Maurice, 1105
Body and Blood of Christ, The (Radbertus), 466
Boehme, Jakob, 958
Boethius, 654, 664, 679–680, 989
bogochelovechestvo (Russian: "Godmanhood"), 1142
Bogomils, 1130
Boleyn, Anne, 579
Bolotov, Vasily, 1197
Bonaventure, 472, 503, 516, 518, 684–685, 690
Bonhoeffer, Dietrich, 1170–1171, 1172
Boniface VIII, 554–555, 784
Book of Common Prayer, 598, 813, 951–952, 958, 1093, 1115
Book of Heraclides (Nestorius), 340, 352–353, 365
Borgia, Cesare, 570
Bossuet, Jacques-Bénigne, 957, 1024
Bourignon, Antoinette, 958, 1042
Bradford, John, 891
Bray, Thomas, 966
Brethren of the Common Life, 825
Brief traité (Amyraut), 915
Brunner, Emil, 1152, 1165–1167, 1172
Bruno of Cologne, 515
Bryennius, Joseph, 702
Buber, Martin, 1076, 1166
Bucer, Martin, 531, 532, 883, 885
Buckley, Michael, 1043–1044
Bulgakov, Mikhail Petrovich, 1136
Bulgakov, Sergei, 1145–1146
Bullinger, Heinrich, 537, 586, 588, 589, 591, 593, 879–880, 925–926
Bultmann, Rudolf, 1083, 1165, 1167–1170, 1172, 1177
Bunyan, John, 725, 873, 942–943, 1146
Butler, Joseph, 1032, 1040–1042
Byzantines, Western view of, 672–673
Byzantium, 394, 1197

Cabasilas, Nicholas, 523–524
Cabasilas, Nilus, 700
Caecilian, 416, 417
Caecilius of Biltha, 457
Caesarea Maritima, 237, 242
Caesarius of Arles, 498, 654
Cain, 53, 544
Calovius, Abraham, 1014
Calvin, John, 508, 531–532, 538–541, 577, 584, 585, 587–589, 591, 592, 593, 598, 712–714, 719, 733–734, 770, 792, 793, 795–796, 797, 799, 800, 843–844, 845–847, 857–860, 869–870, 870–871, 872, 874, 875, 877–882, 914, 920, 926–928, 935, 938, 976, 1000–1006, 1044, 1225; and the doctrine of "aseity," 1005, 1006–1007, 1031; English translations of Calvin's works, 931
Calvinism/Calvinists, 967, 976, 1044, 1111, 1117, 1125, 1128; "four-point" Calvinists, 899; "three-point" Calvinists, 899
Cameron, John, 912–914, 918
canon law, 560
Cappadocian fathers, 278, 279, 637, 641, 643, 646, 647, 658, 712, 817, 987, 1199, 1201, 1202
Cappel, Jean, 800
Cappel, Louis, 800, 913
cardinals, 547
Carmelites, 551
Cassian, John, 349
Cassiodorus, 423
Catenae (Latin: chains), 762
cathedrals, English, 546
Catherine II, 1134
Catholic Faith, The (Thomas), 1115
catholicity, 1139
Celestine I, 349
Celestine of Rome, 350
celibacy, 185, 546–547, 777, 779–781, 789–790, 810
Celsus, 213–214

Cerularius, Michael, 671, 781, 782, 783
Chaadaev, Pyotr, 1137
Chalcedonian Definition, the, 321, 322, 350–365, 371–372, 398
Characters (Theophrastus), 318
charismatic movements, 727, 981–992
Charlemagne (Charles the Great), 398, 659, 663, 771, 783
Charles I, 580, 955, 1144
Charles II (Charles the Bald), 466
Chenu, Marie-Dominique, 1188
Chernyshevsky, Nikolai Gavrilovich, 1145
Childebert I, 664
chiliasm, 749–750
Chillingworth, William, 1011–1012
Chosroes II (Khusraw), 385
chrismation, 483
Christian Faith, The (Schleiermacher), 1067–1069
Christian liberty, 846–847
Christian Library (J. Wesley), 976
Christian perfection, 976, 977–978
Christian vocabulary, 300–311; Christian vocabulary for what God is like (the attributes of God), 311–316; Christian vocabulary for who God is, 316–322
Christianity, 85, 88, 96, 213, 218, 480, 749, 813, 961, 993, 994, 1030, 1034, 1040, 1042, 1052–1053, 1056, 1065–1066, 1075, 1139, 1142, 1171, 1220, 1224; interpretation of Israel's history in, 56–67; and Jewish biblical interpretation, 45–51; legalization of, 141, 416, 543, 608; and the new understanding of Scripture, 137–148; and the prehistory of Israel, 51–56; and the Roman world, 211–220; separation of from Judaism, 27–36. *See also* Old Testament, reappropriation of by Christianity
Christianity Not Mysterious (Toland), 1030
Christianity as Old as the Creation (Tindal), 1032
Christians, 45, 54, 56–57, 58–59, 66, 67, 70–71, 72, 75, 76–77, 78, 84, 86, 87, 91, 92, 93, 95, 107, 114, 115, 121, 139, 147, 160, 192, 193, 218, 230, 235, 341–342, 369, 434, 529, 553, 565, 726, 737, 738, 740, 749, 779, 807, 842, 985, 1035, 1042–1043, 1059, 1159, 1210, 1211, 1220; Gentile Christians, 60; and holiness, 143–144; Jewish Christians, 60; and the new relationship with God, 133–137; persecution of, 411; and the principle of dispensation, 144–145; view of the universe, 72–73
Christology, 220, 240, 332–333, 337, 347–348, 365–366, 386, 399, 402, 461, 676, 1154–1155; Alexandrian Christology, 338, 350–351; Antiochene Christology, 252; two-natures Christology, 767–768
Christology of the Old Testament, The (Hengstenberg), 1110
Christotokos (Greek: Christ-bearer), 343
Christus Victor (Aulén), 439–440
Chrysologus, Peter, 536
Chrysostom, John, 153, 337, 442, 459, 755, 762
church, the: as the body of Christ, 419, 582; as the creation of the Holy Spirit, 847–848; as the image of God, 819–820; and medieval society, 549; the true church, 847–864 passim
church councils/canons, 764–777; admission of the laity to, 874; ecumenical councils, 765, 770–774; in the Middle Ages, 772; provincial councils, 764–765; "reformation councils," 772. *See also specifically listed church councils*
Church Dogmatics (Barth), 1152, 1153–1164, 1181
Church of England, 575, 787, 966, 968, 1020, 1022, 1030, 1093
Church of Ireland, 1111
Church of Scotland, 1022, 1093
churches, "Eastern" and "Western," 43, 205–206, 465–466, 512, 608–611, 666, 743–744, 767, 772–773, 788, 809, 812–813, 987
Cicero, 410
circumcision, 58, 62, 89, 480, 482
Cistercians, 550–551
City of God (Augustine), 544, 747–748, 749, 756
Clarification (Vatican decree), 1218–1219
Clarke, Samuel, 1019–1020
Clement V, 556, 784
Clement XI, 887
Clement of Alexandria, 72, 76, 77, 85, 93, 131–132, 156, 171–172, 202, 737, 762
Clement of Rome, 88–89, 169, 222, 1115
Clementinae (Clement V), 784
clergy, in the Reformation tradition, 865–875
Clericis laicos (decree of Boniface VIII), 554–555
Cocceius, Johannes, 600, 937–938, 969
Codex iuris Ecclesiae Anglicanae (Gibson), 885
coinherence (*perichôrêsis*), doctrine of, 647
Collins, Anthony, 1032–1033
Comestor, Peter, 515
Commentary on the Psalms (Didymus the Blind), 334
Comrie, Alexander, 937
Comte, Auguste, 1135
confession, 475
Confession of Dositheus, 1131

confirmation, 475, 880. *See also* sacraments (the seven specific sacraments)
Congar, Yves, 1188
Congregationalists, 1022
conscience, role of in the Christian life, 847
Consensus Tigurinus, 879–880
Constance, 559
Constans, 257, 258
Constantine, 216, 217–218, 240, 246–247, 249, 254–255, 348, 417, 557, 791
Constantine (Cyril), 666
Constantine Harmenopoulos, 782
Constantine III Lichoudes, 671, 672
Constantine V, 394
Constantine VI, 659
Constantinople, 348, 363, 608, 672, 683, 767, 771, 824, 1196
Constantius I, 255, 258
Constantius II, 257, 258, 263, 265, 269, 275
consubstantiation (Greek: *homoousios*), 228, 250, 251, 254, 256, 260, 261, 262, 269, 270, 274, 275, 277, 278, 281, 307, 308–309, 375, 629, 674, 765
Contra gentes (Athanasius), 266
Coptic language, 295
Corpus Areopagiticum, 812
Corpus Christi, feast of, 473
Corpus iuris canonici, 784, 786–787
Council of Aachen (809), 663
Council of Antioch (341), 256, 257, 274
Council of Ariminum (359), 265
Council of Basel (1438), 569
Council of Carthage (411), 423
Council of Chalcedon (451), 304, 320, 334, 340, 360, 371, 382, 584, 635, 651, 654, 764, 767–768, 1201, 1202, 1218
Council of Constance (1415), 474, 476, 559, 567, 568–569
Council of Constantinople (First Council [381]), 226, 286–287, 315, 317, 328–329, 333–334, 356, 634, 636, 638, 766–767
Council of Constantinople (Second Council [553]), 383, 768
Council of Constantinople (Third Council [680–681]), 387, 388, 392, 400, 651, 768–769
Council of Ephesus (First Council [431]), 340, 349–350, 635, 702, 767, 768
Council of Ephesus (Second Council [449]), 764
Council of Florence (1439), 569, 659, 690, 705, 706, 708, 772, 781, 791, 1100
Council of Lyon (First Council [1245]), 474
Council of Lyon (Second Council [1274]), 474, 569, 685, 690, 772, 1100
Council of Milan (313), 257
Council of Nicea (First Council [325]), 226, 228, 307–308, 356, 373, 474, 620, 625–626, 651, 765, 1188
Council of Nicea (Second Council [787]), 397, 769–770
Council of Seleucia (358), 265
Council of Serdica (344), 253, 254, 255, 256–257
Council of Sirmium (First Council [357]), 258
Council of Sirmium (Second Council [358]), 259, 282
Council of Sirmium (Third Council [359]), 259–260
Council of Soissons (853), 665
Council of Toledo (Third Council [589]), 655
Council of Trent (1545–1563), 885–886, 1091
Council of Trent (first session [1545]), 841
Council of Trent (fourth session [1546]), 43, 792–793
Council of Trent (sixth session [1547]), 841–843, 926
Council of Trent (eleventh session [1551]), 472
Council of Trent (fourteenth session [1551]), 487
Council *in Trullo*. *See* Quinisext (Greek: *Penthektê*) Council (the Council in *Trullo*)
Council of Tyre (335), 255
Councils of Toledo (seventeen councils), 765
Count von Zinzendorf. *See* Ludwig, Nikolaus (Count von Zinzendorf)
Cowper, William, 979–980
Cranfield, Charles, 424
Cranmer, Thomas, 598, 794–795, 799, 857, 866, 867–868, 870, 883–885, 951–952, 1205
creation, 77–81, 407, 751–752, 1172; as an act of divine speech, 78; Christian doctrine of, 164–174; creation *ex nihilo*, 166; goodness of, 78–79, 164–165; hierarchies in, 807–809; order in, 79–90, 165–166. *See also* God, as Creator; Jesus Christ, as Creator
Creed of Epiphanius, 641
Crell, Johan, 1014
Crime and Punishment (Dostoevsky), 1140
Cromwell, Oliver, 942, 945, 946, 948, 949
Cross, the, glory of, 525–535
Crusades, the, 393, 549, 550, 672–673, 682–683
Crutched friars, 551
Cum occasione (bull of Innocent X), 887
Cur Deus homo (*Why God Became Man*), 443–451
Curcellaeus, Stephanus, 1014
Cydones, Demetrius, 699, 700, 824
Cydones, Prochorus, 824
Cyprian of Carthage, 75, 200, 419, 425, 457, 465, 555, 776, 854

Cyril of Alexandria, 321, 335, 343, 348, 349, 350, 353, 354, 355, 365, 375, 377, 383, 652–653, 655, 686, 694, 767, 768, 1202
Cyril of Jerusalem, 275, 623–624, 742, 743
Cyrus, 386, 796

da Fiore, Joachim, 848, 849, 850
Damasus I, 332, 333, 763, 766
Damian, Peter, 671, 899–900, 903
Darby, John Nelson, 750
Darwin, Charles, 1076, 1077–1078, 1079
Darwinism, 1078, 1124, 1126
Davenant, John, 905–909, 910, 911, 913
David, 63, 64, 67, 107–108, 143, 1213–1214
Day of Atonement, 896
De Anima (Justin Martyr), 214
de Bourg-Dieu, Hervé, 515
de Chateaubriand, François René, 1072
De decretis (Athanasius), 269
De Deo uno Patre (*The One God the Father* [Crell]), 1014
De doctrina Christiana (Augustine), 479, 756
De incarnatione (Athanasius), 266, 324, 325
De incarnationis Dominicae sacramento (*On the sacrament of the Lord's Incarnation* [Ambrose of Milan]), 478
de LaMennais, Hugues-Félicité Robert, 1073, 1094
de Lentini, Thomas, 506
de Lubac, Henri, 1188
de Maistre, Joseph, 1098–1099, 1137
de Molina, Luis, 887
de Molinos, Miguel, 957
De mysteriis (Ambrose of Milan), 477
De praedestinationis modo et ordine (Perkins), 891–892
De principiis (*On First Principles* [Origen]), 751
De regno Christi (*The Kingdom of Christ* [Bucer]), 883
de Régnon, Théodore, 987
de Ries, Hans, 861
De sacramentis (Ambrose of Milan), 477
De sacramento regenerationis (*On the sacrament of regeneration* [Ambrose of Milan]), 478
De Spiritu Sancto (Basil of Caesarea), 283, 287, 610–611, 630
De synodis (Athanasius), 270
De Trinitate (Augustine of Hippo), 288–291, 644, 651, 987, 989
deacons, 488, 489, 780, 809, 870, 874
Dead Sea Scrolls, 37
Decretum Gelasianum de libris recipiendis et non recipiendis (Gelasius I), 776–777
Decretum Gratiani (Gratian), 784, 788
Defensor pacis (*Defender of the Peace* [Marsilius of Padua]), 556
deism/deists, 1033, 1034, 1037, 1038, 1041, 1042, 1050
Delitzsch, Franz, 1110
Demiurge, the, 162, 163, 176–177, 179, 219
Democritus, 1174
Descartes, René, 1018, 1025, 1033, 1047
determinism, 73
Devils, The (Dostoevsky), 1140
devotional life, in the Reformation tradition, 951–974 passim
devotional literature, 875–876
d'Huisseau, Isaac, 1024
Dialogue with Trypho (Justin Martyr), 44
Dialogus (Anselm of Havelberg), 678
Dictionnaire historique et critique (Bayle), 1025
Diderot, Denis, 1046–1047
Didymus the Blind, 334, 335, 338, 358, 626–627, 761, 762
Die kosmische Liturgie (von Balthasar), 817
Diocletian, 216, 240, 416
Diodore of Tarsus, 333
Dionysius of Alexandria, 205
Dionysius the Areopagite, 307, 495, 804
Dioscorus of Alexandria, 354, 355–356, 365, 374
Discalced Carmelites, 957
Discourse of Free-thinking (Collins), 1032–1033
dispensationalism, 191, 750
Dissenters, 954–955, 970
divine fatherhood, non-Jewish conceptions of, 104–107
Divine-human Encounter, The (Brunner), 1166
divine passions, 1210–1211
divorce, 882–885
Dobrolyubov, Aleksandrovich, 1145
Docetism, 219–220
Doctoris angelici (decree of Pius X), 1102
Dominic of Caleruega, 551
Dominicans, 518, 551, 857
Donation of Constantine, 570, 782, 791
Donatism/Donatists, 141, 218, 417, 419, 420, 422–423
Donatus, 186, 218
Dositheus II, 1131
Dostoevsky, Fyodor, 1140, 1141, 1146, 1148
Drozdov, Filaret, 1135–1136
dualism, 85, 162
Duns Scotus. *See* Eriugena, John Scotus (John Duns Scotus)
Dutch Reformed Church (*Hervormde Kerk*), 1124–1125

Easter, date of, 248, 463
Eastern Orthodox Church, 341, 392, 506, 512, 659, 727–728, 732, 767, 772–773, 781, 824, 1219
Eastern Orthodoxy, and the crisis of authority, 1129–1149 passim
Ebionites, 228
ecstasy/*ekstasis* (Greek: stepping out), 806–807
"ecumenical" (Greek: *oikoumené*), 250
ecumenism, 15, 1037, 1217–1218
Edict of Nantes (1598), 576, 1023
education, 548, 873
Edward VI, 579
Edwards, Jonathan, 951, 968–969, 970, 1117
elders, 137, 140, 141, 182, 474, 489, 579, 866, 869, 874, 881
election, 88–96, 596, 888, 921, 938, 1156
Elias of Jerusalem, 376
Elijah, 64, 107, 221, 227, 323, 495, 803, 817
Eliot, George, 1070
Elipandus of Toledo, 660
Elizabeth I, 579, 866
Elysian Fields, 161
enhypostasia, painting the person of Christ in human form as an expression of, 396
"enhypostatic" light, 822–823
Enlightenment, the, 1021–1022, 1031–1032, 1037–1038, 1050, 1051, 1187
Enoch, 53–54, 107, 227, 323, 495, 508
Ephraim, 104
Ephrem the Syrian, 613
Epicureans, 159
Epicurus, 1174
Epiphanius of Salamis, 116–117, 130, 260, 282, 332, 335, 619, 626, 639–641, 686
Episcopius, Simon, 1007
Erasmus, Desiderius, 525, 532–533, 745, 792
Erbury, William, 943, 944
Eriugena, John Scotus (John Duns Scotus), 466, 473, 519, 665, 805
Erskine, Ebenezer, 936–937
Esau, 89
Essay on the Development of Christian Doctrine (Newman), 1113–1114
Essenes, 221
essentia (Greek: essence), 309
Esther, book of, 40
Eucher of Lyon, 654
Eudoxius of Constantinople, 245
Eugenicus, Mark, 703–704, 704–707
Eugenius IV, 568, 570
Eunomius of Cyzicus, 262, 263, 627
Eusebius of Caesarea, 217, 240, 242, 243, 250, 251, 253, 536, 621, 743
Eusebius of Dorylaeum, 354
Eusebius of Emesa, 331, 333
Eusebius of Nicomedia, 237, 239, 240, 250, 255
Eustathius of Antioch, 252–253, 254, 326, 331–332, 620
Eustathius of Sebaste, 627
Eutyches, 354, 355, 362, 654
Evangelical Theological Society, 1109
evangelicalism, 972, 1115
evangelism, 185
Evangelists, symbols of, 82
Eve, 51–53, 82, 84, 86–87, 88, 167, 168, 178, 184, 431, 438, 490, 882, 1172
evil, 161, 436, 439, 1176, 1179; existence of, 78–79, 1155–1156, 1208; nature of, 84–88; origin of, 167–169
evolution, 1124
excommunication, 91, 474
exegesis, literal, 47
existentia (Latin: existence), 277
Exposition of the Orthodox Faith (John of Damascus), 989
Extravagantes (decretals of John XXII), 784
extreme unction, 881. *See also* sacraments (the seven specific sacraments)

faith, 186, 466, 513–514, 844, 845, 848, 1012, 1150, 1151, 1152, 1167, 1169
"false apostles," 157, 741
False Decretals (anonymous), 782, 784
Familists, 945
Farel, Guillaume, 593
fate, 179
Felix of Urgel, 660
Fénelon, François, 957
Ferguson, Everett, 853
Feuerbach, Ludwig, 1059, 1074–1076, 1079, 1080, 1163, 1166
First Book of Homilies, The, 840, 875
First Vatican Council (1869–1870), 732, 772, 888, 1099–1100
First World War, 1087, 1088, 1147
Fisher, Edward, 967
Flavian, 354–355, 356, 654
flesh (Greek: *sarx*), 368
flesh (Hebrew: *basar*), 368
foedus hypotheticum (Latin: hypothetical covenant), 913
forgiveness, of sins, 504
Formula of Concord (1577), 578, 1109
Formula consensus Helvetica, 800–801
Forty-two Articles (1553), 794–795, 857, 868, 880
Fourth Creed of Antioch, 258
Fox, George, 941, 942, 943, 949
France, 1131
Francis of Assisi. *See* St. Francis
Franciscans, 518, 551, 857
Francke, August Hermann, 960–961, 965

François I, 569
Franklin, Benjamin, 1040
Franks, the, 385, 393, 398, 666
Frederick II, 553, 554, 555, 848
Frederick III, 526
Frederick William III, 1109–1110
free will, 510–512; as *liberum arbitrium*, 512
"free-willers," 891
French Revolution, the, 1051, 1054, 1072
Freud, Sigmund, 1043, 1076, 1187
Froude, Richard Hurrell, 1112–1113
"Fruitful Exhortation to the Reading and Knowledge of Holy Scripture" (Cranmer), 799
Fulgentius of Ruspe, 654, 661

Galen, 553
Galot, Jean, 1213
Gamaliel, 221
Gassendi, Pierre, 1026
Gay, Peter, 1021
Gelasius I, 567
Gennadius of Marseilles, 654
Gentile, Valentino, 1004
George I, 956, 1022, 1023
George II, 1037
George of Laodicea, 263–265, 270, 622
Germinius of Sirmium, 622
Gerritz, Lubbert, 861
Gershenzon, Mikhail, 1145, 1146
Geschichte (German: meaning), 1084
Gibbon, Edward, 1054
Gibson, Edmund, 885
Gilbert de la Porrée, 681
Gilbert of Sempringham, 521, 723
Gilbertines, 551
Gilson, Etienne, 1186–1187
glossolalia, 728
Gnesio-Lutherans, 578
Gnostic Gospels, 219
Gnosticism/Gnostics, 122–125, 127–128, 139, 176–177, 219, 220, 775, 1141
God, 68–77, 99–100, 102–103, 110, 112–113, 117–118, 145, 184, 186, 204, 222–223, 229–230, 234–235, 260–261, 516–518, 528, 562, 603, 719, 737, 738, 750, 785, 960, 976, 985–986, 994–895, 1001, 1034, 1148, 1150, 1156, 1175–1176, 1181, 1182–1183, 1194–1195, 1223, 1225; as the Almighty, 117–119; the believer's relationship to and experience of God, 814–825; communion with, 811; compassion of, 1211; confusion concerning, 814; covenant of with his people, 92–94, 535; as Creator, 105, 107, 121, 131, 132, 136, 163, 174, 268; devotion to, 394; *einai* ("to be") used as the name of, 305; as *El-Shaddai*, 117; "energies" (Greek: *energeiai*) of, 814, 821–822, 1176, 1199; essence of, 814, 1199; as eternal, 73, 74, 199; "feelings" in, 1214–1216; freedom and generosity of, 522; as "God-in-himself" (Greek: *autotheos*), 119–121, 202–203, 1003–1004; as *ho ôn* (masculine), 303; as holy, 74–75, 103, 143; honor of, 448–450; image of, 175–182; immutability of, 989–990, 996; as judge, 173–174; knowledge of, 467–468, 1001, 1002; as love, 648–650, 999–1000, 1211; love for, 808, 811–812; omnipotence of, 466; as one, 68–70; perfection of, 648, 997, 998, 1041, 1211; as a personal God, 71–73, 1173; perspective of on human affairs, 135–136; revelation of, 467–468, 999, 1002, 1048, 1158–1160, 1163, 1180–1181; simplicity of, 990–991, 997; sovereignty of, 167, 367, 541, 967, 1176, 1207, 1211; spiritual nature of, 70–71; suffering of, 246, 1205–1217; transcendence of, 1211; "truce of," 548–549; two persons in (Greek: *prosôpa*), 200; as unbegotten and uncreated, 268–269; the work of God the Father from a Christian perspective, 155–164; the work of God the Father from a Jewish perspective, 151–155; as *YHWH*, 68, 72, 305–306, 1003. *See also* Christian vocabulary; God, doctrine of; reconciliation, between man and God through Jesus Christ; Trinity, the
God, doctrine of, 1176; and classical philosophy, 991–1000; and the patristic synthesis, 985–991; in the Reformation tradition, 1000–1007
"God-fearers," 69, 157
Gollwitzer, Helmut, 1180
Goodwin, Thomas, 936, 947
gospel, the, 80–82, 509, 588
Gospel and the Church, The (Loisy), 1105
Gospels, the, 1185–1186
Gosse, Philip Henry, 1078
Goths, 271–272. *See also* Visigoths (Western Goths)
Gottschalk of Orbais, 663–664, 667
government, synodical model of, 577–578
grace, 429, 480, 513, 514, 711, 713, 714, 822, 836, 844, 845, 1012, 1150, 1169
Gratian, 498, 782, 784, 788, 789
Great Tew circle, the, 1012
Greco-Roman society, 159
Greece/Greeks, 72, 147, 162–163, 781, 790–791, 1130, 1135, 1175, 1196. *See also* Greek language; Greek philosophy/philosophers
Greek language, 608, 656; theological context of, 293–300

Greek philosophy/philosophers, 34, 104, 158–159, 160–162, 302, 310, 985–986, 1211
Gregorian calendar, 887–888
Gregorian chant, 462
Gregory I (Gregory the Great), 442–453, 462, 498, 546, 779, 783, 788, 922–923, 926
Gregory II (patriarch) of Cyprus, 693–696, 697, 704, 705
Gregory II (pope), 462, 498
Gregory VII, 550
Gregory IX, 784
Gregory X, 505–506
Gregory XIII, 887
Gregory of Laodicea, 275
Gregory of Nazianzus, 278, 284–285, 330, 335–336, 370–371, 442, 452, 628, 630–632, 634, 637, 639, 642, 643, 645, 667, 804, 816, 820, 1015
Gregory of Nyssa, 116, 278, 285, 336, 441–442, 632–634, 642–643, 674, 694, 695
Gregory Thaumaturgus of Pontus, 205, 633
Gregory of Tours, 495
Grillmeier, Aloys, 325, 327, 363
Groote, Gerhard, 724, 825
Grotius, Hugo, 1010, 1014, 1028
guesthouses, 548
Gunton, Colin, 1183
Gutenberg, Johann, 526

Habets, Myk, 816
Hades, 160–161
Haimo of Auxerre, 514–515
Hamann, Johann Georg, 1051–1052
Hammond, Henry, 1012, 1013
"handers-over" (Latin: *traditores*), 416
Hanson, Richard, 238, 239, 243–244, 256
Harris, Howell, 967
Harte, Henry, 891
Hartshorne, Charles, 1176–1178
Hazard, Paul, 1021
Hebrew language, 985; theological context of, 293–300, 800–801
Hebrews, book of, 730
Hegel, Georg Wilhelm Friedrich, 1053–1060, 1060, 1061, 1062, 1069, 1070, 1072, 1074, 1087, 1141
Heidegger, Martin, 1076, 1168, 1177
Hellenism, 155
Helm, Paul, 1184
Helwys, Thomas, 863–864
Hengstenberg, Ernst Wilhelm, 1110
henotheism, 68–69
Henôtikon (Zeno), 374–376
Henri de Navarre, 576
Henry II (of Germany), 671
Henry III (of Germany), 783
Henry IV (of Germany), 550
Henry VIII (of England), 575, 579, 787, 838, 840, 882
Heraclitus, 1174
Heraclius, 385, 386, 387
Herder, Johann Gottfried, 1052–1053
heresies, 216
Hermann, Wilhelm, 1083
hermits, 724
Herodotus, 759
hesychasm (from Greek *hesychia*), 821
Heterousian teaching, 262
Hexabiblos (Constantine Harmenopoulos), 782
hexaêmeron, the, 164
hierarchies: celestial hierarchies, 808, 813; in creation, 807–808; ecclesiastical hierarchies, 808–810
Hilary of Poitiers, 258, 263, 276, 337, 356, 357–358, 359, 623, 641–642, 643, 646, 668, 760, 815, 987, 989
Hildebert of Tours, 468
Hildegard of Bingen, 724
Hillel, 48, 221
Hippolytus of Rome, 118–119, 130, 165–166, 170, 200–202, 319, 407, 458, 740
Historie (German: facts and events), 1084
"history of religions school" (*die religionsgeschichtliche Schule*), 1086
"history of salvation" (*Heilsgeschichte*), 1086
Hitler, Adolf, 1152
Hobbes, Thomas, 1014–1015
Hodge, Archibald Alexander, 1122–1123, 1126
Hodge, Charles, 1078, 1118–1122
Holcot, Robert, 472, 480
holiness, 135, 143–144
holiness movements, 978
Holy Communion. *See* Lord's Supper, the (Eucharist); sacraments (the seven specific sacraments)
Holy Orders, 487–489
Holy Roman Emperor, election of, 526
Holy Roman Empire of the German Nation, 398, 772
Holy Spirit, the, 112, 142, 146, 190, 191, 193, 195–196, 201, 243, 244, 292, 341, 399, 737, 739–740, 751, 764, 778, 794, 797, 799, 801, 802, 815, 820, 823, 836, 839–841, 962, 974–975, 981–982, 1050, 1140, 1154, 1159, 1160, 1167, 1187, 1198, 1200, 1221, 1225; and baptism, 615–616, 960; controversy concerning double procession (*Filioque*) of, 651–696 passim; controversy concerning double procession (*Filioque*) and the parting of East and West, 696–719 passim, 1218–1219; as depicted in the Bible,

612–617; doctrine of, 400–401, 532, 542, 603, 607; in the Eastern tradition, 609–611, 638; fellowship of, 938–951 passim; and the *Filioque* question today, 709–719; as the indwelling power of God, 728–735; as the Paraclete, 617–620, 646; person of, 401; procession of, 637–643; as represented in the ancient church creeds, 620–636 passim; sending of by God the Father, 154–155; in the teachings of Anselm, 671–678; in the teachings of Augustine, 644–651; in the Western tradition, 610, 611, 638; work of, 134, 723–728, 843–844, 1178. *See also* Trinity, the
Homily against Peril of Idolatry (Jewel), 770
Homoean controversy, 271
Homoean teaching, 261–262
Homoeans, 308
Homoeousian controversy, 271
Homoeousians, 308; Nicene Homoeousians, 308–309
homoousios. *See* consubstantiation (Greek: *homoousios*)
Hormisdas of Rome, 654
Hosius of Córduba, 247–249, 250, 258–259
Hospitallers (Knights of St. John), 551
Howe, John, 939
Hubmaier, Balthasar, 850
Hugh of Cluny, 550
Hugh of St. Victor, 468, 478–479, 481, 498–499
Huguenots, 1023–1024
human beings/human race: as a composite of flesh (*sarx*) and soul (*psyche*) in Greek philosophy, 160; as created in the image of God, 81–83, 171–173, 713, 714; free will of, 510
humanity, definition of, 365–384
Hume, David, 1045–1046, 1047, 1118
Hus, Jan, 476, 520, 566–568, 848
Husserl, Edmund, 1177
Hutterites, 578
hymns/hymn-singing, 958, 971–972
hyparchonta (Greek: exist), 309–310
hyparxis (Greek: existence), 280
hypostasis/hypostases. *See* "identity"/"identities" (Greek: *hypostasis/hypostases*)
hypothetical universalism, 905, 906–907, 909, 914, 919–920

Ialdabaoth, 127–128
Iamblichus, 278, 646
Ibas of Edessa, 383, 768
iconoclasm, 394, 395, 397, 769
iconoclastic controversy, the, 393–398
Idea of a University, The (Newman), 1113
"identity"/"identities" (Greek: *hypostasis/hypostases*), 203, 247–248, 249, 251–252, 253, 254, 264, 268, 275–276, 280, 284, 286, 290, 303–306, 317–318, 320–321, 328, 336, 340, 345, 347, 349, 350, 352, 353, 354, 355, 356, 362, 363, 378, 379–382, 389, 390, 627, 646, 650, 666, 667, 670, 678, 692, 697, 699, 712–713, 823, 1197, 1201, 1202
idolatry, 70, 78, 105, 211, 301, 306, 313, 397, 574, 875, 964, 985, 1001, 1002, 1048, 1051, 1193, 1210
Ignatius of Antioch, 186, 331, 464, 474, 1115
illumination, 658, 714, 798, 806–807, 844, 917–918, 940–941, 1042, 1104, 1120–1121, 1123
Imitation of Christ, The (à Kempis), 825–835
In Praise of Folly (Erasmus), 532
incarnation, the. *See* Jesus Christ, incarnation of
indulgences, 501–502, 507–508, 526, 529
infralapsarianism, 902
Innocent I, 788
Innocent II, 789
Innocent III, 462, 547, 682
Innocent IV, 505
Innocent X, 887
inspiration, 1120, 1121, 1123
Institutes of the Christian Religion (Calvin), 538, 712, 797, 799–800, 1000–1001
Interim of 1548, 575–576
intinction, 476
Irenaeus of Lyon, 52–53, 55, 74, 84, 123, 124–125, 130, 142, 172, 177–179, 195–196, 211, 212, 235, 405, 407, 425, 437, 439, 440, 455–456, 613, 737, 738, 739–740, 741–742, 775, 817, 1100; on the *archontes*, 131; on creation, 163; on recapitulation, 181–182, 444; on reconciliation with God, 174
Irene, 659
Irish Articles (1615), 798, 890, 901
Isaac, 59, 60, 101, 588
Isaiah, 64
Ishmael, 59
Isidore of Kiev, 703, 1132
Isidore of Seville, 989
Islam, 993–994, 1220
Israel, Jonathan, 1021–1022
Israel/Israelites, 80, 180, 612, 985; Babylonian exile of, 64, 294; belief systems of, 32; Christian interpretation of Israel's history, 56–67; exile of, 64; prehistory of, 51–56; tribes of, 59
"I-Thou" relationship, 1173–1174
Ivo of Chartres, 501–502

Jacob, 59, 60, 89, 101
James the Apostle, 817
James I, 580, 893
James II, 576, 954, 1022
James VI (of England), 912
James VI (of Scotland), 580, 893
Jan of Chlum, 567
Jan of Leiden, 849
Jansen, Cornelius, 886–887
Jansenists, 887
Jefferson, Thomas, 1040, 1044
Jenson, Robert, 1183
Jeremiah, 103–104, 594
Jeremias II, 708
Jeroboam I, 122
Jerome, 40, 43, 147–148, 358–359, 423, 484, 560–561, 562–563, 656, 751, 763, 793, 989
Jerusalem temple, 28–29, 60; destruction of, 62
Jesuits, 1095, 1130
Jesus Christ, 27, 48, 49, 53, 107, 112, 115, 147, 151, 184–185, 196, 208, 222–223, 231, 338, 371, 394–395, 528, 533–534, 557–558, 603, 741, 751, 836, 1013, 1039, 1049, 1055, 1150–1151, 1152, 1156, 1169, 1177–1178, 1225; ascension of, 583–584, 1057; "aseity" of, 1005, 1006–1007, 1031; baptism of, 223, 228–229, 658, 1200; communion with, 524; contemporaries of, 220–224; as Creator, 192, 408–409; death of, 1057; as a descendent of Adam, 102; differences of from the rabbis in his day, 30–32; as the divine *logos* in human flesh, 323–329; in early Christian teaching, 224–227; earthly work of as manifestation of heavenly principles, 582–583; eternal reign of, 542–543; "farewell discourses" of, 615, 676–677; as the Great High Priest, 62, 94; as guarantor of God's covenant, 595–596; as *homo deifer* (the God-bearing man), 331–332; humanity of, 766; as the image (*charaktêr*) of the Father's *hypostasis*, 304–305, 316–317; incarnation of, 71, 79, 88, 152–153, 165, 218–219, 224, 251, 253, 327, 366–368, 369–371, 409–410, 1057, 1160; as the Lamb of God, 435; and the law of Moses, 60–61; as the likeness of sinful flesh, 421–429; as the *logos*, 192–193; as the man from heaven, 406–410; as Mediator, 594–595, 756–757, 788; as the Messiah, 94–95; as the "new Adam," 52; nineteenth-century biographies of, 1069; obedience of, 154; as the only sacrifice for sin, 434–442; as a portion of the Godhead, 276; priesthood and kingship in the death of, 64–67; as prophet, priest, and king, 535–541, 595; reality of, 1170–1171; relationship of with believers, 1163–1164; resurrection of, 165, 220, 748, 760; return of (*parousia*), 543, 546, 547; revelation of, 1194–1195; as the second Adam, 180, 430–433; second coming of, 95; similarity of to the Father, 262, 269; sinlessness of, 367; as the "son of David," 63, 539; as the Son of God, 99–100, 107–112, 223–224, 435; as the Son of Man, 109; sovereignty of, 584; suffering of, 1207–1217; transfiguration of, 817–818, 1200; union of believers with, 844–845; will of, 384–393, 1143–1144. *See also* reconciliation, between man and God through Jesus Christ; Trinity, the
Jewel, John, 397, 770
Jews, 33, 37, 54–55, 66, 67, 70, 78, 84, 86, 87, 105, 137, 143, 147, 160, 213, 528, 549, 781, 790, 792, 950, 1065; anti-Christian Jews, 45; "Hellenized Jews," 27; Jewish biblical interpretation, 47–49; view of the universe, 72–73
Job, 151, 427, 508
John VIII, 702, 703
John XI Beccus, 692, 693, 694, 696
John XXII, 848
John XXIII, 1103
John of Antioch, 352
John the Apostle, 803, 817, 820
John the Baptist, 221, 223, 228, 535, 733
John of Caesarea (John the Grammarian), 378
John of the Cross, 956–957
John of Damascus, 313–316, 395, 820, 989
John Duns Scotus. *See* Eriugena, John Scotus (John Duns Scotus)
John of Montenero, 702–703
John of Parma, 684
John of Scythopolis, 812
Joseph (New Testament), 341
Joseph (Old Testament), 59–60
Joseph I, 693
Joseph of Arimathea, 1111
Josephus, 796
Judaism, 85, 88, 96, 145, 156, 992, 1064–1065, 1210, 1220; approach of to Scripture, 137–138; patriarchal nature of, 52; separation of from Christianity, 27–36; symbols of, 157
Judas Iscariot, 729
Julian the Apostate, 244, 265, 271, 333
Julian of Halicarnassus, 378, 384
Julian of Norwich, 724
Julius II, 570
Julius of Rome, 255
Jung, Carl, 1187
Jüngel, Eberhard, 1180–1183, 1184
Jupiter (Roman god), 104
justification, 16, 58, 401, 444, 482–483, 484, 485, 497, 499, 508–525 passim, 528, 836–847, 853, 854, 885, 897, 898, 900, 926,

927, 931, 959, 977–978, 1049, 1080, 1096, 1098, 1117, 1139, 1169, 1219, 1223
Justin I, 376
Justin II, 385
Justinian I, 311, 363, 376, 382–383, 384, 385, 768, 780
Justinian II, 769

Kähler, Martin, 1083–1084
Kaïrês, Theophilus, 1135
Kant, Immanuel, 1047, 1048–1050, 1062, 1094
Keble, John, 1111–1112, 1114
Keil, Johann Karl Friedrich, 1110
Kempe, Margery, 724
Kempis, Thomas à, 825–835, 975
Khomyakov, Aleksei, 1138–1140
Kierkegaard, Søren, 1076, 1088–1090, 1148, 1166
kingdom of God, 547
Kireevsky, Ivan, 1137–1138
Kistyakovsky, Bogdan Aleksandrovich, 1145, 1146
Knights Templar, 551
Knott, Edward, 1011
Knowles, David, 458–459
Knox, David Broughton, 919
Koraês, Adamantios, 1134–1135
Krause, Karl Christian Friedrich, 1177
Kuyper, Abraham, 1125, 1126
Kuyperians, 1127–1128

La liturgie cosmique (von Balthasar), 817
La philosophie du christianisme (Bautain), 1103–1104
Laberthonnière, Lucien, 1105
Lactantius, 172–173
Lambeth Articles (1595), 890
Langton, Stephen, 462
Lateran Council (First Lateran Council [1123]), 474
Lateran Council (Fourth Lateran Council [1215]), 470, 474, 475, 500, 502
Lateran Council (Second Lateran Council [1139]), 474, 546, 789
Lateran Council (Third Lateran Council [1179]), 474
Latin language, 463, 656; theological context of, 293–300, 608–609
"Latinophrones," 683, 691, 695, 696, 700–701, 706–707
latitudinarianism, 955–956, 1013, 1030
Latter-Day Saints. *See* Mormons
Law, William, 956, 966, 975, 1032
Laws of Ecclesiastical Polity (Hooker), 580
lay participation, 876
Lazarus and the rich man (parable of), 496

Le génie du Christianisme (de Chateaubriand), 1072
Le Goff, Jacques, 499, 502–503
Lefèvre d'Etaples, Jacques, 792
Leibniz, Gottfried, 1037–1038
Leo I (Leo of Rome), 349, 356, 360, 361, 363, 374, 392, 653–654, 767, 1201
Leo II, 374
Leo III, 394, 662, 663, 707
Leo IX, 783
Leo X, 572
Leo XIII, 1102–1103
Leontius of Byzantium, 340, 380, 381
Leontius of Jerusalem, 381–382, 398
Lessing, Gotthold Ephraim, 1038–1040
Levites, 59, 462, 488, 790
Liber extra (decretals of Gregory IX), 784, 785–786
Liber sextus (decretals of Boniface VIII), 784
liberalism, 955, 973, 1088, 1096, 1097, 1098, 1103, 1115, 1118, 1124, 1128–1129, 1136, 1155, 1167–1168, 1225
Liberius, 259, 263
Libri Carolini (Theodulf of Orléans), 659, 660–661, 662
Licinius, 240, 246
Life of Jesus (Renan), 1104
Lightfoot, John, 797–798
Lightfoot, Joseph Barber, 1115–1116
Lloyd-Jones, Martyn, 810–811
Llwyd, Morgan, 947
Locke, John, 954, 968, 1019, 1029–1030, 1047, 1137
logos (Greek: word, reason), 195, 229, 245–246, 253, 302, 332, 334–335, 338, 342, 344, 350, 351, 353, 359–360, 361, 377, 379; indwelling logos (*logos endiathetos*), 192, 200; *logos prophorikos* (Greek: the uttered word), 192. *See also* Jesus Christ, as the divine *logos* in human flesh
Loisy, Alfred, 1092, 1105–1108, 1109, 1184
Lollards, 566
Lombard, Peter, 469, 472, 476–477, 493, 498, 499, 520, 696, 797, 989–991, 992, 1157; on the seven sacraments, 479–493 passim
Lombards, 397
Lonergan, Bernard, 1185, 1186, 1187, 1188–1190, 1193
Longenecker, Richard, 49
Loofs, Friedrich, 381
Lord's Prayer, the, 136, 633, 1136
Lord's Supper, the (Eucharist), 411, 412, 483–484, 489, 491, 492, 587, 597–598, 834–835; as "the breaking of the bread," 876; centrality of, 453–476 passim; and the concept of sacrifice, 458; development of the general

consensus on, 455–456; in Eastern churches, 465–466; as "Eucharist," 876; as "Holy Communion," 876; as "Liturgy," 876; as the Mass, 876; modern approach to, 454; in the Reformation tradition, 876–880; traditional approach to, 454. *See also* sacraments (the seven specific sacraments)
Lorenz, Rudolf, 238
Lossky, Nikolai, 1196
Lossky, Vladimir, 709–710, 814, 1196–1200
Louis XIII, 912
Louis XIV, 1023, 1024
Louis XVI, 1144
love, 999–1000; perfect love, 648–650; and religion, 1055–1056
Lucaris, Cyril, 708, 712, 1129–1130
Lucian of Antioch, 233, 239, 240, 243
Ludwig, Nikolaus (Count von Zinzendorf), 963–965
Lumen gentium (decree of the Second Vatican Council), 732
Luther, Martin, 439, 480, 508, 523, 524, 525–535, 537, 538, 552, 570–575, 583–584, 585, 586, 708, 786–787, 794, 797, 836, 837, 839, 841, 842, 843, 850, 851, 854, 857, 866, 869, 876, 880, 923–924, 925, 926, 938, 975, 976, 1000, 1081, 1165, 1225; and the creation of theological opposites, 527–529, 848
Lutheranism/Lutherans, 871–872, 1004, 1044, 1109–1110; Missouri Synod, 1110; "Old Lutherans," 1110
Lyell, Charles, 1076
Lyte, Henry F., 1174

Macarius of Corinth, 1133
Macedonianism/ Macedonians (*Pneumatomachoi* ["Attackers of the Spirit"]), 282–283, 689
Macedonius, 282, 624
Machen, John Gresham, 1124
Madame Guyon, 957, 958, 962
Magnentius, 258
Maimonides, 553
Maistre, Joseph de, 1137
Majorinus, 416
Malebranche, Nicolas, 1026
Man in Revolt (Brunner), 1166
Manners, John, 978–979
Manoah of Zorah, 46
Marburg Articles, 531
Marcellus of Ancyra, 253, 254, 255, 325, 330–331, 620
Marcian, 360
Marcion of Pontus, 36, 139–140
Marcionites, 180
Marcus Aurelius, 302
Marian devotion, 1095–1097
Marinus of Cyprus, 655
Maris of Persia, 768
Marpeck, Pilgram, 850
Marquis de Sade, 1047
"marrow men," 967
Marsilius of Padua, 556–560
Martin I, 387
Martin V, 568, 570
Martin, John, 942
Martyr, Justin, 44, 123, 158, 159, 163, 168–169, 179–180, 192, 194, 195, 212, 214, 436–437, 456
martyrdom, 185–187, 216, 412, 415–416, 420–421
Marx, Karl, 1043, 1059, 1076, 1079–1080
Marxism, 1080, 1126
Mary I, 576, 579, 866, 891
Mary II, 1022
Mary (the Virgin Mary), 327, 341, 350, 353, 363, 517, 524, 1095–1096. *See also* Marian devotion
Masoretes, 37
Mass, the, 463–476, 523, 899; private masses, 494, 953; the Tridentine Mass, 886
matrimony, 141, 183–184, 480, 490, 548, 786–787, 789, 864, 882. *See also* sacraments (the seven specific sacraments)
Matthias, 729
Maurice, 385
Maurus, Rabanus, 483
Maximus the Confessor, 387, 388, 389–392, 398, 513, 655, 657, 658, 697, 700, 703, 719, 805, 812, 816–817, 818–819, 1143; on the will as *thelêton* or *thelêthen*), 391
McCormack, Bruce, 717–718, 1164
Mediator, The (Brunner), 1165–1166
Melanchthon, Philipp, 537, 577, 838, 844, 879, 880
Melchizedek, 65, 536
Meletians, 254, 255, 416
Meletius, 333, 416
Melito of Sardis, 177, 761
Melodus, Romanus, 393
Menander, 123, 124
mendicant orders, 551, 552
Mennonites, 578
Messianic movement, 30
Methodists, 966–967
Methodius, 666
Metrophanes of Smyrna, 666
mia physis (Greek: one nature), 343–344
Michael III, 788–789
Michael VIII, 506, 684, 691, 1100
Middle Ages, 734, 812–813, 985, 1193; church councils during, 772; the church and

medieval society, 549–550; idea of the gentleman in, 549
midrash, 48
millenarianism, 749–750
Milton, John, 885, 943, 946
Minucius, 70
miracles, 993–994, 1039
missionaries, 296, 608, 666, 972–973
modalism. *See* Sabellians/Sabellianism (modalism)
Mogila, Peter, 1131
Möhler, Johann Adam, 1101
Moltmann, Jürgen, 716–717, 1205–1207, 1210, 1213
Monarchianism, 189
monasticism, 545–546, 551–552, 778, 779, 825
monenergism, 386
monks, 545, 724, 734, 777–778, 809–810, 821–822, 1133
monophysitism (miaphysitism)/monophysites, 365, 373, 389, 812
monotheism, 68–70, 190, 670, 992, 1158, 1220
monothelitism, 387–388, 389, 817
Montanists, 141, 143, 144, 184, 190, 617, 730, 733, 776
Montanus, 190
moral perfection, 1049–1050, 1054
Moravians, 963–964, 966, 975
Mormons, 726, 730, 1116
Moses, 46, 56, 57, 60, 67, 70, 93, 107, 127, 184, 221, 323, 759; law of, 60–62, 66, 90, 91, 137, 509, 602, 795, 803, 817
Mount Athos, 821, 1133
Muhammad the Prophet, 385, 733, 994
Muller, Richard, 709
Müntzer, Thomas, 849
Muratori, Ludovico Antonio, 743
Muratorian fragment, 743
Musculus, Wolfgang, 589–591
Muses, the, 740
Muslims, 43, 59, 385, 393–394, 443, 554, 670, 672, 726, 730, 790, 949
Mussolini, Benito, 888
mysticism, 306–307, 805, 812, 950, 956–957, 961, 963, 995, 1150, 1193

Naaman, 90
Nadere Reformatie (Dutch: deeper Reformation), 937, 938
Napoleon III, 1099
Napoleon Bonaparte, 1093, 1098
Nathan, 107–108
Natural History of Religion, The (Hume), 1045
natural selection, 1077
nature, laws of, 76–77
Nature and Grace (Brunner), 1166
naz (Aramaic: riddle), 48
"Nazirite"/"Nazarene" word play, 46–47
neo-Arian Anhomoeans, 264
neo-Calvinism, 1126, 1153, 1184
Neoplatonism, 215, 279, 804–807, 813, 992, 1014, 1142
Neo-Scholasticism, 709, 1101–1102, 1103
Neo-Thomism, 709, 1102–1103, 1188
Nero, 29, 211, 212, 410–411
Nestorianism/Nestorians, 320, 340–350, 364–365, 375, 399, 707
Nestorius, 340–341, 342, 343, 349–350, 351, 352–353, 355, 362, 364–365; assessment of his beliefs, 346–347, 386, 767
New Testament, 29, 41–42, 67, 92, 135, 140, 202, 231, 295–296, 305, 390, 480, 549, 648, 743–745, 775–776, 784, 799, 800, 1169, 1188
Newman, John Henry, 725, 922, 1111, 1112, 1113, 1115
Newton, Isaac, 968, 1019, 1047, 1118
Newton, John, 980
Nicene Creed, 226, 249, 273, 399, 400, 542, 634, 654–655, 718, 1135–1136, 1138, 1185, 1201
Niceno-Constantinopolitan Creed (381), 610, 723, 736
Nicephorus, 506
Nicetas of Byzantium, 670–671, 678
Nicholas I, 670, 788, 789
Nicholas II, 783, 1144
Nicodemus of the Holy Mountain, 1133
Nicol, Donald, 682
Nicole, Roger, 920
Nicomedia, 240
Nietzsche, Friedrich, 1043, 1076, 1090–1092
Nikon (Nikita Minin), 1132, 1133
Ninety-five Theses, 526, 570, 571–572
Noah, 53, 54, 55, 508, 1002
Noetus, 190, 200, 201
nominalism, 1000
Normans, 673
North Africa, 186
Novatian, 131, 201–212, 612–613, 618, 620, 987
Nuttall, Geoffrey, 948–949
Nye, Stephen, 1019

Oberman, Heiko, 521, 522
Of the Cases of Conscience (Perkins), 931
Old Catholic Church, 1101
"old ritualists," 1132–1133
Old Testament, 29, 34, 46, 63, 75, 83, 105, 140, 144, 305, 337, 742–743, 751, 792, 796, 799, 985, 1003, 1053; anthropomorphisms of, 1210; commentaries on, 761–762; as divine self-revelation, 69–70; doctrine of creation in, 157–158; reappropriation of by Christianity, 461–463

Olevianus, Caspar, 593–601, 602, 913
Oliver, John, 978
Olivi, Petrus Johannes, 472
On Christian Liberty (Luther), 572–573
On Religion: To Its Cultured Despisers (Schleiermacher), 1060–1066
On theôsis (Palamas), 822
Ophites (Naassenes), 125
Optatus of Milevis, 420
Orationes contra Arianos (Athanasius), 266
ordination. *See* sacraments (the seven specific sacraments)
Origen, 29, 62, 73, 83, 86, 130, 132, 139, 145, 162, 170, 175, 235, 242, 243, 247, 254, 257, 275–276, 279, 317, 356, 383, 405, 415, 425, 440, 441, 457, 614, 615, 616, 738, 762, 764, 768, 776, 815, 853, 1053, 1141; on angels and the Devil, 168; on the Holy Spirit, 203, 618–620; on the interpretation of Scripture, 751–755; legacy of, 148; misinterpretation of Proverbs, 146–147; on the Trinity, 202, 203–204
Orthodox Faith (John of Damascus), 657–658
Osiander, Andreas, 537, 844–845
Othobon, 785
Ottoman Empire, 1130, 1131, 1135
ousia (Greek: being/essence), 275, 280, 284, 286, 290, 303–306, 317, 320–321, 377, 378, 666, 670, 697, 699, 821, 1198
Owen, John, 718, 934–936, 940, 969, 1015
Oxford Movement, 1112–1115

paganism, 72, 180, 206, 213, 217, 284, 313, 394, 510, 1068, 1074
Palamas, Gregory, 696–699, 703, 704, 705, 708, 710, 711, 713, 714, 821–825
Paley, William, 166, 1076, 1077
Palmer, William, 1111, 1141
panentheism, 1177
Pannenberg, Wolfhart, 717
pantheism, 996–997, 1168–1169
papacy: decline of, 887–888; papal infallibility, 1097, 1099–1101, 1121–1122; Protestant Reformers' view of, 1098
Papal States, 398, 1099
Paraclete. *See* Holy Spirit
Parastron, John, 506
Parmenides (Plato), 811
parousia. *See* Jesus Christ, return of (*parousia*)
Parthenius I, 1131
Pascal, Blaise, 887
passion. *See* divine passions
Passover, 248, 463
Pastor aeternus (decree of the Frist Vatican Council), 731
patripassianism, 189–191
Paul the Apostle, 35, 45, 47, 48, 53, 59, 60, 89, 90, 145, 154, 157, 212, 233, 294, 367, 410, 411, 412, 456–457, 614, 728, 729–730, 734, 741, 754, 803, 804, 900; conversion of, 430–431; and the law of Moses, 61–62; on righteousness and justification, 509–510
Paul of Emesa, 352
Paul of Samosata, 217, 227–229, 231, 233–234, 244, 308, 340, 452, 651
Paulicians, 1130
Paulinus of Aquileia, 332, 333, 660, 669
Peace of Augsburg (1555), 576, 578
Peace of Westphalia (1648), 577, 888, 960
Pelagianism/Pelagians, 423–430; primary beliefs of, 426
Pelagius, 423–424, 432, 453, 512, 761
Pelagius I, 664
penal substitution, 534–535
penance, 464, 507, 881. *See also* sacraments (the seven specific sacraments)
Penn, William, 954
Pensées (Pascal), 887
Pentateuch, the (Genesis–Deuteronomy), 37, 39; Greek Pentateuch, 38
Pentecost, 293, 612, 614, 706, 723, 1057, 1058, 1200, 1210
Pentecostal mission, the, 974–982
Pentecostals, 727, 980–981
Perkins, William, 600–601, 602, 889–892, 901, 904, 907, 910, 919, 931, 933
Perpetua, 497
persecution, 216–217, 411
pesher (Aramaic: solution), 48
Petau, Denis (Petavius), 1014
Peter the Apostle, 49, 222–223, 412, 784, 817, 1173
Peter I (Peter the Great), 1133
Peter Comestor or Manducator, 499
Petto, Samuel, 942
Pharisees, 27, 221, 367, 415
Philip IV, 551
Philo of Alexandria, 38, 44, 47, 107, 156, 1142
Philokalia, 1134
Philosophy of Revelation, The (Bavinck), 1126–1127
Photinus, 331
Photius, 666–670, 674, 677–678, 695, 771–772
physis (Greek: nature), 276, 286, 328, 377, 379
Pia desideria (Arndt), 959
Pierius, 205
piety/pietism/pietists, 958–965, 966, 967, 1001, 1047, 1050, 1093, 1174
pilgrimages, 548
Pius VII, 1098
Pius IX, 1096–1097, 1099, 1111
Pius X, 1102, 1109

Plantinga, Alvin, 1184
Planudes, Maximus, 643
Plato, 105–106, 162, 167, 758, 759, 790, 811
Platonism, 202, 243, 334, 776, 806
Plethon, George Gemistos, 569
Pliny the Younger, 211
Plotinus, 215, 278, 279, 285, 646
Pneumatologia: A Discourse on the Holy Spirit (Perkins), 934
pneumatology, 402
Pneumatomachi. *See* "Spirit-fighters" (Greek: *Pneumatomachi*)
Poiret, Pierre, 958, 962
Poland, 1009, 1131
Polycarp, 74
polytheism, 69, 670
Pontius Pilate, 212
Porphyry, 278, 646, 758
Practicall Cathechisme (Hammond), 1012
Pragmatic Sanction of Bourges (1438), 569
Praxeas, 190, 191, 201, 617
predestination, 179, 180, 182, 185, 186, 401, 432, 596, 888–889, 914, 916, 917, 918–919, 921, 926, 938, 967, 971, 999
Prenter, Regin, 836–837, 839–840
Presbyterians, 1020, 1022, 1023, 1116, 1117, 1125–1126, 1129
presbyters, 457, 474, 475, 483, 488, 489, 766, 769, 775, 777, 780, 789, 870
Prescription of Heretics, The (Tertullian), 738–739, 744, 761
Preston, John, 903, 909–912
presuppositionalism, 1127
Princeton Theological Seminary, 1109, 1117, 1124
Princetonians, 1118, 1125–1126, 1127, 1128
Principles of Theology, The (Thomas), 1115
printing, 746
Priscilla, 741
Priscillian of Avila, 655
Priscillianists, 653, 654
Proclus, 353–354, 355, 805
Procopius of Gaza, 751
prophecy, 733–734, 795–796
propitiation, 438–439
Prosper of Aquitaine, 903
prosôpon (Greek: person), 276, 280, 284, 318, 319, 336, 340, 347, 349, 352, 353, 354, 355, 362
Protestant Episcopal Church, 968
Protestant (Reformed) Orthodoxy, 797, 801–802
Protestantism, 552, 575, 609, 727, 1094, 1137–1138; and the crisis of authority, 1109–1129 passim. *See also* Trinity, the, in post–First World War Protestantism
providence, 166, 187, 1077, 1179
Provincial Letters (Pascal), 887
Pseudo-Aristeas, 38
Pseudo-Dionysius, 307, 637, 804, 805, 806–814, 818, 995, 996, 997
psyche (Greek: world-soul), 302, 368
psychic, as *psychikos* (Greek: soul) versus *pneumatikos* (Greek: spirit), 177
Ptolemy (the Valentinian), 128, 130, 139, 140–142, 553
Pulcheria, 356, 360
Pullen, Robert, 468–469
purgatory, 493–508 passim, 921, 922
Puritans, 579–580, 733, 862–863, 872, 885, 936, 938, 941, 944, 948–949, 950–951, 952, 954, 1012, 1022, 1095, 1116
Pusey, Edward Bouverie, 1114
Pyrrhus of Constantinople, 387

Quakers, 941, 942, 943, 949, 950, 1022
Quicunque vult. *See* Athanasian Creed (Latin title: *Quicunque vult*)
Quietists, 957
Quinisext (Greek: *Penthektê*) Council (the Council in *Trullo*), 392, 394, 768–769, 777, 780, 789, 810
Qumran community, 27, 48

rabbis, 30–31, 32, 36, 44, 46, 47, 48, 49, 61, 93, 137–138, 221, 561, 561–566, 774
Racovian Cathechism, 1009–1010, 1015
Radbertus, Paschasius, 466
Radewijns, Florentius, 825
Rahner, Karl, 1181–1182, 1188, 1193, 1195
ransom (Greek: *lytron*), concept of, 440
rationalism, 940, 968, 1017, 1022–1042 passim, 1044, 1051, 1093, 1109, 1114, 1116, 1118, 1119
Ratramnus of Corbie, 466, 663
reading, 746–747
recapitulation (Greek: *anakephalaiôsis*), 178, 181, 444
reconciliation, 155, 218, 252, 257–258, 333, 374, 376–377, 382, 384, 409, 417, 435, 439, 442–453, 509, 591, 593–594, 847, 908, 1029, 1032, 1055, 1057–1058, 1067, 1080, 1082, 1103, 1140, 1163
redemption, 36, 88–96, 100, 101, 128, 130, 151, 168, 174, 191, 206, 236, 291, 415, 422–423, 429–432, 440, 441, 444, 714, 850, 892–893, 914, 915–916, 959, 969–970, 1067–1068, 1087, 1127, 1137, 1143, 1156, 1163, 1183, 1206
Reformatio legum ecclesiasticarum, 883–885
Reformation, the, 570–571, 724–725, 849, 1098
Reformed, the, 872; in the British Isles, 912

Reformed Episcopal Church, 968
Reid, Thomas, 1118
Reimarus, Hermann Samuel, 1038, 1039
Remonstrance, 892–893
Remonstrants, 895, 1004, 1007, 1010, 1011
Renaissance, the, 1031
Renan, Ernest, 1069, 1070, 1072, 1104, 1105
reprobation, 432, 596
revelation, 1120
Revelation, book of, 749, 803, 804; use of Greek *Pantokratôr* in, 117–119
revivalism, 980
Richard, François-Marie-Benjamin Cardinal, 1105
Richard I, 849
Richard of St. Victor, 679, 685, 686
righteousness, 509–510, 513, 836–847
Ritschl, Albrecht, 1080–1083, 1085, 1086, 1087, 1106
ritualism, 1114
Robinson, John, 862–863, 944
Röell, Herman Alexander, 1007
Roman Catholicism/Roman Catholics, 341, 487, 542, 578, 707–708, 727, 772, 783–784, 948, 1004, 1033, 1035, 1130, 1132, 1137–1138, 1153, 1169, 1217, 1218, 1219; and the crisis of authority, 1092–1109 passim. *See also* Trinity, the, in post–First World War Roman Catholicism
Romanov, Mikhail, 1132
Romantic movement, 1060, 1072
romanticism, 1109
Rome/Roman Empire, the, 95, 201–202, 213, 217, 608, 783, 790, 791. *See also* Christianity, and the Roman world
Rous, Francis, 945
Rousseau, Jean-Jacques, 1033, 1035–1037, 1045, 1064
Rufinus, 147–148, 762
Russia, 1131–1132, 1136–1137, 1196
Russian Orthodoxy, 1132–1133
Rutherford, Samuel, 945–946
Ryle, John Charles, 1115

Sabas, 376
Sabbath, the, 80, 99, 157
Sabellians/Sabellianism (modalism), 189, 201, 229, 258, 270, 273, 307–308, 319, 664, 986, 1162, 1192
Sabellius, 200–201, 308
sacraments (the seven specific sacraments), 476–493 passim, 813, 1142, 1169
sacramentum (Latin: oath), 477
Sadducees, 27, 221
saints, 494–495, 921, 947
Saltmarsh, John, 942, 944
salvation, 1012, 1048–1049; assurance of, 920–938 passim
Samaritans, 28, 29, 122, 221
Samson, 46
Samuel, 495
sanctification, 844–845, 848
Satan/the Devil, 78, 84, 87, 102, 168, 436, 438, 439, 441–442, 444–445, 540; as the Cosmocrator, 129
Satornilus (Saturninus), 124
Saturninus (Satornilus), 124
Savoy Declaration of Faith and Order, 934
Schelling, Friedrich, 1141–1142
Schlegel, Friedrich, 1060
Schleiermacher, Friedrich, 1060–1069, 1072, 1119, 1120, 1158
Schleitheim Confession (1527), 852, 860, 868, 877
Scholarius, George, 703
Scholasticism, 1129, 1157
Schweitzer, Albert, 1092, 1106
Scofield Reference Bible, 750
Scottish commonsense philosophy, 1118
Scripture: as "breathed out by God" (*theopneustos*), 614; inspiration of, 736–741; interpretation of, 751–763; as the "rule of faith," 739, 744, 745–750; wisdom/truth of, 790–802
Scripture Doctrine of the Trinity, The (Clarke), 1019–1020
Second Antiochene Creed, 260
Second Book of Homilies, The, 875
Second Helvetic Confession (1566), 797, 798, 1117, 1157
Second Mennonite Confession. *See* Waterland Confession
Second Vatican Council (1962–1965), 732, 772, 773, 1103, 1185
Second World War, 1205–1206
secularization, 1021
Seneca, 302, 410
sensus (Greek: mind), 332
Sentences (Lombard), 469, 479, 493, 499, 797, 989, 1000, 1157
Septuagint, the (or "Seventy" [LXX]), 37, 38, 40, 41
Serapion of Thmuis, 624
Sergius of Constantinople, 386
Serious Call to a Devout and Holy Life, A (Taylor), 956
Sermon on the Mount, 135, 136
sermons, 875
Servetus, Michael, 874, 1002–1003, 1004
Servites, 551
Seventh-Day Adventists, 1116
Severus, 377–378, 382

Sheol, 160
Shepherd of Hermes, 762
Sherlock, William, 1018–1019, 1020
Shylock, 549
Sibbes, Richard, 936, 938, 939–940, 948–949, 953
Simeon, Charles, 971–972
Simon, Richard, 1024–1025, 1028
Simon the magician, 122, 123
Simons, Menno, 578, 860–861
sin/sinfulness, 82, 84–88, 181, 504, 853, 1001, 1139, 1155–1156, 1172, 1208
Sixtus IV, 1095
skepticism, 1118
Skinner, George, 979
Slavonic language, religious vocabulary of, 296–298
Slavophilism, 1137–1140
Smalcald (Schmalkald) Articles (1537), 573, 857, 876, 877
Smyth, John, 863, 864
sobornost' (Slavic: catholicity or conciliatory), 1139–1140
Society for Promoting Christian Knowledge, 966
Society for the Propagation of the Gospel, 966
Socinianism/ Socinians, 1008, 1009–1010, 1013–1014, 1016–1017, 1018, 1025
Socrates, 158–159, 410
sola scriptura (Latin: Scripture alone), 794, 797, 1000, 1002, 1013, 1017, 1018, 1038, 1200
Solomon, 64
Solovyov, Vladimir, 1140–1144, 1146
Song of Songs, 750
Sophronius, 387
soteriology, 402
soul (Hebrew: *nephesh*), 368, 612
Sozzini, Fausto, 1008–1009
Sozzini, Lelio, 1008–1009
Spangenberg, August Gottlieb, 966
speaking in tongues. *See* glossolalia
Spener, Philipp Jakob, 958–960
Spinoza, Benedict, 1026–1028
spirit (Greek: *pneuma*), 368
spirit (Hebrew: *ruach*), 368, 612
"Spirit-fighters" (Greek: *Pneumatomachi*), 624, 627, 628–629, 631, 634
spiritual gifts, 729–735, 804
Spiritual Guide (de Molinos), 957
"spiritual persons," 552, 786
St. Boniface, 498
St. Christopher, 495
St. Denis, 495
St. Dominic, 472
St. Francis, 472, 551
St. Jude, 495
Stăniloae, Dumitru, 710
Stephen, 412
Stephen of Antioch, 257
Sterry, Peter, 940, 941, 947
Stillingfleet, Edward, 1030–1031
Stoics, 159–160, 170, 192, 302
Strauss, David, 1059, 1069–1070, 1072, 1081
Student Christian Movement (SCM), 973
Stylianos of Australia, 712
Succensus, 343, 344
suffering (Greek: *propatheia*), 334
Summa contra Gentiles (Aquinas), 991
Summa theologiae (Aquinas), 518, 991
supralapsarianism, 889–890
Supreme Being, concept of, 72, 104
survival of the fittest, 1077, 1079
Swinburne, Richard, 1183
Swiss Confederation, 577
Syllabus of Errors, 1096
Syllogistic Chapters (Nicetas of Byzantium), 670
Symeon the New Theologian, 820–821
Symmachus, 39
Synesius of Cyrene, 545
Synod of Aachen (Aix-la-Chapelle [809]), 660
Synod of Dort (1619), 901, 905, 906, 907, 919, 924, 1117; and TULIP, 893–899
Synod of Frankfurt (794), 660
Synod of Friuli (797), 660
Systematic Theology (Hodge), 1118

Targums, 294
Tariq, 393
Tarphon, 44
Tatian, 177, 178, 194
Tauler, Johannes, 959
Taylor, Jeremy, 956, 975, 1013
Teacher of Righteousness, 48
teaching/teachers, 734
Ten Articles (1536), 857, 875, 922
Ten Commandments, the, 842
Teresa of Avila, 957
Tersteegen, Gerhard, 962
Tertullian, 64, 75, 78, 87, 93, 95, 116, 130, 141, 143, 144, 156–157, 161, 167, 182–186, 190, 191, 199–200, 202, 203, 211, 212, 217, 277, 302, 319, 356, 407, 408, 412, 413–415, 477, 543–544, 617, 618, 622, 623, 643, 644, 647, 674, 738–739, 744, 748–749, 756, 761, 776; on angels and the Devil, 168; on the doctrine of the Trinity, 196–198; written defenses of the faith, 214–115
Theodora, 382
Theodore of Mopsuestia, 337, 338, 339, 340, 343, 346, 354, 383, 459, 761, 762, 768
Theodore of Tarsus, 815

Theodoret of Cyrus, 41, 344–345, 352, 355, 383, 653, 686, 762, 768
Theodosius I, 284
Theodosius II, 349, 355, 360
Theodotion, 39
Theodulf of Orléans, 659, 660–661, 662
Theognostus, 204–205
Theological Orations (Gregory of Nazianzus), 284
theology, 33, 253–254, 580, 814, 993, 1181; apophatic theology, 812, 995; Christian theology, 147, 179, 208, 310–311, 774, 986, 1016, 1194, 1219; covenant theology, 585–603, 888–899, 1116; credibility of, 1217–1222; Greek theology, 698, 713; "liberal" theology, 1167–1168; medieval theology, 40–41; mystical theology, 306, 397; natural theology, 166–167, 798, 1152; Palamite theology, 711–712; patristic theology, 1218; Process Theology, 1175–1180, 1223; reconstruction of, 1042–1092 passim; sacramental theology, 812–813; scholastic theology, 553–554; systematic theology, 797, 981, 1118–1119; Trinitarian theology, 1220–1221
Theophan the Recluse, 1134
Theophilus of Alexandria, 335
Theophilus of Antioch, 52, 115–116, 164, 194–195, 737
Theophrastus, 318
theôsis (Greek: deification), 814–817, 823, 825, 837, 1144
Theotokos (Greek: God-bearer), 333, 342, 353, 362
Thirteen Articles (1538), 857
Thirty-nine Articles of Religion, 581, 731, 793, 795, 798–799, 877, 901, 955, 1093, 1115, 1205
Thomas, William Henry Griffith, 1115
Thomas of Chobham, 502
Thomism, 1044
"Three Chapters," condemnation of, 383, 384
"Thrice-holy" (*Trishagion*), 383
Tillich, Paul, 1171–1174
Tillotson, John, 1028–1029
Timaeus (Plato), 131–132, 759
time: cyclical time, 170; linear time, 170–171
Timothy, 53
Timothy II Aelurus, 374
Timothy III Salophakiolos, 374
Tindal, Matthew, 1032, 1034
to apeiron (Greek: the infinite), 313
Toland, John, 1030
Tomus ad Flavianum ("*Tome*" [Leo of Rome]), 356, 361, 374, 392, 654, 767, 1201
Toplady, Augustus, 421, 971
Torah, the, 39
Torrance, Thomas, 816
Torrey, Reuben Archer, 1128
Tractarians, 1112–1113
tradition, in Christian theology, 774–790 passim, 1214, 1224
Trajan, 211
"transfer of properties" (Latin: *communicatio idiomatum*), 372
transubstantiation, 468–476
Transylvania, 1009
Treaty of Tordesillas (1529), 887
Treaty of Zaragoza (1529), 887
Trewe, John, 891
Trinitarians (Mathurins), 551
Trinity, the, 69–70, 112–114, 196–198, 365–366, 630–631, 666–667, 697, 713, 986–988, 1000–1006, 1013, 1014–1015, 1017, 1035, 1050, 1056, 1067–1069, 1093–1094, 1143, 1208, 1219, 1220–1222; and the concepts of *substantia*, *forma*, and *persona*, 197–198, 201, 251, 277, 309, 650; and creation, 188–199; and the divine hierarchy, 199–206; and the eclipse of the Father, 206–208; eternal nature of love within, 1216–1217; and God as three *personae* in one *substantia*, 319; in post–First World War Eastern Orthodoxy, 1196–1204; in post–First World War Protestantism, 1147–1184 passim; in post–First World War Roman Catholicism, 1184–1195; self-communication among the persons of, 1191; suffering of, 1207–1210; the Trinitarian synthesis, 273–292 passim, 1223
Trinitarianism/Trinitarians, 1018–1019, 1020; Augustinian Trinitarianism, 322, 1183; Eastern Trinitarianism, 694, 697, 698; economic Trinitarianism (from Greek *oikonomia*), 191
Trinitarians, 1018–1019
"triumph of Orthodoxy," the, 397
Troeltsch, Ernst, 1086–1088
"True Confession of the Faith, A," 862
Tübingen School, 1071, 1084, 1116
Turibius, 653
Turkey, 64, 394, 1196, 1201
Turretini, François, 969, 1117
Turretini, Jean-Alphonse, 969
typology, 144–145
Tyrrell, George, 1108–1109, 1184

Unam sanctum (bull of Boniface VIII), 555, 559
unction, with holy oil, 810–811
Uniates ("Greek Catholics"), 707, 1130
Unigenitus (bull of Clement XI), 887
Union of Brest, 1130
Unitarianism/Unitarians, 1009, 1017–1020, 1116

United Provinces of the Netherlands, 577
United States, 57–58
universities, European, 1037
University of Halle, 960, 961
Urban II, 550, 673
Ursinus, Zacharias, 591, 913
Ussher, James, 901–905, 909, 910
usury, 549, 786
Utraquists, 530, 568
Uytenbogaert, Johannes, 708

Václav of Dubá, 567
Valentinians, the, 128–130
Valens, 272
Valla, Lorenzo, 570, 791
Van Ruysbroeck, Jan, 701
Van Til, Cornelius, 1127
Vatican City State, 888
Vekhi (*Landmarks*), 1144–1145
Velichkovsky, Païsy, 1133–1134
verzuiling (pillarization), 1125, 1128
Victorinus, Marius, 276–278, 279, 281, 356, 359, 623–624, 646, 987
Virgil, 500
Visigoths (Western Goths), 272, 385, 653, 655
Vitalis, 332
Voetius, Gisbertius, 937
Voltaire, 1033–1035, 1036, 1076, 1093, 1134
von Balthasar, Hans Urs, 817, 1193–1195
von Döllinger, Johann Joseph Ignaz, 1101
von Drey, Johann Sebastian, 1101
von Harnack, Adolf, 985, 1084–1085, 1105, 1106, 1149
Voulgaris, Eugenius, 1134
Vulgate, the, 41, 43, 656, 791

Wahres Christentum (*True Christianity* [Arndt]), 959
Ware, Timothy, 661
Warfield, Benjamin B., 1004, 1122–1124, 1126, 1127
Waterland, Daniel, 1020
Waterland Confession (1580 [or 1581]), 861–862, 868–869
Waterlanders, 860–861, 863
Weigel, George, 728
Weinandy, Thomas, 718, 1207–1210
Weiss, Johannes, 1092
Wesley, Charles, 956, 971
Wesley, John, 725, 873, 956, 958, 965–967, 968, 971–972, 974–978
Wesley, Samuel, 965
Wesleyans, 1111
Westminster Confession of Faith, 581–583, 585, 601, 731, 793–794, 798–800, 932–933, 955, 1093, 1117
Westminster Theological Seminary, 1124
Whitaker, William, 890, 891
Whitefield, George, 967, 968, 969, 1040
Whitehead, Alfred North, 1175–1176
Whitgift, John, 890
Whitson, William, 1019
Wilberforce, William, 980
Wilcox, Thomas, 579
Wilhelm II (of Germany), 1084
will, expressed as *thelêma*, 390–391
William I of Aquitaine, 550
William III, 1022
William of Auvergne, 500–501
William of Auxerre, 515
William of Ockham, 480, 520, 523, 1000
William of St. Thierry, 679
Williams, John Rodman, 981
wisdom (*sophia*), 229, 961–962, 1141; distinction between inner and outer wisdom, 791
witchcraft, 83, 865
Wittenberg Articles (1536), 838–839, 840, 856
Wolff, Christian, 1038
Wolterstorff, Nicholas, 1184
Woodal, Frederick, 942
Word, the divine (the Wisdom of God), 405
Word of God, doctrine of, 1153–1154
World Council of Churches (WCC), 773, 973, 1217
World Missions Conference (1910), 1217
Wright, Shawn, 929
Writings, the (*Ketuvim*), 39
Wulfila (Ulfilas), 271, 622–623
Wyclif (Wycliffe), John, 473–474, 475, 520, 560, 561, 562, 563, 564–565, 567, 848, 865

Young Men's Christian Association (YMCA), 973

Zeno, 374, 375
Zenobia of Palmyra, 217
Zernov, Nicolas, 1146
Zizioulas, Jean, 1201–1203
Zonaras, John, 781–782
Zoroastrians, 85
Zwingli, Huldrych, 530, 585–586, 588, 589, 850, 924–925

Scripture Index

Genesis
1–3 79, 763
1–11 51, 749
1:1 1009
1:2 139, 192, 612
1:28 490
1:31 164
5:24 495
6:2 126
12:3 796
18:18 32
21:20–21 59
25:12–18 59
47:31 42, 801
49:10 796

Exodus
20:4–5 301

Deuteronomy
14:1–2 103
24:1–4 140, 883
25:4 753
32:8 101

Joshua
5:2 752

Judges
13:5 46

1 Samuel
28:11–14 495

1 Kings
18:20–40 32

2 Kings
2:11 495
5:15–17 32

1 Chronicles
17:11–14 108

2 Chronicles
7:18 63
21:7 63
24:20–22 53
33:7 63

Job
19:25–26 151
31:33 101

Psalms
2:6–8 108
22 241, 294
33:6 195, 614
36:9 645
45:13 146
51:11 614
67 32
89:26–27 108
103:10, 13 103
110:4 536

Proverbs
8 236
8:22 194, 235, 279, 405
8:22–36 242, 266
8:35 391
22:20–21 146

Isaiah
6:1, 3 135
7:14 44
14:12–20 84
35:8 32
40:5 329
45:5 126
53:4 1209
53:8 242
55:9 301
61:1–2 538–539
63:16–17 100

Jeremiah
1:5 560
31:20 103–104
31:31–33 588

Ezekiel
2:1 109
11:24 614
18:19–20 511
18:23 391
28:1–19 78
28:12–19 84
47:6 109

Daniel
4:8 614
7:13–14 406

Hosea
6:7 590

Amos
4:13 624, 625

Zechariah
1:1 53

Matthew
2:23 46
5–7 135
5:43–48 135
6:9–13 136
7:11 48
8:4 39
10:28 544
11:27 677
12:32 289, 496
13:23 182
16:13–17 109
16:24–27 409–410
17:3 495
19 883
23:35–37 53
26:41 330
26:63–64 406
27:46 226, 294, 1150, 1205
28:19 635

Mark
1:44 39
3:17 109
10:3 39
10:18 244
12:26 39
15:34 226, 1150, 1205

Luke
11:2–4 136
16:22 495
17:14 521
22:20 587
24:44 39
24:44–47 138

John
1:1 1009
1:1–3 192
1:2 631
1:9 949
1:14 71, 253, 329, 405, 642
1:18 71, 110, 301
1:29 903
2:6 753
3:5 859
3:8 674, 723
3:16 112
4:10 645
4:22 32
4:24 616
4:34 110
5:17 99
5:18 100
5:26 723
5:45–46 39
6:63 645
7:19 39

8:37–38 102
10:18 325
10:30 107
14–16 615, 618
14–17 676
14:6 654
14:17 843
14:26 676
14:28 289
15:26 631, 634, 639, 645, 654, 662, 672, 673, 676, 677, 698, 700, 712
16:13 654
16:13–14 676
16:14–15 642
17 1192
17:1–26 436
17:4–5 407
17:9 904
17:11 114
20:17 133, 245
20:22 645, 652

Acts
1:22 482
2:4 482
2:7–11 293
6:1 28
8 122
17:10–15 259
17:11 747
17:28 104
17:34 307, 495
19:2–6 482

Romans
1:20 995
2:1–24 77
4:15 838
5:1 838
5:12 424
5:16–17 509
5:18–19 424
5:20 515
6:3–4 411
7:6 974
7:15, 18–19 974
8 615
8:3 421
8:15 230
8:16 368, 898
8:28 164, 1169
8:29 686
9:20 758
9:20–21 100–101
10:14 747
13:1–7 544

1 Corinthians
1:17 910
2:10 111, 283
3:6 728
3:11–15 497
6:19 461
7:15 884
9:9 138
9:9–10 753
9:14 138
9:20–22 50
11:28–29 877
12–14 615
13:10 943
13:12 319
14:13–19 48
14:21 40
15:22 181, 424
15:24–26, 28 113
15:27 406
15:35–58 737
15:49 686

2 Corinthians
1:6 411
3:17 634
5:7 1046
5:19 190
6:18 118
12:2–4 803
12:8 1003
13:14 815

Galatians
2:20–21 410
2:21 910
3:1 737
3:6 841
4:6 615, 669

4:21–26 754
4:21–31 48

Ephesians
1:3–10 178
1:10 144–145
2:6 584
4 869
4:3 649
4:5 93

Philippians
2:5–7 1222
2:5–11 357
2:6–11 289
2:7 289, 335
2:9–11 113, 154
2:10–11 406, 544
3:3 283

Colossians
1:3 615
1:17–20 408–409
1:15 194, 256
1:15–16 121
1:24 411–412
2:9 71, 382, 713
2:11–12 858

1 Thessalonians
4:13–18 737
4:16 494
5:23–24 979

1 Timothy
5:21 625

2 Timothy
1:5 35
2:11–12 410
2:12 172, 185, 230
3:16 614, 635, 736

Titus
1:15 135

Hebrews
1:2–3 301
1:3 280, 304, 316, 317, 335
1:13 83
2:5–8 83
4:15 1212
6:4–6 413
11 46
11:10, 16 544
11:21 42, 801

James
1:1 64
1:17–18 114
5:14 881
5:14–15 487
5:16 485

1 Peter
1:1 64
1:3 112

2 Peter
1:3–4 815, 816
1:21 614, 635, 736, 800
2:4 84

1 John
4:16 650
5:7 745

Jude
6 84
14 54

Revelation
1:8 118, 396, 986
13:8 185, 409, 436
15:3 118
16:14 118
19:15 118
20:6 172
21:1–4 134
21:22 461

Also Available from Gerald Bray

A uniquely accessible volume on systematic theology, *God Is Love* is written for the average Christian and traces the theme of God's love through all the major doctrines of the Bible.

"Gerald Bray is one of our leading evangelical scholars and he has given us here a magisterial overview of Christian belief and doctrine. A great example of theology in the service of the church."

TIMOTHY GEORGE
Distinguished Professor of Divinity,
Beeson Divinity School, Samford University

For more information, visit **crossway.org**.